KU-273-769

C 02 0410175

ANTIQUES
PRICE GUIDE 2005

ANTIQUES
PRICE GUIDE 2005

Judith Miller

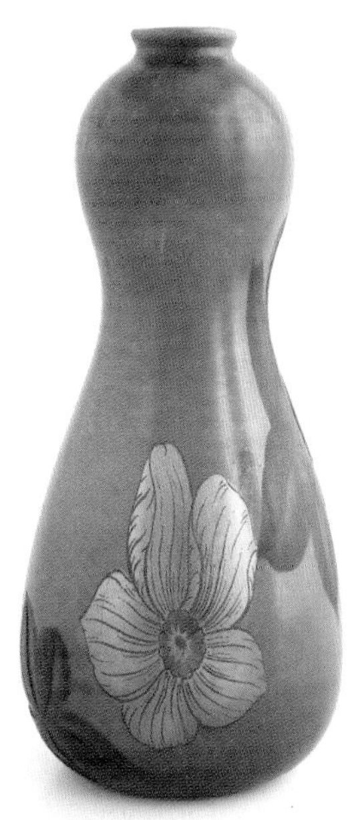

A DORLING KINDERSLEY BOOK

LONDON, NEW YORK,
MELBOURNE, MUNICH, DELHI

A joint production from DORLING KINDERSLEY
and THE PRICE GUIDE COMPANY

THE PRICE GUIDE COMPANY LIMITED

Publisher Judith Miller
Publishing Manager Julie Brooke
Managing Editor Carolyn Madden
European Consultants Martina Franke, Nicolas Tricaud de Montonnière
Assistant Editor Claire Smith
Digital Image Co-ordinator Ellen Spalek
Editorial Assistants Jessica Bishop, Dan Dunlavey, Sandra Lange
Design and DTP Tim Scrivens, TJ Graphics
Photographers Graham Rae, Bruce Boyajian, John McKenzie, Byron Slater, Elizabeth Field, Adam Gault, Heike Löwenstein, Andy Johnson
Indexer Hilary Bird
Workflow Consultant Bob Bousfield
Publishing Advisor Nick Croydon

DORLING KINDERSLEY LIMITED

Category Publisher Jackie Douglas
Designer Martin Dieguez
Managing Art Editor Heather McCarry
Managing Editor Julie Oughton
DTP Designer Mike Grigoletti
Production Sarah Dodd
Production Manager Sarah Coltman

First published in 2004 by
Dorling Kindersley Limited
80 Strand, London WC2R 0RL

Penguin Group

The Price Guide Company (UK) Ltd
Studio 21, Waterside
44–48 Wharf Road
London N1 7UX
info@thepriceguidecompany.com

2 4 6 8 10 9 7 5 3 1

A CIP catalogue record for this book is available from the British Library.

ISBN 1 4053 0542 8

Colour reproduction by Colourscan, Singapore
Printed and bound by MOHN media and Mohndruck GmbH, Germany

Discover more at

www.dk.com

CONTENTS

INTRODUCTION

It's almost impossible to believe that I am writing the Introduction to my third annual *Antiques Price Guide* with DK. The year has just flown by while my team and I have been photographing and compiling information all over the country and overseas. During this period the world of antiques has continued to grow – an expansion substantially fuelled by the Internet, as more and more people log on to the pleasures of buying and selling on-line.

One consequence of this market with fewer geographic limitations is that it has become easier to track down sought-after pieces. Equally, if you want to take full advantage of these new opportunities, a full-colour, annual price guide reflecting all corners and aspects of the market has become even more essential. To this end, we not only change 100% of the antiques shown in the guide every year, but we are also constantly sourcing new locations for our photography – whether it be auction houses, dealers' shops, markets, fairs or private collections.

As to our price bands, they are what we say they are: guides. They give you a low-to-high "ball park" figure of what the market place, checked by our specialist consultants, says you should be paying for an item in similar condition. If in worse condition than the example shown it may be less; if in better condition it may be more.

I am always being asked how good antiques are as an investment. I have usually advised against it, simply because I have always believed you should buy an antique because you love it, because you cannot bear to live without it. However, while stocks, shares and pension funds have suffered some substantial losses during the last couple of years, antiques have performed pretty well. Indeed, while medium quality pieces have been reasonably steady, numerous very good, rare and desirable examples have risen significantly in value.

So, my advice now is still to buy what you love, but with a little more financial confidence. I should, however, point out that whenever I mention to my husband that one of my antiques has risen so much in value, he is always quick to point out that it has not – as I have no intention of selling it. We antique lovers don't take things quite so literally!

Sincerely,

Judith Miller.

LIST OF CONSULTANTS

Ceramics

John Axford
Woolley & Wallis
51-61 Castle Street
Salisbury, Wiltshire
SP1 3SU

Christopher Spencer
Spencer Antiques Services
23a High Street
Falmouth TR11 5AB

Commemoratives

John Pym
Hope and Glory
131a Kensington Church Street
London W8 7LP

Oriental

Clive Stewart Lockhart
Dreweatt Neate
Donnington Priory Salerooms
Donnington, Newbury
Berkshire RG14 2JE

Robert McPherson
R & G McPherson Antiques
40 Kensington Church Street
London W8 4BX

Furniture

Paul Roberts
Lyon and Turnbull Ltd
33 Broughton Place
Edinburgh EH1 3RR

Matthew Smith
Christie's
8 King Street, St. James's
London SW1Y 6QT

Glass

Jeanette Hayhurst
Jeanette Hayhurst Fine Glass
32a Kensington Church Street
London W8 4HA

Horst Ungar
Dr. Fischer Heilbronner
Kunst-und Auktionshaus
Trappensee-Schlösschen
74074 Heilbronn, Germany

Bohemian Glass

Andrew Lineham
Stand G19, The Mall Antiques
Arcade, 359 Upper Street
London N1 0PD

Silver

Trevor Kyle
Lyon & Turnbull Ltd
33 Broughton Place
Edinburgh EH1 3RR

Clocks

Paul Archard
Derek Roberts Fine Antique
Clocks
25 Shipbourne Road
Tonbridge, Kent, TN10 3DN

Jewellery

Joseph H Bonnar
72 Thistle Street
Edinburgh EH2 1EN

Decorative Arts

John Mackie
Lyon & Turnbull Ltd
33 Broughton Place
Edinburgh EH1 3RR

Keith Baker
The Price Guide Company
(UK) Ltd

20th Century

Mark Hill
The Price Guide Company
(UK) Ltd

Toys

Glenn Butler
Wallis and Wallis
West Street Auction Galleries
Lewes
East Sussex BN7 2NJ

We are very grateful to our friends and experts who give us so much help: Sebastian Pryke and Campbell Armour of Lyon and Turnbull; Lennox Cato of Lennox Cato Antiques; Robert McPherson of R. & G. McPherson Antiques; and Michael James of The Silver Fund.

HOW TO USE THIS BOOK

Page tab – This device appears on every spread and identifies the main category heading as indicated in the Contents List on pp.5–6.

The introduction – The key facts about a factory, maker, or style are given, along with stylistic identification points, value tips, and advice on fakes.

Caption – The description of the item illustrated, including, when relevant, the period, the maker or factory, medium, the year it was made, dimensions, and condition. Many captions have **footnotes** which explain terminology or give identification or valuation information.

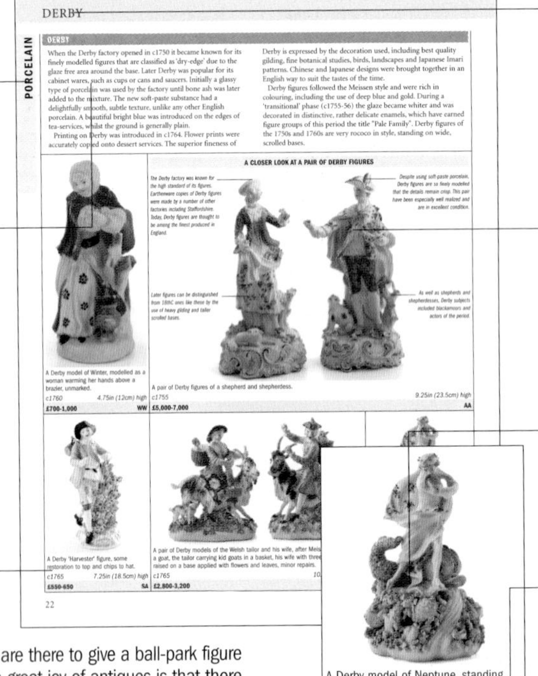

The price guide – The price ranges in the Guide are there to give a ball-park figure of what you should pay for a similar item. The great joy of antiques is that there is not a recommended retail price. The prices guides in this book are based on actual prices – either what a dealer will take or the full auction price – and are then checked by consultants. If you wish to sell an item you may be offered much less; if you want to insure your items the insurance valuation may be considerably more.

A Derby model of Neptune, standing beside a dolphin, raised upon a base of shells and coral, the dolphin's tail lacking and a factory fault where one arm is missing.
c1765 9.25in (23.5cm) high
£200-300 WW

Running head – Indicates the sub-category of the main heading.

A closer look at – Does exactly that. This is where we show identifying aspects of a factory or maker, point out rare colours or shapes, and explain why a particular piece is so desirable.

The object – The antiques are shown in full colour. This is a vital aid to identification and valuation. With many objects, a slight colour variation can signify a large price differential.

The source code – Every item in *Antiques Price Guide 2005* has been specially photographed at an auction house, a dealer, an antiques market, or a private collection. These are credited by the code at the end of the caption, and can be checked against the Key to Illustrations on pages 724–7.

PORCELAIN

At present, the porcelain market is remarkably strong in some areas and struggling in others. Whilst German and Japanese porcelain have become slower to leave the shelves in the last few years, Chinese pieces are popular, partially because more buyers from China have entered the market as its economy expands.

English porcelain is holding up well. Pieces from well-known makers, such as Chelsea and Royal Worcester, remain popular in the UK, but also appeal to the US market, which increases demand and pushes up prices. Pieces by English firms, including Lowestoft and Derby, are less sought after across the water, although exceptional pieces continue to appeal.

Demand for Welsh porcelain has grown over the last few years and prices have risen sharply, with some pieces doubling or tripling in value.

As seems to be the case in recent years, collectors generally favour exceptional and rare pieces of porcelain, and are willing to scour the whole of the market to find them. Buyers can be choosey and damage on some porcelain, such as Early Worcester, can reduce the value by up to 95 per cent, depending on the severity of the damage and rarity of the piece.

John Axford,
European & Oriental Ceramics & Glass, Woolley & Wallis

BERLIN

A KPM porcelain plaque, depicting a scene with nymph seated on rocky cliff, looking at butterfly on her finger, in hand-carved gilt gesso frame.

Plaque 10 x 8in (25.5 x 20cm)

£4,000-6,000 **AAC**

A KPM porcelain plaque, signed "Vagner".

c1880 *9in (23cm) high*

£2,000-3,000 **AL**

A large rectangular Berlin plaque, painted with 'The Penitent Magdalene', after Battoni, inscribed "F. Zapf Dresden", impressed sceptre and KPM mark, broken into several pieces and well restored.

c1880 *20.75in (53cm) wide*

£1,200-1,500 **WW**

Four Berlin octagonal dishes, painted with bouquets of flowers and insects within a border of scrolls divided by puce feuille-de-choux, the pierced rims enriched in puce and green, blue sceptre marks, impressed marks.

c1780 *8.25in (20.5cm) wide*

£500-700 **GORL**

A Berlin porcelain tea caddy, moulded in relief with putti and Pliny doves.

3.25in (8.5cm) high

£180-220 **GORL**

A Berlin model of a finch perched on a stump, naturalistically decorated in coloured enamels, mark in blue, chip to tail.

5in (13cm) high

£40-60 **LFA**

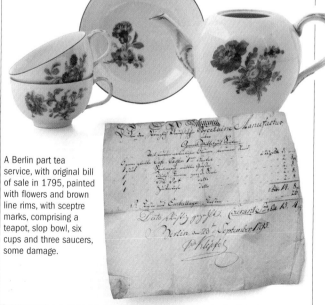

A Berlin part tea service, with original bill of sale in 1795, painted with flowers and brown line rims, with sceptre marks, comprising a teapot, slop bowl, six cups and three saucers, some damage.

£250-350 set **WW**

BOW

An early Bow blue and white vine leaf-shaped pickle dish, painted with peony, a fence and a flowering tree, rim chips.

c1755 *4in (10cm) wide*

£280-320 **WW**

A Bow blue and white vine leaf-shaped pickle dish, painted with trailing flowers, the reverse moulded with veining.

c1760

£220-280 **WW**

A Bow vine leaf-shaped dish, painted with flowers.

c1760 *4in (10cm) wide*

£400-600 **JF**

A Bow blue and white octagonal plate, with central landscape.

c1760 *7.5in (19cm) diam*

£250-350 **AA**

A Bow blue and white fan-shaped dish, from a supper or sweetmeat set, painted with pagoda landscapes in panels on a powder blue ground.

c1765 *6in (15cm) high*

£280-320 **WW**

A Bow saucer dish, painted in underglaze blue, in the Meissen style.

c1760 *8.25in (21cm) diam*

£1,200-1,500 **AA**

A small Bow 'Jumping Boy' pattern blue and white plate.

c1760 *6.5in (16.5cm) wide*

£400-600 **WW**

A Bow blue and white cream boat, painted with flowers in panels on a fluted ground, with a flared foot, a crack at the base of the handle.

c1760 *5in (12.5cm) wide*

£120-180 **WW**

A Bow coffee can, painted in underglaze blue.

c1754 *2.5in (6cm) high*

£1,500-2,000 **AA**

An early Bow blue and white milk jug, painted with three figures, sailing boats and a pine tree at the water's edge, all beneath a wavy blue border, foot rim chips.

c1755 *3.25in (8cm) high*

£700-900 **WW**

An unusual Bow blue and white bowl and cover, painted with large moths and flowers, the interior with a rose spray, unmarked, the cover cracked.

c1760 *8.25in (21cm) wide*

£550-650 **WW**

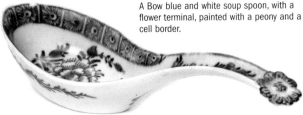

A Bow blue and white soup spoon, with a flower terminal, painted with a peony and a cell border.

c1760 *5.75in (14.5cm) long*

£300-500 **WW**

An early Bow figure of matrimony, by the Muses modeller, standing beside a rockwork fountain wearing a dress painted with flower sprays and holding a birdcage, impressed "T" mark.

c1750 *9.5in (24.5cm) high*

£800-1,200 **WW**

A Bow model of a standing prioress, wearing a black and white lined cowl, some chips.

c1755 *5.5in (14cm) high*

£400-600 **WW**

A Bow model of dancing lady holding her skirt, raised on a scroll-footed base, detailed with coloured enamels, some damage.

c1758 *7.5in (19.5cm) high*

£800-1,200 **WW**

A Bow model of a drummer, sitting on a tree stump, raised on a high scroll footed base, some damage.

c1758 *7.5in (19.5cm) high*

£800-1,200 **WW**

A Bow 'New Dancer' figure, with gilt highlights, some restoration to the back of head.

c1760 *7.5in (19cm) high*

£1,000-1,500 **SA**

A Bow figure, emblematic of Winter.

c1765 *7in (17.5cm) high*

£800-1,200 **AA**

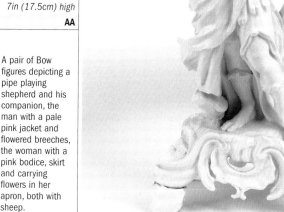

A pair of Bow figures depicting a pipe playing shepherd and his companion, the man with a pale pink jacket and flowered breeches, the woman with a pink bodice, skirt and carrying flowers in her apron, both with sheep.

6.5in (16cm) high

£530-580 **L&T**

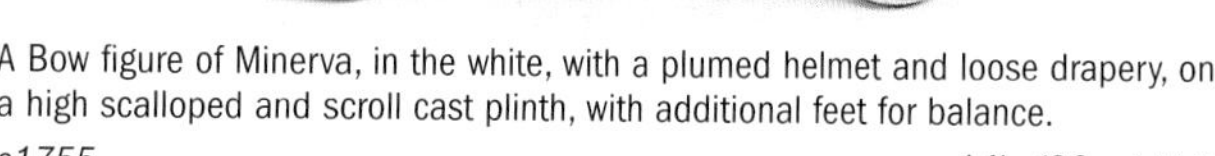

A Bow figure of Minerva, in the white, with a plumed helmet and loose drapery, on a high scalloped and scroll cast plinth, with additional feet for balance.

c1755 *14in (36cm) high*

£1,300-1,600 **L&T**

A Bow figure of Venus, with two doves at her feet, wearing rust and gilt boots and scantily clad in densely flowered drapery with a yellow, pink and green sash, on a raised base with a hole for a candlestick.

10.5in (27cm) high

£800-1,200 **L&T**

A Bow candlestick, in the form of Cupid with a basket of flowers on his head and Venus scantily clad clutching flowers, on a scrolling plinth, lacking sconce.

8.5in (22cm) high

£800-1,200 **L&T**

A Bow figure of Minerva, with a plumed helmet and pink and gold armour, a flowered and striped cloak, on a base with an owl.

12.5in (32cm) high

£1,000-1,500 **L&T**

A Bow figure depicting Air, with a pale pink and blue cloak over a flowered underskirt, with an eagle at her side.

8.5in (22cm) high

£700-1,000 **L&T**

A pair of Bow scallop shell dishes of unusually large size, each painted in Kakiemon palette with the 'Two Quail' pattern, within an iron red and gilt flowerhead and leaf scroll band, one with stress cracks.

c1755 *10.25in (26cm) wide*

£800-1,200 **LFA**

A Bow 'Quail' dish, filled chip to rim.

c1756 *9.5in (24cm) wide*

£1,000-1,300 **SA**

A CLOSER LOOK AT A BOW SWEETMEAT DISH

The yellow panther detail would make this dish more exotic and desirable as panthers would only be known to the public from engravings.

Bow porcelain is a soft-paste porcelain which has a tendency to stain so the excellent condition of this piece contributes to the high price.

The dish uses the delicate famille rose palette of enamels: the opacity of the paint allows for delicate shading of colours.

Sweetmeat dishes were delicately designed and formed to reflect their purpose, to serve candied fruits, dainty pastries and preserves.

A Bow centrepiece sweetmeat dish, of shell form, with a rare yellow panther inside the shell, in the famille rose palette.

c1755 *6.5in (16.5cm) diam*

£5,000-6,000 **JF**

A rare Bow vine leaf-shaped pickle dish, painted in famille rose colours with sprays of flowers, the rim fringed in pink.

c1760 *2.25in (6cm) wide*

£500-800 **WW**

A Bow sauceboat, of silver shape, with a scrolling handle and floral swags moulded to the body and foot, decorated with gilt flowers and leaves, restoration to the handle.

c1750 *8.5in (21.5cm) long*

£700-1,000 **WW**

A small Bow milk jug, printed and painted with Chinese figures in various pursuits, a brown line rim, some faults.

c1760 *3in (7.5cm) high*

£300-500 **WW**

A Bow jug, with green and gilt decoration.

c1768 *4in (10cm) high*

£400-600 **SA**

An early Bow teapot and cover, decorated in the famille rose palette, with peony and rockwork, an incised cross mark.

c1750 *6.75in (17cm) high*

£500-700 **WW**

A Bow coffee cup, moulded with prunus branches.

c1760

£300-500 **JF**

CAUGHLEY

A Caughley blue and white cylindrical mug, printed with the 'Fisherman' pattern, unmarked.

c1780 *5.5in (14cm) high*

£380-420 **WW**

A Caughley 'Royal Flute' shaped coffee cup, with a Chinese style handle, decorated with the 'Pagoda' pattern.

c1785 *2.5in (6.5cm) high*

£80-120 **GAS**

A pair of Caughley blue and white custard cups, printed with the 'Cottage' pattern.

c1790 *2in (5cm) high*

£400-600 **DN**

A Caughley miniature cup and saucer, decorated with an Oriental scene.

c1780 *3in (7.5cm) diam*

£350-400 **SA**

A Caughley blue and white wine-taster or scoop, applied with a leaf handle, the interior printed with the 'Fisherman and Cormorant' pattern.

c1785 *2.75in (7cm) wide*

£200-300 **DN**

A Caughley leaf-shaped butter boat, the interior printed in blue with the 'Fisherman' pattern, the underside moulded with trefoil leaf sprigs.

c1790 3in (7.5cm) long

£150-200 **DN**

A Caughley blue and white bowl, printed with the 'Fisherman' pattern, with an "Sx" mark.

c1780 8.25in (21cm) diam

£220-280 **WW**

A Caughley scalloped plate, painted with root flowers and a butterfly in underglaze blue, a crescent mark, rim chipped.

c1768 7in (18cm) high

£150-200 **GORL**

A Caughley blue and white sugar bowl and cover, with a circular fluted body, printed with pagoda landscapes, with gilt line borders, "Sx" mark.

c1790 4.5in (11.5cm) wide

£180-220 **WW**

A Caughley cabbage leaf moulded mask jug, printed in blue with flower sprays, a "C" mark, crack to the handle.

c1775 7.5in (19cm) high

£220-280 **WW**

A late 18thC Caughley barrel-shaped fluted teapot and cover, decorated with flowersprays in blue and gilt, unmarked, a "M & G.H. Fisher Collection" label, the body cracked, some wear.

8.5in (21.5cm) high

£50-80 **WW**

A Caughley teapot, cover and stand, decorated with gilt rose sprays and with gold and blue borders, unmarked, slight wear.

c1785

£220-280 **WW**

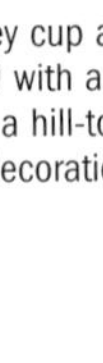

A Caughley cup and saucer, decorated with a scene depicting a hill-top castle, with gilt decoration.

c1795 5.75in (14.5cm) diam

£300-350 **SA**

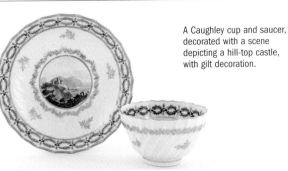

A Caughley tea canister.

c1780 4.75in (12cm) high

£800-900 **SA**

A CLOSER LOOK AT A CAUGHLEY DESSERT DISH

This dish was decorated by the Chamberlain workshop. Chamberlain, known for its high quality, fine designs, purchased a large amount of undecorated Caughley between 1780-95.

Caughley is better known for its blue and white porcelain.

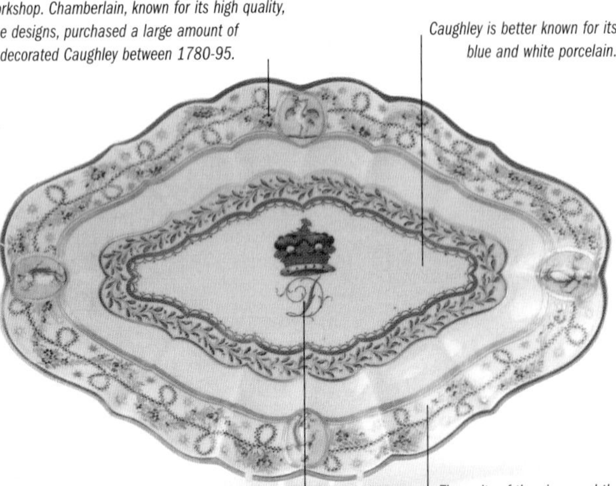

This piece was made for the Marquis of Donegal and is decorated with a crowned "D".

The rarity of the piece and the quality of the decoration makes this piece desirable even when damaged.

A rare Caughley oval dessert dish, decorated with a crowned "D" within floral borders, with oval medallions painted with muses and a bird, a small rim crack.

c1795 10.25in (26cm) wide

£550-650 **WW**

CHELSEA

One of a pair of Chelsea plates, painted with an exotic bird and flowers.

c1775 *9in (23cm) diam*

£800-1,200 pair **SA**

A Chelsea basket, moulded with leaves.

c1760 *11in (28cm) long*

£1,000-1,500 **JF**

A Chelsea dish, of silver shape, painted with two birds.

c1758 *9.75in (24.5cm) long*

£1,500-2,000 **AA**

A Chelsea saucer dish, from the red anchor period.

c1755

£1,300-1,600 **JF**

A Chelsea oval dish, with a leaf moulded border, painted with fruit, leaves and insects, a brown anchor mark, some crazing and two short cracks.

c1760 *9.25in (23.5cm) diam*

£200-300 **WW**

A pair of Chelsea botanical plates, painted in coloured enamels, one with a purple blossoming spray, the other with a red berried spray, the feather moulded borders picked out in turquoise and brown, brown anchor marks.

c1760 *8.25in (21cm) diam*

£3,000-4,000 **AA**

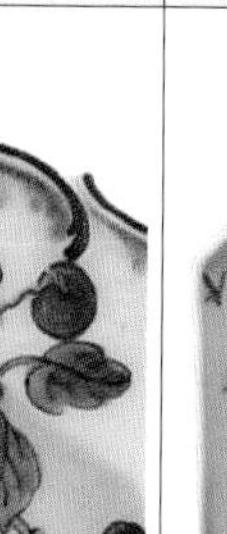

A rare Chelsea octagonal saucer, painted in the Kakiemon style with two colourful birds, one in flight and the other perched on a branch, all amidst bamboo, prunus and rockwork, unmarked, broken into several pieces and well repaired.

c1750 *5.25in (13.5cm) diam*

£350-400 **WW**

A Chelsea saucer, painted in green and black pencilling with a landscape scene, the rim and reverse with gilt dentil borders, a gold anchor mark.

c1760 *5.5in (14cm) diam*

£1,000-1,500 **WW**

One of a pair of Chelsea Derby plates.

c1775 *9in (23cm) diam*

£800-1,200 pair **SA**

A Chelsea figure of a shepherdess, with a gold anchor mark.

c1760 *5.5in (14cm) high*

£1,600-1,800 **AA**

A Chelsea figure, emblematic of autumn, with a gold anchor mark.

c1760 *7in (18cm) high*

£1,000-1,200 **AA**

From left to right -

A mid-18thC Chelsea bust of a goddess, with her waved hair tied back and one shoulder draped.

4.5in (12cm) high

£280-320 **L&T**

A Chelsea bust of Mercury, with a serpent decorated helmet and a breastplate with the head of Medusa, the plinth with a gilt pendant husk, a red anchor mark.

c1760 *5.5in (13.5cm) high*

£260-340 **L&T**

A Chelsea bust of Mercury, with a serpent decorated helmet and a breastplate painted with the head of Medusa, the plinth with a painted puce flowerhead.

c1760 *5in (13cm) high*

£260-340 **L&T**

A mid-18thC Chelsea bust of a goddess, with her dark hair tied back, yellow drapery over one shoulder, on a gilt decorated canted plinth, a red anchor mark.

4.5in (12cm) high

£260-340 **L&T**

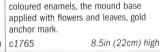

A Chelsea red anchor figure depicting autumn.

11in (28cm) high

£500-700 **L&T**

A Chelsea gold anchor Imperial shepherdess, gold-plated mark.

11in (28cm) high

£3,500-4,500 **L&T**

A pair of Chelsea gold anchor figures depicting Apollo and Celestria, Apollo with a lyre and laurel leaf in hair, red cloak and quiver with arrows, Celestria with gilt decorated skirt but lacking globe, both with painted gold anchor marks.

11in (28cm) high

£500-700 **L&T**

A Chelsea gold anchor hunter's companion, clutching a dead bird, on a rustic base decorated with flowers, with a dog by her side, a feathered hat and with a powder flask, painted gold anchor mark.

11.5in (29cm) high

£500-800 **L&T**

A Chelsea group of two Putti, amidst corn, one leaning on an upturned basket of flowers, picked out in coloured enamels, the mound base applied with flowers and leaves, gold anchor mark.

c1765 *8.5in (22cm) high*

£1,000-1,500 **AA**

A Chelsea vase, decorated with birds and foliage.

c1760 *6.5in (16.5cm) high*

£1,800-2,200 **AA**

A Chelsea vase painted with exotic birds, gold anchor mark.

c1765 *8in (20.5cm) high*

£800-1,200 **AA**

A pair of Chelsea baluster vases, painted with flower sprays and sprigs and with butterflies, unmarked, one with a small restored chip.

c1755 *8in (20cm) high*

£800-1,200 **WW**

A Chelsea red anchor period coffee cup and saucer.

c1756

£1,000-1,500 **JF**

A Chelsea chocolate cup and saucer, red anchor marks.

c1755 *Saucer 5.25in (13.5cm) diam*

£1,800-2,200 **AA**

A Chelsea box and cover, modelled as a pink rose bud, the foot with green buds, unmarked, the cover restored.

c1755 *3.5in (9cm) high*

£600-900 **WW**

A Chelsea scent bottle, in the form of a putto with bird and dog.

c1760 *3in (7.5cm) high*

£2,000-3,000 **AA**

A 'Girl in a swing' factory gilt-metal mounted bonbonnière and hinged cover.

c1750 *2in (5cm) high*

£5,500-6,500 **DN**

GIRL IN A SWING FACTORY

'Girl in a Swing' is the name attributed to a London porcelain factory, established by Charles Gouyn, which ran from 1749 to 1759 from his Bennet Street home. Gouyn was a china retailer and jeweller who specialized in making novelties such as scent bottles, small figures, étuis and bonbonnières. The name was derived from some figures attributed to his factory, which are now in London's Victoria and Albert Museum and the Boston Museum of Fine Arts.

A CLOSER LOOK AT A GIRL IN A SWING ETUI

These pocket-sized decorative cases were popular during the 18thC and 19thC. They were made to hold small, useful items such as scissors, lancets and scent bottles.

Fashionable and carefully treasured items in their day, the fine quality and compact nature of étuis make them highly collectable today. This pushes up the value.

Before it was identified, 'Girl in a Swing' porcelain was often attributed to Chelsea. Although the two factories shared a similar paste, a higher percentage of lead is evident in pieces from Gouyn's St James factory.

This piece, with its feminine floral decoration and gilt mount, is typical of the beautifully decorated novelty 'toys' produced by the 'Girl in a Swing' factory.

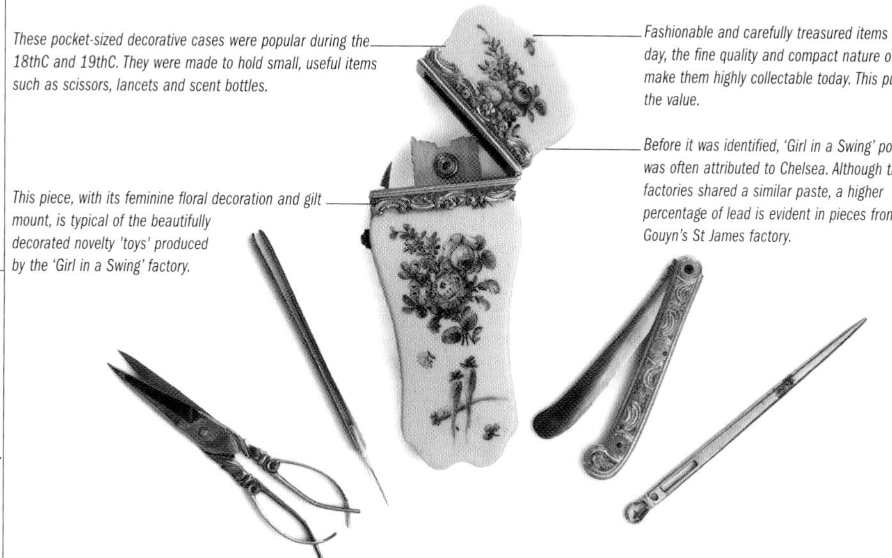

A 'Girl in a Swing' gold mounted étui, of flattened cartouche shape, finely painted in coloured enamels with sprays of European flowers and leaves, scattered flowers and three radishes, the hinged cover with flowers and 'C' scroll cast chased mounts, and a diamond catch, containing a gold mounted fruit knife, scissors, an ivory notecard, a snuff spoon or needle and pincers.

c1755 *3.75in (9.5cm) long*

£15,000-20,000 **AA**

COALPORT

A Coalport plate, decorated with flowers and gilt Greek Key design.

c1805 *8.75in (22cm) diam*

£330-380 **SA**

One of a set of six early 19thC botanical plates, possibly Coalport, each painted with the '690' pattern of different specimen flowers, within four floral ovals on the gilt blue ground of the rims, with four yellow parenthesis brackets at the edges.

8.5in (21.5cm) diam

£800-1,200 set **CHEF**

A Coalport plate, the border moulded with flowers, decorated in the Nantgarw style with flower sprays in overglaze blue, a gilt flowering trail to the border, unmarked.

c1815 *9.75in (24cm) diam*

£150-250 **WW**

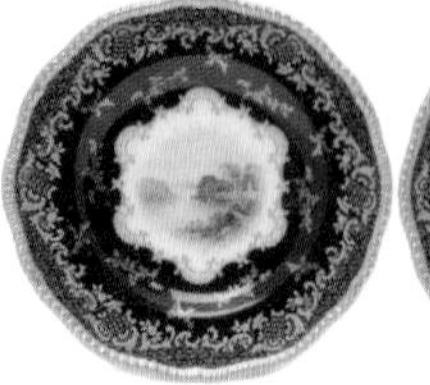

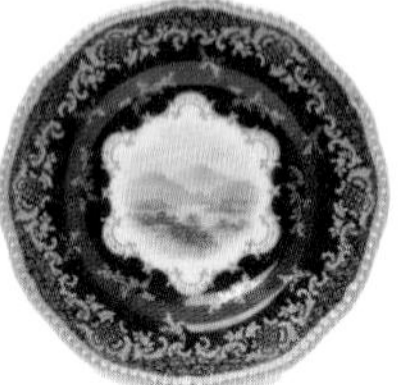

A pair of early 20thC Coalport plates, painted with lake scenes on a deep cobalt blue and gilt ground, the views titled to the reverse, printed and impressed marks.

9.25in (23.5cm) diam

£400-600 **WW**

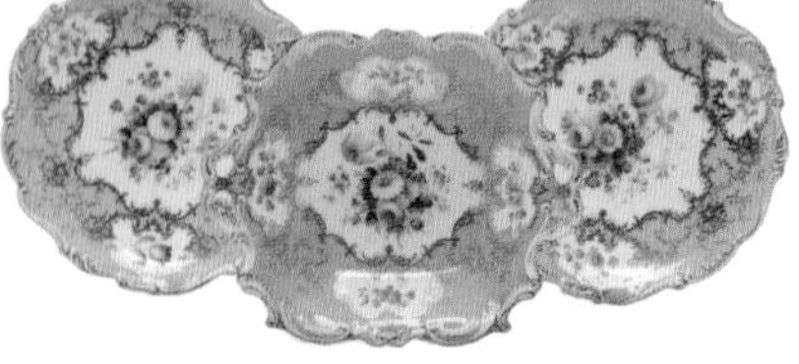

A pair of Coalport plates and a matching dish, painted with flowers, the pale grey borders decorated with gilt leaf scrolls, printed and impressed marks, signed "Howard".

c1910 *Largest 9.75in (25cm) diam*

£400-600 **WW**

A pair of Coalport dishes, painted with flowers, on a gilt decorated blue ground, printed and impressed marks, signed "Howard".

c1930 *10.25in (26cm) diam*

£200-300 **WW**

A Coalport dish, decorated with roses and gilt.

c1820 *11.75in (29cm) diam*

£200-300 **SA**

An early 19thC Coalport comport, in Sèvres style.

c1820

£700-1,000 **AD**

A Coalport 29 piece part dessert service, decorated with an Imari pattern, comprising fifteen plates, four shell-shaped dishes, four oval dishes and a pair of sauce tureens, covers and stands, rubbing and extensive damage.

c1825

£400-600 **WW**

A Coalport coffee can, decorated with floral sprigs.

c1800 *2.25in (5.5cm) high*

£50-100 **GAS**

A pair of Coalport coffee cans, decorated in blue and gold with oak leaves and acorns, unmarked.

c1810 *2.25in (5.5cm) high*

£150-200 **WW**

A Coalport coffee can, decorated with the 'Japan' pattern.

c1810 *2.25in (5.5cm) high*

£150-250 **GAS**

A Coalport coffee can, with an uncommon 'square' handle, border pattern in gold and iron red.

c1815 *2.25in (5.5cm) high*

£100-150 **GAS**

A Coalport miniature coffee can.

c1820 *1.75in (4.5cm) high*

£80-100 **GCL**

A Coalport trio set.

c1815 *5.75in (14.5cm) diam*

£220-280 **SA**

One of a pair of Coalport gold ground cups and saucers, decorated with colourful birds and flowers, registration marks for 1850.

£400-600 pair **WW**

A Coalport vase, painted in the manner of Baxter, with a classical scene of lovers in a woodland on a gilded orange ground and marbled foot, unmarked.

c1810 *8.5in (21.5cm) high*

£800-1,200 **WW**

A Coalport rococo vase, with a blue ground, painted with birds in the manner of Randall and applied with flower heads, unmarked.

c1830 *7in (18cm) high*

£150-250 **WW**

A Coalport demi-tasse cup and saucer.

3.5in (9cm) wide

£120-180 **GCL**

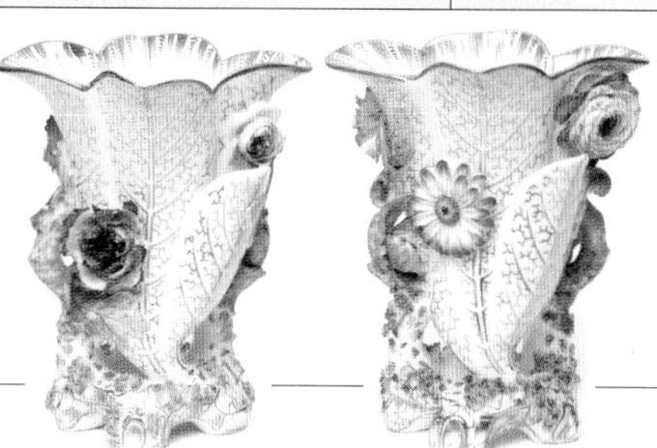

A pair of 19thC Coalport vases, modelled as flowerheads and applied with flowers, raised on rustic bases, unmarked.

6.75in (17cm) high

£200-300 **WW**

A green ground pot pourri vase, possibly Coalport, each side painted with a panel of flowers and applied with flowers, the base with a gilt pebble pattern, unmarked.

c1830 *9.5in (24cm) high*

£200-300 **WW**

A mid-19thC rococo revival vase, possibly Coalport, the gilt handles to the baluster shape modelled as leaves opening from the rim, above floral and landscape reserves on the turquoise body.

10in (25.5cm) high

£70-100 **CHEF**

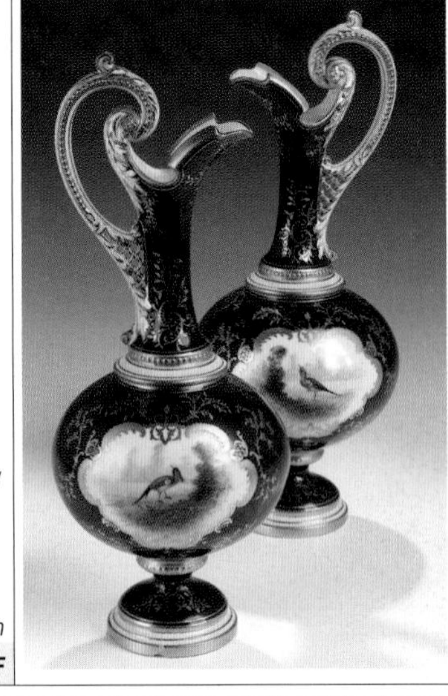

A pair of Coalport ewers, of rococo design, with beaded gilt scroll handles and pierced bracket globular bodies, the royal blue ground with gilt and pale lemon friezes, painted with cartouche panels of a peacock, opposing smaller flower spray panel, green printed mark and brown printed numbers "275" and "500073", gilt painted marks.

11in (28cm) high

£800-1,200 **L&T**

A Coalport floral encrusted blue ground basket, the interior painted with gilt scrolls and flowers, unmarked, a few small chips to the flowers.

c1835 *8.75in (22cm) wide*

£200-300 **WW**

A good pair of Coalport ice pails, covers and liners, with gilt handles and feet, richly decorated with orange and blue gilded bands, unmarked.

c1810 *11in (28cm) high*

£3,000-4,000 **WW**

A gold ground Coalport teapot and cover, decorated with blue birds and bamboo.

c1900 *8in (20cm) high*

£250-350 **WW**

A CLOSER LOOK AT A COALPORT INKWELL

The condition of this piece, even on the more vulnerable sections such as the handles, is remarkably good. Damage would reduce the value considerably.

The shapes of Coalport pieces were widely copied, but other makers struggled to achieve the high quality of decoration and fine gilding found on Coalport porcelain.

Hard-paste porcelain was used by Coalport until c1820, when bone china was introduced.

The decoration on this inkstand and the heavy use of gilt are fine examples of the rich ornate style favoured by Coalport from the 1820s.

A Coalport inkwell, with four removable wells, two marks.

c1825 *9.75in (25cm) diam*

£4,000-6,000 **JF**

A pair of Coalport fruit coolers, with covers and liners, decorated with nasturtium, tulip and sweetpea flowers.

c1825

£800-1,200 **JF**

A Coalport teapot and cover, painted with panels on a green and cream ground, decorated with gilt scrolls and simulated jewels.

c1900 *6.75in (17cm) high*

£550-650 **WW**

DERBY

When the Derby factory opened in c1750 it became known for its finely modelled figures that are classified as 'dry-edge' due to the glaze free area around the base. Later Derby was popular for its cabinet wares, such as cups or cans and saucers. Initially a glassy type of porcelain was used by the factory until bone ash was later added to the mixture. The new soft-paste substance had a delightfully smooth, subtle texture, unlike any other English porcelain. A beautiful bright blue was introduced on the edges of tea-services, whilst the ground is generally plain.

Printing on Derby was introduced in c1764. Flower prints were accurately copied onto dessert services. The superior fineness of Derby is expressed by the decoration used, including best quality gilding, fine botanical studies, birds, landscapes and Japanese Imari patterns. Chinese and Japanese designs were brought together in an English way to suit the tastes of the time.

Derby figures followed the Meissen style and were rich in colouring, including the use of deep blue and gold. During a 'transitional' phase (c1755-56) the glaze became whiter and was decorated in distinctive, rather delicate enamels, which have earned figure groups of this period the title "Pale Family". Derby figures of the 1750s and 1760s are very rococo in style, standing on wide, scrolled bases.

A Derby model of Winter, modelled as a woman warming her hands above a brazier, unmarked.

c1760 *4.75in (12cm) high*

£700-1,000 **WW**

A CLOSER LOOK AT A PAIR OF DERBY FIGURES

The Derby factory was known for the high standard of its figures. Earthenware copies of Derby figures were made by a number of other factories including Staffordshire. Today, Derby figures are thought to be among the finest produced in England.

Despite using soft-paste porcelain, Derby figures are so finely modelled that the details remain crisp. This pair have been especially well realized and are in excellent condition.

Later figures can be distinguished from 18thC ones like these by the use of heavy gilding and taller scrolled bases.

As well as shepherds and shepherdesses, Derby subjects included blackamoors and actors of the period.

A pair of Derby figures of a shepherd and shepherdess.

c1755 *9.25in (23.5cm) high*

£5,000-7,000 **AA**

A Derby 'Harvester' figure, some restoration to top and chips to hat.

c1765 *7.25in (18.5cm) high*

£550-650 **SA**

A pair of Derby models of the Welsh tailor and his wife, after Meissen, each riding a goat, the tailor carrying kid goats in a basket, his wife with three children, each raised on a base applied with flowers and leaves, minor repairs.

c1765 *10.5in (27cm) high*

£2,800-3,200 **WW**

A Derby model of Neptune, standing beside a dolphin, raised upon a base of shells and coral, the dolphin's tail lacking and a factory fault where one arm is missing.

c1765 *9.25in (23.5cm) high*

£200-300 **WW**

A Derby figure of girl holding a basket of grapes, gilt highlights, minor chips.

c1770 *8.5in (21.5cm) high*

£800-1,200 **SA**

A pair of Derby figures, 'French Shepherd and Shepherdess'.

c1775 *7in (18cm) high*

£500-700 **GCL**

A Derby 'Gardener' figure, with gilt highlights.

c1775 *5in (13cm) high*

£220-280 **SA**

A large Derby group of two figures.

c1780 *13.5in (34cm) high*

£1,500-2,000 **AA**

An unusual Derby group, of a couple dancing arm in arm.

c1780 *5.75in (14.5cm) high*

£1,000-1,200 **AA**

A pair of Derby models of the Mansion House dwarves, one with a tall conical hat the other with a wide brimmed hat inscribed "A sale by auction ...", each richly gilded and enamelled and standing on rocky bases, "N227" incised, minor faults.

c1800 *6.25in (16cm) high*

£1,800-2,200 **WW**

A mid-to late 19thC pair of Royal Crown Derby figures, of a young man and woman decorated with pale colours and standing on green bases, printed factory marks.

13.75in (35cm) high

£500-600 **WW**

A Derby figure of Leda and the Swan, with a green cloak and a flowered dress, an arm around the swan's neck, on a tall reed-decorated plinth.

11.5in (29.5cm) high

£1,800-2,200 **L&T**

A Derby figure of Europa and the bull, with an orange flowered dress and a jade coloured sash, the bull with garlands of flowers, on a scroll plinth.

11in (28cm) high

£1,800-2,200 **L&T**

A Derby porcelain figure of Britannia, with a sword and a horn, a bocage back and a naturalistic base.

14.5in (36cm) high

£500-700 **L&T**

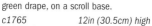

A Derby figure of Justice, the female figure holding scales and a sword, clothed in a floral painted dress and a green drape, on a scroll base.

c1765 *12in (30.5cm) high*

£250-350 **GORL**

A Derby model of Falstaff, with a deep purple jacket and a floral painted waistcoat, brandishing a gilt sword and a shield, on a naturalistic plinth and scroll base.

8in (20cm) high

£120-180 **L&T**

A Derby Pale Family Shepherd, with a pale pink hat and gown, carrying a basket of fruit, with a dog at his feet.

10.5in (27cm) high

£450-550 **L&T**

A pair of porcelain figures, in the style of Derby, of amorini with baskets.

5.5in (14cm) high

£80-120 **CLV**

A pair of Derby birds, on bases decorated with flowers.

c1760 *3.75in (9.5cm) high*

£1,200-1,600 **AA**

A Derby model of a goldfinch, perched on a flower-encrusted base, painted with coloured enamels, some chips and losses.

c1765 *3.25in (8.5cm) high*

£80-100 **DN**

A Derby heart-shaped dish, painted in 'Dodson' style with birds.

c1820 *10in (25.5cm) long*

£650-750 **AA**

A Derby dish, formed as a leaf overlapping a basket, painted with insects and a cherry spray, unmarked, slight wear to rim.

c1760 *10in (25.5cm) long*

£600-900 **WW**

A pair of Derby dishes, painted with butterflies.

c1825 *7in (18cm) long*

£800-1,200 **AA**

A late 19thC Crown Derby large porcelain platter, painted in the Imari style, iron-red painted crowned "D" under crossed baton mark, incised "20".

20.5in (52cm) long

£250-350 **S&K**

A Derby plate from the Duesbury & Kean period.

c1800

£1,800-2,200 **JF**

A Derby botanical plate with a spiral fluted rim, the centre with a flowering blue Gentian, the border with a band of gilt leaves and bell flowers, pattern number 115, the reverse inscribed in blue "Gentiana Acaulis, large-flower'd Gentian" and with blue printed mark.

c1800 *9.25in (23.5cm) diam*

£500-700 **WW**

A Derby plate, painted in 'Dodson' style with birds.

c1820 *8.75in (22cm) diam*

£600-800 **AA**

An early 19thC Bloor Derby part dessert service, each piece painted in the Imari palette with central flowers about a plum tree within swag and palmette border, comprising twelve plates and three dishes.

£500-600 **CHEF**

A Derby, Sampson Hancock small pale-green ground octagonal bowl, painted with floral sprays, iron-red script marks.

c1860 *5in (12.5cm) high*

£60-90 **DN**

A Derby rectangular tray, with a pierced rim, painted with a view of Haddon Hall, Derbyshire, titled to the reverse, with a red painted mark, some restoration.

c1830 *9.5in (24cm) wide*

£250-350 **WW**

A large Derby vase, painted in 'Dodson' style with birds.

c1820 *13.25in (33.5cm) high*

£3,500-4,500 **AA**

A Derby two-handled urn-shaped vase, painted with a panel of colourful birds on a gilt decorated blue ground, red circular Bloor mark, very slight gilt wear.

c1825 *11.5in (29cm) high*

£500-700 **WW**

A large Derby twin handled urn and cover, with a gilt flowerhead finial over a domed lid, with a lappet cast frieze, painted with roses, tulips, poppies in polychrome enamels, the base with ornate ram's head and cornucopiae cast handles and cavetto frieze with gilt anthemion type decoration, over a densely painted frieze of spring and summer flowers, on a gadrooned beaded base, with a square plinth, rust painted mark.

c1810 *15.25in (38cm) high*

£1,400-1,600 **L&T**

An urn and cover, attributed to Derby, painted on one side with a basket of pink roses and other flowers, on a gilt royal blue ground, the gilt handles with lion mask terminals, the socle on square foot.

c1820 *11.5in (29cm) high*

£400-600 **CHEF**

One of a pair of mid-19thC Bloor Derby urn-style fruit coolers, painted with flower sprays.

£1,000-1,500 pair **FRE**

One of a pair of Derby ice pails and covers, with cipher of Philadelphia.

Provenance: These pails were in Derby museum. The granddaughter of William Penn, Hannah Cremone, married Viscount Cremone, a wealthy Irish banker who moved to England from Philadelphia.

9in (23cm) high

£5,000-7,000 pair JF

A Derby oval sugar bowl and cover, with ring handles, decorated with pattern number 333, pink painted and impressed marks.

c1795 *6.25in (16cm) wide*

£400-600 WW

A Derby nightlight, with integral stand, painted by Daniel Lucas.

c1825 *6in (15.5cm) high*

£1,500-1,800 JF

A Derby 'Near Lincoln' coffee can.

c1815 *2.5in (6.5cm) high*

£220-280 SA

A Derby coffee can, with a wishbone handle, polychrome floral decoration.

c1810 *2.5in (6.5cm) high*

£70-90 GAS

A Derby porter mug, with an angled handle and decorated with pink, purple, blue and gilt scrolling foliage, red crowned crossed-batons mark.

c1820 *4.5in (11.5cm) high*

£200-300 WW

A Derby coffee can.

c1825 *2.5in (6.5cm) high*

£80-120 SA

A Derby trio with puce marks.

c1790 *5.5in (14cm) diam*

£220-280 SA

A Royal Crown Derby teapot and cover, decorated with an Imari pattern.

c1887 *10in (25.5cm) high*

£150-250 WW

A Derby cup and saucer.

c1790 *5.5in (14cm) diam*

£250-300 SA

A Derby teapot and stand.

c1815 *11in (28cm) wide*

£320-360 SA

A late 19thC Derby King Street teapot and cover, with a matching milk jug and sugar bowl, decorated with Imari-style patterns.

8.5in (21.5cm) high

£300-400 WW

A Derby milk jug, with a fluted body and a loop handle painted with three coloured flower sprays, a brown line rim, unmarked.

c1760 *4in (10cm) high*

£400-600 **WW**

A Derby ribbed, bucket-shaped cream jug with a wishbone handle, pattern number 68, puce mark.

c1785 *3in (7.5cm) high*

£100-200 **GAS**

A Derby oval sauceboat, with an 'S' scroll handle, painted in purple monochrome with birds and flowering branches, within 'C' scroll moulded cartouches, beneath a gadrooned brown line rim.

c1758 *7.5in (19cm) wide*

£1,500-2,000 **AA**

A CLOSER LOOK AT A DERBY DESK SET

This piece would have been made for the high end of the market. The Derby factory concentrated on producing expensive, fine quality, highly decorative display wares.

George Robertson was one of a group of talented landscape artists employed by the factory during the period. A named and known designer makes this piece desirable.

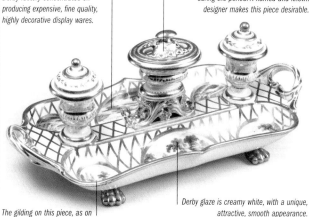

The gilding on this piece, as on other Derby ware, is of very high quality.

Derby glaze is creamy white, with a unique, attractive, smooth appearance. This makes Derby popular today.

A Derby desk set, decorated with topographical views, untitled, but probably by George Robertson.

c1820

£3,500-5,500 **JF**

A composite and extensive Derby tea and coffee set, painted in the Imari palette, with rust painted and Bloor printed circular marks, comprising 12 tea cups, eight coffee cans, 13 saucers, milk jug, slop bowl, twin handled sucrier and cover and a circular bread plate.

£350-450 **L&T**

A Derby blue and white sweetmeat dish, of triple shell form.

c1765 *6.5in (16.5cm) diam*

£2,000-3,000 **JF**

A Derby asparagus tray.

c1765

£300-500 **JF**

DRESDEN

Several porcelain factories, copying and imitating the successful styles of Meissen, operated in and around Dresden in the 19thC. In many cases, the quality of the paste and decoration used by these factories is considered to be lower in quality than the wares they copied. The factories produced a wide range of vases, centrepieces, candlesticks and figures dressed in 18thC costume. Pieces tended to be of the popular Rococo Revival style, ornately decorated with elaborate shells, flowers, scrollwork and figures. On some pieces, real lace was dipped into porcelain and fired to create a distinctive decorative lacework.

One of the most important and productive of the Dresden factories was opened in 1872 by Carl Thieme at Potschappel. Many decorating workshops also opened in the area, such as Donath & Co., Richard Klemm, Oswald Lorenz and Adolph Hammann. Many Dresden pieces are unmarked, although some factories marked their wares with Meissen crossed swords.

A late 19thC Dresden porcelain punch bowl and cover, painted with Watteauesque scenes within ozier moulded borders, the cover surmounted with a bacchic putto, Berlin-type sceptre mark.

10.5in (26.5cm) diam

£400-600 **DN**

A Dresden table centrepiece, in the form of three putti, around a flower applied column supporting a pierced oval basket, painted and applied with flowers and leaves, on a mound base, mark in blue.

16.75in (42.5cm) high

£400-600 LFA

A pair of Dresden salt cellars, each in the form of a putto kneeling beside a shell, the interior painted with a river landscape, the shell and scroll moulded base picked out in puce, marks in blue.

5.5in (14cm) wide

£180-220 LFA

A late 19thC pair of Dresden quatrefoil section two-handled jardinières, with pink grounds, painted with alternate panels of Watteauesque scenes and sprays of flowers, on four scroll feet, Berlin-type marks and one with a Dresden decorator's mark, rivet repaired feet to one.

14.5in (37cm) wide

£1,200-1,800 DN

One of a pair of Dresden flared round jardinières, each with two scroll handles and brightly painted in coloured enamels with birds, flowers and insects.

c1880 *4in (10cm) high*

£150-200 pair LFA

Three of a set of five Dresden pierced dessert plates, painted with floral decoration, the arched borders enriched in gilding, damage.

9in (22.5cm) diam

£220-280 set GORL

LIVERPOOL

A Gilbody's factory porcelain bowl, moulded with flowerheads and scrolls and painted with figures and leaping deer, a rim chip and associated crack.

c1765 *4.75in (12cm) diam*

£450-500 WW

A Chaffers Liverpool blue and white bowl, painted with two figures and a pagoda beside rocky islands, a hatched inner rim.

c1765 *6.25in (16cm) wide*

£280-330 WW

A Chaffers Liverpool 'Jumping Boy' pattern bowl, in blue and white.

c1758 *6in (15cm) diam*

£1,500-2,000 AA

A Chaffers Liverpool 'Jumping Boy' pattern small bowl, moulded with flutes, broken and re-glued.

c1760 *4in (10cm) diam*

£300-400 WW

A Chaffers Liverpool 'Jumping Boy' pattern small plate.

c1758 *5in (12.5cm) diam*

£1,800-2,200 AA

A Chaffers Liverpool coffee can, painted with colourful flower sprays over the bluish green glaze.

c1755 *2.5in (6.5cm) high*

£700-1,000 WW

A Chaffers Liverpool milk jug, painted in blue, iron red and gilt with a man fishing on an island, a tiny restored chip to the spout.

c1760 *3.25in (8cm) high*

£350-400 WW

A Chaffers Liverpool teapot and cover, painted in the famille rose style with peonies and magnolia, small chips to the spout, the cover restored.

c1765 *7.25in (18.5cm) high*

£180-220 **WW**

A rare William Reid Liverpool globular teapot and cover, each side painted in polychrome enamels with a Chinaman at a table, some damage.

c1755 *6.75in (17cm) high*

£800-1,000 **WW**

A rare Pennington's Liverpool teapot and cover, decorated in the atelier of James Giles, with panels of flowers on a blue ground with gilt leaf fronds.

c1770 *8in (20.5cm) high*

£450-500 **WW**

An early 19thC Liverpool large baluster jug, with a loop handle, the flower sprig border above a shield cartouche panel with a monogram, dated 1806.

11in (28cm) high

£500-700 **L&T**

A Pennington's Liverpool high Chelsea ewer, decorated in enamels and underglaze blue with deer in a landscape, the enamels probably added later, a hairline crack and small rim chips.

c1770 *3.5in (9cm) high*

£150-200 **WW**

A Liverpool coffee cup, by Philip Christian, polychrome floral pattern.

c1770 *2.5in (6.5cm) high*

£250-350 **GAS**

LONGTON HALL

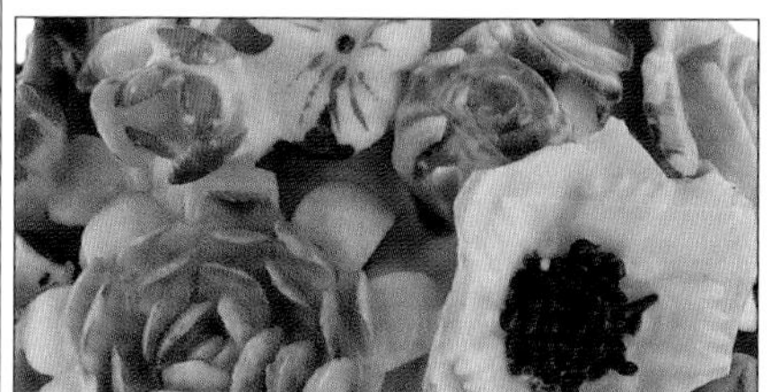

A rare Longton Hall pot pourri vase and cover, formed as a vase of flowers, the rococo vase moulded and painted with colourful butterflies, an insect and flowers, small chips to the flowers, repairs.

c1755 *6.25in (16cm) high*

£600-800 **WW**

One of a pair of rare Longton Hall pugs.

c1755 *3.5in (9cm) high*

£8,000-12,000 pair **AA**

A Longton Hall leaf moulded cup and saucer, with overlapping leaves, painted to the interior by the 'Trembly Rose' painter with a spray of flowers.

c1755 *Saucer 5in (13cm) diam*

£1,800-2,200 **AA**

LOWESTOFT

A Lowestoft globular teapot and cover, painted in polychrome with flowers, a long body crack.

c1770 *7in (17.5cm) long*

£150-200 **WW**

A Lowestoft teapot and cover, painted in blue, iron red and green with flowers and foliage, a buttercup knop, painted crescent mark, restoration to cover.

c1780 *7.5in (19.5cm) high*

£400-500 **WW**

A Lowestoft teapot and cover, painted in blue, iron red and gilt with a Chinese watery landscapes, a flower knop, crescent mark, the knop and the rim to the cover restored.

c1780 *7.5in (19cm) long*

£250-350 **WW**

A Lowestoft blue and white large teapot and cover, painted with pavilions and gardens on islands with sailing boats between.

c1765 *7.75in (20cm) high*

£700-900 **CHEF**

A rare Lowestoft silver-shaped teapot and cover, painted in pink and gilt with flower sprigs and sprays, unmarked, body cracks.

c1790 *10.25in (26cm) wide*

£1,500-2,000 **WW**

A Lowestoft blue and white part tea service, printed with a version of the 'Fence' pattern, comprising a globular teapot and cover, a sparrow-beak hot water jug and cover and a sugar bowl and cover, each with a hatched crescent mark, finial of the jug restored.

c1780 *8.5in (21.5cm) wide*

£1,200-1,800 **DN**

A miniature Lowestoft blue and white teapot and cover, painted with sailing boats in a Chinese pagoda landscape, a painter's mark inside the foot rim, two small chips to the cover and a tiny restored chip to the spout.

c1765 *3in (7.5cm) high*

£1,200-1,800 **WW**

A Lowestoft blue and white baluster coffee pot and domed cover, printed with a version of the 'Fence' pattern, the cover with floriform finial, some minute chips and areas of wear.

c1785 *11.5in (29cm) high*

£800-1,200 **DN**

An 18thC Lowestoft polychrome coffee pot and cover, the baluster sides painted with sprigs and sprays of flowers, the rims and cover finial picked out in iron red.

c1775 *8.25in (21cm) high*

£250-350 **CHEF**

A Lowestoft saucer, painted with peony, bamboo, rockwork and a fence, unmarked.

c1770 *4.75in (12cm) diam*

£150-200 **WW**

A rare Lowestoft trio, with shaped moulded borders and decorated in pink and gold with bands of flowers and leaf sprigs, unmarked, slight wear to the gilding.

c1790

£800-1,200 **WW**

A Lowestoft jug, decorated with flowers.

c1780 *4in (10cm) high*

£400-600 **SA**

A Lowestoft creamboat, of low Chelsea ewer form, with a loop handle, painted in underglaze blue with flowers, leaves and insects, beneath a blue line rim.

c1780 *3.75in (9.5cm) long*

£400-600 **LFA**

A Lowestoft blue and white mug, a "5" mark inside the foot rim.

c1770 *3.5in (9cm) high*

£1,000-1,500 **WW**

An 18thC Lowestoft blue and white butter shell.

c1775 *4.5in (11.5cm) wide*

£350-400 **CHEF**

An English porcelain white glazed model of a seated pug dog, probably Lowestoft, sitting on a chamfered rectangular base, restoration to tail.

£1,500-2,000 **WW**

MEISSEN

A Meissen figure of a woodcutter, by J.J. Kändler, with a crossed swords mark in underglaze blue, restored.

c1740 *5.25in (13cm) high*

£2,200-2,800 **GORL**

A Meissen figure in Oriental dress, with a crossed swords mark in underglaze blue, restored hat and face.

c1745 *5in (12.5cm) high*

£1,000-1,500 **GORL**

A CLOSER LOOK AT A MEISSEN HARLEQUIN

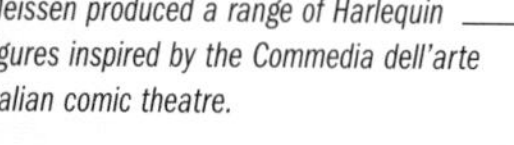

Meissen produced a range of Harlequin figures inspired by the Commedia dell'arte Italian comic theatre.

This figure was made by Johann Joachim Kändler. Made chief modeller from 1733, Kändler was responsible for some of the finest Meissen figures ever made.

This informal figure is full of character and movement, features which typify the extensive range of figures produced in Kändler's time.

The bright colours on the body and the rockwork base show that this is an early piece. Later Meissen figures tended to have softer colours and scrollwork bases.

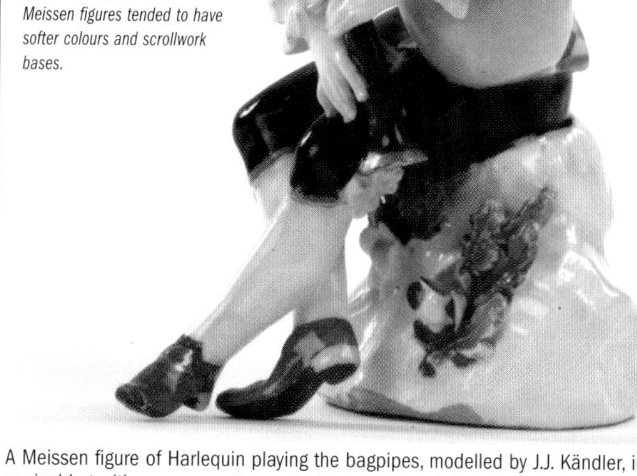

A Meissen figure of Harlequin playing the bagpipes, modelled by J.J. Kändler, in a conical hat with a puce rosette, seated on a rock-work base applied with flowering foliage, impressed "OD45", repair to his hat and top of pipe.

c1740 *5in (12.5cm) high*

£2,500-3,500 **GORL**

A white glazed Meissen model of a hurdy gurdy player, as an old man seated on a grassy mound, crossed swords and "33" impressed, some chips.

c1745 *5.75in (14.5cm) high*

£500-700 **WW**

A Meissen allegorical figure of a classical maiden, probably emblematic of peace and probably modelled by F. Meyer, faint traces of mark, small chips and losses.

c1745 *4.75in (12cm) high*

£450-550 **DN**

A Meissen figure of an old peasant woman, modelled by J.J. Kändler, handle of the basket repaired.

c1750 *7.25in (18cm) high*

£1,200-1,800 **GORL**

A Meissen monkey band drummer, a crossed swords mark to the back of the base, chips to the extremities.

c1760 *5.5in (14cm) high*

£1,000-1,500 **WW**

A Meissen figure of a 'Lemonade Seller' from the 'Cris de Paris', modelled by Kändler and Reinicke, crossed swords mark in underglaze blue, some restoration.

c1755 *6.75in (16.5cm) high*

£1,800-2,200 **GORL**

A Meissen figure of a shepherdess with an apron of flowers, a blue crossed sword mark, minor repairs, chips.

c1755 *6.5in (16cm) high*

£500-700 **GORL**

A Meissen miniature figure of a lady holding a basket of flowers, a blue crossed swords mark to back.

c1755 *3.75in (9cm) high*

£500-700 **GORL**

A Meissen figure of a fisherman, a crossed sword mark in blue, one hand, brim of hat and fishing net restored.

c1760 *6.5in (16cm) high*

£1,500-1,800 **GORL**

A 19thC large Meissen classical marriage group, made in sections with Cupid and the bride and groom around a plinth holding torches, while a maiden reclines holding a cornucopia, the plinth inscribed "Thalasio, Thalasio" in gilt, crossed swords marks to each section.

The words 'Thalasio, Thalasio' formed part of the Roman marriage rite.

12.5in (31.5cm) high

£3,200-3,800 **WW**

A 19thC Meissen figure of a young girl playing a cello, a crossed swords mark.

5in (13cm) high

£250-350 **CHEF**

A pair of Meissen table salts, each in the form of two children holding aloft a flower painted shell, decorated in coloured enamels, the pierced scroll moulded bases picked out in gilt, marks in blue and incised "2926" and "2963", minor restoration.

c1870 *5.75in (14.5cm) high*

£300-350 **LFA**

A mid-to late 19thC pair of Meissen candelabra, one modelled with a father and child collecting eggs, the other with a mother and child picking apples, crossed swords marks and "1160" and "1153" incised, minor damage.

9.25in (23.5cm) high

£700-900 **WW**

A Meissen figure of a young woman, standing, carrying a basket of flowers, and decorated in coloured enamels, beside an ovoid vase of flowers, the scroll moulded base picked out in gilt, cancelled mark in blue, incised "C 68".

c1870 *7.5in (19cm) high*

£220-280 **LFA**

A Meissen group depicting 'Europa and the Bull'.

c1880 *8.75in (22cm) high*

£1,200-1,400 **GCL**

A pair of late 19thC Meissen portrait busts of a boy and girl, each wearing a scarf, encrusted foliage to their sides, on gilded scroll bases, crossed swords marks and incised numeral "2744".

9.25in (23.5cm) high

£700-900 **GORL**

A 19thC Meissen figure representing winter, the grey bearded man standing by a brazier loosely draped in a mauve fur lined cloak, crossed swords mark.

8in (20.5cm) high

£250-350 **CHEF**

A 19thC Meissen group of child apple gatherers, one youth at the top of a ladder throwing apples to a girl with an outstretched apron, on an oval base, chips to branches, one youth with a missing foot, blue crossed swords mark impressed "1898".

10.5in (26cm) high

£600-800 **GORL**

A late 19thC Meissen figure of a rustic maiden, modelled filling a barrel with a funnel and jug, the barrel resting on a tree trunk, the girl wearing rustic dress, blue crossed swords mark, incised "F.80" and Pressnummern, minute chip to hat.

6.75in (17cm) high

£800-1,200 **DN**

A late 19thC Meissen figure of a young girl, modelled standing holding a doll, on a rocaille base, painted in a pale palette and gilt, blue crossed swords mark, incised numerals and Pressnummern, small chips, repairs and losses.

£1,000-1,200 **DN**

A late 19thC Meissen group emblematic of 'Taste' from a series of the 'Senses', modelled as a seated woman beside a table laid with food and a bottle of wine, on a shaped rectangular base, painted in a pale palette and gilt, blue crossed swords mark, incised numerals and Pressnummern, some minute chips.

5in (13cm) high

£1,000-1,300 **DN**

A late 19thC Meissen group of apple gatherers, modelled as a child on a ladder passing fruit to two children below, painted in blue and gilt, blue crossed swords, incised numerals and Pressnummern, small chips and losses.

10.25in (26cm) high

£700-900 **DN**

A late 19thC to early 20thC Meissen porcelain figure of 'The Chocolate Lady', incised "T.5." impressed "3".

7.25in (18.5cm) high

£500-700 **S&K**

A late 19th to early 20thC Meissen-style porcelain figure group of the Seasons, modelled standing and sitting, on a gilt-enriched rocaille mound base, bearing blue crossed swords mark.

6in (15cm) high

£1,000-1,200 **S&K**

A pair of 20thC German porcelain figures of a lady and a gentleman, the lady depicted collecting flowers in her skirt and the gentleman carrying a basket, pseudo Meissen marks.

22in (56cm) high

£1,800-2,200 **S&K**

A Meissen figure of a lady, wearing an elaborate headdress and a feather muff, on a scroll-moulded base, crossed swords mark and incised numeral "D60".

8.25in (21cm) high

£180-220 **GORL**

A German porcelain group of six figures, gardening on a mound, in Meissen style, each decorated in coloured enamels, the flower-applied, drum-shaped base with a gilt roundel and patera band.

9in (23cm) high

£300-500 **LFA**

A matched pair of 19thC Meissen figures of swans, each modelled as a mother with two cygnets, on a circular bulrush base, underglaze blue mark, incised number mark.

c1850 5.25in (13cm) high

£650-750 **L&T**

A Meissen figure of a recumbent tiger, an underglaze blue sword mark.

c1915 10.25in (26cm) long

£400-600 **QU**

One of a pair of Meissen models of quail, each naturalistically decorated in coloured enamels, on a mound base, marks in blue and impressed numerals.

3.5in (9cm) high

£400-600 pair **LFA**

A late 19th to early 20thC large Meissen model of a dove, perched on a grassy mound, crossed swords mark and incised and impressed numbers.

12.5in (32cm) long

£650-850 **WW**

A fine pair of early Meissen gold Chinese teabowls and saucers finely decorated at Augsburg by Bartolomeus Seuter with birds flying above large chinoiserie vignettes, with tall palm trees, one saucer cracked, small chip.

c1725

£1,800-2,200 **GORL**

A pair of Meissen teacups, probably painted by Metzsch, with chinoiserie figures, with Bottger lustre laub-und-bandelwerk and Indianische Blumen, blue crossed swords mark, impressed "2" and gilt "H".

Laub-und-bandelwerk refers to intwined foliate bands.

c1730

£500-700 **GORL**

A pair of Meissen white teabowls and saucers moulded with bands of stiff leaves, blue crossed swords marks, minor chips to saucers.

c1735

£800-1,200 **GORL**

A Meissen octagonal two-handled cup and saucer painted with the quail pattern, with chocolate rims, blue enamel crossed sword marks, minor chip to saucer.

c1738

£700-1,000 **GORL**

A Meissen cup and saucer decorated with panels of battle scenes in purple camaieu within elaborate gilt scrollwork borders, crossed swords in underglaze blue, gilder's marks.

c1740

£800-1,200 **GORL**

A Meissen yellow-ground teabowl painted with merchants in river landscapes within shaped quatrefoil cartouches, the saucer similarly decorated within puce and iron-red laub-und-bandelwerk cartouches, blue crossed swords marks and gilt "27" marks.

c1740

£800-1,200 **GORL**

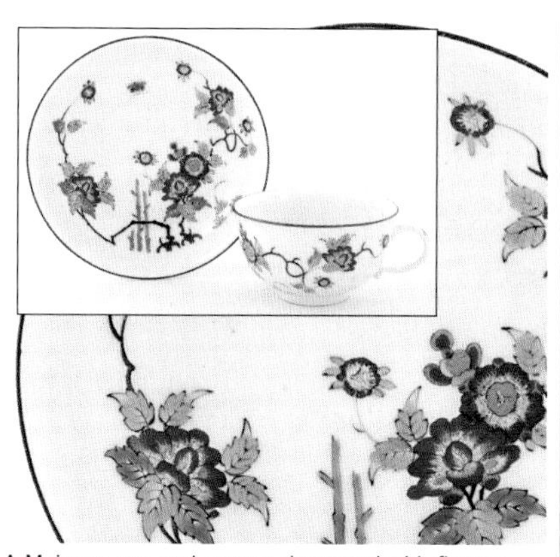

A Meissen cup and saucer, decorated with flowers.

c1740 *5in (13cm) diam*

£1,200-1,600 **SA**

A Meissen teacup and saucer, with a loop handle, painted in purple monochrome with figures shooting ducks or hunting boar in wooded landscapes, above gilt 'C' scroll bands, entwined with flowers and fruits in coloured enamels, gilt line borders, painted marks in blue, impressed numerals and painted initial "A" in purple, tiny rim nick to cup, small rim nick to saucer.

c1750

£300-500 **LFA**

An 18thC Meissen cup and saucer painted after Rugendas, with a battle scene and martial trophies with gilt dentil rims, the cup with blue crossed swords and dot mark, the saucer with blue crossed swords mark and Pressnummer "2".

£800-1,200 **GORL**

A Meissen two-handled beaker and saucer painted en camaieu rose with lovers in a landscape, vignettes divided by branches of moulded prunus, the handles enriched in gilding, a blue crossed swords mark, Pressnummer "2".

c1760

£550-650 **GORL**

A Meissen teacup and saucer painted en camaieu rose with a hound guarding dead game and two deer in a wooded landscape vignette, within a puce chequer-pattern border edged with gilt 'C' scrolls, crossed swords and a dot mark.

c1765

£350-450 **GORL**

A Meissen teacup and saucer painted with flower-sprays within a Dulong pattern border, the cup marked with blue crossed swords and a dot, the saucer marked with blue crossed swords and a star.

c1775

£220-280 **GORL**

Two Meissen miniature teacups and saucers, one printed in coloured enamels with harbour scenes within gilt cartouches on a yellow ground, with marks in blue, the other similarly decorated on a blue ground with blue cancelled marks.

c1880 *2.5in (6.5cm) diam*

£280-320 **LFA**

An early Meissen Hausemalerei circular bowl painted probably in Dresden with two panels of peasant figures in landscapes, within a gilt and iron-red laub-und-bandelwerk cartouche enriched with Bottger lustre, the interior similarly painted in iron-red, restored.

c1725 *5.25in (13cm) wide*

£800-1,200 **GORL**

A Meissen cup, cover and stand, with a loop handle and flower knop, painted in coloured enamels with flowers, fruits and leaves, within gilt scroll and puce scale borders, cancelled marks in blue.

4.25in (11cm) high

£400-600 **LFA**

A Meissen fluted tea bowl, painted in coloured enamels with fruit, a nut and insects, the basket moulded border with gilt line rim, painted mark in blue.

c1750 *3in (7.5cm) diam*

£300-400 **LFA**

A Meissen saucer, painted with figures and a horse in a landscape within a shaped quatrefoil iron-red, puce and gold laub-und-bandelwerk cartouche, rim chips, blue crossed swords mark, gilder's mark.

c1740

£270-300 **GORL**

A Meissen blue and white plate decorated in colours and gilt with Indianische Blumen, blue crossed swords and star marks and impressed "12", chip to foot ring.

c1740 *9.25in (23cm) diam*

£220-280 **GORL**

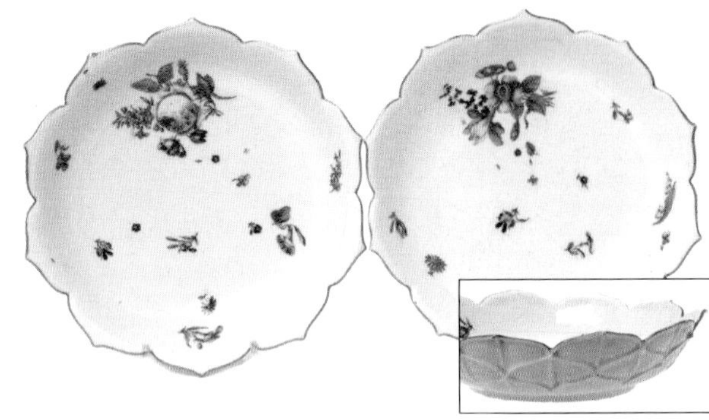

A pair of Meissen dishes, moulded as lotus flowerheads, the interiors painted with Deutsche Blumen, the rims gilded, crossed swords marks and "21" impressed.

c1750 *9.75in (25cm) wide*

£1,200-1,800 **WW**

An 18thC Meissen plate in white, the moulded rim pierced with 'Ausgeschnittenem' pattern of a trellis alternating with flowering branches, crossed swords mark in underglaze blue.

9.25in (23cm) diam

£180-220 **GORL**

A pair of Meissen Marcolini plates, each painted in coloured enamels with fruits and leaves, the border with flower garlands, suspended from blue ribbon ties, gilt line border, marks in blue.

c1780 *9in (23cm) diam*

£400-600 **LFA**

A pair of Meissen Marcolini deep plates, each boldly painted in coloured enamels with birds in trees, and scattered insects, within gilt leaf scroll borders, marks in blue, one with small rim chip.

c1780 *9in (23cm) diam*

£280-320 **LFA**

A Meissen plate, decorated in coloured enamels with exotic birds in a landscape, the pierced basketwork border painted with birds, within gilt scroll cartouches, mark in blue.

9.5in (24cm) diam

£100-150 **LFA**

A Meissen Marcolini shaped oval two-handled tureen stand, painted with a jay, a bullfinch and a blue tit within landscape vignettes, the foliage moulded handles enriched in gilding, with a blue crossed swords and star mark, some heavy staining and repair to one handle.

c1780 *24in (60cm) wide*

£1,000-1,300 **GORL**

A mid-18thC Meissen teapot and cover, with ozier moulded borders and painted with figures in gilt-edged panels and with scattered flowers, crossed swords mark, the handle re-glued.

7in (18cm) long

£750-850 **WW**

A Meissen Marcolini shaped oval spoon tray painted in puce, iron-red and gilt with Indianische Blumen below a gilt rim, with a blue crossed swords and star mark.

c1785 *6.75in (17cm) wide*

£180-220 **GORL**

A Meissen Hausmalerei globular teapot and cover with a pine cone finial, angular handle and faceted spout, painted by Mayer von Pressnitz with figures by a table within a classical landscape, above a band of stiff leaves, with gilt calligraphy to the borders, the spout with a silver mount, blue crossed swords mark.

c1745 *5.25in (13cm) wide*

£800-1,200 **GORL**

A Meissen lobed melon-shaped teapot and cover with a wishbone handle, fruit knop and mask spout, painted in coloured enamels with European flowers and leaves, alternating with moulded sprays of flowers, within gilt borders, mark in blue and gilder's numeral "3", cracked.

c1750 *5.25in (13.5cm) high*

£180-220 **LFA**

A Meissen globular teapot and cover with a rosebud finial, a branch handle and spout, painted with bouquets of flowers en camaieu verte within ozier borders, blue crossed swords and dot mark.

c1765 *7in (17.5cm) wide*

£300-500 **GORL**

A Meissen teapot and cover moulded with a trellis and swags of flowers and painted with fruit and flowers, within a gilt trellis and rococo scroll cartouches, with an entwined handle and blue flower finial, blue crossed swords and dot marks, two small chips.

c1770 *6.75in (17cm) wide*

£280-320 **GORL**

A late 18thC Meissen Marcolini coffee pot and cover of slender ovoid shape, painted with isolated coloured flower sprays, entwined foliate handle and high domed cover with flower finial, crossed swords and asterisk mark in underglaze blue.

9in (22.5cm) high

£150-250 **GORL**

A Meissen pear-shaped octagonal coffee pot and cover in the Kakiemon style, painted with tied bouquets of stylized flowers and with insects, with a chocolate rim, blue enamel crossed swords mark, repair to finial and handle.

c1732 *9in (22.5cm) high*

£700-1,000 **GORL**

A Meissen milk jug and cover decorated with quatrelobed panels of lake-side scenes on a turquoise blue ground, an applied scrolling handle, crossed swords in underglaze-blue, cover restored.

c1748 *5.5in (13.5cm) high*

£800-1,200 **GORL**

A late 19thC Meissen miniature vase, with dolphin handles.

3in (8cm) high

£180-220 **AD**

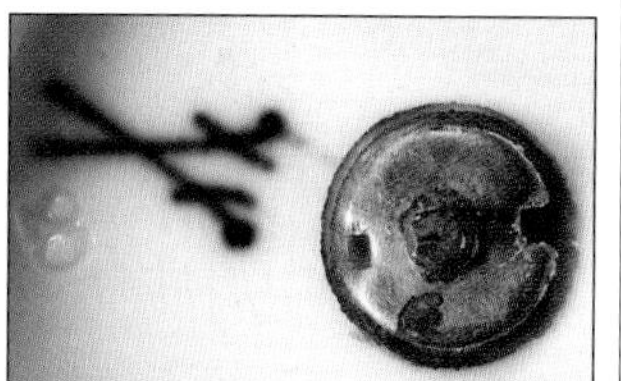

A Meissen pâte-sur-pâte vase, with two handles and a square base, the front decorated with an oval panel depicting two figures, lacking cover, a crossed swords mark.

c1900 *7in (17.5cm) high*

£800-1,200 **BMN**

A Meissen two-handled vase, of Etruscan shape, painted with Deutsche Blumen in polychrome enamels, on a pedestal stem and square base, crossed swords and incised numeral.

11.5in (29cm) high

£120-180 **GORL**

An early Meissen cream pot and cover, decorated at the Seuter workshop of Augsburg with three chinoiserie scenes, each resting on a trellis diaper bracket, in gilding with engraved details, all below a gilt scrollwork border, applied with three paw feet and scroll-moulded handle.

c1720 *4.25in (10.5cm) high*

£1,800-2,200 **GORL**

A Meissen spirally gadrooned oval two-handled tureen and cover with putto finial, moulded with alt-Brandenstein ozier borders and painted with bouquets of Deutsche Blumen, one handle restored.

c1745 *16in (40cm) wide*

£1,000-1,500 **GORL**

A Meissen oval sauce tureen, cover and fixed stand, with putti and cornucopia finial, painted in enamels with sprays of European scattered flowers and leaves, within gilt line borders, mark in blue, chip to rim of stand.

c1880 *6.75in (17cm) high*

£300-350 **LFA**

A pair of late 19thC Meissen-style 'Schneeballen' vases and covers, each with a parrot alighting on a fruiting branch finial, the domed cover and baluster vase applied overall with flowerheads and large balls linked by vine stems, on circular base.

31.25in (78cm) high

£4,000-6,000 **L&T**

A Meissen floral-encrusted pot and cover, painted with insects in bright enamels, crossed swords mark.

4.25in (11cm) high

£120-180 **GORL**

A Meissen box and cover, decorated with flowers.

c1900 *3in (7.5cm) diam*

£120-180 **AD**

A Meissen two-handled double-lipped sauceboat on four scroll feet, painted with flower sprays and enriched with gilding, blue crossed swords mark, minor chip to foot.

c1750 *10in (25cm) wide*

£600-900 **GORL**

A Meissen salt, with basketweave and gilt decoration.

c1760 *4.5in (12cm) long*

£200-250 **SA**

A Meissen needle case, in the form of a baby in swaddling clothes, decorated in coloured enamels and picked out in gilt, and with gilt metal hinged cover, marked in blue.

c1870 *2.5in (6.5cm) long*

£400-600 **LFA**

Part of a ten-piece set of 20thC Copenhagen blue and white porcelain, comprising of a coffee-pot with faux Meissen marks, two square vegetable dishes, a platter by Bing & Grondahl, a circular platter, an oval platter and four luncheon plates by Royal Copenhagen, various maker's marks.

Largest 16in (40.5cm) long

£300-350 set **S&K**

MINTON

A biscuit porcelain model of a girl, sitting in a large chair, her hat on a scrolling irregular base, unmarked, probably Minton, one hand chipped.

c1835 *5in (12.5cm) high*

£40-60 **WW**

A Minton figure of a seated lady.

c1840 *4.75in (12cm) high*

£150-200 **GHA**

A mid-19thC Minton Parian figure designed by John Bell, depicting 'Dorothea' dressed as a young man, resting from her travels, marks in raised cartouches.

c1850 *13.75in (35cm) high*

£200-300 **CHEF**

A mid-19thC Minton Parian figure designed by John Bell, depicting 'Miranda', loosely draped and seated on a wave lapped rock, incised marks.

c1850 *15.25in (39cm) high*

£200-300 **CHEF**

A CLOSER LOOK AT A MINTON PARIANWARE MODEL

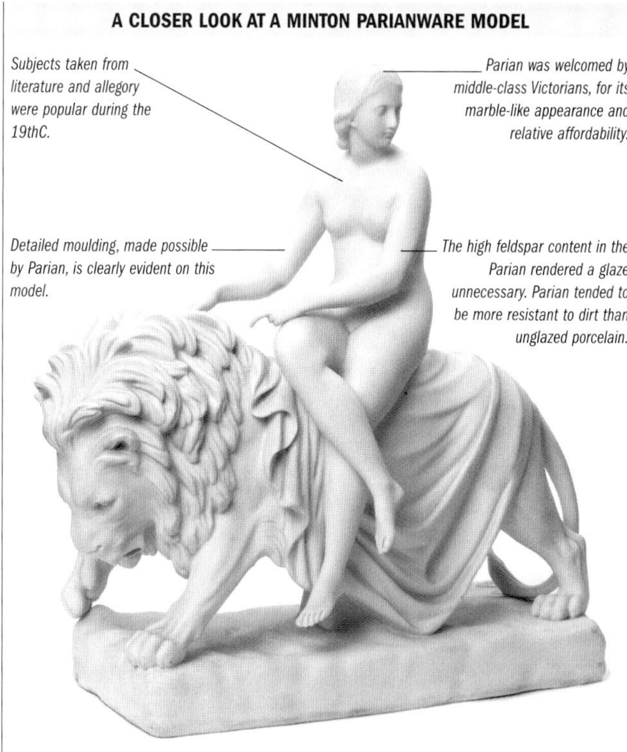

Subjects taken from literature and allegory were popular during the 19thC.
Parian was welcomed by middle-class Victorians, for its marble-like appearance and relative affordability.
Detailed moulding, made possible by Parian, is clearly evident on this model.
The high feldspar content in the Parian rendered a glaze unnecessary. Parian tended to be more resistant to dirt than unglazed porcelain.

A Minton Parian model of Una and the Lion, modelled by John Bell, the subject from Spencer's Faerie Queene, moulded Minton mark and registration mark.

1847 *14.25in (36cm) high*

£800-1,200 **WW**

Two of fourteen Minton gilt and white luncheon plates, retailed by Davis Collamore, Co. Ltd., New York, each with a gilt band chased with rinceaux enclosing flowerheads, puce and impressed marks, pattern no H 1325/4.

c1925 *9in (23cm) diam*

£140-180 set **S&K**

A Minton porcelain cream-ground part service, retailed by Tiffany & Co., New York, each with elaborate raised gilt foliage and flowerheads in panels on the rim, including three dinner plates, six salad plates, six soup plates, six bread and butter plates, puce crowned globe marks, pat. No. H4027.

c1929

£280-320 **S&K**

A Minton plate with a landscape painting, date mark for 1859.

9.75in (25cm) diam

£300-500 **GCL**

A Minton plate with a stag, by Henry Mitchel.

9.75in (25cm) diam

£300-500 **GCL**

A Minton dessert service, each piece painted with birds perched on flowering or fruiting branches, within turquoise and gilt reticulated borders, comprising two low stands and six plates, impressed marks, one plate with a clean body crack.

c1881 *9in (23cm) diam*

£800-1,200 set **WW**

A Minton pâte-sur-pâte plate, the border with three classical panels signed 'A. Birks', divided by panels of elaborate scrollwork, gilt retailers mark for Tiffany & Co. and impressed factory marks.

c1882 *8.75in (22.5cm) diam*

£400-600 **WW**

A Minton bone china teapot, cover and stand, in pattern number 867, richly decorated with panels of flowers on a gilt leaf decorated blue ground, blue painted mark, minor faults.

c1820 *10.25in (26cm) long*

£180-220 **WW**

A miniature Minton floral encrusted teapot and cover, with a rose knop and a green handle and spout, crossed swords mark, a hair crack.

c1835 *2.25in (6cm) high*

£100-150 **WW**

A mid- to late 19thC Minton teapot and cover, in pattern number 7631, decorated with raised enamel and gilding with flowering prunus branches on a pale green ground.

8in (20cm) high

£120-180 **WW**

A small bone china teapot and cover, probably Minton, the handle moulded with leaves and small blue flowers, a faint registration mark.

4.5in (11.5cm) high

£150-250 **WW**

A Minton milk jug, pattern number 854, moulded with vine leaves and grapes and painted with a building in a landscape and with flower sprays.

c1825 *5.5in (14cm) long*

£200-300 **WW**

A Minton flower encrusted ink stand and cover, of sarcophagus shape on an integrated stand.

c1835

£800-1,200 **JF**

A Minton flower encrusted desk set, with water pails for ink and a candlestick sand box cover.

c1835

£700-1,000 **JF**

A CLOSER LOOK AT A MINTON POT POURRI

The body, decoration and overall quality of the piece are extremely good. The applied flowers on the front panel and the detail in the flower to the top of the cover are especially fine.

The perforations would have allowed the aroma to fill the room.

The ornate, gilded decoration is typical of Minton pieces of the period. The factory concentrated on producing high quality original pieces as well as copies of earlier wares from other makers.

Many ceramic makers produced pot pourri containers during the 18th and 19th century, after they first appeared in the French Court. In the early years, pot-pourri was used to mask smells caused by poor hygiene but they later became a fashionable home accessory.

A fine Minton pot pourri.

c1840 *12.75in (32.5cm) high*

£1,500-2,000 **GHA**

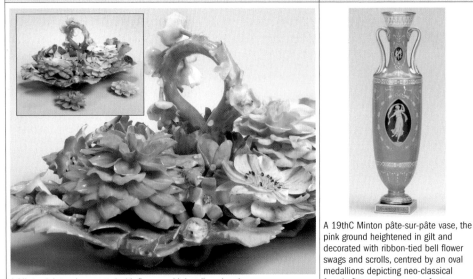

A Minton inkstand encrusted with flowers, with handle, minor losses.

c1840 *9.5in (24cm) long*

£650-750 **GHA**

A 19thC Minton pâte-sur-pâte vase, the pink ground heightened in gilt and decorated with ribbon-tied bell flower swags and scrolls, centred by an oval medallions depicting neo-classical female figures, on a square foot.

17in (43cm) high

£1,800-2,200 **FRE**

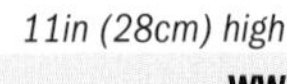

A pair of Minton ewers, painted and signed by Anton Boullemier, with oval panels of children sitting in branches, on a pink ground decorated with raised gilt flowers and foliage, gold printed marks, each with minor restoration.

c1900 *11in (28cm) high*

£1,000-1,500 **WW**

A pair of Minton celador vases.

6.75in (17cm) high

£300-500 **GHA**

A 'Babes in the Wood' spill vase, probably by Minton.

c1835 *5.75in (14.5cm) high*

£700-1,000 **AD**

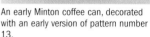

An early Minton coffee can, decorated with an early version of pattern number 13.

c1800 *2.5in (6.5cm) high*

£120-180 **GAS**

NEW HALL

Richard Champion, who initially achieved some success at Bristol c1770 producing a white porcelain similar to that at Meissen, persuaded a consortium of manufacturers to use his patented formula for hard-paste porcelain. Spotting the potential, the consortium set up the New Hall factory in Staffordshire in c1781 to utilize an improved version of Champion's formula.

However, this hard-paste porcelain, known as 'hybrid hard-paste', did not achieve a satisfactorily white body. In 1815 New Hall began making bone china and concentrated on popular, mass-market items such as tea wares, decorating them with simple Chinese floral patterns, under key decorator Fidelle Duvivier, and avoiding more expensive figures and vases. In the 1830s, the factory closed. The later pieces from this factory are not as collectable as its earlier output.

New Hall's porcelain pieces are identifiable by the thinly potted body with a thick, dull, green-tinged glaze. The tea and coffee services are most frequently found, and other items by this factory are very rare. New Hall was the first manufacturer to introduce pattern numbers in order to facilitate the reordering of its services and these help to identify the factory's work.

A New Hall tea bowl and saucer, of 'Hamilton Flute' shape, pattern number 64.

c1790 *5.25in (13.5cm) diam*

£70-90 **GAS**

A New Hall tea bowl and saucer, decorated with 'Knitting Wool' pattern, pattern number 195.

c1795 *5in (12.5cm) diam*

£100-150 **GAS**

A New Hall cup and saucer, pattern number 171.

c1795 *5in (12.5cm) diam*

£120-180 **GAS**

A New Hall tea bowl and saucer, with 'Boy and the Butterfly' pattern, pattern number 421.

c1795 *5in (12.5cm) diam*

£100-130 **GAS**

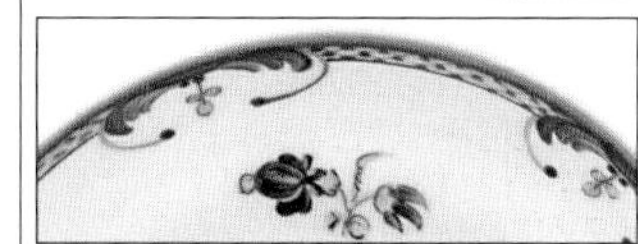

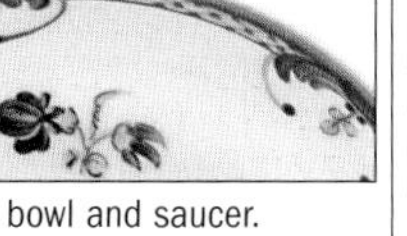

A New Hall tea bowl and saucer.

c1800 *5.25in (13.5cm) diam*

£100-130 **SA**

A New Hall cup and saucer.

c1790 *5.25in (13.5cm) diam*

£140-160 **SA**

A New Hall cup and saucer.

c1805 *5.25in (6cm) diam*

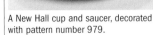

£100-120 **SA**

A New Hall cup and saucer, decorated with pattern number 979.

c1810 *5.5in (14cm) diam*

£50-80 **GAS**

A New Hall tea cup and saucer, of bute shape, with pattern number 1219.

c1815 *5.5in (14cm) diam*

£150-200 **GAS**

A New Hall tea cup and saucer, decorated with pattern number 1235.

c1812 *5.5in (14cm) diam*

£80-120 **GAS**

A New Hall coffee cup and saucer, with 'Ribbon' pattern number 186.

c1795 *5.25in (13.5cm) diam*

£100-150 **GAS**

A New Hall clip handle coffee cup and saucer, decorated with 'Basket of Flowers' pattern number 171.

c1785 *5in (12.5cm) diam*

£150-200 **GAS**

A New Hall coffee cup, decorated with 'Twisted Tree' pattern.

c1790 *2.75in (7cm) high*

£70-100 **GAS**

A New Hall coffee can, decorated with pattern number 446.

c1800 *2.25in (5.5cm) high*

£100-150 **GAS**

A New Hall coffee can, decorated with pattern number 441.

c1805 *2.25in (5.5cm) high*

£100-150 **GAS**

A New Hall coffee can, decorated with pattern number 1153.

c1815 *2.25in (5.5cm) high*

£150-200 **GAS**

A New Hall teapot, decorated with scattered flowers.

c1800 *10in (25cm) wide*

£420-480 **SA**

A New Hall teapot, cover and stand, pattern number 631, in blue and gold with a fruiting grapevine.

c1810 *10.75in (27cm) high*

£450-550 **WW**

An early 19thC New Hall commode-shaped teapot, cover and stand, printed in blue with chinoiserie scenes of a building in a river landscape.

£400-500 **DN**

Part of an extensive New Hall-style porcelain part tea and coffee service, the oval section teapot with loop handle and a faceted scroll spout painted with lines of husks, the neck similarly decorated above a narrow apricot ground frieze in gilt, with a continuous flowerhead and trellis design, comprising a teapot, cover and stand, milk jug, circular slop bowl, oval twin handled sucrier and cover, nine tea cups, ten coffee cans and eleven saucers.

£300-400 set **L&T**

A New Hall style tea and coffee part service, comprising an oval teapot, cover and stand with all over rust concentric circles, gilt flower sprigs and blue dots with continuous gilt flowerhead border, a helmet shaped milk jug, an oval twin handled sucrier and cover, a circular slop bowl, five coffee cans, ten tea cups, eight saucers, and two bread plates.

£220-280 set **L&T**

A New Hall jug, with a floral motif.

c1800 *4.25in (11cm) high*

£400-450 **SA**

A New Hall jug, decorated with flowers.

c1800 *4.5in (11.5cm) high*

£280-320 **SA**

A New Hall bowl, pattern number 157, painted in polychrome with Chinese figures, one with a mandolin the other with a parasol, some wear.

c1800 *6in (15.5cm) high*

£150-250 **WW**

A CLOSER LOOK AT A NEW HALL TEAPOT

This teapot is decorated and marked with pattern number "566". Many other items, such as saucers, coffee cans and cups, were produced in this pattern.

New Hall specialized in producing mass-market porcelain tea and coffee services in a limited range of patterns.

The rich decoration is fine and the shape is attractive, making this piece desirable.

New Hall was the first company to assign pattern numbers to porcelain designs.

A New Hall teapot and stand, some wear on gilt on stand.

c1805 *11in (28cm) wide*

£400-600 **SA**

A New Hall sucrier, painted mark on base "Warbuton's patent" with crown.

c1805 *7.25in (18.5cm) wide*

£500-800 **SA**

A New Hall oval sugar bowl and cover, pattern number 446, decorated in the Imari palette with a fruiting leafy tree.

c1805 *5.25in (13.5cm) wide*

£250-350 **WW**

A New Hall porcelain part dessert service, comprising a fruit stand, a pair of sauce tureens and covers with fixed stands, four shaped oval dishes and twenty-two plates, each printed in the centre with a figural scene, architectural or landscape view, the fruit stand titled, "View of Greenwich from Deptford", the rim relief-moulded with floral sprays in white on a periwinkle-blue ground.

c1825 *Plate 8in (20cm) diam*

£1,200-1,800 **NA**

PARIS

Paris became an important centre of porcelain production from the 1780s. The heyday of the high quality hard-paste Paris factories was from the 1790s to the 1820s. Noble patrons, who included the Duke of Angouleme and Marie Antoinette, offered influence, protection from the authorities, and a secure source of business.

The appeal of Paris porcelain comes from its form and decoration. The factories of the 18th and 19thC were attuned to the fashions of the times and produced a tremendous variety of tablewares and decorations. Gothic, Rococo and Neo-classical styles all melded together. Among at least 15 factories and large workshops four factories were of major importance. The Dihl Factory, founded in 1781 by Christophe Dihl and Antoine Guérhard under the protection of the Duke of Angoulême. The Nast Factory, founded in 1783 by the Austrian Nepomucene-Jean-Hermann Nast. The three Darte brothers founded the Darte Factory in c1795 and another factory trading under the name 'Darte Frères' in 1808. The best-known products of the Dagoty and Honoré factories were richly gilded and decorated dessert, tea and coffee services.

Jacob Petit was the most prominent porcelain manufacturer in Paris from the 1830s. He produced simple wares with meticulously modelled or painted flowers. Petit's factory in Fountainebleau produced pieces that combined Rococo influences with the Gothic and Renaissance revival styles.

Most Paris pieces are unmarked. However, Jacob Petit's factory usually marked its wares with an underglaze blue "J.P.".

An early 19thC Paris 'Rue de Montmartre' plate, 'hulley' in iron-red, incised repairer's mark, minor rubbing.

9.25in (23cm) high

£220-280 **GORL**

A set of four Paris porcelain plates, each printed in coloured enamels with figures in extensive landscapes on a gilt ground, with a flowerhead diaper band.

c1820 7in (18cm) diam

£120-180 **LFA**

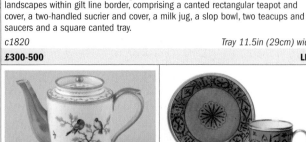

A Paris porcelain cabaret set, each piece printed en grisaille with figures in landscapes within gilt line border, comprising a canted rectangular teapot and cover, a two-handled sucrier and cover, a milk jug, a slop bowl, two teacups and saucers and a square canted tray.

c1820 Tray 11.5in (29cm) wide

£300-500 **LFA**

Part of an Art Deco forty-eight piece Haviland Limoges porcelain part service, retailed by Stonier & Co., Liverpool, decorated with a chateau on a hillock with clouds in black alternating with pink-flowering trees, within gilt rims, comprising eight dinner plates, twelve soup plates, ten salad plates, 12 dessert plates, a covered sauce tureen on a fixed stand, a circular soup tureen, and four graduated platters, green and red printed marks "Edition Exposition/Paris-1925".

c1925

£300-500 set **S&K**

An early 19thC Nast à Paris coffee pot and cover, the cylindrical sides painted with two birds perched in trees.

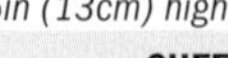

5in (13cm) high

£150-200 **CHEF**

A early 19thC Paris porcelain coffee can and saucer, decorated with leaves, trophies and arrows on a coral ground, unmarked.

£100-150 **WW**

A mid-19thC Paris porcelain punch bowl with a nautical theme.

11in (28cm) diam

£150-200 **DN**

A 19thC Paris porcelain bowl painted overall with sprays and sprigs of flowers.

11in (28cm) diam

£80-120 **CHEF**

Three Paris porcelain round plaques, each decorated in coloured enamels with Napoleonic battle scenes, with chased gilt metal mounts on a mahogany rectangular panel.

Panel 25in (64cm) wide

£500-700 **LFA**

SAMSON

A mid-to late 19thC Samson armorial teapot and cover, modelled as a duck, the cover with a water lily knop, seal mark.

8.75in (22cm) high

£400-450 **WW**

A pair of early 20thC Samson 'Meissen' hoopoes, the exotic black, brown and white birds perched in white tree trunks with a green leaf and pink lichen, pseudo crossed swords marks.

11.25in (28.5cm) high

£80-120 **CHEF**

A pair of Samson porcelain figures of male and female fruit sellers, each holding baskets of apples and grapes, on cushion bases.

9in (23cm) high

£200-300 **GORL**

A pair of Samson porcelain and biscuit figural stands, each navette-shaped reticulated bowl surrounded by a gilt-heightened moulded border of leaf tips centring flowerheads, raised on four partially robed Neoclassical female figures set on a matching base, printed "M Imp le de Sevres" in iron-red, one with gilder's "X" mark in gold.

***Provenance:** A Louisburg Square estate, Boston.*

16.75in (42.5cm) high

£5,000-8,000 **NA**

SÈVRES

In 1756, the Vincennes porcelain factory moved to the Chateau of Sèvres, near Paris. The company's patron, King Louis XV, ensured that high standards were maintained and passed several laws to protect the factory's monopoly, such as banning foreign imports and forbidding other firms use of multi-coloured and gilded decoration. The success of Sèvres was not simply due to its royal patronage. The company employed the finest artists, sculptors and goldsmiths to produce increasingly elaborate and ambitious porcelain ware. After brilliant coloured grounds were introduced in the 1760s, decorators tended to leave little white porcelain showing, although functional services were more sparsely decorated.

By the late 1770s, Neo-classical styles and subtle colours were favoured at Sèvres. Pieces such as the 'Arabesque' service were inspired by ancient vases, urns or recently unearthed frescoes from Pompeii, and were decorated with classical garlands and acanthus leaves. The introduction of hard-paste porcelain at the end of the 18thC enabled new colours to be used. Pieces from this period have gold patterns and enamel 'jewels', but are fairly rare.

From 1793, when the factory came under state control, undecorated pieces were sold to other decorators, making them difficult to identify accurately today. Rich 'Empire' style pieces, with more complex forms, were produced in the early 18thC. Early Sèvres pieces are marked with interlinked Ls, while the mark "RF Sèvres" was used between 1793 and 1800.

A Sèvres dish, by Francois Binet, decorated with gilt edges.

c1769 *9in (23cm) diam*

£380-420 **SA**

A Sèvres two-handled tray, decorated with animals and hounds amongst floral rinceaux, dated 1846, with Louis Phillippe monograms, printed marks and Chateau de Fontainbleau stamps, with a restored cup with similar decoration, dated 1872.

10.5in (27cm) wide

£150-200 set **CHEF**

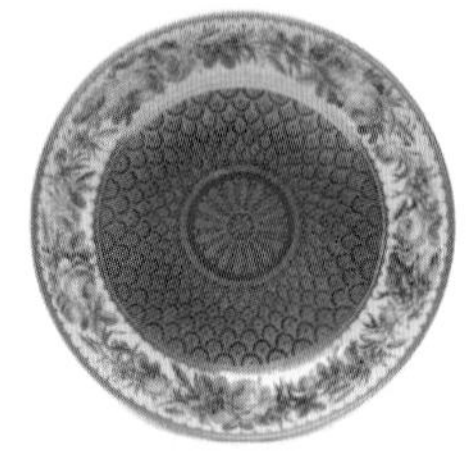

A 19thC Sèvres hard-paste saucer, printed and incised marks.

7in (17.5cm) high

£150-250 **WW**

A 19thC Sèvres style plate, the centre painted with fruit, flowers and leaves, the border with colourful birds in panels on a gilded blue ground, interlaced 'L's.

9.25in (23.5cm) diam

£200-300 **WW**

An 18thC Sèvres plate, painted by Theodore Buteux, with central flowers within a wreath and gilt detailed basket-moulded petal edged rim, marks in blue.

9.25in (23.5cm) diam

£70-100 **CHEF**

A CLOSER LOOK AT A SÈVRES STYLE PANEL

Many factories imitated the Sèvres style and use of brilliant ground colours. Undecorated items were often sold off to be decorated elsewhere, making it difficult to identify pieces.

The piece has a blue Sèvres mark with mock date letters 'L' and 'S'. The Sèvres mark is the one most commonly faked on porcelain.

This panel depicts Louis XVI surrounded by eight portraits of contemporary female figures, including Marie Antoinette, Leczinska, Dubocage, Genlis, Dumoulin, Louise, Elisabeth and Berry.

This panel will appeal to both collectors of porcelain and of commemorative wear, increasing the value.

A large circular Sèvres style panel, the turquoise blue background decorated with eight painted circular portrait panels, all surrounding a central circular portrait panel of a portly Louis XVI wearing crimson gold braided jacket, each portrait within an ornate gilt border, blue painted Sèvres style mark with letters 'L' and 'S'.

20in (50cm) diam

£700-1,000 **L&T**

A Sèvres gilt plate depicting 'Mme de Saraballe', inscribed to base.

c1880 *9.25in (23.5cm) diam*

£300-500 **GCL**

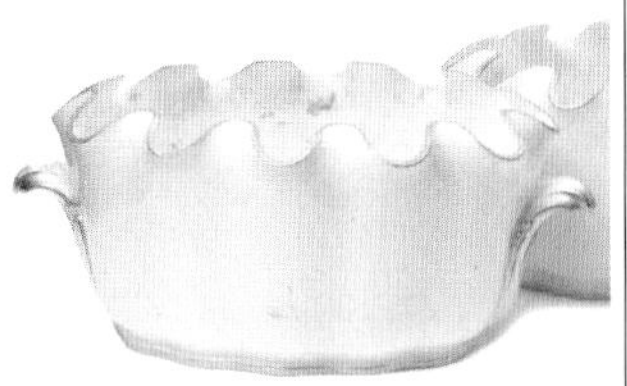

One of a pair of Sèvres oval monteiths, with leaf scroll side handles and wavy rims, decorated with gilt borders and detailing, interlaced 'L's in blue.

c1770 *11.5in (29.5cm) high*

£1,200-1,800 pair **WW**

A Sèvres oval bowl, painted by Hirel de Choisy, with bands of flowers, scrolls and ribbons, interlaced 'L's enclosing 'BB' for 1779 and above the painter's ermine mark, repaired cracks.

10.75in (27cm) wide

£200-300 **WW**

A pair of Sèvres oval sucrier and covers, decorated with gilt dentil borders, interlaced 'L' marks.

c1775 *9.5in (24cm) high*

£500-700 **WW**

A Sèvres oval box and cover, with an angled handle, decorated with bands of roses, violets and buttercups within blue and gilt oeil-de-perdrix borders, rubbed painted mark, some damage.

c1792 *5.5in (14cm) high*

£100-200 **WW**

A Sèvres 'Cuvette a Fleurs Verdun' flower vase with a green ground, painted with two panels of flowers and fruit and with gilt flowers and laurel leaves, interlaced 'L's enclosing 'R' for 1770, a firing fault.

10.5in (26.5cm) high

£1,200-1,800 **WW**

One of a pair of 19thC Sèvres round two-handled jardinières, each painted in coloured enamels with putti in landscpapes, and with flowers and leaves, within gilt flower and leaf scroll cartouches, with a 'jewelled' band, on a turquoise ground, marks in blue.

6.25in (16cm) high

£1,000-1,500 pair **LFA**

A small Sèvres cup and saucer, with roses and turquoise borders, with gilt bands, 'L's mark, the cup cracked.

c1775

£400-500 WW

A late 18thC Sèvres hard-paste cup and saucer, decorated in tooled gilding and platinum with birds and insects, flowers and foliage, all on a powder blue ground, crowned interlaced 'L's above 'LG', small chip to the cup and slight wear.

£800-1,200 WW

A Sèvres coffee cup and saucer, the cup with a scroll handle, painted in coloured enamels with birds in landscapes, within gilt oval panels, the blue ground with gilt flower garlands, the rims painted with continuous bands of birds and trees, painted marks in blue for 1793 and decorator's mark for Evans.

This cup and saucer is reputed to have belonged to Queen Mary.

£1,800-2,200 LFA

A Sèvres custard cup, painted by La Roche, with bands of flowers entwined with blue ribbons, gilt marks, some gilt wear.

This custard cup was made for Princess Kinsky.

c1790 *2in (5cm) diam*

£280-320 WW

A Sèvres teapot, the associated cover with a flower knop, painted with flowers within blue feuilles-de-choux borders, interlaced 'L's enclosing 'R' for 1770.

7.25in (18.5cm) high

£400-500 WW

A CLOSER LOOK AT SÈVRES TEAPOT

Sèvres gilding has a reputation for quality. The gilding process was strictly controlled and many pieces were rejected and destroyed.

Scattered stylized flower patterns were often used on more functional items and large services.

In contrast to later wares, this early Sèvres piece uses a more delicate palette and is decorated with sprays of flowers.

Other Sèvres pieces from this period often had heavily coloured grounds or filled in reserve panels, in keeping with the Neo-Classical style.

A Sèvres small ovoid teapot and cover, with an ear-shaped handle and gilt fruit knop, painted in coloured enamels with scattered cornflowers, within gilt dentil borders, incised and painted marks in blue for 1780.

4.25in (10.5cm) high

£800-1,200 AA

A pair of French vases in the Sèvres style, probably Samson.

c1865 *6.5in (16.5cm) high*

£500-600 GCL

SPODE

A Spode coffee can, bat printed in grey with a country scene.

c1805 *2.5in (6.5cm) high*

£80-120 GAS

A Spode coffee can, 'Japan' border pattern, number 1645.

c1810 *2.5in (6.5cm) high*

£100-160 GAS

A Spode porcelain cup and saucer with a 'serpent' handle.

c1825 *6in (15cm) diam*

£100-150 **GFA**

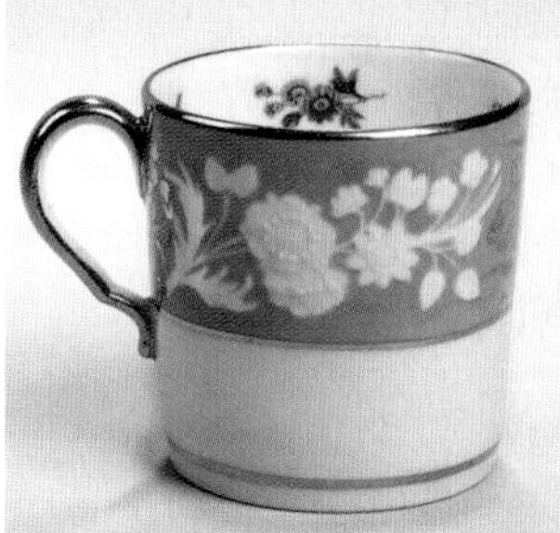

A Spode coffee can, decorated with embossed pattern number 2019.

c1812 *2.5in (6.5cm) high*

£100-150 **GAS**

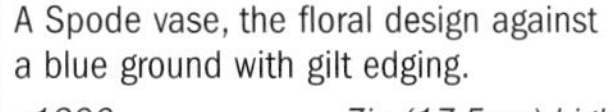

A Spode vase, the floral design against a blue ground with gilt edging.

c1820 *7in (17.5cm) high*

£400-600 **AA**

A Spode spill vase, of everted form printed and enamelled with flowers.

c1830 *5.25in (13.5cm) high*

£100-200 **GORL**

A Spode comport, decorated with flowers and gilt.

c1820 *4.75in (12cm) high*

£1,800-2,200 **AD**

A Spode bowl, the interior with panels.

c1800 *6.5in (16.5cm) diam*

£80-120 **GCL**

An early 19thC Spode plate painted with the '3883' pattern of sprays and sprigs of flowers, in the Welsh style, within shaped gilt rim with dentil line, marks in red.

10in (25.5cm) diam

£70-100 **CHEF**

A Spode tea pot and stand.

c1815 *10in (25.5cm) wide*

£400-600 **GCL**

A Spode octagonal jug, with kakiemon-style decoration of hydrangea.

c1815 *11.5in (29cm) high*

£100-125 **SA**

STAFFORDSHIRE PORCELAIN

A Staffordshire porcelain fox-mask stirrup cup, mostly painted in shades of iron-red, the collar with gilt inscription "Tally Ho", slight wear.

c1840 *4in (10cm) high*

£100-150 **DN**

A Staffordshire porcelain poodle, on a tasselled base, the tail and part of the bone restored.

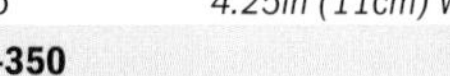

c1835 *4.25in (11cm) wide*

£300-350 **AD**

A Staffordshire porcelain crouching poodle.

c1835 *2.5in (6.5cm) high*

£350-400 **AD**

A Staffordshire porcelain begging poodle.

c1840 *4in (10cm) high*

£350-400 **AD**

A Staffordshire porcelain begging dog.

c1840 *3.75in (9.5cm) high*

£350-450 **AD**

A Staffordshire porcelain seated dog.

c1845 *3.25in (8.5cm) high*

£200-300 **AD**

A Staffordshire porcelain dog.

c1840 *2.25in (5.5cm) high*

£200-250 **AD**

A Staffordshire porcelain dog.

c1845 *2.25in (5.5cm) high*

£250-300 **AD**

A Staffordshire porcelain bull.

c1840 *2.5in (6.5cm) high*

£300-350 **AD**

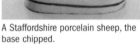

A Staffordshire porcelain sheep, the base chipped.

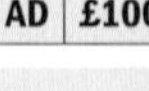

c1840 *3in (7.5cm) high*

£100-150 **AD**

A mid-19thC Staffordshire porcelaineous penholder of a recumbent hound, probably a Great Dane, painted in pale-yellow enamels and on a blue gilt-line base, tips of ears restored.

4.25in (11cm) wide

£100-150 **DN**

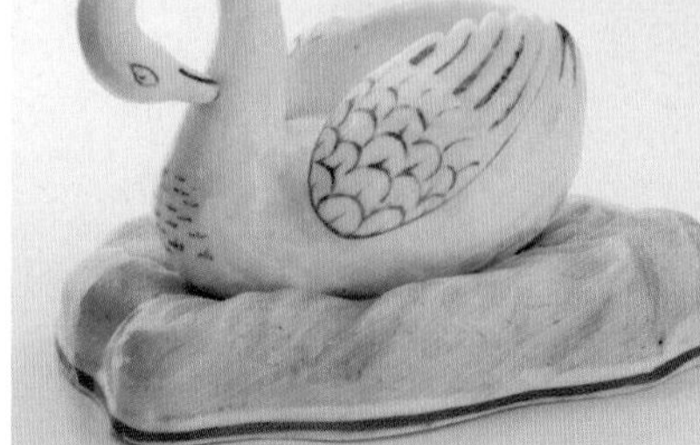

A Staffordshire porcelain swan, by Samuel Alcock.

c1835 *3.75in (9.5cm) high*

£700-900 **AD**

A rare mid-19thC pair of English porcelain Aesop's fable groups, illustrating the fable of the fox and the stork, set before tree spill vases and with quill holders to the backs, no marks.

7in (17.5cm) high

£400-600 **WW**

A Staffordshire porcelain miniature figure of a man in a blue coat.

c1835 *2.75in (7cm) high*

£200-230 **AD**

A Staffordshire porcelain figure of 'Winter'.

c1840 *9in (23cm) high*

£350-450 **AD**

A Staffordshire porcelain Sheep Shearer.

c1840 *6.25in (16cm) high*

£400-500 **AD**

A Staffordshire porcelain shepherdess group, bocage restored.

c1845 *3.75in (9.5cm) high*

£80-120 **AD**

A CLOSER LOOK AT A STAFFORDSHIRE PORCELAIN FIGURE

It is likely that this unusual Staffordshire piece depicts a character taken from a folktale that is unknown today. Figures were often modelled on popular subjects, which mean little in the 21stC, such as the characters Lubin Log or Sam Swipes, played by the 19thC actor John Liston.
This piece has minor restoration to the extremities. It would be rare to find a piece like this with no damage, so the value is not greatly affected. Major damage would reduce the value of the piece substantially.
Figures depicting an almost identical subject were made by at least one other factory during the period.
This figure was inexpensive when new. Items for the higher end of the market tended to be produced by factories such as Minton or Derby.

A rare Staffordshire porcelain figure of a man with a snake.

c1840 *4.25in (11cm) high*

£500-600 **AD**

A Staffordshire porcelain spill vase, in the form of two children, with lambs and a hound before a tree stump, decorated in coloured enamels and picked out in gilt.

c1855 *7in (18cm) high*

£70-100 **LFA**

A Staffordshire porcelain compressed round 'bachelor' teapot and flat cover, with an angular handle and button knop, painted in coloured enamels with flowers and leaves, within gilt cartouches, the blue ground decorated in yellow and gilt with vines.

c1820 *3in (7.5cm) high*

£220-280 **LFA**

A Staffordshire spill vase, decorated with a cottage by a river and a bridge in a landscape.

c1820 *4.75in (12cm) high*

£120-160 **SA**

A Victorian Staffordshire two-handled vase and cover, painted with game birds.

6.25in (16cm) high

£150-200 **GORL**

A Staffordshire rare porcelain cosmetic box and cover, with a screw on lid.

c1825

£800-1,200 **JF**

A pair of unusual Staffordshire porcelain ovoid custard cups, each with a ring handle and flared rim, decorated in raised paste gilding with Chinese pagodas and trees, on a puce ground, the rim with a yellow and gilt trellis band, one with tiny rim nick.

c1830 *3.25in (8.2cm) high*

£80-120 **LFA**

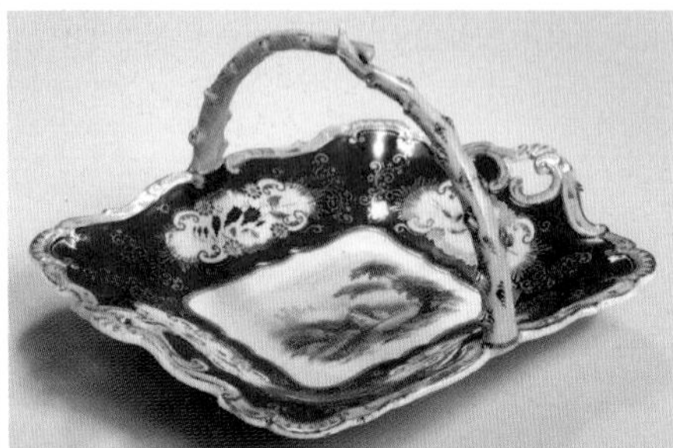

A Staffordshire porcelain bread basket.

c1835 *11in (28cm) wide*

£300-400 **GCL**

A mid-19thC Staffordshire porcelain pastille burner, modelled as a two tier pagoda and applied with morning glory flowers, a few tiny chips.

8in (20cm) high

£500-600 **WW**

VAUXHALL

A Vauxhall saucer, painted in the Imari palette, with a bird perched upon rockwork, an insect and a flowering shrub.

c1760 *4.5in (11.5cm) high*

£350-400 **WW**

A Vauxhall mug.

c1760 *3.75in (9.5cm) high*

£1,500-2,000 **AA**

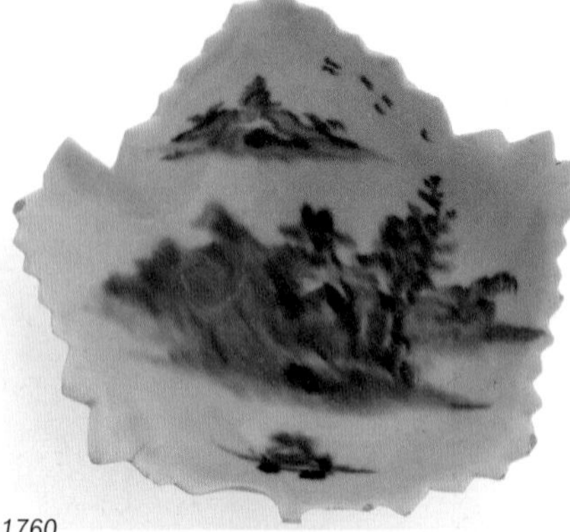

A Vauxhall leaf-shaped pickle dish, painted in underglaze blue with a Chinese river landscape, within a serrated rim, on three tapering feet.

c1760 *3.75in (9.5cm) wide*

£1,800-2,200 **AA**

A Vauxhall blue and white teabowl, painted in the Chinese Kangxi style with a hut beneath trees in a watery landscape, a tiny rim chip.

c1755

£300-500 **WW**

A Vauxhall coffee cup, brightly painted with flowers and leaves issuing from a banded hedge.

c1758 *2.5in (6cm) high*

£500-600 **WW**

WORCESTER BLUE & WHITE

Since the founding of the company in 1751, Worcester has been famous for the variety and quality of its blue-and-white designs, in particular the chinoiserie designs introduced in the early 1750s. Early blue-and-white Worcester shows the influence of the Bristol factory, with shapes derived from British silver. Teawares, sauceboats and pickle-dishes were decorated with blue and white copies of Chinese wares and polychrome chinoiseries. The factory had perfected its blue-and-white ware by eliminating heavy blurring and made fine tea services. Worcester invented the process of printing on porcelain. It used this technique extensively to produce overglaze black enamel and underglaze blue printed decoration. By 1770 Worcester even exported blue-and-white ware to the Netherlands. The factory perfected a deep, underglaze blue ground, invented its famous 'scale blue' and developed other coloured grounds. Many blue-and-white wares bear a workman's mark, usually a simple sign of uncertain meaning, prior to the adoption of the crescent mark.

A mid-to late 18thC pair of Worcester plates with the 'Kangxi Lotus' pattern.

7.5in (19cm) diam

£800-1,000 **AA**

A Worcester blue and white Blind Earl dish, with a stalk handle and two moulded rose buds, the leaves, handle and buds detailed in blue, and with four insects, open crescent mark, a restored rim chip.

c1760 *6in (15cm) diam*

£450-550 **WW**

A rare Worcester blue and white plate, after a Bow original.

c1765 *6.75in (17cm) diam*

£1,200-1,500 **AA**

A Worcester blue and white 'Willow Bridge Fisherman' pattern basin, the exterior with a flowering leaf scroll, open crescent mark, a long body crack.

c1770 *10.75in (27.5cm) wide*

£280-320 **WW**

A Worcester blue and white dish, with deep serrated edge painted in a soft shade of blue with the 'Prunus Root' pattern, workman's mark and letter in underglaze blue.

c1755 *5.75in (14.5cm) wide*

£1,800-2,200 **AA**

A Worcester blue and white leaf dish.

c1755 *7.5in (19cm) wide*

£1,500-2,000 **AA**

A Worcester blue and white leaf-shaped pickle dish, painted with floral sprays, open crescent mark, minor chips.

c1765 *3.5in (9cm) wide*

£100-150 **WW**

A mid-to late 18thC Worcester blue and white leaf-shaped pickle dish, with an angled handle and painted with flowers and leaves within a complex border.

3in (7.5cm) wide

£320-380 **WW**

A Worcester dish, in the shape of a single deep shell, with moulding under the rim and a scroll handle, painted with bamboo in a fenced enclosure.

c1755 *5in (13cm) wide*

£1,500-2,000 **AA**

A good early Worcester pickle dish in the shape of a shell, painted in blue with bamboo, a fence and pointed rockwork, unmarked.

c1754 *3.25in (8cm) long*

£2,500-3,000 **WW**

A Worcester 'Root' pattern blue and white fluted teabowl and saucer, workmen's marks.

c1760

£380-420 **WW**

A Worcester 'Landslip' pattern blue and white teabowl and saucer, the saucer with a workman's mark, the teabowl with a crescent mark, the bowl slightly later.

c1760

£400-500 **WW**

A Worcester 'Fruit and Wreath' pattern blue and white teabowl and saucer, hatched crescent marks.

c1775

£200-250 **WW**

A Worcester 'Prunus Root' pattern blue and white coffee cup, the inner rim with two flower sprays and an insect, a workman's mark at the base of the handle.

c1755 *2.5in (6.5cm) high*

£450-550 **WW**

A Worcester 'Gazebo' pattern coffee cup.

c1756 *2.25in (6cm) high*

£800-1,200 **AA**

A Worcester coffee cup.

It is rare to find gilding combined with underglaze blue decoration on Worcester pieces. Only one such tea and coffee service appears to be recorded.

c1770 *2.5in (6.5cm) high*

£500-700 **AA**

A Worcester 'Warbler' pattern blue and white sparrow beak jug, a workman's mark, hairline to rim and crack to handle.

c1755 *3.25in (8.5cm) high*

£500-700 **WW**

A large Worcester 'Heavy Naturalistic Floral' pattern cabbage leaf moulded mask jug, a small decorator's mark.

c1760 *10.5in (26.5cm) high*

£700-1,000 **WW**

A Worcester 'Macclesfield' pattern sparrow beak cream jug, decorated with underglaze blue painted.

c1770 *3in (7.5cm) high*

£280-320 **GAS**

A pair of Worcester 'Triangular Platform' pattern oval sauceboats, of silver shape, each with loop handle, with scroll thumbpiece, painted in underglaze blue in a Chinese style, the interior with a bird perched on a flowering branch.

c1755 *7.5in (19cm) long*

£2,000-2,500 **AA**

A Worcester blue and white sauceboat.

c1755 2.75in (7cm) high

£1,000-1,500 **AA**

A rare Worcester 'Mission Church' pattern sauce boat.

c1765 8.5in (21.5cm) wide

£1,000-1,300 **SA**

An 18thC Worcester blue and white cylinder mug, with printed floral decoration, N. A. Rose collection label.

4.75in (12cm) high

£300-330 **GORL**

An 18thC Worcester blue and white baluster mug, printed with Oriental figures, cracked.

3.5in (9cm) high

£150-200 **GORL**

An 18thC Worcester blue and white cylinder mug, decorated with ducks swimming before a house.

c1760

£450-550 **GORL**

A Worcester mug, painted in blue with 'Long Eliza' figures.

c1765 5.75in (14.5cm) high

£600-800 **AA**

A Worcester 'Walk in the Garden' pattern blue and white tapering cylindrical mug, painted with a Chinese boy and a 'Long Eliza' figure, the reverse with two birds in the branches of a pine tree, crescent mark.

c1760 5.75in (14.5cm) high

£650-750 **WW**

A First Period Worcester 'peonies and fence' pattern blue-painted six-person tea service, decorated with a pair of flying ducks over a hut on an island, all in the chinoiserie manner, blue crescent mark, comprising globular teapot with flowerhead finial, sparrow neck milk jug, sugar bowl, slop basin, six tea bowls and six saucers, one tea bowl associated 18thC Chinese.

£800-1,200 **L&T**

A Worcester teapot, of angled barrel shape, the inset cover with open flower finial, painted with peonies and associated scroll and diaper cartouche border, workman's mark under handle.

This shape is very uncommon.

c1755

£800-1,200 **AA**

A Worcester blue and white mustard pot.

This pot has a flat lid, which is found on earlier Worcester. Later lids are domed.

c1755 2.5in (6.5cm) high

£2,000-3,000 **AA**

A rare Worcester salt spoon, after a silver original, with a foliate moulded stem, the rounded bowl painted with a flower in the centre and surrounded by a cell pattern.

c1760 4in (10cm) long

£1,500-2,000 **AA**

A Worcester blue and white egg cup, painted with trailing sprays of flowers and foliage, below a lattice work border, workman's mark.

c1758 *2.5in (6.5cm) high*

£1,500-2,000 **AA**

A Worcester blue and white sugar bowl and cover, with a flower knop, printed with flowers and a fence design, crescent mark.

c1770 *4.75in (12cm) wide*

£200-250 **WW**

A Chamberlain's Worcester honey pot in the form of a beehive.

c1800 *4.25in (10.5cm) high*

£500-800 **AA**

A Worcester 'Willow Bridge Fisherman' pattern blue and white guglet, blurred crescent mark, clean body cracks.

c1760 *10in (25.5cm) high*

£450-500 **WW**

A Worcester blue and white 'Three Flowers' pattern spitton or cuspidor, the globular body with broad flat range and uncommon double 'C' scroll handle, printed with flowers, leaves and butterflies, printed hatched crescent mark.

c1770 *4.25in (11cm) high*

£700-900 **AA**

A Worcester blue and white 'Pine Cone' pattern chamber pot, hatched crescent mark, crack to the handle.

c1775 *6.5in (22cm) wide*

£500-800 **WW**

A Worcester 'Fortune Teller' scratch cross coffee cup, transfer printed in black, with a grooved loop handle, a scratch cross mark, cracked.

c1755

£320-380 **WW**

A rare Worcester 'Tea party' coffee cup with a wish bone handle, printed in black, with a garden scene to the reverse, signed "R. Hancock fecit".

c1760 *2.5in (6cm) high*

£600-700 **WW**

An 18thC Worcester mug, transfer-printed with the 'Milkmaids' and 'May Day', after Hancock, restored.

6in (15cm) high

£180-220 **GORL**

A CLOSER LOOK AT A WORCESTER WALL VASE

Wall vases were used to display flowers and store household items from the 18thC onwards.

This piece is very early and is in excellent condition. This increases the value. The cornucopia shape is also attractive.

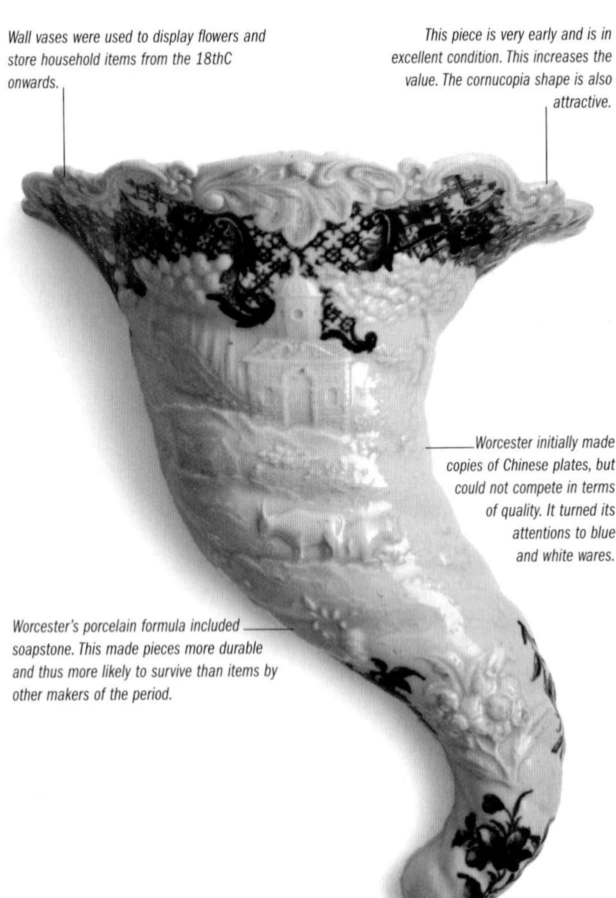

Worcester initially made copies of Chinese plates, but could not compete in terms of quality. It turned its attentions to blue and white wares.

Worcester's porcelain formula included soapstone. This made pieces more durable and thus more likely to survive than items by other makers of the period.

A Worcester blue and white wall vase, of cornucopia shape, moulded in relief with a cowherd seated beneath a tree near European buildings, watching two cows in a hilly rural landscape, with an irregular painted border of latticework and foliate scrolls and at the base painted flower sprays.

c1755 *8.5in (21.5cm) high*

£2,000-3,000 **AA**

A Worcester coffee can, transfer printed in black with the 'Tea Party' pattern.

c1756 *2.5in (6.5cm) high*

£1,000-1,500 **AA**

A large and rare Worcester leaf moulded mask jug, inscribed 'Success to the Crosby Hunt', transfer printed in black with a continuous fox hunting scene, the neck with two vignettes, no mark, repaired cracks.

c1770 *9in (23cm) high*

£1,200-1,800 **WW**

A Worcester 'Tea Party' teapot and cover, with a flower knop, the reverse printed with 'La Diseuse d'Adventure', the cover with three vignettes of buildings, tiny chips to the tip of the spout and to the rim of the cover.

c1760 *7in (18cm) long*

£350-450 **WW**

A Worcester teapot stand, transfer printed in black with the 'Old Dutch Inn' pattern.

c1765 *5.5in (13.5cm) wide*

£280-320 **WW**

A Worcester 'Milkmaids' tea bowl and saucer, transfer printed in black, with black line rims, unmarked.

c1760

£380-420 **WW**

A Worcester 'L'Amour' coffee cup and saucer, printed in black with black line rims, unmarked.

c1775

£180-220 **WW**

A Worcester 'cabbage leaf' jug, printed in black.

c1770 *7.75in (20cm) high*

£1,500-2,000 **AA**

A Worcester 'Tea Party' sugar bowl and cover, with a buttercup knop, transfer printed in black with ladies in a garden and with vignettes of ruins, unmarked.

c1760 *4.5in (11.5cm) high*

£500-700 **WW**

A small Worcester bowl, in the 'Boy on a Buffalo' pattern, the interior with a flower spray, a workman's mark.

This piece bears an Albert Amor exhibition label for the Vincent Townrow collection.

c1755 *4.75in (12cm) diam*

£520-580 **WW**

A Worcester saucer dish, printed in black with 'L'Amour' pattern, a black line rim.

c1765 *7.25in (18.5cm) wide*

£180-220 **WW**

A Worcester plate decorated in the London atelier of James Giles.

c1770 *9in (23cm) diam*

£1,800-2,200 **AA**

An unusual Worcester plate, decorated in the Imari style with a central vase of flowers encircled by flowers and scrolls, unmarked, two tiny rim chips.

c1770 *8.75in (22.5cm) wide*

£280-320 **WW**

A Worcester Blind Earl dish, with a stalk handle and two moulded rose buds, painted in puce camaieu with a chinoiserie scene, unmarked, a small repaired rim chip.

c1760 *6.25in (16cm) wide*

£400-600 **WW**

A Worcester leaf dish, with a polychrome floral pattern.

c1760 *10in (25.5cm) wide*

£1,200-1,800 **SA**

A Worcester quatrefoil dish, painted with floral sprays, within a blue border edged with a gilt C-scroll band, open crescent mark.

c1785 *8.5in (21.5cm) wide*

£250-300 **DN**

A Worcester dessert dish, with a blue scale ground.

c1775 *11.5in (29.5cm) long*

£1,500-2,000 **AA**

A Worcester blue scale ground dish.

c1770 *10.5 (26.75cm) long*

£500-700 **AA**

A Worcester lozenge-shaped spoon tray, painted in black and gold with flowers and line borders, no mark.

c1770 *6in (15.5cm) high*

£250-300 **WW**

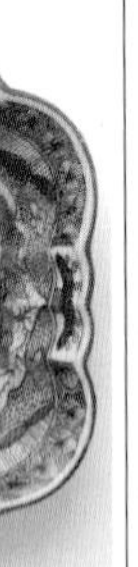

A Worcester hexagonal teapot stand, painted in famille verte palette with the 'Dragon in Compartments' pattern, the fluted border with gilt line rim.

c1775 *5.5in (14cm) wide*

£600-800 **AA**

A Worcester hexagonal teapot stand, painted in kakiemon style with the 'Jaberwocky' pattern, within turquoise, iron red and gilt borders.

c1775 *5.5in (14cm) wide*

£700-900 **AA**

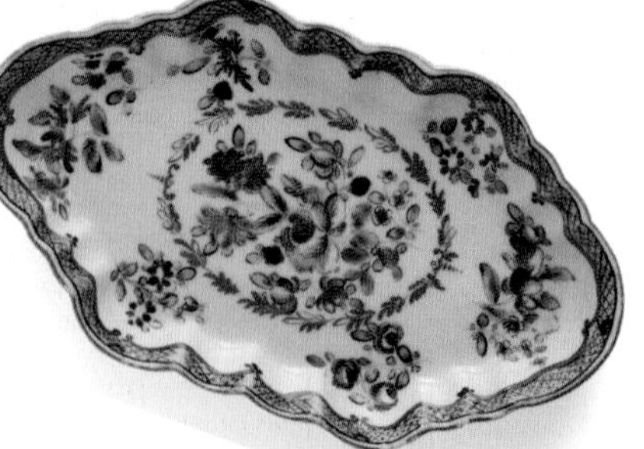

A Worcester lozenge shaped spoon tray, painted in 'Compagnie des Indes' style with flowers and leaves, within a gilt stiff leaf band, and scattered flowers and leaves, within a lavender ground diaper border.

c1780 *6.5in (16.5cm) wide*

£600-800 **AA**

A Worcester octagonal teabowl and saucer, brightly painted with insects, chrysanthemums and rockwork, unmarked.

c1760

£3,500-4,500 **WW**

A Worcester teacup and saucer, painted in the atelier of James Giles, with flower sprays and sprigs, gilt dentil rims, crossed swords marks with a "9" between the blades.

c1770

£550-650 **WW**

A Worcester 'Queen Charlotte' pattern cup and saucer, with a shaped rim, unmarked.

c1770

£280-320 **WW**

A Worcester scratch cross mug, with a grooved loop handle and a short flared foot, painted in underglaze blue, enamelled in red and green with flowers, a fence and rockwork, a blurred workman's mark and two incised lines to the base, the enamels slightly later.

c1755 *3.75in (9.5cm) high*

£1,000-1,500 **WW**

An early Worcester scratch cross 'Stag Hunt' pattern coffee cup, with a grooved loop handle, a scratched cross mark, a chip to the inner rim.

c1755 *2.5in (6.5cm) high*

£280-320 **WW**

A Worcester coffee cup, with a notched loop handle, painted in the famille verte palette with three Chinese figures, one playing a pipe, together with a young boy in a garden, and a moth in flight, the interior with an iron red flowerhead.

c1760 *2.25in (5.5cm) high*

£800-1,200 **AA**

A Worcester coffee cup with a loop handle, decorated in the 'Red Bull' pattern, the saucer in the same pattern, the saucer cracked and chipped.

c1760

£350-450 **WW**

A Worcester fluted cup and saucer, painted with colourful birds and insects, with gilt dentil borders, square seal marks.

c1770

£350-450 **WW**

A Worcester teabowl and saucer, brightly painted in coloured enamels with sprays of European scattered flowers and butterflies, within brown line borders.

c1760 *4.5in (11.5cm) diam*

£500-700 **AA**

A Worcester fluted coffee cup, decorated in the famille verte palette with trailing flowers and leaves, unmarked, a small rim nick.

c1755 *2in (5.5cm) high*

£450-550 **WW**

A Worcester coffee cup, painted in puce camaieu with a chinoiserie scene, the inner border with flowers and foliage.

c1760 *2.5in (6cm) high*

£450-550 **WW**

A Worcester coffee cup, with notched loop handle, painted in the famille rose palette with two Chinese figures in a garden, beneath a gilt scroll band, decorated in iron red and black with flowers and leaves.

c1770 *2.5in (6.5cm) high*

£400-500 **AA**

A Worcester 'Red Bull' pattern cylindrical mug, with a loop handle, decorated in polychrome, unmarked.

c1760 *4.75in (12cm) high*

£1,500-2,000 **WW**

A Worcester coffee cup, with an entwined loop handle, moulded and painted in green with scrolling scolopendrium leaves, interspersed with flowers and leaves, a brown line rim.

c1770 *2.5in (6.5cm) high*

£600-800 **AA**

A Worcester 'Kempthorne' pattern teapot and cover.

c1765 *4.5in (11.5cm) high*

£700-900 **AA**

A Worcester 'Lady at the Loom' pattern globular teapot and cover, with a loop handle and flower knop, painted in famille rose palette in a Chinese style, within iron red loop and dot borders.

c1770 *4.75in (12cm) high*

£1,000-1,500 **AA**

A Worcester teapot and cover, with floral stripes, the knop restored.

c1775 *6.25in (16cm) high*

£1,000-1,500 **AD**

A Worcester teapot, small chip to spout.

c1775 *5.5in (14cm) high*

£500-700 **SA**

A Worcester coffee pot, decorated with flowers.

c1765 *8.5in (21.5cm) high*

£1,000-1,500 **SA**

A fluted Worcester coffee pot and cover, decorated with a Japan pattern, square seal mark, restored knop and a long vertical body crack.

c1770 *9.75in (24cm) high*

£200-250 **WW**

An early Worcester scratch cross coffee pot and cover, painted in colourful enamels with Chinese figures, tables and animals within elaborate gilt scrolling borders, incised line marks, the gilding slightly later, damage to the cover.

c1755 *7in (17.5cm) high*

£1,000-1,500 **WW**

A Worcester sucrier and cover, painted in the style of James Rogers.

c1760 *4.75in (12cm) high*

£1,800-2,200 **AA**

A Worcester fluted sugar bowl and cover, decorated with a Japan pattern, square seal mark.

c1770 *4.75in (12cm) wide*

£450-500 **WW**

A Worcester sugar bowl and cover, with a flower knop, painted with flowers in shaped panels, in the Kakiemon style, on a scale blue ground, a square seal mark, a clean hairline crack.

c1770 *4.75in (12cm) diam*

£180-220 **WW**

A Worcester 'Putai' pattern milk jug, of High Chelsea ewer form, painted in the famille rose palette, the interior with an iron red and gilt looped and dot band.

c1760 *3.5in (9cm) high*

£1,000-1,500 **AA**

A Worcester ewer of High Chelsea form, the acanthus and spiral moulded body painted with flowers and leaves, possibly by the Giles workshops, unmarked, a small foot rim chip.

c1770 *3.5in (9cm) high*

£3,000-5,000 **WW**

A Worcester reticulated basket, the exterior moulded with flowerheads, the interior painted in the manner of Rogers with a flower spray and floral border, unmarked, some good restoration.

c1770 *8.25in (21cm) wide*

£350-450 **WW**

A Worcester ovoid tea canister and cover, painted with flowers in shades of green in the manner of Giles, unmarked, the cover damaged.

c1770 *6in (15.5cm) high*

£500-600 **WW**

A CLOSER LOOK AT A PAIR OF WORCESTER BASKETS

The fine potting and thin, even glaze are typical of Worcester.
Pierced baskets had a tendency to crack during firing. To cover any faults, small flowers were often applied to any vulnerable sections and can be seen on the intersections to the outer side of this pair.
The decoration is fine and the pieces are in excellent condition. As a pair, they are very valuable.
These baskets date from a Worcester period that favoured light flower decoration and chinoiserie design. By the end of the 1760s, Worcester had moved on to a more opulent style inspired by Sèvres.

A pair of Worcester small pierced baskets, painted in the style of James Rogers.

c1760 *4in (10cm) diam*

£3,500-4,500 **AA**

Worcester: The Flight period (1783-1792)

- In 1783 the Worcester Warmstry House factory was purchased by its London agent, Thomas Flight, for his two sons Joseph and John. Although the Flights initially struggled with technical problems, their fortunes slowly began to change.
- John Flight travelled to France to study the latest French porcelain designs and the introduction of new spiral fluted shapes and French sprig patterns. He had seen the exciting new styles and realized that Worcester had relied too heavily on the Rococo style. Instead, Neo-classical styles were in demand.
- In 1789 Mrs. Charlotte Hampton was brought from London to take charge of the decorating departments, introducing a new method of gilding using mercury. The new gold had a flat, mirror-like finish different to anything produced at Worcester before.

A Flight Worcester trio set, decorated with gilt and blue.

c1785

£200-230 **SA**

A late 18thC Flight Worcester tea cup and saucer.

3.5in (9cm) diam

£180-220 **SA**

A Flight Worcester spiral fluted sugar bowl and cover, decorated in blue and gilt with flower sprigs, crescent mark.

c1790 *5in (12.5cm) wide*

£220-280 **WW**

An English porcelain sugar bowl and cover, probably Flight Worcester, unmarked, a small foot rim chip.

c1795 *5.5in (14cm) wide*

£220-280 **WW**

Worcester: The Flight & Barr period (1792-1804)

- Following the death of John Flight, Joseph Flight teamed up with Martin Barr.
- By the end of the 18thC the Worcester Company had developed a new harder body and glaze that compared well with the best French porcelain.
- Monochrome sprays and borders enjoyed great popularity and the artist John Pennington mastered the art of painting landscapes and other scenes in monochrome. He supervised the painting department and worked for the firm for over 50 years.

A Worcester Flight & Barr coffee can, decorated with the 'Royal Lily' pattern.

c1795 *2.25in (5.5cm) high*

£100-150 **GAS**

A Worcester Flight & Barr coffee can, painted in colours with feathers, beneath a gilt Greek key band, impressed mark, light wear to gilding.

c1800

£600-800 **DN**

A Worcester Flight & Barr coffee can, border pattern in gilt.

c1800 *2.5in (6.5cm) high*

£70-100 **GAS**

A Worcester Flight & Barr sucrier.

c1800 *5.75in (15cm) wide*

£200-300 **SA**

Worcester: The Barr, Flight & Barr period (1804-1813)

- In 1804 Martin Barr Junior joined in partnership with his father and Joseph Flight. The following years were to be extremely successful with some of the finest quality British porcelain being made at the factory.
- Porcelain services were decorated with views of customer's properties and grounds. Fashionable places such as Cheltenham, Worcester and Malvern were depicted on the wares.
- Due to the increasing popularity of botanical recording, rare specimens were painted on porcelain, usually copied from printed books. Flowers were painted in a more traditional style from Dutch Still Life paintings.
- Since Chinese porcelain decorated with the family Coat of Arms was a great status symbol and shipping from China was very unreliable, Worcester produced a magnificent alternative. The body was whiter with brighter colours and became the height of fashion in the early 19thC. Personalized services were made for royalty such as Tsar Alexander I, King George III and King William IV.

A Worcester Flight & Barr small oval sucrier and shaped cover, with two scroll handles and urn knop, painted in brown monochrome and gilt with strawberry and stiff leaf bands, within gilt line borders.

This rare shape would have been part of a Solitaire tea service.

c1795 *3.5in (9cm) high*

£600-800 **AA**

A Worcester Barr, Flight & Barr coffee can.

c1805 *2.5in (6.5cm) high*

£200-250 **SA**

A Worcester Barr, Flight and Barr coffee can, border pattern in gilt.

c1805 *2.25in (5.5cm) high*

£70-100 **GAS**

A Worcester Barr, Flight & Barr sucrier.

c1805 *7in (18cm) wide*

£200-250 **SA**

A Worcester Barr, Flight and Barr inkwell, gilt decorated with anthemion and leaf designs, applied goat's head masks and raised on claw feet on a triform base, impressed mark.

c1810 *4in (10cm) wide*

£450-550 **WW**

A CLOSER LOOK AT A BARR, FLIGHT & BARR EGG CUP STAND

Under Barr, Flight & Barr, Worcester excelled at producing items in sumptuous versions of Japanese Imari designs.

Meticulously painted and lavishly gilded, this set is typical of high-end Worcester pieces of the period.

During the early 19thC egg cups were commonly bought in sets that came complete with matching stands.

The good condition of this decorative egg cup stand makes it desirable as the extremities are vulnerable to damage.

A Worcester Barr, Flight and Barr round egg cup stand, with a central loop handle and six egg cups, decorated in Imari style with birds, flowering branches, bamboo and fences, within iron and gilt flowerhead panelled borders, impressed marks.

c1805 *8.25in (21cm) diam*

£2,500-3,000 **AA**

Worcester: The Flight, Barr & Barr period (1813-1840)

- After Martin Barr's death Joseph Flight became the principal shareholder with George and Martin Barr junior in partnership.
- The factory's great success continued and was boosted by the employment of the talented artist Thomas Baxter from 1814 to 1816. He painted flowers, shells, landscapes, portraits and figure subjects in Classical style.
- In the 1830s the Neo-Rococo style became popular with up-and-coming industrialists. The demand for rich classical porcelain diminished but the factory was resistant to change designs that had been so successful.
- In 1840 the Flight, Barr & Barr factory had to join its former rival Chamberlain. Between them they evolved new products and ideas, which were to establish the Worcester Company in the Victorian era.

A Worcester Flight, Barr & Barr campana-shaped small vase, with a gilt eagle head and ring handles, painted in coloured enamels with teal, within a gilt cartouche, on a purple ground, above a beaded band on square base.

c1820 *3.5in (9cm) high*

£800-1,200 **AA**

A early 19thC Worcester two-handled vase, painted with figures in a continuous landscape between beaded borders, probably Flight, Barr & Barr, unmarked, the cover lacking.

5.5in (14cm) wide

£200-250 **WW**

A Worcester, Flight Barr & Barr cup and saucer.

c1815 *Saucer 6in (15cm) diam*

£80-100 **SA**

A Worcester Flight, Barr & Barr coffee can, border pattern of leaves and flowers in greens, reds and golds.

c1815 *2.5in (6.5cm) high*

£80-120 **GAS**

A Chamberlain's Worcester plate, brightly decorated on a gilt vermiculated blue ground, script mark.

c1820 *8.5in (21.5cm) diam*

£60-90 **WW**

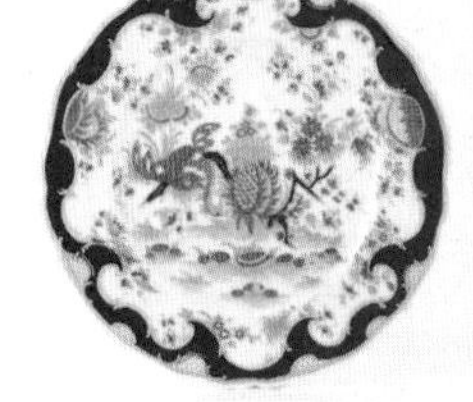

One of a pair of Chamberlain's Worcester plates, marked "2".

c1820 *9in (23cm) diam*

£100-150 pair **SA**

A Chamberlain's Worcester plate painted with birds and fruits, a black printed mark.

c1825 *7.25in (18.5cm) diam*

£300-400 **AA**

One of a pair of Chamberlain's Worcester plates, decorated with the crest of Arkwright of Cromford and Willersley Hall, Derbyshire.

Richard Arkwright was the inventor of the spinning jenny.

c1825 *9in (23cm) diam*

£120-180 pair **SA**

One of a pair of Chamberlain's Worcester lobed dessert dishes, painted with colourful flower sprays, gilded borders, printed marks.

c1825 *9.75in (24cm) wide*

£380-420 pair **WW**

Part of a set of 18 Chamberlain's Worcester dinner plates, the circular scalloped border painted with continuous six sided frieze interspersed with orange and lime green cartouche panels, painted in the 'Dragon in Compartments' pattern, depicting opposed dragons and opposed precious objects, puce and sepia printed marks.

10in (25cm) diam

£1,800-2,200 set **L&T**

A large Chamberlain's Worcester vase and cover, painted with birds.

c1815 *21.75in (55cm) high*

£5,000-7,000 **AA**

A Chamberlain's Worcester vase and cover, painted with a panel of flowers on a lavender ground, marked inside the cover, the knop re-glued.

c1830 *6.5in (16.5cm) high*

£220-280 **WW**

A Chamberlain's Worcester bottle, painted with a view of Worcester on a blue ground, printed mark, a metal and cork stopper.

c1830 *6.75in (17cm) high*

£220-280 **WW**

A Chamberlain's Worcester shallow D-shaped bough pot, with a pierced cover, the side painted with a classical scene entitled "Cornelia, Mother of the Gracchi", probably by John Wood, on a pale orange ground decorated with gilt flowerheads, inscribed "Chamberlains Worcester" in gilt, together with a 20thC Italian version.

Provenance: *Ex. Mottahhedeh collection, cf G. Godden, 'Chamberlain Worcester Porcelain' plate 337 and colour plate XXII.*

c1800 *8.5in (22cm) long*

£2,000-2,500 **WW**

A CLOSER LOOK AT A PAIR OF CHAMBERLAIN'S WINE COOLERS

Robert Chamberlain initially worked at the Worcester factory, but set up on his own c1786. The finely painted flower decoration and gilding is typical of Chamberlain's high quality work.

As a pair, the value of the wine coolers is increased. The fact that they retain their liners and covers in good condition also adds to the value.

Wine coolers were produced from the 15thC. The marbled liner in this container would have been filled with ice and the bottles placed inside to chill.

The term 'gadrooning' refers to decorative borders of convex flutes, often applied to a curved surface as an edging. This decorative technique has been used since the Renaissance.

A fine pair of Chamberlain's Worcester wine coolers, covers and liners, with richly gilded knops and gadrooned borders, the sides painted with botanical sprays titled 'Tulips', 'Flowering Raspberry', 'Moss Rose' and 'Superb Corn-Flag', the liners decorated inside and out with veined yellow marbling, a script mark to inside of one cover.

c1815 *13in (33cm) high*

£8,000-12,000 **WW**

A Chamberlain's Worcester cup and saucer, painted with views titled 'Park Place' and 'Nuneham', on a mauve ground, painted script marks, faint hairlines to the rims.

c1815

£220-280 **WW**

A Chamberlain's Worcester cup and saucer, decorated with flowers and gilt highlights.

c1820 *6in (15cm) diam*

£150-170 **SA**

A Chamberlain's Worcester miniature cup and saucer, painted with flowers and leaves on a gold ground, script mark to the cup.

c1825 *3.75in (9.5cm) diam*

£400-600 **WW**

A mid-19thC Chamberlain's Worcester small two-handled cup and saucer, painted with a view of Malvern on a blue ground, script mark to the cup.

4.25in (10.5cm) diam

£280-320 **WW**

A mid-19thC Chamberlain's Worcester cup and saucer decorated in 'Jaberwocky', pattern number 275.

£220-280 **WW**

A Chamberlain's Worcester flared beaker, finely painted in coloured enamels with Sappho and Phaon, within a titled gilt oval panel, the orange ground decorated in gilt with oval and lozenge shaped panels, flowerheads and garlands.

c1795 *3.5in (9cm) high*

£1,000-1,500 **LFA**

A Chamberlain's Worcester 'Charborough Park' part tea service, finely painted in coloured enamels with named views, on an orange and gilt vermicelli ground, with a gilt diamond border, comprising an oval teapot and stand, two teacups and saucers, two coffee cups, an oval milk jug and a plate.

c1810 *Teapot 6.5in (16.5cm) high*

£7,000-9,000 **AA**

A Chamberlain's Worcester fluted oval sugar bowl and cover, painted in polychrome with huts and trees on rocky islands.

c1795 *5.5in (14cm) wide*

£120-180 **WW**

A Chamberlain's Worcester teapot, cover and stand, decorated with a wide band of gilt and enamel foliage and stylized flowers, a chip inside the rim.

c1810 *10.5in (27cm) high*

£180-220 **WW**

An English porcelain 'lion-in-compartment' bowl, possibly Chamberlain's Worcester, with flaring gilt rim and colourful decoration.

c1820 *7in (18cm) diam*

£80-120 **S&K**

A Chamberlain's Worcester shell-moulded basket, the interior painted with flowers, the exterior with naturalistic details, black crowned mark.

c1820 *5in (13cm) long*

£450-500 **WW**

A Chamberlain's Worcester egg cruet, decorated with a rich Imari pattern, unmarked, one egg cup cracked.

c1825 *6.5in (16.5cm) wide*

£500-600 **WW**

A Grainger's Worcester coffee can, with a deep border pattern of white flowers, green and gold leaves in blue ground.

c1810 *2.5in (6.5cm) high*

£120-160 **GAS**

A Grainger's Worcester pot pourri.

c1825 *5in (13cm) high*

£250-350 **AD**

A Grainger's Worcester reticulated teapot and cover, pierced with scrolling foliage, within gilt band borders, printed marks.

c1880

£280-320 **DN**

PORCELAIN

OTHER FACTORIES

A Belleek moulded teapot and cover, the handle and knop formed as coral, with green shaded details, a second period mark.

c1900 *8in (20cm) high*

£200-300 **WW**

A Charles Bourne vase, with gilt lion head handles, a hairline crack.

c1820 *5.5in (14cm) high*

£400-450 **SA**

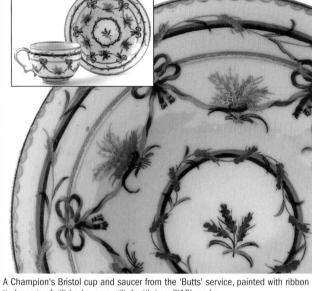

A Champion's Bristol coffee cup, with a moulded handle, painted in polychrome with scrolls and leaves, overglaze crossed swords and cross mark.

c1775

£350-450 **WW**

A Champion's Bristol cup and saucer from the 'Butts' service, painted with ribbon tied swags of gilt barley ears, gilt dentil rims, 'X10' marks.

c1775

£1,200-1,800 **WW**

A Coalbrookdale rococo vase, modelled with flowers and leaves, painted with panels of flowers, unmarked, some chips.

c1835 *9.75in (25cm) high*

£150-200 **WW**

A Copeland cup and saucer.

c1890 *5.5in (14cm) diam*

£30-50 **GCL**

A Copeland 'jewelled' porcelain plate painted by S. Alcock, the reverse inscribed "'I have a song to sing oh! W.S. Gilbert'", signed lower right, printed marks, impressed date code for 1895.

'I have a song to sing oh!' appears in the operetta by W.S. Gilbert and Sir A. Sullivan, 'The Yeoman of the Guard', which opened at the Savoy Theatre in 1888. It was first sung by Elsie and Jack Point.

9in (23cm) diam

£400-500 **DN**

A Copeland 'jewelled' porcelain plate painted by S. Alcock, with a bust portrait of a woman wearing a broad brimmed hat with a feather, within an elaborate rocaille border of turquoise 'jewelling' and gilt C-scrolls, signed lower right, impressed date code for 1896.

9in (23cm) diam

£300-400 **DN**

One of a pair of early 20thC Copenhagen porcelain plates, painted with sprigs and sprays of flowers within sinuous ribbing, osier moulding and gilt dog tooth lines on the rims, printed and painted marks.

9in (23cm) diam

£60-80 pair **CHEF**

A pair of Davenport pot pourri vases and covers, pattern number 6066, decorated in the Imari style, with pierced covers on dolphin supports, printed mark, one with a faint hairline to the rim.

c1835 *6in (15.5cm) high*

£200-300 **WW**

A Davenport part coffee service, decorated in the Imari style, printed factory marks, comprising seven cups, saucers and small plates, two cake plates, a slop bowl and a milk jug.

£150-250 set **WW**

A 19thC Davenport circular teapot and cover, decorated with an Imari pattern, number 2617, printed mark, the spout restored.

7in (18cm) high

£100-150 **WW**

A pair of Frankenthal figures of a peasant boy and girl, the boy wearing a red cap, puce lemon lined jacket and white breeches, the girl with a puce shawl, lemon apron with gilt and puce floral painted skirt, a pair of scissors hanging to one side, each standing with outspread arms, she is shading her eyes, blue underglaze mark.

6.25in (15.5cm) high

£350-400 **GORL**

A Herculaneum jug with gilt decoration of vines.

c1805 *6in (15cm) high*

£100-150 **SA**

A large 20thC Herend porcelain cockerel, brightly coloured and raised on an oval base.

15.75in (40cm) high

£500-700 **WW**

A pair of 20thC Herend porcelain owl bookends, brightly coloured and perched upon books.

11.5in (29.5cm) high

£500-700 **WW**

A Höchst pear-shaped hot-milk jug and cover, a blue crowned wheel mark, the handle, cover and spout restored.

c1765 *6in (15cm) high*

£120-180 **GORL**

A Höchst figure of a boy leaning forward with an outstretched arm, holding a bird and wearing a pale blue and yellow hat, a pale pink tailcoat, striped breeches, white stockings and black shoes, standing on a naturalistic base, a wheel mark in underglaze-blue, incised "N" and "18".

c1770 *4.25in (10.5cm) high*

£500-700 **GORL**

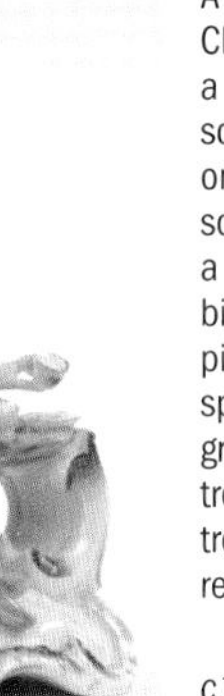

A Höchst figure of a Chinaman shown seated on a rocky base with a scrolling edge, a tree on one side and a table with scroll support on the other, a cup in his left hand a bird in his right, he wears a pink hat and a robe sprigged with pink and green flowers over green trousers, gilt wheel mark, tree and both wrists restored.

c1865 *6in (15cm) high*

£2,000-2,500 **GORL**

An Isleworth blue and white teabowl, printed with figures on a boat, a hut beside rocks and a pine tree on an island.

c1770 *3in (7.5cm) wide*

£200-300 **WW**

A Limbach figure of 'Autumn' from a set of the 'Four Seasons', represented as a gallant standing holding a bunch of grapes in his left hand and wearing a purple suit, with a long coat over a white waistcoat, a black tricorn hat and shoes, a basket full of grapes resting on a tree trunk beside him, on a mound base, minor damage to left hand.

c1775 *6.75in (16.5cm) high*

£700-900 **GORL**

A Ludwigsburg cup and saucer, with raised and painted decoration.

c1760 *5.25in (13.5cm) diam*

£300-350 **SA**

A Ludwigsburg figure of a farmer's wife with a basket and apron of fruit and vegetables and a chicken, in a white mob-cap, iron-red bodice and marbled purple skirt, the base with gilt scrolls, repair to basket and head, blue interlaced "C" mark to back.

c1770 *5.75in (14.5cm) high*

£350-450 **GORL**

A Ludwigsburg teabowl and saucer, painted marks in blue and "N.S." in iron red.

Saucer 5in (13cm) diam

£220-280 **LFA**

A Miles Mason sucrier.

c1805 *7.5in (19cm) wide*

£300-500 **SA**

A Miles Mason cup and saucer.

c1805 *5.25in (13.5cm) diam*

£130-190 **SA**

A Miles Mason teacup and saucer, pattern number 244.

c1810 *5.5in (14cm) diam*

£80-120 **GAS**

A Mennecy knife, decorated with Oriental scenes.

c1740 *11in (28cm) long*

£200-300 **SA**

Two of six Mennecy custard cups and covers, with finely spiral fluted bodies and fruit finials, painted with flower sprays, some with incised "DV" marks, some small chips.

c1760 *3.5in (9cm) high*

£1,000-1,500 set **WW**

A Nantgarw cup and saucer, painted with flowers and gilt leaves, the cup with a band of flower heads on a gilt ground, unmarked.

c1820

£2,000-2,500 **WW**

A Nantgarw oval stand, from the Marquise of Exeter service, decorated in London with a wide band of flowers on a gilt ground and a central rose spray, "Nant-garw C.W." impressed, cracks and some staining.

c1820 *14.25in (36cm) wide*

£450-550 **WW**

A pair of late 18thC Niderviller porcelain plates, each painted with figures and buildings in landscape vignettes, the borders with flower sprigs, crowned crossed 'C's marks.

9.5in (24cm) diam

£200-300 **WW**

A Niderviller figure of an apple vendor in a hat, a blue interlaced "C" mark.

c1775 *6in (15cm) high*

£250-300 **GORL**

A Nymphenburg bucket-shaped cup and saucer painted with floral monogram and scattered flower sprays with iron-red rim, impressed Bavarian shield marks and painter's mark ST, minor chip and crack to saucer.

c1775

£100-150 **GORL**

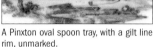

A Pinxton oval spoon tray, with a gilt line rim, unmarked.

c1800 *7.25in (18.5cm) wide*

£300-500 **WW**

A Plaue mantel clock, the pierced and moulded scroll base applied with coloured flowers, leaves and angel heads, surmounted by a putti supporting a cartouche, the eight day striking movement with round white enamel dial, marks in blue, some damage.

17.25in (44cm) high

£300-500 **LFA**

A square dish, probably by Ridgway.

c1815 *8.5in (21.5cm) wide*

£180-220 **SA**

A Ridgway Coalbrookdale-style pot and cover.

c1830 *5.5in (14cm) high*

£280-330 **GHA**

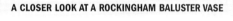

A Ridgway tureen.

c1840 *11.5in (29cm) wide*

£200-250 **GCL**

A Rosenthal circular white glazed dish, in three colour gilt, painted with a figure of a Chinaman after a design by Bjorn Winblad.

13in (32.5cm) diam

£70-100 **GORL**

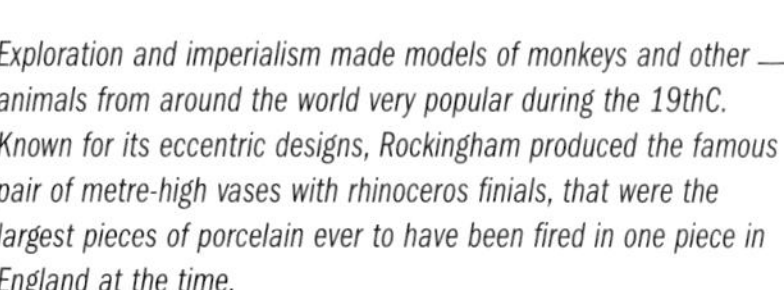

Part of a Victorian English porcelain Rockingham-style tea service, the Rococo baluster teapot with a domed lid and cast rose finial, the body on scrolling quadripartite base, a painted pattern number "2/5526", comprising a teapot and cover, a baluster milk jug, a footed slop bowl, a twin handled sucrier, 12 shallow cups with scroll handles, 11 saucers and a pair of twin handled bread plates.

£300-500 set **L&T**

A CLOSER LOOK AT A ROCKINGHAM BALUSTER VASE

Exploration and imperialism made models of monkeys and other animals from around the world very popular during the 19thC. Known for its eccentric designs, Rockingham produced the famous pair of metre-high vases with rhinoceros finials, that were the largest pieces of porcelain ever to have been fired in one piece in England at the time.

The large size, appealing shape and decoration of this vase makes it a substantial and attractive piece. This increases its value.

This vase is unmarked. During the 19thC, a great deal of unmarked porcelain, such as Coalport, Ridgway and Staffordshire, was incorrectly attributed to Rockingham.

It can be difficult to correctly identify Rockingham, making it necessary for collectors to understand shapes and pattern numbers.

A large Rockingham hexagonal baluster vase and cover, with a gilt monkey finial, printed in blue with birds and insects amid flowering branches, no mark, minor damage.

c1830 *25in (64cm) high*

£1,800-2,200 **WW**

A pair of Sitzendorf candelabra.

c1880 *13.25in (33.5cm) high*

£500-700 **GCL**

A pair of early to mid-19thC St Petersburg plates, the borders with eagle crests, gilt monograms and panels of flowers, all on a gilt decorated blue ground, blue factory marks, both with rim chips, one with a crack.

9.5in (24cm) diam

£600-900 **WW**

A Paul Hannong figure of a boy, Strasbourg or Frankenthal, "PH" impressed, some repairs.

c1755 *5.5in (14cm) high*

£300-500 **WW**

A Swansea cabinet cup and saucer, the cup with a scroll handle and raised on three paw feet, painted with a view of Coningsburgh Castle, the saucer with a view of Bicknacre Priory Essex, elaborate gilt scrolling borders, painted factory marks, a repair to the handle.

c1820

£2,200-2,800 **WW**

A matched Swansea porcelain trio, with fluted bodies and gilt borders, the centres with flower head motifs, red painted marks.

c1820

£200-300 **WW**

A Venice Cozzi blue and white plate, painted in iron-red and gilt with a bouquet of flowers and a butterfly, within a flowerhead border reserved with panels of birds and flowering plants, an iron-red anchor mark.

c1765 *8.75in (22cm) diam*

£150-200 **GORL**

A small Venice Cozzi figure of a young man, wearing a purple jacket with a tricorn hat at his side, some chips.

c1770 *4.25in (11cm) high*

£300-500 **WW**

A continental vase in Vienna style.

c1880

£250-300 **GCL**

A late 19thC Vienna plate painted with 'Mione and Amor', loosely robed in blue and yellow, Mione sleeps below a tree as Amor approaches with a green scarf, the rim gilt with alternating foliate panels and animal ovals, bindenschild mark in blue.

9.5in (24.5cm) diam

£220-280 **CHEF**

Two late 19thC porcelain cabinet plates in the style of Vienna, finely painted with half-length portraits of Catherine the Great and Elisabeth of Russia within elaborate panelled rims, blue beehive marks.

9.75in (25cm) diam

£800-1,200 **S&K**

One of a pair of Vincennes plates, incised and blue interlaced 'L's marks.

c1750 *9in (23cm) high*

£1,500-2,000 pair **WW**

An early 20thC blue-ground two-handled porcelain vase and cover in the Vienna style, on a stand, the cover with a gilt finial above angular handles, the centre painted with a continuous allegorical scene on a gilt ground, raised on a flaring socle and square plinth, with further scenes in arched reserves, with a blue beehive mark, signed "Seller".

21.75in (55.5cm) high

£2,000-3,000 **S&K**

A Keeling Factory X coffee cup, with floral pattern and a half wheel border.

c1795 *2.5in (6.5cm) high*

£60-80 **GAS**

A Yates teapot, in a rare shape, marked "No 231", crack to lid.

c1815 *11in (28cm) wide*

£320-380 **SA**

A Factory Z coffee can, a border pattern of orange ribbon and gold sprigs.

c1805 *2.5in (6.5cm) high*

£60-80 **GAS**

Part of a Yates bone china 16 piece part tea service, pattern number 1201, painted with flowers in panels on a gilt decorated blue ground, comprising five cups and saucers, a sugar bowl and cover, a milk jug, a slop bowl and two plates.

c1820-30

£600-900 set **WW**

A pair of English porcelain spill vases, painted with bands of pink roses within blue and gilt borders, one with a small foot chip.

c1820 *4.25in (11cm) high*

£100-150 **WW**

An English porcelain spill vase.

c1830 *4.25in (11cm) high*

£150-200 **AD**

Two 19thC English porcelain spill vases, decorated in the Sèvres style with panels of birds on a blue and gilt decorated ground, interlaced 'L's marks, one cracked and worn.

3.25in (8cm) high

£100-150 **WW**

A pair of English porcelain shaped vases.

c1835 *3.75in (9.5cm) high*

£300-350 **AD**

A small pair of English porcelain vases, formed as tulip flowers and leaves, raised on oval mound bases, unmarked, some restoration.

c1830 *3.75in (9.5cm) high*

£100-150 **WW**

An unusual English porcelain flask, of flattened form, each side painted with landscapes and bands of flowers, some damage.

c1815 *5in (13cm) high*

£180-220 **WW**

A mid-19thC porcelainous Toby jug in the Yorkshire style, modelled seated with a jug and beaker, painted with coloured glazes, some damage, lacks cover.

9.75in (25cm) high

£200-250 **DN**

An early to mid-19thC miniature English porcelain watering can, pattern number 221, with a gilt butterfly knop and colourful flower sprays to the sides.

2.5in (6.5cm) high

£180-220 **WW**

An English porcelain circular sugar bowl and cover, with a gilt ball finial and decorated with yellow bands and gilt foliage.

c1800 *6in (15cm) wide*

£180-220 **WW**

An English porcelain sucrier, decorated with flowers and gilt.

c1835 *6.75in (17cm) wide*

£120-180 **GFA**

An early to mid-19thC English porcelain double inkwell, in the form of a flower tub on a pierced base, painted with flowers, unmarked, some chips.

5.5in (14cm) wide

£200-250 **WW**

An English porcelain D-shaped bough pot, painted with three panels of flowers on a gold ground, within elaborate border patterns above a yellow band, the cover pierced with seven circular holes, unmarked, the cover repaired, slight wear.

c1805 *8.75in (22cm) high*

£450-550 **WW**

An English porcelain rectangular plaque, bat printed and painted with Scottish figures in a landscape with mountains beyond a lake, mounted in a glazed gilt frame, unmarked.

c1830 *6.75in (17cm) wide*

£280-320 **WW**

An English porcelain spill vase, painted with a panel of flowers on a gilt decorated blue ground, some wear to the gilding.

c1820 *4.25in (10.5cm) high*

£60-100 **WW**

A late 18thC French pottery figure group, depicting a shepherd with bagpipes, crowned with wreaths by a shepherdess, with a sleeping dog.

9.5in (24cm) high

£280-330 **L&T**

A pair of French bisque porcelain figures of hunters, each standing with a shotgun, the male beside a dead deer, the female beside dog.

13in (33cm) high

£70-100 **GORL**

A late 19thC French porcelain vase and cover, of Meissen style.

32in (80cm) high

£1,500-2,000 **L&T**

A late 18thC Continental figure of Clio.

9.5in (24.5cm) high

£220-280 **L&T**

A late 18thC German porcelain figure of a merchant, after a Meissen original.

8.5in (21cm) high

£150-200 **L&T**

A large French porcelain rectangular plaque, titled 'Le Printemps', painted by M.N. Shearman after Pierre Auguste Cot (1837-1883), depicting young lovers on a swing beside a forest pool, initialled "M.N.S.", the reverse inscribed with a Howell & James Paris Exhibition label for 1878, mounted in a gilt frame.

'Springtime', an oil on canvas by Pierre Auguste Cot sold on 1st November 1995 at Sotheby's New York for $50,000 (around £33,000).

c1875 *15.5in (39.5cm) high*

£6,000-8,000 **WW**

QUEEN VICTORIA

A Minton octagonal plate, made to commemorate the golden jubilee of Queen Victoria.

c1887 *10in (25.5cm) wide*

£250-300 **H&G**

A plate made to commemorate the golden jubilee of Queen Victoria, probably by Burgess and Leigh.

The bright colours of this piece are unusual. Most pieces made for the golden jubilee were in dark colours to reflect Victoria's reluctance to celebrate the jubilee following the death of Albert.

c1887 *9in (23cm) diam*

£100-150 **H&G**

An octagonal plate, made to commemorate the golden jubilee of Queen Victoria.

c1887 *10in (25.5cm) diam*

£250-300 **H&G**

A bone china plate, made to commemorate the diamond jubilee of Queen Victoria.

c1897 *9.5in (24cm) diam*

£100-150 **H&G**

A Doulton earthenware mug, made to commemorate the diamond jubilee of Queen Victoria, in near mint condition.

c1897 *3.5in (9cm) high*

£100-150 **H&G**

An earthenware mug by Maling, made to commemorate the diamond jubilee of Queen Victoria.

c1897 *3.5in (9cm) high*

£100-150 **H&G**

A pressed copper plaque, made to commemorate either the golden or diamond jubilee of Queen Victoria.

It is likely that this plaque was once originally part of a larger, dated, commemorative piece made in c1887 or c1897.

16in (13.25cm) diam

£180-220 **H&G**

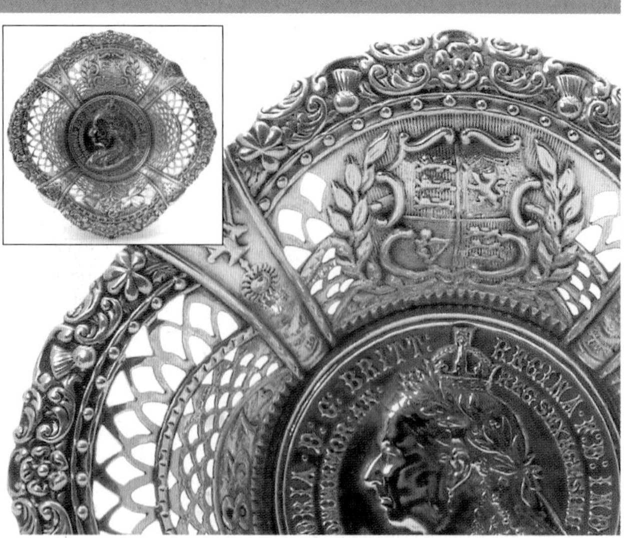

An unusual pressed sterling silver dish, made to commemorate the diamond jubilee of Queen Victoria, the detailed work in fine condition.

c1897 *5in (13cm) wide*

£150-200 **H&G**

A Doulton Lambeth jug, *in memoriam* of Queen Victoria.

c1901 *8in (20.5cm) high*

£550-650 **H&G**

EDWARD VII

A pair of bone china plates by Hammersley, made to commemorate the coronation of Edward VII and Queen Alexandra.

c1902 *9in (23cm) diam*

£350-450 **H&G**

A bone china trio, made to commemorate the coronation of King Edward VII and Queen Alexandra.

This trio bears the date August 9th, the actual date of the coronation. Most commemorative pieces produced for this event are dated 26th June because they were made before the coronation was postponed as a result of the King's appendicitis. Items bearing the August date often command a premium.

c1902 *6in (15cm) diam*

£100-150 **H&G**

An enamel beaker, made to commemorate the coronation of King Edward VII and Queen Alexandra.

These beakers are fairly common but vulnerable to damage, this one is unusually in near mint condition with no chips and all the gold decoration remaining. A damaged version is likely to be worth £30-40.

c1902 *4in (10cm) high*

£80-120 **H&G**

EDWARD VIII

A bone china loving cup with lion handles, made to commemorate the proposed coronation of Edward VIII, by Paragon China, a limited edition of 1,000 in each of four sizes.

There is a general misconception that Edward VIII coronation pieces must be rare as Edward was never crowned. However, many factories produced wares in preparation for the coronation prior to his abdication, so commemorative items are not scarce.

c1936 *5.25in (13.5cm) high*

£350-400 **H&G**

A Minton bone china beaker, made to commemorate the proposed coronation of Edward VIII, a limited edition of 2,000.

c1936 *4.25in (11cm) high*

£220-280 **H&G**

An earthenware beaker, made to commemorate the proposed coronation of Edward VIII, by Wedgwood & Co.

This beaker was made by the lesser-known Wedgwood company.

c1936 *4.25in (11cm) high*

£50-80 **H&G**

An earthenware Toby jug, made to commemorate the proposed coronation of Edward VIII, the handle in the shape of an initial 'E', by Bretby pottery.

c1936 *4in (10cm) high*

£60-70 **H&G**

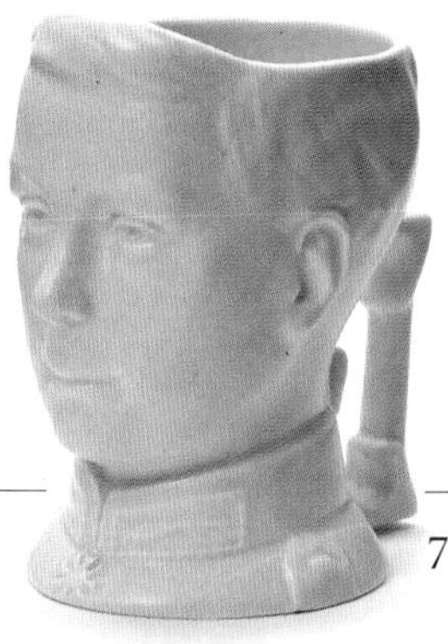

GEORGE V & GEORGE VI

A Copeland Late Spode whisky decanter for Andrew Usher & Co. distillers, Edinburgh, made to commemorate the coronation of George V.

This decanter was also made in green with beige decoration, but this blue version is less common. To find one in such good condition is unusual as the cross to the stopper is very vulnerable to breakage. Any damage will reduce the value of the bottle by 50 per cent or more.

c1911 *10in (25.5cm) high*

£120-180 **H&G**

A Coalport bone china blue transfer plate, made to commemorate the coronation of King George V and Queen Mary.

c1911 *10.5in (26.5cm) diam*

£150-180 **H&G**

A bone china mug by Hammersley, made to commemorate the silver jubilee of George V.

c1935 *5.5in (14cm) high*

£50-80 **H&G**

A bone china cup and saucer by Grafton China, made to commemorate the silver jubilee of George V.

c1935 *5.5in (14cm) high*

£50-80 **H&G**

A Copeland Spode jumbo cup and saucer, made to commemorate the coronation of George VI and Queen Elizabeth.

c1937 *9in (23cm) diam*

£280-320 **H&G**

A bone china cup, saucer and plate, with a green ground, made to commemorate the coronation of George VI, by Aynsley.

This set was also produced in white, which is less desirable.

c1937 *Plate 7in (18cm) diam*

£100-150 **H&G**

An earthenware mug, made to commemorate the coronation of George VI, by Bristol Pountney.

c1937 *4.75in (12cm) high*

£100-150 **H&G**

A Tuscan China bone china loving cup, made to commemorate the coronation of George VI.

c1937 *3.5in (9cm) high*

£60-90 **H&G**

An earthenware egg cup, made to commemorate the coronation of George VI.

c1937 *2.5in (6.5cm) high*

£25-30 **H&G**

A rare comport by Paragon, made to commemorate the coronation of George VI.

With the six matching plates the value of the set rises to £600-800.

c1937 *8.5in (21.5cm) diam*

£350-450 **H&G**

A bone china plate, made to commemorate the coronation of George VI, by Paragon.

c1937 8.5in (21.5cm) diam

£80-120 **H&G**

A pair of Wedgwood Queensware plates, made to commemorate the visit of George VI and Queen Elizabeth to the US, made exclusively for Plummers of New York, a limited edition of 3,000.

'Limited edition' means a promise not to make more than the stated number. In practice, less were often made.

c1939 9.5in (24cm) diam

£180-220 **H&G**

OTHER COMMEMORATIVES

A saucer *in memoriam* of Princess Charlotte, with pink lustre decoration.

The pink lustre makes this saucer appealing to collectors of lustre ware as well as of commemorative ware. Charlotte died in childbirth at the age of 21.

c1817 5.5in (14cm) diam

£80-120 **H&G**

A Copeland parian bust of Princess Alexandra, made to commemorate her wedding to Prince Albert Edward, later Edward VII.

This bust was produced for several years, but had earrings for only the first two years of production. This version has earrings and commands a premium. As the damage on this bust is limited to the base, the value is not greatly affected. A bust of the Prince was also produced.

c1863 12in (30.5cm) high

£500-700 **H&G**

A CLOSER LOOK AT A PRINCE ALBERT TAZZA

Commissioned from Copeland by The Art Union of London, this tazza would have been given away as a high quality 'ballot' prize.

The tazza was produced in two colourways. This orange-brown version is less common than the green and cream type although they are both valuable.

This is one of the most impressive and detailed pieces produced in memoriam to Prince Albert's death.

The three panels depict Albert's achievements and are entitled "Albert, promoter of the Arts", "President of societies for science" and "Chancellor of an university".

A Copeland tazza *in memoriam* of Prince Albert, produced for the Art Union of London, made in 1863.

16in (40.5cm) diam

£800-1,200 **H&G**

An octagonal plate by Wallace Gimson, made to commemorate the Emin Pacha relief exhibition.

c1887 9.5in (24cm) diam

£300-350 **H&G**

A Parian bust of Princess Mary made at the time of her wedding to the Duke of York, by Robinson and Leadbetter.

c1893 8.5in (21.5cm) high

£220-280 **H&G**

A Spanish-American War commemorative plate, entitled "Remember the Maine", with a gilt decorated edge.

c1898 6.25in (16cm) diam

£30-40 **BCAC**

A bone china mug *in memoriam* of Princess Alice, Countess of Athlone.

Princess Alice was the last surviving grandchild of Queen Victoria.

c1981 3.5in (9cm) high

£50-80 **H&G**

BLUE & WHITE

A Spode 'Caramanian' series oval well-and-tree dish printed with 'The Castle of Boudron in the Gulf of Stancio', printed and impressed upper-case marks, a riveted crack through the well.

18.25in (46.5cm) long

£300-500 **DN**

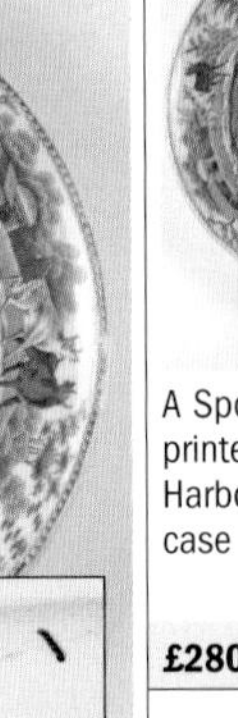

A Spode 'Caramanian' series oval dish printed with 'Principal Entrance to the Harbour of Cacamo', impressed lower-case mark.

15in (38cm) long

£280-320 **DN**

A Spode 'Indian Sporting' series small patty dish of deep oval shape, printed with a section adapted from 'Common Wolf Trap', untitled, printed upper-case mark.

5.5in (13.5cm) long

£500-700 **DN**

A Spode 'Caramanian' series oval dish, printed with 'Caramanian Castle', impressed lower-case mark.

9.75in (24.5cm) long

£300-350 **DN**

A Spode 'Caramanian' series oval dish, printed with 'Part of the Harbour of Macri', impressed lower-case mark, some discolouration.

10.75in (27.5cm) long

£220-280 **DN**

A Spode 'Caramanian' series large circular dish or charger, printed with a variant of 'Antique Fragments at Limisso', impressed upper-case mark, the rim glued.

16.75in (42.5cm) diam

£600-900 **DN**

A Spode 'Indian Sporting' series small dish printed with 'Battle Between a Buffalo and a Tiger', printed title and printed and impressed upper-case marks.

9.25in (23.5cm) long

£1,500-2,000 **DN**

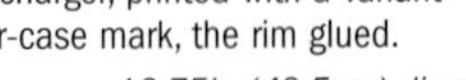

A Spode 'Indian Sporting' series square salad bowl, printed with 'Driving a Bear out of Sugar Canes', untitled, impressed upper-case mark.

9.75in (24.5cm) wide

£1,200-1,800 **DN**

A Spode 'Indian Sporting' series dish, printed with 'Shooting at the Edge of a Jungle', printed title and impressed upper-case marks, some staining.

14.75in (37.5cm) long

£500-800 **DN**

A Spode 'Caramanian' series rectangular dish or stand of deeper than usual form, printed with 'Caramanian Castle', impressed lower-case mark.

8.5in (22cm) long

£500-700 **DN**

A Spode pearlware deep canted rectangular dish, printed in underglaze blue with the 'Lady at the Well' pattern, impressed and printed mark in blue.

12.5in (31.5cm) long

£150-200 **LFA**

A Spode 'Indian Sporting' series dessert dish or comport, of lobed diamond shape, printed with 'Hunting a Hog Deer', printed and impressed upper-case marks, small chip behind one handle.

10.5in (27cm) long

£2,200-2,800 **DN**

A Spode 'Indian Sporting' series dessert dish or comport, of lobed diamond shape, printed with 'Hunting a Civet Cat', printed title and upper-case mark, small filled chips beneath rim.

10.5in (27cm) long

£1,500-2,000 **DN**

A Spode 'Caramanian' series dessert dish of lobed and cusped diamond shape, printed with 'Citadel near Corinth', impressed upper-case mark, hair crack.

10.5in (27cm) long

£500-700 **DN**

A Spode pearlware lozenge shaped dish, printed in underglaze blue with 'A Domestic Ceremony' from the 'Greek' series, small chip.

c1810 *9.75in (25cm) wide*

£70-100 **LFA**

A Spode 'Caramanian' series circular footed comport and cover, printed with 'Citadel Near Corinth' inside, 'Caramanian Vase' outside, and 'Caramanian Castle' on the cover, possibly the centrepiece from a supper set, some discolouration, small filled chip to edge of the cover.

8.25in (21cm) diam

£700-1,000 **DN**

A Spode 'Caramanian' series divided vegetable dish and cover, the cover with 'A Colossal Sarcophagus at Cacamo in Caramania' and 'A Colossal Vase Near Limisso in Cyprus', the divided liner with 'Principal Entrance to the Harbour of Cacamo', and the base with a composite scene derived from the 'Indian Sporting' series engravings, impressed lower-case marks, base broken and riveted, liner cracked and riveted with some staining, cover with hairline crack and riveted knop.

12.5in (32cm) long

£200-250 **DN**

A Spode 'Caramanian' series square vegetable dish, printed with a variant of 'Principal Entrance to the Harbour of Cacamo', impressed lower-case mark, no cover.

9.25in (23.5cm) wide

£280-320 **DN**

A rare Spode 'Musicians' pattern washbowl, printed and impressed upper-case marks, minor cracks within footrim.

13in (33cm) diam

£1,800-2,200 **DN**

A Spode 'Filigree' pattern footbath, of banded oval shape, printed and impressed upper-case marks, star cracks to base.

20.5in (52cm) long

£700-1,000 **DN**

A Spode 'Tower' pattern bidet, printed on both inner and outer surfaces, printed and impressed upper-case marks.

21in (53cm) long

£400-600 **DN**

A Spode 'Indian Sporting' series covered soap box of three pieces with an inner draining tray, the cover printed with a section adapted from 'Common Wolf Trap', the tray with the usual border, the base with larger parts of the border, untitled, the printed upper-case marks also impressed on the base, a hairline crack to base, filled chip on cover.

4.5in (11cm) long

£1,000-1,500 **DN**

A rare Spode 'Tower' pattern sponge box, of low circular form with a separate pierced drainer cover, printed upper-case marks, cracks to both pieces.

11in (28cm) wide

£320-380 **DN**

A Spode 'Caramanian' series small ewer, printed with a composite design derived from the 'Indian Sporting' engravings, printed lower-case mark, fine glaze cracks to base.

6.5in (16cm) high

£500-700 **DN**

A Spode 'Caramanian' series wash ewer of new shape, printed with 'A Colossal Sarcophagus Near Castle Rosso', printed lower case mark.

9in (23cm) high

£280-320 **DN**

A rare Spode 'Tower' pattern suckling pot, of churn bottom shape, printed upper-case mark.

3.5in (9cm) high

£500-700 **DN**

A Spode 'Tower' pattern dog dish, printed upper-case mark, cracks, damage to one foot.

6.75in (17cm) long

£500-700 **DN**

A Spode 'Indian Sporting' series meat dish printed with 'Dooreahs Leading Out Dogs', printed title and printed and impressed upper-case marks, some staining.

18.5in (47cm) long

£700-1,000 **DN**

A Spode 'Caramanian' series meat dish of the later new indented shape, printed with 'A Triumphal Arch of Tripoli in Barbary', impressed upper-case mark, kiln dust to back.

20.5in (52cm) long

£600-900 **DN**

A Swansea Baker, Bevans & Irwin 'Castle' pattern meat dish, printed in blue with a copy of the Spode design, printed mark with "Opaque/China" and maker's initials.

c1825 *16.5in (42cm) long*

£200-300 **DN**

A Spode 'Caramanian' series meat dish of the later new indented shape, printed with 'Antique Fragments at Limisso', impressed lower-case mark.

16.5in (42cm) long

£400-600 **DN**

A Spode 'Aesop's Fables' series meat dish, printed with 'The Dog in the Manger', a printed title mark "SPODE" and impressed upper-case mark, broken and glued.

18.5in (47cm) long

£100-150 **DN**

A Spode 'Indian Sporting' series drainer, printed with 'Hunting a Buffalo', printed title and printed and impressed upper-case marks, chip to drainage hole.

11.5in (29cm) long

£700-1,000 **DN**

A Spode 'Caramanian' series oval drainer, printed with 'Antique Fragments at Limisso', an impressed lower-case mark, some staining.

13.25in (33.5cm) long

£500-700 **DN**

A Spode 'Caramanian' series drainer of the later new indented shape, printed with 'The Castle of Boudron in the Gulf of Stancio', an impressed lower-case mark, some staining, minor chipping to drainage holes.

14.75in (37.5cm) long

£400-600 **DN**

A Spode stone china pierced oval drainer, printed in underglaze blue with the 'Grasshopper' pattern, a printed mark in blue.

c1820 *14.75in (37.5cm) wide*

£180-220 **LFA**

A Spode 'Indian Sporting' series soup tureen, cover and stand, the body printed with 'The Hog at Bay', the cover and stand with 'Hunting a Buffalo', printed titles and printed and impressed upper-case marks, glued crack to tureen body.

Stand 17in (43.5cm) long

£1,500-2,000 **DN**

A Spode 'Caramanian' series covered soup tureen, of the later 'Tower' pattern shape, the body with 'A Colossal Sarcophagus Near Castle Rosso' and the cover with 'A Colossal Sarcophagus at Cacamo in Caramania' and 'A Colossal Vase near Limisso in Cyprus', impressed lower-case marks, repair to foot at one end, the knop glued.

14.25in (36.5cm) long

£220-280 **DN**

A Spode 'Indian Sporting' series oval soup tureen stand, printed in blue with 'Hunting a Buffalo', a printed title and printed and impressed upper-case maker's marks.

c1825 *17.25in (43.5cm) long*

£700-1,000 **DN**

A Spode armorial soup tureen stand, of circular gadroon shape, printed with the arms of Alderman Thompson MP and the motto "Spectemur Agendo" (Let us be judged by our actions), within a border from the 'Jasmine' pattern, printed and impressed upper-case marks, filled chips behind rim.

13.5in (34.5cm) diam

£100-150 **DN**

Part of a Spode 'Geranium' pattern circular supper set, comprising a low circular centrepiece with reversible segmented cover and four quadrant dishes, impressed upper-case marks, some restoration, four covers missing.

c1825 *18.25 (46.5cm) diam*

£400-600 set **DN**

A Spode 'Flower Cross' pattern oval supper set in a mahogany tray, comprising four segment dishes with covers and a covered centrepiece containing a pierced tray, four eggcups and a divided salt and pepper dish, two covers with scroll marks, one dish and the centrepiece handle repaired, no alternate inner bowl.

23.25in (59cm) wide

£600-900 **DN**

A pair of Spode pearlware plates, each printed in underglaze blue with 'Zeus in his Chariot', from the 'Greek' series.

c1810 *9.75in (25cm) diam*

£120-180 **LFA**

A rare Spode bone china 'Shepherdess' pattern pierced basket and stand of oval shape with oval piercing, printed lower-case marks.

Stand 10.75in (27.5cm) long

£800-1,200 **DN**

A Spode 'Caramanian' series pierced basket and stand of oval shape with oval piercing, both pieces printed with 'A Sarcophagus at Cacamo', printed lower-case marks, the stand broken and riveted.

Stand 9.25in (23.5cm) long

£350-400 **DN**

A Spode 'Caramanian' series syllabub or custard cup, of bell shape, printed with part of 'Sarcophagi and Sepulchres at the Head of the Harbour of Cacamo', unmarked.

2.25in (5.5cm) high

£180-220 **DN**

A Spode 'Indian Sporting' series custard cup, of pail shape, printed with 'Death of the Bear', printed upper-case mark, hairline crack to base.

2.5in (6.5cm) high

£800-1,200 **DN**

A Spode 'Caramanian' series porter mug, printed with 'A Colossal Sarcophagus Near Castle Rosso', printed lower-case mark.

5.5in (14cm) high

£800-1,200 **DN**

A Spode 'Forest Landscape' pattern cheese cradle, unmarked, small repaired chip to foot.

12.25in (31cm) long

£700-1,000 **DN**

A Spode 'Caramanian' series sauce ladle, printed with an animal design derived from the border of 'Indian Sporting', printed lower-case mark.

6.5in (16.5cm) long

£600-900 **DN**

A Thomas Godwin plate, from the 'Indian Scenery' series, printed in underglaze blue with 'Supseya Chart, Khanpore', printed title mark.

c1845 *10.25in (26cm) diam*

£70-100 **LFA**

A Thomas Godwin plate, from the 'Indian Scenery' series, printed in underglaze blue with 'Tombs near Etaya on the Jumna River', printed title mark.

c1845 *9in (23cm) diam*

£70-100 **LFA**

A pearlware plate, printed in underglaze blue with the 'Beemaster' pattern, the rim panelled with animals alternating with flowers.

10in (25.5cm) diam

£280-320 **LFA**

A pair of pearlware plates, each printed in underglaze blue with 'A Wreath for the Victor' from the 'Greek' series, one with a small rim chip.

c1810 *8in (20.5cm) diam*

£60-90 **LFA**

A Minton 'English Scenery' series meat dish, printed in blue with a scene identified as Castle Gantully in Perthshire, a printed series title mark.

c1830 *18.5in (47.5cm) long*

£700-1,000 **DN**

A pair of pearlware small canted rectangular dishes, each printed in underglaze blue with the Devonshire serpent crest beneath a coronet, the motto "Cavendo Tutus" on a peony and lotus ground, brown line rims, one dish with a glaze chip.

c1880 *6.25in (16cm) wide*

£150-200 **LFA**

A Minton 'Chinese Marine' series meat dish, with gadrooned rim, printed in blue with a typical chinoiserie scene within the usual floral scroll border, printed mark with cursive initial "M".

c1835 *20.5in (52cm) long*

£400-600 **DN**

A Wedgwood pearlware canted and rectangular meat dish, printed in underglaze blue with the 'Crane' pattern, within a border of Gothic tracery, flowers and leaves, an impressed mark.

c1820 *16.5in (42cm) wide*

£280-320 **LFA**

A large Wedgwood 'Absalom's Pillar' pattern meat dish, printed in blue with the Middle Eastern scene and a floral border, impressed mark, some wear and staining.

c1820 *22.75in (57.5cm) long*

£220-280 **DN**

A Swansea 'Monopteros' pattern meat dish printed in blue with the variant of the 'Daniell scene depicting an Ancient Building near Firoz Shah's Cotilla, Delhi', unmarked, small area of restoration behind rim.

c1815 *19in (48.5cm) long*

£280-320 **DN**

A Henshall & Co. 'Temple of Friendship' pattern meat dish from the 'Fruit and Flower Border' series, printed in blue with the titled scene within the usual series border of fruit and flowers, printed title mark.

c1820 *20.25in (51.5cm) long*

£700-1,000 **DN**

A Don Pottery 'Named Italian Views' series meat dish, printed in blue with 'Cascade at Isola' within the usual border of flowers and flying putti, unmarked, minor crazing to one end of the well.

c1825 *17in (42.5cm) long*

£500-700 **DN**

A Goodwin & Ellis 'Peruvian hunters' well-and-tree meat dish, printed in blue with a scene of four deer hunters within a border of related vignettes on a floral and leafy ground, a printed title mark with maker's initials.

c1840 *21.75 (55.5cm) long*

£320-380 **DN**

A pearlware helmet shaped jug, with a loop handle, printed in underglaze blue with mounted figures before ruins, within stiff leaf and anthemion bands.

c1820 *7.5in (19cm) high*

£400-600 **LFA**

A pearlware compressed baluster shaped jug, with a scroll handle, printed in underglaze blue with the 'Genevese' pattern and inscribed in black "Janet Scott, Park Foot".

c1845 *6in (15cm) high*

£120-180 **LFA**

A blue and white frog puzzle jug printed with a view of the Pulteney Bridge in Bath from a wooded landscape with a deer, incised "JBD" mark, attributed to Dillwyn, Swansea.

7.5in (19cm) high

£2,200-2,800 **CHEF**

A Wedgwood pearlware small compressed round teapot and cover, with a loop handle, everted rim and button knop, printed in underglaze blue with the 'Blue Bamboo' pattern, impressed mark, the tip of the spout restored.

c1815 *3.5in (9cm) high*

£120-180 **LFA**

A Brougham and Russell reform bill commemorative teapot, of globular shape with a recessed cover, printed in purple with portraits of "Lord John Russell" and "Baron Brougham & Vaux" separated by union sprays and crowns, unmarked.

c1835 *9.25in (24cm) long*

£180-220 **DN**

A Joseph Meyer and Sons cylindrical spitoon and liner from the 'Northern Scenery' series, printed in underglaze blue with Loch Katrine, printed title mark.

3.5in (9cm) high

£150-200 **LFA**

An early Victorian blue and white teabowl and saucer, the facetted sides printed with a band of flowers enclosing a scene of a European couple docking in China on the saucer.

£30-40 **CHEF**

A Staffordshire black printed octagonal tureen, cover and stand, printed with the 'Rhone Scenery' pattern, with foliate crown finial bracket, scroll handles, marks for T.J. & J. Mayer.

c1850 *Stand 16.75in (42.5cm) wide*

£250-350 **S&K**

A mid-19thC Staffordshire ironstone large octagonal bowl, by J. Clementson, decorated with the 'Corea' pattern of sepia-printed pavilions in a landscape.

13.5in (33cm) diam

£100-150 **S&K**

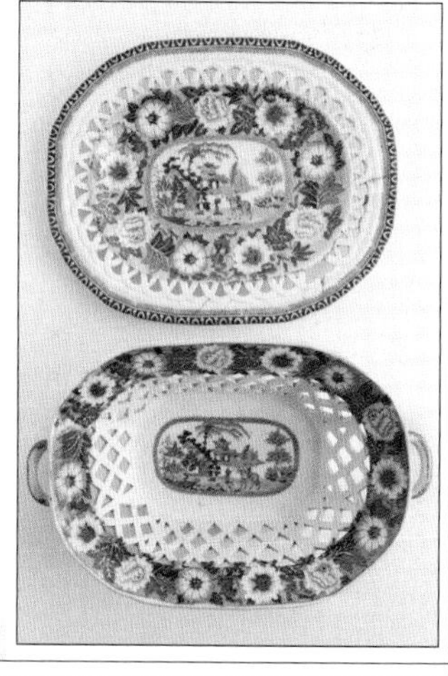

A John Rogers pearlware pierced two handled basket and stand, of canted rectangular form, printed in underglaze blue with the 'zebra' pattern, within a broad band of flowers and leaves, impressed marks, the stand glued.

c1820 *10in (25.5cm) wide*

£280-320 **LFA**

An Andrew Stevenson 'Netley Abbey' pattern soup tureen and cover, with blue moulded lion handles, printed in blue with the identified view within the usual border of flowers and scroll-framed vignettes, impressed maker's ship mark, a fine hairline crack.

c1825 *13.75in (35cm) long*

£300-400 **DN**

A General Steam Navigation company chamber pot, of ornate lobed shape with moulded handle, printed in blue with a sheet floral ground and large reserves on either side comprising a belt inscribed "General Steam Navigation Company, 1824", surrounding the globe with superimposed compass points, the motif repeated inside, unmarked.

Founded in 1824 and incorporated in 1831, the General Steam Navigation Co. was one of the first commercial steamship lines. Based in London, it developed an important trade with British North Sea ports and with Hamburg, Rotterdam, Antwerp and le Havre. It was taken over by P&O in 1920.

8in (20.5cm) diam

£600-900 **DN**

POTTERY

The English pottery market has witnessed a decline in the price of common pieces at the lower end of the market and many pottery dealers have suffered a downturn in business from the US. In the UK, pottery enthusiasts tend to have been collecting for many years, and are thus only looking for the most exclusive pieces to complete their collections. The fall in prices does however mean that it is a good time for the new collector to enter the field.

Portrait figures of royalty, military, theatrical and religious personalities have been particularly affected by this general slump, although rare pieces continue to attract high prices, as do certain niches within the general market. Staffordshire figures of exotic jungle animals, such as zebras and tigers, for example, are finding buyers who are drawn to their whimsical qualities. The demand for the classic dogs, cats, rabbits, cows and other domestic pieces has remained fairly stable.

Pottery that is rare and of exceptional quality will most likely continue to rise in value. At the lower end of the market prices will remain undervalued unless new collectors discover the charm of British pottery, as is beginning to happen in the US.

John Howard

An 18thC Liverpool creamware jug, printed in black by Joseph Johnson with the 'Farmer's Arms' on one side of the baluster shape and with verses on the other.

7.25in (18.5cm) high

£400-500 **CHEF**

A CLOSER LOOK AT A GREATBATCH CREAMWARE JUG

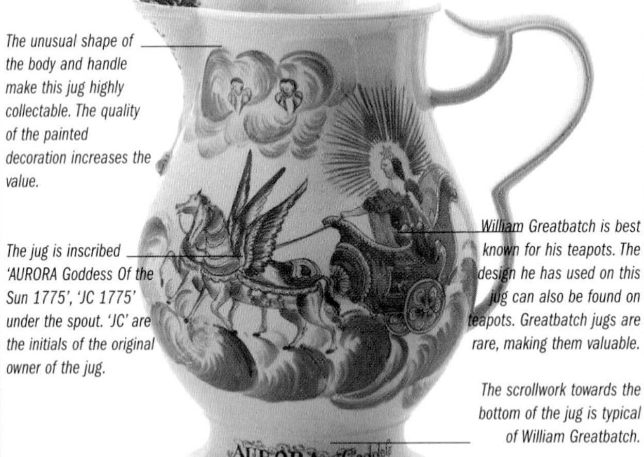

The unusual shape of the body and handle make this jug highly collectable. The quality of the painted decoration increases the value.

The jug is inscribed 'AURORA Goddess Of the Sun 1775', 'JC 1775' under the spout. 'JC' are the initials of the original owner of the jug.

William Greatbatch is best known for his teapots. The design he has used on this jug can also be found on teapots. Greatbatch jugs are rare, making them valuable.

The scrollwork towards the bottom of the jug is typical of William Greatbatch.

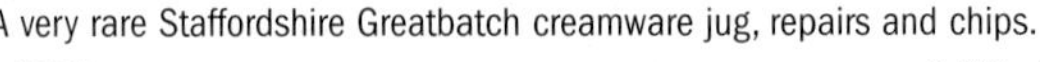

A very rare Staffordshire Greatbatch creamware jug, repairs and chips.

c1775 *8.75in (22cm) high*

£5,500-6,500 **JHOR**

An English creamware pitcher, with a restored spout.

c1780 *7in (17.5cm) high*

£400-600 **JHD**

An English creamware jug, with a strap handle.

c1780 *6in (15cm) high*

£300-400 **JHD**

A good creamware flag jug, with a green line rim, one side printed in black with a sailing ship, the other displaying fifty-two flags and titled "An East View of Liverpool Light House & Signals on Bidston Hill", the tip of the spout repaired, crack to rim.

c1790 *7.25in (18.5cm) high*

£600-900 **WW**

A creamware jug, of ovoid shape with a simple strap handle, overglaze printed with "Jack Spritsail's Frolic" on one side, a British three-mast frigate and "Success to trade" on the reverse, a framed verse beneath the spout, unmarked, some damage.

c1800 *8.5in (22.5cm) high*

£550-650 **DN**

A late 18thC creamware masonic jug, the printing in black, attributed to "Sadler and Green", the London arms of the Antients or the Athol Grand Lodge on each side and the spout.

6.75in (17.5cm) high

£400-500 **CHEF**

A late 18thC creamware punch pot and cover, possibly Liverpool, the near spherical sides printed in black with an oval stipple engraving of a girl squeezing grapes into a funnel, a number seven above and "Summer" below, the other side with an oval titled "Plenty".

6.75in (17cm) high

£300-400 **CHEF**

A late 18thC creamware jug, printed in black and overpainted on one side with a ship over "Success to the Pilchard Fishery", the other side with an oval scene of a lady with an olive branch and a cornucopia titled "Peace and Plenty", "Michael and Jane Donkin" inscribed below the spout.

5.75in (14.5cm) high

£1,200-1,800 **CHEF**

A late 18thC creamware jug printed in black with an oval scene on one side titled "Separation of Louis XVI from his family" the scene on the other side titled "Massacre of the French King in 1793".

7in (18cm) high

£1,300-1,800 **CHEF**

A late 18thC creamware jug, printed in terracotta on bellied cylindrical sides, with an oval scene titled "Paddy Bull's expedition" on one side and verses describing his sea trip to England.

6in (15cm) high

£600-700 **CHEF**

A Liverpool jug, printed with the 'Death of Wolfe'.

6.75in (17.5cm) high

£3,500-4,500 **JHOR**

An English 'Farmer's Arms' creamware jug named "William Fowles", restoration to spout.

c1790 *11.5in (29cm) high*

£700-1,000 **JHD**

An early 19thC creamware jug, the bellied shape printed in black with a portrait of "Sir Francis Burdett Bart. MP. The determined enemy of Corruption & the constitutional friend of his SOVEREIGN", a note that he was committed to the Tower in 1810 on the other side within a laurel wreath.

5.5in (14cm) high

£200-300 **CHEF**

An early 19thC Liverpool creamware jug, printed in black on one bellied side with an oval scene of a lady waving goodbye to a distant ship, below a banner inscribed "Returning Hopes", and above a verse, the reverse with a three-masted warship.

7in (18cm) high

£600-700 **CHEF**

An early 19thC commemorative Nelson creamware jug, printed in black with a map and description of the battle of Trafalgar on one bellied side, with an oval portrait of "Adml Lord Nelson" above a banner bearing his dates of birth and death on the other.

6.75in (17.5cm) high

£2,200-2,800 **CHEF**

An early 19thC creamware jug, printed in black on one side with Apollo riding his chariot of the sun across the sky, a rain cloud below, all within guilloche enclosed star sign, the reverse with Diana in a deer-drawn chariot drawing the moon.

11.75in (30cm) high

£700-800 **CHEF**

An early 19thC creamware jug printed in black with scenes and verses from "Palemon and Lavinia", one side with fields and a stately home, depicting their first meeting while harvesting, printed with his words "The fields, the master, all my fair! Are thine".

8.75in (22.5cm) high

£500-600 **CHEF**

A creamware small ovoid teapot, with an ear shaped handle and a leaf moulded spout, splashed in green, brown, yellow and black, the everted rim pierced with hearts and trellis, no cover.

c1770 *3in (8cm) high*

£180-220 **LFA**

A mid-18thC Staffordshire saltglazed teapot, with applied leaves, flowers and berries, traces of painted enamels and size gilt, with a matched creamware lid, chips and body cracks to teapot.

7in (18cm) high

£180-220 **WW**

A rare early Staffordshire creamware teapot, with applied reliefs.

c1755 *3.75in (9.5cm) high*

£1,000-1,500 **JHOR**

A late 18thC creamware teapot and cover, possible by Neale & Co., with a floral knop and strap handle, printed with birds in a landscape and with Minerva and three cherubs, titled "Let Wisdom Unite Us", restoration to cover and spout.

8.25in (21cm) high

£400-500 **WW**

An enamelled creamware coffee pot, probably Staffordshire, chip to lid.

c1770 *9in (23cm) high*

£1,800-2,200 **JHOR**

A creamware teapot, probably Leeds, chips to rim.

c1780

£1,800-2,200 **JHOR**

An English creamware teapot, with a red, pink, yellow, green and purple floral design on either side and around the lid, relief designs to spout and handle.

c1780 *5.75in (14.5cm) high*

£800-1,200 **JHD**

A late 18thC lidded creamware pot.

4.75in (12cm) high

£500-700 **JHD**

A creamware coffee pot, with floral decoration in relief to the pair of entwined handles, a flower knop to lid, restoration to hairline crack to rim.

8in (20.5cm) high

£600-900 **JHD**

A late 18thC creamware teapot and cover, printed and overpainted by William Greatbatch with two scenes from 'The Prodigal Son', "The Prodigal Son Receives His Patrimony" and "The Prodigal Son Taking His Leave", gilt beading below the pierced gallery, the cover with a purple sponge band and angel heads.

£1,300-1,800 **CHEF**

A late 18thC blue and white creamware coffee pot and cover, possibly Liverpool, the baluster shape painted with Chinese pavilions on islands to both sides of the handle and spout.

9.5in (24.5cm) high

£350-400 **CHEF**

A late 18thC blue and white creamware coffee pot, the baluster shape painted with trained and trailing vines about four moulded roundels of a Chinese man with a parasol below a pine tree.

8.25in (21cm) high

£100-150 **CHEF**

A creamware coffee pot, with floral decoration in relief to the pair of entwined handles, a flower knop to lid.

10.75in (27.5cm) high

£800-1,200 **JHD**

An English 18thC creamware coffee pot, with floral decoration in relief to the pair of entwined handles.

c1790 *10.25in (26cm) high*

£700-1,000 **JHD**

A large Chaffers Liverpool cylindrical mug, with a strap handle, printed by Sadler with 'The Triple Plea', the satirical print of a lawyer, doctor and priest discussing their fees, above a verse attacking the hypocrisy of their vows, a small area of restoration to the handle.

c1760-65 *6.5in (17cm) high*

£800-1,200 **WW**

A Leeds creamware cylindrical mug, the reeded entwined loop handle with flower and leaf terminals, painted in coloured enamels with a spray of flowers and leaves, and scattered flowers.

c1770 *4in (10cm) high*

£350-400 **LFA**

A Staffordshire creamware mug, decorated with a scene of a lady strolling in landscape, small chips.

c1780 *5in (13cm) high*

£1,000-1,500 **JHOR**

A late 18thC Liverpool creamware mug, printed in black with the "East view of Liverpool Light House & Signals On Bidston Hill", all fifty signals flying and the ship's owners identified in the legend below.

c1790 *6in (15.5cm) high*

£1,200-1,800 **CHEF**

A late 18thC creamware mug, printed in black and overprinted with 'British Slavery', the cartoon showing a man eating and exclaiming against taxes making "...Slaves of us All".

5in (12.5cm) high

£1,200-1,800 **CHEF**

A late 18thC creamware mug, printed in terracotta on the cylindrical sides with a cartoon of John Bull spoiling the dance of "Master Boney" across Europe.

4.75in (12cm) high

£400-500 **CHEF**

A late 18thC creamware frog mug, printed in black and overpainted with verses on each side "May Peace and Plenty..." and "Tyrants are Cruel...", below ships and within vine and hop swags.

c1790 *5.75in (14.5cm) high*

£700-800 **CHEF**

A Dawson & Co., Low Ford creamware mug printed and overpainted with a ship in full sale in a garrya oval flanked by figures of 'Peace' and 'Plenty' and over a verse "May Peace and Plenty on our Nation Smile...", the initials "WC" in the printing to one side.

5.5in (14cm) high

£550-650 **CHEF**

An early 19thC creamware quart mug, printed and painted with a cavalry skirmish, bearded lancers in tall red hats spring from behind a fence to attack two cavalrymen in blue uniform.

6in (15cm) high

£450-550 **CHEF**

A creamware Bacchus mask mug, with a loop handle, picked out in coloured enamels on a stiff moulded round base, some damage.

c1800 *4.5in (11.5cm) high*

£80-120 **LFA**

An English creamware pierced basket and stand.

c1780 *Stand 9.75in (24.5cm) wide*

£1,000-1,500 **JHD**

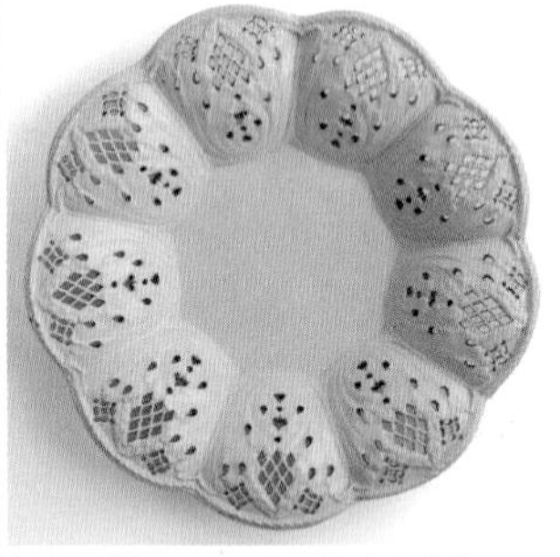

An English creamware basket dish.

c1780 *9.75in (24.5cm) diam*

£500-700 **JHD**

A creamware ozier-moulded quatrefoil footed basket, with a pierced rim and two leaf-scroll handles.

c1785 *11in (28cm) wide*

£450-550 **DN**

A creamware basket, with two handles.

c1785 *9.25in (23.5cm) wide*

£400-600 **JHD**

A creamware basket and stand.

This basket may be the work of James and Chas Whitehead of Staffordshire.

c1890 *Stand 9in (23cm) wide*

£1,000-1,500 **JHD**

A Wedgwood creamware orange basket and cover, one handle restored.

c1790 *11in (28cm) wide*

£1,000-1,500 **JHD**

A rare pair of Wedgwood creamware lidded pots.

c1800 *7in (17.5cm) high*

£800-1,200 **JHD**

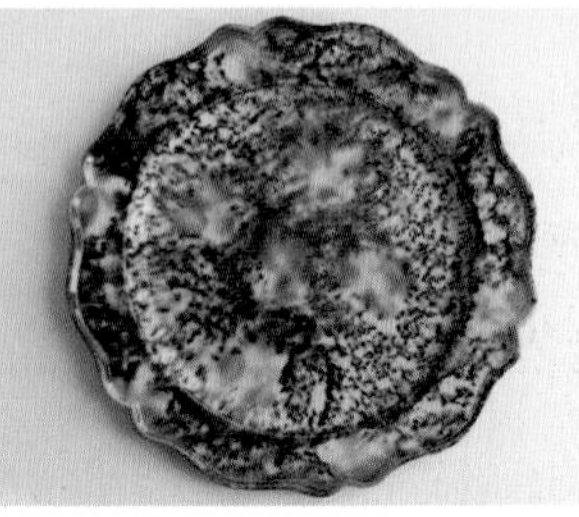

An English creamware 'Whieldon' type plate with coloured glazes.

c1770 *9.5in (24cm) diam*

£320-380 **JHD**

A Staffordshire enamelled creamware plate, minor repairs.

c1770 *12.75in (32.5cm) long*

£1,800-2,200 **JHOR**

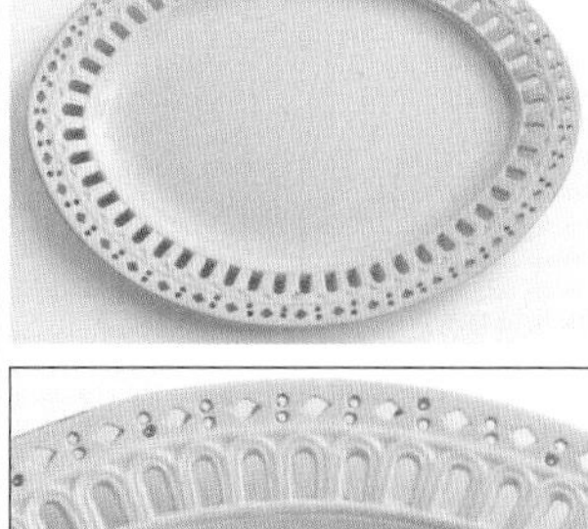

A Shorthose creamware oval dish.

c1790 *10in (25.5cm) wide*

£200-250 **JHD**

A Liverpool transfer-printed creamware nursery plate.

c1800 *5.25in (13.5cm) diam*

£250-300 **RDER**

An English creamware egg strainer.

c1780 *3.5in (9cm) diam*

£200-300 **JHD**

A Wedgwood creamware drainer and stand.

c1810 *Stand 5in (13cm) diam*

£300-400 **JHD**

A pair of green-glazed creamware plates, each moulded in relief with a basket of flowers, the pierced basketwork border moulded with fruits and leaves.

c1820 *8.25in (21cm) diam*

£120-180 **LFA**

An English creamware bowl with floral decoration and a red band to rim.

c1785 *5.75in (14.5cm) diam*

£300-350 **JHD**

A Wedgwood creamware mustard pot.

c1800 *Saucer 2.75in (7cm) diam*

£200-300 **JHD**

A Wedgwood creamware tureen with stand and ladle.

c1800 *Stand 14.25in (36cm) long*

£1,000-1,500 **JHD**

A 19thC creamware tureen and cover in the form of a dressed chicken, the breast applied with a parsley leaf band and scattered leaves.

9.5in (24cm) wide

£300-400 **CHEF**

An 18thC creamware figure.

4.5in (11.5cm) high

£550-650 **AD**

A creamware cylindrical tea canister, painted in coloured enamels with flowers and leaves, within iron red leaf scrolls, the shoulder with flower sprays.

c1770 *4in (10cm) high*

£350-400 **LFA**

An early 19thC creamware wine cistern, the half baluster shape with shells and scrolls raised behind the open neck, a band of guilloche floral chains above cut sprays painted on the gadrooned sides, the metal spigot amongst moulded acanthus and oak leaves painted green and brown.

17in (43cm) high

£600-700 **CHEF**

A Wedgwood creamware 'Mr Punch' set.

c1875 *13.5in (34cm) diam*

£1,500-1,800 **AL**

A creamware pierced round cruet stand, the central knopped handle with a coloured finch terminal, the stiff leaf moulded borders picked out in green, puce and blue, and fitted with three jars and covers, the two pierced bun top castors titled in black, within an iron red scroll cartouche, on three leaf scroll feet, some damage.

c1810 *9.5in (24cm) high*

£900-1,200 **LFA**

A Castleford Dunderdale and Co. creamware ink stand and cover, with four sections for bottles and a central candle sconce, the shaped cover with a recumbent hound finial, impressed marks, cracks.

c1800 *7.75in (20cm) wide*

£1,200-1,800 **DN**

An English creamware veilleuse or nighlight.

c1800

£500-700 **JHD**

A late 18thC Neale and Wilson creamware wine barrel, the moulded coopering bound with green withies and applied with grapes above the metal spigot, all supported on a detachable socle, impressed marks.

13in (33cm) high

£500-600 **CHEF**

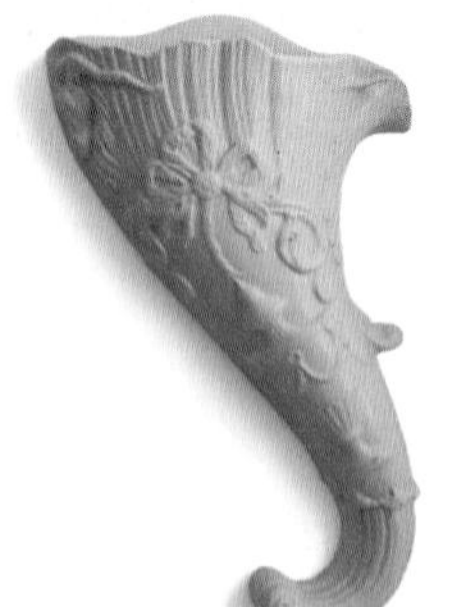

An English creamware wall pocket, a hairline crack to back, minor chips to rim.

c1785 *8.5in (22cm) high*

£700-1,000 **JHD**

A pair of creamware candlesticks.

c1790 *10.25in (26cm) high*

£2,000-2,500 **JHD**

An extremely rare creamware spoon, probably Yorkshire.

c1780 *7.75in (20cm) long*

£1,200-1,800 **JHOR**

DELFTWARE

The Netherlands began to produce tin-glazed earthenware in the late 15thC. Although many potteries were founded in Amsterdam, Haarlem and Rotterdam, by the late 17thC, Delft had become the most important centre of production and was home to nearly 30 companies. Initially, potteries moved into disused breweries and took advantage of the cessation of imports of Chinese porcelain c1650, by producing reproductions of popular Chinese ware in blue and white. When imports resumed after 1680, Delft potters introduced a wider variety of colours to their ware, and used yellow, purple, blue, red, green and black. Dutch Delft ware is commonly decorated with Chinese and Japanese designs, Dutch scenes, biblical subjects or repeating patterns. Important Delft factories included The Greek A factory, which marked pieces with an "AK", The Metal Pot, The Porcelain Claw factory and The Golden Flowerpot factory.

Dutch Delft ware often has a gritty texture, thick glaze and 'peppering' on the surface, caused by air bubbles exploding during firing. The condition of pieces varies and chips, especially around the rim, are common.

Tin-glazed delftware, influenced by Dutch and Chinese designs, was also produced in Britain from the mid-16thC, in areas such as Southwark, Aldgate, Lambeth, Norwich, Liverpool and Bristol. From the early 18thC, British delftware became more distinctive. Typical 18thC British pieces are more delicate than earlier items and have a smoother glaze than Dutch wares of the same period. Most pieces are blue and white and are decorated with British landscapes, leaves or bold flowers. Polychrome, inscribed and dated pieces are rarer.

British delftware is typically less finely potted than Dutch Delft ware and the glaze is often tinged with blue or pink. Colours tend to be more muted due to the absorbency of the tin-glaze used and marks are rare.

ENGLISH DELFTWARE

A London delftware chinoiserie plate.
c1680 *8.5in (21.5cm) diam*
£900-1,100 **JHOR**

A London or Bristol flared delftware plate, some chips to rim.
c1690 *8.5in (21.5cm) diam*
£2,000-2,500 **JHOR**

A London delftware plate, with flowers.
c1700 *8.25in (21cm) high*
£900-1,100 **JHOR**

A London delftware plate, painted with a peacock and foliage.
c1730 *9in (23cm) diam*
£2,000-2,500 **JHOR**

A London delftware plate, hair crack, restoration.
c1730 *8.5in (21.5cm) diam*
£450-550 **JHOR**

A London delftware plate dated 1731.
8in (20.5cm) diam
£2,500-3,000 **JHOR**

A London delftware plate, painted with a figure and a bird beside a hut, in blue, green and iron red, with some restoration.
c1740 *9in (23cm) diam*
£180-220 **WW**

An English delftware plate, possibly London, painted in underglaze blue with a seated figure holding a falcon, in a Chinese landscape with bamboo, a fence and rockwork, the rim with a simple trellis-panelled band.

c1750 *8.75in (22cm) diam*

£400-600 **LFA**

A London or Bristol delftware plate, decorated with a landscape of a lake in front of a castle and trees, the rim with flower designs.

c1780 *8.5in (21.5cm) diam*

£500-600 **JHOR**

A London/Bristol delftware blue dish, with painted bird and foliage, rare size.

c1695 *8.5in (21.5cm) high*

£9,000-11,000 **JHOR**

A delftware dish, probably London, decorated with a basket of flowers, the rim with flower pattern, crack restored.

c1765 *12.75in (32.5cm) diam*

£800-1,000 **JHOR**

A delftware deep round charger, probably London, boldly painted in underglaze blue with flowering branches, issuing from rockwork, the rim panelled with flowerheads.

c1700 *11.75in (30cm) diam*

£500-700 **LFA**

A London or Liverpool delftware charger, with rare figure and building design.

c1760 *13in (33cm) diam*

£650-750 **JHOR**

A London delftware blue and white bowl, painted with a naïve fruit design, a few faint cracks.

c1725

£280-320 **WW**

A delftware bowl, probably London, decorated with fish, pattern to rim.

c1720 *8.75in (22cm) high*

£2,000-2,600 **JHOR**

A rare pair of London polychrome delftware flower bricks, the sides decorated with foliage, the pierced top section with repeating pattern.

c1735 *6in (15cm) high*

£6,500-7,500 **JHOR**

A London delftware brick with a European landscape scene.

c1750 *6.25in (16cm) long*

£1,800-2,200 **JHOR**

An English delftware blue and white commemorative posset pot, probably London or Bristol, painted with birds and flowering shrubs, inscribed beside the spout "EIP" and dated "1689", slight damage and restoration.

9.75in (25cm) diam

£3,000-4,000 **DN**

A London or Liverpool delftware puzzle jug, some restoration.

c1770

6.75in (17cm) high

£1,800-2,200 **JHOR**

A London delftware blue and white gallipot, of cylindrical form with everted foot and rim and painted with a band of crosses within bands of four horizontal lines, minor rim chips.

Gallipots were used for storing medicines.

c1725 *5.5in (14cm) high*

£700-900 **DN**

A London delftware tile, depicting 'Christ Speaking to the Blind Man'.

c1750 *5in (13cm) high*

£120-180 **JHOR**

A CLOSER LOOK AT A DELFTWARE HAND-WARMER

Hand-warmers were filled with hot water or embers. This one would have been filled through the hole at the top.

Delftware pieces are typically dinnerware. Rare forms, such as this hand-warmer, are very valuable.

Hand-warmers had been made since the middle ages, and were especially popular during the 17thC. They were typically used by ladies to keep their hands warm in cold weather, at church or whilst travelling in carriages.

The piece is in good condition and has had no restoration. This increases its value. It is also unusually large.

A rare late 17thC delftware tin-glazed hand-warmer, probably London, in the shape of a book.

6in (15cm) high

£15,500-16,500 **JHOR**

A mid-18thC delftware blue and white plate, probably Lambeth, painted with two figures, a cottage and sponged tree, cracked.

9in (23cm) diam

£120-180 **WW**

A pair of Lambeth delftware plates, unusually painted with a mill and a church in a landscape in underglaze blue, with blue line borders, minor chips.

c1755 *8.5in (21.5cm) diam*

£400-600 **LFA**

A Lambeth delftware plate, painted in underglaze blue with bamboo, flowering trees, a fence and rockwork, in Chinese style, the scroll border with pendant leaves, brown line to rim.

c1780 *9in (23cm) diam*

£80-120 **LFA**

A Lambeth delftware plate, decorated with a balloon scene and floral pattern.

c1785 *8.75in (22cm) diam*

£1,200-1,800 **JHOR**

A Lambeth delftware plate, in a rare small size.

c1760 *7.25in (18.5cm) diam*

£600-700 **JHOR**

A pair of Lambeth delftware plates, painted in famille verte palette, with a parrot, flowering branches and rockwork, in Chinese style, the rim with trailing flowers, fruits and leaves, minor rim chips.

c1780 *8.75in (22cm) diam*

£300-500 **LFA**

A Lambeth delftware small plate, painted in famille verte palette with a parrot, flowering branches and rockwork, in Chinese style, the rim with flowers, fruits and leaves, rim chips.

c1780 *7.5in (19cm) diam*

£180-220 **LFA**

A Lambeth delftware charger, minor rim chips.

c1765 *13.5in (34.5cm) diam*

£1,500-2,000 **JHOR**

A Lambeth delftware charger, boldly painted in blue with a Chinese river landscape, the powdered manganese border with sgraffito flowers and leaves, minor rim chips.

c1770 *12in (30.5cm) diam*

£700-1,000 **LFA**

A Lambeth delftware charger, painted in the famille verte palette, with bamboo in a fenced garden, the border with flower garlands, within a feathered border, minor rim chips.

c1780 *13.5in (34.5cm) diam*

£500-800 **LFA**

A Lambeth delftware shallow round dish, boldly painted in blue with a fenced garden, in a Chinese river landscape, within a broad, flower-panelled, diaper border.

c1780 *9in (23cm) diam*

£180-220 **LFA**

A Lambeth delftware blue and white wet-drug jar, of globular form with short spout to the back, on a conical foot, named for "O:SAMBUC", within a strapwork cartouche surmounted with flowers and putti, some chips.

c1780 *7.75in (20cm) high*

£1,200-1,500 **DN**

A Lambeth delftware blue and white wet-drug jar, of globular form with short spout to the back, on a conical foot named for "O:LAURIN", within a strapwork cartouche surmounted with flowers and putti, some chips.

c1780 *7.75in (20cm) high*

£1,200-1,500 **DN**

A delftware blue and white jar, Lambeth or Brislington, with a ogee body and two side handles, painted with birds perched on flowering branches between jui bands, Lipski Collection label, slight damage.

c1715

£1,300-1,800 **WW**

A Bristol delftware plate, inscribed with initials "AR" for Queen Anne.

1719 *8.5in (21.5cm) high*

£2,800-3,300 **JHOR**

A Bristol delftware 'Farmyard' plate, a particularly fine example, painted in iron-red, ochre and blue with a peacock between trees, small rim chips.

c1730 *7.75in (20cm) diam*

£3,500-4,500 **DN**

A Bristol 'Farmyard' delftware plate, painted with a peacock and sponged trees.

c1730 *7.75in (20cm) diam*

£2,000-2,400 **JHOR**

A Bristol delftware plate, with floral design.

c1730 *8.75in (22cm) high*

£550-650 **JHOR**

A Bristol delftware plate, decorated with a bird and foliage.

c1740 *9in (23cm) diam*

£500-600 **JHOR**

A Bristol delftware plate, boldly painted in underglaze blue with a stylized flower, the rim with alternating flowerheads and leaves.

c1745 *9in (23cm) diam*

£180-220 **LFA**

A delftware blue and white plate, probably Bristol, painted with a man and a woman beneath trees with a cottage in the distance, a well repaired long curving crack.

c1750 *9in (23cm) diam*

£180-220 **WW**

A Bristol delftware plate, painted in underglaze blue with a flowerhead medallion in a roundel, the rim with pendant flowers and leaves, rim chips.

c1750 *9in (23cm) diam*

£100-150 **LFA**

An English delftware polychrome plate, probably Bristol, painted in the Fazackerley manner with scattered floral sprays, chips and hairline fracture.

c1760 *9in (23cm) diam*

£300-350 **DN**

A Bristol delftware plate, painted in underglaze blue with two figures in a boat, in a Chinese river landscape, within a flower-panelled diaper band, and diaper rim.

c1770 *9.25in (23.5cm) diam*

£150-200 **LFA**

An initialled and dated Bristol delftware plate.

1736 *9in (23cm) diam*

£2,200-2,800 **JHOR**

A pair of 18thC delftware plates, with fluted rims and painted in blue with baskets of flowers, perhaps Bristol, one damaged.

7.5in (19.5cm) diam

£300-400 **WW**

An early 18thC English delftware blue and white two-handled bowl and domed cover, possibly Bristol, painted in the Transitional style with figures in landscapes, the interior with a pierced strainer, some chips.

9.75in (25cm) wide

£700-1,000 **DN**

A CLOSER LOOK AT A DELFTWARE CHARGER

The condition of this charger is exceptionally good. This increases the value.

The charger was made at a Bristol pottery. Operating from the late 17thC, Bristol potters are best known for their tin-glazed earthenware and blue-dash chargers.

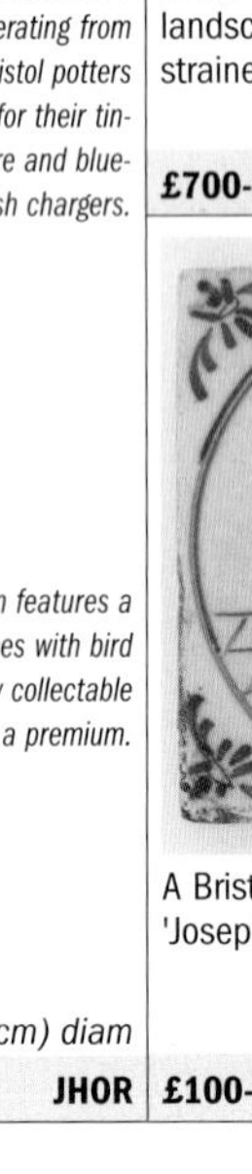

Chargers were produced both for display and for serving food. The design and colour on this piece are attractive, making the charger visually appealing.

The decoration features a painted bird. Pieces with bird designs are highly collectable and command a premium.

A Bristol delftware charger.

c1760 *13.25in (34cm) diam*

£3,000-3,500 **JHOR**

A Bristol delftware tile, depicting 'Joseph's Coat Brought to Isaiah'.

5in (13cm) high

£100-130 **JHOR**

A Liverpool delftware tile, depicting 'Esther before Ahasuerus'.

c1740 *5in (13cm) high*

£80-120 **JHOR**

A Liverpool delftware tile, depicting a peasant having a tooth extracted.

c1765 *4.75in (12cm) high*

£450-500 **JHOR**

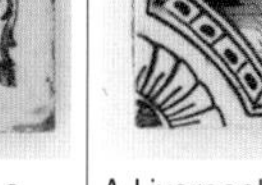

A Liverpool delftware tile, depicting 'The Mocking of Elisha'.

c1770 *5in (13cm) high*

£80-100 **JHOR**

A Liverpool delftware tile, 'Harlequin between Rogonda and Columbine'.

c1740 *5in (12.5cm) high*

£80-120 **JHOR**

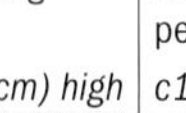

A Liverpool delftware tile, depicting 'Mr. Moody in the Character of Teague'.

c1775 *4.5in (11.5cm) high*

£600-650 **JHOR**

A Liverpool delftware plate, with a bird perched in foliage.

c1760 *8.5in (21.5cm) diam*

£800-1,200 **JHOR**

A Liverpool delftware char dish.

c1770 *7in (18cm) diam*

£2,000-2,500 **JHOR**

A Liverpool delftware ship plate, depicting a ship flying the flag of Bremen.

c1760 *8.75in (22.5cm) diam*

£6,500-7,500 **JHOR**

A Liverpool delftware shallow round dish, painted in blue with a Chinese river landscape, within a roundel, the rim with a diaper band.

c1780 *9in (23cm) diam*

£180-220 **LFA**

An English delftware puzzle jug, probably Liverpool, of typical form, inscribed "Here Gentlemen come try your skill, I'll hold a wager if you will That you don't drink this liquor all Without you spill or let some fall", painted with flower sprays, repairs and small chips and wear.

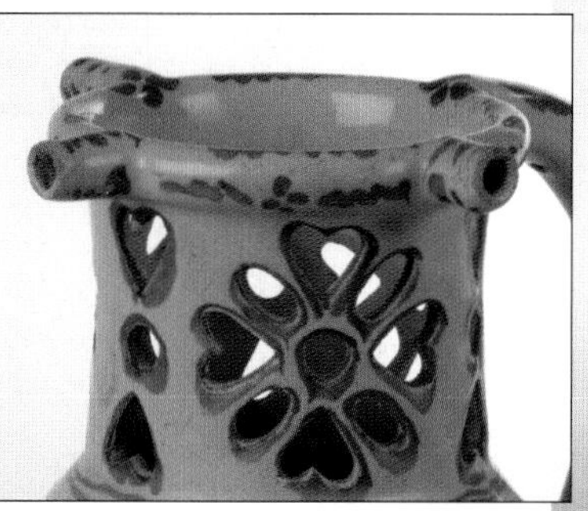

c1760 *7in (18cm) high*

£1,000-1,500 **DN**

OTHER DELFTWARE

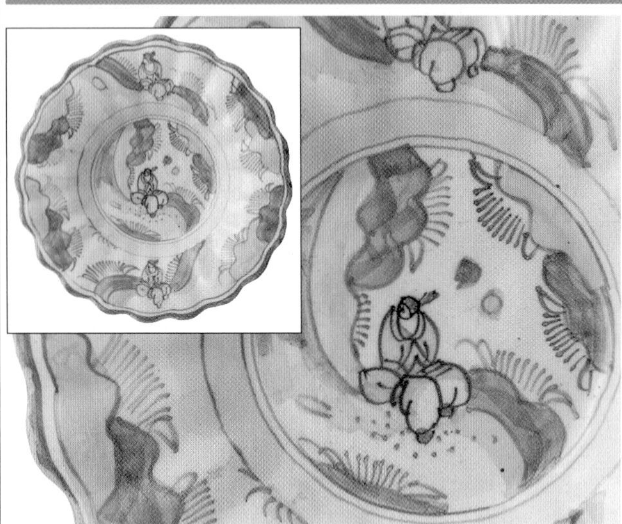

A delftware plate, with rare yellow colouring.

c1685 *8.25in (21cm) high*

£1,800-2,200 **JHOR**

An English delftware blue and white plate, the centre decorated with the 'IHS' insignia within a star burst, hair cracks.

c1720 *8.5in (21.5cm) diam*

£280-320 **WW**

An early to mid-18thC delftware plate, painted in polychrome with a bird in a bush between flowers, a manganese chequered border, a hair crack.

8.25in (21cm) diam

£150-200 **WW**

A delftware blue and white plate, painted with a lady carrying a basket on her head between two sponged trees, a few small rim chips and flakes.

c1730 *7.5in (19cm) diam*

£350-400 **WW**

A mid-18thC delftware plate, probably Wincanton, painted in manganese with a lady standing beneath a tree in parkland with a building in the distance, long hair crack.

8.5in (21.5cm) diam

£350-400 **WW**

A delftware plate, possibly made in Glasgow, painted in underglaze blue, with an alternating diaper and flower medallion, the rim with two bold sprays of flowers and leaves.

c1760 *8.75in (22cm) diam*

£180-220 **LFA**

An English delftware plate, possibly made in Wincanton, painted in underglaze blue with a shepherd seated by a fence, within a flower panelled diaper band, the rim with leaves, bamboo and fences.

c1770 *9in (23cm) diam*

£250-300 **LFA**

An Irish delftware plate, painted in underglaze blue with a Chinese river landscape and birds in flight, some restoration.

c1770 *9.25in (23.5cm) diam*

£150-200 **LFA**

A delftware plate, with spouting whale design.

8.75in (22.cm) diam

£1,800-2,200 **JHOR**

A delftware oak leaf charger, rim repaired.

c1700 *13in (33cm) diam*

£4,500-5,000 **JHOR**

A mid-to late 17thC large delftware charger, moulded with concentric lappets beneath a creamy white glaze, minor faults.

17.5in (44.5cm) diam

£1,800-2,200 **WW**

A delftware round charger, possibly made in Glasgow, painted in underglaze blue with an exotic bird perched on rockwork, in a fenced garden, in Chinese style, the rim with bold flowers and leaves, rim chips.

c1780 *13.75in (35cm) diam*

£180-220 **LFA**

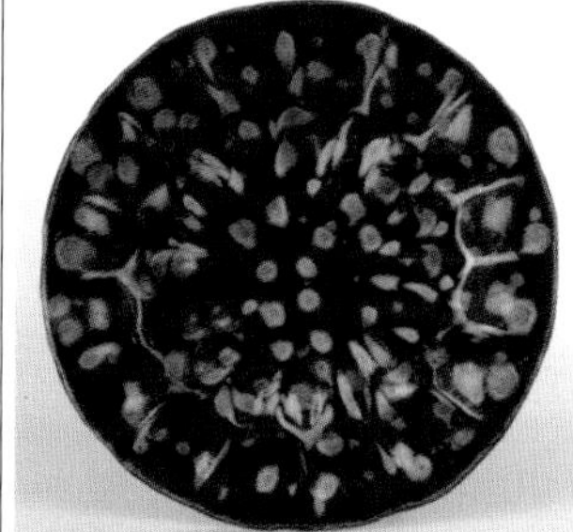

A delftware 'Bleu Persan' lobed bowl, splashed with white spots on a blue ground.

c1700 *8.25in (21cm) diam*

£900-1,100 **DN**

A delftware blue and white bowl, the exterior painted with two Chinamen, one in a fishing boat, the other on a river bank, the reverse with a scruffy bird, the interior with an artemisia leaf, faint body cracks.

c1740 *9in (23cm) diam*

£350-400 **WW**

An English delftware flared round bowl, the exterior painted in blue and yellow with flowers and leaves, on a powdered manganese ground, the interior with a flowerhead in blue, restored.

c1750 *10.25in (26cm) diam*

£300-350 **LFA**

A late 17thC delftware commemorative lobed dish, painted in shades of blue, green and ochre with a portrait bust of William III within initials "KW", restored section to rim.

8.5in (21.5cm) diam

£800-1,200 **DN**

A large Vauxhall delftware dish, painted in polychrome with the 'Bending Chinaman' pattern, the border with flowers and leaves, broken and repaired.

c1725 *13in (33cm) diam*

£280-320 **WW**

A delftware two handled ovoid vase, polychrome decorated with flowers and scrolling foliage, painted "N" mark, faint body cracks.

c1720 *4.75in (12cm) wide*

£1,200-1,800 **WW**

A mid-18thC delftware blue and white two handled vase, painted with cattle, houses and haystacks, a rim chip, a scroll to one handle lacking and a hairline crack.

c1750 *11in (28cm) high*

£7,000-8,000 **WW**

An 18thC delftware blue and white vase, the urn shape painted with churches either side of lion mask handles, the trumpet foot with a star of lanceolate leaves.

c1750 *6in (15cm) high*

£1,000-1,500 **CHEF**

An 18thC tin glazed drug jar, possibly French, the cylindrical sides painted in blue with a cartouche surmounted by a vase flanked by peacocks and inscribed "FI.SALVIAE", with brass top.

c1750 *6.5in (16.5cm) high*

£800-1,000 **CHEF**

A CLOSER LOOK AT A DELFTWARE LAYETTE BASKET

The intricate and finely crafted pierced work makes this an attractive piece. This type of openwork is often found on pot-pourri vases and bouquetieres, and was used for both decorative and functional purposes.

Although the basket has chips, losses and is missing its original rope handles, it remains valuable because it is rare.

The centre panel is painted with an angel before shepherds and the four sides are painted with landscape panels.

The large size of the basket increases its value.

A mid-to late 17thC large and imposing delftware blue and white layette basket, the sides, flared foot and centre border pierced with floral and geometric designs, the centre panel painted with an angel before shepherds, the four sides painted with landscape panels, unmarked, the rope twist handles lacking, other small chips and losses.

The purpose of these large and rare baskets is unclear. It is said they were given to mothers of newborn babies perhaps for holding gifts, as were the contemporary beadwork baskets of this shape. It is also possible that they were used to hold fruit.

19in (48.5cm) long

£4,500-5,500 **WW**

DUTCH DELFT WARE

A commemorative Delft ware (De Paeuw) blue and white plate, painted with a shield with three lions with human masks and inscribed "IR" for James II and dated "1698", restored.

10.25in (26cm) diam

£1,000-1,500 **DN**

A rare Dutch Delft ware tile, with Roman warrior, restored.

c1630 *5in (12.5cm) wide*

£400-450 **JHOR**

A 17thC Dutch Delft ware polychrome tile.

5in (12.5cm) wide

£150-200 **JHOR**

A Dutch Delft ware sugarbowl with lid, with a grey-white glaze and blue chrysanthemum pattern, of cylindrical shape with two ear handles, a flat lid with a button knop, marked to the lid and base, damaged.

4.25in (10.5cm) high

£350-450 **LPZ**

An early 19thC Dutch Delft ware vase, the flattened baluster shape painted in blue with flowers in a rococo frame on one side and within a pendant swag on the other.

7.75in (20cm) high

£80-120 **CHEF**

A pair of early 20thC Dutch Delft ware blue and white candlesticks, the square sectioned baluster columns painted with yachts and flowers below diaper panels, the four feet with leaves, marked "Delft".

9.5in (24cm) high

£80-120 **CHEF**

EARTHENWARE & STONEWARE

Earthenware is lightly fired, porous pottery that retains the red, brown and buff hues of raw clay. Some earthenware was cast in relief-moulded shapes, a practice that led to the production of decorative items such as Toby and character jugs. Stoneware is a similar type of pottery, made by combining clay with a fusible stone, such as feldspar, to achieve a similar effect.

There are as many different types of earthenware as there are treatments that have been applied to it through the years. One of the most basic methods of sealing earthenware is to apply semi-liquid slip clay to the finished surface. Often, this slip is trailed or piped on carefully to make an item more attractive as well as more practical. Similarly, salt glaze is achieved simply by throwing salt into the kiln as the pottery is fired. Manufacturers added colour by mixing other compounds with the salt. This technique developed further with the introduction of lustreware, where earthenware was fired with metallic pigments.

More specialized still is the perennially popular mocha ware – earthenware daubed with coloured slip and decorated with complex patterns – which is especially sought-after in the US, so much so that it can be hard to find in the UK these days.

The quest to recreate Chinese porcelain led to ever-more refined forms of earthenware, such as creamware and pearlware.

An early 17thC green glazed Border ware jug.

Border ware is a type of English earthenware that comes from the area along the border of the counties of Surrey and Hampshire.

5in (13cm) high

£1,000-1,500 **JHOR**

A green jug, probably Yorkshire, chips to spout.

c1770 *6.75in (17.5cm) high*

£4,000-4,500 **JHOR**

A Nottingham bear-baiting jug with applied ground clay and repaired foot.

c1745

£4,000-4,500 **JHOR**

A CLOSER LOOK AT A RALPH WOOD PITCHER

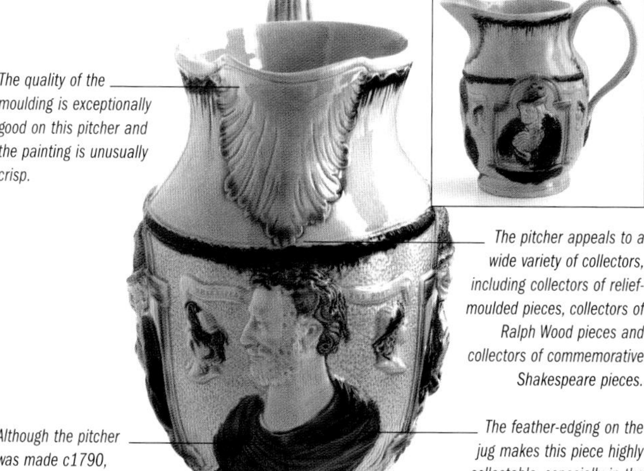

The quality of the moulding is exceptionally good on this pitcher and the painting is unusually crisp.

The pitcher appeals to a wide variety of collectors, including collectors of relief-moulded pieces, collectors of Ralph Wood pieces and collectors of commemorative Shakespeare pieces.

Although the pitcher was made c1790, it has survived in excellent condition.

The feather-edging on the jug makes this piece highly collectable, especially in the US, where shell-edging is popular.

A Ralph Wood relief moulded pitcher with three panels inscribed "Shakespeare the Poet", "Spendthrift" and "The Miser", with blue feather edging.

c1790 *9.25in (23.5cm) high*

£800-1,200 **JHD**

An unusual smear-glazed white ovoid jug, with leaf scroll handle, moulded with vases of flowers and leaves, boldly picked out in blue, green, brown and puce, on a fluted ground, beneath a swag and flowerhead band, blue line borders.

c1800 *4.75in (12cm) high*

£300-400 **LFA**

A Mackin and Potter relief-moulded jug, spout in the form of Robert Burns, with mark.

c1845 *7.75in (20cm) high*

£400-600 **JHD**

A Copeland jug with a rugby scene, relief moulded on a blue jasper ground.

Sporting scenes add value to ceramics as they will appeal to sport enthusiasts.

c1895 *6in (15cm) high*

£1,000-1,500 **JHD**

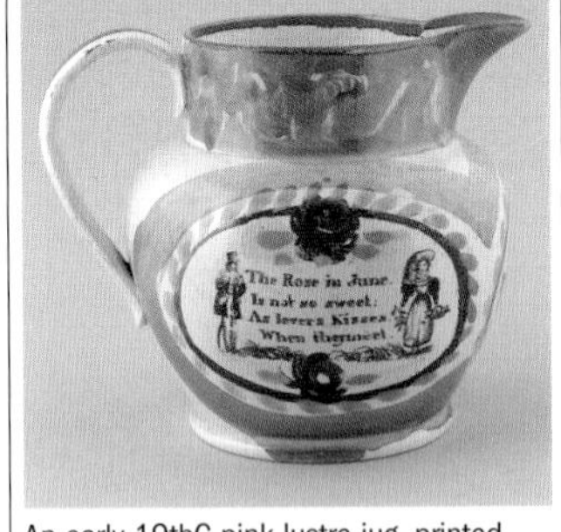

An early 19thC pink lustre jug, printed with a ship below the spout, flanked by a marine verse on one side and on the other by "The Rose in June is Not so Sweet as Lover's Kisses When They Meet".

8.5in (21.5cm) high

£220-280 **CHEF**

A Sunderland pink lustre pitcher, inscribed "When this you see remember me And keep me in your mind Let all the world say what they will Speak of me as you find."

c1845 *8.25in (21cm) high*

£800-1,200 **JHD**

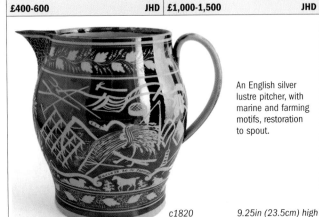

An English silver lustre pitcher, with marine and farming motifs, restoration to spout.

c1820 *9.25in (23.5cm) high*

£1,800-2,200 **JHD**

A moulded jug, with hunting scene and pink lustre decoration.

c1825 *5.5in (14cm) high*

£320-380 **AD**

A 17thC Yorkshire block-glazed Cistercian-ware mug, top part restored.

6.25in (16cm) high

£700-800 **JHOR**

An early 18thC Vauxhall saltglazed stoneware beer mug, with a portrait of Queen Anne.

8in (20.5cm) high

£2,200-2,800 **JHOR**

An English Mocha ware tankard with a small hairline crack.

c1820 *6in (15cm) high*

£800-1,200 **JHD**

A Copeland tankard decorated with a hand-painted dog.

c1840 *3in (7.5cm) high*

£180-220 **JHD**

A 19thC green-glazed tureen, in an organic design with scrolled handles.

5in (12.5cm) high

£220-280 **AD**

A peafowl teabowl, with a light blue glaze and a design of a peafowl in a tree.

c1800 *3in (7.5cm) diam*

£120-180 **JHD**

A Staffordshire earthenware two-handled baluster-shaped crock and cover, painted in coloured enamels with mountainous landscapes, within gilt line borders.

c1870 *16in (40.5cm) high*

£60-90 **LFA**

An English pottery flower pot, with applied decoration of a woman, with yellow slip foliage decoration, inscribed "MR", dated.

1821 *13in (33cm) high*

£2,500-3,500 **SG**

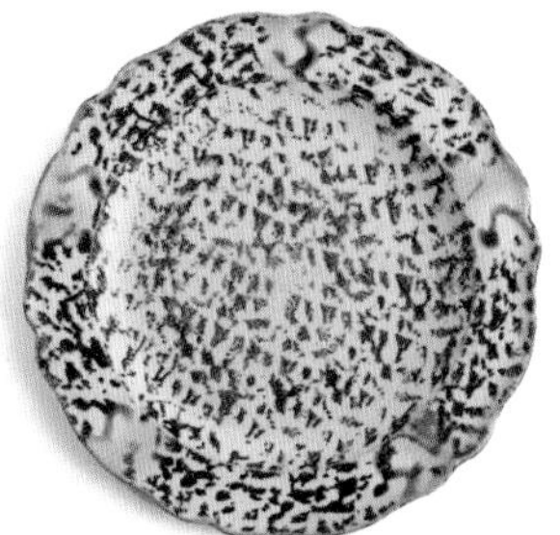

An English colour-glazed plate in brown, green and yellow, with raised, pinched rim.

9.5in (24.5cm) diam

£300-500 **JHD**

A Swansea pottery arcaded plate, with heron and dragonfly.

c1815 *7.75in (20cm) diam*

£800-1,200 **JHD**

A pair of Welsh transfer-printed nursery plates, with inscriptions "Lying is the vice of a Slave" and "Example is the best of Sermons".

c1850

£300-350 **RDER**

A Minton buff earthenware round plaque, painted in underglaze blue with a view of Balmoral Castle, impressed marks for 1876.

16.75in (42.5cm) diam

£280-320 **LFA**

Two early 19thC Continental tin-glazed earthenware models of recumbent lions, with ochre, manganese and iron-red colouring, on rectangular bases.

5.75in (14.5cm) wide

£400-500 **S&K**

A Yorkshire figure of a reclining ram.

c1825 *5in (13cm) high*

£800-1,000 **JHOR**

A Yorkshire pottery deer.

c1820 *4.5in (11.5 cm) high*

£550-600 **AD**

One of a pair of Scottish deer spill vases, one ear restored.

c1825 *6in (15.5cm) high*

£1,500-2,000 pair **JHOR**

A very rare Yorkshire figure of St George, in Pratt colours, dated 1838.
11in (28cm) high
£4,500-5,500 **JHOR**

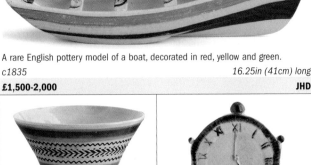

A pair of English pearlware boats with black and green decoration.
c1820 *16.25in (41cm) long*
£3,000-4,000 **JHD**

A rare English pottery model of a boat, decorated in red, yellow and green.
c1835 *16.25in (41cm) long*
£1,500-2,000 **JHD**

A pottery darning egg, from north-eastern England, decorated with birds and foxes.
c1850 *2.5in (6.5cm) high*
£320-380 **JHD**

A pottery darning egg, probably from the north-east, sponged decoration.
c1850 *2.25in (6cm) high*
£150-200 **JHD**

One of a pair of Mocha ware vases with blue and orange banding and a brown horizontal pattern bands.
c1820 *4.75in (12cm) high*
£1,800-2,200 pair **JHD**

An English pottery longcase clock, blue staining to edges.
c1810 *6.5in (16.5cm) high*
£400-600 **JHD**

A darning egg from north-eastern England, decorated with 'The Dull Scholar' and 'Hoops'.
c1850 *3in (7.5cm) high*
£220-280 **JHD**

A British north country smoking companion in five pieces, tip of snuffer restored.
11in (28cm) high
£800-1,200 **JHD**

A large brown saltglazed stoneware flask modelled as the head of a man wearing a night cap, its end forming the spout, a loop handle applied to the back, cork stopper, small chip to his nose and his collar.
c1830 *9.5in (24cm) high*
£280-320 **WW**

A red stoneware tea kettle, probably Yorkshire, tip of spout restored.
c1775 *9in (23cm) high*
£3,500-4,000 **JHOR**

FAIENCE

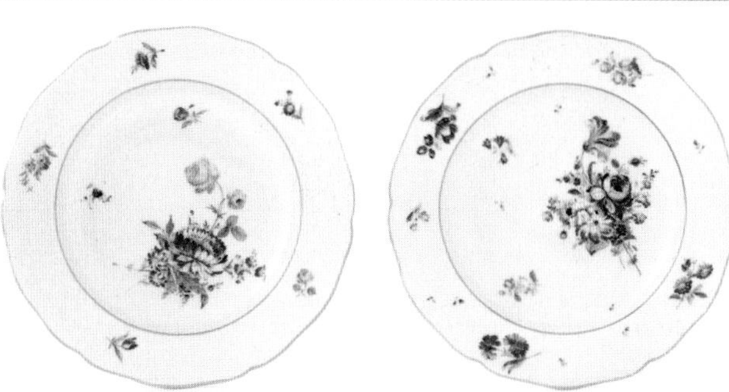

A pair of Cozzi plates, decorated with sprays of flowers.

c1775 *9in (23cm) diam*

£900-1,000 pair **SA**

One of a pair of Strasbourg plates, decorated with flower sprays.

c1870 *9.25in (23.5cm) diam*

£550-650 pair **SA**

An 18thC Italian faience plate, painted with a strutting bird and sprays of foliage.

7.5in (19.5cm) diam

£350-450 **WW**

Three of a 20thC set of twelve Gien plates, each printed in black with a humorous aviation scene, the scroll moulded border washed in purple, printed black marks.

8in (20.5cm) diam

£180-220 set **LFA**

A Niderviller dish, finely painted with European flowers, mark to base.

c1840 *12.5in (32cm) wide*

£400-450 **SA**

A Nast cup and saucer, decorated in sepia tones with gilt rim.

c1795 *5in (12.5cm) diam*

£150-200 **SA**

A French faience jardinière, decorated with blue foliage.

c1760 *13.5in (34.5cm) wide*

£800-1,000 **SA**

A Frankfurt faience cylindrical jar, with two scroll handles, painted in blue with Chinese figures in a landscape, the handles dashed in blue, missing cover, some glaze flakes.

c1700 *3.75in (9.5cm) high*

£300-350 **LFA**

An Italian faience fluted drum-shaped sander, painted in green and black with landscapes and ruins, within beaded borders.

c1770 *2.75in (7cm) diam*

£150-200 **LFA**

IRONSTONE

Part of a 19thC Mason's Ironstone dinner service, printed and painted in the chinoiserie manner with a central lotus flower, the border with meandering flowers, the puce printed ground with apple green, rust, blue, lemon and purple decoration, puce printed mark "Mason's Patent Ironstone China" and impressed mark, comprising a large twin-handled tureen and cover with twin-handled stand, three twin-handled serving dishes and covers, a large ashet, a deep bowl on four feet, a twin-handled sauce tureen and cover with a twin-handled stand, 16 dinner plates, 10 soup plates, 16 fish plates and 10 side plates.

c1850

£1,500-2,000 set **L&T**

A Mason's Ironstone octagonal jug, decorated with panels of figures on a coral coloured Y-diaper ground, black printed mark, the handle cleanly re-glued.

c1835 *8in (20cm) high*

£100-150 **WW**

A Mason's Patent Ironstone China bowl, the fluted sides painted with butterflies within gilt rims, impressed marks.

14.25in (36cm) diam

£400-500 **CHEF**

An extensive 19thC Mason's Ironstone dinner service, the painted chinoiserie decoration with overpainted details, depicting a bird amongst blossom, comprising a twin-handled soup tureen, cover and stand, a pair of canted rectangular vegetable dishes and covers, a sauce tureen, cover and stand, a sauce boat, twelve soup, meat, fish, side and dessert plates.

£1,500-2,000 **L&T**

A pair of late 19thC English Ironstone tin-glazed terracotta bottle vases, with a globe and shaft form, painted in sgraffito in a Near Eastern style with scrolling vines and stylized motifs.

7.25in (18.5cm) high

£120-180 **GORL**

A mid-19thC English Imari pattern Ironstone platter, with scalloped edge, decorated with a tree, flowers and leaves.

17in (43cm) wide

£250-300 **S&K**

A Mason's Ironstone canted rectangular meat dish, printed in underglaze blue with a scroll depicting a Chinese landscape amidst flowers and leaves, the details in coloured enamels, the printed mark in blue.

c1820 *16.5in (42cm) wide*

£200-250 **LFA**

An early 19thC Mason's Ironstone pint mug, the tapering cylindrical sides printed and painted with blue birds amongst chinoiserie vases of flowers, the crown and banner mark overpainted in green.

4.5in (11.5cm) high

£150-200 **CHEF**

An Ironstone square canted vegetable dish and cover, with scroll knop, printed in the famille rose style with birds in flowering branches, within turquoise ground borders, probably by Stephen Folch.

c1820 *9.25in (23.5cm) wide*

£150-200 **LFA**

An Ironstone vase, with mask handles and a flared foot, the twelve sides decorated in blue and iron red with flowers and foliage, unmarked, a rim section re-glued.

c1810 *9.75in (24.5cm) high*

£400-600 **WW**

MAIOLICA

An 18thC northern Italian waisted maiolica albarello jar, probably Savona, painted with St John the Evangelist, with scattered flowers and buildings, script shield mark, a "TARC" monogram beneath the crown, cracked.

8.25in (21cm) high

£600-700 **DN**

A late 17thC to early 18thC Italian maiolica albarello, repaired.

An albarello jar was used to store dry drugs.

10.25in (26cm) high

£800-1,000 **JHOR**

A late 17thC to early 18thC northern Italian maiolica albarello jar, probably Turin or Savona, painted in blue with armorial bearings, scrolling foliage, birds, hares, lions and buildings, with a waisted central section inscribed "Lonfs. amech.", with the arms of Savoy.

8in (20.5cm) high

£1,000-1,200 **DN**

A late 17thC to early 18thC northern Italian maiolica albarello jar, painted in blue with armorial bearings, scrolling foliage, birds, hares, stags and buildings, with a waisted central section inscribed "Dia Liacinti", with the arms of Savoy.

8in (20.5cm) high

£1,000-1,200 **DN**

A late 17thC to early 18thC Italian maiolica wet-drug jar, painted in shades of blue, manganese and ochre, with a figure, probably St John the Evangelist, inscribed in a banner "SY: D. Eris: mo", some chips.

8.5in (22cm) high

£800-1,200 **DN**

An 18thC maiolica bottle vase, possibly Spanish, of globular form with a slender neck, painted with a ship with furled sails, in shades of blue, green and ochre, some glaze chips.

11in (28cm) high

£700-1,000 **DN**

An 18thC Italian maiolica vase, probably Savona, with a narrow neck, decorated in blue with mythological scenes enclosed by borders.

12in (33cm) high

£320-380 **BMN**

An 18thC Savona maiolica tazza, painted with a winged putto flying within an Italianate landscape, script "A.C" mark to base, restored rim chip.

11.25in (28.5cm) diam

£200-250 **DN**

An 18thC Nevers maiolica model of a putto seated upon a dolphin, partially painted in shades of blue and ochre, with repaired tail.

6.75in (17cm) high

£220-280 **DN**

PEARLWARE & PRATTWARE

Pearlware was introduced by Wedgwood in 1779 as an improvement on its creamware range. Higher proportions of white clay and calcined flint were used in the body and cobalt oxide was added to the glaze giving it a bluish tinge. Other factories also copied Wedgwood in making pearlware.

Early items were decorated in a painted underglaze blue, while later pieces were typically transfer-printed. Teapots, coffee pots and dinner services were produced alongside ornamental vases and animal figures. Designs included English landscapes, classical style or versions of the famous 'Willow' pattern. Pieces were sometimes decorated with pink, orange or silver lustre. Pearlware ranges were produced in Staffordshire, Yorkshire and Wales, but pieces are often unmarked and difficult to attribute.

Similar to pearlware in weight and colour, Prattware was introduced c1775 by the Pratt family in Staffordshire and was produced at a number of factories around the country. Prattware pieces differ from pearlware in the decoration, which uses the high-temperature colours of ochre, yellow, brown, green and blue. Jugs, teapots and figures were factory-produced and, from the 1840s, Pratt became famous for its multicoloured printing.

An unusual Ralph Wood pearlware vicar and parson pulpit group, in the white, the vicar sleeping as his parson preaches, the reverse incised "R. Wood" and dated.

1794 *9in (23cm) high*

£400-600 **LFA**

A Staffordshire pearlware dandies group, restored chip to hat.

c1820 *6.25in (16cm) high*

£500-800 **JHD**

A pair of Staffordshire pearlware putti on cushions, restoration to some flowers, minor chips and flakes.

c1820 *4.25in (11cm) long*

£1,000-1,500 **JHD**

An early 19thC Staffordshire pearlware gardener group, of a man seated on rocks before a tree and a woman sitting holding a rake, raised on a square base, minor damage.

10.25in (26cm) high

£400-500 **WW**

A Staffordshire pearlware tree trunk spill vase, with an owl and a parrot in the branches and a boy to the base, minor repairs.

c1830 *10.5in (27cm) high*

£400-600 **WW**

A pair of pearlware groups of the flight to and return from Egypt, the Holy Family modelled with an ass and facing left and right before bocage, each applied with a plaque inscribed "FLIGHT & RETURN", some small areas of restoration.

c1825 *9.5in (24cm) high*

£1,200-1,800 **DN**

A Staffordshire pearlware bear group, with a tethered bear, a lion and a performer, all standing before a tree on a base detailed in red and blue, minor restoration.

c1825 *9in (23cm) high*

£1,800-2,200 **WW**

A small Staffordshire pearlware model of a bird, picked out in ochre, on a green glazed mound base, crack to base.

c1790 *3.5in (9cm) high*

£300-350 **LFA**

A Staffordshire pearlware tree trunk, serpent and sheep group.

c1820 *9in (23cm) high*

£2,000-2,500 **JHD**

A Staffordshire pearlware figure of a cow, with chips to the bocage tips.

c1820 *7in (18cm) high*

£1,800-2,200 **JHD**

A Staffordshire pearlware sheep and lamb group.

c1825 *4in (10cm) high*

£220-280 **JHD**

A pair of Walton pearlware models of a ram and ewe, standing before flowering trees on high green bases each with a lamb below, "Walton" impressed on straps to the backs, minor faults.

c1830 *6.5in (16.5cm) high*

£700-1,000 **WW**

A Staffordshire pearlware model of a recumbent doe, before a flowering tree.

c1830 *4in (10cm) high*

£180-220 **WW**

An English pearlware longcase clock, in Pratt colours with an unhappy face on the dial.

c1800 *8.5in (21.5cm) high*

£800-1,200 **JHD**

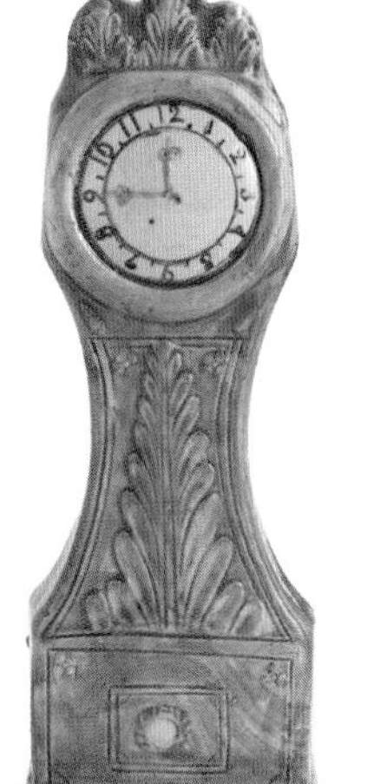

A pearlware clock in Pratt colours, with a honey yellow glaze.

c1810 *9.25in (23.5cm) high*

£500-800 **JHD**

An English pearlware watch holder, featuring a longcase clock and a pair of regal figures, replaced finial.

c1800 *9.75in (25cm) high*

£1,200-1,800 **JHD**

An English pearlware pottery cradle, restored.

c1800 *13in (33.5cm) long*

£800-1,200 **JHD**

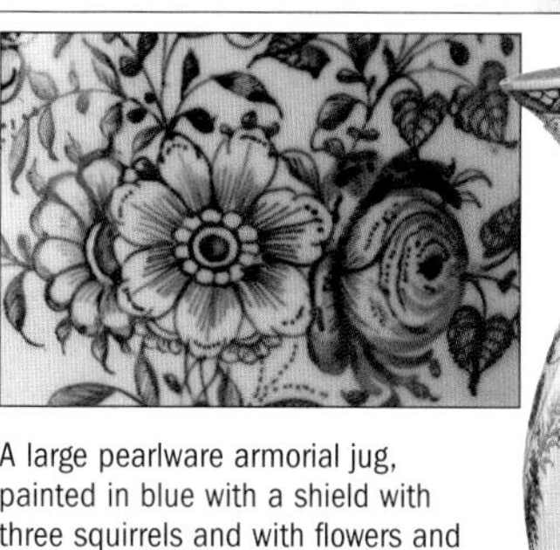

A large pearlware armorial jug, painted in blue with a shield with three squirrels and with flowers and scattered leaves, the spout damaged.

c1790 *12.5in (31.5cm) high*

£300-400 **WW**

A late 18thC pearlware commemorative jug of Pratt type, moulded in relief and painted in colours with profile busts of Admiral Nelson and Captain Berry, the neck inscribed with their names, repaired spout.

7.5in (19cm) high

£1,000-1,500 **DN**

A pearlware ovoid jug with 'C' scroll handle and straight neck, moulded in relief with a farmer chasing a fox, a shepherd and a woman with a hound, picked out in blue, green, yellow, brown and ochre, beneath an entwined leaf and ribbon band, rim cracks.

c1805 *5in (13cm) high*

£400-600 **LFA**

An English Pratt pearlware jug, restoration to the beak.

c1800 *4.5in (11.5cm) high*

£350-400 **JHD**

A rare Spode pearlware bat-printed jug of Dutch shape, with a green ground to the rim and handle, the sides decorated with two large bat prints of country houses, the front with an enamelled colour spray of roses, unmarked.

One of the country houses has been identified as West Clandon Place, near Guildford in Surrey.

c1810 *6.75in (17cm) high*

£300-500 **DN**

An English peafowl jug with pearlware glaze, design includes stylized peafowl and a distant horizon.

c1820 *5in (13cm) high*

£500-800 **JHD**

A pearlware commemorative ovoid jug, with straight neck and loop handle, printed and painted with William of Orange, masonic emblems and verses, and the cypher "GR", and with flowers and leaves, beneath a pink line rim, some restoration to lip and lower terminal of handle.

c1825 *8.75in (22cm) high*

£180-220 **LFA**

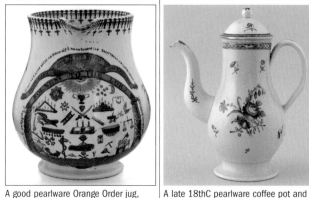

A good pearlware Orange Order jug, decorated with William III and Orangemen holding up a crown and emblems of the order.

c1830 *6in (15.5cm) high*

£320-380 **WW**

A late 18thC pearlware coffee pot and cover, the latter with pierced ball knop and green trellis diaper rim band repeated on the rim of the baluster body, above scattered sprays and sprigs of flowers.

10in (25.5cm) high

£120-180 **CHEF**

A late 18thC pearlware teapot and cover of Leeds type, the pierced ball-knopped cover fitting into a crimped gallery above the spherical pleat-moulded body, painted in Chinese export style with flowers, some damage.

5.5in (14cm) high

£60-90 **CHEF**

A pearlware serpentine-sided teapot and cover, with leaf moulded loop handle and flower knop, painted in blue, green, yellow, brown and ochre with flowers and leaves, within stiff moulded borders, the shaped rim decorated with flowerheads, cover has restored chip to inner rim.

c1795 *5.75in (14.5cm) high*

£550-650 **LFA**

A pearlware lozenge-shaped teapot and cover, with leaf moulded scroll handle and swan knop, the stiff leaf moulded borders picked out in gilt, chips to rim of cover.

c1800 *5.25in (13.5cm) high*

£220-280 **LFA**

A late 18thC blue and white pearlware mug, possibly Caughley, the cylindrical sides printed with a variation of the willow pattern and the handle with a coral diaper.

c1790 *5.75in (14.5cm) high*

£150-200 **CHEF**

A pearlware Reform Bill mug, printed in pink with four figures holding a scroll inscribed "Grey, Brougham, Russel, Althorp, Burdett, Norfolk" beneath a banner inscribed "We are for our King and our People", printed mark.

c1830 *4in (10cm) high*

£150-200 **WW**

A pearlware round bowl, painted in underglaze blue with a Chinese figure and buildings, in a fenced river landscape, the interior inscribed "Drink round about" within a diaper band, probably made in Swansea, small chip to rim.

c1780 *8.5in (21.5cm) diam*

£300-500 **LFA**

An English pearlware 'Earthworm' pattern sugar bowl and cover, losses.

4.5in (11.5cm) high

£1,000-1,500 **DAW**

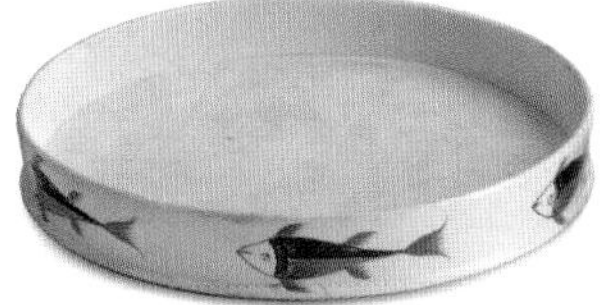

An English pearlware char dish in Pratt colours, with a pattern of fish around the rim, restored rim chip.

c1800 *12in (30.5cm) diam*

£800-1,200 **JHD**

A pearlware botanical oval meat dish, painted in coloured enamels with a Convolvulus Major, within green line borders, restored.

c1810 *19.25in (49cm) wide*

£100-150 **LFA**

An English pearlware child's plate in Pratt colours, floral relief pattern around the lip, central blue and white design of a mother and child, inscribed "Perfect Innocence".

c1815 *7.5in (19cm) diam*

£280-320 **JHD**

A child's pearlware commemorative plate, printed and painted with a figure and an angel at an urn and inscribed "To the memory of Queen Caroline, the Injured Queen of England", the rose and honeysuckle moulded border picked out in colours, brown line to rim.

c1825 *6.25in (16cm) diam*

£400-600 **LFA**

One of a pair of pearlware plaques depicting cherubs and celestial maidens surrounded by foliage borders.

9in (23cm) wide

£1,800-2,200 pair **JHD**

One of a pair of Staffordshire pearlware plaques depicting fighting horses, one inscribed on the back "A. Hall, Spotted Cow, Hanley 1836", some paint loss.

9.25in (23.5cm) wide

£1,800-2,200 pair **JHD**

A Staffordshire pearlware small character jug, the Toby figure holding a glass and a bottle decorated in coloured enamels, on a mound base.

c1830 *4.5in (11.5cm) high*

£60-90 **LFA**

An English pearlware caddy, bearing a stylized design of a peafowl in a tree.

4in (10cm) high

£500-700 **JHD**

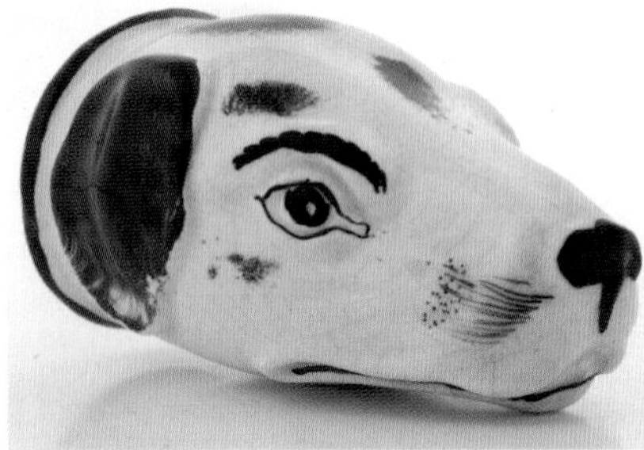

A Staffordshire pearlware hound's head stirrup cup, picked out in black and brown.

c1820 *4.5in (11.5cm) long*

£300-500 **LFA**

A pearlware sauceboat, in the form of a fox mask, with swan loop handle, boldly decorated in ochre and yellow, on green glazed leaf moulded foot.

c1800 *6.25in (16cm) long*

£600-700 **LFA**

PRATTWARE

A Prattware cockerel, crack and minor chips.

c1790 *3.75in (9.5cm) high*

£800-1,000 **AD**

A Prattware cat, both ears chipped.

c1800 *6in (15cm) high*

£2,500-3,000 **JHOR**

An English Prattware pug dog.

c1810 *3.25in (8cm) high*

£400-600 **JHD**

A fine and richly coloured early 19thC Prattware figure of a cockerel.

9in (23cm) high

£4,000-5,000 **JHOR**

A Staffordshire pearl-glazed rural group in Pratt colours, depicting squirrels, sheep and birds around a farmer and his wife, replaced sheep, restored ears, squirrel and stick.

7.25in (18.5cm) high

£2,500-3,000 **JHD**

An early 19thC Prattware model of a young girl riding on a nanny goat, decorated in yellow, manganese, blue and green, probably Scottish, small chips.

5.5in (14cm) high

£250-350 **WW**

An early 19thC Prattware figure inscribed "Spring".

8.5in (21.5cm) high

£700-800 **JHOR**

A Prattware figure, depicting winter.

c1800 6.25in (16cm) high

£300-350 **AD**

A Prattware clock, painted in blues and yellows.

c1800 8in (20.5cm) high

£800-900 **JHOR**

A pottery longcase clock, in Pratt colours with toffee-coloured glaze and green floral decoration.

c1810 8.75in (22.5cm) high

£1,000-1,500 **JHD**

A mid-18thC Prattware pipe, modelled as a lady seated with her cat smoking a pipe with male mask bowl, her dress spotted in blue and brown and lined in ochre, the mouthpiece behind her modelled as a snake.

c1750 4.75in (12cm) high

£280-320 **CHEF**

A CLOSER LOOK AT PRATTWARE COILED PIPE

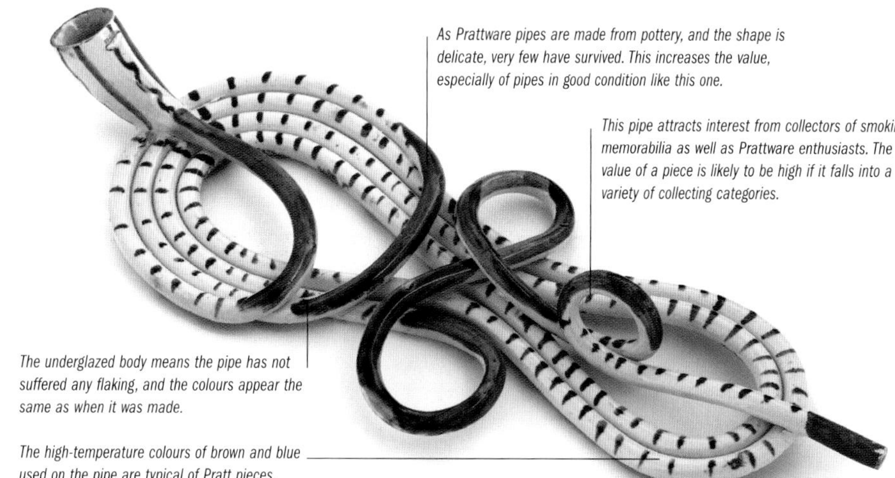

As Prattware pipes are made from pottery, and the shape is delicate, very few have survived. This increases the value, especially of pipes in good condition like this one.

This pipe attracts interest from collectors of smoking memorabilia as well as Prattware enthusiasts. The value of a piece is likely to be high if it falls into a variety of collecting categories.

The underglazed body means the pipe has not suffered any flaking, and the colours appear the same as when it was made.

The high-temperature colours of brown and blue used on the pipe are typical of Pratt pieces.

An English Prattware coiled pipe in blue and brown on a cream ground.

c1800 11in (28cm) long

£1,800-2,200 **JHD**

An English Prattware 'Farmer's Arms' tankard with a blue rim, design features a wheatsheaf surrounded by farm tools.

c1800 4.5in (11.5cm) high

£500-700 **JHD**

An 18thC Prattware circular plaque, moulded and painted with Diana the huntress holding an arrow, her brown spotted ochre robe falling from one shoulder and covering her knees.

7.5in (19.5cm) diam

£280-320 **CHEF**

An early 19thC Prattware oval plaque, relief moulded with the head of a classical maiden, decorated in blue, brown, green, yellow and ochre, good restoration to the rim.

9.5in (24cm) diam

£350-400 **WW**

A Prattware teapot, with side panels depicting rural scenes.

c1800 5.5in (14cm) high

£1,200-1,800 **JHOR**

STAFFORDSHIRE POTTERIES

For centuries, the heart of British pottery production lay in the five towns of the Staffordshire potteries. Stoke-on-Trent, Burslem, Hanley, Tunstall, and Longton were home to almost 1,000 firms by the end of the 19thC, including the famous Wedgwood, Spode and Ridgway companies. Early Staffordshire ware included slip decorated, functional household items produced by notable potters such as Thomas Toft (d.1689). During the 18thC, Thomas Whieldon's brightly coloured tea and coffee pots and chimney ornaments were highly regarded.

The Staffordshire companies became increasingly well known for their decorative pottery figures during the 19thC. Potters met the widespread demand by producing exact copies of high-quality porcelain figures in large quantities. During the early part of the century, pieces were often inspired by Derby and Chelsea, and depicted rustic, allegorical or biblical scenes. Victorian figures, typically of children or lovers, were largely designed for the mantelpiece and were left undecorated at the back. From c1840, depictions of famous people, such as politicians, royalty or sportsmen, became popular, as well as pairs of animals.

Pairs of figures, and early pieces are especially valuable to collectors. Most Staffordshire ware is unmarked, making it difficult to identify, and there are many fakes on the market.

ANIMALS

A pair of Staffordshire spaniel dogs, 'Grace and Majesty', with pink and green bases.

c1850 *10in (25.5cm) high*

£3,000-5,000 **JHD**

A pair of Staffordshire hearth spaniels.

c1860 *16.25in (41cm) high*

£2,500-3,000 **JHD**

A pair of Staffordshire brown and white spaniel dog jugs.

c1860 *10in (25.5cm) high*

£1,000-1,500 **JHD**

A pair of Staffordshire black and white King Charles spaniel jugs.

c1860 *10in (25.5cm) high*

£800-1,200 **RDER**

A rare Scottish pottery spaniel.

10in (25.5cm) high

£2,200-2,800 **JHD**

A Staffordshire spaniel on a base.

c1845 *7.5in (19cm) high*

£800-1,200 **JHD**

A pair of Staffordshire poodle kennel groups.

c1860 *8.25in (21cm) high*

£1,000-1,500 **JHD**

A pair of Victorian Staffordshire poodles.

c1860 *5in (13cm) high*

£500-700 **AD**

A pair of Staffordshire poodles.

c1865 *10.25in (26cm) high*

£400-600 **JHD**

An unusual Staffordshire brown poodle.

c1835-40 *4in (10cm) high*

£300-400 **AD**

A Staffordshire poodle family group pen holder.

c1850 *6.75in (17cm) high*

£500-800 **JHD**

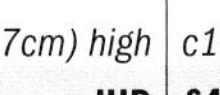

A Staffordshire pug dog.

c1820 *3.5in (9cm) high*

£400-600 **JHOR**

A Staffordshire pottery pug.

c1825 *3.25in (8.5cm) high*

£300-500 **AD**

A Staffordshire pug dog, with transfer-printed decoration and glass eyes.

c1890 *11.5in (29cm) high*

£1,200-1,800 **RDER**

A pair of Staffordshire pug dogs.

c1880 *9.5in (24cm) high*

£700-1,000 **JHD**

A pair of Staffordshire pugs, a hairline crack to one leg.

c1885 *11in (28cm) high*

£1,000-1,500 **JHD**

A pair of Staffordshire Newfoundlands.

c1850 *5.5in (14cm) high*

£2,500-3,000 **JHD**

A pair of Staffordshire sporting dog spill vases, restoration to tip of one vase.

c1855 *6.75in (17cm) high*

£1,800-2,200 **JHD**

A pair of Staffordshire greyhounds on turquoise bases.

c1855 *11in (28cm) high*

£800-1,200 **JHD**

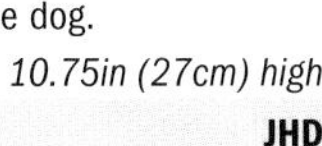

A Staffordshire pipe dog.

c1850 *10.75in (27cm) high*

£1,500-2,000 **JHD**

A rare Staffordshire Italian greyhound.

c1850 *7in (18cm) high*

£1,000-1,500 **JHD**

A pair of rare Staffordshire greyhounds, with rabbits at their feet.

c1880 *11.5in (29cm) high*

£1,000-1,500 **RDER**

A Walton Staffordshire lion and unicorn pair with regal attributes, reclining at the base of trees.

6.25in (16cm) high

£2,500-3,000 **JHD**

One of a pair of Lloyd of Shelton Staffordshire lion and lambs on cream plinth bases with gold decoration.

c1835 *4in (10cm) high*

£2,500-3,500 pair **JHD**

One of a rare pair of Staffordshire lions, minor chips and flaking and some restoration.

c1880 *8.75in (22.5cm) high*

£3,000-4,000 pair **JHD**

A very fine Staffordshire Wood family figure of a lion, with excellent colour glaze and crisp modelling, restoration to tail.

c1790 *9.5in (24.5cm) high*

£8,000-12,000 **JHOR**

An unusual early 19thC Staffordshire model of a lion before a flowering tree, its paw resting on a ball, raised on a green rocky base.

5.5in (14cm) high

£1,200-1,800 **WW**

A rare Staffordshire leopard with cubs and a snake spill vase, restoration to the snake's head.

c1850 *9.75in (25cm) high*

£1,500-2,000 **JHD**

A Staffordshire leopard and cub group.

c1840 *5in (12.5cm) high*

£400-600 **JHD**

A pair of Staffordshire leopard spill vases, one restored and with a hairline crack.

6.75in (17cm) high

£2,500-3,000 **JHD**

A rare Staffordshire panther, with some restoration.

c1820 *6in (15.5cm) high*

£1,200-1,800 **JHOR**

A Staffordshire Romulus and Remus group, minor damage.

c1820 *8.75in (22.5cm) high*

£1,200-1,800 **JHOR**

A North Yorkshire cow creamer, with a new stopper, repair to an ear.

c1800 *6in (15.5cm) high*

£800-1,200 **JHOR**

A Swansea-type Prattware cow creamer.

c1800 *5in (13cm) high*

£700-1,000 **AD**

An early 19thC North Yorkshire cow creamer, a new stopper, repair to ear.

5.5in (14cm) high

£1,000-1,500 **JHOR**

A Staffordshire brown and white cow creamer with attendant.

c1860 *7.75 (20cm) high*

£500-800 **JHD**

A Staffordshire black and white cow creamer with attendant, restoration to legs and lid.

c1860 *7.75in (19.5cm) long*

£500-700 **JHD**

A pair of early 19thC North Yorkshire cow creamers with attendants, the horns repaired.

6in (15cm) high

£2,200-2,800 **JHOR**

One of a pair of Prattware cow creamers.

c1810 *5.25in (13cm) high*

£1,800-2,200 pair **AD**

One of a pair of Scottish cow creamers.

c1820 *5.25in (13.5cm) high*

£1,000-1,500 pair **AD**

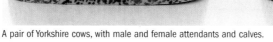

A pair of Yorkshire cows, with male and female attendants and calves.

c1820 *5.5in (14cm) high*

£3,500-4,500 **JHOR**

A pair of Yorkshire cow creamers, with attendants.

c1830 *5.5in (14cm) high*

£1,200-1,800 **JHOR**

A Staffordshire bull standing before a tree trunk spill vase, a restored horn.

c1820 *7.5in (19cm) high*

£1,800-2,200 **JHD**

An Obadiah Sherratt Staffordshire cow and snake on a rainbow base, minor hairline crack to base.

c1830 *7.75in (20cm) high*

£1,500-2,000 **JHD**

An early 19thC Staffordshire bull baiting group, with a bull and terrier on a green and brown rustic base, restoration to the horns and tails.

6in (15cm) high

£220-280 **WW**

A Staffordshire figure of a water buffalo, restoration to head.

c1755 *5.25in (13.5cm) high*

£5,000-7,000 **JHOR**

One of a pair of Staffordshire cow and calf groups, with horns and flowers, a restored base.

c1820 *6.25in (16cm) high*

£1,200-1,800 pair **JHD**

A pair of Staffordshire cows with attendant figures.

c1860 *7in (18cm) high*

£500-700 **JHD**

A Ralph Wood colour-glazed ram, finely detailed.

c1790 *7in (18cm) wide*

£2,200-2,800 **JHD**

An English colour-glazed ram on a green base.

c1790 *4.75in (12cm) high*

£1,800-2,200 **JHD**

A Staffordshire or Yorkshire sheep figure.

c1880

£700-1,000 **JHOR**

A Staffordshire ewe with a lamb reclining beneath a tree.

c1860 *5.5in (14cm) high*

£320-380 **JHD**

A rare Staffordshire spill vase group, repair to horns.

c1820 *7.25in (18.5cm) high*

£1,800-2,200 **JHOR**

A Staffordshire bocage figure of a ewe and lamb, chips to ear and leaf.

c1820 *7.5in (19cm) long*

£600-900 **JHD**

A Staffordshire agate ware cat with stylized black banding, a small hole above rear leg.

4.75in (12cm) high

£2,200-2,800 **JHD**

A mid-18thC Whielden type cat, the dark brown eyed feline reclining, its cream coat with rust slip hatching, blue and dark brown spots.

3.75in (9.5cm) wide

£300-350 **CHEF**

A naïve English seated cat, slight damage and scuffing to paintwork.

8.25in (21cm) high

£600-900 **JHD**

A Staffordshire cat, with transfer-printed decoration and glass eyes.

c1890 *14in (35.5cm) high*

£1,200-1,800 **RDER**

An English pottery cat with attractive vertical banding.

10.75in (27.5cm) high

£500-700 **JHD**

One of a pair of 19thC treacle-glazed cats.

c1850 *6in (15cm) high*

£800-1,200 pair **AD**

A pair of Staffordshire zebras.

c1860 *7.75in (20cm) high*

£700-1,000 **JHD**

A pair of Thomas Parr Staffordshire zebras with detailed foliage to base.

c1860 *5in (13cm) high*

£700-1,000 **JHD**

A pair of Staffordshire zebras mounted by children, restored ear and leg.

c1860 *6in (15.5cm) high*

£500-700 **JHD**

A pair of Staffordshire zebra spill vases.

c1875 *11in (28cm) high*

£1,800-2,200 **JHD**

A pair of Staffordshire white horse spill vases.

c1870 *10.5in (27cm) high*

£800-1,200 **JHD**

A pair of Staffordshire stag and doe spill vases with fawns.

c1860 *12.25in (31cm) long*

£1,000-1,500 **JHD**

A Staffordshire elephant spill vase.

c1855 *6in (15cm) high*

£700-1,000 **JHD**

A Staffordshire elephant spill vase.

c1855 *6.75in (17cm) high*

£700-1,000 **JHD**

One of a pair of small Staffordshire elephants.

c1860 *2.75in (7cm) high*

£500-700 pair **JHD**

One of a pair of Staffordshire exotic birds, small chips to beak and tail.

c1850 *8.25in (21cm) high*

£1,000-1,500 pair **JHD**

A Staffordshire figure of a bird, repair to tail.

This piece is possibly a copy of a Meissen original.

c1765 *7.75in (19.5cm) high*

£3,500-4,500 **JHOR**

A Staffordshire roc bird saving a child from a waterfall.

c1855 *13.5in (34cm) high*

£1,000-1,500 **JHD**

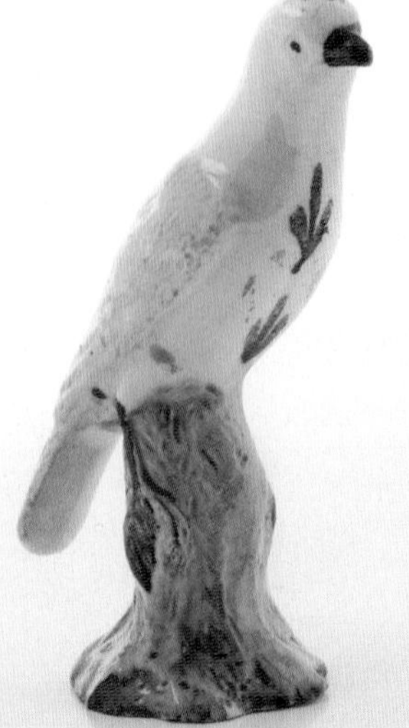

A late 18thC Staffordshire bird in Pratt colours.

4.75in (12cm) high

£800-1,200 **JHOR**

A rare Staffordshire fox spill vase.

c1850 *9in (23cm) high*

£1,000-1,500 **JHD**

A Staffordshire figure of a squirrel.

c1780 *6.5in (17cm) high*

£3,500-4,500 **JHOR**

A Staffordshire bear baiting jug, the head forming the cover, he sits on his hind legs and grasps a yellow dog which fiercely bares its teeth, all decorated in overglaze enamels, some damages.

c1810 *12in (30.5cm) high*

£800-1,200 **WW**

A Scottish pottery goat in cream and brown with a bright polychromatic base.

c1845 *7in (18cm) high*

£1,200-1,800 **JHD**

CANARYWARE

Canaryware is a rare, brightly decorated, yellow glazed pottery, which was produced in Staffordshire, Yorkshire, the North East of England and South Wales during the short period from c1815-1830. Although popular at the time, the cost of production was extremely high, making it financially inviable. The glaze used had a tendency to burn during firing and leave black marks on the surface, meaning a large proportion of pieces were wasted. Surviving pieces often show evidence of kiln damage, even items considered to be in good condition.

Typically, canaryware pieces are tableware. Decoration varies from naïve painting to more formal designs, using lustre and polychrome enamel. The size of items also varies, with pieces on the market ranging from 2in (5cm) to over 24in (61cm) in height. The rarity of canaryware makes it valuable, although smaller pieces are generally more affordable. A jug can cost between £300-£3,000, more if it is in perfect condition.

One of a pair of English canary yellow plates, with botanical decoration.

c1820 *6.25in (16cm) diam*

£500-800 pair **JHD**

A small English canary yellow plate, decorated in polychrome colours with relief moulded borders.

c1820 *6.25in (16cm) diam*

£400-600 **JHD**

An English canary yellow plate, decorated with exotic birds and a pink lustre.

c1820 *7.5in (19cm) diam*

£280-320 **JHD**

An English canary yellow bowl, decorated with polychrome colours.

c1820 *4.5in (11.5cm) diam*

£320-380 **JHD**

An English canary yellow bowl, decorated with a flower and leaves.

c1820 *5.25in (13.5cm) diam*

£320-380 **JHD**

An English canary yellow shallow dish, decorated with ivy leaves.

c1820 *4.75in (12cm) long*

£300-500 **JHD**

An English canary yellow mug, with naïvely painted houses.

c1825 *4.75in (12cm) high*

£800-1,200 **JHD**

An English canary yellow soldier on horseback.

c1815 *4.25in (10.5cm) high*

£500-800 **JHD**

An English canary yellow mug, with silver resist band.

c1820 *3.25in (8.5cm) high*

£400-600 **JHD**

An English canary yellow pot with stand.

c1820 *Pot 4.5in (11.5cm) diam*

£600-900 **JHD**

A CLOSER LOOK AT A CANARYWARE BACCHUS PITCHER

Very little canaryware was produced. It was made for a short period at the beginning of the 19thC. Most of it was functional tableware for everyday use, meaning few pieces survived. This increases the value.

The relief moulding of Bacchus on the spout and grapes on the body is especially well defined, and is rarely seen in canary yellow.

This jug is in very good condition. It has not been restored and the polychrome colours are original and bright.

The shape of the jug is rare, making it highly collectable.

An English canary yellow pottery Bacchus pitcher.

c1820 *5.5in (14cm) high*

£1,000-1,500 **JHD**

An English canary yellow child's tea set, chip to lid of sucrier.

c1820 *Teapot 3.25in (8.5cm) high*

£1,500-2,000 **JHD**

An English canary yellow whistle.

c1820 *4in (10cm) long*

£500-700 **JHD**

An English canary yellow egg cup.

c1820 *2.25in (5.5cm) high*

£300-500 **JHD**

An English canary yellow cottage money box.

c1835 *28in (11cm) high*

£500-700 **JHD**

PASTILLE BURNERS

An Alcock Staffordshire Warwick Castle pastille burner with a detachable top.

c1840 *6.75in (17cm) high*

£600-900 **JHD**

A Staffordshire cottage pastille burner.

c1845 *4in (10cm) high*

£150-250 **AD**

A Staffordshire pottery cottage pastille burner with dogs.

c1855 *7.75in (20cm) high*

£500-800 **JHD**

A Staffordshire pottery pastille burner, with minor chips.

c1860 *7in (17.5cm) high*

£300-500 **JHD**

A Staffordshire ceramic castle.

c1845 *4.75in (12cm) high*

£280-320 **JHD**

A Staffordshire ceramic castle.

c1845 *6.75in (17cm) high*

£280-320 **JHD**

A Staffordshire garden house pastille burner, old repairs to finial.

c1830 *9.75in (25cm) high*

£500-800 **JHD**

A Staffordshire lodge pastille burner with slide, old repair to one chimney and replaced slide.

c1840 *5.25in (13.5cm) wide*

£600-900 **JHD**

A mid-19thC Staffordshire gothic cottage.

7.75in (20cm) high

£300-500 **JHD**

An Alcock Staffordshire pastille burner.

c1830 *6in (15cm) high*

£500-700 **JHD**

An Alcock Staffordshire umbrella roof cottage.

c1830 *8in (20.5cm) high*

£500-800 **JHD**

A Staffordshire cottage pastille burner.

c1840

£300-400 **AD**

STAFFORDSHIRE FIGURES

A CLOSER LOOK AT A STAFFORDSHIRE FIGURE

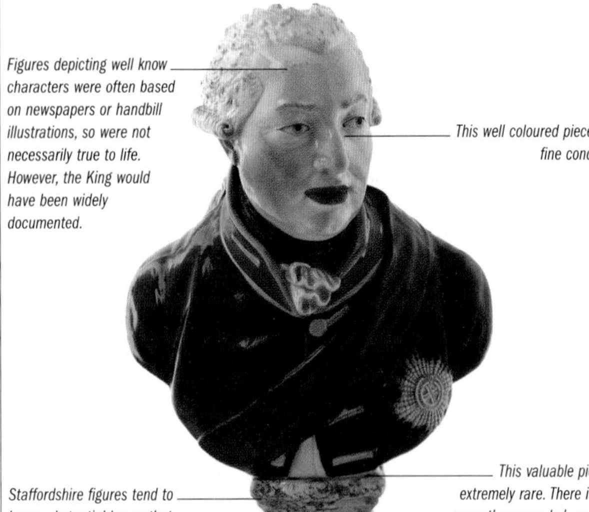

Figures depicting well know characters were often based on newspapers or handbill illustrations, so were not necessarily true to life. However, the King would have been widely documented.

This well coloured piece is in fine condition.

Staffordshire figures tend to have substantial bases that are uneven to the underside. This is because they were hand pressed into a mould.

This valuable piece is extremely rare. There is only one other recorded example, which is in the Victoria and Albert Museum.

A very fine Staffordshire figure of George III, possibly by E. Wood.

c1790 *12.5in (32cm) high*

£16,000-18,000 **JHOR**

A pair of Staffordshire figures depicting the Tailor of Gloucester and his wife.

c1820 *6.75in (17cm) high*

£700-1,000 **JHD**

A Staffordshire Hercules and the bull.

c1800 *5.25in (13.5cm) high*

£1,000-1,500 **JHOR**

A Staffordshire pottery 'Roger Giles' pepper pot.

c1825 *4.75in (12cm) high*

£400-600 **AD**

A Staffordshire Ralph Wood-type figure of King David.

c1795 *12.25in (31cm) high*

£2,500-3,500 **JHOR**

A rare Staffordshire 'Jim Crow' figure.

c1830

£2,000-3,000 **JHOR**

A rare Staffordshire spill vase group, of a boy with a pair of leopards.

c1820 *8.5in (21.5cm) high*

£4,000-5,000 **JHOR**

A Portobello pottery horse-drawn carriage with rider.

c1820 *3.75in (9.5cm) high*

£400-600 **JHD**

An early 19thC Staffordshire spill vase group, of a shepherd playing his horn to two recumbent sheep, with a pigeon perched in the tree trunk above him, his dog tries to attract his attention.

7.5in (19cm) high

£280-320 **CHEF**

A Staffordshire spill or quill holder, depicting a girl and a sheep.

c1840 *4.5in (11.5cm) high*

£320-380 **AD**

A pair of Staffordshire children feeding chicks.

c1845 *5.5in (14cm) high*

£500-700 **JHD**

A pair of Staffordshire children with pets, restoration to boy's neck.

c1845 *7in (18cm) long*

£800-1,200 **JHD**

A Yorkshire pottery watch group depicting a longcase clock, male and female figures and a dog.

c1790 *8.75in (22.5cm) high*

£1,800-2,200 **JHD**

A Staffordshire 'Dandies' group.

c1820 *7.5in (19.5cm) high*

£1,200-1,800 **JHOR**

An early 19thC Staffordshire group, marked "Tittensor".

6.5in (16.5cm) high

£1,200-1,800 **JHOR**

A Staffordshire 'Dandies' group, with restored hairline cracks to neck, right hand and bag.

c1825 *6.75in (17cm) high*

£500-700 **JHD**

A Staffordshire saltglazed stoneware figure of a monkey dressed as a soldier.

c1750 *5.25in (13.5cm) high*

£1,000-1,500 **JHOR**

A rare Staffordshire 'Sailor's Farewell' and 'Sailor's Return' pair, depicting a sailor in fine dress with booty, pipe and ale, and a reclining sailor with forlorn expression respectively.

c1820 *6.75in (17cm) high*

£1,800-2,200 **JHD**

A small Staffordshire figure of a parson.

c1820 *3.5in (9cm) high*

£500-700 **JHOR**

A pair of Staffordshire monkey musicians, some restoration.

c1850 *2.25in (6cm) high*

£500-800 **JHD**

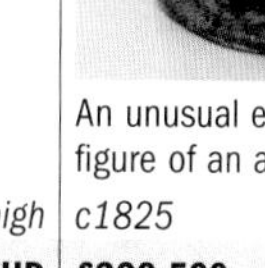

An unusual early 19thC Staffordshire figure of an archeress.

c1825 *6in (15cm) high*

£300-500 **AD**

A pair of fine quality early 19thC 'Sailor and Lass' figures, probably Staffordshire or Yorkshire.

7.75in (20cm) high

£3,500-4,500 **JHOR**

A Staffordshire model of a huntsman, with his gun and powder flask standing before a tree with his hound, repairs to the tree.

c1830 *7in (17.5cm) high*

£280-320 **WW**

A very rare English figure of a boy's head.

9.5in (24cm) high

£2,500-3,000 **JHD**

A very rare Staffordshire figure, of 'Dr. Syntax on Horseback'.

c1820 *6in (15.5cm) high*

£3,500-4,500 **JHOR**

A rare pair of Staffordshire portrait figures of Sir John and Lady Franklin from the Alpha factory, he with a telescope, she with a head-dress and shawl, some restoration.

c1850 *11in (28cm) high*

£1,000-1,500 **GORL**

A pair of Staffordshire horses, with the Duke and Duchess of Cambridge.

The Duke was the son of George III.

c1850 *13.5in (34cm) high*

£800-1,200 **RDER**

A Staffordshire 'Prince of Wales' pen holder.

c1850 *4in (10cm) high*

£300-500 **JHD**

Two Staffordshire 'Railway Children' spill vases with restored hands.

c1860 *9.5in (24cm) high*

£1,000-1,500 **JHD**

A Staffordshire figure depicting Lady Hestor on a camel, by Thomas Parr.

c1850 *7in (18cm) high*

£1,000-1,500 **JHD**

A Staffordshire 'Euston Station' group.

c1855 *10.5in (27cm) high*

£1,200-1,800 **JHD**

A Staffordshire pottery group of 'Topsy and Eva', kneeling, holding hands, and picked out in coloured enamels, the oval base titled in gilt.

c1860 *8.75in (22cm) high*

£500-700 **LFA**

A Victorian Staffordshire figure group, 'Eva and Uncle Tom', from Uncle Tom's Cabin.

8.5in (21.5cm) high

£100-150 **GORL**

A rare Staffordshire pottery figure, entitled "The First Ride".

c1860 *13.5in (34cm) long*

£1,000-1,500 **JHD**

A rare Staffordshire circus group, of performers on horseback.

c1855 *8.5in (21.5cm) high*

£600-900 **JHD**

A Staffordshire group of figures with pets.

c1855 *8in (20.5cm) high*

£500-700 **JHD**

A rare Staffordshire pair of spill vases, featuring children with foxes.

c1855 *8.75in (22.5cm) high*

£700-1,000 **JHD**

A pair of Staffordshire children with swans, in the form of spill vases.

c1855 *7in (18cm) high*

£500-800 **JHD**

A pair of diminutive Staffordshire figures with sheep, restored hairline cracks.

c1860 *7.5in (19cm) high*

£600-900 **JHD**

A Staffordshire shepherd with his flock and sheepdog.

c1860 *9.75in (25cm) high*

£500-700 **JHD**

A 19thC Staffordshire figure of a Scottish huntsman in a kilt, with one arm around a fawn standing on rocks above a waterfall, some restoration.

16.75in (42.5cm) high

£50-80 **CHEF**

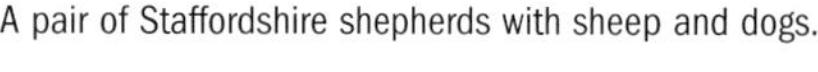

A pair of Staffordshire shepherds with sheep and dogs.

c1860 *7.75in (20cm) high*

£600-900 **JHD**

A Staffordshire harlequin figure.

c1830 5in (13cm) high

£500-800 **JHOR**

A Staffordshire Prince and Princess group.

c1850 7.25in (18.5cm) high

£1,000-1,500 **JHD**

A 19thC Staffordshire clock group, the clock face surrounded by grape vines, a bagpiper and his lass sit above.

15in (38cm) high

£50-80 **CHEF**

A Staffordshire sailor with sweetheart, restored hairline crack.

c1860 9.75in (25cm) high

£350-400 **JHD**

A Staffordshire model of a tavern wench, standing and holding a bottle, modelled in detail beneath her skirt.

c1875 8in (20cm) high

£180-220 **WW**

A Staffordshire group of angels with sleeping children, restored chip to hat.

c1855 9in (23cm) high

£300-500 **JHD**

A Staffordshire tobacco box in the form of an Eastern gentleman, possibly theatrical.

c1855 7in (17.5cm) high

£220-280 **JHD**

A Staffordshire scratch blue saltglazed stoneware teapot, restoration to spout.

c1750 4in (10.5cm) high

£3,000-4,000 **JHOR**

A Staffordshire saltglazed stoneware miniature globular teapot.

c1750 2.5in (6.5cm) high

£220-280 **LFA**

A Staffordshire red stoneware small globular teapot and cover, with a loop handle and turned knop, applied with numerous Chinese figures in gardens, and scattered leaf scrolls, inner rim chips.

c1750 3.5in (8.5cm) high

£500-700 **LFA**

A Staffordshire teapot with chinoiserie panels, repairs to spout.

c1765 5.75in (14.5cm) high

£3,000-4,000 **JHOR**

A mid-18thC saltglazed teapot and cover, the latter pierced through the acorn knop, the spherical pot painted with flowers, the crabstock handle and spout detailed in red.

c1750
£400-500 **CHEF**

A Staffordshire cauliflower teapot, the handle and knop restored.
c1765 *5.25in (13.5cm) high*
£1,200-1,800 **JHOR**

A Staffordshire mottled green and brown teapot.
c1770 *4.75in (12cm) high*
£1,200-1,800 **JHOR**

A Staffordshire redware pottery bullet-shaped punch pot, sprigged en rocaille with two panels of a Chinese figure within C-scroll foliate borders, traces of old lacquer or varnish.

c1760 *6.75in (17cm) high*
£800-1,200 **DN**

A Staffordshire dove tureen, with a restored beak.
c1835 *8.25in (21cm) long*
£500-800 **JHD**

A Staffordshire hen on nest, with polychrome decoration.

c1870 *8in (20.5cm) long*
£300-500 **RDER**

A Staffordshire duck tureen, restored hairline crack to basket.

c1840 *7in (18cm) long*
£700-1,000 **JHD**

A Staffordshire duck tureen.

c1850 *10.5in (26.5cm) long*
£500-800 **RDER**

A Staffordshire duck tureen with a restored beak.

c1860 *9in (23cm) long*
£800-1,200 **JHD**

A pair of Staffordshire dove tureens, one with a restored beak.
c1860 — *8.25in (21cm) long*
£1,200-1,800 **JHD**

A Staffordshire pineapple tea canister.
c1765 — *4.25in (11cm) high*
£2,000-2,500 **JHOR**

A Staffordshire cabbage leaf bowl.
c1765 — *3in (8cm) high*
£1,200-1,800 **JHOR**

A Staffordshire canister in the manner of Whieldon.
c1765 — *6.75in (17.5cm) high*
£3,500-4,500 **JHOR**

A very rare Staffordshire 'Welshman' Toby jug.

c1780 *9.75in (25cm) high*

£6,000-7,000 **JHOR**

An enamelled Staffordshire sailor Toby jug.

c1800 *11.25in (28.5cm) high*

£2,500-3,500 **JHOR**

A 19thC Staffordshire table condiment set, in the form of portly gentlemen, with blue printed 'willow pattern' decoration, wearing red jackets and yellow breeches.

c1850

£300-500 **L&T**

A Ralph Wood type Staffordshire sailor Toby jug, the hat restored.

c1790 *11.5in (29cm) high*

£2,000-2,500 **JHOR**

A CLOSER LOOK AT A STAFFORDSHIRE POSSET POT

Posset pots were produced in England and Holland from the 16thC to the 18thC, usually in tin-glazed earthenware.

This piece is very rare as so few slipware posset pots were produced.

Posset pots are drinking vessels for posset (a mixture of milk, spices and beer or wine). They usually have two handles, like this one, and sometimes a cover and spout for drinking.

Considering its age, the piece is in exceptionally good condition, and has not been restored.

A very rare Staffordshire posset pot, with slip decoration and an inscription around the rim which reads: "The Best is not too good for you".

c1690 *5in (13cm) high*

£30,000-40,000 **JHOR**

A Staffordshire Burslem slipware charger, probably decorated by Ralph Simpson, restored.

c1680 *12.5in (32cm) diam*

£12,000-18,000 **JHOR**

A Staffordshire nursery plate, with alphabet.

c1880 *6in (15cm) diam*

£150-200 **RDER**

A Staffordshire Pratt pipe with whistle.

c1820 *10.25in (26cm) long*

£2,000-3,000 **JHOR**

CHINESE DYNASTIES & MARKS

ORIENTAL

CHINESE CERAMIC MARKS

Imperial reign marks were adopted during the Ming dynasty, and some of the most common are reproduced here. Certain emperors forbade the use of their own reign mark, lest they should suffer the disrespect of a broken vessel bearing their name being thrown away. This is where the convention of using earlier reign marks comes from – a custom that was enthusiastically adopted by potters as a way of showing their respect for their predecessors. It is worth remembering that a great deal of Imperial porcelain is marked misleadingly and pieces bearing the reign mark for the period in which they were made are therefore especially sought after.

EARLY DYNASTIES

Xia Dynasty	*c2000 - 1500BC*
Shang Dynasty	*c1500 - 1028BC*
Zhou Dynasty	*c1028 - 221BC*
Qin Dynasty	*221 - 206BC*
Han Dynasty	*206BC - AD220*
Three Kingdoms	*221 - 280*
Jin Dynasty	*265 - 420*
Northern and Southern Dynasties	*420 - 581*
Sui Dynasty	*581 - 618*
Tang Dynasty	*618 - 906*
The Five Dynasties	*907 - 960*
Song Dynasty	*960 - 1279*
Jin Dynasty	*1115 - 1234*
Yuan Dynasty	*1260 - 1368*

EARLY MING DYNASTIES

Hongwu	*1368 - 1398*
Jianwen	*1399 - 1402*
Yongle	*1403 - 1424*
Hongxi	*1425 - 1425*
Xuande	*1426 - 1435*
Zhengtong	*1436 - 1449*
Jingtai	*1450 - 1457*
Tianshun	*1457 - 1464*
Chenghua	*1465 - 1487*
Hongzhi	*1488 - 1505*
Zhengde	*1506 - 1521*

LATER MING DYNASTY MARKS

大明嘉靖年製
Jiajing
1522 – 1566

大明隆慶年製
Longqing
1567 – 1572

大明萬曆年製
Wanli
1573 – 1619

大明天啟年製
Tianqi
1621 – 1627

崇禎年製
Chongzhen
1628 – 1644

QING DYNASTY MARKS

大清順治年製
Shunzhi
1644 – 1661

大清康熙年製
Kangxi
1662 – 1722

大清雍正年製
Yongzheng
1723 – 1735

大清乾隆年製
Qianlong
1736 – 1795

嘉慶年製
Jiaqing
1796 – 1820

大清道光年製
Daoguang
1821 – 1850

大清咸豐年製
Xianfeng
1851 – 1861

大清同治年製
Tongzhi
1862 – 1874

大清光緒年製
Guangxu
1875 – 1908

大清宣統年製
Xuantong
1909 – 1911

REPUBLIC PERIOD

崇禎年製
Hongxian (Yuan Shikai)
1915 – 1916

ORIENTAL CERAMICS

The continuing boom in the Chinese economy has given the Oriental art market new buoyancy. Demand for Chinese antiques in particular is now very high in their home country and prices have been increasing commensurately. The segment currently most affected by this phenomenon is porcelain from the mid-17thC transitional period, which is similar to, yet more affordable than, the fêted Imperial porcelain.

Previously largely ignored, Oriental artefacts in damaged condition are attracting more attention today. As the availability of pristine examples dwindles, collectors are now more willing to consider damaged goods, at least at the top end of the market. As restoration techniques become more sophisticated and prices for the best pieces become prohibitive, the stigma associated with damaged items is being eroded. This curious development is so far confined to cases where undamaged examples are nigh-on impossible to locate except for astronomical sums of money.

Antique Oriental ceramics salvaged from the ocean floor continue to fascinate many collectors and attract high prices. Salerooms are quick to exploit the media attention that large sales of shipwreck cargoes attract. The romance surrounding these finds shows little sign of abating.

More specialist markets, such as those in netsuke or lacquer boxes and furniture, remain strong. Oriental antiques are generally less susceptible to regional price fluctuations than many other artefacts because of the global nature of the market. A downturn in the US economy, for instance, might have serious repercussions for the folk art market, yet Oriental art would still attract buyers in Europe and Asia.

Robert McPherson

ANCIENT CERAMICS

A large Chinese neolithic pottery vessel, with the shoulders boldly painted in dark red and black with circular reserves and linear bands.

c3000BC *14in (35.5cm) high*

£1,200-1,800 **S&K**

A neolithic two-handled earthenware jar, cold painted with a red ground and black pattern.

c2500BC *3.75in (9.5cm) high*

£200-250 **R&GM**

A rare Chinese neolithic earthenware stem jar, of bombé form, with two loop handles and everted, reticulated foot, brown geometric decoration, Majiayao culture, Gansu province.

c2500BC

£280-320 **S&K**

A Chinese neolithic pottery vessel, painted with swirling spirals, with two loop handles, Majiayao culture.

2500BC *9.75in (25cm) high*

£350-400 **S&K**

A Chinese neolithic pottery vessel, with geometric decoration flanked with two loop handles, Majiayao culture.

c2250BC *10in (25.5cm) high*

£1,000-1,500 **S&K**

A Chinese neolithic pottery bottle, of ovoid form, with a waisted neck, painted with geometric motifs, flanked by two loop form handles, Majiayao culture, Gansu province.

2250BC *10in (25.5cm) high*

£350-400 **S&K**

A rare Chinese neolithic pottery jar, of ovoid form with a garlic neck, loop handle, painted to depict scrolling and dot motif, Majiayao culture, Gansu province.

c2400BC *7in (10cm) high*

£800-1,200 **S&K**

A rare Chinese pottery vessel, the neck with four loop handles, Qijia culture, Qinghai province.

c2000BC *6.75in (17cm) high*

£120-180 **S&K**

A large Chinese neolithic pottery vessel, Qijia culture.

c3000BC *18.5in (47cm) high*

£500-700 **S&K**

A Chinese neolithic pottery vessel painted black with swirling spirals and linear bands.

c3000BC *11in (28cm) high*

£1,800-2,200 **S&K**

A Chinese neolithic pottery bowl, Majiayao culture, of ovoid form, the interior with three faces and scroll motifs.

c2500BC *9.5in (24cm) diam*

£350-450 **S&K**

A Chinese neolithic earthenware bowl, of bombé form, with brown geometric decoration, Majiayao culture, Gansu-Qinghai province.

c2500BC

£350-400 **S&K**

A large Chinese neolithic pottery bowl, of circular form, with geometric decoration, Majiayao culture.

The dating of this bowl is consistent with the result of a thermo-luminescence test, Oxford, number C102J24.

c2250BC *11.5in (29cm) diam*

£3,500-4,500 **S&K**

A Chinese neolithic pottery vessel, the shoulders boldly painted in dark brown and cream with circular reserves and linear bands, Majiayao culture, Gansu-Qinghai province.

c2200 BC *11.25in (28cm) high*

£1,200-1,800 **S&K**

A Neolithic pottery bird-form vessel, Qijia culture, standing on three feet, the wings and tail painted in brown with a net pattern.

c2000BC *9.5in (24cm) long*

£500-700 **S&K**

A rare Chinese neolithic pottery figural ewer, Qijia culture, of globular outline with a cock's-head handle and cylindrical spout.

c2000BC *7in (18cm) high*

£1,800-2,200 **S&K**

A Chinese neolithic pottery bowl, of ovoid form, the interior painted with a band depicting three reserves with five figures of dancers.

c2500BC

£450-500 **S&K**

A pair of Chinese green glazed pottery figural candle holders, Han dynasty, each moulded to depict seated figures.

cAD100 *7.5in (19cm) high*

£400-600 **S&K**

A pair of Chinese grey pottery figures of men, Han dynasty, standing with a static pose.

The arms for these figures, which were probably wooden, have disappeared, as have the clothes they would originally have been wearing.

c50BC *24.25in (61.5cm) high*

£1,800-2,200 **S&K**

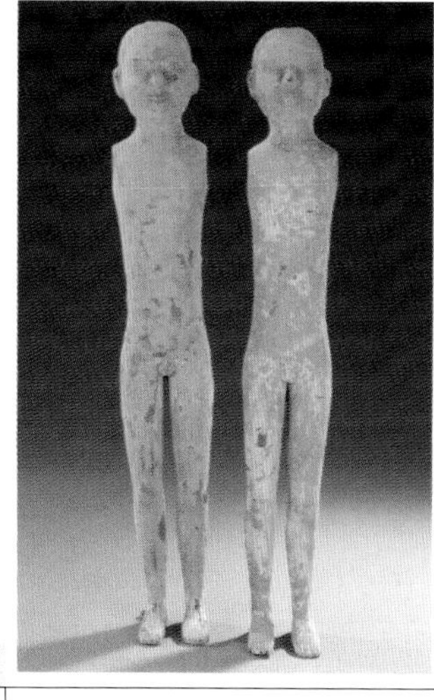

A large and fine grey pottery figure of a man with a drum, Eastern Han dynasty.

c50BC *20.25in (54cm) high*

£700-1,000 **S&K**

A Chinese Han figure.

c200BC *6.25in (16cm) high*

£400-450 **DB**

A large Chinese pottery figure of a dog, Eastern Han dynasty.

c50BC *17in (43cm) high*

£800-1,200 **S&K**

A Chinese Han dynasty ox.

c50BC *10in (25cm) long*

£320-380 **DB**

A large Chinese pottery figure of a dog, Eastern Han dynasty.

c50BC *17in (43cm) high*

£800-1,200 **S&K**

A Chinese red pottery head of a horse, Western Han dynasty.

c100BC *7.5in (19cm) high*

£180-220 **S&K**

A Chinese iridescent green glazed pottery ram pen, Han dynasty, of rectangular form with six moulded rams.

c50BC *8in (20cm) high*

£1,200-1,800 **S&K**

A Chinese green pottery lian, Han dynasty, of circular form with a band of moulded animals, hill shaped cover representing the isles of the Taoist Immortals, the base is supported by three crouching bears.

These lian were used as boxes for cosmetics. A similar piece is at the Victoria and Albert Museum in London.

c50BC *12in (30.5cm) high*

£2,500-3,000 **S&K**

A Chinese green glazed red pottery granary, Han dynasty, of cylindrical form, raised on three feet with a conical open cover.

AD100 *10in (25.5cm) high*

£400-600 **S&K**

A Chinese green glazed pottery censer, Han dynasty, of circular form with a domed cover moulded in low relief with animals, raised on bear-form feet.

cAD100 *7in (18cm) high*

£1,200-1,800 **S&K**

A Chinese iridescent green glazed pottery hu, of globular form standing on sprayed foot, the body encircled by two intervals of concentric ribs, the sloping shoulder set with moulded taotie mask and ring handles beneath the tall neck and flared mouth, covered with a silver iridescent and green glaze, Han dynasty.

c50BC *13.5in (34cm) high*

£320-380 **S&K**

A Chinese ash glazed stoneware vase, Hu dynasty, of ovoid form, the neck incised with two bands of wavy designs, the shoulders with two bands flanked by two taotie masks and ring handles.

cAD100 *16.75in (42.5cm) high*

£2,500-3,000 **S&K**

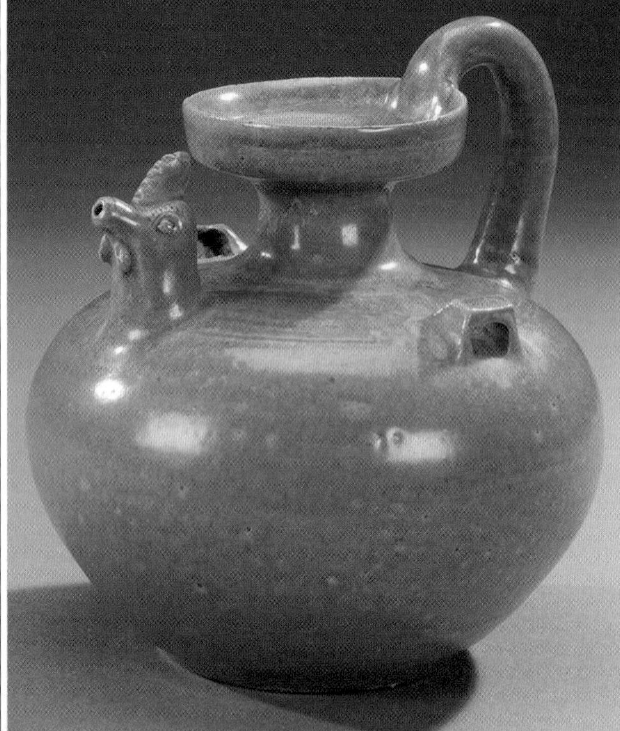

A Chinese celadon yue stoneware ewer, of ovoid form, with a cock's-head spout and 'C'-form handle, Six Dynasties period.

cAD400 *6.5in (16.5cm) high*

£1,200-1,800 **S&K**

A Chinese grey pottery vessel, of ovoid form, the sides impressed with a pattern of squares, short neck flanked by loop handles, Warring States period.

c350BC *6.25in (16cm) high*

£400-600 **S&K**

A Chinese green glazed pottery water well, Han dynasty.

c50BC *11.5in (29.2cm) high*

£200-350 **S&K**

A Chinese painted grey pottery box and cover, Han dynasty.

7in (18cm) diam

£80-120 **S&K**

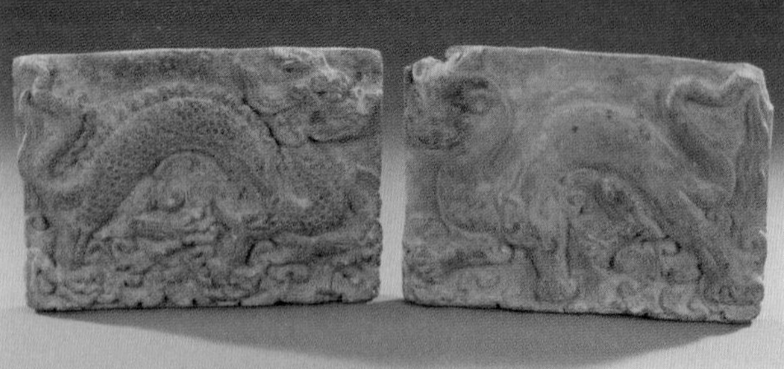

A rare pair of Chinese pottery tiles, with dragon and tiger decoration, Warring States period.

c350BC *10in (25.5cm) long*

£1,000-1,500 **S&K**

A Chinese Sancai pottery brush washer, Tang dynasty, of bombé form, the shoulders with yellow, green and ochre enamel.

cAD750 4in (10cm) d.

£80-120 **S&K**

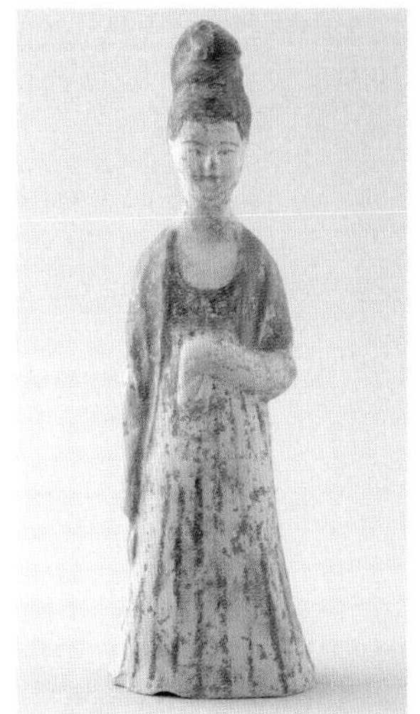

A Chinese Tang dynasty figure of a lady.

cAD750 *10in (25.5cm) high*

£500-700 **DB**

A Chinese Tang dynasty figure, with green glaze.

cAD750 *8in (20.5cm) high*

£120-180 **DB**

A Chinese Tang dynasty green-glazed figure, with red hat.

cAD750 *8.25in (21cm) high*

£120-180 **DB**

A Chinese Tang dynasty figure of a dwarf.

cAD750 *4.75in (12cm) high*

£300-400 **DB**

A fine Chinese pottery figure of a guardian (Lokapala), standing atop a demon wearing an elaborate phoenix-form head-dress with traces of polychrome pigment, Tang dynasty.

cAD750 *20in (50cm) high*

£2,200-2,800 **S&K**

Two Chinese sancai Tang dynasty-style figures of court ladies, each wearing a yellow and green robe, their hands clasped at the chest.

8in (20cm) high

£200-300 **S&K**

A Chinese Tang dynasty ceramic camel.

cAD750 *6in (15cm) high*

£200-250 **DB**

A Chinese straw glazed pottery figure of a camel, standing on a rectangular plinth, Tang dynasty.

cAD750 *13in (33cm) high*

£500-800 **S&K**

A Chinese Tang dynasty ceramic horse.

cAD750 *4.75in (12cm) high*

£200-250 **DB**

A Chinese pottery figure of a horse, well moulded and standing four-square with head slightly turned to the left, open mouth, pointed ears, the saddle with gathered cloth over a blanket, Tang dynasty.

cAD750 *20in (51cm) high*

£1,000-1,500 **S&K**

A Chinese Tang dynasty glazed pig.

cAD750 *4.25in (11cm) high*

£200-300 **DB**

A Chinese stoneware amphora, the well potted body with a pair of double-strap handles applied on the shoulders, rising to the dragon-head terminals, biting the rim of the cup-shaped mouth, Tang dynasty.

cAD750 *10.5in (27cm) high*

£300-400 **S&K**

A Chinese stoneware ewer, of ribbed ovoid form with cylindrical neck and everted mouth, ribbed handle and short spout, painted in green enamel with a bird on a flowering branch against an ochre ground, late Tang dynasty.

cAD900 *7in (18cm) high*

£300-400 **S&K**

A Chinese straw glazed pottery jar, of ovoid form, with short waisted neck and everted lip, covered with a straw glaze over white lip, buff pottery revealed at the foot, Tang dynasty.

cAD750 *12.25in (31cm) high*

£150-200 **S&K**

A large and fine Chinese amber glazed pottery jar, of ovoid form, flat base, short neck with rounded lip, Tang dynasty.

cAD750 *12in (30.5cm) high*

£800-1,200 **S&K**

A rare Chinese Changsha stoneware bowl, the interior with a painted floral design in green and brown phosphatic glaze, Tang dynasty.

cAD750 *6in (15cm) diam*

£550-650 **S&K**

A rare Chinese Changsha iron red and celadon barbed stoneware bowl, of lotus form, the cavetto with lotus petal form reserves, the centre with four lotus flowerheads, Tang dynasty.

The lotus flower is a Buddhist symbol of purity.

cAD750 *5.5in (14cm) diam*

£350-400 **S&K**

An 11thC Northern Song ding or ding-type ware.

6.75in (17cm) diam

£1,200-1,800 **R&GM**

An 11thC Song Qingbai dish, with carved decoration.

6in (15cm) diam

£550-650 **R&GM**

A 12thC Song Qingbai bowl with combed and carved peony, small crack.

6.5in (16.5cm) diam

£300-350 **R&GM**

A Chinese Qingbai porcelain bowl, with carved cloud decoration, Song dynasty.

c1200 *7in (18cm) diam*

£220-280 **S&K**

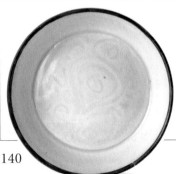

A 12thC Song Qingbai dish, with carved decoration and a later copper rim.

5.25in (3.5cm) diam

£320-380 **R&GM**

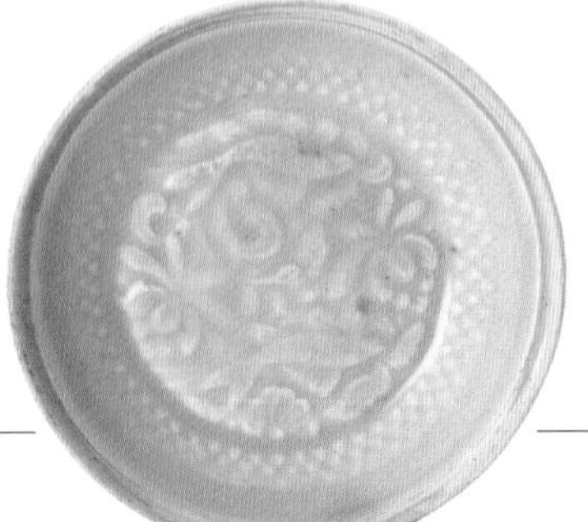

A 13thC Southern Song twin fish Qingbai dish, tiny rim crack.

4.25in (11cm) diam

£200-300 **R&GM**

A Longquan celadon charger, of fluted dish form, Song dynasty.

c1250 *15in (37.5cm) diam*

£800-1,200 **FRE**

A 13thC Song or Jin dynasty Henan type tea bowl.

4.5in (11cm) diam

£150-200 **R&GM**

A Chinese Henan glazed bowl, the shallow conical sides becoming cylindrical at the rim, the treacle black glaze stopping short of the oatmeal foot, possibly Song dynasty.

6.75in (17cm) diam

£100-150 **CHEF**

A Chinese celadon bowl, the exterior moulded with lotus motif, Song dynasty.

cAD450 *6in (15cm) diam*

£200-250 **S&K**

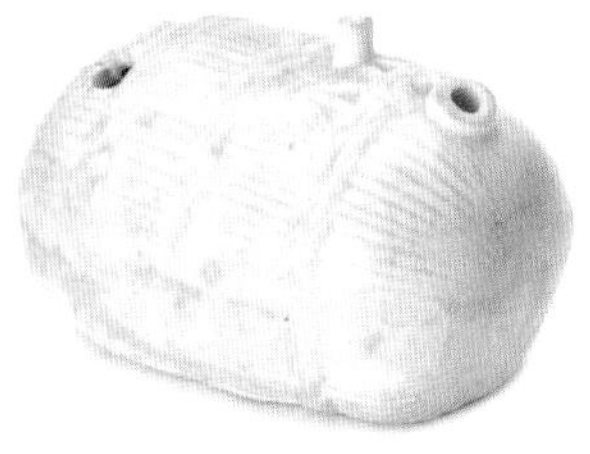

A Song water dropper in the form of a barrel, part missing.

c1250 *2in (5cm) wide*

£220-280 **R&GM**

A CLOSER LOOK AT A JUN WARE BOWL

Many of these Jun pieces with purple splashes were thrown away after they were made, as the purple colour often misfired

If this item did not have a purple splash and it was in this condition it would only be worth about £300.

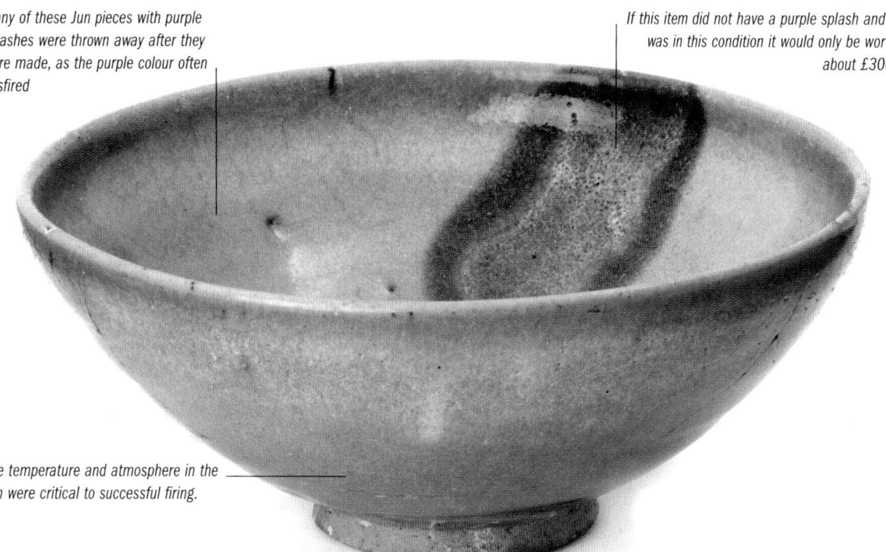

The temperature and atmosphere in the kiln were critical to successful firing.

A Yaun Jun ware bowl with purple splash, two large sections of the side restuck.

Jun ware with purple splashed decoration was an invention of the Northern Song period (in use from the 11thC), the purple was a difficult colour to control in the kiln and is not common.

c1300 *7.25in (18.5cm) diam*

£1,000-1,500 **R&GM**

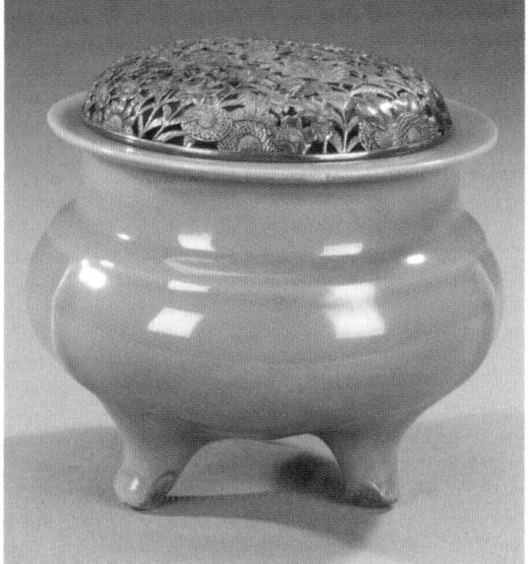

A Chinese Longquan celadon porcelain tripod censer with pierced silver cover, the cover Meiji period, potted in the form of an archaic bronze li vessel, applied overall with an even green glaze, the cover pierced with floral sprays, Southern Song dynasty.

5.25in (13cm) high

£3,000-4,000 **S&K**

A Chinese Qingbai glaze ewer, of lobed ovoid form with a curving spout, double strap handle and cylindrical neck, Song dynasty.

c1100 *6.25in (16cm) high*

£500-800 **S&K**

A 13thC Song Dynasty vase.

9in (23cm) high

£60-90 **R&GM**

A Chinese Song dynasty Yingqing water dropper.

cAD1200 *2in (5cm) high*

£120-180 **DB**

A Sin or Jin miniature Cizhou monkey.

cAD400 *2in (5cm) high*

£120-180 **R&GM**

A Southern Song or Yuan unglazed tortoise, with coiled snake on his back.

Many legends are associated with the tortoise, which was thought to be immortal. It was believed that there were no male tortoises and that the females mated with snakes. Combined with a snake, the tortoise represents the North in Chinese cosmology. Similar snake and tortoise groups can be seen in Blanc De Chine figures of the 17thC and 18thC, at the foot of the God of the North.

cAD450 *4.5in (11.5cm) wide*

£120-180 **R&GM**

A 10thC/11thC box and cover, possibly Liao.

3.75in (9.5cm) diam

£500-800 **R&GM**

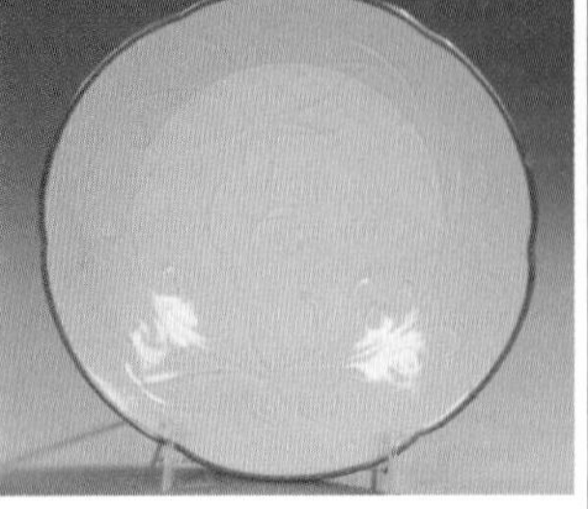

A late 11thC/early 12thC fine Chinese dingyao dish, with incised floral and scrolling foliate decoration, scalloped rim with a copper ring.

7in (17.5cm) diam

£2,500-3,000 **S&K**

A Chinese crackled glaze stoneware vase, of conical form with flat shoulders and folded mouth, Yuan-Ming dynasty.

c1370 *6.25in (16cm) high*

£200-300 **S&K**

A Chinese Ming dynasty stem cup.

c1550 *3.5in (9cm) high*

£800-1,200 **DB**

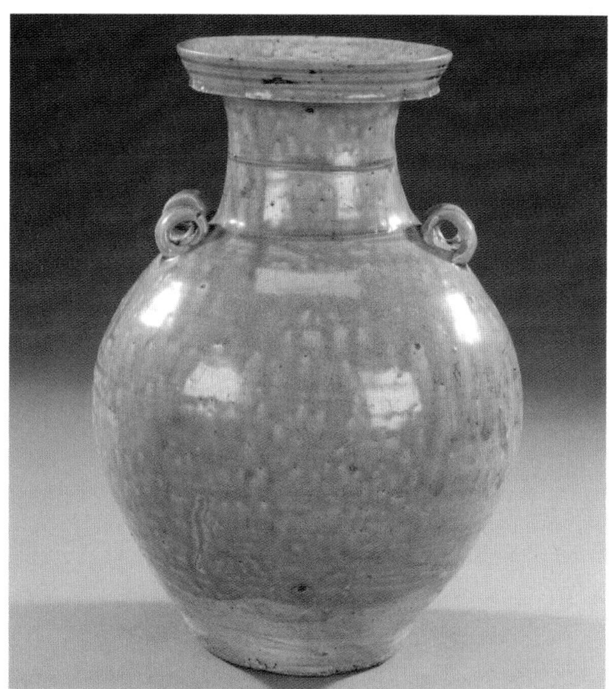

A rare Chinese celadon stoneware vase, Jin dynasty, of ovoid form, with dish shaped mouth and four loop handles on the shoulder.

cAD350 *10in (25.5cm) high*

£2,000-3,000 **S&K**

A Yuan Qingbai ewer.

c1250 *4.25in (11cm) high*

£280-320 **R&GM**

A Chinese green glazed stoneware cockscomb vase, Liao dynasty, of ovoid form with a straight neck and handle, light green crackled glaze.

c1000 *10in (25.5cm) high*

£650-750 **S&K**

A Chinese pottery model of a horse, standing on a rectangular base, the saddle and trappings glazed, Ming dynasty, old wear and repairs.

12.25in (31cm) high

£400-450 **WW**

BLUE & WHITE PORCELAIN

Underglaze blue decoration was first used in China in the mid-14thC. The method of painting cobalt oxide onto white porcelain before the final firing is still used today. By the Ming dynasty (1368-1644), Chinese potters had developed a very fine painting style. The cobalt blue did still tend to filter through the glaze at times, causing a pooled effect known as 'heaped and piled'. This was imitated in the Qing period (1644-1911) as a sign of high quality, and is collectable today.

Unmarked pieces can be dated by their style, date and colour, as well as the nature of the porcelain and its potting. For example, while Ming pieces often have a blue tinge to the white body, later Qing porcelain tends to be a pearly white colour. Dated pieces with a genuine date mark can be worth ten times as much as unmarked pieces of the same age, quality and condition. Conversely, Chinese copies of Ming pieces made in the 18thC are now becoming more collectable.

By the end of the Ming dynasty large quantities of blue and white wares were being shipped to Europe. These pieces are known as kraak porcelain after the Portuguese carrack ships that carried the cargoes west. Transitional ware, dating from the end of the Ming dynasty, is heavier, better potted and more refined than much kraak porcelain.

At the end of the 17thC, Chinese potters were making mainly blue and white garnitures and dinner and tea services for export to Europe. Some polychrome pieces were made but these were more expensive. Chinese porcelain from this period can be distinguished by the orange tint to the body, visible where the glaze has been removed on feet and teapot rims, for example. This has never been seen in European porcelain of any date.

A Chinese blue and white Swatow porcelain bowl, Ming dynasty, floral decoration.

12in (30.5cm) diam

£150-200 **S&K**

A Chinese blue and white porcelain box and cover, of octagonal form painted with a rabbit, precious objects, flowers and birds, Ming dynasty.

3.75in (9cm) diam

£180-220 **S&K**

A Chinese blue and white porcelain tripod censer, painted to depict immortals, Ming dynasty, Wanli period.

c1600 *5in (12.5cm) high*

£400-600 **S&K**

A CLOSER LOOK AT A JIAJING BOWL

Ming bowls can range in price from £80 to well over £1,000,000.

Bowls like this would have been prestigious vessels, probably used for food.

This large bowl with its dramatic dragons, is the sort of object that was made for the Middle and Near Eastern markets.

Many of these large bowls were damaged when they were used, making it unusual to find one in such good condition.

Similar examples can be seen in the Topkapi Saray museum in Istanbul.

The seal type mark to the base, in common with many marks on Chinese porcelain, does not indicate a specific date.

A large Jiajing bowl with dragon design, small chip, rim fritting.

c1550

£4,200-4,800 **R&GM**

A late Ming kraak porcelain crow cup.

c1620 *5in (12.5cm) diam*

£650-750 **R&GM**

A Chinese blue and white porcelain dragon bowl, Yongzheng mark and period, painted to depict a dragon chasing the flaming pearl of wisdom.

c1730 *7in (18cm) diam*

£800-1,200 **S&K**

A Late Ming dish for Japanese market, rim frits, grit from kiln, imprinted mark.

c1630 *8.5in (21.5cm) diam*

£420-480 **R&GM**

A rare Late Ming miniature kendi of slender form.

c1625 *5.25in (13.5cm) high*

£1,200-1,800 **R&GM**

A Wanli period kraak porcelain plate.

c1600 *8.75in (22cm) diam*

£400-500 **R&GM**

A Wanli period blue and white jar, chip to burst bubble, filled.

c1600 *7in (18cm) high*

£700-800 **R&GM**

A Transitional or late Ming Kraak dish, kiln grit on base.

c1640 *14.25in (36cm) diam*

£2,200-2,800 **R&GM**

A Chinese kraak porcelain dish, decorated in underglaze blue with birds and rockwork within radiating panels of flowers and antiques, Wanli period, cracked.

c1600 *14.25in (36cm) diam*

£400-500 **DN**

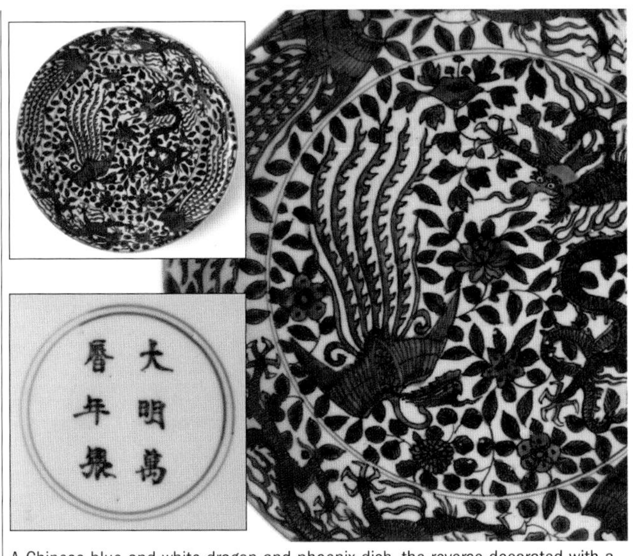

A Chinese blue and white dragon and phoenix dish, the reverse decorated with a continuous lotus scroll, Wanli, six character mark.

11.25in (28.5cm) diam

£3,000-4,000 **WW**

A wine ewer, decorated with two panels, one with birds in a watery landscape with lotus plants flowering among reeds and a scholar rock, reverse with a bird on a rock among flowering plants, chipped.

Scholar rocks were resonant stones used to focus the contemplative energies.

c1645 *10in (25.5cm) high*

£700-800 **R&GM**

A Transitional blue and white gourd-shaped ewer, sealed crack to bracket.

c1640 *8in (20.5cm) high*

£1,200-1,800 **R&GM**

A Transitional blue and white ewer, small chip to rim.

c1645 *7.25in (18.25cm) high*

£1,200-1,800 **R&GM**

A CLOSER LOOK AT A BLUE & WHITE BRUSH POT

The well-executed painting on this pot remains bright and clearly defined. The subject depicted provides a fascinating insight into life in the Kangxi period.

This brush pot is virtually in mint condition and has no faults - this sort of preservation is most unusual with ceramics.

If this pot had a good Kangxi mark, its value might be double.

Prices for Chinese ceramics have risen dramatically in the last two years, due in no small part to the economic boom in mainland China.

This pot was owned by Lord Kitchener, an important collector of Oriental art. Such a strong provenance can only increase the value of an object like this, and also provides crossover appeal to historians and military enthusiasts.

A good Chinese blue and white cylindrical brush pot, well painted with a dignitary and nine further figures on a veranda, no mark, Kangxi period.

c1680 *6.75in (17cm) wide*

£17,000-20,000 **WW**

A Transitional brush pot with flowers and calligraphy.

c1655 *5.75in (14.5cm) high*

£1,500-2,000 **R&GM**

A Chinese blue and white jar, Kangxi period, painted with three quatrefoil reserves of Buddhist objects on a prunus and cracked ice ground.

7.75in (20cm) high

£150-200 **CHEF**

A Chinese blue and white porcelain bowl, the interior painted to depict a flower-filled basket, the exterior with lotus-form reserves enclosing flowering branches, Kangxi period.

c1710 *9in (23cm) diam*

£300-400 **S&K**

A Chinese blue and white porcelain bowl, painted to depict court scenes, Kangxi mark.

8in (20.5cm) diam

£600-900 **S&K**

A Chinese spice dish, of deeply waisted form with a deep central depression on top, the sides decorated with flowers and scrolls.

The recess would probably have contained expensive spices such as nutmeg or pepper, the flared plain border would have prevented spillage.

c1700

£120-180 R&GM

A deep Kangxi blue and white bowl.

c1700 *5.5in (14cm) diam*

£400-450 R&GM

A Kangxi bowl, of klapmuts form, Chenghua mark.

c1700 *8in (20.5cm) diam*

£1,500-2,000 R&GM

A Chinese Kangxi period bowl.

c1600 *10.5in (27cm) diam*

£800-1,200 DB

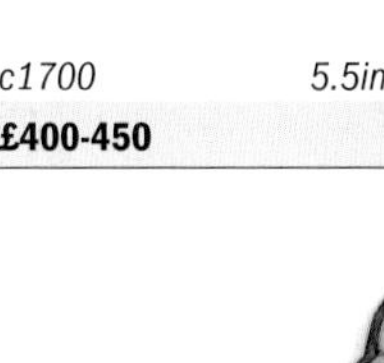

One of a pair of rare lotus form wine cups and leaf shape saucers, Kangxi.

Dealers have not been able to find any reference to these extraordinary rare cups and saucers. It is likely that this shape would have been used for wine in China, however the style of decoration is more in keeping with export ware, so they may have been novelty tea bowls and saucers made for the European Market.

c1700 *saucer 5.25in (13.5cm) wide*

£2,800-3,200 pair R&GM

A Chinese blue and white porcelain jar, floral decoration, Kangxi period.

c1700 *6in (15cm) high*

£200-300 S&K

A Kangxi pot and cover, with 19thC mounts.

c1700 *6.75in (17cm) high*

£500-800 R&GM

A Kangxi blue and white water sprinkler, small chips.

c1710 *8in (20.5cm) high*

£500-800 R&GM

A late Kangxi or Yongzheng blue and white bottle vase, with extensive watery landscape.

c1720 *8in (20.5cm) high*

£1,500-2,000 R&GM

A pair of 19thC Chinese underglaze blue and red Meiping vases, decorated with writhing dragons amidst cloud scrolls, six character Kangxi marks.

14in (35.5cm) high

£1,000-1,500 WW

One of pair of blue and white Yongzheng dishes, three small chips to one dish.

c1730 *13.75in (35cm) diam*

£2,200-2,800 pair R&GM

One of a pair of Yongzheng blue and white ewers and covers.

c1730 *4.75in (12cm) high*

£1,200-1,800 pair R&GM

A Qianlong miniature basket.

c1745 *3in (7.5cm) high*

£620-680 R&GM

A Chinese blue and white porcelain hot water dish, with urn decoration, made for the American market, Qianlong.

c1790 *9.5in (24.1cm) diam*

£100-150 S&K

A pair of early 18thC Chinese blue and white shell dishes, the pecten shapes painted centrally with radiating plants within a lotus vine rim band and café au lait lined rims.

7.75in (19.5cm) wide

£1,000-1,500 **CHEF**

One of a set of four late 18thC Nanking blue and white plates, each painted with a crane flying over a pavilion on an island, and a boat approaching from another island with a distant pagoda.

8.75in (22.5cm) diam

£220-280 set **CHEF**

A Chinese blue and white porcelain vase, from the Fang Hu area, Qianlong seal mark.

c1900 *12.5in (32cm) high*

£450-550 **S&K**

A Chinese blue and white porcelain covered vase, of baluster form painted to depict prunus flowering branches on crackle ice ground, Qing dynasty.

c1850 *15.25in (38.5cm) high*

£200-300 **S&K**

A 19thC Chinese blue and white porcelain vase, of baluster form, painted to depict two dragons facing the flaming pearl of wisdom, four fu dog-form loop handles moulded in high relief, Qing dynasty.

14.25in (36cm) high

£200-300 **S&K**

A 19thC Chinese underglaze blue and red vase, the Meiping shape painted with five clawed dragons chasing flaming pearls through clouds above waves, six character mark of the Kangxi period.

5.75in (14.5cm) high

£60-90 **CHEF**

A large 19thC Chinese blue painted vase and cover, with four geometric motifs painted on a leafy scroll ground.

17.25in (43cm) high

£550-650 **L&T**

A large 19thC Chinese blue painted globular vase and cover, with dog of fu finial over domed lid, the neck with four applied dog of fu masks.

26in (65cm) high

£1,000-1,500 **L&T**

A Chinese blue and white porcelain covered vase, of baluster form with floral and calligraphy decoration.

17in (42.5cm) high

£100-150 **S&K**

A pair of late 19thC Chinese blue painted vases and covers, with dog of fu finial over domed lid, the shoulder with opposed landscape and blossom panels on a cellular ground, above dense scrolling flowerheads, painted four character mark, damaged.

16.5in (41cm) high

£100-150 **L&T**

A Chinese export Canton tea caddy and cover, rectangular with cut corners and a round lid.

5.25in (13cm) high

£1,200-1,800 **FRE**

A Chinese blue and white porcelain jar and cover, of ovoid form with two quatrefoil reserves enclosing feather-filled jar, scrolls, baskets on a prunus blossom and cracked ice ground, openwork wood cover, Qing dynasty.

8in (20cm) high

£150-200 **S&K**

A Chinese blue and white porcelain jar and cover, of ovoid form with prunus blossoms on cracked ice ground, drilled, late Qing dynasty.

c1900 *9in (22.5cm) high*

£50-70 **S&K**

A Chinese blue and white porcelain covered jar, of ovoid form, painted to depict flowerheads and scrolling foliage, Qing dynasty.

c1870 *10.5in (26.5cm) high*

£220-280 **S&K**

A Chinese blue and white porcelain vase, Qing dynasty.

c1870 *13in (33cm) high*

£280-320 **S&K**

A 19thC Chinese blue painted baluster vase, the deep cylindrical neck with stiff leaf frieze, with serrated leaf and blossom decoration.

19.25in (48cm) high

£180-220 **L&T**

A 20thC large Chinese blue and white porcelain vase, of baluster form with floral decoration.

18in (45cm) high

£250-350 **S&K**

A 20thC Chinese blue and white vase, of ovoid form painted with shaped cartouches enclosing mountainous landscape.

17in (42.5cm) high

£70-100 **S&K**

A Chinese Guangxu vase.

c1890 *14in (36cm) high*

£1,200-1,800 **DB**

A Chinese Canton blue and white porcelain tureen undertray.

c1770 *13in (33cm) long*

£70-100 **S&K**

A 19thC Canton reticulated basket and undertray.

basket 4.5in (11.5cm) high

£500-600 **FRE**

One of a set of sixteen Chinese Canton blue and white porcelain luncheon plates, riverscape decoration, Qing dynasty.

c1880 *9in (23cm) diam*

£180-220 set **S&K**

A 19thC Canton covered tureen, of typical form, rim chip to cover.

9in (23cm) high

£800-1,200 **FRE**

SHIPWRECK CARGOES

A shipwreck olive ceramic dish with incised decoration, Yuan period.

c1320 *10.75in (27.5cm) diam*

£280-320 **R&GM**

A shipwreck ceramic dish with shell encrustation, Yuan period.

c1320 *6.5in (16.5cm) diam*

£50-70 **R&GM**

A shipwreck ceramic vase, Yuan period.

c1320 *4in (10cm) diam*

£30-40 **R&GM**

A shipwreck ceramic dish with shell encrustation, Yuan period.

c1320 *6.75in (17cm) diam*

£50-70 **R&GM**

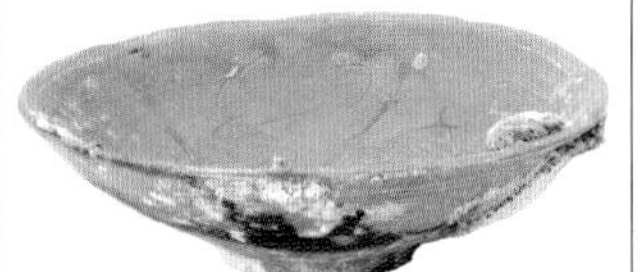

A shipwreck ceramic dish, Yuan period.

c1320 *6.25in (16cm) diam*

£50-70 **R&GM**

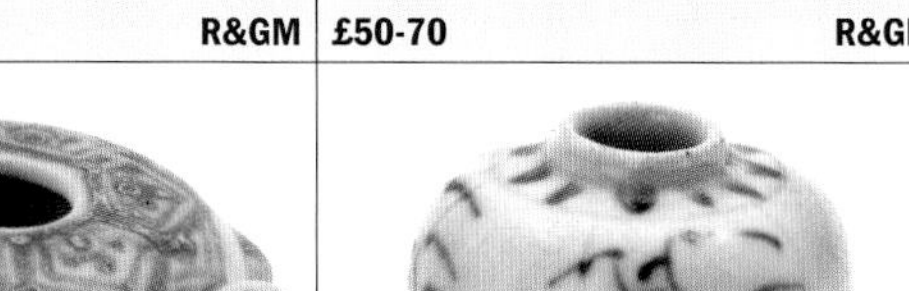

A Hoi An Hoard Vietnamese pot.

c1450-1500 *1.5in (4cm) diam*

£250-300 **R&GM**

A Hoi An Hoard Vietnamese small jar.

c1450-1500 *1.25in (3cm) diam*

£40-60 **R&GM**

A Hoi An Hoard Vietnamese pot.

c1450-1500 *2.5in (6.5cm) wide*

£400-450 **R&GM**

A Hoi An Hoard Vietnamese box, with flower decoration.

c1450-1500 *2.5in (6.5cm) high*

£200-250 **R&GM**

A Hoi An Hoard Vietnamese pot.

c1450-1500 *2.5in (6.5cm) diam*

£400-600 **R&GM**

A Hoi An Hoard Vietnamese shallow bowl, of compressed baluster form, on a wide shallow foot, the sides decorated with petals drawn in simple lines, a border of ruyi or diaper below the unglazed rims.

c1450-1500 *4in (10cm) diam*

£70-90 **R&GM**

A Hoi An Hoard Vietnamese pottery aubergine, hollow, with a hole towards the top, glaze in good condition.

c1450-1500 *3in (7.5cm) high*

£350-450 **R&GM**

A CLOSER LOOK AT A HOI AN HOARD VASE

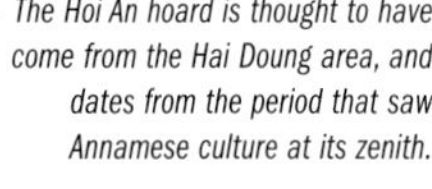

The vessel, carrying around a million ceramic artefacts, was probably bound for Cham Island when it sank off the Hoi An coast in Vietnam.

The Hoi An hoard is thought to have come from the Hai Doung area, and dates from the period that saw Annamese culture at its zenith.

There were many exceptional objects among the more ordinary ones and it is possible to buy a good object from this wreck for under £100.

Although there were over 250,000 pieces recovered from the Hoi An wreck, many were rather ordinary. There were not so many of these large, good quality vases among the cargo.

There were more pieces of Vietnamese ceramics of this period recovered from this one hoard than all the pieces known to exist at the time.

The British Museum in London has several examples from this wreck on display.

A Hoi An Hoard Vietnamese vase, decorated with birds and vegetation.

c1450-1500 *17.5in (44.5cm) high*

£850-950 **R&GM**

A Hoi An Hoard Vietnamese dish, decorated with a fish.

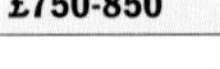

c1450-1500 *9.5in (24cm) diam*

£750-850 **R&GM**

A Hoi An Hoard Vietnamese dish, decorated with a fish and scrolling flowers.

c1450-1500 *9.5in (24cm) diam*

£500-800 **R&GM**

A Hoi An Hoard Vietnamese dish, decorated with a bird.

c1450-1500 *9in (23cm) diam*

£420-480 **R&GM**

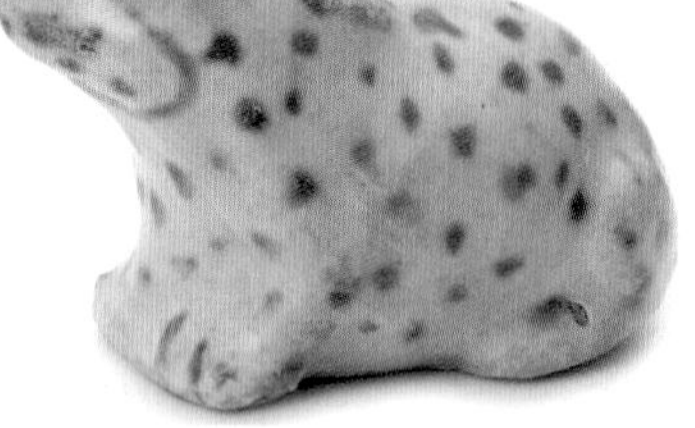

A Hoi An Hoard Vietnamese blue and white toad form water pot, with the blue dots representing the warty marking on their backs, good glaze condition.

A toad of this type was exhibited in the Oriental Ceramics Society Exhibition: 'The World in Blue and White', item 38, p.18. The British Museum, London, also has a toad water pot of this type.

c1450-1500 *2.75in (7cm) wide*

£220-280 **R&GM**

A Hatcher Cargo Chinese wine cup, decorated with a dragon.

c1645 *6in (15cm) diam*

£200-250 **R&GM**

A Hatcher Cargo Chinese 'Red Cliff' bowl, decorated with scenery and calligraphy, chips.

c1645 *6in (15cm) d.*

£200-250 **R&GM**

A Hatcher Cargo Chinese 'Three Friends' cup.

c1645 *2.5in (6.5cm) diam*

£100-150 **R&GM**

A Hatcher Cargo Chinese kraak porcelain dish, cracked, with Christie's lot label.

c1645 *10.75in (27.5cm) diam*

£100-150 **R&GM**

A Hatcher Cargo small Chinese Kraak porcelain kendi, decorated with panels.

c1645 *5.25in (13.5cm) high*

£580-620 **R&GM**

A Hatcher Cargo Chinese large vase and cover, with octagonal neck.

c1645 *14.25in (36cm) high*

£1,800-2,200 **R&GM**

A pair of early 17thC Hatcher Cargo pots with covers.

2.25in (6cm) diam

£700-1,000 **DB**

A large Vung Tau Cargo teabowl, cover and saucer, painted with birds perched on peony sprays and trees.

c1690

£300-500 **RB**

A large Vung Tau Cargo octagonal tea bowl and saucer, painted with panels of flowers.

c1690 *5in (13cm) diam*

£300-500 **RB**

A Vung Tau Cargo tea bowl and saucer, of octagonal form divided into panels containing flowers, the borders of diaper pattern, with flower mark on base.

c1690 *4.5in (11.5cm) diam*

£150-180 **R&GM**

A small Vung Tau Cargo tea bowl and saucer, with floral panels.

c1690 *3.75in (9.5cm) diam*

£320-380 **RB**

A Vung Tau Cargo saucer, cracked.

c1690 *6.25in (11.5cm) diam*

£50-70 **R&GM**

Four Vung Tau Cargo provincial blue and white dishes.

c1690 *4.75in (12cm) diam*

£60-90 each **RB**

A Vung Tau Cargo baluster vase and domed cover, with amusing figures in a rocky landscape, with pines and the sea below.

c1690 *4.5in (11.5cm) high*

£300-500 **RB**

A Vung Tau Cargo blue and white baluster vase and cover, four panels of stylized flowers and foliage.

c1690 *7in (18cm) high*

£550-580 **RB**

A Vung Tau Cargo vase and cover.

c1690 *6.25in (16cm) high*

£320-380 **R&GM**

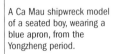

A Ca Mau shipwreck box and cover, from the Yongzheng period.

c1730 *2.75in (7cm) diam*

£50-75 **R&GM**

A Ca Mau shipwreck model of a seated boy, wearing a blue apron, from the Yongzheng period.

c1730 *3in (7cm) high*

£320-280 **R&GM**

A Vung Tau Cargo brown dish, depicting a hare in a landscape.

c1690 *5in (13cm) diam*

£60-80 **RB**

A Ca Mau shipwreck plate, after a design by Frederik van Fryton, from the Yongzheng period.

c1730 *10.75in (4.25in) diam*

£480-520 **R&GM**

A large Nanking Cargo Batavian tea bowl and saucer, with willow and peony.

c1750 *5.5in (14cm) diam*

£350-400 **RB**

A Nanking Cargo Imari 'Pine Tree' tea bowl and saucer.

c1750 *4.5in (11.5cm) diam*

£320-380 **RB**

A Nanking Cargo 'Pagoda Riverscape' pattern tea bowl and saucer.

c1750 *4.75in (12cm) diam*

£220-280 **RB**

A large and rare Nanking Cargo Batavian tea bowl and saucer, with decoration of a pavilion and trees on an island.

c1750 *5.25in (13.5cm) diam*

£350-400 **RB**

A Nanking Cargo Batavian 'Bamboo and Peony' pattern tea bowl and saucer.

c1750 *4.75in (12cm) diam*

£220-280 **RB**

A Nanking Cargo 'Blue Pine Tree' pattern tea bowl and saucer.

c1750 *4in (10cm) diam*

£200-250 **RB**

A Nanking Cargo 'Peony Rock' pattern blue, white and enamel tea bowl and saucer.

c1750 *5.25in (13.5cm) diam*

£200-400 **RB**

A Nanking Cargo 'Daisy Terrace' teacup and saucer painted with daisy and camellia issuing from a terrace.

It is likely that the decoration was copied from drawings sent from Europe.

c1750 *5in (13cm) diam*

£100-150 **RB**

A Nanking Cargo 'Flying Geese' pattern bowl, depicting a flock of geese flying above a pagoda landscape, with trees.

c1750 *4.5in (11.5cm) diam*

£250-300 **RB**

A Nanking Cargo Batavian chrysanthemum pattern bowl.

c1750

£300-400 **RB**

A Nanking Cargo blue and white 'Scholar on the Bridge' pattern bowl, with scholar crossing bridge, pavilion and trees.

c1750 *7.5in (19cm) diam*

£380-420 **RB**

A Nanking Cargo Batavian bowl with landscape decoration.

c1750 *9.75in (25cm) diam*

£280-320 **RB**

A Nanking Cargo Batavian bowl.

c1750 *6.5in (16.5cm) diam*

£180-220 **R&GM**

A large Nanking Cargo bowl.

c1750

7.25in (18.5cm) diam

£200-250 **R&GM**

A Nanking Cargo bowl.

c1750 *4.5in (11.5cm) diam*

£50-70 **R&GM**

A Nanking Cargo blue, white and enamel 'Scholar on the Bridge' bowl, some enamel missing, in places the pattern can only be seen in ghost form.

c1750 *7.25in (18.5cm) diam*

£220-280 **RB**

A Nanking Cargo 'Peony Rock' pattern bowl.

c1750 *6in (15cm) diam*

£200-250 **RB**

A Nanking Cargo bowl, with Christie's lot number sticker.

c1750 *4.5in (11.5cm) diam*

£100-150 **R&GM**

A Nanking Cargo provincial blue and white bowl, freely painted with flowers and other motifs.

c1750 *4in (10cm) diam*

£100-150 **RB**

A Nanking Cargo blue and white carved bowl, incised with stylised chrysanthemums and foliage.

c1750 *6in (15cm) diam*

£150-200 **RB**

A large Nanking Cargo floral bowl, with enamels, virtually all the pattern in ghost form, leaving grey glaze.

c1750 *7.5in (19cm) diam*

£220-280 **RB**

A Nanking Cargo blue, white and enamel beer mug, painted with flowers and trees on a rocky terrace.

c1750 *5.5in (14cm) high*

£500-800 **RB**

A Nanking Cargo blue and white condiment pot with loop handle, the domed cover decorated with pavilions surrounded by a lattice fence and trees, the body with peonies.

c1750 *4.25in (11cm) high*

£2,000-2,500 **RB**

A rare Nanking Cargo Chinese milk pourer.

c1750 *7.25in (18.5cm) diam*

£600-900 **R&GM**

A Nanking Cargo milk pourer.

c1750 *8.25in (21cm) diam*

£500-800 **RB**

A Nanking Cargo 'Three Pavilion' pattern soup dish, in blue and white with enamel.

c1750 *9in (23cm) diam*

£320-380 **RB**

A Nanking Cargo 'Willow Terrace' pattern soup dish painted with willow, peony, bamboo and rockwork on a terrace.

c1750 *9in (23cm) diam*

£350-400 **RB**

A large Nanking Cargo 'Three Pavilions' pattern dish, in blue, white and ghostly enamels, with some gold remaining.

c1750 *14.25in (36cm) diam*

£1,500-2,000 **RB**

A Nanking Cargo 'Boatman' pattern plate, in underglaze blue, with applied coloured enamels.

Shipwreck ceramics with a lot of enamel intact are more valuable than worn pieces.

c1750 *9in (23cm) diam*

£350-450 **RB**

A Nanking Cargo 'Boatman' pattern plate in underglaze blue and white.

c1750 *9in (23cm) diam*

£350-400 **RB**

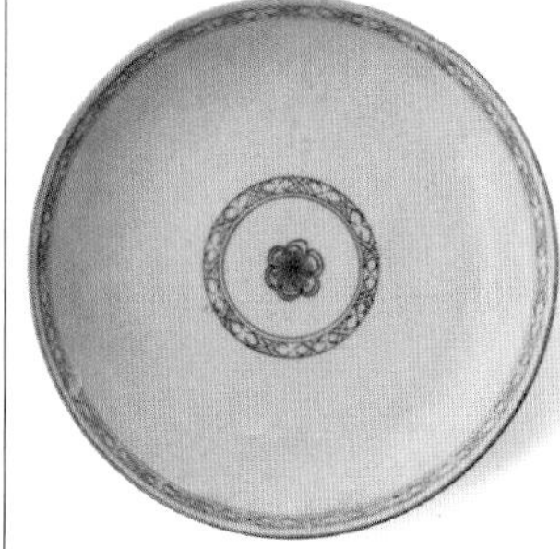

A Nanking Cargo blue and white carved saucer dish, carefully incised with chrysanthemums and foliage.

c1750 *9in (23cm) diam*

£200-250 **RB**

A Nanking Cargo provincial 'Dragon' pattern dish.

c1750 *7.75in (19.5cm) diam*

£125-150 **RB**

A Nanking Cargo blue and white dish.

c1750 *4.5in (11.25in) diam*

£320-380 **R&GM**

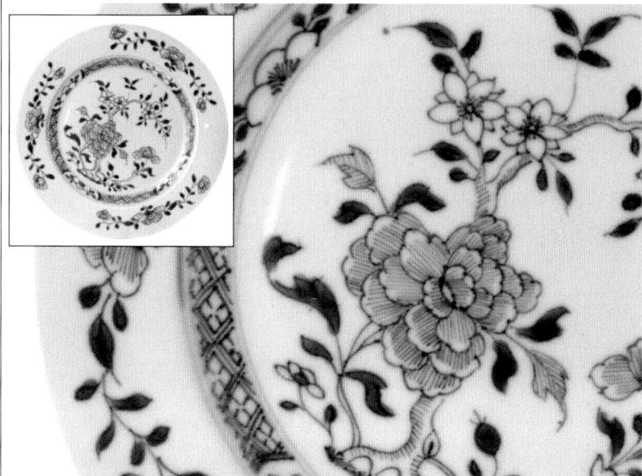

A Nanking Cargo plate, with flower decoration.

c1750 *9.25in (23.5cm) diam*

£150-200 **R&GM**

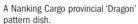

A Nanking Cargo bullet-shaped teapot, decorated with enamels.

c1750 *9in (23cm) wide*

£300-500 **RB**

A Nanking Cargo globular teapot in enamels, with flowers and terrace.

c1750 *8.75in (22cm) wide*

£300-500 **RB**

A Nanking Cargo 'Lattice Fence' pattern plate, with pagoda, willow and pine trees.

c1750 *16.5in (42cm) diam*

£4,000-4,500 **RB**

A Nanking Cargo blue and white 'Trellis' pattern sauceboat of European silver shape, painted with foliage and a fence, decorated with long life symbols.

c1750 8in (20.5cm) d.

£2,000-2,500 **RB**

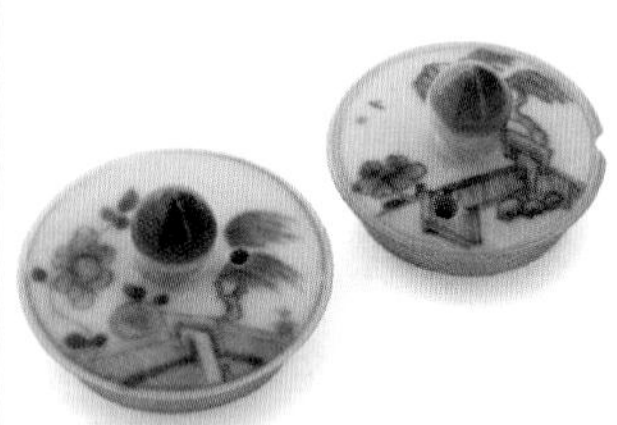

A pair of Nanking Cargo blue, white and enamel teapot lids for a globular teapot.

c1750 2.25in (6cm) diam

£30-40 each **RB**

Five Nanking Cargo floral enamel teapot lids, for a bullet-shaped teapot.

c1750 2.25in (6cm) diam

£20-30 each **RB**

Three Nanking Cargo blue, white and enamel teapot lids, for a globular teapot.

c1750 3.25in (8.5cm) diam

£30-40 each **RB**

A Nanking Cargo Chinese butter tub, of circular form with two raised flanges, with holes, the handle painted blue, made in imitation of wooden milk tubs with loops for carrying, restored.

Approximately 235 round and oval butter tubs were recovered from the sunken Geldermalsen (the Nanking horde) in seven different shapes. These unusual objects were sometimes included in dinner services. Similar examples were made at Delft and at Meissen.

c1752 4.75in (12cm) diam

£600-700 **R&GM**

A Nanking Cargo pair of salt stands, of shallow type, for rock salt.

c1750 3.25in (8cm) wide

£3,500-4,000 **RB**

A CLOSER LOOK AT A NANKING TUREEN

This tureen would have been one of a number placed in the centre of a large dining table. The 'Lattice Fence' pattern was used to decorate magnificent dinner services for over 100 people.

The pomegranate finial is delicate and prone to damage. It is incredible that this one has survived in such good condition. A Nanking piece in this condition is unusual and valuable.

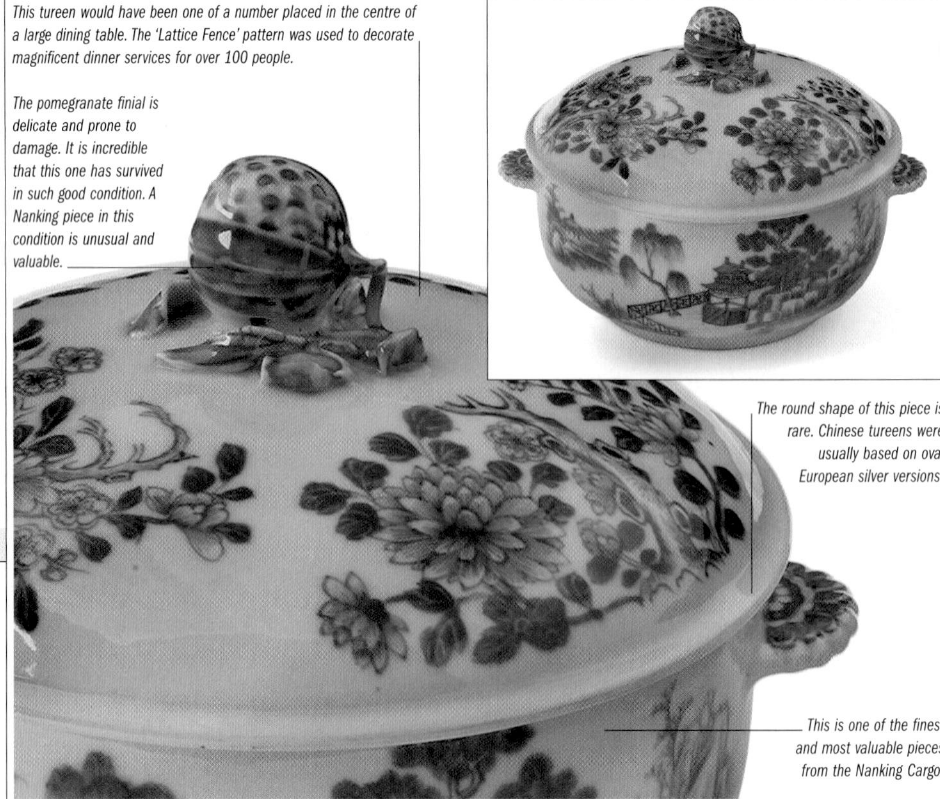

The round shape of this piece is rare. Chinese tureens were usually based on oval European silver versions.

This is one of the finest and most valuable pieces from the Nanking Cargo.

A Nanking Cargo 'Lattice Fence' pattern tureen, with pavilions, trees and flower, finely crafted pomegranate finial.

c1750 9in (23cm) diam

£5,000-7,000 **RB**

A Nanking Cargo collection of five daoist immortals in various poses, one without a head.

c1750

£500-600 **RB**

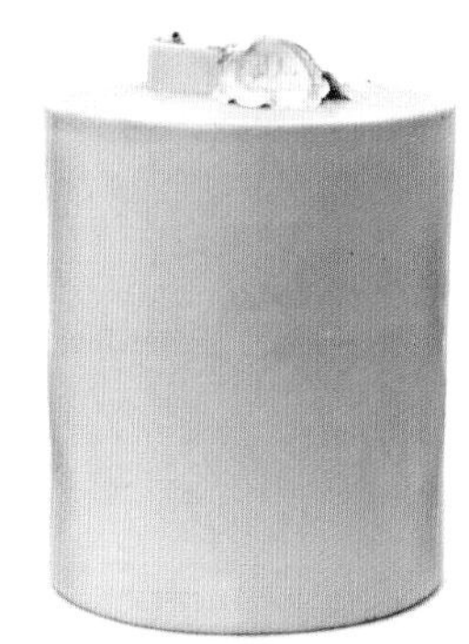

A large Diana Cargo Chinese storage jar, of cylindrical form, lacking cover.

Approximately half of the rim is missing, covered by shell growth.

c1815 *10.75in (27.5cm)high*

£420-480 **R&GM**

A Diana Cargo cover, with fruit knop.

c1815 *3in (7.5cm) diam*

£20-30 **R&GM**

A Diana Cargo dish.

c1815 *11in (28cm) diam*

£70-100 **R&GM**

A Diana Cargo green glass bottle, part of cork inside.

c1815 *11in (28cm) high*

£70-100 **R&GM**

A Tek Sing Cargo orchid leaf dish, with poetic inscription.

c1820 *7.75in (20cm) diam*

£350-400 **RB**

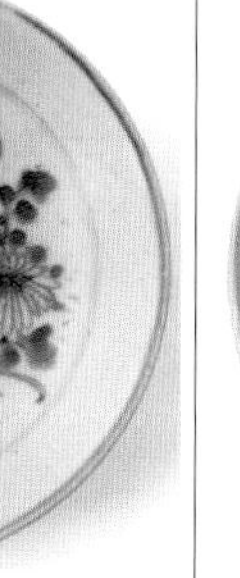

A Tek Sing Cargo dish, with chrysanthemum and rockwork design, with poetic inscription.

c1820 *7.75in (19.5cm) diam*

£300-350 **RB**

A large Tek Sing Cargo dish, decorated with chrysanthemums.

c1820 *6.25in (16cm) diam*

£100-130 **RB**

A large Tek Sing Cargo peony dish, with flower sprays, dots and crosses.

c1820 *8.25in (21cm) diam*

£250-300 **RB**

A Tek Sing Cargo 'Magnolia' pattern dish.

c1820 *7.75in (20cm) diam*

£250-300 **RB**

A Tek Sing Cargo basket of flowers dish.

c1820 *4.25in (10.5cm) diam*

£60-90 **RB**

A large Tek Sing Cargo 'Spiral Lotus' dish, decorated with lingzhi fungus, fruiting peach and flowering lotus spray.

c1820 *7in (18cm) diam*

£180-220 **RB**

A medium-sized Tek Sing Cargo 'Spiral Lotus' dish.

c1820 *6in (15cm) diam*

£100-150 **RB**

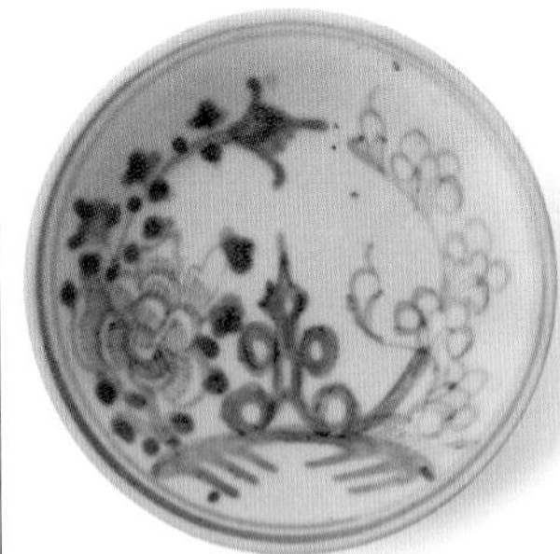

A large Tek Sing Cargo 'Peony and Magnolia' pattern dish.

c1820 *6.35in (16cm) diam*

£100-150 **RB**

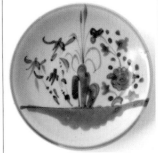

A Tek Sing Cargo dish, painted with reeds, bamboo and flowers.

c1820 *6in (15cm) diam*

£80-120 **RB**

A Tek Sing Cargo small dish, decorated with a basket of chrysanthemums, the underside with three stylized flower sprays.

c1820 *4.25in (11cm) diam*

£50-80 **RB**

A Tek Sing Cargo 'Asta Flower' pattern saucer in blue and white with aster flower spray and dot-dash ring decoration.

c1820 *4.25in (11cm) diam*

£30-50 **RB**

A Tek Sing Cargo ogee-shaped 'Hare' bowl, the interior decorated with band of three panels and a hare in the well, the exterior with stylized characters, chrysanthemums and bamboo leaves.

c1820 *6.75in (17cm) diam*

£180-220 **RB**

A Tek Sing Cargo 'Scholar' bowl, with a figure standing beside a fence, with prunus blossoms.

c1820 *6.75in (17cm) diam*

£200-250 **RB**

A Tek Sing Cargo 'Boy' bowl, with a boy holding a lotus bloom in front of a garden fence, between flowers issuing from rockwork.

c1820 *6.25in (16cm) diam*

£200-250 **RB**

A Tek Sing Cargo bowl, with peony, magnolia and rockwork decoration, with insect on reverse.

7in (17cm) diam

£150-200 **RB**

A Tek Sing Cargo bamboo bowl, with bamboo, peony bunches and rockwork.

c1820 *5in (12.5cm) diam*

£80-120 **RB**

A Tek Sing Cargo bamboo bowl, with bamboo, peony bunches and rockwork.

c1820 *5in (12.5cm) diam*

£80-120 **RB**

A Tek Sing Cargo Chinese cup.

c1820 *3in (7.5cm) diam*

£20-40 **R&GM**

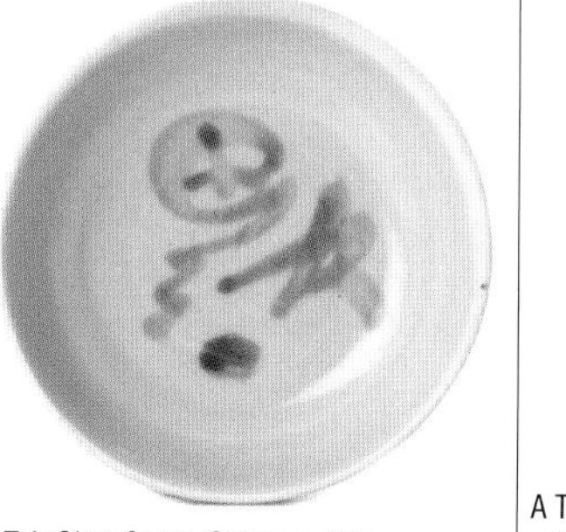

A Tek Sing Cargo Chinese dish.

c1820 *3in (7.5cm) diam*

£50-70 **R&GM**

A Tek Sing Cargo encrusted storage jar, originally in brown pottery.

c1820 *8.25in (21cm) high*

£400-600 **RB**

A Tek Sing Cargo olive glaze bowl of bombé form, the cover with fish knop.

c1820 *5.5in (13.5cm) high*

£400-600 **RB**

A set of three Tek Sing Cargo porcelain spoons, with white and reddish glaze.

c1820 *4.5in (11.5cm) long*

£15-25 each **RB**

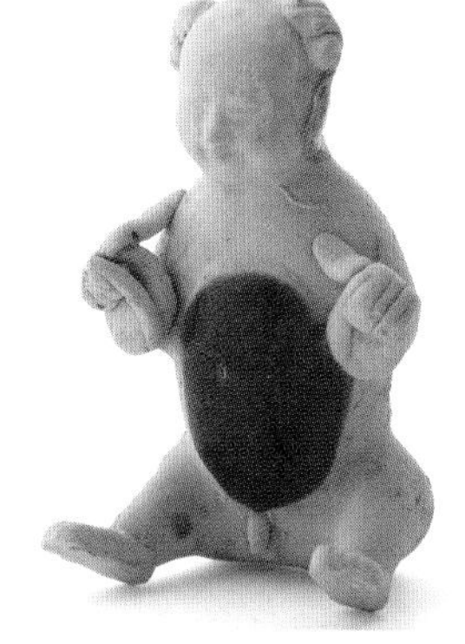

A Tek Sing Cargo unglazed figure of a seated boy with underglaze blue apron.

c1820 *3in (7.5cm) high*

£1,000-1,500 **RB**

A Tek Sing Cargo set of sixteen sake cups.

c1820 *2in (5cm) diam*

£50-80 each **RB**

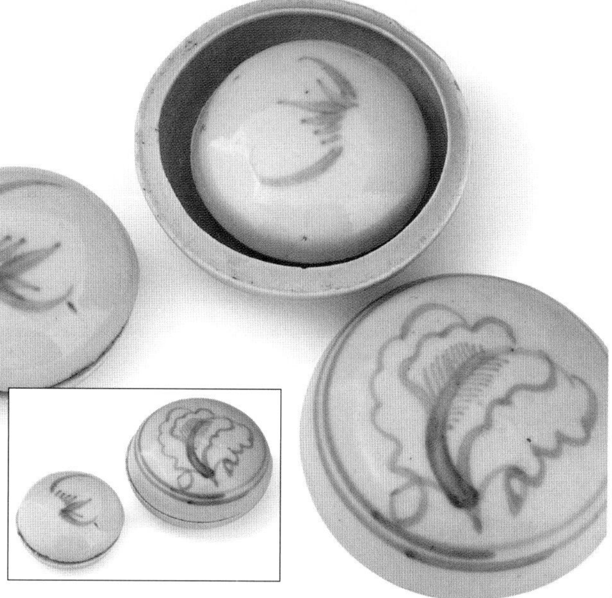

Two Tek Sing Cargo porcelain boxes, with lids.

c1820

£220-280 **RB**

BLANC-DE-CHINE

A Chinese Blanc-de-Chine figure of Guanyin, standing wearing loose robes, a high chignon and beaded necklace, Republic period.

c1930 *14in (35.5cm) high*

£200-300 **S&K**

A Chinese Blanc-de-Chine Guanyin, seated holding a child with a ruji sceptre, wearing a high chignon, loose robes and a beaded necklace.

c1900 *8.5in (21.5cm) high*

£150-200 **S&K**

A 18thC Chinese Blanc-de-Chine porcelain incense holder, moulded to depict a fu lion on an oval plinth.

4.5in (11.5cm) high

£160-200 **S&K**

A Chinese Blanc-de-Chine porcelain vase, pierced floral decoration, late Qing dynasty, early Republic period.

c1910

£100-150 **S&K**

A pair of 18thC Chinese Blanc-de-Chine libation cups.

2in (5.5cm) high

£500-700 **DB**

One of pair of Blanc-de-Chine beakers.

c1700 *2.5in (6.5cm) high*

£800-1,200 pair **R&GM**

EXPORT

The arrival of Jesuit missionaries in the early 17thC opened up the trade route between China and Europe. Silks and spices were the first Chinese exports, exchanged for silver bullion. The mid-17thC saw an explosion in trade, sparked by Europe's new-found passion for tea. Tea chests containing porcelain teapots in amongst the dried leaves began to arrive on European shores, soon followed by tea sets and dinner services. Despite being cheaper than contemporary European earthenware, this Chinese porcelain was of a higher quality.

Chinese ceramics rapidly became fashionable and services were made to order for aristocratic families, with their coat of arms picked out in the famille rose palette. A cheaper alternative was the porcelain decorated in underglaze blue with Chinese landscape and river scenes. Today famille rose pieces tend to be worth three to five times as much as blue and white.

The European market for Chinese porcelain continued into the 18thC, with blue and white tableware making up the bulk of the trade. However, by the end of the century trade was dwindling as tastes changed and competition from industrialized Europe began to bite.

In the 19thC highly decorative Canton porcelain was exported to Europe but quality was slipping. This was later surpassed by blue and white wares in the Kangxi style. Throughout the 20th century, copies of earlier Chinese porcelains have been exported.

A Chinese green porcelain dragon dish, underglaze blue six character mark probably of the period, Chenghua period.

c1480 *8in (20cm) diam*

£450-550 **S&K**

A large Chinese celadon porcelain charger, the cavetto with a ribbed band, Ming dynasty.

c1600 *19.5in (49.5cm) diam*

£1,200-1,800 **S&K**

A pair of Chinese export Imari porcelain plates, floral and brocade decoration, Kangxi period.

c1720 *9in (23cm) diam*

£180-220 **S&K**

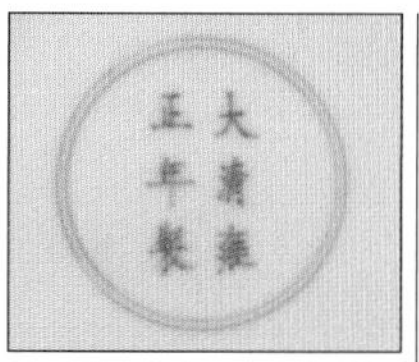

A Chinese iron red and blue porcelain dish, underglaze blue six character mark, the centre with two dragons chasing the flaming pearl of wisdom, the rim with a wave band, Yongzheng period.

8.5in (21cm) diam

£180-220 **S&K**

A Chinese 18thC export armorial part dinner service, each piece painted with motto "PRO.PATRIA" in a gilt banner, above a figure of a warrior holding a sword, with loose peony sprays in blue enamel, the sides with continuous rouge-de-fer barbed frieze, comprising one large deep bowl and one similar smaller, three large platters, four large shallow bowls and four similar smaller, thirteen meat plates, and sixteen soup plates.

£1,500-2,000 set **L&T**

A set of four Chinese 18thC armorial export salts, of canted rectangular trencher form, the central well with motto "PRO.PATRIA" and painted warrior figure wearing wide pantaloons, holding a sword in his right hand and wearing a plumed hat, the sides painted with sprigs of flowers and the spreading plinth with gilt and rouge-de-fer barbed frieze.

3in (7.5cm) wide

£3,000-3,500 set **L&T**

Part of a Chinese 18thC export armorial part dinner service, with central large armorial device, with pink banner enclosing motto "PRO.PATRIA", above a small helmeted warrior brandishing a sword, with rouge-de-fer shield enclosing a banner with armour helmet surmount and shell apron, within gilt swag cartouche and meandering gilt and rouge-de-fer border, the rim with gilt barbed frieze, comprising: one serving plate, 28 meat plates and eight soup plates.

£6,000-9,000 set **L&T**

One of a set of four large circular Chinese 18thC export armorial chargers, with central large armorial device with pink banner enclosing motto "PRO.PATRIA" above a helmeted warrior brandishing a sword, with rouge-de-fer shield enclosing banner, with armour helmet surmount and shell apron within gilt swag cartouche, within meandering gilt and rouge de fer border, the rim with gilt barbed frieze.

£1,200-1,800 set **L&T**

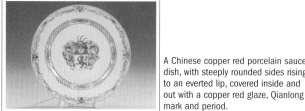

A Chinese export grisaille armorial porcelain plate, Qianlong period.

c1750 *9in (23cm) diam*

£320-380 **S&K**

A Chinese copper red porcelain saucer dish, with steeply rounded sides rising to an everted lip, covered inside and out with a copper red glaze, Qianlong mark and period.

8.5in (21.5cm) diam

£1,000-1,500 **S&K**

A Chinese monochrome blue porcelain charger, incised with a lotus decoration, Qing dynasty.

3.25in (33.5cm) diam

£500-600 **S&K**

A pair of Chinese export armorial bowls, with the arms of Altena accolé with Pierson, the border with a floral garland, Qianlong period.

c1760 *6.25in (16cm) diam*

£500-700 **S&K**

A pair of Chinese puce and gilt porcelain barbed dishes, with puce and purple floral decoration, Qianlong period.

c1760 *9.5in (24cm) diam*

£180-220 **S&K**

Two Chinese export rectangular porcelain dishes, with central gilt "JNS" monogram flanked by ribbon-tied flowering branches held by billing dove, the rims with puce bamboo interlaced with garlands, Qianlong period.

c1775 *11.5in (29cm) wide*

£1,200-1,800 pair **S&K**

A Chinese porcelain lozenge dish, dragon and bat decoration on a dark blue ground, Qing dynasty.

c1780 *10.25in (26cm) long*

£120-180 **S&K**

A Chinese export gilt and blue porcelain plate, made for the Persian market, the centre with calligraphy, foliate border.

c1800 *9.75in (25cm) diam*

£150-200 **S&K**

A set of seven Chinese famille noire porcelain plates, with floral decoration on the black ground, Guangxu iron red six character mark and of the period.

£240-260 set **S&K**

A Chinese iron red and white porcelain charger, painted to depict two dragons chasing the flaming pearl of wisdom, Guangxu mark and period.

3.5in (43cm) diam

£350-450 **S&K**

A late 19thC Chinese export porcelain 'Thousand Butterfly' pattern platter, oval, painted in colours with overlapping butterflies.

16in (40.5cm) long

£320-380 **S&K**

A late 19thC Chinese Canton dish, centrally decorated with figures, within a star-shaped panel, the carved ground decoration with birds and flowers, short rim crack.

13.5in (34.5cm) diam

£100-150 **LFA**

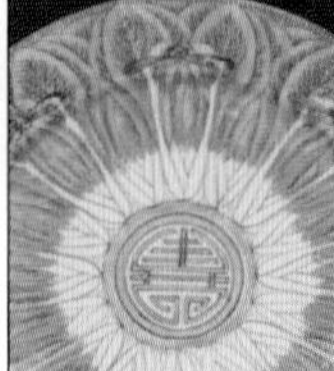

A 20thC Chinese porcelain 'Cabbage Leaf' pattern assembled part dinner service, comprising teapot, sugar and cover, creamer, waste bowl, four teacups, eight saucers, seven dinner plates, one luncheon plate, eight salad plates, two bread and butter plates, stamped "Hong Kong" and "China", together with two similar saucers.

Teapot 9in (23cm) long

£100-150 **S&K**

A 19thC Chinese copper red porcelain water pot, floral decoration, Kangxi mark.

3in (7.5cm) diam

£800-1,200 **S&K**

A Chinese Imari porcelain bowl, floral decoration, Kangxi period.

c1690 7.75in (19.5cm) diam

£150-200 **S&K**

A Chinese armorial chamfered rectangular tureen and cover, decorated in underglaze blue, with famille rose flower sprays and with the arms of Danne, cracks to tureen and damage to the cover handle.

c1755 14.5in (36.5cm) long

£1,500-2,000 **WW**

A CLOSER LOOK AT A CHINESE EXPORT PUNCHBOWL

As hongs became increasingly elaborate and westernised during the 18thC, they began to be depicted on China trade bowls such as this.

These punchbowls were made from about 1764, initially with a view in a single panel, later followed by two panels and from c1780 with a continuous scene.

The shoreline is crowded with Chinese 'chop' boats and many Europeans fill the courtyards in front of the factories, the balconies, the doorways and the windows.

Punch bowls were used to serve alcoholic punch in the 18thC. Punch, a word derived from the Hindi word for five, often contained five ingredients - sugar, water, lime juice, spices, and wine or spirits.

A rare and important Chinese export porcelain punchbowl, with enamelled exterior depicting the hongs at Canton, with western figures and the flags of Denmark, France, Sweden, Britain and Holland, ornate inner borders, the foot is decorated with keyfret and spearhead borders.

In the late 18thC Canton (Guangzhou) was the only port in China at which Western nations were allowed to trade. The 'hongs', or factories, were groups of Chinese-built buildings that included living quarters, storage and offices for the western merchants.

c1780 14.5in (37cm) diam

£30,000-40,000 **NA**

A Chinese flambé porcelain vase, pear-form with elongated neck, chips on foot rim, age crack on the body, Qing dynasty.

c1780 *20.5in (52cm) high*

£300-400 **S&K**

A Chinese tea-dust glazed porcelain double gourd vase.

14.5in (37cm) high

£200-250 **S&K**

A pair of early 19thC Chinese globular vases and covers, the domed lid with cone finial, painted in underglaze blue and turquoise and rouge-de-fer enamels with figures in a landscape, above a continuous frieze of stylized palm trees and various figures, including a boy with a duck in a basket and a lady with a fan, together with carved hardwood stands.

12.5in (31cm) high

£1,500-2,000 **L&T**

Two Chinese green glazed porcelain garden seats, of barrel form, with floral and butterfly decoration, Qing dynasty.

c1900 *16in (40.5cm) high*

£350-450 **S&K**

A pair of Chinese monochrome green porcelain vases, of ovoid form, moulded to depict cartouches enclosing a figure under a tree, flanked by a fu dog head and ring handles, electrified.

9.25in (23.5cm) high

£200-250 **S&K**

A pair of Chinese green-glazed bottle-shaped table lamps, with coiling dragon about the mid-section.

16.5in (42cm) high

£220-280 **S&K**

A Kutani porcelain figural group, depicting an immortal riding a shi shi, Showa period.

8.5in (21cm) high

£180-220 **S&K**

A lead glazed ridge tile depicting General Han Hsin on horseback.

Although the face and outline of this equestrian figure are moulded, there is an exceptional amount of carving and applied decoration. An inscription names the rider as Han Hsin, a famous general from the early part of the Han dynasty. The rest of the inscription relates to the area and maker. The figure also has a two-character inscription on his back.

c1550 *15in (38cm) high*

£2,800-3,200 **R&GM**

A Chinese polychrome pottery figural tile, moulded to depict a warrior on the back of a phoenix.

10.5in (26.5cm) high

£300-400 **S&K**

A large Jiajing figure, hands restored, foot restuck.

c1810 *21.75in (55cm) high*

£2,000-2,500 **R&GM**

A small pair of Chinese biscuit models of parrots, standing on rockwork, Kangxi period.

c1690 *3in (7.5cm) high*

£220-280 **WW**

A pair of 19thC Chinese turquoise glazed models of cockatoos, each perched on a tall tree stump on pierced scrolling ormolu mounts, one re-glued through the base.

17in (43cm) high

£800-1,200 **WW**

A pair of Chinese sancai pottery figures of fu dogs.

9.5in (24cm) high

£250-300 **S&K**

A Chinese 18thC export globular teapot and cover, with rustic gilt-decorated spout and handle, painted in rouge-de-fer with opposed European scenes of lovers in a woodland bower, looked over by a winged putti holding a torch in one hand and a garland in the other.

6in (15cm) high

£1,500-2,000 **L&T**

A Chinese export globular teapot, with flat cover, reeded scroll handle and spout.

c1780 *5.75in (14.5cm) high*

£300-400 **S&K**

An 18thC Chinese Yixing tea pot, moulded in low relief with flowering prunus tree decoration.

4in (10cm) high

£180-220 **S&K**

A CLOSER LOOK AT A FAMILLE VERTE BOWL

This bowl was made in the reign of the Qing dynasty emperor Kangxi (1662-1722). This era saw many developments in Chinese ceramics including the introduction of the famille verte palette, used to decorate this bowl.

This bowl is of a large size and relatively thickly potted. The depiction of figures is common in Kangxi pottery, and this fascinating processional decoration is detailed and lively.

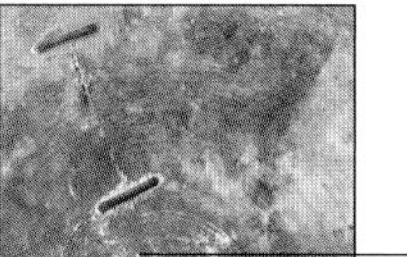

The fact that this bowl has been repaired and not simply thrown away, as other broken everyday porcelain items would have been, suggests that it was important and precious at the time.

For many years rivetting was the only available method of repairing ceramics. Originating in China and widely used in Europe, it required a great deal of skill. Holes were drilled into the pot and a brass or iron rivet cut to size and threaded through to clamp the break.

A large Chinese famille verte bowl, thickly potted, the exterior decorated with three standing figures approaching a sage seated by the waterfront, a procession of banner men in a rocky wooded landscape beyond, the interior with many swimming fish and crustacea amidst water plants on a yellow ground, Kangxi period, cracked in half and rivetted.

c1700 *13in (33.5cm) diam*

£2,500-3,500 **WW**

A Chinese famille verte porcelain bowl, phoenix and floral decoration, Kangxi mark, Guangxu.

10in (25.5cm) diam

£220-280 **S&K**

A large circular Chinese famille verte bowl, with two rows of two concentric rings, painted with central panel of the sorceress Magu fleeing to the mountains after quarrelling with her father, in a chariot pulled by a spotted deer, and attendant, the underside with three rows of Chinese character marks in brown, the one hundred characters of longevity, Ch'eng Hua mark but Kangxi period.

c1690 *16in (40cm) diam*

£15,000-18,000 **L&T**

A large famille verte dish decorated with a dragon, Kangxi, repaired.

c1690

£420-480 **R&GM**

A Yongzheng rouleau vase, painted in famille verte palette, on a coral ground.

c1730 *18in (45.5cm) high*

£6,000-7,000 **R&GM**

A large pair of Chinese baluster vases, each with a tall flared neck over swollen baluster body, painted in bright polychrome enamels with fuchsia and passion flowers issuing leafy tendrils, reserved on an incised jade green ground decorated with meandering scrolls, the neck with applied relief-cast puce, brown, yellow and rouge-de-fer painted dragons, Qianlong period.

22.25in (55.5cm) high

£18,000-22,000 **L&T**

An early 18thC famille verte jar and jadeite mounted wood cover, the rounded sides painted with aubergine and yellow horses flying through green scroll clouds between waves on the shoulders and waves and rocks on the base.

9.25in (23.5cm) high

£800-1,200 **CHEF**

A Chinese famille verte slender bottle vase, decorated with mythological beasts on a ground carved with waves and enamelled with flames, wood stand, six character Kangxi mark but 19thC.

18.5in (47cm) high

£1,500-2,000 **DN**

A 20thC Chinese famille verte porcelain vase, of baluster form, painted to depict a warrior holding a sword perched on rockery.

18in (45.5cm) high

£400-600 **S&K**

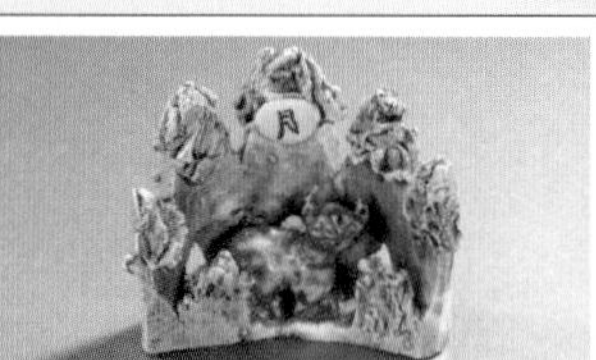

A Chinese famille verte porcelain brush holder, Kangxi period.

c1690 *3in (7.5cm) high*

£300-350 **S&K**

An 18thC Chinese famille verte tea pot and cover.

4.75in (12cm) high

£220-280 **CHEF**

A 19thC Chinese sancai figure of an immortal, seated on rockery wearing a long beard and loose robe.

8.5in (21.5cm) high

£100-150 **S&K**

One of a set of four mid-18thC Chinese famille rose plates, each centrally painted with peonies and cherries flowering on a mound within gilt vine band with four sprays on the rim.

8.75in (22.5cm) diam

£300-400 set **CHEF**

A mid-18thC Chinese famille rose plate, painted with a reclining dignitary being offered sake by a kneeling attendant while another fans the air above.

8.75in (22.5cm) diam

£100-150 **CHEF**

A Chinese famille rose porcelain plate, floral decoration on celadon ground, Qianlong mark and period.

c1765 *8in (20.5cm) diam*

£280-320 **S&K**

A Chinese export plate, centrally decorated in iron red and gilt with a vase, a scroll and flowers, the famille rose border with flowers and lappet heads, Qianlong period.

c1765 *9in (23cm) diam*

£60-90 **LFA**

A Chinese export dinner service, each piece painted in famille rose palette with floral sprays and insects on a white ground, comprising a large platter, a covered soup tureen and stand, two smaller platters, a serving dish, a covered sauce tureen and stand, seven plates and four soup bowls, a soup tureen, a serving dish, three soup bowls and two plates.

c1775 *Platter 17.5in (44.5cm) long*

£2,000-2,500 set **FRE**

A pair of famille rose armorial porcelain plates, with the arms of Thwaite, underglaze blue brocade border, Qianlong.

c1785 *9in (23cm) diam*

£800-1,200 **S&K**

A pair of Chinese famille rose porcelain plates, with the arms of Johnstone impaling Gordon, floral border, Jiaqing.

c1805 *7.5in (19cm) diam*

£600-900 **S&K**

A Chinese rose medallion porcelain charger, painted with alternating reserves enclosing figures and flowers.

c1850 *16in (40.5cm) diam*

£500-700 **S&K**

Two of a set of seven 19thC rose mandarin porcelain plates, together with ten rose medallion plates.

9.5in (24cm) diam

£480-520 set **S&K**

One of a pair of 19thC Chinese famille rose porcelain dishes, each painted to depict a warrior on horseback and calligraphy, Yongzheng mark.

5.5in (14cm) diam

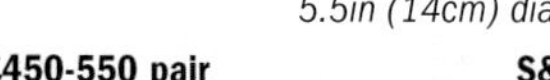

£450-550 pair **S&K**

A 19thC Chinese famille rose porcelain plate, the celadon ground painted with flowers and butterflies, gilt accents.

10.25in (25.5cm) diam

£100-150 **S&K**

A Chinese famille rose porcelain erotic dish, painted to depict an embracing couple, Yongzheng mark.

c1900 *7in (18cm) diam*

£280-320 **S&K**

A late 18thC or early 19thC Chinese famille rose saucer dish, painted with peony, pomegranate and rockwork.

13.5in (34cm) diam

£220-280 **WW**

A Chinese export porcelain famille rose decorated charger and five matching plates, each rim with four reserves of palmetto and floral sprays on a whorl and floral ground, the centre with landscape vignettes of the Great Wall and a pavilion.

Charger 13.75in (35cm) diam

£1,800-2,200 **NA**

Part of a collection of forty-two pieces of Chinese rose medallion porcelain, including two graduated quatrelobed footed dishes, a cylindrical jar, fifteen dinner plates, nineteen saucers and five teacups.

£400-600 set **S&K**

A Chinese famille rose porcelain bowl, floral decoration on apple green ground, Qianlong mark and period.

c1765 *6in (15cm) diam*

£250-300 **S&K**

A 19thC Chinese famille rose porcelain cup and cover, phoenix and dragon decoration, six character Qianlong seal mark.

4.5in (11.5cm) diam

£250-350 **S&K**

An 18thC Chinese export famille rose porcelain butter dish and cover, with floral decoration.

4.75in (12cm) diam

£100-150 **S&K**

A Chinese rose medallion punch bowl, painted with alternating reserves enclosing figures and flowers.

c1850 *16in (40.5cm) diam*

£1,000-1,500 **S&K**

A Chinese rose medallion punch bowl, painted with alternating reserves enclosing figures and flowers.

c1850 *16in (40.5cm) diam*

£1,000-1,500 **S&K**

A large early 20thC Chinese porcelain 'Cabbage Leaf' pattern punch bowl, with an overlapping leaf decoration, butterflies and famille rose floral borders

15.75in (40cm) diam

£500-700 **S&K**

A 20thC Chinese rose medallion pierced porcelain chestnut basket and undertray, painted with figural and bird reserves.

£400-600 **S&K**

A pair of Chinese famille rose porcelain bowls, with floral decoration, Guangxu mark and period.

5in (12.5cm) diam

£350-450 **S&K**

A Chinese famille rose porcelain vase and cover, of baluster form painted to depict peonies, fu lions and scrolling foliage on apple green ground, Qing dynasty, Daoguang period.

c1835 *18in (45.5cm) high*

£400-600 **S&K**

A 19thC pair of rose medallion porcelain vases, painted with floral and figural reserves, applied with qilin and fu dog handles.

25in (63.5cm) high

£1,800-2,200 **S&K**

A mid-19thC large Chinese Canton famille rose cylindrical vase with a flared neck, brightly painted with four panels of figures in various pursuits on a gold ground enamelled with butterflies, insects, flowers and fruits.

24in (61cm) high

£800-1,200 **WW**

A pair of 19thC Chinese rose medallion porcelain vases, each of club form with fu dog handles.

12in (30.5cm) high

£450-550 **S&K**

A 19thC Chinese famille rose porcelain vase, painted to depict figures under a tree in a mountainous landscape.

22.5in (57cm) high

£150-200 **S&K**

A large pair of Chinese Canton famille rose vases, decorated with panels of figures, birds, insects and flowers, one with restoration to the rim.

c1875 *25in (62.5cm) high*

£600-700 **WW**

A pair of Chinese famille rose porcelain vases, each of double gourd form, with medallions enclosing dragons in high relief, dragon-form handles, early Republic period

c1910 *9.5in (24cm) high*

£180-220 **S&K**

A near pair of large 20thC Chinese famille rose porcelain vases and covers, each of baluster form, with flower-filled vase decoration.

22in (56cm) high

£800-1,200 **S&K**

A Chinese famille rose porcelain meiping vase, painted to depict peaches, flowers, scrolling foliage and calligraphy on a yellow ground, Jiaqing mark, Republic period.

c1930 *9.5in (24cm) high*

£1,800-2,200 **S&K**

A large Chinese Imari baluster vase and cover, decorated in blue, gilt, iron red and famille rose enamel with vertical bands of foliage, minor faults.

£1,500-2,000 **WW**

A 20thC pair of Chinese famille rose porcelain jars and covers, of baluster form with floral decoration.

20in (50cm) high

£600-650 **S&K**

A Chinese famille rose figure of a lady standing holding a vase, Qianlong period, some damage.

c1765 *15in (38cm) high*

£1,500-2,000 **WW**

Two early 20thC Chinese famille rose porcelain figures of immortals, each wearing long loose robes, long black beard and diadem.

16.5in (41cm) high

£250-350 **S&K**

Two early 20thC Chinese famille rose porcelain figures of an immortal and a meiren, the immortal holding a peach and a sceptre with animal-head finial, the meiren with a deer, holding a flower-filled basket.

15in (37.5cm) high

£120-180 **S&K**

An early 18thC Chinese famille rose mug of bell shape and painted with figures, damaged.

9.5in (24cm) high

£60-90 **CHEF**

An early 20thC Chinese famille rose porcelain plaque, entitled 'Children at Play'.

17in (43cm) wide

£500-700 **S&K**

A pair of Chinese famille rose porcelain brush handles, floral decoration, Qianlong mark, Republic period.

c1930 *8in (20.5cm) long*

£550-650 **S&K**

JAPANESE CERAMICS

JAPANESE CERAMIC STYLES & DATES

Arita
In the late 16thC, the Japanese invaded Korea and brought back with them Korean potters who, settling in Arita, manufactured the first Japanese porcelains from c1620. The early products, decorated in blue and white, showed Korean influence whereas later goods from c1650 were influenced by Chinese styles. Arita porcelain splits into three types: Arita blue and white; Imari blue and white; and Kakiemon.

Hirado
This town near Arita also produced some of the earliest blue-and white and plain white porcelain at the start of the 17thC, using very pure clay from the island of Amakusa which allowed for fine potting and detailed modelling and gave an icing-sugar finish.

Imari
Named for the port from which it was exported, this porcelain developed from the 1650s, and was widely copied from the 18thC by the Meissen and Delft factories. Imari's definitive palette uses underglaze blue, iron red and gilding, but can also employ green, yellow, manganese brown and turquoise.

Kutani
This porcelain came from the Kaga region from the 19thC. It falls into two types: dark washes using green, purple, yellow and black; and Red Kutani, well-known in the West, which has a red ground and grisaille decoration, with romantic subject matter. Teawares were the most common form of Kutani ware.

Satsuma
Porcelain was produced in this region from the 16thC but the name is synonymous with that which was produced from c1850 onwards. The key feature is cream-coloured earthenware with a crackled glaze and heavy enamel and gilded decoration. The finest of these wares caught the imagination of Aesthetic Movement followers in the UK and US. Wares are usually signed.

Key periods
Edo 1615-1868
Meiji 1868-1912
Taisho 1912-1926
Showa 1926-1989

A 18thC Japanese Arita blue and white saucer dish, decorated with iris, Kin mark.

9in (22.5cm) diam

£320-380 **WW**

A CLOSER LOOK AT A JAPANESE ARITAWARE DISH

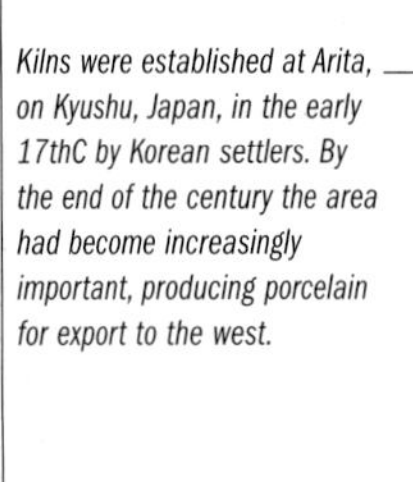

Kilns were established at Arita, on Kyushu, Japan, in the early 17thC by Korean settlers. By the end of the century the area had become increasingly important, producing porcelain for export to the west.

The large size of the plate makes this an impressive piece and the fact that the pattern can be displayed on a large area increases the value.

The fine craftsmanship of the lavish decoration and attention to detail make this plate visually attractive. Japanese ceramics are highly sought after, especially pieces with fine decoration.

Arita, Imari and Kakiemon ceramics all come from the same area of Japan. The term Arita is often associated with cobalt blue and white porcelain, but polychrome enamels were frequently used.

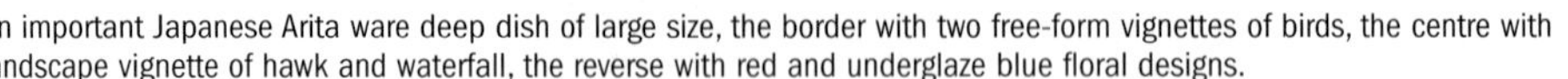

An important Japanese Arita ware deep dish of large size, the border with two free-form vignettes of birds, the centre with landscape vignette of hawk and waterfall, the reverse with red and underglaze blue floral designs.

c1710 *21in (52.5cm) diam*

£3,000-4,000 **NA**

A Japanese Arita bottle.

c1800 *10.75in (27.5cm) high*

£400-500 **DB**

A good Japanese Hirado cylindrical vase and cover with a pine cone knop, painted in a soft blue with figures beneath a pine tree examining a scroll.

c1800 *8in (20.5cm) high*

£1,200-1,800 **WW**

A Japanese Hirado ceramic dog.

4.25in (11cm) high

£500-700 **DB**

An early 18thC Japanese Imari plate.

8.5in (21.5cm) diam

£150-200 **CHEF**

A pair of Japanese Imari porcelain chargers, with a central medallion depicting flowerheads surrounded by a band enclosing floral and brocade decoration, Meiji period.

c1890 *22in (56cm) diam*

£1,200-1,800 **S&K**

One of a set of six early 20thC Japanese Imari plates, stencilled with central blue flower within alternating panels painted with gardens and flowers on fluted sides, within wavy rims.

8.25in (21cm) diam

£100-150 set **CHEF**

An early 18thC Japanese Imari vase, the baluster shape painted with two exotic birds flying above red flowers growing on spindly blue stems.

10in (25cm) high

£200-300 **CHEF**

A large Japanese Meiji period Imari vase, of baluster form with short flared neck painted with flowers, over tapered body decorated with opposed shaped panels of three ladies in a garden, on a ground of diaper decoration with panels of cranes above six opposed shaped bird and flower panels.

c1890 *18.5in (47cm) high*

£220-280 **L&T**

A CLOSER LOOK AT A LARGE JAPANESE IMARI BOWL

Imari porcelain was made at Arita, Japan, from the late 17thC and shipped to Europe from the port of Imari.

Imari shapes and designs were extensively copied and adapted in Europe during the 19thC by factories such as Meissen, Delft, Derby and Mason's Ironstone.

The large size of the bowl makes it an impressive and desirable piece.

The rich palette of underglaze blue as well as iron red and gilt is typical of Imari pieces.

A late 19thC large Japanese Imari bowl, of scalloped form, each panel with foliate and geometric decoration in polychrome and gilt, signed in underglaze blue.

16.5in (41cm) diam

£1,500-2,000 **FRE**

A large pair of Japanese Imari baluster vases, with flared rim over narrow neck and pear shaped body, the black ground painted with scrolling peonies, gilt and apricot Greek collar.

37.5in (95cm) high

£500-800 **L&T**

A Japanese Kutani porcelain charger, with bird, floral and architectural decoration, Meiji period.

c1890 *12in (30cm) diam*

£150-200 **S&K**

A Japanese Kutani porcelain charger, painted overall with flying cranes on gilt ground, brocade motif rim on red ground, Showa period.

c1960 *15in (37.5cm) diam*

£600-800 **S&K**

A 19thC Japanese Kutani figure.

11.75in (30cm) high

£500-800 **DB**

A Japanese Kutani ceramic cat.

14in (36cm) long

£2,000-2,600 **DB**

A Japanese Satsuma earthenware vase, of ovoid form, with an elongated neck, with three roundels enclosing figures on a flowerhead and cloud ground, Meiji period.

c1890 3.5in (9cm) high

£350-450 **S&K**

A pair of Japanese Satsuma earthenware vases, each painted to depict samurai on horseback, the elongated neck moulded with a dragon in high relief, Satsuma mon, Meiji period.

c1890 10in (25.5cm) high

£1,200-1,800 **S&K**

A pair of Japanese Satsuma vases, by Kinkozan.

5.75in (14.5cm) high

£500-800 **DB**

A CLOSER LOOK AT A SATSUMA VASE

These handles have been fashioned in the form of dragons – in Japan and China dragons symbolize power and excellence.

Satsuma wares are often decorated with panels featuring scenes of everyday life. Here, Japanese figures interact in a busy scene. Flowers and animals were also popular forms of decoration.

High quality Satsuma wares were often signed and bought by wealthy collectors. More mediocre, unsigned pieces were usually sold in department stores in the West. The difference in value is still apparent today.

Complex patterns and overlapping designs are common on Satsuma pieces.

A massive Satsuma vase on stand, decorated with panels of figures with foliate reserves in rich polychrome and gilt, the handles in the form of dragons, signed in gilt, Meiji period.

c1890 47in (117.5cm) high

£2,000-3,000 **FRE**

A large Japanese Satsuma vase, decorated with five storks beneath flowers and foliage, the inner rim with four Satsuma mon, gilt signature, Meiji period.

c1890 12in (31cm) high

£400-600 **WW**

A Japanese Satsuma baluster vase, each side decorated with figures beneath bamboo and wistaria on a gilt floral blue ground, no mark, Meiji period.

c1890 9.5in (24.5cm) high

£300-500 **WW**

A late 19thC Japanese Satsuma vase.

6in (15cm) high

£800-1,200 **DB**

A Satsuma tapered vase, decorated with a pagoda and numerous figures.

9.5in (24cm) high

£2,000-3,000 **GORL**

A Japanese Satsuma hexagonal section vase, decorated with panels of figures in gardens on blue ground, no mark, Meiji period, slight wear to gilt.

c1890 10in (25cm) high

£250-350 **WW**

A pair of Japanese reticulated Satsuma vases, with narrow flared neck above the shoulders with brocade frieze and cylindrical body, the centre surrounded by three rows of pierced friezes separated by bands of brocade.

9.5in (24cm) high

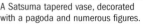

£500-800 **L&T**

A Satsuma box and cover, decorated with a warrior deflecting arrows, signed.

4.25in (10.75cm) diam

£180-220 **GORL**

A Japanese Satsuma earthenware vase, of ovoid form, the exterior painted to depict shaped cartouches enclosing flowering branches on a brocade and cobalt blue ground, the interior with a geisha in a garden, Meiji period.

c1890 *2.75in (7cm) high*

£1,500-2,000 **S&K**

A large Japanese Satsuma punch pot, painted to depict figures, shi shi, flowers and brocade, shi shi finial.

c1860 *15in (38cm) high*

£1,000-1,300 **S&K**

A large Japanese moulded dish, depicting figures on a shore landscape.

c1900 *15in (38cm) diam*

£70-100 **R&GM**

A Japanese polychrome porcelain charger, phoenix and floral decoration, Meiji period.

c1890 *16in (40cm) diam*

£280-320 **S&K**

A Japanese 'Rose Medallion' porcelain charger, the central medallion with a bird amongst peonies within a double iron red ring, the cavetto with four cartouches with alternating figural and floral decoration.

c1850 *18in (45cm) diam*

£100-150 **S&K**

A Japanese figure of the poet Kakinomoto No Hitomaro.

8.5in (22cm) high

£1,000-1,500 **DB**

One of a pair of late 19thC or early 20thC Japanese vases.

8.5in (22cm) high

£400-600 pair **DB**

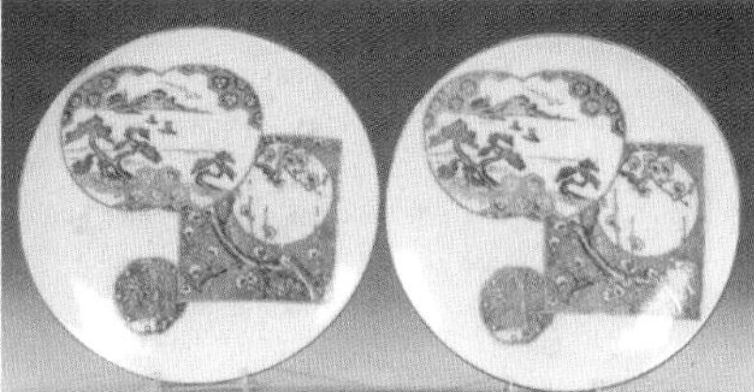

Two Japanese blue and white chargers, with transfer floral and brocade decoration, Meiji period.

13in (32.5cm) diam

£120-180 **S&K**

Nine Japanese blue and white porcelain plates, painted to depict horses and clouds, Showa period.

c1960 *8in (20cm) d.*

£160-200 set **S&K**

ANNAMESE CERAMICS

Annam was the name given by the ancient Chinese, and later by the imperial French, to regions in what we now know as Vietnam. Ceramics were so important to ancient Vietnam that the country has a temple dedicated to the first Annamese potter, Troung Trung Ai, and his Chinese instructor. The similarities between Annamese and Chinese ceramics are striking, although Annamese ware also shares many characteristics with pottery from Siam, or Thailand.

Characteristically fashioned of coarse, heavily potted, grey clay, Annamese ceramics are frequently painted in underglaze blue or coated with enamel. Yuhuchun, or pear-shaped bottles, are clearly derived from similar wares made under the Chinese Yuan dynasty.

The peak of Annamese ceramic production came between the 12thC and 15thC, during a culturally rich period also marked by relative peace and prosperity for most of the nation. Quality was high and consistent enough that export trade to Japan and the Middle East thrived, and many Annamese articles have survived as family heirlooms and burial pieces.

A late 15th or early 16thC Annamese blue and white yuhuchun bottle, good condition, glaze worn.

9.25in (23cm) high

£400-600 **S&K**

A late 15thC or early 16thC Annamese blue and white Yuhuchun bottle, of pear form, decorated with overglaze enamel, marine encrustation and wear.

9in (23cm) high

£400-600 **S&K**

A late 15thC/early 16thC Annamese blue and white yuhuchun bottle with overglaze enamel decoration, glaze degradation, clouds clearly depicted, very small chip to rim, several chips to base.

8.5in (21.5cm) high

£300-500 **S&K**

A CLOSER LOOK AT AN ANNAMESE EWER

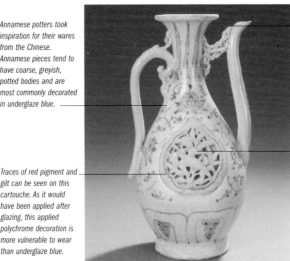

Annamese potters took inspiration for their wares from the Chinese. Annamese pieces tend to have coarse, greyish, potted bodies and are most commonly decorated in underglaze blue.

Traces of red pigment and gilt can be seen on this cartouche. As it would have been applied after glazing, this applied polychrome decoration is more vulnerable to wear than underglaze blue.

The delicate and skillfully crafted openwork decoration enhances the appeal of this fine ewer. Despite the vulnerability of the shape, the piece has survived in remarkably good condition.

The parrot was a popular Annamese motif and was often used figuratively and in decoration on Annamese ceramics.

A late 15thC/early 16thC fine Annamese blue and white ewer with openwork panels, each side with an unglazed cartouche bearing traces of red pigment and gilt, reticulated as a parrot standing amid foliage, surrounded by rich cobalt blue painted lotus scrolls.

9.75in (25cm) high

£800-1,200 **S&K**

A late 15thC/early 16thC Annamese blue and white jar and cover, small chips to rim of cover and one chip to body, crazing.

6.75in (17cm) high

£200-250 **S&K**

A 12thC/14thC Annamese stoneware cylindrical bowl, carved on the exterior with panels of lotus flowers, leaves and geometric designs, old damage and restoration.

5.5in (14cm) wide

£220-280 **WW**

A late 15thC/early 16thC Annamese blue and green dish, rim chips, wear to the enamel and glaze, cracks.

17.5in (44.5cm) diam

£800-1,200 **S&K**

A late 15thC/early 16thC large Annamese blue and white dish, painted beneath the lustrous glaze with a flowering lotus plant, a leafy spray band around the cavetto, glaze worn.

13.5in (34.5cm) high

£700-1,000 **S&K**

A late 15thC/early 16thC large Annamese blue and white dish, the reverse with large loosely painted lotus-form lappets enclosing cloud scrolls, glaze worn, staining, crazing.

13.25in (33cm) diam

£400-600 **S&K**

A late 15thC/early 16thC Annamese blue and white bowl, the shallow bowl decorated at the well with a stylized chrysanthemum blossom, a floral meander around the cavetto.

12.5in (32cm) diam

£400-600 **S&K**

An late 15thC/early 16thC Annamese blue and white bowl, the shallow dish with a central lotus blossom amid scrolling tendrils, the cavetto with an alternating floral and leafy spray.

13.5in (34.5cm) diam

£300-500 **S&K**

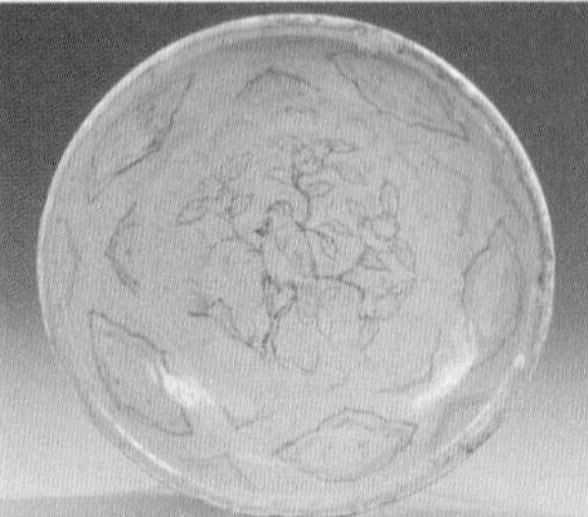

A late 15thC/early 16thC large Annamese underglaze blue and enamelled dish, with traces of original enamels.

13.25in (33.5cm) diam

£300-500 **S&K**

A late 15th/early 16thC large Annamese underglaze blue and enamel dish, the exterior lacking most of the original glaze, glaze and enamel degradation, staining, overall crazing.

13.25in (33cm) diam

£400-500 **S&K**

Two of a set of ten early 19thC Vietnamese blue and white porcelain bowls, painted to depict a rabbit and insects, Nguyen dynasty.

£200-300 set **S&K**

A Vietnamese crackled ivory glazed pottery jar, of ovoid form with a domed cover, Ly dynasty.

£350-450 **S&K**

A 15thC Vietnamese dish, repaired.

16in (40.5cm) wide

£320-380 **R&GM**

OTHER ORIENTAL CERAMICS

A Korean celadon bowl, Koryo dynasty.

4in (10cm) diam

£150-200 **S&K**

A CLOSER LOOK AT A MEIPING VASE

Meiping translates from the Chinese as 'prunus branch'. These vases were originally decorative pieces, designed to hold a single branch of the prunus fruit tree blossoms so beloved in the Far East.

The graceful 'S' shaped bend sweeping from the neck, past the shoulder and down to the base is a classic feature, defining this type of vase.

Korean ceramicists were influenced by their Chinese counterparts, and their wares often have similar forms.

The milky, almost pearlescent, glaze on this Meiping vase is unusual and makes it a particularly attractive and desirable piece.

The wooden base on which this vase stands is original. This is very important if a vase is to retain its value on the market.

A 19thC Korean white glazed porcelain Meiping vase, Choson dynasty.

20in (51cm) high

£4,000-6,000 **S&K**

A 19thC Korean blue and white porcelain Meiping vase, with dragon decoration, Choson dynasty.

15in (38cm) high

£3,000-4,000 **S&K**

A pair of Korean white glazed vases, elephant head form handles, mounted as lamps.

9.5in (24cm) high

£200-300 **S&K**

A Korean blue glazed porcelain water dropper, moulded to depict a fish, Choson dynasty.

3in (7.5cm) long

£120-180 **S&K**

A large Chinese stone head of Buddha, Qing dynasty.

c1890 *16in (40.5cm) high*

£500-700 **S&K**

PRINTS

Kano Tanyu, (Japanese, 1602-1674), 'Monkey', ink and colour on silk scroll, signed with two seals.

35.75in (91cm) high

£480-520 **S&K**

Toyokuni III (Japanese, 1823-1880), 'Warriors', colour triptych, signed and sealed.

c1850 *13.75in (38cm) high*

£180-220 **S&K**

Toyokuni III, 'Warriors', colour diptych, signed and sealed.

c1850 *13.75in (38cm) high*

£180-220 **S&K**

Toyokuni (Japanese, 19thC), 'Actor', colour woodcut, framed.

13.5in (34.5cm) high

£150-200 **S&K**

Utagawa Kuniyoshi (Japanese, 1797-1861), 'Historical Battle Scene', colour triptych depicting battle scenes, signed and sealed, framed.

c1850 *14in (35.5cm) high*

£350-450 **S&K**

Toyokuni I, 'Actor', colour woodcut, framed.

13.5in (34.5cm) high

£150-200 **S&K**

Toyokuni I, 'Actor', colour woodcut, framed.

13.5in (34.5cm) high

£180-220 **S&K**

Hiroshige (Japanese, 19thC), 'Battle Scene'.

12.75in (32.25cm) high

£320-380 **S&K**

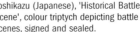

Yoshikazu (Japanese), 'Historical Battle Scene', colour triptych depicting battle scenes, signed and sealed.

c1855

£180-220 **S&K**

Hakuin Tanaka (Japanese, 19thC), 'Mountainous Landscape with Pavilions', two ink and colour on silk scrolls, signed and sealed.

51in (129.5cm) high

£120-180 **S&K**

Utagawa Kuniyoshi (Japanese), 'Monagaku Shonin na chi Waterfall', colour vertical triptych, sealed with a kiri seal, published by Sumiyoshi-ya Masagoro, dated, censor seals for Mera and Kinugosa.

1851 *41.5in (105.5cm) high*

£1,200-1,800 **S&K**

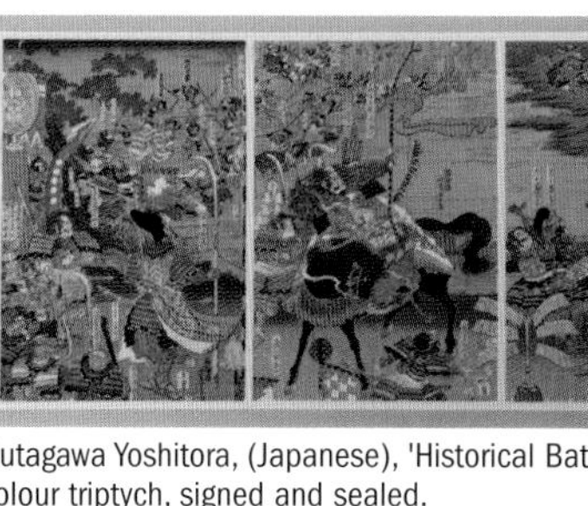

Dutagawa Yoshitora, (Japanese), 'Historical Battle Scene', colour triptych, signed and sealed.

c1860 *14.5in (37cm) high*

£320-380 **S&K**

Yoshikata (Japanese), 'Historical Battle Scene', colour triptych depicting battle scenes, signed and sealed, framed.

c1860 *13.5in (34.5cm) high*

£150-200 **S&K**

Anonymous (Japanese, 19thC), 'Warriors', colour diptych, with publisher's seal, date and censor seals, unidentified carver's seal.

1867 *14in (35.5cm) high*

£150-200 **S&K**

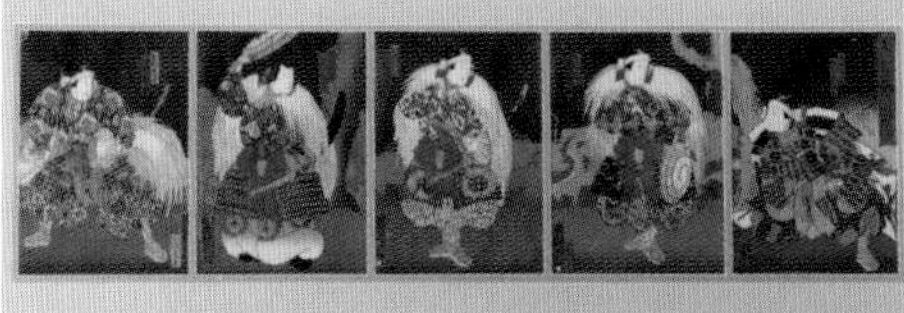

Yoshitaki, five colour woodcuts, framed.

c1870 *Woodcuts 11in (28cm) high*

£280-320 **S&K**

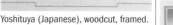

Yoshituya (Japanese), woodcut, framed.

c1885

£180-220 **S&K**

Utagawa Kokunimasa (Japanese, 19thC), 'Actors', colour triptych depicting warrior on horseback, signed and sealed.

c1890 *14.75in (37.5cm) high*

£320-380 **S&K**

Tsuchiya Koitsu (Japanese, 1870-1949), 'Sino-Japanese War Peace Treaty', colour triptych depicting Chinese ambassadors Riko-sho and Rikeiho, Japanese Ministers Ito and Mutsu, and a foreign mediator, signed and sealed.

c1895 *13.25in (33.5cm) high*

£150-200 **S&K**

Beisaku (Japanese, 19thC), 'Sino-Japanese War of 1894-1895', colour triptych, signed and sealed.

c1895 *14in (35.5cm) high*

£280-320 **S&K**

Anonymous (Japanese, early 20thC), 'Paintings from Daily Life', ink and colour on silk hand scroll, with seal.

50in (127cm) high

£300-500 **S&K**

Hiratsuka (Japanese), 'Home of Lafcaido Hearn', dated.

c1948 *21in (52.5cm) wide*

£700-1,000 **S&K**

A CLOSER LOOK AT A JAPANESE PRINT

Beautiful young women are typical subject matter for the artist. His style made him popular at home and in the West.

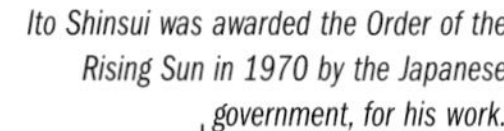

Ito Shinsui was awarded the Order of the Rising Sun in 1970 by the Japanese government, for his work.

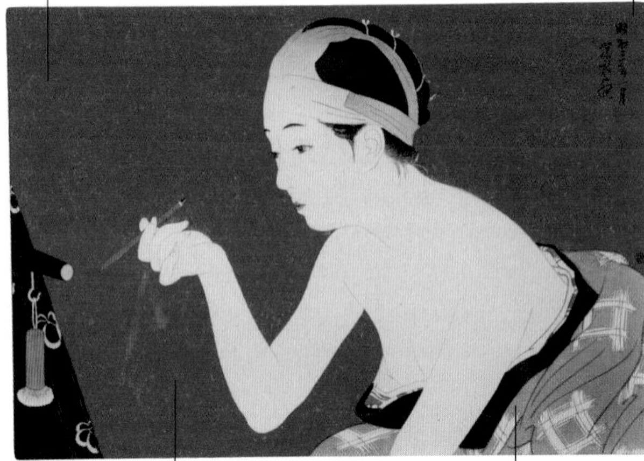

The Tokyo publisher of this print, Watanabe Shozaburo, was a key figure in the highly regarded shin hanga (new print) movement.

The image is bold and striking and full of character, making this a desirable print.

Ito Shinsui (Japanese, 1898-1972), 'A Woman Penciling her Eyebrows (Mayu Zumi)', signed 'Shinsui ga' with artist's seal 'Shinsui' and publisher seal 'Watanabe', dated January 1928 and numbered on reverse 69/200.

15.5in (39.5cm) wide

£5,000-7,000 **S&K**

Sadao Watanabe, (Japanese, b. 1913), two colour woodcuts, the first dated 1959, numbered 38/50; the second dated 1963, numbered 2/50, framed.

£600-800 **S&K**

Sadao Watanabe, two colour woodcuts, the first, 'Three Women', dated 1962, numbered 7/50, the second, 'King and two Women', dated 1968, numbered 13/50, framed.

£400-600 **S&K**

Hiroshi Yoshida, 'Tokugawa Peony Garden', colour woodcut, tape stains verso, signed.

£600-650 **S&K**

Hiratsuka (Japanese), 'Pagoda of Joruki-Ji Yamato Temple', woodcut, dated.

1960 *24in (60cm) high*

£700-1,000 **S&K**

Eizan Ikeda (Japanese), 'Geisha', two colour woodcuts, brown spots.

£300-400 **S&K**

Foujita Tsuguji (Tsuguharu Leonard, Japanese), 'Child with Bird', colour woodcut, backed, faded with multiple professional repairs, signed.

15.25in (38cm) high

£350-450 **S&K**

Foujita Tsuguji, 'Portrait de Femme', colour woodcut, backed, faded with multiple professional repairs, signed.

15.25in (38cm) high

£450-550 **S&K**

One of six anonymous 19thC Chinese ink and colour on paper court scenes, framed.

Provenance: *ex-collection Lady Sarah (Amherst) Williams, wife of the English Ambassador to China.*

15.5in (39.5cm) x 23in (58.5cm)

£1,800-2,200 set **S&K**

A 19thC Chinese school ink and colour on scroll, depicting a mandarin with female attendants.

39in (99cm) x 16in (40.5cm)

£200-300 **S&K**

A Chinese ink and colour on silk, after Shimin, depicting a mountainous landscape, signed and sealed, framed.

35in (89cm) x 16in (40.5cm)

£450-550 **S&K**

An anonymous Iranian Qajar miniature picture, gouache on paper, depicting a battle in a mountainous landscape.

8in (20.5cm) x 4.75in (12cm)

£400-600 **S&K**

A pair of anonymous Iranian miniature battle scenes, gouache on paper.

11in (28cm) x 6.25in (16cm)

£80-120 **S&K**

An anonymous Iranian Qajar miniature picture, gouache on paper, depicting a man in a garden, framed.

9.5in (24cm) x 5.5in (14cm)

£180-220 **S&K**

An anonymous Indian Mughal period miniature picture, gouache on paper, depicting a nobleman and horse consulting a sage, framed.

8in (20.5cm) x 5.5in (14cm)

£350-450 **S&K**

An anonymous Iranian Qajar miniature picture, gouache on paper, depicting three men at rest with a horse.

7in (18cm) x 4in (10cm)

£300-400 **S&K**

An anonymous Indian Mughal period miniature picture, gouache on paper, inspired by Bellini's visit to India, framed.

8in (20.5cm) x 5in (12.5cm)

£2,500-3,000 **S&K**

CLOISONNÉ

A rare Japanese cloisonné vase, by Ando.

7.75in (20cm) high

£3,000-4,000 DB

A Japanese cloisonné vase, by Ando.

8.25in (21cm) high

£1,000-1,500 DB

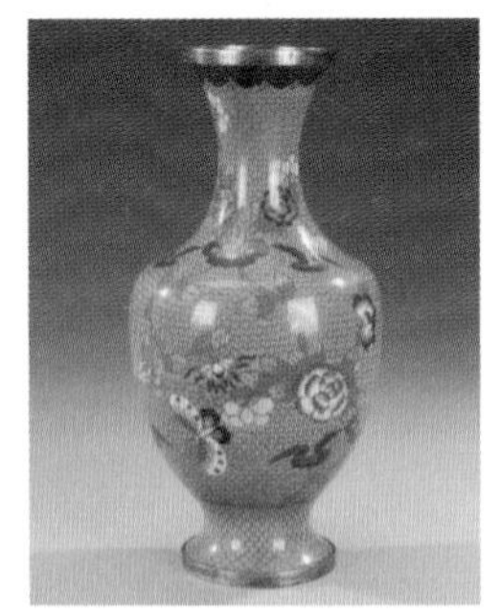

A 20thC Chinese cloisonné enamel vase, of ovoid form with floral decoration on a blue ground.

13in (32.5cm) high

£70-100 S&K

A pair of Japanese Meiji period cloisonné enamel vases, with prunus flowering tree decoration on turquoise blue ground, signed, probably Ota Kichisaburo.

7.5in (19cm) high

£500-700 S&K

A pair of Japanese cloisonné black ground baluster vases, decorated with cranes in flight, with a stiff leaf frieze to neck and foot and matched hardwood stands.

4.5in (11.5cm) high

£450-500 L&T

One of a pair of Chinese cloisonné dishes, decorated with butterflies, birds and foliage on a key fret ground, the rims and bases gilt.

c1800

£700-900 pair WW

A Japanese Meiji period cloisonné enamel charger.

Provenance: *Ex collection of LTC Kenneth White, Baltimore.*

14.5in (36cm) diam

£280-320 S&K

A Chinese cloisonné 'elephant' incense burner, with a vase on its back.

9in (23cm) wide

£320-380 GORL

A CLOSER LOOK AT A CLOISONNÉ INRO

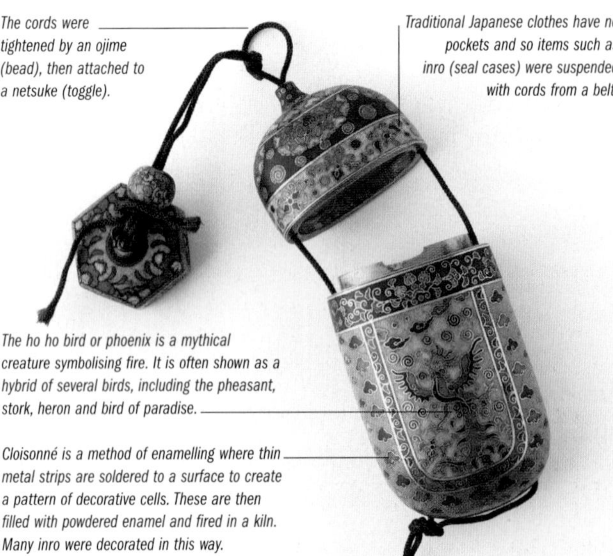

The cords were tightened by an ojime (bead), then attached to a netsuke (toggle).
Traditional Japanese clothes have no pockets and so items such as inro (seal cases) were suspended with cords from a belt.
The ho ho bird or phoenix is a mythical creature symbolising fire. It is often shown as a hybrid of several birds, including the pheasant, stork, heron and bird of paradise.
Cloisonné is a method of enamelling where thin metal strips are soldered to a surface to create a pattern of decorative cells. These are then filled with powdered enamel and fired in a kiln. Many inro were decorated in this way.

An early to mid-19thC rare Japanese cloisonné inro, of oval section, the top concealing a single chamber decorated with a ho ho bird on one side and a bouquet of flowers to the reverse, on a scroll ground in turquoise green, blue, white and brown, a related ojime and netsuke.

c1825

£4,500-5,000 WW

IVORY

A late 19thC carved ivory tusk, depicting three figures and a cockerel, with an inset signed red tablet and carved naturalistic hardwood plinth.

12.5in (32cm) high

£180-220 L&T

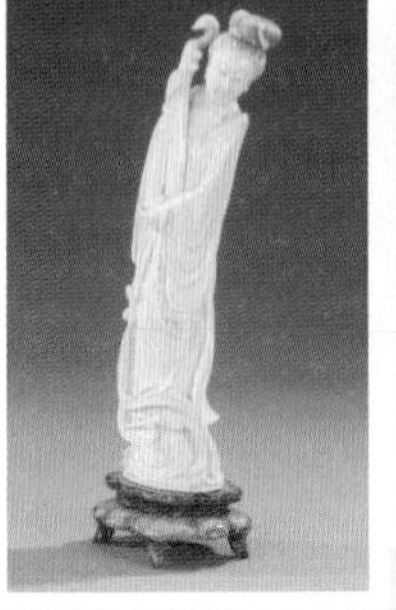

A 20thC Chinese ivory figure of a female musician, with a high chignon, wearing loose robes and holding a musical instrument.

10in (25.5cm) high

£280-320 S&K

A Chinese late Qing dynasty, early Republic period, ivory figure of a female warrior, carved standing holding a sword.

12in (30.5cm) high

£1,000-1,500 **S&K**

A Chinese ivory figure of a Goddess, standing with one hand raised and a scrolled brush, on a lotus leaf base.

10in (25.5cm) high

£100-150 **GORL**

An early 20thC Chinese polychrome ivory figure of an immortal, wearing long, loose robes, holding a peach and a stick with a dragon-form head.

7.75in (19.5cm) high

£280-320 **S&K**

Two Chinese ivory figures of a meiren, or beautiful woman, and an immortal.

12in (30.5cm) high

£500-800 **S&K**

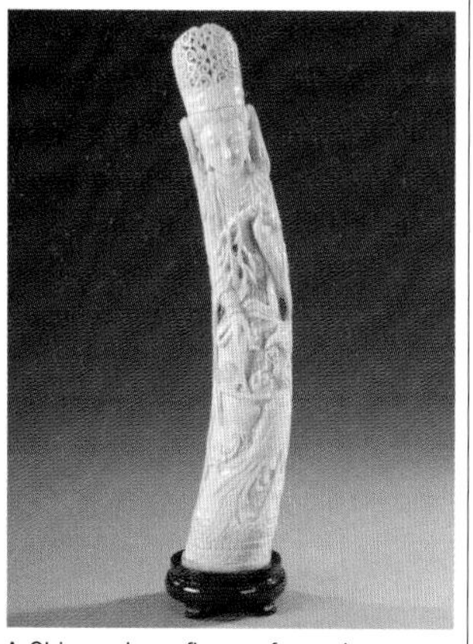

A Chinese ivory figure of a meiren, wearing a pierced headdress and loose robes.

15.25in (38.5cm) high

£600-700 **S&K**

A late 19thC to early 20thC Chinese ivory figure of a meiren, wearing loose robes, holding a hoe and a flower-filled basket, with attendant, on a pine tree-form plinth.

9.5in (24cm) high

£450-550 **S&K**

An early 20thC Chinese ivory figure of a meiren, standing wearing loose robes and holding a peony branch.

14in (35.5cm) high

£600-700 **S&K**

A pair of Chinese ivory figures of a standing emperor and empress.

Larger 15.5in (39.5cm) high

£800-1,100 **S&K**

A 20thC Chinese ivory head of a meiren, wearing a floral diadem and a high chignon.

5in (12.5cm) high

£300-400 **S&K**

A Chinese ivory figure of Buddha, seated on a lotus throne.

5.5in (14cm) high

£280-320 **S&K**

A Chinese ivory figure of a horse.

8in (20cm) high

£300-500 **S&K**

An early 20thC Japanese ivory group, of a mother with one child on her back as she passes a bowl of rice to another seated beside her, a kettle on a drum shaped table to the other side, lacquer seal mark.

3.5in (9cm) high

£250-350 **CHEF**

An early 20thC Japanese ivory and Shark's tooth group of two women, one standing holding a basket of lotus on his back and the other seated on his bundle, smoking a pipe.

4.5in (11.5cm) high

£150-200 **CHEF**

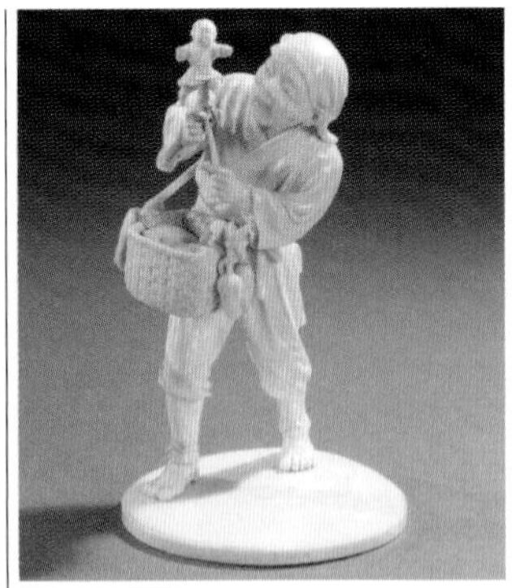

A Japanese Meiji period ivory okimono, carved to depict a noh mask carver standing on a circular plinth.

6in (15cm) high

£480-520 **S&K**

An early 20thC Japanese ivory and shark's tooth figure, caught in the moment of raising a knife to ward off an attacking snake.

7.5in (19cm) high

£150-200 **CHEF**

A Japanese Showa period ivory figure of a Geisha, wearing a kimono and holding a lantern, signed.

7in (18cm) high

£350-450 **S&K**

A Japanese carved ivory figure of a woodsman, with large rolls of sticks on his back, standing holding a long axe at his feet and next to a young boy holding a hare and a gourd, on a shaped naturalistic plinth, signed on an inset red tablet.

9in (22.5cm) high

£3,000-4,000 **L&T**

A large Japanese carved ivory figure of a fisherman, with one hand to his mouth and carrying a net, on an oval naturalistic plinth, signed, damage, and another smaller segmented carved ivory figure of a stick gatherer, wearing a wide brimmed hat with his head cocked to one side, carrying a large bundle of sticks under one arm, on oval plinth, signed.

Largest 12in (30cm) high

£2,000-3,000 **L&T**

A Japanese ivory okimono, carved to depict an inkwell.

4in (10cm) diam

£220-280 **S&K**

From left to right: A Japanese carved ivory exotic fruit, with leafy stalk and cut-away side panel revealing erotic scene of two naked figures, the other side carved with netsuke holes and signed.

2in (5cm) wide

£180-220 **L&T**

A Japanese carved ivory almost life-size red stained apple, the interior hollowed out and carved with a scene of landscape with a central fir tree and figures, indistinctly signed.

2.5in (6cm) diam

£300-400 **L&T**

A Japanese carved ivory exotic fruit, in the form of a pomegranate with flowered top, partly opened to reveal textured interior, one side with cut-away panel revealing an erotic scene of two naked figures, the other side with netsuke carved holes and signed.

2in (5cm) wide

£180-220 **L&T**

A Japanese carved ivory banana, with two strips almost wholly peeled back, and a long stalk, and another smaller, decorated with a winged insect.

Largest 5in (12.5cm) long

£220-280 **L&T**

From left to right: A Japanese carved ivory shibyama decorated bunch of eight cherries, with long, minutely observed, stained stalk and applied with ten insects, signed in rust.

4.5in (11cm) long

£250-300 **L&T**

A Japanese carved ivory shibyama decorated bunch of seven cherries, with minutely observed stained stalk and six applied insects, signed in rust.

3in (7cm) long

£220-280 **L&T**

From left to right: A small Japanese carved ivory shibyama decorated pineapple, the sides decorated with eight applied insects and another on the flattened base, signed in rust.

2.5in (7cm) high

£480-520 **L&T**

A Japanese carved ivory shibyama decorated pineapple, the tall flared crown decorated with applied insects, including a centipede and various beetles, the base decorated with two insects, signed in rust.

5in (13cm) high

£3,000-4,000 **L&T**

From left to right: A Japanese carved ivory shibyama decorated gourd, with broad stalk, seven applied insects and carved skin breaks, signed in rust.

1.5in (4cm) high

£180-220 **L&T**

A Japanese carved ivory shibyama decorated flattened gourd, with tall carved stalk, nine applied insects and carved skin breaks, signed in rust.

2in (5cm) diam

£300-350 **L&T**

A pair of Japanese carved ivory shibyama decorated cherries, with long twin stalk, each decorated with three insects, signed in rust.

3in (8cm) long

£180-220 **L&T**

From left to right: A Japanese carved ivory shibyama decorated mushroom, with a plump stalk and a textured underside, applied with six various insects, signed in rust.

2.5in (6cm) wide

£180-220 **L&T**

A Japanese carved ivory shibyama decorated mushroom of flattened form, the stalk with one applied beetle and the cap with four insects, including a dragonfly, signed in rust.

2in (5cm) diam

£120-180 **L&T**

A Chinese ivory tusk, carved to depict dragons chasing the flaming pearl of wisdom.

21.5in (54.5cm) long

£1,200-1,800 **S&K**

A Chinese ivory tusk, carved to depict a court scene with figures and a pagoda under a pine tree.

12.25in (31cm) long

£350-450 **S&K**

An Indian hollowed ivory tusk, carved to depict an animal procession.

20in (51cm) long

£500-700 **S&K**

Two Chinese ivory carvings, carved to depict figures in a mountainous landscape.

Largest 7.25in (18.5cm) high

£400-600 **S&K**

A 19thC Cantonese carved ivory jewel casket, the rectangular hinged lid with a central vacant oval surrounded by densely carved figures, animals and birds, the sides with shaped cartouche panels of figures and flowers, grotesque mask feet, velvet lined, tray top interior.

6in (15cm) wide

£600-800 **L&T**

A Chinese Qing dynasty ivory card case, carved with a shaped cartouche enclosing a garden scene.

4.5in (11.5cm) high

£350-450 **S&K**

A Chinese Qing dynasty ivory card case, carved to depict a garden scene.

4.5in (11.5cm) high

£300-400 **S&K**

A Chinese ivory brush pot, carved to depict a mountainous landscape with figures, Qianlong mark.

5.75in (14.5cm) high

£450-550 **S&K**

An early 20thC Chinese ivory teapot, carved with birds under a pine tree and animal decoration.

3in (7.5cm) high

£200-300 **S&K**

An early 20thC Chinese ivory chess set, in a fitted box.

£400-600 **S&K**

JADE

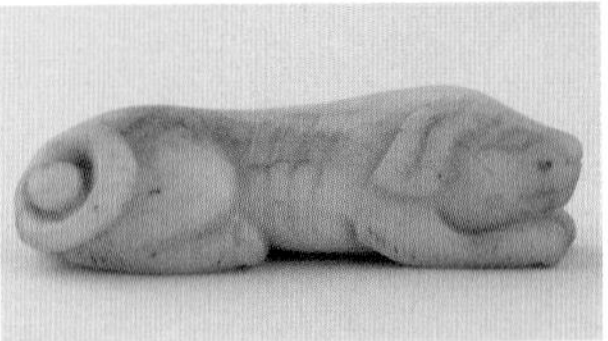

A Chinese Song dynasty jade hound.

2.75in (7cm) long

£1,000-1,500 **DB**

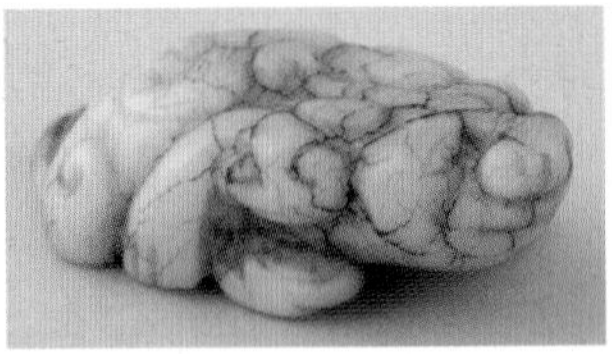

A Chinese Ming dynasty jade toad.

2.75in (7cm) long

£1,500-2,000 **DB**

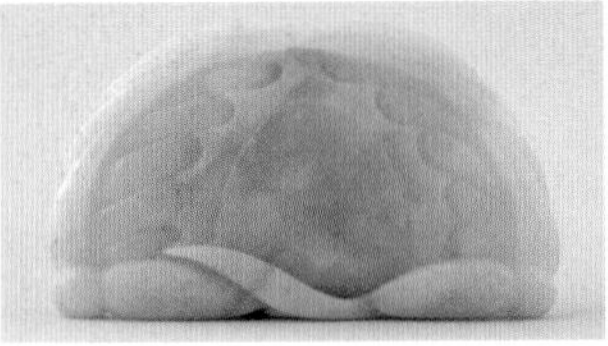

A Chinese Ming dynasty jade crab.

2in (5.5cm) long

£300-500 **DB**

A Chinese Ming dynasty jade goat.

2.75in (7cm) long

£1,000-1,500 **DB**

A Chinese late Ming dynasty jade elephant.

3in (8cm) high

£3,000-4,000 **DB**

An 18thC Chinese jade cat and kitten.

2in (5.5cm) long

£2,200-2,800 **DB**

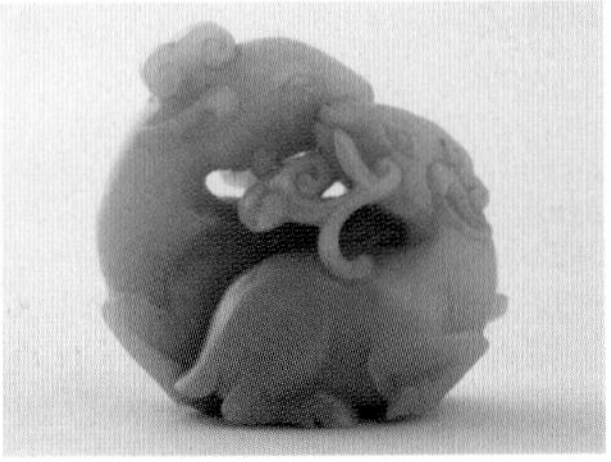

An 18thC Chinese jade deer and young.

3in (7.5cm) long

£2,000-3,000 **DB**

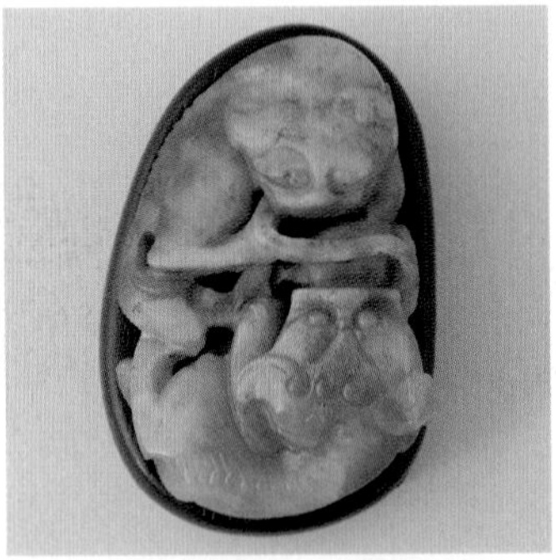

An 18thC Chinese jade shishi dog.

2.75in (7cm) high

£700-1,000 **DB**

A Chinese jade figure of a meiren, wearing loose robes and a high chignon, holding a fan and a bird.

c1945 *6in (15cm) high*

£150-200 **S&K**

A Chinese serpentine figure of a meiren, carved wearing long robes, holding a mirror and a flowering branch.

7.75in (19.5cm) high

£150-200 **S&K**

A large Chinese spinach jade table screen, carved to depict a pavilion and figures under pine trees.

c1930 *21in (53cm) high*

£4,500-5,500 **S&K**

A Chinese jade and wood ruyi sceptre, late Qing dynasty, early Republic period, each plaque carved to depict a dragon chasing the flaming pearl of wisdom.

21.5in (54.5cm) long

£600-900 **S&K**

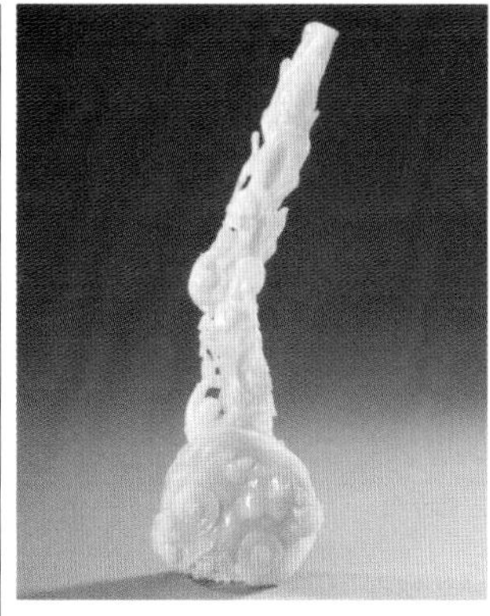
A Chinese white jade ruyi sceptre, late Qing dynasty, early Republic period, carved in the form of a lingzhi with figures and bats.

13.5in (34.5cm) long

£800-1,200 **S&K**

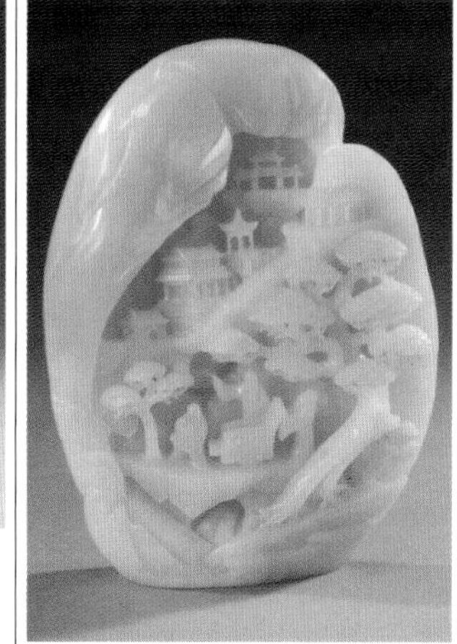
A Chinese white carved jade boulder, late Qing dynasty, early Republic period, carved to depict a garden scene with figures under pine trees and pavilions.

8in (20.5cm) high

£1,000-1,500 **S&K**

A Chinese jade Ming dynasty vase.

4.75in (12cm) high

£700-1,000 **DB**

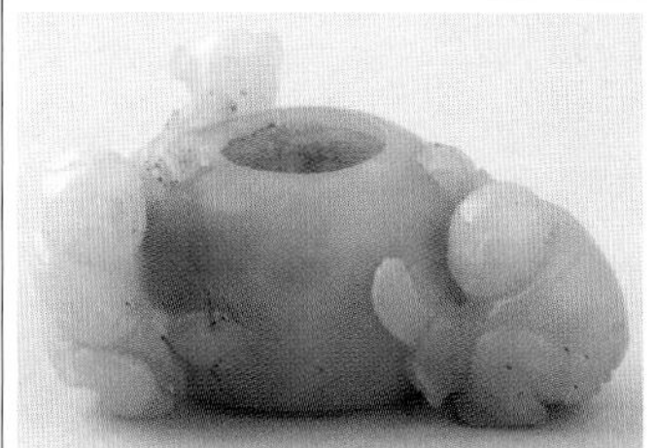
A Chinese jade brush pot.

3in (8cm) wide

£700-1,000 **DB**

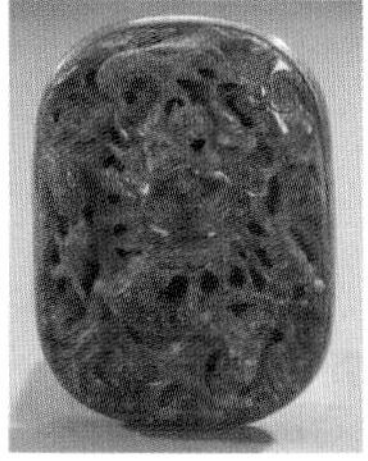
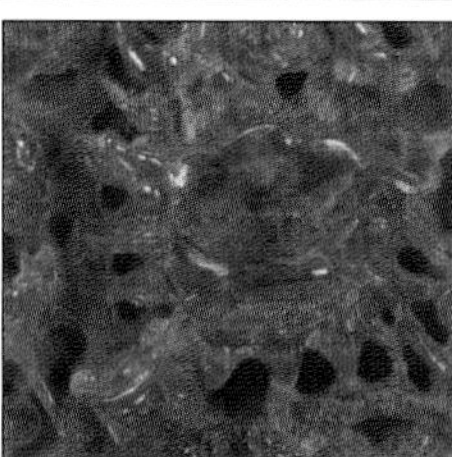
A Chinese apple green jadeite belt buckle, carved to depict a dragon, with brass mounts.

3in (7.5cm) high

£200-250 **S&K**

METAL

A 17thC Chinese bronze model of Guanyin, wearing a flowing robe inlaid with silver wire and raised on a cloud scroll and plinth base, a seal mark within a gourd inlaid, signed "Shi Sou", crack to the robe, a hair ornament lacking.

It is unusual to find a Shi Sou figure with its contemporary stand.

19in (48.5cm) high

£4,000-5,000 **WW**

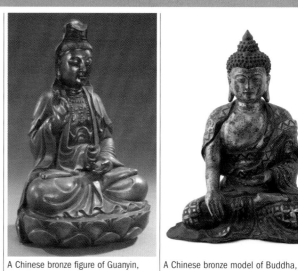

A Chinese bronze figure of Guanyin, Republic period, seated in dhyanasana on a lotus base, her right hand in vitarka mudra, wearing log pleated robes and veil cast with a brocade motif, beaded necklace with a rosette pendant.

17in (43cm) high

£200-300 **S&K**

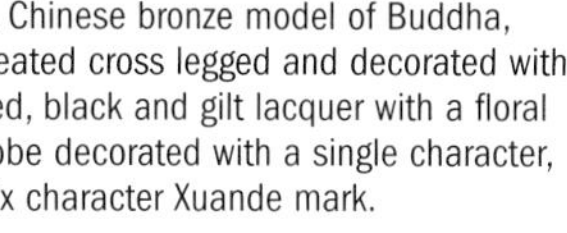
A Chinese bronze model of Buddha, seated cross legged and decorated with red, black and gilt lacquer with a floral robe decorated with a single character, six character Xuande mark.

16.25in (41cm) high

£700-1,000 **WW**

A Chinese gilt bronze figure of Buddha, seated in dhyanasana, his hands resting in his lap in dhyana mudra, the face with a serene expression.

19in (48.5cm) high

£300-400 **S&K**

A Chinese late Qing dynasty gilt bronze two-part censor, formed as a Taoist dignitary and a horse, the horse shown standing foursquare with head facing forward, mouth closed and ears pricked, an aperture on his back seating the separate figure of a Taoist dignitary holding a scroll.

20in (51cm) high

£800-1,200 **S&K**

A 19thC Chinese archaistic bronze vase, cast with taotie masks and flanked by two floral handles.

6.75in (17cm) high

£80-120 **S&K**

A Chinese gilt bronze figure of a Fu lion, Tang dynasty.

0.75in (2cm) high

£80-120 **S&K**

A rare Chinese Han dynasty gilt bronze tripod censer and cover, of circular form, a domed cover with three animal-shaped finials, flanked by two upright handles.

c220BC *5in (12.5cm) diam*

£2,500-3,000 **S&K**

A Chinese Han dynasty bronze covered vase, of square baluster form, the cover with a band of geometric design, three loop handles with loose rings.

7.5in (19cm) high

£500-700 **S&K**

A Chinese Ming dynasty water dropper, depicting a deer.

3.25in (8.5cm) long

£500-700 **DB**

A Chinese bronze censer.

12.5in (32cm) high

£800-1,200 **DB**

A Chinese Ming dynasty water dropper.

4in (10cm) long

£500-700 **DB**

A Chinese Ming dynasty bronze water dropper.

2.25in (6cm) high

£400-600 **DB**

A rare Chinese Warring States period archaic bronze vessel, the neck cast with thunder cloud above a wide band of snakes, with grey patina and some green encrustation.

6.25in (16cm) high

£3,000-4,000 **S&K**

A pair of Japanese Meiji period bronze Miyao style Samurai warriors, one standing on one foot with a sword held over his head, his robe decorated in gilt with mon, signed on a raised tablet, the other with open coat and pantalon, holding a long spear, signed "Joshimitsu", both on carved hardwood plinths.

13in (32.5cm) high

£6,000-8,000 **L&T**

A Japanese bronze figure of a warrior, in attacking posture, carrying a long nailed club aloft, on a rectangular ebonised plinth, bearing a "Gyoko" signature on his left side.

22.5in (56cm) high

£7,000-9,000 **L&T**

A Japanese Meiji period bronze boar.

14.5in (37cm) long

£2,000-3,000 **DB**

A Japanese Meiji period bronze elephant.

8.75in (22cm) long

£2,000-3,000 **DB**

A Japanese Meiji period Kirlin.

9.75in (25cm) long

£2,000-3,000 **DB**

A Japanese Meiji bronze tiger.

3.5in (9cm) high

£700-900 **DB**

A Japanese incense burner, in the shape of a hare.

6in (15cm) high

£800-1,200 **DB**

A Japanese bronze fish.

6.75in (17.5cm) long

£800-1,200 **DB**

A Japanese reticulated bronze crab, of realistic appearance with moving pincers and legs with naturalistic engraved decoration.

9in (23cm) long extended

£320-380 **L&T**

A Japanese bronze shouldered vase, with relief and incised silver decoration of two bears by a stream, the base with oval impressed mark.

10in (25cm) high

£280-330 **L&T**

A pair of Japanese Meiji period metal and bronze vases, each with gold, copper, and a shakudo bird perched on a flowering branch, signed.

6in (15cm) high

£300-350 **S&K**

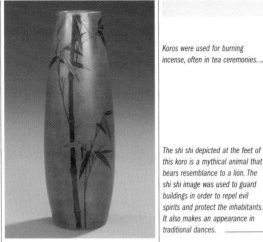

A Japanese Meiji period bronze vase, of ovoid form with bamboo branch motif, signed.

7in (17.5cm) high

£150-200 **S&K**

A CLOSER LOOK AT A SILVER KORO

Koros were used for burning incense, often in tea ceremonies.

Despite, its small size and missing finial, this is a very valuable piece. It was made by the highly regarded Katsuyoshi (1830-1909).

The shi shi depicted at the feet of this koro is a mythical animal that bears resemblance to a lion. The shi shi image was used to guard buildings in order to repel evil spirits and protect the inhabitants. It also makes an appearance in traditional dances.

The globular shape of the body, the pierced lid and the three supporting feet are typical of koro design. The fine decoration on this example is highly intricate.

A Japanese silver and mixed metal tripod Koro, of ovoid form cast with cockerels, the cover with flower head, shi shi head legs.

5in (12.5cm) high

£28,000-32,000 **S&K**

A Japanese Meiji period fine silver and Shibayama bowl, of Kikugata form, decorated with a central kinji panel depicting a Shojo balancing an enormous sakazuki on his head, with a large saki ladle behind, the exterior chased with a profusion of overlapping flowerheads, signed "Watanabe Katsutoshi".

9.25in (23cm) diam

£8,000-12,000 **L&T**

A Japanese Showa period silver dish, of petal form, chased to depict a flowering branch, with a bamboo shaped upright handle, signed.

£100-150 **S&K**

A Japanese bronze water dropper.

2.75in (7cm) high

£400-500 **DB**

A 12thC-13thC Burmese bronze figure of Buddha, seated in dhyanasana on a tall shaped pedestal, his right hand in bhumisparsa mudra, the left in dhyana mudra, wearing a sanghati.

9.75in (25cm) high

£300-400 **S&K**

A Tibetan gilt bronze figure of Buddha, sitting cross legged on a lotus throne, six character Yongle mark.

7in (18cm) high

£800-1,200 **WW**

A Thai Bangkok period bronze crowned head of Buddha, Ayutthaya style, his face with a benign expression, his hair arranged in a high chignon and crowned with a diadem.

7in (18cm) high

£250-350 **S&K**

A Vietnamese Dong Son culture bronze vessel, cast with geometric designs, double loop handles.

c750BC *9.5in (24cm) high*

£2,200-2,800 **S&K**

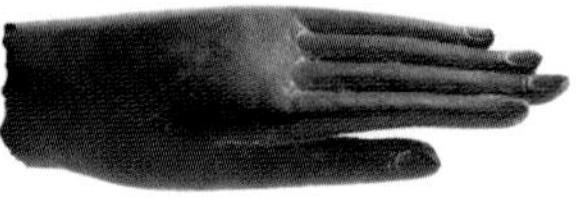

A 15thC Thai bronze Buddha hand, with a wooden stand.

9in (22.5cm) high

£300-400 **TA**

NETSUKE

Netsuke (toggles) were in everyday use throughout the Edo and Meiji periods of Japanese history. From them were suspended 'sagemono', receptacles hung below the sash of a kimono for storage. Although functional, netsuke were also highly decorative, and the netsukeshi craftsmen produced innumerable designs in materials as diverse as wood, stone, ivory and amber. Very few were signed, so it is often impossible to trace the pedigree of a particular piece unless the craftsman had a particularly distinctive oeuvre. Netsuke fall into four broad categories: katabori are the most common, compact netsuke; sashi are long and thin; kagamibuta are spherical and lidded; and manju are rounder and flat. The single most important factor governing the value of a netsuke is the quality of the carving, although subject matter is also influential. Netsuke gradually fell out of use along with the kimono, and many of the best examples are now in western collections.

An 18thC Japanese ivory netsuke, depicting a monkey trainer.

2in (5cm) long

£1,000-1,500 **DB**

A Japanese ivory netsuke mask, by Sigkogyoko.

1.25in (3cm) wide

£700-900 **DB**

A 19thC japanese ivory netsuke of an Oriental man making his escape with a huge tobacco pouch which he has purloined, signed Ickiya, one toe chipped.

1.75in (4.5cm) high

£220-280 **WW**

A 19thC Japanese ivory netsuke group, of Ashinaga and Tenaga.

3.25in (8.5cm) long

£2,000-2,500 **DB**

A Japanese ivory netsuke, by Sig Gyokusai.

1.5in (3.5cm) wide

£400-450 **DB**

An 18thC Japanese ivory netsuke, of a shishi dog.

1.75in (4.5cm) long

£1,500-2,000 **DB**

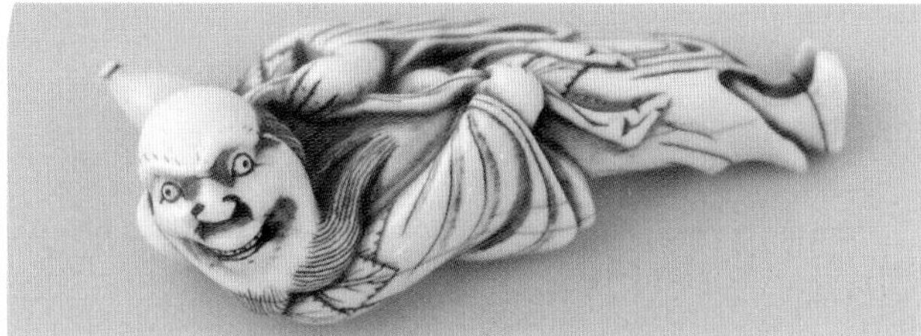

A Japanese ivory netsuke, by Sennin.

3in (7.5cm) long

£1,500-2,000 **DB**

An 18thC Japanese ivory netsuke, depicting a shishi dog.

2in (5cm) long

£1,200-1,800 **DB**

A Japanese ivory netsuke, depicting an elephant, inset with diamonds and rubies.

2.25in (6cm) long

£3,200-3,800 **DB**

An early 19thC Japanese ivory netsuke carved as the dried body of a large fish, its jaw being nibbled by a rat with inlaid eyes, the cord holes running from one side up through the fish's mouth.

5.5in (14cm) long

£500-700 **CHEF**

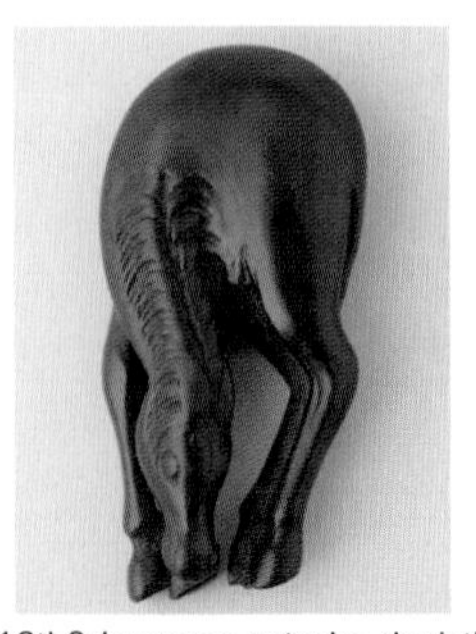

An 18thC Japanese netsuke, depicting a grazing horse.

3in (8cm) high

£2,000-2,500 **DB**

A Japanese wood netsuke, depicting a rat.

2in (5.5cm) long

£1,500-2,000 **DB**

A Japanese netsuke, depicting a toad on a leaf.

2in (5.5cm) long

£2,000-2,500 **DB**

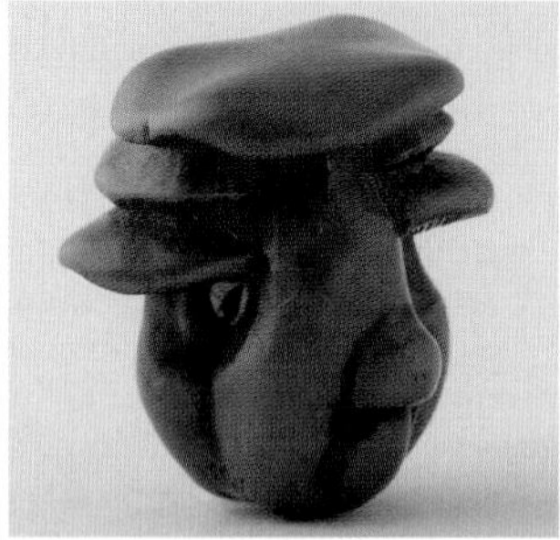

A 19thC Japanese wood netsuke, by Masanao, depicting a cluster of mushrooms.

1.5in (3.5cm) high

£800-1,200 **DB**

A 19thC Japanese wood netsuke mask.

1.5in (4cm) long

£320-380 **DB**

A Japanese wood netsuke mask, by Yuki Chika.

1.5in (4cm) long

£400-500 **DB**

A Japanese kutani porcelain cat, medium size.

These cats were made in four sizes: small, medium-small, medium and large.

2in (5cm) long

£800-1,200 **DB**

A Japanese Showa period hornbill netsuke, carved to depict a Chinese boy perched on a fruiting branch.

2.5in (6.5cm) long

£300-400 **S&K**

SNUFF BOTTLES

A 19thC Chinese amber snuff bottle.

2in (5.5cm) high

£2,000-2,500 **DB**

A 19thC Chinese agate snuff bottle.

2.5in (6.5cm) high

£600-900 **DB**

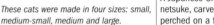

A CLOSER LOOK AT A CHINESE SNUFF BOTTLE

Chinese snuff bottles are typically cylindrical or flattened ovoid in form and were made from glass, porcelain, amber, coral, jade or laquer.

Snuff bottles were popular throughout the 18thC, but most date from the Daoguang period (1821-50) or later. Beware of modern replicas, new bottles and fakes.

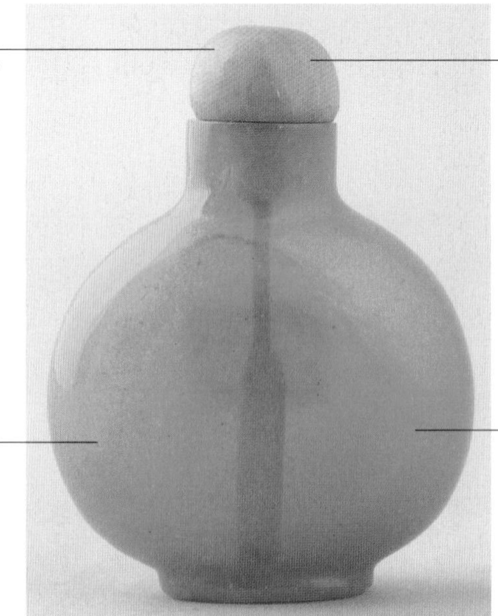

The imperial yellow colouring gives the bottle a distinctive finish.

As luxury items for wealthy individuals, snuff bottles were well made and attractively decorated. They remain very sought after by collectors today.

An 18thC Chinese Imperial yellow Peking glass snuff bottle.

2.25in (6cm) high

£3,000-3,500 **DB**

A 19thC Chinese agate snuff bottle.

2.75in (7cm) high

£1,200-1,800 **DB**

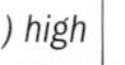

A Chinese inside-painted smoky crystal snuff bottle, by Ye Zhongsa.

2.25in (6cm) high

£700-1,000 **DB**

A Chinese hair crystal snuff bottle.

2in (5.5cm) high

£700-900 **DB**

A Chinese red overlay glass snuff bottle.

2.25in (6cm) high

£700-1,000 **DB**

A Chinese cloisonné snuff bottle.

2.5in (6.5cm) high

£600-800 **DB**

A Chinese porcelain snuff bottle.

2.25in (6cm) high

£300-500 **DB**

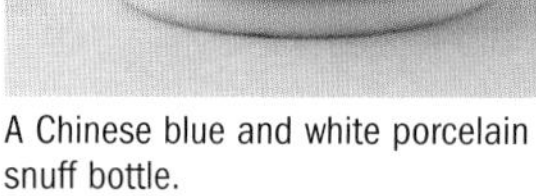

A Chinese blue and white porcelain snuff bottle.

3.25in (8.5cm) high

£400-500 **DB**

TEXTILES

A pair of Chinese arm bands, with hand-embroidered blue silk.

c1870 *33.5in (85cm) long*

£2,200-2,800 **S&K**

A pair of hand-embroidered Chinese cuffs.

c1890

£50-70 **ATL**

A Chinese embroidered silk rank badge.

c1870 *10.5in (27cm) high*

£330-50 **ATL**

A yard of fully embroidered silk, decorated with bats and chrysanthemums.

c1890 *38.5in (98cm) long*

£150-200 **ATL**

A Chinese embroidered magenta rose dragon coat, worked with couched gold threads on the front and back, depicting dragons chasing the flaming pearl of wisdom.

40.5in (101cm) long

£300-400 **S&K**

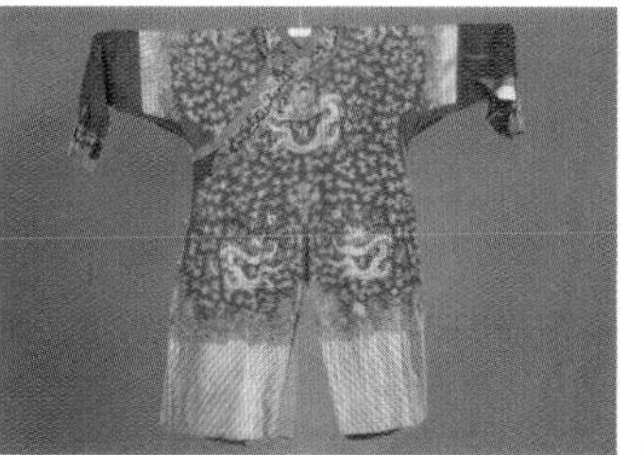

A Chinese embroidered blue silk dragon robe, worked with couched gold threads on the front and back, depicting dragons chasing the flaming pearl of wisdom.

52in (130cm) long

£450-550 **S&K**

OTHER WORKS OF ART

A Chinese Peking blue overlay glass vase, carved cartouches, a four character Qianlong mark.

£1,200-1,800 **S&K**

A 20thC Chinese Peking enamel vase, with floral decoration on a light blue ground.

11in (28cm) high

£80-120 **S&K**

A Chinese Qing dynasty red cinnabar lacquer vase, of pear form.

12.5in (31.5cm) high

£500-700 **S&K**

A Japanese carved wood figure of a terrapin, with young on its back, signed.

4.75in (12cm) wide

£400-600 **GORL**

Two Japanese Meiji period gilt lacquer boxes, of square form, one two tier, one three tier, each gilt with flowering branches and grasses, two on Nashiji ground.

18in (45.5cm) wide

£280-320 **S&K**

An early 20thC Chinese wood figure of an Immortal, standing holding a stick.

Provenance: *acquired in Japan in the 1940s.*

12in (30.5cm) high

£100-150 **S&K**

A 20thC Chinese lavender stone carving, depicting two dragons and the pearl of wisdom.

4.25in (11cm) high

£200-300 **S&K**

A 20thC Chinese serpentine bird, carved perched on a flowering branch.

8.5in (21.5cm) high

£120-180 **S&K**

A Chinese rock crystal carved figure of a monk.

4in (10cm) high

£180-220 **GORL**

A Chinese carved white soapstone vase and cover, carved in high relief to depict pavilions under pine trees, electrified.

11.5in (29cm) high

£250-300 **S&K**

A Chinese Qing dynasty wood birdcage, with two blue and white porcelain feeding bowls.

c1900 *32in (80cm) high*

£120-180 **S&K**

A 20thC Chinese Qing dynasty brass gong and beechwood stand, the stand carved with stylized dragon openwork.

32in (80cm) high

£250-300 **S&K**

CABINETS

A Tibetan polychrome wood cabinet, of rectangular outline, with two rows of three panels opening to an interior with one shelf, painted to depict flowering branches.

c1800 *52.75in (134cm) wide*

£350-450 **S&K**

A Tibetan polychrome wood cabinet, of rectangular section, with two panel doors flanked by two panels, opening to an interior with one shelf, above three panels and a straight apron, with floral decoration on red ground.

c1810 *49.5in (126cm) wide*

£350-450 **S&K**

A Tibetan polychrome wood cabinet, of rectangular outline, with two panels and two panel doors above three panels, the doors opening to an interior with one shelf, painted overall with animal motifs on red ground.

c1830 *56in (142cm) wide*

£300-400 **S&K**

TIBETAN FURNITURE

- Tibetan antique furniture was not widely available in the West until the 1990s.
- Most Tibetans live nomadic lifestyles and do not need much furniture. In ancient Tibet, the ownership of wooden furniture was restricted to monasteries and the wealthy. Many of these pieces were destroyed during the Chinese Cultural Revolution, making it even scarcer.
- Most of the furniture available today consists of chests, cabinets and finely carved tables. It may be decorated with paintings of animals, religious symbols, dragons or scenes of everyday life.
- Chests and cabinets are usually decorated on the front; low tables were used for tea or reading; taller tables were altar tables.
- There are many fakes about. From the late 18thC, cabinets became more popular, due to the influence of China on the country.
- Although the market for Tibetan furniture is growing, it is still believed to be undervalued, making it affordable.

A CLOSER LOOK AT A TIBETAN WOOD CABINET

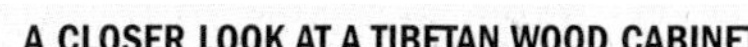

The colours on the cabinet have remained bright and clear, but some wear is visible. Beware of cabinets in perfect condition as many on the market have been retouched, repainted, or may even be less-valuable reproductions.

This piece is of typical construction, with fixed and opening panels, a single shelf and a skirt between the body and the floor.

Cabinets were used for storage. They were often placed next to each other, so rich decoration generally appears on the front and is less frequently seen to the sides.

The compact size of the cabinet makes it a suitable addition to a modern home.

A Tibetan polychrome wood cabinet, of rectangular section, with two rows of two panel doors flanked by two panels, each opening to an interior with one shelf, with floral decoration on red ground.

c1810 *49in (124.5cm) wide*

£700-900 **S&K**

A Tibetan polychrome wood cabinet, of rectangular section, with two rows of two panel doors flanked by two panels, each opening to an interior with one shelf, with floral decoration on red ground.

c1850 *52.5in (133.5cm) wide*

£350-450 **S&K**

A Tibetan polychrome wood cabinet, of rectangular outline, with two panels and two doors above three panels, on legs of square section, painted overall with floral decoration.

c1850 *47.5in (120.5cm) wide*

£600-700 **S&K**

A Tibetan polychrome cypress cabinet, the rectangular top above three drawers and two doors, with floral decoration.

c1850 *50.5in (126cm) wide*

£500-800 **S&K**

A Tibetan polychrome cypress altar table, of rectangular outline with two doors, fu dog decoration on ochre ground.

c1850 *28.5in (71cm) wide*

£200-250 **S&K**

A Tibetan polychrome cypress altar table, of rectangular outline with one long side drawer, panels with floral decoration.

c1850 *27in (67.5cm) wide*

£200-250 **S&K**

A Tibetan polychrome cypress altar table, the rectangular outline above one long side drawer, a shaped apron, floral decoration.

c1850 *30.5in (76cm) wide*

£320-380 **S&K**

A Tibetan polychrome wood low cabinet, of square outline, the side with two panel doors opening to an interior of one shelf, the other three sides with two panels, painted all over with floral motif on red ground.

c1880 *27.75in (70.5cm) wide*

£350-450 **S&K**

A Chinese red lacquered wood cabinet, of rectangular outline, with two drawers over two doors opening to an interior with one shelf, painted with figural and mountainous landscape decoration, Shanxi Province, Qing dynasty.

c1850 *33.25in (84.5cm) high*

£350-550 **S&K**

A Chinese red lacquered wood cabinet, of square outline, with two doors and a panel apron, painted to depict precious objects and with floral and bird motifs, Qing dynasty.

c1850 *43.25in (110cm) wide*

£300-500 **S&K**

A Chinese gilt and red lacquered wood chest, of rectangular form, painted to depict figures and a pavilion in a garden, Qing dynasty.

c1860 *27in (68.5cm) wide*

£250-350 **S&K**

LACQUERWARE

- The lacquer tree (Rhus vernicifera) is native to China, Japan and Korea. Very thin layers of its sap can be used to create a highly resistant surface.
- The process is very time consuming as every layer must be allowed to dry before the next one is applied.
- From c206BC Chinese craftsmen developed increasingly elaborate forms of decoration for what was originally a protective coating. Variations included red lacquer (created by adding cinnabar), gold lacquer, carving and mother-of-pearl inlay.
- Lacquerware was highly prized in China, and in the 16thC lacquer items started to be imported to the West as luxury goods.
- It was used to decorate furniture, trays, boxes and vases. Lacquerware should not be confused with Japanning, which is European painting and varnishing in the style of Oriental laquer.

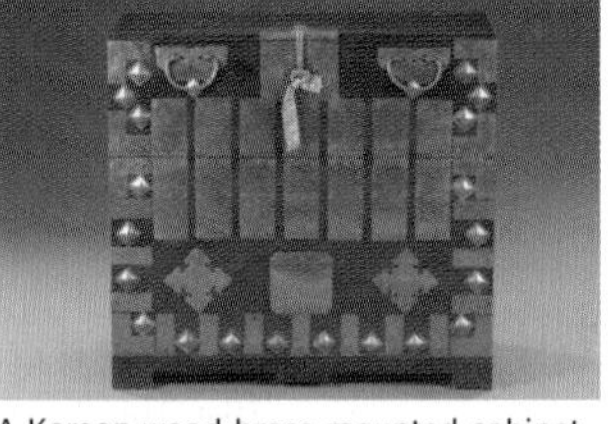

A Korean wood brass mounted cabinet, the rectangular hinged top above a panel à abattant.

33in (84cm) wide

£350-450 **S&K**

A 19thC Japanese mixed wood miniature cabinet, with a rectangular overhanging top above four small drawers and one deep drawer on bracket feet.

22in (55cm) wide

£120-180 **S&K**

A small Chinese red lacquered elm chest, with two drawers above an apron of scrolling foliage, Qing dynasty.

c1850 *40.25in (102cm) wide*

£120-180 **S&K**

A Korean wood brass mounted cabinet in two sections, the rectangular top above four small drawers and two doors, with a shaped skirt.

45.5in (115.5cm) high

£180-220 **S&K**

A late 16thC to early 17thC Chinese Nanmu cabinet, of rectangular outline composed of strikingly figured timber, on rectangular legs with a straight apron, the interior opening to two shelves and two drawers, Ming dynasty.

84in (213.5cm) high

£3,500-4,500 **S&K**

A Chinese black lacquered elm cabinet, of rectangular outline, with an open shelf with a stylized dragon apron and spandrels, above two panel doors opening to an interior with two drawers above one shelf, supported on cabriole legs, Ming dynasty, Wanli.

c1650 *75.5in (192cm) high*

£450-550 **S&K**

A large Chinese gilt and red lacquered cabinet, of rectangular outline, with two panel doors opening to an interior with one shelf, above a shaped apron, painted to depict precious objects, Ming dynasty, Wanli.

81in (205.5cm) high

£800-1,200 **S&K**

A Chinese red lacquered elmwood cabinet, of rectangular outline with four doors painted with medallions on a brocade ground, Shanxi province.

c1750 *79.5in (202cm) high*

£700-1,000 **S&K**

A Chinese red lacquered elmwood cabinet, of rectangular outline with two doors opening on two shelves, painted to depict a mountainous landscape, the apron carved in high relief with two dragons.

c1750 *77.5in (197cm) high*

£800-1,200 **S&K**

A Chinese lacquered elmwood cabinet, in two parts, the top with two openwork doors, above two doors opening on two drawers and one shelf, Shanxi province.

c1820 *39in (99cm) high*

£650-750 **S&K**

A Chinese gilt and red lacquered wood cabinet, of rectangular outline, with two doors opening to an interior with one shelf, painted with floral decoration, Shanxi province, Qing dynasty.

c1830 *45in (114cm) high*

£350-450 **S&K**

A Chinese gilt and red lacquered wood cabinet, of rectangular outline, with two panel doors opening to an interior with one shelf, painted overall to depict flower filled vases and precious objects, Qing dynasty.

c1830 *55.75in (141.5cm) high*

£300-400 **S&K**

A Chinese gilt and red lacquered wood cabinet, of rectangular outline, with two doors opening to an interior with two shelves, above a shaped apron, painted to depict children at play, Shanxi province, Qing dynasty.

c1830 *57in (145cm) high*

£300-400 **S&K**

A Chinese gilt and red lacquered wood cabinet, of rectangular outline, with two panel doors opening to an interior with one shelf above a shaped apron, painted overall to depict a garden and mountainous landscape, Qing dynasty.

c1830 *50.75in (129cm) high*

£300-400 **S&K**

A Chinese red lacquered wood cabinet, of rectangular outline, the two doors opening to an interior with one shelf, painted with figural and mountainous landscape decoration, Shanxi province, Qing dynasty.

c1850 *41in (104cm) high*

£400-600 **S&K**

A Chinese red lacquered elm cabinet, of rectangular outline, with two doors above three small drawers, Qing dynasty.

c1850 *62in (157.5cm) high*

£200-300 **S&K**

A Chinese lacquered elm medicine chest, of rectangular section with multiple small square drawers, Shanxi Province, Qing dynasty.

c1850 *66in (168cm) high*

£250-350 **S&K**

One of a pair of Chinese red lacquered elmwood cabinets, of rectangular outline with two doors opening on one shelf and two drawers, Shandong Province, the lacquer is 20thC.

c1850 *70in (178cm) high*

£700-1,000 pair **S&K**

A 19thC Chinese red lacquered elmwood cabinet, of rectangular outline with two doors opening on two shelves, painted to depict children at play, Shanxi province.

71in (180.5cm) high

£500-700 **S&K**

A Chinese gilt and red lacquered wood cabinet, of rectangular outline with two doors over a panel, opening to an interior with one shelf, painted overall with floral and bird motif, Qing dynasty.

c1860 *68in (173cm) high*

£600-800 **S&K**

A Chinese black lacquered elm cabinet, of rectangular outline with two doors, painted to depict flowering trees and birds, Qing dynasty.

c1860 *73in (185.5cm) high*

£180-220 **S&K**

A Chinese Art Deco hardwood cabinet, of rectangular outline, with two doors opening on two sections, one with two shelves.

Provenance: *acquired from Hillcrest, Lattingtown, Long Island, Mrs Chiang Kai Shek's estate.*

c1930 *49in (124.5cm) high*

£180-220 **S&K**

A Chinese lacquered cabinet on stand, the cabinet with two cupboard doors decorated with figures amongst pagodas and birds with foliage, with ornate brass mounts enclosing various similarly decorated drawers, on a later base fitted with five drawers, the chamfered square legs joined by a shaped galleried undertier.

19.5in (50cm) wide

£1,000-1,500 **L&T**

TABLES

A pair of Chinese elmwood wine tables, each with a rectangular top above a straight beaded apron, the legs of square section ending in hoof feet and joined by a high arched stretcher, Shanxi province.

c1720 *36.5in (92.5cm) wide*

£650-750 **S&K**

A Chinese walnut altar table, the rectangular top with everted ends, with rectangular legs jointed by a pierced panel, Shanxi province.

c1750 *72.5in (184cm) long*

£550-650 **S&K**

A pair of Chinese beechwood stands, the square top above one drawer, Shanxi province.

c1750 *33in (84cm) high*

£350-450 **S&K**

A Chinese rosewood square side table, made for the English market, with a carved apron and circular legs, the stretcher depicting prunus blossoms, Qing dynasty.

24in (61cm) high

£150-200 **S&K**

A Chinese black lacquered wood altar table, of rectangular form, with spandrels above joined legs and cut out sides, Qing dynasty.

c1800 *63.75in (162cm) wide*

£300-500 **S&K**

A Chinese elmwood altar table, of rectangular outline, with a panel top over rectangular legs, Qing dynasty.

c1800 *61.25in (155.5cm) wide*

£250-350 **S&K**

A Chinese elmwood altar table, of rectangular outline, the panel top supported by a pierced shaped apron and rectangular legs joined by a frame and stretchers, Qing dynasty.

c1850 *94in (229cm) wide*

£300-500 **S&K**

A Chinese lacquered elm side table, the rectangular top above one drawer above two panels, apron and spandrels with scrolling foliage motif, Shanxi Province, Qing dynasty.

c1850 *38.75in (98cm) wide*

£150-200 **S&K**

A Chinese lacquered elmwood low table, the rectangular top above three drawers, the skirt with open work depicting a dragon, Shanxi province.

c1800 *53.5in (136cm) long*

£250-350 **S&K**

A Chinese elmwood bench, the rectangular top above a beaded apron with scroll spandrels, on rectangular legs with two stretchers, Shanxi province.

c1820 *63in (160cm) long*

£200-300 **S&K**

A Chinese beechwood stand, the square top above one drawer and a crackle ice shelf, Shanxi province.

c1850 *30.5in (77.5cm) high*

£180-220 **S&K**

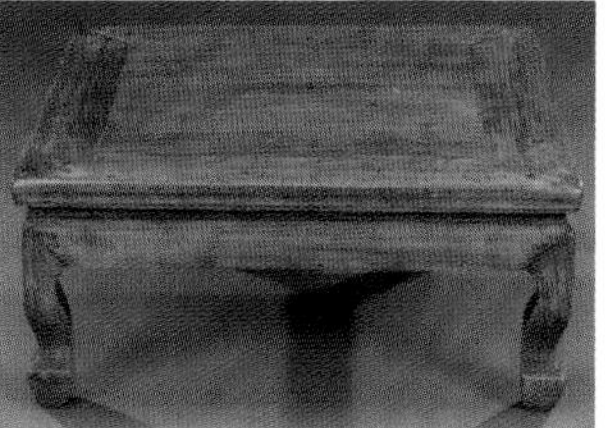

One of a pair of Chinese elm low tables, each with a curved apron and cabriole legs, Qing dynasty.

c1850 *27in (68.5cm) wide*

£180-220 pair **S&K**

A Chinese beechwood desk, the rectangular top above three drawers and a carved apron, Shuzhou province.

c1850 *45.5in (115.5cm) long*

£350-450 **S&K**

A Chinese elmwood table, the rectangular top above two drawers, carved to depict a dragon and a phoenix, Shanxi province.

c1850 *40in (101.5cm) wide*

£500-600 **S&K**

A Chinese elmwood bench, the rectangular top above a shaped and beaded apron, the shaped rectangular legs ending on tiger paw feet, Shanxi province.

c1880 *43in (109cm) long*

£180-220 **S&K**

A Japanese lacquer rectangular tray and stand, Meiji period, with mon and calligraphy decoration.

12.5in (31cm) wide

£100-150 **S&K**

A Chinese red lacquered wood D-form table, with wide rounded apron with angular scrolling motif on cabriole legs ending in scroll feet, Qing dynasty.

c1890 *38.5in (98cm) wide*

£280-320 **S&K**

A Chinese hardwood altar table, the panelled rectangular top with scrolled ends above an apron frieze carved with dragons to both sides, enclosed by scrolled brackets and opposed side drawers, the whole raised on moulded supports linked by stretchers.

48in (122cm) high

£300-500 **L&T**

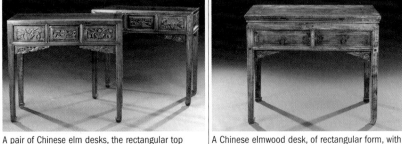

A pair of Chinese elm desks, the rectangular top above three drawers carved in high relief to depict floral sprays, supported on legs of square section, Shanxi province, Qing dynasty.

c1850 *37.75in (96cm) wide*

£480-520 **S&K**

A Chinese elmwood desk, of rectangular form, with two drawers over a straight apron, with spandrels of scrolling foliage, Qing dynasty.

c1880 *40in (102cm) wide*

£200-300 **S&K**

A Chinese red lacquered wood desk, the rectangular top above three drawers supported on square legs, Qing dynasty.

c1890 *45.25in (115cm) wide*

£400-500 **S&K**

A Chinese elmwood desk, of rectangular outline, with two drawers over an open work apron, spandrels carved to depict stylized dragons, Qing dynasty.

c1880 *40in (101cm) wide*

£200-300 **S&K**

CHAIRS

A Chinese elmwood official's hat chair, Shanxi province.

c1750

£280-320 S&K

A pair of Chinese lacquered elmwood official's hat armchairs, inscribed on the splat, from the private temple of the Lee family, Shanxi province.

c1780

£400-600 S&K

A pair of Chinese elmwood official's hat chairs, each with a shaped crest rail, curved back splat and shaped apron, Qing dynasty.

c1850

£350-450 S&K

A pair of Chinese black lacquered wood chairs, each with a shaped crest rail, curved back splat with lotus motif, Qing dynasty.

c1850

£180-220 S&K

A pair of Chinese Ming style elmwood chairs, each with a shaped crest rail, curved back splat with open work cartouches above a beaded apron, Qing dynasty.

c1850

£450-550 S&K

A near pair of Chinese beechwood stools, the square top above a beaded apron, on rectangular legs and stretchers, Shanxi province.

c1850 *18.5in (46cm) high*

£180-220 S&K

A pair of Chinese children's red lacquered wooden chairs, each with a back splat with a cartouche enclosing floral decoration, above a green glazed apron, on legs of circular section, Qing dynasty.

c1860

£180-220 S&K

Two of a set of six Chinese hardwood folding chairs, each with cane back and seat, crest rail with carved scrolling motif, Qing dynasty.

c1880

£600-700 set S&K

A Chinese stained hardwood armchair, the shaped rectangular back with a vase shaped splat carved in relief with fruiting branches, the arms filled with similarly carved panels above a solid seat on square stepped legs linked by stretchers.

£180-220 L&T

A CLOSER LOOK AT A PAIR OF HUANGHUALI ARMCHAIRS

Furniture made from Huanghuali, or 'yellow flowering pear' wood, was introduced during the Ming dynasty. The wood was prized for its attractive grain and durability. and was usually used to produce high quality items.

The splat, the central vertical member of a chair back, is made from a network of criss-crossing straight pieces of wood, forming a lattice.

Chairs need to be checked for restoration or strengthening, especially at the vulnerable junction between the stile and the top rail.

Chinese furniture became popular in Europe during the late Qing period, and a successful export trade developed.

A pair of rare Chinese Huanghuali horse-shoe armchairs, each with a 'U'-shaped bamboo-form carved crest rail and cane seat, with a lattice splat.

£4,000-6,000 S&K

SCREENS

A Chinese black coromandel lacquer twelve-panel screen, depicting a palace garden with figures within a border of fan-shaped reserves enclosing a riverscape.

108in (274.5cm) high

£2,200-2,800 **S&K**

A Chinese red lacquered elm four panel screen, of rectangular outline, with open work to depict birds, animals and scrolling foliage, Qing dynasty.

c1800 *82.5in (210cm) high*

£220-280 **S&K**

A Chinese black, red and gilt lacquered elm wood six panel screen, Qing dynasty, each upper section with open work, the solid lower section with a narrow panel above a larger panel.

c1810 *79in (200.5cm) high*

£450-550 **S&K**

One of a pair of Japanese six panel screens, the panels with a continuous landscape, Edo period.

c1750 *67in (167.5cm) high*

£1,800-2,200 pair **S&K**

OTHER ORIENTAL FURNITURE

A pair of Chinese elmwood benches, each of rectangular shape, supported on legs of square section joined by high stretchers, Qing dynasty.

c1860 *47.5in (120.5cm) wide*

£300-400 **S&K**

A pair of Chinese walnut wood benches, the rectangular top supported on legs of square section joined by high stretchers, Qing dynasty.

c1880 *44.5in (113cm) wide*

£220-280 **S&K**

A pair of Chinese lacquered elm stands, each with a drawer above legs of square section, Shanxi Province, Qing dynasty.

c1830 *33.5in (85cm) high*

£300-400 **S&K**

A large Tibetan polychrome wood trunk, of rectangular outline painted to depict two confronting dragons holding the pearl of wisdom amongst flowering branches, the side panels with faux tiger skin decoration, iron mounts.

c1850 *53.25in (135cm) wide*

£550-650 **S&K**

An early 19thC small Tibetan polychrome wood box.

19in (48cm) wide

£220-280 **S&K**

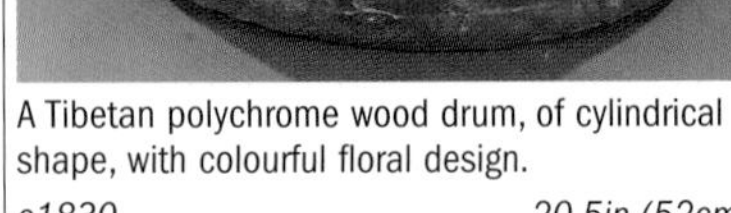

A Tibetan polychrome wood drum, of cylindrical shape, with colourful floral design.

c1830 *20.5in (52cm) high*

£350-450 **S&K**

FURNITURE

Media and technology are changing the face of the furniture market. Thanks to the influence and popularity of makeover and antiques programmes, people are better informed and no longer content to buy pieces simply because they are old. More demanding buyers are looking for good quality pieces in excellent condition. People are seeking unusual or unique furniture and only special pieces realise very high prices.

The lower end of the market is moving slowly, although towards the top end, furniture is still selling well. However, condition is critical: buyers are much less willing to spend extra money and time restoring items in poor condition and only really good, museum-quality pieces fetch the top prices.

Always a difficult area, bedroom furniture is selling badly, as more than ever, buyers are looking for modern, streamlined, fitted pieces to maximise on space and to create a 'look'.

Bureaux are down to less than half their previous value because buyers are choosing purpose-built pieces to hold all the computer components required in the modern office or study. This has had a major impact on kneehole desks, which are not selling well unless they are unusual and in prime condition. As offices modernise, large pieces are coming on to the market but unless they are in pristine condition, they are not selling.

There is a good deal of movement in the Eastern-influenced furniture market. Pieces are proving popular here and demand is increasing as buyers in the countries of origin are beginning to enter the market too.

With the dollar struggling, American buyers are not spending much money in Europe. The effect that this will have on the market as a whole is yet to be seen.

Paul Roberts, Lyon & Turnbull

BOOKCASES

A German Baroque walnut bookcase secrétaire, in two parts, with an interior fitted with shaped shelves and drawers, centring an arched prospect door, the lower section fitted with three long drawers above a moulded base, raised on bracket feet.

46in (117cm) wide

£5,000-8,000 **NA**

A George II walnut slant-front secrétaire, the moulded cornice above a pair of panelled doors opening to a fitted interior, the slant-lid opening to a stepped fitted interior, above two short and two long drawers, raised on a moulded base and with bracket feet.

38in (96.5cm) wide

£3,000-5,000 **NA**

An 18thC Dutch walnut and marquetry bombe bureau bookcase, inlaid with exotic birds, cherubs, urns and foliage, the glazed panel doors enclosing shelves and candle slides, the lower section with a fall-front enclosing a fitted interior with pigeonholes, drawers, a central cupboard door and a covered well, above three drawers, on carved hairy claw and ball feet joined by a wavy apron.

48in (122cm) wide

£2,000-3,000 **FRE**

A George III mahogany secrétaire bookcase, the associated top above two glazed doors enclosing adjustable shelves, the lower section with a secrétaire drawer, fitted with a writing surface and various pigeon holes, above three graduated long drawers on splayed bracket feet.

42in (107cm) wide

£500-800 **L&T**

A CLOSER LOOK AT A GEORGE III LIBRARY BOOKCASE

The moulding to the doors has a semicircular section known as 'astragal', or bead moulding. This shape is often found on the glazing bars of bookcases.

Large quantities of mahogany were imported into Europe from Jamaica and South America from c1730. The width of its boards and its strength made it a popular material for larger items of furniture like this bookcase.

During the 1780s furniture form became more refined. Imported woods were used for decorative effects such as veneering.

Secrétaire drawers open to create a writing surface. This one also conceals a variety of drawers and pigeonholes for safely storing papers.

A good George III mahogany library bookcase, the raised top above an arch-moulded cornice and four astragal-glazed doors, opening to adjustable shelves, the lower section with a central secrétaire drawer with a satinwood-veneered, fitted interior of pigeonholes, drawers and an inset leather writing surface, four oval-panelled cupboard doors enclosing drawers and shelves, raised on a plinth base.

c1780 *101in (256.5cm) wide*

£10,000-15,000 **FRE**

A George III mahogany bureau bookcase of small proportions, the moulded cornice above astragal-glazed doors enclosing adjustable shelves and candle slides, the tall front with a fitted interior above four long graduating drawers and lopers, with shaped bracket feet.

31in (80cm) wide

£800-1,200 **L&T**

A George III mahogany secrétaire bookcase, the moulded dentilled cornice above twin astragal-glazed doors enclosing adjustable shelves, the secrétaire drawer with a false front opening to reveal an interior fitted with drawers and pigeonholes, above three long graduated drawers, bracket feet.

45.5in (116cm) wide

£5,000-8,000 **L&T**

A George III secrétaire bookcase, with astragal-glazed doors enclosing an interior with adjustable shelves, below a dentilled cornice and swan neck pediment, the base with three boxwood-strung graduated drawers and a crossbanded secrétaire drawer, the interior fitted with drawers and pigeonholes, shaped bracket feet, a later mirror back.

44in (112cm) wide

£3,000-5,000 **L&T**

A late George III mahogany bureau bookcase, the moulded, fluted cornice above twin astragal-glazed doors, enclosing adjustable shelves above a sloping fall, enclosing a fitted interior, with four long graduated drawers, on bracket feet.

50.75in (129cm) high

£1,200-1,800 **L&T**

A George III mahogany bureau bookcase, the swan neck pediment with pierced lattice fretwork, above two astragal-glazed doors enclosing adjustable shelves, the sloping fall enclosing a fitted interior with drawers and pigeonholes above four graduated drawers, on ogee bracket feet.

45.75in (116cm) wide

£4,000-6,000 **L&T**

A George III mahogany bookcase, the moulded cornice above a pair of astragal-glazed doors enclosing adjustable shelves, raised on a deeper base with a pair of panelled doors and splayed bracket feet.

42in (107cm) high

£2,500-3,000 **L&T**

A Georgian walnut slant-lid secrétaire in two parts, the upper mirrored doors opening to three shelves above compartments and candle slides, the lower case with a channel-moulded lid with banded inlay, the stepped interior with a central prospect door, flanked by document drawers with half-round, burled columns and compartments, above small drawers over two drawers, on bracket feet.

41.5in (105.5cm) wide

£3,500-4,500 **NA**

A George III mahogany slant-front secrétaire bookcase, in two parts, the rectangular dentilled cornice above a pair of bevelled mirrored doors opening to a shelved interior, over a pair of candle slides, the slant-front opening to reveal a series of drawers and compartments, above drawers, raised on bracket feet.

38in (96.5cm) high

£3,500-4,500 **NA**

A George III small mahogany break-front bookcase secrétaire, in two parts, the moulded pediment crest and cornice over a pair of astragal-glazed doors and single doors, opening to shelved interiors, the lower section with a hinged drawer opening to a tooled leather writing surface and a fitted interior, two lower panelled doors, opening to a shelved interior, flanked by two banks of five graduated drawers, raised on a moulded plinth.

55in (140cm) wide

£4,000-6,000 **NA**

A Regency mahogany secrétaire bookcase, with ebony stringing, the projecting cornice with a reeded frieze above twin glazed doors with reeded astragals, enclosing adjustable shelves, the base with reeded edge above a panelled secrétaire drawer, enclosing an inset tooled leather writing surface and satinwood veneered drawers and pigeonholes, above two panelled doors enclosing sliding shelves and raised on curved feet, frieze to cornice reduced.

50.5in (128cm) wide

£3,000-5,000 **L&T**

An early 19thC ebonised and gilt bookcase cabinet, the waterfall open shelved top raised on a base with a single drawer above a panelled door enclosing a shelved interior, on a shaped apron with splayed bracket feet.

17.75in (45cm) wide

£600-900 **L&T**

An early 19thC Scottish reverse break-front mahogany bookcase, the central section with a pair of astragal-glazed doors enclosing adjustable shelves, flanked by taller corresponding sections, all with bead and reel moulded cornice above a base with doors enclosing shelves, the central section with a shallow drawer fitted with writing slope.

100.5in (255cm) wide

£8,000-12,000 **L&T**

A late Regency mahogany bookcase, the upper section with two sets of open adjustable shelves divided by horizontally fluted projecting columns, raised on a corresponding deeper base with four projecting doors on a plinth with bun feet, with ebonised mouldings.

87.25in (218cm) wide

£3,500-4,500 **L&T**

A 19thC mahogany bookcase, the projecting and moulded cornice above four glazed doors with arched mouldings, enclosing adjustable shelves, the base with a moulded rim above four moulded panel doors, fitted with shelves and drawers and raised on a plinth.

89in (226cm) wide

£4,000-6,000 **L&T**

A 19thC mahogany break-front library bookcase, in the Chinese Chippendale manner, the dentil cornice and blind fret-carved frieze above four astragal-glazed doors enclosing adjustable shelves, the lower section with four further panelled cupboard doors enclosing shelves, raised on a plinth base, lacks pediment.

93.5in (234cm) high

£4,000-6,000 **FRE**

A CLOSER LOOK AT A VICTORIAN BREAK-FRONT BOOKCASE

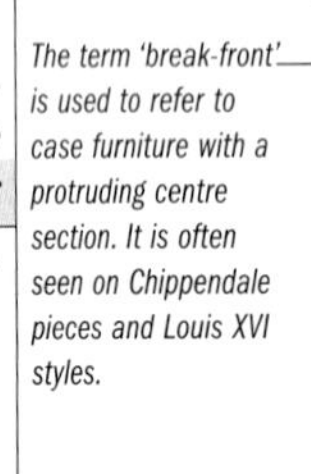

The term 'break-front' is used to refer to case furniture with a protruding centre section. It is often seen on Chippendale pieces and Louis XVI styles.

Book ownership increased during the 19thC and the private library became more fashionable. Grand storage furniture was created to meet the increased demand of the nouveau riche.

Rosewood is a hard, heavy wood from the tropical Dalbergia tree. Used sparingly for decorative finishes in the 18thC, it became an increasingly popular material for solid furniture during the 19thC.

The substantial size and high quality of the workmanship make this a valuable piece.

An early Victorian rosewood break-front bookcase, bearing the label of William Johnson, Cabinet Maker, Sheffield, the moulded ogee cornice above a crossbanded frieze and three pairs of doors with arched glazed panels enclosing adjustable shelves, the deeper corresponding base with solid panelled doors enclosing shelves and drawers, on a plinth base.

122cm (310in) wide

£15,000-20,000 **L&T**

An Edwardian mahogany break-front bookcase, the moulded dentil cornice and plain frieze above four astragal-glazed doors enclosing adjustable shelves, raised on a deeper serpentine base with panelled cupboard doors enclosing shelves and drawers, on a plinth base.

102.25in (261cm) wide

£8,000-12,000 **L&T**

An early 20thC mahogany bookcase, the dentilled cornice above three astragal-glazed doors enclosing adjustable shelves, on a deeper base with three panel doors, a plinth base.

73in (186cm) wide

£2,500-3,500 **L&T**

A late 19thC Renaissance Revival walnut and burr-walnut cabinet bookcase, in two parts, the upper section with a moulded cornice and a pair of panelled doors above two small drawers, the lower section with a fossil-marble top over a slide, two frieze drawers and two panelled doors.

47.5in (120.5cm) wide

£1,800-2,200 **S&K**

A George III-style tall mahogany open bookcase, with satinwood crossbanding, the inverted-arch top with a fan medallion and inlaid flutes, above adjustable shelves and a bowfront door enclosing a shelf, splayed bracket feet.

17.75in (45cm) wide

£1,000-1,500 **L&T**

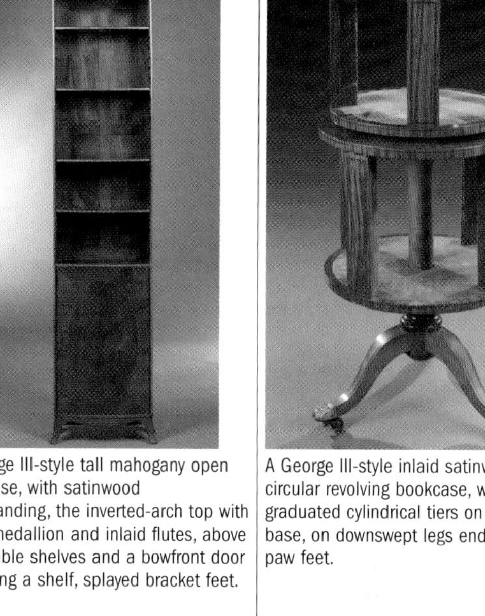

A George III-style inlaid satinwood circular revolving bookcase, with two graduated cylindrical tiers on a tripod base, on downswept legs ending in lion-paw feet.

17.75in (45cm) diam

£1,000-1,500 **S&K**

An unusual Regency mahogany and satinwood veneer enclosed bookcase, each side with a sliding panel opening to a central shelf.

c1800 *84cm (33in) high*

£2,000-4,000 **RGA**

An unusual George III mahogany and boxwood strung multi-drawer writing table, with ivory turned handles and a rear hinged flap, on four turned supports with an undertier.

c1800 *29in (73.5cm) high*

£3,500-4,500 **RGA**

A Regency rosewood and brass open bookcase, the four graduated shelves with spreading brass column supports and rear pilasters, with applied half columns, a pierced brass gallery to top shelf, on brass ball and claw feet.

40.75in (102cm) wide

£800-1,200 **L&T**

A late Regency rosewood open bookcase, the rectangular top above three compartments of adjustable shelves, with carved consoles, on a plinth base.

60in (153cm) wide

£2,000-2,500 **L&T**

A pair of Regency inlaid-mahogany small bookcases, each fitted with four graduated shelves centred by line-inlaid sides of conforming shape, raised on reeded bulbous feet, on casters.

27in (68.5cm) wide

£4,000-6,000 **NA**

A mahogany graduated bookcase, in the Regency style, with open shelves to each side, turned double-end supports and two stretchers, on square tapering feet with brass terminals and casters.

36in (9.5cm) wide

£500-700 **DN**

A Victorian walnut break-front bookcase, the raised back above adjustable shelves enclosed by glazed doors within carved flowers, on a plinth base, some locks stamped "Hobbs & Co, London".

78.75in (200cm) wide

£400-600 **WW**

An Edwardian mahogany revolving octagonal bookcase, with satinwood crossbanding, the chequer-strung top and undershelf divided by turned baluster supports, on a pedestal with four sabre legs.

22in (56cm) wide

£800-1,200 **L&T**

BUREAUX

A German Baroque mahogany slant-front desk, with bone or ivory marquetry, the top inlaid with a putto mask and vines, the slant-front with a chariot, putti, dragons and dolphins, the fitted interior with a sliding compartment, over three serpentine-fronted drawers inlaid with swans, serpents and grotesque masks, the sides inlaid with harpies, putti and urns, a moulded base and bracket feet.

45.5in (114cm) wide

£3,000-4,000 **NA**

An early Georgian-style walnut veneered slant-front desk, the slant-front opening to a fitted interior with two banks of three stepped drawers with wooden pulls, flanking five open compartments, the bead-moulded apron with an arched centre, raised on bead-moulded and tongue-carved cabriole legs ending in hoof feet, one pull missing.

40in (100cm) wide

£2,000-3,000 **S&K**

A rare mid-18thC walnut and box-strung miniature bureau, the stepped interior fitted with drawers and pigeonholes about a small mirror and chequer board inlay, five assorted small drawers below, lacks base.

10in (25.5cm) wide

£4,000-6,000 **WW**

A Louis XV-style rosewood bureau-de-dame, with kingwood-banding and marquetry, the fall front enclosing a fitted interior with shelves and three small drawers.

27.5in (70cm) wide

£400-600 **S&K**

A George III mahogany dwarf bureau, the fall front enclosing a fitted interior with a well above false drawers to front and sides, on square section tapering legs joined by an H-stretcher.

13in (33cm) wide

£600-900 **L&T**

A Georgian mahogany bureau, the fall front enclosing a fitted interior above lopers and four long graduated drawers, on bracket feet.

38in (96cm) wide

£600-900 **L&T**

A mid-19thC mahogany and crossbanded cylinder bureau, fitted interior with satinwood drawers and pigeonholes above baize lined pull-out slide, three small drawers above later square tapering legs and china casters.

34.25in (87cm) wide

£700-1,000 **WW**

A 19thC kingwood bureau-de-dame, the double serpentine, marble-inset top with a pierced gilt-metal gallery, above two serpentine doors enclosing shelves and inset with Sèvres-style porcelain panels, painted with putto and gilding, with porcelain pilasters and two further drawers, the base with a serpentine top, inlaid with a shaped Sèvres-style panel depicting a mother and her children, above a slide-out panel with a leather writing surface, a porcelain-inlaid panel and drawers, on square tapering cabriole legs with cast sabots.

27.5in (77cm) wide

£7,000-10,000 **L&T**

A 19thC walnut bureau, with crossbanding and chequer stringing, the fall front enclosing a burr-walnut veneered interior with a cupboard flanked by pigeonholes and drawers, above drawers with lopers, bracket feet.

39.75in (101cm) wide

£1,200-1,800 **L&T**

A late 19thC Louis XV-style kingwood and parquetry bureau, with gilt-metal mounts, the fall front enclosing pigeonholes and six stepped drawers.

35in (77cm) wide

£1,000-1,500 **S&K**

A late 19thC transitional Louis XV or XVI-style kingwood bureau-de-dame, inlaid with floral marquetry decoration and with gilt-brass mounts, the cylinder bureau inlaid with a harp, enclosing an interior with drawers and open shelves, above a leather-inset writing slide, with a pagoda top and a guilloche frieze, a marble top and brass gallery, the drawers above a shaped apron and tapering legs with sabots.

27.5in (70cm) wide

£3,000-4,000 **L&T**

CABINETS

An early 17thC oak press, with naive relief carving of vines and stylized flowers, the later dentil cornice above a frieze and a pair of twin fielded panel doors, above three further panels, the sides with four plain and fielded panels, raised on stile feet.

£1,200-1,800 **L&T**

A CLOSER LOOK AN OAK CUPBOARD

The turnings would have been made using a lathe that enabled the craftsman to cut a number of similar pieces.

The top of the cupboard supports a very good example of hand cut saw marks. This suggests the piece is early.

The colour of the surface, the patina, is built up through centuries of exposure to the environment, dust and repeated polishing.

Until the late 17thC, furniture makers tended to use indigenous materials. This cupboard is made of oak, which was favoured for its resistance to rot and woodworm, until it was superseded by walnut in the early 18thC.

A late 17thC English oak two tier hanging turner's cupboard, comprised of ring and baluster turnings and two central doors.

26.5in (67.5cm) wide

£10,000-15,000 **POOK**

A 17thC carved oak court cupboard, the moulded cornice above a scroll-carved frieze and a triple-panelled front, carved with flowerhead motifs and with two cupboard doors, the lower section with two further triple-panel, foliate-carved doors, raised on scroll feet, some restoration.

51in (129.5cm) high

£1,800-2,200 **FRE**

A late 17thC wall cabinet, marked "EM", probably for the maker or owner.

20in (51cm) high

£1,800-2,200 **EP**

An early 18thC wall cabinet, with a central hinged door and a lock.

c1720 *18.5in (47cm) wide*

£1,200-1,800 **EP**

A small 18thC oak press.

c1730 *66.5in (169cm) high*

£2,500-3,500 **EP**

A fine oak press, of exceptional quality, the moulded cornice above two cupboard doors separated by a central panel, above a lower section with four drawers and two further cupboard doors.

c1740 *88in (223.5cm) wide*

£8,000-12,000 **EP**

A Georgian oak press, the moulded cornice above two cupboard doors with ogee-arched, fielded panels, separated by a central circled panel, enclosing a pegged interior, the lower section with three fielded panels above three drawers, on block feet.

61in (155cm) wide

£3,000-5,000 **L&T**

A 19thC carved Gothic-style oak side cabinet, with some earlier components, the moulded top above a pair of tracery carved cupboard doors, centred by a coat of arms, with two conforming apron drawers below, raised on square legs, united by an undertier with a linen-fold panelled back.

46in (117cm) high

£1,200-1,800 **FRE**

DRESSERS

A George II dresser, with three drawers on cabriole legs.

c1750 *78in (198cm) wide*

£5,500-7,500 **DL**

An oak dresser base, lacking rack.

c1770 *73in (185.5cm) wide*

£5,000-7,000 **EP**

A George III oak dresser base, the rectangular top with a moulded edge above an arrangement of two short and six long raised panel drawers.

76in (193cm) wide

£4,000-6,000 **L&T**

An early 19thC South Wales oak dresser and rack, the moulded projecting cornice above three elm shelves with hand-wrought hooks, three frieze drawers above a pot board base.

62.5in (159cm) wide

£1,800-2,200 **WW**

An early 19thC oak dresser, with an associated shelved rack, the base with a planked top above two frieze drawers and a pair of panelled doors, flanking a ogee-arched panel, later adaptation.

65in (165cm) wide

£1,200-1,800 **WW**

An early 19thC oak and mahogany crossbanded dresser and plate rack, the cornice above a pierced frieze, the three concave racks with serrated aprons, enclosed by doors and with single drawers below, above three further drawers on square tapered legs.

76.75in (192cm) wide

£2,500-3,500 **L&T**

An early 19thC English painted pine double dresser, with four drawers, the whole with green, ochre and yellow sponge and grain decoration.

71in (180cm) wide

£3,000-5,000 **POOK**

A French provincial walnut dresser, the corniced plate rack with three shelves, on a base with a moulded edge above a frieze drawer and a pair of panelled doors, with shaped apron and stile feet.

49.5in (126cm) wide

£1,800-2,200 **L&T**

An English oak Welsh dresser, in two parts, the moulded cornice above three open shelves, the base with a rectangular top over three drawers, raised on turned columnar legs joined by a shelf, ending in block feet.

55in (140cm) high

£4,500-5,500 **NA**

A pine Welsh dresser, the shelved superstructure with a moulded cornice, the base with a short drawer over a false front inset panel, flanked by a pair of inset-panel cupboard doors, enclosing a shelved interior.

55in (140cm) high

£600-900 **S&K**

CUPBOARDS & CABINETS

An English oak hanging corner cabinet, with an ogee moulded cornice over a turkey breast front, with two raised arched panel cupboard doors.

c1690 *28in (71cm) wide*

£3,500-4,500 **POOK**

An 18thC walnut hanging corner cupboard, the dentil cornice above a double-fielded panel door, enclosing shaped shelves, with canted sides.

31.5in (80cm) wide

£600-900 **WW**

An 18thC painted pine hanging corner cupboard, decorated with a biblical scene.

20in (51cm) wide

£300-500 **FRE**

An 18thC japanned bow-fronted hanging corner cupboard, with figures and buildings in gilt on a black ground, the concave cornice above two doors enclosing shelves.

23in (59cm) wide

£600-900 **DN**

A George III mahogany inlaid two-piece corner cupboard, the moulded cornice over a lattice-glazed door, flanked by canted stiles above a base with a single panel door, with overall line inlays and banding.

c1800 *28in (71cm) wide*

£1,500-2,000 **POOK**

An early 19thC corner cabinet, with satinwood banding and ebony stringing, the arched top with inlaid decoration above a pair of astragal-glazed doors, enclosing a shaped apron and bracket feet.

44in (112cm) wide

£1,000-1,500 **L&T**

A 19thC mahogany hanging corner cupboard, with an astragal-glazed door and box stringing, enclosing later interior shelves.

28.5in (72.5cm) wide

£400-600 **WW**

An American glazed and panelled yellow pine corner cupboard, from the Eastern Shore of Virginia, the moulded cornice with dentils, above double glazed doors opening to three shelves, above two panelled doors flanked by fluted chamfered sides, on bracket feet with a shaped centre foot, old breaks and repairs.

Provenance: This corner cupboard was included in the 'Eastern Shore Virginia Raised-Panel Furniture 1730-1830' exhibition at The Chrysler Museum, Norfolk, Virginia, in 1982.

c1820 *86.5in (220cm) high*

£3,000-5,000 **FRE**

A mid-19thC Dutch Baroque-style walnut and marquetry corner display cabinet, in two parts, the upper section with an arched cornice and a glazed conforming door, the lower with a panelled door, profusely decorated with floral marquetry.

33.5in (85cm) wide

£2,000-3,000 **S&K**

A 20thC Victorian-style figured mahogany corner cupboard, with a mullioned glazed door opening to a blue-painted two shelved interior, the lower section with an arched panelled cupboard door, the whole with spiral, baluster and ring-turned pilasters on a plinth base.

42in (107cm) wide

£500-800 **S&K**

A Louis XV provincial armoire with clock, the foliate-carved raised top centred by a 30-hour clock, striking on a bell with a silvered dial and roman numerals, the shaped, fielded, panel doors enclosing hanging space, centred by a conforming panel with a pendulum window, with two apron drawers, raised on scroll carved bracket feet.

63in (160cm) wide

£1,000-1,500 **FRE**

An early 19thC mahogany wardrobe, the moulded cornice above a plain frieze and eight graduated drawers, flanked by twin panelled full-length doors enclosing hanging space and further drawers, raised on a plinth base.

74.5in (189cm) wide

£3,500-4,500 **L&T**

A mid-19thC Biedermeier satin walnut and ebonized armoire, the moulded cornice above two shaped panelled doors, enclosing hanging space and an apron drawer, flanked by turned split pilasters, on splayed bracket feet.

57in (145cm) wide

£1,500-2,000 **FRE**

A late 19thC English walnut two door armoire, the moulded cornice above a pair of inset, shaped, panel doors, opening to an open interior of two small drawers with wooden pulls on a plinth base, above a pediment.

48in (122cm) wide

£480-520 **S&K**

A fine Victorian 'Plum Pudding' break-front armoire, attributed to Maple & Co., with a foliate scroll inlaid dentil cornice, the pair of glazed, foliate-carved panel doors enclosing sliding trays, two short and three long conforming drawers, centred by oval inlaid panels, with two full length doors enclosing hanging space and two apron drawers, on a panelled plinth base.

c1880 *99.5in (249cm) wide*

£2,200-2,800 **FRE**

An Edwardian mahogany display cabinet, with satinwood crossbanding, boxwood and ebony stringing, the inlaid cornice and frieze above a pair of astragal doors enclosing shelves, above a deeper bow front base with a pair of panelled doors, on square section tapering legs with spade feet.

40in (102cm) wide

£1,800-2,200 **L&T**

An Edwardian mahogany break-front wardrobe, part of a bedroom suite, with satinwood banding, boxwood and ebony stringing, inlaid with Neo-classical marquetry, with drawers and mirrored doors, the suite also comprising a double bed, a dressing table, a pot cupboard and a pair of side chairs.

51in (130cm) wide

£1,800-2,200 suite **L&T**

An Edwardian wardrobe, part of a mahogany and chequer-banded bedroom suite, the centre section with an inlaid panel door and open shelf, with graduated drawers and two panelled doors, the suite also comprising a dressing table and two pairs of single bed ends.

83.75in (213cm) wide

£2,000-3,000 suite **L&T**

An early 20thC French oak wardrobe, with foliate cast brass mounts, the arched moulded cornice above a corresponding mirror door flanked by shaped, parquetry, panelled narrow doors, enclosing adjustable shelves and further mirrors, raised on a moulded plinth with turned feet.

74in (188cm) wide

£800-1,200 **L&T**

An early Georgian-style break-front wardrobe, part of a walnut and gilt bedroom suite, by Maple and Co., London, the moulded leaf carved cornice above a central panel door enclosing a shelf and carved with a winged cherub, flanked by two arched and bevelled mirror doors, enclosing four long graduated drawers, raised on leaf-carved bracket feet, the suite also comprising a dressing table, a pair of bedroom chairs, a pot cupboard, a pair of double bed ends and an associated dressing stool.

This suite comes with its original invoice and pattern sheet, the total cost in the late 1920s was £300.

81in (206cm) wide

£2,200-2,800 suite **L&T**

An oak wardrobe, moulded cornice above hanging space enclosed within pair of arcaded panel doors, the base with single drawer, stile supports.

50in (127cm) wide

£300-400 **WW**

A George II mahogany linen press, the shallow moulded cornice above a pair of folded, panelled doors enclosing hanging space, on a base with two short and one long drawers and ogee bracket feet.

54.25in (138cm) wide

£600-900 **L&T**

A George III mahogany dwarf linen press, with a moulded edge above a pair of boxwood strung doors with star medallions enclosing sliding trays, on a base with drawers and shaped bracket feet.

49.25in (125cm) wide

£2,200-2,800 **L&T**

A George III mahogany linen press, with satinwood crossbanding and chequer stringing, the moulded cornice above panelled doors centred by shell medallions, enclosing shelves, on a base with drawers, on ogee bracket feet.

51in (130cm) wide

£2,200-2,800 **L&T**

An early 19thC satinwood linen press, the moulded cornice above doors with mahogany mouldings, enclosing a mahogany interior with sliding trays, on a base with drawers and turned mahogany handles.

50.5in (128cm) wide

£2,200-2,800 **L&T**

A Scottish George III mahogany linen press, with rosewood crossbanding and boxwood stringing, the moulded cavetto cornice with a panelled frieze centred by a geometric inlaid tablet, the oval-panelled doors enclosing sliding trays, the base with four long graduated drawers on splayed bracket feet, with a inlaid tablet to the apron.

49.25in (125cm) wide

£4,000-6,000 **L&T**

An early 19thC linen press, the moulded cornice above a pair of panelled doors enclosing sliding trays, raised on a base with drawers, a shaped apron and splayed bracket feet.

49in (124cm) wide

£800-1,200 **L&T**

A 19thC mahogany linen press, the moulded cornice above a pair of panelled doors enclosing sliding trays, raised above drawers, on shaped bracket feet.

30in (140cm) wide

£500-800 **L&T**

A 19thC mahogany linen press, the flat, arched and moulded top with a central tablet and roundel terminals, above panelled doors enclosing sliding trays, with a reeded plinth and turned feet.

47.25in (120cm) wide

£800-1,200 **L&T**

A 19thC mahogany linen press, inlaid with boxwood and chequer stringing, the moulded cornice above a panelled frieze and panelled doors centred by Neo-classical urns, enclosing sliding trays, on a base with drawers, shaped bracket feet.

49.5in (126cm) wide

£2,800-3,200 **L&T**

A Victorian 'plum pudding' mahogany linen press, the moulded cornice above a pair of panelled doors enclosing hanging space, two short and two long drawers below, stamped "Heal and Son".

51.5in (131cm) wide

£500-800 **WW**

An Empire mahogany vitrine cabinet, with gilt-metal mounting, the brass-bound arched crest applied with a charioteer and putti, the frieze applied with swans, suspending wreaths, putti and swags, the bevelled glass door concealing shelves, over a drawer and door mounted with a silk embroidered, watercolour and ink picture depicting a couple and Cupid, the canted sides applied with female figures, raised on brass paw feet, the whole applied with ram's head, swag, wreath and trophy mounts.

32in (81cm) wide

£3,500-4,500 **NA**

A mid-19thC Italian stained pear wood and ivory inlaid display cabinet, in the Renaissance style, the glazed door enclosing two glass shelves and flanked by fluted columns, on turned front feet.

26.75in (68cm) wide

£1,800-2,200 **L&T**

A late 19thC ebonized display cabinet, with brass mounts, the glazed top above a reverse break-front surmount, with glazed panels and a central door enclosing shaped shelves covered with velvet, the break-front lift-up top with a glazed panel, enclosing a velvet-lined display surface with glazed sides, on turned and tapering legs, with pot casters.

41in (104cm) wide

£600-900 **L&T**

A late 19thC continental mahogany vitrine cabinet, mounted with gilt-metal and fitted with porcelain plaques depicting couples in rural scenes, the galleried pillow top with a moulded frieze, the glazed door enclosing a mirror back and glass shelves, the shaped apron on cabriole legs.

13.5in (35cm) wide

£400-600 **L&T**

A late Victorian mahogany and bronze-mounted hexagonal display cabinet, with a circular glass tier on six scrolling acanthus cast supports, above a moulded top over six bevelled glass doors, on cabriole legs headed by cast shells with harebells and pad feet.

31.5in (80cm) wide

£1,000-1,500 **L&T**

An Edwardian Louis XVI-style mahogany and ormolu mounted vitrine cabinet, the cornice with egg and dart moulding, above a floral swag frieze centred by two fauns carrying Bacchus, above a glazed door enclosing shelves, on toupie feet.

36in (92cm) wide

£2,800-3,200 **L&T**

An Edwardian mahogany break-front display cabinet, with boxwood stringing, the moulded caddy top centred by marquetry conches, above central glazed door flanked by glazed sides, enclosing glass shelves, on chamfered legs with scroll toes and toupie feet.

52in (132cm) wide

£2,000-3,000 **L&T**

An Edwardian cylinder front secretary bookcase, in two parts, the upper with a fan-pierced broken pediment above two glazed doors with gothic arch mullions, the base with a cylinder front, opening to a fitted interior of drawers and pigeonholes above an adjustable tooled-leather writing slope, the drawers inlaid with laurel swags and with lion's head circular pulls, all on square tapering, bellflower-inlaid legs ending in spade feet.

37.25in (94.5cm) wide

£5,000-7,000 **S&K**

An Edwardian mahogany display cabinet, with boxwood stringing and an arched, moulded cornice above a corresponding glazed central door flanked by glazed quadrant sides, on square section tapering legs and spade feet.

49.5in (126cm) wide

£800-1,200 **L&T**

A Louis XVI style kingwood vitrine cabinet, with gilt brass mounts, the rouge marble top above a frieze with a central panel of cherubs, the glazed door with a parquetry panel centred by an applied trophy, enclosing an interior with glazed sides and a mirror back, on turned tapering legs.

32.25in (82cm) wide

£1,500-2,000 **L&T**

A William and Mary oyster veneered walnut chest-on-stand, the crossbanded top inlaid with a geometric boxwood pattern corresponding to the veneering, above ogee moulding and crossbanded drawers, above an ogee moulded plinth, on a stand with a drawer and five barley twist legs joined by a shaped stretcher with bun feet, the legs and feet probably later.

54.5in (97cm) wide

£4,000-6,000 **L&T**

A CLOSER LOOK AT A RED JAPANNED CABINET

Japanned cabinets became popular from the late 17thC. They are an imitation of fashionable Chinese lacquered cabinets of the period. The technique involved coating objects with varnish, which is allowed to dry and then sanded before more layers are added.

European japanned decoration is commonly in black, blue, green or red

This magnificent piece is intricately decorated with scenes from Stalker and Parker's Treatise on Japanning, a well-known reference text on the subject dating from c1688.

Damage or restoration to japanned cabinets will affect the value. Gilt bases are also susceptible to damage so require thorough checking.

A late 17thC red Japanned cabinet on a gilt stand, decorated with scenes from Stalker and Parker's 'Treatise on Japanning', the pair of doors with gilt brass, pierced and engraved strapwork hinges and drop handles to sides, enclosing an arrangement of eight large drawers around three smaller recessed drawers, on a stand carved and pierced with cherubs at the centre, the four 'C' scrolled legs splayed at the front with scroll toes, formerly silvered.

This cabinet was ordered by Sir James Dick, London, in 1688/9 along with a State Coach.

51.25in (130cm) wide

£30,000-40,000 **L&T**

A Queen Anne walnut and burr-walnut veneered chest-on-stand, with feather banding, the rectangular crossbanded top above an ogee cornice and two short over three long graduated drawers, the base with a moulded top and a single drawer, with squat cabriole legs and pad feet.

42.5in (108cm) wide

£1,800-2,200 **L&T**

A George III japanned cabinet on stand, the doors with gilt metal engraved hinges and escutcheon, enclosing an interior with ten small drawers, the whole decorated with Chinoiserie figures and animals in landscape settings, on a later stand.

38.5in (98cm) wide

£1,500-2,000 **WW**

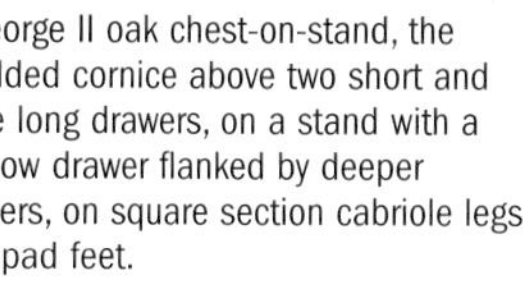

A George II oak chest-on-stand, the moulded cornice above two short and three long drawers, on a stand with a shallow drawer flanked by deeper drawers, on square section cabriole legs with pad feet.

41.5in (105cm) wide

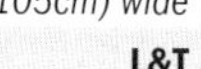

£2,000-3,000 **L&T**

A George III mahogany writing cabinet.

c1800 *58.5in (148.5cm) high*

£5,000-8,000 **DL**

An early 19thC rosewood and marquetry inlaid cabinet on stand, the top with a central panel of inlaid flowerheads enclosed by a border, the drawers with applied mouldings and inlaid with nine marquetry panels of baskets of fruit, the side panels inlaid with fruit, flowers and four urns, the associated mahogany stand with turned legs and lappet brackets.

24.5in (62cm) wide

£450-550 **L&T**

An early 19thC Colonial padouk cabinet, the doors enclosing four small drawers, one with a zinc liner, above three long drawers, with turned knob handles, on a later stand.

24.25in (61.5cm) wide

£200-300 **WW**

A 19thC lacquer chest, decorated with figures and buildings in a landscape on a black ground, the pair of doors with pierced and engraved strap hinges enclosing shelves, on a later stand with square section legs and scroll toes, joined with a stretcher.

38.5in (98cm) wide

£1,000-1,500 **L&T**

A late 19thC French ebony, ebonized and ivory strung secretaire cabinet on stand, inlaid with putti, birds and animals and foliate scrolls in a Neo-classical style, the rectangular top with outset corners, above three drawers and a fall front drawer, the interior veneered in amboyna and flanked by turned and carved pillars, the stand with a flat interlaced stretcher on leaf carved feet, stamped to lock plate "Hunsinger and Wagner a Paris".

Charles Hunsinger (1823-93) took part in the Paris Exhibitions of 1865, 1867, 1868 and 1889. He went into partnership with Charles Adolphe Frederic Wagner in 1872 and they won a gold medal at Brussels in 1881. Examples of their work can be found in the Musée d'Orsay and in the Österreichisches Museum für Angewandte Kunst in Austria.

33.75in (86cm) wide

£7,000-9,000 **DN**

An Edwardian mahogany cocktail cabinet, the divided, hinged top enclosing a rising interior with crystal decanters, glasses and a cigarette box, on square section tapered legs with brass caps and casters, three glasses missing.

23in (59cm) wide

£500-700 **L&T**

A French satinwood and marquetry break-front side cabinet, the raised top with two glazed panel doors enclosing shelves, supported by turned pilasters and a later mirrored panel back, the lower section with geometric veneers, opening to reveal a shelf, on slender square tapered legs.

c1910 *67in (170cm) wide*

£1,000-1,500 **FRE**

An Edwardian serpentine break-front satinwood cabinet, with boxwood stringing and inlaid oval and lozenge panels, the moulded cornice above a central door with concave flanks, enclosing a fabric-lined shelved interior, raised on a deeper corresponding base with a pair of doors, and square section tapering legs with spade and an undershelf.

45.5in (116cm) wide

£3,000-5,000 **L&T**

A Louis XV-style bijouterie cabinet, the gilt ground with Vernis Martin decoration, gilt metal mounts, the serpentine rectangular hinged glazed top enclosing a lined interior, above a door painted with lovers, on splayed legs with sabots.

15.5in (40cm) wide

£300-500 **L&T**

A Louis XV-style parquetry kingwood cabinet, with cast gilt metal mounts, stamped "Krieger, 74 Fauberg St. Honore, Paris".

29in (74cm) wide

£3,000-5,000 **L&T**

A William and Mary-style flat-top figured maple high chest of drawers, in two parts, the upper section with a moulded cornice above drawers, the base with a small drawer flanked by two deep drawers, all drawers with herringbone banding, above a bead-moulded shaped skirt on trumpet turned legs and bun feet, connected by a shaped stretcher.

38.5in (97.5cm) wide

£1,200-1,800 **S&K**

A Continental early Baroque ebonized and ivory inlaid valuables cabinet, the case with twin doors and engraved ivory panels, opening to a fitted interior with similar engraved ivory panels.

22in (56cm) wide

£3,000-5,000 **NA**

A Georgian mahogany cabinet, the rectangular top with a dentilled cornice, above a pair of panelled doors, enclosing an interior fitted with pigeonholes, on ogee bracket feet.

23in (58cm) wide

£700-900 **L&T**

A 17thC Italian walnut side cabinet, the fluted dentil frieze above a drawer and a panelled cupboard door, centred by a cartouche and flanked by caryatids, opening to a shelf, raised on carved paw feet.

£1,200-1,800 **FRE**

A George III mahogany secrétaire chest, with brass stringing, the false-fronted secrétaire drawer enclosing a baize-lined tray and lifting writing slide, revealing a well with carved and lidded stationery compartments, above doors enclosing a sliding tray, on shaped and moulded bracket feet, the top with a silver plaque engraved "Left to Gabriella Cunninghame Graham of Gartmoor by Anna Lady Erskine 1885".

43in (109cm) wide

£2,200-2,800 **L&T**

An Anglo-Chinese collector's cabinet.

c1800 *18in (45.5cm) wide*

£1,200-1,800 **DL**

An early 19thC Scandinavian waxed pine Neo-classical convex corner cabinet, with a low gallery, dentil frieze, reeded door and bracket feet.

40.5in (103cm) wide

£800-1,200 **S&K**

A Regency dwarf lacquered Gothic cabinet, the crenellated upper section with octagonal corner towers, flanking a glazed door enclosing a velvet-lined interior with shelves, raised on a deeper base with a pierced quatrefoil gallery above a pair of tracery panelled doors flanked by clasping buttresses.

28.75in (73cm) wide

£4,000-6,000 **L&T**

A Regency rosewood and brass inlaid collector's cabinet, in the manner of George Bullock, the reverse break-front top surmounted by a rectangular plinth, inlaid with brass banding, the single drawer above a pair of panelled doors enclosing shelves, flanked by two glazed doors enclosing a bank of six drawers on one side and sliding shelves on the other, each with turned ivory handles, the whole raised on a plinth with an ebonized base.

53.25in (133cm) wide

£8,000-12,000 **L&T**

An early 19thC Dutch walnut and chequer-banded side cabinet, the top inlaid with a central shell, above a drawer and two doors flanked by turned pillars on plinth base.

39.25in (100cm) wide

£1,000-1,500 **DN**

A Regency rosewood and brass-inlaid dwarf side cabinet, with a frieze drawer and pleated cupboard door, decorated with a brass grille, on sabre supports.

c1810 *91cm (35.75in) high*

£3,500-4,500 **RGA**

An early 19thC Regency penwork side chiffonier with a single drawer.

c1815 *32in (81cm) wide*

£6,000-9,000 **JK**

A late Regency tortoiseshell and brass-inlaid boulle cabinet, with stained wood veneers and gilt brass cast mounts, the rectangular slate top above a leaf cast cornice and a boulle frieze, the glazed doors enclosing a velvet-lined, shelved interior flanked by panelled pilasters, on brass strung plinth with bracket feet.

44.5in (113cm) wide

£3,500-4,500 **L&T**

An early Victorian rosewood cabinet, with rounded outset corners and a three-quarter gallery, with fluted supports and slender spindles above two grille doors, on turned feet.

36in (91.5cm) wide

£1,200-1,800 **DN**

A 19thC Empire-style bird's eye maple and parcel gilt side cabinet, the Carrara marble top above a pair of silk panelled doors with entwined serpent motifs flanked by canted angles with acanthus consoles, on a moulded plinth base.

45.25in (113cm) wide

£4,500-5,500 **L&T**

A 19thC tortoiseshell, mother-of-pearl and walnut Spanish cabinet, the rectangular parquetry top above nine drawers around a central drawer, with a tabernacle front centred by a convex mirror, on a later moulded plinth base and turned feet.

45.5in (114cm) wide

£5,500-6,500 **L&T**

A 19thC Regency burr-walnut side cabinet, in a French-style, with a deep cornice above a single glazed door enclosing shelves, on a bracket base with a serpentine apron.

36in (91.5cm) wide

£1,000-1,500 **S&K**

A Victorian rosewood table book cabinet, with a three-quarter balustraded brass gallery above a glazed door flanked by barley twist columns, enclosing shelves and a false fronted drawer, on turned feet.

21.25in (54cm) wide

£500-800 **L&T**

A Victorian tortoiseshell and ebonized boulle cabinet, the Carrara marble top raised above a tortoiseshell frieze and a single door, enclosing a mahogany-veneered shelved interior flanked by canted angles with cherub mask capitals, on a plinth base with a shaped apron, the whole with gilt brass mounts.

30.75in (78cm) wide

£1,800-2,200 **L&T**

An Edwardian mahogany cabinet, with boxwood and ebony stringing and with crossbanding, the rectangular top with an astragal edge above panelled doors and a drawer, on splayed bracket feet.

22in (56cm) wide

£450-550 **L&T**

An Edwardian mahogany and satinwood-banded cabinet, with two frieze drawers above an interior with adjustable shelves enclosed by astragal glazed doors.

58.75in (149.5cm) high

£550-650 **WW**

An early 20thC demi-lune side cabinet inlaid with walnut, calamander, mahogany and amboyna, with a moulded frieze and a long drawer, centred by marquetry tablet depicting a bowl of fruit, above two cupboard doors flanked by carved and gadrooned demi columns, on gadrooned block feet.

52in (130cm) wide

£1,200-1,800 **L&T**

A 20thC Italian polychrome painted side cabinet, the rectangular coved top above a conforming case, the cupboard doors opening to shelves, the moulded base with bracket feet, decorated with arabesques, swags, flowers, birds, figures and masks on a light green and off-white crackled ground.

67.25in (168cm) wide

£2,200-2,800 **S&K**

A 20thC Italian polychrome painted side cabinet, with a rectangular stained fruitwood top above two small drawers over a pair of cupboard doors, opening to a shelved interior, the front and sides decorated with coral bellflowers, shells and scrolls on a cream coloured ground.

55in (137.5cm) wide

£800-1,200 **S&K**

A Victorian ebonized credenza, with gilt metal mounts, the moulded break-front D-shaped top above a cupboard door fitted with a cental Sèvres style plaque, flanked by two curved, glazed doors, enclosing shelves, on a plinth base with bun feet.

58.5in (149cm) wide

£500-800 **L&T**

A Victorian rosewood, ebonized and gilt Rococo-style chiffonier, the three tier open-shelved back with mirror panels and carved and pierced C-scroll consoles, with corresponding cresting, raised on pair of drawers and a deeper base with a pair of arched panelled doors enclosing shelves, a shaped apron and scroll feet.

42.5in (108cm) wide

£800-1,200 **L&T**

A George III mahogany cabinet.

c1800 *55.5in (139.5cm) high*

£4,000-5,000 **DL**

A Victorian walnut, inlaid and gilt metal-mounted credenza, the lugged serpentine top above a panelled cupboard door, flanked by glazed serpentine doors, enclosing shelves, on a shaped plinth base.

51.25in (128cm) wide

£3,500-4,500 **L&T**

A Regency mahogany break-front side cabinet, the top with rounded angles and one frieze drawer flanked by two false drawers, above a pair of glazed doors enclosing drawers, flanked by open shelves between reeded and ring turned columns, on toupie feet.

51in (129cm) wide

£2,000-2,500 **L&T**

A Victorian walnut credenza, the shaped top above a frieze and a break-front panelled door, with gilt brass mounts and boxwood marquetry, flanked by convex glazed cupboard doors, on a plinth, incorporating later fitted three drawer canteen.

60.75in (152cm) wide

£2,500-3,000 **L&T**

A large Regency mahogany chiffonier, the boldly shaped and scrolled surmount with a single open shelf, raised on break-front base with beaded moulding and four panelled doors, on a plinth.

68in (173cm) wide

£1,800-2,200 **L&T**

A pair of Victorian mahogany bedside cupboards, each with a three quarter gallery above a single-shelved interior within a panel door, on a plinth base.

15in (38cm) wide

£800-1,200 **WW**

A Victorian mahogany bedside cupboard, on reeded tapering legs, with a later handle.

14in (35.5cm) wide

£180-220 **WW**

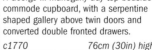

A George III mahogany tray-top bedside commode cupboard, with a serpentine shaped gallery above twin doors and converted double fronted drawers.

c1770 *76cm (30in) high*

£2,500-3,500 **RGA**

A George III mahogany tray-top commode with crossbanded doors and a shaped apron and rim, with original brass fittings.

c1780 *75.5cm (29.75in) high*

£2,200-2,800 **RGA**

A George III mahogany double-sided pot cupboard, with pierced handles.

c1800 *28in (71cm) high*

£2,200-2,800 **DL**

A George III mahogany tray-top night commode, with pierced side handles and two doors above the pull-out section, on straight legs.

22in (56cm) wide

£500-800 **DN**

A George III mahogany bedside commode, the rectangular top with a shaped gallery and pierced handles above a pair of doors and a drawer-shaped apron, converted from close-stool, square section chamfered legs.

20.5in (52cm) wide

£1,800-2,200 **L&T**

An early George III mahogany bedside serpentine commode, the shaped gallery with pierced handles, above a boxwood and mahogany tambour door enclosing a pull out close-stool with a basin and turned lid, on chamfered legs, with leaf cast brass handles to front and sides.

22in (56cm) wide

£2,500-3,500 **L&T**

An 18thC Dutch walnut and later marquetry-inlaid bureau cabinet, the arched and moulded cornice with a central C-scroll and a rosette-carved cartouche above twin astragal-glazed doors enclosing shelves, the sloping fall opening to reveal an interior fitted with drawers and pigeonholes, with a well below and an inset writing surface, above a bombe chest of two short and two long drawers, raised on bracket feet.

50.75in (129cm) wide

£8,000-12,000 **L&T**

A late 18thC South German or North Italian walnut and parquetry cabinet-on-chest, the arched cabinet with a pair of glazed doors, the reverse-serpentine chest with three drawers and bun feet.

48in (123cm) wide

£5,000-8,000 **S&K**

A late 18thC Dutch mahogany secrétaire à abattant, with a frieze drawer above fall front, enclosing a fitted interior, inlaid with shell patera, with twin cupboards below, similarly inlaid, the whole enclosed by canted angles inlaid with a zig-zag design on square tapered feet.

42.5in (108cm) wide

£2,000-3,000 **L&T**

A Regency mahogany cabinet.

c1810 *68in (172.5cm) high*

£7,000-10,000 **DL**

A George III and later mahogany and marquetry serpentine cabinet-on-chest, with an architectural dentil pediment, the doors with central oval paterae, the corners with inlaid huaka, base with a leather slope, panel bracket feet.

£10,000-13,000 **WW**

A late Victorian mahogany and polychrome cabinet, with all over painted decoration of foliage, trophies, birds and cherubs.

45in (114.5cm) wide

£1,800-2,200 **WW**

An Empire gilt-metal-mounted mahogany secrétaire à abattant, the slate top above a frieze drawer, the mirrored fall front flanked by female term figures, opening to an interior fitted with two shelves over two banks of three drawers and a baize-lined writing surface, with three drawers, raised on square moulded feet, the whole applied with griffin and putti, with stylized leaf tip and flowerhead mounts.

31.25in (79.5cm) wide

£1,200-1,800 **NA**

A late 19thC walnut and kingwood veneered secrétaire à abattant, with marquetry inlay, the fall with an inset writing surface, enclosing pigeonholes and drawers and a mirrored void, on square cabriole legs with cast sabots.

29.5in (75cm) wide

£2,200-2,800 **L&T**

An unusual late 19thC Continental satinwood and grained mahogany watchmaker's cabinet, probably Austrian, the 15 drawers with carved acorn handles, the sides painted with panels depicting river landscapes, raised on a plinth base.

14.5in (37cm) wide

£320-380 **FRE**

An early 20thC French walnut cabinet, the upper section with a balustraded gallery, centred by a broken pediment above a panelled frieze, the panelled doors centred by rosettes, flanked by turned columns, an open shelf below, on a deeper base and plinth and bun feet.

63.75in (162cm) wide

£700-1,000 **L&T**

A Louis XVI-style provincial slant-front secrétaire, with arched ogee cornice above panelled cupboard doors, the desk with a slant front, enclosing a fitted interior, above two cupboard doors, raised on short scroll legs.

44in (259cm) wide

£1,500-2,000 **S&K**

A black Chinoiserie decorated cabinet, with a pair of arched doors, opening to a shelved interior, on bun feet, modified as an entertainment centre.

64in (162.5cm) wide

£1,200-1,800 **S&K**

CANTERBURIES

An early 19thC mahogany canterbury, the three open compartments with baluster-turned corner supports, roundel terminals and downswept top rails, a single drawer below and corresponding turned feet, brass caps and casters.

19.5in (49cm) wide

£900-1,100 **L&T**

A late Regency rosewood canterbury, the three open compartments with X dividers, with a wreath to front and ribbon supports, ring and baluster turned rails, a base drawer with applied acanthus carving and acorn finials, on ring and baluster turned legs with brass caps and casters.

20in (51cm) wide

£2,200-2,800 **L&T**

An early 19thC mahogany canterbury, with three open compartments and downswept top rails, a single cock-beaded drawer, turned tapering legs with brass caps and casters.

18.75in (48cm) wide

£1,200-1,800 **L&T**

A Regency rosewood canterbury, the three divisions with laurel wreath carved facings, above an apron drawer, raised on slender turned legs ending in brass cappings and casters.

A Canterbury is a small stand, popular in the 18thC. Those with racks were used for holding sheet music, others had trays for holding cutlery.

c1820 *18in (46cm) wide*

£2,500-3,000 **FRE**

A Regency mahogany canterbury, with five concave dividers and slatted sides, the turned and blocked uprights with finial surmounts above a single drawer, brass caps and casters.

17in (43cm) wide

£600-800 **L&T**

A Regency mahogany canterbury, with four concave dividers, the baluster turned and blocked upright supports with finial surmounts above a drawer, on baluster turned legs, terminating in brass caps and casters.

19.25in (49cm) wide

£320-380 **L&T**

A 19thC mahogany canterbury, with four open compartments divided by downswept top rails, one with a pierced handle, turned and blocked corner uprights with finials, a drawer, turned legs with brass caps and casters.

£1,200-1,800 **L&T**

A Victorian burr walnut canterbury, the shaped rectangular top with a border inlaid with meandering foliage, turned and carved supports, on turned feet with brass caps and casters.

25.25in (64cm) wide

£2,500-3,500 **L&T**

CELLARETS

A Queen Anne walnut cellaret, of cylindrical form, fitted with a drawer, mounted with brass carrying handles and fitted with a liner, the cyma curved and scalloped skirt raised on cabriole legs ending in pad feet.

17.5in (44.5cm) diam

£2,000-3,000 **NA**

A George III mahogany and box-strung cellaret, of serpentine outline, with carrying handles to the sides, on tapering legs, lacking casters and with repairs to rear legs.

22in (56cm) wide

£1,500-2,000 **WW**

A George III mahogany wine cooler, of oval tapered section and staved construction, with two broad brass bands and carrying handles, raised on a moulded base, the outset square legs with chamfered inside edges, wooden casters, decorated with scrolling brackets, a later zinc liner.

28in (70cm) wide

£2,800-3,200 **L&T**

A George III mahogany cellaret, the ogee moulded hinged lid enclosing a baize-lined compartmented interior, with side carrying handles, raised on ogee bracket feet and casters, the baize later.

c1790 *15in (38cm) wide*

£1,800-2,200 **FRE**

A George III mahogany cellaret, of square form with a hinged lid, the interior formerly divided, brass carry handles to sides, a later attached stand with square section legs.

15.25in (39cm) wide

£800-1,200 **L&T**

Left: A Regency mahogany cellaret, the rectangular hinged top raised on turned and reeded tapering legs, with brass caps and casters, ivory escutcheon and brass carry handles.

18in (46cm) wide

£700-1,000 **L&T**

Right: A George III mahogany cellaret, with boxwood stringing, the hinged rectangular top centred by a fan patera, raised on square section tapered legs, with spade feet, brass caps and casters, brass carry handles to sides.

18in (46cm) wide

£800-1,200 **L&T**

A Regency black lacquered cellaret, with side handles and a base, decorated with landscapes.

Cellarets were used to cool wine.

c1810 *30in (76cm) high*

£5,000-7,000 **DL**

A 19thC mahogany cellaret, the hinged rectangular top with a beaded edge, enclosing a lead-lined divided interior, on chamfered square section legs.

15.75in (40cm) wide

£400-600 **L&T**

A Regency mahogany wine cooler, the leaf and berry carved handle above a fluted cover, zinc lined interior, with applied reeded balusters. turned feet, brass cappings and casters.

27.5in (70cm) wide

£4,000-6,000 **WW**

A Regency mahogany sarcophagus wine cooler, the tapered rectangular top surmounted by a panel carved with fruits in relief, above tapering sides and enclosing a lead-lined interior, the whole raised above a moulded base, on bun feet.

30in (75cm) wide

£800-1,200 **L&T**

A Regency mahogany cellaret, with Gonzalo Alves crossbanding, of rectangular tapering brim, the hinged lid with a cavetto border and reel moulding, enclosing a lead-lined interior, the panelled body with rosette bosses and wooden ring handles to the sides, on paw feet with sunk casters.

29.25in (74cm) wide

£5,000-8,000 **L&T**

A Scottish Regency mahogany cellaret, of sarcophagus form, the rectangular pagoda lid with a reeded finial above tapering panelled sides, with bead and reel moulding and paw feet, on a rectangular panelled base with casters.

31in (79cm) wide

£3,500-4,500 **L&T**

A 19thC George II-style mahogany cellaret, the hinged rectangular caddy top enclosing a plain interior, above panelled sides with carry handles, the relief carved front with cherubs in a Rococo framework, on leaf-carved cabriole legs with pad feet.

28in (70cm) wide

£1,200-1,800 **L&T**

A Regency mahogany cellaret in the architectural style, with diamond-shaped line inlay decoration.

c1820 *23.5in (60cm) wide*

£2,500-3,500 **RGA**

A 19thC mahogany cellaret, of rectangular sarcophagus form, the hinged pyramidal lid enclosing a lead-lined interior, raised on carved paw feet, on casters, a brass drainage tap to rear.

32in (81cm) high

£3,000-4,000 **L&T**

A 19thC 'plum pudding' mahogany cellaret, of sarcophagus form, the hinged lid with a gadrooned finial, enclosing a fitted interior, on carved paw feet and plinth base, the lock stamped "D Cormack, Edinbro'".

31.25in (78cm) wide

£4,000-6,000 **L&T**

A mahogany cellaret, of tapering rectangular form with canted corners and gilt-metal side handles, the hinged top enclosing interior divisions, turned legs with brass terminals and casters.

20.5in (52cm) wide

£500-700 **DN**

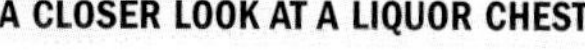

A CLOSER LOOK AT A LIQUOR CHEST

Sheraton's refined style was widely taken up after the publication of his 'The Cabinet Maker's and Upholsterer's Drawing Book, in 1791.

The delicate straight lines and elegant Neo-classical shape are typical of the period.

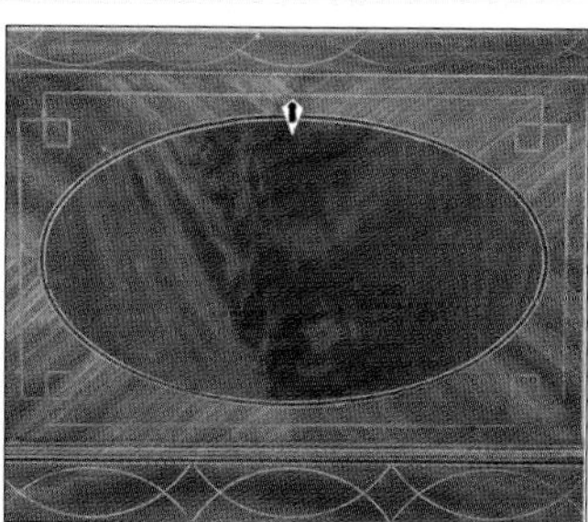

The fine decoration makes use of the natural grain of wood. Sheraton is known for his preference for veneers and inlaid ornamentation. The value reflects the excellent condition of the piece.

A small 19thC Sheraton-period mahogany arched top liquor chest.

c1800 *17.5in (45cm) wide*

£15,000-20,000 **NOA**

COUNTRY CHAIRS

An early 18thC wooden chair, from Ile D'Orleans, Quebec.

See Palandy's 'Early Furniture of French Canada' for similar examples.

29.5in (75cm) high

£300-400 BP

A George III open oak and elm country armchair, the serpentine top rail above a vase splat and outscrolled open arms, with a plank seat, on chamfered square legs linked by an 'H' stretcher.

£400-600 L&T

A yew wood low-back Windsor chair, with a spindle back and shaped seat.

c1830 *35in (89cm) high*

£1,200-1,800 EP

An oak ladder-back chair, with shaped splats and a rush seat.

c1840 *44.75in (121.5cm) high*

£300-400 EP

A yew wood broad armchair, with a pierced splat and shaped seat.

c1850 *45.5in (115.5cm) high*

£1,200-1,800 EP

Two of a set of six 19thC ash and elm ladder-back chairs, each with a simple curved top rail above three shaped splats, the rush seat with facings, with turned club front legs.

£1,500-2,000 set L&T

Two of a set of eight 19thC Lancashire ash ladder-back dining chairs, with rush seats, including a pair of elbow chairs, some damage.

£1,500-2,000 set WW

A pair of Victorian fruitwood Windsor armchairs, the splat backs pierced with initials, above elm saddle seats, turned legs united by H-stretchers.

A similar pair of chairs, attributed to High Wycombe, are illustrated in "The English Regional Chair", page 88, by Dr B Cotton.

£800-1,200 WW

Left: A 19thC Charles II-style oak panelled-back armchair, the arched scroll carved cresting with chequered banding and a diamond motif, with two open scroll arms above a chip carved solid seat, raised on turned legs, joined by a peripheral stretcher.

£650-750 FRE

Centre: A late 19thC Charles II style carved oak panelled-back armchair.

£650-750 FRE

Right: A 19thC Charles II style oak panelled-back armchair, inlaid with checker banding, carved with stylized plant forms, with open scroll arms and a ship-carved solid seat, raised on turned legs joined by stretchers.

£700-900 FRE

A late 19thC pair of French 'Gothic Revival' armchair, the tracery-carved, panelled backs with conforming arched crestings, with moulded outswept arms above solid tri-form seats, supported by spiral turned legs joined by stretchers.

£600-900 FRE

A 20thC walnut elbow chair in the early 18thC style, with shepherd crook arms and shell-carved cabriole legs, stamped with "D.S".

£450-550 WW

A mid-20thC ash and elm high-back Windsor chair, with a pierced splat and shaped seat.

41.25in (105cm) high

£700-800 EP

An oak metamorphic chair and library steps, supporting a brass plaque inscribed with "Evans Matthews...80 Bull Street, Birmingham".

£280-320 WW

An Italian walnut hall settle, of Renaissance style, the back with two scrolled crestings carved with dragons flanking a lion mask, above two grotesque-carved fielded panels, the hinged seat flanked by scrolled, carved, armrests, above a grotesque-carved frieze, on paw feet.

62in (155cm) wide

£2,000-2,500 L&T

An early 19thC oak settle, the five-panel rectangular back above a slatted seat with squab, open arm to one end and an outscrolled padded rest with a rosette terminal to the other, on club legs.

77in (196cm) wide

£280-320 L&T

DINING CHAIRS

A set of eight English Queen Anne mahogany dining side chairs, each with a carved yoke crest over a pierced vasiform splat, flanked by ribbon carved stiles, over a compass seat frame, supported on cabriole legs with shell-carved knees and voluted returns, resting on modified trifid feet.

c1700

£12,000-18,000 POOK

One of a set of four Flemish carved walnut chairs, each with an ornate scrolled back and fabric seat, above cabriole legs and a shaped stretcher.

c1740 *41in (104cm) high*

£3,000-4,000 set DL

A walnut dining chair, 18thC and later, the arched top rail above a vase splat, flanked by curved uprights above a drop-in seat and shaped seat rail, on cabriole legs with scroll-carved brackets and terminating in claw and ball feet.

£350-450 L&T

A Chippendale period carved mahogany chair, with a carved back.

c1760 *37.5in (95.5cm) high*

£1,800-2,200 **DL**

A set of five George III carved mahogany shield-back dining chairs, each with a racquet-form splat carved with Prince of Wales feathers, a stuff-over serpentine-fronted seat, with square section tapering legs joined by an H-stretcher.

c1775

£3,200-3,700 set **S&K**

Two of a set of four George III mahogany dining chairs, each with a yoked top rail above a pierced, tapering splat, the serpentine drop-in seat on reeded tapering legs, with stretchers.

£300-400 set **L&T**

Two of a set of six George III Scottish mahogany dining chairs, of brander back form, each with three vertical spars centred by roundels, with stuff-over leather seat and square section tapering legs joined by an H-stretcher.

£2,500-3,500 set **L&T**

Two of a set of eight George III mahogany dining chairs, including one carver, each with an arched back with three carved splats, the central one with Prince of Wales feathers, above stuff-over seat and square section tapering legs joined by an H-stretcher.

£1,800-2,200 set **L&T**

A set of eight George III-style inlaid satinwood dining chairs, each with an arched and crossbanded back, a sheaf splat, caned seat and ring-turned legs.

£1,000-1,500 set **S&K**

A set of ten Regency mahogany dining chairs, each with slightly curved top rails with padded upholstered panels, above a carved and pierced latticed splat flanked by fluted Corinthian columns, the stuff-over seats raised above panelled rails, turned and fluted front legs terminating in toupie feet.

£4,000-6,000 set **L&T**

Two of a set of six early 19thC mahogany dining chairs, each with yoke back and mid rail above a leather stuff-over seat and square section tapered legs joined by H-stretcher.

£400-600 set **L&T**

Two of a set of ten Regency mahogany dining chairs, including one carver, each with a top rail with a moulded edge above an interwoven back lower rail with a turned boss, stuff-over seats, square tapering legs, with spade feet.

£3,000-4,000 set **L&T**

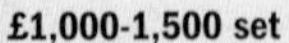

Two of a set of four Regency mahogany dining chairs, each with a carved yoke back with a central tablet and scroll terminals, above a corresponding pierced mid rail, the drop-in seat with carved side panels and a moulded seat rail, on turned and reeded front legs.

£1,000-1,500 set **L&T**

Two of a set of eleven Regency simulated rosewood and brass inlaid dining chairs, each with a scrolled, carved, top rail centred by an inlaid tablet above a corresponding mid rail, the drop-in stuffover seat raised above a similarly panelled seat rail, on turned and reeded tapering front legs.

Provenance: The Dukes of Hamilton.

£4,000-6,000 set **L&T**

Two of a set of six early 19thC satin birch dining chairs, each with a curved top rail above a pierced mid rail, above a drop-in seat, on turned and reeded tapering front legs.

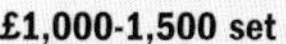

£1,000-1,500 set **L&T**

One of a pair of mahogany sabre leg chairs, with a carved top rail.

c1810 *34in (86.5cm) high*

£1,000-1,500 pair **DL**

One of a pair of Regency mahogany lyre back chairs.

c1810 *33.5in (85cm) high*

£1,800-2,200 pair **DL**

Two of a set of six Regency mahogany dining chairs, including one carver, each with a scroll-over entablature top rail, the leaf-carved mid rail centred by a roundel, supported by scrolling curved uprights above a needlework drop-in seat, raised on sabre legs.

£800-1,200 **L&T**

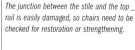

A CLOSER LOOK AT REGENCY DINING CHAIR

The junction between the stile and the top rail is easily damaged, so chairs need to be checked for restoration or strengthening.

The broad masculine proportions of this chair and the dark colouring are typical of Regency furniture. This chair has stained decoration, resembling ebony. The technique of ebonizing was first used in the late 17thC.

This chair is made from solid mahogany. Regency dining chairs were often made from softwood and veneered with mahogany.

Look for wear to the base of the back legs where the chair has been repeatedly pushed back along the floor to allow the occupant to leave the table.

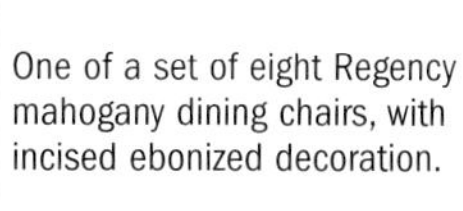

One of a set of eight Regency mahogany dining chairs, with incised ebonized decoration.

c1810 *33.5in (85cm) high*

£45,000-50,000 set **B&I**

A set of five Regency rosewood chairs, including one carver, each chair with a leaf-carved yoke back with scroll terminals and centred by rosettes, and panel inlaid with scrolling frieze in boxwood, above corresponding carved and pierced mid rail and seat rail with a corresponding inlaid central and flanking panels, squab upholstered in self stripe green horse hair, ring-turned and reeded tapering front legs.

£2,200-2,800 set **L&T**

A set of eight early 19thC mahogany dining chairs, each with reeded back-swept uprights, with a panelled bar back and three mid rails divided by ball spacers, a stuff-over seat and ring-turned tapered front legs.

£3,500-4,500 set **L&T**

Two of a set of twelve Regency mahogany dining chairs, including two carvers, each with a panelled yoke back and pierced mid rail, centred by a roundel, on moulded scrolled uprights, with a stuff-over seat and turned tapering front legs.

£8,000-12,000 set L&T

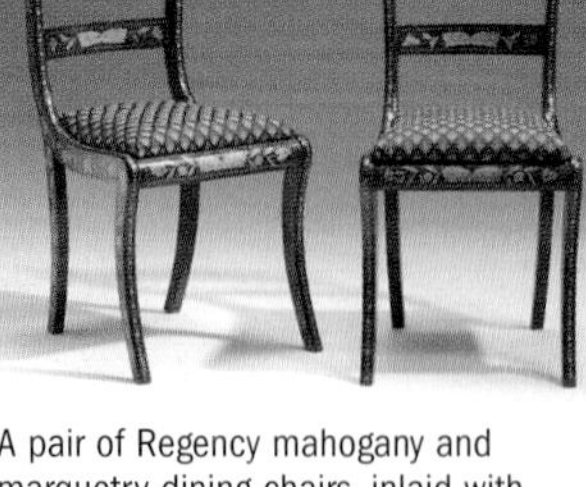

A pair of Regency mahogany and marquetry dining chairs, inlaid with scrolling foliage, the bar centred by a coat of arms, above Trafalgar drop-in seats, raised on sabre legs.

c1815

£700-1,000 FRE

One of a set of four George IV mahogany dining chairs, each with a crest rail and a rope twist back rail, with a wool work drop-in seat and sabre legs, one with arms.

£1,200-1,800 set DN

Two of a set of six late Regency mahogany dining chairs, each with a yoke back above a carved mid rail and drop-in squab, above a moulded seat rail and octagonal turned front legs.

£800-1,200 set L&T

Two of a set of six William IV mahogany dining chairs, including one carver, each with a broad leaf-carved top and mid rails, the leather upholstered seats on turned and reeded front legs, toupie feet.

£1,200-1,800 set L&T

One of a set of six early Victorian mahogany open back chairs, with a scroll-carved back rail, an upholstered serpentine seat and cabriole legs, stamped "Gillows Lancaster".

£800-1,200 set DN

Two of a harlequin set of six 19thC mahogany dining chairs, including two elbow chairs, each with a rope twist top rail above a floral carved mid rail, drop-in seats, on moulded sabre legs.

£800-1,200 set WW

Two of a set of six 19thC Empire-style painted dining chairs, including two armchairs, with gilt brass castings, the square backs with inset raised squab above bow front stuff-over seats, square section front legs and brass paw feet.

£2,000-3,000 set L&T

One of a set of eight 19thC dining chairs with pierced splats and square legs in George III style, each with a carved, pierced and interlaced splat, an upholstered serpentine fronted seat, on straight moulded legs with an 'H' stretcher, two with arms.

38.25in (97cm) high

£3,500-4,500 set DN

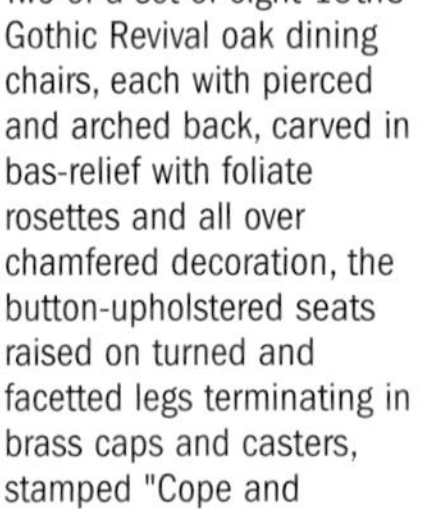

Two of a set of eight 19thC Gothic Revival oak dining chairs, each with pierced and arched back, carved in bas-relief with foliate rosettes and all over chamfered decoration, the button-upholstered seats raised on turned and facetted legs terminating in brass caps and casters, stamped "Cope and Collinson Patent".

Provenance: Arden House, Loch Lomond, Dunbartonshire.

£800-1,000 set L&T

Two of a set of six 19thC Italian provincial walnut dining chairs, each with an in-curved pierced lattice back, above a rectangular leather seat, on tapering square fluted legs, headed by paterae.

£1,500-2,000 set S&K

One of a set of twenty-one late Victorian walnut chairs, by GM and HJ Storey, each with a curved back rail, solid splat and upholstered bow-fronted seat, on turned tapering legs, with metal labels, the attached plaque reading "GM & HJ Storey, Cabinet Makers, 35 London Wall".

33.25in (87cm) high

£2,200-2,800 set **DN**

Two of a set of fourteen early 20thC Chippendale-style mahogany dining chairs, including two carvers, each with a moulded top rail and an interlaced vase splat and drop-in seats, front cabriole legs, claw and ball feet.

£5,000-8,000 set **L&T**

Two of a set of six early 20thC Regency style mahogany side chairs, each with an incised and scroll-carved shaped crest rail, downcurving stiles and a lotus-carved back splat, the padded slip seat on similarly carved, turned, tapered legs, ending in button feet.

33.75in (84cm) high

£800-1,200 **S&K**

Two of a set of eight 20thC French provincial-style white-painted dining chairs, each with a padded back and seat, on cabriole legs ending in slipper feet, the two armchairs with lime green and blue striped upholstery, the side chairs upholstered in lime green velvet.

44.5in (111cm) high

£700-1,000 **S&K**

Two of a set of eight mahogany dining chairs, in a late 18th century-style, including two carvers, each with leaf-carved top rails above chamfered spandrels, the drop-in seats on square moulded legs with stop feet.

£2,500-3,500 **L&T**

Two of a set of six George III-style mahogany dining chairs, each with an interlaced pierced splat back, drop-in seat and square section legs joined by an H-stretcher.

£700-1,000 set **L&T**

Two of a set of six mahogany dining chairs, including one carver, each with an interlaced pierced splat back, drop-in seat and cabochon-carved cabriole legs, with ball and claw feet.

£500-700 set **L&T**

Two of a set of eight Hepplewhite-style mahogany dining chairs including two carvers, each centred by a pierced splat carved with ears of wheat, with a stuff-over seat and moulded square section legs joined by an H-stretcher.

£2,000-3,000 set **L&T**

One of a set of six mahogany ladder-back chairs, in the George III-style, including one carver, each with leaf-carved serpentine rails with pierced and moulded decoration, above a drop-in seat, raised above moulded square legs united by stretchers.

£1,200-1,800 set **L&T**

One of a set of six dining chairs, each with a shaped top rail, with a brass lyre motif back and a cane seat, raised on sabre legs.

33in (84cm) high

£20,000-25,000 set **B&I**

Six of a set of twelve George I-style burl walnut or elmwood dining chairs, comprising two arm and ten side chairs, each vase-form splat above a compass-shaped slip seat, raised on cabriole legs carved at the knees with shells and bellflowers and ending in ball and claw feet.

£10,000-15,000 set NA

Two of a set of eight mahogany dining chairs in the Hepplewhite style, including a pair of elbow chairs, each with a shield back carved with Prince of Wales feathers, above a brass-studded red leather seat, square tapering legs.

£3,000-3,500 set WW

Two of eight Queen Anne-style mahogany dining chairs, including two arm and six side chairs, each with an applied shell crest above a vasiform splat, a balloon-shaped slip seat, on shell-carved cabriole legs with pad feet.

£2,200-2,800 set S&K

One of a set of eight mahogany dining chairs, in the George III-style, including two with arms, each with a shaped crest and a carved and pierced splat, with a drop-in seat, on leaf-carved cabriole legs, with claw and ball feet.

38.25in (97cm) high

£2,500-3,500 set DN

One of a set of twelve beech and parcel gilt dining chairs, in the Regency-style painted to simulate rosewood, including two with arms, each with a rope twist crest rail and an 'X' shaped back, a drop-in seat and sabre legs, with gilt patera mounts.

33.25in (84.5cm) high

£2,000-2,500 set DN

A set of eight burr-walnut veneered George I-style dining chairs, including two carvers, each with a vase splat above a stuff-over seat, on cabriole legs with shell-carved knees and ball and claw feet.

29.5in (75cm) high

£6,000-8,000 set L&T

SIDE CHAIRS

An Irish Queen Anne mahogany side chair, with a solid vasiform splat, over a slip seat within a shaped apron, resting on cabriole legs joined by turned stretchers, terminating in pad feet.

c1740

£700-1,000 POOK

A matched pair of George I-style walnut side chairs, each with a square back with a shaped top rail and a vase splat, above a drop-in seat and cabriole front legs with pad feet, one with elm rear legs and uprights.

£300-500 L&T

An early George I walnut veneer side chair with a shaped back.

c1720 *40in (101.5cm) high*

£10,000-15,000 B&I

One of a pair of George III oak corner chairs, with square section legs.

c1800 *32in (81.5cm) high*

£3,000-5,000 pair DL

Two of a set of four Regency mahogany and brass-inlaid side chairs, each with a tablet top rail above a C-scroll and ball mounted mid rail, over-stuffed seat on ring turned tapering legs, repairs.

£400-500 set **WW**

Two from a set of four early Victorian simulated rosewood side chairs, possibly Scottish, leaf and knurl carved decoration to top and mid-rails, with turned tapering legs.

£250-300 set **WW**

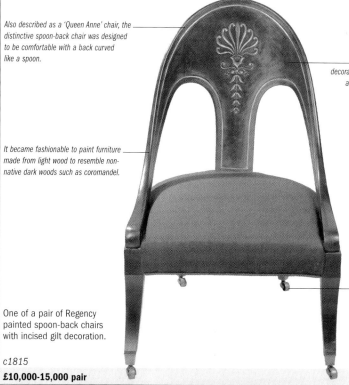

A CLOSER LOOK AT REGENCY SPOON-BACK CHAIR

Also described as a 'Queen Anne' chair, the distinctive spoon-back chair was designed to be comfortable with a back curved like a spoon.

The dark colours and opulent incised gilt decoration reflect the Regency love of the exotic and the bold curved shape is typical of the period.

It became fashionable to paint furniture made from light wood to resemble non-native dark woods such as coromandel.

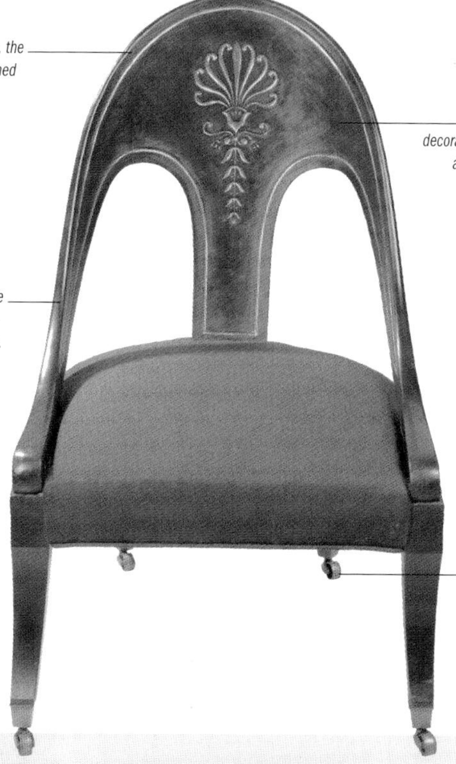

Casters were first applied to the end of furniture legs in the 16thC. They made pieces more versatile as they could be moved around the room to cater for different occasions.

One of a pair of Regency painted spoon-back chairs with incised gilt decoration.

c1815

34.5in (87.5cm) high

£10,000-15,000 pair **B&I**

An early Victorian mahogany library armchair, with carved scroll supports above a serpentine seat, turned and ribbed legs, later leather upholstery.

£500-800 **WW**

A 19thC Spanish Baroque-style carved walnut side chair, with a studded leather backrest and seat, with a decorative front stretcher.

£80-120 **S&K**

A mid-19thC Continental fruitwood piano chair, possibly Russian, with a lyre-shaped back above a circular padded seat, on sabre legs terminating in black-painted paw feet, the back stamped "NI".

£1,000-1,500 **S&K**

A 19thC stained oak library reading chair, with a buttoned, leather upholstery seat, above a carved frieze with pull-out compartments, the leaf-carved splat flanked by facetted columns and incorporating a frieze drawer and a reading stand, on four curved leaf-carved struts, bracket feet.

£1,200-1,800 **L&T**

Two of a set of six Scottish Victorian rosewood chairs, each with a moulded oval back, with cartouche and husk cresting, a stuff-over serpentine velvet seat with a carved apron and cabriole legs, with scroll toes and thistle carving.

£800-1,200 set **L&T**

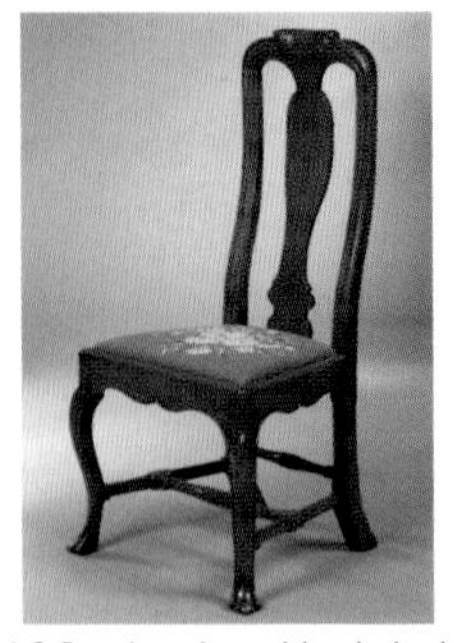

A 19thC Dutch walnut side chair, the tall rectangular moulded back with a vase splat above a drop-in floral needlework seat, shaped seat rails, cabriole front legs joined by turned and block H-stretchers.

£150-200 **L&T**

Two of a set of six Scottish Victorian rosewood chairs, each with a moulded oval back, a stuff-over serpentine velvet seat with a carved apron and cabriole legs, scroll toes and thistle carving.

£800-1,200 set **L&T**

A pair of Victorian papier mâché bedroom chairs, with cane seats, mother of pearl inlaid decoration and gilt highlights.

£180-220 **WW**

A pair of Victorian side chairs, with shaped padded backs and serpentine stuff-over seats, on scroll legs.

£120-180 **S&K**

One of a set of four Victorian rosewood balloon back chairs, each with a stuffover serpentine seat, moulded cabriole front legs with scroll toes.

£450-550 set **L&T**

A pair of late 19thC French Gothic Revival oak side chairs, raised on a tripod base.

31.5in (80cm) high

£2,200-2,800 pair **B&I**

A late 19thC satinwood and painted side chair, with a lyre back and caned seat.

£500-700 **DN**

Two of a set of five Victorian spoon-back parlour chairs, each with an open moulded back, a pierced scrolled splat, stuff-over seat and cabriole front legs with scroll toes and casters.

£1,800-2,200 set **L&T**

Two of a late 19thC set of four Louis XV-style giltwood chaises, each with shell cresting, a rocaille-pierced splat and an upholstered seat, on cabriole legs headed by foliage.

£800-1,200 **S&K**

A mahogany shell-top side chair, with ornate carving, on a tripod base.

25.5in (64.5cm) high

£4,000-6,000 **B&I**

A carved oak 'Burgomaster' chair, the back with three pierced ovals within turned supports, the brass studded leather seat on six leaf-capped short cabriole legs united by turned stretchers, paw feet and casters.

£500-800 WW

Two of a set of four Louis XV-style carved walnut chairs en cabriolet, comprising two fauteuils and two chaises, each with a button-upholstered cartouche-form back and cabriole legs.

£400-600 set S&K

Two Louis XV-style fruitwood chaise à la reine, each with a cartouche-shaped padded back, carved with ruffled C-scrolls and leaf tips, the over-upholstered serpentine-fronted seat raised on shell and leaf-carved cabriole legs.

£2,000-3,000 pair NA

HALL CHAIRS

A Regency carved mahogany hall chair, with a scrolled and shaped solid back, centring a painted armorial inscribed "Quo Vadis Sequinur", above a balloon-shaped seat on ring-turned tapering legs ending in peg feet.

c1815 *34.25in (85.5cm) high*

£180-220 S&K

One of a pair of George III mahogany hall chairs.

c1780 *39in (99cm) high*

£1,800-2,200 pair DL

A CLOSER LOOK AT PORTUGUESE HALL CHAIR

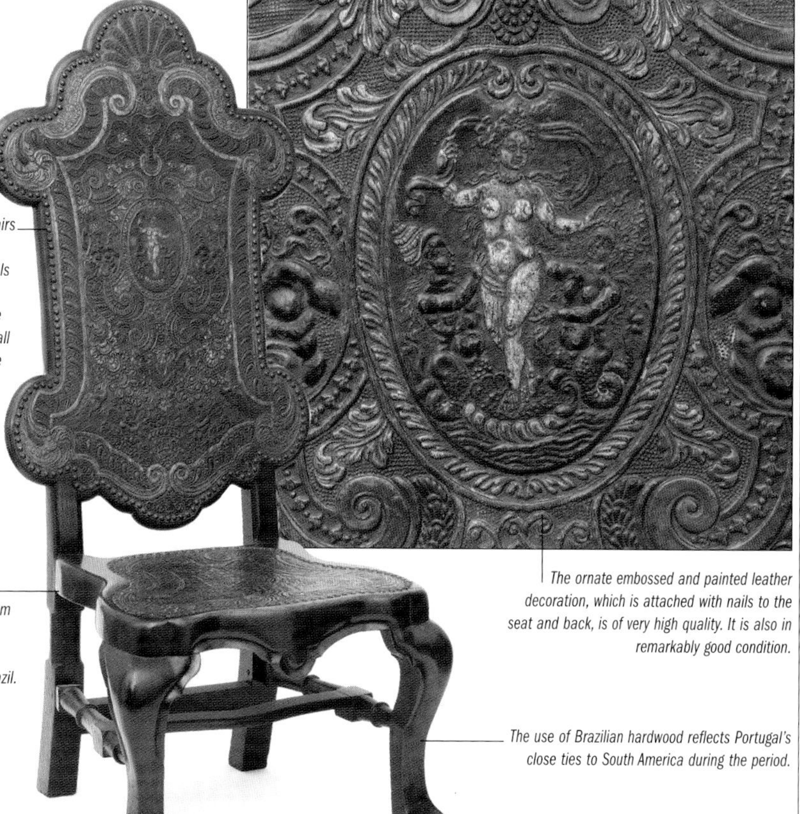

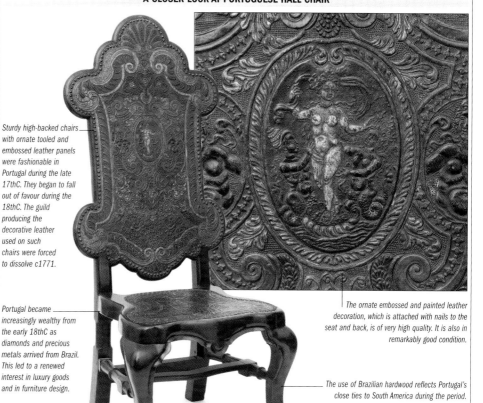

Sturdy high-backed chairs with ornate tooled and embossed leather panels were fashionable in Portugal during the late 17thC. They began to fall out of favour during the 18thC. The guild producing the decorative leather used on such chairs were forced to dissolve c1771.

The ornate embossed and painted leather decoration, which is attached with nails to the seat and back, is of very high quality. It is also in remarkably good condition.

Portugal became increasingly wealthy from the early 18thC as diamonds and precious metals arrived from Brazil. This led to a renewed interest in luxury goods and in furniture design.

The use of Brazilian hardwood reflects Portugal's close ties to South America during the period.

One of a pair of 18thC Portuguese hall chairs, of carved Brazilian hardwood with original embossed and painted leather seat and back.

c1720 *53in (104cm) high*

£10,000-12,500 pair JK

One of a set of three Sheraton mahogany hall chairs.

c1790 *38in (96.5cm) high*

£3,000-4,000 set **DL**

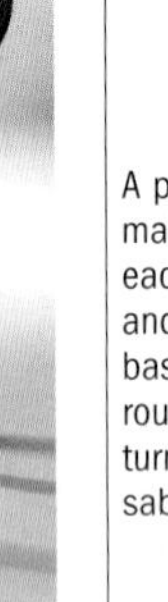

A Regency mahogany hall chair, with a panelled oval back on a waisted support, on ring turned front legs.

£400-450 **L&T**

A pair of early 19thC mahogany hall chairs, each with an oval back and shell motif, carved in bas relief, raised on rounded solid seats on turned tapering front legs, sabre legs to the rear.

£1,000-1,500 **L&T**

A George IV mahogany hall chair, the crescent shaped back carved with paterae and foliage, centred with a horse crest, with a solid seat, on ring turned tapering legs, repairs to leg.

33.75in (86cm) high

£400-600 **DN**

An Anglo-Indian ebonized mahogany hall chair.

c1835 *40in (101.5cm) high*

£2,000-3,000 **B&I**

A harlequin set of four 19thC Italian walnut hall chairs, in a medieval Gothic manner, each of pegged construction with stretchers below the seat, with solid, pierced, carved backs of different designs, the spreading seats with moulded and carved edges, on spreading chamfered front legs and single rear support.

£4,000-6,000 **L&T**

A Victorian oak hall chair, the pointed Gothic carved back surmounted by a fleur-de-lys, flanked by chamfered columns, the solid seat on octagonal tapering legs, with similar feet.

£400-600 **L&T**

A pair of late Victorian Gothic oak hall chairs, each with a pointed arch back enclosing two similar panels and rosette roundels, above a spreading seat and arcaded rail, on turned and tapering front legs, with bosses.

£600-900 **L&T**

A pair of Flemish Henry II-style carved oak hall armchairs, each with a tall panelled back, balustraded arms, a hinged seat and box base.

£1,200-1,800 **S&K**

One of a pair of mahogany Gainsborough-style elbow chairs, each with an upholstered back, arms and seat, with blind fret arm supports, legs and brackets, with H-stretchers.

37.5in (95cm) high

£10,000-12,000 pair **DN**

OPEN ARMCHAIRS

An early 18thC Louis XIV walnut and upholstered open armchair, the padded back and stuff-over seat covered in foliate-patterned tapestry fabric, with open S-scroll arms and conforming legs, joined by a wavy H-stretcher.

£1,000-1,500 **FRE**

A Chinese traditional open armchair, in solid padouk.

c1740 *43in (109cm) high*

£7,000-10,000 **B&I**

A mid to late 18thC Louis XVI Provincial cherrywood fauteuil à la reine, with an arched rectangular back, downswept arms, a bow-fronted stuff-over seat and turned tapering legs, channelled throughout.

£650-750 **S&K**

A matched pair of George III mahogany hall or drunkard chairs.

c1775 *87cm (34.25in) high*

£2,500-3,500 **RGA**

One of a set of six 18thC Adam-period armchairs, each painted and gilded with an oval stuffed back.

c1775 *37in (94cm) high*

£100,000-125,000 set **NOA**

Left to right: A George III mahogany armchair, with a yoked swag-carved top rail and a tapering pierced splat, the outscrolled arms above an upholstered seat on square tapering legs with spreading feet, joined by stretchers.

£400-600 **L&T**

A George III mahogany armchair, with a pierced ladder-back and scrolled arms, above an upholstered seat on square legs joined by stretchers.

£400-600 **L&T**

Left to right: A George III mahogany Raeburn chair, the serpentine top rail above padded open arms with down-scrolled moulded supports, on moulded chamfered legs with casters, joined by an H-stretcher.

£3,000-5,000 **L&T**

A George III mahogany Raeburn chair, the serpentine top rail above padded open arms with down-scrolled moulded supports, a serpentine seat rail and front legs with carved brackets joined by an H-stretcher, later casters.

£2,800-3,200 **L&T**

A George III mahogany armchair, with a shaped rail, over a pierced splat with scroll arms, all resting on square legs.

c1790

£700-1,000 **POOK**

A pair of late 18thC of Louis XVI carved beechwood fauteuils à la reine, each arched and padded back with downswept arms, the bow-fronted seat on turned, tapering, stop-fluted legs.

£2,000-3,000 **S&K**

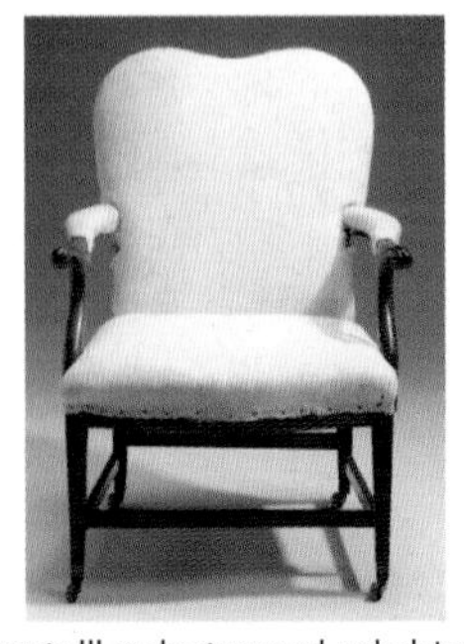

A George III mahogany and upholstered open armchair, the shaped back with outswept scroll arms above a stuff-over seat, raised on square tapered legs, joined by a stretcher and terminating in brass cappings and casters.

c1790

£500-800 **FRE**

An early George III mahogany chair back settee, the 'C' and 'S' scrolled top rail above two pierced vase splats and stuffover seat on chamfered square section legs joined by stretchers, with open outscrolled arms.

57.5in (147cm) wide

£2,000-3,000 **L&T**

A CLOSER LOOK AT AN HEPPLEWHITE-PERIOD ARMCHAIR

The term 'Hepplewhite period' refers to the last quarter of the 18thC. Hepplewhite's influential pattern book 'The Cabinet-maker and Upholsterer's Guide' was published posthumously in 1788. Highly regarded at the time, the Prince Regent owned many Hepplewhite pieces.

Chairs in the Hepplewhite style have distinctive shield or heart-shaped backs.

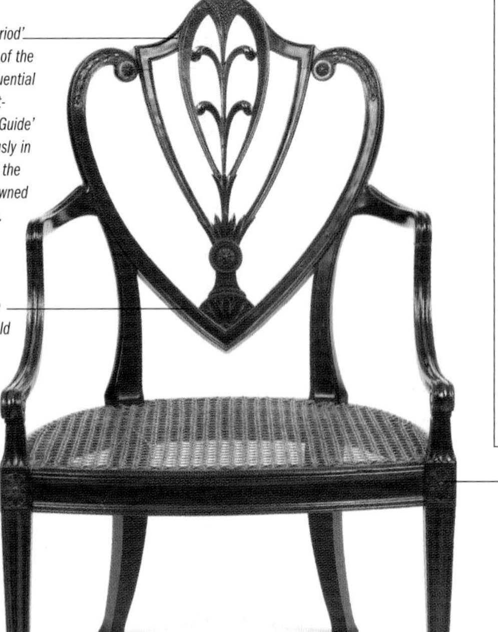

These pieces are typical of Hepplewhite's designs, which feature slender, elegant furniture with inlaid rather than carved decoration.

The spade foot was used from the end of the 18thC and was incorporated into pieces by leading furniture designers such as Hepplewhite and Sheraton.

One of a set of four Hepplewhite-period carved mahogany armchairs, en suite pair of window seats, the 'Harvey Suite'.

c1780 *37.5in (95cm) high*

£170,000-200,000 set **NOA**

A 19thC mahogany X-frame chair, designed by Thomas Hope in the manner of the ancient curule chair.

c1805 *38in (96.5cm) high*

£15,000-18,000 **JK**

One of a pair of George III mahogany cockpen-backed armchairs.

c1800 *35.25in (89.5cm) high*

£6,000-9,000 pair **DL**

One of a pair of Regency brass-inlaid armchairs.

c1820 *33in (84cm) high*

£2,200-2,800 pair **DL**

A late Regency mahogany gentleman's armchair, the buttoned, upholstered back between moulded scrolling uprights, above open arms with padded rests and scrolling terminals, raised on baluster turned front legs, the back and seat reclining together.

£400-600 **L&T**

One of a pair of George IV mahogany library chairs.

c1825 *40in (101.5cm) high*

£10,000-15,000 pair **DL**

A pair of American classically-figured mahogany gondola chairs, from New York, each with a curved back and vasiform solid splat, the downswept stiles continuing into shaped sabre front legs, with a padded slip seat.

c1830

£500-600 **S&K**

A 19thC Colonial planter's chair, possibly English, carved oak with leather upholstery, on brass casters.

c1840 *39in (100cm) high*

£5,000-7,000 **JK**

A pair of early 19thC Scottish mahogany library armchairs, each with a buttoned back and open downscrolled arms, with turned supports and squabs, a stuff-over buttoned seat and ring turned front legs with brass caps and casters.

£2,000-3,000 **L&T**

One of a pair of 19thC George II-style walnut 'shepherd's crook' library armchairs.

40.5in (103cm) high

£28,000-32,000 pair **B&I**

A mid-19thC Indian open armchair, with sadeli work decoration within ebony and ivory borders, losses to decoration.

£350-450 **WW**

A 19thC Dutch colonial rosewood open armchair, the foliage carved splat back above scroll-over arms, with a scroll-carved rail, on sabre legs, a later leather covered seat.

£600-900 **WW**

A Victorian rosewood open armchair, with outsplayed arms, knop turned legs, brass cappings and casters.

£400-600 **WW**

A pair of 19thC Empire-style mahogany fauteuils, with curved open arms with gilded leaf collars and carved dolphin head terminals, raised on square cabriole front legs.

£2,500-3,000 **L&T**

A 19thC Selanese ebony planter's chair, with a leaf and flower-carved back and seat rails, with downscrolled open arms, shaped front legs terminating in stylized claw feet, the deep upholstered seat formerly caned.

£1,800-2,200 **L&T**

A 19thC Italian calamander and ivory-inlaid chair, in late 16thC colonial style, with a tapestry fabric back and seat, the square supports, scrolled arms and pierced hinged stretchers inlaid with the Greek key pattern.

£3,000-4,000 **L&T**

One of a pair of late 19thC Louis XV-style carved giltwood and upholstered fauteuils, the shaped backs and serpentine stuff-over seats covered in red fabric, with outswept carved cabriole scroll legs.

£650-750 pair **FRE**

A late 19th to early 20thC fruitwood elbow chair, with a caned back and seat, raised on square tapering legs, with an H-stretcher.

34in (86.5cm) high

£350-450 **DN**

An Edwardian satinwood elbow chair in the Hepplewhite-style, the heart-shaped back carved with 'Prince of Wales' feathers, on square tapering legs.

£800-1,200 **DN**

A George II mahogany open armchair, the carved serpentine top rail above a pierced interlaced splat and scrolling arms, the stuff-over seat with woolwork panel, cabriole legs with shell carving and ball and claw feet.

£1,000-1,500 **L&T**

Left to right: A Queen Anne style walnut open armchair, the back with a vase splat inlaid with neo-classical motifs, outscrolled arms and a drop-in needlework seat, cabriole legs with pad feet, shaped H-stretcher.

£500-700 **L&T**

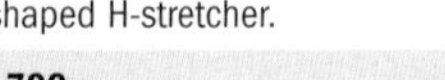

A Queen Anne style walnut open armchair, the back with a pierced vase splat, outscrolled open arms and a drop-in needlework seat, cabriole legs with pad feet

£300-500 **L&T**

A Continental mahogany grotto-style armchair.

37in (94cm) high

£3,000-5,000 **B&I**

A pair of Louis XVI-style giltwood fauteuils à medallion à la reine, with padded oval backs, outcurved arms, stuff-over seats and turned, tapering, fluted legs, frame channelled throughout and carved with feuillage and ruban enroulé, covered in old figural Aubusson panels.

£800-1,200 **S&K**

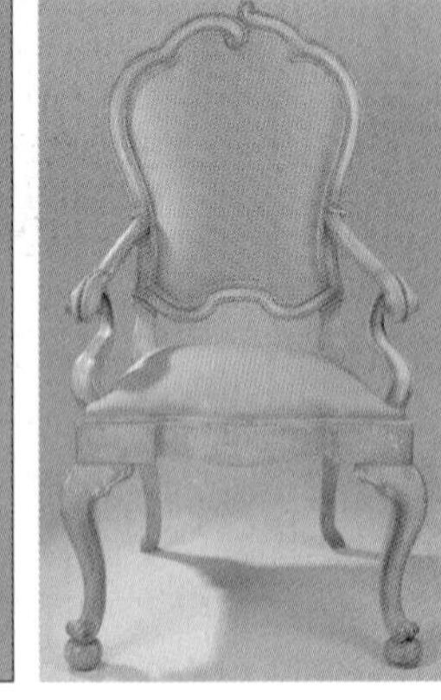

One of a pair of Continental painted and parcel-gilt armchairs.

41.5in (105.5cm) high

£5,000-7,000 pair **B&I**

One of a set of six Louis XV Provincial-style beechwood dining chairs, comprising two fauteuils and four chaises, each with a padded cartouche-form back, stuff-over serpentine-fronted seat and cabriole legs, joined by a shaped H-stretcher, the frame moulded throughout.

£1,000-1,500 set **S&K**

A stained beech and upholstered bergère, in the style of Syrie Maugham, upholstered in rust-red striped Lelievre 'Cauchois velour' fabric, with scrolling open arms, with squab and short cabriole legs.

£2,000-3,000 **L&T**

A pair of giltwood fauteuils, of North Italian-style, each with an arched acanthus and harebell carved cresting above a cream velvet, upholstered back, arms and seat, on carved cabriole legs and cup feet.

£2,000-3,000 L&T

A pair of Louis XV-style walnut fauteuils, each moulded, upholstered, cartouche-shaped backrest carved with a floral spray, above padded armrests set on moulded, voluted supports, the over-upholstered seat above a serpentine-fronted apron carved to match, raised on moulded cabriole legs, upholstered in floral needlepoint.

£2,500-3,000 NA

A pair of Elizabethan-style carved oak open arm chairs, each with a rectangular back with foliate finials, fleur-de-lys and gothic arch carving on a stippled ground, a brown leather upholstered seat on ring and block turned legs, ending in bun feet, connected by a flowerhead-carved front stretcher.

£700-1,000 S&K

A William and Mary-style oak armchair, with a rectangular back, scroll-carved arms, the block-and-baluster turned legs connected by a similarly carved stretcher, chamfered rear legs.

40in (100cm) high

£100-150 S&K

A baroque-style walnut arm chair, with an oval padded back and seat, on turned and block legs, joined by an arched pierced rayed stretcher and further turned H-stretchers, on ball feet, with tapestry upholstery.

£180-220 S&K

A Louis XV-style carved beechwood open arm chair, with velvet upholstery.

£300-400 S&K

A French provincial-style brass-inlaid fruitwood double cane-back armchair, with a concave back, a brass-inlaid centre splat above a cane seat, on cabriole legs, a red damask cushion.

31in (77.5cm) high

£350-450 S&K

A French Louis XV-style beech open armchair, the shield-shaped back with a leaf-carved crest, the down-swept arms carved with leaves, with a padded woolwork back, armrests and seat, on turned and fluted legs.

24.5in (62cm) wide

£300-400 DN

A set of eight Regency style black-and-gilt-painted open armchairs, with cane seats, Neo-classical decoration, bamboo-style tapering, with slightly flared legs and fitted cushions.

£1,800-2,200 set S&K

A walnut framed Carolean style armchair, with moulded scrolling frame and upholstered back and sides, open arms, legs joined by stretchers.

£250-350 L&T

ARMCHAIRS

An English Queen Anne mahogany wing chair, with scrolled arms supported by cabriole legs and pad feet.

c1730

£2,000-3,000 **POOK**

A George III wing chair, the upholstered back with lugged sides and outscrolled arms, raised on square section chamfered legs, with brackets and an H-stretcher.

£800-1,200 **L&T**

A Regency fruitwood library armchair, the curved top rail with thumbnail mouldings, above down-swept arms, with beast head terminals, the carved hide upholstered back with a studded border, an upholstered seat with a squab cushion, on tapering sabre legs, with block feet.

£1,800-2,200 **L&T**

Left to Right: An Edwardian Regency Revival satinwood bergère library armchair, the square cane back with a formerly painted central tablet, above cane arms and seat, on round ogee square section tapering legs.

£1,200-1,800 **L&T**

A Regency mahogany bergère library armchair, the square back with moulded frame, with turned and reeded upright arm supports and legs, on brass casters.

£1,500-2,200 **L&T**

An early 19thC mahogany framed settee, of small proportions, the upholstered back with sloping arms, above an upholstered seat, on square legs with blind fretwork carving and curved bracket supports, linked by pierced stretchers.

38.75in (97cm) wide

£1,200-1,800 **L&T**

A pair of ebonised early 19thC library armchairs, each with applied square and down-swept upholstered arms, with a separate squab to the seat, raised on turned tapering front legs, brass caps and casters.

£2,200-2,800 **L&T**

A CLOSER LOOK AT AN REGENCY BERGÈRE

This bergère is finely ornamented with crisp, carved and inlaid decoration. The fluted design to the centre of each leg reflected contemporary classical tastes.

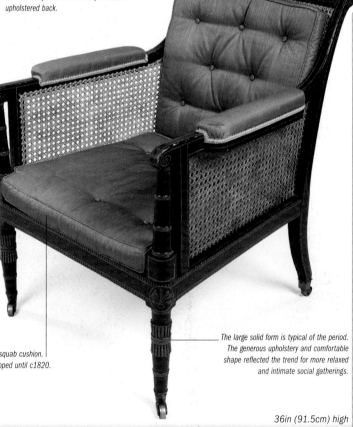

Popular in the 19thC and 20thC, the bergère is an informal easy chair with a deep seat and upholstered back.

This chair supports a removable stuffed squab cushion. Coiled upholstery springs were not developed until c1820.

The large solid form is typical of the period. The generous upholstery and comfortable shape reflected the trend for more relaxed and intimate social gatherings.

A Regency decorated bergère.

c1810 *36in (91.5cm) high*

£3,500-4,500 **DL**

An early 19thC mahogany library armchair, with a reeded frame and arm supports, the caned back and seat with loose cushions, on reeded turned legs with brass casters, restoration.

24.75in (63cm) wide

£1,200-1,800 **DN**

A late Regency mahogany library armchair, with solid upholstered arms with pomegranate terminals, the sides carved with rosette and palmette panels on turned tapering front legs with casters, with applied carpet upholstered panels.

£2,500-3,000 **L&T**

A 19thC mahogany bergère armchair, the square cane back and lower arms with turned front supports and buttoned squab cushions, raised on turned front legs with brass caps and casters.

£800-1,200 **L&T**

A 19thC Louis XV-style white-painted bergère, with a moulded, arched floral-carved crest, the curved padded arms with scroll-carved grips, the padded back and sides upholstered in rose velvet with nailhead trim, a squab cushion, on moulded cabriole legs.

37.5in (94cm) high

£500-700 **S&K**

A pair of Napoleon III carved walnut and parcel-gilt bergères en cabriolet, each with an arched, curved and padded back continuing into down-swept arms, the bow-fronted seat on cabriole legs with scroll toes, carved throughout with rose heads, guilloche-banding and feuillage.

c1860

£1,500-2,000 **S&K**

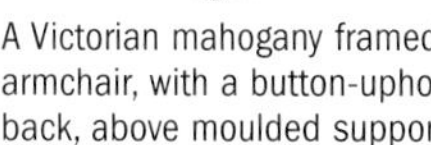

A Victorian mahogany framed easy armchair, with a button-upholstered back, above moulded supports and a serpentine seat.

£500-700 **WW**

A late Victorian walnut gentleman's library armchair with leather upholstery, the buttoned back between moulded uprights, a stuffover seat and padded arms, on baluster supports.

£300-500 **L&T**

A pair of armchairs from an early 20thC mahogany parlour suite, with carved Neo-classical decoration, also comprising a two-seat sofa, each piece with a stuff-over back, square section legs and casters, modern upholstery.

£1,000-1,500 set **L&T**

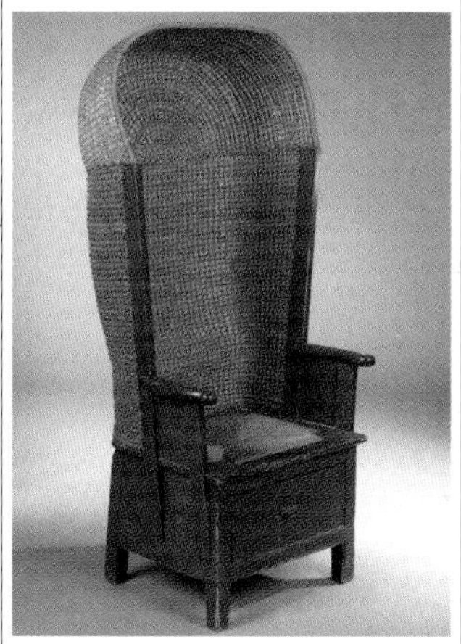

A late 19thC Orkney chair, the hooded cowl back above typical panelled arms and a drop-in rush seat, with a drawer below, square legs with beaded edges.

£1,500-2,000 **L&T**

A late 19thC Victorian gilt wood armchair, the tufted back with gilt, foliate and scroll-carved stiles, above a padded seat and outward scrolling padded arms, turned legs and casters.

£180-220 **S&K**

An early 20thC George III-style mahogany upholstered easy chair, the curved crest above rolled arms, raised on cabriole legs with claw and ball feet, rose and beige silk damask upholstery.

39in (97.5cm) high

£400-600 **S&K**

An early 20thC pair of Italian Renaissance Revival carved walnut palazzo chairs, each with a shaped padded back and seat, carved with lion-head terminals, dolphin-form feet and acanthus foliage.

£2,000-2,500 S&K

A 20thC George III style mahogany wing chair, with outward scrolling armrests and a squab cushion, on square legs connected by stretchers, with striped upholstery.

47in (117.5cm) high

£500-800 S&K

A 20thC Louis XVI-style parcel-gilt white-painted fauteuil, with a square moulded back and an arched crest, continuing to down-swept arms above a trapezoidal seat with a down-filled loose cushion on fluted legs, cream silk damask upholstery.

36.5in (91cm) high

£200-300 S&K

A Regency-style leather wing armchair, the barrel back with outscrolled arms and squat seat, on moulded front legs.

£500-700 L&T

A pair of easy armchairs, of low form, upholstered in apricot fabric with a tasselled fringe, on square tapering mahogany legs and brass casters, upholstered in Colefax & Fowler's 'Dalmatian' fabric.

£1,500-2,000 L&T

An Empire-style mahogany and gilt metal-mounted tub chair, with a wrap around back, with moulded square tapering legs and paw feet.

£450-650 WW

A gilt wood fan-back fauteuil, with leaf-carved decoration above padded arms and seat, on turned and fluted legs.

£600-900 WW

A William IV-style mahogany bergère, down-swept arms and cannon-ball feet.

£600-900 S&K

A Louis XV-style double cane-back child's arm chair, with a striped and floral silk cushion.

£200-300 S&K

A French provincial-style white-painted wing chair, upholstered with brown cotton sateen fabric.

£220-280 S&K

A Chippendale-style wing chair, with moulded legs and an H-stretcher, trellis-pattern upholstery.

£300-400 S&K

An opposing pair of armchairs by Lutyens Design Associates, the out-scrolled back and arms upholstered in horsehair, on fluted square section tapered legs with brass casters.

These chairs were originally designed by Sir Edward Lutyens for his own personal use after a model he had seen in a print of Napoleon. These modern reproductions were made by a firm set up by his granddaughter to recreate his designs.

£2,800-3,200 **L&T**

A mahogany tub chair, the shaped, incised back in the form of a stylized flower, on cabriole legs.

£600-900 **L&T**

A Louis XV carved beech canape, the serpentine moulded crest rail carved with flowerheads and foliate sprays, continuing to padded armrests raised on incurved moulded supports, the bow-fronted fluted seat rail applied with carved rosettes, raised on circular tapered stop-fluted legs.

76in (190cm) wide

£2,500-3,000 **NA**

A late 18thC gilt wood settee, the upholstered serpentine back within a moulded frame with carved foliage decoration, on cabriole legs.

58in (147.5cm) wide

£4,000-6,000 **WW**

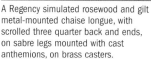

A Regency simulated rosewood and gilt metal-mounted chaise longue, with scrolled three quarter back and ends, on sabre legs mounted with cast anthemions, on brass casters.

80in (200cm) wide

£1,200-1,800 **L&T**

A Louis XV-style beech double cane bergère chair, the moulded and carved scrolling frame with a tub back and cabriole legs.

£350-450 **L&T**

A tub armchair, the leather upholstered back and seat with shaped lugs and out-scrolled arms, on square section tapering legs with block feet and casters.

£1,000-1,500 **L&T**

A Louis XVI painted beechwood love seat, with a curved back.

41.5in (105.5cm) wide

£3,000-4,000 **DL**

A George III mahogany Hepplewhite sofa, with a padded rectangular back and arms, square section tapering legs, brass caps and casters.

c1780 *62in (157.5cm) wide*

£1,000-1,500 **S&K**

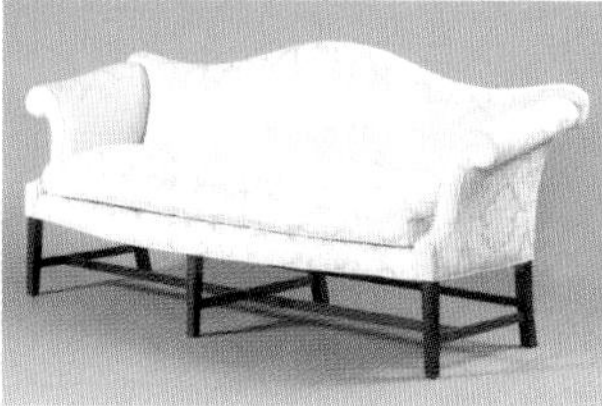

A George III mahogany camel-back sofa, the serpentine back above outscrolled arms and a loose seat cushion, raised on moulded square legs, joined by a recessed box stretcher.

85in (212.5cm) wide

£2,200-2,800 **NA**

A Regency ebonized framed sofa, the scroll-over back and arms upholstered in a Regency stripe fabric above a squab cushion with two bolsters, the moulded and bobbin-inset frame with brass roundels to the terminals, raised on reeded sabre legs, brass caps and casters.

74in (185cm) wide

£2,000-2,500 **L&T**

A Regency settee, overpainted in verdis gris and gilt, the back comprising four lattice backs, with musical trophy panels and out-scrolled top rail, caned seat with squab and down-scrolled open arms, turned front legs with brass caps and casters.

73in (185cm) wide

£600-900 **L&T**

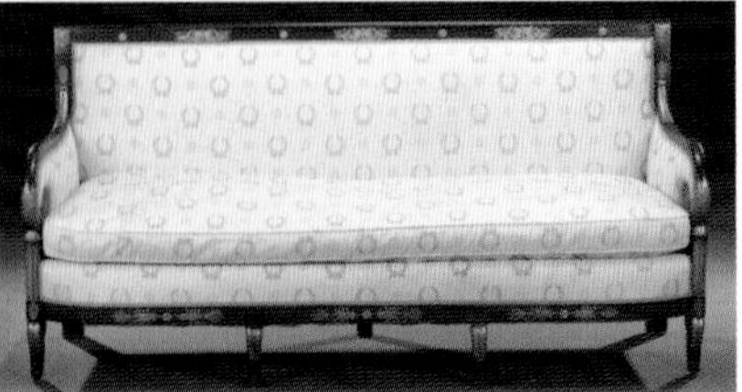

An early 19thC Empire ormolu-mounted mahogany settee, the gilt-bronze mounts with figures, hounds, urns, rosettes and palmettes, the scrolled arms enriched with carved and gilt leaf tips and scrolls, raised on short scroll feet carved with leaves.

72in (180cm) wide

£1,000-1,500 **S&K**

A Regency simulated rosewood chaise longue, with gilt metal mounts and upholstered sides, back and seat, on sabre legs with brass acanthus-cast terminals and casters, some worn.

78.75in (200cm) wide

£400-600 **DN**

An early 19thC Continental walnut show frame sofa, with serpentine crest, the outswept arms with roundels and outswept feet.

69.25in (176cm) wide

£300-500 **DN**

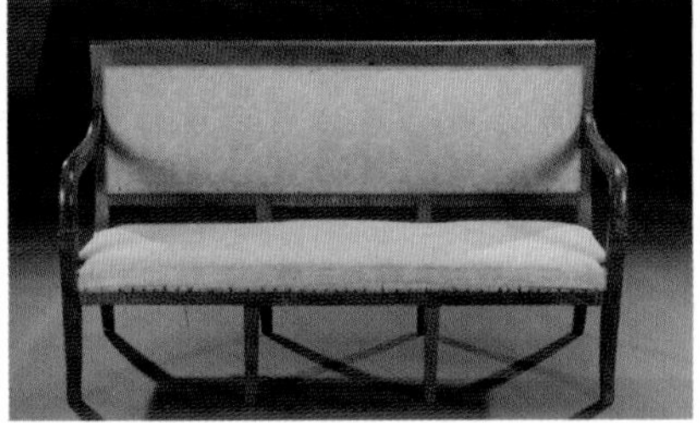

An early 19thC French Empire walnut country canapé à la reine, with a padded rectangular back, downswept arms, stuff-over seat and eight sabre legs.

64in (162cm) wide

£800-1,200 **S&K**

A pair of early 19thC sofas, each with a square back and arms and slightly scrolled top rails, on square section tapered mahogany legs and casters, one with original folding base converting to a bed, both with original linen upholstery and horse hair squabs.

77.25in (196cm) wide

£4,000-6,000 **L&T**

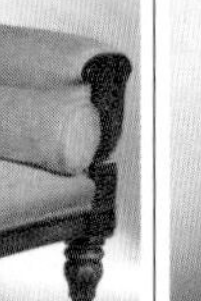

A William IV mahogany sofa, with brass stringing, the panelled top rail flanked by leaf-carved scrolling terminals, the upholstered lower arms with leaf-carved urn terminals, on turned and carved tapering feet, with brass caps and casters, a pair of bolsters.

80.25in (204cm) wide

£1,800-2,200 **L&T**

A 19thC Russian mahogany-framed sofa, the ornately scroll-carved top rail with anthemion motifs above down-swept solid arms, with scroll-carved terminals enclosing an upholstered back and seat on sabre front and rear legs.

83.5in (212cm) wide

£1,800-2,200 **L&T**

A mid-19thC Continental Empire carved walnut canapé, the slightly arched padded back continuing to padded arms, the serpentine-fronted seat on scrolled legs joined by a scrolled skirt.

86in (218.5cm) wide

£300-400 **S&K**

A Victorian carved walnut settee, the shaped back centred by a flower and grape-carved crest, out-scrolling arms, serpentine apron on cabriole legs.

70in (175cm) wide

£180-220 **S&K**

A Victorian ebonized and upholstered parlour suite, covered in a gold, buttoned fabric comprised of a settee window seat, two side chairs and two further matched side chairs, each with tasselled aprons raised on turned legs, terminating in casters.

c1890

£1,500-2,000 set **FRE**

A CLOSER LOOK AT A MOORISH SETTEE

The Western Moorish style is based on the architecture and design principles of North African Muslims.

This settee exhibits classic elements of Moorish design such as a geometric form, arches, the use of symmetry and inlaid decoration.

This settee is inlaid with mother of pearl and ivory.

The seat is upholstered with Tekke carpet. The Tekke tribal group produced a large volume of important patterned carpets and other artefacts in West Turkestan. They were highly regarded during the 19thC.

A mid-19thC Moorish walnut settee, made in Spain, carved with Cyrillic characters, the seat upholstered with Tekke carpet.

c1860 *53in (135cm) wide*

£5,000-8,000 **JK**

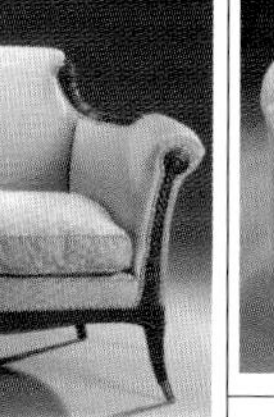

A Continental Classical-style carved walnut and parcel-gilt sofa, with a padded over-scroll back, out-curved over-scroll arms, a serpentine-front squab-cushion seat and splayed turned legs, with rope carved decoration throughout.

c1900 *84in (210cm) wide*

£600-900 **S&K**

A late Victorian walnut club sofa, with a low, over-scroll padded back, continuing into similar arms, a stuff-over seat and short ring-turned legs.

c1900 *70in (178cm) wide*

£400-600 **S&K**

A late 19th to early 20thC Classical-style mahogany and upholstered settee.

78in (198cm) wide

£300-500 **S&K**

A walnut-framed two seater settee, finely carved with leaf scrolls and flowers, on four cabriole supports, in the French style.

c1900 *122cm (48in) wide*

£2,500-3,500 **RGA**

A 20thC Louis XVI-style carved walnut canapé, the moulded and ribbon-carved frame with a floral-carved crest, above a three-section padded back, with a cushioned seat over a similarly carved apron, on fluted, tapered legs, headed by floral-carved patera, ending in peg feet.

50in (125cm) wide

£1,000-1,500 **S&K**

A George I-style stained mahogany sofa, the straight paper-scrolled back with carved and scrolled ends, flanked by padded arms with out-scrolled lions' head terminals, cabriole legs, with paw feet and casters.

£700-900 **L&T**

A Louis XVI-style walnut window seat, with a caned seat and out-scrolled ends, on leaf-clasped and fluted, turned, tapered legs, with toupie feet.

36in (91cm) wide

£320-380 **L&T**

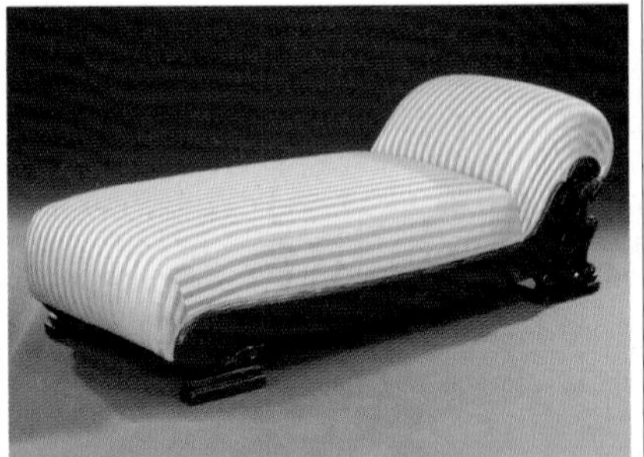

An Empire-style mahogany recamier, with a scrolled, padded head and rectangular, padded seat, the frame carved with griffin supports, on bracket feet.

80in (203cm) wide

£800-1,200 **S&K**

A Louis XVI-style painted recamier, with an over-scroll backrest, a bolster cushion and sabre legs, the frame channelled throughout.

55in (139.5cm) wide

£3,000-4,000 **S&K**

A Louis XV-style gilt wood canapé en cabriolet, with an arched and padded back continuing into down-curved arms, a serpentine-fronted squab seat and cabriole legs, the frame channelled throughout and carved with flowerheads.

81.5in (207cm) wide

£600-900 **S&K**

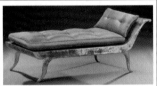

A Regency-style silvered recamier, of whimsical, angled, rectangular form, with an over-scroll backrest, sabre legs and mink-coloured squab cushion.

81.25in (206.5cm) wide

£280-320 **S&K**

A Louis XIV-style tabouret longue, with a padded rectangular stuff-over seat, square-section tapering gadrooned legs, bun feet and X-stretchers.

£400-600 **S&K**

A gilt wood and upholstered settee, of Louis XVI style, with a harebell-carved frame, the out-scrolled arms and serpentine seat upholstered in pink damask fabric, on acanthus carved and fluted tapering legs.

98in (245cm) wide

£1,500-2,000 **L&T**

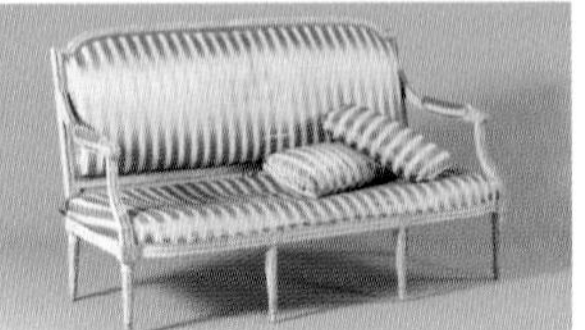

A Louis XVI-style grey-painted canapé, the moulded crest rail above a padded back and armrests, set on moulded supports, the over-upholstered seat raised on stop-fluted, circular, tapered legs.

63in (157.5cm) wide

£1,200-1,800 **NA**

A pair of Continental Biedermeier carved fruitwood small settees, each with a rectangular crest and twin-carved, interlaced splats with scrolls, above an upholstered slip sear, with flanking armrests on supports, continuing to square tapering legs.

5in (87.5cm) wide

£3,000-5,000 **NA**

A 17thC oak stool, the rectangular top above moulded frieze rails and turned and blocked legs, joined by stretchers, a split to top.

11in (28cm) wide

£400-600 **L&T**

A Queen Anne walnut stool, the rectangular stuff-over top above moulded rails and cabriole legs, with shell-covered knees and with pointed-toe feet.

26.5in (67cm) wide

£3,500-4,500 **L&T**

A pair of 18thC Italian wrought iron and leather upholstered savonarola chairs, with brass ball finials, on x-form bases ending in bun feet.

£600-900 **FRE**

A late 18thC to early 19thC American footstool, with original red paint, the seat with an original needlework cover, with a fruit and floral design.

11.5in (26cm) wide

£800-1,200 **PH**

A 19thC early George III-style mahogany stool, the rectangular top with a stuff-over seat, square section chamfered legs with 'C' scroll brackets, a pierced H-stretcher.

21.25in (54cm) wide

£350-450 **L&T**

A Regency mahogany X-frame stool, the rectangular top with a leather seat raised on incised scrolling splats, joined by a turned stretcher, with applied gilt brass on the anthemion mounts.

20.75in (52cm) wide

£700-1,000 **L&T**

A Regency mahogany stool.

c1810 *20in (51cm) wide*

£3,000-4,000 **DL**

A Georgian milking stool.

c1810 *13in (33cm) high*

£100-150 **EP**

A Georgian stool, original paint finish.

c1820 *10in (25.5cm) high*

£50-70 **EP**

An early 19thC simulated rosewood footstool, wormed and lacking original ball feet.

15in (38cm) wide

£100-150 **WW**

A mid-19thC simulated rosewood stool, the rectangular stuff-over seat above plain rails and lappet-carved, turned, tapering legs with casters.

27.5in (70cm) wide

£600-900 **L&T**

A 19thC Italian cast iron and upholstered savonarola chair, with a lobed brass cup and cover finials, rope twist arms above a padded seat with foliage-patterned fabric, cabriole legs.

42in (105cm) high

£700-1,000 **FRE**

A pair of mid-19thC Anglo-Indian rosewood stools, each with rectangular flamework squab above a moulded curvilinear apron, legs with scroll toes.

22in (56cm) wide

£1,200-1,800 **L&T**

A Victorian walnut stool, the rectangular stuff-over woolwork top with shaped aprons and moulded cabriole legs.

38.75in (97cm) wide

£1,500-2,000 **L&T**

A Victorian walnut log stool, the rectangular drop-in seat above a shaped and moulded seat rail and cabriole legs, with scroll toes.

44in (112cm) wide

£1,500-2,000 **L&T**

A Victorian rosewood Rococo-style stool, the rectangular stuff-over top above a moulded rail and cabriole legs, with scroll toes.

43.25in (110cm) wide

£1,500-2,000 **L&T**

A late 19thC cream painted Thebes stool.

16in (40.5cm) wide

£1,500-2,000 **B&I**

A late 19thC carved rosewood stool, the burgundy velvet-covered stuff-over top above a frieze, the cabriole legs richly carved with foliage and C-scrolls, with knurled toes.

39.75in (101cm) wide

£2,200-2,800 **WW**

A late 19thC Italian gilt gesso footstool, in Rococo style, the raised back moulded with a shell and foliate scrolls, above a padded seat, on 'X' shaped supports and decorated with garrya.

25.5in (65cm) high

£350-450 **DN**

An early 20thC gilt wood stool, with fluting and acanthus decoration, the rectangular stuff-over seat with raised out-scrolled open ends, turned legs, overgilt.

26in (66cm) wide

£500-800 **L&T**

A George I-style walnut stool, the rectangular stuff-over seat raised on shell-carved cabriole legs, with ball and claw feet.

20in (50cm) wide

£700-1,000 **L&T**

A George I-style ebonized stool, with a padded oval seat, cabriole legs and hoof feet.

£350-400 **S&K**

A Louis XV-style gilt metal-mounted walnut piano stool, the stuff-over adjustable seat with shaped concave-moulded rails, on cabriole legs, gilt metal, floral and foliate mounts.

£500-800 **S&K**

An English mahogany back stool, with a crewelwork-upholstered straight back and seat, over square legs, joined by an H-stretcher.

£350-450 **POOK**

A pair of George II-style mahogany footstools, each over-upholstered seat raised on scroll-carved cabriole legs, carved at the knees with an acanthus leaf and ending in hairy paw feet.

19in (47.5cm) high

£1,800-2,200 **NA**

A William and Mary-style walnut stool, the needlepoint-upholstered seat with serpentine apron above trumpet-form legs, carved with blocks, joined by C-stretchers centring an urn, on bun feet.

19.25in (48cm) wide

£700-1,000 **S&K**

A Chippendale-style mahogany tufted brown leather-top footstool, the serpentine top above a fret-carved apron on down-curving, tapering legs ending in ball and claw feet.

25in (62.5cm) wide

£500-800 **S&K**

A mahogany-framed square stool, the stuff-over seat upholstered in Howard fabric, on square section legs with brass casters, stamped "Howard & Sons".

22.75in (58cm) wide

£700-900 **L&T**

COFFERS

An early to mid-17thC oak coffer, with carved detail.

38in (96.5cm) wide

£1,800-2,200 EP

A 17thC oak dough bin, of plank construction, the hinged lid above a front with incised lozenge decoration, crimped corners, cut-out trestle ends.

38in (97cm) wide

£400-600 L&T

A 17thC oak kist, the three-panelled front with guilloche carvings and a frieze of acorns and animals, stile feet, some later carving.

53.5in (136cm) wide

£600-900 L&T

A 17thC Spanish wrought-iron polychrome-painted coffer, the rectangular top inset with leather, beneath the wrought-iron straps, the intricate lock lifting to an intricately incised and pierced panel, decorated with flora and fauna above a well, with cast-iron bail handles and decorative hasps, floral painted decoration, on lion's head-carved oak supports.

32in (80cm) wide

£1,500-2,000 S&K

A 17thC oak coffer, with carved detail.

c1660 *48in (120cm) wide*

£2,000-2,400 EP

A late 17thC Italian carved walnut cassone, the hinged lid opening to a storage well above a foliate panelled front, with a later cupboard door, enclosing three later drawers, the gadrooned apron raised on paw feet, restoration and alterations.

54.75in (139cm) wide

£1,200-1,800 S&K

An 18thC North European oak chest, with a moulded rectangular top and base, vertical sides and with a decorative iron escutcheon.

33.5in (85cm) wide

£700-1,000 S&K

A Charles II carved oak lap desk, the chip-carved sloped top opening to reveal a partially fitted interior, the front carved with stylized Celtic knots and foliage.

c1680 *18.5in (46cm) diam*

£250-300 FRE

A Charles II oak coffer, the hinged plank top above a lunette-carved frieze and triple-panelled front, raised on tall stile feet.

c1680 *48in (120cm) wide*

£400-600 FRE

A 17thC oak mule chest, with a fine dark colour and patina.

c1690 *45.5in (115.5cm) wide*

£2,500-3,500 EP

A Georgian mahogany dwarf chest, the hinged rectangular top with a moulded edge, enclosing a divided interior, brass carry handles, plinth base.

23in (58cm) wide

£250-300 **L&T**

An early 19thC mahogany brass-bound jewellery case, by G. Palmer of James Street, London, with a coronet, the lid with panel engraved "Lord Kinnaird", an engraved brass trade plate and printed trade label to the interior, the interior fittings now removed.

14.5in (37cm) wide

£120-180 **L&T**

A 19thC Zanzibar brass-mounted teakwood marriage chest, with a hinged lid, with a candle till, three external drawers and turned feet, brass studs and decorative straps throughout.

46in (117cm) wide

£250-300 **S&K**

A 19thC Spanish Colonial painted pine dowery chest, with a hinged, vaulted lid, decorated with polychrome landscapes, inscriptions and heraldic devices on a black ground.

32.75in (83cm) wide

£500-700 **S&K**

A 19thC bird's-eye maple and mahogany parquetry coffer, with a cubic-veneered, panelled front, raised on shaped bracket feet.

36.5in (91cm) wide

£500-800 **FRE**

A 17thC-style chest, the panelled top above three front panels, floral and rosette motifs, later carved.

48in (122cm) wide

£150-200 **L&T**

A Continental painted pine chest, with a hinged lid, the front decorated with panels of flowers in vases, metal side handles, on bracket feet.

50in (127cm) wide

£300-400 **WW**

An early 18thC chest, with panelled sides, the rectangular top above two short drawers over three long drawers, with a fine coloured patina.

39in (99cm) wide

£2,500-3,500 **EP**

An English Jacobean yew chest of drawers, the rectangular top above two short drawers, over three drawers with elaborately moulded panelled fronts, raised on bun feet.

37in (94cm) wide

£5,000-7,000 **NA**

A George II mahogany metamorphic bachelor's chest, the rectangular top above a brushing slide and a long drawer, with an arrangement of six short drawers flanking a kneehole with four sliding forward drawers, the pedestals with bracket feet.

33.5in (84cm) wide

£6,000-9,000 **L&T**

A George III mahogany serpentine gentleman's fitted dressing chest, the shaped top with mahogany and satinwood cross-banding, serpentine sides, the fitted drawer with brushed slide, inside compartments and pigeonholes, above three drawers, on scroll-carved bracket feet.

c1765 *44in (110cm) wide*

£3,000-4,000 **FRE**

A CLOSER LOOK AT A QUEEN ANNE CHEST

The restrained style favoured during the Queen Anne period of 1702-14 contrasted markedly with earlier, ornate, Baroque design. Part of the appeal of furniture rested on the beautiful colouring of the wood.
This piece has a particularly fine patina.
Feather banding was adopted for chests in the late 17thC. Two strips of veneer are banded together to form a feather or herringbone effect.
Bun feet were often replaced with bracket feet at a later date. Check for old holes in the base of furniture indicating that feet have been replaced.

A rare Queen Anne burr elm chest of two short and three long feather-banded drawers, the top quarter-veneered and with ebony strung borders and yew wood crossbanding, the mouldings and bun feet also in yew wood, the sides quarter-veneered and crossbanded in burr wood, possibly field maple, with arched ebony stringing.

c1705 *38in (96.5cm) wide*

£10,000-15,000 **RGA**

A George III mahogany bow front chest of drawers, the shaped top above two short and three long graduated drawers, on bracket feet.

43.5in (110cm) wide

£350-400 **L&T**

A Scottish George III mahogany chest of drawers, with boxwood and ebony stringing, the rectangular top above a crossbanded frieze and three short drawers above three long graduated drawers, a shaped apron and bracket feet.

45.5in (116cm) wide

£400-600 **L&T**

A George III mahogany chest of small proportions, the projecting top above a slide and two short and three graduated long drawers, on ogee bracket feet, splits and replaced handles.

32.5in (82.5cm) wide

£1,200-1,800 **WW**

A matched pair of George III mahogany serpentine commodes, each with a line-inlaid top, above a baize-lined slide, over three drawers, raised on flared feet.

41.75in (106cm) wide

£7,000-9,000 **NA**

A late 18thC Dutch mahogany bombé chest, of four long graduated drawers, the whole inlaid with panels of flowers and urns issuing flowers, in stained specimen woods highlighted with penwork, raised on bracket feet.

42.5in (106cm) wide

£2,500-3,500 **L&T**

A George III mahogany serpentine chest of drawers, the shaped top above three graduated drawers, flanked by blind fretwork panels, raised on bracket feet.

48.5in (121cm) wide

£1,500-2,000 **L&T**

A George III mahogany chest, of exceptionally small size, with two short and three long cock-beaded drawers, with brass swan-neck handles, on ogee bracket feet.

c1780 *24.75in (63cm) wide*

£7,000-9,000 **RGA**

A George III mahogany bow-front chest of drawers, the crossbanded top above four graduated cock-beaded drawers, over a serpentine apron and raised on flared feet.

36.75in (92cm) wide

£1,800-2,200 **NA**

A George III mahogany chest of drawers, with a serpentine front and four long graduated drawers, with brass handles, on bracket feet and casters, old repairs to two feet.

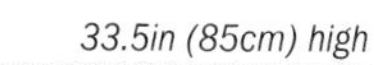

33.5in (85cm) high

£4,000-6,000 **DN**

A George III mahogany chest of drawers, with boxwood stringing, the rectangular top with a moulded edge, above two short drawers and three long graduated drawers, on shaped bracket feet.

45.25in (115cm) wide

£500-800 **L&T**

A George III mahogany bow-front chest of drawers, by James Mein of Kelso, the top with a reeded edge, above three short and three long graduated drawers, with blue lining paper and label, on splayed bracket feet.

£1,500-2,000 **L&T**

A George III mahogany secrétaire chest, with brass stringing, the false-fronted secrétaire drawer with a lifting writing slide and carved hinged stationery compartments, panelled doors enclosing a sliding tray, on shaped and moulded bracket feet.

Provenance: *The top bears a silver plaque engraved "Left to Gabriella Cunninghame Graham of Gartmoor by Anna Lady Erskine 1885".*

43in (109cm) wide

£2,200-2,800 **L&T**

A Regency mahogany chest of drawers, the rectangular top with a reeded edge, over three long drawers, raised on splayed bracket feet.

c1810 *34in (85cm) wide*

£1,500-2,000 **FRE**

An early 19thC mahogany bow-front chest, the crossbanded top with boxwood stringing, above two short and two long drawers, with brass ring handles and bracket feet.

35.25in (89.5cm) wide

£1,200-1,800 **DN**

An early 19thC Dutch mahogany commode, with three frieze drawers and a pair of panelled tambour doors carved with laurel swags, enclosing a shelved interior, flanked by fluted pilasters, on fluted spade feet.

46.5in (118cm) wide

£800-1,200 **L&T**

An early 19thC mahogany chest, with a reeded edge, above four long drawers, raised on turned feet, later handles.

36.5in (93cm) wide

£400-600 **WW**

An early 19thC padouk and brass-bound campaign chest, the rectangular top inset with brass caps to the angles, above two short and one long drawer, the lower section with two further long drawers, the whole raised on removable turned feet, with inset flush handles.

47.75in (119cm) high

£1,200-1,800 **L&T**

An Empire mahogany chest of drawers, with two short and one deep drawer, over three stepped-back drawers, flanked by turned tapering columns, on ring and ball-turned feet.

c1830 *49.25in (123cm) high*

£800-1,200 **S&K**

An early Victorian mahogany bow-front chest, the shaped rectangular top with a moulded edge, above four long graduated drawers flanked by panelled pilasters, on turned feet.

39.25in (100cm) wide

£2,000-3,000 **L&T**

A 19thC mahogany campaign chest, the rectangular top above two short and three long graduated drawers, on turned feet.

36.25in (92cm) wide

£500-700 **L&T**

A 19thC mahogany campaign chest, in two parts, with two short and three long drawers, with brass-bound corners and sunken handles.

59.75in (152cm) wide

£1,200-1,800 **L&T**

A 19thC Dutch satinwood chest, the canted rectangular top with mahogany and feather crossbanding, above three long drawers, on square tapering legs.

40in (100cm) wide

£2,200-2,800 **L&T**

A 19thC French provincial bow-front kingwood commode, the marble top with a moulded edge, above four long drawers, divided and flanked by brass lined flutes, a shaped apron with gilt mounts.

32in (82cm) wide

£1,200-1,800 **L&T**

A 19thC William and Mary-style oak chest, with step-moulded drawers, all with rectangular and diamond-shaped medallions, above a moulded base on bracket feet, replacement brass bail handles.

38.5in (96cm) wide

£800-1,200 **S&K**

A 19thC George III-style mahogany chest of drawers, the top with a thumb-moulded edge, above three short drawers, the centre inlaid with a bird's-eye maple shaped panel, above three graduated long drawers on bracket feet.

45.5in (114cm) wide

£1,500-2,000 **S&K**

A Scottish Victorian bird's-eye maple chest of drawers, the rectangular top with rounded angles, above four long graduated drawers with turned handles on plinth base.

Provenance: *The Dukes of Hamilton, Hamilton Palace.*

48in (120cm) wide

£1,200-1,800 **L&T**

A late 19thC rosewood chest of drawers, the serpentine, moulded top above three long graduated drawers, enclosed by canted angles, with scroll-carved brackets, raised on a moulded base and bracket feet with scroll carving.

48.75in (122cm) wide

£3,000-4,000 **L&T**

An early 20thC miniature Sheraton-style mahogany and crossbanded chest of drawers, with three long drawers, raised on bracket feet.

15.5in (39cm) high

£220-280 **FRE**

A George II-style satinwood veneered chest of drawers, with chequerbanding, the rectangular top with canted angles and a moulded edge, above four long graduated drawers, on a plinth, with shaped bracket feet.

20.5in (52cm) wide

£400-600 **L&T**

An oak chest of drawers, the rectangular moulded top above two short and two long crossbanded drawers, on shaped feet, adapted.

23in (58cm) wide

£400-600 **L&T**

A late 19thC Continental fruitwood and burl-walnut high chest of drawers, with seven small herringbone-inlaid drawers and a cupboard door, the fitted interior with a checker-board surface and three long drawers, the sides quarter-inlaid, on square legs.

54in (135cm) high

£2,200-2,800 **S&K**

A CLOSER LOOK AT A WELLINGTON CHEST

Allegedly designed for the Duke of Wellington c1820, this popular style of chest was similar to earlier narrow French linen chests.

Wellington chests tend to have a single flap locking mechanism for the whole piece. The simple turned handles on this piece are also typical.

Although this fine piece has seven graduating drawers, Wellington chests can be found with up to twelve.

Check the runners correspond with any marks to the bollom of drawers to ensure that they are original. Any extra screw holes as well as sections of timber that do not match the rest of the piece may also be signs of alteration.

A 19thC highly figured walnut Wellington chest, with seven drawers, carved brackets and turned wooden handles, raised on a plinth base.

c1850

124cm (48.75in) high

£5,000-8,000 **RGA**

A Victorian burr walnut Queen Anne-style cabinet chest, with feather banding, the crossbanded rectangular fold-over top hinged at the front and resting on lopers, above three graduated drawers and a door, on a plinth and bracket feet.

43in (109cm) high

£1,500-2,000 **L&T**

A 19thC Anglo-Indian coromandel wood Wellington chest.

c1880 *18in (45cm) wide*

£4,500-5,500 **JK**

An early 20thC Spanish Renaissance Revival oak chest of drawers, with painted and parcel-gilt decoration, profusely carved with Gothic and Renaissance architectural, foliate and floral motifs.

48in (122cm) high

£500-800 **S&K**

CHEST-ON-CHEST

A Georgian mahogany chest-on-chest, the dentilled cornice above three short and three long graduated drawers, flanked by fluted angles, the base with a brushing slide and three long graduated drawers, shaped bracket feet.

70in (178cm) high

£1,800-2,200 **L&T**

A George III mahogany chest-on-chest, the moulded cornice above a blind fret frieze, over two short and three long graduated drawers, flanked by chamfered blind fret angles, on a base with three long graduated, with shaped bracket feet.

73.25in (183cm) high

£2,500-3,000 **L&T**

A CLOSER LOOK AT A CHEST-ON-CHEST

The chest-on-chest is often referred to as a double chest-of-drawers. This form of storage furniture was developed in the second half of the 17thC.

Chest of drawers were often made in an inexpensive wood and veneered. This one however is solid mahogany, increasing its value. Mahogany replaced walnut as the most commonly used quality wood c1740.

Look for evidence that the feet, handles or drawers have been replaced, such as inconsistent wear and colouring. Also check for bruising where handles have damaged the wood.

The ogee bracket feet and the simple rectangular form are typical of this period.

An early George III mahogany chest-on-chest, with canted corners, the crossbanded and chequer-strung moulded cornice above two short and six long graduated drawers, on ogee bracket feet.

76.5in (194cm) high

£6,000-9,000 **L&T**

A George III oak and pollard oak veneered chest-on-chest, the rectangular top with dentilled cornice above two short and three long graduated drawers, flanked by fluted quarter columns, the base with three long graduated drawers and plinth, on shaped bracket feet.

38in (97cm) wide

£5,000-6,000 **L&T**

A George III oak chest-on-chest, in two parts, the moulded rectangular cornice above two short over three long drawers flanked by fluted quarter columns, the lower section with two short over three long drawers, raised on a moulded base with shaped bracket feet.

38in (96.5cm) wide

£1,800-2,200 **NA**

A George III mahogany chest-on-chest, in two parts: the moulded rectangular cornice above two short over three long cock-beaded graduated drawers, above three graduated long drawers, raised on a moulded base with ogee bracket feet.

41in (104cm) wide

£4,000-6,000 **NA**

COMMODE

A Régence period rose marble-top tulipwood and amaranth parquetry commode, three rows of drawers, top drawers with drop handles, original bronze mounts.

46.75in (119cm) wide

£1,800-2,200 **S&K**

A mid-18thC Italian-style burr walnut commode, of exaggerated bombe form, the serpentine cross-banded top above three long drawers with applied c-scrolled Rococo panels on swept scroll feet, corresponding sides.

49.5in (124cm) wide

£4,500-5,500 **L&T**

A mid-18thC Louis XV gilt metal-mounted provincial walnut commode, with moulded serpentine-fronted top, three panelled graduated drawers, over a moulded shaped apron, fitted with foliate and pierced ruffled c-scrolled keyhole escutcheons, handles and mounts, raised on scroll feet.

55.5in (139cm) wide

£5,000-7,000 **NA**

An 18thC decorated marble-top Tuscan commode, twin doors enclosing an interior with a shelf, one narrow door-fronted compartment at each end.

56in (143cm) wide

£12,000-14,000 **BL**

A Maltese 18thC walnut commode, with boxwood stringing, the splayed rectangular top with cross-banding and radiating veneers centred by shaped panels, above corresponding sides and three long similar graduated drawers, on cabriole feet with carved toes.

50in (127cm) wide

£3,000-4,000 **L&T**

A Louis XV/XVI gilt metal-mounted mahogany parquetry commode, the moulded 'breche d'Alep' marble top of breakfront outline, case with two drawers, veneered 'sans traverse' in a circular fan pattern with interlocking geometric borders, canted corners fitted with swag mounts, raised on hipped cabriole legs fitted with cast leaftip chutes and sabots, signed "L. Aubry" on the case.

49.5in (124cm) wide

£5,000-7,000 **NA**

A Louis XV/Louis XVI parquetry and marquetry marble-top commode, with rectangular mottled grey marble top of slight breakfront outline above a conforming case with two drawers on cabriole legs, marquetry front depicting musical instruments and a foliate motif.

45in (112.5cm) wide

£4,000-6,000 **S&K**

An early George III mahogany serpentine commode, shaped top with moulded edges above four long graduated drawers with leaf-cast brass handles, a divided top drawer, carved canted corners, shaped and panelled bracket feet, straight sides.

44in (112cm) wide

£4,500-5,500 **L&T**

A Louis XVI marble-topped mahogany and ormolu mounted commode, stamped "B. Molitor", rounded rectangular grey-veined marble top above four long graduated drawers between reeded column angles, on turned tapering feet.

54.5in (136cm) wide

£5,000-8,000 **L&T**

A Louis XVI walnut provincial commode, with rectangular moulded top and serpentine front above a conforming base with two long serpentine drawers, embellished with moulded fronts, raised side panels, on tapered cylindrical legs.

50in (125cm) wide

£3,000-4,000 **NA**

A Louis XVI-style brass-mounted mahogany commode, the moulded rectangular grey marble top with canted corners inlaid with brass fluting above three brass-banded drawers, raised on matching square tapered legs ending in brass caps.

43.25in (108cm) wide

£3,000-4,000 **NA**

A George III mahogany serpentine commode, moulded edge top above four graduated long drawers with later swan-neck brass handles within blind fret-carved corners, raised on large bracket feet.

38.75in (98.5cm) wide

£7,000-10,000 **WW**

A George III mahogany serpentine commode, shaped top above four long graduated drawers with ebony stringing, top drawer later fitted for cutlery, raised on shaped bracket feet.

48in (122cm) wide

£2,500-3,500 **L&T**

An early 19thC Scandinavian walnut commode, with three long drawers, the upper drawer outset, with later embossed brass ring handles, raised on block feet.

50in (127cm) wide

£2,000-3,000 **DN**

A Regency gilt metal-mounted parquetry rosewood commode, the moulded serpentine-fronted white-veined grey marble top mounted above the conforming case fitted with two top drawers aligned over two long drawers, case foliate handles, raised on cabriole legs fitted with pierced c-scroll chutes and sabots.

49in (122.5cm) wide

£6,000-9,000 **NA**

A French Empire mahogany commode, black marble top mounted above a secret frieze drawer, three further long drawers flanked by turned gilt-metal capped pilasters, raised on bun feet.

c1820 *48in (120cm) wide*

£1,800-2,200 **FRE**

A converted oak commode, with four long drawers, raised on square bracket feet.

c1820 *27.5in (70cm) high*

£550-650 **EP**

A Louis Phillipe mahogany commode, rectangular grey fossilized marble top above a concave frieze drawer and three long drawers with matching flame veneers, on a plinth and square bun feet.

52.75in (132cm) wide

£3,500-4,500 **L&T**

A pair of small 19thC Continental painted commodes, each with a moulded faux marble top, four drawers and a carved foliate skirt, foliate arabesque carvings throughout.

32in (81.5cm) high

£1,200-1,800 **S&K**

A mid-19thC Louis XV/XVI-style kingwood marble top commode, inlaid with checker-banding, black marble top mounted above an inverted breakfront with three rows of ring-pull drawers, raised on square cabriole legs with sabots.

50in (125cm) wide

£1,200-1,800 **FRE**

A 19thC Louis XVI-style figured mahogany commode, with a grey-veined marble top and outset corners above three mounted gilt bronze long drawers with floral-embossed ring pulls flanked by stop-fluted supports, brass-mounted inset panelled sides, on turned tapering legs with brass caps.

46in (115cm) wide

£1,200-1,800 **S&K**

A late 19thC miniature Italian burl walnut cross-banded commode, with gilt-metal mounts, of inverted breakfront form, three rows of drawers set with two framed porcelain panels each, painted with scenes of courting couples, raised on bracket feet joined by a wavy apron.

13.5in (34cm) wide

£450-550 **FRE**

A French kingwood and gilt-metal mounted marquetry commode, of serpentine outline with red marble top mounted above two small drawers.

19.5in (49.5cm) wide

£600-900 **WW**

A Continental gilt-decorated lacquer commode, the rectangular top mounted above a bombe case fitted with three long drawers over the apron relief, carved on each side with a shell, decorated overall with Chinoiserie figures and landscape views, raised on hoof feet.

47in (117.5cm) wide

£7,000-10,000 **NA**

PARTNERS' DESKS

A mid-18thC mahogany kneehole partners' desk, with later carvings, the sides and central drawer are characterized by a ratchetted slope and small compartments above a kneehole panel door framed by six small drawers, pedestals enclosed within ogee panelled doors, on bracket feet with casters.

50in (127cm) wide

£15,000-17,000 **WW**

A George III mahogany kneehole partners' desk with one long drawer over a shallow cupboard, flanked on either side by three-drawer pedestals, bracket feet.

c1770 *37in (94cm) wide*

£4,800-5,200 **RGA**

A George III mahogany kneehole partners' desk, with rectangular top and moulded edges above a frieze drawer, kneehole cupboard flanked by six drawers, on bracket feet.

31.25in (78cm) wide

£1,800-2,200 **L&T**

A George III mahogany partners' desk, with rectangular moulded top and inset writing surface mounted above three drawers, opposing twin pedestals with three graduated drawers each, raised on plinths.

65.25in (163cm) wide

£5,000-7,000 **L&T**

A mahogany pedestal partners' desk, with inset leather writing surface decorated with a later foliate carved edge, above six opposing frieze drawers, each pedestal with a panelled door and three more drawers, on raised bracket feet.

c1840 *59in (147.5cm) wide*

£2,500-3,500 **FRE**

A 19thC mahogany partners' desk, bearing the label of 'S & H Jewell, London', the rectangular top with moulded edges and gilt-tooled leather skiver, six opposing frieze drawers raised on pedestals with three graduated drawers and opposing cupboards, shaped bracket feet.

Provenance: *Formerly the property of Sir Stanley Baldwin, British Prime Minister 1923-29 & 1935-37.*

£6,000-9,000 **L&T**

A 19thC Chippendale-style mahogany partners desk, each pedestal with three opposing drawers, raised on plinths.

55in (140cm) wide

£400-600 **S&K**

A 19thC mahogany partners desk, with rectangular moulded top and inset-tooled leather skiver mounted above three opposing frieze drawers and twin pedestals, fitted with three graduated drawers each and opposing a panelled door enclosing a shelf, raised on plinths.

61.5in (154cm) wide

£2,000-3,000 **L&T**

A 19thC Georgian-style oak pedestal partners desk, in three parts: rectangular green tooled-leather inset top with moulded edges above three small drawers supported on two three-drawer pedestals, plinth bases raised on casters.

£1,200-1,800 **S&K**

A George III mahogany pedestal desk, with shaped rectangular top and inset gilt-tooled leather skiver above six frieze drawers and conforming serpentine pedestals, each with three graduated drawers and opposing dummy-fronted cupboard doors, raised on plinth bases

66.5in (169cm) wide

£4,500-5,500 **L&T**

An early 19thC Continental walnut twin pedestal partners desk, with rectangular top, inset leather skiver and moulded edges mounted above three frieze drawers on twin pedestals with four graduated drawers each, hinged locking pilasters and opposing dummy drawers, raised on ebonized block feet.

55.5in (139cm) wide

£1,800-2,200 **L&T**

A 19thC mahogany campaign desk, projecting tripartite rectangular top double-hinged at the centre and sides, above false fronted drawers on pedestals with two drawers each, flush fitted brass handles, raised on ball feet.

47in (120cm) wide

£2,200-2,800 **L&T**

A Louis XVI-style kingwood walnut and brass-mounted bureau plat, with rectangular top and leather inset writing surface, above five drawers surrounding a kneehole, on turned fluted tapering legs with gilt brass sabots.

68in (170cm) wide

£2,500-3,000 **L&T**

A Victorian walnut 'Dickens' pedestal desk, stepped top with later gilt-tooled leather insets, eight real and one dummy drawer about the kneehole, later handles, plinth base on concealed casters.

47.25in (120cm) wide

£800-1,200 **WW**

An 18thC Scottish Sheraton-period mahogany and bonheur du jour marquetry desk with a single drawer and panelled cabinet superstructure, on tapering legs.

c1790 *28.5in (72cm) wide*

£42,000-46,000 **NOA**

An Edwardian mahogany and boxwood strung writing desk, with a pair of George II knife boxes as a superstructure, fitted for stationery and centred with a lidded compartment and serpentine back, inset tooled-leather writing surface above five rows of drawers and twin pedestals, with arc en arbelette fronts and graduated silver-handled drawers, on reciprocal plinths.

45.5in (114cm) high

£1,200-1,800 **L&T**

A mid-19thC walnut marquetry bureau plat, in the mid-18thC French style, moulded outline top and inset writing surface bordered by a florate band on a stained pearwood background, above a panelled serpentine fringe, opposing frieze drawers, square cabriole legs, gilt-metal c-scroll cartouches and cast sabots.

58.75in (147cm) wide

£2,500-3,000 **L&T**

A Louis XVI-style kingwood inlaid bonheur du jour, with marble top and pierced brass gallery, above three frieze drawers, fall front enclosing a fitted interior with small drawers, shelf and writing surface (now missing), bottom apron drawer, on square tapered legs ending in brass cappings.

c1900 *43in (107.5cm) high*

£1,800-2,200 **FRE**

A late Victorian Adam-style satinwood writing desk, with Neo-classical marquetry, of bowed breakfront form with gilt-tooled Morocco skiver, superstructure with flip-top fitted stationery box at centre flanked by drawers and lidded cupboards, three-quarter brass galleries, central frieze drawer flanked by deeper drawers on the square section, tapered legs on brass casters.

46.75in (117cm) wide

£2,800-3,200 **L&T**

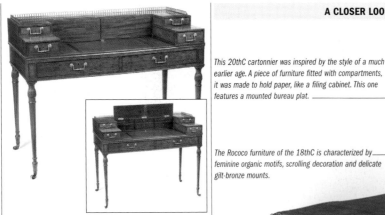

A 19thC Sheraton-period mahogany 'Carlton House' writing table with brass gallery along the top.

c1800 *46.5in (118m) wide*

£54,000-56,000 **NOA**

An early 20thC Louis XVI-style cylinder desk, inlaid with checker-banding and lateral apron drawers, the roll top enclosing a fitted interior with pigeonholes, drawers, a brushing slide and central cupboard door, raised on turned tapered fluted legs capped in toupie feet.

48.5in (121cm) high

£1,200-1,800 **FRE**

A CLOSER LOOK AT A KINGSWOOD CARTONNIER

This 20thC cartonnier was inspired by the style of a much earlier age. A piece of furniture fitted with compartments, it was made to hold paper, like a filing cabinet. This one features a mounted bureau plat.

The Rococo furniture of the 18thC is characterized by feminine organic motifs, scrolling decoration and delicate gilt-bronze mounts.

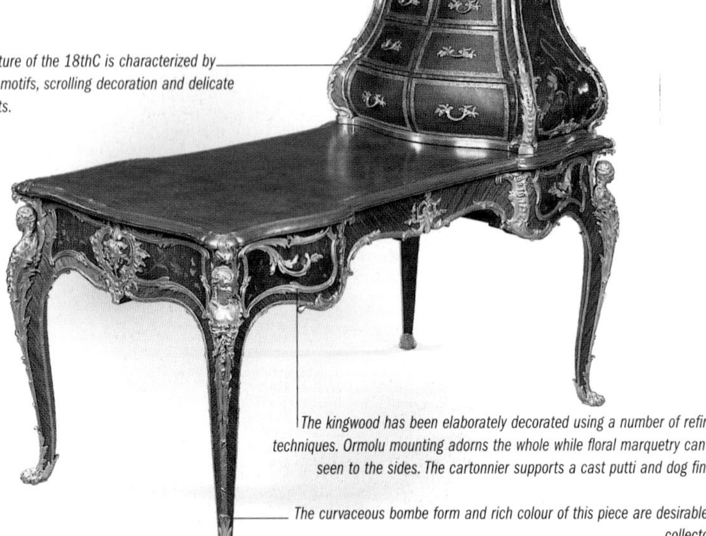

The kingwood has been elaborately decorated using a number of refined techniques. Ormolu mounting adorns the whole while floral marquetry can be seen to the sides. The cartonnier supports a cast putti and dog finial.

The curvaceous bombe form and rich colour of this piece are desirable to collectors.

An early 20thC French kingwood, marquetry and ormolu-mounted bureau plat and associated cartonnier, in the Louis XV style, the bombe cartonnier with cast putti and dog finial, a clock with white enamelled dial, eight leather-fronted drawers, the back and sides decorated with floral marquetry, the bureau with shaped rectangular leather inset top above a shaped bombe ormolu-mounted frieze, fitted with two drawers to one side and two false drawers to the other, on cabriole legs headed by cast female caryatid busts and with lion's paw feet, stamped under one mount "CZ".

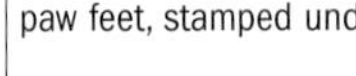

64.75in (162cm) wide

£40,000-50,000 **L&T**

A Hepplewhite harewood and yew writing desk, on cabriole legs, perhaps by John Linnel.

c1775 *42in (106.5cm) high*

£7,000-10,000 **DL**

A Victorian burr walnut and amboyna-banded music desk, with a raised top above a fitted interior, partitioned frieze drawer above an oval-panelled door, on china casters.

24.75in (63cm) wide

£800-1,200 **WW**

A Victorian mahogany corner desk by John Taylor and Sons, Edinburgh, with curved arched superstructure, foliate carved panels above a shelf over two panelled cupboard doors flanked by six drawers, the curved leather inset writing surface above a carved foliate frieze flanked by a real drawer and a false drawer, on fluted supports, panelled rear.

63.75in (159cm) high

£3,000-4,000 **L&T**

A Directoire-style fall-front desk, with gilt-metal mounts, the fall with an inset felt writing surface that opens onto a shelved interior with drawers.

42in (106.5cm) high

£400-600 **S&K**

A Regency mahogany Davenport, the top with pierced brass gallery, pull-out pen drawer and sloping hinged fall, inset writing surface, interior fitted with drawers and pigeonholes, the whole sliding forward to form a desk, the base, panelled to the front and rear, sides with opposed slides and four graduated drawers opposed by dummy drawers, raised on divided bun feet with casters.

23.5in (60cm) wide

£1,000-2,000 **L&T**

A 19thC Regency mahogany Davenport desk, the top with pierced brass gallery, pull-out pen drawer and sloping hinged fall, inset writing surface, interior fitted with drawers and pigeonholes, the whole slides forward, panelled base to the front and rear, sides with opposed slides and four graduated drawers opposed by dummy drawers, on L-shaped square bracket feet.

c1810 *15in (38cm) wide*

£12,000-14,000 **NOA**

A late Regency period mahogany library Davenport, the sliding upper portion with calf writing slope over ejecting penslide, the base with five graduated side drawers, the panelled front with half pilaster columns over turned feet on brass casters.

21.25in (54cm) wide

£2,500-3,500 **L&T**

A Victorian rosewood Davenport, galleried top above tooled leather inset slope, fitted interior with hidden pen drawer above spiral twist supports, side panelled door enclosing four graduated drawers, disc feet on sunken casters.

34.25in (87cm) wide

£550-650 **WW**

A Victorian carved oak Davenport, ornate foliate-carved decoration throughout, the raised back with two glass inkwells above an inset leather fall enclosing small drawers, the pedestal containing four real and four opposing dummy drawers with fox mask handles, raised on a shaped plinth base with casters, stamped "W. Williamson & Sons, Guildford".

c1880 *32.5in (81cm) high*

£1,200-1,800 **FRE**

MIRRORS

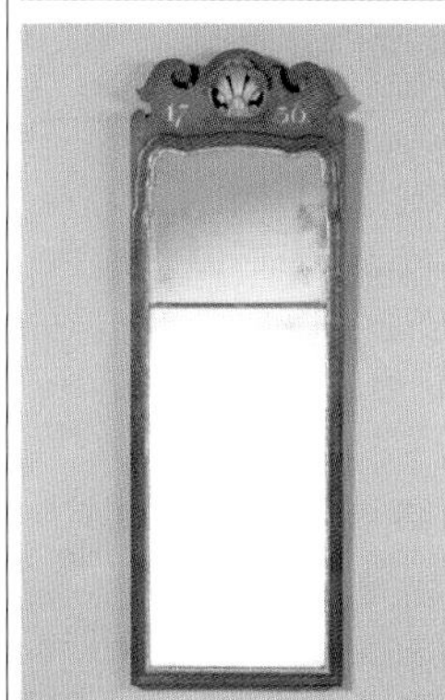

A walnut and gilt wall mirror, with crest centred by a gilded plume in an open circle, flanked by scrolled volutes and bearing the date, mirrored glass split into two sections, the top with bevelled edges, the glass bordered by a carved and gilded inner outline and a segmented walnut moulded ogival outer border and upper outline.

1736 *56in (140cm) high*

£4,000-6,000 **NA**

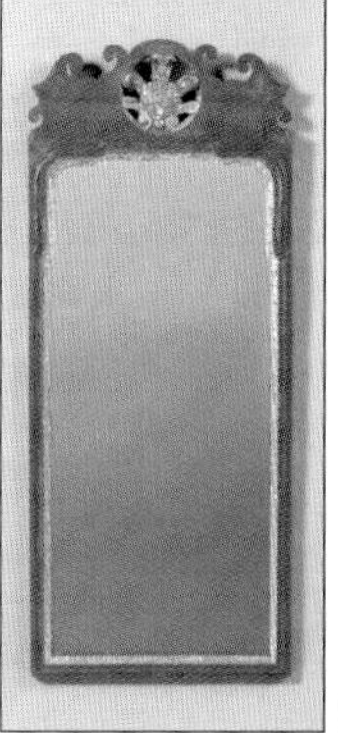

A Queen Anne walnut and parcel-gilt two-plate bevelled mirror, the scroll-carved crest centring a plumed gilt cartouche within an open circle, the moulded frame with ogival upper outline and conforming gilt liner enclosing mirror glass plates bevelled to follow the shape of the frame.

45in (112.5cm) high

£3,000-5,000 **NA**

An George II walnut mirror, with scrolling crest, plumed cartouche and candlearms.

c1730 *21.5in (54.5cm) wide*

£16,500-18,500 **NOA**

A George II mahogany and giltwood two-plated mirror.

c1750 *63in (160cm) high*

£7,000-10,000 **DL**

A CLOSER LOOK AT A PIER GLASS

Pier glasses were designed to hang on the wall between two windows (the pier). They were often placed above pier tables, after the influence of Scottish architect, Robert Adam, who believed that furniture should be an integral part of the decoration of a room.

Gesso is a paste-like substance made from chalk or plaster of Paris and glue or gelatin. It was often used as a base for carved and gilded decoration to hide the grain of the wood and even out imperfections.

The solid, symmetrical form and scrolling decoration are typical of the late 17th and early 18thC.

The large size, great age and fine quality of this piece makes the glass very valuable.

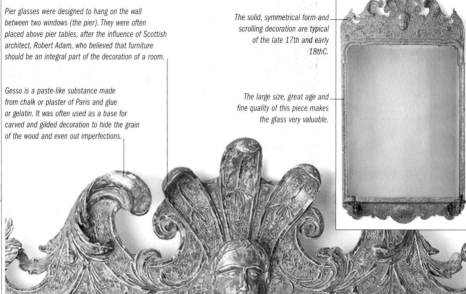

An fine George I carved and gilded gesso pier glass.

c1720 *26in (66cm) wide*

£28,000-32,000 **NOA**

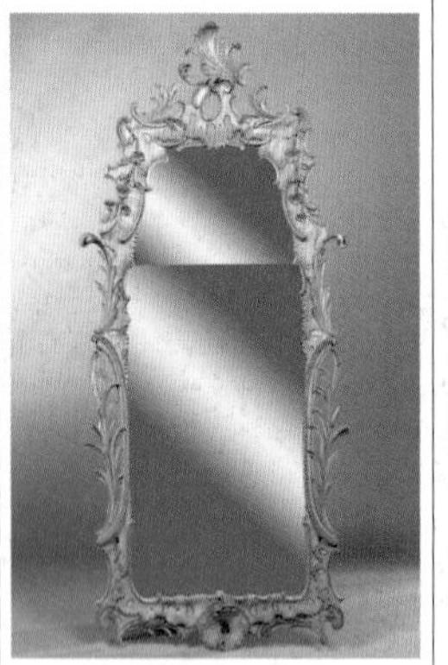

A George II-style carved and overpainted pier mirror, the split bevelled plate enclosed by a frame carved and pierced with c-scrolls and rocaille work embellished with bulrushes and floral sprays, the surround a leafy cartouche, overpainted grey with gilt.

36.25in (93cm) wide

£2,500-3,500 **L&T**

A mid-18thC giltwood mirror, the plate encased within rectangular mirrored panels and borders carved with scrollwork and foliage, the arched crest centred by feathers and flanked by foliage and flowerheads, all-over copper patina.

23.5in (59.5cm) wide

£2,200-2,800 **S&K**

A small ornate 18thC Chippendale-period cartouche-shaped mirror in carved wood and gilt, with a feathered crest.

c1760 *18.5in (47cm) wide*

£10,000-15,000 **NOA**

An Italian giltwood girandole mirror with embellished surround.

c1770 *34in (86.5cm) high*

£2,000-2,500 **DL**

A George III parcel-gilt and mahogany mirror, the rectangular mirror plate within a moulded surround, the eared crest applied with ruffled c-scrolls and surmounted by a phoenix, the sides with pendant flowers and leaf tips, the shaped pendant below applied with c-scrolls.

26in (66cm) wide

£3,200-3,800 **NA**

A George III mahogany and giltwood wall mirror, the rectangular plate surrounded by leaf-moulded gilt slip and a shaped frame with a scrolling crest embellished by a giltwood and gesso eagle surmount and c-scroll mounts.

45.25in (113cm) high

£600-900 **L&T**

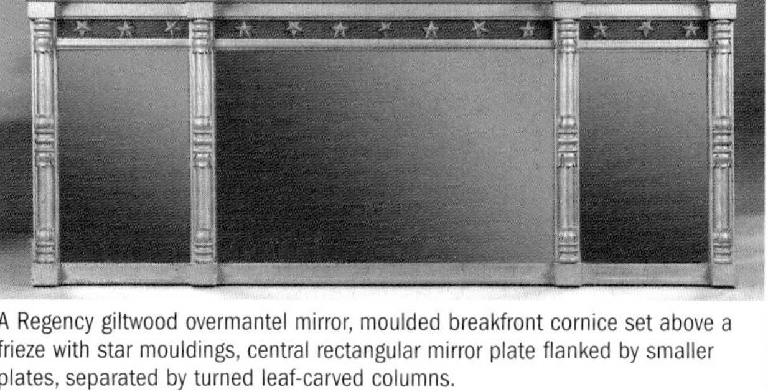

A Regency giltwood overmantel mirror, moulded breakfront cornice set above a frieze with star mouldings, central rectangular mirror plate flanked by smaller plates, separated by turned leaf-carved columns.

56in (143cm) wide

£350-450 **L&T**

A Regency gilt bronze convex wall mirror, the circular plate and reeded slip set within a moulded concave frame with ball spacers, surmounted by a bronze eagle on a rocky base and plinth, foliate crestings, similar leaf-carved pendant below.

21.75in (55cm) wide

£1,500-2,000 **L&T**

A 19thC Continental marquetry mirror, rectangular bevelled plate encased in a frame with floral decoration, centred by a bird to the top and a mask below, bordered by chevron stripes.

21.75in (55cm) wide

£500-700 **L&T**

A Regency giltwood and gesso pier glass, of rectangular form with concave cornice above ring and leaf frieze, the eleven original rectangular plates divided by astragals and including two larger central ones, flanked by fluted and reeded Corinthian half columns with plinth base.

46.75in (117cm) wide

£3,500-4,500 **L&T**

A 19thC Louis XV-style giltwood mirror, the asymmetrical frame robustly carved with an anthemion crest and both c-scroll and foliate borders enclosing a conforming plate engraved with a running wolf and pennant, losses to the mirror plate.

23in (58.5cm) wide

£600-900 **S&K**

A 19thC overmantel mirror, with a rectangular plate and rounded top angles set within a bold rope twist-carved oak frame, surmounted by knotted cresting.

77in (196cm) wide

£400-600 **L&T**

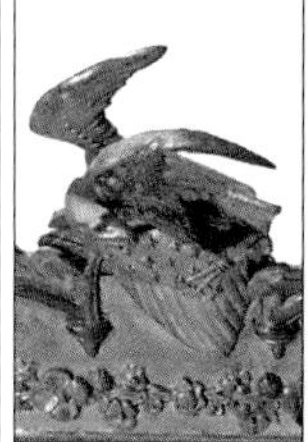

An American carved and gessoed gilt wall mirror, rectangular bevelled plate with scrolled pediment centring on an eagle and American shield, enclosed by moulded frame, back board missing, old repairs.

c1865 *58in (147cm) high*

£1,800-2,000 **FRE**

A 19thC Victorian carved giltwood tripartite overmantel mirror, in the Chinese Chippendale manner with a pierced crest and arched foliate pagoda-shaped canopy above the three-part mirror plate, sides with pierced c-scroll and foliate detail, base framed by a pierced foliate and c-scroll pendant.

62in (155cm) wide

£1,200-1,800 **S&K**

A late 19thC gilt brass-mounted mirror with cresting, of waisted arched form with a scrolled foliate and husk framing surmounted and flanked by flaming urns and centred by engraved flowers within a laurel wreath.

32.75in (82cm) wide

£600-900 **L&T**

A late 19thC Adam-style gilt wall mirror, bevelled rectangular plate flanked by two panels with ribbon-tied husk pendants, urn and anthemion surmount with floral swags and scrolling foliage, husk swags and pendant centred by a rosette.

19.25in (49cm) wide

£800-1,200 **L&T**

A late 19thC Empire-style gilt bronze satinwood and kingwood mounted mirror crowned by a coved crest and a gilt-bronze foliate-mounted frieze over an arched plate, enclosed by an inlaid frame centring on a star, with classical figural spandrels, flowerhead and Grecian urn gilt-bronze mounts on the sides.

20.75in (52.5cm) wide

£2,200-2,800 **S&K**

A late 19thC Victorian mahogany mirror, the rectangular plate encased by a moulded gilded frame.

33.75in (84.5cm) high

£300-400 **S&K**

A 20thC Rococo giltwood pier mirror, a rectangular bevelled plate set within mirrored panels, ornately carved frame with scrolling foliage, shells, floral-filled urns and crowned by a plumed crest.

63in (157.5cm) high

£1,000-1,500 **S&K**

A late 19th/early 20thC Louis XVI-style carved and gessoed giltwood mirror, oval bevelled mirror plate set within an inner mirror surround, frame with beading, egg-and-dart moulding, foliage decorations and pierced crest.

51in (127.5cm) high

£1,000-1,500 **S&K**

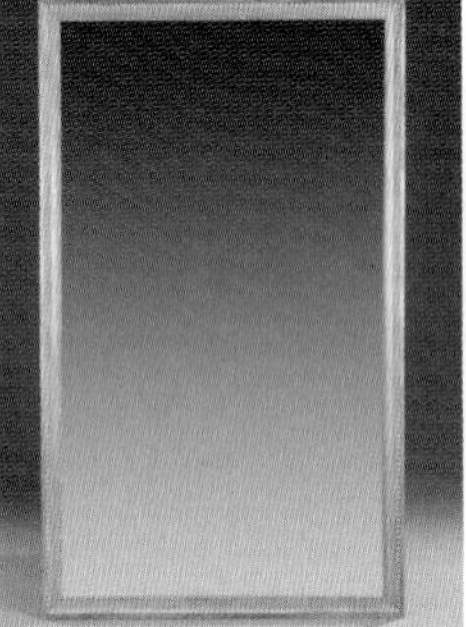

A 20thC Louis XVI-style giltwood mirror, the rectangular plate encased within an egg-and-dart double-bordered frame.

66in (165cm) high

£500-800 **S&K**

A 20thC carved giltwood mirror, the bevelled rectangular plate enclosed in a coved frame, the corners and sides decorated with applied giltwood shell and scrolling foliate motifs.

47in (117.5cm) high

£150-200 **S&K**

An English/American Neo-classical-style giltwood and partly ebonized convex wall mirror, with reeded slip frame, spherules, an eagle-carved crest and foliate pendant.

30.75in (78cm) high

£700-1,000 **S&K**

A Victorian-style gilt-gesso picture frame wall mirror, with rectangular plate in a moulded frame, applied scrolling foliage and marguerites all around.

51in (129.5cm) high

£300-500 **S&K**

A George III-style carved parcel-gilt wall mirror, with c-scrolls, volutes, leaf swags and fully sculpted floral blossoms for decoration.

61.5in (156cm) high

£1,000-1,500 **S&K**

A Continental Rococo-style giltwood rectangular wall mirror, surmounted by a flower-carved rocaille crest and tapered with a pendant frieze.

30.25in (77cm) high

£200-300 **S&K**

A Continental giltwood rectangular mirror, plate bordered by a continuous band of deeply ornate scrolling acanthus foliage.

39in (99cm) high

£500-700 **S&K**

An Italian walnut wall mirror, in the Renaissance style, the broken pediment carved with cherub heads on either side of a female bust and fruiting swags, the oval mirror plate encased by carved caryatids with more cherub heads below.

59.25in (148cm) high

£1,500-2,000 **L&T**

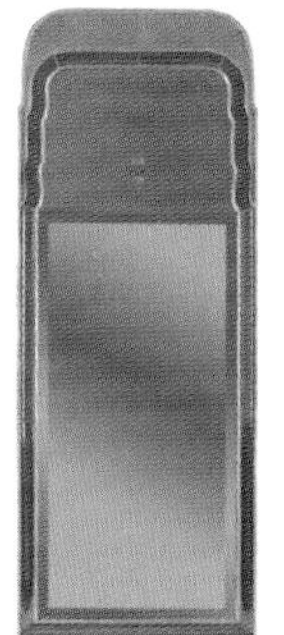

A giltwood framed pier glass, of early 18thC style, the arched frame enclosing two bevelled mirror plates, the top section engraved with a coronet above a star.

60.75in (152cm) high

£1,500-2,000 **L&T**

A Rococo giltwood mirror, with cartouche-shaped crest and pierced shell and foliate carvings centred above a rectangular plate mounted on a similarly decorated shell and foliate frame.

67in (167.5cm) high

£10,000-15,000 **NA**

A Masonic carved mirror frame, with a spread-winged eagle flanked by commerce symbols, the central keystone inscribed "HTWSSTKS".

The letters are the Masonic mark of the Ancient Grand Master.

32in (80cm) high

£700-1,000 **NA**

A George III-style black-painted and parcel-gilt girandole mirror with a lion mask crest, two serpentine-shaped candlelights, reclining seahorse and lotus bud pendant below.

38.5in (96cm) high

£1,500-2,000 **S&K**

One of a pair of Baltic walnut veneer gilt mirrors, each with an arched crest and urn with flowers and leaves, above a mirror glass arch over a rectangular frame encasing a bevelled rectangle, gilded beading and segmented walnut frame, upper glass fronted by rosette with trailing ribbons, base embellished by gilded carved leafage, excellent condition.

45in (112.5cm) high

£6,000-9,000 pair **NA**

A Louis XIV-style carved giltwood and gessoed sunburst mirror, with central circular convex plate and radiating spiked tiers.

59in (147.5cm) diam

£2,200-2,800 **S&K**

A matching pair of mahogany and giltwood mirrors with Rococo details, scrolled pediment and gilded rosette with leafage centring a leafy openwork finial above an applied foliate scroll ornament, the rectangular frame and gilded slip moulding enclosing a mirror plate, over a pendant apron with similar applied ornament.

62in (155cm) high

£12,000-18,000 each **NA**

A Baroque-style repoussé silvered metal mirror, the bevelled plate within a shaped scrollwork frame decorated with trellis and foliage, the shaped arched crest centred by an armorial flanked by crowned lions.

48in (120cm) high

£1,000-1,500 **S&K**

A Regency-style ebonized and giltwood convex mirror, the outer moulding decorated with spherules, the crest centred by a foliage-flanked dragon, pendant with two seahorses.

46in (115cm) high

£1,500-2,000 **S&K**

An Italianate carved giltwood pier mirror, the rectangular plate within a laurel rosette and trailing foliage carved frame with pendant ball-and-claw feet, the crest centred by an oval figural reserve with fanciful birds on either side.

72in (180cm) high

£1,500-2,000 **S&K**

A rare George I carved gilt gesso easel mirror.

c1725 *23in (58.5cm) wide*

£15,000-17,000 **NOA**

A George III mahogany shaving mirror, the oval plate between serpentine stiles above a serpentine-fronted base with three drawers, on bracket feet.

c1790 *20in (51cm) high*

£300-400 **S&K**

A George III mahogany toilet mirror, the oval plate within a cross-banded frame and scrolling supports on carved plinths, raised on splayed feet with apron-shaped front and sides.

26.25in (67cm) high

£3,000-4,000 **L&T**

A George III mahogany and satinwood cross-banded toilet mirror, the shield-shaped framed plate with finial supported by shaped uprights on a serpentine-fronted base with three drawers, raised on ogee bracket feet.

19.25in (49cm) wide

£500-800 **L&T**

A George III stained satinwood shaving mirror, crest inlaid with floral motifs, the serpentine-fronted base inlaid with a fan patera, inside a bellflower husk border, matching inlaid drawers, bun feet.

20.75in (52.5cm) wide

£1,200-1,800 **NA**

A 19thC rosewood and ivory inlaid Vizagapatnam dressing table mirror, the cartouche-shaped mirror with flowers and leafy motifs, on boxwood string-shaped supports and base.

26.75in (68cm) high

£500-800 **DN**

An English mahogany campaign mirror with fruitwood and ebony stringing and oval and circular mirrors.

By turning the mirrors back on themselves, this flat mirror can be made to stand upright.

7in (18cm) wide

£150-200 **ET**

A Regency mahogany cheval mirror with satinwood inlaid panels, with turned supports and stretchers.

c1815 *64.5in (164cm) high*

£2,500-3,500 **RGA**

A George IV mahogany cheval mirror, with a ring-turned frame and cross-banded rectangular frame, on reeded outswept legs with brass paw terminals and casters.

67in (170cm) high

£1,000-1,500 **DN**

A pair of pier mirrors with console tables, in the Gothic style, the ornate pierced scroll tops centred by grotesque masks above arched mirrored plates flanked by moulded stylized pilasters, serpentine consoles with red velvet tops above blind fret friezes centred by shells, on turned and tapered legs.

c1880 *120in (300cm) high*

£2,200-2,800 **FRE**

A George III mahogany cheval mirror, in the manner of Gillows, the double baluster-turned top rail above a rectangular mirror plate flanked by turned supports and similar stretcher, on splayed reeded legs with brass caps and casters.

57.75in (144cm) high

£1,000-1,500 **L&T**

An early 18thC gilt gesso and wood cresting, probably from a pier glass, of pierced arched strapwork form, centred by a cherub holding flaming urns, surmounted by a floral vase.

30.75in (77cm) wide

£600-900 **L&T**

SIDEBOARDS

A Scottish George III mahogany breakfront sideboard, with satinwood cross-banding, boxwood and ebony stringing, on square section tapering legs with round dot terminals and spade feet.

73.25in (183cm) wide

£1,200-1,800 **L&T**

A George III mahogany serpentine sideboard, with cross-banding, marquetry medallions and chequer stringing, on square section tapering legs with spade feet, lion mask handles, probably Scottish.

59.5in (149cm) wide

£6,000-9,000 **L&T**

A George III mahogany sideboard, with purplewood banding, the rectangular top above a central drawer and kneehole flanked by two smaller side drawers and corresponding false-fronted drawer, on ring-turned tapering legs with bun feet.

74.75in (187cm) wide

£800-1,200 **L&T**

A George III mahogany twin-pedestal sideboard, with semi-bowed top, with a deep cellar drawer, on hairy paw feet, stamped "H. Mawer and Stephenson, London".

86.75in (217cm) wide

£2,000-3,000 **L&T**

A George III mahogany sideboard, the semi-bowed top with boxwood stringing and satinwood banding above a rosewood veneered edge, the drawers with inset satinwood panels, on square tapering curved legs with inset dart inlay, spade feet.

80.75in (202cm) wide

£5,000-7,000 **L&T**

A George III mahogany bowfront sideboard, the rectangular top above a central drawer and kneehole flanked by two smaller side drawers, on spade feet.

c1800 *58in (147.5cm) wide*

£6,500-7,500 **DL**

A George III bird's-eye maple and mahogany sideboard, inlaid with fans and raised on square tapered legs.

61.75in (154cm) wide

£7,000-9,000 **NA**

A George III mahogany bowfront sideboard, with satinwood cross-banding and boxwood stringing, one drawer with lift-out tray, on square section tapering legs with spade feet.

59.75in (152cm) wide

£2,000-3,000 **L&T**

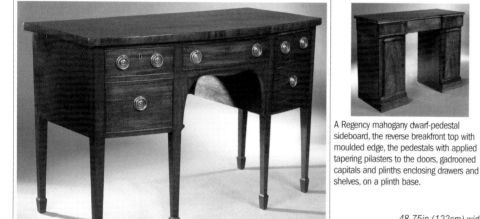

A George III mahogany bowfront sideboard, the rectangular shaped top above a frieze drawer flanked by deeper false-fronted drawers, one with secondary lift-out tray, shaped kneehole, on square section tapering legs with spade feet.

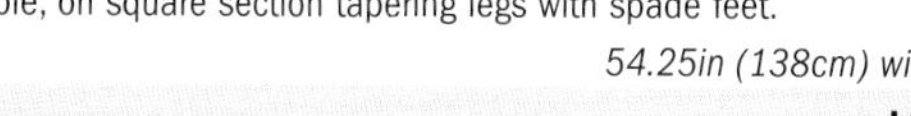

54.25in (138cm) wide

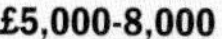

£5,000-8,000 **L&T**

A Regency mahogany dwarf-pedestal sideboard, the reverse breakfront top with moulded edge, the pedestals with applied tapering pilasters to the doors, gadrooned capitals and plinths enclosing drawers and shelves, on a plinth base.

48.75in (122cm) wide

£1,800-2,200 **L&T**

A Regency mahogany sideboard, rectangular breakfront top with brass rail to the rear, raised on ring-turned tapering legs.

60in (152cm) long

£1,500-2,000 **L&T**

A Scottish Regency mahogany sideboard, with ebony stringing, the stage back with projecting flanks and corresponding brass rail above the bowfront, with long frieze drawers on reeded ring-turned tapering legs and toupie feet.

88in (224cm) wide

£1,800-2,200 **L&T**

An early 19thC mahogany bowfront sideboard, the shaped top above a frieze drawer flanked by deeper cupboard doors on turned tapering legs and toupie feet.

60in (152cm) wide

£1,500-2,000 **L&T**

A Scottish Regency sideboard with ebony stringing, the stage back with sliding panels, raised on ring-turned and ebonized tapering legs.

71in (180cm) wide

£1,500-2,000 **L&T**

An early 19thC mahogany sideboard, originally fitted with a brass gallery rail, ebonized banded top with plate groove, with later brass handles, on ring-turned legs.

75in (190.5cm) wide

£1,500-2,000 **WW**

A Scottish Regency mahogany sideboard, with ebony stringing, raised stage back with sliding doors and projecting bowfront, on turned and reeded legs.

91.25in (232cm) wide

£2,500-3,500 **L&T**

An early 19thC mahogany bowfront sideboard, the shaped top above a central frieze drawer flanked by deeper cupboard doors, on ring-turned tapering legs.

60.75in (152cm) wide

£800-1,200 **L&T**

An early 19thC mahogany side table, the rectangular top with ledge back and a three-quarter gallery shelf raised on turned columns, above four short cross-banded drawers, on ring-turned tapering legs.

48.75in (124cm) high

£400-600 **L&T**

A late George III mahogany sideboard with rosewood cross-banding and boxwood and ebony stringing, with a central drawer with deep cellaret drawer containing a dummy drawer front, raised on ring-turned tapering legs.

84.25in (214cm) wide

£2,800-3,200 **L&T**

A Scottish Regency mahogany sideboard, with cross-banding and ebony stringing, the stage back with breakfront and sliding doors, on square section tapering legs with spade feet.

29in (74cm) wide

£2,200-2,800 **L&T**

A CLOSER LOOK AT A REGENCY SIDEBOARD

This magnificent Regency sideboard is a good example of the epitome of Scottish work from the period. It has Scottish features, such as the sunken bead-and-reel panels, the stage back and the use of ash to line the drawers.

It bears the signature "Aberdeen 1819" on the underside in pencil.

Sideboards were designed to be used as serving tables by the Scottish architect Robert Adam c1760. They were often produced en suite with other types of dining furniture.

This piece of furniture would have been used for storing cutlery, table linen and condiments.

A Scottish Regency mahogany sideboard, cross-banded with ebony stringing, sunk panels with bead moulding, the reverse breakfront stage with shaped ledge back and pagoda-topped pedestal with sliding cupboard fronts, central section with lifting door above a breakfront frieze drawer flanked by cupboards enclosing two drawers, tapering corner pedestals with ring-turned and reeded columns, on a plinth base with bronzed paw feet centred by palmettes.

Provenance: *Straloch House, Aberdeenshire.*

1819 *79.25in (201cm) wide*

£7,000-10,000 **L&T**

STANDS

A 20thC variegated green marble Doric column pedestal.

43in (107.5cm) high

£220-280 **S&K**

An 18thC pair of Italian parcel-gilt spiral-carved Corinthian columns with tops and bases later painted black.

45in (112.5cm) high

£800-1,200 **S&K**

A 20thC carved painted and gilded Corinthian pedestal, with a spiral-turned shaft on a carved circular lotus and egg-and-dart base, on three flattened ball feet.

55.5in (139cm) high

£600-900 **S&K**

A pair of 19thC reeded and tapered mahogany Doric columns, moulded with brass collars, top and bottom, on square stone bases.

90in (225cm) high

£5,000-8,000 **FRE**

A 20thC variegated green marble Doric columnar pedestal.

43in (107.5cm) high

£200-300 **S&K**

A pair of Louis XVI-style black marble and gilt pedestals, the square columns with applied flaming torch, ribbon-tied drapery and foliate swag decorations.

43in (107.5cm) high

£600-900 **FRE**

A Flemish rosewood torchere.

c1690 *38.5in (98cm) high*

£2,500-3,500 **DL**

An Adam-period giltwood torchere, on a three-legged base.

c1790 *51in (129.5cm) high*

£3,200-3,800 **DL**

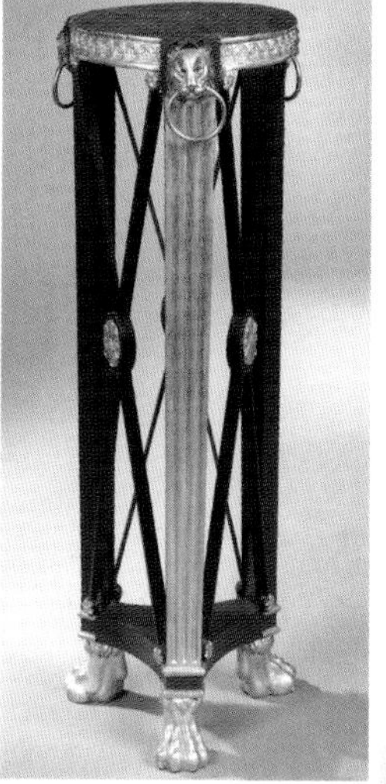

A Regency bronzed-and-gilt wooden torchere stand, the circular top above guilloche moulded frieze, three gilt reeded supports with later gilt brass lions masks, joined by X-supports with applied rosettes, on a concave base with three gilt paw feet.

39.5in (99cm) high

£600-900 **L&T**

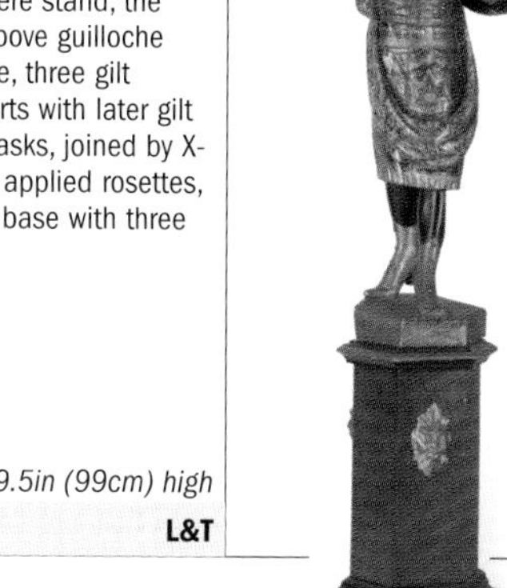

An early 19thC carved and painted blackamoor figure of a woman wearing an elaborately painted floral dress with gold highlights, one arm stretched overhead to hold a torch, the other hand lowered to receive cards, lacking torch.

81in (205.5cm) high

£3,500-4,500 **POOK**

A 19thC blackamoor torchere female figure in polychrome and gilt costume, one arm holding a cornucopia aloft, a shell tray in the other, on a hexagonal pedestal with an applied wreath suspended from masks, on a plinth.

63.25in (158cm) high

£800-1,200 **L&T**

An overpainted composition of a polychrome tobacco Highlander figure taking a pinch of snuff, inscribed on the base 'Snuff fig. by R. Waine', raised on a square section tapering base.

70in (178cm) high

£250-350 **L&T**

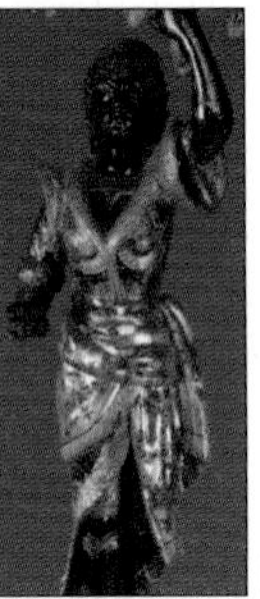

A Venetian-style ebonized and parcel gilt blackamoor standing figure in polychrome costume, the left arm supporting a canopy, the right hand outstretched, on a drapery-painted conical pedestal, circular moulded base on bun feet.

49in (122.5cm) high

£1,500-2,000 **S&K**

A CLOSER LOOK AT A PAIR OF BLACKAMOORS

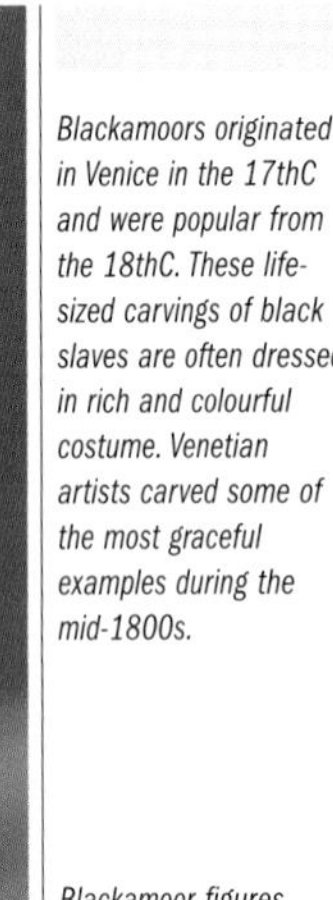

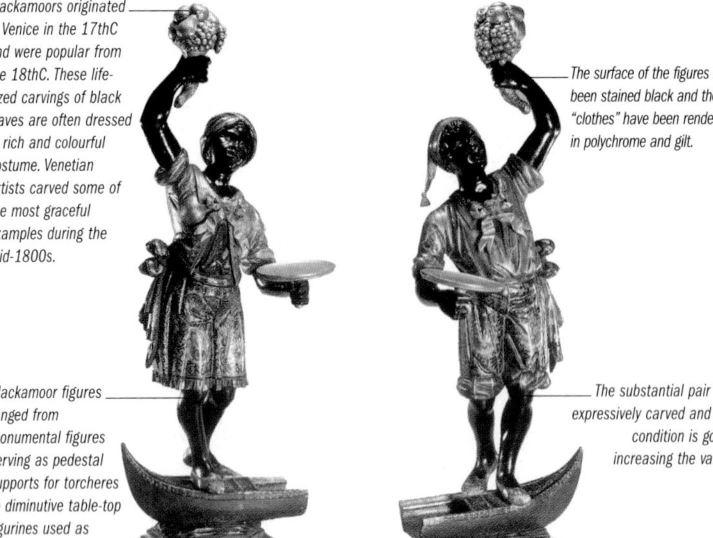

Blackamoors originated in Venice in the 17thC and were popular from the 18thC. These life-sized carvings of black slaves are often dressed in rich and colourful costume. Venetian artists carved some of the most graceful examples during the mid-1800s.

The surface of the figures has been stained black and the "clothes" have been rendered in polychrome and gilt.

Blackamoor figures ranged from monumental figures serving as pedestal supports for torcheres to diminutive table-top figurines used as candleholders. The raised arm is typical.

The substantial pair are expressively carved and the condition is good, increasing the value.

A pair of Italian ebonized blackamoors, painted in polychrome and gilt, each with an arm held aloft, holding a fruit-filled cornucopia in one hand, a tray in the other, standing on the end of a gondola, on an octagonal faux marble pedestal with a shaped base and three gilt paw feet.

65.35in (166cm) high

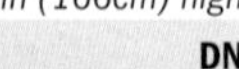

£4,500-5,500 **DN**

A George III mahogany basin stand, with an open ring, overturned supports and two drawers, resting on cabriole legs terminating in ball-and claw-feet.

33.5in (85cm) high

£800-1,200 **POOK**

A George III Hepplewhite period bowfront West Indian satinwood veneered bowl stand, banded in purpleheart and line inlaid, veneered legs.

Veneered legs are a rare feature which contribute to the value of this piece.

c1790 *79cm (31in) wide*

£3,000-4,000 **RGA**

A George III mahogany washstand.

37.5in (95.5cm) high

£300-400 **EP**

A George III mahogany corner basin stand, shaped shelf above a bowed top fitted for three receptacles, lower shelf with one working drawer raised on flared supports connected by a shaped stretcher.

44in (110cm) high

£300-400 **S&K**

A George III mahogany washstand, with a shaped apron, above a drawer and an 'X'-shaped undertier.

32.25in (82cm) high

£300-400 **DN**

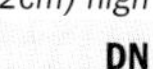

A George III mahogany washstand, with a shaped apron, above a drawer and an 'X'-shaped undertier.

32.25in (82cm) high

£300-400 **DN**

An early 19thC mahogany corner washstand, splashback above a later rosewood panel-filling basin recess, square supports united by a radially veneered shelf with a single frieze drawer, outsplayed legs.

30in (76cm) high

£220-280 **WW**

An early 19thC mahogany corner washstand, splashback with later top covering recesses, central frieze drawer flanked by pair of dummy drawers.

26in (66cm) high

£350-400 **WW**

An early Victorian rosewood stand, the circular petal edge top inset with white marble, ring-turned and ribbed stem on a triform base, scroll feet.

13in (33cm) diam

£600-900 **WW**

An Edwardian mahogany plant stand, with a brass liner.

33in (84cm) high

£100-150 **WW**

An early 20thC Empire-style ebonized jardinière, with three incurved legs ending in hoof feet, joined by an undertier and hung with weighted chains.

53in (134.5cm) high

£200-300 **S&K**

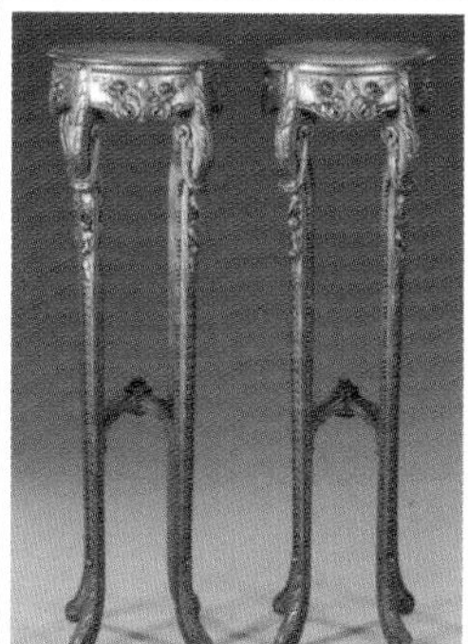

A pair of 20thC Louis XVI-style carved giltwood plant stands, circular with floral, foliate and bead-and-reel carving, on square supports with scroll feet.

43.25in (108cm) high

£200-300 **S&K**

A bentwood plant stand, with brass liner and open basket top on a tripod base.

36in (92cm) high

£120-180 **L&T**

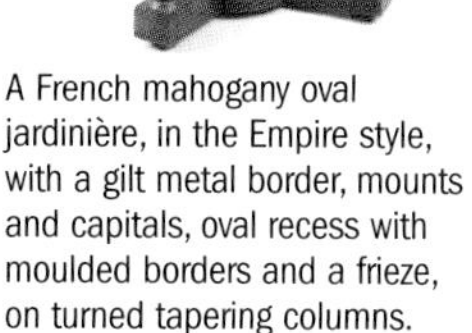

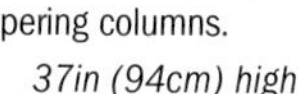

A French mahogany oval jardinière, in the Empire style, with a gilt metal border, mounts and capitals, oval recess with moulded borders and a frieze, on turned tapering columns.

37in (94cm) high

£2,500-3,500 **DN**

A 19thC walnut jardinière and stand, in the 17thC Venetian style, the circular bowl carved with fruits and flowers, with three pendants raised on a tall Renaissance-style baluster pedestal with Green Man masks, acanthus leaf clasps, festoons and tied fruit, on a concave triangular base with winged caryatids and cherubs, raised on a conforming carved plinth and saucer feet.

70in (175cm) high

£4,500-5,500 **L&T**

A French mahogany, box strung and gilt metal-mounted planter, lift-off lid above a zinc liner, on cabriole legs.

27.5in (70cm) wide

£300-400 **WW**

A giltwood pot stand, the circular top with moulded edge, raised on three scrolled leaf-and-husk carved consoles.

18.75in (47cm) high

£500-700 **L&T**

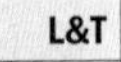

A CLOSER LOOK AT A REGENCY PORTFOLIO STAND

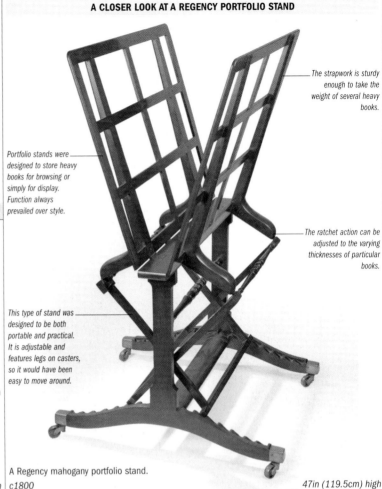

The strapwork is sturdy enough to take the weight of several heavy books.

Portfolio stands were designed to store heavy books for browsing or simply for display. Function always prevailed over style.

The ratchet action can be adjusted to the varying thicknesses of particular books.

This type of stand was designed to be both portable and practical. It is adjustable and features legs on casters, so it would have been easy to move around.

A Regency mahogany portfolio stand.

c1800 *47in (119.5cm) high*

£5,000-8,000 **B&I**

An American Victorian white-painted duet stand, with fretted lyre-shaped slopes, turned standard, on a tripod base.

c1870 *56in (143cm) high*

£200-300 **S&K**

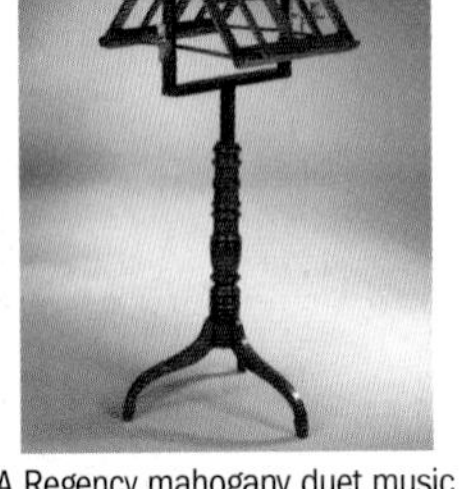

A Regency mahogany duet music stand, the opposed hinged and sloping falls with applied rests, on a rectangular frame with two scrolling brass candlebranches to the sides, on an adjustable support with a ring-turned column on a tripod base with curved tapered legs, spade feet.

56.5in (141cm) high

£1,500-2,500 **L&T**

A 19thC English papier-mâché music stand, inlaid with mother-of-pearl and depicting Windsor Castle.

c1850 *31.5in (80cm) high*

£4,000-4,500 **JK**

A George II carved mahogany tripod pole screen, with silk needlework panel of floral arabesques, urns and birds within a carved frame with ribbons and flowerheads, finial fluted and lobed baluster standard, acanthus-carved downswept and moulded legs with scroll toes.

c1750 *65.75in (167cm) high*

£2,000-3,000 **S&K**

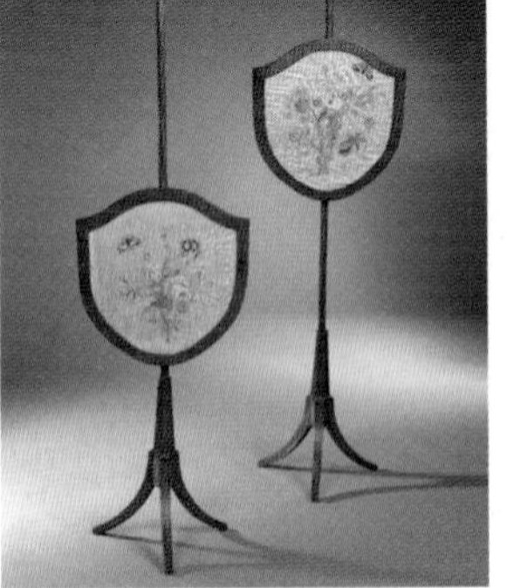

A pair of early 19thC satinwood and ash polescreens, with shield-shaped cross-banded panels containing silkwork with spray flowers and butterflies, supported by satinwood poles and faceted ash tripod bases on sabre legs.

55.25in (138cm) high

£300-400 **L&T**

A Victorian rosewood polescreen, the rectangular woolwork panel encased in a moulded frame with four corner rosettes, the pole with carved finial and knop on a tripod base with scrolling legs.

57.75in (144cm) high

£400-600 **L&T**

An early 19thC mahogany coatstand, with a central ring-turned baluster column, one shelf with four circular apertures for canes, the other with restraining gallery, on square section sabre legs with ball feet.

59in (150cm) high

£800-1,200 **L&T**

A William IV carved mahogany serpentine-shaped pedestal, with shell and foliate decoration, the top with later ring inset above the door, on brass casters.

19.5in (49.5cm) wide

£1,200-1,800 **WW**

A pair of 19thC bronze stands, in the Louis XIV style, each with circular top above a dentilled frieze and strapwork-cast basket, on three scrolled shell-cast legs joined by stretchers with shell-cast surmounts, later ebonized wooden covers.

31.25in (78cm) wide

£6,000-9,000 **L&T**

A late Victorian rosewood workbox, with boxwood stringing, the top with hinged sloping glazed falls enclosing a satin-lined interior, above a shaped apron and undershelf, supported by square section tapered splayed legs.

32in (81cm) high

£600-900 **L&T**

A folding mahogany three-tiered muffin stand, painted with roses.

c1910 *36in (91.5cm) high*

£80-120 **PS**

DINING TABLES

A large oak dropleaf table on cabriole legs and pad feet.

c1680 *28.5in (72.5cm) high*

£2,500-3,500 **EP**

A William and Mary gateleg table on baluster legs.

39.5in (100.5cm) wide

£2,800-3,200 **EP**

A 17thC gateleg table on baluster legs.

c1690 *29in (73.5cm) high*

£2,500-3,500 **EP**

A Queen Anne gateleg table with moulded edge to the top, on bun feet.

c1710 *29.5in (75cm) high*

£1,800-2,200 **EP**

A walnut gateleg table.

c1720 *28.25in (72cm) high*

£2,200-2,800 **EP**

A George II mahogany gateleg table, the oval top with moulded edge above a frieze drawer and arched aprons, raised on cabriole legs with hoof feet.

42.75in (107cm) wide

£1,500-2,000 **L&T**

A George II mahogany gateleg table, with oval top, raised on cabriole legs and pad feet.

39.25in (100cm) long extended

£300-500 **L&T**

A CLOSER LOOK AT A SLEDGE FOOT TABLE

During the 17thC smaller, more compact and flexible tables, such as the gateleg table, replaced traditional trestle-style pieces. They could be expanded and reduced in size, and became very popular.

Tops on early examples tend to be thick and uneven, like the one on this table. The handcarved balusters also tend to be slightly uneven in shape.

The colour is especially fine and dark. A patina builds up through years of exposure to the environment, repeated polishing and everyday wear. The underside tends to be lighter in colour.

Check for replacement drop leaves and hinges as they are vulnerable to damage. Wear on the underside of the table should be consistent with the movement of the supporting legs underneath.

An oak sledge foot table with oval top, on baluster-turned and blocked legs joined by stretchers.

c1690 *34.75in (88.5cm) wide extended*

£3,000-4,000 **EP**

A George III mahogany gateleg table, the oval top with satinwood cross-banding and rounded edge, on turned legs with club feet.

45in (114cm) wide

£600-900 **L&T**

A Georgian mahogany gateleg table, the hinged twin-flap oval top, on turned legs with pad feet.

14in (35cm) wide

£400-600 **L&T**

A 19thC oak gateleg table, the oval top above a single drawer, on turned and blocked legs joined by stretchers.

50in (127cm) wide

£500-800 **L&T**

A 19thC oak gateleg table, the oval top raised on baluster-turned and blocked legs joined by stretchers, drawer missing.

42in (106cm) wide

£300-350 **L&T**

A 19thC oak gateleg table, the oval top above a frieze drawer, on turned and block legs joined by stretchers.

41.5in (106cm) wide

£400-600 **L&T**

A 16thC English oak extending table, with four demi-lune folding leaves, rectangular top with breadboard ends above four bulbous baluster-turned supports, on bun feet connected by a circular moulded stretcher.

78in (195cm) wide

£8,000-12,000 **S&K**

A 17thC oak refectory table, carved frieze, on restored feet.

c1680 *45in (114.5cm) wide*

£1,000-2,000 **EP**

A Queen Anne oak table with drawer.

c1715 *48in (122cm) long*

£4,000-5,000 **EP**

A Queen Anne mahogany extension dining table, rectangular top, drop leaves, on circular tapered legs with pad feet.

28.25in (70.5cm) high

£1,800-2,200 **NA**

A mid-18thC mahogany rectangular dropleaf table, on turned tapering legs with ball-and-claw feet.

61.5in (156.5cm) long extended

£700-1,000 **DN**

A George III mahogany dining table, comprising a pair of D-form ends and single-hinged leaf, the frieze with boxwood stringing, on square section tapering legs.

71.75in (182cm) long extended

£2,800-3,200 **L&T**

A late 18thC Pennsylvania Queen Anne walnut dining table, the rectangular top with conforming hinged leaves on a shaped apron and cabriole legs ending in pointed pad feet, old repairs.

50in (125cm) wide

£1,200-1,800 **FRE**

A Regency mahogany metamorphic dining table, with repeating scissor action and four leaves, the rectangular fold-over top with moulded edge and rounded angles, above a frieze with central tablet and roundels, on turned and reeded legs with brass caps and casters.

125in (317cm) long

£6,000-9,000 **L&T**

An early 19thC mahogany dining table, with D-form ends and central drop-leaf section, reeded edge and plain frieze with ebony ring-turned legs on toupie feet.

106in (270cm) long

£4,500-5,500 **L&T**

An early 19thC mahogany patent extending dining table, comprised of a pair of swivel top ends with rounded corners, three extra leaves, one end with a draw frame, on ring-turned reeded tapering legs, with brass cappings and casters.

97in (277cm) long extended

£2,500-3,500 **WW**

A Regency mahogany metamorphic extending dining table, with repeating scissor action and four leaves, the rectangular fold-over top with moulded edge and rounded angles, above a frieze with central tablet and roundels, on turned and reeded legs with brass caps and casters.

126.75in (317cm) long

£3,500-5,500 **L&T**

A Regency mahogany three-part banquet table, the rectangular three-section top with D-form ends and surrounded by reeded edges, on bulbous ring-turned pedestals and reeded downswept legs terminating in brass caps, on casters.

90.5in (226cm) long

£12,000-14,000 **NA**

A 19thC walnut extending dining table, rectangular canted top with moulded angles above a plain frieze, on turned swollen legs with spirally incized decoration, brass caps and casters, includes three additional leaves.

121in (307cm) long

£1,000-1,500 **L&T**

A 19thC Georgian-style mahogany twin-pedestal dining table, the rectangular top with rounded angles, on turned pedestals with three sabre legs, brass caps and casters, includes one additional leaf.

78in (195cm) long

£1,800-2,200 **L&T**

A 19thC mahogany dining table, with a central gateleg section and D-form ends, on square section tapering legs with spade feet, bears label of "Weir and Hamilton, 9 Grafton Street, Glasgow".

114.25in (290cm) long extended

£1,500-2,000 **L&T**

A 19thC mahogany dining table, with pair of D-form ends and rectangular centre section, with frieze and turned tapering legs, three additional leaves.

166.25in (422cm) long extended

£6,000-9,000 **L&T**

A Victorian oak extending dining table, the moulded rectangular top with rounded angles above a plain frieze on turned and tapering legs, with carved cabochon knees and fluted decoration, brass caps and pot casters, includes four additional leaves.

155in (394cm) long

£2,500-3,500 **L&T**

A CLOSER LOOK AT A TELESCOPIC DINING TABLE

The design for an extending table was first introduced in the early 19thC and incorporated a telescopic frame that could accommodate extra leaves to extend the length of the table.

It is important to check that no sections of the extending table are missing as the additional leaves were often removed to make separate tables.

During the 19thC, middle class homes began to fill up with tables for every occasion. Dining took place at a large central table that could usually be extended.

Mahogany became popular during 18thC, when supplies of walnut declined. The strength of the wood and the width of its boards were ideal for producing large table leaves made from a single piece.

A 19thC mahogany telescopic dining table, the rectangular top with moulded edge and rounded angles, raised on boldly turned and reeded tapering legs with brass caps and casters, stamped "Lewty's Patent", of extending box construction, with five additional leaves.

172in (430cm) long

£7,000-10,000 **L&T**

A Victorian mahogany extending dining table, by John Taylor & Sons, Edinburgh, the top with demi-lune ends and moulded edges above a plain frieze, on turned and tapered legs with brass caps and casters, with six additional leaves.

185in (460cm) long

£7,000-10,000 **L&T**

A European Baroque oak draw-leaf refectory table, the rectangular panelled top above a panelled frieze, raised on bulbous legs headed by stop-fluted stiles and pierced brackets, joined by a box stretcher, on bun feet.

31in (79cm) wide

£1,200-1,800 **NA**

A George III-style inlaid mahogany twin-column extending dining table, by Kittinger, with a cross-banded edge, rounded corners and urn-form standards, on quadruped bases with lion paw feet.

113.5in (288cm) wide

£1,500-2,500 **S&K**

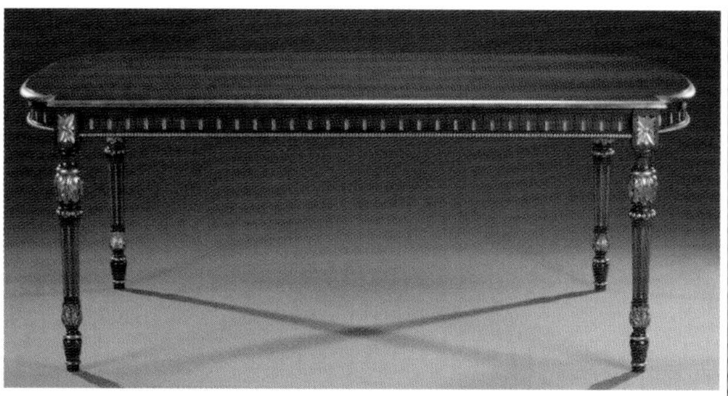

A Louis XVI-style mahogany dining table, the rectangular top with gilded rounded ends above a fluted apron with a gilt rope border on gilt foliate-carved fluted tapering legs on turned feet, with two additional leaves.

43.5in (109cm) wide

£800-1,200 **S&K**

A George II mahogany dropleaf breakfast table, possibly American, with rounded corners, shaped frieze and turned legs on stockinged pad feet.

47in (119.5cm) wide

£700-1,000 **S&K**

BREAKFAST TABLES

A late 18thC George III mahogany breakfast table, labelled "Alfred Bullard", circular hinged top half supported by a swing leg or folded into D-form drop-leaf table, satinwood and ebony inlay, on square reeded tapered legs.

47.5in (119cm) diam

£1,200-1,800 **S&K**

A Regency rosewood breakfast table, the rectangular cross-banded top with rounded angles and brass-stringing above a plain frieze raised on a rectangular tapered pedestal with a gilt collar on concave quadruped base with four canted sabre legs terminating in cast brass paw terminals and casters.

61.25in (153cm) wide

£1,800-2,200 **L&T**

A Regency mahogany breakfast table, stamped "Wilkinson, Ludgate Hill, 14582", rectangular tilt top on turned and reeded stem and four hipped scroll legs, leaf and shell cappings, on casters.

62.5in (159cm) wide

£800-1,200 **WW**

A CLOSER LOOK AT A TELESCOPIC MAHOGANY BREAKFAST TABLE

The introduction of veneer in the 18thC encouraged the development of a wide range of new, lighter and more versatile table designs.

Care should be taken to ensure that each section of the table is original and no married part is present.

The opposite of fluting, reeding refers to the convex moulded decorations to the edges of this table, which were derived from Classical columns.

The sabre leg, with its concave curve, was popular during the period and carved acanthus leaf decoration also appeared frequently on furniture.

A George III mahogany breakfast table, the rectangular framed veneered top a with ribbon-tied reeded edge and rounded angles, fluted frieze separated by oval rosettes, tilting with rest, baluster pedestal with foliate carving, raised on four sabre legs with acanthus leaf and ram's head terminals, leaf-cast gilt brass caps and casters.

59in (150cm) long

£15,000-20,000 **L&T**

A Regency mahogany circular extending breakfast table, the circular top with a fluted frieze reserved with carved urns in rectangular cartouches above a large knopped pedestal support and four square tapering legs carved with bellflowers and paterae, on brass casters, with three additional leaves.

54in (135cm) wide

£1,200-1,800 **S&K**

A Regency mahogany octagonal breakfast table, cross-banded tilt top on a baluster support, four angular outswept legs with brass terminals on casters.

51.5in (131cm) diam

£800-1,200 **DN**

A Regency rosewood breakfast table, the circular top with a plain frieze raised on a bulbous octagonal column, concave triform base with paw feet on brass casters.

50.5in (128cm) diam

£2,800-3,200 **L&T**

A Scottish Regency rosewood breakfast table, circular top with shallow frieze and beaded edge, raised on a triangular spreading pedestal with beaded sunk panels, on a concave triform base similarly panelled, with scrolled console and reeded bun feet on sunk casters.

34.75in (88cm) diam

£2,200-2,800 **L&T**

An early Victorian mahogany breakfast table, the circular tilt top on a faceted bulbous column support, ending in a platform base with scroll-carved feet on casters.

c1840 *57in (142.5cm) diam*

£1,200-1,800 **FRE**

A Victorian mahogany breakfast table, the moulded oval top above a plain frieze, on turned and button moulded column with three stiff leaf-carved cabriole legs, adapted on casters.

31in (79cm) wide

£500-800 **L&T**

A Victorian rosewood breakfast table, the rectangular top with moulded edge and rounded angles,on a turned and carved pedestal and circular base with four flat legs and leaf-carved scroll feet on casters.

56in (140cm) wide

£2,000-3,000 **L&T**

A 20thC French Empire-style mahogany circular extending breakfast table, with outset top, conforming frieze with fluted tablets and a dividing hexagonal standard with four downswept square-section legs on casters.

54in (138cm) diam

£500-700 **S&K**

A Regency rosewood and brass inlaid breakfast table, circular top with banding, scrolling foliage and brass line to the edge, above a turned column with finely reeded knop, on a turned base with four sabre legs terminating in brass caps cast as rams' heads on casters.

49.5in (124cm) diam

£1,200-1,800 **L&T**

A mid-18thC walnut tavern table, Delaware Valley, the overhanging rectangular top with breadboard ends on a frieze with a single drawer and scalloped apron, raised on vase and ring-turned legs joined by moulded and scalloped stretchers.

48in (120cm) wide

£800-1,200 **FRE**

An early George III mahogany serving table, rectangular top above two frieze drawers with engraved silvered handles flanked and divided by oval rosettes.

59.75in (152cm) wide

£7,000-9,000 **L&T**

A George III mahogany serving table, with boxwood stringing, the rectangular top with rounded angles and three frieze drawers raised on turned and tapering reeded legs terminating in toupie feet.

77in (195cm) wide

£10,000-15,000 **L&T**

A George IV mahogany two-tier buffet.

c1825 *31in (78.5cm) high*

£2,200-2,800 **DL**

An early Victorian mahogany metamorphic buffet, the rectangular top with moulded angles and corresponding counterbalanced undershelf opening to provide three tiers, raised on panelled trestle supports with scrolled console brackets, on scrolling moulded feet with casters.

48in (120cm) wide

£1,200-1,800 **L&T**

A mahogany carved serving table, in the George II style, moulded rectangular top above a scrolling frieze and acanthus-carved apron centred by a pierced shell, cabriole legs with shells and harebells, on pad feet.

64in (160cm) wide

£3,000-5,000 **L&T**

A 19thC Selanese stained hardwood table, long rectangular top with beaded edge raised above an ornate carved frieze with vine panels, on six corresponding turned tapering baluster legs.

84in (210cm) long

£2,000-3,000 **L&T**

A mahogany serving table, reeded edge above four drawers, ring-turned tapering legs, brass cappings on casters.

48in (122cm) wide

£1,200-1,800 **WW**

A Spanish Baroque walnut table, the rectangular top above three panelled frieze drawers opposing faux drawers, each carved with flowerheads and diamond-shaped escutcheons, raised on baluster-turned legs joined by a box stretcher.

66.5in (166cm) long

£3,500-4,500 **NA**

CENTRE TABLES

An 18thC German walnut centre table, shaped moulded rectangular top with central parquetry inlay above a frieze with s-scrolled mouldings, on cabriole legs with scrolled feet.

37.5in (95cm) long

£500-700 **L&T**

A Regency amboyna, ebony and ivory centre table.

c1810 *38in (96.5cm) wide*

£7,000-11,000 **DL**

An early 19thC Anglo-Indian coromandel veneered and bronzed library table, with rosewood cross-banding, three panelled frieze drawers opposed by reciprocal panels, reeded columnar supports with acanthus-carved terminals centred by a foliate roundel linked by a turned stretcher, on leaf-carved bases with turned feet.

49.75in (124.5cm) wide

£3,500-4,500 **L&T**

A George III mahogany revolving drum table with leather inset surface, incorporating four frieze drawers, one with adjustable slope for writing, a pen drawer and four dummy drawers on a turned centre column to four inlaid sabre legs terminating in brass casters.

c1810 *109.5cm (43in) diam*

£15,000-17,000 **RGA**

An early Victorian walnut octagonal centre table, tilt top with burr panel and elaborate marquetry and specimen wood decoration, on a triangular pedestal with carved and turned columns and strapwork decoration on corresponding tripod base with moulded cabriole legs and scroll toes on casters.

48in (122cm) wide

£5,000-7,000 **L&T**

A 19thC Dutch oak centre table, the rectangular moulded top inlaid with a chequer-parquetry panel in coromandel and ebony, above a moulded frieze applied with coromandel tablets, raised on eight boldly turned supports and stepped plinth base linked by a stretcher, on flattened disc feet.

60.75in (152cm) wide

£1,000-1,500 **L&T**

An early 19thC rosewood centre table by William Trotter, Edinburgh, the circular tilt top with plain cross-banded frieze raised on octagonal spreading pedestal and concave triform base with carved scrolling paw feet on sunken casters.

54in (135cm) diam

£2,800-3,200 **L&T**

A mid-19thC William IV Derbyshire marble centre table, the top inset with coloured marble pieces and enclosed by a marquetry border, gadrooned edge above a bead-moulded frieze, on three reeded cabriole supports with anthemion and scroll-carved brackets and paw feet, a tripod medial shelf over a plinth base, each corner with a carved boss.

36in (90cm) high

£1,200-1,800 **S&K**

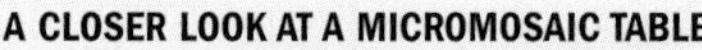

A CLOSER LOOK AT A MICROMOSAIC TABLE

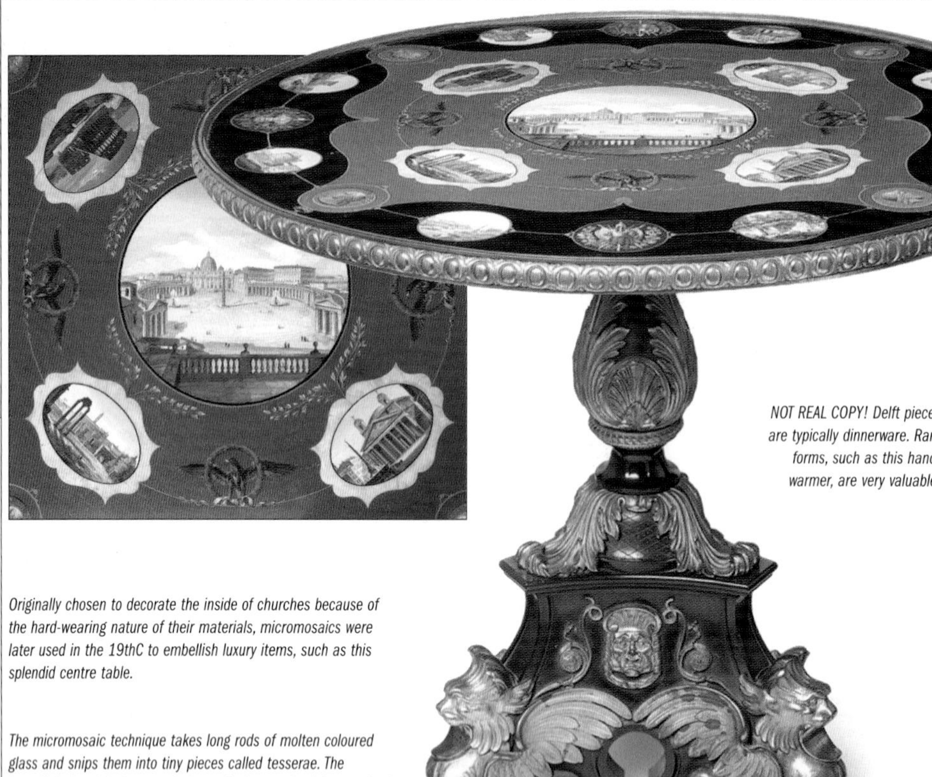

NOT REAL COPY! Delft pieces are typically dinnerware. Rare forms, such as this hand-warmer, are very valuable.

Originally chosen to decorate the inside of churches because of the hard-wearing nature of their materials, micromosaics were later used in the 19thC to embellish luxury items, such as this splendid centre table.

The micromosaic technique takes long rods of molten coloured glass and snips them into tiny pieces called tesserae. The incredible detail in the mosaic image is the result of thousands of these pieces of brilliantly tinted glass being compressed, assembled and secured with adhesive.

An Italian micromosaic 'Chronological Rome' round table by Michaelangelo Barberi, with an ebony and ormolu base, the micromosaic top on a square red cartouche and black marble ground, the roundels and ovals representing the four epochs of Rome, the inner circle with pink marble cartouches, an ormolu border with egg-and-dart type band, the base with an ebonized oak cruciform support, on an ebony baluster column, with masks on three griffon supports and paw feet with recessed brass casters, signed "Cav Barberi, 148 Via Rasella".

Provenance: *By family repute purchased by Robert Frederick Brownlow Rushbrooke while on grand tour c1850, for Rushbrooke Hall, Suffolk, thence by descent.*

c1845 *40.25in (102cm) diam*

£300,000-400,000 **DN**

A 19thC and later marble topped giltwood and gesso pier table, in the manner of William Kent, the shaped grey and red-veined rectangular marble top above an acanthus-carved and fluted frieze, centred by a scrolled shell, flanked by s-scrolls and oak leaf swags, raised on scrolling acanthus and fish scale-carved legs with scrolled feet.

78in (195cm) wide

£16,000-18,000 **L&T**

A 19thC pollard oak centre table, by James Schoolbred & Co, the moulded rectangular top with D-form ends above a plain frieze and turned leaf-carved spirally reeded legs on casters.

54.25in (138cm) wide

£800-1,200 **L&T**

A late 19thC Italian satin mahogany centre table, the top with calamander cross-banded frieze, inlaid with trailing leaves raised on an octagonal base with four barley twist supports and arcaded frieze, moulded lobed base with ribbon carving and sunken grass casters.

40in (102cm) diam

£2,000-3,000 **L&T**

A Victorian oak, pitch pine and specimen wood centre table, the octagonal top with central starburst and pollard oak border raised on an octagonal beehive and four-drip carved cabriole legs on casters.

47in (120cm) wide

£1,000-1,500 **L&T**

A late 19thC marble-topped centre table, in the manner of William Kent, the rectangular verde antico marble top with lugged canted angles raised on a stained gilt wood and gesso base, the ogee acanthus-carved and fluted frieze centred by shells to the long sides with oak leaf and acorn swags and drops, on canted acanthus, guilloche and fish scale-carved console supports.

56.75in (142cm) wide

£3,500-4,500 **L&T**

A late 19thC kingwood purple heart marquetry inlaid and gilt metal mounted centre table, serpentine rectangular top with central floral bouquet above a single frieze drawer, raised on cabriole legs.

43in (109cm) wide

£1,200-1,800 **WW**

A late 18thC mahogany oval centre table with shell pattern and kingwood banding, from the Low Countries.

95cm (37.5in) wide

£2,200-2,800 **RGA**

An Edwardian mahogany centre table, rectangular top with concave edge, fluted and carved frieze raised on trestle supports formed as opposing scrolled consoles with leaf-carved reeded columns at the centre, on Vitruvian scrolled bases with corresponding feet joined by stretcher and columnar supports.

73.5in (184cm) wide

£1,800-2,200 **L&T**

A George II-style mahogany centre table, moulded rectangular top above a frieze centred by a carved acanthus motif, on cabriole legs headed by a similar carving, with ball-and-claw feet.

28.5in (73cm) wide

£500-700 **L&T**

An Edwardian sabicu, mahogany and satinwood centre table, the galleried octagonal top inlaid with a central rosette, above a frieze with inlaid drapery swags on four square section tapering legs with gilt brass capitals joined by shaped X-stretcher.

32in (80cm) high

£800-1,200 **L&T**

A Louis XVI-style mahogany centre table, with gilt brass mouldings, the circular quarter veneered top with cross-banding above a panelled frieze, fluted tapering turned legs with brass capitals and toupie feet.

33.5in (83.5cm) diam

£1,000-1,500 **L&T**

A Regency-style mahogany round table, with galleried undertier, curved sabre legs ending in animal paw feet.

36in (91.5cm) wide

£1,000-2,000 **S&K**

An amusing figural circular marble-top low pedestal table, with a variegated pink top raised on a pedestal formed from a pair of white-painted human booted legs on a cloud-carved base.

36in (91.5cm) diam

£400-600 **S&K**

A Regence-style parquetry and parcel gilt twin-pedestal extending dining table, the top with rounded corners and a lambrequin-carved edge, each quadruped pedestal with incurved foliate scroll legs centred by a foliate boss, includes two additional leaves.

147in (373cm) wide

£2,000-3,000 **S&K**

An early 19thC Anglo-Indian ebony sofa table, with two drawers centred by a relief-carved palmette, opposing dummy drawers, on a turned and spirally reeded baluster pedestal with panelled plinth and concave square base with reeded edge, on four canted ball-and-claw feet.

51.5in (129cm) wide

£12,000-14,000 **L&T**

A Hepplewhite mahogany inlaid centre table, rectangular top with tray edge above a conforming apron joining square tapering legs with oval inlaid patera, joined by a cross stretcher.

Provenance: *Stair & Anderson, London, label.*

30in (75cm) high

£10,000-15,000 **NA**

A Louis XV-style kingwood centre table, with gilt metal mounts, mottled marble top above a shaped panelled frieze, on square cabriole legs surmounted by caryatids.

c1900 *30in (75cm) diam*

£1,500-2,000 **FRE**

SOFA TABLES

A Regency rosewood sofa table, the rounded rectangular top with boxwood stringing above two frieze drawers and opposing dummy drawers, on a simulated rosewood base with arched cross supports linked by a turned stretcher and terminating in leaf cast caps and casters, restorations.

65.5in (166cm) wide

£600-900 **L&T**

A Regency rosewood sofa table, the rectangular hinged top with rounded angles above two drawers with beaded panelling and turned brass handles, opposing dummy drawers, raised on turned and tapering moulded legs terminating in brass caps and casters.

61.5in (154cm) wide

£2,500-3,000 **L&T**

A Regency rosewood sofa table, the rectangular top with rounded angles and brass stringing above two drawers and opposing drawers, raised on trestle supports and reeded sabre legs with brass caps and casters.

60in (150cm) wide

£2,000-3,000 **L&T**

A Sheraton mahogany sofa table.

c1790 *63.5in (161.5cm) wide*

£18,000-20,000 **DL**

A Regency mahogany boxwood and ebony strung sofa table, rosewood cross-banding, rectangular hinged top with rounded angles above two frieze drawers, opposing dummy drawers over rectangular section supports and stretcher, inlaid sabre legs in brass cups and casters.

58.75in (147cm) wide

£1,000-1,500 **L&T**

An early 19thC mahogany and boxwood ebony strung sofa table, satinwood cross-banded top with rounded corners above two drawers and opposing dummy drawers on lyre-shaped supports carved with acanthus, sabre legs with brass paw terminals on casters.

64.5in (164cm) wide

£4,500-5,500 **DN**

A Regency mahogany sofa table, rectangular top with rounded corners above two boxwood strung drawers on end supports high stretcher and square tapering downswept legs with brass terminals on casters.

57.75in (147cm) wide

£1,000-1,500 **DN**

A Regency rosewood dwarf sofa table, by Gillows of Lancaster, rectangular top with drop flaps and rounded angles above a frieze with a stamped cockbeaded drawer and opposing dummy drawer, on panelled rectangular trestle supports joined by a turned stretcher, with sled base and console supports on cast gilt brass paw feet with casters.

28.75in (73cm) wide

£10,000-15,000 **L&T**

PEMBROKE TABLES

A George III mahogany Pembroke table, twin dropleaf top above a single frieze drawer with later brass drop handles, on square tapering legs united by an X-stretcher.

20.25in (51.5cm) wide

£400-600 **WW**

A George III rosewood and satinwood cross-banded Pembroke table with boxwood stringing, single frieze drawer, on four square tapering legs with casters, stamped "Edwards & Roberts" who retailed the piece in the 19thC.

c1795 *31.75in (80.5cm) wide*

£3,500-4,500 **RGA**

A George III harewood Pembroke inlaid table.

c1780 *37in (94cm) wide*

£9,000-11,000 **DL**

A George III mahogany figured oval Pembroke table, cross-banded in tulipwood, the frieze containing one bow-fronted drawer opposed by a dummy drawer, on four tapering legs with shell inlays to the tops and stringing, original barrel casters.

c1795 *37.5in (95cm) wide extended*

£5,500-6,500 **RGA**

A George III mahogany Pembroke inlaid table, rectangular top with two D-form drop leaves, one faded, above an inlaid ebony and satinwood line apron, one working drawer, one dummy drawer, tapered legs ending in brass caps on casters.

c1800 *29.75in (74cm) wide*

£600-900 **S&K**

A Regency mahogany Pembroke table, rectangular top with moulded edge and rounded angles above a frieze drawer and opposing dummy drawer, on turned and reeded tapering legs with brass caps and casters.

36.5in (91cm) wide

£1,500-2,000 **L&T**

A George II mahogany dropleaf table, rectangular top above a frieze drawer and square section legs with tassel feet, later H-stretcher.

39.5in (100cm) wide

£500-800 **L&T**

WRITING TABLES

A George II mahogany drawing table, tilting rectangular top with retracting rest, turned pedestal and tripod base with cabriole legs on casters.

30.75in (78cm) wide

£1,200-1,800 **L&T**

A Scottish George III mahogany writing table with boxwood stringing, rectangular hinged top with rosewood cross-banding and pinned rest, above a frieze centred by a panelled tablet, side drawer fitted for pens, on square section tapered legs.

This table is almost certainly from Edinburgh, and it is typical of the work of Bruce and Burns.

36.25in (92cm) wide

£2,000-3,000 **L&T**

A Sheraton period mahogany writing table.

c1790 *40in (101.5cm) wide*

£7,000-10,000 **DL**

An early 19thC writing table, rectangular top with rising central section and leather skiver, above a fitted drawer to one end, on trestle supports with opposing s-scrolls and turned roundels, each with reeded sabre legs and cast brass terminals on casters.

31.25in (78cm) wide

£2,800-3,200 **L&T**

A Regency mahogany writing table.

c1820 *46in (117cm) wide*

£4,500-5,500 **DL**

A George IV mahogany writing table.

c1825 *55.5in (139.5cm) wide*

£5,500-8,500 **DL**

A William IV satinwood writing table, rectangular top with rounded angles and overhanging ends with console supports above a pair of cockbeaded frieze drawers with opposing dummy drawers, on trestle ends framed by fluted columns with similar consoles, sled bases with turned feet on sunk casters.

44in (112cm) wide

£3,500-4,500 **L&T**

An early Victorian rosewood library table, two frieze drawers with later handles opposed by dummy drawers, faceted lotus-carved dual supports united by a turned pole stretcher, on bold paw feet.

52in (132cm) wide

£1,200-1,800 **WW**

A 19thC bureau plat, shaped and moulded top with an inset tooled leather skiver enclosed by an inlaid frieze, bone and mother-of-pearl, above two marquetry inlaid frieze drawers on square cabriole legs with gilt brass mounts and cast sabots, one missing.

54.75in (139cm) wide

£2,500-3,000 **L&T**

An early Victorian Louis XV-style bureau plat, with gilt brass mounts and marquetry decoration, the rectangular serpentine top with inset leather skiver above frieze drawers, on square section cabriole legs with sabots.

£9,000-11,000 **L&T**

A late 19thC kingwood and floral marquetry writing table, boxwood stringing and rosewood cross-banding with acanthus and c-scroll gilt metal mounts and border to the leather inset top, three frieze drawers and opposing false drawers, on slender cabriole legs.

48.5in (123.5cm) wide

£4,000-6,000 **DN**

A Hispano-Mooresque inlaid writing table, profusely decorated with ivory, ebony and specimen wood geometric inlay, rectangular top above frieze drawer and curved X-supports joined by mid and lower stretchers, on bun feet.

48.75in (122cm) wide

£4,000-6,000 **L&T**

A mahogany serpentine front writing table, stamped "Holland & Sons Ltd, Mount Street, London", tooled leather inset top with leaf-carved edge, above an arrangement of five drawers with cast brass handles, pierced spandrels to the kneeholes, one missing, on acanthus and husk-carved square tapering legs and block feet.

42in (107cm) wide

£400-600 **WW**

CARD & GAMES TABLES

A mid-18thC mahogany card table, baize-lined folding top with rounded outset corners, counter wells above a frieze drawer, on turned tapering legs with pad feet, drawer is a later addition.

33.25in (84.5cm) wide

£1,200-1,800 **DN**

A George III mahogany fold-top games table, rectangular top with outset square corners opening on to a baize-lined playing surface, above a frieze drawer and raised cabriole legs ending in ball-and-claw feet.

35in (87.5cm) wide

£2,200-2,800 **NA**

A George II mahogany architects table, rectangular double foldover top with a fluted edge opening to reveal a surface for cards, a drawing slope with two drawers below and a fold-down pen tray, raised on square chamfered legs.

37in (90.5cm) wide

£2,800-3,200 **L&T**

A Chippendale period mahogany carved concertina action card table with hollow square section legs in the Gothic style, shown extended.

c1770 *29in (73.5cm) high*

£6,500-8,500 **DL**

A pair of George III mahogany card tables, attributed to James Newton, each with rectangular swivelling foldover top with rounded edge enclosing a quarter-veneered interior inset with blue baize oval and raised moulded edge, above a plain cockbeaded frieze drawer and curved square section tapering X-frame supports with brass caps and casters joined by a turned stretcher.

28.75in (73cm) high

£6,000-8,000 **L&T**

A George III inlaid mahogany foldover tea/card table, the hinged rectangular top with inset rounded corners, the conforming frieze centred by a satinwood diamond-form reserve, on square-section tapering legs, stringing and rosewood crossbanding throughout.

c1800 *36in (91.5cm) wide*

£1,200-1,800 **S&K**

A Regency mahogany Channel Island card table, rectangular fold-over top with rounded angles above a boxwood strung frieze with central tablet raised on a baluster pedestal and canted rectangular base with applied half spheres and carved paw feet on casters.

36.5in (91cm) wide

£1,200-1,800 **L&T**

An early 19thC mahogany card table, canted rectangular hinged foldover top with satinwood banding, later baize to interior, tablet frieze on ring-turned tapering legs.

36in (91.5cm) wide

£500-800 **WW**

A Regency partridge wood card table, hinged swivelling top above four square supports with turned terminals, shaped quatreform base on moulded legs, brass cappings and casters.

35.75in (91cm) wide

£600-900 **WW**

An early 19thC mahogany card table, the foldover top with canted corners, cross-banded, with boxwood stringing, single frieze drawer and square section tapering legs, legs adapted.

£500-800 **L&T**

A George IV rosewood card table, rectangular folding top with brass inlay and rounded corners, on an octagonal tapering column with a nulled collar, round platform and four outswept legs with brass terminals and casters, the top warped, some veneers detached.

36in (91.5cm) wide

£1,000-1,500 **DN**

A William IV burr elm card table of unusually small size, with baize playing surface.

c1830 *29in (73.5cm) high*

£6,000-7,000 **DL**

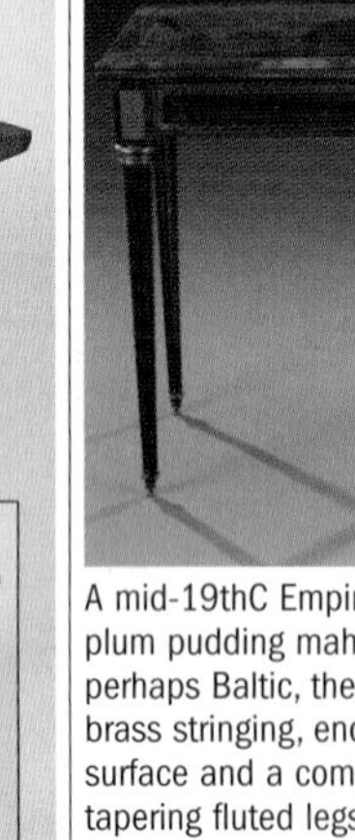

A mid-19thC Empire-style brass-inlaid plum pudding mahogany games table, perhaps Baltic, the hinged top with brass stringing, enclosing a baize-lined surface and a compartment, on tapering fluted legs with brass capitals and feet

£1,200-1,800 **S&K**

A matched pair of mid-19thC walnut turnover card tables, in the French mid-18thC style, each with serpentine moulded and hinged tops with boxwood stringing, kingwood cross-banding and opening to reveal one blue and one green baize-lined interior, with card compartment below, serpentine frieze, cabriole legs with gilt metal mounts, cast sabots.

38.25in (95.5cm) wide

£8,000-10,000 **L&T**

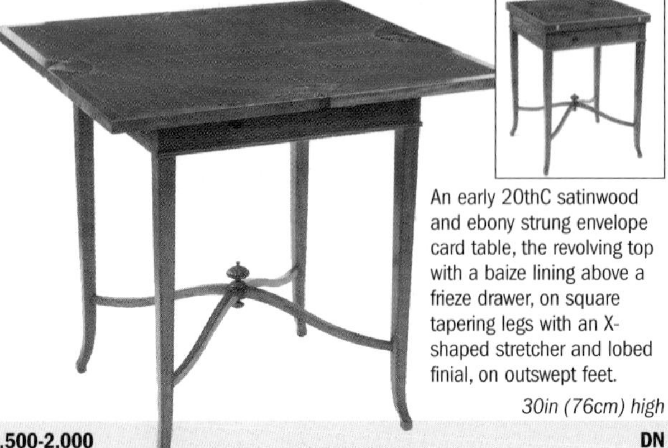

An early 20thC satinwood and ebony strung envelope card table, the revolving top with a baize lining above a frieze drawer, on square tapering legs with an X-shaped stretcher and lobed finial, on outswept feet.

30in (76cm) high

£1,500-2,000 **DN**

A George II-style mahogany foldover card table, shaped top with rounded angles, raised on club legs with shaped knees and pad feet.

32in (81cm) wide folded

£320-380 **L&T**

A late 19thC walnut and marquetry envelope card table, segmented top with chinoiserie inlaid decoration depicting figures in an architectural landscape, opening to reveal a baize playing surface, conforming frieze with one drawer, raised on spiral-turned legs joined by an X-shaped stretcher.

25in (63.5cm) wide

£1,200-1,800 **FRE**

An 18thC Anglo-colonial hardwood table, rectangular top with a satinwood chequered banding, moulded lipped edge above a shaped frieze with a leaf carving at each corner, on faceted legs with ebony and boxwood line inlay to the feet.

c1740 *30in (76cm) wide*

£15,500-17,000 **RGA**

A George III mahogany tea table, the D-shaped foldover top with cross-banding above a frieze drawer and square section tapered legs with spade feet.

29in (74cm) high

£450-550 **L&T**

TEA TABLES

A George I Virginia walnut fold-over tea table with good rich colour, deep frieze with a single drawer following the elegant line of the top, on cabriole legs with generous scroll-carved knees terminating on pad feet.

c1725 *84cm (33cm) wide*

£7,000-10,000 **RGA**

A George II mahogany tea table, rectangular fold-over top with rosette carved edge above frieze drawer and fretwork lattice apron, on square section chamfered legs.

32.75in (83cm) wide

£1,500-2,000 **L&T**

A George III mahogany tea table, D-shaped fold-over top with reeded edge above a boxwood strung frieze, on square section tapered legs.

35.5in (90cm) long

£300-500 **L&T**

A George III mahogany foldover tea table, in the Hepplewhite style, the serpentine top with moulded edge above a serpentine frieze raised on double gate action, carved cabriole legs.

40in (102cm) wide

£6,000-9,000 **L&T**

An early George III mahogany fold-over tea table, rectangular top with projecting rounded corners above frieze drawers and cabriole legs with carved knees and ball-and-claw feet.

35.25in (88cm) wide

£2,500-3,000 **L&T**

A George III mahogany tea table with unusual extending mechanism, red baize top and hollow legs.

c1800 *36in (91.5cm) wide*

£1,500-2,000 **DL**

A Regency mahogany foldover tea table with ebony stringing, rectangular hinged top with canted corners on a square column and stepped splayed quadriform base, brass caps and casters.

37.5in (95cm) long

£500-800 **L&T**

A Scottish Regency mahogany tea table, rectangular foldover top with rounded angles raised on a concave tapering square pedestal with gadrooned base, concave quadriform base with bead and reel moulding, four leaf-carved scrolled legs with paw feet on casters.

36.5in (93cm) wide

£3,000-4,000 **L&T**

An early 19thC mahogany tea table, foldover top with box strung edging, square tapering legs topped with inlaid marquetry shells.

35.25in (89.5cm) wide

£400-600 **WW**

A George IV rosewood patience table on carved end supporters.

c1825 *27in (68.5cm) wide*

£3,000-3,500 **RGA**

A 19thC Continental walnut tea table, shaped cross-banded fold-over top with rounded angles and moulded edge, raised on four square section cabriole legs, opening with concertina action.

33in (84cm) wide

£300-500 **L&T**

A Victorian rosewood tea table, serpentine swivelling fold-over top on an octagonal baluster stem, scrolling cabriole legs on china casters.

36in (91.5cm) wide

£500-700 **WW**

A Victorian rosewood tea table, rectangular swivelling foldover top above an ogee frieze, on six scrolled supports with carved shell terminals, turned feet with casters.

36in (91.5cm) wide

£700-1,000 **WW**

An 18thC Queen Anne mahogany tray-top tea table, rectangular top above a shaped frieze applied with flowerheads, on shell-carved cabriole legs ending in leaftip-carved drake feet, restored.

27.5in (69cm) high

£5,000-8,000 **NA**

A mahogany foldover tea and game table, rectangular top above a single frieze drawer to one end and fluted square section tapering legs with brass caps and casters inlaid with chequer and backgammon boards.

32.25in (82cm) wide

£500-800 **L&T**

A Victorian walnut game table, swivel twin drop leaf top with central chess and backgammon board above a single frieze drawer, spiral incized turned stem on carved cabriole legs.

29in (73.5cm) wide

£280-320 **WW**

A Sheraton mahogany games and work table.

c1790 *29in (73.5cm) high*

£3,000-4,000 **DL**

A Regency mahogany, rosewood and penwork games table.

17.5in (44.5cm) wide

£8,000-12,000 **B&I**

A George III casuarina wood work table.

c1780 *28.5in (72.5cm) wide*

£3,500-4,500 **DL**

A George III mahogany silver table, rectangular top with pierced fretwork gallery above a plain frieze and moulded square section chamfered legs joined by later arched and pierced X-shaped stretcher with frame finial.

29.5in (74cm) high

£2,000-2,500 **L&T**

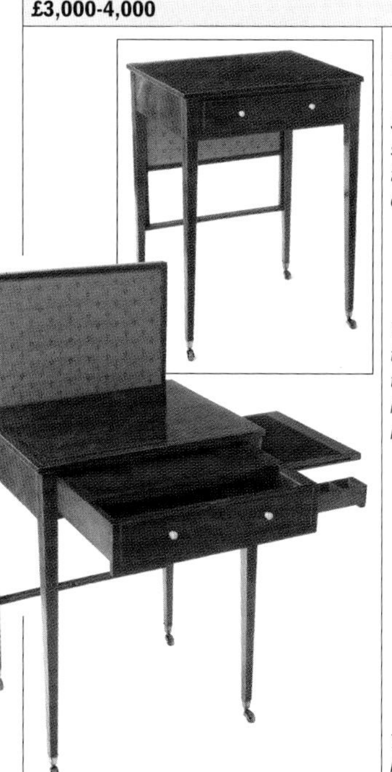

A Sheraton rosewood lady's writing/work table with rising screen and boxwood and satinwood line inlays, the top banded in purpleheart, pen and ink drawer to the side of writing drawers.

c1795 *56cm (22in) wide*

£4,000-6,000 **RGA**

A CLOSER LOOK AT AN ITALIAN MARBLE TABLE TOP

Strapwork decoration, so called for its resemblance to leather straps, was first used by Rosso Fiorentino in the late 16thC for framing paintings at Fontainebleau. It became increasingly elaborate during the 17thC and 18thC.

The fine central tablet of this table has been inlaid with specimen marbles.

The oak base of this table dates from the 19thC and is later than the top. Although the two sections have been matched, the piece remains valuable because of the desirability of the top.

The table top is early and has survived in excellent condition thus greatly increasing its value.

An 18thC Italian inlaid specimen marble table top, the rectangular top with moulded edge and a central tablet inlaid with strapwork panelled decoration in specimen marbles, on an early 19thC oak base.

55in (137.5cm) wide

£28,000-30,000 **L&T**

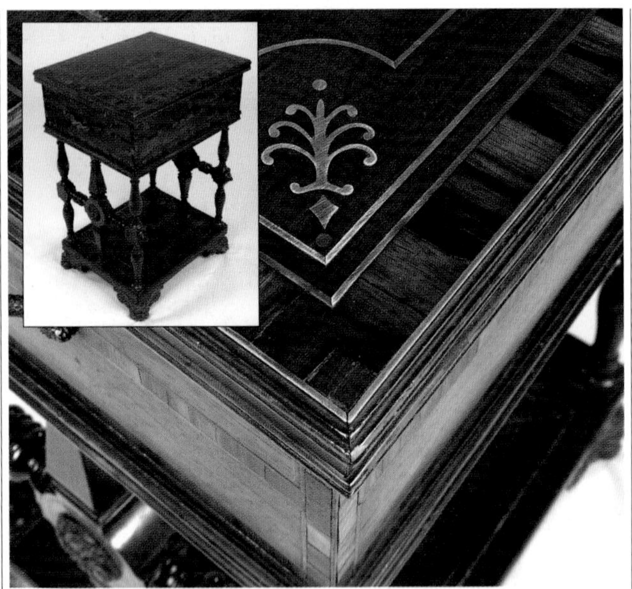

A Regency brass inlaid rosewood work table.

c1810 *32in (81.5cm) high*

£5,000-7,000 **DL**

An English regency satinwood and ebony work table, the slender turned legs of solid ebony, the hinged box over a drawer and slide, in the manner of George Oakley.

c1810 *31.5in (80cm) high*

£3,000-5,000 **RGA**

A late George III mahogany work table, with boxwood and ebony stringing, the rectangular top with rounded corners above a frieze drawer with ivory turned handles, on slender square tapering legs, lacking a sliding wool bag.

30in (76cm) high

£1,200-1,800 **DN**

A Regency mahogany work table, the rectangular top with drop flap ends above two drawers and ring turned legs with brass caps and casters.

30.25in (77cm) high

£400-600 **L&T**

An early 19thC mahogany deception work table, the hinged rectangular top above false drop flaps and square section tapering legs.

29.25in (74cm) high

£500-800 **L&T**

An early Victorian mahogany work table, the rectangular top with drop flaps and moulded edge above frieze drawer with divided interior raised on leaf carved trestle supports joined by stretcher, sled base with scroll toes on casters.

30in (76cm) high

£400-600 **L&T**

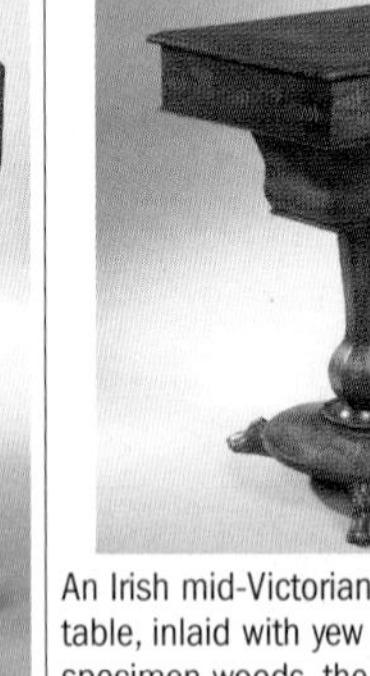

An Irish mid-Victorian Killarney work table, inlaid with yew and other specimen woods, the hinged rectangular top with moulded edge centred by panel of ruined abbey, leafy spandrels and frieze, enclosing interior with lift-out divided tray above wool bin, interior of lid inlaid with harp and shamrock motifs, on bulbous octagonal column and saucer base with three paw feet.

28.75in (73cm) high

£3,000-3,500 **L&T**

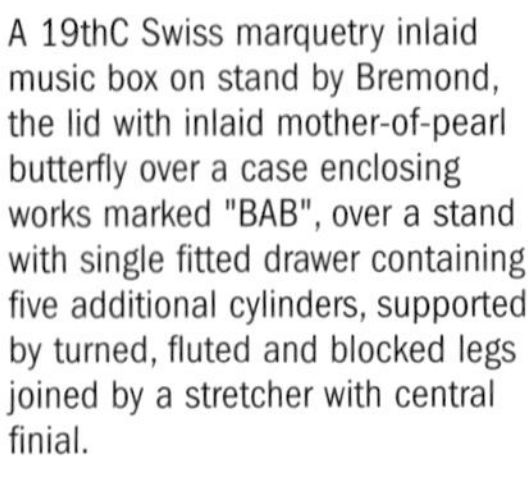

A 19thC Swiss marquetry inlaid music box on stand by Bremond, the lid with inlaid mother-of-pearl butterfly over a case enclosing works marked "BAB", over a stand with single fitted drawer containing five additional cylinders, supported by turned, fluted and blocked legs joined by a stretcher with central finial.

33in (84cm) high

£3,500-4,000 **POOK**

A Victorian walnut and ebonized work table, in the manner of Daniel Pabst, with a frieze drawer, carved grotesque mask animals and a domed work drawer, ring turned legs, on casters.

c1880 *30in (75cm) high*

£2,000-2,500 **FRE**

A late 19thC Victorian 'Aesthetic' parquetry and ebonized centre table, the geometric veneered square top with a conforming frieze, raised on openwork X-form base.

28in (70cm) high

£200-300 **FRE**

An Edwardian satinwood worktable, with rosewood crossbanding and ebony and boxwood stringing, the divided hinged bowfront top enclosing fitted interior with lidded compartments above chimney drawer and twin cupboard doors, on square section tapering legs.

14in (35cm) wide

£350-450 **L&T**

A Queen Anne gilt gesso pier table, the rectangular top with moulded edge and cusped corners, relief decorated with grotesque panel and borders, above frieze with shells and similarly decorated cabriole legs with scroll toes.

38.25in (97cm) wide

£5,000-8,000 **L&T**

An 18thC Italian Rococo console table, pine carcass, primed, painted silver and gilded, faux marble top and gilding original.

c1770 *54.5in (136cm) wide*

£14,000-16,000 **JK**

A late 18thC Italian decorated console table with gilt scroll and rosette decoration to frieze on leaf clasped tapered circular stop-fluted legs.

c1780 *43.5in (110.5cm) wide*

£14,000-16,000 **BL**

A Sheraton mahogany console table.

c1790 *42in (106.5cm) high*

£6,000-7,000 **DL**

A George III mahogany half round console table.

c1790 *36in (91.5cm) wide*

£6,000-7,000 **DL**

A 19thC Scottish oak lobby table, the rectangular top with moulded edge and panelled ledge back centred by rosette, moulded frieze on scrolled truss front legs and turned back legs.

48in (122cm) long

£500-800 **L&T**

A 19thC pair of Louis XVI-style gilded marble-top console tables, each with a shaped mottled brown/black marble-top, the bowed front with a frieze hung with foliate swags centring a figural medallion on foliate and drape carved fluted tapering legs.

45in (112.5cm) wide

£3,000-4,000 **S&K**

A Swedish painted and gilt console table.

c1790 *32in (81.5cm) high*

£4,000-5,000 **DL**

A Scottish Regency mahogany lobby table, in the manner of William Trotter, the rectangular top above ogee frieze and palmette carved scrolling front console legs with bun feet, panelled rear legs.

58in (148cm) wide

£3,000-3,500 **L&T**

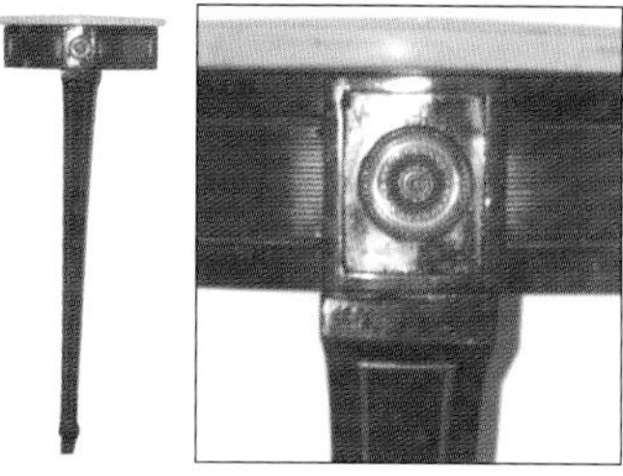

A 19thC pair of Russian marble-top corner consoles, each with a white marble-top and two ribbed gilt-bronze inset panels centring a floral roundel on a gilt-bronze mounted downcurving support ending in squared peg foot.

42in (105cm) high

£1,500-2,000 pair **S&K**

CONSOLE TABLES

A Victorian Rococo-style giltwood console table, serpentine rouge marble top on a profusely carved leaf and c-scrolled support, on two tapering cabriole square legs.

38.5in (98cm) high

£500-700 L&T

A late 19thC pair of Louis XVI-style carved, painted and parcel gilt marble-top demi-lune console tables, with pierced acanthus-carved friezes, turned fluted legs and interlaced stretchers.

30.75in (78cm) high

£1,200-1,800 S&K

A 20thC Spanish Colonial-style silver-veneered console table, on cabriole legs joined by shaped X-form stretcher, repousse with flowers, foliage and shells.

39.5in (100cm) wide

£2,500-3,000 S&K

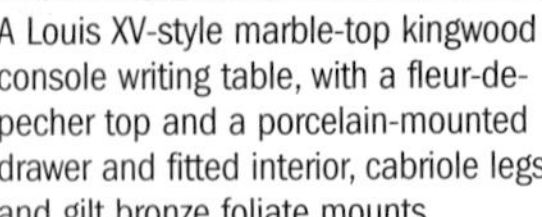

A Louis XV-style marble-top kingwood console writing table, with a fleur-de-pecher top and a porcelain-mounted drawer and fitted interior, cabriole legs and gilt bronze foliate mounts.

47.75in (121cm) wide

£3,500-4,000 S&K

An Italian green and cream painted marble-top console table, with relief-carved giltwood lion's head, female bust and foliate spray, on fluted turned tapering supports with block and peg feet connected by an H-stretcher.

44in (110cm) wide

£700-900 S&K

A George III mahogany rosewood cross-banded and marquetry ladies' dressing table, hinged divided top inlaid with floral sprays and riband tied bellflower ovals, rosewood interior of a ratcheted sliding mirror, eight lidded compartments, on slender cabriole legs.

c1770 *24.5in (62cm) wide*

£15,000-17,000 RGA

A 19thC Hispano-Mooresque walnut and ebony dressing table, inlaid with geometric bone and ivory decoration, cabinet with reverse breakfront top, mirror and turned bone balustrading, moulded plinth, block feet on casters.

76.75in (195cm) high

£1,500-2,000 L&T

A Queen Anne inlaid walnut dressing table, rectangular moulded top, shaped skirt with acorn pendants, cabriole legs ending in pad feet.

33.25 (83cm) wide

£12,000-14,000 FRE

A late 19thC Victorian faux tortoise shell bamboo dressing table and chair, pedimented rectangular mirror plate, on bamboo rod supports with outswept feet connected by a lower shelf, chair with heart-shaped open back and brown velvet upholstered seat.

62in (155cm) high

£700-1,000 S&K

A mahogany serpentine front dressing table, stamped "Holland & Sons Ltd, Mount Street, London", cross-banded top with Vitruvian scroll-carved edge, with cast brass handles, on acanthus and husk-carved square tapering legs and block feet.

51in (129.5cm) wide

£450-550 WW

A George II mahogany cabriole leg lowboy, with pierced detail.

c1770 30in (76cm) wide

£10,000-12,000 **DL**

A George II mahogany cabriole leg lowboy.

c1770 30in (76cm) wide

£10,000-12,000 **DL**

SIDE TABLES

A William IV mahogany lobby table, rectangular slate top raised on a base with a frieze and a pair of scrolled and leaf-carved consoles with panelled rear pilasters.

72in (183cm) wide

£700-900 **L&T**

A Charles II oak side table.

c1680 29.5in (75cm) wide

£3,500-4,500 **EP**

A William and Mary oak side table.

c1695 33in (84cm) wide

£2,500-3,500 **EP**

A William and Mary oak side table with tapered twisting legs.

c1690 40in (101.5cm) wide

£4,500-5,500 **DL**

A Queen Anne oak side table.

28in (71cm) high

£2,500-3,500 **EP**

An Irish walnut cabriole leg side table.

c1750 41in (104cm) wide

£5,000-7,000 **DL**

An 18thC French provincial walnut side table, quarter-veneered with boxwood stringing and cross-banding, serpentine top with moulded edge above a single long drawer, raised on c-carved cabriole legs with toupie feet, later stretchers.

44in (112cm) wide

£3,500-4,500 **L&T**

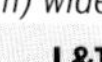

A George III mahogany side table, D-shaped top with satinwood and tulipwood cross-banding and boxwood and ebony stringing above a plain frieze with panelled terminals to the reeded and fluted turned tapering legs.

43.25in (108cm) wide

£4,000-6,000 **L&T**

A George III mahogany side table, rectangular rouge marble top with moulded edge, raised on stand with Vitruvian scroll frieze and square chamfered legs with curved brackets.

Provenance: *The Dukes of Hamilton.*

54.5in (136cm) wide

£7,000-10,000 **L&T**

An early 19thC chestnut and rosewood banded table, with rounded rectangular top on a scrolling X-frame, united by a faceted pole stretcher.

33.5in (84cm) wide

£1,500-2,000 **L&T**

A Regency mahogany side table, three-quarter galleried top above a central frieze drawer flanked by two further deep drawers carved with lobed rondels, raised on spiral-fluted turned legs.

c1820 *42in (105cm) wide*

£800-1,200 **FRE**

A William IV burr walnut table, rectangular veneered top above a concave frieze on panelled trestle tapering supports joined by a leaf-carved and turned stretcher, on sled bases with scroll toes and casters.

30.25in (77cm) high

£1,500-2,000 **L&T**

A 19thC Anglo-Indian octagonal table, with specimen wood radiating inlay over a carved frieze and base, on turned supports and platform base.

c1850 *30in (76cm) high*

£550-650 **L&T**

One of a pair of 19thC Continental inlaid side tables, probably Italian, inlaid with classical motifs, the single drawer with an ebony inlaid scene of a charioteer, on square tapering legs and spade feet.

36.5in (91cm) wide

£2,000-3,000 pair **S&K**

An Anglo-Indian carved hardwood side table, with marble inset top over a carved frieze, on bold scrolling legs terminating in scrolled toes.

72in (183cm) wide

£3,500-4,500 **L&T**

An Anglo-Indian rosewood and brass inlaid library table, rectangular top with petal inlay, on lyre end supports with arched stretcher, scrolling legs with brass paw cappings on casters.

60in (152.5cm) wide

£2,200-2,800 **WW**

A rare matched pair of Colonial oval Sutherland tables, tops inlaid with radiating exotic specimen wood with a leaf-carved moulded edge, solid ebony base profusely carved with leaves and scrolls.

c1860 *63cm (24.75in) high*

£12,000-15,000 **RGA**

A pair of Scandinavian satin birch demi-lune tables, each top above an angled frieze, on three square-section tapered legs.

34.75in (87cm) wide

£1,200-1,800 **L&T**

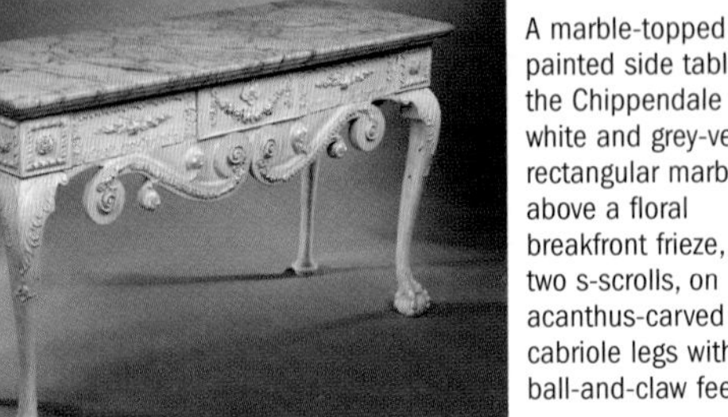

A marble-topped white painted side table, in the Chippendale style, white and grey-veined rectangular marble top above a floral breakfront frieze, over two s-scrolls, on acanthus-carved cabriole legs with ball-and-claw feet.

50.75in (127cm) wide

£2,000-3,000 **L&T**

A Louis XVI-style marble-top and parquetry table en chiffoniere.

28in (71cm) high

£300-500 **S&K**

A Louis XV marquetry inlaid kingwood table.

c1770 *27in (68.5cm) high*

£2,200-2,800 **DL**

A Regency marble inlaid occasional table, rectangular scagliola top with marble inlay and central panel of musical trophies, ebonized base with bobbin-turned column, on three cabriole legs.

19.5in (49cm) wide

£2,800-3,200 **L&T**

A Regency mahogany specimen table, circular marble specimen top with slate ground resting on corresponding table top with ring-turned and stiff leaf-carved column on a concave triform base with acanthus-carved scroll feet, adapted.

20in (51cm) diam

£800-1,200 **L&T**

A Regency rosewood occasional table, rectangular top, scrolled and pierced end supports, turned pole stretcher, on arched feet.

c1810 *28.75in (73cm) high*

£700-1,000 **S&K**

A 19thC mahogany patience table, cross-banded with inlaid stringing, on spliced front legs.

18in (46cm) wide

£300-400 **WW**

A 19thC Italian Classical inlaid fruitwood table en chiffoniere, with a three-quarter gallery, two drawers with chevron banding, and square section tapering legs, top was formerly lined.

27in (65.5cm) high

£280-320 **S&K**

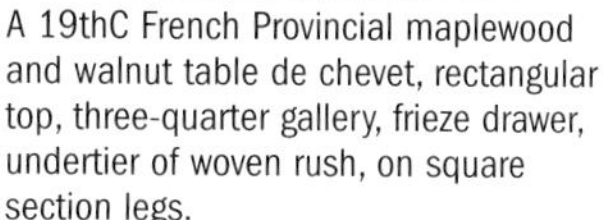

A 19thC French Provincial maplewood and walnut table de chevet, rectangular top, three-quarter gallery, frieze drawer, undertier of woven rush, on square section legs.

29.75in (75.5cm) high

£120-180 **S&K**

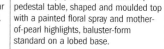

A Victorian papier-mâché oval tilt-top pedestal table, shaped and moulded top with a painted floral spray and mother-of-pearl highlights, baluster-form standard on a lobed base.

c1860 *27.5in (70cm) high*

£180-220 **S&K**

A pair of Victorian rosewood and burr walnut occasional tables, in the style of Louis XV, serpentine rectangular tops above a shaped frieze and moulded carved cabriole legs with scroll toes and toupie feet joined by undershelves.

25.5in (65cm) high

£2,500-3,500 **L&T**

A late 19thC Louis XV-style kingwood mahogany and gilt bronze-mounted gueridon, possibly by Francois Linke, cross-banded fan veneered top with an engine-turned edge above a panelled frieze applied with mask motifs and cornucopia, on slender cabriole legs joined by an X-form stretcher with a fruit and flame finial, terminating in hoof sabots.

30in (75cm) high

£3,000-4,000 **FRE**

One of a pair of George IV mahogany circular tables, on casters.

c1820 *27in (68.5cm) high*

£6,000-8,000 pair **DL**

An Edwardian ebonized occasional table, circular top above a pierced arcaded frieze, on four turned block legs each comprising a cluster of ring-turned columns joined by a concave undertray with similar pierced arcaded gallery, on turned feet with brass casters.

27.5in (70cm) high

£100-150 **L&T**

An early 20thC pair of Classical-style mahogany marble-top tables, each with square grey-veined white marble top above an apron with gilt figural mount on turned tapering legs with gilt bronzes collars connected by a flat stretcher.

24in (60cm) high

£300-400 **S&K**

A 20thC pair of Louis XVI-style gilt bronze-mounted veneered end tables, each with a shaped square top decorated with flowers above a frieze mounted with putti, on cabriole legs with foliage.

33in (84cm) high

£900-1,100 **S&K**

A 20thC Louis XV-style kingwood and checker inlaid marble-top side table, with gilt metal mounts.

27in (65.5cm) high

£350-450 **S&K**

A 20thC Louis XVI style giltwood marble-top side table, inset marble-top above a frieze with tied ribbon suspending a floral swag on each side, raised on fluted tapering legs ending in toupie feet.

28.5in (71cm) high

£500-800 **S&K**

One of a pair of Louis XVI-style bouillote tables with breche d'Alps marble tops.

20.75in (52.5cm) high

£4,500-5,500 pair **B&I**

A pair of satin birch occasional tables, each with radially veneered circular top on faceted stem, triform base and turned feet.

17.25in (44cm) diam

£400-600 **WW**

A mahogany and gilt metal mounted bijouterie table, serpentine top with floral marquetry, on slender cabriole legs united by an undertier.

25in (63.5cm) wide

£500-700 **WW**

A French kingwood and foliage marquetry lamp table, serpentine galleried top above a slide drawer and opposing drawer, on slender cabriole legs united by an undertier.

13.75in (35cm) wide

£350-450 **WW**

A French mahogany gilt metal mounted table, inverted breakfront marble top with trellis gallery, on turned and fluted legs united by undertier.

21in (53.5cm) wide

£180-220 **WW**

A Charles X-style mahogany and marble-top parcel gilt gueridon, moulded fossil marble top, reeded frieze, on three incurved legs with ram head capitals and hoof feet.

27.5in (70cm) high

£280-320 **S&K**

A Biedermeier-style part-ebonized glass-top oval occasional table, with a moulded gallery, banded frieze, conforming undertier, raised on square-section tapering legs.

30in (76cm) high

£400-600 **S&K**

A Louis XVI-style kingwood marquetry table a ecrire, hinged top with rounded ends and a pierced three-quarter gallery, opening to a fitted interior, frieze with a drawer, turned tapering fluted legs joined by a shaped H-stretcher.

30in (76cm) wide

£300-400 **S&K**

TRIPOD TABLES

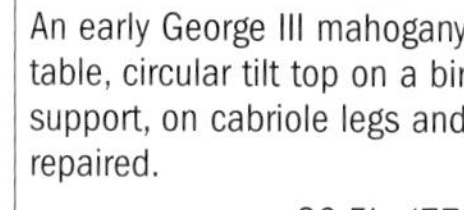

An early George III mahogany tripod table, circular tilt top on a birdcage support, on cabriole legs and pad feet, repaired.

30.5in (77.5cm) diam

£500-700 **WW**

A George III yew wood tripod table, on cabriole legs with pad feet.

c1770 *28.25in (72cm) wide*

£4,000-5,000 **DL**

A George III mahogany cricket table.

c1770 *28.5in (72.5cm) high*

£2,000-2,500 **DL**

An early George III mahogany tripod table, circular tilt top on a barrel turned stem, on cabriole legs with pad feet.

30in (76cm) diam

£600-900 **WW**

A George III Chippendale-style mahogany tea table with shaped top and applied moulded edge over elaborately scrolled turned and fluted shaft, supported by three cabriole legs with acanthus carved knees and scrolled feet terminating in brass casters.

The base of this table is derived from designs by Mayhew and Ince. The top does not sit well on the base and the comparatively low value of this piece would suggest that the table has been altered or a later top been added.

c1760 *28in (71cm) high*

£4,000-6,000 **POOK**

An early George III-style mahogany tripod table, shaped circular top with pie crust edge, on a bird cage turned pedestal with spirally fluted knop, leaf-carved cabriole legs on ball-and-claw feet.

29.25in (74cm) high

£600-900 **L&T**

A Georgian mahogany tripod table, circular tilt top, raised on turned pedestal and cabriole legs.

23in (58cm) high

£350-450 **L&T**

A George III mahogany occasional table, moulded cross-boarded rectangular tilt-top with canted corners, on ring and baluster-turned column, tripod base with spade feet.

31in (79cm) wide

£350-400 **L&T**

A George III mahogany tilt top tripod table, circular top with rounded edge on a turned pedestal and cabriole legs.

30.5in (78cm) high

£200-300 **L&T**

A late 18thC Chippendale mahogany tilt-top candlestand, from Philadelphia, circular dished top on a turned standard above a compressed ball, cabriole legs ending in slipper feet, some restoration.

27.5in (70cm) high

£2,000-3,000 **FRE**

A George III mahogany tripod table, tilt top on tapering stem and spiral-turned knop, tripod base, replacements to bearers and repair to one foot.

36in (91.5cm) diam

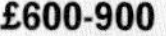

£600-900 **WW**

A George III tripod table, circular mahogany tilt top on an oak base with chamfered cabriole legs.

21in (53.5cm) diam

£400-600 **WW**

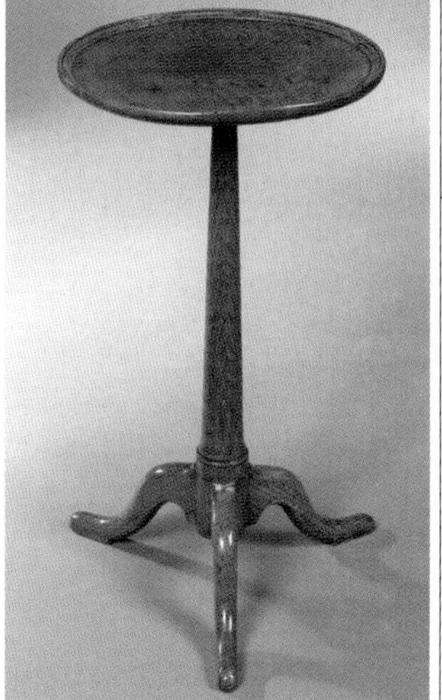

A George III oak country tripod table, round top with thumbnail rim raised on a turned pedestal and tripod base with cabriole legs.

27.5in (70cm) high

£250-300 **L&T**

A late George III mahogany tripod table, tilt top on baluster-turned stem, cabriole legs and pad feet.

31.5in (80cm) diam

£350-450 **WW**

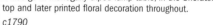

A George III mahogany tripod lamp table, in the Sheraton style, with canted tilt top and later printed floral decoration throughout.

c1790 *72cm (28.5in) high*

£3,000-3,500 **RGA**

An early 19thC ebonized and parcel gilt table, papier-mâché rectangular top with rounded corners and painted in red and gilt with Oriental figures, on a turned leaf-carved support and triform with paw feet, top cracked.

28.25in (72cm) high

£450-550 **DN**

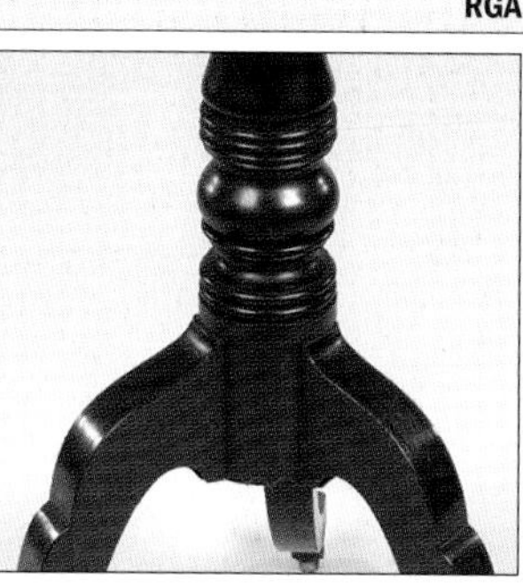

A Regency mahogany adjustable height reading table, missing rail.

c1820 *31.5in (80cm) high*

£2,200-2,800 **DL**

A William IV painted armorial tripod table.

c1835 *27.5in (70cm) high*

£2,000-2,500 **DL**

A mid-19thC oak cricket table with circular planked top.

28in (71cm) diam

£400-600 **WW**

A mid-19thC oak cricket table, circular planked top with reeded edge.

28in (71cm) diam

£300-500 **WW**

A Victorian papier-maché painted tripod table, ornate-shaped mother-of-pearl inlaid and gilt scroll-decorated top centred by a panel painted with an architectural mountainous landscape scene, turned column support ending in three cabriole legs with pad feet.

c1860 *26in (65cm) high*

£500-800 **FRE**

A Black Forest carved walnut and inlaid tripod table, shaped oval top inlaid with oval panels of stags, raised on a turned column support ending in three foliate carved cabriole legs.

c1860 *30.5in (76cm) high*

£400-600 **FRE**

A Victorian ebonized polychrome painted tilt-top table, square top painted with floral sprays on an urn-turned pedestal, on four feet downcurving supports.

27in (67.5cm) wide

£300-350 **S&K**

TRAY TABLES

A Regency papier mâché tray on a modern stand.

31.5in (80cm) wide

£2,800-3,200 **DL**

An ornate lacquered black paper mâché tray by Henry Clay of Covent Garden, London.

c1815 *18.75in (47.5cm) wide*

£2,200-2,800 **TCS**

A late Georgian mahogany folding butler's tray with well figured timber, on a modern stand.

c1820 *89cm (35in) wide*

£3,000-3,500 **RGA**

A 19thC mahogany butler's tray, galleried rectangular top with pierced handles, on turned and blocked supports.

30.5in (78cm) long

£300-500 **L&T**

A Victorian papier mâché tray on a stand, shaped tray with gilt border and forest scene with birds of paradise raised on an attached gilt and ebonized faux bamboo stand.

26in (66cm) long

£800-1,200 **L&T**

A toleware tray painted with a church scene.

While reminiscent of Fountains Abbey in Yorkshire, the scene does not appear to represent a specific location.

c1830 30in (77cm) wide

£700-1,000 **DL**

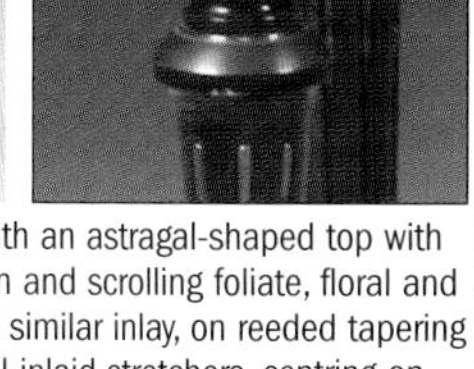

A Napoleon III ebony and marquetry centre table, with an astragal-shaped top with gilt bronze and mother-of-pearl boulle inlay of an urn and scrolling foliate, floral and bird-in-flight details, gilt-bronze edge, the apron with similar inlay, on reeded tapering legs with gilt collars and bases connected by c-scroll inlaid stretchers, centring on an ebonized parcel gilt urn, raised on toupie feet ending in brass caps.

c1860 *51in (127.5cm) wide*

£700-1,000 **S&K**

A nest of three burr walnut and crossbanded occasional tables with ring-turned spindle supports.

c1890 *largest 20.75in (53cm) wide*

£2,000-2,500 **RGA**

A nest of four mahogany tables, the rectangular tops crossbanded and ebony strung, raised on ring turned supports and downscrolled sled bases.

Largest 14in (35cm) wide

£600-900 **L&T**

A part nest of two rosewood occasional tables, rectangular tops on ring turned supports and out scrolled standard ends.

Largest 16.5in (42cm) wide

£120-180 **WW**

An Italian olivewood fire screen table.

c1780 *27in (68.5cm) high*

£4,000-4,500 **DL**

A late 18thC French maple and rosewood dressing table, with three false drawers above five drawers, pull-out tray, on conical legs with bronze sabots, the top opens out into three sections, inlayed with an unusual knotted wood veneer, original locks and mounts, some restoration.

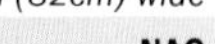

32.25in (82cm) wide

£2,200-2,800 **NAG**

An early 19thC mahogany-cased Bagatelle table, the rectangular hinged lid opening to reveal a baize lined interior fitted with inset numbered cups for balls, and a moveable target for balls, the edges inset with interior holes, the whole raised on a base with turned and leaf carved legs with tapering feet, stamped 'Thurston, 14 Catherine St, London', includes cue, balls, markers.

48.75in (122cm) long

£1,200-1,800 **L&T**

A Victorian mahogany metamorphic buffet, the moulded serpentine top rising on a square column to reveal a second smaller tier, on octagonal column and acanthus carved and scrolled quadriform base.

17.5in (45cm) wide

£1,500-2,000 **L&T**

WHATNOTS

A George III mahogany whatnot.

c1800 *48in (122cm) high*

£2,800-3,200 **DL**

A Regency simulated rosewood whatnot, with three rectangular galleried shelves, turned and blocked supports above a single drawer, corresponding feet with brass caps and casters.

54.75in (137cm) high

£1,800-2,200 **L&T**

A 19thC rosewood etagere.

28.5in (72.5cm) high

£2,200-2,800 **DL**

A Victorian walnut whatnot, pierced gallery above three shelves on spiral twist supports, single drawer to base, brass casters.

26.25in (67cm) wide

£800-1,200 **WW**

A late 19thC French rosewood and floral marquetry three-tier etagere, top with a brass three-quarter gallery above a drawer with turned supports and legs.

30in (76cm) high

£380-420 **DN**

Left to Right: A Victorian burr walnut three-tier whatnot, rectangular shelves with moulded edge and rounded edge and rounded angles raised on turned and fluted supports, base with a single drawer on turned feet with brass caps and casters.

36in (91cm) high

£2,500-3,000 **L&T**

A 19thC rosewood whatnot with four open serpentine shelves raised on barley twist supports and turned feet with brass caps on casters.

48.5in (123cm) high

£1,000-1,500 **L&T**

A George II mahogany three-tier dumb waiter, graduated circular tiers with thumbnail rims supported by turned pedestals with spirally fluted knops, tripod base with plain pedestal and cabriole legs with cobs.

46in (115cm) high

£2,500-3,000 **L&T**

A George III mahogany dumb waiter with two revolving graduated tiers supported on a turned centre column on a tripod base with casters.

c1780 *83cm (32.75in) high*

£3,000-3,500 **RGA**

A pair of George III mahogany dumb waiters, possibly Irish, each surmounted by a turned urn finial, above three circular and graduating tiers, with moulded rim supported by turned urn uprights, tripod base with square section curved legs with boxwood stringing, each terminating in brass caps and casters.

61.25in (153cm) high

£3,000-4,000 **L&T**

A 19thC French carved walnut and upholstered day bed, in the Louis XVI style, reeded and foliate-carved scroll arms and loose cushion seat covered in beige fabric, raised on turned and stop-fluted legs, surmounted by paterae and joined by a rope-carved apron.

83in (207.5cm) wide

£1,000-1,500 **FRE**

BEDS

A William IV mahogany four-poster bed, moulded cornice with carved frieze raised on turned, reeded and leaf-carved foot posts and plain head posts enclosing a panelled headboard, formerly the foot board.

Provenance: *Straloch House, Aberdeenshire.*

107.5in (273cm) high

£2,500-3,500 **L&T**

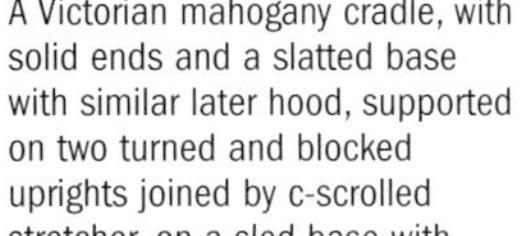

A Victorian mahogany cradle, with solid ends and a slatted base with similar later hood, supported on two turned and blocked uprights joined by c-scrolled stretcher, on a sled base with scroll toes.

Provenance: *Straloch House, Aberdeenshire.*

48in (122cm) high

£500-800 **L&T**

A Victorian mahogany caned cradle, with ogee hood and turned finials with blocked uprights, on bun feet.

49.25in (125cm) high

£250-350 **L&T**

A late Victorian oak and mahogany child's bed, shaped head and foot boards with turned finials, slatted base on turned legs.

38.75in (98.5cm) long

£40-60 **DN**

An English 'New Celestial Globe', by Cary, on a mahogany stand.

c1800 *36in (91.5cm) high*

£7,000-10,000 **B&I**

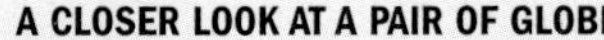

A CLOSER LOOK AT A PAIR OF GLOBE

John and William Cary founded their firm c1790 and it became one of the leading English globe-making companies of the period. They prided themselves on achieving geographical accuracy. Smith set up in competition c1799.

Globes were a common feature in the private libraries of the wealthy and the educated. They reflect the era's growing interest in British colonial expansion and astronomy.

The "G" and "J" marks mean this globe was made after 1821, when the firm had been taken over by John's two sons, George and John.

This pair is matched. Although terrestrial and celestial globes were often sold together, it is difficult to find original pairs. Had these two globes formed an original pair, their estimated price would be higher.

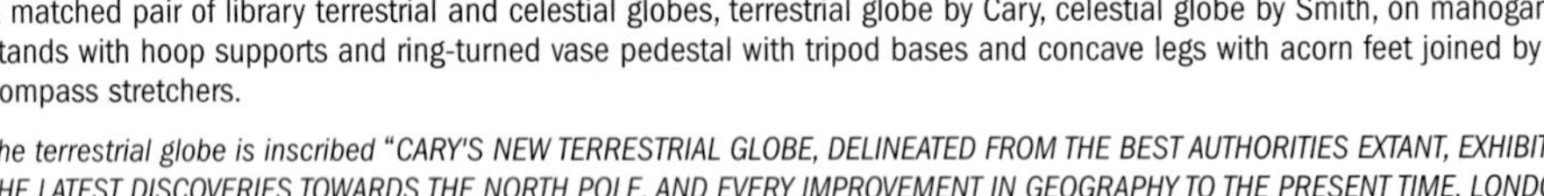

A matched pair of library terrestrial and celestial globes, terrestrial globe by Cary, celestial globe by Smith, on mahogany stands with hoop supports and ring-turned vase pedestal with tripod bases and concave legs with acorn feet joined by compass stretchers.

The terrestrial globe is inscribed "CARY'S NEW TERRESTRIAL GLOBE, DELINEATED FROM THE BEST AUTHORITIES EXTANT, EXHIBITING THE LATEST DISCOVERIES TOWARDS THE NORTH POLE, AND EVERY IMPROVEMENT IN GEOGRAPHY TO THE PRESENT TIME, LONDON" with later inscribed autograph note "SOLD BY G & J CARY, 80 St James's St, London, 1825". The celestial globe is inscribed "SMITH'S CELESTIAL GLOBE, CONTAINING ALL THE KNOWN STARS, NEBULAE, & C, COMPILED FROM THE WORKS OF ... [and] THE TRANSACTIONS OF THE ASTRONOMICAL SOCIETY OF LONDON & C & C LONDON, SOLD BY C SMITH & SON, 172 STRAND".

12in (30.5cm) diam

£10,000-15,000 **L&T**

A pair of early 19thC celestial and terrestrial globes, by J. & W. Cary of London, stand with quadriform cradle and baluster pedestal with tripod base and cabriole legs, the celestial globe missing meridian ring and stand and dated 1800, the terrestrial inscribed "Cary's New Terrestrial Globe, deliniated from the best Authorities extant; Exhibiting the different Tracks of Captain Cook, and the New Discoveries made by him and other Circumnavigators, London: Made and Sold by J&W Cary, Strand, Jan. 1st 1812".

12in (30.5cm) diam

£4,500-5,500 **L&T**

A pair of Cary's terrestrial and celestial globes, probably George IV, each on a turned mahogany base with brass meridian ring, losses.

13in (33cm) diam

£5,000-8,000 **DAW**

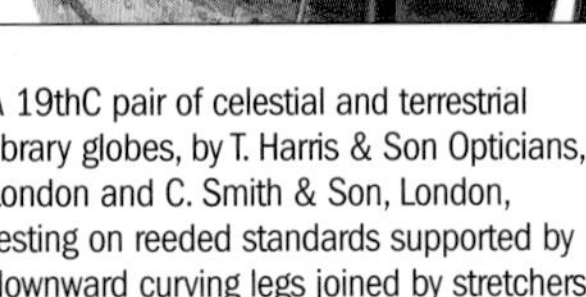

A 19thC pair of celestial and terrestrial library globes, by T. Harris & Son Opticians, London and C. Smith & Son, London, resting on reeded standards supported by downward curving legs joined by stretchers centring on a compass.

18in (46cm) diam

£7,000-10,000 **POOK**

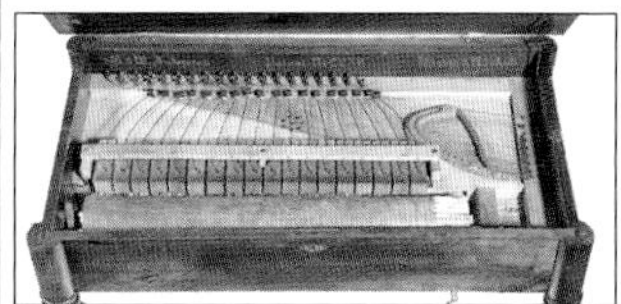

A Swedish harp piano, by G. & W. Andersson, hand-cranked drum-operated mechanism, eighteen notes, including one drum with twelve tunes, working condition.

c1840 *37in (94cm) wide*

£500-700 **ATK**

A 19thC walnut carved polyphone, mechanism inside burr veneered case, moulded lid inset, marquetry floral panel and frieze open to reveal glazed print verso scene, panelled sides above leaf-carved frieze, bracket feet, includes 44 playing discs.

23.25in (58cm) wide

£1,500-2,000 **L&T**

A CLOSER LOOK AT A MUSIC BOX

The first musical box was made by Swiss watchmaker Antonine Favre in 1796. Keith, Prowse & Co. produced and sold musical instruments from Cheapside in London between c1830 and c1950.

The condition of the piece is excellent and the attention to detail in the decoration of the bird finial and painted butterfly striker make this desirable to collectors.

As designs improved, various features were often incorporated. This box features nine visible chased bells and a reed organ, as well two cylinders. It plays six airs that are detailed on the label at the base.

The comb-shaped metal piece has teeth of varying lengths and pitch which are plucked by pins on a revolving cylinder to produce a melody.

A large 19thC burr walnut-cased Swiss musical box, with nine chased bells in sight, each with bird finial and painted butterfly striker, mandolin and flute cylinders and seventeen-note reed organ playing six airs, case with canted corners, tulipwood banding and marquetry decoration, ebonized mouldings, cast handles to the sides, on plinth base with feet, bearing the label of "Keith Prowse Manufacturers, Cheapside, London".

35.75in (91cm) wide

£3,200-3,800 **L&T**

A Polyphon 'Excelsior' musical box, with 15.5in (40cm) disc and comb with 77 teeth, complete with one disc.

c1900 *21in (53cm) wide*

£800-1,200 **ATK**

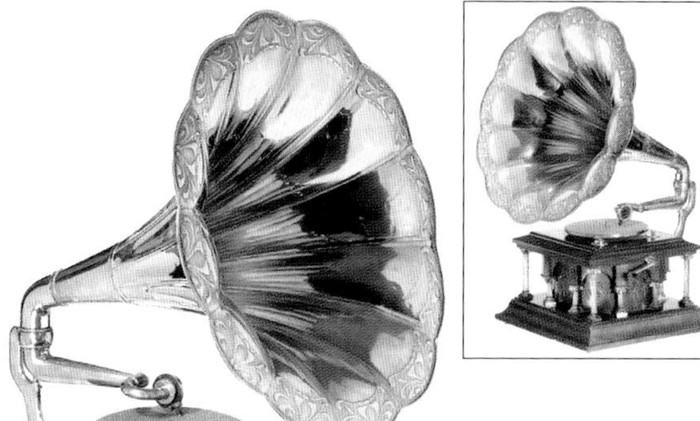

An extraordinary Paillard gramophone, richly decorated walnut case with twelve brass pillars and applied metal flower decorations, polished brass horn, nickel-plated cast-iron support, double spring motor, Swiss-made 'Expression' soundbox, very good condition.

c1905 *18.5in (47cm) wide*

£1,500-2,500 **ATK**

A Thorens gramophone, with Swiss spring motor and English soundbox, oak case, tin horn with original colouring, working condition.

c1920

£300-400 **ATK**

A rare and unusual American gramophone, in the form of a decorative table lamp, made by The Endlessgraph Manufacturing Co. of Chicago.

1919

£2,200-2,800 **ATK**

An early 20thC Victrola XI quartered oak record player and cabinet, with an ogee-moulded hinged platform top over a front with two short over two long, scribed doors opening to shelves, flanked by keeled stiles, with Victrola Talking Machine Company labels and plaques; comes with a music cabinet.

44in (112cm) high

£350-450 **S&K**

A German cabinet gramophone, oak case, automatic stop lever, dealer's engraved label "Musikhaus Merkur, Dortmund".

41.75in (106cm) wide

£150-200 **ATK**

An unmarked cabinet gramophone, probably German, oak cabinet, horn behind double doors with record compartment below, stop lever.

35.5in (90cm) long

£150-200 **ATK**

A rare French Pathé gramophone with horizontal horn, large paper cone diaphragm, mahogany case with segmented lid for sound regulation.

c1930 *21in (53cm) wide*

£800-1,200 **ATK**

A George III japanned set of hanging shelves, the black ground decorated with figures and buildings in a landscape, two principal shelves with concave canted ends and two drawers below surmounted by a smaller shelf on tapering square columns and turned finials.

41.25in (103cm) wide

£1,500-2,000 **L&T**

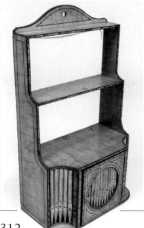

A set of Regency painted wallshelves.

c1820 *30.5in (77.5cm) high*

£3,000-3,500 **DL**

A George III set of mahogany and harewood open hanging shelves, with satinwood banding, three stepped shelves and two drawers below with floral marquetry decoration and turned ivory handles.

35in (89cm) high

£800-1,200 **L&T**

A George III mahogany plate bucket.

c1770 *15in (38cm) high*

£1,000-1,500 **DL**

An early 19thC pair of leather fire buckets, of circular tapering form, with leather carrying strap, copper-banded rim with riveted seams, front decorated with the Royal Coat of Arms, and another taller bucket, of similar construction, with an Earl's crest.

12.75in (32cm) high

£600-900 **L&T**

A 19thC mahogany peat bucket, of staved construction, with brass hoops and carrying handle.

18in (46cm) high

£800-1,200 **L&T**

Right: A mahogany and beech log bucket, of staved and ring-turned tapering form, with ebonized bands, brass liner and carrying handle.

13in (33cm) high

£400-450 **L&T**

Left: A walnut log bucket, of ring-turned tapering form, turned plinth base, brass liner and carrying handle.

13.5in (34cm) high

£450-500 **L&T**

A Kimball figured wood baby grand piano, retailed by Junius Hart Piano House Ltd., New Orleans, on ring-turned tapered legs with brass caps on casters, wooden bench with sheet music.

67in (167.5cm) wide

£400-600 **S&K**

A London Regency inlaid mahogany piano by John Broadwood & Sons, registration number 23534, together with a piano stool on reeded legs, hinged rectangular lid with ebonized line decoration, lifting to a pierced satinwood panel with the maker's inscription and 68-note keyboard, on tapering ring-turned cylindrical legs with rollers and single foot pedal.

Provenance: *Historic Deerfield, Inc.; Purchased by Edmund Morewood, New York City, for his daughter Helen Grace, who married John Ferguson, Stamford, Connecticut.*

£1,800-2,200 **NA**

An ebonized baby grand piano, by William Knabe of Baltimore, with impressed mark "AX" on the harp, mechanical elements have been altered to accommodate post-manufacture installation of a QRS Pianomation 200CD + Device, includes six discs.

68in (170cm) deep

£3,000-5,000 **S&K**

An early 19thC set of metamorphic mahogany library steps, closing to form a stool, rectangular upholstered suede seat with studded decoration, applied steps verso and set of steps with hinged strut above, raised above a plain frieze on square section tapering legs.

36.75in (92cm) high

£4,000-4,500 **L&T**

A set of mahogany library steps, upright supports with brass ball finials and side loop handles, each sloped side with seven steps on later casters, bears the ivorine label "Maple & Co., London".

76in (190cm) high

£1,500-2,000 **FRE**

An 18thC pair of early rare George III papier-mâché brackets by Bromwich and Leigh, 1764.

Provenance: *Stoneleigh Abbey, Warwickshire.*

10in (244.5cm) high

£15,000-17,000 **NOA**

An 18thC Venetian gessoed and gilt carved overmantel frame, with robust floral, foliate and scrolling details centring a c-scroll crest within a cartouche, lower right floral pendant missing.

70in (175cm) wide

£1,200-1,800 **S&K**

A brass extending club fender, stuffover L-shaped seats upholstered with Caucasian-style woodwork, on plain column supports with moulded base.

65.25in (166cm) wide extended

£1,000-1,500 **L&T**

An early 19thC pine spoon rack.

28.25in (72cm) high

£420-480 **EP**

A 19thC fruitwood linen press, top bar stamped "Thomas Bradford & Co., No.3, Manchester and London", screw with acorn finial, single frieze drawer on square legs.

26.25in (67cm) wide

£500-700 **WW**

An Edwardian mahogany table vitrine, form based on The Burns Monument, Ayr, turned finial on columns and gadrooned top, hexagonal glazed case with shelves, circular moulded base on bun feet.

40.75in (102cm) high

£3,000-3,500 **L&T**

A 19thC painted dummy board, in the figure of a 17thC girl with lace collar holding a rose.

36in (90cm) high

£800-1,200 **L&T**

CANDLESTICKS & CANDELABRA

A pair of 18thC brass candlesticks, each with a ridged, lobed base, a narrow stem, a cylindrical nozzle and a fixed flared drip pan with a wavy edge.

8.5in (21cm) high

£1,000-1,500 **FRE**

A pair of Charles X bronze and ormolu candelbra, each with urn and basket of fruit finial, surrounded by five scrolled candle branches with urn shaped sconces, on a tapering reeded and acanthus cast column, on a tripod base with claw feet and a cast, stepped plinth.

43.5in (109cm) high

£8,000-12,000 **L&T**

A pair of Empire gilt bronze candelabra, each with five branches held aloft by a Middle Eastern figure above a baluster column, on a hexagonal base.

22in (55cm) high

£3,000-4,000 **L&T**

A pair of 19thC gilt-brass table candelabra, each with four scrolling branches cast with ivy leaves and with removable drip trays, centred by a fifth branch cast with leaves and flowers, the whole held by a naked putto on a naturalistic base, on a black slate and verde antico socle.

23.25in (58cm) high

£1,000-1,500 **L&T**

A 19thC Continental cobalt-blue glass and gilt-bronze three-light candelabrum, the two-handled vase issuing floral branches hung with rock crystal and amethyst glass drops, raised on a square pedestal foot, electrified.

25in (63.5cm) high

£1,800-2,200 **S&K**

A pair of 19thC moulded glass dolphin candlesticks, possibly Baccarat, in clear and frosted glass and hung with prisms.

14.5in (37cm) high

£1,200-1,800 **S&K**

A pair of 19thC bronze and ormolu candelbra, of Renaissance style, each with an urn shaped socle above four grotesque scrolling branches, on a column cast with a seated cherub above two grotesque scrolling supports and gadrooned bun feet, on a black marble plinth.

24.75in (62cm) high

£2,000-2,500 **L&T**

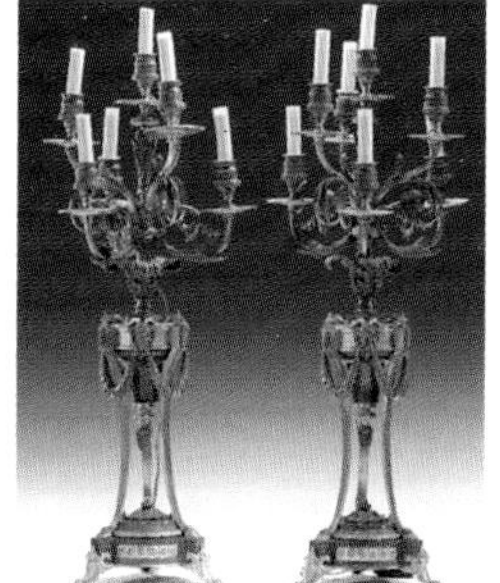

A pair of 19thC French Empire-style bronze candelabra, the reeded columns surmounted by six candle nozzles, raised on three acanthus cast claw feet, ending in red marble triform bases.

31in (77.5cm) high

£2,000-3,000 **FRE**

A pair of 19thC French gilt bronze candelabra, each with nine scrolling branches and ten cast nozzles with pierced drip trays, the support modelled as a winged angel with a snake.

33.25in (83cm) high

£1,800-2,200 **L&T**

A mid 19thC pair of Continental Neo-classical-style four-light candelabra, with bronze figures of Diana and Paris holding ormolu branching arms, mounted as table lamps.

26in (65cm) high

£2,500-3,500 **S&K**

A Victorian five-candle girandole, with an Egyptian gentleman holding a palm leaf fan, the flowing floral arms with hanging crystal prisms, on a heavy marble base.

21in (53.5cm) high

£200-300 **JDJ**

A late 19thC gilt-metal and alabaster candelabrum, with a flame finial and seven branches issuing from a fluted urn on splayed acanthus cast legs, headed by a cast ram's head, on hoof feet and a canted triangular plinth with a scrolled frieze.

43.25in (108cm) high

£2,500-3,500 L&T

A pair of late 19thC gilt-metal torchères, each with twenty four graduated scrolling candlebranches, issuing from a beaded and swag-hung column, on a pierced tripod base with feet cast as winged mythical creatures.

90in (225cm) high

£3,000-5,000 L&T

A pair of late 19thC Louis XV-style patinated bronze and gilt-bronze candelabra, with three naturalistic branches supported by cherubs, raised on openwork rococo scroll bases.

14in (35cm) high

£1,200-1,800 FRE

A pair of late 19thC Louis XVI-style gilt-bronze candelabra, with three scroll candelabra arms supported by three cherubs, raised on fluted marble bases with toupie feet.

16in (40cm) high

£2,200-2,800 FRE

A pair of late 19th to early 20thC Baccarat frosted and clear glass candlesticks, with tulip shades etched with flowerheads above cross-hatched candleholders, held aloft by scantily draped putti, on gadrooned bases, raised mark under bases.

23in (58.5cm) high

£200-300 S&K

A pair of late 19th to early 20thC Louis XV-style gilt-bronze four-light candelabra, each with a spire finial above tiers of glass stars, beaded glass chains and large drops, the four candle holders above foliate drip pans, on circular domed bases.

25.75in (65.5cm) high

£600-900 S&K

A late 19th to early 20thC pair of small gilt metal candlesticks, each modelled as a bacchic putto seated on a grapevine, on a scroll base.

7in (17.5cm) high

£120-180 S&K

A pair of brass candlesticks, each with a slightly domed base with a flat shaped rim, a turned stem and cylindrical nozzle with a small fixed flared drip pan.

7.25in (18cm) high

£800-1,200 FRE

A pair of modern sawfish jaw and brass sconces.

29.25in (74.5cm) high

£3,000-4,000 B&I

A pair of Edwardian cut-glass table candelabra, each with scrolling branches with lobed drip trays, with lustre drops and fluted nozzles, the central triangular section upright with a strawberry-cut finial supporting riviere garlands, the facetted and knopped base with a spreading foot.

19.25in (48cm) high

£1,800-2,200 L&T

A Louis XVI-style gilt-metal and alabaster three-light candelabrum, with rose branch arms held aloft by two putti, on a waisted plinth, electrified.

27in (68.5cm) high

£400-600 S&K

A pair of cast-bronze four-light candelabra, on tripod bases.

43.5in (110.5cm) high

£5,000-8,000 B&I

A Venetian gold-flecked glass three-light candelabrum, with petal drip pans, spiral-reeded arms and a flaming ball spire, fitted with leaves and flowers, on a circular base, electrified.

23.75in (60.5cm) high

£480-520 S&K

CHANDELIERS

A Victorian brass and rose medaillon porcelain gas chandelier.

£500-800 SK

A late 19thC five-light cast-brass chandelier, attributed to Cornelius and Baker, Philadelphia, the shaped shaft and arms ornamented with cast leafage and decorative bosses, restored and electrified.

46in (117cm) high

£3,000-4,000 FRE

A Louis XV-style gilt-bronze chandelier.

£600-900 S&K

A Louis XV-style gilt-bronze and glass three-light chandelier, the cylindrical candleholders on spade-shaped arms joined by beaded chain swags, issuing from a circular pierced frame, hung with rows of prisms forming a basket and with spear prisms, electrified.

15in (38cm) diam

£350-450 S&K

A Louis XV-style chandelier, with fruit.

£300-500 S&K

An Empire-style gilt-metal and glass six-light chandelier, the scroll arms on a circular frame fitted with a diamond-patterned glass bowl, suspended from an urn, surmounted by a prism crown, electrified.

26in (66cm) diam

£300-400 S&K

LAMPS

A pair of American bronze Argand lamps, with foliate finials, pendant prisms and frosted glass shades, the base with applied masks on lion's paw feet, one labelled "J.I. Cox, New York", the other "S. Gardiner, New York", missing prisms.

c1845 *23in (57.5cm) high*

£1,000-1,500 S&K

A pair of 19thC Empire-style gilt-bronze lamps, in the form of the Three Graces, raised on bronzed metal waisted circular bases, with claw feet.

31in (77.5cm) high

£2,000-3,000 FRE

A Victorian figural smoking lamp, with a metal base depicting a woman playing croquet and an open tree trunk match holder, with two embossed cigar holders, the hammered brass shade set with multicoloured, faceted glass jewels, and adorned with a glass bead fringe, some wear.

15.5in (39.5cm) high

£700-1,000 JDJ

A Victorian cranberry glass kerosene lamp, with a brass stem resting on a black glass base, the lamp topped with a frosted clear to cranberry ruffled shade with clear areas depicting sunflowers, repairs.

22.5in (57cm) high

£150-200 JDJ

A pair of early 20thC verde antico and gilt-metal-mounted lamp bases, in the manner of Matthew Boulton, each urn-shaped base with applied acanthus leaf handles and swag decoration, on leaf-clasped bases and moulded square plinths.

17.75in (44.5cm) high

£2,000-3,000 L&T

A pair of 20thC French Sèvres-style cobalt blue porcelain vases, in the Louis XV style, with dore bronze mounts, mounted as lamps.

17in (42.5cm) high

£800-1,200 **S&K**

A 20thC pair of Continental tole ware canisters, decorated with gilt figures on a green ground, mounted as lamps.

16in (40cm) high

£250-350 **S&K**

A pair of oil lamps with art glass shades, each brass base with a yellow and white glass oil font and surmounted by a yellow glass shade, with iridescent trailings.

14in (35.5cm) high

£200-300 **S&K**

A large brass and glass banquet lamp, the base with three nude figures of hunters and game, with faces to handles, the cut-glass font with ruby highlights, the swirl, ribbed, clear to cranberry glass shade with a ruffled top, slight damage.

33in (84cm) high

£250-350 **JDJ**

A Louis XVI-style floor lamp in the form of a torchère, with an acanthus-carved capital, turned and fluted standard and a scrolled tripod base hung with floral garlands.

75in (190.5cm) high

£300-500 **S&K**

A late Victorian extending brass lamp, the gadrooned reservoir on a reeded Corinthian column and stepped square base, with paw feet.

£200-300 **L&T**

An Empire-style bronze and ormolu table lamp, with four light fittings on a baluster column, cast with stiff leaf, trefoil and acanthus decoration, on a stepped plinth cast with wreaths and columns, on paw feet.

43.25in (108cm) high

£2,000-3,000 **L&T**

A Victorian jewel hall lamp, with a ribbed ruby glass globe in a brass frame, the six vertical brass bands with multicoloured jewels, electrified.

28in (71cm) high

£1,200-1,800 **JDJ**

A Victorian cranberry hobnail parlour lamp, with an embossed brass frame supporting a cranberry hobnail glass shade with crystal prisms, with a smoke bell.

£500-800 **JDJ**

A Victorian hall lamp, with six flat panels, topped with a pressed design of gold-stained leaf panels and cranberry teardrops, the frosted shade handpainted with a chalet near a lake with mountains.

20in (51cm) high

£250-350 **JDJ**

WALL LIGHTS

One of a very fine pair of 18thC Chippendale-period carved gilded girandoles, after Thomas Johnson.

c1760 *21in (53cm) wide*

£130,000-150,000 pair **NOA**

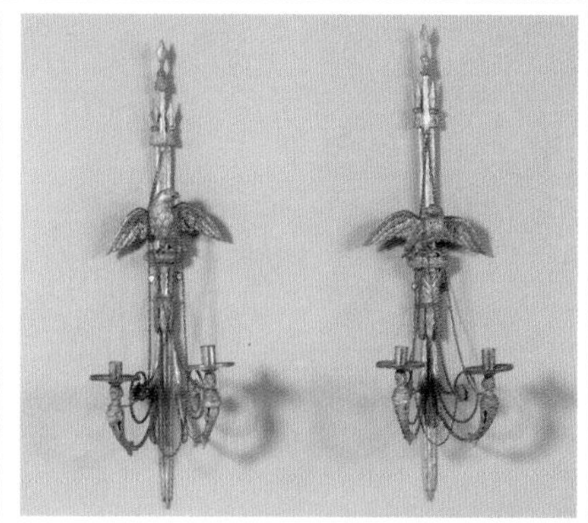

Two pairs of late 18thC Federal carved and gilded eagle wall sconces, each with a columnar back formed of a cluster of arrows centring a spreadwing eagle, with an acanthus carved plinth and demilune beaded shelf.

30.5in (77.5cm) high

£16,000-20,000 set **NA**

One of a pair of 19thC Louis XV style bronze wall lights, the cornucopia shaped acanthus carved support with four ornate S-scroll branches, centred by a further candle branch.

13.5in (34cm) wide

£1,500-2,000 pair **FRE**

A 19thC pair of Louis XV style gilt bronze wall sconces, in the form of satire caryatids from which issue five ornate acanthus cast scroll branches with conforming candle nozzles.

23.5in (59cm) high

£2,000-2,500 **FRE**

A pair of late 19th to early 20thC Louis XVI-style gilt-bronze wall lights, formed as tiers of gilt-bronze icicles above putti hippogryphs, electrified.

25in (63.5cm) high

£3,000-4,000 **S&K**

One of a pair of Louis XIV-style gilt-wood three-light sconces, modelled as foliate scroll cartouches with three floral lights.

37.25in (93cm) high

£600-900 pair **S&K**

OTHER LIGHTING

A Regency mahogany ship's-style lantern, the hexagonal case with a bobbin turned frame, urn finials and bun feet, fitted with a brass liner with a tray and sconce, with scrolling brass cresting and chain.

19.5in (50cm) high

£4,000-6,000 **L&T**

A Louis XVI-style gilt bronze ceiling light, the painted ovoid body applied with three female caryatids from which issue six naturalistic branches, three terminating in frosted glass shades.

c1900 *33in (82.5cm) high*

£1,500-2,000 **FRE**

A bronze glazed octagonal lantern, with bevelled plates and a surmount of open scrolling leaves.

18.5in (46cm) high

£1,000-1,500 **L&T**

CADDIES

A set of three George II Sheffield plate tea caddies, each of rectangular section with hinged caddy lids, engraved with a crest, the plain sides with a moulded base, stamped marks, enclosed within a later Victorian mahogany box, of sarcophagus form.

10.5in (26.5cm) wide

£2,200-2,800 **L&T**

A Georgian mahogany boxwood, ebony inlaid large tea caddy.

12in (30.5cm) wide

£200-250 **MB**

A CLOSER LOOK AT A ROLLED PAPER TEA CADDY

During the late 18thC, ladies could purchase plain caddies to decorate at home as a pastime. A favourite method of ornamentation was strips of coloured paper rolled, cut and glued to the surface of the caddy.

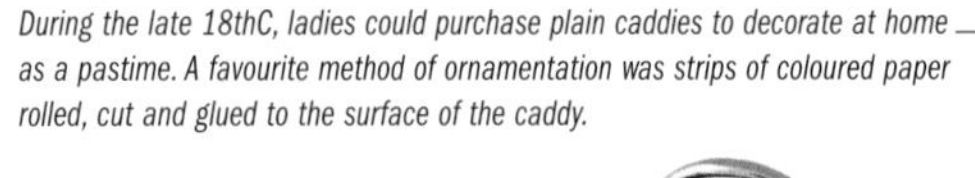

This caddy features a lock. Tea was relatively expensive during the 18thC and many caddies of the period were made secure from servants.

New designs for caddies were introduced as tea consumption increased. Late 18thC tea caddies tend to be oval, rectangular or octagonal, like this one. They often have flat tops and no feet.

This tea caddy has survived in good condition considering it is over 200 years old, was a functional object and is made from a material vulnerable to damage and deterioration.

An 18thC octagonal rolled paper tea caddy.

c1790 *7in (18cm) wide*

£1,200-1,800 **RDER**

A late 18thC mahogany tea caddy, the plain top with a gilt metal handle, the interior with gilt paper, cracks, the bottom edge replaced.

5.5in (14cm) high

£180-220 **FRE**

A George III burr-yew tea caddy, with boxwood stringing to the edges, of sarcophagus form, with a stepped hinged lid enclosing an interior fitted with two lidded compartments, ivory escutcheon, brass handles to sides, brass ball feet with vine ornaments.

8in (20cm) long

£300-500 **L&T**

A George III octagonal satinwood tea caddy, inlaid with shell and thistle paterae, with a lock.

6.25in (16cm) wide

£400-600 **GORL**

A George III fruitwood tea caddy, in the form of an apple with a stalk, with a hinged lid.

5.25in (13cm) high

£4,000-6,000 **L&T**

A George III fruitwood tea caddy, in the form of a melon, the lobed body with a stalk and green tinged patination, an oval escutcheon.

5.75in (14.5cm) high

£3,500-4,500 **L&T**

A George III fruitwood tea caddy, in the form of a melon, the lobed body with a stalk and green tinged patination, shaped escutcheon.

5.5in (13.5cm) high

£2,500-3,500 **L&T**

A George III fruitwood tea caddy, in the form of a pear with a stalk, the hinged lid with oval escutcheon.

7.25in (18cm) high

£2,000-3,000 **L&T**

A George III fruitwood tea caddy, in the form of a pear with stalk, the hinged lid with shaped escutcheon.

7.25in (18cm) high

£2,200-2,800 **L&T**

A George III mahogany scrollwork tea caddy, of hexagonal lozenge form with a boxwood-strung hinged lid enclosing a divided interior, the body decorated with glazed panels containing gilt-edged scrollwork in the form of flowers, on a coloured foil ground.

8.5in (21cm) wide

£400-600 **L&T**

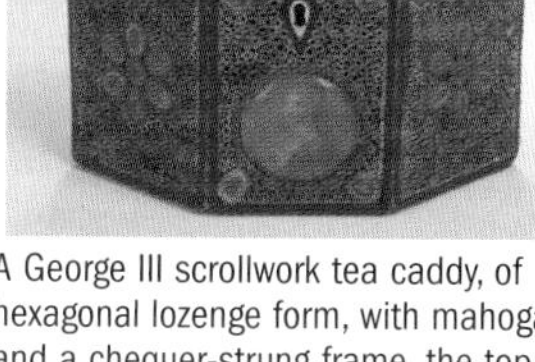

A George III scrollwork tea caddy, of hexagonal lozenge form, with mahogany and a chequer-strung frame, the top and sides filled with gilt-paper scrolls, the front centred by a printed miniature portrait of a lady under a domed glass cover, a hinged lid enclosing a paper lined interior with a lid.

7.5in (19cm) wide

£350-450 **L&T**

A 19thC Regency mahogany tea caddy, the tapering sides and top with line inlay, on four ball feet, losses, cracks.

5.75in (15cm) high

£700-900 **FRE**

A Regency mahogany sarcophagus tea caddy, with two canisters and a glass bowl.

11.5in (29cm) wide

£180-220 **GORL**

A Regency boxwood strung mahogany tea caddy, of sarcophagus form.

12in (30.5cm) wide

£70-100 **GORL**

A Regency mahogany sarcophagus tea caddy, with side handles.

12in (30.5cm) wide

£120-180 **GORL**

An early 19thC rosewood tea caddy, the corners of the sarcophagus shape lined in boxwood.

7.5in (19cm) wide

£180-220 **CHEF**

An early 19thC rosewood tea caddy, the sarcophagus shape with circular brass key escutcheon, bun feet, two canisters and a cut-glass mixing bowl.

12.25in (31cm) wide

£120-180 **CHEF**

A double-cut marquetry tea caddy, with original glass mixing bowl and canisters, turned satinwood handles.

c1820 *12in (30.5cm) wide*

£1,200-1,800 **RDER**

A penwork tea caddy, with a removable cushion.

c1820

£1,000-1,500 **RDER**

A blond tortoiseshell octagonal tea caddy, strung with ivory and silver, the lid with a silver finial.

c1820 *7in (18cm) wide*

£3,000-4,000 **RDER**

A William IV brass-inlaid mahogany tea caddy, of sarcophagus form, the domed rectangular lid with brass banding and diamond inlay, the slanted sides similarly decorated, on brass ball feet.

c1830 *12in (30cm) wide*

£280-320 **S&K**

An early Victorian tortoiseshell tea caddy, the sarcophagus shape with veneers separated by white metal lines, the rectangular lid closing on ivory fillets about two compartments, on four brass ball feet.

5.75in (14.5cm) wide

£800-1,200 **CHEF**

An early Victorian tortoiseshell tea caddy, the lid with a wavy front and back, closing on ivory fillets, the compartment cover knops and four bun feet of vegetable ivory, the veneers separated by a white metal line inlay.

5in (13cm) wide

£1,200-1,800 **CHEF**

A 19thC tortoiseshell tea caddy, the fitted interior with covers, with a spherical knop and feet.

6.75in (17cm) wide

£1,000-1,500 **CLV**

A 19thC mahogany tea caddy, the rounded edges of the hinged, diamond-shaped lid in ebony line, enclosing a marquetried butterfly, the front of the single compartment caddy with conch shell ovals, with a white metal spoon.

7.25in (18.5cm) wide

£400-600 **CHEF**

A late 19th century burr-yew wood tea caddy, a diamond-shaped ebony key escutcheon below the rectangular lid, the interior with three tinned canisters.

8.75in (22cm) wide

£80-120 **CHEF**

A late 18thC inlaid mahogany writing box, probably English, the rectangular form with a hinged lid inlaid with a fan and quarter-fans, brass handles to sides, the fitted interior with two silver-capped ink bottles, discolouration to top, veneer loss.

18.5in (46cm) long

£1,000-1,500 **FRE**

WRITING BOXES

A mahogany brass-banded writing box, with original ink wells, in mint condition.

c1790

£500-700 **RDER**

A Regency writing casket.

11.5in (29cm) wide

£500-700 EP

A Regency inlaid mahogany travelling writing box, with satinwood banding and inlay, centring satinwood and ebony inlaid compass stars, the fitted interior with folding doors enclosing a long document compartment, the base with two compartments fitted for writing implements, a secret drawer that pulls out to reveal four more secret drawers.

17.5in (44cm) wide

£400-600 S&K

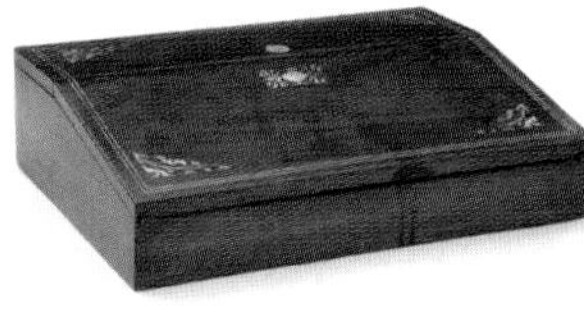

A mid-19thC rosewood writing slope, the hinged fall sloping away from a lid covering compartments and two glass inkwells, the mother-of-pearl spandrels within a double line of white metal.

13.75in (35cm) wide

£200-250 CHEF

A mid-19thC mother-of-pearl inlaid papier-mâché stationery box, the floral painted lid opening about the central gilt metal handle to reveal two glass inkwells flanking a central stamp box, with a pen trough to one side and stationery compartments to the other.

9.75in (25cm) wide

£250-300 CHEF

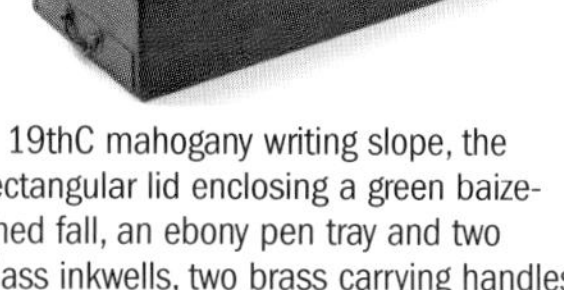

A 19thC mahogany writing slope, the rectangular lid enclosing a green baize-lined fall, an ebony pen tray and two glass inkwells, two brass carrying handles and a drawer at one end.

24in (61cm) wide

£280-320 CHEF

A mid-late 19thC American burled walnut travelling desk, the lid inlaid with a metal shield monogrammed "K.E.B.", bordered with ebony and mother-of-pearl, retailed by Wurdemann & Co., Washington, DC.

14in (35cm) wide

£350-450 S&K

A Victorian walnut veneered and coromandel brass-bound deskstand, the surmount with a stationery box, the hinged serpentine lid enclosing a fitted interior flanked by ink bottles, the sloping fall opening to reveal a velvet surface, with a leather-lined well below, fitted with pigeonholes, damage.

14.75in (37cm) wide

£600-900 L&T

A Victorian brass-mounted walnut writing slope.

12in (30.5cm) wide

£100-150 GORL

A Victorian brass-banded burr-walnut writing slope.

11.5in (29cm) wide

£180-220 GORL

A green leather stationery box, the rectangular lid releasing the fall front, with integral writing slope and compartment, the two hinged compartments behind it with notepad fronts, over an ebony pen trough and an inkwell compartment, compartments above, marked "Jessie Dean, April 11th 1882".

9.5in (24cm) wide

£80-120 CHEF

A late 19thC Continental mother-of-pearl, ebony and brass inlaid burr-wood lap desk, the hinged rectangular top inlaid with a jardinière of Spring flowers with ebony and brass bands, the canted edge with alternating ebony floral plaques and mother-of-pearl and brass stripes, enclosing a fitted interior.

15in (37.5cm) wide

£320-380 **S&K**

A late Victorian brass-bound walnut writing slope, the rectangular lid enclosing an ebonized pen trough and compartments, containing two brass-topped inkwells.

14in (35.5cm) wide

£250-300 **CHEF**

A rosewood and mother-of-pearl inlaid travel writing desk, by W. T. Fry, Philadelphia, the case with a black leather-covered writing surface over two hinged compartments, a section fitted with lidded compartments, the top with small slots for letters, two lids with paper labels reading "MANUFACTURED BY/W.T. FRY & CO./9Nth. 6th ST./PHILADELPHIA, damage, lacking ink bottles.

16in (40.5cm) long

£350-450 **FRE**

An early 20thC oak stationery box, the rectangular lid releasing the fall front writing slope before a drawer, leather and wooden compartments.

£200-300 **CHEF**

WORK BOXES

A French straw work boite à mouches, the lid with a shepherd in a rural scene, the interior fitted with two compartments, with an original mirror.

c1780 *3in (7.5cm) long*

£350-450 **HD**

An early 19thC penwork box, the rectangular lid of the sarcophagus shape decorated with a Gothic tower in a wood on a satinwood ground within a guilloche band with birds and insects, rinceaux on the tapering sides above bun feet.

c1810 *11.5in (29cm) wide*

£250-350 **CHEF**

An early 19thC Prisoner of War straw work casket, the arched lid worked with five stars and the sides with geometric designs, the yellow paper lining stencilled with blue and red flowerheads.

12.5in (31.5cm) wide

£150-200 **CHEF**

A Biedermeier burr-walnut and mother-of-pearl inlaid sewing box, the lid inset with an oval mother-of-pearl panel and decorated with incised penwork depicting a fishing boat, with mother-of-pearl spandrels and musical, military, garden and architectural trophies and a band of scrolling, with applied steel studs, the interior with a lift-out tray of sewing equipment, the ogee-moulded sides on sphere feet.

8.5in (21.5cm) long

£600-900 **L&T**

An early Victorian Vizagapatnam stag-horn workbox, the exterior of the sarcophagus shape nailed with stag-horn batons, the rectangular lid closing on horn fillets and enclosing a tray with various spools and fittings, the ivory lids to the four compartments engraved with floral borders picked out in black.

13in (33cm) wide

£1,800-2,200 **CHEF**

A mid-19thC Coromandel workbox, with an unusual mechanical operation, of rectangular shape with rounded corners and ripple moulding, the hinged lid operates a plinth drawer and two cavities in the corner mouldings simultaneously, the interior with mother-of-pearl and other fittings.

£600-900 **GORL**

A 19thC Vizagapatnam rosewood and ivory inlaid workbox, profusely inlaid inside and out with trailing foliage, the rectangular hinged top with internal strapwork hinges, enclosing an interior with tortoiseshell panels, hinged lidded compartments and drawers surrounding a well, on a plinth base.

Vizagapatnam, a town in South-East India, lends its name to the pieces of furniture and smaller items made from hardwood inlaid with ivory, which were produced in the area for the British market in the 18thC-19thC.

18.5in (46cm) wide

£3,500-4,000 **L&T**

A Victorian mahogany workbox, with a base drawer, on lion's paw feet.

10.5in (26.5cm) wide

£50-80 **GORL**

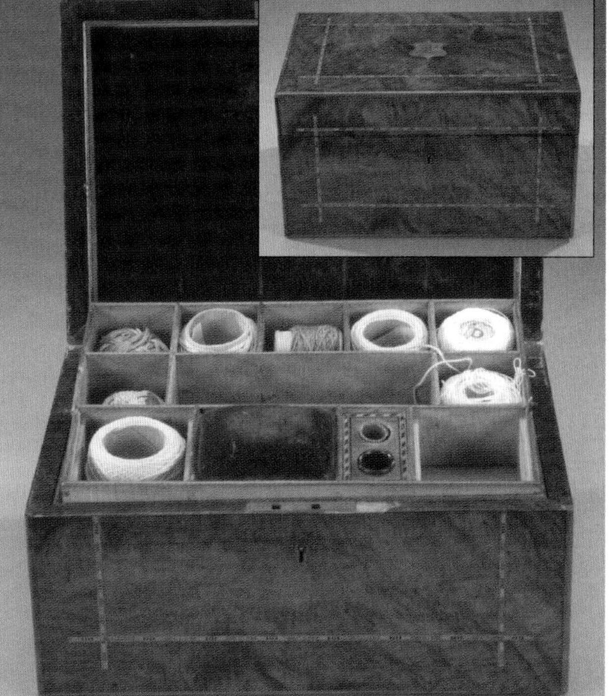

A Victorian burl-walnut and satinwood inlaid sewing box, the lid inset with a brass monogram "L", a compartmented interior.

c1870 *12in (30cm) wide*

£400-600 **S&K**

ASSORTED WOODEN BOXES

A Victorian carved oak tantalus and games box.

14.5in (37cm) wide

£400-500 **CSA**

A Victorian rosewood toilet box, the cover with brass and mother-of-pearl inlay, the interior with a lift-out compartmented tray and assorted fittings above one long drawer.

11in (27.5cm) wide

£300-500 **GORL**

A 19thC Louis XV-style kingwood, burl-walnut and gilt metal-mounted tantalus, the lid surmounted by two winged cherubs holding a cartouche bearing the initials "M. M.", opening to reveal a fitted interior with four gilt-enhanced liquor decanters and fifteen matched glasses, the shaped front centred by a Sèvres-style porcelain panel, raised on toupie feet.

£1,800-2,200 **FRE**

An early 19thC apothecary set, by Hume, 103 Longacre, London, the rectangular lid enclosing twelve bottles above a drawer with a tray, over a glass pestle and mortar and two small bowls.

8.35in (21cm) wide

£600-900 **CHEF**

A 17thC table box on a later stand.

33.5in (85cm) wide

£500-700 **EP**

A Regency satinwood-inlaid oval box.

c1800 *17.75in (44cm) wide*

£1,000-1,500 **S&K**

A rare early 18thC Russian carved ivory and wood miniature desk, with painted decoration, the upper section with a large drawer concealing an interior with two small drawers above a case with three drawers, with hunt scenes depicting dogs, stags, horses and rabbits.

This piece comes from the Kholmogory region in Russia. Another fine example can be found in the Hermitage, St Petersburg.

8.75in (22cm) wide

£3,000-4,000 **POOK**

A George III mahogany candle box, the tapering rectangular front marquetried with a knife and fork within chequer banding, the back extended into a bell shape, pierced for suspension, above the hinged sloping lid.

19.75in (50cm) high

£150-200 **CHEF**

A George III mahogany knife box, of serpentine form, the lid finely inlaid with a satinwood and ebony patera on an olivewood ground, bordered overall with satinwood and ebony stringing, the shield-form escutcheon engraved with the mongram "JM", the interior later fitted for cutlery.

c1800 *14.5in (36cm) high*

£450-550 **S&K**

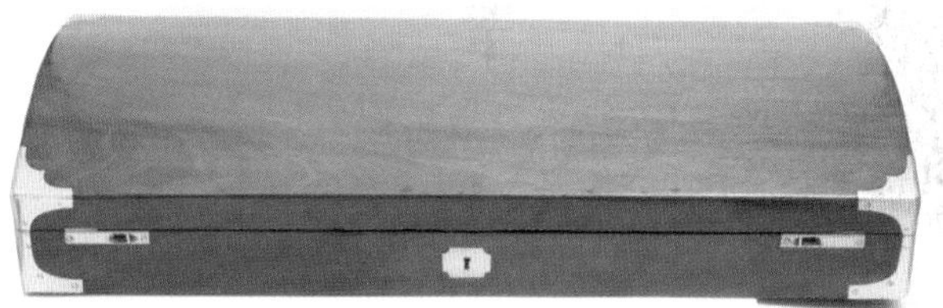

An unusual Georgian mahogany domed-top gun case, with brass ban, relined interior.

c1820 *47in (120cm) long*

£400-500 **MB**

A CLOSER LOOK AT A P.O.W WATCH HUTCH

During the Napoleonic Wars, some prisoners became highly regarded for their work and were commissioned to make individual pieces with specially supplied materials.

This watch hutch is made from bone. Prisoners were forced to use the limited materials available to them including bone and straw.

Watch hutches were initially designed to hold pocket watches at night. They gradually became more decorative for display and were made out of a range of materials including porcelain, wood and ivory.

Producing this ornate piece would have been a time-consuming task. The detail and quality of the decoration are high.

A rare continental Prisoner of War carved bone watch hutch, dated "1807", with decorations of a lion, swags, vases of flowers, birds and hearts, on a case with a single drawer, enclosing an Irish silver pocket watch marked "Geo. Rycroft Dublin".

6in (15cm) wide

£1,800-2,200 **POOK**

An early to mid-19thC American maplewood document box, with a hinged and vaulted lid opening to a painted interior, the front applied with a lock, the sides with bail handles.

24in (61cm) wide

£300-500 **S&K**

An early Victorian tortoiseshell trinket box, the slightly domed rectangular lid with radiating white metal line inlay, the four acorn feet of ivory.

4in (10cm) wide

£200-300 **CHEF**

A rare 19thC birchwood dresser sugar box, with a tray to collect small granules.

12.5in (32cm) long

£320-380 **EP**

A mid-19thC burr-walnut sewing and writing box, the rectangular hinged lid crossbanded in kingwood and edged in coromandel, the interior fitted for sewing, the folding writing slope fitting as a drawer to back.

13.75in (35cm) wide

£300-400 **CHEF**

A Victorian burr-walnut games compendium, with a brass plaque inscribed "H.Rodricues, 42 Piccadilly, London", the interior fitted with a leather folding chess and backgammon board, with two lift-out trays containing cards, a cribbage board, turned ivory draughts, bezique score markers, treen dice shakers, carved ivory markers, natural and stained chess pieces, bone dominoes, a registration lozenge for 29th November, 1869, a brass Bramah lock.

14.25in (36.5cm) wide

£1,500-2,500 **WW**

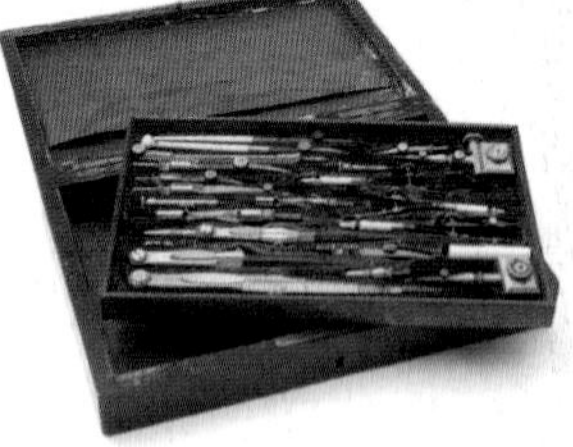

A Victorian geometry set, in a brass-inlaid rosewood case, the well-figured rectangular lid with brass line inlay, the velvet-lined tray fitted with a selection of instruments.

10.25in (26cm) wide

£80-120 **CHEF**

A Victorian tortoiseshell trinket casket, the slightly arched lid inset with facetted iron studs, brass ball feet.

2.5in (6.5cm) wide

£150-200 **CHEF**

A Victorian brass-bound mahogany box, the rectangular lid enclosing a compartment, above a drawer to one side, with a recessed brass handle.

13.5in (34cm) wide

£150-200 **CHEF**

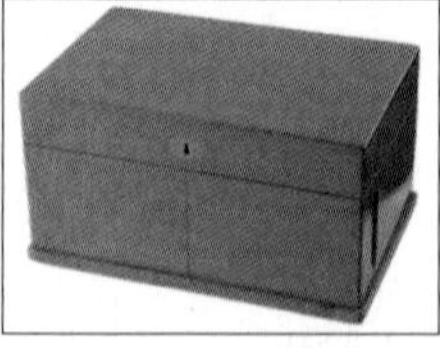

A late Victorian mahogany games compendium, the rectangular hinged lid containing a leather games board, opening to release front doors bearing a black and white wood staunton-style chess set, three trays containing games markers, draughtmen, bone dominoes and a horse racing game.

13in (33cm) wide

£300-400 **CHEF**

A Continental walnut valuables box, the cover carved with a bearded lion and opening to a plain interior, the front with two roundels enclosing crosses.

19.25in (48cm) wide

£280-320 **NA**

A Continental oak slant-front box, the hinged cover inscribed "IA 1710" in a rectangular cartouche, flanked by foliage, the deep interior fitted with a shelf, the front with a band of scrolling acanthus.

29.5in (74cm) wide

£320-380 **S&K**

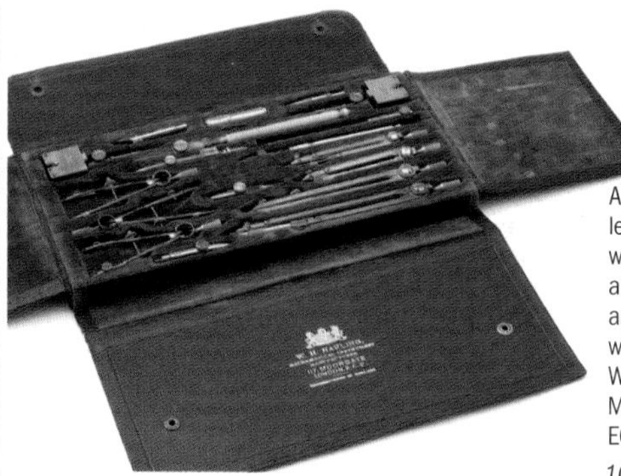

A geometry set in a leatherette folding wallet, two pens amongst the nickel and steel instruments with ivory handles, by W H Harling, 117 Moorgate, London EC2.

10.5in (26.5cm) wide

£70-100 **CHEF**

SNUFF BOXES

A late 18thC to early 19thC snuff box, depicting three Alsace salesmen.

4in (10cm) long

£700-900 **SAPH**

A George III mounted wooden novelty snuff box, with piquework inlay, the sliding cove hallmarked for Joseph Wilmore, Birmingham 1810.

4in (10cm) long

£300-350 **WW**

An early 19thC tortoiseshell double snuff box.

3in (7.5cm) wide

£180-220 **BJ**

A Mauchline ware hand-painted snuff box.

c1830 *3.25in (8.5cm) wide*

£300-400 **RDER**

A Mauchline ware boxwood snuff box, with an inscription.

c1840 *1.5in (4cm) wide*

£150-200 **RDER**

A tartan ware snuff box, with lake scene decoration.

c1840 *3in (7.5cm) wide*

£300-500 **RDER**

A Victorian snuff box, the lid painted with a scene of a deer in snowy woodland.

£40-50 **PC**

A Penwork snuff box, the domed cover and body painted with a pattern of oak leaves and acorns, the top with an oval reserve of a crest and motto belonging to either the Borrington or Critchley family, translates to "Honour rather than splendour".

3in (8cm) wide

£180-220 **B**

EARLY TUNBRIDGEWARE

An early Tunbridgeware box, containing eighteen smaller boxes, with a Thomas Barton label.

c1820 *2.75in (7cm) high*

£200-300 **RDER**

A rare early Tunbridgeware mirror box, in turned boxwood and burr walnut.

c1820 *4.5in (11.5cm) diam*

£300-400 **RDER**

An early Tunbridgeware box, decorated with garlands of flowers, the centre with a rare enamelled plaque, inscribed "A present from Bath".

c1820 *6in (15cm) wide*

£450-550 **RDER**

An early Tunbridgeware nutmeg grater, the screw lid decorated with a view of Chain pier, Brighton.

c1820 *3.5in (9cm) diam*

£400-500 **RDER**

An early Tunbridgeware clamp, with six attachments.

c1820 *8in (20.5cm) long*

£500-800 **RDER**

An early Tunbridgeware clamp, with seven houses, inscribed "The absent not forgotten", one house restored.

c1820 *8in (20.5cm) long*

£500-800 **RDER**

An early Tunbridgeware clamp, painted with line decoration, with a pin cushion to top and a screw to base.

c1820 *3.5in (9cm) long*

£150-200 **RDER**

A set of four early Tunbridgeware trays, decorated with scenes of Brighton.

c1820 *Largest 6in (15cm) wide*

£600-900 **RDER**

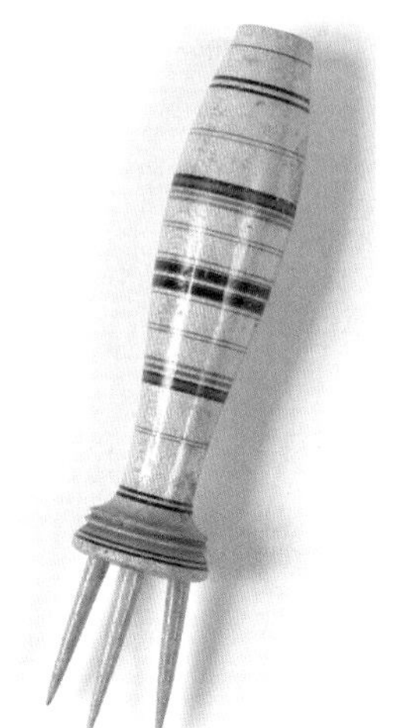

A rare early Tunbridgeware tool for silk winding.

c1820 *5in (13cm) long*

£400-600 **RDER**

A rare early Tunbridgeware tipstaff, with a painted crown and poppet.

c1820 *6.75in (17cm) long*

£500-800 **RDER**

An early 19thC tulip wood veneered box, the top with perspective cube decoration.

10.25in (26cm) wide

£220-280 **B**

TUNBRIDGEWARE

A mid-19thC Tunbridgeware double tea caddy, with waisted rectangular sides and a raised panel to the slightly domed hinged lid, decorated with flowers, the interior with four canisters and two mixing bowls.

16.5in (43cm) wide

£2,500-3,500 **CHEF**

A mid-19thC Tunbridgeware workbox, the rectangular lid with a rounded band of flowers outside abbey ruins, inlaid on satinwood, the waisted sides with a floral band on walnut, the interior with fitted tray and yellow silk lining.

10.5in (26.5cm) wide

£250-300 **CHEF**

A mid-19thC Tunbridgeware writing box, the rectangular lid inlaid with a central bunch of flowers on rosewood, within a rounded edge, chequer-inlaid with a floral band, the interior with a tray, ebony ruler, inkwell, stamp and lidded compartments.

10in (25cm) wide

£300-400 **CHEF**

A mid-19thC Tunbridgeware writing slope, the rectangular lid inlaid with a ruined abbey scene within a band of flowers, the sides of rosewood and the front with a further band of flowers, the interior with two rosette-topped inkwells.

14in (36cm) wide

£250-350 **CHEF**

A mid-19thC Tunbridgeware playing card box, the rectangular cribbage board lid marquetried with flowers on satinwood, the interior with two compartments for playing cards and another central compartment.

10in (25cm) wide

£120-180 **CHEF**

A mid-19thC Tunbridgeware box, the rectangular top inlaid with a castle, on a satinwood ground within a rounded edge band of oak leaves, on an ebony ground, the waisted rosewood sides with a vine band.

10.5in (27cm) wide

£300-400 **CHEF**

A Victorian Tunbridgeware stamp box, inlaid with a stamp on rosewood ground.

1.5in (4cm) wide

£120-180 **GORL**

A Victorian Tunbridgeware square casket, inlaid with a floral spray.

6in (15cm) wide

£220-280 **GORL**

A Tunbridgeware coromandel box, possibly by Barton, the central panel with a tesserae mosaic flower spray within a running rose banding, the base with rose spray broad band.

8in (20.5cm) wide

£280-320 **B**

An unusual Tunbridgeware ebony-veneered and geometric-inlaid cigarette box by Thomas Barton, with a circular label to base, corner moulding missing.

6.25in (16cm) wide

£400-600 **B**

An early Tunbridgeware burr-walnut box, the top with a rounded-end oblong half square panel, with chequer and rosewood crossbanding, the key escutcheon with an eight-point star.

7in (18cm) wide

£300-500 **B**

A Tunbridgeware coromandel glove box, probably by Barton, the dome cover with an oblong perspective cube panel, within a tesserae mosaic stylised flowerhead band, the sides with a broad band of running flowers.

9.5in (24cm) wide

£280-320 **B**

A Tunbridgeware ebony ground ring box, the top with a micro-mosaic dog panel, within stylized tesserae mosaic bands.

3.5in (9cm) wide

£400-600 **B**

A Tunbridgeware ebony jewellery casket, possibly by Barton, the domed cover with a polychrome rose spray on a whitewood ground within a geometric border, the sides with a broad running band of flowers.

8in (20.5cm) wide

£350-450 **B**

A Tunbridgeware rosewood scent bottle box, the domed top with a gauge work view of Eridge Castle, the walls with tesserae mosaic leaf banding, possibly by James and George Burrows, the interior with three divisions for now missing scent bottles, the lid slightly warped.

6in (15cm) wide

£220-280 B

A Tunbridgeware rosewood cribbage box, the top with a running tesserae mosaic rose band, crossbanded by peg holes, the sides decorated with a smaller running rose band.

10in (25.5cm) wide

£250-300 B

A Tunbridgeware rosewood box, the pin hinged top with a tesserae mosaic of a moth, with tartan paper to base.

6in (15cm) wide

£250-350 B

An early Tunbridgeware bird's-eye maple netting box, the lid with an oblong perspective cube panel, within half square crossbanding, the interior fitted with a Cantonese ivory tape measure and three thread wheels, the tops of which are carved and pierced with figures, two of which are red stained, also with a ratchet and pull and lead weight, faults to mosaic on top corners.

10.25in (26cm) wide

£500-800 B

A Tunbridgeware rosewood games box, with a cribbage board top, housing fitted divisions for playing cards.

11in (28cm) wide

£60-90 B

A Tunbridgeware rosewood tangram puzzle box, the top with a lozenge panel centred on an eight point star, with green chequered crossbanding, one of the seven puzzle pieces missing.

2in (5cm) wide

£120-180 B

A Tunbridgeware rosewood tangram puzzle box, the top with a mosaic lozenge centred on a mosaic device, within green chequered crossbanding, housing complete seven piece puzzle.

2.25in (5.5cm) wide

£120-180 B

A Tunbridgeware ebony-ground elongated octagonal games box, possibly by Thomas Barton, with a central tesserae mosaic flower spray on a light wood ground, within a broad stylized banding, with a fitted interior complete with a key, the walls with crossbanding and stylized flower banding, the lid slightly warped.

10.75in (27cm) wide

£500-800 B

A Tunbridgeware coromandel box by Edmund Nye, the lid with a perspective cube panel of specimen wood, including palm wood, within a geometric tesserae mosaic band, the walls with a rose and leaf tesserae band, with an Edmund Nye paper label to base.

10in (23cm) wide

£300-400 **B**

NYE & BARTON

Tunbridgeware is a type of wooden inlaid marquetry which originated in Tunbridge Wells in Kent. It became highly popular as a souvenir ware during the Victorian era, and pieces often depicted popular tourist sites as well as more traditional decorative motifs including flowers, animals and geometric designs. The technique involved making decorative pictures from strands of differently coloured woods which were glued together, then cut across the length into pieces. A wide variety of items were decorated in this way, from tiny boxes to table tops.

Edmund Nye and Thomas Barton were major manufacturers of Tunbridgeware. Barton was Nye's chief apprentice and developed the business in Tunbridge Wells following Nye's death in 1863.

Initially, Nye and Barton both used standard marquetry. However, the ultimate Tunbridgeware technique, developed by James Burrows in the early 1830s, was tessellated mosaic, consisting of tiny square tesserae. Nye was quick to adopt it for his own work.

So popular was the technique that even the young Princess Victoria bought Tunbridgeware as gifts for her family and it was exhibited by three manufacturers at the Great Exhibition of 1851: Nye, Robert Russell and Henry Hollamby. However, by the end of the 19thC, tastes had changed and the industry fell into decline.

Many specialists regard Barton's work as some of the finest Tunbridgeware ever made.

A Tunbridgeware ash stationery box, by Edmund Nye, the domed cover with a flower spray on a whitewood ground, within a geometric ebony ground border, the lid with a divided interior, the walls with a running wild rose mosaic band, with a paper label to base.

9in (23cm) wide

£600-900 **B**

A pair of Tunbridgeware whitewood boxes, with sliding rosewood lids, with lozenge, half-square mosaic panels and turned ebony handles.

2.5in (6.5cm) wide

£80-120 **B**

A Tunbridgeware rosewood box, the pin-hinged lid with a tesserae panel depicting a recumbent dog, missing knop and smiling joints.

5.5in (14cm) wide

£180-220 **B**

A Tunbridgeware rosewood glove box, by Edmund Nye, the pin-hinged lid with a rose and scrolling leaf mosaic band, within geometric crossbanding, with an original turned ivory peg handle, the base with a paper label.

9.25in (23.5cm) wide

£280-320 **B**

A small Tunbridgeware rosewood box, with a tesserae panel of a young boy, possibly Edward, Prince of Wales, on a light wood ground, within geometric tesserae mosaic cross banding.

4in (10cm) wide

£280-320 **B**

A Tunbridgeware rosewood box, the top with tesserae panel of a seated King Charles spaniel.

2.25in (5.5cm) wide

£200-300 B

A Novelty Tunbridgeware rosewood matchbox, modelled as a book, the top with tesserae mosaic lettering, spelling "A Present from Tunbridge Wells", now missing its three book spine drawers.

3.75in (9.5cm) wide

£180-220 B

A Tunbridgeware rosewood stamp box attributed to Thomas Green of Rye, the top with a tesserae mosaic view of a windmill.

1.75in (4.5cm) wide

£220-280 B

A Tunbridgeware rosewood box, the cover with tesserae mosaic lettering spelling "Studs", damage.

£200-300 B

A Tunbridgeware rosewood box, the top decorated with a tesserae panel depicting a rabbit.

2.5in (6cm) wide

£150-200 B

A Tunbridgeware rosewood box, the top with a tesserae mosaic panel of a cat on cushion, missing crossbanding.

2.25in (5.5cm) wide

£180-220 B

A Tunbridgeware rosewood tea caddy, the domed cover with a flower spray on a whitewood ground, within stylized flowerhead banding, with two lidded divisions, the base with a running band of flowers and chequer stringing.

8in (20cm) wide

£400-600 B

A large Tunbridgeware rosewood tea caddy, the domed cover with a tesserae view of Penshurst Castle, within a narrow band of tesserae mosaic running roses, enclosing a velvet-lined sugar bowl aperture, between a pair of lidded caddies, the waisted sides with a running acorn and oak leaf band, damage and losses.

13in (33cm) wide

£450-550 B

A Tunbridgeware box, the top with a tesserae mosaic of a King Charles spaniel on a cushion, above chequer-strung walls.

2.25in (5.5cm) wide

£220-280 B

A Tunbridgeware rosewood work box, the cushion-shaped top with a tesserae mosaic view of Dover Castle, within a broad band of flowers, the interior with a divided tray with a tesserae mosaic, chamfered edges and one stickware-handled division, the waisted sides with a broad ebony-ground tesserae mosaic of a running band of roses, splits and losses.

9.5in (24cm) wide

£600-900 B

A Tunbridgeware ebony-ground sewing box, the rectangular cushion-shaped lid with a tesserae view of Hever Castle, on a black ground within a broad flower and berry tesserae mosaic border, the box with waisted sides, with a broad tesserae flower band, the divided interior with a chamfered tesserae mosaic frame and one stickware-handled lidded well, slight damage.

10.75in (27cm) wide

£700-1,000 **B**

A Tunbridgeware walnut workbox, the top with a tesserae view of Tonbridge Castle, the front with a pair of small tesserae mosaic flower panels, the interior with a divided removable tray.

£280-320 **B**

A Tunbridgeware rosewood workbox, the domed cover with a view of Battle Abbey gatehouse, within a flower and leaf tesserae mosaic band, the waisted walls with similar rose and leaf tesserae mosaic banding, damage, tray missing.

9.5in (24cm) wide

£450-550 **B**

A Tunbridgeware walnut workbox, the cushion-shaped cover with central tesserae mosaic view of Eridge Castle, within band work stringing, the interior with a removable divided tray, with a working key.

9.75in (25cm) wide

£250-350 **B**

A Tunbridgeware walnut sewing box, inlaid with two geometric stripes and a rectangular reserve and escutcheon, the fitted interior lined with green satin.

c1850 *20in (25cm) wide*

£150-200 **S&K**

A Tunbridgeware rosewood stationery box, the sloping panel with tesserae mosaic view of girl, cat and peacock within geometric banding, the sides with broad oak leaf and acorn tesserae band, the interior divided, the lock now missing and some damage around key escutcheon.

6.25in (16cm) wide

£600-900 **B**

A Tunbridgeware rosewood writing slope, the sloping fall with a view of Dover Castle below an oblong panel of perspective cubes, all within a broad band of tesserae mosaic roses, the bright interior including one ink well with an eight point star cap and a geometric tesserae mosaic lidded box, some losses.

12.25in (31cm) wide

£800-1,200 **B**

A Tunbridgeware burr-walnut folding writing slope, the top with a tesserae of Tonbridge Castle, the front with two small tesserae flower panels, the interior with a pair of plated ink bottles.

15.75in (40cm) wide

£280-320 **B**

A Tunbridgeware rosewood folding writing box, the top with a tesserae view of Hever Castle within a broad band of stylized flowers and leaves, the front with a broad banding of roses, the interior complete with two ink bottles with eight point stars caps, slight damage.

14.25in (36cm) wide

£500-800 **B**

A Tunbridgeware cylindrical needle case, with a tesserae mosaic shaft and turned stickware ends.

4in (10cm) long

£250-300 **B**

A Tunbridgeware stickware thimble case, the nut-shaped body housing a yellow-banded white metal thimble.

1.5in (4cm) long

£150-200 **B**

A Tunbridgeware needle wallet, one cover with a tesserae flower mosaic and the other with perspective cubes.

2.5in (6cm) long

£80-120 **B**

A Tunbridgeware white wood sewing companion, the cylindrical body mounted with a tape measure and pin cushion, the underside with a coloured print of York Place, Tunbridge Wells, with a green ribbon necklace.

2in (5cm) diam

£180-220 **B**

A Tunbridgeware rosewood sewing companion, possibly by Nye or Barton, with a fitted removable reel tray and two pin cushions, one housing a thimble, the sloping sides with a broad band of tesserae mosaic roses, on turned bun feet, evidence of paper label, the three reels now missing.

8.75in (22cm) wide

£300-400 **B**

Three Tunbridgeware stickware thread wheels and a tesserae mosaic thread cross.

1.75in (4.5cm) wide

£500-800 **B**

Two pairs of Tunbridgeware thread crosses, minor splits and losses.

1.75in (4.5cm) wide

£350-450 **B**

Six Tunbridgeware thread wheels, with half-square and eight point star mosaic, with one damaged tesserae mosaic thread cross.

1.75in (4.5cm) diam

£800-1,200 **B**

A Tunbridgeware chalybeate spring stained bird's-eye maple dressing table stand, with a hinged pin cushion enclosing a mosaic-strung removable tray, the splayed sides with a broad tesserae mosaic running band of flowers, on stickware bun feet, together with a key, missing scent bottles.

9in (23cm) wide

£280-320 **B**

A large circular Tunbridgeware weighted pin cushion, with stickware sides, the base with an Edmund Nye paper label, a segment missing.

11.75in (8cm) diam

£150-200 **B**

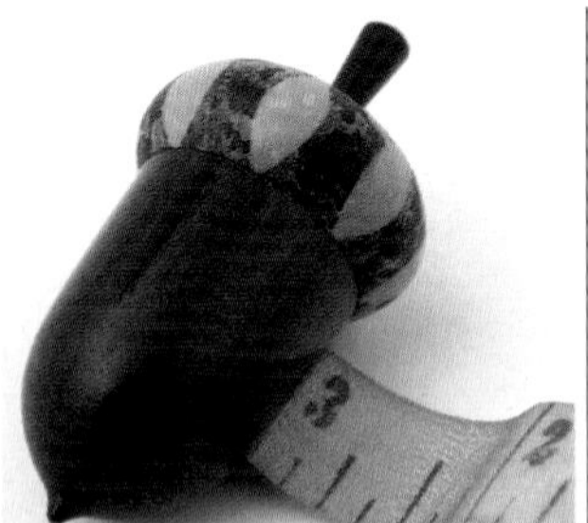

A Tunbridgeware rosewood tape measure, modelled as an acorn with a stickware cup.

2in (5cm) long

£150-200 **B**

A Victorian Tunbridgeware and rosewood lap desk, the hinged lid with inlaid bands and an inlaid diamond shape, some restoration.

c1840 *12in (30cm) wide*

£350-450 **S&K**

A Tunbridgeware propelling pencil, the rectangular stem with tesserae mosaic bands and an eight point star stickware finial, with original uncut cedar pencil lead, with a similar rosewood propelling pencil with a half square mosaic top, the neck cracked.

Largest 4.75in (12cm) long

£150-200 **B**

A Tunbridgeware dip pen, the slight baluster-shaped shaft with a tesserae mosaic.

6.25in (16cm) long

£150-200 **B**

A Tunbridgeware dip pen, the cylindrical shaft with a geometric tesserae mosaic.

6.25in (16cm) long

£100-150 **B**

A Tunbridgeware rosewood sealing wax outfit, the drum-shaped body with a half square mosaic top, with turned rosewood sconce and bone match cup, crack and losses.

4.5in (11cm) high

£180-220 **B**

A Tunbridgeware rosewood sealing wax outfit, with a tesserae mosaic top, the octagonal body with running geometric bands over a threaded step base, some faults and the sconce missing.

3.5in (9cm) high

£120-180 **B**

A Tunbridgeware octagonal ebony stamp dispenser, the circular eight point star top with a revolving handle on a tesserae mosaic panelled body.

1.75in (4.5cm) diam

£250-350 **B**

An early Tunbridgeware circular inkstand, the tesserae mosaic banded plinth with a reeded edge, housing a central moulded inkwell with a half square mosaic top, between two pen stands.

4.25in (11cm) diam

£350-400 **B**

A Tunbridgeware folding wallet, one cover with a tesserae mosaic of a cornucopia of flowers and the other cover with a rose spray, both within geometric crossbanding, the pencil holding together the two covers missing.

4in (10cm) wide

£150-200 **B**

A Tunbridgeware sealing wax outfit by Edmund Nye, the ebony top inlaid with an eight point star and a stickware candle sconce, with a turned bone match stand, the interior with a circular Edmund Nye label, the octagonal stem with stylized tesserae mosaic bands.

5.75in (14.5cm) high

£700-1,000 **B**

A Tunbridgeware magnifying glass, with tesserae and vandyke inlay, set on a stickware handle.

6.25in (16cm) width

£220-280 **B**

A Tunbridgeware rosewood book slide, one end with a view of Tonbridge Castle and the other of Penshurst Place, the ends with tesserae mosaic banding.

13in (33cm) wide

£150-200 **B**

A Tunbridgeware rosewood book slide, one end with a gaugework view of Eridge Castle and the other with a gaugework view of Hurstwood Cottage, both within geometric tesserae mosaic crossbanding, some damage.

10.75in (27cm) wide

£150-200 **B**

A Tunbridgeware book slide, both folding ends with perspective cube panels, crossbanded with geometric tesserae mosaics.

15.5in (39cm) wide

£80-120 **B**

A CLOSER LOOK AT A TUNBRIDGEWARE BOOK SLIDE

Tunbridgeware is associated with intricate wooden decoration. On this fine book slide, small, tessellating pieces of coloured wood have been carefully laid together to compose a magnificent image of a ruin to one end, and a butterfly to the other.

Book slides are typical of the small, domestic Tunbridgeware items made in the 19thC. A number of larger items, including tables, were also produced.

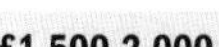

This book slide is attributed to Edmund Nye. His work tends to command a premium.

A rare Tunbridgeware rosewood book slide possibly by Nye, one end with a gaugework butterfly, and the other side gauge work view of ruins with Victorian figures in foreground, both on satin birch grounds.

13in (33.5cm) wide

£1,500-2,000 **B**

A Tunbridgeware rosewood book stand, by Russell, with a perspective cube central panel, within a broad border of stylized leaves on a light wood ground.

12in (30cm) wide

£800-1,200 **B**

A mid-19thC Tunbridgeware rosewood book stand, each side inlaid with foliate sprays within a foliate border, a shelf below, damaged.

13in (32.5cm) high

£180-220 **GORL**

An unusual Tunbridgeware bookmark, with perspective cubes.

3.25in (8.5cm) wide

£150-200 **B**

An unusual Tunbridgeware bookmark, the pear-shaped body with a chalybeate spring face, with a flower spray mosaic, the underside of tulipwood.

3.25in (8.5cm) wide

£150-200 **B**

A Tunbridgeware pin tray, the oblong base with a gaugework view of a small cottage, on a satinbirch ground, the satinwood sloping walls with a single tesserae mosaic band, some damage.

6.75in (17cm) wide

£120-180 **B**

A Tunbridgeware whitewood pin tray, the rectangular body with a print of Brighton Pavilion with figures in the foreground, the sloping sides painted with stylized pink flowers, damage to varnish of print.

3.75in (9.5cm) wide

£50-80 **B**

A small Tunbridgeware basket, the base with perspective cubes, turquoise silk walls and a tesserae mosaic frame, with a rosewood swing handle, the original silk torn and the varnish worn.

6in (15cm) diam

£180-220 **B**

A Tunbridgeware whitewood coaster, printed with Eridge Castle.

4in (10cm) diam

£80-120 **B**

An unusual Tunbridgeware Cleopatra's needle thermometer stand, by Thomas Barton, the ebony-veneered needle and plinth with chequer mosaic stringing, the plinth with flower wreath mosaic panels, the ivory scale signed, with minor losses.

8.75in (22cm) high

£400-600 **B**

A mid-19thC Tunbridgeware compass and thermometer stand, the octagonal sides topped by a compass, inscribed "T Barton Tunbridge Wells" on the thermometer scale.

5in (13cm) high

£300-400 **CHEF**

A Tunbridgeware whitewood nutmeg grater, with a coloured print of Brighton Pavilion.

2.75in (7cm) diam

£300-400 **B**

A Tunbridgeware ebony sovereign ball, with eight point star roundels, two cracks to smaller aperture.

2in (5cm) diam

£300-400 **B**

A Tunbridgeware stickware spinning top, and a round Tunbridgeware tesserae mosaic button.

Top 1in (3cm) high

£120-180 **B**

A pair of Tunbridgeware cloak buttons, each with a half square and eight point star mosaic.

1in (2.5cm) diam

£250-300 **B**

A small Tunbridgeware caddy spoon, with a stickware bowl and handle.

1.5in (4cm) diam

£400-600 **B**

A Tunbridgeware stickware vesta, modelled as a capstan with a tesserae mosaic top.

2in (5cm) high

£70-100 **B**

An unusual Tunbridgeware circular rosewood hand mirror, with a perspective cube back.

3in (7.5cm) diam

£180-220 **B**

A Tunbridgeware hat brush, with a rose and leaf tesserae mosaic back.

6.25in (16cm) wide

£20-30 **B**

A Tunbridgeware rosewood rouge pot, the top with a tesserae mosaic.

8in (3.5cm) diam

£70-100 **B**

A rare Tunbridgeware necklace, with nine tesserae mosaic and stickware buttons, with various bead spacers.

£300-400 **B**

A Tunbridgeware rosewood banjo, decorated with tesserae mosaic panels and bandings.

£500-800 **B**

MAUCHLINEWARE

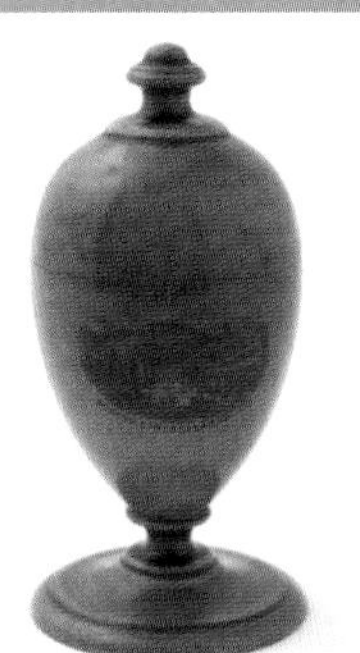

A Mauchlineware egg-shaped vesta and cover, with a transferred view of Mostyn Street, Llandudno.

3.75in (9.5cm) high

£80-120 **B**

A Mauchlineware string box, the circular body, transferred with "The Sands, Margate".

3.5in (9cm) diam

£50-80 **B**

A Mauchlineware photograph frame, made from wood grown at Abbotsford, engraved with Nelson's monument, Walter Scott's monument, Edinburgh Castle and Holyrood Palace.

8.75in (22cm) high

£180-220 **B**

A Mauchlineware money box, the cylindrical body engraved with "New Chelsea suspension bridge" and "Horseguards from St James' Park".

3.75in (9.5cm) high

£120-180 **B**

A Mauchlineware spectacle case, transfer-decorated with St Margaret's Church, Lowestoft, housing a pair of gold plated spectacles, the case cracked.

6in (15cm) long

£50-80 **B**

A Victorian Tartanware holder.

c1890 *2in (5cm) high*

£50-80 **BJ**

A Tartanware chamberstick with McPherson tartan.

3.5in (9cm) diam

£400-600 **B**

TARTANWARE

A rare Victorian Tartanware thimble bottle.

c1890 *3in (7.5cm) high*

£200-280 **BJ**

A Victorian Tartanware marker, with numbered panels.

2.75in (7cm) high

£70-100 BJ

A Tartanware night light, the barrel-shaped body with a tartan ground, the top with a turned bone match holder.

2.5in (6cm) high

£80-120 B

A Tartanware spinning dice, the numbered sides on a Fraser tartan ground.

2in (5cm) high

£280-320 B

A Tartanware egg timer, with McGregor tartan, damage.

3in (7. 5cm) high

£80-120 B

A Tartanware box magnifying glass, the McPharlen tartan body open to one end.

1.25in (3cm) high

£250-300 B

A Tartanware needle case, the slip top finely painted with a fox's head, the octagonal walls with Royal Stuart tartan.

2.25in (5.5cm) high

£280-320 B

A Tartanware needle case, one side finely painted with a duck, the other side with a partridge.

4in (10cm) long

£350-400 B

A Tartanware cleopatra's needle thermometer stand, with ivory gauge, the ground of McDuff tartan, crazed varnish.

6.25in (16cm) high

£150-200 B

A Victorian tartanware 'Go to bed', with a match holder.

2.5in (6.5cm) high

£120-180 BJ

A Tartanware heart-shaped pin cushion, both faces with Louise tartan, one side with a Victorian registration diamond, with red velvet walls.

2.5in (6cm) wide

£150-200 B

A Tartanware whistle, the tapering body with Prince Charlie tartan, an ebonised turned finial and mouth piece.

2.5in (6.5cm) long

£250-300 B

A Tartanware needle case, the elongated octagonal top finely painted with a sporting dog, the walls with McPherson tartan.

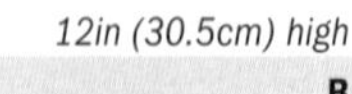

12in (30.5cm) high

£220-280 B

A late 17thC staved wood quaich, the body with willow binding and a central silver disc, the lug with silver mounts, engraved with Dutch -style tulips and initials "II/MF", the later foot rim with marks for Ferguson and McBean, some restoration and later feet.

c1680 9in (23cm) diam

£1,000-1,500 L&T

TREEN

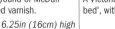

An early 18thC Scottish laburnum quaich, the large bowl of staved form with three plain wood lugs, a central boss to the base, engraved with a crest of an erased bear's head, within a C-scroll cartouche, an engraved upper band "Andrew Burnett, Writer to the Signet and Margaret Mowat, his wife, September 21st 1731", the foot rim with a further engraved band, "May the Beggars Benizon attend my owner".

9.5in (24cm) diam

£3,000-4,000 L&T

A rare late 17thC laburnum quaich, of stave form with silver corded and reeded bands, the three shaped lug handles with silver mounts, variously engraved initials and dates, the centre with an engraved disc "DS ML 1670".

8.75in (22cm) diam

£1,800-2,200 **L&T**

An burl-ash food-working scoop.

c1720 *8.5in (22cm) long*

£500-800 **RAA**

A rare mid-18thC tortoiseshell and mother-of-pearl banded capstan snuff mull, engraved silver mounts and an oval disc engraved "Jas Hope", the thumbpiece formed as a winged heart.

2.5in (6.5cm) high

£2,200-2,800 **L&T**

An 18thC Dutch pewter-inlaid treen shoe snuff box, the lift-off cover inlaid with the date "1760".

3.75in (9.5cm) wide

£400-600 **GORL**

A Norwegian peg tankard, the hinged dome cover with a knop finial central to a carved rope band, the ring-turned cylindrical sides above three ball feet, dated "1761".

8.75in (22cm) high

£600-900 **CHEF**

An ebony capstan snuff mull, with a silver butterfly hinge, engraved "JM", with another in bog oak, brass-bound and engraved "GC 1761".

£250-300 **L&T**

A late 18thC to early 19thC coconut cup, carved in low relief with 'Daniel in the lion's den', a head of 'Christ and David triumphing over Goliath', the ovoid bowl on three brass paw feet.

4in (10cm) high

£200-300 **CHEF**

A walnut cake mould, marked by maker John Conger and retailer J.Y. Watkins, New York, depicting a Hessian soldier with a rifle and flower.

John Conger was an accomplished carver who designed the New York State of Arms. He signed very few pieces.

c1835 *6in (15cm) long*

£1,000-1,500 **RAA**

A maple sugar mould, depicting a bucket of seed with a feeding bird.

c1840 *4.25in (10.5cm) high*

£500-700 **RAA**

An early 19thC papier-mâché box.

3.25in (8.5cm) diam

£80-120 **BJ**

A 19th century 'bugbear' carved coconut, geometrically-carved with a mask of eyes and an open mouth to one end of the ovoid shape.

4.75in (12cm) wide

£80-120 **CHEF**

A Victorian mounted vari-coloured agate piggin, for the Scottish market, of coppered construction with two small lug handles and an engraved upper and lower frieze of scrolls, unmarked.

c1860 *3.75in (9.6cm) wide*

£3,000-4,000 **WW**

A 19thC boxwood spice box, of turned form with four screwed tiers and overhanging lid, paper labels for Mace, Cloves, Ginger and All-Spice.

8.75in (22cm) high

£280-320 **L&T**

GLASS

Glass enthusiasts have had a good year, with a number of important collections going under the hammer and releasing high quality pieces back onto the market. This has not, however, been on a large enough scale to sufficiently bolster the availability of top quality items, and prices for these pieces remain extremely high and continue to climb.

Wine bottles from the 18thC have been hot commodities in the past year, with prices rising very quickly for good quality examples, especially those with seals. Unusual collector's wine glasses from the same period have enjoyed similar popularity, as have heavy baluster glasses. Increases in value within these sectors of the market have a lot to do with rarity: relatively little glass survives this long and when a number of collectors express interest in the same scarce stock, prices surge upwards. Similarly, styles that catch the public's imagination and become fashionable will inevitably become more expensive. This seems to have happened to glasses with colour-twist stems recently, and the increased market attention they have been attracting has had a commensurate effect on value.

Glass decanters remain relatively overlooked unless they have some crossover appeal, such as Irish or ship's decanters, which are popular. This may be an area to watch for in the future as the market can be fickle and, as stocks of bottles and glasses dry up, eyes may well begin to turn to this hitherto neglected cousin.

BOTTLES

A rare early English dark green glass wine bottle, onion-shaped with a seal.

c1690 *6.75in (17.5cm) high*

£700-900 **CSA**

A Middle Temple wine bottle, from a three-part mould, with "Lamb & Flag" seal on shoulder and applied lip.

c1820 *12in (30.5cm) high*

£60-90 **AG**

A small 18thC Alpine region bottle, with melted stripes of spiralling milk-glass decoration on a brown body.

4.5in (11.5cm) high

£300-400 **FIS**

A 'Wellspring' water carafe, designed by Richard Redgrave.

c1850 *6.25in (16cm) high*

£500-800 **AL**

A mid-19thC Nailsea-type shaft and globe carafe, with white and pink inclusions.

9.5in (24cm) high

£100-150 **AG**

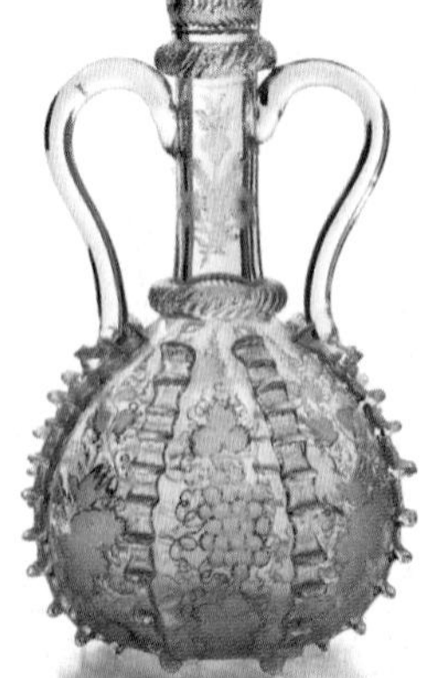

A 19thC globular flask, probably English, engraved and gilded with fruiting vines, with loop handles.

8.5in (21.5cm) high

£100-150 **AG**

A pair of 19thC flat octagonal spirit bottles, engraved with birds, fruit and flowers, with associated stoppers.

10in (25.5cm) high

£150-200 **AG**

A pair of 19thC panel-cut and gilded toilet bottles, with hollow facet-cut stoppers.

7.25in (18.5cm) high

£70-100 **AG**

DECANTERS

A pair of late 18thC green mallet-shaped decanters and flattened disc stoppers, each with gilt cartouche with ribbands and chains named for "BRANDY" and "RUM".

9in (23cm) high

£400-600 **DN**

Three late 18thC blue mallet-shaped cruet decanters and flattened disc stoppers, named in gilding for "KETCHUP", "SOY" and "KYAN", within gilt borders decorated as bottle labels.

5.5in (14cm) high

£300-500 **DN**

A late 18thC blue mallet-shaped decanter and stopper, named in gilt script for "BRANDY", the stopper with letter "B", some wear to gilding.

12in (30cm) high

£300-400 **DN**

A decanter, with four cut neck-rings, flute-cut base and original lozenge stopper.

c1800 11.25in (28.5cm) high

£180-220 **JH**

A decanter, with triple neck-ring, slice-cut shoulders, flute-cut base and mushroom stopper.

c1820 9.5in (24cm) high

£180-220 **JH**

An Irish moulded decanter, with pinched stopper.

c1820 9in (23cm) high

£40-60 **AG**

One of a pair of decanters, diamond- and flute-cut with blown stopper.

c1830 10in (25.5cm) high

£300-500 pair **JH**

A decanter, with step-cut neck and slice-cut body.

c1830 9.5in (24cm) high

£120-180 **JH**

A 19thC oval and round shouldered spirit decanter, cut with printies, with star base and cut stopper.

c1830 11.5in (29cm) high

£50-70 **AG**

A Friedrich Egermann decanter with stopper, clear glass with Schwarzlot-enamel paint on golden fond, hairline crack to handle.

c1840 14in (35cm) high

£400-600 **FIS**

A fine 19thC panel-cut green spirit decanter, with single ring neck and spire stopper.

c1840 14in (35.5cm) high

£150-250 **AG**

A decanter, slice- and lens-cut, with stopper.

c1845 14in (35.5cm) high

£60-90 **JH**

A late 19thC Baccarat moulded Amberina glass drinks set, comprised of a decanter and a pair of glasses on a circular tray, each spirally moulded in amber shading to pink glass, both glasses and tray moulded "Baccarat Deposé".

11in (28cm) diam

£400-600 **S&K**

A mid-19thC pair of pale green slender club-shaped pillar-cut decanters and ball stoppers, the pillars with three notches, one chipped.

c1850 *13in (33cm) high*

£200-300 **DN**

A late 19thC step-cut ship's decanter, with two moulded and faceted neck rings, star-cut base and cushion mushroom stopper.

8.5in (21.5cm) high

£150-200 **AG**

A 19thC Irish style four-ring decanter, with etched motif and associated stopper.

10.5in (26.5cm) high

£70-100 **AG**

A pair of mid-19thC decanters, cut all-over with deep printies, with star base and matching printie-cut stoppers.

c1850 *13.5in (34.5cm) high*

£30-40 **AG**

A 19thC amber blown-glass spirit decanter bottle, with loop handle.

8.5in (21.5cm) high

£30-40 **AG**

A Victorian pillar decanter, with hollow-blown stopper.

c1865 *11in (28cm) high*

£20-40 **AG**

A mid-Victorian pair of emerald green decanters, with bull's-eye stoppers.

11.5in (29cm) high

£500-800 **AL**

A Victorian shaft and globe decanter, facet-cut with star base and original matching stopper.

c1870 *12in (30.5cm) high*

£60-90 **AG**

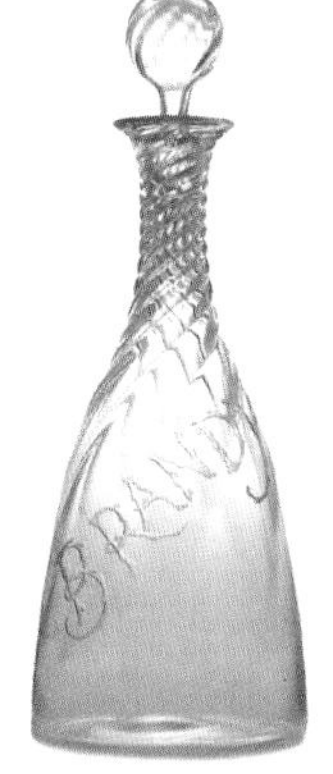

An unusual Wrythen decanter, engraved "Brandy" and with blown stopper.

c1900 *12in (30cm) high*

£150-200 **JH**

A pair of early 20thC continental silver and enamel mounted glass liqueur jugs, the necks and handles decorated with red guilloche and enamel banding, the domed lids with scroll thumbpiece, engraving to one.

8.75in (22cm) high

£600-800 **L&T**

A glass claret decanter, modelled as a pig, with silver mounted stopper to the snout and a silver collar.

10.75in (27cm) long

£300-400 **L&T**

A Webb Corbett ship's decanter, with step-cut cone body, two moulded neck rings and cut mushroom stopper.

9in (23cm) high

£100-200 **AG**

A pair of moulded cut-glass decanters, each of globular form with a tall narrow neck and spherical stopper.

11.5in (29cm) high

£150-200 **S&K**

A pair of etched glass decanters, each hexagonal with waisted neck and conforming stopper, etched with vines.

15in (38cm) high

£100-150 **S&K**

A late 19thC/early 20thC Napoleon II-style brass and mother-of-pearl inlaid tantalus, the hinged cover and front inlaid with cartouches, enclosing a caddy fitted with four spirit decanters and two glasses.

13.5in (34cm) wide

£300-500 **S&K**

A CLOSER LOOK AT A DECANTER

This decanter was made in Stourbridge, in the West Midlands, which was the centre of English glassmaking in the mid-19thC.

This is not the original stopper. This decanter may well have been produced without one.

This decanter would have been used by a hunting meet, hence the remarkable and whimsical novelty form.

The engraved design features various items associated with the hunt, including a horn, a riding crop, a horseshoe, a stirrup and the head of a fox.

The pontil is polished rather than broken, indicating high-quality and careful craftsmanship.

An unusual Stourbridge decanter in the form of a hunting horn, decorated with a fox's head and inscribed "Tally Ho".

c1880 *14.5in (37cm) high*

£600-900 **AL**

WINE GLASSES

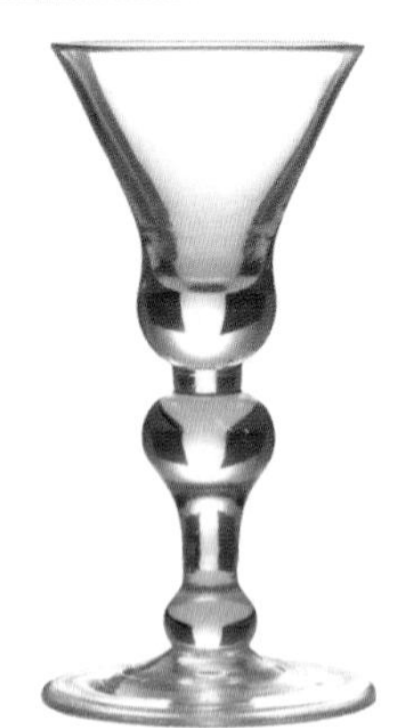

A bell bowl heavy baluster wine glass, with folded foot.

The heavy weight of this wine glass adds to its value.

c1715 *6in (15cm) high*

£800-1,200 **JH**

A baluster wine glass, of drawn trumpet form, the stem with a tear inclusion above a baluster section, on a domed foot.

c1720 *7in (17.5cm) high*

£700-1,000 **DN**

A baluster wine glass, the bell bowl supported on an annular knop above an inverted baluster section and a basal knop, on a folded conical foot.

c1720 *7in (18cm) high*

£1,200-1,800 **DN**

A bell bowl baluster wine glass, with tiered stem and folded foot.

c1725 *6in (15cm) high*

£400-600 **JH**

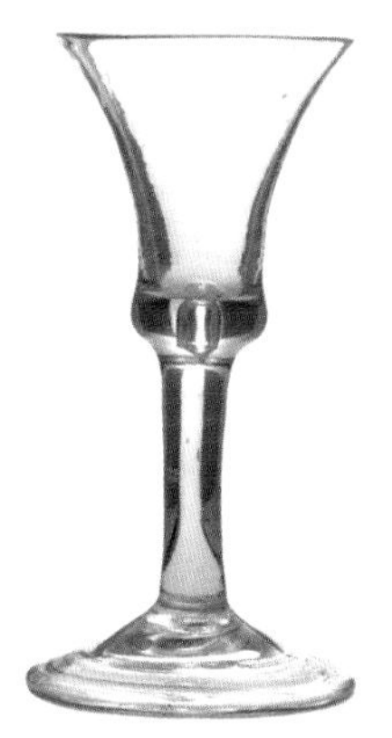

A bell-bowl wine glass, with tear in base, plain stem and folded foot.

c1725 *6in (15cm) high*

£120-180 **JH**

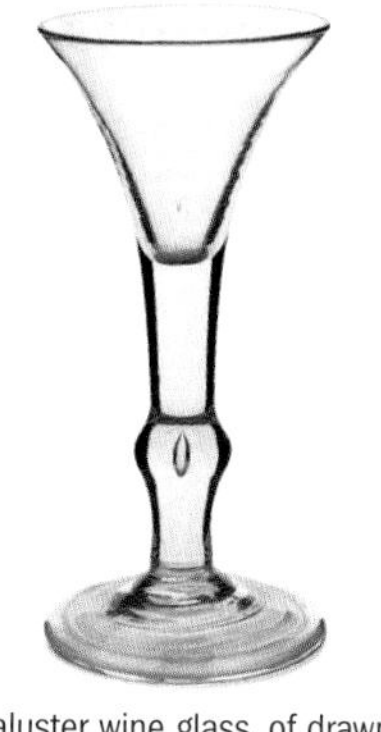

A baluster wine glass, of drawn trumpet form, supported on a centrally knopped stem with small tear inclusion, on a folded conical foot.

c1730 *7in (18cm) high*

£400-600 **DN**

A baluster wine glass, the bell bowl with solid lower section and bead inclusion, supported on an inverted baluster with bead inclusion and a basal knop, on a folded conical foot.

c1730 *6.75in (17cm) high*

£700-1,000 **DN**

A composite-stemmed wine glass, the bell bowl above a plain stem and knop, supported on a large knop filled with beads, on a domed foot.

c1730 *7in (18cm) high*

£800-1,200 **DN**

A balustroid wine glass, the bell bowl supported on an inverted stem and basal knop with two tear inclusions, on a folded conical foot.

c1730 *7.35in (18.5cm) high*

£700-1,000 **DN**

A baluster wine glass, the bell bowl with solid lower section, supported on a stem with a beaded knop above an inverted baluster and basal knop, on a conical foot.

c1730 *6.25in (16cm) high*

£600-900 **DN**

A balustroid wine glass, of drawn trumpet form with solid lower section and tear inclusion, supported on an inverted baluster section with bead inclusion, on a folded conical foot.

c1730 *6.5in (16.5cm) high*

£500-700 **DN**

A baluster wine glass, of drawn trumpet form, the stem with a plain section above a beaded knop and basal cushion knop, on a conical foot.

c1730 *7in (18cm) high*

£500-700 **DN**

A balustroid wine glass, of drawn trumpet form, supported on a centrally knopped stem with tear inclusion, on a folded conical foot.

c1730 *6.25in (16cm) high*

£300-500 **DN**

A wine glass, with teared drawn trumpet and folded foot.

c1730 *6.5in (16.5cm) high*

£220-280 **JH**

A light baluster wine glass, the round funnel bowl supported on a multi-knopped stem, the lower baluster section with a bead inclusion, on a folded conical foot.

c1740 *7.5in (19cm) high*

£600-900 **DN**

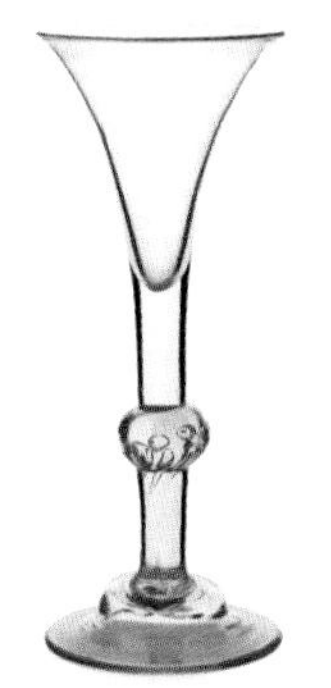

A balustroid wine glass, of drawn trumpet form with a central knop with bead inclusions, on a domed foot.

c1740 *7in (18cm) high*

£500-700 **DN**

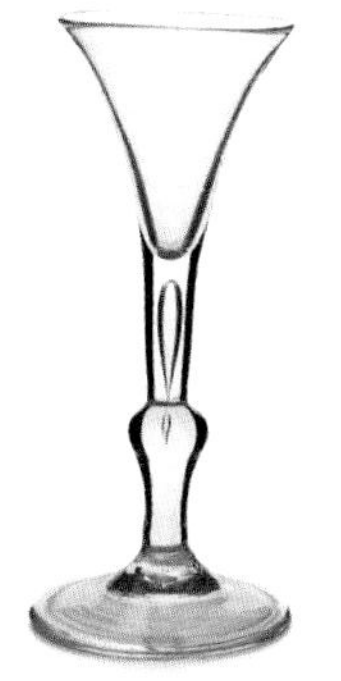

A balustroid wine glass, of drawn trumpet form, supported on a stem with a tear inclusion above an inverted baluster section, on a folded conical foot.

c1740 *6.5in (16.5cm) high*

£500-700 **DN**

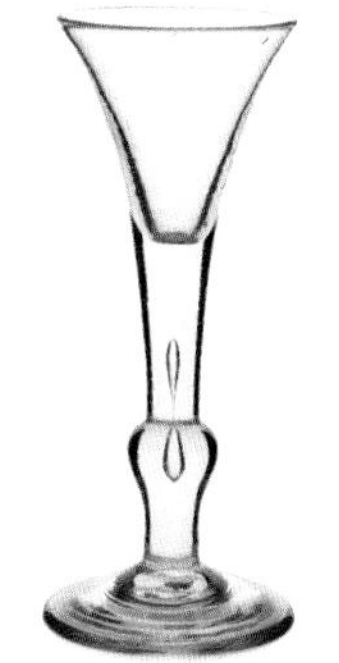

A kit-cat wine glass, the drawn trumpet bowl with a solid lower section and elongated tear inclusion, supported on an inverted baluster stem and conical foot.

c1740 *6.5in (16.5cm) high*

£500-700 **DN**

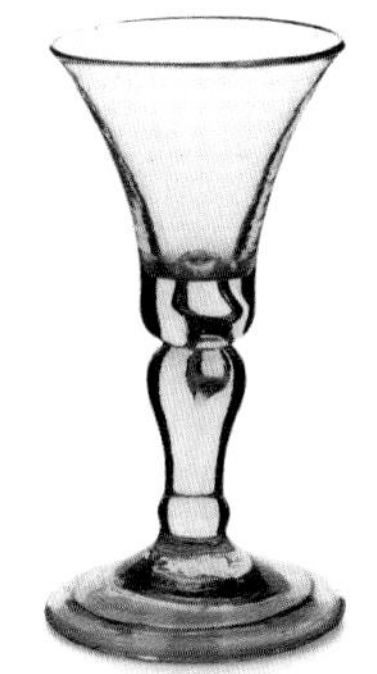

A baluster gin glass, the bell bowl with a solid lower section and tear inclusion, supported on an inverted baluster stem with tear inclusion, on a folded conical foot.

c1740 *4.5in (11.5cm) high*

£500-700 **DN**

A kit-cat wine glass, the drawn trumpet bowl with a solid lower section and elongated tear inclusion, supported on a short inverted baluster stem with a bead inclusion, on a domed foot.

c1740 *7in (17.5cm) high*

£1,000-1,500 **DN**

A pair of hollow-stemmed wine glasses, the round funnel bowls supported on double-knopped stems.

c1740 *6in (15cm) high*

£600-800 **DN**

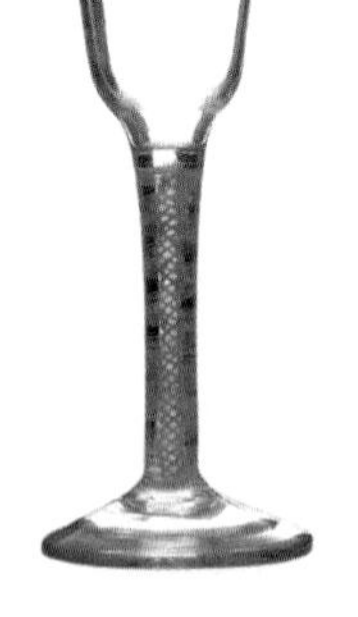

A wine glass, with bell bowl and multi-spiral air-twist stem.

c1745 *7.5in (19cm) high*

£400-600 **JH**

A wine glass, with bell bowl, domed folded foot and multi-spiral air-twist stem.

c1745 *6.5in (16.5cm) high*

£300-400 **JH**

A mid-18thC plain-stemmed wine glass of Jacobite significance, the drawn trumpet bowl engraved with a rose, rosebud and a sunburst, the plain stem with a tear inclusion, supported on a conical foot.

6.75in (17cm) high

£800-1,200 **DN**

A mid-18thC plain-stemmed wine glass, of drawn trumpet form with a single bead inclusion, on a conical foot.

7in (18cm) high

£100-150 **DN**

A mid-18thC air-twist toasting glass, of drawn trumpet form.

7.25in (18.5cm) high

£400-600 **DN**

An incised-twist wine glass, the round funnel bowl with a hammered flute lower section, the stem with an elongated tear, on a conical foot.

c1750 *5.5in (14cm) high*

£500-700 **DN**

A Newcastle light baluster goblet, the round funnel bowl supported on a multi-knopped stem, the inverted baluster section with bead inclusions, on a conical foot.

c1750 *8in (20.5cm) high*

£1,000-1,500 **DN**

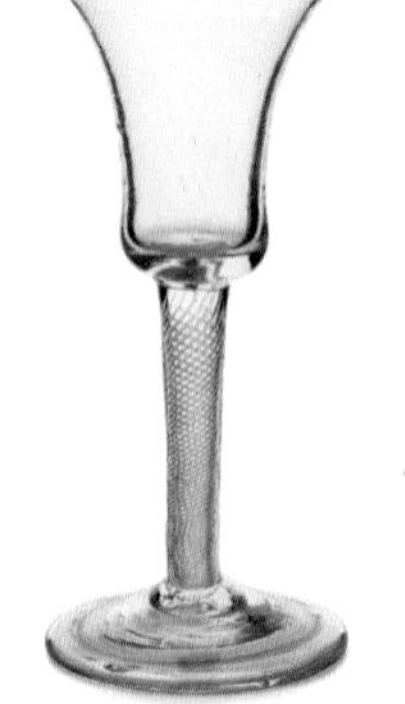

An air-twist wine glass, the bell bowl supported on a stem filled with spiral threads and a folded conical foot.

c1750 *6in (15.5cm) high*

£200-300 **DN**

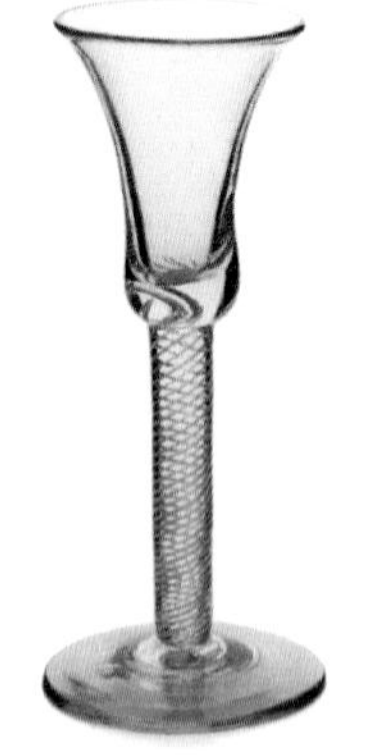

A mid-18thC air-twist wine glass, the bell bowl supported on a stem filled with spiral threads and a conical foot.

c1750 *6.5in (16.5cm) high*

£120-180 **DN**

An engraved light baluster goblet, the funnel bowl with a border of scrolling foliage, supported on an inverted baluster stem, the knop filled with bead inclusions, on a conical foot.

c1750 *7in (18cm) high*

£800-1,200 **DN**

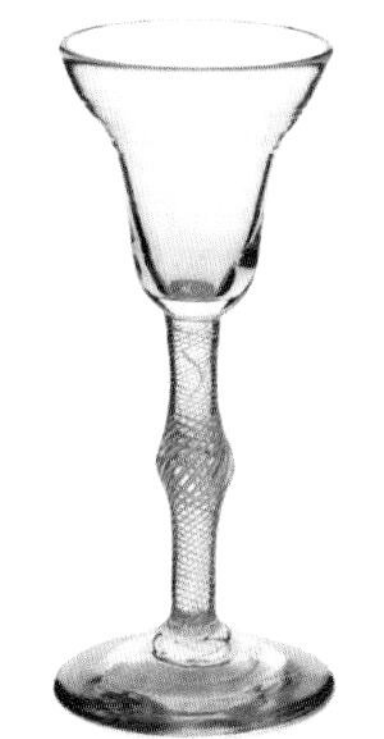

An air-twist wine glass, the pan-topped bowl supported on a stem with a swelling central knop and a conical foot.

c1750 *6.25in (16cm) high*

£300-500 **DN**

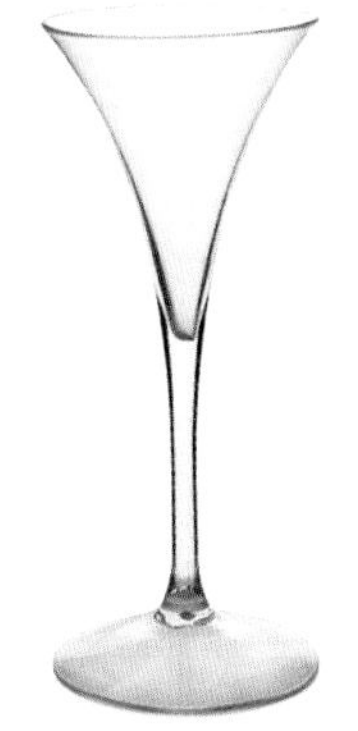

A mid-18th century plain-stemmed toasting glass, of drawn trumpet form.

c1750 *7in (18cm) high*

£200-300 **DN**

A mid-18thC air-twist wine glass of Jacobite significance, of drawn trumpet form, the stem with a tear inclusion, on a conical foot.

c1750 *6.25in (16cm) high*

£800-1,200 **DN**

A mid-18thC plain-stemmed wine glass, of drawn trumpet form, the stem with a tear inclusion, on a domed foot.

c1750 *6.75in (17cm) high*

£200-300 **DN**

A mid-18thC air-twist wine glass, the ogee bowl supported on a stem filled with spiral threads and a conical foot.

c1750 *6.25in (16cm) high*

£200-300 **DN**

A mid-18thC balustroid wine glass, the round funnel bowl supported on a knopped stem and folded conical foot.

c1750 *6in (15cm) high*

£220-280 **DN**

An air-twist wine glass, the bell bowl supported on an inverted baluster stem and conical foot.

c1750 *6.25in (16cm) high*

£400-600 **DN**

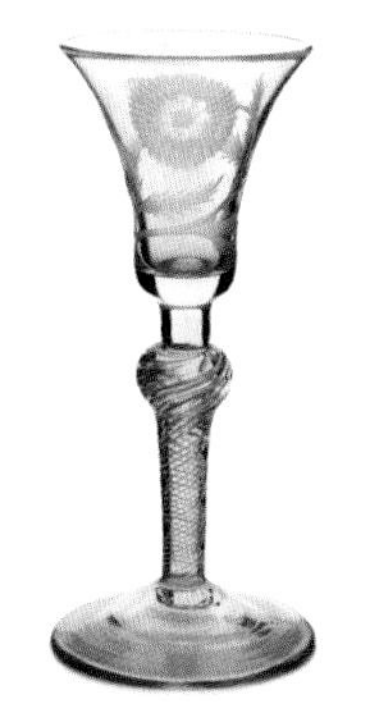

An air-twist wine glass of Jacobite significance, the thistle bowl engraved with a moth and a flower above a solid section and shoulder-knopped stem filled with spiral threads.

c1750 *6.25in (16cm) high*

£1,000-1,500 **DN**

A CLOSER LOOK AT A BALUSTER GOBLET

The arms on this glass are unidentified, but are more likely to be that of a guild, city or Dutch province than of a family.

Very early wine glasses like this one tend to be of baluster form. Due to their fragile nature and great age, there are a limited number available on today's market.

Glasses as finely engraved as this were probably made to special commission in very small quantities, further enhancing their rarity and value.

Glass is notoriously easy to restore and present as new. This piece, however, appears to be in wholly original condition save for one tiny chip.

A Dutch engraved light baluster goblet, the round funnel bowl engraved with arms depicting four lions rampant beneath a coronet and flanked by lion supporters, supported on a bobbin-knopped stem, the central knop filled with bead inclusions, on a conical foot, minute foot-rim chip.

Provenance: *Exhibited at 'Strange and Rare: 50th Anniversary of The Glass Circle' at Broadfield House Glass Museum in September 1987, and thereafter at the Pilkington Glass Museum in St. Helens, Lancs.*

c1750 *7.5in (19cm) high*

£3,000-5,000 **DN**

An air-twist wine glass, with a bucket bowl supported on a stem filled with spiral threads, on a conical foot.

c1750 *7in (17.5cm) high*

£280-320 **DN**

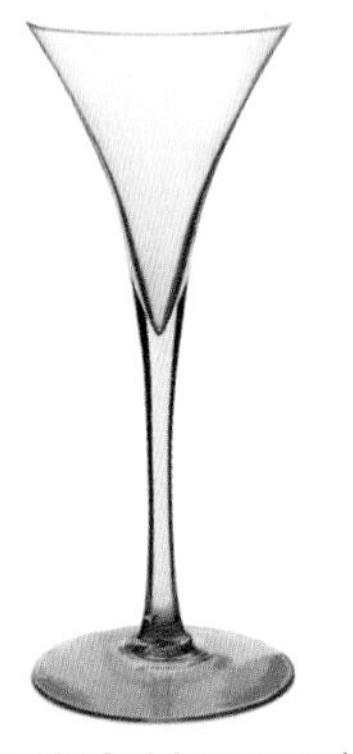

A mid-18thC plain-stemmed toasting glass, of drawn trumpet form.

c1750 *7.5in (19cm) high*

£300-500 **DN**

An air-twist wine glass, the round funnel bowl supported on a double-series stem and conical foot.

c1750 *6in (15cm) high*

£300-500 **DN**

An air-twist wine glass, the round funnel bowl with a hammered lower section, supported on a stem with multi-spiral cable, on a conical foot.

c1750 *6.75in (17cm) high*

£500-700 **DN**

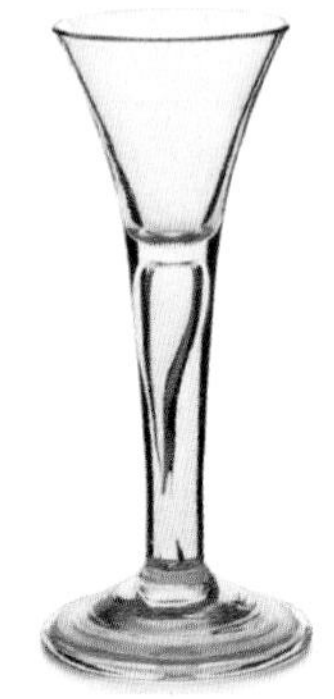

A mid-18thC plain-stemmed wine glass, of drawn trumpet form, the stem with an elongated tear, on a folded conical foot.

c1750 *6in (15.5cm) high*

£180-220 **DN**

A wine glass, with bell bowl and double-knopped, multi-spiral air-twist stem.

c1750 *6.5in (16.5cm) high*

£400-600 **JH**

A mid-18thC emerald green wine glass, the cup bowl supported on a swollen knop stem moulded with vertical flutes and a folded conical foot applied with trailed spiral ornament, chips to trailed ornament of foot.

c1750 *5in (13cm) high*

£320-380 **DN**

An emerald green wine glass, the generous ovoid bowl supported on a plain stem and a conical bowl.

c1760 *6.5in (16.5cm) high*

£200-300 **DN**

A wine glass, with tulip border and coarse incised-twist stem.

c1760 *6.5in (16.5cm) high*

£400-600 **JH**

A wine glass, with fluted ogee bowl and double-series opaque-twist stem.

c1765 *6.75in (17cm) high*

£300-400 **JH**

A firing glass, with ogee bowl, double-series opaque-twist stem and thick, heavy foot.

c1765 *4.5in (11.5cm) high*

£350-400 **JH**

An emerald green air-twist wine glass, the generous ogee bowl moulded with broad flutes, supported on a stem with a gauze core within spiral tapes, on a conical foot.

c1760 *7.5in (18.5cm) high*

£2,800-3,200 **DN**

A Beilby enamelled opaque-twist wine glass, the round funnel bowl decorated with a band of fruiting vine, supported on a double-series stem and a conical foot.

c1765 *6in (15cm) high*

£2,000-3,000 **DN**

A wine glass, with ogee bowl and double-series opaque-twist stem.

c1765 *5.5in (14cm) high*

£220-280 **JH**

A wine glass, with bell bowl and double-series opaque-twist stem.

c1765 *6.75in (17cm) high*

£220-280 **JH**

A wine glass, with ribbed round funnel bowl and double-series opaque-twist stem.

c1765 *5.75in (14.5cm) high*

£280-320 **JH**

A wine glass, with facet stem and rare cut foot.

c1765 *5.5in (14cm) high*

£280-320 **JH**

A wine glass, with pan-top bowl and single-series opaque-twist corkscrew cable stem.

c1765 *6in (15cm) high*

£400-600 **JH**

A wine glass, with fluted bowl, mixed air- and enamel-twist stem, and plain foot.

c1765 *7.5in (19cm) high*

£700-900 **JH**

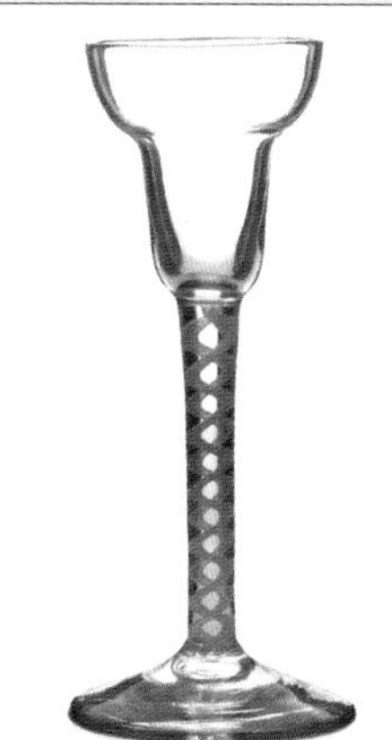

A wine glass, with ogee bowl and enamel-twist stem.

c1765 *6.25in (16cm) high*

£220-280 **JH**

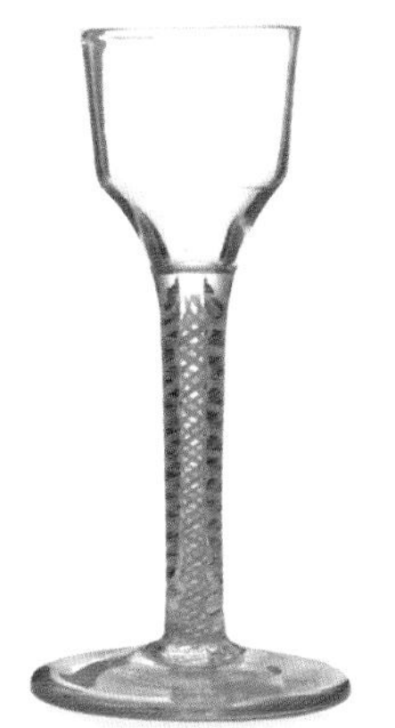

A wine glass, with fluted bowl and single-series opaque-twist stem.

c1765 *6.5in (16.5cm) high*

£300-400 **JH**

A wine glass, with honeycomb moulded bowl and double-series opaque-twist stem.

c1765 *5.75in (14.5cm) high*

£300-400 **JH**

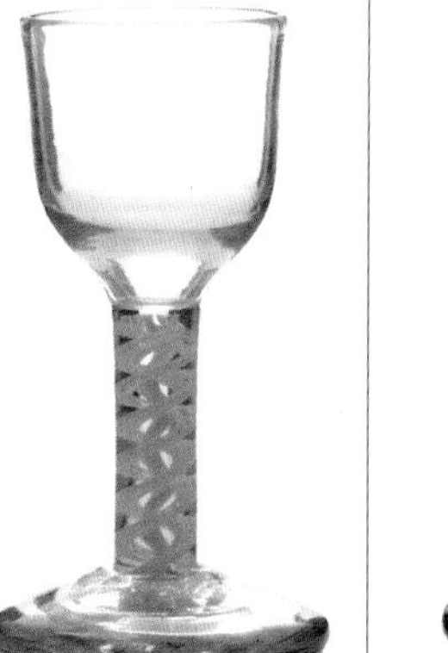

A wine glass, with drawn trumpet bowl and double-series opaque-twist stem.

c1765 *7in (17.75cm) high*

£300-400 **JH**

An opaque-twist wine glass, the ogee bowl supported on a double-series stem and conical foot.

c1770 *5.75in (14.5cm) high*

£200-300 **DN**

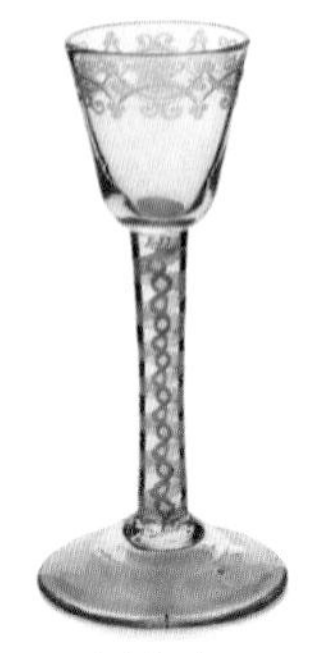

An opaque-twist wine or cordial glass, the round funnel bowl engraved with a stylized foliate band of cross-hatched ovals, the stem with a pair of spiral tapes with multi-ply spirals, on a conical foot.

c1770 *6in (15cm) high*

£400-600 **DN**

An engraved opaque-twist wine or ale glass, the ogee bowl with a hop sprig and ears of barley, supported on a double-series stem and conical foot.

c1770 *6.25in (16cm) high*

£300-500 **DN**

An opaque-twist wine glass, the bucket bowl supported on a double-series stem and a conical foot.

c1770 *5.5in (14cm) high*

£220-280 **DN**

An opaque-twist goblet, the generous ogee bowl with hammered flute lower section, on a double-series stem and conical foot.

c1770 *7.75in (19.5cm) high*

£400-600 **DN**

An emerald green wine glass, the ovoid bowl supported on a plain stem and conical foot.

c1770 *6in (15cm) high*

£200-300 **DN**

An engraved opaque-twist wine glass, the ogee bowl engraved with a band of fruiting vine, supported on a double-series stem and conical foot.

c1770 *5.75in (14.5cm) high*

£500-700 **DN**

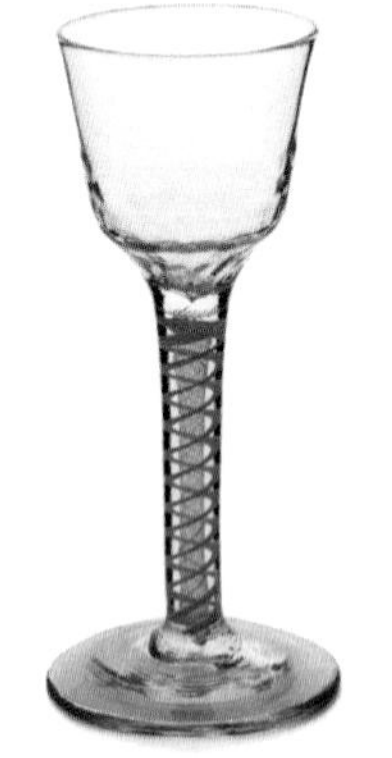

An opaque-twist wine glass, the ogee bowl with a hammered lower section, on a double-series stem and conical foot.

c1770 *6in (15cm) high*

£300-400 **DN**

An opaque-twist wine glass, the round funnel bowl supported on a double-series stem, and a conical foot.

c1770 *6in (15cm) high*

£300-400 **DN**

An opaque-twist wine glass, the round funnel bowl with hammered lower section, supported on a double-series stem and a conical foot.

c1770 *6in (15cm) high*

£400-600 **DN**

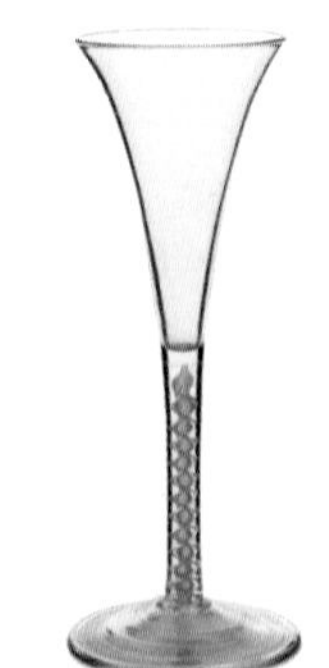

A mixed-twist wine flute, of drawn trumpet form, the stem with a gauze core within a pair of air-twist spiral threads, on a conical foot.

c1770 *7.5in (19cm) high*

£600-900 **DN**

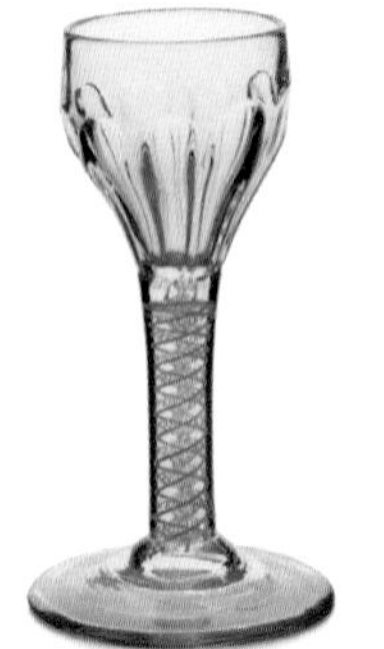

An opaque-twist wine glass, the flute-moulded ogee bowl supported on a double-series stem and conical foot.

c1770 *5.25in (13cm) high*

£400-600 **DN**

An engraved facet-stemmed wine glass, the generous ovoid bowl engraved and polished with stars and 'oxo' band swags, supported on a stem cut with diamond facets, on a conical foot.

c1780 *6in (15.5cm) high*

£250-300 **DN**

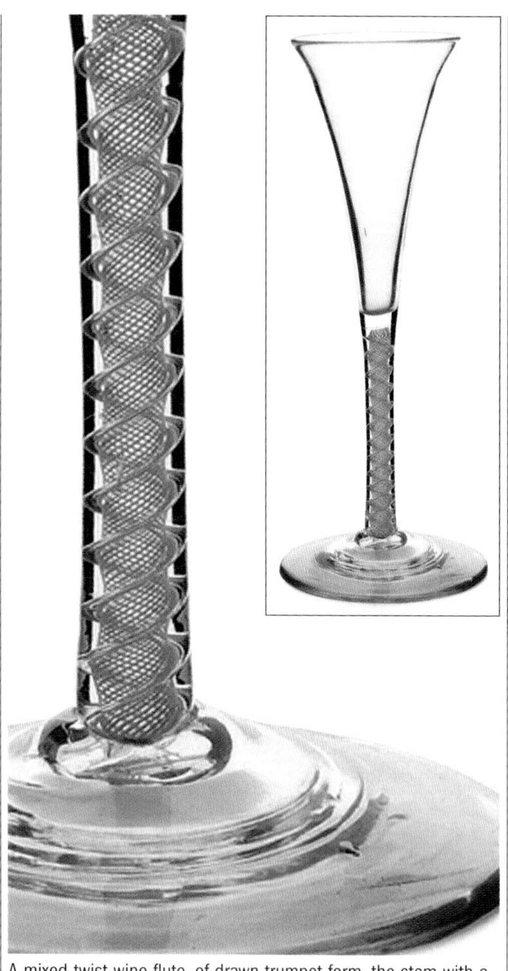

A mixed-twist wine flute, of drawn trumpet form, the stem with a gauze core within a pair of air-twist spiral threads, on a conical foot.

c1770 *7.75in (19.5cm) high*

£700-1,000 **DN**

An engraved facet-stemmed wine glass, the round funnel bowl engraved and polished with a band of fruiting vine, the waist-knopped stem cut with hexagonal facets, on a conical foot, small chips to facets of knop.

c1780 *7.5in (14cm) high*

£200-300 **DN**

A pale green tinted 'export' wine glass, the ovoid bowl supported on a knop above a hollow stem, on a conical foot.

c1780 *6in (15.5cm) high*

£100-150 **DN**

A late 18thC engraved facet-stemmed glass, the round funnel bowl decorated with floral sprigs and a bird in flight, supported on a stem cut with hexagonal facets, on a conical foot.

c1790 *5.5in (14cm) high*

£200-300 **DN**

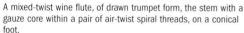

A pair of late 18thC facet-stemmed short wine glasses, each round bowl engraved and polished with an 'oxo' swag band above a scale-cut basal section, the stem cut with diamond facets, on conical foot.

c1790 *6in (15.5cm) high*

£400-600 **DN**

A late 18thC facet-stemmed wine glass, the ovoid bowl supported on a stem cut with hexagonal facets, on a conical foot.

c1790 *6.25in (16cm) high*

£100-150 **DN**

A late 18thC facet-stemmed wine glass, the round funnel bowl with a flared rim, the lower section cut and polished with a band of roundels, the waist-knop stem cut with diamond facets, on a conical stem.

c1790 *6.5in (16.5cm) high*

£300-500 **DN**

A late 18thC engraved facet-stem wine glass, the ovoid bowl decorated with ears of barley and hops, the stem with diamond facets, on a conical foot.

c1790 *5.25in (13cm) high*

£220-280 **DN**

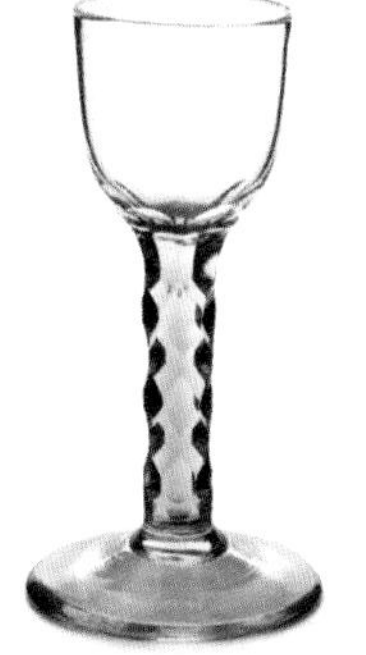

A late 18thC facet-stemmed wine glass, the ovoid bowl supported on a stem cut with hexagonal facets, on a conical foot.

c1790 *5.25in (13.5cm) high*

£120-180 **DN**

A late 18thC engraved facet-stemmed wine glass, the ogee bowl with an everted rim and decorated with stylized flowers and foliage above a petal-cut lower section, the stem with hexagonal facets, on a conical foot, minute chips to stem.

5.5in (14cm) high

£220-280 **DN**

A late 18thC facet-stemmed wine glass, the ovoid bowl engraved with sprays of rose and lily-of-the-valley, supported on a stem cut with hexagonal facets, on a conical foot.

c1790 *6in (15.5cm) high*

£200-300 **DN**

A late 18thC facet-stemmed wine glass, the ovoid bowl supported on a stem cut with hexagonal facets, on a conical foot.

c1790 *5in (12.5cm) high*

£150-200 **DN**

A wine glass, with facet-cut stem.

c1790 *6in (15cm) high*

£120-180 **JH**

A gilded amethyst wine glass.

c1850 *6in (15cm) high*

£300-400 **AL**

Two 19thC printie-cut wine glasses, engraved with fruiting vines, on plain stems with large feet.

c1840 *4.75in (12cm) high*

£15-20 each **AG**

ALE GLASSES

A mid-18th century engraved air-twist ale flute, the funnel bowl decorated with hops and barley, supported on a stem filled with spiral threads, on a conical foot.

c1750 *8in (20cm) high*

£400-600 **DN**

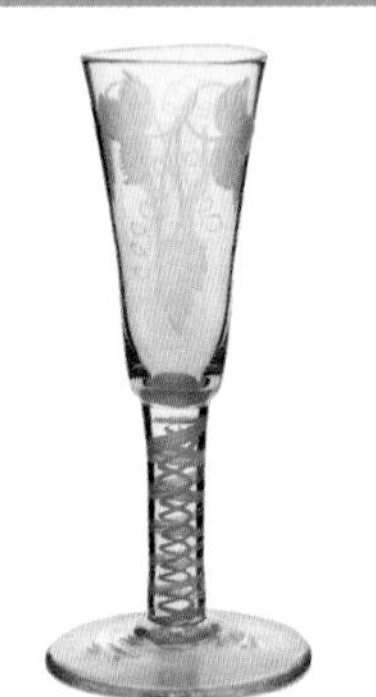

An engraved opaque-twist ale flute, the funnel bowl engraved with ears of barley and hops, supported on a double-series stem and a conical foot.

c1770 *6.75in (17.5cm) high*

£220-280 **DN**

An opaque-twist ale glass, the funnel bowl engraved with ears of barley and a stylized floral sprig, supported on a double-series stem and a conical foot.

c1770 *7.75in (19.5cm) high*

£400-600 **DN**

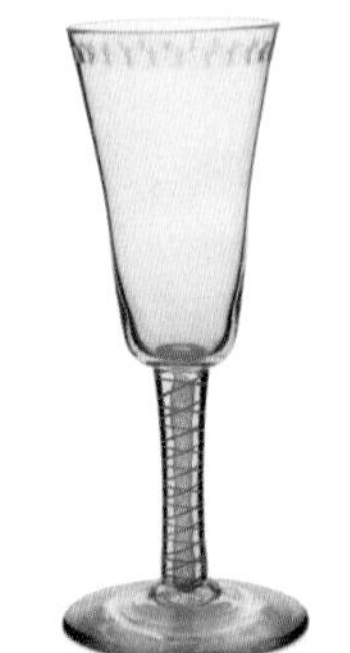

An opaque-twist ale flute, the funnel bowl cut and polished with an 'oxo' band, supported on a double-series stem, minute foot-rim chips.

c1770 *7in (18cm) high*

£220-280 **DN**

An ale glass, with centre-knopped facet-cut stem.

c1770 *7in (17.75cm) high*

£200-300 **JH**

A facet-stemmed ale glass, the funnel bowl with vertical flutes above a scale-cut lower section, supported on a stem with hexagonal facets.

c1780 *7in (18cm) high*

£400-600 **DN**

A drawn trumpet hops and barley ale glass.

c1780 *6in (15cm) high*

£70-90 **JH**

A late 18thC facet-stemmed ale flute, the funnel bowl engraved and polished with an 'oxo' band and a scale-cut basal section, the stem cut with diamond facets, on a conical foot.

c1790 *7.25in (18.5cm) high*

£300-500 **DN**

A hops and barley ale glass with knopped stem.

c1800 *5in (12.75cm) high*

£50-70 **JH**

A petal-moulded ale glass.

c1800 *4.75in (12cm) high*

£50-70 **JH**

CHAMPAGNE GLASSES

A Georgian champagne flute, with high panel-cutting, on collar and blade knop stem.

c1820 *7in (18cm) high*

£30-50 **AG**

A 19thC champagne flute, panel-cut bowl on blade knop stem.

7in (18cm) high

£30-50 **AG**

A 19thC printie-cut champagne bowl, on hollow faceted baluster stem.

5in (12.5cm) high

£10-20 **AG**

A slice-cut, hollow stem champagne glass.

c1890 *5in (12.75cm) high*

£20-30 **JH**

RUMMERS & GOBLETS

A commemorative goblet, the rounded bucket bowl with gently everted rim, engraved with flower sprays and named for "BASTIAAN KAT", on a baluster stem and 'lynn' foot.

c1760 *6.25in (16cm) high*

£500-700 **DN**

A rummer, engraved with fruiting vine on a lemon squeezer foot.

c1800 *6.5in (16.5cm) high*

£120-180 **JH**

A petal-moulded capstan-stem rummer.

c1800 *5.5in (14cm) high*

£60-90 **JH**

An early 19thC engraved commemorative rummer, depicting a Highlander or Highland Division officer standing between a barrel and a windmill, beneath the inscription "G. SMITH", on a lemon squeezer foot, small foot-rim chips.

8in (20.5cm) high

£1,500-2,000 **DN**

An early 19thC engraved commemorative rummer, the ovoid bowl with a plough above the inscription "SPEED THE PLOUGH", the reverse with monogram "FEB", supported on a short stem and moulded pedestal base.

5.25in (13.5cm) high

£320-380 **DN**

An early 19thC engraved rummer, the round funnel bowl engraved and polished with an egg and tulip band, on a moulded and stepped stem and square base.

c1810 5.75in (14.5cm) high

£120-180 **DN**

A 'Sunderland Bridge' rummer, the tapered bucket bowl engraved with a barque sailing beneath Iron Bridge, above the inscription "SUNDERLAND BRIDGE", the reverse with a square panel within foliate borders with monogram "RMH", supported on a capstan stem and conical foot.

c1820 5.75in (14.5cm) high

£400-600 **DN**

A pair of 'Sunderland Bridge' rummers, the tapered bucket bowls engraved with a brig sailing beneath Iron Bridge, above the inscription "SUNDERLAND BRIDGE", the reverse with a square panel within foliate borders with monogram "RA", supported on capstan stems and conical feet.

c1820 5.25in (13.5cm) high

£800-1,200 **DN**

A rummer, with slice- and flute-cut bucket bowl.

c1820 5in (12.5cm) high

£50-70 **JH**

A commemorative rummer, the tapered bucket bowl engraved with initials "JMC" within a wreath border, the reverse with hops and ears of barley, supported on a short annular stem and circular foot.

c1825 6.25in (16cm) high

£220-280 **DN**

A commemorative rummer, the tapered bucket bowl engraved with a rectangular panel with initials "EMG", the reverse with a rose and a thistle sprig, on a capstan stem and conical foot.

c1825 5in (13cm) high

£180-220 **DN**

A large engraved rummer, the round funnel bowl engraved with a band of swags and stars, above a fluted lower section, on a plain stem and conical foot.

c1830 7.75in (19.5cm) high

£280-320 **DN**

A CLOSER LOOK AT A MARRIAGE GOBLET

This goblet features a very fine engraving of Edinburgh Castle, done at John Ford's Edinburgh atelier.

This cup is comprised of three different colours - cobalt blue, clear and ruby. It was very expensive to produce glass in more than one colour, and so this was reserved for special commissions.

Within the hollow ballast stem is encased a silver threepence, dated 1868.

Relatively little good quality coloured glass was produced in Scotland, making this piece an unusual and valuable example.

A Victorian marriage goblet by John Ford of Edinburgh.

1868 9.5in (24cm)

£2,000-3,000 **AL**

A dimple-moulded rummer.

c1850 *6in (15cm) high*

£25-35 **JH**

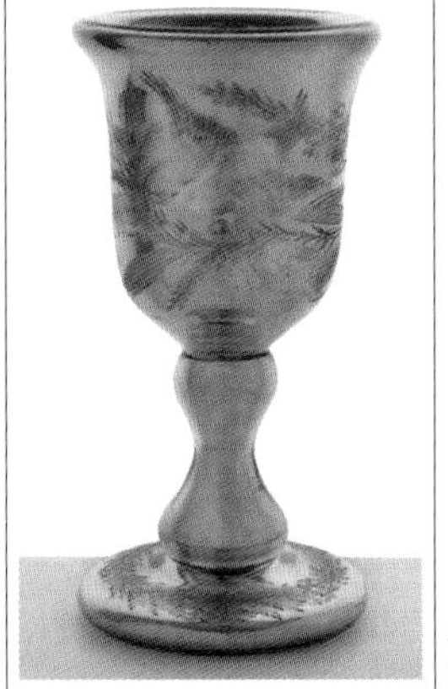

A Varnish & Co. lustre goblet.

c1850 *9in (23cm) high*

£1,500-2,000 **AL**

A 19thC 'U'-bowl tavern rummer, on faceted drop-knop stem, with gadget mark.

c1870 *5.5in (14cm) high*

£25-35 **AG**

A Victorian 'U'-bowl tavern rummer, with gadget mark.

c1870 *5.5in (14cm) high*

£25-35 **AG**

A Victorian panel-cut tavern rummer.

5.25in (8cm) high

£10-20 **AG**

A large Victorian cup and bowl tavern rummer, with gadget mark on large foot.

5in (12.5cm) high

£30-50 **AG**

A small Victorian 'U'-bowl tavern rummer.

4.25in (11cm) high

£10-20 **AG**

A small Victorian bucket-bowl tavern rummer, on large foot.

c1880 *4in (10cm) high*

£12-22 **AG**

A late 19thC heavy rummer, on elaborate dumb-bell knop stem.

6in (15cm) high

£25-35 **AG**

An engraved goblet, with rope-twist stem.

c1870 *8in (20cm) high*

£80-120 **JH**

One of a pair of goblets, acid-etched with classical scenes after Flaxman.

c1875 *8in (20cm) high*

£400-600 pair **JH**

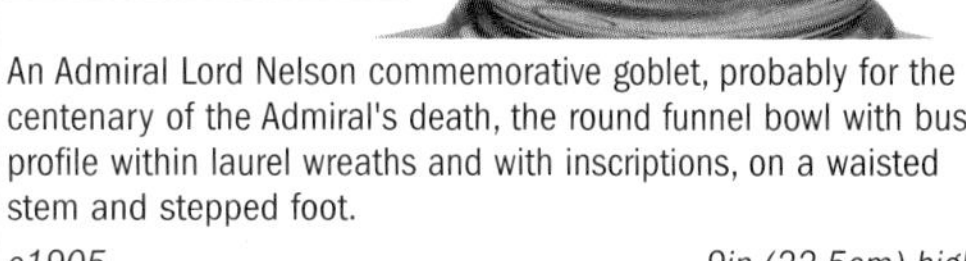

An Admiral Lord Nelson commemorative goblet, probably for the centenary of the Admiral's death, the round funnel bowl with bust profile within laurel wreaths and with inscriptions, on a waisted stem and stepped foot.

c1905 *9in (22.5cm) high*

£400-600 **DN**

TUMBLERS

A mid-18thC plain glass tumbler, of gently tapered form.

c1750 *6in (15.5cm) high*

£100-150 **DN**

An engraved commemorative tumbler, of tapered cylindrical form and fluted lower section, engraved with swagged band and the monogram "JAO".

c1800 *4.75in (12cm) high*

£220-280 **DN**

An engraved tumbler, of tapered cylindrical form with scale-cut lower section, engraved with a stylized foliate band suspending polished stars.

c1800 *5in (13cm) high*

£300-400 **DN**

An engraved commemorative tumbler, of tapered cylindrical form, engraved with a two-masted ship under sail, the reverse engraved with "GL Junr. Leeds".

c1800 *4.75in (12cm) high*

£280-320 **DN**

A pair of 19thC whisky tumblers, panel-cut with star-cut bases.

c1830 *3.75in (9.5cm) high*

£50-80 **AG**

Two of a set of ten heavy mid-19thC panel-cut whisky tumblers, hand-blown with polished pontils.

4.25in (11cm) high

£20-30 set **AG**

A pair of panel-cut and engraved tankards, probably 19thC, with loop handles, pictures of 'Spring in Karlsbad' and the 'Market Fountain in Karlsbad', inside heart cartouches.

4.75in (12cm) high

£60-90 **AG**

Two 19thC panel-cut whisky tumblers, with star-cut feet, polished rims.

3.5in (9cm) high

£20-30 each **AG**

A 19thC spa glass from Marienbad, engraved with the Cross Spring building, with panel-cut sides.

5.25in (8cm) high

£25-35 **AG**

One of a pair of Victorian tumblers, intricately acid-etched with birds and butterflies in bushes.

c1870 *4.25in (11cm) high*

£40-60 pair **AG**

A 19thC Historismus beaker, possibly by Fritz Heckert, with coat-of-arms of Prince Conty, white enamel decoration, with date 1612.

c1880 *4.5in (11.5cm) high*

£60-90 **AG**

SWEETMEATS

A baluster sweetmeat glass, the round funnel with an everted rim, supported on a beaded knop stem and a domed and folded foot.

c1740 *5in (13cm) high*

£220-280 **DN**

A mid-18thC pedestal-stemmed sweetmeat glass, the ogee bowl supported on a spirally fluted octagonal stem and a domed foot.

c1750 *7in (17.5cm) high*

£280-320 **DN**

A mid-18thC plain-stemmed sweetmeat glass, the round funnel bowl with an everted rim supported on a centrally knopped stem and a domed foot.

c1750 *6.25in (16cm) high*

£150-200 **DN**

A mid-18thC pedestal-stemmed sweetmeat glass, the ogee bowl supported on a fluted octagonal stem and a domed and folded foot.

c1750 *6in (15.5cm) high*

£220-280 **DN**

A mid-18thC pedestal-stemmed sweetmeat glass, the vertically fluted ogee bowl supported on a tapered octagonal stem and lightly pincered conical foot.

c1750 *6in (15.5cm) high*

£320-380 **DN**

A mid-18thC pedestal-stemmed sweetmeat glass, the ovoid bowl with broad vertical flutes and a scalloped rim, on a tapered octagonal stem and a domed and pincered foot.

c1750 *5.75in (15cm) high*

£320-380 **DN**

A 19thC sweetmeat dish, cut with swags and stars.

2.5in (6.5cm) high

£15-25 **AG**

MISCELLANEOUS

A mid-18thC plain-stemmed firing glass, the ogee bowl with a hammered flute lower section, the short stem on a terraced foot.

c1750 *3.5in (9cm) high*

£220-280 **DN**

A jelly glass, with panel-moulded bowl and domed foot.

c1750 *3.75in (9.5cm) high*

£80-120 **JH**

A jelly glass, with ribbed bell bowl.

c1760 *3.5in (9cm) high*

£50-70 **JH**

A dram glass, with facet-cut stem and tavern foot.

c1770 *4.25in (10.75cm) high*

£80-120 **JH**

A dram glass, with oversewn foot.

c1770 *3.75in (9.5cm) high*

£120-180 **JH**

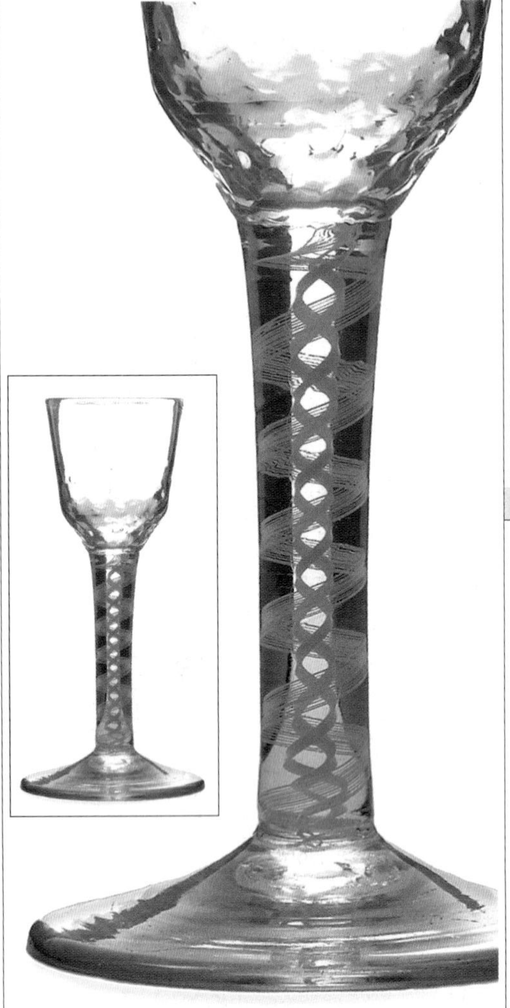

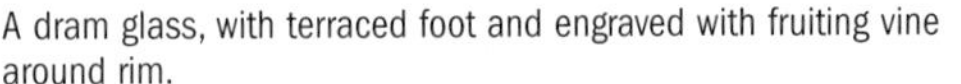

A dram glass, with terraced foot and engraved with fruiting vine around rim.

c1765 3.75in (9.5cm) high

£400-600 JH

An opaque-twist firing glass, the round funnel bowl supported on a double-series stem and a terraced foot.

c1770 4.5in (11.5cm) high

£320-380 DN

A jelly glass with flange rim.

c1770 4in (10cm) high

£30-40 JH

A hexagonal jelly glass.

c1770 3.5in (9cm) high

£80-120 JH

A celery vase, with strawberry diamond-, lens- and flute-cutting.

c1825 8.25in (21cm) high

£220-280 JH

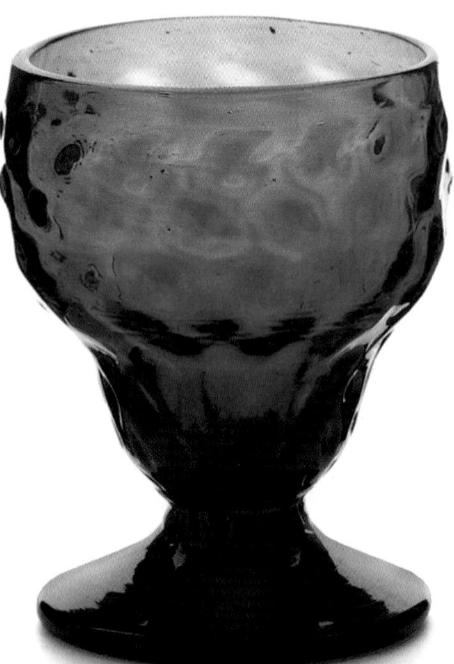

A late 18thC blue bonnet glass, the honeycomb-moulded ogee bowl supported on a conical foot.

c1790 3.25in (8cm) high

£220-280 DN

A Victorian 'U'-bowl celery vase, engraved with ferns and an acid-etched grouse in woodland, baluster knop stem.

c1875 9in (23cm) high

£80-120 AG

A pair of small 19thC flute-moulded port or liqueur glasses.

2.75in (7cm) high

£30-50 AG

JEANETTE HAYHURST

FINE GLASS

32A Kensington Church St. London W8 4HA. 0207 938 1539

A group of rare 18th Century drinking glasses.

We specialise in glass of all ages including Roman vessels, 17th, 18th, 19th century drinking glasses, cut, coloured and engraved glass for the table.

Open: Monday-Friday 10AM-5PM
Saturday 12PM-5PM

MEMBER OF THE BRITISH ANTIQUE DEALERS ASSOCIATION

JUGS

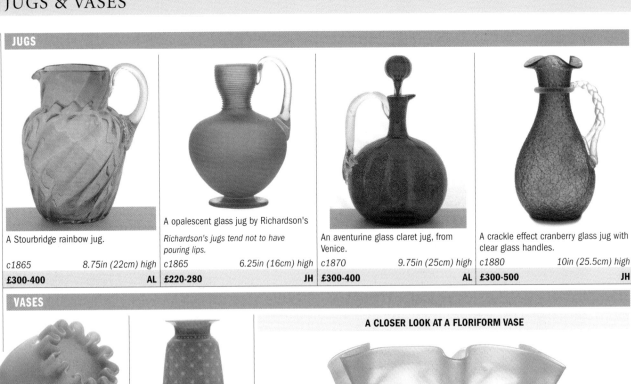

A Stourbridge rainbow jug.

c1865 8.75in (22cm) high

£300-400 **AL**

A opalescent glass jug by Richardson's

Richardson's jugs tend not to have pouring lips.

c1865 6.25in (16cm) high

£220-280 **JH**

An aventurine glass claret jug, from Venice.

c1870 9.75in (25cm) high

£300-400 **AL**

A crackle effect cranberry glass jug with clear glass handles.

c1880 10in (25.5cm) high

£300-500 **JH**

VASES

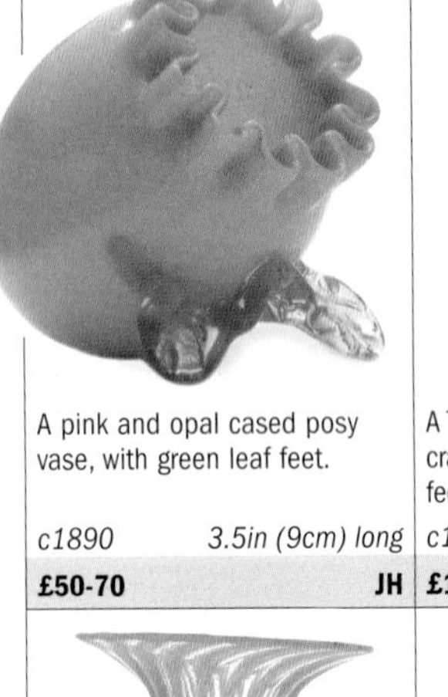

A pink and opal cased posy vase, with green leaf feet.

c1890 3.5in (9cm) long

£50-70 **JH**

A Thomas Webb white and cranberry glass vase, on three feet.

c1890 7.75in (19.5cm) high

£180-220 **JH**

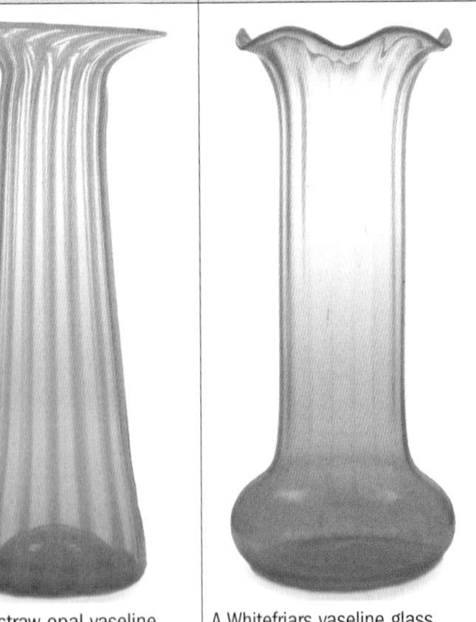

A ribbed straw opal vaseline glass vase.

c1890 10in (25.5cm) high

£150-180 **JH**

A Whitefriars vaseline glass vase.

c1890 12.5in (31.75cm) high

£200-300 **JH**

A CLOSER LOOK AT A FLORIFORM VASE

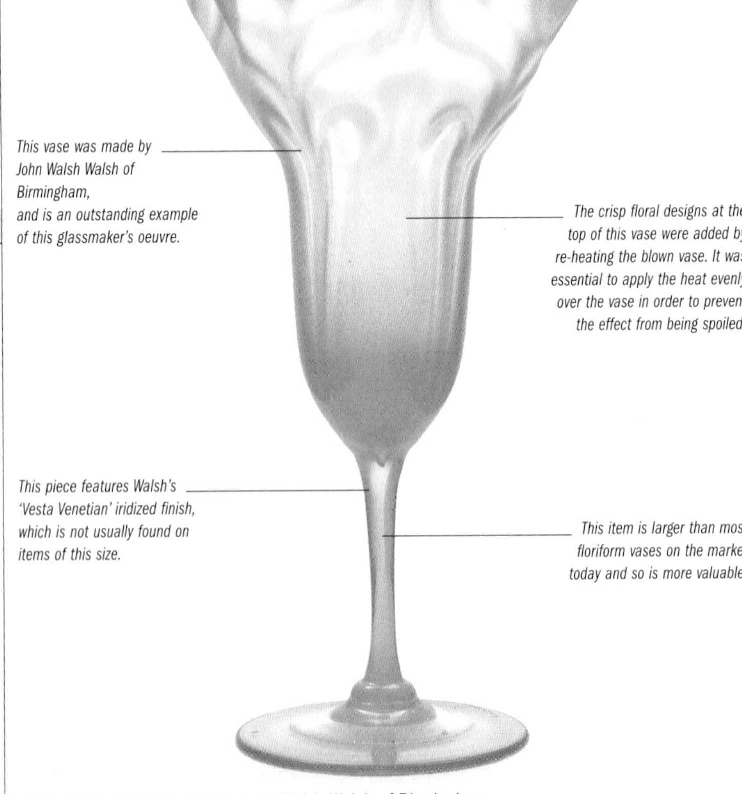

This vase was made by John Walsh Walsh of Birmingham, and is an outstanding example of this glassmaker's oeuvre.

The crisp floral designs at the top of this vase were added by re-heating the blown vase. It was essential to apply the heat evenly over the vase in order to prevent the effect from being spoiled.

This piece features Walsh's 'Vesta Venetian' iridized finish, which is not usually found on items of this size.

This item is larger than most floriform vases on the market today and so is more valuable.

A late 19thC floriform vase by John Walsh Walsh of Birmingham.

12.5in (31.5cm) high

£500-700 **JH**

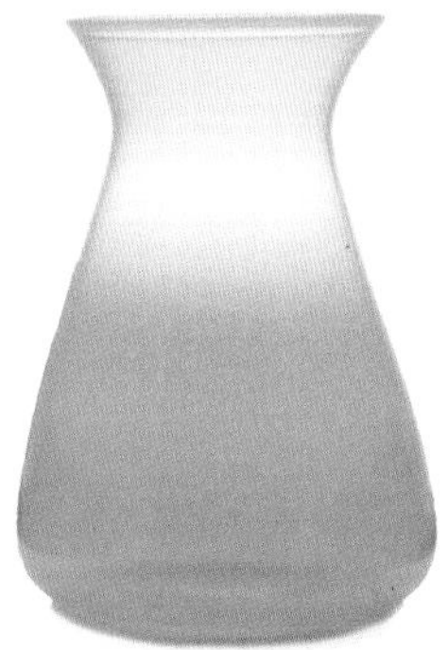

A late 19thC James Powell for Whitefriars vaseline glass vase.

7.5in (19cm) high

£120-180 **JH**

A glass vase, yellow with white trailed feathering.

c1890 *5in (12.5cm) high*

£120-180 **JH**

An olive green glass vase.

c1890 *4.5in (11.5cm) high*

£50-80 **JH**

An opal over blue vase, with applied leaf decoration.

c1890 *4in (10cm) high*

£40-60 **JH**

A green glass vase, with a blue trailed snake.

c1900 *4.75in (12cm) high*

£50-70 **JH**

BOWLS & TAZZAS

A pedestal-stemmed tazza, the galleried circular dish supported on an inverted baluster stem of fluted form, on a folded conical foot.

c1750 *9in (22.5cm) diam*

£200-300 **DN**

A pedestal-stemmed tazza, the galleried circular dish on a broad spirally fluted stem and a domed and folded foot.

c1790 *10.5in (26.5cm) diam*

£280-320 **DN**

An Irish canoe-shaped cut pedestal bowl, possibly Cork, with a serrated rim above a lozenge band, on an inverted baluster stem and moulded gadroon lemon squeezer foot, small polished areas to the rim.

c1800 *9in (23cm) wide*

£1,000-1,500 **DN**

An Irish cut pedestal bowl with turnover rim, the rim cut with a diamond band, the bowl with a central faceted band, on a knopped stem and square lemon squeezer foot.

c1800 *10.75in (27cm) wide*

£800-1,200 **DN**

An Irish cut pedestal bowl with turnover rim, the rim cut with three lozenge-fluted bands, the bowl with a central three-strand lozenge band, on a knopped stem and square lemon squeezer foot, minute foot-rim chips.

c1800 *12in (30cm) wide*

£1,000-1,500 **DN**

A cut-glass footed bowl.

c1825 *5in (12.75cm) high*

£220-280 **JH**

A cut-glass salt, with scalloped rim.

c1825 *3in (7.5cm) diam*

£25-35 **JH**

An oval cut-glass bowl.

c1825 *10in (25.5cm) long*

£80-120 **JH**

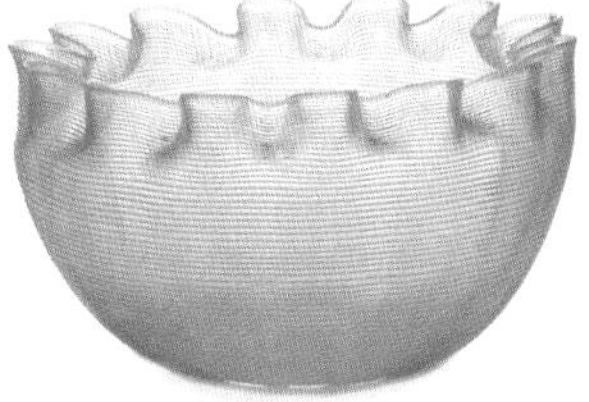

A blue and opal threaded bowl, with frilled rim.

c1880 *5cm (12.5cm) diam*

£80-120 **JH**

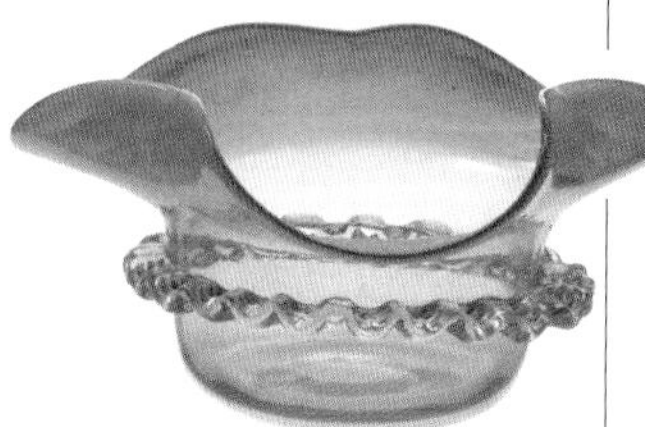

A green and ruby opalescent bowl.

c1890 *5.5in (14cm) diam*

£80-120 **JH**

A Powell feather pattern bowl.

c1900 *4in (10cm) diam*

£80-120 **JH**

One of a set of six scallop-moulded finger bowls, with intaglio engraving of swags and bunches of grapes.

c1925 *4.25in (11cm) diam*

£280-320 set **JH**

Two of a set of six bowls on stands, pink and gold lustre, with crimped and threaded decoration.

5.25in (8cm) diam

£320-380 set **AG**

A CLOSER LOOK AT A CRANBERRY BOWL

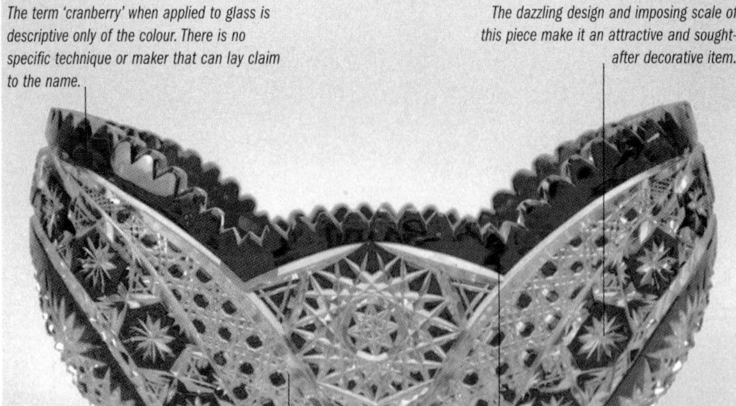

The term 'cranberry' when applied to glass is descriptive only of the colour. There is no specific technique or maker that can lay claim to the name.
The dazzling design and imposing scale of this piece make it an attractive and sought-after decorative item.
The cranberry glass is used as an overlay here, with the clear glass underneath showing through where it has been cut.
Glass of this colour was originally made using gold, although this was eventually replaced by copper and other agents.

A cranberry cut to clear bowl, heavily cut 'Hobb Star' decoration with scalloped edge, minor rim roughage, otherwise excellent condition.

12in (30.5cm) long

£1,500-2,000 **JDJ**

BOHEMIAN GLASS

A Bohemian goblet, engraved with a stag in an architectural landscape.

c1680 *9in (22.5cm) high*

£800-1,200 **FIS**

A Bohemian goblet, engraved with foliage, vine, grain and inscriptions, green and rubi-flash bands in stem, chip to lip.

c1700 *8.5in (21cm) high*

£700-1,000 **FIS**

A Bohemian goblet, depicting a battle scene, of baluster form with faceted cup, on a conical foot.

c1730 *7.25in (18cm) high*

£3,000-4,000 **FIS**

An 18thC Bohemian 'apostle' goblet, decorated with oval medallions depicting the twelve apostles, inscribed "MD".

10in (25cm) high

£700-1,000 **FIS**

A Bohemian amber glass goblet, with scenes of the city of Aachen, inscribed "Elsienbrunn bei Aachen', stepped rim.

c1840 *7in (17.5cm) high*

£600-900 **FIS**

A Bohemian yellow glass goblet, with scenes of the river Rhine, stepped rim.

c1840 *6in (14cm) high*

£300-400 **FIS**

A tall Bohemian clear and amber glass cup with scenes of the river Rhine, signed.

c1845 *18in (27cm) high*

£500-700 **FIS**

A Bohemian red glass beaker, with gilded leaf pattern and six medallions engraved with scenes of the city of Salzbrunn, gilded rim, dated.

1845 5.75in (14.5cm) high

£500-700 **FIS**

A late 19thC north Bohemian goblet with a portrait of Karl VI, inscribed "CAROL VI DGRISACHIHBREX".

12in (30cm) high

£600-900 **FIS**

A Bohemian ruby-flashed and clear goblet, the thistle-shaped bowl with alternate flashed and clear flutes, with a shaped rectangular raised panel engraved with figures in a landscape, on a faceted knop stem and scalloped rim foot, some minute chips.

c1875 6.5in (16.5cm) high

£220-280 **DN**

A Bohemian clear and colour-flashed goblet, the round bowl with a pink-flashed oval panel engraved with a pair of galloping horses, the reverse with an oval amber-flashed panel cut with concentric circles and engraved panels of flowers, on a fluted stem and shaped foot, minute chips.

c1875 6.5in (16.5cm) high

£180-220 **DN**

A Bohemian painted and parcel-gilt cut glass large goblet, finely painted with a portrait of a gentleman wearing a military medal above a laurel wreath, with a gilt rim and German inscription on reverse, dated.

1905 13.5in (34.5cm) high

£300-400 **S&K**

A set of 20thC engraved Bohemian glasses, comprising a clear glass decanter in the form of a horn and a set of six wine glasses, the decanter with pewter cover and engraved with a stag in woodland, the glasses with clear bowls and ruby stems, engraved with foliage.

Decanter 10.5in (26.5cm) high

£180-220 set **S&K**

A Bohemian beaker, with associated cover.

c1700 10.5in (26cm) high

£1,500-2,000 **FIS**

An early Bohemian flared beaker.

5.25in (13cm) high

£400-600 **AL**

A Bohemian glass tankard with pewter mount, depicting a woman with a purple cape, flower bouquets, restored, on a pewter base, signed "JPJ".

c1740 9.25in (23cm) high

£800-1,200 **FIS**

An enamelled Bohemian overlay beaker, purple cut to clear glass, engraved with floral motifs and birds, with a gilded rim.

c1830 5.25in (13cm) high

£600-900 **FIS**

A Bohemian beaker, engraved with allegorical scenes, from northern Bohemia.

c1830 5.5in (14cm) high

£1,200-1,800 **FIS**

A Carlsbad Bohemian two-colour flared beaker.

c1835 6.25in (16cm) high

£500-800 **AL**

A Bohemian beaker with cover, depicting the baptism of Jesus, from northern Bohemia.
1836 7.75in (19.5cm) high
£500-700 **FIS**

A Bohemian double overlay beaker, with blue glass and enamel overlay cut to clear glass, with oval roundels enclosing polychrome enamelled flower sprays, insects and birds, gilded rim.
c1840 4.5in (11.5cm) high
£1,000-1,500 **FIS**

A Bohemian beaker with a male portrait, Karlsbad, signed.
c1850 5.5in (14cm) high
£2,200-2,800 **FIS**

A very rare Masonic double overlay Bohemian beaker, inscribed with lodge number.
c1860 6.25in (16cm) high
£1,000-1,500 **AL**

A 20thC Bohemian white, blue and clear overlay glass beaker, painted with a full-length portrait of Maria Theresa, the reverse depicting the Schonbrun Palace, the sides and base with roses and circlets.
5in (7.5cm) high
£120-180 **S&K**

A Bohemian Iranian glass decanter, with stopper.
c1840 13in (33cm) high
£300-400 **AL**

A Bohemian cranberry glass claret jug with cast pewter mounts, stopper and base.
13in (33cm) high
£1,200-1,800 **JDJ**

A Bohemian decanter with stopper and beaker, opaline glass decorated with branches and flowers in silver.
Decanter 10.5in (26cm) high
£600-900 **FIS**

A pair of Bohemian flash overlay decanters, with engraved Oriental scenic decoration, sterling silver tops and matching overlay stoppers.
14in (35.5cm) high
£180-220 **JDJ**

A CLOSER LOOK AT A BOHEMIAN BOTTLE

The gold and silver raised gilding on this bottle is an indication its high quality.

The quality of this piece is far higher than anything that was produced in the Middle East at the time. Few export pieces have survived in this region, making it more valuable.

This bottle has an amethyst band over the green glass body. Dual colour glass is more difficult and expensive to make than single colour.

This frieze has Persian motifs, designed to increase the appeal of this bottle to the Middle Eastern export market.

A very rare Bohemian overlay bottle for the Turkish or Islamic market.
c1870 10.25in (26cm) high
£3,000-5,000 **AL**

A late 19thC Bohemian engraved glass drinks set, comprising a panel-cut decanter and eight panel-cut tapering tumblers, each finely engraved with a stag hunt scene.

Decanter 10in (25.5cm) high

£320-380 **S&K**

A Bohemian coloured cut-glass vase, by Egermann.

c1835 *9.5in (24cm) high*

£400-600 **AL**

A north Bohemian milk glass vase, on a round base with a trumpet-shaped neck, gilded foot and rim.

c1870 *8.75in (22cm) high*

£500-800 **FIS**

A late 19thC Bohemian green glass overlaid vase and cover, decorated with alternate panels of flowers and diamond-cutting on a ground decorated with gilt foliage and dots.

16.5in (41cm) high

£2,000-3,000 **WW**

A late 19thC or early 20thC Bohemian overlaid and enamelled glass vase, in white cut to clear and ruby glass, painted with colourful flowers, gilt rim.

10in (25.5cm) high

£120-180 **S&K**

A Bohemian vase with floral engraved design, Austrian.

c1905 *10.5in (26.5cm) high*

£100-200 **MW**

OTHER GLASS

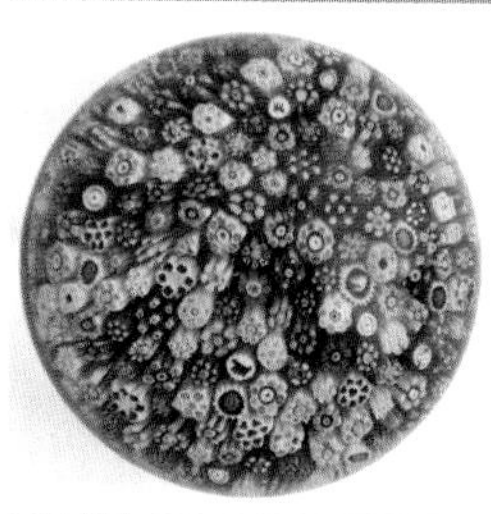

A Baccarat multi-cane millefiori paperweight, inscribed "B1848" on diamond-cut base.

1848 *2.5in (6.5cm) diam*

£600-900 **FIS**

A St. Louis French crystal paperweight, fuchsia encased in clear glass, pentagon form, with paper label.

3in (7.5cm) diam

£120-180 **AAC**

A Victorian green 'metallic' glass witches' ball.

c1875 *4.75in (12cm) diam*

£50-70 **JHD**

A Victorian glass witches' ball with red swirl.

c1880 *4.75in (12cm) diam*

£80-120 **JHD**

A large stained and leaded Victorian window, with a dancing woman holding a tambourine over her head, the background glass is frosted crackle glass and is stained with flowers on both the front and back to give a three-dimensional effect, the bordered design is set with faceted jewels.

37.5in (95.5cm) high

£4,000-6,000 **JDJ**

A late 19thC model of a hand bell, the clear handle fixed to a ruby bell.

c1890 *9in (23cm) high*

£100-150 **DN**

A late 19thC model of a hand bell, the uranium yellow handle with opaque white finial and fixed to a ruby bell with opaque white rim.

10.5in (27cm) high

£100-150 **DN**

A late 19thC model of a hand bell, the clear handle fixed to a blue bell.

c1890 10.25in (26cm) high

£100-150 DN

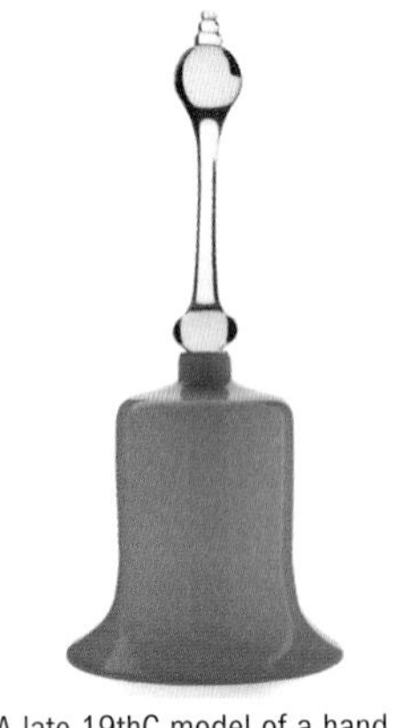

A late 19thC model of a hand bell, the clear handle fixed to an opaque white bell.

11in (28cm) high

£100-150 DN

A Victorian cranberry glass epergne, the central and three flanking trumpet vases with frilled wavy rims and trailed with clear glass spirals above the fluted circular underdish.

13.5in (34cm) high

£300-400 CHEF

A large Venetian ruby glass goblet and matching dish, decorated with wide gilt bands of Cupid and Psyche amidst scrolling foliage, the foot inscribed 'Amore E Psiche Giovanni da San Giovanni'.

c1900 14.25in (36.5cm) high

£400-600 WW

A rare 17thC alpine German purple glass powder flask.

6in (15cm) high

£1,200-1,800 FIS

An early 18thC Georgian linen smoother, with seven bobbin knop stem.

4.5in (11.5cm) high

£100-150 AG

A rare and unusual late 18thC Georgian 'peg' lamp, made to fit into a candlestick.

6in (15cm) high

£50-70 AG

A late 18thC Georgian triangular bodied lamp, on pedestal foot with loop handle and pierced thumb rest.

3in (7.5cm) high

£120-180 AG

A mid-18thC Georgian 'lace makers' oil lamp, on heavy foot.

4in (10cm) diam

£30-50 AG

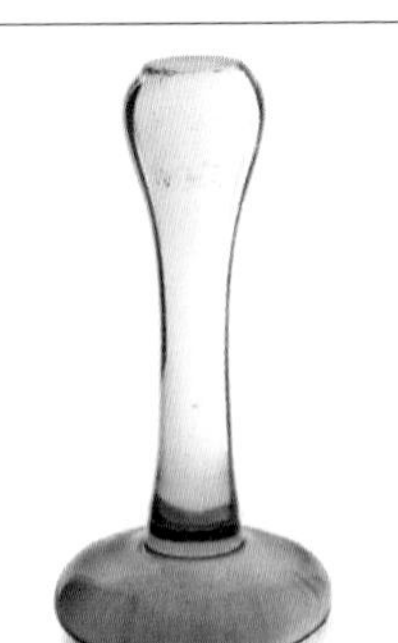

A 19thC mushroom-shaped glass muller.

5in (12.5cm) high

£30-40 AG

A 19thC wythern glass funnel.

6in (15cm) high

£15-25 AG

A Georgian 'lace makers' lamp, with spherical oil reserve and drip tray, hollow teardrop baluster stem, conical foot.

c1800 8.5in (21.5cm) high

£150-200 AG

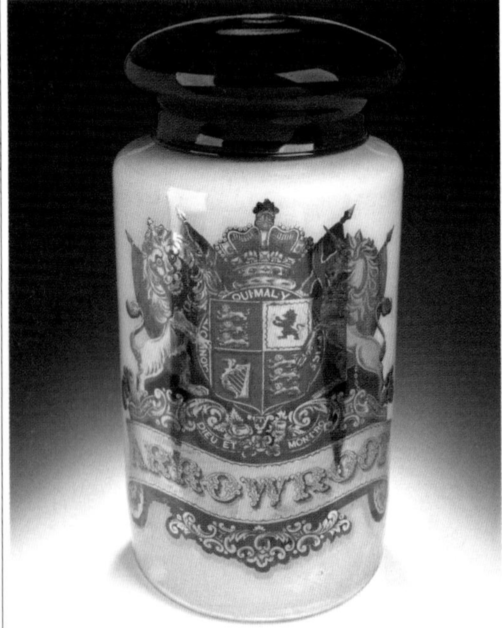

A large 19thC glass pharmacist's drug jar, with blue mushroom-shaped cover over cylindrical body with painted gilt scroll banner inscribed "Arrowroot", with lion, unicorn and crown insignia surmounted by motto and heraldic shield.

27in (70cm) high

£600-900 L&T

SILVER

Holloware (bowls, pitchers, jugs etc) is currently commanding a higher price by weight than flatware (cutlery, utensils etc), which is more often bought by those who are newer to the market. Within the holloware sector, items that fit well into contemporary homes and lifestyles are faring particularly well; picture frames, mirrors and vinaigrettes are commanding more interest than tea sets and bed pans.

Buyers are becoming more interested in the historical context of their silver, so pieces that have a good provenance or a strong link with a historical figure will attract a premium, sometimes in spite of the quality of the silver itself. An armorial mark that links a piece of silver to a well-known family will have a significant effect on its value. The market for Irish silver is busy, thanks in no small part to the US interest in Irish history but more particularly due to the current boom in the Irish economy. Another regional sector attracting greater market interest than in recent years is Scottish provincial silver, with prices for the best examples rising steadily as demand increases.

As always, any marks should be clear and legible to get the best prices, and items with a demonstrable link with a respected silversmith will attract a premium. Rare or unusual designs are valued more highly than the mundane. Remember that silver with unsightly staining, holes or bends will not fare as well on the market. Buyers will invariably overlook these pieces in favour of examples in better condition.

Trevor Kyle, Lyon & Turnbull

BASKETS

A George III silver sweetmeat basket by Edward Aldridge of London, with chased foliate and pierced decoration on an oval body with beaded edge and shell-clasped decoration, panelled, pierced and engraved base with a lion rampant crest, all on a pierced and chased C-scroll frame with scroll feet.

1770 *6.5in (16cm) wide*

£1,200-1,800 **L&T**

A George III silver cream pail, by Richard Meach of London, of tapering form with a lattice swing handle and bead borders, pierced and embossed around the sides with cranes and a parrot amongst foliage, with a vacant oval cartouche and maker's mark.

1775 *2.25in (5.5cm) high*

£350-450 **WW**

A George III silver cake basket, by William Plummer of London, with a pierced swing handle, the body of shaped oval outline with embossed beaded swirls and a cast border of flowers and gadrooning, the sides pierced with reserves of diaper work, scrolls and ovolo motifs, stamped with the mark "DESPREZ", possibly a retailer.

1768 *14in (35.5cm) long*

£1,800-2,200 **WW**

A late 18thC Irish silver sugar bowl, possibly by William Bond of Dublin, of navette form, the body embossed and chased with flowers below a bail handle, indistinct date mark.

8in (20.5cm) long

£400-600 **CHEF**

A George III silver swing handled sugar basket, by Peter and Ann Bateman of London, with a pedestal foot, reeded borders and gilt interior, engraved with a crest and coat of arms.

1791 *6.75in (17cm) wide*

£1,000-1,500 **WW**

A George III silver cake basket, by 'WK' of London, of lobed oval form with chased C-scroll and floral border, pierced and chased handle, engraved with a crest, motto and initials, on a lobed foot.

1800 *11.25in (28cm) wide*

£220-280 **L&T**

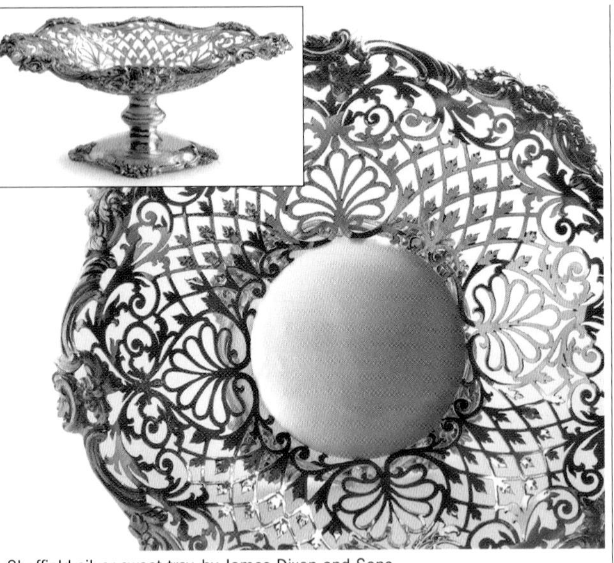

A Sheffield silver sweet tray, by James Dixon and Sons.

1906 *3.25in (8.5cm) high*

£380-420 **JBS**

A London silver basket, by Jackson and Fullerton.

1911 *7.5in (19cm) high*

£800-1,200 **JBS**

BOWLS

A late 17thC quaich of traditional form, with simple incised simulated staves and banded withies, the lugs engraved with betrothal initials "MN" and "IM", indistinct date mark.

c1690 *2.75in (7cm) diam*

£1,500-2,000 **L&T**

A 17thC two-handled parcel gilt sweetmeat dish, maker's mark "W" over "SS", indistinct date mark.

6in (15cm) wide

£700-1,000 **WW**

An early 18thC silver quaich, unmarked, the lug bearing child's teething marks, and engraved "A" and "Mc".

2.25in (5.5cm) diam

£200-250 **L&T**

A George I silver porringer, by James Goodwin of London, embossed with a ropework girdle and swirl fluting around the lower body, resting on a small flared foot, scratched on the base with the initials "I.F".

1718 *3.25in (8.5cm) high*

£700-900 **WW**

A mid-18thC Scottish silver quaich, the shaped lugs with engraved border, engraved crudely to the underside, "D MT, I MP", on a spool foot.

5.5in (13.5cm) wide

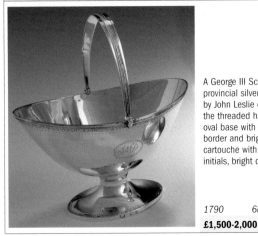

£600-900 **L&T**

A George III Scottish provincial silver sugar bowl, by John Leslie of Aberdeen, the threaded handle onto an oval base with threaded border and bright cut detail, cartouche with engraved initials, bright cut oval foot.

1790 *6in (15cm) wide*

£1,500-2,000 **L&T**

A George III Scottish provincial silver sugar bowl, by Robert Dickson of Perth, of inverted vase form, with beaded border, simple circular foot with beaded edge and engraved initials.

1790 *4.75in (12cm) diam*

£4,000-6,000 **L&T**

A Scottish George III silver quaich, by J. MacDonald of Edinburgh, the lug handles engraved "AMcL" and "RMcL".

1802 *2.75in (7cm) diam*

£700-1,000 **L&T**

A Victorian silver porringer by Wakely and Wheeler of London, of plain waisted form, indistinct date mark.

3in (7.75cm) wide

£70-100 **CHEF**

A London silver 'Britannia' bowl, by the Goldsmiths and Silversmiths Co. Ltd.

1905 *2.5in (6.5cm) high*

£300-400 **JBS**

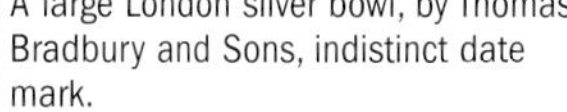

A large London silver bowl, by Thomas Bradbury and Sons, indistinct date mark.

11.75in (30cm) diam

£1,800-2,200 **JBS**

A Scottish George III silver quaich, of traditional form, with one lug, engraved crests and mottos for MacPherson, MacIntosh and others.

1800 *2.75in (7cm) diam*

£800-1,200 **L&T**

BOXES

A William III silver snuff box, by John Tongue of Birmingham, of rectangular shape, chequer engraved, the cover with scrolled cartouche, initialled, indistinct date mark.

2.75in (7cm) wide

£120-180 **CHEF**

A fine and rare Jacobite snuff box, with partial pseudo marks, possibly Dutch, the domed oval lid finely engraved and emblematic to the Stuarts, the interior with a concealed hinged panel cast and chased with dogs gnawing at bones.

The box is engraved with emblems that relate directly to the Stuarts. Presumably the intention, if the box can be dated on stylistic grounds to about 1700, is to imply that what happened to Charles II would probably apply to James II. This box would have belonged to an ardent Jacobite.

c1700 *3.25in (8cm) wide*

£10,000-15,000 **L&T**

A George III mounted cowrie shell snuff box, with an engraved coat of arms on the cover, probably provincial, possibly by John Walker of Newcastle, no date mark.

c1770 *3.25in (8cm) long*

£550-560 **WW**

A George III silver bougie box, by Susannah Barker of London, of circular form, with sliding cutter, bright cut engraved border to the lid with concealed hinge and swivel handle, engraved with a crest.

1785 *2in (5cm) diam*

£1,200-1,800 **L&T**

A fine George III silver mounted cowrie shell snuff mull, with marks for Perth, by William Ritchie, the mount finely engraved with a coat of arms and motto for Dick, Baronet of Prestonfield, the hinge well concealed in the pattern of bright cut work, marked "WR" and with two double-headed eagles.

1795 *3in (7.5cm) long*

£3,500-4,000 **L&T**

A Dublin silver snuff box, made by W. M. Law.

1821 *2in (5cm) diam*

£700-900 **JBS**

A Birmingham silver snuff box, inscribed "Presented to Brother William Graham Commander of the Ship Anglo-Saxon".

1860 *3in (7.5cm) long*

£400-600 **JBS**

A silver heart-shaped box with an embossed lady's head with a grinning, devilish expression, hallmark for London.

1889 *2.5in (6.5cm) wide*

£200-300 **GS**

A late 19thC Continental Victorian circular box and cover, engraved "To Stephen Ronan from Richard Everard Webster Attorney General Parnell Commission 25 December 1889".

1889 *2.25in (5.5.cm) diam*

£350-450 **L&T**

A pair of late Victorian silver pin boxes by Gibson and Langman of London, each of oval shape, with fluted body and cover, indistinct date mark.

4.5in (11cm) diam

£100-150 **CHEF**

A late 19thC Continental snuff box, oblong cushion-shaped and decorated in the mid-18thC manner, with chased sides and classical figures in a wooded glade on the cover, the gilt interior inscribed "Nicholas Peter Hawtrey from Radclyffe Hall and Una Troubridge", with English import marks for London.

1899 *3.25in (8cm) long*

£250-350 **WW**

A London silver snuff box, in the shape of a brazil nut.

1896 *2in (5cm) long*

£280-320 **JBS**

A George III silver vinaigrette by Philips and Robinson of London, of oval shape with bright cut edge, grille unmarked.

1797 *1.5in (4.5cm) long*

£300-400 **CHEF**

A George III silver vinaigrette by Matthew Linwood of Birmingham, shaped as a scallop shell, marked on inner rim only, grille decoratively pierced.

1808 *1in (2.5cm) long*

£180-220 **CHEF**

A George III silver vinaigrette, by Joseph Ash of London, of plain rectangular shape, bright cut engraved, initialled, foliate grille.

1812 *1.25in (3.5cm) long*

£150-200 **CHEF**

A silver vinaigrette, by Thomas Willmore of Birmingham, with swirling decoration, reeded sides and engraved cartouche.

1823 *1.5in (4cm) wide*

£300-350 **GS**

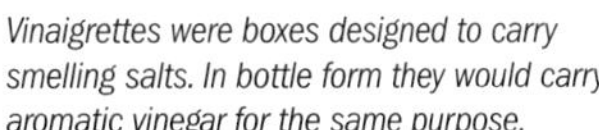

A Birmingham silver vinaigrette, inscribed "A. Gordon".

Vinaigrettes were boxes designed to carry smelling salts. In bottle form they would carry aromatic vinegar for the same purpose.

1828 *1.75in (4.5cm) long*

£600-650 **JBS**

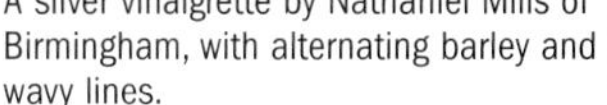

A silver vinaigrette by Nathaniel Mills of Birmingham, with alternating barley and wavy lines.

1836 *1.75in (4.5cm) wide*

£300-350 **GS**

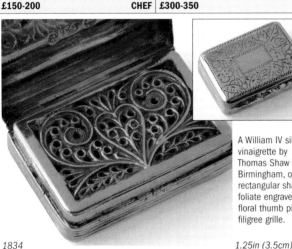

A William IV silver vinaigrette by Thomas Shaw of Birmingham, of rectangular shape, foliate engraved, floral thumb piece, filigree grille.

1834 *1.25in (3.5cm) long*

£200-250 **CHEF**

An early Victorian parcel gilt vinaigrette, by Nathaniel Mills of Birmingham, oblong with waisted sides and pricked borders, the cover engraved centrally with the all-seeing eye emblem of the Odd Fellows and the inscription "May it watch over you", flanked by foliage and a raised floral border.

1837 *1.25in (3cm) long*

£280-320 **WW**

An early Victorian vinaigrette, by Nathaniel Mills of Birmingham, of shaped oval outline, engraved on the cover with sailing boats in the bay of a small seaside town against a coastal backdrop, with promenading figures.

1846 *1.75in (4.5cm) long*

£380-420 **WW**

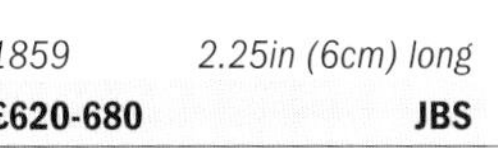

A Birmingham silver vinaigrette.

1859 *2.25in (6cm) long*

£620-680 **JBS**

A Victorian silver vinaigrette, by C. H. Cheshire of Birmingham, of oval shape with serpentine edge, engine-turned diaper band within a floral border, foliate pierced grille, suspension ring.

1868 *1.5in (4.5cm) long*

£180-220 **CHEF**

A Victorian silver gilt vinaigrette by George Unite of Birmingham, of rectangular cushion shape, serpentine edged, with foliate pierced grille and suspension ring, indistinct date mark.

1.25in (3.5cm) long

£120-150 **CHEF**

A Victorian novelty mounted glass scent bottle or vinaigrette in the form of a champagne bottle, by S. Mordan and Co., with a hinged cover on the base concealing the vinaigrette and a simulated 'foiled' neck and wired cork screw cap, with applied registration lozenge, incised marks.

c1870 *5in (12.5cm) high*

£2,500-3,000 **WW**

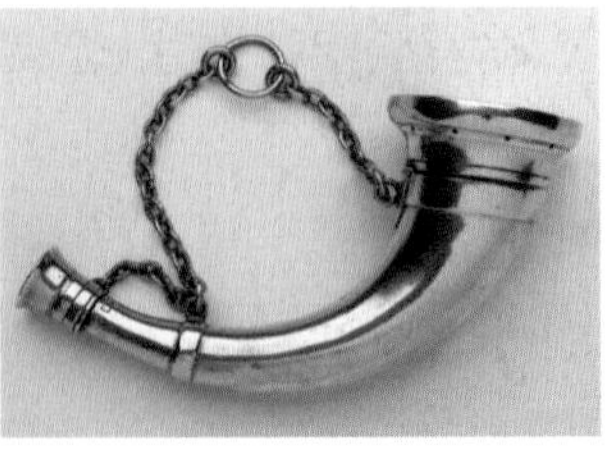

A rare and unusual Storr and Mordan silver cornucopia vinaigrette, with hallmark for London.

1871 *4in (10cm) long*

£300-400 **GS**

A silver card case with intricate barley pattern and two initials in the cartouche, hallmark for Birmingham.

1858 *4in (10cm) long*

£320-380 **GS**

A Dutch silver card case with repoussé decoration showing a lady on a swing to one side and a lady and gentleman drinking wine to the other.

c1890 *4in (10cm) long*

£200-300 **GS**

A Birmingham silver cigarette case, by Saunders and Shepherd, entitled "A Gentleman in Khaki".

1899 *3.25in (8.5cm) long*

£700-1,000 **JBS**

A Russian silver cigarette case.

1869 *4in (10cm) long*

£600-800 **JBS**

A Russian silver cigarette case.

c1870 *4.25in (10.5cm) long*

£700-900 **JBS**

A London silver cigarette case, painted with a hunting scene on the cover.

1888 *5in (12.5cm) long*

£2,200-2,800 **JBS**

A French 18ct gold cigarette case.

c1890 *3.75in (9.5cm) long*

£800-1,200 **JBS**

A silver cigar case with repoussé herringbone design in the form of five cigars, with London hallmark for "JC".

c1890 *4.75in (12cm) long*

£300-500 **GS**

A Continental silver cigarette case, painted with a horse's head.

c1900 *3in (7.5cm) long*

£400-600 **JBS**

An Austrian silver cigarette case, painted with a dog's head.

c1900 *3.25in (8.5cm) wide*

£400-600 **JBS**

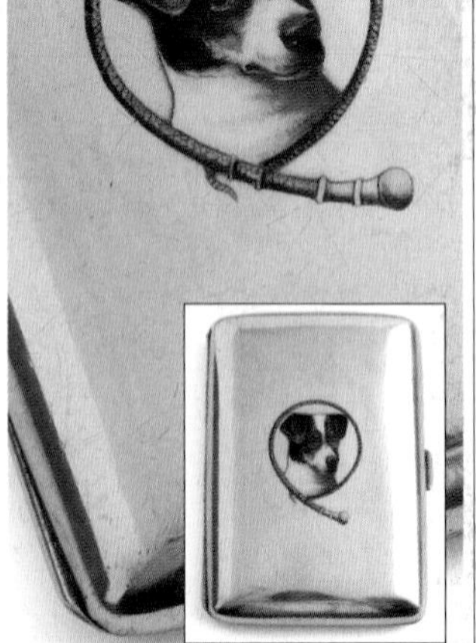

A Continental cigarette case.

c1900 *3.25in (8.5cm) long*

£400-600 **JBS**

A Birmingham silver cigarette case, painted with a hunting scene.

1906 *3.25in (8.5cm) long*

£1,000-1,500 **JBS**

A Birmingham silver cigarette case, painted with a horse, a ballerina, a hand of cards and a bottle of champagne.

1913 *3.25in (8cm) long*

£700-900 **JBS**

A silver cigarette case, the enamel cover with floral decoration, indistinct date mark.

c1920 *3.5in (9cm) long*

£400-500 **JBS**

A silver cigarette case, with engraved foliate design and shield-shaped cartouche, hallmark for WW Ltd of Birmingham, damaged.

1925 *3.5in (9cm) long*

£40-60 **GS**

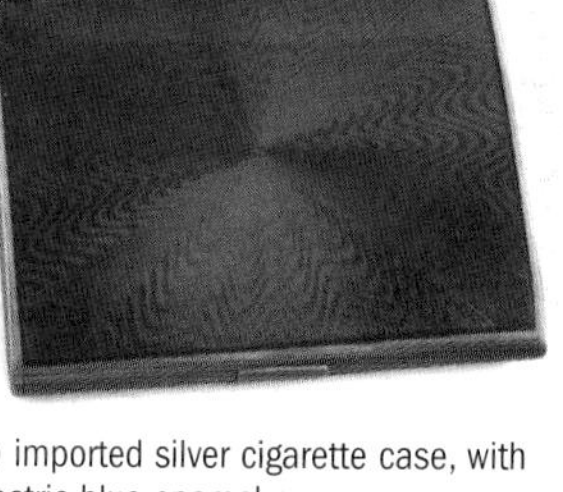

An imported silver cigarette case, with electric blue enamel cover.

1926 *3.25in (8.5cm) long*

£280-320 **JBS**

A Victorian vesta case and whistle, by Stokes and Ireland of Birmingham, oval tubular section with a hinged cover and suspension ring, struck with French duty marks.

1886 *2.5in (6.5cm) long*

£200-250 **WW**

A Birmingham silver vesta case.

1890 *2in (5cm) long*

£400-500 **JBS**

A late Victorian oblong vesta case, by H. Matthews of Birmingham, with a stamped border of scrollwork.

1898 *2in (5cm) long*

£70-100 **WW**

A Victorian novelty vesta holder, by Deakin and Francis of Birmingham, in the form of a caricature dwarf figure with a pig-tail and a pointed cloth hat, standing with his hands in his pockets on a domed circular base, ridged for striking purposes, his hat hinged to reveal the vesta compartment.

c1890 *4.5in (11.5cm) high*

£600-900 **WW**

A silver vesta case, with shield design, made in Birmingham.

1909 *2in (5cm) long*

£40-60 **SSP**

An Edwardian novelty heart-shaped vesta case, with scroll engraving and a vacant cartouche, maker's mark "S.M.L. Birmingham", struck with French duty marks.

1904 *2.5in (6.5cm) high*

£150-200 **WW**

A Birmingham silver vesta case.

1911 *3.25in (8.5cm) long*

£320-380 **JBS**

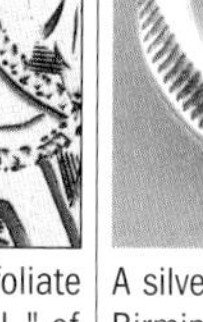

A silver vesta case, with engraved foliate and star design, hallmark for "S.M.L." of Birmingham.

1903 *1.5in (4cm) wide*

£40-60 **GS**

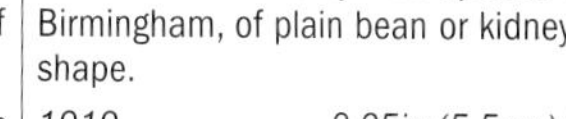

A silver vesta case by W.H. Sparrow of Birmingham, of plain bean or kidney shape.

1919 *2.25in (5.5cm) long*

£40-60 **CHEF**

CANDLESTICKS

A George II taper stick, by John Cafe of London, of conventional form with a knopped stem and spreading foot.

1745 *5.5in (14cm) high*

£700-1,000 **L&T**

An exceptional pair of George II Scottish candlesticks, by Kerr and Dempster of Edinburgh, marked by assaymaster Hugh Gordon, the cast sticks with hexafoil bases with shells, an inner border of roses, fluted baluster stems, spool-shaped sockets and shell-decorated nozzles.

The unusual addition of the band of roses is probably a Jacobite symbol.

1745 *8.5in (21.5cm) high*

£15,000-20,000 **L&T**

One of a set of three Scottish George II casters, by Ebenezer Oliphant of Edinburgh, marked by assaymaster Hugh Gordon, the plain baluster body on spreading feet, with pierced covers and turned finials, one blind.

1746 *8in (20cm) high*

£3,800-4,200 set **L&T**

A pair of mid-18thC German candlesticks, by Nicolaus Titkens of Hannover, on domed and canted square bases with octagonal baluster columns and cylindrical capitals, with detachable nozzles.

c1750 *8.25in (21cm) high*

£3,000-4,000 **WW**

A pair of George II table candlesticks, by John Cafe of London, cast in conventional form, with spreading bases, scalloped corners, and engraved crests with crown surmounts.

1751 *7.75in (19.5cm) high*

£1,800-2,200 **L&T**

A set of four George II or George III cast candlesticks, by Daniel Smith and Robert Sharp of London, on stepped square bases with knopped columns, decorated with swirl-fluting and gadrooning, detachable nozzles.

1760 *10.75in (27.5cm) high*

£6,500-7,500 **WW**

A pair of late 18thC German candlesticks, on domed and wrythen bases with wrythen baluster columns and campana-shaped capitals, the bases with later loading, maker's mark "I" over "IB" in a trefoil, Augsburg.

c1760 *6.75in (17cm) high*

£1,200-1,800 **WW**

A pair of George III table candlesticks, by John Carter of London, the removable sconces with gadrooned and leaf-clasped circular stems, on spreading hexagonal leaf-clasped bases.

1769 *10.5in (26cm) high*

£1,500-2,000 **L&T**

A pair of George III table candlesticks, with marks for Sheffield, of baluster form, with beaded borders, acanthus-clasped columns, gadroon bases and turned mahogany undersides.

1814 *11.5in (29cm) high*

£1,500-2,000 **L&T**

A pair of George IV silver candlesticks, by John Green and Co., with fluting throughout, lions rampant engraved on the bases, Sheffield hallmarks.

1834 *12.75in (32.5cm) high*

£2,200-2,800 **S&K**

A pair of Russian silver candlesticks, made in Chernigov, chased with leaves and scrolls throughout.

1838 *9.5in (24cm) high*

£1,500-2,000 **S&K**

A pair of late Victorian lyre candlesticks, by George Heath of London, on fluted oval bases with fluted, vase-shaped capitals.

1899 *8in (20.5cm) high*

£800-1,200 **WW**

A pair of Edwardian candlesticks, by G. Nathan and R. Hayes of Birmingham, in the Neo-classical style, decorated with bead borders and bat's-wing fluting.

1908 *9.5in (24cm) high*

£400-600 **WW**

A pair of George III chambersticks, by John Crouch and Thomas Hannam of London, with conical snuffers, vase-shaped capitals and bead borders, with detachable nozzles, crested.

1782 *5.25in (13.5cm) diam*

£1,200-1,800 **WW**

A pair of Scottish George III chamber candlesticks by William Robertson, with marks for Edinburgh, the sconces with threaded rings, the scroll handles and conical snuffers with engraved crests.

1799 *5.5in (13.5cm) diam*

£1,800-2,200 **L&T**

A George III chamberstick, by Robert Makepiece and Richard Carter of London, circular with bead borders, conical snuffer and detachable nozzle, crested.

1777 *5.25in (13.5cm) diam*

£400-600 **WW**

A pair of Scottish silver candle holders, marks for Edinburgh.

1814 *4.25in (10.5cm) high*

£3,000-3,500 **JBS**

A pair of Victorian silver chamber candlesticks, with marks for London, possibly by James Alldridge, each of lobed circular form, engraved crest within a belt, complete with snuffers.

The crest is for the Green family.

1859 *5.5in (14cm) diam*

£1,200-1,800 **L&T**

A pair of heavy silver gilt chamber candlesticks, by C.S.G. and Co. of London, after a model by Paul Storr, the large leaf-clasped sconce on a bowl with shaped leaves to the base, the rim and handle modelled as a coiled snake.

1985 *6.75in (17cm) wide*

£800-1,200 **L&T**

A Scottish George III silver mustard pot, with marks for Edinburgh, of oval form, with threaded rims and scroll handle to rear, the domed cover with plain finial and inscribed "B.G.L.".

1802 *3.25in (8cm) high*

£200-300 **L&T**

CONDIMENTS

A William IV Irish cast silver mustard pot, probably by William Nelson of Dublin, of squat circular form on three lion mask and paw feet below a floral rim, decorated around the sides with chased work, the hinged cover with a knop finial.

1831 *3.5in (9cm) high*

£1,000-1,500 **WW**

A George III silver drum mustard pot, by Rebecca Emes and Edward Barnard of London, the angular handle with a shell thumbpiece, part-fluted lower body, crested, with a blue glass liner.

1810 *2.75in (7cm) high*

£380-420 **WW**

A George IV silver mustard pot, possibly by Thomas Ross of London, of drum form with part-fluting, gadrooned border, shell thumbpiece and a blue glass liner, crested.

c1825 *2.5in (6.5cm) diam*

£220-280 **WW**

An early Victorian drum mustard pot, by Messrs Barnard of London, with engraved and scroll-pierced sides, openwork thumbpiece and blue glass liner.

1845 *3in (7.5cm) high*

£250-300 **WW**

A Birmingham silver salt, with blue glass liner, by Williams.

1908 *2.75in (7cm) high*

£500-550 **JBS**

A set of four London silver shell and hoof feet dishes, by David Hennell.

Apprenticed to Edward Wood in 1728, David Hennell established his own firm of silversmiths in 1735 and was the first of several generations of Hennell silversmiths who were renowned for their fine silverwork in the 18th and 19thC.

1754 *2.25in (6cm) high*

£2,000-2,500 **JBS**

A pair of George III silver salts, maker's mark "DH", made in London, each of a plain compressed circular shape, raised on three hoof feet, indistinct date mark.

2.5in (6.25cm) diam

£120-180 **CHEF**

A pair of English silver salts, retailed by Tiffany and Co., each with rocaille edge, on three shell-capped scroll legs and hoof feet, together with two Tiffany and Co. silver salt spoons, monogrammed, London hallmarks.

1917 *2.5in (6.5cm) diam*

£150-200 **S&K**

A London silver sugar pot, with glass liner, by Charles and George Fox.

1856 *2in (5cm) high*

£420-480 **JBS**

A London silver sugar sifter, by Finley and Taylor.

1891 *6.5in (16.5cm) high*

£320-380 **JBS**

A London Stabler silver sugar sifter, by Goldsmiths and Silversmiths Co. Ltd.

6in (15cm) high

£400-450 **JBS**

A London silver sugar pot, with glass liner, by Charles and George Fox.

1856 *2in (5cm) high*

£420-480 **JBS**

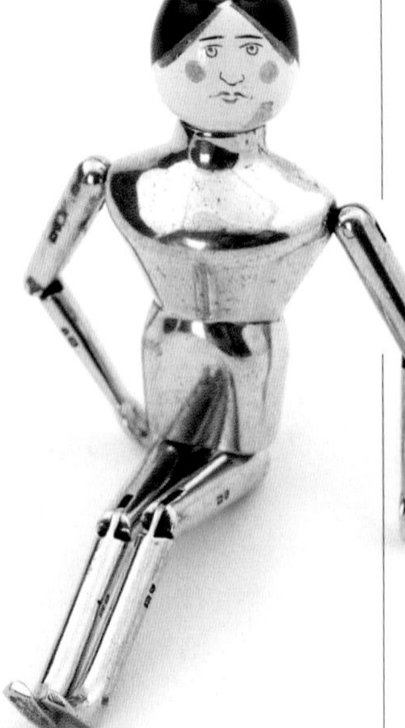

An Edwardian novelty pepperette, by Louis Willmott of London, in the form of an articulated doll with enamelled head, minor chip.

1907 *4.75in (12cm) long*

£800-1,200 **WW**

A late George II silver cruet stand, by Jabez Daniell and James Mince of London, of trefoil form with C-scroll handle, C-scroll supports to the bottle frame and an armorial cartouche, on four stylized web feet, the two lidded cut-crystal bottles with silver collars, scroll handles, and engraved armorial crests, the crystal caster with pierced silver lid, with a miniature spice label and chain marked "Kyan".

1759 *8.5in (21cm) high*

£1,500-2,000 **L&T**

A George III silver cruet set, by Robert Hennell I and David Hennell II of London, the boat-shaped frame fitted for two large bottles, two casters and a mustard pot, with loop handle, wooden base, bright cut frieze and cartouche with initials, all on fluted spade feet.

1799 *9.5in (24cm) high*

£1,800-2,200 **L&T**

A George IV silver eight-bottle cruet frame, by William Elliot of London, on a square base and four paw feet with gadrooned and foliate borders, fitted with two mounted and six other stoppered cut-glass bottles, crested.

1820 *9in (23cm) wide*

£800-1,200 **WW**

A late Victorian trefoil-shaped silver breakfast condiment set, by Horace Woodward and Co. of London, with gadrooned borders and three lift-out condiments.

1896 *5.25in (13.5cm) high*

£200-300 **WW**

A London silver condiment stand, by Edward Barnard.

1868 *8.25in (21cm) long*

£800-1,200 **JBS**

CUPS

A rare pair of Queen Anne Scottish silver mugs, by John Luke of Glasgow, of traditional thistle shape, engraved with initials "RH" and "AS", dated 1688 and engraved with the Forrester coat of arms.

The earlier engraved date possibly indicates that this was an 18th birthday present.

1707 *3in (7.5cm) high*

£12,000-18,000 **L&T**

A George I Scottish silver half-pint mug, by Charles Dickson of Edinburgh, of good gauge, with engraved crest and motto for Lockhart.

1719 *3.5in (9cm) high*

£1,800-2,200 **L&T**

A Scottish silver dram cup, of traditional thistle form, with applied lobing beneath a moulded band, reeded strap handle and engraved initial "M" to the base, indistinct date mark.

c1720 *1.5in (4cm) high*

£2,500-3,000 **L&T**

A scarce George II Scottish provincial pattern heavy-gauge dram cup, with marks for Tain, by Hugh Ross, of traditional thistle shape, the lobed body below a moulded central band, with strap handle, engraved with betrothal initials "AS" over "MF", marked with conjoined initials "HR" to the base, indistinct date mark.

c1720 *1.75in (4.5cm) high*

£24,000-30,000 **L&T**

A George I Scottish silver half-pint mug, by James Kerr of Edinburgh, marked for assaymaster Edward Penman, with scroll handle.

1727 *3.5in (8.5cm) high*

£1,500-2,000 **L&T**

A George II silver beer mug, maker's mark indistinct, made in Exeter, of plain baluster shape with moulded foot ring and S-scroll handle, initialled "IGB".

1731 *4in (10cm) high*

£350-450 **CHEF**

An early George II West Country mug, by Philip Elston of Exeter. with moulded girdle, tucked-in base and scroll handle, scratched underneath with initials and date "WD 1729" and the later inscription "Bernard on his eighteenth birthday from his Punch Friends".

1729 *4.5in (11.5cm) high*

£400-600 **WW**

A George II Scottish silver half-pint mug, by Milne Campbell of Glasgow, of plain form, with leaf-capped scroll handle.

1750 *3.5in (9cm) high*

£800-1,200 **L&T**

A George II baluster mug, by William Shaw and William Preist of London, with scroll handle, initialled.

1753 *5in (12.5cm) high*

£300-400 **WW**

A George II North Country provincial silver mug, by John Langlands I of Newcastle, of tapering form with skirted base and S-scroll handle, scratched "T" over "J.A.".

1757 *4.75in (12cm) high*

£500-700 **WW**

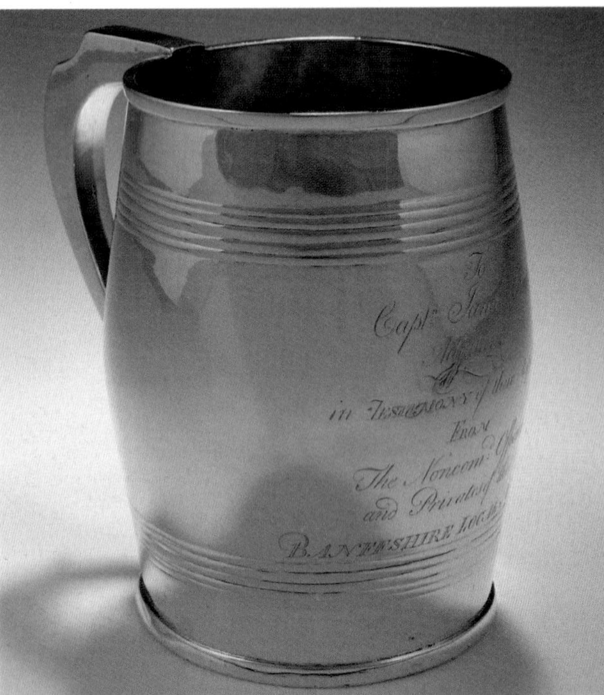

A George III Scottish provincial beer mug, by John Keith of Banff, of large size with simple rounded angular handle, the bellied body with threaded bands and engraved inscription "To Capt. James Reid Adjutant in Testimony of their respect from the Noncom'd Officers and Privates of the Banffshire Local Militia 1810".

1810 *4.75in (12cm) high*

£12,000-18,000 **L&T**

A George III Scottish provincial silver half-pint mug, by William Jamieson of Aberdeen, with reeded hooped bands, engraved crest and motto for Elder, leaf-capped scroll handle and five marks "WJ", "A", "B", "D" and "WJ".

1815 *3.5in (9cm) high*

£1,800-2,200 **L&T**

A London silver mug, by Reily and Storer.

1845 *3.75in (9.5cm) high*

£500-600 **JBS**

A London silver mug, by G. Angel.

1858 *4.25in (10.5cm) high*

£600-650 **JBS**

Two similar Edwardian cast reproductions of ancient drinking vessels, by G. Nattan and R. Hayes of London and Chester respectively, the first silver gilt with a frieze of wild bulls goring their captors, the second with a similar frieze depicting the captured bulls, both with lug and spool handles.

1904 *3in (7.5cm) high*

£350-450 **WW**

A Queen Anne silver tankard by Humphrey Payne of London, of plain tapering cylindrical shape with moulded foot, girdle and edge below a stepped and domed cover with scroll thumbpiece with rounded spade terminal.

1713 *7in (18cm) high*

£1,200-1,500 **CHEF**

A George II silver tankard, by Richard Bayley of London, the baluster-shaped body with reeded girdle, domed cover with chairback thumbpiece, double-scroll handle and moulded foot.

1742 *7.75in (19.5cm) high*

£2,500-3,000 **CHEF**

A George III lidded tankard, by Thomas Parr II of London, the domed lid with scroll thumbpiece and clasped handle, the body with moulded band, engraved armorials and monogram, on a spreading foot.

1771 *7.5in (18.5cm) high*

£2,200-2,800 **L&T**

An Edwardian tankard, by S.W. Sissons and Co. of London, of plain tapering form, with a skirted base, broad reeded brim and a cast volute thumbpiece.

1905 *7in (18cm) high*

£600-900 **WW**

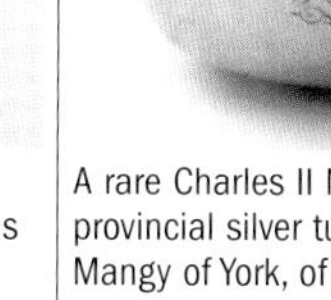

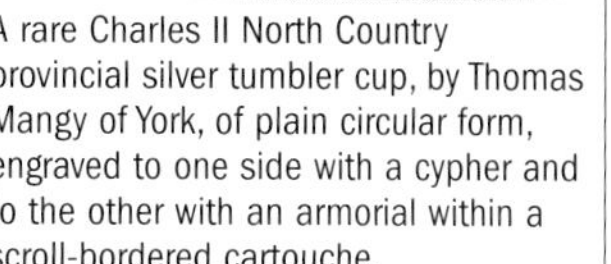

A rare Charles II North Country provincial silver tumbler cup, by Thomas Mangy of York, of plain circular form, engraved to one side with a cypher and to the other with an armorial within a scroll-bordered cartouche.

1679 *3.5in (9cm) diam*

£2,800-3,200 **WW**

A late 17thC silver tumbler cup, of plain form with a curved base and near-vertical sides, with maker's mark "TP" within a quatrefoil, probably English provincial, indistinct date mark.

2.75in (7cm) diam

£800-1,200 **WW**

A London silver cup, by Richard Bayley.

1733 *5.5in (14cm) high*

£800-1,200 **JBS**

A mid-18thC Russian beaker, by G. Serebrenikov of Moscow, of tapering form, embossed and chased in high relief around the sides with birds amongst fruiting scrolls and husks, on a matte ground.

c1760 *3.5in (9cm) high*

£250-300 **WW**

A London silver cup, possibly by Benjamin Mountigue.

1786 *6.75in (17cm) high*

£800-1,200 **JBS**

A George III Scottish provincial wine goblet, by James Erskine of Edinburgh, with plain stem, spreading foot with beaded edge and gilt interior, the plain body engraved with "M" and "E" in script, with duty mark.

1785 *6.5in (16.5cm) high*

£800-1,200 **L&T**

A pair of Irish George III two-handled loving cups, by Richard Tudor of Dublin, the body with central moulded band, engraved armorial and a later crest, with acanthus-clasped scrolled handles, on pedestal feet.

1768 *7.25in (18cm) wide*

£1,800-2,200 **L&T**

A London silver cup, by George Fox.

1865 *3.5in (9cm) high*

£500-800 **JBS**

A pair of George III goblets, by John Wakelin and Robert Garrard I of London, on pedestal bases with part-fluted bowls, decorated with a frieze of chased vitruvian scrolls between two applied rope borders, with the engraved motto "Pretium Recti", the interiors gilt, with inset-turned wooden bases.

1796 *6.5in (16.5cm) high*

£3,000-4,000 **WW**

An early 19thC Scottish provincial horn beaker, by George Elder of Banff, with engraved silver rim inscribed "Jas. Brower, Duff House" above an applied shield with a crest and motto.

c1820 *4.25in (10.5cm) high*

£1,000-1,500 **L&T**

A London silver cup, by Houle and Houle.

1869 *7in (18cm) high*

£350-450 **JBS**

CUTLERY

A George III caddy scoop, by George Smith and William Fearn of London, with bright cut crescent-shaped handle and plain circular bowl.

1787 *2.25in (5.5cm) long*

£250-300 **WW**

A London silver shell-shaped tea caddy spoon.

1788 *2.75in (7cm) long*

£300-350 **JBS**

A George III silver bright cut caddy spoon, no maker's mark, made in London, with shell bowl.

1792 *3.5in (9cm) long*

£70-100 **CHEF**

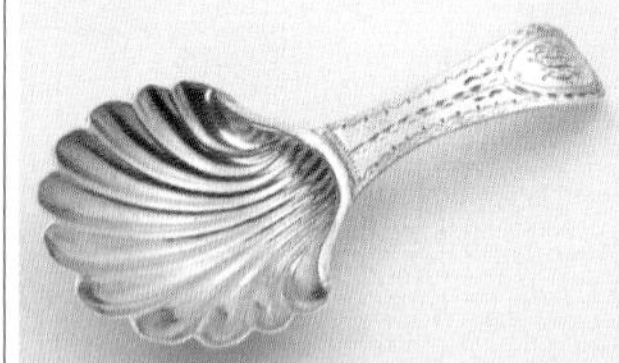

A George III bright engraved caddy spoon, with a fluted scallop-shell bowl, initialled by Peter and Ann Bateman of London.

1793 *3.25in (8cm) long*

£380-420 **WW**

A Birmingham silver tea caddy spoon.

1795 *3.25in (8.5cm) long*

£150-200 **JBS**

A Birmingham silver tea caddy spoon.

1810 *2.5in (6.5cm) long*

£250-300 **JBS**

A George III caddy spoon, by William Pugh of Birmingham, with a heart-shaped handle and plain leaf-shaped bowl.

1809 *3.25in (8.5cm) long*

£100-150 **WW**

A small George III bright engraved caddy spoon, with a circular bowl and a vacant shield cartouche in the centre, maker's mark partially distorted, Birmingham.

1812 *2.25in (5.5cm) long*

£150-200 **WW**

A George III fiddle caddy spoon, by Thomas James of London, with exaggerated shoulders, heptagonal bowl with jagged edge and a circular panel of vermicelli in the centre, crested, indistinct date mark.

c1815 *3.75in (9.5cm) long*

£280-320 **WW**

A George III 'pastern hoof' type engraved caddy spoon, by John Bettridge of Birmingham, with hollow decorated stem and pierced gallery around the bowl, together with another 'pastern hoof' spoon, by Cocks and Bettridge of Birmingham, with bright engraving.

1809, 1818 *3in (7.5cm) long*

£350-400 **WW**

A George III engraved caddy shovel, by Joseph Taylor of Birmingham, with a fan-shaped bowl and a vacant oval cartouche at the top of the stem.

1817 *2.5in (6.5cm) long*

£80-120 **WW**

A George III fiddle caddy spoon, by Francis Powell of London, with exaggerated shoulders and circular pan bowl, initialled.

1818 *3in (7.5cm) long*

£80-120 **WW**

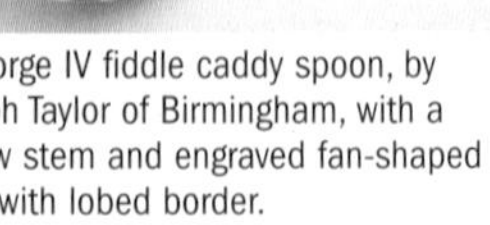

A George IV fiddle caddy spoon, by Joseph Taylor of Birmingham, with a hollow stem and engraved fan-shaped bowl with lobed border.

1823 *3.5in (9cm) long*

£150-200 **WW**

A William IV fiddle caddy spoon, by Joseph Wilmore of Birmingham, with a hollow stem, the kidney-shaped bowl engraved with a fruiting plant, initialled "H".

1831 *3in (7.5cm) long*

£180-220 **WW**

A Birmingham silver tea caddy spoon, with engraved floral decoration.

1844 *3in (7.5cm) long*

£150-200 **JBS**

A London silver tea caddy spoon, by Charles Horner.

1927 *2.5in (6.5cm) long*

£220-280 **JBS**

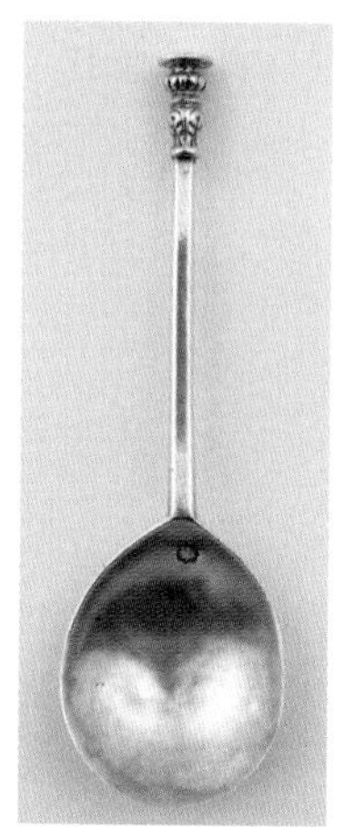

An Elizabeth I seal-top spoon, the chased and fluted terminal with traces of gilding, anchor and maker's mark, London.

1594 *6.25in (16cm) long*

£1,200-1,800 **WW**

A Charles I slip-top spoon, probably by Thomas Brothwell of London, with a short tapering stem, engraved on the back of the bowl with a mullet and three cinquefoils.

1627 *6in (15cm) long*

£1,000-1,500 **WW**

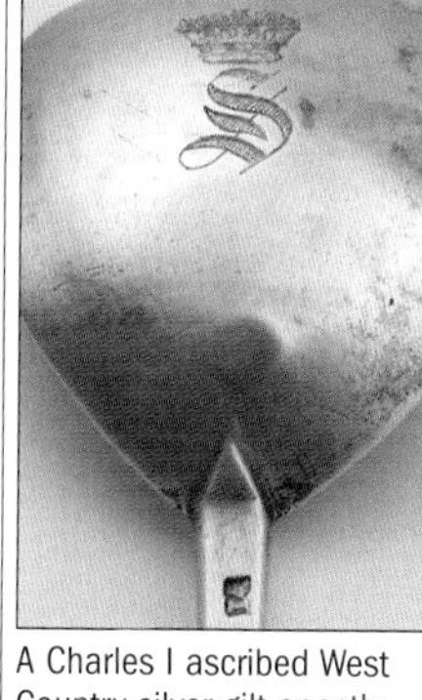

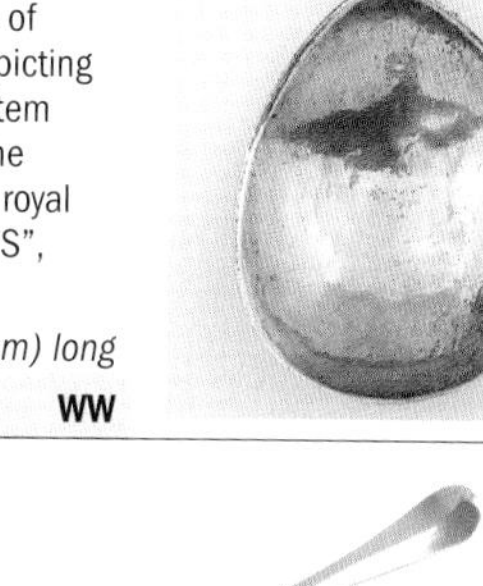

A Charles I ascribed West Country silver gilt apostle spoon, by Joseph Arden of Sherborne, probably depicting St Paul, on a tapering stem with a small V rat-tail, the reverse engraved with a royal crown above the initial "S", indistinct date mark.

c1635 *7in (18cm) long*

£1,200-1,800 **WW**

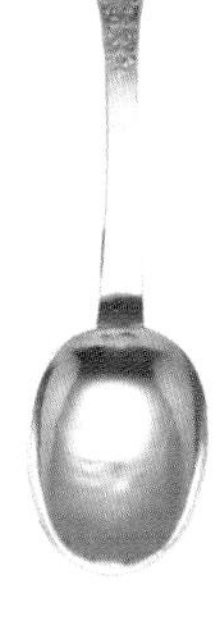

A Charles II trefid table spoon, by Robert King of London, the rear of the bowl and handle terminal decorated with C-scrolls, owners initials "S" over "IM" crudely engraved to rear of handle.

1680 *7.5in (19cm) long*

£450-550 **L&T**

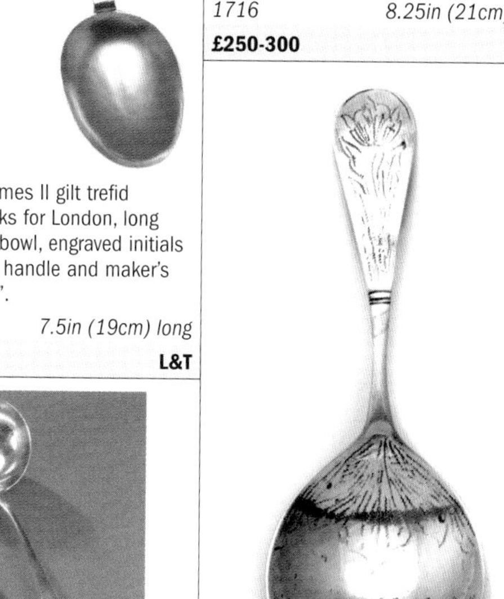

A good pair of James II gilt trefid spoons, with marks for London, long rat-tail to rear of bowl, engraved initials to the rear of the handle and maker's mark "S" over "W".

1685 *7.5in (19cm) long*

£700-900 pair **L&T**

A London silver spoon, by Richard Edwards.

1716 *8.25in (21cm) long*

£250-300 **JBS**

A London silver spoon, by Richard Edwards.

1718 *8in (20.5cm) long*

£250-300 **JBS**

A London silver serving spoon, by William Soame.

1733 *14.5in (37cm) long*

£800-1,200 **JBS**

A George III 'Old English' pattern silver sauce ladle, by Hester Bateman of London, with duty mark.

1785 *7in (18cm) long*

£300-400 **S&K**

A Norwegian spoon with floral engraving, assaymaster's mark "P" and maker's mark "HB", Bergen.

1779 *6in (15cm) long*

£80-120 **WW**

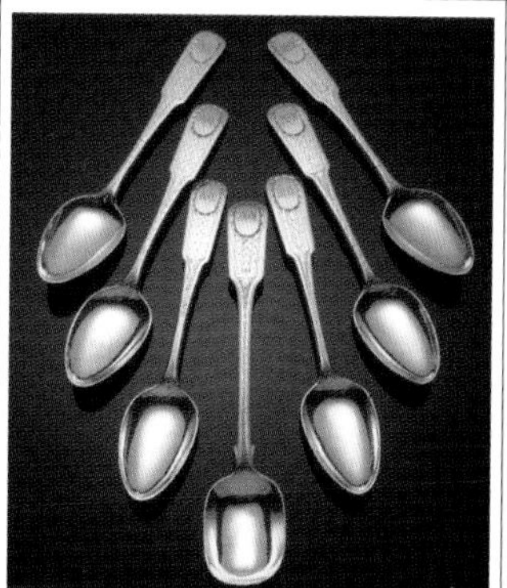

A Scottish provincial composite set of six teaspoons and a sugar spoon, the teaspoons by Charles Fowler, the sugar spoon by Thomas Stewart of Elgin, all of fiddle pattern with bright cut engraved decoration and oval cartouche with engraved initials, the sugar spoon with rounded rectangular bowl, no date marks.

c1790 *6.5in (16.5cm) long*

£400-600 set **L&T**

An original cased set of six Scottish provincial teaspoons and one masking spoon, by Nathaniel Gillet of Aberdeen, of plain form, with engraved interlinked initials "JMD", contained in a late 18thC laburnum case of pinched oval form, with initials "JMD" to the lid.

1790 *Case 7in (17.5cm) long*

£400-600 **L&T**

A Scottish provincial soup divider, by Benjamin Lumsden of Montrose, with unusually long oar section to the handle and broad elliptical bowl.

1800 *11in (28cm) long*

£500-800 **L&T**

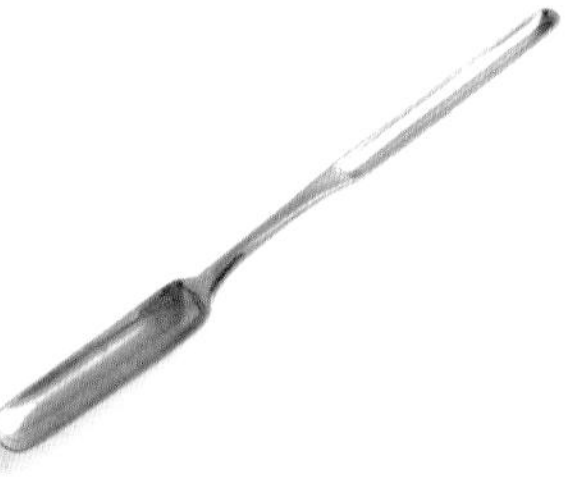

An Irish silver marrow scoop, made by Sam L. Neville.

1811 *9.5in (24cm) long*

£300-350 **JBS**

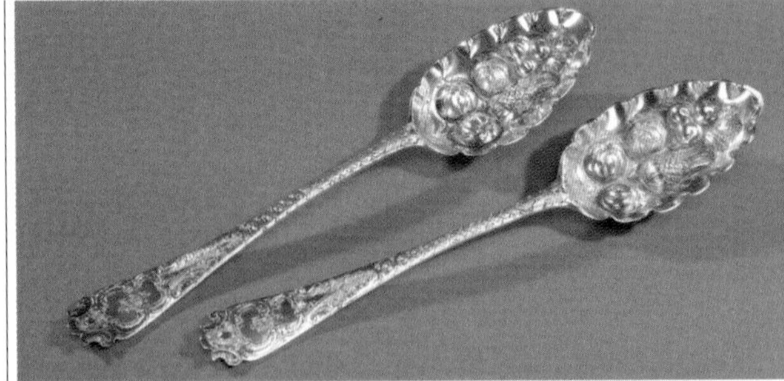

A pair of George IV silver serving spoons, by Hester Bateman of London, the bowls with scalloped edges raised with fruits, the handles etched with scrolls and acanthus, monogrammed "C".

1827 *9.5in (24cm) long*

£350-450 **S&K**

Left: A Scottish provincial masking spoon, with marks for John McQueen, with plain engraved initials and wrythen stem.

1830 *8in (20.5cm) long*

£500-800 **L&T**

Right: A Scottish provincial sugar spoon, by George Elder of Banff, of 'Old English' pattern, with plain engraved initials and wrythen stem.

1830 *7.75in (19.5cm) long*

£280-320 **L&T**

Two stuffing spoons, the first by Simon Harris of London, the second by Thomas Stone of Edinburgh, dates unclear.

9.5in (24cm) long

£100-150 **S&K**

A London silver serving spoon, by George Adams.

1879 *12in (30.5cm) long*

£200-250 **JBS**

An Aesthetic Movement silver ladle and serving spoon, the handles with raised flowering prunus branches, stamped in a roundel "Sandrik a S", date unclear.

Ladle 12.25in (31cm) long

£180-220 **S&K**

A London silver fish slice, by William Knight.

1816 *11.75in (30cm) long*

£220-280 **JBS**

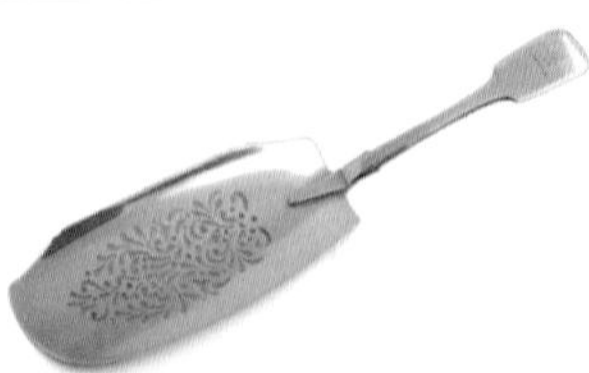

An Exeter silver fish slice, by George Turner.

1830 *11in (28cm) long*

£200-250 **JBS**

A Birmingham silver and ivory page turner, by Deakin and Francis.

1889 *17in (43cm) long*

£400-450 **JBS**

A pair of London silver scissors, by Charles Boyton.

1885 *7.25 (18.5cm) long*

£400-450 **JBS**

A pair of 19thC Austrian silver sugar tongs, cast with a couple harvesting grapes below the handles, their heads by the pivot of the scissor action, the blades cast as vine leaves.

5.5in (14cm) long

£80-120 **CHEF**

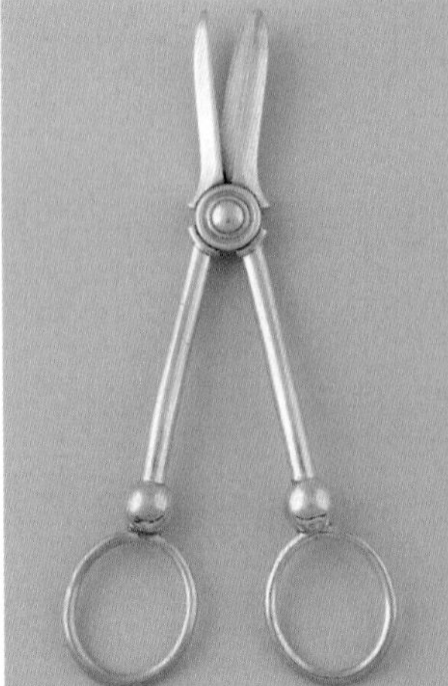

A pair of silver grape shears by James Dixon and Sons of Sheffield, of plain design with ball and ring handles.

1913 *5.5in (13.5cm) long*

£120-180 **CHEF**

TAZZAS & TRAYS

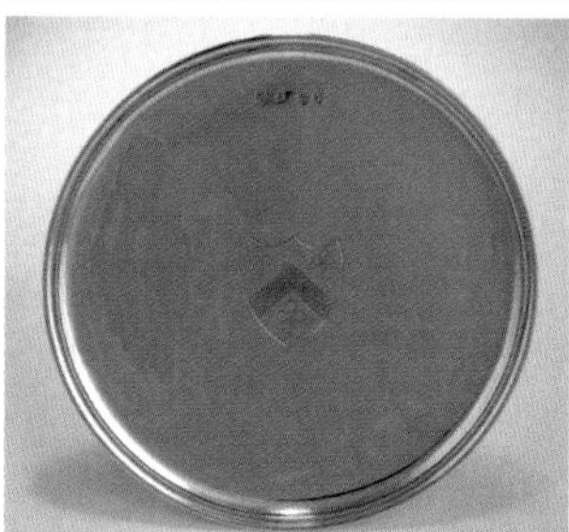

A Queen Anne Britannia standard tazza, by Francis Garthorne of London, of conventional form, with engraved crest, slight raised rim and spool foot.

1706 *9in (22.5cm) diam*

£1,800-2,200 **L&T**

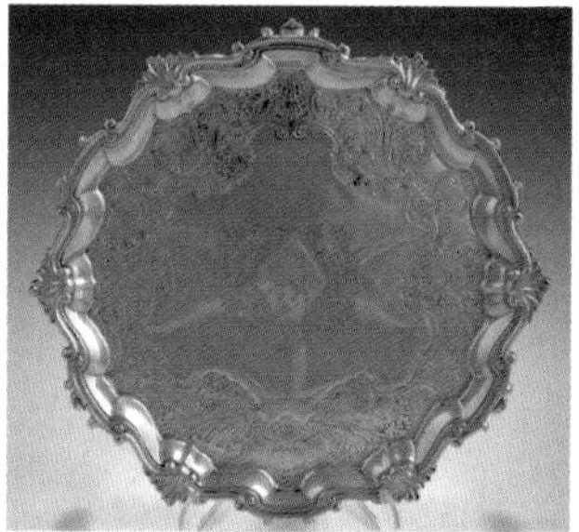

A George II salver, by William Justus of London, the bold C-scroll border with shell-clasping, the flat with central cartouche and engraved ram with a principal outer chased border of C-scrolling foliate and fish-scale panels, all on three bold scroll feet.

1747 *11.5in (28.5cm) diam*

£1,200-1,800 **L&T**

A George II circular silver salver, by William and Robert Peaston of London, the shaped rim with scrolls and shells, on three hoof feet, the centre later decorated with flowers, scrolls and monogram.

1757 *7in (18cm) diam*

£350-400 **S&K**

A George III silver footed tray, maker's mark "EC", the shaped circular rim with shell and gadroon border, centred by a coat of arms bearing the inscription "Steer Steady", London hallmarks.

1773 *13.25in (33.5cm) diam*

£1,000-1,500 **S&K**

A rare 18thC Colonial waiter, with marks for Kingston in Jamaica, by Anthony Danvers, of circular form with a shell-cast border and flat chased band, on three feet, alligator's head mark and "AD" mark.

c1760 *13in (33cm) long*

£800-1,200 **L&T**

A rare London silver teapot stand, by Peter and Jonathan Bateman.

1790 *7in (18cm) wide*

£1,200-1,800 **JBS**

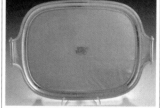

A Scottish George III coffee tray, by George McHattie of Edinburgh, with bold threaded rim, bright cut with engraved Greek key border, further inner border and central group of initials, on four threaded feet.

1806 *17.5in (44cm) wide*

£2,800-3,200 **L&T**

A George III coffee tray, by Edward James of London, the oval tray with threaded border, scroll handles, bright cut inner border and shaped cartouche with crest to the centre.

1791 *19.5in (48.5cm) wide*

£2,800-3,200 **L&T**

A good two-handled tea tray by Matthew Boulton, the heavy gadroon border with bold acanthus and shell-clasped handles, with inset silver plaque for engraving, date unclear.

27.25in (68cm) wide

£800-1,200 **L&T**

A George III London silver tea tray, with maker's mark "W.B.", of rounded rectangular form, with deep gadroon border and handles and engraved armorial crest to centre featuring the arms of Kearsley, originally of Lancashire and London, quartering those of Harvey of Yorkshire.

1810 *28.25in (70.5cm) wide*

£2,200-2,800 **L&T**

An 18thC Irish silver miniature strawberry dish, marks indistinct, of plain circular shape with lobed edge, crested with an arrow, marks for Dublin.

1750 *4.75in (12cm) diam*

£300-350 **CHEF**

A set of four second course plates, by Thomas Henning of London, each of shaped outline, with heavy gadroon edge, engraved armorial crest, scratch weights and inscribed number.

1768 *9.5in (24cm) diam*

£1,200-1,800 **L&T**

A German silver dinner plate, of shaped circular outline with a gadrooned border and an engraved coat of arms, made in Augsburg, maker's mark "CD".

c1795 *9.75in (24.5cm) diam*

£300-400 **WW**

Left: A small Victorian London silver waiter, with rocaille serpentine border and acanthus and C-scroll engraving, on three leaf-clasped C-scroll feet.

c1840 *8.5in (21cm) diam*

£350-450 **L&T**

Right: A Victorian London silver salver, of circular form, with acanthus-clasped shaped rim, and engraved shell and floral border, on acanthus feet.

1840 *12.5in (31cm) diam*

£300-400 **L&T**

A pair of George III shell dishes, by Rebecca Eames and Edward Barnard of London, the scallop shells with cast gadroon and shell border and engraved crest, on three shell feet.

1819 *5.5in (13.5cm) long*

£1,000-1,500 **L&T**

A Victorian pierced dish, by R. Martin and E. Hall of London, of lobed oval outline with embossed decoration and a shaped bead border.

1872 *12.75in (32.5cm) diam*

£500-800 **WW**

A Victorian silver bowl, by the Goldsmiths and Silversmiths Company of London, in the manner of Paul de Lamerie, modelled as a large scallop shell with pierced decoration, the handle as a mermaid, on dolphin feet.

1898 11in (28cm) d.

£1,800-2,200 **L&T**

JUGS

An early George II silver cream jug, with marks for London, maker indistinct, the upright rim on a plain spherical body with reeded handle.

1729 *3in (7.5cm) high*

£220-280 **L&T**

A George III Scottish provincial silver cream jug, by Charles Allan, the baluster body with shaped rim, bold acanthus-clasped scroll handle, all on three 'C'-scroll legs and hoof feet.

1750 *4.75in (11.5cm) high*

£1,200-1,800 **L&T**

A George II baluster cream jug, by William Garrard, on three feet, with a wavy rim and scroll handle, the body embossed with a pheasant and a dog chasing a fox amongst flowers, with a vacant cartouche, indistinct date mark.

3.75in (9.5cm) high

£380-420 **WW**

A George III silver cream jug, on a circular pedestal with an embossed wrythen-fluted body and ropework borders, maker's mark partially worn "?W", London.

1770 *4in (10cm) high*

£200-300 **WW**

A pair of George III silver pitchers by William Cripps of London, each raised from a circular foot with plain spherical body below a ribbed neck and with a double-scroll handle, crested.

1760, 1761 *5in (12.5cm) high*

£1,000-1,500 **CHEF**

A George III silver cream jug, by Robert Sallam, the well-shaped jug with gadroon rim and clasped handle, fluted wrythen body and pedestal foot.

1771 *5in (12.5cm) high*

£450-550 **L&T**

A Victorian silver water jug, by Richard Martin and Ebenezer Hall of London, of plain bulbous form with simple handle, on three ball feet.

1876 *9.25in (23cm) high*

£1,000-1,500 **L&T**

A George III Scottish provincial silver cream jug, of traditional helmet form, with C-scroll handle and raised foot on square base, the body engraved with two tulips and an inscription framed within tulip leaves "Presented to Mr. John Gardener by Greenock Florist Society for First Prize of Tulips 24 May 1798", the base with what appear to be four different maker's marks.

1798 *5.25in (13cm) high*

£1,500-2,000 **L&T**

A late 19thC/early 20thC Austrian silver hot milk jug, of spiral-moulded pear shape, with short curved spout and scroll handle, the rim with feuille-de-choux, on three foliate scroll feet, maker's mark "SH".

5.5in (14cm) high

£200-300 **S&K**

A silver creamer by Garrard and Co. of London, of plain compressed circular shape with leaf-decorated spout and double-scroll handle.

1959 *3.75in (9.5cm) diam*

£220-280 **CHEF**

A pair of George III silver boat-shaped salts, by Paul Storr of London, with oval pedestal bases, reeded borders and loop handles, the interiors gilt, engraved on one side with a coat of arms.

1792 *5in (13cm) wide*

£1,200-1,800 **WW**

A pair of London silver sauce boats, by Henry Chawner.

1795 *4.75in (12cm) high*

£1,500-2,000 **JBS**

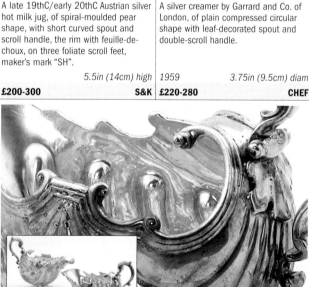

A pair of George II fluted silver sauceboats, probably by Eliza Godfrey of London, of bellied oval form on cast oval bases with leaf-capped scroll handles and applied, shell and scroll borders, maker's marks worn.

1756 *8.5in (21.5cm) long*

£3,000-4,000 **WW**

TEA, COFFEE & CHOCOLATE POTS

A rare George II Scottish silver bullet milk pot, by James Ker of Edinburgh, assaymaster Edward Penman, the spherical body with V-shaped spout, orb finial and scroll handle.

1729 *4in (10cm) high*

£2,000-3,000 **L&T**

A Victorian teapot for a travelling set designed by Christopher Dresser, by Johnathan Wilson Hukin and John Thomas Heath of London, of squat circular form, the flat lid with simple loop finial, engraved crest and straight spout, together with a teaspoon with later engraved crest, Victorian Diamond registration mark to base.

The crest is for a continental Marquis and is French or Dutch in style.

1882 *10in (25.5cm) wide*

£220-280 **L&T**

A George II Scottish bullet teapot, by John Main of Edinburgh, assaymaster Archibald Ure, the spherical body with a straight tapering spout, chased band of scrolls, shells and flowers, orb finial and scroll handle.

1729 *6.25in (16cm) high*

£2,500-3,500 **L&T**

A Scottish George III teapot, by James McEwan of Glasgow, the domed lid with pineapple finial, the inverted bombé body with chased floral decoration, C-scroll cartouches with engraved crests, bird-cast spout and simple handle, on an oval foot.

1783 *10.5in (26cm) wide*

£1,500-2,000 **L&T**

A George III bright cut silver oval teapot, by Thomas Pratt and Arthur Humphreys of London, with corrugated sides, matching oval stand with bead borders and ball and claw feet, both initialled.

1781 *10.5in (26.5cm) wide*

£1,000-1,500 **WW**

A George III teapot, with marks for London, possibly by John Robins, the spherical demi-fluted body with flared rim, engraved crest and armorial bearings, straight tapering spout, the removable fluted lid with ivory finial.

1798 *11in (27cm) wide*

£450-550 **L&T**

A George III teapot, by John Edwards of London, of circular squat form, with everted rim enclosing lift-off lid with ivory finial, the body with engraved crown of plums and tapering straight spout, on ball feet.

1799 *10in (25cm) long*

£380-420 **L&T**

A London silver teapot, by William Fountain.

1800 *10.5in (26.5cm) high*

£1,200-1,800 **JBS**

A George III silver teapot and cover, unidentified maker's mark, of panelled oval shape, with scroll spout and wood handle decorated with bands of flower heads and circlets, London hallmarks.

1800 *6.75in (17.5cm) high*

£350-450 **S&K**

A George III teapot, by John Robertson of Newcastle, of tall serpentine oval outline, with domed lid with wooden finial, simple wooden handle and straight tapering spout, the body with floral bright cut border and two armorial bearings.

c1800 *11.5in (29cm) wide*

£800-1,200 **L&T**

A George III miniature teapot, with marks for London, maker's mark worn, the domed lid with ivory finial and scroll handle, plain tapering spout.

1801 *6.5in (16cm) wide*

£180-220 **L&T**

A George III silver oval teapot and cover, by Peter and William Bateman of London, with flattened urn finial, hollow loop handle, ivory insulators and scroll spout, the shoulder and hinged cover chased with bands of stylized foliage.

1805 *11in (28cm) wide*

£300-500 **S&K**

A George III teapot, by William Birwash and Richard Sibley I of London, the oval squat body with shaped rim, engraved crest, demi-fluted slight domed lid with finial, and short stub spout.

1806 *9.5in (24cm) wide*

£400-600 **L&T**

A George III teapot, by Thomas and Rowland Hastings of London, the squat circular body with gadrooned edge, curved band and demi-fluted lower section, straight tapering spout.

1804 *10.5in (26.5cm) wide*

£380-420 **L&T**

A William IV melon-fluted teapot, by Joseph and John Angell of London, with ornate feet, applied border of flowers and flower finial.

1834 *6in (15cm) wide*

£450-550 **WW**

Left: A Victorian teapot, with marks for London, maker "J.F.", of squat ribbed form, with floral finial, acanthus-chased handle, ornate feet and shaped apron.

1840 *6.5in (16.5cm) high*

£250-350 **L&T**

Right: A Scottish William IV silver teapot, by Marshall and Sons of Edinburgh, of inverted pear form, with chased floral decoration, leaf-capped scroll handle, domed flush lid and knopped melon finial.

1836 *7in (17.5cm) high*

£350-450 **L&T**

A William IV tea service, comprising a teapot and sugar bowl, with marks for London and an Edinburgh cream jug and pair of tongs, all of lobed form with well-chased floral borders, floral chased panels and figural terminals.

c1830 *Teapot 7in (18cm) high*

£450-550 **L&T**

An early Victorian four-piece tea and coffee service, by Charles Lias of London, of melon-fluted form on ornate feet with scroll handles, the two pots with flower finials, the cream and sugar with gilt interiors.

1839 *Coffee pot 8in (21.5cm) high*

£1,500-2,000 **WW**

A George III Scottish Rococo silver coffee pot, by Lothian and Robertson of Edinburgh, the domed lid with cast fruiting branch, the tapering cylindrical body with a stained wooden handle, the spout of bold curved form with leaf chasing and figural mouth, on a circular spreading base, the whole with bold C-scroll, foliate and acanthus decoration with two cartouches, one with engraved crest and motto.

1760 *10.75in (27cm) high*

£4,000-6,000 **L&T**

A George II tapering coffee pot, by John Kincaid of London, with tucked-in base, leaf-capped swan-neck spout and spreading circular foot, the body partly chased and crested, the low-domed cover with knop finial and ivory handle.

1744 *9.5in (24cm) high*

£800-1,200 **WW**

A George III coffee pot, with marks for London, maker indistinct, the domed lid with vase finial, the spout with beaded edge, the body with beaded border and engraved armorial, all on pedestal feet with beaded rim.

1780 *12.25in (30.5cm) high*

£800-1,200 **L&T**

A George III silver water pot, by Samuel Harris of London, the tall cylindrical pot with removable lid, the body with engraved crest and one-third fluted, short spout, circular foot.

1812 *9.25in (23cm) high*

£450-550 **L&T**

A George III Scottish silver chafing dish and cover, by Ker and Dempster of Edinburgh, assaymaster Hugh Gordon, of circular form, with ebony turned handle, knopped handle to cover, crested to lid and interior.

1753 *9.25in (23cm) diam*

£5,500-6,500 **L&T**

An unusual silver brandy saucepan, probably either provincial or colonial, with turned wooden handle, baluster body with large spout, crested, with lion passant, marked "EE", indistinct date mark.

c1815 *3.5in (9cm) high*

£400-450 **WW**

A George III Scottish provincial brandy pan, by George Elder of Banff, the bulbous plain body with spout and double-hinged lid with dome and turned wooden finial, the angular handle with turned mahogany section and silver knop with hanging ring.

1820 *5in (12cm) high*

£5,000-8,000 **L&T**

A pair of George II Scottish provincial silver tea caddies, with marks for George Cooper, the rectangular upright bodies with canted corners with later engraved floral sprays and cartouches with initial, the pull-off domed lids with turned finials, scratched initials "G.J.B." in script to the base.

1730 *4.75in (12cm) high*

£5,000-8,000 **L&T**

VASES

A George III vase, with marks for Newcastle, probably by Thomas Watson, of campana form, the upper edge with applied stylized shells and a continuous band of naturalistic leaf-clasping around the base and column, on a spreading circular foot.

1809 *7in (17.5cm) high*

£350-450 **L&T**

A pair of late Victorian silver specimen vases, by H. Matthews of Birmingham, each raised on a square foot below a lobed part-fluted flaring body.

1894 *8in (20.5cm) high*

£100-150 **CHEF**

A pair of London silver vases, by Gibson and Langman.

1890 *8in (20.5cm) high*

£700-1,000 **JBS**

A Birmingham silver photo frame vase.

1900 *6.25 (16cm) high*

£600-650 **JBS**

A garniture of three vases and covers, with stretched globular bodies with applied rosette and harebell swags engraved with a crest and motto and scrolling wire handles, the lids with flame finials, on plain stems and stepped square bases with beaded edges and ball feet, the covers with lions passant, the bodies unmarked.

9.75in (24.5cm) high

£600-900 **L&T**

WINE ACCESSORIES

A George II escutcheon wine label, by John Harvey of London, with a flat-chased border of fruiting vines, incised "W-WINE", maker's mark struck twice, no date mark.

c1740 *1.75in (4.5cm) wide*

£180-220 **WW**

A George III plain oblong wine label, probably by Thomas Woodhouse of London, incised "WHITEWINE", with maker's mark and lion passant, no date mark.

c1770 *2in (5cm) wide*

£180-220 **WW**

A unusual George III bright engraved openwork wine label, probably provincial or colonial, with Prince of Wales feathers issuing from a crown, above festoons of foliage and the title "HOCK", maker's mark "JB. F" struck thrice, no date mark.

c1775 *2in (5cm) wide*

£380-420 **WW**

A George III large oblong wine label, by Margaret Binley of London, with incurved corners and reeded borders, incised "MADEIRA", with maker's mark struck twice, no date mark.

c1780 *1.75in (4.5cm) wide*

£180-220 **WW**

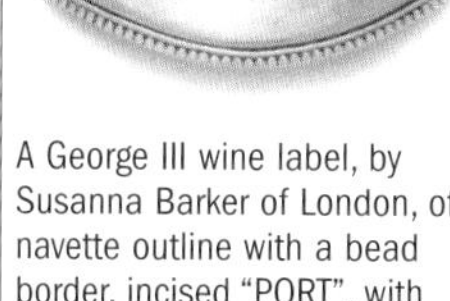

A George III wine label, by Susanna Barker of London, of navette outline with a bead border, incised "PORT", with duty mark, no date mark.

c1785 *1.5in (4cm) wide*

£120-180 **WW**

A set of three George III Scottish provincial wine labels by Edward Livingstone of Dundee, each of crescent shape, engraved "RUM", "GIN" and "SHERRY", marked "EL" and with a vase of lilies.

1780 *1.75in (4.5cm) wide*

£500-800 **L&T**

A scarce pair of George III wine labels, by Peter and Jonathan Bateman of London, in the form of shaped crescents, incised "GIN" and "RUM", no date marks.

c1790 *2in (5cm) wide*

£500-700 **WW**

A scarce Maltese wine label, by Gioacchino Lebrun, of canted oblong form with a neck ring and reeded borders, pierced "MADEIRA".

1790 *1.75in (4.5cm) wide*

£400-600 **WW**

A George III bright cut provincial silver wine label, with a curved title area surmounted by Prince of Wales feathers, incised "HOCK", maker's mark "IM", no date mark.

c1790 *1.75in (4.5cm) wide*

£200-300 **WW**

A George III wine label, probably provincial, with bright cut zig-zag border and an arched surmount pierced with a bunch of grapes, incised "SHERRY", unmarked.

c1790 *1.75in (4.5cm) wide*

£150-200 **WW**

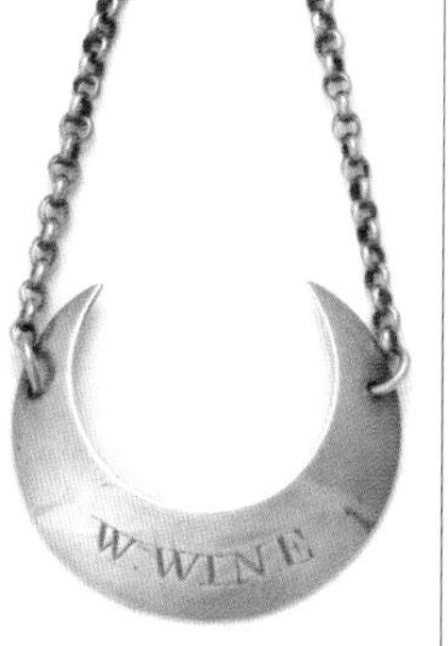

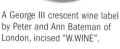

A George III crescent wine label by Peter and Ann Bateman of London, incised "W.WINE".

1797 *2in (5cm) wide*

£120-180 **WW**

A rare George III Irish wine label, by John Teare of Dublin, of canted oblong form with a vacant shield surmount, incised "MADEIRA", no date mark.

c1800 *2in (5cm) wide*

£180-220 **WW**

A composite set of three early 19thC Edinburgh silver wine labels, each formed as engraved capital letters, no date marks.

2in (5cm) high

£150-200 L&T

A George III wine label, by Alice and George Burrows of London, in the form of a shaped crescent, incised "MADEIRA".

1810 2.25in (5.5cm) wide

£80-120 WW

An early 19thC Continental silver oval wine label, with a bright cut border and a vacant slot for inserting a title, no date mark.

c1810 1.75in (4.5cm) wide

£120-180 WW

A George III Irish silver wine label, probably by John Teare of Dublin, of canted oblong shape with gadrooned border, incised "PORT".

1813 2in (5cm) wide

£150-200 WW

A George III stamped-out wine label, by Soloman Hougham, Solomon Royes and John East Dix of London, decorated with a border of fruiting vines, a shell and scrolls below on oval surmount, incised "MADEIRA".

1817 2in (5cm) wide

£220-280 WW

A George III large wine label, by Charles Rawlings of London, in the form of a shaped escutcheon, profusely decorated in relief with flowers, grapes, scrolls and a shell, with a scroll title area, pierced "SHERRY".

1819 2in (5cm) wide

£250-300 WW

A pair of George IV escutcheon wine labels, by John Reiley of London, with shell and foliate borders, pierced "MADEIRA" and "SHERRY".

1825 2in (5cm) wide

£180-220 WW

A George IV canted oblong wine label, by John Reily of London, with reeded borders, pierced "VIDONIA".

1823 2in (5cm) wide

£180-220 WW

A set of three George IV canted oblong wine labels, by Joseph Wilmore of Birmingham, with reeded borders, incised "BUCELLAS", "MOSELLE" and "HOCK".

1826 1.75in (4.5cm) wide

£280-320 WW

A William IV West Country wine label, probably by William Woodman of Bristol, of canted oblong form with a moulded border, incised "SHERRY", no date mark.

c1835 1.75in (4.5cm) wide

£120-180 WW

An early Victorian cut-out letter "P" wine label, by C. Rawlings and W. Summers of London, with a thread border.

1839 1.75in (4.5cm) high

£80-120 WW

An early Victorian engraved cut-out letter "C" wine label, by Charles Reily and George Storer of London.

1839 *1.75in (4.5cm) high*

£80-120 **WW**

An early Victorian Scottish provincial wine label, by Robert Keay II of Perth, of canted oblong shape with an incised border, titled "SHERRY", maker's mark, no date mark.

c1840 *1.75in (4.5cm) wide*

£80-120 **WW**

A Victorian hexagonal wine label, by James Dixon and Sons of Sheffield, with a stamped foliate border, incised and filled "BRANDY".

1847 *1.5in (4cm) wide*

£80-120 **WW**

A mid-19thC colonial wine label stamped "SHERRY", the central section flanked by two cut-out exotic birds with chased decoration, probably Indian or Chinese.

1.75in (4.5cm) wide

£70-100 **WW**

A Victorian Scottish cut-out letter "G" wine label, by Mackay and Chisholm of Edinburgh, with foliate engraving, no date mark.

c1850 *1.5in (4cm) high*

£200-300 **WW**

A pair of Victorian engraved, cut-out letter "P" and "S" wine labels, by Charles Rawlings and William Summers of London.

1855 *1.75in (4.5cm) high*

£100-150 **WW**

A Victorian stamped-out Bacchanalian wine label, by C. Rawlings and W. Summers of London, with a shaped scroll border interspersed by grape bunches and surmounted by a mask pierced "SHERRY".

1860 *1.75in (4.5cm) wide*

£150-220 **WW**

A rare Victorian vine-leaf wine label, by George Unite of Birmingham, pierced "SOLFERINO".

1872 *2in (5cm) wide*

£500-700 **WW**

A rare Victorian cast wine label, by William Evans of London, of escutcheon form with a scroll and foliate border, pierced "BITTERS".

1876 *1.5in (4cm) wide*

£350-400 **WW**

A pair of modern Birmingham silver commemorative wine labels, by British Airways, given to passengers on the 10th anniversary of Concorde in 1986, with incurved corners, incised "BOURBON, CONCORDE" and "RYE, CONCORDE".

1986 *1.75in (4,5cm) wide*

£300-400 pair **WW**

A Birmingham silver souvenir neck-tag wine label, presented to passengers by British Airways as a reminder of their flight on Concorde.

c2000 *1.5in (4cm) wide*

£30-40 **WW**

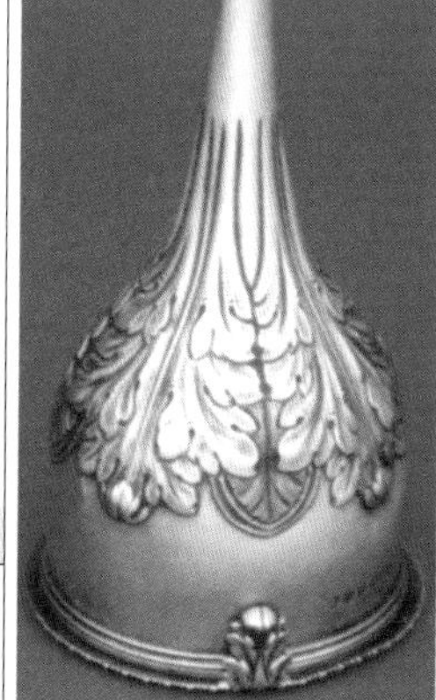

A late George III wine funnel, by Robert Hennel II of London, with crest and leaf clip and gadrooned border, embossed with acanthus.

c1815 *6in (15.5cm) high*

£1,000-1,500 **DN**

A George III wine funnel, by John Cowie of London, with a tapering spout, the bowl decorated with part-fluting and a band of reeding, initialled "M".

1814 *6.25in (16cm) high*

£500-700 **WW**

A George III wine funnel, by William Abdy II of London, with a slender spout and reeded borders, initialled "A".

1792 *5.25in (13.5cm)*

£700-1,000 **WW**

A George III wine funnel, possibly by Henry Notting of London, of conventional demi-fluted form with gadroon edge and engraved crest.

1813 *6.25in (15.5cm) high*

£700-1,000 **L&T**

A pair of London silver wine coasters, by James Mince.

1799 *6in (15cm) d.*

£2,200-2,400 **JBS**

Left: A George III coaster, possibly by Edward Aldridge, with wavy gadroon rim and well-pierced sides with blank cartouches, on a turned mahogany base, no date mark.

4.75in (12cm) diam

£400-600 **L&T**

Right: A George III wine coaster, by John Roberts and Co. of Chester, the gadroon rim above a band of pierced, chased and engraved trailing vine branch with leaves and grapes, on a turned base.

1809 *5.5in (14cm) diam*

£500-800 **L&T**

A Victorian gilt silver mounted clear glass claret jug, by Robert Harper of London, with a bulbous star-cut base and a cylindrical body, the embossed mount decorated with grotesque masks and fruiting vines, with a rampant lion and shield thumbpiece and a simulated tendril handle, hinge pin replaced.

1861 *10.5in (27cm) high*

£500-800 **WW**

A London silver decanter, by Barnards.

1864 *12.75in (32.5cm) high*

£700-1,000 **JBS**

A London silver and glass decanter, by George Fox.

1898 *11.5in (29cm) high*

£1,800-2,200 **JBS**

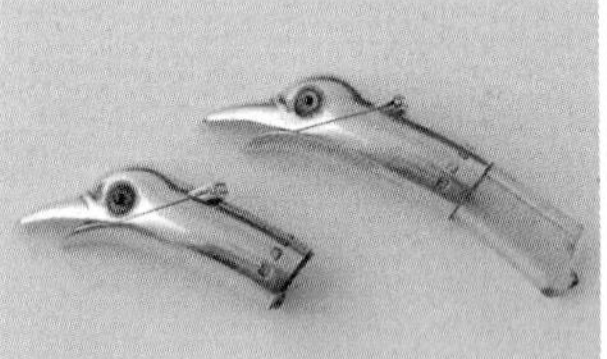

A pair of Victorian silver bottle pourers by Heath and Middleton of Birmingham, each modelled as a bird's head with hinged covers and beaded eyes, broken away from original glass.

1895 *2.75in (7cm) high*

£40-60 pair **CHEF**

A London silver wine cooler, by William Hutton and Sons Ltd.

1904 *6.5in (16.5cm) high*

£600-900 **JBS**

OTHER SILVER

A William IV toast rack, by Messrs Barnard of London, with a ring handle and seven curved bars, crested.

1835 *6.5in (16.5cm) long*

£350-400 **WW**

A London silver toast rack, by Robert Harper.

1870 *5.5in (14cm) high*

£400-600 **JBS**

A late Victorian toast rack, by the Goldsmiths and Silversmiths Co. of London, with seven Gothic arched bars and octagonal feet.

1899 *5.5in (14cm) long*

£180-220 **WW**

A small silver toast rack with ball feet and Sheffield hallmark.

1919 *2.75in (7cm) long.*

£40-60 **GS**

A Georgian ornate silver rattle, with original bells, whistle and coral teether, indistinct date mark.

3.75in (9.5cm) long

£120-180 **SSP**

A silver baby's rattle, by Yapp and Woodward of Birmingham, of pagoda-style form, with a red coral handle, and bells, terminating in a whistle.

1835 *6.25in (16cm) long*

£400-450 **GS**

A Victorian silver and ivory baby rattle, with a whistle at one end, six bells surrounding the centre section and an ivory ring at the other end, no date mark.

5in (12.5cm) long

£380-420 **JDJ**

A silver baby's rattle, by George Unite of Birmingham, with a coral handle, silver bells and repoussé floral decoration.

1863 *6in (15cm) high*

£300-500 **GS**

A silver baby's rattle with silver bells, mother of pearl handle and repoussé decoration, hallmark for "E.S.B." of Birmingham.

1900 *6in (15cm) high*

£300-400 **GS**

A Queen Anne miniature or toy mug, of tapering form with a reeded girdle and foot and a coiled scroll handle, no apparent maker's mark, London.

1712 *1.5in (3.5cm) high*

£400-450 **WW**

A George I miniature or toy teapot and cover, by David Clayton of London, pear-shaped with a straight spout and scroll handle, maker's mark and lion passant, indistinct date mark.

c1725 *1.5in (4cm) high*

£300-400 **WW**

A Victorian miniature or toy teapot, by Yapp and Woodward of Birmingham, of cuboid form with panels of stamped chinoiserie decoration and a hinged cover with a flower finial.

1848 *1.5in (4cm) high*

£180-220 **WW**

An Edward VII silver miniature tea service, maker's mark for "J and JM Ltd", comprising coffeepot, cream jug, sugar bowl and cartouche-shaped tray, inscribed "Phyllis", with Sheffield hallmarks.

1910 *Tray 5.5in (14cm) long*

£180-220 **S&K**

A George III silver gilt 'Pitt' inkwell, by John Robbins of London, the urn finial opening to reveal a fitted interior with a pounce pot, inkwell and a small jar and cover, the lower support with a floral frieze and threaded curved supports on a spreading circular base.

1791 *5.75in (14.5cm) high*

£3,000-4,000 **L&T**

A rare George III lady's inkstand, by Samuel Meriton II of London, on four paw feet, with an openwork handle, the oval base fitted with two mounted glass bottles and three other receivers, decorated all over with bead borders.

1782 *4.5in (11.5cm) wide*

£2,000-3,000 **WW**

A George IV oblong inkstand, by Messrs Barnard of London, the rounded corners and gadrooned borders with shell and foliate corners, fitted with two mounted glass bottles and a central box with a detachable cover in the form of a small chamberstick, with detachable nozzle and conical snuffer.

1829 *8in (20cm) wide*

£2,000-3,000 **WW**

A Sheffield silver and glass inkwell, by Brook and Son.

1920 *3.25in (8cm) high*

£320-380 **JBS**

A scarce Scottish George III dish cross, by Fraser Howden of Edinburgh, of traditional cross form, with adjustable lamp holder, the supports sliding along the arms, one support with engraved initials "WD" in script, lamp missing.

1794 *14in (35cm) wide*

£800-1,200 **L&T**

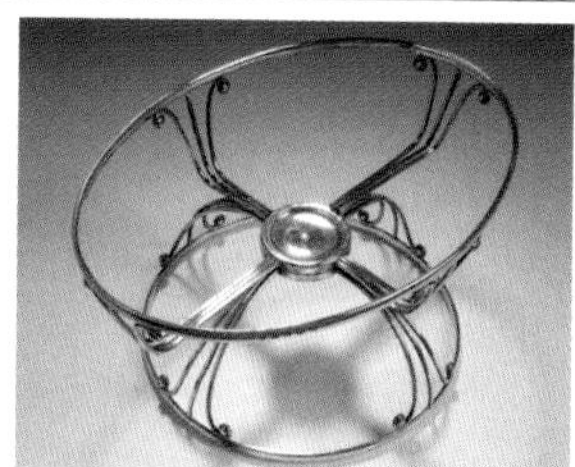

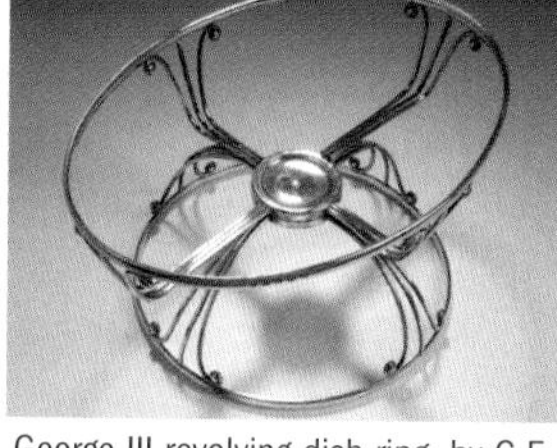

A George III revolving dish ring, by G.E. and Co. of Sheffield, with upper oval frame and engraved central boss, on a circular foot.

1803 *11.75in (29.5cm) wide*

£220-280 **L&T**

A Britannia London silver standard dish ring, with maker's mark "HF", of traditional form, with well-reticulated chased decoration in the chinoiserie taste.

1909 *8in (20cm) diam*

£1,000-1,500 **L&T**

A pair of French silver and enamel flowered lorgnettes.

c1900 *6in (15cm) long*

£220-280 **SSP**

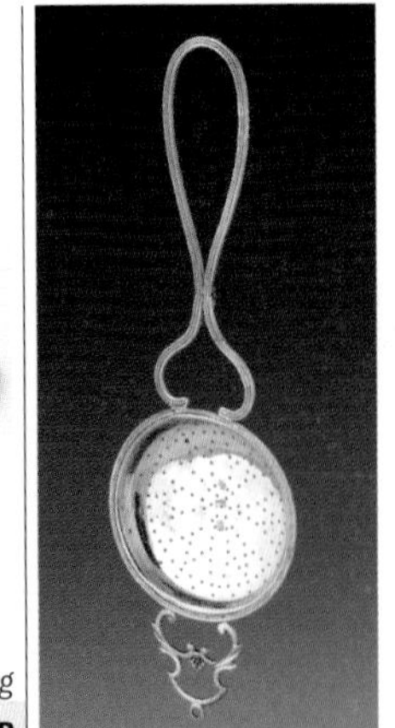

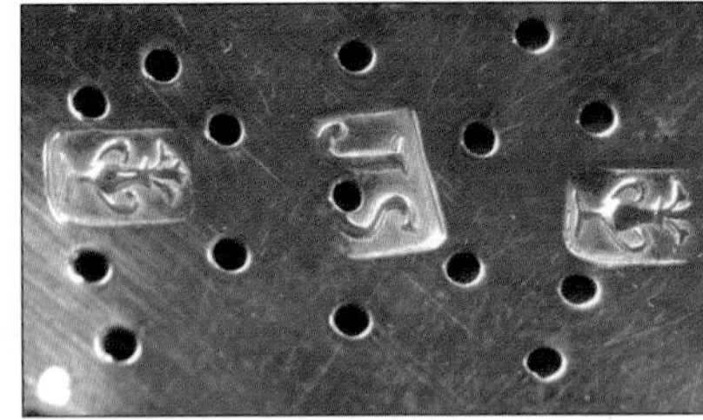

A rare Scottish George III provincial punch strainer, probably by John Steven, with marks for Dundee, the circular shallow bowl with scrolled clip, the open reeded handle hinged and folding, three marks to the bowl including a vase of lilies.

1760 *11.75in (30cm) long*

£2,000-3,000 **L&T**

A George III lemon strainer, by Charles Aldridge and Henry Green of London, with twin beaded loop handles and a beaded rim, the shallow bowl pierced with a flowerhead pattern of drilled holes.

1785 *11in (28cm) long*

£700-1,000 **WW**

A George III Scottish nutmeg grater, by Robert Gray and Sons of Glasgow, with marks for Edinburgh, engraved with crest for Stirling of Keir.

1814 *3.5in (9cm) high*

£400-600 **L&T**

A London silver and glass paperweight, with pig knop, engraved "JWB".

1890 *3.5in (9cm) high*

£320-380 **JBS**

A London silver picture frame, by William Hutton and Sons Ltd.

1903 *3.75in (9.5cm) high*

£600-700 **JBS**

A Birmingham silver and glass box, by Hukin and Heath.

1909 *7in (18cm) high*

£520-580 **JBS**

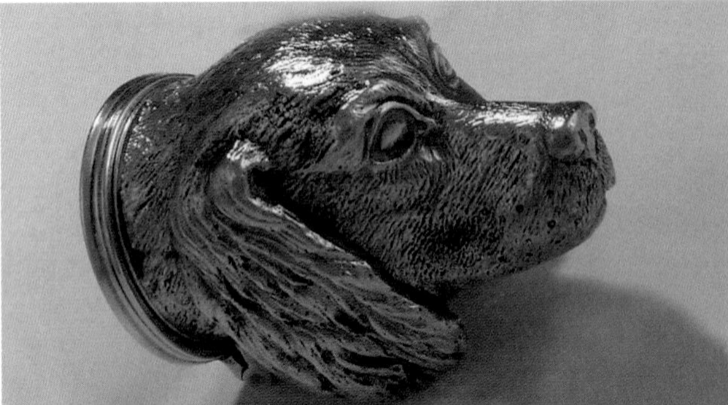

A silver pill box, by Robert Garrard of London, modelled as a setter's head.

2000 *4.5in (11.5cm) long*

£200-300 **L&T**

A hanging paper clip, with marks for London and maker's mark "WW", modelled as a duck's head, with parcel gilt beak, glass eyes and a sprung clip with a hole for hanging.

2000 *5.25in (13cm) long*

£220-280 **L&T**

A late Victorian silver scent funnel, by Deakin and Francis of Birmingham, of plain conical form with a scrolled edge.

1900 *2.5in (6.5cm) long*

£50-80 **CHEF**

SILVER PLATE

A pair of middle period Old Sheffield Plate wine coolers, of squat form with part-fluting, rope borders and drop-ring handles with Bacchanalian masks, complete with liners and collars and engraved with a coat of arms.

c1815 *9in (23cm) high*

£800-1,200 **WW**

A late period Old Sheffield Plate wine cooler, with a part-fluted campana-shaped body and foliate handles, crested, complete with collar and liner.

c1820 *9.25in (23.5cm) high*

£500-800 **WW**

A pair of late period Old Sheffield Plate wine coolers, of square vase form on shaped square bases with borders of embossed part-fluting, gadrooned with shells and foliage, engraved on one side with a coat of arms below the motto "Fide Sed Vide", complete with large collars and liners.

c1825 *10.25in (26cm) high*

£1,800-2,200 **WW**

A pair of 19thC Sheffield Plate wine coolers, each campana-shaped body with flaring sides engraved with a coat of arms, the spreading moulded foot with a band of lobing above a gadrooned rim, the top with a plated insert, wear to all areas, minor dents to lobed section of bodies.

9.5in (24cm) high

£600-900 **FRE**

One of a pair of late period Old Sheffield Plate wine coolers, of campana form with part-fluting, twin foliate handles, gadrooned and shell borders, a frieze of repeating anthemion motifs, and engraved with a coat of arms and a crest above the motto "Stabit Quocunque Jeceris", complete with collars and liners, maker's mark a single sunburst motif, possibly for Mappin Brothers.

c1845 *10in (25.5cm) high*

£2,500-3,000 pair **WW**

A set of five early period Old Sheffield Plate oval salts, on ball and claw feet with pierced sides, bead borders and star-cut blue glass liners, crested.

c1780 *2.75in (7cm) long*

£280-320 set **WW**

A set of three George III wine coasters, by John Roberts and Co. of Sheffield, with gadrooned borders and turned wooden bases with inset bosses, initialled.

c1810 *5.75in (14.5cm) diam*

£1,200-1,800 **WW**

A George III silver-plated chamberstick, by George Eadon and Co. of Sheffield, with an oblong base and nozzle and conical snuffer, crested.

c1805 *5.5in (14cm) wide*

£400-600 **WW**

A pair of George IV silver-plated wine coasters, by John and Thomas Settle of Sheffield, with part-fluted sides, gadrooned borders and turned wooden bases with inset bosses, crested.

c1830 *6in (15cm) diam*

£1,500-2,000 **WW**

A pair of middle period Old Sheffield Plate three-light candelabra, by Matthew Boulton and Co., with torch finials, reeded scroll branches and circular bases with gadrooned borders.

c1815 *17.75in (45cm) high*

£1,200-1,800 **WW**

A late period Old Sheffield Plate centrepiece, on a triform base, the column in the form of three Classical maiden figures, standing back to back supporting aloft a lattice basket, fitted with a cut-glass bowl.

c1825 *21in (53cm) high*

£800-1,200 **WW**

A pair of late period Old Sheffield Plate candlesticks, profusely decorated with flowers, husks and scrolls.

c1825 *10.5in (26.5cm) high*

£250-300 pair **WW**

A pair of late period Old Sheffield Plate chambersticks, with foliate borders, circular pans and ejector bolts, complete with nozzles and conical snuffers.

c1830 *6.5in (16.5cm) diam*

£300-500 **WW**

Two pairs of middle period Old Sheffield Plate wine labels, one pair crescent-shaped with drapery surmounts titled "CLARET", and "SHERRY", the other pair with openwork and urn surmount with foliate borders titled "MADEIRA" and "LISBON".

c1785 *1.75in (4.5cm) wide*

£400-600 **WW**

An early period Old Sheffield Plate two-handled cup, on a raised gadrooned foot, the waisted body embossed with a rocaille cartouche, wrythen fluting and a rope girdle, crested below the motto "Mea Gloria Fides".

c1765 *7in (18cm) high*

£350-400 **WW**

Two middle period Old Sheffield Plate tankards, of tapering form with domed covers, applied girdles and inset wooden bases.

c1785 *7.5in (19cm) high*

£300-400 pair **WW**

A middle period Old Sheffield Plate oval tea caddy, with bead borders and a flower finial, engraved on the front with a crest and a foliate wreath.

c1785 *5.25in (13cm) high*

£300-400 **WW**

A late period Old Sheffield Plate soup tureen, oblong with a gadrooned border and reeded handles with mask decoration, the cover and warming base embossed and part-fluted, with engraved coat of arms.

c1820 *13.5in (34.5cm) long*

£400-600 **WW**

Two large Victorian plate spirit kettles and stands, of ornate Rococo form.

14in (35.5cm) high

£200-300 **L&T**

A 19thC American miniature silver-plated tea set, comprising a teapot, covered sugar bowl, creamer, waste bowl, six cups and saucers, and five spoons, the fitted box bearing label "Manufactured by James W. Tufts, 33 to 39 Bonker St. Boston".

12.5in (32cm) wide

£250-300 **POOK**

CLOCKS

Antique clocks have suffered from the same mood of uncertainty that has been affecting so many other areas of the antiques market in the last couple of years. Combined with the weakness of the dollar, this has meant that many prices have remained static or even dropped over the last year. Until recently, any clock with a good, interesting mechanism would find a buyer: today, the case must also be striking if a clock is to sell.

Elegance, however, will always sell, and a clock with a good mechanism in an elegant case can be relied upon to attract interest. Exceptional and early examples of the horologist's art are similarly impervious to market fluctuations – a clock by Vulliamy is unlikely to be affected by the adverse conditions at the lower end of the market. Marquetry cases are also perennially popular, and attracting more interest today.

Dark wood furniture does not fit comfortably into many modern interiors, and this has affected the market for long case clocks, especially those made from walnut, mahogany and dark oak. Traditionally the mainstay of the clock dealer's inventory, longcase clocks are far less important today.

Clock collectors tend to be in middle age and, as they get older and their collections become more comprehensive, they tend to buy less at the bottom and middle of the market. With a lack of young collectors coming into the bottom of the market, the prognosis for all but the most exceptional antique clocks can only be for modest price increases at best.

Paul Archard at Derek Roberts Fine Antique Clocks

LONGCASE CLOCKS

A late 17thC marquetry eight-day longcase clock, by Joseph Saer, London, the five pillar, twin train movement with an anchor escapement, striking on a bell, with a silver chapter ring and cast spandrels, inscribed "Jos Saer, Porpoole Lane, London".

94.5in (236cm) high

£8,000-12,000 **L&T**

An early 18thC burr-walnut eight-day longcase clock, by Andrew Dickie of Stirling, with a twin train movement and anchor escapement, striking on a bell.

85.5in (217cm) high

£2,500-3,000 **L&T**

A CLOSER LOOK AT A 17THC LONGCASE CLOCK

Clocks in largely unrestored condition are very much in demand. Their rarity means that they command high prices.

The provenance of this clock was solid, having been in the same family for generations.

The twin train movement is in working order and is unrestored, preserving the integrity.

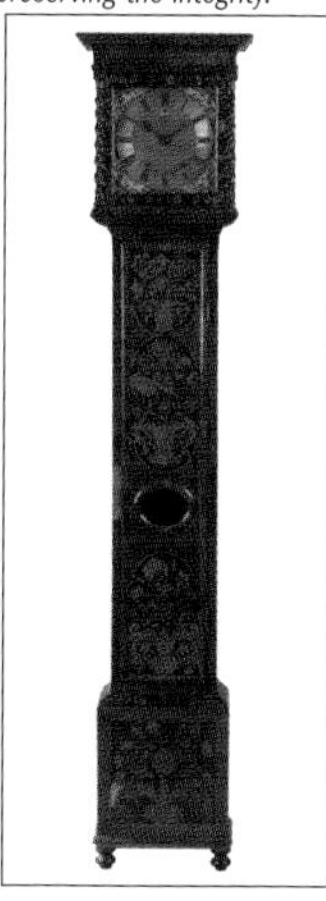

A 17thC walnut and marquetry-inlaid eight-day longcase clock, the twin train movement with an inscribed square brass dial, with a silvered chapter ring and Roman chapters, enclosing a date aperture, with a glazed lenticle and marquetry panelling, the whole raised on turned feet.

80.75in (202cm) high

£30,000-40,000 **L&T**

A George I mahogany eight-day longcase clock, the twin train movement with an anchor escapement, striking on a bell, the brass dial with a silvered chapter ring, cast spandrels, a subsidiary seconds dial and date aperture.

92in (234cm) high

£1,200-1,800 **L&T**

A George I Japanned eight-day longcase clock, the twin train movement with an anchor escapement, striking on a bell, the arched brass dial with cast spandrels and with a strike/silent dial.

86.5in (216cm) high

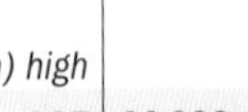

£2,500-3,000 **L&T**

A George II mahogany eight-day longcase clock by William Drysdale, Edinburgh, the twin train movement with an anchor escapement, the painted dial with Roman chapters and a subsidiary date aperture.

89in (222.5cm) high

£4,000-6,000 **L&T**

An 18thC carved oak longcase clock, the eight-day twin train movement with an anchor escapement, striking on a bell, the dial signed "William Gill, Maidstone".

80.5in (201cm) high

£1,200-1,800 **FRE**

A mid-to late 18thC brass-mounted and mahogany-inlaid longcase clock, by Henry Biddle, London, with a strike/silent feature.

81.25in (206.5cm) high

£2,000-3,000 **S&K**

A George III mahogany eight-day longcase clock, by Robert Croal, Alyth, the twin train movement with an anchor escapement.

84.75in (212cm) high

£3,000-4,000 **L&T**

A George III mahogany eight-day longcase clock, by Robert Hay, the twin train movement with an anchor escapement, the painted dial with Roman numerals, with seconds and date dials.

82.5in (206cm) high

£1,200-1,800 **L&T**

A George III mahogany eight-day longcase clock, by John Carmichael, Greenock, the twin train movement with an anchor escapement, striking on a bell.

83.25in (208cm) high

£1,200-1,800 **L&T**

A George III mahogany eight-day longcase clock, by Moses Abraham, Frome, the twin train movement with an anchor escapement, striking on a bell.

94in (235cm) high

£3,500-4,500 **L&T**

An early 19thC Provincial mahogany-inlaid oak longcase clock, inscribed with "Huband/Evesham".

82.75in (210cm) high

£700-1,000 **S&K**

A Georgian inlaid burl walnut longcase clock, the silvered dial with pierced corner spandrels and the maker's name "Charles Loundes, Pall Mall, London".

86in (215cm) high

£10,000-15,000 **NA**

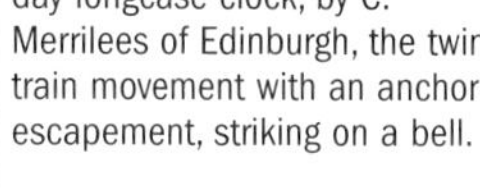

A George III mahogany eight-day longcase clock, by C. Merrilees of Edinburgh, the twin train movement with an anchor escapement, striking on a bell.

84.25in (214cm) high

£2,500-3,000 **L&T**

An early 19thC oak and mahogany eight-day longcase clock, by Hugh Russell, Moffat, the twin train movement with an anchor escapement, the enamelled dial indistinctly signed.

88.75in (222cm) high

£600-900 **L&T**

An early 19thC mahogany eight-day longcase clock, by James McOwan, Crieff, the twin train movement with an anchor escapement.

87.25in (218cm) high

£2,200-2,800 **L&T**

An early 19thC eight-day drumhead mahogany longcase clock, by A. Breckenridge & Son, Kilmarnock, the twin train movement with an anchor escapement.

87.75in (219cm) high

£1,500-2,000 **L&T**

An early 19thC Irish George III pine longcase clock, inscribed "Jos. Andrew/Dublin".

77.75in (197.5cm) high

£800-1,200 **S&K**

A Regency inlaid mahogany longcase clock, the brass face enclosing musical works with seven bells, a moon phase and the inscription "Tempus Fugit".

c1800 95in (241.5cm) high

£3,000-4,000 **POOK**

A George IV mahogany and oak longcase clock, with an eight-day movement, striking on a bell, signed "A. THOMAS".

c1825 93in (232.5cm) high

£800-1,200 **FRE**

A 19thC mahogany eight-day longcase clock, the twin train movement with an anchor escapement, the painted dial with Roman chapters and subsidiary seconds and date dials.

87.5in (219cm) high

£1,500-2,000 **L&T**

A 19thC mahogany eight-day longcase clock, the twin train movement striking on a bell, the enamelled, arched dial painted with flowers, the hood with a swan neck pediment and columns, the shaped trunk door flanked by quarter columns, on a plinth base.

82.5in (206cm) high

£600-900 **L&T**

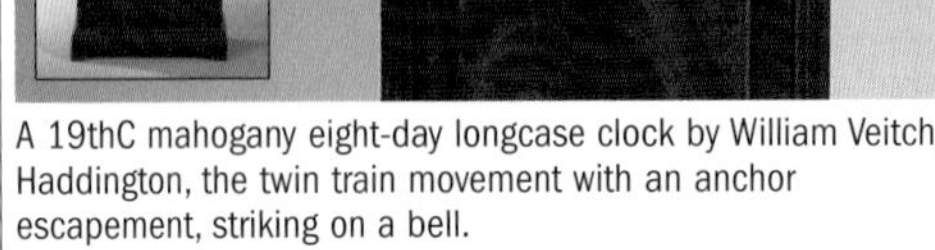

A 19thC mahogany eight-day longcase clock by William Veitch, Haddington, the twin train movement with an anchor escapement, striking on a bell.

90.75in (227cm) high

£7,000-10,000 **L&T**

A 19thC French Gothic-style carved oak longcase clock, with an eight-day movement, striking on a bell, the white enamel dial signed "a Aigueperse".

92.5in (231cm) high

£2,200-2,800 **FRE**

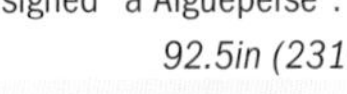

A 19thC carved and stained oak longcase clock by William Miller, Edinburgh, the twin train movement with an anchor escapement, striking on a bell.

89.5in (224cm) high

£700-1,000 **L&T**

An Edwardian mahogany longcase clock, by John Colet, the eight-day movement striking on a bell.

86in (215cm) high

£600-900 **FRE**

A Japanned Queen Anne-style eight-day longcase clock, the associated twin train movement with an anchor escapement, adapted.

99.5in (253cm) high

£700-1,000 **L&T**

A mahogany eight-day longcase clock by Bryson & Sons, Dalkeith, the twin train movement with an anchor escapement, the painted dial with Roman chapters and subsidiary seconds and date dials.

89.5in (224cm) high

£1,200-1,800 **L&T**

A Dutch marquetry walnut longcase clock, the eight-day movement with an anchor escapement, striking on a bell, signed "Joseph Parish, Broughton".

101in (252.5cm) high

£4,000-6,000 **FRE**

An eight-day longcase clock by Thomas Powley, the twin train movement with an anchor escapement, striking on a gong, the case with carved decoration.

82in (205cm) high

£600-900 **L&T**

BRACKET CLOCKS

A small late 17thC ebonised bracket clock, by Richard Colston of London, with a fine repoussé basket top surmounted by a decorative carrying handle, surrounded by four Rococo finials, the unusual side panels with glazed inner panels, on brass bun feet, the engraved back plate decorated with tulips and signed in a cartouche, the faceted blued steel hands with chasing.

c1690 *12.5in (32cm) high*

£20,000-30,000 **DR**

An unusual mahogany balloon-shaped automaton bracket clock, by Joseph Dudds, with a pineapple urn finial, the silk-covered sides with brass fish scale frets, the dial painted with a scene of a girl and musicians, the two train striking movement with a restored verge escapement, with a profusely engraved back plate.

c1760 *19in (48.5cm) high*

£10,000-15,000 **DR**

An elegant mahogany-cased bell top bracket clock, by John Mitchell of London, with gilded caryatids to the corners and gilded frets to either side of the arch, with flambeau finials to the top, standing on ogee bracket feet, the rectangular plated fusee striking movement with a verge escapement, the back plate profusely engraved with a floral pattern, signed to silvered dial disc.

c1770 *19in (48.5cm) high*

£10,000-15,000 **DR**

A mahogany bell top bracket clock, by Charles Geddes of London, the dial with a strike/silent disc, a twin gut fusee movement, reconverted verge escapement striking on a bell, a presentation signature dated 1855.

As Charles Geddes moved to Nova Scotia in 1776, it is possible that this clock was signed 'London' to make it saleable, or it may have been made in London, Nova Scotia.

c1780 *17.5in (44cm) high*

£10,000-15,000 **DR**

A George III ebonised musical bracket clock, by Edward Tomlin of London, the inverted bell top case with pineapple finials, the large cast brass frets with human figures to the sides, a fine three train fusee movement playing four tunes, employing ten bells and 16 hammers, with a substantial pin barrel, the back plate with fine oriental-style engraving, the brass dial with a recessed name plaque in the arch and decorated with engraving.

c1780 *24in (61cm) high*

£10,000-15,000 **DR**

A CLOSER LOOK AT A BRACKET CLOCK

Lacquered clocks were only available to the very richest in society and were in vogue for a short period. Most were a dark colour – this very pale lacquer is extremely rare.

Bracket clocks of a certain size, small enough to fit on a modern mantelpiece, are particularly sought after by today's market.

The chinoiserie decoration on this clock is lively, and is exquisitely accomplished. This clock is in excellent condition, further enhancing the value.

A very rare English cream ground bracket clock, with a lacquered case, by Robert and Peter Higgs of London, with an eight-day verge movement.

c1775

£30,000-40,000 **CATO**

An 18thC Dutch mahogany table clock, the four pillar movement into twin train fusee movement, striking the quarters on two steel bells, the arch with strike/silent and fast/slow dials.

18.5in (46cm) high

£1,500-2,000 **L&T**

A George III walnut and brass-mounted striking table clock, by John Prichard, London, the five pillar twin fusee movement striking the half hours on a brass bell, the back plate bearing the inscription "No 508", with a strike/silent dial to the arch.

20.75in (52cm) high

£5,000-8,000 **L&T**

A George III mahogany-cased bracket timepiece by Matthew Powell, London, the single train fusee movement with a silvered dial, inscribed to the arch "Matthew. Powell, London".

14.75in (37cm) high

£1,500-2,000 **L&T**

A late 18thC mahogany pad top bracket clock, by William Jordan of Chesham, the sturdily constructed movement with a verge escapement, striking the hours on a bell.

£5,000-8,000 **DR**

A late 18thC mahogany pad top bracket clock, by William Jordan of Chesham, the sturdily constructed movement with a verge escapement, striking the hours on a bell.

£5,000-8,000 **DR**

A mahogany pad top bracket clock, by Jno. Bryan of Shadwell, with cast spandrels and engraving to the moon arch, the moon disc with a finely painted sky, the moon faces edged with a silvered border, the twin gut fusee movement with a re-converted verge escapement, with an unusual engraved back plate depicting the Half Moon public house.

c1790 *15in (38cm) high*

£12,000-18,000 **DR**

A Regency rosewood bracket clock, by J. & M. Mitchell, Glasgow, the twin train movement with an anchor escapement, striking on a bell, the square, silvered, dial engraved "J & M Mitchell, 80 Argyll Street, Glasgow".

15.25in (38cm) high

£2,000-3,000 **L&T**

A late George IV to early William IV English brass-inlaid mahogany bracket clock.

22in (56cm) high

£5,000-8,000 **B&I**

A 19thC oak bracket clock, quarter repeating, with twin train fusee movement, a brass dial.

29.25in (73cm) high

£800-1,200 **L&T**

A 19thC mahogany and brass-inlaid bracket clock, the eight-day striking fusee movement with an anchor escapement.

18in (45cm) high

£1,800-2,200 **FRE**

A 19thC mahogany bracket clock, with a subsidiary strike/silent ring, an eight-day twin train, the five pillar fusee movement striking on a bell, signed "Jn. Carter, London".

22in (55cm) high

£2,200-2,800 **FRE**

A late 19thC rosewood-cased chiming mantel clock, the triple train movement striking on five gongs, the brass dial inscribed "Goldsmiths & Silversmiths Company, 112 Regent Street, London" stamped "M&H".

15.25in (38cm) high

£1,800-2,200 **L&T**

A George III mahogany break-arch bracket clock, by James McCabe of London, the brass-bound pad top with a carrying handle, with fishscale frets to either side, the brass dial with a silvered chapter ring and a maker's name plaque, the verge escapement movement on a knife edge, the back plate engraved with Prince of Wales feathers.

c1790 *15in (38.5cm) high*

£10,000-15,000 **DR**

A lancet shaped mahogany and ebony-strung bracket clock, with a twin fusee striking movement, on brass ball feet with two carrying handles to the sides, the painted dial with an original background, the two train fusee movement of typical quality, striking hours on a bell.

c1840 *19in (48.5cm) high*

£3,000-4,000 **DR**

A fine striking mahogany bracket clock, by James McCabe of London, with a gilded dial, the arched mahogany case with a recessed ebony-bound panel, the gilded dial with an engine-turned centre and a matt-gilded chapter ring with light roman numerals, the substantial fusee movement with a signed and numbered circular plate.

c1850 *13in (33.5cm) high*

£5,000-8,000 **DR**

A superb three train mahogany balloon-shaped bracket clock, by Patrick Hutton, London, chiming the quarters on ten bells, strikes the hours on a further bell, a three train chain fusee movement with shaped plates to conform with the shape of the case, the long steel rod pendulum employed with a heavy and shaped bob, with a pendulum clamp, signed by the maker on the back plate.

79in (197.5cm) high

£8,000-12,000 **DR**

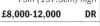

An inlaid figured walnut veneer musical bracket clock, by Samuel Whichcote, London, the brass and steel dial with maker's name.

18in (45cm) high

£8,000-12,000 **NA**

A mahogany double fusee bracket clock, an engraved back plate, the dial signed "S & C Joyce, Lombard Street, London".

15in (38cm) high

£2,500-3,000 **GHOU**

An English mahogany triple fusee bracket clock chiming on eight bells.

23in (58.5cm) high

£1,800-2,200 **GHOU**

A double fusee verge bracket clock, with regulator and strike/silent dials, the mated centre with false bob pendulum, the brass dial signed "John Elliott, Plymouth" to the arch.

22.5in (57cm) high

£4,000-6,000 **GHOU**

A rosewood double fusee bracket clock, by James McCabe of Royal Exchange, London, the movement with dead beat escapement, a pull repeat and striking on a bell, the dial with strike/silent to the arch, number "2376", signed to the dial and back plate.

17in (43cm) high

£3,000-5,000 **GHOU**

A George III-style mahogany bracket clock, by Hamilton and Inches of Edinburgh, the twin train movement striking on a gong with anchor escapement.

15.25in (39cm) high

£800-1,200 **L&T**

A mahogany double fusee bracket clock, with a shaped and engraved back plate.

20in (51cm) high

£1,200-1,800 **GHOU**

CARRIAGE CLOCKS

A 19thC brass-cased carriage clock by Auguste, Paris, the twin train movement with a lever platform escapement, a stamped mark to the back plate "Auguste à Paris".

6.75in (17cm) high

£700-1,000 **L&T**

A substantial twin chain fusee gilded carriage clock, by John Carter of London, the lever escapement with a gilded platform and a compensated split bi-metallic balance.

c1850 *7.75in (19.5cm) high*

£18,000-20,000 **DR**

A giant Drocourt Cannelee cased striking and repeating carriage clock, No. 7439, with an alarm, strikes and repeats on a gong, large platform and lever escapement.

c1870 *8.5in (21cm) high*

£6,000-9,000 **DR**

A giant grande sonnerie striking gorge-cased carriage clock, by Henri Jalot, with a calendar work, the engine-turned gilt mask surrounding the four dials, a large lever escapement with a bi-metallic balance.

c1870 *8.25in (21cm) high*

£12,000-18,000 **DR**

A French miniature corniche-cased carriage clock, No. 23815, with an enamelled dial and a good lever escapement.

c1880

£600-900 **DR**

A Drocourt grande sonnerie striking gorge-cased carriage clock, No. 11329, with a travelling box and key, the lever escapement with a gilded platform, striking on two gongs, bears the maker's stamp and serial number, repeated on the engraved case, key and base plate, also marked with regulation for "Petite Sonnerie - Silence & Grande Sonnerie".

c1880 *6.5in (16cm) high*

£5,000-8,000 **DR**

A CLOSER LOOK AT A CARRIAGE CLOCK

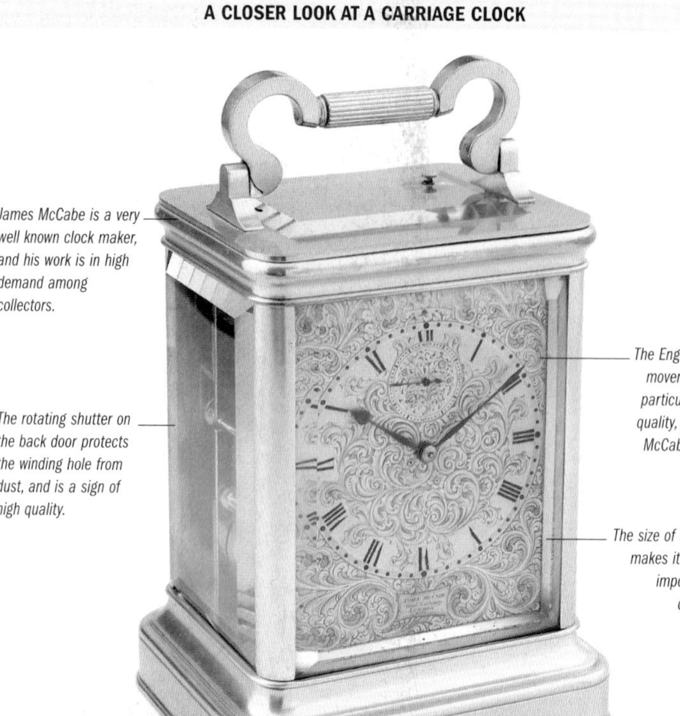

James McCabe is a very well known clock maker, and his work is in high demand among collectors.
The rotating shutter on the back door protects the winding hole from dust, and is a sign of high quality.
The English fusee movement is of particularly high quality, typical of McCabe's work.
The size of this clock makes it unusual, imposing and desirable.

A giant carriage clock, by James McCabe of London, with a fine twin chain fusee movement, lever escapement and a large plain balance, signed in full on the back plate, with maker's signature and number to base.

c1850 *9.5in (24cm) high*

£20,000-30,000 **DR**

A Lindsay Locke fine English twin chain fusee carriage clock, No. 1925, with a free-sprung lever escapement, the movement with a finely spotted back plate, striking the hour on a gong, with maintaining power to both trains.

c1880 *8in (20cm) high*

£5,000-8,000 **DR**

A rare giant rococo cased striking and repeating carriage clock, by Leroy & Fils, the back plate marked with Leroy's number "2748" and number "6466", possibly Henry Lamaille's number.

c1880 *8in (20.5cm) high*

£15,000-20,000 **DR**

A grande sonniere striking gilt and silver carriage clock, with three Limoges enamel panels, the substantial movement with a large and impressive silvered platform, striking on two gongs, numbered to back plate.

c1885 *10in (25.5cm) high*

£20,000-25,000 **DR**

A striking three-quarter size carriage clock, with a bamboo case and porcelain panels, by Henri Jacot, the top with a repeat button and a bevelled edge glass, eight-day duration and striking and repeating on a coiled blue gong, stamped with "6330", signed.

c1890 *5.5in (14cm) high*

£4,000-6,000 **DR**

An Anglaise-cased gilded carriage clock, with an original lever escapement, striking and repeating on a gong, the movement numbered "668", with a velvet-lined leather carrying case.

c1890 *5.25in (13cm) high*

£4,000-6,000 **DR**

£6,000-9,000 **DR**

A rare late 19thC bow-sided gilded carriage clock, with five enamelled panels, striking and repeating on a gong, as does the alarm, the movement numbered "3818".

7.25in (18cm) high

An E.M & Co. porcelain-panelled grande sonnerie striking carriage clock, No. 1030, with a box and key, striking on two gongs, the platform signed "T. Martin & Co. Regent Street".

c1890 *7.75in (19cm) high*

£5,000-8,000 **DR**

A Louis Fernier grande sonnerie striking carriage clock, No. 4439, the three porcelain panels decorated with figures, striking on two gongs.

c1890 *7.75in (19cm) high*

£6,000-9,000 **DR**

A Drocourt, Paris three-quarter size gong cased carriage clock, striking and repeating on a gong, the movement and case stamped with the number "31691", with its original travelling case.

c1890 *5.25in (13cm) high*

£3,000-3,500 **DR**

A grand sonnerie carriage clock, with cloisonné enamel, an alarm and centre sweep seconds hand, the movement with a silvered lever platform, striking on two coiled gongs, with a selection lever in the base for silent, quarters only and hours and quarters, with a button for repeating the hours and quarters, numbered "582".

c1890 *7.75in (19cm) high*

£5,000-7,000 **DR**

A carriage clock, by William Comyns, London, with inlaid tortoiseshell panels and a domed cover.

c1910 *4.75in (12.2cm) high*

£2,000-3,000 **WW**

An early 20thC French brass-cased repeating carriage clock, the twin train movement with a lever platform escapement, striking on a gong, the faded Morocco leather travelling case with a purple velvet lining, a glazed window and cover.

7.25in (18cm) high

£1,500-2,000 **L&T**

An early 20thC French carriage clock, retailed by Furber and Son, Cheltenham, the case with a beaded oval about the carrying handle.

4.75in (12cm) high

£80-120 **CHEF**

An early 20th century French carriage clock, retailed by Cockburn, Richmond, the glazed brass obis case with an enamel dial.

4.75in (12cm) high

£50-80 **CHEF**

A rosewood twin train carriage clock, by James Gorham, maker to the Queen, with chain fusee and standing barrel mechanisms, both wound through the dial, a well executed lever escarpment, the dial and back plate with the maker's signature.

James Gorham's great talent led him to become clockmaker to Queen Victoria and the Prince of Wales as well as the Duke of Sussex, who amassed what was probably the finest collection of clocks in the country. Gorham is best known for his group of three skeleton clocks, each incorporating a celestial and terrestrial globe, one of which recently changed hands at Christies for over £300,000.

c1835 *9in (23cm) high*

£15,000-20,000 **DR**

MANTEL CLOCKS

A spring clock, by John Holmes of London, the movement with an engraved back plate, a tic-tac escapement and a roller suspension to the half seconds pendulum, employing a cradle with a regulating nut supporting a suspended bob.

c1780 *15.25in (38.5cm) high*

£10,000-15,000 **DR**

An Empire ormolu mantel clock, the twin train movement striking the half hours on a steel bell, enclosed within a case cast as a draped table with a seated classical maiden, above a verde antico marble base with turned feet.

13.25in (33cm) high

£3,500-4,500 **L&T**

An Empire gilt brass mantel clock, the case with a seated classical youth holding a ball, the dial with a porcelain chapter ring.

19.25in (48cm) high

£2,000-3,000 **L&T**

An Empire ormolu mantel clock, the movement with a silk suspension and an outside count wheel, striking on a bell, the dial signed "Foucquet Noel, Tours" flanked by figures depicting 'The Soldier's Return'.

15.5in (39.5cm) high

£1,000-1,500 **GHOU**

A miniature rosewood mantel clock, by Thwaites & Reed of London, single train chain fusee four pillar movement, with arched plates and anchor escapement.

c1825 *9in (23cm) high*

£7,000-10,000 **DR**

A 19thC Continental Empire mahogany mantel clock, the circular enamel clock face in an architectural case.

14.25in (36cm) high

£150-200 **S&K**

A Louis-Philippe gilt-bronze mounted mantel clock, surmounted by two cherubs supporting a conch shell, raised on rococo feet, headed by satire masks, the eight-day striking movement signed "Deniere A Paris".

c1840 *17in (42.5cm) high*

£800-1,200 **FRE**

A 19thC French gilt brass mantel clock, the twin train movement striking on a bell, the enamelled circular dial in a drum case.

15.5in (39cm) high

£700-1,000 **L&T**

A 19thC French ormolu and champleve enamel mantel clock, with an urn finial, the eight-day movement stamped "Japy Freres et Cie".

17.5in (45cm) high

£1,200-1,800 **WW**

A 19thC brass mantel clock, the twin train movement striking the half hours on a coiled gong, the circular dial with inset enamelled chapters.

22.5in (56cm) high

£500-800 **L&T**

A 19thC Louis XV-style Boullework mantel clock, with an enamelled dial and a Marti & Cie gong striking movement, in a boullework case with ormolu mounts.

11.75in (30cm) high

£300-500 **GORL**

A 19thC mantel clock, with an enamelled dial, a walnut case and a Winterhalder & Hoffmeier gong-striking movement.

8.25in (21cm) high

£120-180 **GORL**

A 19thC Louis XV-style bronze mantel clock, the white enamel dial with a striking eight-day barrel movement, within an ornate ogee form case, surmounted by a bronze figure of Diana, signed "MERCIER".

23in (57.5cm) high

£2,000-3,000 **FRE**

A 19thC French porcelain mantel clock, by Jacob Petit, the eight-day movement striking on a bell.

15.5in (39cm) high

£1,000-1,500 **FRE**

A 19thC Louis XVI-style gilt bronze and white marble mantel clock, the white enamel dial with a 30-hour movement surmounted by a gilt nude female figure.

18.5in (46cm) high

£600-900 **FRE**

A 19thC bronze Neo-classical mantel clock, modelled as a Greek warrior, the gilt dial cast as a shield resting against a tree, the naturalistic bronze base on a stepped Sienna marble plinth, with applied wreaths and leaf cast mouldings.

24.5in (62cm) high

£3,000-5,000 **L&T**

A Victorian fluted slate and red marble mantel clock, by Claude Michel Clodion, inscribed "Clodion", with two Bacchantes and an infant satyr bronze group, with gold patina.

31in (77.5cm) high

£2,500-3,500 **FRE**

A late 19thC French gilt-metal mantel clock, with a Sèvres-style porcelain dial, urn finial and inset plaques, the movement striking on a bell, in a Louis XVI-style case, on a shaped wood plinth.

14.5in (37cm) high

£400-600 **GORL**

A late 19thC Continental 'Four Seasons' porcelain mantel clock, with an eight-day movement, striking on a bell, an underglaze blue star and cross sword marks.

19in (47.5cm) high

£500-800 **FRE**

A Moore Brothers clock case, with cherubs, floral decoration and gilt to base.

1890 *10in (25.5cm) high*

£300-500 **AL**

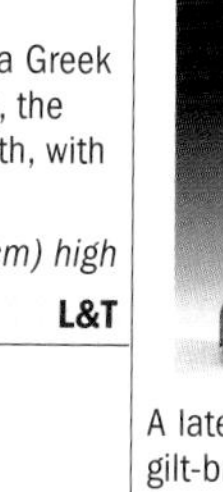

A late 19thC French onyx and gilt-bronze mantel clock, by H. Journet et Cie, Paris, with an agate dial, an eight-day barrel movement, striking on a bell.

33in (82.5cm) high

£3,500-4,500 **FRE**

A late 19thC French gilt-bronze and brass mantel clock, the eight-day movement striking on a bell, within an oval case moulded in a relief with two panels of cherubs.

22in (55cm) high

£3,500-4,500 **FRE**

A late Victorian novelty clock modelled after Henry V's helmet, by Elkington of Leeds, with a twin train movement within a shaped copper case, on a marble plinth.

14.25in (36cm) high

£2,500-3,500 **L&T**

A Wedgwood Jasperware clock case, in dark blue with white decoration, with original movement.

c1895 *6.75in (17cm) high*

£500-700 **AL**

A Neo-classical-style mantel clock, by Harris & Schafer, Washington, formed as a temple in onyx, the dial with an elaborate gilt bronze mount with a central phoenix.

c1900 *10in (25cm) high*

£300-500 **S&K**

An Edwardian mahogany mantel clock, in an arched case with a visible escapement.

12in (30.5cm) high

£150-200 **GORL**

An early 20thC porcelain and gilt-bronze mounted carriage clock, for Tiffany & Co., New York, the circular clock face on a Sevres-style plaque, painted on a turquoise ground, one side with a gallant and the other depicting his companion, on similar plaques, signed "L. Malpass".

7.5in (19cm) high

£3,000-5,000 **S&K**

An early 20thC French gilt-bronze and glass mantle clock, the works by Japy Freres, Paris, retailed by Bailey, Banks and Biddle, with a circular porcelain clock face.

10.75in (27.5cm) high

£180-220 **S&K**

An English inlaid mahogany electric mantel clock, by Eureka, model No. 4440, the arched case with a projecting moulded cornice and a plinth base, on brass feet.

c1910 *11.75in (29cm) high*

£600-900 **S&K**

An early 20thC mahogany-cased balloon clock, the French eight-day movement with a platform escapement, the enamel dial above a marquetried rosette, the plinth on four brass bun feet.

8.75in (22cm) high

£150-200 **CHEF**

An early 20thC Negretti and Zambra oak mantel clock, the eight-day timepiece with a silvered dial within a round oak frame resting on a stepped rectangular plinth.

8.75in (22cm) high

£100-150 **CHEF**

A 20thC French brass mantel clock, the enamel dial inscribed with retailer's name "Tiffany & Co./FRANCE", twin train movement, coil gong and mercury regulator pendulum.

13in (32.5cm) high

£1,500-2,000 **S&K**

An early Georgian-style red lacquered mantel clock, with chinoiserie decoration and an engraved, arched brass dial, with Smiths movement.

9.25in (23.5cm) high

£120-180 **GORL**

A German musical clock, by E.M. Wherle & Cie, with a cylinder musical box accompanied by musical pipes, driven by a mechanical bellows, the pipe mechanism with a paper label reading "E.W.Co Marke".

In order to make the mechanism play music, a penny must be dropped into the slot on the side. When the pipes play, the doors under the clock open and a small German piper moves out.

34in (86.5cm) high

£3,000-5,000 **ET**

A German oak ting tang mantel clock, with Winterhalder and Hofmeier movement.

16in (40.5cm) high

£280-320 **GHOU**

A German oak ting tang mantel clock, with Winterhalder and Hofmeier movement.

19in (48cm) high

£150-250 **GHOU**

A large Black Forest trumpeter mantle clock, with a metal skeletonised plate movement, sounding the hours and halves on three trumpets, the emerging figure holding a barrel, within a fretwork and pillared case.

28.5in (72.5cm) high

£600-900 **GHOU**

A Black Forest mantel timepiece, with a small printed circular dial and Junghans movement, supported between four columns, with a gilt-metal cone finial.

12.75in (32.5cm) high

£150-200 **GORL**

A French four glass clock, the movement striking on a gong, with mercury compensated pendulum.

15.75in (40cm) high

£500-800 **GHOU**

A French tortoiseshell mantel clock, the gilt dial with porcelain cartouche numerals, within a shaped case with foliate gilt metal mounts.

15.5in (39.5cm) high

£400-600 **GHOU**

A carved oak mantel clock, with a silvered chapter ring and a Japy Frères gong-striking movement, the case inlaid with boxwood spandrels and a bats-wing oval.

15.25in (38.5cm) high

£200-300 **GORL**

An early electric Bulle mantel clock, with a silvered dial, on a circular mahogany plinth.

9.5in (24cm) high

£120-180 **GORL**

SKELETON CLOCKS

A triple-framed arabesque skeleton clock, by Evans of Handworth, with seven turned pillars, anchor escapement and a chain fusee with clickwork, exposed on the front of the spring barrel, the white marble base with a plaque bearing the name of the retailer "Staniland, Malton", with original dome.

c1865 *20in (50cm) high*

£5,000-7,000 **DR**

An English skeleton timepiece, in the shape of the Scott Memorial, by Evans in Edinburgh, with a balance wheel, on a marble base, the movement with five turned pillars, all the wheelwork with six crossings.

c1850 *21in (52.5cm) high*

£4,000-6,000 **DR**

A French 'Great Exhibition' timepiece, with alarm and engraved, inverted, 'Y' shaped plates, the central alarm disc of silvered brass, with an eight-day movement, the alarm set and wound via two pull cords.

c1850 *10in (25.5cm) high*

£2,000-3,000 **DR**

A 20thC English brass skeleton clock, with a scalloped dial and black Roman chapters, two train movement, on a velvet and wood base beneath a glass dome.

11.5in (29cm) high

£300-500 **S&K**

A Scott Memorial double fusee skeleton clock, striking on a gong, within a square brass-edged dome, mounted on a rosewood base.

20in (51cm) high

£2,200-2,800 **GHOU**

A giant wheel skeleton timepiece, with a passing strike and a white enamel dial, raised on a marble base, under a glass dome.

22in (56cm) high

£800-1,200 **GHOU**

A single fusee skeleton timepiece, on an ebonised base, under a glass dome.

16in (40.5cm) high

£500-800 **GHOU**

A Scott Memorial skeleton timepiece, the single fusee movement with a balance wheel escapement, on a marble and rosewood base, lacks dome.

19in (48.5cm) high

£1,200-1,800 **GHOU**

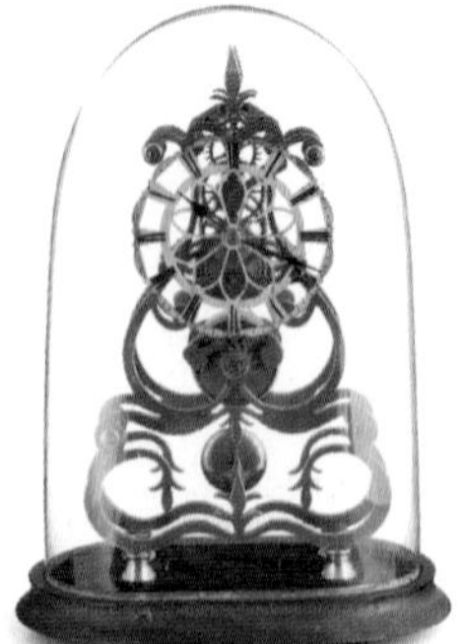

A single fusee skeleton timepiece, on an oval base, under a glass dome.

16.5in (42cm) high

£450-650 **GHOU**

A brass skeleton clock, with a silvered chapter ring, an anchor escapement and a single train fusee movement, raised on an oval ebonised plinth, under a glass dome.

13.25in (33.5cm) high

£450-650 **GORL**

A CLOSER LOOK AT A SKELETON CLOCK

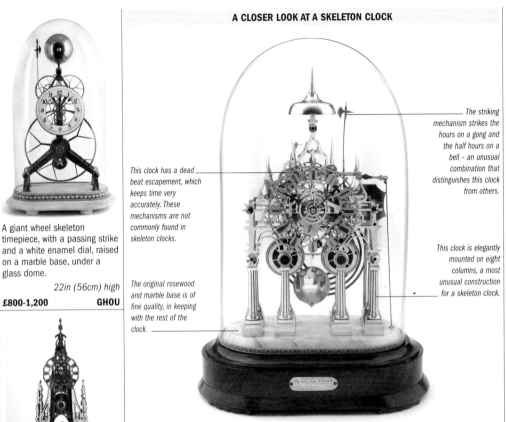

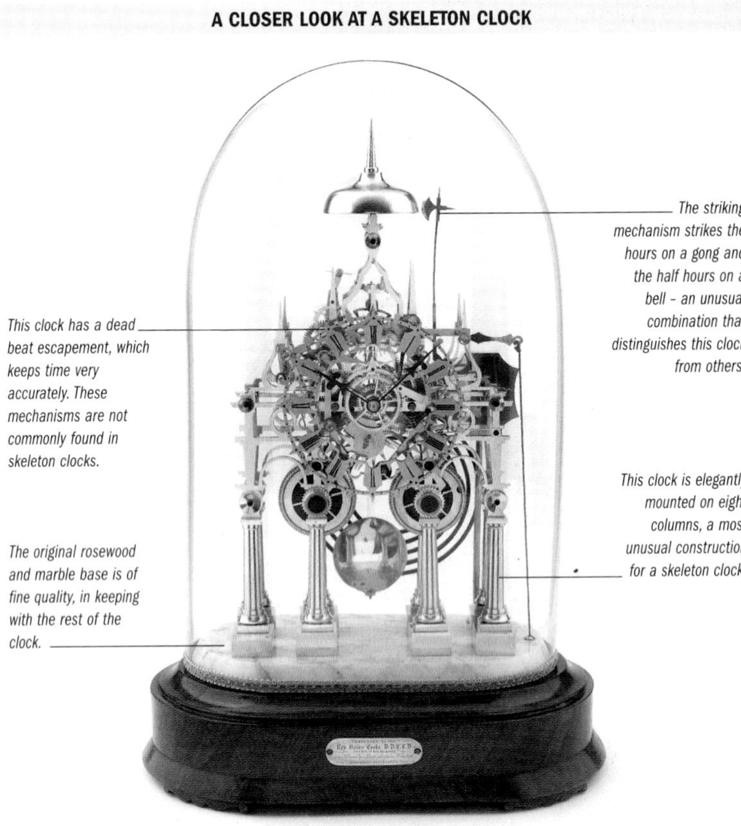

This clock has a dead beat escapement, which keeps time very accurately. These mechanisms are not commonly found in skeleton clocks.
The original rosewood and marble base is of fine quality, in keeping with the rest of the clock.
The striking mechanism strikes the hours on a gong and the half hours on a bell - an unusual combination that distinguishes this clock from others.
This clock is elegantly mounted on eight columns, a most unusual construction for a skeleton clock.

A striking architectural brass skeleton clock, with a dead beat escapement, the frame surmounted with four spires and a bell, mounted on eight Doric columns, the movement striking the hours on a gong and half hours on a bell, the fretted, silvered, brass dial with blued steel spade hands, the frontal plaque recording the presentation of the clock to the Reverend Henry Cooke in October 1853.

c1850 *22.5in (56cm) high*

£5,000-7,000 **DR**

CLOCK GARNITURES

A 19thC French gilt-brass clock garniture, comprising a mantel clock with twin train movement, within a waisted case, with Rococo and scroll castings, on a stand, and a pair of twin branch candelabra.

Clock 14in (35cm) high

£1,500-2,000 **L&T**

A French black slate and gilt metal clock garniture, in the Egyptian Revival style, the clock with an eight-day movement, striking on a bell, the pyramid-form case with a songbird finial, the matching candelabra each supporting three ornate openwork branches and four candle nozzles.

c1880 *Clock 17in (42.5cm) high*

£350-450 **FRE**

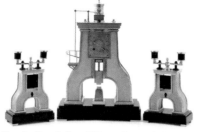

A French gilt and silvered 'Steam Hammer' clock garniture, by Guilmet, the clock with an inverted 'Y' shaped form, the platform to the left of the clock linked via a mock steam whistle handle to the imitation vent and whistle to the top of the case, the steam hammer rising and falling with the pendulum.

c1880 *Clock 18in (45cm) high*

£5,500-8,500 **DR**

A late 19thC American gilt-bronze assembled mantel garniture, the central piece with three prism-hung candleholders above a relief of Paul and Virginia, the flanking candlesticks each with a figure of Virginia.

Tallest 16.5in (42cm) high

£180-220 **S&K**

A French late 19thC slate and enamel assembled clock garniture, in the Egyptian Revival style, the enamel dial with Roman numerals and an eight-day movement, together with a pair of matched urn shaped candelabra.

22in (55cm) high

£3,500-4,500 **FRE**

An Empire-style bronze-mounted marble clock garniture, with a flaming urn finial and drum case, the candelabra of elongated urn form with pierced stylized foliate branches.

Clock 18.75in (47.5cm) high

£500-800 **S&K**

A late 19thC small Louis XV-style gilt metal assembled clock garniture, the barrel movement with a white enamel dial, within a gilt-enhanced cobalt blue ceramic case, supported by a cherub on a ornate scroll base, together with two matched figural vases.

9.25in (23cm) high

£700-1,000 **FRE**

WALL CLOCKS

A George III black lacquer and gilt Parliament timepiece, by John Merrigeot, London, the single train movement with an anchor escapement, a moulded frame and rectangular trunk, painted with a chinoiserie scene, above a bulbous base with a glass lenticle.

60in (150cm) high

£8,000-12,000 **L&T**

An early 19thC Dutch mahogany Staartklok, with a 30-hour movement, striking the half hours on a coiled gong, the arch painted with a military scene.

50.5in (126cm) high

£800-1,200 **L&T**

An English bulkhead timepiece, by W. Johnson, the silvered dial signed "W. Johnson, Strand, London", the engraved gilt brass case with a lockable bezel, English fusee movement with a lever escapement.

William Johnson is best known for his association with Grimaldi & Johnson, the marine chronometer makers. This piece was possibly commissioned by a yacht owner whose chronometers had been made by that firm.

c1840 *9in (22.5cm) high*

£4,000-6,000 **DR**

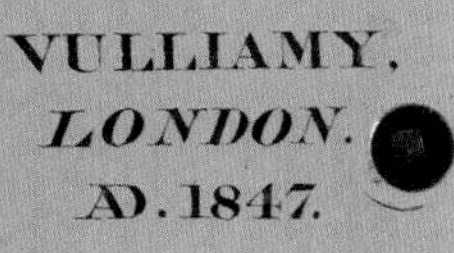

A bulkhead timepiece, the single fusee movement with a platform lever, signed "Vulliamy" and numbered "1819", the silvered dial signed and dated "1847", now with a brass bulkhead case, alterations.

£2,000-3,000 **GHOU**

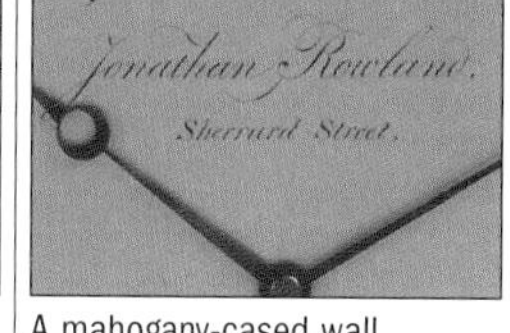

A mahogany-cased wall timepiece, by Jonathan Rowland, Sherrard Street, St James's, with a single train fusee movement, within a moulded circular case, with a brass key engraved "Jonathan Rowland No 105".

14.5in (36cm) diam

£2,800-3,200 **L&T**

OTHER CLOCKS

An Austrian small Zappler clock, in the shape of a desk, covered in engraved mother-of-pearl, with two integrated ink wells and fire-gilded bronze mounts, the small 30-hour-movement with an anchor escapement and a pendulum to the front of the clock case.

c1825 *5.25in (13cm) high*

£3,000-5,000 **DR**

A 30-hour strut clock, by Howell James & Co. to the Queen, London, the engraved and silvered oval dial with decorative engraving, the rope twist bezel extensively inlaid with blue stones, an engraved border, signed and numbered "7075", with dust covers.

c1870 *4in (10cm) high*

£1,000-1,500 **DR**

A mid-19thC French automata and novelty clock, in the shape of a windmill, in gilded brass and bronze, with one miller turning the face to the wind and a second miller carrying a sack of flour, the white enamel clock face signed "Frisard à Paris", with an early pendule de Paris movement.

19in (49cm) high

£8,000-12,000 **DR**

A 'lighthouse' clock, powered by a movement concealed in the simulated stone base, a French timepiece movement mounted within one side, thermometers and a barometer to the other sides.

c1880 *17in (43cm) high*

£3,500-4,500 **DR**

A 17thC style double fusee lantern clock, quarter strike on two bells, within a typical case.

15.5in (39.5cm) high

£1,200-1,800 **GHOU**

WATCHES

An early 18thC French verge oignon brass pocket watch, the circular pierced balance cock with regulating dial, enamelled dial and a winding hole, the outer case engraved with a classical urn, with bullseye glass, signed "Marc Merlier, Paris", the dial restored.

2.25in (5.5cm) diam

£700-1,000 **GHOU**

An early 18thC Continental crucifix verge pocket watch, the silvered case with hinged, bevelled, glazed panels and a pierced balance cock, with Egyptian pillars, the silvered dial engraved with Adam and Eve and three saints, back plate signed "Etienne Bordier, Fecit".

2.75in (7cm) long

£1,000-1,500 **GHOU**

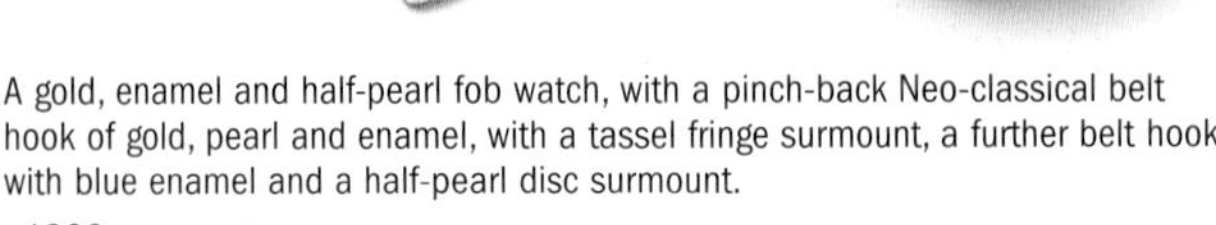

A gold, enamel and half-pearl fob watch, with a pinch-back Neo-classical belt hook of gold, pearl and enamel, with a tassel fringe surmount, a further belt hook with blue enamel and a half-pearl disc surmount.

c1800

£600-900 **WW**

A George III tortoiseshell silver pair-cased pocket watch, hallmarked London 1818, the movement signed "John Crawley, Stoke Newington", number "1784", a converted verge.

2in (5cm) diam

£180-220 **GHOU**

A George III silver pair-cased verge pocket watch, hallmarked for London 1801, the gilt-engraved movement with a regulating dial signed "Adley & Brown, London" and "8114", a silver dust cover, the outer case with a release button.

2.25in (6cm) diam

£300-400 **GHOU**

A George IV 18ct duplex pocket watch, the engraved, balanced cock with a diamond endstone, within a rubbed engine-turned case with a facetted edge, hallmarked for London 1820, the movement signed "Wiltshire & Sons, Cornhill, London" and "2145", a faint hairline crack to dial.

2in (5.5cm) diam

£1,800-2,200 **GHOU**

A William IV silver pair-cased verge pocket watch, the white enamelled dial painted with a sailing boat, with a plain outer case, the watch hallmarked for London 1831, the movement signed "G. Graham, London", numbered "2152".

2.25in (5.5cm) diam

£280-320 **GHOU**

A French gold key-wound pocket watch, by Le Roy, the dial with an engraved centre and a black-enamelled chapter ring, the cover decorated with a bouquet of flowers in a translucent green enamel guilloche, surrounded with half-pearls to the front and back, the movement signed "Le Roy Paris", numbered "763".

c1850

£800-1,200 **WW**

A Thomas Yates silver fusee lever pocket watch, with a diamond-set endstone, key wound with maintaining power and half-second beat, the dust cover engraved "Yates patent", hallmarked for Chester 1853, the movement signed "Thos Yates, Preston" and number "1663" the plain outer case rubbed.

2in (5cm) diam

£400-600 **GHOU**

A Charles Frodsham silver lever hunter pocket watch, key wound, with a diamond-set engraved balance cock, within an engine-turned case, hallmarked for London 1868, the movement signed "84 Strand, London" and numbered "16870".

1.75in (4.5cm) diam

£200-300 **GHOU**

A Victorian silver Masonic pocket watch, with a blue and yellow enamel dial.

c1880 *2.5in (6.5cm) long*

£350-450 **SSP**

A J.W. Benson 18ct hunter lever pocket watch, inscribed cuvette, the plain outer case engraved with a crest, hallmarked for London 1929, the movement and dial signed "The Bank S.3293", together with the original boxes and purchase receipt from J.W. Benson Ltd, dated "1st February 1933".

2in (5cm) diam

£450-550 **GHOU**

An 18ct Patek Philippe yellow gold open-face pocket watch, the off-white enamelled face with Arabic numerals at quadrants of the chapter ring, with a sweep seconds hand, a short chain and a 10ct yellow gold mesh chain.

£1,800-2,200 **FRE**

A Patek Philippe 18ct lever pocket watch, the movement number "93254", dial and cuvette signed and numbered, the hinged back with an engraved monogram, case number "221284".

2in (5cm) diam

£650-850 **GHOU**

An 18ct pocket chronometer, with a detent escapement, key wound with a going barrel, with a helical balance spring and a plain case.

2in (5cm) diam

£400-600 **GHOU**

A tortoiseshell gilt pair-cased verge pocket watch, with a finely pierced balance cock, regulating dial and square tapered pillars, within a brass studded outer case, the movement signed "John Ginger, London" and numbered "216".

2in (5cm) diam

£400-600 **GHOU**

A gilt pair-cased verge pocket watch, with a fine pierced balance cock and round pillars, the dial with black Roman numerals and bullseye glass, within a plain outer case, with a key, signed "Reeves (Richard), 208 Shoreditch".

2in (5cm) diam

£300-400 **GHOU**

A Vacheron & Constantin 18ct lever pocket watch, movement and cuvette signed, number "388063", the white dial with black Roman numerals and subsidiary seconds within a plain case with hinged back, case number "244891".

2in (5cm) diam

£600-900 **GHOU**

A Sorley of Glasgow steel lever pocket watch, the silvered dial with Arabic Breguet numerals and subsidiary seconds with moon hands, nickel finish jewelled movement with Patek layout, the hinged back engraved with initials "IFH", original box.

1.75in (4.5cm) diam

£220-280 **GHOU**

A Thomas Russell & Sons 18ct 'Chronograph' pocket watch, the movement and dial signed "Liverpool", number "101711", the dial with black Roman numerals and centre seconds within a plain outer case.

2.25in (5.5cm) diam

£350-450 **GHOU**

A Hamilton gold-filled lever pocket watch, No. "1151200", with a nineteen jewel movement, adjusted five positions, within a keystone engraved screw case, the dial and movement signed "Motor Barrel 952".

2in (5cm) diam

£280-320 **GHOU**

An 18ct lever hunter pocket watch, with a Swiss twenty-one jewel movement, the dial with black Roman numerals and a subsidiary seconds dial, within a plain outer case.

2in (5cm) diam

£300-400 **GHOU**

A Waltham 'Vanguard' pocket watch, number "14104642", with a nineteen jewel adjusted five position movement, subsidiary constant seconds dial with outer minute numerals, screw cashier case engraved with a steam locomotive.

2.25in (5.5cm) diam

£180-220 **GHOU**

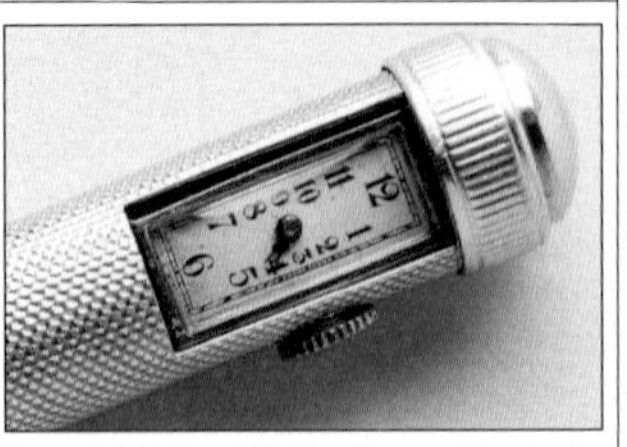

A 9ct gold watch pencil, by Sampson Mordan, with engine-turned decoration.

£1,200-1,800 **TAG**

BAROMETERS

A late 18thC Louis XVI gilt-wood barometer, with a rectangular glazed thermometer aperture, above a circular glazed-front barometer, indistinctly inscribed "CHa B1813 A Paris Rue le Noir No. 8 Faubourg, St. Antoine".

40in (100cm) high

£1,200-1,800 **S&K**

A George III mahogany stick barometer, the brass back plate with temperature and vernier scales, the chequer-strung and moulded column with mercury glass, inscribed "Deo Stampa & Co., No.14 Leith Street, Edinburgh".

38.75in (97cm) high

£800-1,200 **L&T**

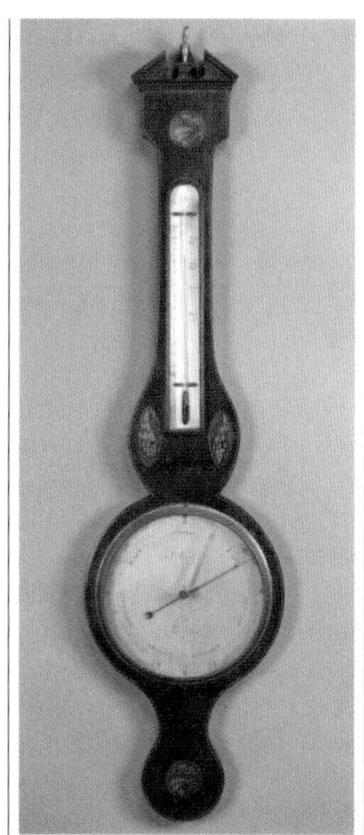

A George III inlaid mahogany wheel barometer, the baluster case with shell patera, the silvered thermometer and dial signed "J. Steele, Liverpool".

39in (97.5cm) high

£500-800 **S&K**

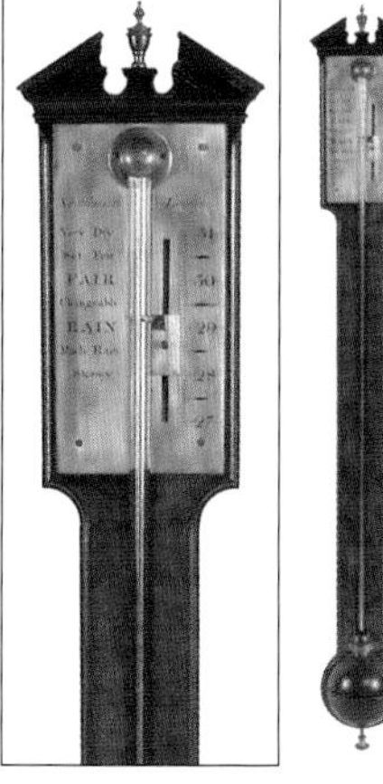

A mahogany stick barometer, the case with a globular mercury reservoir, the silvered rectangular register inscribed "Shuttleworth London".

39in (99cm) high

£2,800-3,200 **DN**

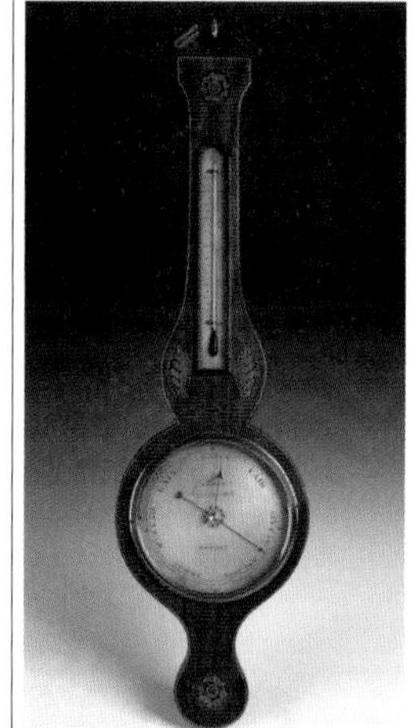

An early 19thC mahogany-cased banjo barometer, by J. Pastorelli, London, with a glazed, arched, silvered thermometer and a boxwood-strung case, with a broken pediment and inlaid rosette and shell motifs, the dial inscribed "J Pastorelli, Grays Inn Lane, Holborn, London".

39.25in (98cm) high

£500-800 **L&T**

An early 19thC mahogany-cased banjo barometer by Della Torre, Perth, the silvered dial surmounted by a convex mirror, an arched thermometer and a dry/damp dial, the case with boxwood stringing and swan neck pediment, inscribed "J Della Torre, Perth, Warranted".

39.5in (99cm) high

£320-380 **L&T**

An early 19thC mahogany-cased stick barometer, with a silvered vernier and thermometer, the squared case with a pagoda-topped moulded cornice, above a glazed scale and slender body with an applied thermometer, with a drum reservoir, on a brass gimbel with a circular plate, inscribed "Cary, London".

36.25in (92cm) high

£2,000-3,000 **L&T**

A mahogany and line-inlaid wheel barometer, with a timepiece with an enamelled dial, a thermometer, hygrometer and spirit level, the case with a swan-neck pediment, the level engraved "L. Gianna Salop".

'The Salopian' magazine of March 1816 noted at his passing, "Death of Mr L Gianna barometer maker of Salisbury, his death imputed to his sleeping in a damp bed".

c1810 46.75in (119cm) high

£1,800-2,200 **DN**

A 19thC mahogany-cased banjo barometer by Galletti, Glasgow, the dial surmounted by an enamelled clock, with an arched silvered thermometer and a dry/damp dial, the level below inscribed "Galletti, Glasgow, Warranted".

42.75in (107cm) high

£500-800 **L&T**

A mahogany wheel barometer, the round silvered register with a central sweep hand, with a convex mirror, hygrometer and spirit level, the latter inscribed "Chas. Pensotti Gravesend".

42.25in (107cm) high

£400-600 **DN**

A mahogany and line-inlaid wheel barometer, the silvered round register with a central sweep hand, with thermometer, hygrometer and spirit level, the latter inscribed "WARRANTED CORRECT", some damage.

35.75in (91cm) high

£180-220 **DN**

A mahogany aneroid wheel barometer, with a round silvered register and Fahrenheit thermometer, the case inlaid with rosettes and shell motifs, register inscribed "E Johnson & Son Ltd, Derby".

38in (96.5cm) high

£250-300 **DN**

The market for luxury goods, including antique jewellery, is very much tied to the performance of the economy as a whole. In recent years, uncertainty about the economy, falling City bonuses and shaky consumer confidence have led to a decline in interest in the more expensive end of the antique jewellery market, although certain pieces continue to sell well.

Jewellery for regular use, to be worn during the day as well as in the evening, is currently more sought after than ornate trophy pieces to be worn in the evening only. Gold continues to be the most popular material, although some gem pieces also sell well. Signed pieces by the well-known French fashion houses, such as Cartier, usually retain their value, as do those of exceptionally good quality or fine design. Rings are the most popular type of jewellery in terms of what is sold, followed by earrings, bracelets, pendants and brooches.

A growing area of interest is jewellery from the 1960s and 70s in contemporary styles. As genuine Edwardian and Art Deco pieces have become increasingly expensive, these newer pieces have been reassessed and have become popular whilst remaining affordable. This trend is likely to continue in the future, and as relatively few quality pieces were produced in this period, prices should rise.

Joseph Bonnar

SCOTTISH AGATE JEWELLERY

A CLOSER LOOK AT A SCOTTISH AGATE BROOCH

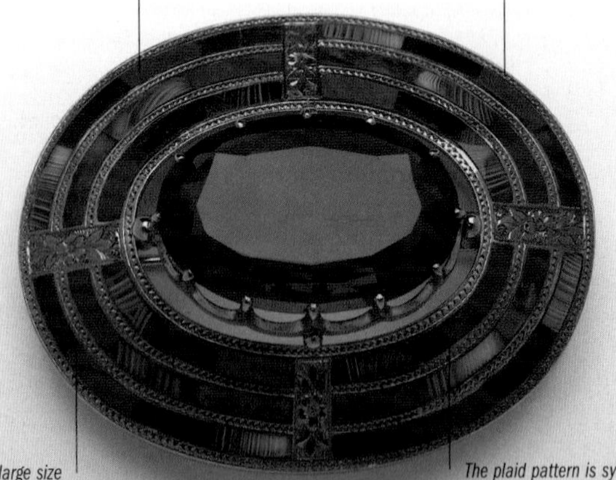

Brooches were the most widely produced type of jewellery in the 19thC and agate has been used as an ornamental hardstone for centuries.
The dark muted tones are typical of Victorian Scottish agate jewellery, which utilised local minerals to encapsulate the landscape into the item of jewellery.
The large size and attractive shape of the brooch make it valuable.
The plaid pattern is symbolic of the tartan worn by Scottish clans, which became fashionable during the 19thC.

A gold mounted Scottish agate and quartz plaid brooch.

c1860 *2in (5cm) long*

£3,000-3,500 **JHB**

A gold, Scottish agate and quartz set plaid brooch.

c1860 *2in (5.25cm) wide*

£800-1,000 **JHB**

A silver and Scottish agate set brooch.

c1865 *2.5in (6.25cm) long*

£350-450 **JHB**

A silver mounted Scottish agate bow brooch.

c1865 *5in (3.5cm) wide*

£250-350 **JHB**

A silver and Scottish agate kilt pin of Dirk design set with paste 'Cairngorms'.

c1865 *4in (10.5cm) long*

£600-700 **JHB**

SCOTTISH AGATE JEWELLERY

Scottish jewellery made with agate, a banded form of chalcedony, became popular in the mid-19thC, when Queen Victoria purchased Balmoral Castle in Scotland. Known as 'pebble jewellery', many pieces included granite or other stones in earthy hues, set into silver or gold. Inspiration came from traditional Celtic designs and motifs such as thistles, harps, shields and crosses featured heavily. Circular brooches and dagger pins were also popular, although a wide variety of shapes were individually commissioned.

Scottish agate jewellery is generally unmarked, but signed pieces by Sangster of Aberdeen are sought-after, as are those signed by J.P. Hutton (not be confused with less valuable agate pieces made in later years by Hutton in Birmingham).

Agate jewellery can be expensive to repair, so collectors tend to look for pieces in good condition.

A silver mounted Scottish agate brooch.

c1865 *1.75in (4.5cm) diam*

£250-300 **JHB**

A Scottish agate ware bar pin by Sangster of Aberdeen in silver inlaid with agates.

c1885 *3.25in (8.25cm) l.*

£500-700 **LYNH**

A Scottish agate ware butterfly brooch by J. P. Hutton, with red and Montrose blue agate set in a silver frame.

c1885 *3in (7.5cm) wide*

£700-1,100 **LYNH**

A Scottish agate ware brooch with interlaced panels of silver-set Montrose blue agate.

c1885 *3in (7.5cm) wide*

£700-1,000 **LYNH**

A Scottish agate ware engraved silver brooch with central thistle motifs and four panels of dark and pale blue agate.

c1870 *2in (5cm) diam*

£500-550 **RBRG**

A Scottish agate ware silver harp motif brooch with engraved flowers and red and black agates.

c1885 *2.25in (5.75cm) diam*

£800-1,000 **LYNH**

A Scottish agate ware silver shield brooch with a large citrine paste and inlaid with red, black and Montrose blue agate.

c1885 *2.25in (5.5cm) diam*

£700-1,000 **LYNH**

A Scottish agate ware brooch with shield motifs in silver with citrine stones and red and black agate.

1880 *2.75in (7cm) diam*

£1,000-1,500 **LYNH**

A Scottish agate ware silver garter brooch set with Montrose blue agate and a topaz.

c1885 *2.5in (6.5cm) long*

£500-800 **LYNH**

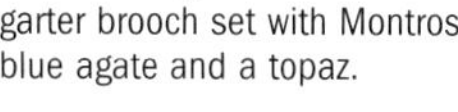

A Scottish agate ware buckled bracelet with silver links and mounts set with various agates.

c1885 *8.5in (22cm) long*

£1,000-1,500 **LYNH**

A gold mounted Scottish agate bracelet and padlock.

c1865

£800-1,000 **JHB**

BROOCHES & PINS

A Georgian floral motif brooch in gilt metal set with rings of faux diamond pastes.

c1780 *1.75in (4.5cm) diam*

£550-600 **CSAY**

A Late Georgian floral cross pin with round- and navette-cut emerald pastes in gold metal.

c1820 *1.5in (4cm) wide*

£450-500 **CSAY**

A Late Georgian sprig of flowers pin of gilt metal with faux diamond pastes.

c1820 *2.5in (6.25cm) long*

£550-600 **CSAY**

A Georgian commemorative brooch diamond paste border and J W. woven hair cypher.

c1850 *1.75in (4.5cm) long*

£280-320 **CSAY**

A Victorian steel shield-shape pin set with oval-cut ruby and round-cut clear pastes.

c1855 *2.75in (7cm) long*

£150-180 **PC**

A Victorian garnet beehive-shape brooch.

c1880 *1.5in (4cm) diam*

£250-300 **SSP**

A Victorian Rococo-revival brooch of gilt metal with a variegated black and red paste cabochon.

c1865 *2.2in (5.5cm) long*

£100-120 **MARA**

A Victorian Rococo-revival brooch of gilt metal with a large citrine paste centre.

c1865 *2.5in (6.25cm) long*

£50-100 **MARA**

A Victorian love knot 'REGARD' pin with faux ruby, emerald, garnet, amethyst, ruby and diamond.

c1860 *1.75in (4.5cm) wide*

£300-350 **CSAY**

A Victorian twin-hearts and bow brooch in gilt metal with diamond and emerald pastes.

c1885 *0.75in (2cm) wide*

£150-200 **LYNH**

A Vauxhall glass flowerhead motif hair pin with clear glass navette petals.

c1875 *Flower 2in (5cm) diam*

£100-120 **LYNH**

A Vauxhall glass bee pin and earrings with ruby and turquoise glass and gilt metal.

c1875 *Pin 1.5in (4cm) long*

£350-550 **LYNH**

A Vauxhall glass crown brooch with ruby and dark amethyst glass stones and gold pin.

c1890 *1.5in (4cm) high*

£200-250 **CSAY**

A 19thC Russian silver and gold brooch set with diamonds, rubies, sapphire and pearls.

1.5in (4cm) long

£1,500-1,800 **JHB**

A CLOSER LOOK AT A DIAMOND DEMI-PARURE

Decorative jewellery was usually worn in the evening, for special social events.

The striking appearance and fine quality of this piece makes it valuable, and the design remains appealing today.

It is likely this suite started off life as part of a five star tiara, versions of which were worn by Ducia, Countess of Rosse, Marchioness of Cambridge and Princess Beatrice of Battenberg.

Diamonds became more widely available in the 1870s as supplies from South Africa increased. In this period jewellery makers began to include more diamonds in their designs.

A late 19thC gold and silver set suite of three diamond-set stars with removable brooch fittings and earrings.

c1870 *Brooch 1.5in (3.5cm)*

£5,500-6,500 **JHB**

An Edwardian 18ct gold and silver-set exceptional diamond brooch/pendant with a square set emerald.

c1910 *1in (2.5cm) wide*

£2,000-2,200 **SSP**

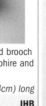

A Continental brooch of white metal with crystal diamanté and an aquamarine paste.

c1905 *1.5in (4cm) long*

£300-400 **MARA**

An Edwardian platinum Cartier-style emerald and diamond brooch, with articulated centre piece as a posy holder.

c1910 *2.25in (6cm) long*

£1,000-1,200 **SSP**

A platinum Edwardian diamond flower spray brooch.

c1910 *1.75in (4.5cm) long*

£700-800 **SSP**

A dolphin brooch set with rubies and diamonds.

c1965 *2.5in (6.25cm) long*

£1,500-2,000 **JHB**

A flower spray brooch set with zircon, amethyst and citrine.

c1965 *3.25in (8.25cm) long*

£1,500-1,800 **JHB**

A feather brooch set with rubies and diamonds.

c1965 *2in (5cm) long*

£1,000-1,300 **JHB**

A Continental gem set butterfly brooch, the body with central oval cut emerald and circular cut sapphires, emeralds and rubies, with articulated diamond set wings.

2.25in (6cm) wide

£300-400 **F**

A platinum set marquise, brilliant and baguette cut 4ct diamond brooch, European marks.

2in (4.5cm) long

£3,500-4,500 **JHB**

A Roman solid gold cloak pin in the shape of the cross.

c100-200AD *2.5in (6.25cm) long*

£20,000-27,000 **LNXG**

A 19thC pinchbeck brooch with clear and emerald green pastes.

c1840 *1.75in (4.5cm) long*

£100-200 **MARA**

A 19thC pinchbeck shield brooch with floral motifs, tassels and emerald green paste cabochons.

c1840 *2.4in (6cm) long*

£200-300 **MARA**

A 19thC pinchbeck feather motif brooch with emerald green paste cabochons.

c1840 *2.5in (5cm) long*

£200-300 **MARA**

A 19thC French, gold and enamel fringed brooch, set with rubies and pearls.

2.5in (7.5cm) long

£1,000-1,500 **JHB**

A gold brooch with applied detail and locket back.

c1860 *1.75in (4.25cm) wide*

£300-350 **JHB**

An Etruscan-revival gold brooch and earring set.

c1865

£600-800 **JHB**

A Victorian 9ct gold horseshoe brooch, set with diamonds spelling "Good Luck".

1.25in (3cm) long

£180-220 **SSP**

A late 19thC gold and silver brooch set with diamonds and pearls.

1in (2.5cm) wide

£900-1,100 **JHB**

A late 19thC 15ct gold, pearl set acorns brooch.

1.75in (4cm) long

£150-200 **JHB**

An Edwardian 18ct gold golf club brooch, set with a diamond in the centre.

c1910 *1.5in (4cm) long*

£180-220 **SSP**

A gold new moon brooch set with opals and pairs of old cut diamonds with inscription for 1911.

1.5in (3.5cm) diam

£750-900 **JHB**

An early 20thC 15ct gold and seed pearl crescent brooch, set with graduated seed pearls.

1in (2.5cm) long

£100-150 **F**

A 9ct gold peridot and cultured pearl crescent brooch.

1.75in (4.5cm) long

£70-100 **F**

A three-colour gold 'rooster' brooch set with rubies and rose cut diamonds.

1960 *3in (8cm) long*

£600-750 **JHB**

A European gold brooch set with demantoid garnet, old and rose cut diamonds.

2in (4.5cm) long

£2,000-2,400 **JHB**

A brooch in the style of a basket of flowers, set with rubies and diamonds, with a ribbon bow to the handles, stamped "750".

2in (5cm) high

£200-250 **F**

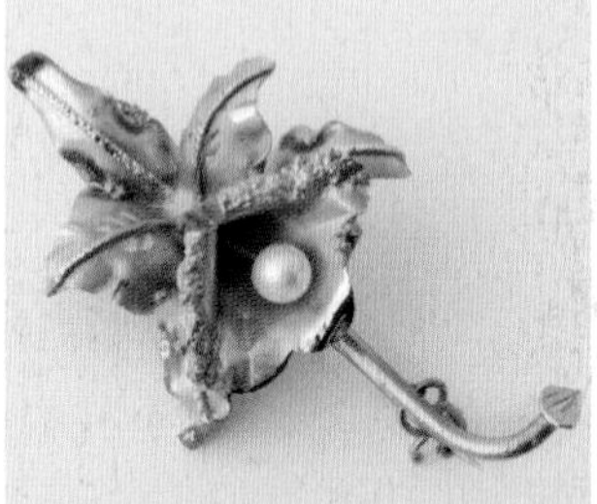

A Continental brooch in the form of an orchid, set with a single pearl and stamped "18k".

£70-100 **F**

A 14ct yellow gold diamond set brooch, realistically modelled as an open flowerhead with diamond detail and textured finish.

1.5in (4cm) diam

£100-150 **F**

A curb link bar brooch, with central heart motif and chain swags.

£30-50 **F**

A 9ct gold brooch, in the form of a bow.

£40-60 **F**

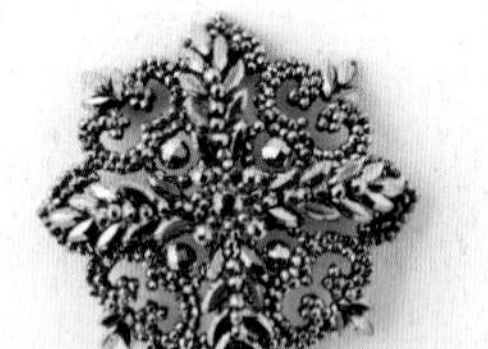

A floral, fruit and foliate motif brooch of cut steel.

c1840 *1.75in (4.5cm) diam*

£300-350 **CSAY**

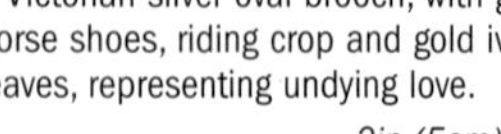

A Victorian silver oval brooch, with gold horse shoes, riding crop and gold ivy leaves, representing undying love.

2in (5cm) long

£40-50 **SSP**

A Victorian silver heart-shaped brooch with ivy leaves, reading in gold "Forget-Me-Not".

2in (5cm) long

£40-50 **SSP**

A Victorian cuffed hand and anchor pin cast in, respectively, silver and bronze.

c1890 *1.5in (4cm) wide*

£100-200 **LYNH**

A Victorian silver croquet mallet brooch, with a hat with forget-me-not detail.

c1900 *2in (5cm) long*

£100-130 **SSP**

A Georgian seed pearl mother-of-pearl backed ornate brooch, with stylized tulips on the sides and flower cluster in centre.

c1825 *2.5in (6cm) long*

£300-350 **SSP**

A Georgian seed pearl mother-of-pearl backed brooch in the shape of a feather.

c1825 *2.75in (7cm) long*

£200-250 **SSP**

A late 19thC split pearl and diamond brooch, pendant in original case.

1.25in (3cm) long

£800-1,000 **JHB**

A Victorian Etruscan 15ct gold, turquoise and pearl fringe brooch, with matching earrings.

Brooch 1.5in (4cm) long

£400-500 **SSP**

A Wedgwood brooch with a white on blue carved cameo in a cut steel frame.

c1770 *2.75in (7cm) long*

£900-1,100 **RBRG**

An early Victorian butterfly pin of cut steel rivetted to brass.

c1830 *1.5in (4cm) wide*

£100-150 **MARA**

A Victorian silver and two-tone blue enamel butterfly brooch, with green enamel tips.

2.5in (6cm) wide

£100-150 **SSP**

An Egyptian-revival silver scarab pin with turquoise, purple, green, blue and red enamel.

c1925 *1.5in (4cm) wide*

£150-200 **MARA**

A Victorian gold brooch with a lock of hair with hair and enamel flowers over chalcedony.

c1850 *2.25in (5.5cm) long*

£150-200 **MARA**

A Victorian winged insect pin carved from horn.

c1900 *3.75in (9.5cm) wide*

£100-200 **LYNH**

A Victorian commemorative brooch with gold frame, black enamel and hair picture over chalcedony.

c1850 *2.25in (5.75cm) wide*

£150-200 **MARA**

A Victorian kingfisher pin of carved horn with a pearlised finish.

c1900 *3in (7.5cm) long*

£100-150 **LYNH**

A Victorian hand and flower love token pin in mother-of-pearl.

c1900 *2in (5cm) long*

£100-200 **LYNH**

A Victorian cuffed hand and rose pin in mother-of-pearl.

c1890 *2in (5cm) long*

£100-200 **LYNH**

A crescent moon tortoiseshell pin with inlaid gold and silver floral motifs.

c1880 *1.5in (3.75cm) long*

£400-450 **LYNH**

A Whitby jet pin and pendant earrings with angel coral cameos.

c1900 *2in (5cm) long*

£300-400 **MARA**

PENDANTS, CHAINS & NECKLACES

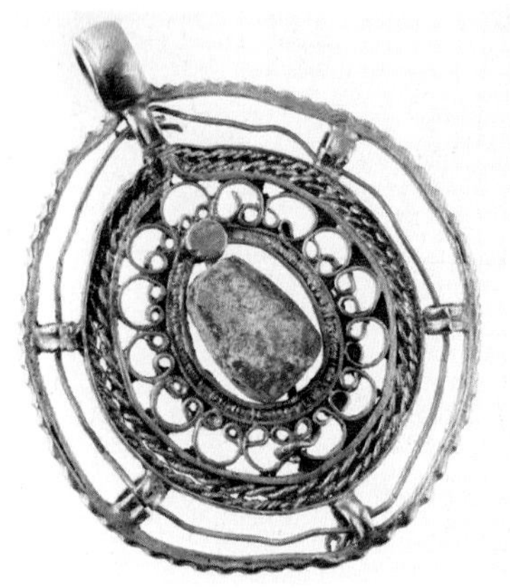

A Byzantine filigree gold wire pendant with coloured glass stone centre, originally with pearls.

c500-600AD

£3,500-4,000 **LNXG**

A Continental 18ct gold framed portrait miniature, of contemporary design, depicting a young woman with dark upswept hair, set with three small paste stones.

£220-280 **F**

An 18thC style portrait miniature, hand-painted on ivorine, contained within an oval base metal pendant locket, with seed pearl border and mother-of-pearl reserve, some seed pearls deficient.

£80-100 **F**

A 15ct gold, Etruscan-revival style locket set with a pearl.

1865 *2.5in (6cm) long*

£600-800 **JHB**

A 15ct gold strap design locket.

c1870 *2in (5cm) long*

£400-450 **JHB**

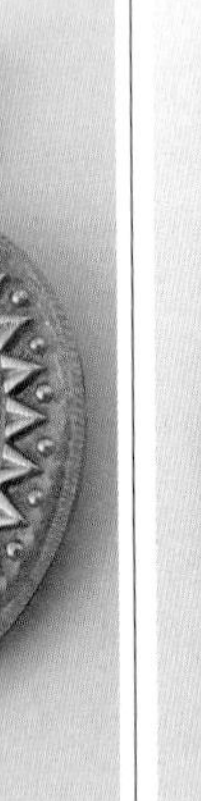

A Victorian 9ct oval grand tour locket, with forget-me-not spray, with arrow head and canon ball surround, the forget-me-not with turquoise stone.

2in (5cm) long

£200-250 **SSP**

An early 20thC gold and enamel pendant set with rubies, emeralds, diamonds and pearls, with locket back.

c1900 *2in (5.5cm) long*

£2,000-2,500 **JHB**

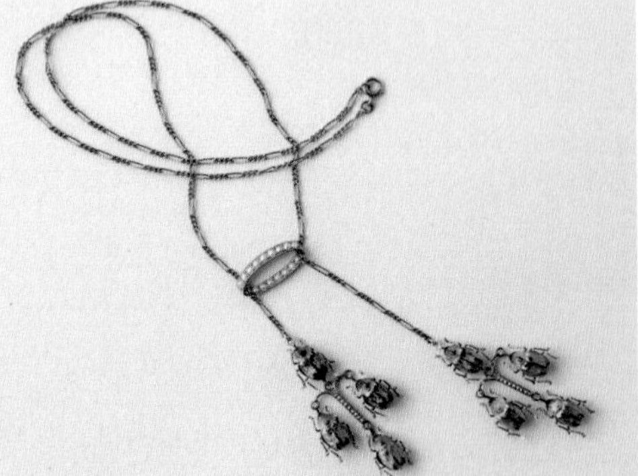

A gold twin-pendant necklace, each with a quartet of fluorescent blue beetles.

c1900 *Pendants 1.5in (4cm) long*

£800-1,200 **LYNH**

An Edwardian 9ct gold citrine single stone pendant, with fine belcher chain, the cushion cut pale yellow citrine in simple wire frame.

£120-180 **F**

A 19thC Swiss gold and enamel long chain.

33.5in (86cm) long

£2,200-2,800 **JHB**

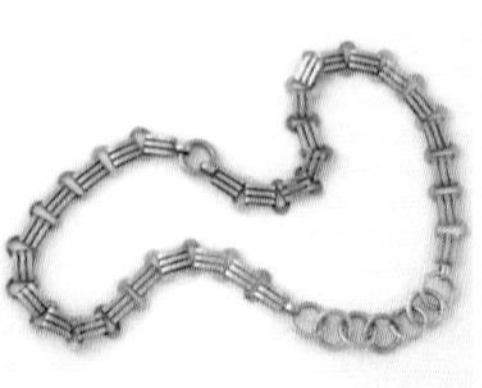

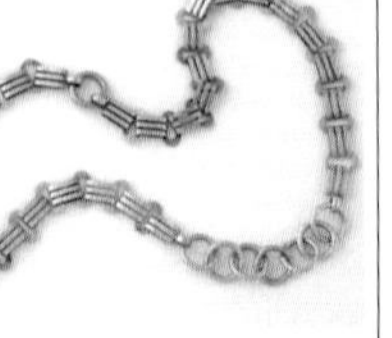

A Victorian 15ct gold collar, with flat links for a pendant or swivel seal.

c1890 *16.5in (42cm) long*

£350-450 **SSP**

A gold chain necklace with multiple fluorescent green moth pendants.

Thanks to the work of Darwin, the Victorians had a love of natural history which they even extended to their jewellery. Here, real insects from distant corners of the British Empire have been lacquered and applied to a gold chain.

c.1900 *Pendants 0.75in (2cm) long*

£350-450 **LYNH**

A Victorian 18ct gold bead necklace, on original chain.

c1900 *15.5in (39cm) long*

£600-700 **SSP**

A mid-20thC 18ct gold collar with French marks.

£1,500-2,000 **JHB**

A late Georgian cut steel necklace with pearl drops and red velvet tie.

c1820 *17in (44cm) long*

£600-700 **CSAY**

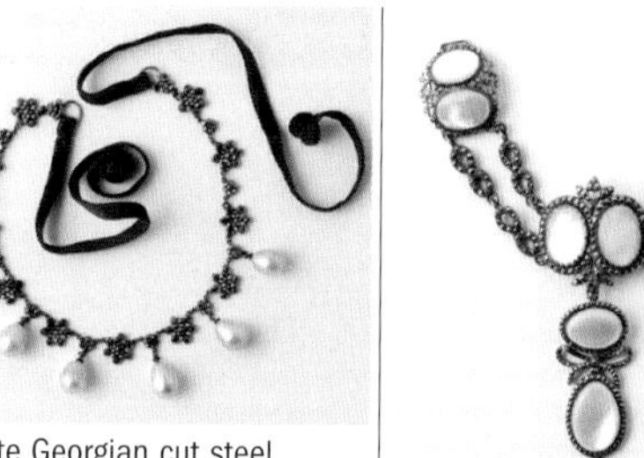

A Georgian cut steel pendant necklace with mother-of-pearl cabochons, by Munsy & Co. of Cambridge, England.

c1780 *Pend: 3in (7.5cm) long*

£1,100-1,300 **CSAY**

A Georgian drapé seed pearl necklace, consisting of oval-shaped plaques with drops.

c1800 *15.75in (40cm) l*

£800-1,000 **SSP**

A CLOSER LOOK AT A GEORGIAN SEED PEARL PARURE

This parure, or set of jewellery designed to be worn together, is unique as each one was made to a different design.

The grape decoration is in keeping with the period, as this motif became very fashionable in the Georgian era.

This would have been a wedding gift to a wealthy bride, possibly from the bride's parents or the groom.

The seed pearls have been carefully hand-stitched onto a mother-of-pearl backing, a time-consuming task that has prevented this 200 year-old piece of jewellery from disintegrating or losing its shape.

A Georgian seed pearl parure, backed on mother-of-pearl, consisting of necklace with matching grape and drop earrings and brooch, in original box.

c1800 *17.75in (45cm) long*

£1,000-1,200 **SSP**

An early 19thC gold set Roman micro-mosaic necklace with pearl spacers.

c1820 *15in (38cm) long*

£4,500-5,500 **JHB**

A torsade necklace, consisting of sixteen strings of Georgian baby seed pearls, with original split pearl clasp.

17in (43cm) long

£800-1,000 **SSP**

A five strand natural pearl necklet on an antique diamond and emerald set centrepiece, diamond 5.25ct, emerald 9.00ct.

Centrepiece 1.25in (3cm) long

£14,000-17,000 **JHB**

A Georgian seed pearl lace work necklace, with double flower drop in the centre.

c1825 *14.25in (36cm) long*

£600-700 **SSP**

A triple row Georgian seed pearl twist necklace, with important star pendant.

c1800 *15.5in (38cm) long*

£600-700 **SSP**

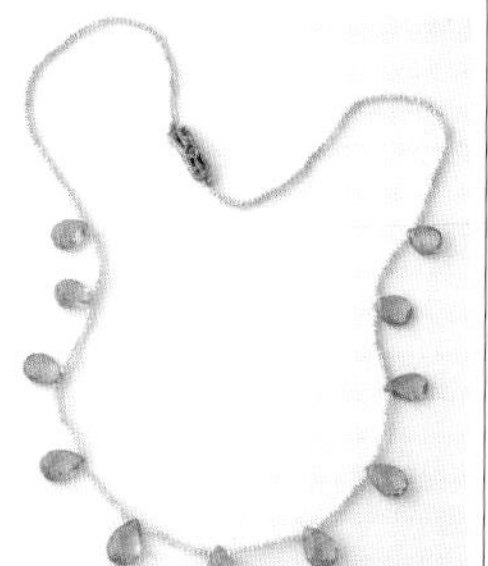

A Victorian seed pearl necklace, enhanced with peridot tear drops.

£200-300 **SSP**

Late 18thC Queen Anne pendant necklace and earrings demi-parure, with ruby paste cabochons.

Pendant 2.5in (6.25cm) long

£2,500-3,500 **LB**

A Whitby jet carved bead necklace with pendant Maltese cross.

c1860 Pendant 2in (5cm) long

£200-300 **MARA**

A Whitby jet pendant with carved Egyptian pharaoh motif.

2.5in (6.5cm) long

£100-200 **MARA**

A gold and silver pendant set with diamonds, a pearl and a Ceylonese sapphire.

1.5in (3.5cm) long

£800-1,000 **JHB**

An Indian silver wirework necklace, sewn with Persian Gulf seed pearls and set with hand-cut rubies.

This would not have been made for domestic sale, but rather for sale to Western residents or tourists.

c1900 Drop 2.5in (6.5cm) long

£750-850 **TAB**

An opal rivière necklace with diamond accents and clasp, in fitted case.

1870

£3,500-4,500 **JHB**

A Suffragette silver pendant necklace with green, white and violet pastes.

Suffragette jewellery was worn as a political statement. The green, white and violet-coloured gems stood for 'Give Women the Vote'.

c1900 Pendant 1.4in (3.5cm) long

£250-350 **LYNH**

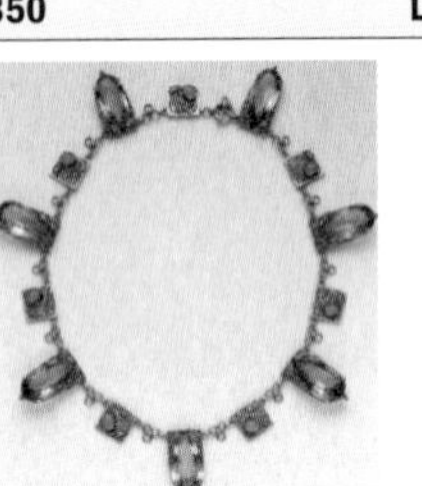

A silver necklace set with amethysts and chrysoprase green stones, by George Hunt.

c1930

£1,000-2,000 **VDB**

A Georgian 18ct gold longard, with hand clasp with turquoise stone on finger.

c1800 29.5in (75cm) long

£1,500-2,000 **SSP**

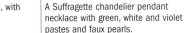

A Victorian 18ct gold necklace, with moonstone drops.

15in (38cm) long

£250-350 **SSP**

A Suffragette basket-of-flower pendant necklace with green, white and violet pastes.

c1900 Pendant 1.4in (3.5cm) long

£250-350 **LYNH**

An engraved silver locket, in the Aesthetic Movement style, Birmingham.

1881 2.5in (6.5cm) long

£200-300 **JHB**

A Victorian 9ct rose gold chased open curb link double Albert, with original T-bar.

16.5in (42cm) long

£350-450 **SSP**

A Suffragette chandelier pendant necklace with green, white and violet pastes and faux pearls.

c1900 Pendant 2.2in (5.5cm) long

£250-350 **LYNH**

An 15ct gold, brooch/pendant set with aquamarines and half pearls on a gold neckchain.

2.25in (6cm) long

£1,000-1,200 **JHB**

A Victorian silver flat line curb collar, with original plain oval locket.

c1880 11.75in (30cm) long

£220-280 **SSP**

A Victorian 9ct gold chased double Albert, with original T-bar.

16.25in (41cm) long

£500-700 **SSP**

BRACELETS

A Victorian woven horsehair bracelet with gilt metal clasp engraved with a floral motif.

c1840 *6.75in (17.5cm) circ*

£100-200 **MARA**

A 19thC French gold and diamond set bangle, part engraved.

£800-1,000 **JHB**

A Victorian 18ct gold turquoise bangle, with engraving either side of the stones.

c1880 *2.5in (6cm) wide*

£250-350 **SSP**

A Victorian 18ct gold opal and diamond bangle.

2.5in (6.5cm) wide

£2,500-3,000 **SSP**

A Victorian 18ct gold bangle, with a pearl flower.

2.5in (6.5cm) wide

£250-300 **SSP**

A Victorian oval-shaped garnet bangle.

2.5in (6.5cm) wide

£220-280 **SSP**

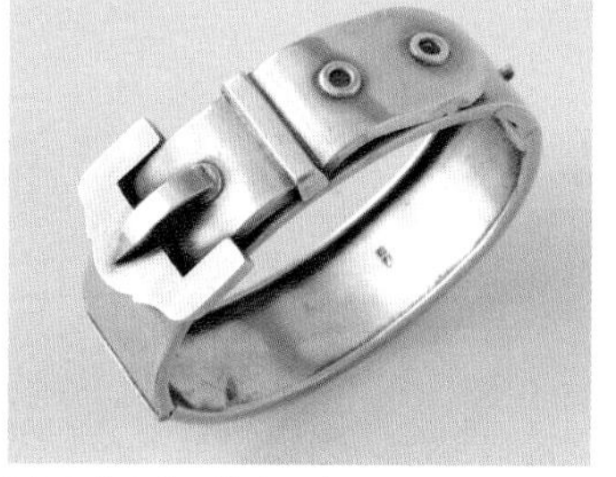

A Victorian silver buckle bangle.

2.5in (6.5cm) wide

£80-120 **SSP**

A 1920s silver Egyptian bangle, with rope effect on top.

c1910 *2.75in (7cm) wide*

£60-80 **SSP**

A 9ct gold bangle of weave and bead design.

1900

£400-800 **JHB**

A 15ct gold bangle set with sapphires and a pair of diamonds.

£2,500-3,000 **JHB**

An 18thC genuine pinchbeck bracelet with oval links and barrel clasp.

c1770 *7in (18cm) long*

£350-400 **RBRG**

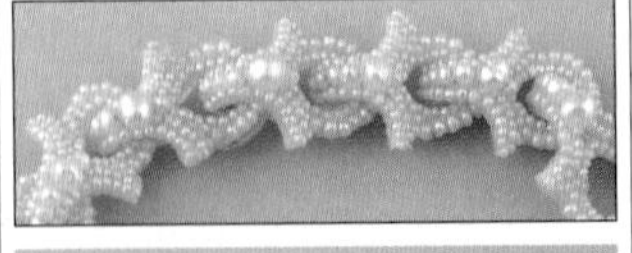

A Georgian seed pearl mother-of-pearl backed articulated bracelet, with original split pearl gold clasp.
6.75in (17.5cm) long
£400-500 **SSP**

A Georgian seed pearl bracelet, with lovers knots, with split pearl gold clasp.
7in (18cm) long
£200-250 **SSP**

A Victorian 18ct gold diamond and peridot bracelet.
c1890 *7.5in (19.5cm) long*
£800-1,000 **SSP**

A late Regency/early Victorian bracelet of cut steel rivetted to brass.
c1820-30 *6.75in (17cm) long*
£200-300 **MARA**

A Victorian 15ct gold turquoise and pearl curb bracelet.
c1890 *6.25in (16cm) long*
£650-750 **SSP**

A Victorian lozenge-shaped garnet bracelet.
c1880 *7.25in (18.5cm) long*
£300-400 **SSP**

Egyptian-revival pharaoh heads bracelet in goldtone metal with turquoise glass stones.
c1925 *7in (18cm) circ*
£60-100 **MARA**

RINGS

A Roman solid gold ring with a carved blue agate cameo of a female bust.
c100-200AD *0.5in (1.25cm) wide*
£3,500-4,000 **LNXG**

A Georgian rose-cut diamond ring.
Stone 0.75in (2cm) wide
£700-900 **SSP**

A Georgian 18ct chased shank gold ring, with decorative pearl cluster ring, set with ruby in centre.
0.5in (1cm) diam
£220-280 **SSP**

A Georgian 18ct gold decorative chased shank, with surround of split pearls with large garnet in centre.
0.5in (1cm) diam
£220-280 **SSP**

A Georgian 18ct gold chased shank, set with four split pearls and emeralds.
0.5in (1cm) wide
£300-350 **SSP**

A George III gold mourning ring, set with enamel and split pearls, inscribed 1814.
£550-650 **JHB**

A Georgian gold eternity ring, with Georgian-cut diamonds set in silver.
c1800 *0.75in (2cm) diam*
£800-1,000 **SSP**

A Victorian 18ct diamond round ring, set with a large ruby.
0.5in (1cm) diam
£350-450 **SSP**

An 18ct Victorian opal ring, with diamonds either side.

c1890 *0.75in (2cm) long*

£650-750 **SSP**

An 18ct Victorian vibrant three-stone opal ring, set with diamonds in between.

c1890 *0.75in (2cm) diam*

£150-200 **SSP**

A CLOSER LOOK AT A RUSSIAN GOLD RING

The cut of the diamond is of a type largely favoured before the era of this ring, making this piece unusual. Russian jewellers, like the maker of this ring, continued to use earlier cuts of diamonds into the 20thC.
The purpose of the cut is to reflect the maximum amount of light to make the stone sparkle. A poor cut can reduce the value of a stone by up to 50 per cent.
Diamonds were first mined in India in ancient times, but did not appear in European jewellery until the middle ages. They became more widely available in the 18thC and 19thC.
Antique diamond rings tend to be popular today and are often purchased as engagement rings.

A late 19thC Russian gold ring, set with seven old cut diamonds, est. 1.75ct.

1890

£2,500-3,500 **JHB**

A Victorian 18ct gold large oval vibrant opal ring set with four diamonds.

c1880 *0.75in (2cm) wide*

£800-1,000 **SSP**

A Victorian 18ct gold diamond oval ring, set with a moonstone.

c1890 *0.5in (1.5cm) wide*

£450-550 **SSP**

A Victorian 15ct gold flower-shaped 'Dearest' ring.

The first letter of each stone on the ring spells 'Dearest'.

c1880 *0.5in (1cm) diam*

£350-450 **SSP**

A Victorian 18ct gold double heart diamond ring, set with amethyst hearts.

c1890 *0.75in (2cm) long*

£700-800 **SSP**

A Victorian black enamel memorial ring, inscribed "In Memory Of".

c1890 *0.75in (2cm) diam*

£150-200 **SSP**

A Victorian black enamel memorial ring.

c1880 *0.75in (2cm) diam*

£180-220 **SSP**

A Victorian 15ct gold black enamel memorial ring, inscribed "In Memory Of", with five split pearls either side.

c1890 *0.75in (2cm) diam*

£220-280 **SSP**

An Edwardian 18ct platinum and three stone ring, with one fine Columbian emerald with diamonds either side.

Stone 0.5in (1.5cm) diam

£900-1,100 **SSP**

A 1920s platinum day and night ring, set with rubies, diamonds and sapphires.

The diamond band flips over to allow a choice of colour.

0.75in (2cm) wide

£700-900 **SSP**

A six stone sapphire and diamond ring.

1935

£600-700 **JHB**

A 1940s platinum and diamond ring, set with sapphire baguettes.

0.75in (2cm) wide

£900-1,100 **SSP**

EARRINGS

Late Roman–Byzantine gold pendant earrings with large sapphires and low-grade pearls.
c400-500AD *2.25in (5.75cm) long*
£12,000-18,000 **LNXG**

Late Georgian floral motif earrings with of gold wire with round- and pear-cut French jet stones.
c1720 *1.5in (4cm) diam*
£650-750 **CSAY**

Regency earrings with large diamond-cut sapphire blue pastes and four round-cut clear pastes.
c1780 *1in (2.5cm) long*
£600-700 **CSAY**

A pair of pendant hoop earrings of cut steel.
c1780 *2in (5cm) long*
£500-600 **CSAY**

A pair of Georgian seed pearl mother-of-pearl backed earrings, with a flower top supporting snail shell drops.
c1800 *1.75in (4.5cm) long*
£300-350 **SSP**

A pair of Georgian seed pearl mother-of-pearl backed daisy flower earrings.
1.5in (3.5cm) long
£300-350 **SSP**

A pair of Berlin ironwork floral motif earrings with gilt highlights.
c1825 *2.25in (6cm) long*
£1,000-1,200 **CSAY**

A pair of Georgian 18ct gold silver-set diamonds with pink tourmaline drops.
1.75in (4cm) long
£400-500 **SSP**

A late 19thC Turkish ottoman earrings set with rose cut diamonds.
c1880
£3,500-4,500 **JHB**

A gold and garnet set earrings, slight damage.
1860 *2in (5cm) long*
£500-600 **JHB**

A pair of pendant hoop earrings of black and red tortoiseshell with bands of gold inlay.
c1880 *1.75in (4.5cm) long*
£700-1,000 **LYNH**

A pair of pendant elongated hoop earrings with inlaid gold floral and foliate motifs.
c1880 *1.75in (4.5cm) long*
£700-1,000 **LYNH**

A pair of Edwardian platinum diamond and natural pearl earrings.
c1910 *1.75in (4cm) long*
£1,000-1,500 **SSP**

A pair of platinum and old mine-cut diamond claw-set stud earrings.
c1910
£1,200-1,800 **SSP**

COSTUME JEWELLERY

Costume jewellery collectors are buying up named designer pieces, the more expensive the better, as the public becomes increasingly aware of the collectability of vintage jewellery.

At present the costume jewellery market is buoyant, with collectors buying more expensive, more elaborate and larger pieces, signed by key names, with necklaces and earrings perennially popular.

After a recent period of interest, the market for retro pieces from 1930s-40s is suppressed and people are buying to create a look. Strong, dramatic, large pieces are selling well, but subtly coloured, pearl pieces are not as highly sought after as in previous years. Trifari's enamel pieces especially have to be in excellent condition to attract much attention. Key designers such as Dior and Chanel tend to become over-priced, but reasonably priced pieces are still available to the determined hunter and are highly collectable.

Collectors are snapping up diamanté bracelets in a bid to create the Marlene Dietrich / Madonna look. Mixing and matching pieces is now in fashion too. Christmas tree pins have lost none of their sparkle as the trend for bright colours and rhinestones gains momentum.

Names to look out for are the perennially popular Miriam Haskell and Lea Stein; Regency and Weiss are currently in demand too. Pieces by Hattie Carnegie are still reasonably priced and avidly sought-after. The high-quality and finely crafted jewellery of Vendome is currently attracting a great deal of interest, as are Coro Duettes. Stanley Hagler's unusual, bold and colourful creations are also popular.

by Yai Thammachote at Cristobal

MIRIAM HASKELL

A Miriam Haskell Edwardian-style pendant necklace, with multiple looped and interlaced strands of baroque pearls, the clasp and head of the pendant encrusted with rings of tiny baroque pearls and rose montées.

c1950 *Pendant 4in (10cm) long*

£1,550-1,750 **SUM**

A Miriam Haskell two-strand faux pearl necklace with floral pendant of pink, blue and red glass beads, seed pearls, clear rose montées and amethyst poured glass leaves.

c1960 *14in (35.5cm) long*

£1,500-1,700 **SUM**

A Miriam Haskell necklace with a chain of gilt metal and clear rhinestone navettes, and a fruit-and-leaf motif pendant of faux pearl beads, seed pearls and clear rose montées.

c1960 *Pendant 3.75in (9.5cm) long*

£900-1,000 **SUM**

A Miriam Haskell necklace and hoop earrings with baroque pearls and jade, decorated with emerald poured glass beads and emerald poured glass cabochons, encircled with swirls of clear rose montées.

c1960 *Earrings 2in (5cm) long*

£1,000-1,200 **SUM**

MIRIAM HASKELL

- From her modest childhood home in Indiana, USA, Miriam Haskell (1899-1981) moved to New York in 1924 and set up her first costume jewellery shop in the McAlpin Hotel.
- Haskell was not trained in jewellery design: her genius lay in her ability to choose designers, designs and materials. When she saw the work of Frank Hess, a window designer for Macy's, she appointed him Chief Designer of the new Miriam Haskell Company, which she founded in 1926. Hess worked there until 1960, establishing stylish, innovative and affordable designs for the company.
- Later talented designers, including Robert Clark and Larry Vrba, continued in Hess' footsteps. Their work was made by highly skilled European craftsmen who executed the complex and intricate designs to high standards, using exceptional quality materials which Hess and Haskell sourced from all over the world, including beads from Murano, Italy, and crystals from Austria.
- Her signature material was the baroque pearl, which was made exclusively for her in Japan. These pearls were given their extraordinary lustre by several layers of 'essence d'orient' a mixture of fish scales, cellulose and resins. The details of this secret process went with Haskell to her grave.
- Other signs of Haskell's quality include hand-wired beads, antiqued filigree metal and rose montées mounted in pierced metal cups.
- Haskell pieces are always popular, but condition affects the price as parts are difficult to replace.

A Miriam Haskell open bangle of gilt metal with filigree metal, seed pearls and clear rose montées.

c1950 *6.75in (17cm) circ*

£700-800 **SUM**

A Miriam Haskell Art Nouveau-style, floral motif bracelet of antiqued gilt metal bordered with clusters of faux seed pearls.

c1950 *6.5in (16cm) circ*

£500-600 **SUM**

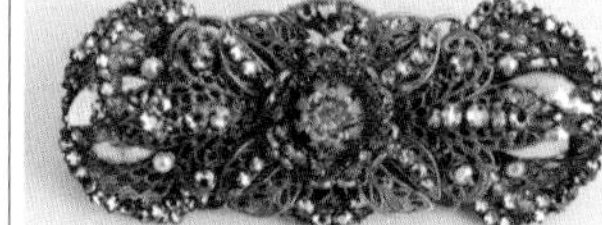

A Miriam Haskell floral-motif pin of filigree antiqued gilt metal, studded with faux pearls and clear rose montées.

c1950 *3.25in (8.25cm) wide*

£450-550 **SUM**

A Miriam Haskell floral and foliate pin, with antiqued gilt metal leaves, chained petals and clear rose montées.

c1950 *3.75in (9.5cm) long*

£600-700 **SUM**

A Miriam Haskell floral motif stick pin with bird and turtle figures, of antiqued gilt metal with clear crystal beads and rose montées.

c1950 *3.75in (9.5cm) long*

£500-600 **SUM**

A CLOSER LOOK AT A MIRIAM HASKELL PIN

Stones and beads are built up to create a three-dimensional effect.
This piece incorporates Haskell's signature materials: rose montées, cabochons and baroque pearls.
Check that baroque pearls are not scratched as they flake easily once damaged.
The materials are hand-wired onto a gold-plated filigree backing.

A Miriam Haskell floral pin, of gilt metal with coral poured glass beads, faux seed and baroque pearls and clear rose montée highlights.

c1940 *4in (10cm) long*

£650-750 **SUM**

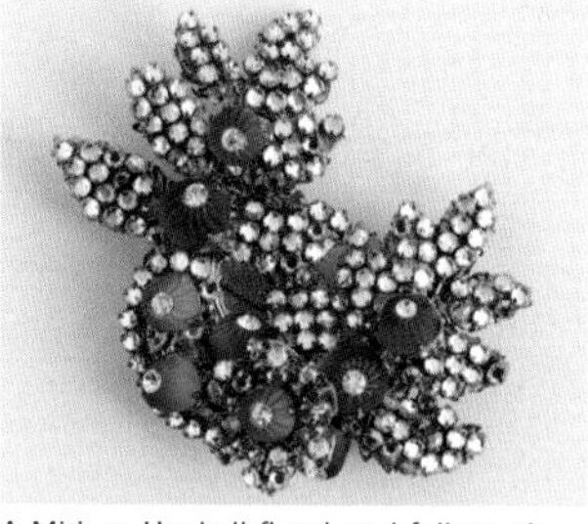

A Miriam Haskell floral and foliate pin of antiqued gilt metal with melon-cut emerald beads and clear rose montées.

c1960 *3in (7.5cm) long*

£450-500 **SUM**

A Miriam Haskell pendant fruit drop necklace and earrings with faceted citrine glass beads, filigree gilt findings and clear rose montées.

c.1950 *Pendant 14.5 (37.5cm) long*

£800-900 **SUM**

A Miriam Haskell hinged bracelet and earrings by Frank Hess, of silvered metal with filigree metal, clear rose montées, faux baroque pearls and polychrome poured glass beads.

c1950 *7in (18cm) circ.*

£800-900 **SUM**

A Miriam Haskell floral necklace and earrings with amber, pear-cut, poured glass cabochons, citrine poured glass oval beads and citrine and amber rhinestones.

c1950 *Pendant 2.75in (7cm) long*

£1,000-1,250 **SUM**

A Miriam Haskell floral wreath necklace and earrings with smoky amethyst and violet poured glass petals and leaves, and gilt findings.

c1960 *Necklace 16in (40.5cm) long*

£1,000-1,200 **SuM**

A Miriam Haskell hinged bracelet of gilt and filigree metal, clear rose montées and emerald green poured glass beads.

c1950 *7in (18cm) circ*

£500-600 **SUM**

A Miriam Haskell floral motif pin, with dark amber poured glass petals, set under an antiqued gilt metal shell motif, with five pendants and poured glass amber leaves.

1930s *6.25in (16cm) long*

£200-250 **SUM**

CHANEL

COCO CHANEL

- Coco Chanel (1883-1971) opened a millinery shop in Paris in 1909 and went on to launch her own couture houses in Paris, Deauville and Biarritz. From humble origins, she became one of the greatest icons of fashion in the 20thC.
- The creator of the little black dress and Chanel No.5, Chanel pioneered a new style of women's clothes, combining simplicity and comfort with elegance, to create an unmistakable style which had a great influence over the fashions of the 1920s and 30s.
- Her innovations in costume jewellery were introduced through her Paris salon, where she opened a boutique specializing in accessories and jewellery. Instead of copying the style of fine jewellery, her costume jewellery was designed specifically to reflect the elegant simplicity of her clothes and to compliment and 'finish' an outfit. The simple but effective use of multiple strings of faux pearls with a black pullover epitomises this style.
- Other key pieces for Chanel include gold tone chains, pâte-de-verre jewellery from Maison Gripoix and classic Maltese cross cuffs designed by Verdura.
- Chanel closed her business when she was exiled to Switzerland during WWII, following her affair with a Nazi officer. She reinvented her name throughout the 1950s and into 1960s, working with designer Robert Goossens, producing long, rosary-style necklaces, with chains of pearls and beads, and Maltese cross brooches decorated with glass cabochons in her signature colours of red and green.

A rare Chanel Mr Punch pin with *en tremblant* head, in lead with white, red and black enamel, the head also with pavé-set clear crystal rhinestones.
c1920s *2.5in (6cm) high*
£1,500-2,000 **BY**

A Chanel stylized floral pin with green, red and blue poured glass stones, faux pearls and pavé-set clear crystal rhinestones.
c1920s *4in (10.5cm) high*
£1,000-1,200 **BY**

A late 1920s Chanel 'Bijoux de Fleurs' orchid pin, pot metal decorated with pink and red enamel, with smoky brown crystal rhinestones.
3in (7.5cm) wide
£600-700 **CRIS**

A 1930s Chanel pendant-pin with red and dark and light green glass stones, faux pearls and clear crystal rhinestones, in gilt metal settings.
3.75in (9.5cm) long
£280-320 **RITZ**

A 1940s Chanel dragon pin by Maison Gripoix, with a gold-plated wire frame set with green, red and black poured glass.
4in (10.5cm) wide
£250-300 **RITZ**

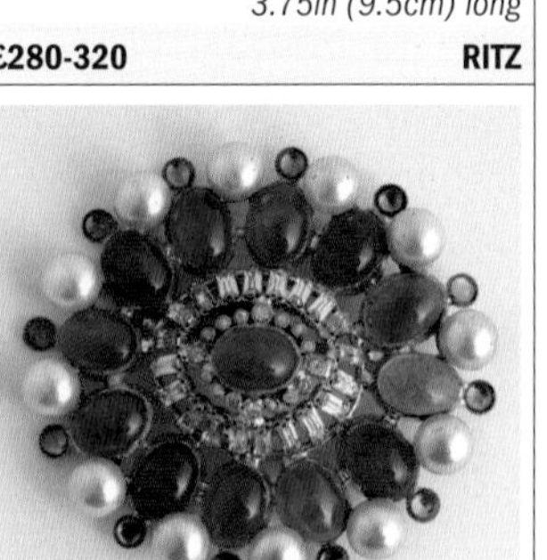

A Chanel oval pin with red, green and blue glass cabochons, faux pearls and round and baguette clear crystal rhinestones.
c1970 *2.75in (7cm) wide*
£400-500 **SUM**

A CLOSER LOOK AT A CHANEL PIN

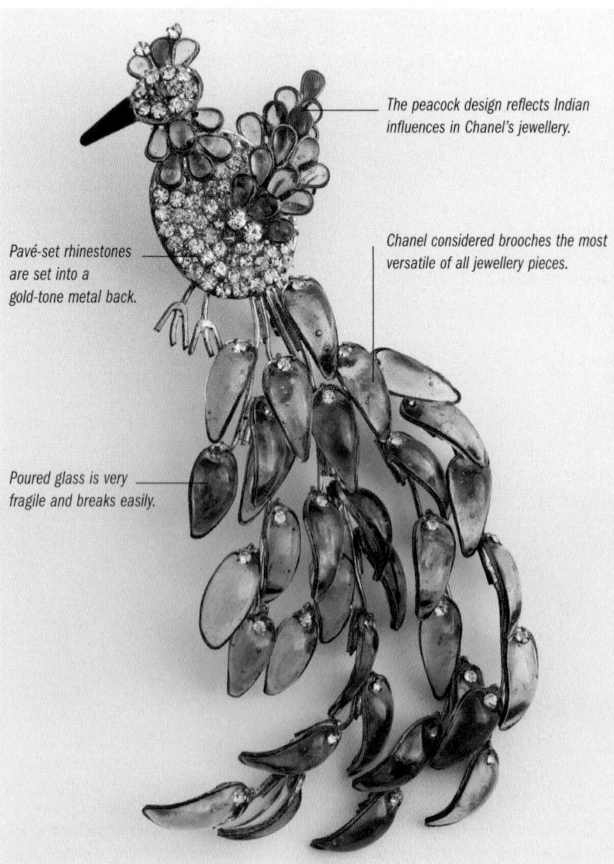

The peacock design reflects Indian influences in Chanel's jewellery.
Pavé-set rhinestones are set into a gold-tone metal back.
Chanel considered brooches the most versatile of all jewellery pieces.
Poured glass is very fragile and breaks easily.

A rare 1930s Chanel peacock pin with turquoise, aquamarine and red poured glass feathers and pavé-set clear crystal rhinestones.
5.5in (14cm) long
£1,800-2,600 **BY**

A Chanel Maltese Cross pin with green, red and pink poured glass cabochons in gilt metal settings.

c1990s *2.5in (6.5cm) wide*

£80-100 **PC**

A Chanel round flower pin and pendant, with turquoise, amethyst and pastel green French poured glass beads, and clear crystal rhinestone highlights, on a gold-plated wire frame.

1995 *2.75in (7cm) diam*

£350-400 **CRIS**

A Chanel necklace with multiple pendants of faux pearls, blue, red and green poured glass beads, some carved, and clear crystal rhinestones.

c1970 *Longest pendant 4in (10.5cm) long*

£1,800-2,200 **SUM**

A pair of Chanel floral motif earrings, of gold-plated metal with green poured glass and pavé-set clear crystal rhinestone petals and red glass cabochon centres.

c1980s *1.5in (4cm) diam*

£275-300 **SUM**

COPPOLA E TOPPO

A Coppola e Toppo choker necklace with blue, red, amber and clear Bohemian crystal beads and similarly beaded clasp.

c1950s *2in (5cm) wide*

£450-500 **WAIN**

A Coppola e Toppo necklace with gilt metal clasp and multiple interlaced strands of baroque pearls and clear glass beads.

c1950s *13.75in (35cm) long*

£1,600-1,800 **FM**

A Coppola e Toppo necklace with four strands of black and clear plastic beads and a black-beaded oval clasp.

1960s *19.5in (49.5cm) long*

£500-600 **FM**

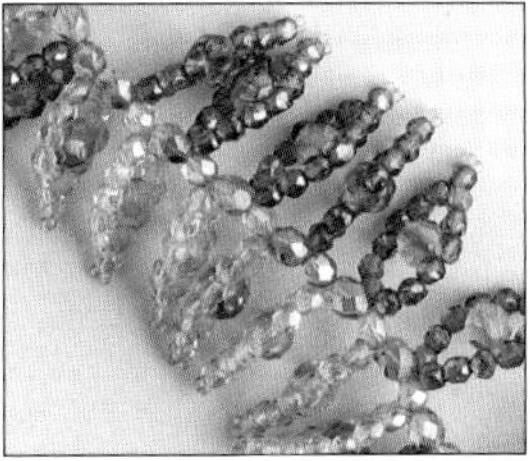

An early 1960s Coppola e Toppo necklace with stylized floral motifs of dark blue, pale green and turquoise glass beads hand-wired within a chain of similarly coloured glass beads.

28.5in (72.5cm) long

£1,400-1,500 **FM**

A 1960s Coppola e Toppo necklace with multiple interlaced strands of pink and cranberry red plastic beads, terminating in a gilt metal clasp embellished with glass beads in the same colours.

3in (7.5cm) wide

£700-800 **SUM**

A 1960s Coppola e Toppo necklace with gilt metal clasp and strands and pendants of clear crystal and citrine and green plastic stones.

2.5in (6.25cm) wide

£400-500 **SUM**

A 1960s Coppola e Toppo necklace with a bow motif and five strands of turquoise, mauve and black glass beads, with matching earrings.

Necklace 13in (33cm) long

£1,300-1,400 **FM**

COPPOLA E TOPPO

- In the late 1940s, brother and sister designers, Bruno Coppola and Lyda Toppo, began designing fashion jewellery in Milan. They came to the attention of fashion houses Dior and Balenciaga, who commissioned designs both for the catwalk and for retail. They also produced pieces under their own trademark 'Made in Italy by Coppola e Toppo'. Early pieces were stamped for Lyda's dog, 'Mikey'.
- Their work for Italian couturier Valentino helped to reinforce his standing as 'king of fashion' with celebrities such as Jackie Kennedy and Elizabeth Taylor.
- Coppola e Toppo is known for its elaborate pieces composed of brightly coloured plastic, Murano glass and crystal beads. Turning away from earlier costume jewellery designs which used 'old fashioned' pearls and gilt, their key pieces utilized faux pearls and gilt metals as highlights rather than core materials, creating striking, modern pieces which were in tune with the glamour of the late 1950s and the 1960s.
- Coppola e Toppo is best known for the bright, elaborately strung, multi-strand crystal necklaces.

A 1960s Coppola e Toppo necklace with multiple interlaced strands of amber, topaz and citrine coloured crystal beads.

2.5in (6.25cm) wide

£750-850 **SUM**

A 1960s Coppola e Toppo necklace with multiple strands of red glass beads, gathered on one side within a ring of darker red glass beads and terminating in gilt metal and red bead clasps.

26in (66cm) long

£600-750 **ROX**

A 1960s Coppola e Toppo necklace with twin and quadruple strands of lava stone beads, and ornaments of gilt metal with similar beads and faux pearls.

19.5in (49.5cm) long

£700-800 **FM**

A Coppola e Toppo pendant necklace and earrings, designed for Valentino, with faceted sapphire blue and clear Swarovski crystal stones set in gilt metal.

c1970 *Necklace 13in (33cm) long*

£1,800-2,000 **WAIN**

CORO

A 1930s-40s Coro Duette, with hearth and overmantel motifs of white metal, with clear crystal rhinestones and ruby glass 'fires'.

3in (7.5cm) long

£100-150 **MIIIB**

A 1930s-40s Coro Duette, of silver leaves in rhodium-plated metal with round and baguette clear crystal rhinestones.

2.5in (6cm) wide

£100-150 **CRIS**

A 1940s Corocraft diamanté, glass and faux pearl pin.

2.25in (5.5cm) wide

£100-130 **ROX**

A 1940s Coro Duette, of putti with crowns in vermeil sterling silver with ruby and emerald crystal rhinestones and faux pearls.

1.5in (3.5cm) high

£200-250 **CRIS**

A Coro basket of fruits pin, of white metal with clear crystal rhinestones and pale blue and moonglow Lucite cabochons.

c1940 *1in (2.5cm) long*

£30-40 **JJ**

A 1940s Coro Duette, of parrots in yellow metal with green, blue and pink enamelling and pavé-set clear crystal rhinestones.

2.5in (6cm) long

£100-150 **ABIJ**

A 1940s Coro goldtone metal badge and shield pin with matching earrings, the shields with white and red enamelling.

Pin 2in (5cm) diam

£30-50 **ABIJ**

A 1950s-60s Coro horse's head pin with matching earrings, of bright, goldtone metal castings with aquamarine navette-cut rhinestone eyes, fuchsia pink navette-cut rhinestone ears and red enamelled flowers and green enamelled leaves.

Pin 2in (5cm) long

£150-170 **ABIJ**

A 1950s Coro floral motif necklace with matching earrings, in goldtone metal with faux coral beads, clear crystal rhinestones and white enamelling to some of the leaves.

Necklace 16in (40.5cm) long

£55-75 **MIIIB**

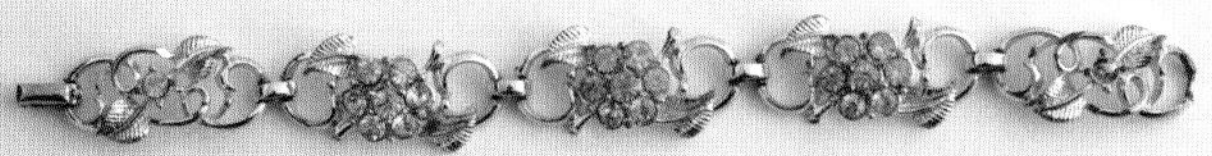

A 1950s Coro bracelet with silvertone metal links and leaves and jonquil-coloured crystal rhinestones.

7in (18cm) long

£30-40 **MIIIB**

TRIFARI

A 1930s Trifari flower pin, rhodium-plated with small clear baguette and round rhinestones.

4in (10cm) long

£150-225 **ROX**

A 1950s Trifari leaves and berries pin and earrings, of matte-finish gold alloy with faux pearls.

Pin 4in (10cm) long

£140-160 **CRIS**

A 1950s matte-finish, gold alloy Trifari leaves and berries pin with faux pearls and tiny pavé-set clear rhinestones.

4in (10cm) long

£90-100 **CRIS**

A 1950s Trifari gold-plated leaf pin with channel-set and pavé-set clear rhinestones.

7.75in (20cm) long

£75-95 **LB**

A rare Trifari plant motif pin of sterling silver with green and brown enamelling and pavé-set clear rhinestones.

c1940 *7in (18cm) long*

£1,200-1,300 **SUM**

A mid-1950s Trifari basket-of-flowers pin, gold-plated with amethyst-blue, jonquil and rose-pink rhinestones.

1.75in (4.5cm) long

£35-45 **CRIS**

A 1940s Trifari necklace and earrings, of stylized ivy leaf motifs in sterling silver with pale blue chalcedony paste leaves.

Necklace 0.5in (1.25cm) wide

£170-250 **ROX**

A 1950s Trifari lily-of-the-valley necklace and earrings.

Earring 1in (2.5cm) long

£100-170 **ROX**

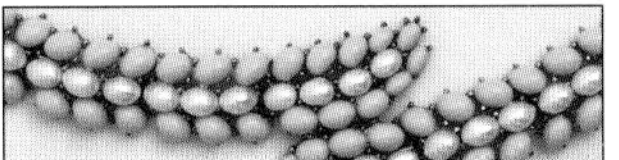

A 1960s Trifari necklace set, with faux turquoise and pearls.

Necklace 17in (43cm) long

£70-90 **RG**

A Trifari bracelet, with clear navette-cut rhinestone flowerheads with faux pearl centres.

c1950 *6in (15cm) diam*

£150-250 **LB**

MADE IN AUSTRIA

A 1940s Austrian fruit pin and earrings, with red glass strawberries, green glass and gilt leaves, and gilt metal stalks.

Pin 2.75in (7cm) long

£60-90 **ROX**

A 1950s Austrian fruit pin with red glass cherries, yellow glass leaves, japanned metal stalks and a red crystal rhinestone.

2.25in (5.5cm) long

£50-80 **CRIS**

A 1950s Austrian fruit pin, with pink glass bunches of grapes, green glass leaves, japanned metal stalks and a pink crystal rhinestone.

2.5in (6.5cm) long

£40-60 **BY**

A 1950s Austrian fruit pin, with opaque blue glass pears, yellow glass leaves, japanned metal stalks and an aquamarine crystal rhinestone.

2.75in (7cm) long

£50-60 **BY**

A 1950s Austrian fruit pin with opaque green glass pears, green glass leaves, japanned metal stalks and a green crystal rhinestone.

2.5in (6.5cm) long

£45-55 **BY**

A 1950s Austrian fruit pin, with a single clear glass strawberry, clear glass leaves and japanned metal stalks.

2in (5cm) long

£45-55 **BY**

A 1950s Austrian fruit pin, with a yellow glass apple, green glass leaves and yellow diamanté.

3.5in (6cm) high

£45-55 **BY**

OTHER MAKERS

A Marcel Boucher ballerina pin, of rhodium-plated casting with selected gilt highlights and round-cut and pavé-set clear crystal rhinestones.

c1950 *2in (5cm) long*

£115-130 **ABIJ**

A 1960s Marcel Boucher floral motif pin, of antiqued silvertone metal casting with pale blue round and striated crystal cabochons.

2.5in (6.5cm) long

£55-65 **ABIJ**

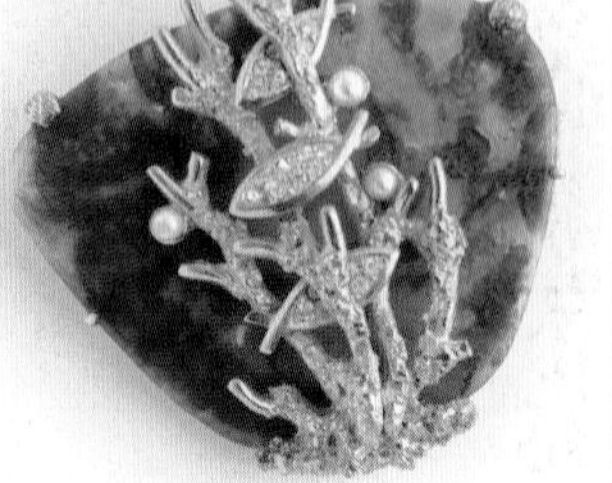

A 1950s Boucher glass and diamanté pin.

The stamped signature on this piece is in capitals which identifies its period of manufacture.

2.25in (5.5cm) high

£80-120 **ROX**

A rare 1940s Marcel Boucher poured glass, diamanté and faux pearl necklace.

Pendant 4.75in (12cm) wide

£2,000-2,500 **BY**

A 1970s Marcel Boucher bird on a branch pin, of goldtone metal casting with blue enamelling and clear crystal rhinestone highlights.

2.5in (6.5cm) long

£50-60 **JJ**

A 1950s Hattie Carnegie pearlescent enamel pin.

4in (10cm) long

£100-150 **ROX**

A 1970s Hattie Carnegie pansy pin with large 'cabochon' centre, all of base metal coated with metallic-yellow cold enamel.

2in (5cm) diam

£50-60 **ABIJ**

A late 1990s Cristobal bouquet-of-flowers pin from their 'Secret Garden' collection, comprising polychrome French poured glass and a clear rhinestones set in a brass wire frame.

3.5in (9cm) high

£300-350 **CRIS**

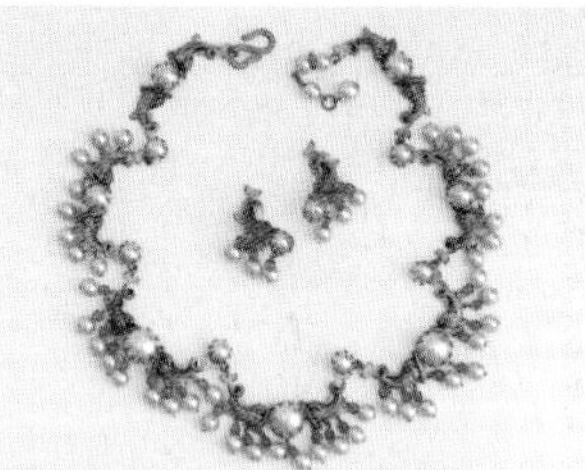

An extremely rare Christian Dior necklace and earrings, with gilded metal mythical sea creatures set with faux pearls and green glass, marked 'Christian Dior 1959'.

Necklace 14.5in (37cm) long

£800-900 **RG**

A 1960s Kramer for Dior rhodium-plated flower pin, with pavé-set and large central clear rhinestones.

1.5in (3.5cm) long

£140-160 **FM**

A Dior floral motif necklace and earrings, with lapis lazuli glass beads and cabochons and clear rhinestones.

1959 Necklace 14in (35.5cm) long

£900-1,100 **FM**

A late 1930s Eisenberg Original pin, of rhodium-plated metal with prong-set, round- and pear-cut Swarovski crystal clear rhinestones, a round faux pearl and nine faux pearl drops.

3in (7.5cm) long

£130-170 **ABIJ**

An early 1940s Eisenberg Original fur clip, of with tiered scrolls of sterling silver with prong- and bezel-set Swarovski crystal clear rhinestones.

2.25in (5.5cm) long

£190-225 **ABIJ**

A 1940s Eisenberg Original white metal and diamanté pin, the back of one mount stamped "STERLING".

3.25in (8.5cm) wide

£200-225 **ROX**

A 1980s Stanley Hagler floral and figural pin, with a central carved ivory oriental head encircled by rose quartz and green faux seed pearl leaves, rose quartz and violet pressed glass petals and jade green rhinestones.

2.5in (6.25cm) wide

£200-250 **CRIS**

A 1960s Stanley Hagler stylized camellia pin, with pearlised metal blue petals, pressed red glass, red faux seed pearls and clear crystal rhinestones.

3.25in (8cm) diam

£200-250 **PC**

A 1960s necklace and earrings by Stanley Hagler, with frosted pressed glass flowers and Russian gold plated stamping.

The price of Stanley Hagler has doubled in the last two years.

1in (2.5cm) long

£300-400 **CRIS**

A 1980s Stanley Hagler floral motif necklace and earrings, with faux coral glass petals, beads, cabochons and drops hand-wired to filigree gold-plated backings.

Necklace 22.5in (57cm) long

£500-600 **CRIS**

A 1950s-60s Hobé bib necklace, bracelet, pin and earrings parure, in gilt metal with strings of faceted faux topaz and red aurora borealis beads with overlaid spherical blue and pink Venetian glass beads.

Necklace 2.5in (6.5cm) wide

£320-380 **BY**

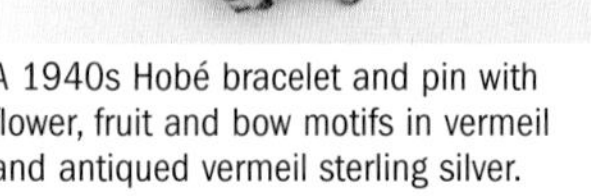

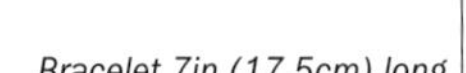

A 1940s Hobé bracelet and pin with flower, fruit and bow motifs in vermeil and antiqued vermeil sterling silver.

Bracelet 7in (17.5cm) long

£100-150 **BY**

A 1950s pair of Hobé earrings of antiqued gilt metal castings with pink and white faux pearls and clear crystal rhinestones.

1.75in (4.5cm) long

£65-100 **LB**

A mid-1990s Iradj Moini *en tremblant* flower pin, with prong-set clear and emerald-green rhinestones set in a brass wire frame.

6.3in (16cm) long

£850-950 **CRIS**

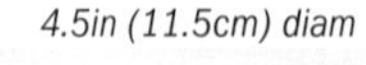

A 1940s Joseff floral motif pin, with aquamarine crystal lozenges and clear rhinestones set in Russian gold-plated metal.

4.5in (11.5cm) diam

£800-900 **SUM**

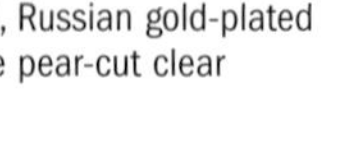

A 1940s large Joseff floral pin with pendant tassel, Russian gold-plated with three large pear-cut clear rhinestones.

6in (15cm) long

£300-350 **SUM**

A pair of 1950s Joseff Russian gold-plated and faux pearl pendant earrings, as worn by Grace Kelly in the film 'High Society'.

4in (10cm) long

£150-200 **SUM**

A 1940s Joseff patriotic American eagle and flag pin, Russian gold-plated with prong-set ruby, clear and sapphire rhinestones.

2.25in (5.5cm) wide

£100-150 **CRIS**

A 1940s Joseff floral motif pendant necklace and earrings, Russian gold-plated with faux topaz and clear rhinestones.

Pendant 3in (7.5cm) diam

£500-600 **SUM**

A L'Atelier de Verre pendant rose necklace with faux pearls and emerald poured glass and mother-of-pearl leaves.

c2000 Necklace 15.25in (39cm) long

£400-500 SUM

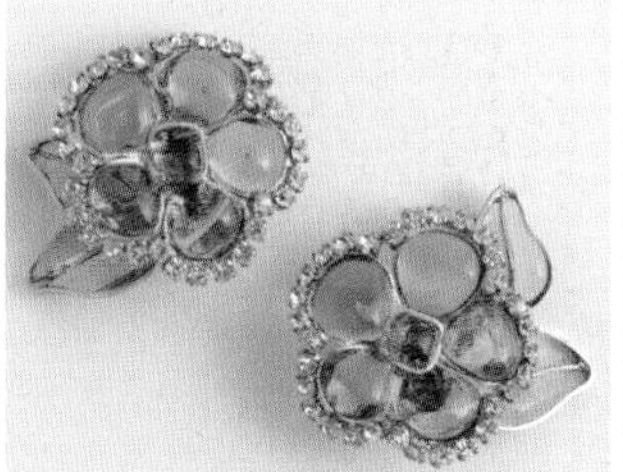

A pair of L'Atelier de Verre floral earrings of green poured glass and clear crystal rhinestones in gold-plated settings.

c2000 2.2in (5.5cm) long

£200-250 SUM

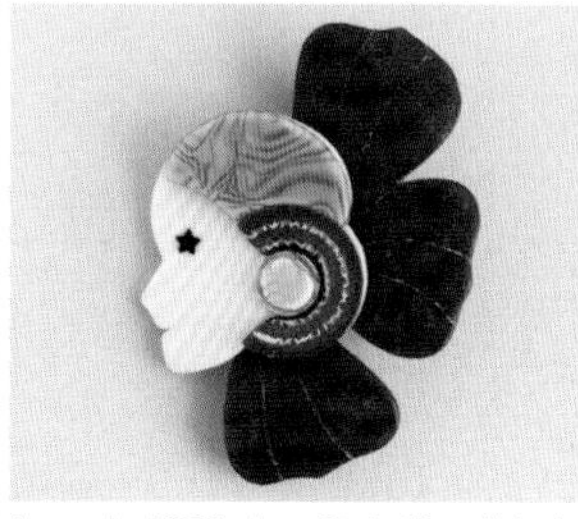

An early 1980s Lea Stein 'Corolle' pin, made of laminated rhodoid.

2.5in (6cm) high

£60-70 CRIS

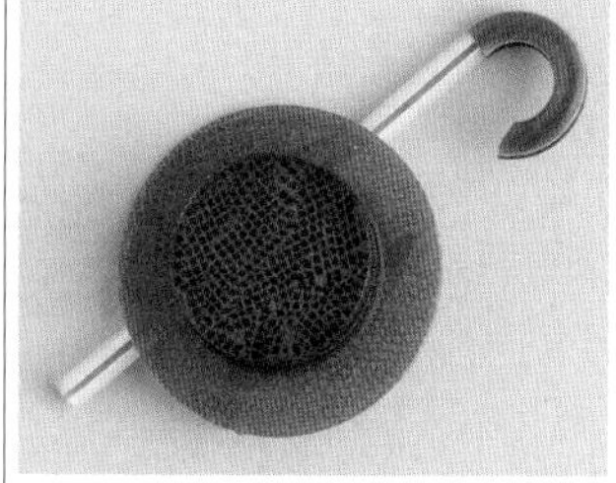

A 1980s Lea Stein 'Hat and Cane' pin, made from laminated rhodoid.

2.75in (7cm) high

£45-55 CRIS

A 1980s Maison Gripoix spray of flowers pin, with polychrome poured glass petals and leaves set in gilt wire, with clear crystal rhinestone highlights.

3.25in (8cm) diam

£200-240 RITZ

A Maison Gripoix flower pin, with green poured glass petals and leaves set in gilt wire, and with a ruby glass centre.

c2000 2.75in (7cm) diam

£200-240 RITZ

A Maison Gripoix floral motifs necklace, with amber and topaz poured glass leaves in japanned metal frame with clear crystal rhinestone stigmas.

c2000 Large flower 2.75in (7cm) diam

£450-500 RITZ

A mid-1940s Pennino Bros vermeil sterling silver pin, with aquamarine and rose-pink crystal rhinestones.

3.75in (9.5cm) long

£200-230 CRIS

A mid-1940s Pennino Bros stylized flower pin with trailing trendrils, of vermeil sterling silver with rose-pink and clear crystal rhinestones.

2.75in (7cm) long

£200-250 CRIS

A mid-1940s Pennino Bros bow and spray-of-flowers pin, of vermeil sterling silver with aquamarine and small rose-pink crystal rhinestones.

2.5in (6cm) long

£200-250 CRIS

A Pennino Bros flower pin and earrings of vermeil sterling silver with deep aquamarine and pavé-set clear crystal rhinestones.

c1940 Pin 2.75in (7cm) long

£250-350 SUM

A Regency butterfly pin, with crystals and prong-set Bakelite cabochon body.

2in (5cm) long

£55-65 CRIS

A 1940s Nettie Rosenstein minstrel pin, of vermeil sterling silver, with turquoise glass cabochons and pavé-set clear crystal rhinestones.

2.75in (7cm) high

£180-200 ROX

A 1950s Elsa Schiaparelli necklace, bracelet and earrings demi-parure, with rhodium-plated links, prong-set blue and green glass stones and aurora borealis rhinestones.

Necklace 15in (38cm) long

£1,000-1,200 CRIS

A 1950s Elsa Schiaparelli diamanté and faux pearl bracelet and earrings.

Necklace 7.5in (19cm) long

£100-150 ROX

A 1950s Elsa Schiaparelli pin and earrings, with prong-set leaves of pale green and pink Lucite on a gold-plated backing.

Pin 3.5in (9cm) long

£275-350 PC

A 1950s Elsa Schiaparelli frog-on-a-leaf pin, the leaf gold-plated, the frog with dark blue cabochon body, ruby red, kite-shaped glass feet and faux pearl eyes.

2.5in (6.5cm) long

£150-200 **CRIS**

A 1940s Schreiner Lucite and glass trembler pin.

3in (7.5cm) high

£80-100 **ROX**

A 1940s Schreiner pin, pale green glass cabochon surrounded by dark green rhinestones and pale green glass petals.

2.25in (6cm) wide

£180-200 **ROX**

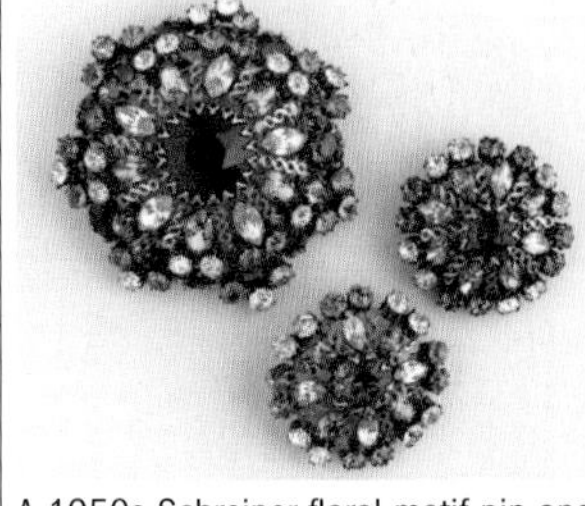

A 1950s Schreiner floral motif pin and earrings, of gunmetal plating with olivine and aquamarine crystal rhinestones and amethyst cabochons.

Pin 2.5in (6.25cm) diam

£200-250 **CRIS**

A late 1940s to early 1950s Weiss flower pin, of gold-plated metal, with prong-set, navette-cut aquamarine, emerald and jade green Austrian crystal rhinestone petals and leaves, and a faceted sapphire blue crystal centre.

3in (7.5cm) long

£100-150 **JJ**

A mid-1960s-early 1970s Weiss flower pin with white enamel petals and green enamel leaves and stem.

3in (7.5cm) long

£15-20 **MILLB**

A 1950s Weiss floral motif pin and earrings, with smoky quartz and aurora borealis crystal rhinestones in antiqued goldtone metal settings.

Pin 2in (5cm) diam

£50-60 **ABIJ**

A 1940s Weiss necklace, of silvertone white metal set with Austrian crystal rhinestones.

17in (43cm) long

£70-75 **JJ**

UNMARKED PIECES

A 1940s unsigned vase of flowers pin, of vermeil sterling silver with faceted ruby, emerald and apple green glass stones and clear crystal rhinestones.

3.25in (8.25cm) high

£220-280 **BY**

An unsigned 1940s flamingo pin of vermeil sterling silver with faceted yellow glass body and pavé-set clear crystal rhinestones.

3.5in (9cm) long

£220-280 **BY**

An unsigned 1940s elephant watch pin in vermeil sterling silver with faceted glass faux sapphire body and clear crystal rhinestones.

2.75in (7cm) wide

£100-120 **BY**

An unsigned flower and leaf pin made in Canada in the style of the Regency company, with lime green navettes and carved powder blue glass stones.

c1965 *3in (7.5cm) wide*

£55-65 **CRIS**

An unsigned 1940s ballerina pin and earrings in vermeil sterling silver with faceted aquamarine and sapphire glass stones, and clear crystal rhinestones.

Pin 3.5in (9cm) high

£240-280 **BY**

A rare 1930s gold-plated white metal Vogue glass and diamanté lily corsage pin, the clip marked 'STERLING'.

3.25in (8cm) long

£100-115 **ROX**

An unsigned 1940s bouquet of flowers pin with prong-set pale and dark faux amethysts, polychrome enamelled highlights and clear crystal rhinestones.

4in (10cm) long

£100-150 **BY**

An unsigned 1940s 'Retro style' floral motif pin, of sterling silver with sapphire glass cabochons and clear crystal rhinestones.

2.5in (6.5cm) long

£60-90 **RG**

An unsigned 1950s pin in the form of a bonsai tree, the branches set with multicoloured diamanté and with enamel flowers and leaves.

2.5in (6cm) high

£100-130 **BY**

An unsigned pin in the form of a pendulous lily, the leaves inset with pink-faceted diamanté, the flower enamelled with baguette-cut diamanté.

3.5in (9cm) high

£180-220 **BY**

An unsigned 1930s cricket-playing-a-violin pin, of gold-plated metal with enamelling and pavé-set clear crystal rhinestones.

2.25in (6cm) high

£100-130 **BY**

An unmarked peacock pin, in white metal, with pavé-set diamanté and faux amethysts.

4.75in (12cm) long

£380-420 **TR**

An unsigned 1950s pin, of floral form, with coloured enamelling and inset diamanté to the petals, with 'night and day' panel flipping over to reveal further similarly decorated flowers.

This piece is attributed to Corocraft.

2in (5cm) wide

£120-180 **BY**

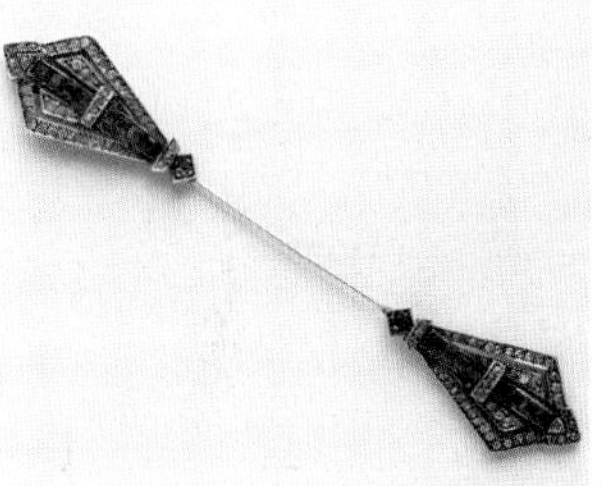

A 1930s French pin, decorated with paste stones.

1.75in (4.5cm) long

£600-900 **TR**

A 1930s French ring, in white metal, with clear and pink paste stones.

£650-750 **TR**

An unsigned 1920s/30s faceted green and clear glass and diamanté necklace, the clasp stamped '935', possibly French.

16.5in (42cm) long

£220-280 **BY**

A 1930s Czechoslovakian ruby glass and diamanté necklace, stamped "CZECHOSLOVAKIA".

10.5in (27cm) long

£100-200 **ROX**

An unsigned, late 1940s West German necklace and earrings with japanned metal links and sapphire blue crystal stones in round, pear and navette cuts.

Necklace 1.5in (39.5cm) long

£450-550 **ROX**

A 1960s, unusual, unsigned high-relief bracelet and earrings, with inset Venetian-style coloured glass with gold inclusions.

Bracelet 7in (18cm) long

£100-150 **BY**

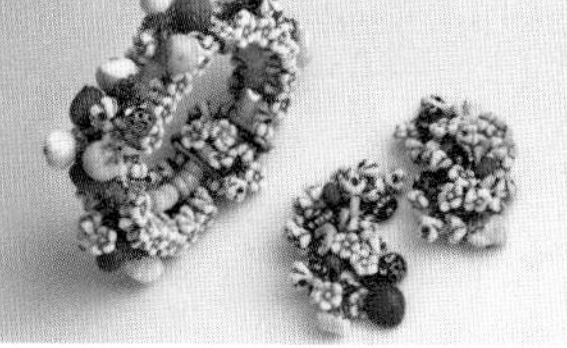

A 1960s unsigned, glass, sprung bracelet and earrings set, with white glass flowers, faux natural pearls, coloured glass fruits and diamanté inset spheres and bars.

Bracelet 3.5in (8.5cm) wide

£40-60 **BY**

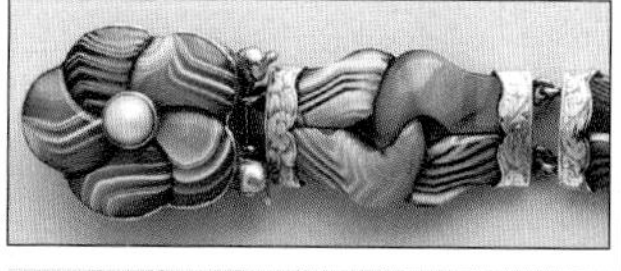

An 1890s Scottish agate ware bracelet with gold-capped links of Montrose blue agate, and a single pearl highlight.

9.5in (24cm) long

£400-450 **CRIS**

A pair of 1930s Czechoslovakian inset diamanté and glass fruit clips.

2.25in (6cm) wide

£120-180 **ROX**

BOXES

A 19thC Russian lacquer box, decorated with a troika group.

7.75in (19.5cm) long

£320-380 **S&K**

A 19thC Russian lacquer box, decorated with a troika group.

10.5in (26.5cm) long

£300-400 **S&K**

A Russian vishniakov box, with a milk maid.

c1860 2.75in (7cm) diam

£350-450 **RDER**

An Alexander III Russian box, with a boy serenading a spinner.

c1880 3.5in (9cm) diam

£600-900 **RDER**

A rare Ivan Golikov battle scene cigarette case, Palekh School.

c1925 5in (12.5cm) wide

£2,200-2,800 **TA**

A rare pre-revolution Russian vishniakov papier-mâché tray, decorated with children at play.

7.25in (18.5cm) square

£500-700 **RDER**

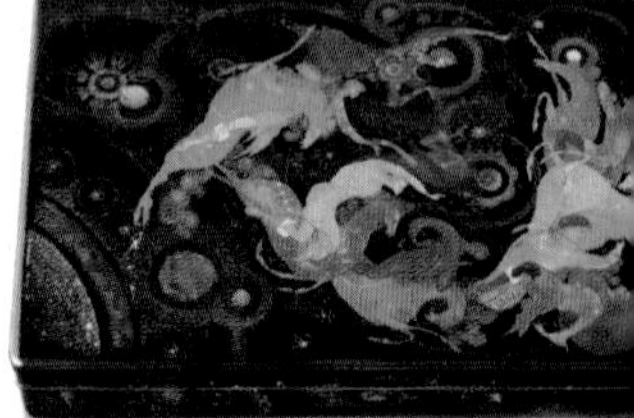

A Russian lacquer box 'Dance of the Galaxies' by N. Lopatin, Palekh School.

c1970 7.25in (18cm) wide

£1,800-2,200 **TA**

A Russian lacquer box 'Tzar Saltan' by O. An, Palekh School.

c1975 9.5in (23.5cm) wide

£1,200-1,800 **TA**

A Russian lacquer box 'Dobrina' by V. Korovkin, Palekh School.

c1980 8in (20cm) wide

£550-750 **TA**

A Russian lacquer box 'Alexander Nevsky' by B. Velichko, Palekh School.

c1980 8in (20cm) wide

£550-750 **TA**

A Russian lacquer box 'The Magic Carpet Meets Sputnik' by A. Koslova, Fedoskino School.

c1990 10in (25cm) wide

£220-280 **TA**

A Russian tea caddy, with six medals of merit, decorated with a scene of children.

c1860 6in (15cm) wide

£600-900 **RDER**

A Russian box, decorated with woodcutters and a pony in a forest.

c1870 8in (20.5cm) wide

£300-500 **RDER**

A 19thC Continental painted and gilt metal box, the cover painted with women bathing by a cliff with architectural ruins, the sides painted with continuous landscape.

6.5in (16cm) wide

£280-320 **S&K**

A late 19thC German Imperial presentation jewel gold snuff box, cartouche shaped with waisted sides, engraved and decorated with applied rocaille floral scroll work, the base engraved with the German Imperial eagle on a trompe l'oeil ground, the cover applied with a diamond monogram "W" for Emperor Wilhelm II entwined with a diamond floral spray, the rose coloured interior inscribed "Presented to Lord Edward Pelham Clinton by the German Emperor William II at Windsor Castle November 24th 1899".

Lord Edward Pelham Clinton (1836-1907), younger brother of the 6th Duke of Newcastle, was Master of Queen Victoria's household from 1894-1902.

7.75in (10cm) wide

£6,000-9,000 **WW**

A malachite jewel box 'Mistress of Copper Mountain' by E. Zhiriakova, Palekh School.

c1990 *8.75in (22cm) wide*

£2,000-3,000 **TA**

A pietre dure mounted, rectangular bijouterie box, the floral inlaid panels set in a gilt-metal bead-moulded frame, raised on ornate scroll feet.

Pietre dure is an expensive form of inlay using thin slivers of semi-precious stones.

9in (23cm) wide

£1,200-1,800 **FRE**

A pietre dure jewel box, with oval pietre dure floral medallions on four sides, top inset with large square pietre dure panel, on four looped rope legs, some staining to satin lining and snap-catch missing.

2in (5cm) wide

£550-650 **JDJ**

A pietre dure box, small jewel box has four side medallions inset with round pietre dure floral medallions, hinged top is also set with floral pietre dure medallion, box rests on four legs and is lined with green satin.

3in (7.5cm) high

£450-550 **JDJ**

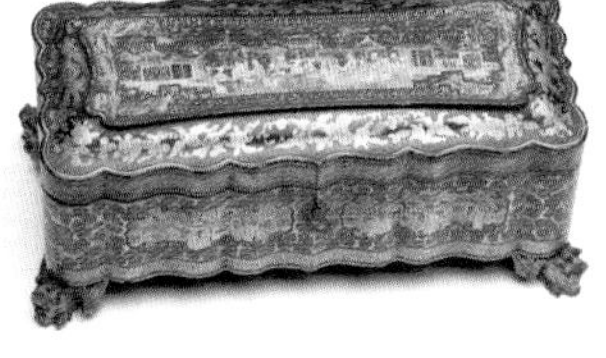

A Chinese black lacquer jewellery box, the shaped rectangular body painted in red and yellow gold with figures in front of temples in shaped reserves with floral borders, the hinged lid opening to an interior with a removable tray, all on four carved and gilt dragon feet, minor losses to finish and feet.

11.25in (28.5cm) long

£300-400 **FRE**

An early 19thC tortoiseshell card case, the top of the rectangular lid bearing a white metal tablet initialled "CMS".

3in (8cm) high

£50-70 **CHEF**

A Victorian mother-of-pearl card case, with abalone inlay.

3.5in (8.5cm) long

£40-60 **GORL**

A leather card case.

c1875 *5in (12.5cm) long*

£60-90 **BCAC**

An 18thC gold mounted dendritic agate snuff box, in pale mocha brown, of cartouche form with bombe sides decanted with an enamelled border, thumbpiece and vertical straps, unmarked probably English.

c1740 *3.5in (8.5cm) wide*

£3,000-5,000 **WW**

A late 18thC French two colour gold snuff box and cover, of circular form decorated with engine turning and chiselled foliate borders, marks distorted, probably Paris, 2.4oz gold.

c1785 *2.5in (6.5cm) diam*

£700-1,000 **WW**

A late 18thC silver and gilt metal inlaid tortoiseshell snuff box, circular with a two colour vase of flowers on a regular ground of pellets and mullets, the interior unscrews to reveal a concealed miniature painting on ivory, depicting a boudoir scene (behind glass), indistinctly signed.

c1785 *3.5in (8cm) diam*

£800-1,200 **WW**

An early 19thC Neo-classical snuff box, the lid with a plaque depicting the Capitoline or 'Pliny's' doves, with monogram 'G.N', the interior gilt plate engraved "To Lieu (Charles Moore R.N. for Heroism and Humanity at Calais on the 16th April 1817)".

£2,200-2,800 **WW**

A late 19thC French snuff box, of shaped oblong form decorated with enamel on the cover and engine 'turning', gilt interior.

c1880 *3.25in (8.5cm) long*

£80-120 **WW**

A mid-18thC shagreen and silver mounted box, with a 17thC gold medal, the circular plaque to the top of the case engraved "Donum In Memoria J. Skene De Dyce Qui Obijt prs Decembrs 1746" and to the base "Accepi Acceptum Seruabo Alexr Bannerman", the box velvet lined and containing the gold medal to commemorate the investiture of Charles XI of Sweden as a Knight of The Garter in 1669, the medal issued in 1671, by Roettiers, MI 549-206.

£1,000-1,500 **L&T**

An early 19thC French musical box, the oval lid with central watch, the offset small circular engraved dial within a shagreen inlaid ground, bright cut oval border, sides and base, musical action within the watch movement.

£1,500-2,000 **L&T**

A late 18thC French gold mounted lacquer necessaire de voyage, the cover set with a chased urn of flowers with birds and dog, the cover latch with diamond set thumbpress, the interior fitted with five glass bottles with stoppers modelled as birds and animals, mounted items include a pair of steel scissors, a tortoiseshell and steel penknife, a tortoiseshell and ivory note case, and a pencil, the interior spring loaded, forming a boite à surprise and revealing an enamelled portrait of a young lady, indistinctly signed and dated, sitter probably a member of the French aristocracy, struck with two indistinct marks.

c1770 *3.5in (9cm) high*

£12,000-18,000 **WW**

An Irish George III circular gold box and cover, with marks for Dublin 1780, maker Richard Tudor, engraved leaf border and inscription "From the L. Derry Battalion to Sir Edwd Bannerman Bart Major of the 36th regt as a Grateful Mark of Esteem for the Obliging Attention he has always shown them both as a Commanding Officer and a Gentleman".

1780 *2.5in (6.5cm) diam*

£8,000-12,000 **L&T**

A George III silvergilt oviform nutmeg grater, with bright engraving and later grille, by Samuel Pemberton, Birmingham.

c1795 *1.5in (4cm) high*

£220-280 **WW**

A late 19thC Continental novelty box in the form of a flexible fish with red glass eyes, a hinged head and a hinged mouth, with English import marks for London.

c1895 *3.5in (9cm) long*

£220-280 **WW**

A Chicago World Fair commemorative pillbox.

1895 *1.5in (4cm) diam*

£60-90 **BCAC**

A round turquoise and white French moiré enamelled covered box, with gold plated interior, minor losses to enamel on rim.

2.25in (6cm) diam

£220-280 **JDJ**

ENAMEL

An 18thC Staffordshire enamel round patch box, decorated with an architectural scene and floral cartouches against a purple ground, lid damaged.

1.75in (4.5cm) wide

£40-60 **GORL**

A pair of Staffordshire enamel rectangular boxes and covers, the covers and sides painted in coloured enamels with figures in landscapes on white ground decorated with raised white and gilt scrolls.

c1765 *3.5in (9cm) width*

£8,000-12,000 **WW**

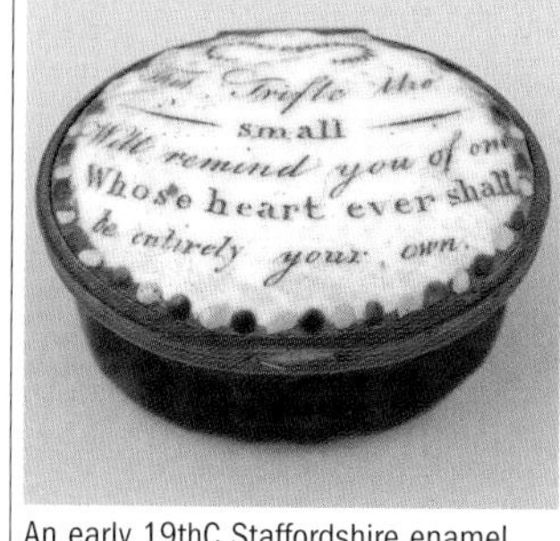

An early 19thC Staffordshire enamel patch box, with a "Trifle" inscription oval cover.

1.75in (4.5cm) wide

£150-200 **GORL**

An enamel box, with miniature portrait.

c1880 *2.5in (6.5cm) long*

£750-850 **JBS**

A Continental enamel box.

c1890 *4in (10cm) diam*

£1,200-1,800 **JBS**

A Continental silver and green enamel box.

c1920 *1.75in (4.5cm) long*

£120-180 **JBS**

A French red and green enamelled octagonal box, with gold decoration, minor wear and discolouration to top enamel.

£180-220 **JDJ**

A French oval enamel patch box, with central enamel floral decoration with outer rim of blue and turquoise coloured enamel with gold wash interior and mirror on upper lid, minor wear to gold finish and to enamel.

2in (5cm) diam

£250-300 **JDJ**

A late 19thC French enamel plaque, painted in colours with a cavalier admiring himself in a dressing table mirror, his red cloak with foil backing, in a conforming gilt-bronze Rococo scroll frame, signed monogram "S.T".

Plaque 5.25in (13.5cm) high

£700-1,000 **S&K**

A Fabergé enamelled and gem set silver kovsh, decorated with an opaque green enamel applied with imperial eagles in seed pearls, set front and rear with a cabochon garnet, interior silver gilt, in original silk and velvet lined fitted oak box, the cover applied with the cypher of the city of St. Petersburg, Moscow, numbered 31045.

1896-1908 *6.5in (16cm) long*

£6,000-9,000 **WW**

An early to mid-19thC French enamelled gilt metal tubular etui, with a screw cover in the form of a thimble, the interior with a faceted glass scent bottle and stopper, the exterior inscribed "Sincer en amitie".

3.25in (8cm) long

£800-1,200 **WW**

A Birmingham silver and green enamel belt buckle and buttons, made by James Freeman.

1910 *5.5in (13.5cm) long*

£200-250 **JBS**

INKSTANDS

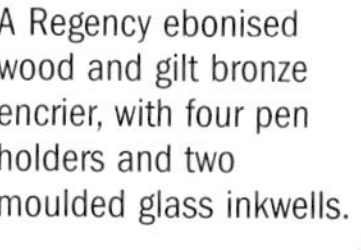

A Regency ebonised wood and gilt bronze encrier, with four pen holders and two moulded glass inkwells.

9.75in (25cm) wide

£1,000-1,500 **GRO**

An 18thC French kingwood and ormolu mounted inkstand, of curvilinear outline with scrolling auricular and foliate cast mounts, the three lidded wells above sloping parquetry front on cast feet.

12.5in (31cm) wide

£400-600 **L&T**

A 19thC ebony and boulle rectangular inkstand, with a brass handle, two glass inkpots and two tortoiseshell-lined pen trays, with a boulle frieze on ormolu stiff leaf and hairy paw feet, with paper retainers label for "John L..., Sloane Street, Knightsbridge, by appointment."

13.25in (34cm) wide

£1,200-1,800 **DN**

A 19thC malachite rectangular inkstand, with a gilt-bronze bell, on a scroll and bird cast stand, flanked by urn-shaped ink and pounce pots, with a recess for pens, on four acanthus feet.

10.75in (27.5cm) wide

£1,800-2,200 **DN**

A 20thC bronze and marble inkstand, the bronze cast after a model by Thomas-François Cartier, the cartouche-shaped black and brown mottled marble base surmounted by a bronze figure of a mountain lion on rockwork, flanked by cylindrical inkwells, raised on toupie feet.

17in (43cm) wide

£800-1,200 **S&K**

ICONS

An 18thC Russian icon 'Our Lady of Kazan', wood panel.

12.25in (30.5cm) wide

£1,000-1,500 **TA**

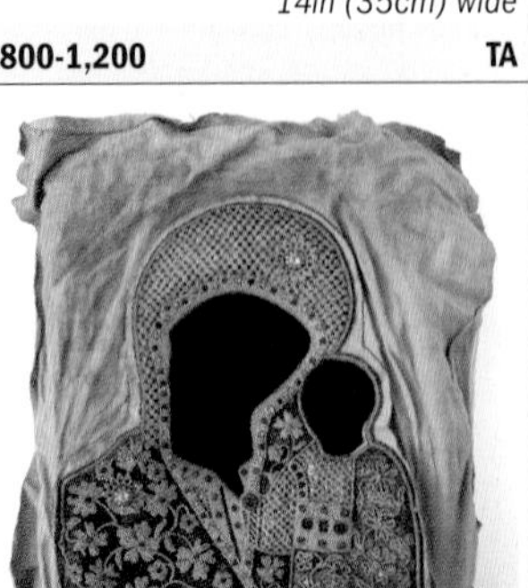

An 18thC Russian icon 'Three Prelates, Ionne Zlatoust, St. Gregory, St. Vasily', panel.

14in (35cm) wide

£800-1,200 **TA**

An 18thC Russian icon 'Our Lady of Vladimir', with earlier wood panel.

10.75in (26.5cm) wide

£1,800-2,200 **TA**

An 18th/19thC Russian icon of the Virgin and child, with a brass oklad.

12.5in (31cm) high

£200-300 **S&K**

A 19thC Russian icon with Riza fitting, with woven pearls, jewelled and silver detailing.

£180-220 **TA**

A 19thC Riza 'Birth of Christ' icon, gilt metal, three crowns.

12in (30cm) wide

£100-150 **TA**

A 19thC Riza, selected saints icon, gilt metal, three crowns.

12in (30cm) wide

£100-150 **TA**

A 19thC Russian icon 'Our Lady of Kazan', wood panel.

11.25in (28cm) wide

£1,000-1,500 **TA**

A 19thC silvered and silver gilt Riza 'Virgin of Sorrows' icon, five crowns.

13.5in (33.5cm) wide

£100-150 **TA**

A 19thC Russian icon of St. Nicolas, oil on wood panel, with elaborately chased and stipple engraved silver Riza.

22in (55cm) wide

£500-800 **TA**

A 19thC Riza 'Virgin of the Burning Bush' icon, gilt metal, gilt crown.

14in (35cm) wide

£100-150 **TA**

A 19thC Riza 'Virgin of Vladimir', silvered metal icon, gilt crown.

14in (35cm) wide

£80-120 **TA**

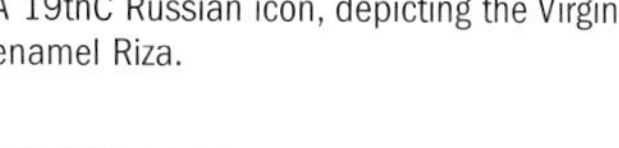

A 19thC Russian icon, depicting the Virgin of Vladimir, in a gilt metal and enamel Riza.

46in (117cm) high

£12,000-18,000 **TA**

A 19thC Greek icon of the archangels Michael and Gabriel.

17in (42.5cm) high

£100-200 **S&K**

A late 19thC Russian icon of the Virgin Mary, oil on wood panel.

28in (70cm) wide

£150-200 **TA**

A late 19thC Russian icon of John the Baptist, oil on wood panel.

28in (70cm) wide

£220-280 **TA**

A late 19thC Russian icon of Christ the Saviour, oil on wood panel.

28in (71cm) high

£150-200 **TA**

A Russian icon of Saint Nicholas, made in Moscow, silver-gilt oklad with richly enamelled halo.

1893 *12.5in (31.5cm) high*

£700-1,000 **S&K**

A late 19th/early 20thC Russian icon of Christ Pantocrator, featuring Christ Pantocrator surrounded by 14 scenes from the Gospel.

12.5in (31cm) high

£150-200 **S&K**

A late 19th/early 20thC Greek icon of the Holy Trinity.

12.75in (32cm) high

£280-320 **S&K**

An early 20thC Russian icon of Christ on the Cross, with silvered metal oklad, featuring a cloisonné Christ on the Cross surrounded by saints, archangels and God the Father.

11.75in (29cm) high

£150-220 **S&K**

An early 20thC Russian icon of two saints, with silver oklad, featuring a saint holding keys and one holding a sword, each with cloisonné halo.

8.75in (22cm) high

£300-400 **S&K**

A 20thC Russian silvered and enamelled icon triptych, opening to depict Christ and the Mother of God flanked by archangels.

13in (32.5cm) high

£180-220 **S&K**

A Russian icon of the mother of God and child with kneeling saint, silver oklad and richly enamelled halos and corners.

12.5in (31.5cm) high

£1,000-1,500 **S&K**

DESK SEALS

A mid-17thC brass swivel seal, engraved intaglio with an unidentified prelate's coat of arms below a Bishop's mitre.

2.75in (7cm) long

£300-350 **WW**

A late 17thC Continental steel desk seal, spool shaped with a mushroom cap, the large matrix with intaglio Continental arms and mantling.

2.5in (6cm) high

£150-200 **WW**

A mid-18thC agate mounted, polished steel desk seal, decorated with swirl fluting, the cushion matrix with intaglio armorial.

2.4in (6cm) high

£60-90 **WW**

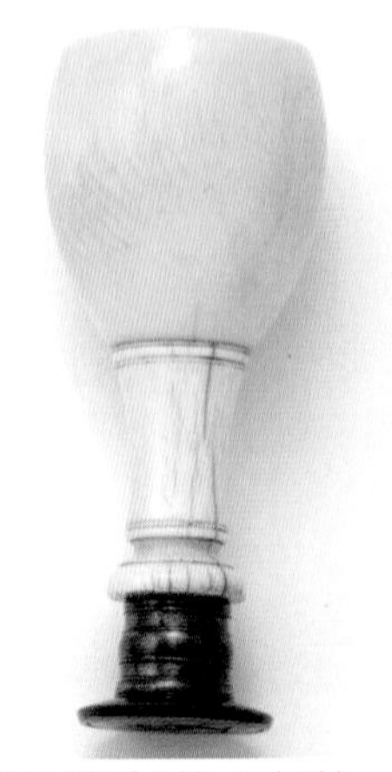

A late 18thC table seal, with ivory baluster handle and polished steel collar and matrix with crest of a demi-griffin segreant, crest of Adams, Akarys and other families.

3.5in (9cm) high

£180-220 **WW**

An early 19thC table seal, with moulded ivory handle and large silver mount, with foliate decoration and a carnelian matrix with an eagle volant, script initials "TM" and motto "Tout ou Rien".

2in (10.5cm) high

£220-280 **WW**

An early 19thC double ended desk seal, with ivory baluster handle and silver matrices, one hatched, one set with carnelian with an owl intaglio.

3.75in (9.5cm) high

£150-200 **WW**

A 19thC table seal, with ivory baluster handle and silver collar and matrix, coat of arms of the London family of Fisher.

3.5in (9cm) high

£220-280 **WW**

A 19thC carved ivory seal, of baluster form with a spreading eraser matrix.

2.75in (7cm) high

£60-90 **WW**

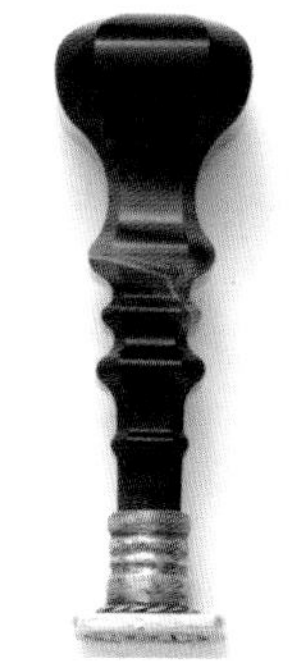

A 19thC Dutch silver mounted desk seal, with a banded agate, baluster handle and an oblong matrix with intaglio crest and two mottos "Floreant Lauri" and "Virtus Semper Viridis".

3.5in (8.5cm) high

£100-150 **WW**

A 19thC French silver mounted ruby-in-zoisite desk seal, with a turned, domed handle, the oval matrix with intaglio armorials.

3in (8cm) high

£220-280 **WW**

A mid-19thC French desk seal, with a small ivory baluster handle, engraved with the arms of the French Republic and "MINISTERE de la Guerre".

2.5in (6cm) high

£200-250 **WW**

A 19thC desk seal, with a baluster rosewood handle and a steel matrix, engraved intaglio with a strap and buckle cartouche the initials "MTH" and the name "ST. AGNES".

3.5in (9cm) high

£60-90 **WW**

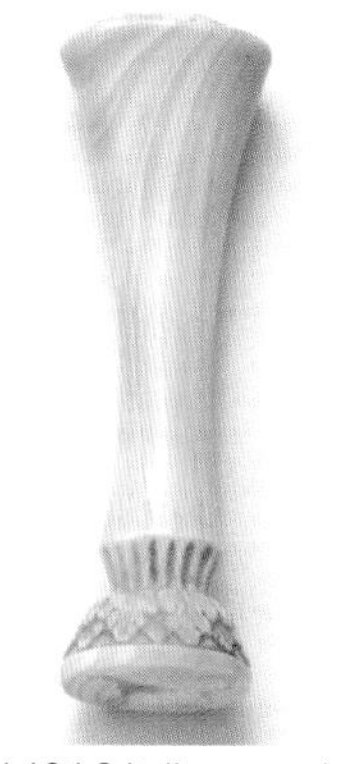

A mid-19thC Italian carved helmet-shell seal, of waisted form with an acanthus matrix, crested, the terminal carved with a vignette of Romulus and Remus, probably from Rome.

c1850 *3.5in (8.5cm) high*

£100-130 **WW**

A mid-19thC desk seal, with a turned and figured laburnum wood handle and a steel collar and matrix with a full achievement of arms below a Count's coronet and motto "Sine Fraude" intaglio.

4in (10cm) high

£100-130 **WW**

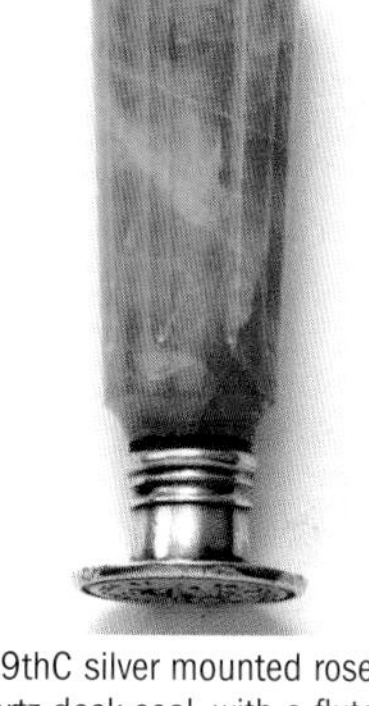

A 19thC silver mounted rose quartz desk seal, with a fluted tapering handle and an oval matrix with intaglio initials, crest and motto "In Deo Omnia".

3in (7.5cm) high

£150-200 **WW**

A late 19thC Continental silvergilt mounted rock crystal seal, of tapering faceted form with cagework mounts and a finial in the form of the bust of a gentleman in a powdered wig, the matrix plain.

3.5in (9cm) high

£250-300 **WW**

A Victorian silver mounted desk seal, with a turned ivory handle, engraved intaglio with crest, initials and motto "FIDE ET FORTITUDINE" Crest & motto for Capel or Capell, Earls of Essex.

c1880 *3.5in (8.5cm) high*

£120-180 **WW**

A late 19thC smoky quartz desk seal, with a faceted, tapering handle, the oval matrix with intaglio coat of arms.

2.5in (6cm) high

£150-200 **WW**

A late 19thC Continental silver mounted desk seal, with carved mother-of-pearl handle as a cuffed hand grasping a reeded column, with intaglio armorials, probably Dutch/Low Countries.

3.75in (10cm) high

£100-150 **WW**

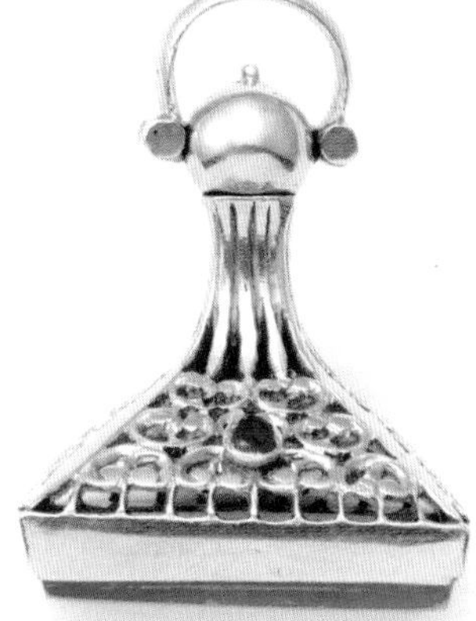

A large Persian qajar, gold mounted pale-green stone seal, inscribed "Mohammed Husayn Ilkhani Bakhtiyari 1322 AH" (1904 AD) the mount finely pierced with swivel attachment and set with a small ruby.

1.75in (4cm) high

£1,000-1,500 **WW**

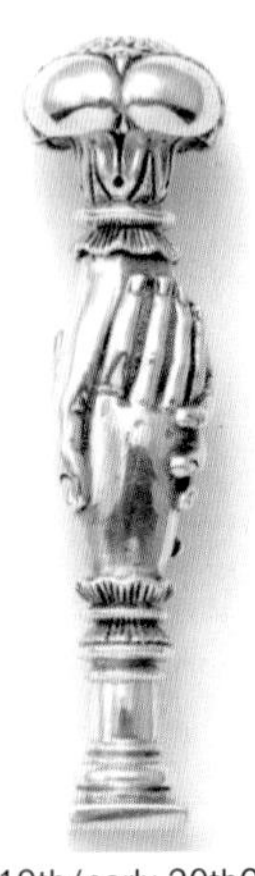

A late 19th/early 20thC French cast silver seal, with a blank matrix, cast in the form of two clasped hands below a large, lobed rosette finial, 5.75oz.

c1900 *4in (10cm) high*

£300-330 **WW**

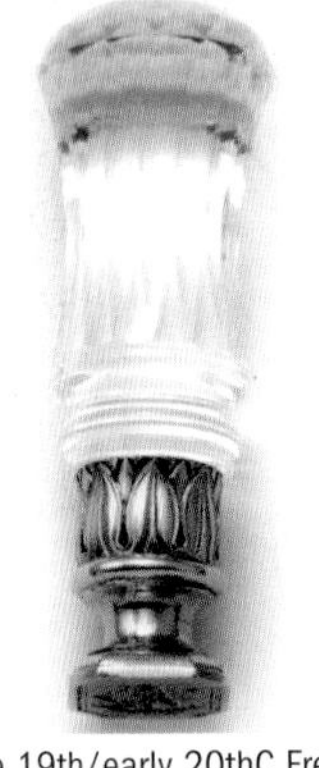

A late 19th/early 20thC French gold mounted rock crystal desk seal, with a waisted, faceted handle, a canted oblong matrix with intaglio monogram, the collar formed as a stiff leaf calyx.

3.25in (8.5cm) long

£450-550 **WW**

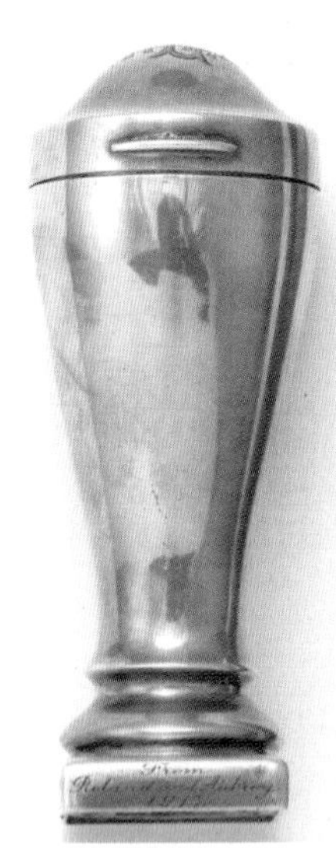

A silver combined desk seal/container, with a vase shaped body and hinged cover, a gilt interior, the large oblong matrix with the arms of Leeds of Crockton Park, Cambridge intaglio monogrammed and inscribed "From Roland and Aubrey 1917" maker's mark mis-struck, probably by the Goldsmiths and Silversmiths Co Ltd, London, 5.5oz gross.

c1915 *3.5in (9cm) high*

£320-380 **WW**

A rare WWII Nazi party desk seal, with brass collar and copper matrix, with the Swastika emblem and the circumscription "Portagentur Schlampirz" intaglio.

Perhaps a harbour master's seal.

4in (10cm) high

£80-120 **WW**

An 18ct large bloodstone swivel seal.

2in (5cm) high

£200-300 **SSP**

A 9ct gold double-sided Masonic bloodstone seal.

1in (2.5cm) diam

£150-200 **SSP**

A 15ct gold shield-shape opening seal, with bloodstone.

1.25in (3cm) long

£220-280 **SSP**

A late 18thC marble figure of a Classical maiden.

75in(190.5cm) high

£10,000-12,000 **POOK**

A 19thC Continental school marble figure, 'Young Shepherd', on a variegated dark green marble pedestal.

56in (142cm) high

£5,000-8,000 **FRE**

A 19thC English school marble bust of a lady, head slightly downcast, her shoulders draped above a leafy frieze and socle base, raised on a veined marble column with plinth.

Bust 27.5in (70cm) high

£4,000-6,000 **L&T**

A 19thC Italian marble figure of a fisherman, in the form of a young fisherman holding a net by his side, raised on a naturalistic circular base.

33in (82.5cm) high

£1,500-2,000 **FRE**

A late 19thC white marble bust of Octavia, after the Antique, the head and shoulders above a scrolled leaf fringe, raised above a socle and standing on cylindrical marble column.

70.75in (177cm) high

£5,000-8,000 **L&T**

A 19thC marble bust of Admiral Sir David Milne, the three stars confirm he is modelled as an Admiral of the White (1840) and he is also wearing the GCB (1841) and the Order of St Januarius.

24in (61cm) high

£5,000-8,000 **L&T**

A marble bust of George Washington together with a companion column, modelled with draped Classical robe, the column marbleized.

68in (170cm) high

£6,000-9,000 **NA**

A marble bust of Machiavelli by M. Michelozins, signed.

22in (55cm) high

£4,000-6,000 **L&T**

A white marble sculpture of Magdalene, after Lorenzo Bartolini, sculpted in a seated pose, gazing upwards, and raised on oval base.

20in (50cm) high

£1,800-2,200 **L&T**

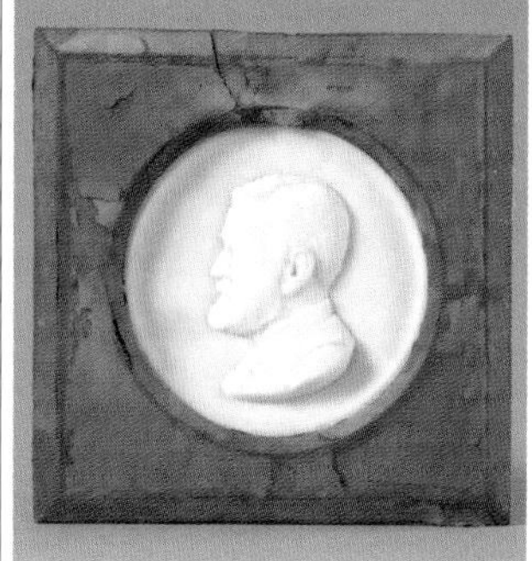

An American bas relief marble portrait plaque of President Ulysses S. Grant, framed.

10in (25cm) diam

£350-450 **NA**

A marble sculpture of a young girl.

30.5in (76cm) high

£1,200-1,800 **FRE**

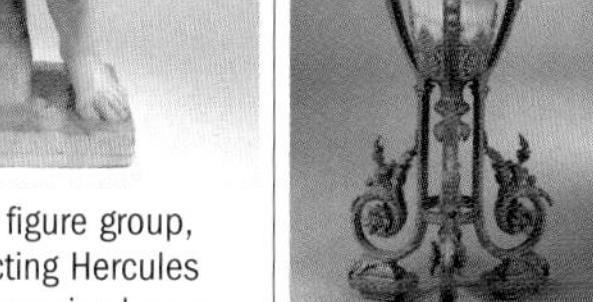

A late 19thC alabaster figure group, after the Antique, depicting Hercules and the Aromythian Boar raised on a square base.

30.5in (76cm) high

£2,800-3,200 **L&T**

A pair of Italian 19thC alabaster lions, each sleeping lion set on integral rectangular plinth.

£350-450 **GORL**

A late 19thC alabaster and ormolu mounted urn, with pierced cast rim above slender baluster body, with three scrolled swag hung handles and acanthus cast base suspending a finial, on three scrolled acanthus and flower cast legs with block feet.

57.25in (143cm) high

£2,800-3,200 **L&T**

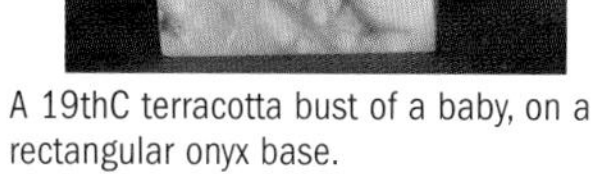

A 19thC terracotta bust of a baby, on a rectangular onyx base.

9.75in (25cm) high

£280-320 **SL**

A French 18thC-style patinated terracotta bust, modelled as an aristocratic lady, her hair tied up with a string of pearls and with drapery around her shoulders.

28.5in (72cm) high

£1,200-1,800 **L&T**

A terracotta figure of Lorenzo de'Medici after Michelangelo Buonarroti.

28in (70cm) high

£1,200-1,800 **L&T**

A pair of late 17thC Italian giltwood figures of saints.

33in (82.5cm) high

£5,000-7,000 **S&K**

Two 17th/18thC Iberian carved wooden figures, one a bishop and the other a female figure with polychrome and gilt decoration.

c1700 *Female: 26in (66cm) high*

£500-700 **FRE**

A 19thC Russian carved and painted wood figure of St Nils Stolbinski.

15in (38cm) high

£1,800-2,200 **S&K**

A 17thC Italian provincial carved wood and parcel gilt panel, probably formerly the centre of a triptych, the pediment surmount of the Virgin and Child, a triple window frame depicting Christ, Madonna with saints, breakfront plinth base carved with a shield within a quatrefoil roundel, supported by a pair of standing birds and two male heads, an iron candle bracket to lower plinth, remains of an iron hinge to sides.

18.5in (47cm) wide

£4,500-5,500 **DN**

A pair of 17thC Spanish painted and giltwood carved panels, formerly part of a vagueño, the twin-panelled doors each carved with mask motifs within cartouches.

23in (58cm) high

£600-900 **FRE**

CANES

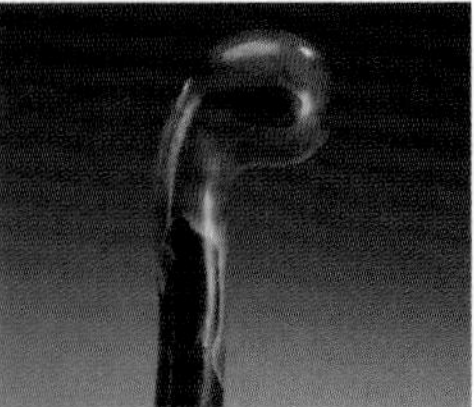

A mid-19thC Victorian briarwood sword walking stick, with curved knob handle, the shaft concealing a gilt-decorated steel sword.

34.75in (88.5cm) long

£180-220 **S&K**

A silver-mounted horn-handled briar dagger walking stick, with heron's head handle and silver collar, "LP" monogram, dated 1882-8 London, maker's "GC".

37in (94cm) long

£350-450 **S&K**

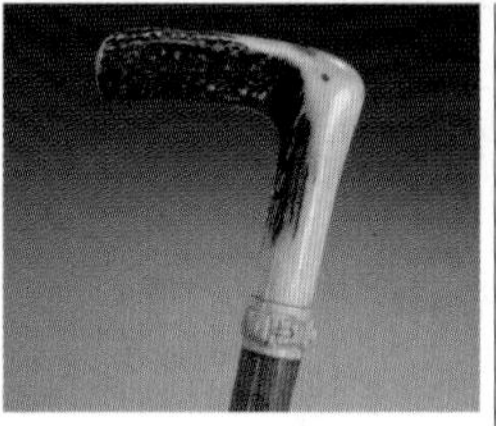

A late 19th/early 20thC Russian stag horn and yew wood dagger walking stick, the shaft concealing a dagger, original ferrule, shaft marked.

33.5in (85cm) long

£600-900 **S&K**

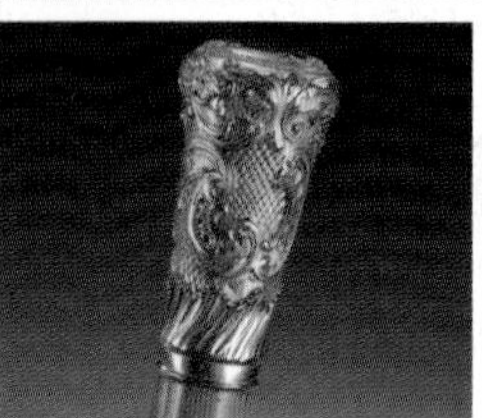

A late 19th/early 20thC gilt-copper mounted walking stick, with scrolls, trellis cartouches and feuille-de-choux, horn ferrule, marked "Dou... or".

36.25in (92cm) long

£220-280 **S&K**

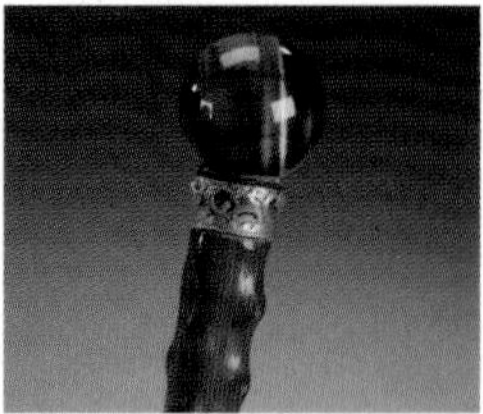

A late 19th/early 20thC tiger's eye-mounted briarwood walking stick, with tinted blue stone, ball knob, pewter collar and original ferrule.

35.5in (90cm) long

£220-280 **S&K**

A late 19th/early 20thC Continental briarwood double-headed walking stick, original ferrule, marked "JH.D".

35.5in (90cm) long

£180-220 **S&K**

A late 19th/early 20thC Alpine carved stag horn and briarwood walking stick, the handle formed as a bearded man, original ferrule.

34.5in (87.5cm) long

£350-450 **S&K**

A 20thC carved wood walking stick, the handle as a long-haired terrier's head with glass eyes above the wood shaft and horn ferrule.

36.75in (95.5cm) long

£150-200 **S&K**

A early 20thC ivory and briarwood walking stick, the handle carved as a jester's head above a woven wire collar.

35in (89cm) long

£350-450 **S&K**

An early 20thC carved briarwood walking stick, the angled handle carved as a stalking fox above snail and caterpillar, original ferrule.

36in (91.5cm) long

£220-280 **S&K**

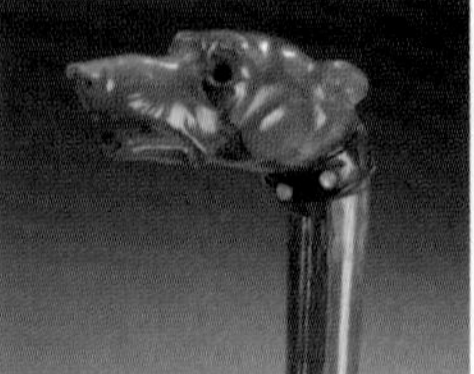

An early 20thC carved horn and yewwood walking stick, carved as a whippets head with moonstone studded colour, original ferrule.

34.25in (87cm) long

£500-600 **S&K**

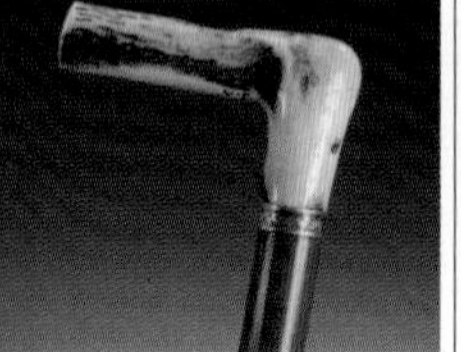

An early 20thC stag-horn mounted bamboo gun walking stick, with pewter collar and concealed mechanism, marked "J.A.", removable ferrule.

34.75in (88.5cm) long

£70-100 **S&K**

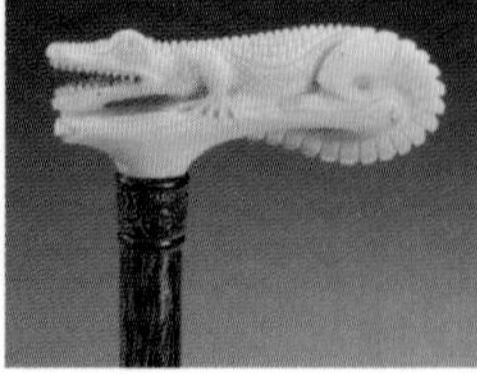

An early 20thC carved bone and stained wood walking stick, the crocodile handle possibly a later replacement, with silver copper collar.

36.25in (92cm) long

£200-300 **S&K**

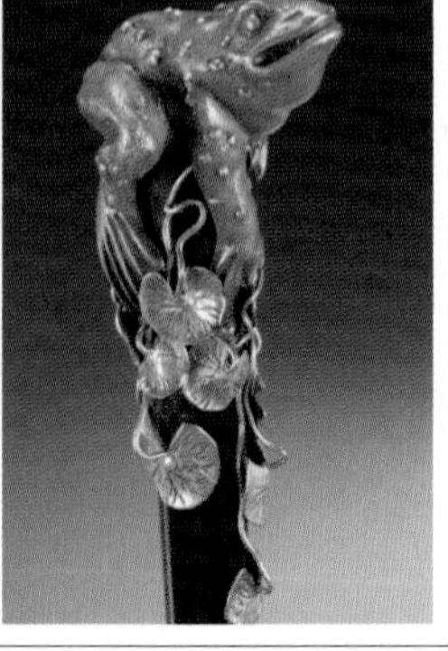

An early 20thC silver-mounted mahogany cane, the handle realistically modelled as a toad perched on lily pads.

34in (86.5cm) long

£800-1,200 **S&K**

STUFFED ANIMALS

An early 20thC pair of stuffed and mounted Capercaille, one male, one female, each perched on pine branches in a naturalistic setting and enclosed within an oak framed and glazed case.

44.5in (111cm) wide

£1,200-1,800 **L&T**

A stuffed albino pheasant, mounted in a naturalistic setting, with label "K. Clarke, Weston-under-Wetherby, Jan 14 1950", in an ebonised glazed case, bears label of Peter Spicer and Son, Victoria Terrace, Leamington.

1950 *34.5in (86cm) wide*

£450-550 **L&T**

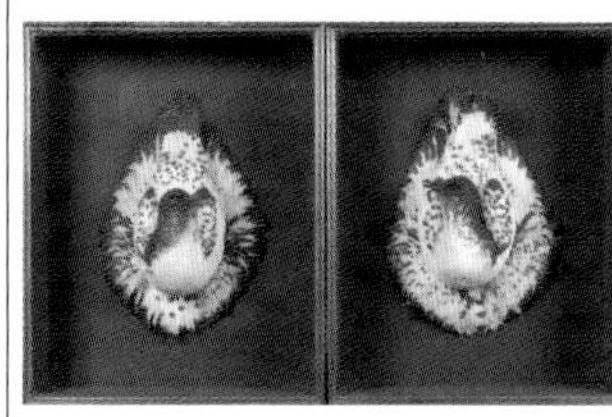

A pair of Cape pigeons, each mounted vertically in a baize lined case, the glazed cases with moulded gilt frames.

23.35in (58cm) high

£180-220 **L&T**

A stuffed swan, in a naturalistic setting, in a glazed ebonised case with gilt slip, on turned feet.

40in (100cm) high

£400-600 **L&T**

A pair of stuffed greylag geese, in an ebonised glazed case, bears label of H. Murray & Son, Naturalists, Bank Buildings, Carnforth.

41.5in (104cm) wide

£350-450 **L&T**

A pair of large stuffed ducks, in a naturalistic rocky setting, in ebonised glazed case.

34.75in (87cm) wide

£180-220 **L&T**

A stuffed common eider, mounted on a sea shore setting, the ebonised case with naturalistically painted interior.

£220-280 **L&T**

A stuffed fighting cock and hen, in a naturalistic setting, and canted glazed case.

25.25in (63cm) wide

£350-300 **L&T**

A 20thC mounted moose head trophy.

41in (102.5cm) high

£280-320 **S&K**

A 20thC mounted buffalo head trophy.

36in (91.5cm) high

£250-300 **S&K**

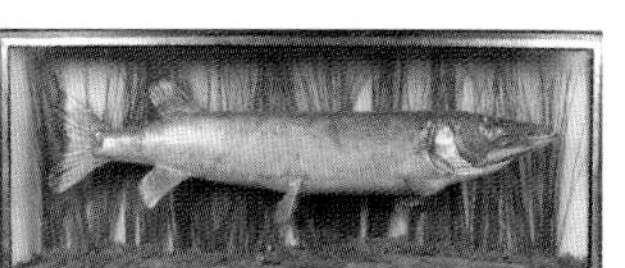

A stuffed pike in a naturalistic riverbed setting, in bow-front ebonised glazed case, inscribed in gilt "Pike, 20lb, caught by C H Turner, August 31st, 1935, Castle Lack, Lochmaben, Scotland".

1935 *53.5in (134cm) wide*

£800-1,200 **L&T**

A stuffed echidna, in an ebonised glazed case.

22.5in (56cm) wide

£300-400 **L&T**

A stuffed parrot, mounted on a branch, on an ebonised plinth, with glass cover.

20in (50cm) high

£280-320 **L&T**

A stuffed bush cat, mounted with tree stump, in a glazed ebonised case.

26.75in (67cm) wide

£280-320 **L&T**

A 19thC model of a bone spinning jenny, the hand-operated winding mechanism contained between two platforms, with figure of a lady with moving head and arm, some damage.

4.5in (11.5cm) high

£180-220 **F**

A 19thC model of a bone spinning jenny, the hand-operated winding mechanism contained between two platforms, with a figure of a lady with moving head and arm, some damage.

3.5in (9cm) high

£280-320 **F**

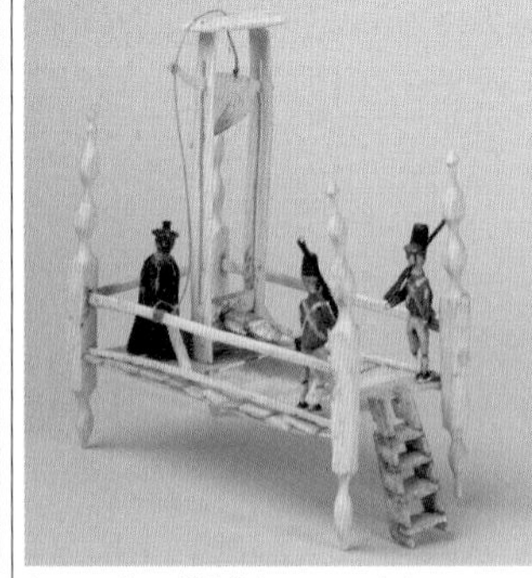

A macabre 19thC bone model guillotine, raised on a platform base and complete with a conforming carved decapitated figure, figures of a priest and two guardsmen, some damaged.

6.25in (16cm) long

£500-800 **F**

A pair of silver mounted ivory pepper mills, of waisted form, made in Birmingham by Hukin & Heath.

c1935 *3.25in (8.5cm) high*

£380-420 **DN**

A late 19thC engine turned ivory thermometer tower, with hexagonal tapering stem and turned dished top supporting a pricket.

£40-60 **GORL**

An Edwardian ivory six-draw spy glass, with engine-turned case and eye-piece inscribed "Smith, Royal Exchange, London".

£100-150 **GORL**

A 19thC Dieppe ivory mirror, applied all over with ivory leaves and sea serpents, cherubs and feathers, banner inscribed "SGOTUM" above the plate, gold painted chamfered edge and ivory border to sides.

33.25in (83cm) high

£1,000-1,500 **L&T**

A pair of Japanese Shibayama opera glasses, each side inlaid with engraved mother-of-pearl and painted with gilding and enamelling with flowering plants and birds.

£600-900 **GORL**

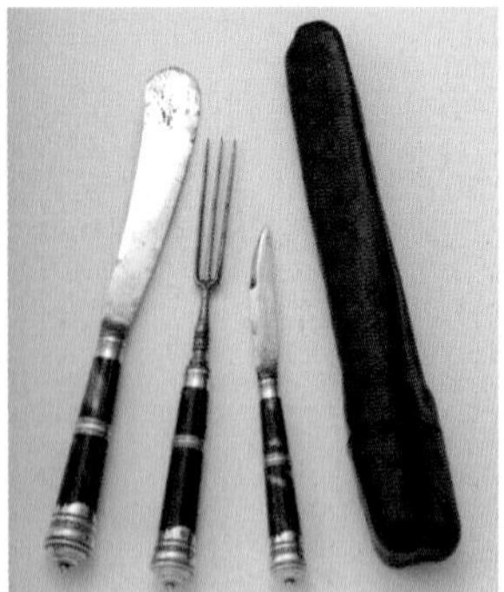

An extremely rare William III Scottish provincial knife, fork and by-knife, decorated with corded wire inlay, blades with cutler's mark, the silver end caps with maker's mark ("DB" within a heart shaped punch) for David Bigger or Biggart of Kilmaurs, in original fitted, tooled leather travelling case.

Knife 8.25in (21cm) long

£5,000-8,000 **WW**

A late 19th/early 20thC Ottoman gold and jewelled cup holder, zarf, in presentation case, the scalloped gem set cup featuring river-cut diamonds, emeralds and rubies accented with etched designs and jewelled base, accompanied by two Paris porcelain demi-tasse coffee cups, in original fitted box.

2.75in (7cm) high

£4,000-4,500 **S&K**

A George III wax jack, on a beaded circular base with ring handle, the central stem with an acorn finial and bright engraved sprung clamp, crested by Burrage, Davenport, London, complete with a coil of wax.

1785 *5.5in (14cm) high*

£2,500-3,000 **WW**

A conch shell cameo, surface carved with Classical scene of female gods and attendants in an Elysian setting with buildings and trees.

9.5in (24cm) long

£800-1,200 **L&T**

PERSIAN

A fine Afshar rug from south-west Persia.

c1880 58.25 x 46in (148 x 117cm)

£1,200-1,800 JW

An Afshar rug from south-west Persia.

c1900 79.25 x 62.25in (201 x 158cm)

£1,200-1,800 JW

A 20thC Bakhtiari rug.

180in x 149in (457 x 378cm)

£2,500-3,000 S&K

A particularly fine example of an Afshar rug from south-west Persia.

c1860 69 x 48.5in (175 x 123cm)

£4,000-4,500 JW

A 20thC Bakhtiari garden carpet.

158 x 127in (401 x 322cm)

£800-1,000 S&K

A Bakhtiari rug from west Persia.

c1920 80.25 x 53.25in (204 x 135cm)

£800-1,200 JW

A Bakhtiari rug from Kurdish north-west Persia.

c1910 82.25 x 51.5in (209 x 131cm)

£700-900 JW

A Bakhtiari carpet.

120in (300cm) wide

£700-1,000 S&K

A mid-20thC Belouch rug from eastern Persia.

44in x 74in (112 x 187cm)

£100-150 S&K

A 20thC Belouch rug.

30in x 48in (76 x 122cm)

£80-120 **S&K**

A Bidjar rug from north-west Persia.

c1920 68in (170cm) long

£500-800 **FRE**

An antique Bidjar Triclinium carpet, from north Persia, the deep indigo primary field with a polychrome palmette floral lattice, flanked by yellow arabesque spandrels, with two red herati ground runners and a blue herati ground 'carpet'.

227in (567.5cm) long

£4,000-6,000 **NA**

An Esfahan rug from central Persia.

c1910 85.5 x 57.5in (217 x 146cm)

£1,500-2,000 **JW**

An Esfahan rug from central Persia.

c1910 80.25 x 53.25in (204 x 135cm)

£800-1,200 **JW**

An Esfahan rug from central Persia.

c1910 82.25 x 51.5in (209 x 131cm)

£800-1,200 **JW**

A Ghashghai rug from south-west Persia.

c1870 75.25 x 63in (191 x 160cm)

£2,500-3,000 **JW**

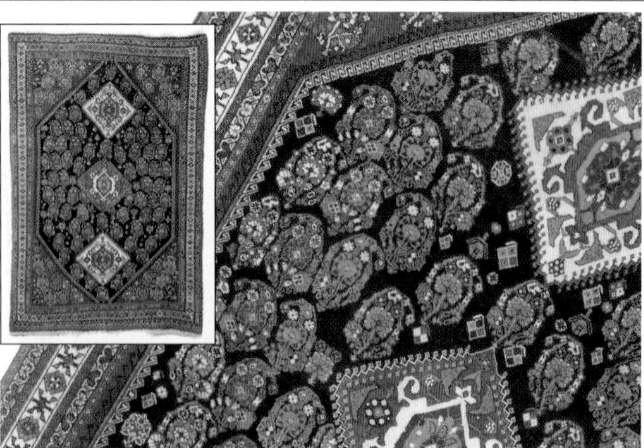

A very fine example of a Kashkouli Ghashghai rug from south-west Persia.

'Ghashghai' is the name of a Persian tribe, and 'Kashkouli' is a sub-group within that tribe.

c1900 52 x 80.25in (132 x 204cm)

£3,000-5,000 **JW**

A Ghashghai rug from south-west Persia.

c1890 3.75 x 48.5in (238 x 123cm)

£1,200-1,800 **JW**

A Ghashghai rug from south-west Persia.

c1890 78.75 x 59in (200 x 150cm)

£2,000-3,000 **JW**

A Kashkouli Ghashghai rug from south-west Persia.

c1890 65.25 x 45.75in (166 x 116cm)

£1,200-1,800 **JW**

A 20thC Hamadan rug.

76.5 x 44in (194 x 192cm)

£200-300 **S&K**

A late 19th to early 20thC Hamadan rug from Persia.

48 x 62in (122 x 157cm)

£300-400 **S&K**

A Hamadan rug.

c1900 66 x 41in (168 x 104cm)

£300-400 **S&K**

A Hamadan runner from north-west Persia.

c1900 114.5 x 39.25in (291 x 100cm)

£500-800 **JW**

A Hamadan rug.

90in (225cm) wide

£200-300 **S&K**

A Karaja rug from north-west Persia.

c1880 55 x 42.25in (140 x 107cm)

£500-800 **JW**

A Karaja rug from north-west Persia.

c1890 57.75 x 34.75in (147 x 88cm)

£400-600 **JW**

A Kashan rug.

86in (215cm) wide

£220-280 **S&K**

A late 19thC Mohtashem Kashan carpet.

136 x 100in (345 x 254cm)

£4,000-6,000 **S&K**

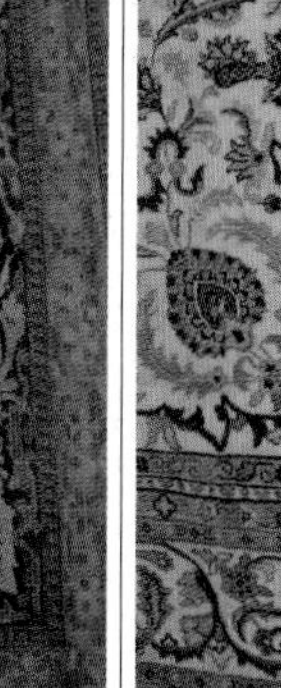

A 20thC Indian Kashan ivory ground rug.

122 x 150in (310 x 381cm)

£300-500 **S&K**

A 20thC Kashan rug from Iran.

120in x 96in (305 x 244cm)

£150-200 **S&K**

An early 20thC Kashan rug from central Persia.

78in (195cm) long

£1,000-1,500 **FRE**

A Kashan carpet.

134in (335cm) wide

£300-500 **S&K**

A Kashan carpet.

152in (380cm) long

£600-900 **S&K**

An Indian Kashan rug.

106in (265cm) wide

£400-600 **S&K**

A Persian Kashan carpet.

c1950 *156in (390cm) wide*

£600-900 **S&K**

An early 20thC Mahal carpet from west Persia.

151in (383.5cm) long

£3,000-4,000 **FRE**

A 20thC Mahal rug from Iran.

83in x 49in (213 x 124cm)

£200-300 **S&K**

A Mahal carpet from west Persia.

c1920 *149in (372.5cm) long*

£2,000-3,000 **FRE**

A Mahal carpet from west Persia.

c1920 *171in (427.5cm) long*

£3,000-5,000 **FRE**

A fine Sarough Faraghan rug from central Persia, slightly worn.

c1880 *80.25 x 52.75in (204 x 134cm)*

£1,500-2,000 **JW**

A Sarough runner from central Persia.

c1920

£1,200-1,800 JW

A Sarouk carpet from west Persia.

c1945 *214in (535cm) long*

£2,800-3,200 FRE

A Sarouk carpet from west Persia.

c1945 *319in (797.5cm) long*

£4,000-6,000 FRE

An early 20thC Sarouk Fereghan carpet from west Persia.

244in (610cm) long

£10,000-15,000 FRE

A Sarouk Malayer carpet, with a central cobalt medallion on a rust field, with green and ivory borders.

c1910 *106 x 137in (269 x 348cm)*

£4,000-6,000 POOK

A late 19th to early 20thC Serab rug.

64in x 35in (163 x 89cm)

£600-900 S&K

A room-sized Serapi rug, with a central medallion on a peach field, with blue corners and a crab border, even sun fading.

c1910 *148 x 233in (376 x 591cm)*

£7,000-10,000 POOK

A late 19th to early 20thC Serab rug.

80 x 46in (203 x 117cm)

£200-300 S&K

A room-sized Serapi rug, with a cobalt medallion on a rust field with blue corners.

c1930 *132 x 96in (335 x 244cm)*

£2,500-3,000 POOK

A room-sized Serapi rug, with a large rust medallion, with blue corners, some losses.

c1900 168in (426cm) long

£4,000-6,000 **POOK**

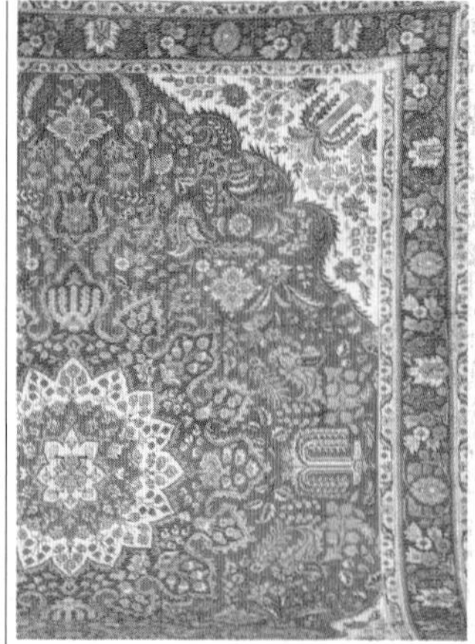

A Tabriz carpet.

148in (370cm) long

£800-1,200 **S&K**

A 20thC Tabriz carpet from Iran.

180in x 120in (457 x 305cm)

£800-1,200 **S&K**

A Tabriz carpet from north-west Persia.

c1935 161in (402.5cm) long

£300-500 **FRE**

A large Tabriz garden carpet, with a cruciform field, central foliate roundel and fifteen rectangular tree and vase panels to each quarter, within an indigo scrolling floral vine border, between palmette bands.

240in (610cm) long

£4,500-5,000 **L&T**

A Persian Tabriz carpet.

c1960 156in (390cm) wide

£500-800 **S&K**

An Abadeh rug from south-west Persia.

c1910 79.25 x 59in (201 x 150cm)

£1,200-1,800 **JW**

A fine Abadeh rug from south-west Persia.

c1910 100 x 63.75in (255 x 162cm)

£1,800-2,200 **JW**

A north-west Persian carpet.

c1960 *156in (390cm) wide*

£600-900 **S&K**

A modern silk Ghom rug from central Persia.

78.25 x 54in (199 x 137cm)

£3,000-3,500 **JW**

A silk Esfahan prayer rug, the cream field with a blue vase of palmettes and scrolling foliate vines, with claret spandrels and a claret palmette and scrolling vine border, refringed.

78in (198cm) long

£1,200-1,800 **L&T**

A late 19thC Laver Kerman carpet from south-east Persia.

187in (467.5cm) long

£4,000-6,000 **FRE**

A Persian Kerman carpet.

c1960 *156in (390cm) wide*

£400-600 **S&K**

A Khamseh rug from south-west Persia.

c1880 *65 x 45in (165 x 115cm)*

£2,000-2,500 **JW**

A CLOSER LOOK AT A PERSIAN RUG

Tree of Life rugs are more associated with urban regions. The angular form of this tree can be attributed to its tribal provenance, and makes it an unusual piece.

It is likely that the weaver of this rug had seen a Tree of Life design and been inspired to reproduce it according to his own aesthetic.

This rug would almost certainly have been woven from memory rather than copied from a plan.

A Khamseh 'Tree of Life' rug from south-west Persia.

This ascending tree design is an important motif in Persian weaving, symbolic of eternal life.

c1900 *81 x 63.5in (206 x 161cm)*

£2,800-3,200 **JW**

A Persian Lilihan rug.

c1950 *156in (390cm) wide*

£1,500-2,000 **S&K**

A Malayer rug from the Hamadan district of west Persia.

c1910 *76 x 49.5in (193 x 126cm)*

£800-1,200 **JW**

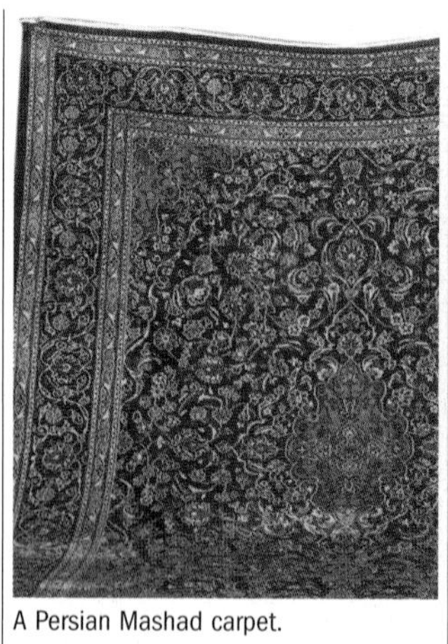

A Persian Mashad carpet.

c1970 *56in (390cm) wide*

£500-800 **S&K**

A Persian Mashad carpet.

152in (380cm) wide

£600-900 **S&K**

A 20thC Indo-Persian rug.

48in x 72in (122 x 183cm)

£400-600 **S&K**

A 20thC Indo-Persian rug.

72in x 48in (183 x 122cm)

£200-300 **S&K**

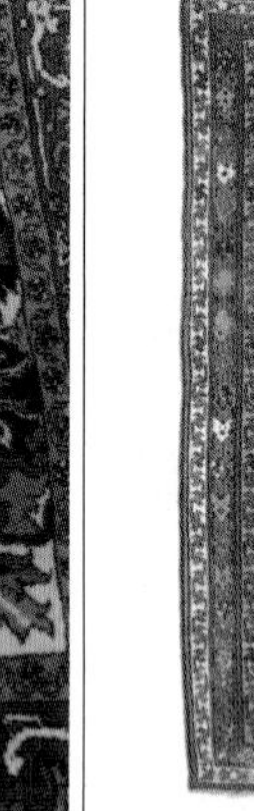

A Persian rug from Kurdistan.

c1870 *92.5 x 51.25in (235 x 130cm)*

£1,500-2,000 **JW**

A Sarab runner from north-west Persia.

c1890 *196 x 38.25in (497 x 97cm)*

£800-1,200 **JW**

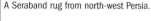

A Seraband rug from north-west Persia.

c1910 *29.5 x 22in (75 x 56cm)*

£150-200 **JW**

A Sewan rug, with a red field and a large lobed polychrome medallion, within an ivory hooked border with blue and ivory bands.

55in (140cm) long

£1,200-1,800 **L&T**

A Persian Shiraz corridor rug.

121in (302.5cm) wide

£300-400 **S&K**

A Persian Sultanabad carpet.

c1950 *156in (390cm) wide*

£800-1,200 **S&K**

A Sultanabad carpet, with an indigo field and allover pattern of large polychrome palmettes, rosettes and leaves, within a rust palmette and scrolling vine border, between multiple green and ivory bands.

226.5in (566cm) long

£7,000-9,000 L&T

A Tehran rug from north Persia.

c1900 76.5 x 56in (194 x 142cm)

£3,500-4,500 JW

A late 19th to early 20thC south-west Persian rug.

84 x 55in (213.5 x 140cm)

£300-500 S&K

CAUCASIAN RUGS

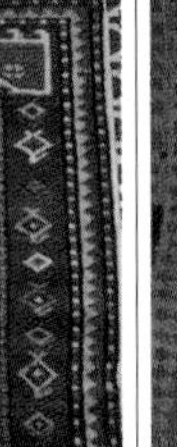

A late 19thC to early 20thC Kazak rug from Caucasus.

51 x 63in (130 x 160cm)

£1,200-1,800 S&K

An early 20thC Kazak Prayer rug, Southwest Caucasus.

34 x 48in (86 x 122cm)

£350-450 S&K

A Garabagh runner from south-east Caucasus.

c1890 134 x 40.5in (340 x 103cm)

£700-1,000 JW

A late 19thC to early 20thC Kazak Prayer rug.

66 x 34in (168 x 86cm)

£1,200-1,800 S&K

A late 19thC Borjalou Kazak prayer rug, from south-west Caucasus.

63in (157.5cm) long

£1,800-2,200 FRE

A late 19thC Kazak throw rug, with four central medallions flanked by trees of life, on a rust field with multiple blue and red borders.

78 x 58in (198 x 147.5cm)

£2,500-3,000 POOK

A Farchalo Kazak prayer rug, with a rare sea foam green field and red Mihrab, within a running dog border.

64 x 42in (162 x 106cm) long

£2,200-2,800 POOK

A Kuba rug from east Caucasus.

c1900 78in (195cm) long

£2,800-3,200 FRE

A Kuba rug from north-eastern Caucasus.

c1880 *70.75 x 40.25in (180 x 105cm)*

£6,000-8,000 **JW**

A late 19thC Shirvan prayer rug, from east Caucasus.

63in (157.5cm) long

£1,000-1,500 **FRE**

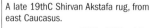

A late 19thC Shirvan Akstafa rug, from east Caucasus.

110in (275cm) long

£2,500-3,000 **FRE**

A Shirvan runner, with a vibrant overall floral and diamond design and a multiple border, small reweaves.

c1910 *131 x 40in (333 x 101.5cm)*

£3,000-4,000 **POOK**

A late 19thC Daghestan prayer rug, from north-east Caucasus.

67in (167.5cm) long

£800-1,200 **FRE**

A large 20thC Afghan carpet.

176in x 134in (447 x 340cm)

£1,800-2,200 **S&K**

A late 19th to early 20thC Daghestan Prayer rug, from south-west Caucasus.

33in x 62in (84 x 157cm)

£180-220 **S&K**

A Caucasian rug.

c1905 *73in x 37in (185 x 94cm)*

£350-450 **S&K**

An Antique Caucasian Kelim carpet.

174in (435cm) wide

£800-1,200 **S&K**

CHINESE RUGS

A Chinese carpet, with floral motifs.

c1900 *150in (375cm) long*

£1,200-1,800 **FRE**

A late 19thC to early 20thC Chinese rug.

116 x 96in (294 x 243cm)

£300-400 **S&K**

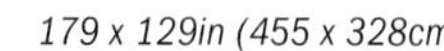

A 20thC Chinese rug.

179 x 129in (455 x 328cm)

£400-600 **S&K**

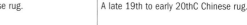

A late 19th to early 20thC Chinese rug.

115 x 98in (292 x 248cm)

£300-500 **S&K**

A Chinese rug, with a floral design.

c1930 *132 x 164in (335 x 416cm)*

£220-280 **S&K**

A Chinese needlepoint rug, in the French Aubusson style.

93 x 117in (236 x 297cm)

£250-300 **S&K**

A Chinese carpet, with foliate motifs.

c1900

£1,200-1,800 **FRE**

An Oriental Kelim corridor rug.

165in (412.5cm) wide

£500-800 **S&K**

A Chinese sculpted celadon rug.

102in (255cm) wide

£180-220 **S&K**

An Indo-Chinese Ming design carpet.

120in (300cm) wide

£180-220 **S&K**

A 20thC Kashmiri rug.

77.5 x 46in (197 x 117cm)

£150-200 **S&K**

A Kashmir rug.

c1920 *108 x 142in (274 x 360cm)*

£350-400 **S&K**

KASHMIR CARPETS

A fine silk Kashmir carpet.

122in (305cm) wide

£1,800-2,200 **S&K**

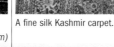

OTHER RUGS

A Kurdish rug bag, together with a small Kurdish rug.

Bag 17in (43cm) wide

£100-150 set **S&K**

A 20thC Kurdish rug.

89 x 50in (226 x 127cm)

£600-900 **S&K**

A silk Kashgar carpet, from east Turkestan, the rust red field with diagonal rows of muted stylized pomegranate sprays, within a wide pale blue-green border of Chinese rosettes and brackets.

110in (275cm) long

£2,500-3,000 **NA**

A late 19th to early 20thC Turkoman Tekke rug.

50.5 x 43.5in (128 x 110cm)

£50-80 **S&K**

A Turkish Kilim rug.

c1850 *75 x 48in (190 x 122cm)*

£150-200 **S&K**

A 19thC Beshir Turkoman rug.

125 x 69in (317 x 175cm)

£300-500 **S&K**

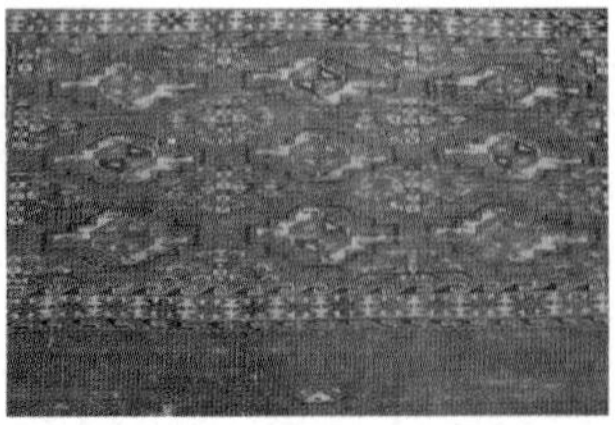

One of two late 19thC Yomud Turkoman Matrash, from west Turkistan.

35 x 57in (88 x 145cm)

£100-150 pair **S&K**

A 20thC Turkish Silk prayer rug.

26 x 47in (66 x 119cm)

£700-1,000 **S&K**

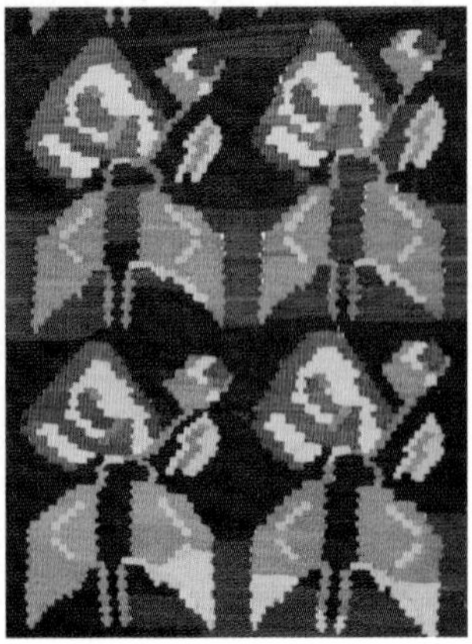

A Turkish Kilim rug, with tulips on a black field.

108 x 73in (274 x 185cm)

£150-200 **S&K**

A 20thC Turkish rug.

52 x 36in (132 x 91cm)

£180-220 **S&K**

A Turkish Kazak rug.

72in (180cm) wide

£280-320 **S&K**

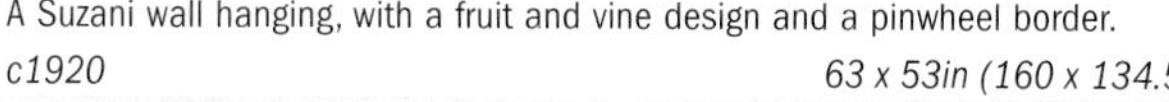

A Suzani wall hanging, with a fruit and vine design and a pinwheel border.

c1920 *63 x 53in (160 x 134.5cm)*

£1,200-1,800 **POOK**

A 20thC Indian Keshan rug.

120 x 168in (304 x 426cm)

£150-200 **S&K**

An Agra carpet from north-west India.

c1900 *138in (345cm) long*

£1,200-1,800 **FRE**

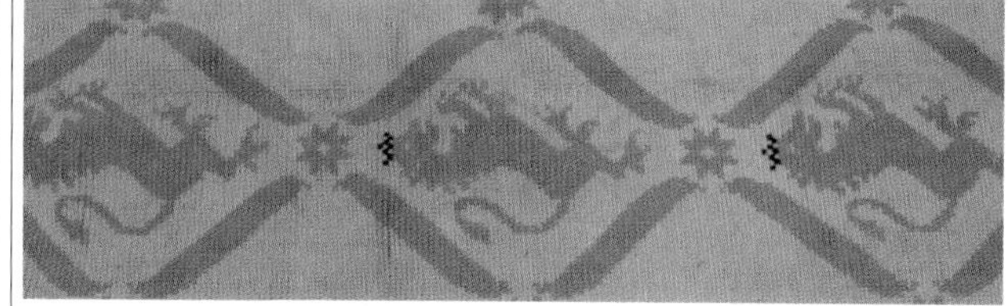

A 20thC Spanish-Continental carpet.

103 x 70in (262 x 178cm)

£350-400 **S&K**

A 20thC Anatolian rug.

43 x 57in (109 x 145cm)

£400-600 **S&K**

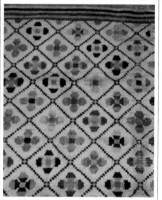

A late 19thC Tibetan horse blanket.

33 x 51in (83 x 129cm)

£1,200-1,800 **S&K**

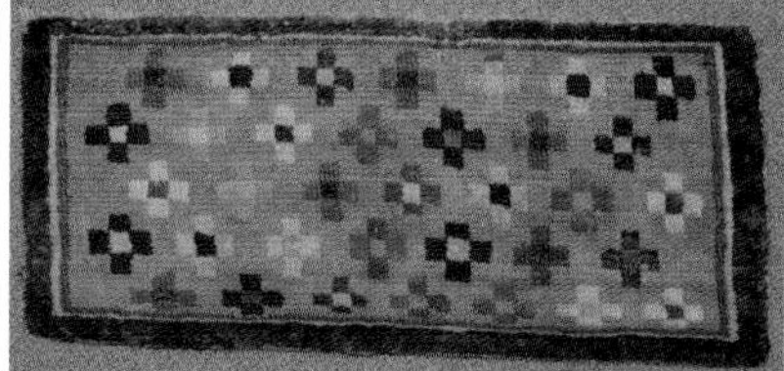

A late 18th to 19thC Tibetan pillow cover, with a geometric pattern, and a trapping fragment.

Pillow cover 12 x 24in (30 x 61cm)

£120-180 set **S&K**

A 19thC Uzbekistan suzani, the linen field with a central floral medallion surrounded by large floral boteh, spandrels and fans, within a leafy vine and floral border.

99.25in (284cm) wide

£500-800 **L&T**

TEXTILES

FOLK RUGS

A 19thC circular wool hooked rug, possibly Shaker, with bands of multicoloured diamond-shaped segments radiating from a central red eight-point star, with an applied wool braided edge, some wear.

79in (197.5cm) diam

£5,000-8,000 **SK**

An American hooked rug, from New England, in Waldoboro style.

c1930 *39.5 x 27.5in (100 x 70cm)*

£700-1,000 **BCAC**

A hooked rug by Ruth Hasendy, from New York, with an overall diamond pattern of 'Lamb's Tongue' or 'Fish Scale', worked in wool, maker's initials "R.H 60" worked into corner.

1960 *76in (190cm) long*

£600-900 **FRE**

A American custom hook rug with a Maryland motif.

216in (540cm) wide

£500-800 **S&K**

An American pictorial hooked rug, with a central white rooster on a blue ground, with red and white stripes.

33 x 18in (84 x 45.5cm)

£500-800 **POOK**

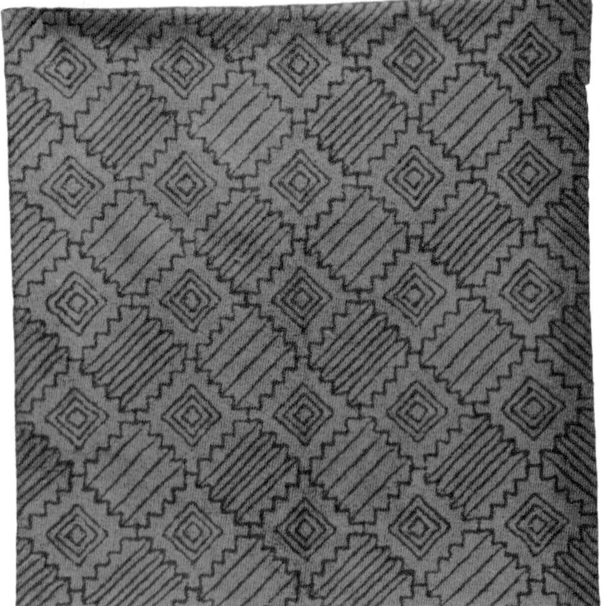

A hooked rug, by Green Mountain Rug Mills, North Carolina, worked with dark blue and bittersweet wool yarns in a overall geometric design.

This is a reproduction of a rug in the collection of the Henry Ford Museum, Michigan.

c1965 *104in (260cm) long*

£300-500 **FRE**

A Folk Art hooked rug, with a medallion of a grey cat with a floral border, wear and losses, unmarked.

32in (80cm) wide

£220-280 **DRA**

A Navajo textile, of commercially and naturally dyed homespun wool, with an asymmetrical stepped diamond and cross pattern.

74in (185cm) long

£450-550 **DRA**

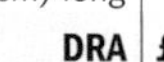

A Navajo textile, of commercially and naturally dyed homespun wool, with diagonal serrated stripes on an ivory ground, the ends with further stripes.

78.75in (197cm) long

£350-400 **DRA**

A Pennsylvania Mennonite raised-work carriage throw, the field of dark twill, plaid and tweed wool squares embroidered with tufted flowerheads, in brightly coloured wool, within a green wool felt border.

c1925 *70in (175cm) wide*

£180-220 **FRE**

A Delaware wool-on-linen overshot table runner, possibly by Lancaster Co., the hand embroidered borders with birds and flowers, dated.

1791

£180-220 **POOK**

A 20thC machine-made American rug.

136 x 98in (345 x 249cm)

£150-200 **S&K**

QUILTS

A mid-to late 19thC North Country pieced 'strippy' quilt, with seven different quilting motifs on the strips.

80 x 80in (205 x 205cm)

£220-280 **DN**

A 19thC Pennsylvanian quilt piece.

16.5in (42cm) wide

£50-70 **BCAC**

A Baltimore pieced cotton quilt, in pink and green on a white ground.

c1850 *88in (220cm) wide*

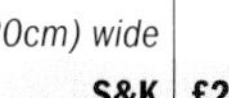

£400-600 **S&K**

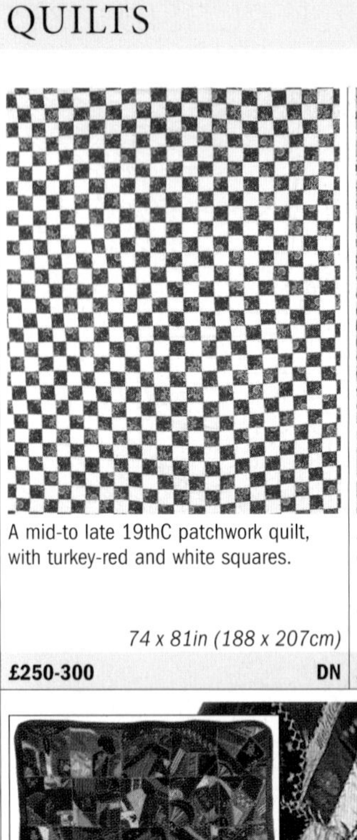

A mid-to late 19thC patchwork quilt, with turkey-red and white squares.

74 x 81in (188 x 207cm)

£250-300 **DN**

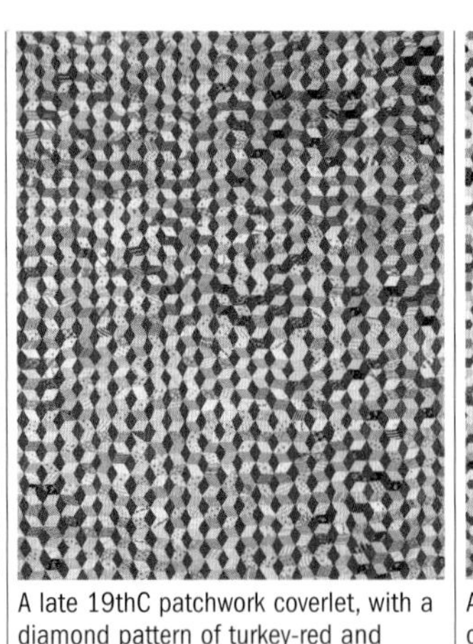

A late 19thC patchwork coverlet, with a diamond pattern of turkey-red and printed cottons, with Oxford shirting and a 'strippy' back.

89 x 59in (227 x 152cm)

£200-300 **DN**

A late 19thC unfinished patchwork quilt, of hexagon design with a defined centre, with printed cottons including plain and turkey-reds.

91 x 81in (232 x 206cm)

£120-180 **DN**

A late 19thC American patchwork quilt, of Ocean Waves design.

64 x 71in (163 x 180cm)

£220-280 **DN**

An American silk and velvet embroidered crazy quilt, embellished with a variety of embroidery stitched and painted motifs, a black satin border, stitched date.

1885 *64in (160cm) wide*

£800-1,200 **SK**

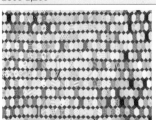

A late 19thC Star of Bethlehem patchwork quilt, probably Pennsylvania, patches to back.

88in (224cm) high

£550-650 **FRE**

A late 19thC wholecloth quilt, using a cheater cloth, quilted in 'strippy' style.

80 x 83in (203cm x 210cm)

£250-300 **DN**

A late 19thC patchwork quilt, of lozenge and turkey-red square with zig-zag quilting, with a variety of printed cottons including some from sample books, possibly Isle of Man or Ireland.

74 x 93in (187cm x 235cm)

£250-300 **DN**

An early 20thC pieced quilt, with a design of squares and triangles, in printed cottons and chintz.

90 x 95in (229cm x 241cm)

£500-800 **DN**

TAPESTRIES

A 17thC Flemish mythological tapestry, woven in wools, depicting a young child in a wooded landscape and surrounded by soldiers with spears, the background with buildings, tents and hills beyond.

96.75in (242cm) long

£3,000-5,000 **L&T**

A 17thC Continental tapestry, with a fountain in a wooded landscape.

99in (247.5cm) long

£3,000-4,000 **FRE**

A CLOSER LOOK AT A TAPESTRY

Very little is known about the Shaerbeck factory that produced this piece, although it was probably set up by George Chaudoir specifically to make tapestries.

This is a verdure depiction of a wild garden, hence the dense, varied flora and variety of birdlife.

The scale of the plants in the foreground is larger than in the background. This gives the tapestry its characteristic layered effect.

Unsigned tapestries cannot be attributed to a particular maker with certainty. The monogram and signature give this tapestry a definite provenance.

A fine 18thC verdure tapestry by Chaudoir, manufactured by the Schaerbeck factory in Brussels, signed "Mture Chaudoir" in brown to the bottom right hand corner and with "CG" monogram featuring a serpent coiled around a spear.

Verdure tapestries typically fall into four categories: formal gardens, wild gardens, game preserves and game parks. This piece depicts a wild garden, although it is probably based on the garden of an estate. Giant foreground leaves create a three-dimensional effect and there is no focal point in the composition; numerous independent vignettes combine to form a whole.

78.75 x 104in (200 x 264cm)

£7,000-10,000 **JW**

A 17thC Beauvais tapestry fragment made into a bell pull, depicting fruits and foliage.

£200-300 **S&K**

A late 19th to early 20thC Continental machine-made tapestry, probably French, depicting a stag and deer in a wooded landscape, within a rich border of fruits and flowers.

112in (284.5cm) wide

£700-1,000 **S&K**

SAMPLERS

A Massachusetts needlework family register, of Benjamin Norton and Sarah Wyatt, married 1775, and their twelve children, with repeating alphabets above the list of names and dates, with hillocks and animals centring a vase of flowers, wrought by "Hannah" in 1785, Newburyport.

21.75in (54cm) high

£7,000-10,000 **NA**

A rare late 18thC Pennsylvania silk on silk and linen sampler purse, with a black silk exterior opening to a floral embroidered spray, and multicoloured alphabet, wrought by "M. Morton", probably Chester County.

9in (23cm) high

£5,000-8,000 **POOK**

A Rhode Island silk on linen sampler, with a central verse above a house and trees, within a blue scrolling and floral border, wrought by "Ruth Smith...Bristol...1799".

15in (38cm) high

£4,000-6,000 **POOK**

An American silk on linen sampler, with a central verse above a tree with birds, animals and baskets of fruit, with a floral border, wrought by "Anna Hansell done in November 1800".

19in (48.5cm) high

£1,800-2,200 **POOK**

An English silk on linen sampler, with a verse, house and a girl within a scrolling border, wrought by "Eliza Haynes...done in her Ninth Years".

17.75in (45cm) high

£1,500-2,000 **POOK**

A George III sampler, in coloured silk with a verse entitled "Religion", birds, trees and deer, by "Charlotte Cuthbert" and dated "May 10, 1809", framed.

15.75in (40cm) high

£600-900 **KBON**

A Pennsylvania Philadelphia needlework sampler, in silk threads on a linen ground, with a floral border enclosing the alphabet, a verse, a pictorial panel and the inscription "Mary Headman's work in the 8th Year of her age 1805," framed, some ageing.

17in (42.5cm) wide

£1,000-1,500 **FRE**

An English silk on linen sampler, with a verse, alphabet, crowned cherubs and Adam and Eve, within a floral border, wrought by "Mary __man 1809".

22in (56cm) high

£800-1,200 **POOK**

An early 19thC New England silk on linen sampler, wrought by the Frazier family, with a verse and a house flanked by trees, within a strawberry border.

24.25in (61.5cm) high

£1,500-2,000 **POOK**

A New Hampshire needlework sampler, with silk threads on a linen ground, inscribed "Sarah Hobb's Sampler" and "1822," framed, some ageing.

16in (40cm) high

£2,500-3,000 **FRE**

An English or Irish silk on linen sampler, with a verse above a mansion, over Adam and Eve, within a strawberry border, by "Jeanie Robertson 1824".

16.75in (42.5cm) high

£1,200-1,800 **POOK**

A Philadelphia needlework sampler, worked with silk threads on a linen ground, a floral border encloses the names "Henry Gravel" and "Mary Gravel" and the pious verse "An Infant's Prayer," a pictorial panel with house, trees, child and sheep, the edges bound in blue silk, inscribed "Ellenor Gravel Nov. 15 1825", framed, some fading.

17in (42.5cm) wide

£7,000-10,000 **FRE**

An Ohio silk on linen sampler, with a central green lawn with a sheep, and birds, surrounded by a large rooster, a couple flanking a well and other designs, wrought by "Ann Brook Aged 10 1825".

26.25in (66.5cm) wide

£3,000-5,000 **POOK**

A needlework sampler, Province of New Brunswick, worked with silk threads on a linen ground, inscribed "Clarissa Keillor Aged 13 years April 30th 1827", framed, darkened ground, some fading.

17.5in (36cm) wide

£400-600 **FRE**

An American silk on linen sampler, possibly Maryland, depicting a Federal home with people, animals and a floral vine, wrought by "Eliza Ann Newman... Mrs. Brown's Seminary 1828".

16.5in (42cm) high

£7,000-10,000 **POOK**

A New Jersey silk on linen sampler, with an alphabet and flowers above a wooded landscape with a house, wrought by "Ann Sophia Beckwith, 1829, Ag. 11 yrs, Poplar Grove".

16in (40.5cm) high

£5,000-8,000 **POOK**

A New England silk on linen sampler, with central alphabets, within a double sawtooth border surmounted by floral vines, wrought by "Susan E. Cutter aged 12".

16.25in (41.5cm) high

£1,500-2,000 **POOK**

A needlework sampler, Chester County, Pennsylvania, with a bold floral border and a pious verse, with the inscriptions "Parents William and Elizabeth Beale", "Teacher Mary M. Rutherford" and "Lydia Ann Beale's Work, 1832", above a hillock with animals, worked in silk threads on gauze ground, framed.

£10,000-15,000 **FRE**

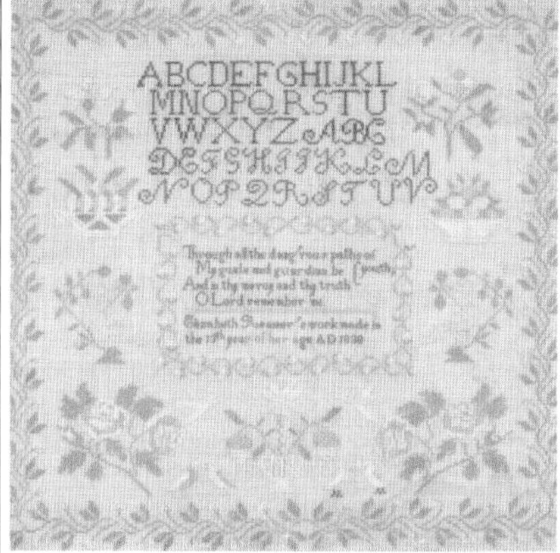

A needlework sampler, in silk threads on a linen ground, with the alphabet and a verse enclosed by flower, bird and basket spot devices and a floral border, inscribed "Elizabeth Reamer's work made in the 13th Year of her age AD 1838," framed, some ageing.

17.5in (44cm) wide

£600-900 **FRE**

An American silk on linen sampler, possibly Pennsylvania, with the alphabet and a verse above floral sprays, potted flowers, birds and a vine border, wrought by "Mary Mercer...1838 Aged 12 years".

19in (48.5cm) high

£1,200-1,800 **POOK**

A Maine woolwork 'friendship' sampler, with images of the American flag, a locomotive and tender, two figures in a row boat, several black figures, animals, flowers and other designs.

19in (48.5cm) high

£700-1,000 **POOK**

NEEDLEWORK

An early 19thC English needlework picture, depicting a woman mourning at Shakespeare's tomb, worked in a variety of stitches with painted highlights.

11.25in (28cm) high

£500-800 **S&K**

An early 19thC English needlework picture, depicting a milkmaid greeting an aristocrat, worked in a variety of stitches on a silk ground with painted details.

9.75in (24cm) high

£300-400 **S&K**

A late 19thC American needlework picture, depicting the seal of the United States with an eagle, flags and motto, stitched in multicoloured threads and surrounding a painted paper silhouette of George Washington.

21in (52.5cm) wide

£300-400 **S&K**

A 20thC framed needlework picture of CGS Vigilant warship, built by Polson's of Toronto in 1904.

CGS Vigilant may be regarded as the first 'modern' warship to be built in Canada.

28in (71cm) wide

£800-1,200 **WAD**

A silk painted and needlework mourning picture, attributed to Abby Wright's School, South Hadley, Massachusetts, depicting a young couple leaning on a plinth inscribed "M.W.B., Died Febr. 16th, AE 8yrs.".

£3,000-4,000 **NA**

A silk painted and needlework wedding picture, possibly New Jersey, depicting a couple, preacher and an attendant, all with painted details, the backboard with partial pencil inscription "Mrs. Judge Everett, Jersey City, 1797".

16.5in (41cm) high

£2,500-3,500 **NA**

A silk double memorial, with eglomise mat, depicting a woman in Empire dress beside urns in a hilly setting, with painted details, inscribed "Sally K. Druce".

19.5in (49cm) wide

£1,500-2,000 **NA**

A Pennsylvania needlework picture, worked with polychrome wool yarns on a linen ground, with an outdoor scene of a woman, inscribed "Ruth Ann Watkins 1839," framed, dated.

28.5in (71cm) wide

£400-600 **FRE**

A late 19thC printed children's cotton handkerchief, probably Germantown Print Works, the square form printed in black and red in 'Blowing Bubbles' design, framed.

10.25in (25.5cm) wide

£150-200 **FRE**

An important Pennsylvania silk on silk needlework memorial, by Mary Ann Mitchell, student at Bethlehem Female Seminary, for "George Mitchell departed this life the 14th day of June 1793".

c1805 *20.5in (52cm) wide*

£3,000-5,000 **POOK**

An American needlepoint picture, worked with colourful wood yarns, depicting a scene with birds, holly branches, a stone wall and an urn, initialled and dated "E L C 1896".

14in (35cm) wide

£150-200 **FRE**

SILKS

A 17thC English silk on silk stumpwork purse, worked in crewel with sequins and silver and gold thread, probably depicting Moses in the rushes on one side and a bearded man with sun rays on the other, with intricate flowers, birds and trees.

£5,000-8,000 **POOK**

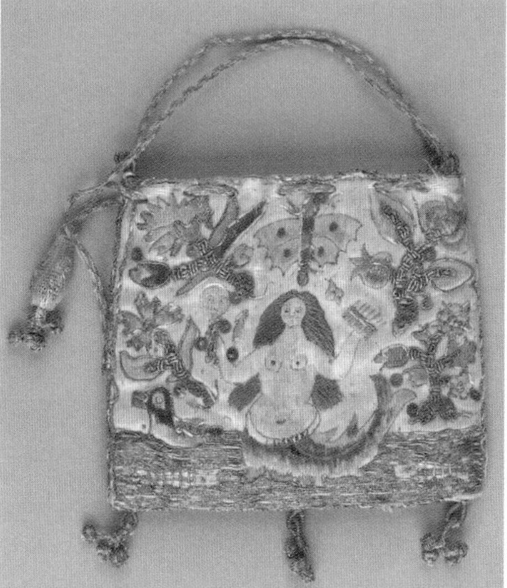

A late 17thC to early 18thC English intricate silk on silk embroidered purse, one side with a mermaid flanked by a butterfly, bird and other designs, the other side with Archangel Michael flanked by animals, overall crewel with metallic braid and sequins.

5.25in (13.5cm) wide

£15,000-20,000 **POOK**

An early 20thC embroidered silkwork picture, probably Japanese, worked with silk and metallic threads, heightened with watercolour, framed, minor discolouration.

19.75in (50cm) high

£400-600 **FRE**

A Maine silk memorial needlework, by Sarah E. Sawyer, in pencil, paint and ink, with an elaborate landscape of Portland and a memorial to her son William, who was lost at sea, in a reverse painted mat, dated 1833, some damage.

25.25in (64cm) wide

£3,000-4,000 **POOK**

A 19thC English oval silk on silk needlework, of a bird perched in a tree with a butterfly, with reverse painted frame.

16in (40.5cm) high

£600-900 **POOK**

A woolwork picture, probably Chester County, Pennsylvania, with a wreath of roses enclosing a bowl a fruit worked in wool yarns, by "Elizabeth Swartz 1839", edged in green wool tape, framed.

17.5in (44cm) wide

£1,500-2,000 **FRE**

A 19thC Berlin woolwork sampler, worked in coloured wools with an image of a spaniel seated on a cushion, above the inscription "Sarah Harris Her Work, September 14th 1869".

31in (79cm) high

£350-450 **DN**

WOOLWORK & OTHER TEXTILES

A late 18thC Boston or English wool and silk on linen needlework picture, with a reclining shepherdess and a shepherd, in a wooded landscape with a house, woodcutter, animals and flowers.

20.75in (52.5cm) high

£20,000-25,000 **POOK**

A 19thC woolwork picture, depicting a lady in medieval dress, holding a dove beside a cloister, worked in petit point in coloured silks and wools.

13in (34cm) high

£80-120 **DN**

A woolwork panel, depicting medallions surrounded by flower sprays, worked in cross-stitch in coloured wools.

48in (123cm) high

£150-200 **DN**

A 19thC woolwork picture, depicting a first-rate man o' war flying the White Ensign, worked in coloured wools in long and short stitch, in a maple frame.

22in (56.5cm) wide

£3,500-4,500 **DN**

A late 19thC woolwork picture of a British ship, worked in colourful wool and cotton yarns, in a bird's-eye maple frame, some fading.

20.5in (51cm) wide

£300-500 **FRE**

A large woolwork picture, depicting the taking of a manor house by soldiers, worked in coloured wools.

39in (98.5cm) wide

£200-250 **DN**

A large circular Hawaiian tapa cloth, painted with an American flag.

32in (80cm) diam

£6,000-9,000 **NA**

A Massachusetts silk embroidered coat-of-arms of the Russell family of Salem, on a black silk ground with a sailing vessel above a shield, worked in metallic threads, in original gilded and ebonized frame.

18.25in (46.5cm) high

£18,000-22,000 **NA**

COSTUME

A late Victorian silk skirt, top and bolero.

£150-200 **JV**

A black lace dress, with hand-beaded decoration.

c1910 *55in (140cm) long*

£200-250 **HP**

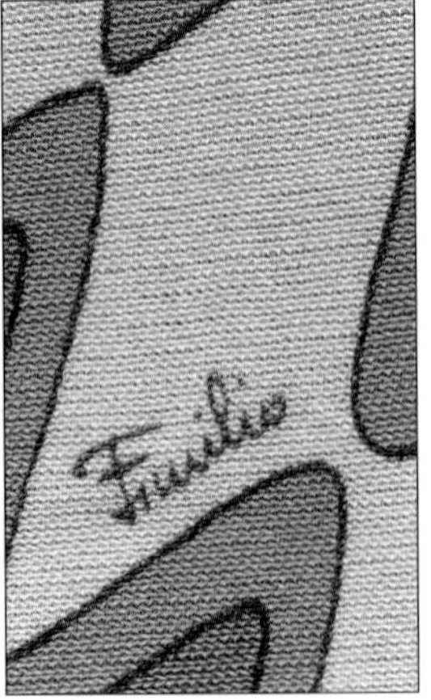

A Pucci printed silk dress.

The 'Emilio' signature, which is integral to the pattern of the dress, indicates the authenticity of the garment.

£200-250 **HP**

A 1920s pale blue silk chiffon dress, with white hand-beaded decoration.

48in (122cm) long

£180-220 **RR**

A 1920s Macclesfield silk dress.

40in (102cm) long

£50-80 **JV**

A 1920s printed silk dress, with a matching scarf.

45in (114cm) long

£250-300 **RR**

A 1930s silver lamé wedding dress, with a long train.

£220-280 **JV**

A 1920s black velvet jacket, with a white fur collar.

35in (89cm) long

£120-180 **JV**

A 1920s Triguard velvet fringed jacket.

35in (89cm) long

£300-350 **JV**

A 1930s silver lamé wedding dress, with a long train.

£220-280 **JV**

A 1940s Skirt Deluxe blue satin two-piece suit.

45in (114cm) long

£80-120 **RR**

A 1930s Colin Becke two-piece dress, with velvet trim and flowers.

60in (152cm) long

£400-450 **HP**

EVENING BAGS

A rare French cut steel microbeaded handbag, with an engraved frame.

c1900 *14in (35.3cm) long*

£500-600 **STE**

An iridescent beaded handbag, in a crochet fabric.

c1915 *6.5in (16.5cm) long*

£150-200 **AHL**

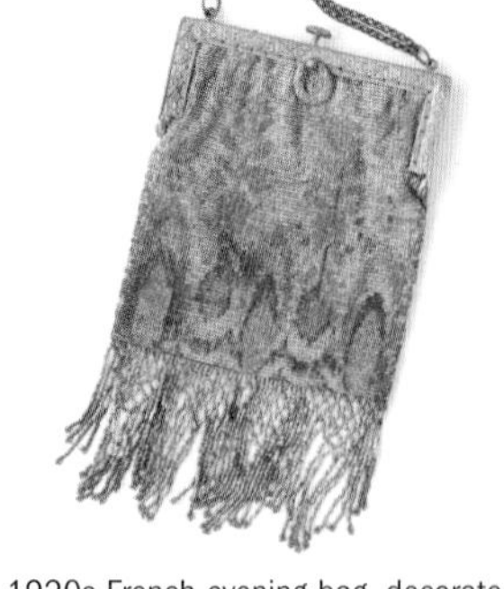

A 1920s French evening bag, decorated with microbeading, with a beaded fringe, chain handle and metal closure.

11in (28cm) wide

£300-350 **AHL**

A 1920s beaded bag, with an abstract ethnic design, tortoiseshell-effect Lucite clasp and strap, with a black-and-white beaded fringe.

8.5in (21.5cm) high

£300-350 **AHL**

A 1920s silk purse, woven with gold thread and overlaid with draping rows of clear yellow beads and vertical rows of orange rhinestones, with a concealed gilt metal frame and a spherical clasp, lined with cream silk.

7in (17.5cm) high

£70-100 **BY**

A 1920s celluloid-framed handbag, with a linked strap, decorated with blue iridescent beads.

11in (28cm) long

£250-350 **AHL**

A CLOSER LOOK AT A 1920S BEADED BAG

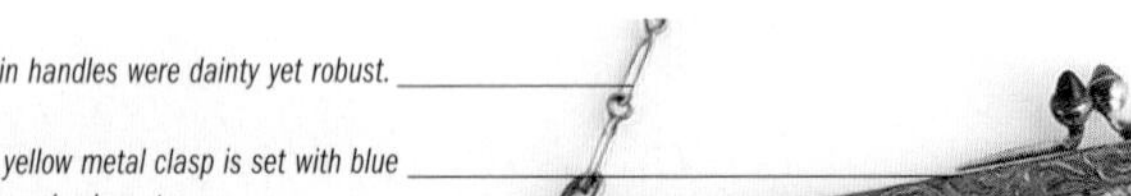

Chain handles were dainty yet robust.
The yellow metal clasp is set with blue glass cabochon stones.

This floral design is typical of early 20thC bags. The glass beads were painstakingly knitted together on fine steel needles.

The beaded fringe was a popular finishing touch.

A 1920s beaded evening bag, decorated with a beaded floral design, the brass clasp with a bead-decorated fastening, a beaded fringe and chain strap.

7in (18cm) wide

£250-300 **AHL**

An Art Deco evening bag, decorated with cut steel beads and finished in gold and silver, with a Spanish fringe and chain handle.

9in (22.5cm) high

£40-60 **TA**

An Art Deco bag, with beaded decoration, probably 1930s.

8in (20.5cm) wide

£100-150 **TDG**

A 1930s multicoloured beadwork bucket bag, with silk rope handles, a beadwork collar and tassels, lined with cream silk, stamped "Saks Fifth Avenue MADE IN FRANCE" in gilt.

£80-120 **BY**

A 1930s French two colourmetal beadwork and diamanté purse, with a fretted foliate and floral gilt metal clasp, the hinged clasp with a transfer-printed porcelain oval plaque, with a heavy, gold-plated chain, lined throughout with white silk, a label reading "'MADE IN FRANCE".

9.25in (23.5cm) wide

£80-120 **BY**

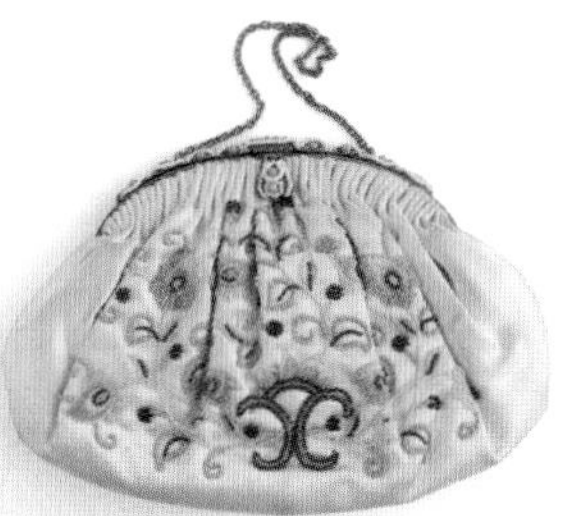

A 1930s French beadwork and silk purse, decorated with paisley forms, the metal frame with a catch, the interior in cream silk, with labels reading "Exclusive Handbags by Ed B. Robinson" and "MADE IN FRANCE".

9in (23cm) wide

£60-80 **ROX**

A 1930s Art Deco beaded peacock handbag, with a fringe and an unusual leather lining.

7in (8cm) long

£150-200 **AHL**

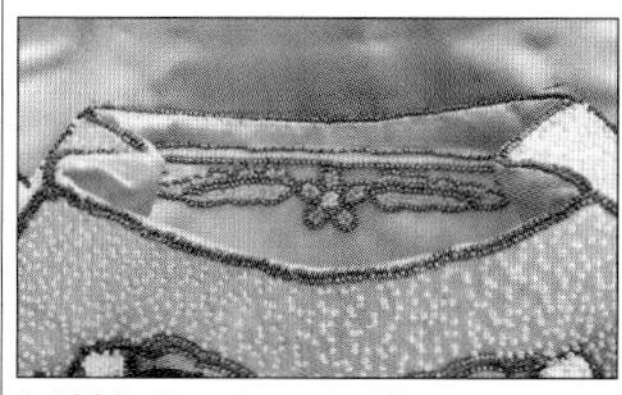

A 1930s French cream silk purse, decorated with multicoloured and metallic beadwork, with two handles, the interior with two silk-lined sections, one with beadwork.

9.5in (24cm) wide

£70-100 **BY**

A 1940s French gold microbeaded evening bag, by Josef, the stitched floral detail in pastel shades, with a beaded and enamelled clasp and a chain handle, the satin-covered purse mirror inside printed "Bag by Josef".

Bags by Josef are as highly sought after by collectors today as they were when they were new.

9.5in (24cm) wide

£300-400 **AHL**

A 1940s small black silk evening bag, the metal clasp with enamelling, beads and faux pearls, with a chain strap.

Heavy Oriental clasps and frames were popular in Italy and France in the early 1920s. They were often embellished with precious, semi-precious or faux jewels and enamelling. However, it was in the 1930s and into the 1940s that clasps and frames were at their most opulent. Exotic materials such as Chinese ivory and Lalique glass were used. Art Deco styles by companies such as Cartier used diamonds, lapis lazuli and gold. Their imitators substituted these with imitation paste and crystals.

8.75in (22cm) wide

£300-350 **AHL**

A 1940s bead box bag, by Fre-Mor, with a relief metal surround and five internal compartments.

Fre-Mor Manufacturing Corp was owned by the same people as ME Products (Morty Edelstein). It merged with Jewel Plastic Corp to form Llewellyn, which manufactured Lucite bags.

8in (20.5cm) high

£150-200 **FAN**

A 1950s beaded and needlepoint embroidered bag, from Hong Kong, with a beaded handle.

The combination of beading and needlepoint decoration is unusual.

8.75in (22cm) wide

£150-200 **AHL**

A 1960s French hand-beaded and silk-embroidered bag, with a black satin lining, unmarked.

9in (23cm) wide

£100-150 **RG**

A 1980s white and multicoloured beaded bag, with a mother-of-pearl clasp and a chain strap.

66.75in (17cm) wide

£150-200 **AHL**

A French beadwork and bargello work purse, with a woven Indian paisley-style design and cream beads, lined with cream silk, together with a small handheld mirror and a pocket covered with similar material, interior stamped "_ de vie Paris France" in gilt.

c1905 *7in (18cm) wide*

£80-120 **BY**

A 1930s American hand-beaded and embroidered clutch bag, with ivory satin lining and a matching satin-covered mirror, marked "Bags by Josef, Hand beaded in the USA".

9in (23cm) wide

£80-90 **RG**

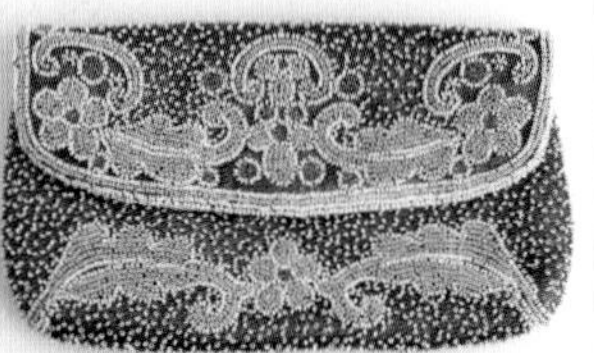

A 1930s French olive green satin clutch bag, with white and grey beadwork and an ivory satin lining, marked 'Made in France for Coblentz'.

7.5in (19cm) wide

£60-70 **RG**

A 1930s French hand-beaded and embroidered evening purse, with pearl decoration and a cream satin lining, marked "Jolle Original".

11.5in (29cm) wide

£50-60 **RG**

A beaded evening bag, with a black and silver design.

c1945 *9in (23cm) wide*

£70-90 **TDG**

A beadwork and embroidered purse, with faux pearl decoration, of circular form, the gilt metal frame with applied pink and blue cabochons, lined with cream silk, probably 1950s.

6.5in (16.5cm) high

£70-100 **ROX**

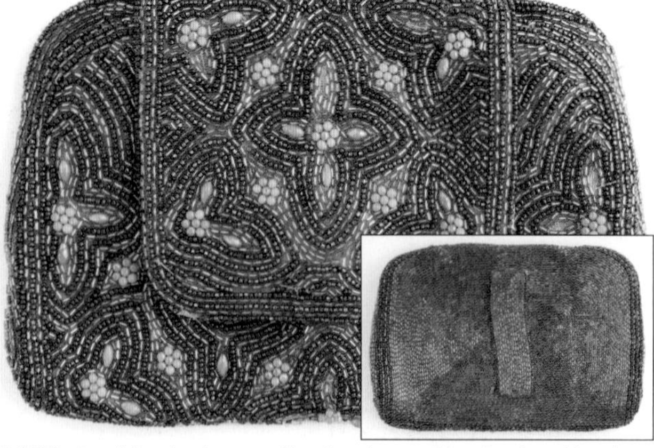

A 1930s French beadwork purse, with a flap closure, silver tube-shaped beads and a fabric handhold to the reverse, lined with cream silk, with a "MADE IN FRANCE" label.

7in (18cm) wide

£60-80 **ROX**

A French cut steel bead handbag.

c1915 *7.5in (19 cm) long*

£200-250 **AHL**

A 1940s black silk moiré evening bag, decorated with cut steel beads.

9.5in (24cm) wide

£300-350 **AHL**

EMBROIDERED BAGS

A silk semicircular clutch bag, the antique-gold ground decorated with oriental-style silk embroidery with a different design to each side, an oriental-style filigree frame and a faux-jade decorated clasp.

c1915 *10.75in (27cm) wide*

£500-600 **AHL**

A 1940s silk-satin evening bag, by Krucker of London, with embroidered appliqué detail in gold and coloured silks and an enamelled frame, with an accompanying 'Krucker's Chinese Embroidered Handbags' booklet, explaining the symbolism of the design.

10in (25cm) wide

£350-450 **AHL**

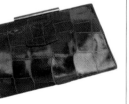

A 1940s French embroidered moiré silk evening bag, with a brass closure and chain strap.

8in (20cm) wide

£200-250 **AHL**

LEATHER BAGS

A 1920s alligator handbag, finished with brass hardware.

10.75in (27cm) wide

£200-300 **AHL**

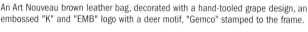

A 1930s English brown crocodile clutch bag, marked "British Made".

10.25in (26cm) wide

£60-90 **RG**

A honey-coloured crocodile handbag.

c1935 *11.5in (29cm) wide*

£70-90 **TDG**

An Art Nouveau brown leather bag, decorated with a hand-tooled grape design, an embossed "K" and "EMB" logo with a deer motif, "Gemco" stamped to the frame.

c1915 *10in (25cm) wide*

£150-180 **AHL**

A 1940s lizardskin clutch bag, by Picard, West Germany, with a brass clasp.

17.75in (45cm) wide

£150-200 **AHL**

A red snakeskin handbag.

c1945 *13in (33 cm) wide*

£100-150 **AHL**

A small 1940s French black suede evening bag, the gold metal clasp decorated with enamel and rhinestones, with a suede strap, the cream satin interior with a small purse attached.

9in (23cm) wide

£200-250 **AHL**

A 1950s American black alligator bag, unmarked.

12.25in (31cm) wide

£180-220 RG

A 1950s Guild Creations leather bag.

10in (25.5cm) wide

£80-120 FAN

A green and black snakeskin handbag, with a narrow handle, opening to three separate compartments, the tie at the bottom drawing the three sections together.

c1950 *6.75in (7cm) long*

£200-250 GOL

FABRIC BAGS

A velvet bag with a 1920s frame.

11in (28cm) wide

£60-90 GMC

An Art Deco evening bag, by Artbag, a carnelian, onyx and marcasite frame, in pleated black silk, with European hallmarks, a replaced chain.

9in (22.5cm) wide

£220-280 TA

A 1940s navy crêpe bag, with an antique-gold filigree frame and a multi-coloured gem floral motif, a gold circle clasp, marked "Gail's Original".

12in (30cm) wide

£250-300 AHL

A 1940s black crêpe rectangular bag, with a gold metal clasp and a porcelain-effect miniature detail, surrounded by rhinestones.

12.75in (32cm) wide

£200-250 AHL

LUCITE BAGS

A CLOSER LOOK AT A LUCITE BAG

The handle is made from plain, extruded plastic.

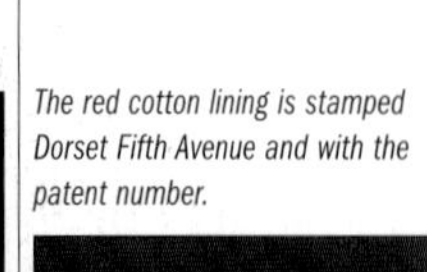

The red cotton lining is stamped Dorset Fifth Avenue and with the patent number.

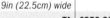

This design was also made in black Lucite. Check that the lid fits properly and is not badly scratched or dented.

The bag has a distinctive S-hook catch.

Woven metal and Lucite bags are usually less valuable than all-Lucite bags.

A 1950s lidded lunchbox bag, by Dorset Fifth Avenue, with an amber Lucite lid and a woven silver and gold metal body, with a brass clasp.

8.75in (22cm) wide

£80-120 AHL

A 1950s bucket bag, a natural straw effect body and a pink Lucite lid with painted, pearl and diamanté floral motifs, with a clear Lucite handle.

10.25in (26cm) wide

£200-250 **AHL**

A 1950s Lucite tortoiseshell-effect oblong bag, by Tyrolean NY, with floral filigree edging.

This classic design is highly sought after by collectors. It has a single, hinged handle and a characteristic snap latch closure.

7.75in (19.5cm) wide

£200-250 **FAN**

A 1950s oblong confetti Lucite bag, by Majestic, with a clear handle.

Ladies would line transparent bags like this one with a piece of fabric that matched their outfit.

9.5in (24cm) wide

£70-100 **FAN**

A 1950s clear Lucite bag, with carved, diamond-shaped moulding and rhinestone detail, with a metal clasp and a clear handle.

10in (19cm) wide

£120-180 **AHL**

A 1950s Lucite clutch bag, with rhinestone decoration.

6.5in (6.5cm) wide

£80-120 **AHL**

A very rare 1950s American Walborg beaded poodle purse.

American manufacturer Walborg is famed for its beaded bags and purses. In the late 1940s it produced a line of black poodle purses hand-beaded in Belgium. It followed these in the 1950s with white poodles, hand-beaded in Japan. Both colours are the same size, equally rare and of similar value.

1955 *13.5in (34cm) high*

£1,000-1,500 **RG**

NOVELTY BAGS

A rare 1950s American wicker parasol purse, unmarked.

1955 *25in (64cm) high*

£250-300 **RG**

An extremely rare 1940s French surreal telephone handbag, in white kid leather, by Anne-Marie of Paris.

Along with Elsa Schiaparelli, Anne Marie produced an exclusive range of surreal handbags. She was known for her bags in realistic yet witty shapes and with intriguing openings. They included champagne buckets, pianos and alarm clocks. Many, such as this telephone, were also available in black.

6.5in (16.5cm) high

£1,500-2,000 **RG**

A CLOSER LOOK AT A NOVELTY BAG

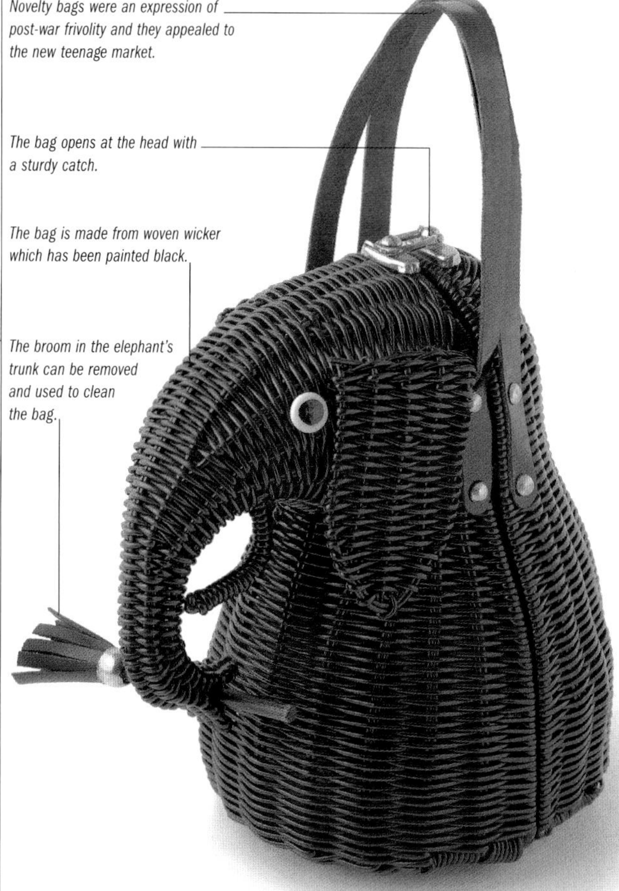

Novelty bags were an expression of post-war frivolity and they appealed to the new teenage market.

The bag opens at the head with a sturdy catch.

The bag is made from woven wicker which has been painted black.

The broom in the elephant's trunk can be removed and used to clean the bag.

A rare 1950s American black wicker elephant purse, unmarked.

10.5in (27cm) wide

£250-300 **RG**

WOODEN DOLLS

An early wooden Queen Anne 'baby' doll, in remains of original costume, with painted features, and nailed wig.

c1700 *9.5in (24cm) high*

£2,000-3,000 **BEJ**

A well-articulated wooden male doll, with two shirts, owned by Rudolph Nureyev.

c1860 *16in (40.5cm) high*

£1,500-2,000 **BEJ**

A CLOSER LOOK AT A GEORGIAN WOODEN DOLL

This doll has inset glass eyes, which were inserted by cutting the wood and soaking it. As the wood dried it closed around the eyes, holding them in place.
The bodies of these wooden dolls were turned by very skilled craftsmen.
This doll is complete with three different costumes, including original underwear and shoes. It is almost unheard of for a doll of this age to be complete with so many accessories.
The face has unrestored gesso painting, with very fine layers of pigment laid over one another. This technique is very prone to cracking and peeling and many examples have been restored, which has a detrimental effect on value.

A very rare early Georgian wooden doll, with turned wooden body, two original outfits and leather shoes, minor damage.

c1730 *13in (33cm) high*

£4,000-6,000 **BEJ**

An American clown squeaker, with a painted bisque face.

c1890 *12in (30.5cm) high*

£220-280 **PST**

A 19thC carved and painted figure of a soldier, with yellow and black painted uniform and jointed arms.

11.75in (30cm) high

£500-600 **POOK**

An American penny wooden doll, with a painted face and jointed limbs, wearing a red cotton dress with a lace collar.

c1910 *11in (29cm) high*

£100-150 **PST**

WAX DOLLS

A tiny wax doll in original outfit, with blue painted eyes, closed perky mouth, brown painted dome head with applied ribbons at sides, sloping shoulders, wax lower arms, composition lower legs, black flat-soled boots, original cotton print dress, apron and straw hat.

c1860 *6in (15cm) high*

£400-600 **SK**

A French bisque swivel-neck lady doll, with light blue stationary eyes, softly outlined closed mouth, original blonde mohair wig over cork pate, gusseted kid body, separated fingers, original commercial ivory silk and net two-piece dress, bronze leather shoes marked "M.G.", impressed mark "3".

c1870 *16in (40cm) high*

£1,800-2,200 **SK**

A rare Kestner 'G' fashion doll with kid body, blonde mohair wig, and original outfit.

c1880 *22in (56cm) high*

£1,200-1,800 **BEJ**

A CLOSER LOOK AT A FASHION DOLL

The moveable swivel head indicates that this is a doll of superior quality.

Purple was the Victorian colour of half-mourning, and it is possible that this doll belonged to a child who was mourning a deceased parent or sibling.

The clothes are completely original, even down to the underwear and straw-filled bustle. The painstaking detail of doll's costumes from this period makes them of great interest to costume collectors and wardrobe professionals.

The body of this doll is made from kid-leather. Each of the fingers has been individually hand-stitched.

A Barrios for Bru fashion doll, in original costume, with kid body and bisque head.

c1875 *17in (43cm) high*

£3,000-4,000 **BEJ**

A French bisque-headed fashion doll, with lace-trimmed silk taffeta costume and kid gloves and shoes.

c1880 *13.5in (34cm) high*

£120-180 **S&K**

A tiny fashion doll with a bisque head and cloth body, in silk outfit, repaired crack to shoulder.

c1890 *7.5in (19cm) high*

£180-220 **BEJ**

A porcelain Queen Louise doll, with porcelain face, fixed eyes and movable painted wooden arms and legs.

c1910 *21in (52.5cm) high*

£180-220 **S&K**

JUMEAU

A French Paris bisque-headed bébé, with brown glass paperweight eyes, closed mouth, pierced ears, original blonde mohair wig over cork pate and pull-string voice mechanism, wearing a green satin dress and hat and brown leather Jumeau 'bee' mark shoes, the fully articulated composition body stamped "Jumeau Medaille d'Or", with red stamp "Paris Bébé Tete Deposee Jumeau production".

c1885 *21in (52.5cm) high*

£2,000-3,000 **SK**

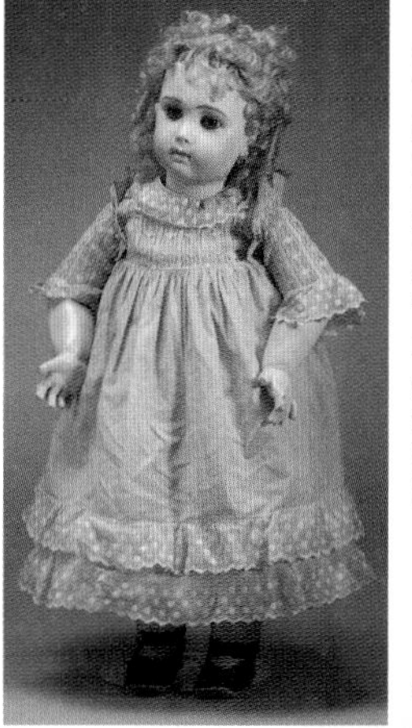

A large French Jumeau Triste or 'long face' bébé, with blue feathered paperweight eyes, lightly outlined closed mouth, large applied ears and original full blonde mohair wig with curls over cork pate impressed "14", wearing old white cotton undergarments and a blue cotton dress, the articulated straight-wristed composition body stamped in blue "Jumeau Medaille d'Or".

c1885 *29in (72.5cm) high*

£10,000-12,000 **SK**

A small French Jumeau bisque-headed bébé, with brown lined paperweight eyes, closed mouth, pierced ears, and original blonde mohair wig over cork pate, wearing a two-tone green wool and silk coat-dress, straw hat and bronze leather Jumeau shoes, the fully articulated eight-ball straight-wristed composition body stamped "Jumeau Medaille d'Or Paris", impressed "DEPOSE E. 3 J." mark.

c1885 *11.5in (29cm) high*

£5,000-6,000 **SK**

A French Tete Jumeau bisque-headed bébé, with original silk dress, stamped "Jumeau Medaille d'Or Paris" in blue.

c1885 *17in (42.5cm) high*

£2,000-3,000 **SK**

A Tete Jumeau French bisque-headed bébé, with human hair wig and paper pate, stamped "Jumeau Medaille d'Or".

c1890 *13in (32.5cm) high*

£3,000-4,000 **SK**

A CLOSER LOOK AT A JUMEAU TRISTE DOLL

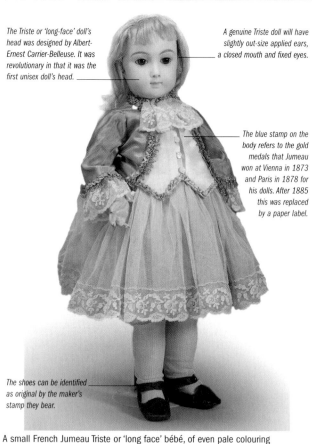

The Triste or 'long-face' doll's head was designed by Albert-Ernest Carrier-Belleuse. It was revolutionary in that it was the first unisex doll's head.

A genuine Triste doll will have slightly out-size applied ears, a closed mouth and fixed eyes.

The blue stamp on the body refers to the gold medals that Jumeau won at Vienna in 1873 and Paris in 1878 for his dolls. After 1885 this was replaced by a paper label.

The shoes can be identified as original by the maker's stamp they bear.

A small French Jumeau Triste or 'long face' bébé, of even pale colouring throughout, with brown lined paperweight eyes, closed mouth, pierced applied ears and blonde mohair wig over cork pate, impressed "10", wearing a blue silk and lace dress and bronze leather shoes signed "E. Jumeau 11", the straight-wristed articulated composition body stamped in blue "Jumeau Medaille d'Or".

c1885 *22in (55cm) high*

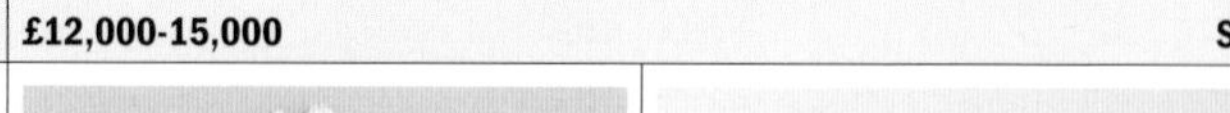

£12,000-15,000 **SK**

A small French closed-mouth Jumeau bébé, with brunette human hair wig and cream cotton satin and lace outfit.

c1890 *12in (30cm) high*

£1,500-2,000 **SK**

A large Jumeau child doll, with bisque head and chunky composition body, paperweight eyes and multi-layer costume.

c1895 *28in (71cm) high*

£3,500-4,500 **BEJ**

A large French S.F.B.J. Jumeau-type bébé with rare flirt eyes and extra clothing.

c1900 *30in (76cm) high*

£3,500-4,500 **BEJ**

A pair of French bébé boots, to fit a size 13 Jumeau doll, in quilted silk and fake fur trim, with leather soles.

c1890 *3.5in (9cm) high*

£300-350 **BEJ**

ARMAND MARSEILLE

An Armand Marseille mould number 1894 schoolgirl, with bisque head and composition body, in original outfit and lambskin wig.

c1895 *16.5in (42cm) high*

£500-700 **BEJ**

An Armand Marseille bisque-headed doll, mould number 1894, with fixed eyes and jointed composition body.

16in (40cm) high

£80-120 **GORL**

An Armand Marseille bisque-headed doll, mould number 390, with sleepy eyes and jointed composition body.

18in (45cm) high

£180-220 **GORL**

An Armand Marseille shoulder bisque doll, mould number 370, with sleepy eyes and jointed composition body.

17in (42.5cm) high

£100-150 **GORL**

An early 20thC Armand Marseille bisque-headed doll, with sleepy eyes, and jointed composition body.

17in (43cm) high

£120-180 **CHEF**

An early 20thC Armand Marseille bisque-headed doll, with sleepy eyes and open mouth, wearing a green tartan dress, impressed marks.

14.25in 36cm high

£180-220 **CHEF**

HEUBACH

A Gebruder Heubach character boy doll, mould number 7602, with intaglio eyes and interesting outfit.

c1915 *14in (35.5cm) high*

£700-1,000 **BEJ**

A rare German Gebruder Heubach for Einco doll, with lever-moving googlie eyes and composition body.

c1915 *12in (30cm) high*

£2,500-3,000 **BEJ**

A Heubach Koppelsdorf bisque-headed doll, mould number 250, with sleepy eyes and jointed wooden body.

18in (45cm) high

£180-220 **GORL**

OTHER NAMED MAKERS

An Alhaver character child, with hip-jointed toddler's body and fixed paperweight eyes, in original linen outfit.

c1910 *18in (45.5cm) high*

£500-800 **BEJ**

A Paris Danel et Cie bébé, with spring stringing to body.

c1880 *21in (53.5cm) high*

£4,000-6,000 **BEJ**

A French Ettiene Denamur 'Ed' bébé, in original schoolgirl's outfit.

c1890 *13in (33cm) high*

£1,600-1,800 **BEJ**

A Hertol Schwab character boy, with expressive face and rare joined wrists.

c1915 *21in (53.5cm) high*

£1,500-2,000 **BEJ**

A CLOSER LOOK AT A CIRCLE DOT BÉBÉ BRU DOLL

The eyes have striations and are layered with crystals to provide a more realistic effect. These 'paperweight' eyes were the first doll's eyes to have three dimensions.
The bisque head and lower arms of this doll are fragile and prone to damage. It is becoming harder to find dolls of this period in good condition.
This doll is dressed mostly in original costume. The clothes are those of a child, in keeping with the body proportions.
This was one of the first dolls to be modelled as a child (bébé) rather than an adult. The body is plump rather than waisted, and the head is bigger in relation to the body.

An early Circle Dot Bébé Bru doll, with bisque head and lower arms, full kid body and lambskin wig, wearing original outfit.

c1880 *16in (40.5cm) high*

£10,000-14,000 **BEJ**

A black Kammer and Reinhardt child doll, with two outfits and original wig.

c1890 *25in (63.5cm) high*

£1,200-1,800 **BEJ**

A Kammer and Reinhardt 'Mien Leibling' doll, with flirt eyes and original outfit.

c1890 *25in (63.5cm) high*

£2,500-3,000 **BEJ**

A Schoenau and Hoffmeister bisque-headed doll, mould number 1909, with sleepy eyes and composition body.

26in (66cm) high

£120-180 **GORL**

A large Schoeneau and Hoffmeister child doll, with a mohair plush teddy bear.

c1890 *32in (81cm) high*

£700-1,000 **BEJ**

A S.F.B.J.-era tiny bébé, mould number 301, with trunk and extra clothes, dressed in nurse's outfit.

c1910 *11in (28cm) high*

£700-1,000 **BEJ**

A Simon and Halbig child doll, with mohair wig, sleepy eyes and pierced ears, wearing original cotton and lace dress and bonnet.

c1890 *15in (38cm) high*

£700-1,000 **BEJ**

A German Simon and Halbig Kammer and Reinhardt bisque doll, with weighted blue glass eyes, impressed "KR" and "Simon and Halbig 76".

1876 *30in (76cm) high*

£400-600 **HAMG**

A Jules Steiner bisque doll, with closed mouth, fixed blue glass eyes, and ball-jointed wood and composition body with paper label reading "Au nain bleu é chauviere Paris", painted red mark "J Steinr Bbe Sg Dg J Bourgin", impressed "S C 3/0".

11.5in (29cm) high

£2,500-3,000 **HAMG**

A Tom lady doll with cloth body, rivetted joints and sleepy eyes, dressed in an Edwardian outfit.

c1900 *14in (35.5cm) high*

£500-700 **BEJ**

UNNAMED MAKES

A German 'Grape Lady' China-headed doll, with blue painted eyes, crisp nose and mouth, deep sloping shoulders, the cloth body with china limbs, wearing original beige silk and wool challis dress and white ruffled gold snood with a cluster of iridescent cobalt blue grapes, restored.

c1860 *17in (42.5cm) high*

£1,500-2,000 **SK**

A German child doll, with original wig and outfit, marked "890 RM".

c1890 *18in (46cm) high*

£500-700 **BEJ**

A small German China 'fortune teller' doll, with a skirt made of paper fortunes.

c1870 *5in (12.5cm) high*

£220-280 **GORL**

A German bisque-headed boy doll, with sleepy eyes, open mouth and jointed composition body.

24in (60cm) high

£120-180 **GORL**

A bisque bridal half doll, in a dress made from the material used on the original owner's wedding dress, comes with a tooled leather volume containing photographs of the wedding.

c1900 *7in (18cm) high*

£300-400 **BEJ**

A biscaloid girl doll, with finely painted features and five piece body, wearing a floral print dress.

c1925 *9in (23cm) high*

£200-300 **BEJ**

An electric automaton, with glass eyes and velvet costume, papier-mâché head turns from side to side, flag waves and teddy bear moves arms.

c1930 *30in (76cm) high*

£1,000-1,500 **BEJ**

A CLOSER LOOK AT A FRENCH CHILD DOLL

Belton was an early partner in Jumeau who designed this type of doll. His name is now used as a generic term for dolls in this French style, although many of them were actually made in Germany.

The colourful lithograph insert is similar to a Victorian scrap, and depicts children playing in a leafy landscape.

The box contains original clothes, as well as additional accessories of the period, possibly hand-made by the owner's family.

The original box has survived in good condition, adding to the value of the doll.

A French child doll, in layette box with coloured lithograph insert in lid, with extra clothes and accessories.

c1880 *Doll 9.5in (24cm) high*

£2,000-2,500 **BEJ**

A baby in cradle squeak toy, with a blonde papier-mâché doll in a wooden cradle, brightly painted in orange and blue, navy print bedding, bellows at base.

c1870 *2.75in (7cm) long*

£180-220 **SK**

A boxed dancing toy with African-American doll, the rectangular storage box holds the carved and painted doll supported by wirework on two shaped wooden paddles and rectangular platform.

13.5in (34cm) high

£700-1,000 **FRE**

DOLL'S HOUSES

A mid-Victorian dark stained wooden doll's house, with two rooms, old oriental carpeting on floors.

26in (66cm) long

£1,500-2,000 **BEJ**

An American Bliss-type doll's house, with a litho-decorated exterior and fully decorated interior, some damage.

c1885 10.25in (260cm) high

£280-320 **PST**

A painted W.P.A. plaster model of the historic Neo-classical house Woodlands in Pittsburgh Pennsylvania, mounted on a plaster plinth inscribed "Late Georgian Woodland House, 1788 Philadelphia, PA," a small W.P.A. District stamp at back, some paint loss.

c1935 15in (37.5cm) wide

£300-500 **FRE**

A CLOSER LOOK AT A NOAH'S ARK SET

There are sixty pairs of animals included with this ark. The number of complete pairs has an affect on its value, but is not as important as the overall quality of the carving and painting.

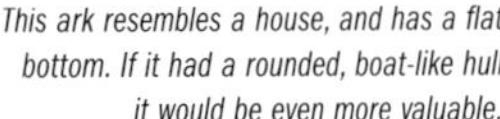

This ark resembles a house, and has a flat bottom. If it had a rounded, boat-like hull it would be even more valuable.

Arks that are heavily or clumsily restored will be worth less than examples in good original condition, like this one.

These arks were made by craftsmen throughout Europe and the US, and appeal to collectors of both toys and folk art.

A late 19thC German carved and painted Noah's Ark set, with sixty pairs of animals and three human figures.

19.5in (49.5cm) long

£4,000-6,000 **POOK**

A late 19thC folk art cut tin and polychrome model building, with glass windows and faux stone painted sides, spread-winged eagle weathervane atop a steeple and dome clock tower, inscribed "Academy of Fine Art", signed "F.A. Wigton" in the clock face, resting on a carved wooden stand.

59in (150cm) high

£1,500-2,000 **POOK**

A 20thC Shaker-style wooden doll's house with miniature Shaker furnishings, the exterior a replica of a Shaker Trustees' Office, with painted sign, the interior rooms furnished with an assortment of miniature handmade Shaker wooden furniture, including tables, chairs, cupboards, desks, counter, beds, and wood boxes, also several Shaker-style stoves, bedding, rugs, and other small accessories, several signed "Don Crossen".

36in (90cm) wide

£5,000-6,000 **SK**

An American wooden Noah's Ark, by Rochers, with litho-print decoration and hinged lid, animals missing.

c1890 12.5in (32cm) long

£200-250 **PST**

DOLL'S HOUSE FURNITURE

A doll's spindle-turned fruitwood chair.

c1880 *13in (33cm) high*

£200-250 **BEJ**

An American contemporary limited edition doll's chair, hand carved by an Appalachian craftsman.

c1960 *11in (28cm) high*

£60-90 **BEJ**

A miniature bureau bookcase in burr walnut, with mirrored upper doors and four drawers.

c1900 *27in (68.5cm) high*

£800-1,200 **BEJ**

A doll's dresser, in dark stained wood with opening doors and drawers.

c1920 *13in (33cm) high*

£80-120 **BEJ**

A late 19thC pine doll's cradle, from Quebec.

19.5in (49.5cm) long

£80-120 **BP**

A French wicker doll's cradle, with original bedding.

c1890 *23in (58.5cm) long*

£300-400 **BEJ**

A doll's bonnet in original hat box, with faint maker's stamp.

c1910 *9in (23cm) wide*

£200-300 **BEJ**

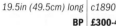

An assembled collection of 19thC and 20thC copper and brass doll's house metalware, including pots, pans, bedwarmer, scuttle, tea kettles, coffee mill and colander.

Provenance: *From the collection of Vivian Greene, wife of author Graham Greene.*

£2,500-3,000 **POOK**

BEARS & SOFT TOYS Steiff

A Steiff bear, with boot button eyes, stitched woollen nose and claws, blank "Steiff" button in ear.

1905 *10in (25.5cm) high*

£1,800-2,200 **HGS**

A Steiff cinnamon bear, pad feet, stitched woollen nose and claws, boot bead eyes.

1905 *16in (40.5cm) high*

£5,000-6,000 **HGS**

A Steiff teddy bear, with pad feet, some exposed straw, stitched woollen nose and claws and boot bead eyes.

c1905 *13in (33cm) high*

£1,500-2,000 **HGS**

A CLOSER LOOK AT A STEIFF BEAR

Fewer Steiff bears were produced in white than in other colours such as brown or black, making this bear a highly prized item.

The boot bead eyes of this bear date him from before 1920, when Steiff introduced glass eyes.

This bear has an appealing face and his stuffing still fills his body well. The overall look of a bear can be an important factor in determining value.

This bear retains his original foot pads and nose stitching whereas many if his counterparts would have these areas restored due to wear.

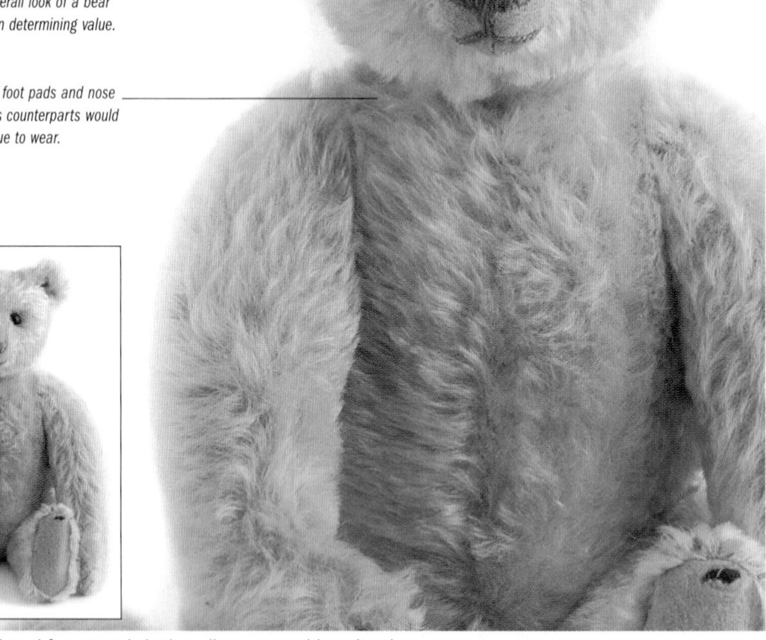

A white Steiff bear, with pad feet, tan stitched woollen nose and boot bead eyes.

18in (45.5cm) high

£6,000-8,000 **TCT**

A dark brown Steiff bear, with glass eyes, pad feet and black woollen nose.

c1920 *18in (45.5cm) high*

£5,000-7,000 **HGS**

A blonde Steiff bear, with brown stitched woollen nose, glass eyes and pad feet.

c1920 *18in (45.5cm) high*

£4,000-6,000 **HGS**

A small blonde Steiff bear, with glass eyes and brown stitched nose and claws.

8.5in (21.5cm) high

£800-1,200 **HGS**

A pair of dark brown Steiff bears, with traditional dress, original paper tags, ear studs with block-printed "Steiff" logo, and "Made in US Zone Germany" tags.

c1945 *9in (23cm) high*

£2,000-3,000 **HGS**

A Steiff koala bear in mint condition, with glass eyes, felt feet and nose, ear stud with raised "Steiff" logo, original fabric tag and paper medallion.

6in (15cm) high

£800-1,200 **HGS**

OTHER BEARS

A large Chad Valley blonde mohair teddy bear, with black stitched snout, amber glass eyes and swivel-jointed body with rexine pads, label on foot.

c1955 *30in (76cm) high*

£200-300 **HAMG**

A Cramer musical bear, the mechanism operated by moving neck up and down, with stitched woollen nose and claws.

c1930 *18in (45.5cm) high*

£3,000-4,000 **TCT**

A Petsy Bear 'Baby Bear', of soft-filled white mohair tipped with red, with distinctive seam along head and across ears.

Steiff only produced the Petsy bear for two years (1928-30), yet it ranks among their most celebrated creations. It was marketed by the company as the 'Baby Bear' due to its bright blue eyes and childish demeanour.

c1930 *12.5in (32cm) high*

£8,000-10,000 **TCT**

An American gold mohair bear, with celluloid weighted eyes, pad feet, and black stitched woollen nose.

c1925 *18in (45.5cm) high*

£3,000-4,000 **TCT**

A 1930s brown teddy bear with a black scarf.

14in (35.5cm) high

£60-90 **GEW**

CLOCKWORK TOYS

An Andre Citröen painted tinplate model open four-seater tourer, the red body with black wings and silvered running boards, with leatherette seats and gearstick linked to the clockwork motor, registration number "142-E-3".

15in (38cm) long

£700-1,000 **CHEF**

A Marklin Constructor clockwork model Mercedes Benz racing car, with single red seat and blue exhaust, the silver body numbered "1".

10.5in (27cm) long

£300-500 **CHEF**

A French C.I.J. tinplate clockwork model Alpha Romeo P2 vintage racing car, with three petrol caps, badge above the grill, starting handle, front suspension, steering wheel, hand brake and spoked wheels with black tyres, the red body with stencilled clover leaf emblems and numbered "2" some losses.

20.5in (52cm) long

£2,000-2,500 **CHEF**

A Kingsbury clockwork model of the record-breaking 'Golden Arrow' car, the pressed metal body with gold finish, Dunlop rubber tyres, and driver.

20in (51cm) long

£700-1,000 **CHEF**

A British tinplate clockwork model sedan car, the orange body with lithographed detail, the boot with an operating lever.

13in (33cm) long

£50-80 **CHEF**

A scarce C.K.O. tinplate clockwork convertible Volkswagen Beetle, model 359, finished in brown and beige, with a mechanism to convert the cab top from open-top to saloon car, with steerable front wheels and key, in original box, made in the US Zone of Germany.

6.25in (16cm) long

£100-150 **W&W**

A large wooden clockwork boat, 'The Scotland', complete with tender, wooden sailors and cargo in hold.

c1910 *35in (89cm) long*

£700-1,000 **BEJ**

A scarce early Sutcliffe clockwork speed boat, with a red and cream hull and a cream deck, wooden hatch cover over the motor, the rear cockpit with brake lever and tiller bar to control rudder.

16in (40.5cm) long

£120-180 **W&W**

A scarce Hornby speed boat, "Number 4 Venture", with a light green hull and a cream deck, saloon style cabin top, brake and rudder steering bar, in the remains of an original box, with original instruction sheet and replacement key, minor wear.

16in (40.5cm) long

£150-200 **W&W**

A scarce Arnold tinplate clockwork single-seat rowing boat, model number 2030, with cream and light blue painted hull with articulated composition figure operating two yellow tinplate oars, in original box with key, marked "Made in US Zone Germany", minor wear and paint loss.

8.5in (21.5cm) wide

£350-400 **W&W**

A tinplate submarine, painted in matt grey, with clockwork four-blade propeller, cannon, rudder, conning tower, gun and bow platforms, moveable dive planes to stern and added weight under the keel, complete with key and hand-made box.

14.5in (37cm) long

£300-350 **W&W**

A Technofix tinplate clockwork car elevator, model number 266, with two cars and an extending track, in original box, made in the US Zone of Germany, some wear to toy and tears to box.

c1945 *16in (40.5cm) wide*

£80-120 **W&W**

A clockwork fur dog, with moving legs and ringing collar bell.

c1920 *6.5in (16.5cm) long*

£70-100 **BEJ**

A tinplate clockwork tortoise, with moving legs.

c1920 *6in (15cm) long*

£30-40 **BEJ**

A clockwork elephant in velvet plush, with lumbering movement.

c1920 *6in (15cm) long*

£200-250 **BEJ**

An Art Deco dog with a magnetic bone toy.

c1930 *5in (12.5cm) high*

£30-40 **BEJ**

A Japanese clockwork puppy with bone, with running movement, in original box.

c1930 *4in (10cm) high*

£150-200 **BEJ**

CORGI

A scarce Corgi Fiat Ghia 600 Jolly, model number 240, in light metallic blue with a red interior and sun canopy, boxed, complete with packing ring.

3.25in (8.25cm) long

£180-220 **W&W**

A Corgi Austin A60 'Motor School' car, model number 236, in light blue, boxed.

3.75in (9.5cm) long

£100-150 **W&W**

A Corgi Mini Cooper 'Monte Carlo', model number 321, with red body and white roof, marked with rally number "2", and red printed panel "The 1965 Monte Carlo Winner", with facsimile signatures for Timo Makinen and Paul Easter, in an earlier 321 box.

c1965 *2.75in (7cm) long*

£200-300 **W&W**

A Corgi Decca Mobile airfield radar, model number 1106, in cream and orange striped livery, boxed.

5.5in (14cm) long

£50-80 **W&W**

A Corgi Midland Red 'Motorway Express' coach, model number 1120, in red with a black roof, boxed.

5.25in (13.5cm) long

£100-150 **W&W**

An early Corgi Riley Pathfinder saloon car, model number 205, in red, boxed.

4in (10cm) long

£60-90 **W&W**

A Corgi 'Chipperfield's Circus Mobile Booking Office', model number 426, in standard livery, boxed.

3.5in (9cm) long

£180-220 **W&W**

An early Corgi 'Batmobile', model number 267, with Batman and Robin figures, gold wheel hubs, rockets, Batman logo, pulsating exhaust flame and aerial, boxed, with an inner display sleeve and operating instructions.

5in (12.75cm) long

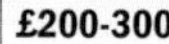

£200-300 **W&W**

A Corgi number 16 gift set, comprising a metallic blue 'Ecurie Ecosse' car transporter, a Vanwall in red, a Mark II Lotus racing car in blue, and a BRM in turquoise, with original box.

Transporter 7.75in (19.5cm) long

£300-500 **W&W**

A Corgi number 17 gift set, comprising a Land Rover with a Ferrari racing car on the trailer, in red and yellow livery, boxed, with insert.

8.25in (21cm) long

£180-220 **W&W**

Two Corgi cars, comprising a Chrysler Imperial, model number 246, in deep red, and a Ford Mustang 'Fastback 2+2', model number 320, in metallic lilac, both boxed.

Largest 4.25in (10.75cm) long

£150-200 **W&W**

Two Corgi cars, comprising a Simca 1000 competition model, model number 315, in a plated finish, and a NSU Sport Prinz, model number 316, in metallic pink, both boxed.

Largest 3.5in (9cm) long

£80-120 **W&W**

Two Corgi vehicles, comprising a Mercedes Benz 220 SE coupe, model number 230, in maroon, and a Volkswagen Kombi, model number 434, in light green, both boxed.

Largest 4in (10cm) long

£120-180 **W&W**

Two Corgi cars, comprising a Studebaker 'Golden Hawk', model number 211S, with plated finish, and a Plymouth sports suburban station wagon, model number 219, in cream with a light brown roof, both boxed.

Largest 4in (10cm) long

£100-150 **W&W**

Two Corgi cars, comprising a Lotus Mk II Le Mans racing car, model number 151, in blue, and a Rover 2000, model number 252, in metallic blue, both boxed.

Largest 3.75in (9.5cm) long

£120-180 **W&W**

Two Corgi TV and film cars, comprising a James Bond Aston Martin DB, model number 261, with a gold body, red interior figure and secret instructions leaflet, and a 'Man from UNCLE Thrush-Buster Oldsmobile', model number 497, in metallic blue, both in original box with inner display sleeve.

Largest 4.25in (10.75cm) long

£300-400 **W&W**

DINKY

A Dinky Jaguar XK 120 coupe, model number 157, in red, boxed, inner flap missing.

3.75in (9.5cm) long

£100-150 **W&W**

A Dinky Riley saloon, model number 158, in cream with green wheel hubs, boxed.

3.5in (9cm) long

£70-100 **W&W**

A Dinky AC Aceca coupe, model number 167, in light grey and red, with spun wheel hubs, boxed.

3.5in (9cm) long

£80-120 **W&W**

A Dinky Singer Gazelle, model number 168, in two-tone light grey and dark green, with spun wheel hubs, boxed.

3.5in (9cm) long

£80-120 **W&W**

A Dinky 'FAB1' Rolls Royce, model number 100, with second edition wheels, complete with rocket and missile.

5.75in (14.5cm) long

£180-220 **W&W**

A Dinky Supertoys Mighty Antar low loader with propeller, model number 986, in red and light grey, with original gold coloured Scimitar propeller, boxed with packaging.

12in (30cm) long

£200-250 **W&W**

A Dinky Supertoys orange lorry mounted cement mixer, model number 960, with blue and yellow drum, boxed.

5in (12.75cm) long

£100-150 **W&W**

A Dinky Supertoys 'Big Bedford' Heinz van, model number 923, in standard livery, with baked bean can design to sides, boxed.

5.5in (14cm) long

£200-250 **W&W**

A Dinky Supertoys B.B.C. TV 'roving eye vehicle', model number 968, complete with detachable aerial, boxed.

4.25in (11cm) long

£80-120 **W&W**

A Dinky Supertoys Marrel 'multi-bucket unit', model number 966, in yellow with a light grey skip, boxed.

4.5in (11.5cm) long

£120-180 **W&W**

Two Dinky Supertoys, comprising a Blaw Knox bulldozer, model number 961, in red, and a Commercial Servicing platform vehicle, model number 977, in cream and red, with paperwork, both boxed.

5.5in (14cm) long

£150-200 **W&W**

A Dinky Austin Seven 'Countryman' Mini, model number 199, in light blue with red interior, and a Spot On BMW Isetta, model number 118, in lilac, both boxed.

Largest 2.75in (7cm) long

£120-180 **W&W**

A French Dinky American DUKW amphibious vehicle, in olive green, complete with all accessories and driver.

6.75in (17cm) long

£50-80 **W&W**

A Dinky Caravelle SE 210 Airliner, model number 997, in silver, white and blue Air France livery, with metal undercarriage wheels, wing markings "F-BGNY", in original picture box with internal packing strip.

6.75in (17cm) long

£50-80 **W&W**

CARS

A C.I.J. tinplate and clockwork Alfa Romeo P2 toy racing car, finished in silver with red numerals, damage.

c1930 *21.25in (54cm) long*

£800-1,200 **HAMG**

A Matchbox Series No22 Vauxhall crester, in pink, no plastic windows, minor chips.

2.5in (6.5cm) wide

£50-80 **W&W**

A Meccano No.1 Constructor Car for the French market, the two seater open tourer in blue and cream with red seats.

8.25in (21cm) long

£200-250 **CHEF**

A scarce Prameta Buick 405 sedan, painted in bright red, complete with key in the shape of a man.

5.5in (14cm) long

£80-120 **W&W**

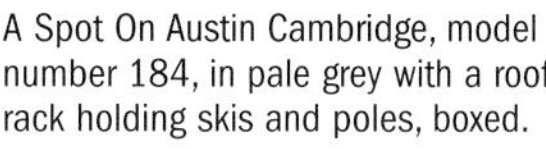

A Spot On Austin Cambridge, model number 184, in pale grey with a roof rack holding skis and poles, boxed.

4.25in (11cm) long

£70-100 **W&W**

A 1960s Tri-Ang pedal car, in the style of a Renault veteran car, with spoked wheels solid rubber tyres, ackerman steering and registration "LBL 4242".

3.5in (9cm) long

£100-150 **W&W**

An early 20thC Pennsylvania carved and painted pull-toy, the figure of an eagle perched on a log painted in shapes of brown, green, yellow, grey, black and red, with hand-made flapping mechanism, paint paint cracking.

13in (32.5cm) long

£1,500-2,000 **FRE**

TRAINS

A French Hornby 'O' gauge Number 1 locotender, marked "ETAT 040", black.

c1925 *10.5in (26.5cm) long*

£150-180 **L&T**

A French Hornby 'O' gauge Number 0 locomotive and tender, with lined splasher and French mechanism, locomotive marked "EST" and tender marked "2710".

c1930 *16.5in (42cm) long*

£400-600 **L&T**

A French Hornby 'O' gauge Number 1 locotender, marked "PLM" and "D20512"in maroon, late body shape.

c1935 *10.25in (26cm) long*

£220-280 **L&T**

A Hornby export E420 'Eton' locomotive, with FCO LNER pattern tender and front bulb, no 'Hornby' transfer, some wear.

c1940 *17in (43cm) long*

£1,000-1,500 **L&T**

An early Lines Brothers wooden toy train.

39in (99cm) long

£800-1,200 **BEJ**

An early Lines Brothers wooden toy train, with original paint work.

c1900 *13in (33cm) long*

£800-1,200 **BEJ**

An early 20thC tinplate electric train set, by American Flyer Mfg Co. lithographed, including 'Lexington' passenger car, 'Paul Revere' passenger car, and 'United States Mail Railway Post Office', with lithographed tin bridge, American Flyer transformer, two illuminated switches, eleven sections of straight track and eight sections of curved track, with original box.

20in (51cm) long

£280-320 **S&K**

A 'Colman's Mustard' covered luggage van.

c1925 *5in (12.5cm) long*

£1,000-1,500 **L&T**

A Hornby Number 2 locomotive and tender, in Southern green.

1928 *16.75in (42.5cm) long*

£500-800 **L&T**

A Hornby Number 2 Special locomotive and tender, with black bogie, cab lined, tender unlined, marked "Southern A759", restored.

1929 *16.75in (42.5cm) long*

£800-1,200 **L&T**

A Hornby E220 Special locomotive and tender, marked "LMS 1185"

c1935 *16.25in (41.5cm) long*

£800-1,200 **L&T**

A CLOSER LOOK AT A HORNBY 'SOUTHERN' LOCOMOTIVE

The Number 2 locomotive was introduced in 1921 and withdrawn in 1929. It was only available in 'Southern' colours between 1928-29.

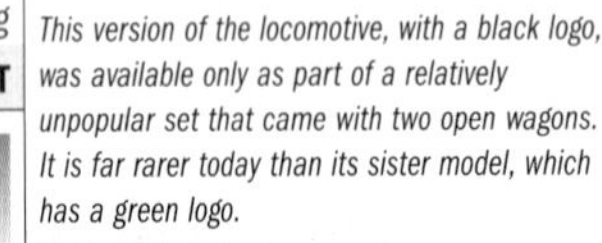

There is some restoration to this train, but it has been done sympathetically by an expert. Every nut and bolt is present and in the correct position.

This version of the locomotive, with a black logo, was available only as part of a relatively unpopular set that came with two open wagons. It is far rarer today than its sister model, which has a green logo.

The Hornby black 'Southern' livery is the rarest of all the liveries they produced for the home market, and is especially hard to find on a Number 2 locomotive.

A Hornby Number 2 locomotive and tender, in black livery, with painted brass dome marked "Southern E510".

1928 *16.75in (42.5cm) long*

£2,000-3,000 **L&T**

A LE220 Swiss type Locomotive, with 1933 brush-cap mechanism, in green and red with cream roof.

This locomotive has been fitted with number 3 pony trucks. This was an enhancement recommended by Meccano Magazine in the early 1930s, but was never adopted by the factory.

1933 *9.5in (24cm) long*

£1,200-1,800 **L&T**

A LE220 Swiss type locomotive, with 1934 fibreboard mechanism, in cream and blue, with blue roof, restored.

1934 *9.5in (24cm) long*

£700-800 **L&T**

A CLOSER LOOK AT A LOCOMOTIVE

Although relatively common, this train raised a very high sum at auction because of its condition, which is very nearly mint.

This version of the No2 locomotive replaced that which was withdrawn in 1929, and was available until 1942. It was only produced in this particular livery during the first year of its production.

Tenders were usually supplied separately from the trains, so many of them did not exactly match their locomotives.

This tender can be ascribed to the second issue as it has a black bogie, as opposed to the earlier models, which had nickel bogies.

A Number 2 Special locomotive and tender, with silver vac pipe, unlined tender, and black bogie, marked "LMS 1185".

1930 *16.75in (42.5cm) long*

£2,500-3,000 **L&T**

A Hornby E220 Special locomotive and tender, 'The Bramham Motor', in dark green livery, marked "LNER 201", tender boxed.

1937 *16.5in (42cm) long*

£1,000-1,500 **L&T**

A Hornby E320 locomotive and tender, in gloss brown livery with brown smokebox and deflectors, marked "Nord 3, 1290", complete with inserts and spanner.

1938 *17in (43cm) long*

£1,800-2,200 **L&T**

A Hornby E220 Special locomotive and tender, marked "Southern 1759 L1".

1938 16in (40.5cm) l.

£1,500-2,000 **L&T**

A No3 Mitropa sleeper coach, with rivetted couplings, and corridor connection, no trade mark.

1940 13in (33cm) long

£1,500-2,000 **L&T**

A Hornby export E320 locomotive and tender, matt black, with FCS LMS pattern tender, marked "1290".

c1940 *16.5in (42cm) long*

£1,500-2,000 **L&T**

A wooden trolley car child's toy.

c1935 *17.5in (44.5cm) long*

£500-700 **BP**

A rare export Number 1 signal box transformer and controller.

6.5in (16.5cm) wide

£300-400 **L&T**

A CLOSER LOOK AT A HORNBY EXPORT LOCOMOTIVE

This is an extremely rare export Hornby engine made for the Argentine market.

This series was produced between 1937-38 in the 'Southern' green livery. It was available in black only by special request to the Hornby factory or, as is the case with this model, as an Argentine export.

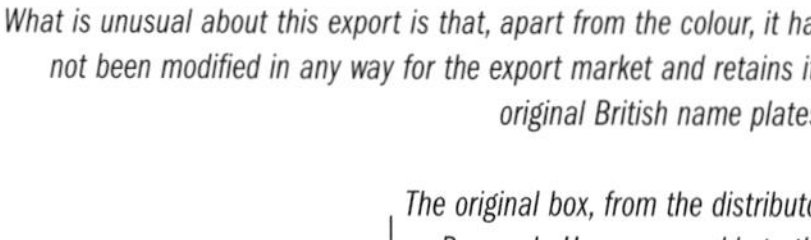

What is unusual about this export is that, apart from the colour, it has not been modified in any way for the export market and retains its original British name plates.

The original box, from the distributor Burnando Hermanon, adds to the value of this locomotive.

A very rare Hornby export E420 'Eton' locomotive, in matt black goods livery, together with 1937 box for Burnando Hermanon of Buenos Aires.

1937

£2,200-2,800 **L&T**

MILITARY

A scarce Hugar British Guard House, set number 1734, with canopied front, opening door three wired windows, removable gabled roof finished in grey and stained walls.

c1940 *8.25in (21cm) wide*

£250-350 **W&W**

A scarce Astra diecast 'Ack Ack' gun, mounted on a four-wheel drop-centre trailer, gun rotates and fires caps, with operating battery searchlight mounted to the rear of the trailer.

11in (28cm) long

£100-150 **W&W**

One of a set of three scarce Bullock model guns, of diecast construction with spring firing action, by MSR Toys Ltd of Brighton, in original boxes.

11in (28cm) long

£100-150 set **W&W**

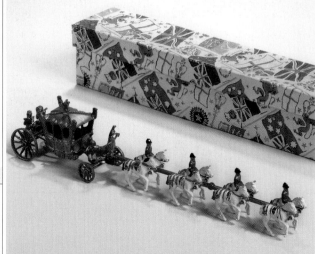

A metal coronation coach, decorated with paint and gilding, complete with original box decorated with flags of the Commonwealth.

c1950 *12in (30cm) long*

£180-220 **BEJ**

MODEL SHIPS

An American wooden shadowbox, by Mr Tucker of Tucker Castle, depicting a steam-sail schooner.
c1870 *35.5in (90cm) wide*
£1,000-1,500 PST

A late 19th/early 20thC shadowbox, with carved and painted three-masted ship.
13.25in (33cm) wide
£400-600 FRE

A 19thC half hull model 'SS Okement', built by Messrs Wm. Pickersgill and Sons Ltd of Southwick Sunderland, set on mirror background, in glazed mahogany case.
60in (150cm) wide
£2,000-3,000 L&T

A model of the Govan Ferry 'Number 1' shipyard, on an ebonized and gilt plinth, with framed perspex cover.
63.25in (158cm) wide
£2,000-3,000 L&T

A mid-19thC unrigged dockyard model of a two-deck 94-gun ship of the line, with three stepped lower masts, and a carved bust figurehead, the hull with decorated quarter galleries, on a mahogany stand, some damage to the keel.
16.25in (41cm) long
£600-900 DN

A model of an 18thC Spanish 'Man of War' naval ship, from a plank-on-frame wooden kit, with two gun decks and open gunports, fully rigged, with a San Juan Nepomuceno nameplate.
38in (96.5cm) long
£180-220 W&W

An American hand-carved folk art boat.
c1880 *22in (56cm) long*
£280-320 BCAC

A 20thC carved wooden model of a galleon, on a trestle base.
42in (106.5cm) wide
£300-400 S&K

A 20thC scale model of the racing yacht 'America', mounted in a plexiglass case.
34in (85cm) long
£400-600 S&K

A 20thC scale model of the riverboat 'Tennessee', mounted in a plexiglass case.
27in (67.5cm) long
£700-1,000 S&K

An early 20thC painted wood and cloth pond yacht, with a wooden stand.
82in (205cm) high
£700-1,000 S&K

MONEY BOXES

A mechanical bank with wooden soldiers, the figures in red uniforms and black hats facing trapezoidal towers with slots, the prototype for a cast-iron mechanical bank.
10in (25cm) high
£1,000-1,500 NA

A 19thC painted cast iron 'Tammany Bank', cast as a seated banker with moving head and arm.
6in (15cm) high
£600-900 S&K

An American painted cast iron mechanical bank, by J. and E. Stevens Co. of Cromwell Connecticut, modelled as a black man with moving arm, tongue and eyes.
7in (18cm) high
£600-900 S&K

OTHER TOYS

A German folk art fabric-covered rocking horse, complete with saddle, on a painted plinth, mounted with wheels that detach from the rails, marked "Bauer 4 Krause".

c1900

£400-600 **WAD**

A rare rattan and cane rocking duck, unknown maker.

c1900 *26in (66cm) wide*

£400-600 **BEJ**

An American wooden horse and cart, by S.A. Smith of Battleboro Vermont, with movable wheels and "Sunnyside Farm" inscription.

c1900 23.5in (60cm) l.

£500-700 **PST**

A pair of Mickey and Minnie Mouse toys by Knickerbocker, with cloth bodies, composition shoes, blue and green polkadot clown outfits and maker's tag.

11in (27.5cm) high

£4,000-6,000 **SK**

An American squeaky wolf puppet, with a papier mâché body, on a wooden and fabric base.

c1885 *5in (13cm) high*

£300-400 **PST**

A Bing painted tin model of a diver, wearing helmet and weighted boots, holding a knife and axe, some losses.

8.25in (21cm) high

£180-220 **CHEF**

An American 'Roly Poly' painted papier mâché Santa toy, by Albert Schoenhut.

c1895 *12in (30.5cm) high*

£800-1,200 **PST**

An American 'cheeky boy' toy target, litho-printed on card with a fabric tongue.

c1900 *16in (41cm) high*

£100-150 **PST**

Two wooden Easter eggs, with silk covering, for holding small treasures and gifts.

c1890 *5in (12.5cm) high*

£200-300 **BEJ**

An early 19thC turned toy top, with red, yellow, blue and green stripes.

3in (7.5cm) high

£500-700 **POOK**

A Pennsylvania painted child's drum, with applied wallpaper band with white, green, yellow, and blue floral decoration.

c1830 *8in (20cm) diam*

£220-280 **POOK**

An early 20thC tin mechanical musical toy, in the form of a cathedral organ, by J. Chein and Co.

9.25in (23cm) high

£150-200 **S&K**

A Masanori Umeda for Memphis limited edition 'Ginza Mobile robot', of plastic, laminated wood, and metal, in original wooden crate, signed to base and numbered 69/500.

1982 11.5in (29cm) h.

£400-600 **DRA**

CHESS SETS

An English ivory chess set.
c1860 *King 2.75in (7cm) high*
£300-400 **CO**

A small English bone chess set.
c1870 *King 2.75in (7cm) high*
£80-120 **CO**

A 19thC bone Selenus chess set, from Nuremberg.
King 4.75in (12cm) high
£400-600 **CO**

A 20thC Goan ivory playing part chess set.
King 3in (7.5cm) high
£220-280 **CO**

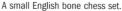

A 20thC carved jade figural chess set, Indian or Chinese.
King 1.5in (4cm) high
£800-1,200 **CO**

A 20thC German carved ivory figural 'Erbach' chess set.
£1,200-1,800 **CO**

A Czechoslovakian glass 'Jan Masaryk' bust chess set.
c1950 *King 3.25in (8cm) high*
£80-120 **CO**

A 20thC Islamic metal chess set, from Agra, the knights with coloured plastic heads.
King 2.25in (5.5cm) high
£500-700 **CO**

A 20thC South American-style bone chess set, from Mexico.
King 5.5in (14cm) high
£100-150 **CO**

A 20thC Italian painted lead chess set, with mythological figures.
King 5in (13cm) high
£800-1,200 **CO**

A hand-carved wooden animal chess set, by Ben Greisham, one side in a darker coloured wood, signed and dated.
1976 *King 3in (7.5cm) high*
£280-320 **FRE**

A carved wooden 'Country' figural chess set, one side in a paler coloured softwood, the pieces on a rural theme.
King 6in (15cm) high
£220-280 **FRE**

An Argentine clay modelled folk art chess set, one side in a darker coloured clay.
King 5in (12.5cm) high
£30-50 **FRE**

A Cretan metal figural chess set, one side a gold colour, the other side black.
King 6in (15cm) high
£100-150 **FRE**

A polychrome decorated ceramic figural 'Broadway versus Hollywood' chess set, by Doug Anderson, number 2 of an edition of 25, the pieces representing musicals and cinema, all on circular gilded bases, the rook signed by the artist.

King 10in (25.4cm) high

£3,000-4,000 **FRE**

A 19thC Italian pietra dura circular specimen chess board, set in a black composition, inlaid with specimen hard stones alternating with black granite and framed with a band of verde antico marble, surrounded by four micromosaic vedute, each depicting a scene in Rome.

18in (45cm) diam

£4,000-6,000 **S&K**

An Italian filigree metal 'Fiorentino' chess set, one side gilded, with an Italian wooden games table, the fitted chess board revealing an inset backgammon board, on a base of stepped square section.

27.5in (69.8cm) high

£150-200 **FRE**

An Italian 'Camelot' metal figural chess set, hand-painted with green and red highlights, together with a blue painted games table, the decorated top over a baluster-knopped column on tri-form base.

King 3.5in (8.8cm) high

£100-150 **FRE**

A carved wooden chess set and table of large size, the pieces in medieval dress, one side with a dark stain, the other side with a light stain, with a wooden chess table.

King 8.7in (22cm) high

£600-900 **FRE**

A 20thC Italian gilt metal figural chess set, the pieces in traditional medieval dress, together with an onyx-mounted chess board on raised feet.

King 6in (15cm) high

£700-1,000 **FRE**

A Mexican polychrome decorated bone 'bust' set, one side with figures stained light blue, the other side pink, in a board that doubles as a box.

Box 17.5in (44.5cm) wide

£500-700 **FRE**

A Pennsylvanian folk art game board.

18in (45cm) wide

£800-1,200 **TA**

ANTIQUITIES

Over the past year the market in ancient art has enjoyed steady growth and is generally looking very healthy. Egyptian artefacts in particular have become significantly more expensive, due in no small part to the activity of a few serious and determined collectors at the high end of the market. Decorative pieces are very much in vogue – a good Greek bowl will look equally at home in a minimalist modern lounge space as in a cluttered panelled library – and prices reflect this.

Perhaps the key to the current popularity of ancient artefacts is that many people perceive them to be very reasonably priced when compared to more recent antiques. There is, however, a finite supply: fewer and fewer new items find their way on to the market and many of the pieces available today are from old collections that have been split up and sold off. As demand rises and supply falls away, prices will inevitably increase.

Recent sales of ancient weaponry have attracted huge interest and made a great deal of money, as have sales of ancient art on the European mainland.

Reputable dealers will usually offer some sort of guarantee that the artefacts they offer for sale are genuine antiquities as described. In some cases, documentation providing carbon-dating results or other scientific proof of age can be supplied. Buyers should be aware that reproductions and fakes are in circulation and they can fool all but the most expert scholars. Members of the Antiquities Dealers Association undertake not to sell any artefacts they believe to have been removed from their country of origin illegally.

Chris Martin, Ancient Art

ROMAN

A Roman pottery lamp, depicting a bust of Mercury, messenger of the gods.

cAD1-200 *4in (10cm) long*

£400-500 **ANA**

A Roman black glazed terracotta discus lamp, with floral pattern.

cAD1-200 *3.25in (8.5cm) long*

£100-150 **ANA**

A Roman red glazed terracotta discus lamp, with gladiatorial scene.

cAD100-200 *4.5in (11.5cm) long*

£1,000-1,500 **ANA**

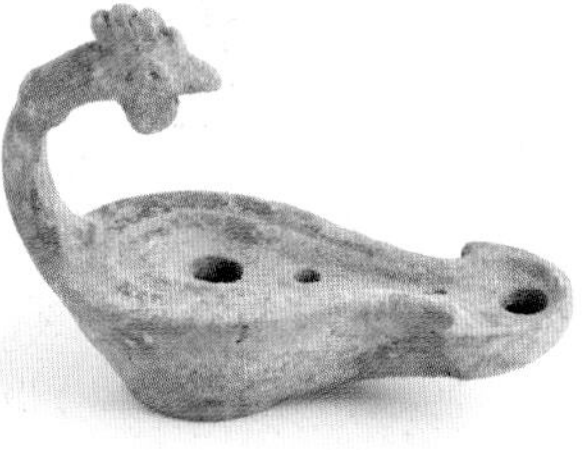

A Roman pottery lamp, the handle in the form of a cockerel.

cAD100-200 *5in (12.5cm) long*

£250-350 **ANA**

A Roman orange glazed terracotta discus lamp, with a Hercules scene on the discus.

cAD100-200 *4in (10cm) long*

£200-250 **ANA**

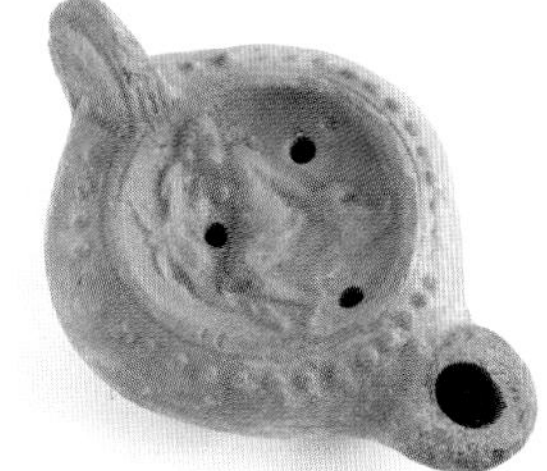

A Roman pottery lamp, the discus depicting a semi-draped seated goddess.

cAD200-300 *4in (10cm) long*

£200-300 **ANA**

A Roman pottery lamp, the discus depicting a boy holding a club.

cAD100-200 *3.5in (9cm) long*

£150-200 **ANA**

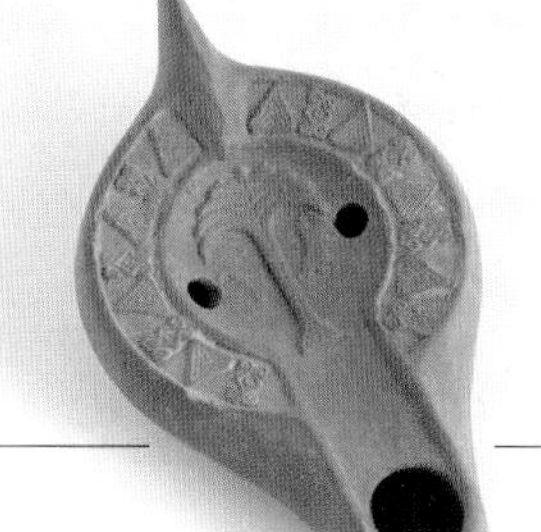

A Roman north African pottery lamp, the discus depicting rabbits running up a palm tree.

cAD400-500 *5.5in (14cm) long*

£150-200 **ANA**

A Roman north African redware pottery wine flagon, with applied figurative design.

cAD100-200 *8.5in (21.5cm) high*

£400-600 **ANA**

A Roman European buff pottery mug, in the form of the head of Dionysus.

cAD100-200 *6.25in (16cm) high*

£1,000-1,500 **ANA**

A Roman north African redware pottery wine flagon.

cAD100-200 *6.25in (16cm) high*

£150-200 **ANA**

A Roman European buffware pottery wine flask, with ribbed body.

cAD200-300 *6.5in (16.5cm) high*

£100-150 **ANA**

A Roman translucent blue and green glass flask, with pear shaped body, excellent iridescence.

cAD200-300 *6in (15cm) high*

£1,000-1,200 **ANA**

A Roman translucent blue and green square bodied flask, with small handle.

cAD300-500 *7.75in (19.5cm) high*

£1,000-1,200 **ANA**

A Roman aubergine sprinkler flask, with pinched glass nodules around the body.

cAD200-400 *4.25in (11cm) high*

£300-500 **ANA**

A Roman translucent green and blue glass jar, with two handles and a ribbed body, good iridescence.

cAD200-400 *4.5in (11.5cm) high*

£800-900 **ANA**

A Roman translucent green and blue glass jar with indented body, good iridescence.

cAD200-400 *3.5in (9cm) high*

£500-600 **ANA**

A Roman translucent green and blue glass jar with two handles, good iridescence.

cAD200-400 *3.25in (8.5cm) high*

£400-600 **ANA**

A Roman translucent blue and green wine cup, with indented body and small foot.

cAD100-300 *3.5in (9cm) high*

£300-350 **ANA**

A Roman disc brooch, decorated and gilded and set with a black gem stone, complete with pin.

cAD100-200 *1in (2.5cm) high*

£200-300 **ANA**

A Roman bronze brooch, in the form of a cross, the arms decorated with ring and dot decoration, complete with pin.

cAD100-200 *1.5in (4cm) long*

£150-200 **ANA**

A Roman bronze lunar and phallic pendant, used to ward off the evil eye, with loop for suspension.

cAD200-300 *2in (5cm) high*

£100-140 **ANA**

A Roman rabbit brooch, the body carved with two baby rabbits.

cAD200-300 *1in (2.5cm) long*

£70-100 **ANA**

A Roman silver fibula brooch with wings, complete with pin.

cAD100-200 *1.25in (3cm) long*

£150-200 **ANA**

A Roman silver brooch, depicting a vessel flanked by a pair of dolphins.

1in (2.5cm) long

£300-350 **ANA**

A Roman iron fibula brooch, finely set with gold and silver inlay.

It is very rare for a brooch of this type to retain its inlay.

1.5in (4cm) long

£600-800 **ANA**

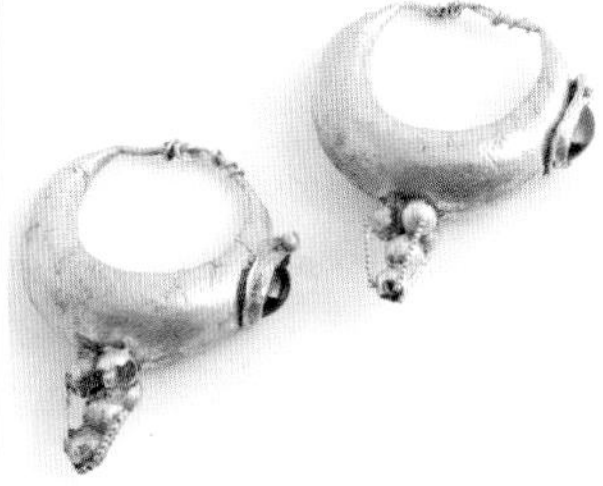

A pair of Roman gold earrings, sheet gold with garnet inlaid stones and granular drops.

cAD300-400 *1in (2.5cm) long*

£400-500 **ANA**

A pair of Roman gold earrings, with filigree work pattern and drops with original beads.

cAD300-400 *1.5in (4cm) long*

£700-1,000 **ANA**

A pair of Roman gold hoop earrings, with gold and bead drops.

cAD200-300 *1.5in (4cm) long*

£300-400 **ANA**

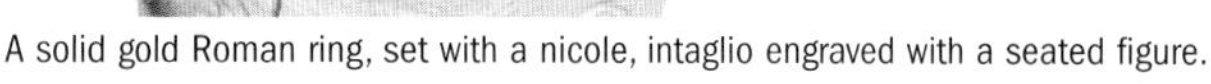

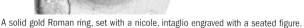

A solid gold Roman ring, set with a nicole, intaglio engraved with a seated figure.

1in (2.5cm) diam

£1,500-2,000 **ANA**

A solid gold Roman ring, the bezel engraved with the figure of victory.

cAD200-400 *0 .75in (2cm) wide*

£900-1,200 **ANA**

A solid gold Roman ring, set with three semi-precious stones.

cAD300-400 *1in (2.5cm) wide*

£1,200-1,500 **ANA**

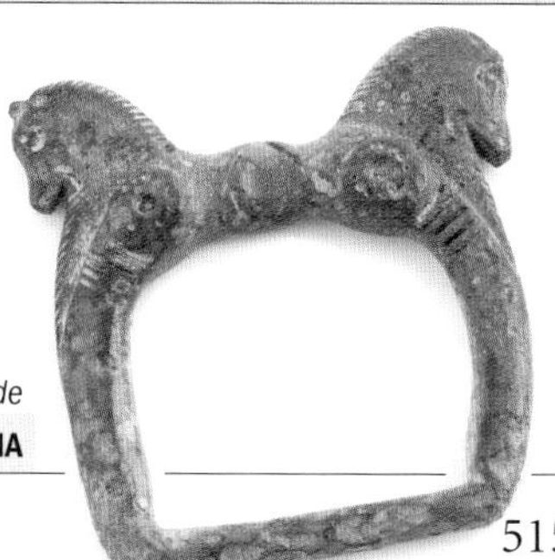

A Roman bronze military buckle, surmounted by two horse heads.

cAD300-400 *1.25in (3cm) wide*

£70-100 **ANA**

A fine Roman bronze applique, in the form of a facing bust of Pan.

3.5in (9cm) high

£1,800-2,200 **ANA**

A Roman bronze applique disc, with a good facing bust of a male wearing a Phrygian cap.

cAD200-300 *1.75in (4.5cm) diam*

£300-350 **ANA**

A Roman bronze applique fragment, depicting the head and shoulders of a young male.

cAD100-200 *1.75in (4.5cm) wide*

£200-300 **ANA**

A Roman bronze applique, in the form of a facing lion's head.

cAD100-200 *1.25in (3cm) high*

£80-100 **ANA**

A Roman bronze key ring, with etched decoration.

cAD100-200 *1in (2.5cm) high*

£50-70 **ANA**

A Roman bronze knife handle, in the form of a statue of Mars, naked, holding a shield and wearing a crested helmet.

cAD100-200 *4.5in (11.5cm) high*

£1,800-2,000 **ANA**

A Roman bronze key with loop.

cAD100-200 *2.25in (5.5cm) long*

£50-60 **ANA**

A Roman bronze ligula, or ear scoop, with decorative shaft.

cAD100-200 *5.75in (14.5cm) long*

£80-120 **ANA**

A Roman bronze scalpel blade, with iron end missing, similar to examples found at Pompeii.

cAD50-200 *3in (7.5cm) high*

£70-100 **ANA**

A Roman silver ligula, or ear scoop, with decorated shaft.

cAD100-200 *4.5in (11.5cm) long*

£200-300 **ANA**

A Roman bronze cyathiscomele and probe.

cAD100-200 *5.75in (14.5cm) long*

£100-200 **ANA**

A Roman silver stylus, with pointed end for writing and flattened end for erasing, twisted shaft.

cAD100-200 *4.75in (12cm) long*

£300-400 **ANA**

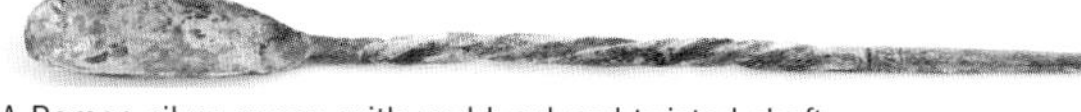

A Roman silver spoon, with oval bowl and twisted shaft.

cAD100-200 *5.5in (14cm) long*

£300-400 **ANA**

A fine bronze Roman hair pin, in the form of a hand holding a ball.

cAD100-200 *5.75in (14.5cm) long*

£100-150 **ANA**

A bronze Roman mirror case, with concentric circles, the interior polished with tinning.

cAD150 *4.5in (11.5cm) diam*

£150-200 **ANA**

A Roman bronze lamp, with the handle in the form of a cockerel.

cAD200-300 *4in (10cm) long*

£600-700 **ANA**

EGYPTIAN

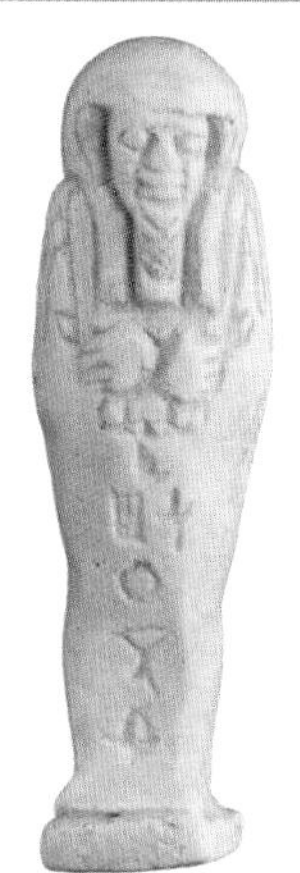

A small Egyptian apple green faience ushabti figure, with hieroglyphics on panel.

c400BC *2.75in (7cm) high*

£150-180 **ANA**

An Egyptian late Dynastic ushbati figure, with panel of impressed hieroglyphics naming the owner.

c500-400BC *4in (10cm) high*

£200-300 **ANA**

An Egyptian late Dynastic ushabti figure, with panel of etched hieroglyphics naming the owner.

c500-400BC *4in (10cm) high*

£200-300 **ANA**

An Egyptian late dynastic ushabti figure, with crook and flail.

c500BC *4.75in (12cm) long*

£200-250 **ANA**

An Egyptian faience amulet of Thoth, scribe to the gods, depicted as an ibis-headed human.

c400BC *2in (5cm) high*

£300-500 **ANA**

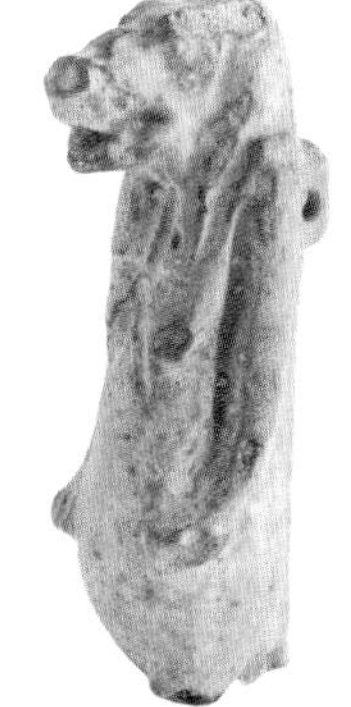

An Egyptian fragmentary faience glazed amulet, depicting the hippopotamus god Thoueris.

c500BC *2in (5cm) high*

£100-150 **ANA**

An Egyptian late dynastic ushabti figure, with a panel of impressed hieroglyphics naming the owner.

c500BC *5in (12.5cm) long*

£500-700 **ANA**

An Egyptian late Dynastic faience pectoral, with figures of Isis standing.

c500BC *2.25in (5.5cm) high*

£400-600 **ANA**

An Egyptian steatite scarab beetle amulet seal, with finely carved underside.

c1800BC *1.5in (4cm) diam*

£100-150 **ANA**

An Egyptian steatite scarab beetle amulet seal, with finely carved underside and original bronze swivel ring attached.

It is very rare to find a seal like this complete with its ring.

c1800BC *0.75in (2cm) long*

£300-400 **ANA**

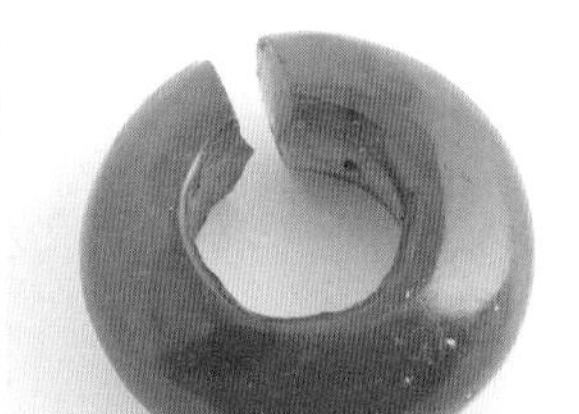

An Egyptian carnelian hair ring.

c1200BC *0.5in (1.5cm) diam*

£50-100 **ANA**

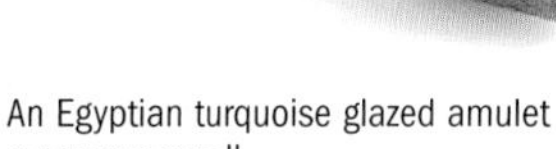

An Egyptian turquoise glazed amulet of a papyrus scroll.

c400BC *1in (2.5cm) long*

£70-100 **ANA**

An Egyptian restrung faience bead necklace, with an amulet of the Djed Pillar, or 'Backbone of Isis'.

c500BC *9.5in (24cm) diam*

£120-180 **ANA**

An Egyptian restrung necklace of blue glass beads, set with a gold pendant with blue glass bead.

cAD200 *5.5in (14cm) diam*

£200-250 **ANA**

An Egyptian bronze statuette of Horus, wearing a crown, his finger to his mouth.

c400BC *6in (15cm) high*

£2,500-3,000 **ANA**

An Egyptian bronze statuette of Horus wearing a cap, his finger to his mouth.

c400BC *4.5in (11.5cm) high*

£1,800-2,000 **ANA**

An Egyptian Coptic period textile comb.

cAD500 *5.5in (14cm) long*

£50-100 **ANA**

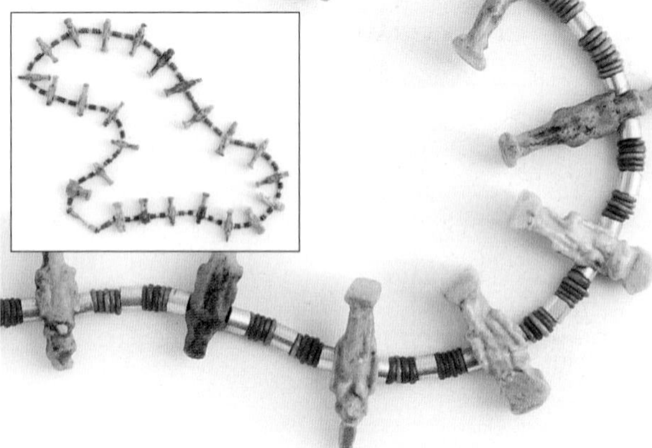

A restrung Egyptian necklace of bright blue faience beads, with interspaced amulets and gold spacers, restrung c1900.

c500BC *6in (15cm) diam*

£800-1,200 **ANA**

GREEK

A Greek Athenian black figureware skyphos wine cup, with scenes on each side and floral palmette decoration.

c400BC *10in (25.5cm) wide*

£1,800-2,200 **ANA**

A Greek Magna Graecia Gnathian ware skyphos wine cup, in black glaze pottery with painted decoration.

5.5in (14cm) high

£250-300 **ANA**

A Greek Magna Graecia apulian miniature kantharos, black glazed pottery with red painted decoration.

c300BC *2.25in (5.5cm) high*

£100-150 **ANA**

A CLOSER LOOK AT A GREEK KRATER

Kraters are two-handled vessels, with wide rim and a foot, that were used for mixing water with wine.

As a large centrepiece, a krater would often be decorated with scenes from Greek mythology.

Pieces like this are much sought after by decorators and designers, to furnish modern living spaces.

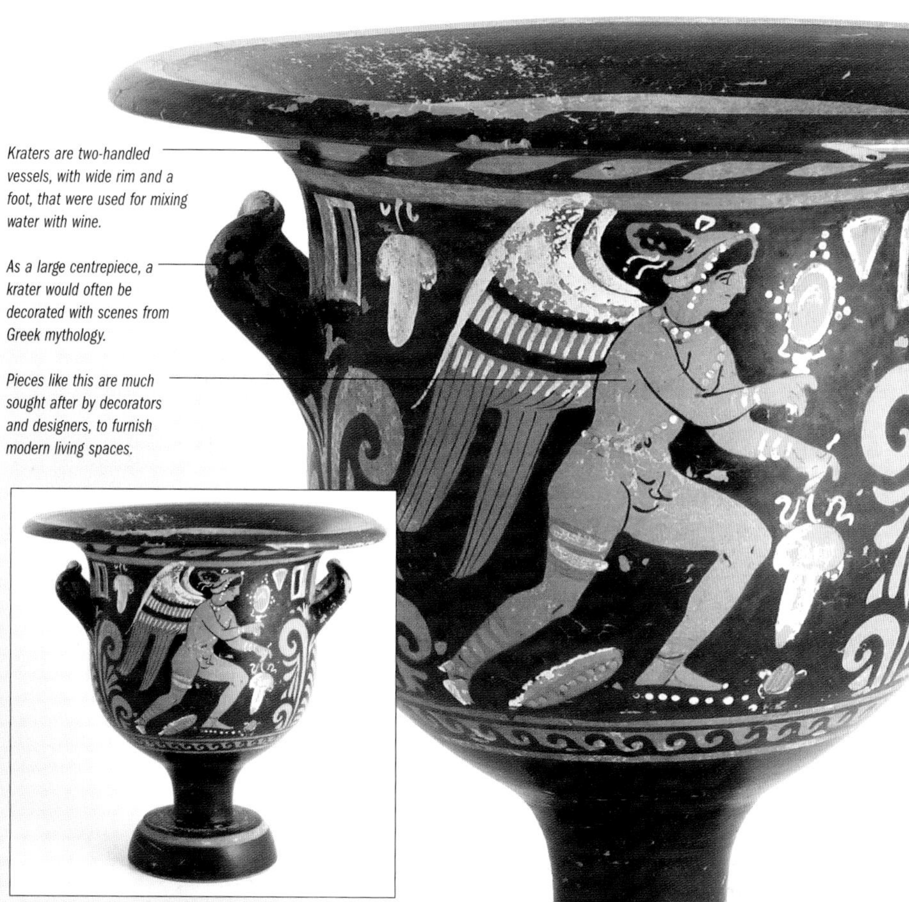

This krater has survived in remarkably good condition for such a large piece. The delicate rim is particularly prone to damage.

A Greek Magna Graecia redware bell krater, with painted scenes on either side, surrounded by decoration.

c400-300BC *12.5in (32cm) high*

£3,000-3,500 **ANA**

A Greek Magna Graecia apulian black glazed trefoil mounted oinochoe, with painted leaf frieze.

4.5in (11.5cm) high

£250-350 **ANA**

A Greek Magna Graecia Gnathian ware beaker, in black glazed pottery with painted decoration.

c300BC *4.5in (11.5cm) high*

£250-350 **ANA**

A Greek Magna Graecia apulia potted wine cup, in buff clay with partial glazing.

c300BC *4.75in (12cm) long*

£50-80 **ANA**

A Greek Gnathian ware prochous, with painted decoration.

c300BC *6.75in (17cm) high*

£450-550 **ANA**

An eastern Mediterranean Greek terracotta fragmentary head of a goddess.

c400-350BC *2.75in (7cm) high*

£150-250 **ANA**

A Greek fragmentary terracotta head.

c200-100BC *1.75in (4.5cm) high*

£100-150 **ANA**

A Greek Hellenistic bronze statue of a reclining horse, finely modelled, with incised decoration.

3.5in (9cm) long

£2,500-3,000 **ANA**

MESOPOTAMIAN

A Mesopotamian cuniform tablet with administrative text, Ur III period.

c2000BC *2.25in (5.5cm) wide*

£250-350 **ANA**

A Mesopotamian cuniform tablet with administrative text, with remains of the envelope in which it was kept, old Babylonian.

c1800BC *2.75in (7cm) wide*

£300-400 **ANA**

A Mesopotamian cuniform tablet tablet with administrative text, old Babylonian.

c1800BC *4in (10cm) wide*

£400-600 **ANA**

A Mesopotamian carved Sumerian stone finial, depicting a cow.

c2700BC *1.5in (4cm) long*

£400-500 **ANA**

A Mesopotamian pottery model of a hunchback bearded man riding a horse, old Babylonian.

c1800BC *4.75in (12cm) high*

£300-400 **ANA**

A Mesopotamian pottery figure of Astarte, seen naked and wearing a necklace, old Babylonian.

c1800BC *4in (10cm) high*

£150-250 **ANA**

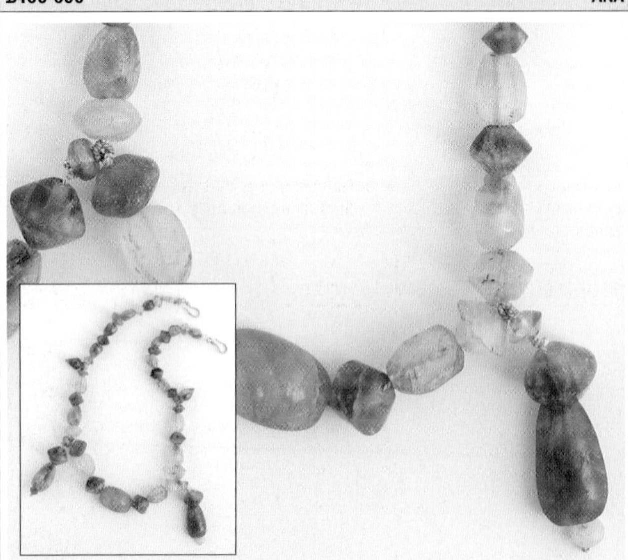

A Mesopotamian or Phoenician restrung necklace, of lapis lazuli beads, scarabs and drop pendants, with a 19thC clasp.

c2000BC *8in (20cm) long*

£750-1,000 **ANA**

LURISTAN

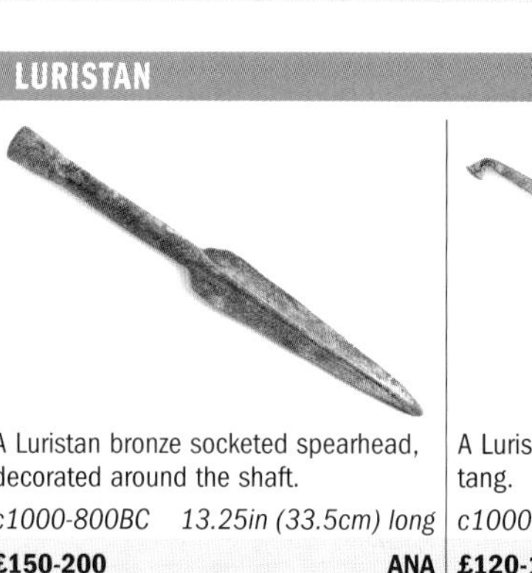

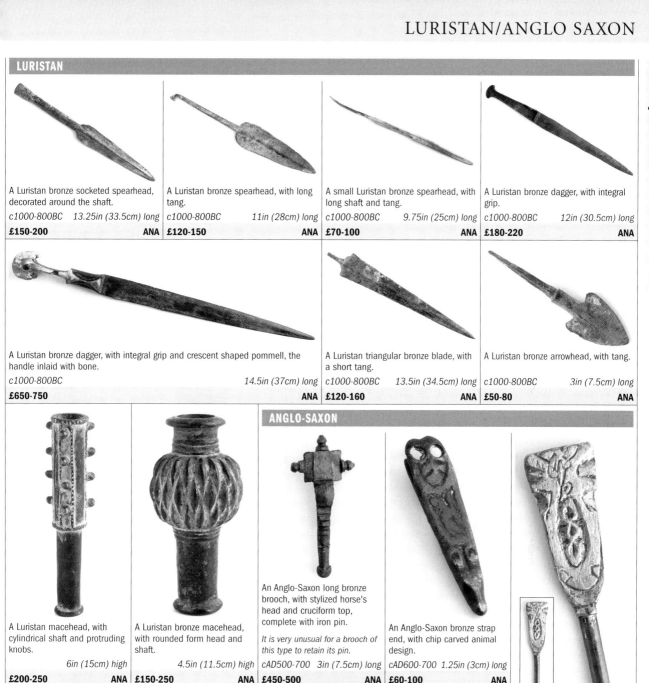

A Luristan bronze socketed spearhead, decorated around the shaft.

c1000-800BC *13.25in (33.5cm) long*

£150-200 **ANA**

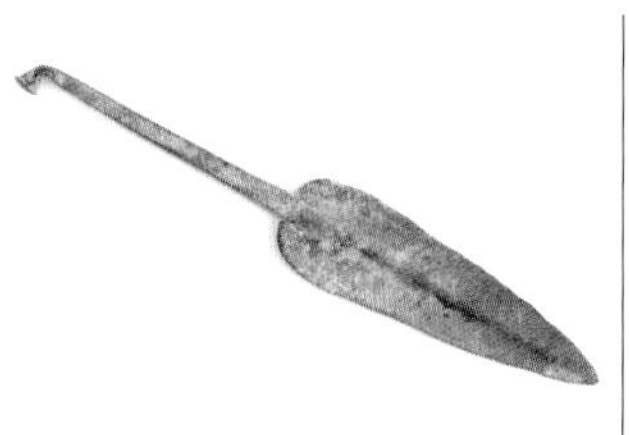

A Luristan bronze spearhead, with long tang.

c1000-800BC *11in (28cm) long*

£120-150 **ANA**

A small Luristan bronze spearhead, with long shaft and tang.

c1000-800BC *9.75in (25cm) long*

£70-100 **ANA**

A Luristan bronze dagger, with integral grip.

c1000-800BC *12in (30.5cm) long*

£180-220 **ANA**

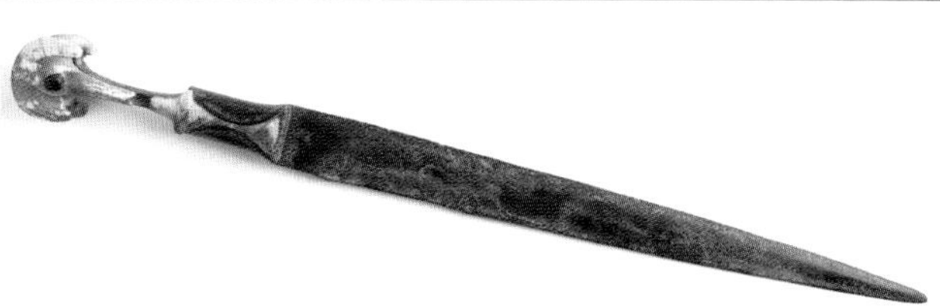

A Luristan bronze dagger, with integral grip and crescent shaped pommell, the handle inlaid with bone.

c1000-800BC *14.5in (37cm) long*

£650-750 **ANA**

A Luristan triangular bronze blade, with a short tang.

c1000-800BC *13.5in (34.5cm) long*

£120-160 **ANA**

A Luristan bronze arrowhead, with tang.

c1000-800BC *3in (7.5cm) long*

£50-80 **ANA**

A Luristan macehead, with cylindrical shaft and protruding knobs.

6in (15cm) high

£200-250 **ANA**

A Luristan bronze macehead, with rounded form head and shaft.

4.5in (11.5cm) high

£150-250 **ANA**

ANGLO-SAXON

An Anglo-Saxon long bronze brooch, with stylized horse's head and cruciform top, complete with iron pin.

It is very unusual for a brooch of this type to retain its pin.

cAD500-700 *3in (7.5cm) long*

£450-500 **ANA**

An Anglo-Saxon bronze strap end, with chip carved animal design.

cAD600-700 *1.25in (3cm) long*

£60-100 **ANA**

A pair of Anglo-Saxon gilt bronze saucer brooches, the interior with fine chip carving.

1.5in (4cm) diam

£2,000-2,500 **ANA**

An Anglo-Saxon gilt bronze button brooch, with a facing male head.

cAD600-700 *0.75in (2cm) diam*

£250-350 **ANA**

A quality Anglo-Saxon silver gilt pin, the finial with chip carved animal and interlaced pattern.

cAD600 *3in (7.5cm) long*

£1,500-2,500 **ANA**

CELTIC

A Celtic bronze bracelet, flattened with pointed terminals, fine patina.

c200BC *4in (10cm) diam*

£50-100 **ANA**

A Celtic bronze neck torc, with hook and eye fastening.

c100BC *5.25in (13.5cm) diam*

£100-150 **ANA**

A Celtic silver pin, the shaft with a modelled figure of a bird with closed wings.

c100BC *4.25in (11cm) long*

£200-250 **ANA**

A Celtic silver bird applique, with finely carved decoration.

c100BC *1.25in (3cm) long*

£70-100 **ANA**

OTHER ANTIQUITIES

A Trans-Jordan early Bronze Age juglet.

c3000BC *5in (13cm) high*

£75-100 **ANA**

A Sumerian black stone cylinder seal, the body carved with a contest scene, Akkadian.

c2300-2200BC *0.75in (2cm) high*

£150-200 **ANA**

An Indus Valley area pytis pot, with geometric design.

c2000 BC *4in (10cm) high*

£150-200 **ANA**

An Iron Age Cypriot pottery wine flagon, with pinched spout and bichromatic painted circles.

c1200BC *8in (20.5cm) high*

£250-350 **ANA**

A Daurian terracotta krater, with a painted geometric design.

c600-400BC

£600-900 **ANA**

A Daurian krater in buff terracotta, painted with geometric patterns.

c600-500BC *8.5in (21.5cm) wide*

£300-500 **ANA**

A Cypriot early Bronze Age polished redware bowl, with vestigal handles.

c200-100BC *5in (12.5cm) wide*

£180-220 **ANA**

A Byzantine bronze cross, with rounded arms and an empty setting for a gemstone.

cAD700-800 *1.25in (3cm) long*

£60-70 **ANA**

A Byzantine bronze cross, part of a reliquary, the front engraved with the Virgin Mary orans, inscribed above.

c1100 *3.25in (8.5cm) long*

£200-300 **ANA**

URNS

A pair of 20thC large patinated bronze urns, of lobed ovoid form, the sides of each moulded in relief with cherubs, fruit and foliage, flanked and divided by satyr masks, raised on a circular pedestal foot.

38.5in (96cm) high

£400-600 **FRE**

A pair of Georgian-style terracotta garden urns.

27in (68.5cm) high

£350-450 **S&K**

A pair of 20thC carved stone garden urns, in three parts, each with an everted rim above a continuous band of scrolling grape clusters, centring a roundel with putti, on a circular fluted base above a square inset-panel pedestal, inscribed "Italgarden", later pedestals.

62in (155cm) high

£1,200-1,800 **S&K**

A pair of 20thC cast-iron black-painted campana form garden urns, each with a continuous band of floral and foliate decoration beneath an egg-and-dart everted rim, on a gadrooned base, flanked by lion mask angular handles.

24.5in (61cm) high

£800-1,200 **S&K**

A pair of English cast-iron garden urns, the handles with mask terminals.

30in (76cm) high

£1,000-1,500 **S&K**

Two of a set of six white-painted cast-iron garden urns, moulded with egg and dart rims, plinth bases, one damaged.

25in (62.5cm) high

£400-600 set **S&K**

A pair of large patinated garden urns, each with bead and mask decorative details, on a plinth base.

27in (67.5cm) high

£1,200-1,800 **S&K**

A pair of sandstone flaming urn finials, the circular urns with scroll handles, issuing vigorously carved flames.

32.75in (82cm) high

£800-1,200 **L&T**

One of three cast-iron campana-form garden urns, damaged.

20in (50cm) high

£180-220 set **S&K**

One of a pair of large patinated metal two-handled garden urns, each with lion handles, lotus base on shallow plinth.

27in (67.5cm) high

£1,000-1,500 pair **S&K**

A pair of cast iron garden urns, each with a waisted body, applied scrolling foliage, loop handles and a fluted socle base, with square plinths.

31.5in (79cm) high

£1,000-1,500 **L&T**

PLANTERS

A wirework plant stand, with three tiered semi-circular trays.

40in (100cm) wide

£150-200 **L&T**

A matched pair of wirework plant stands, each with rounded ends to tray and splayed stands.

38in (95cm) wide

£250-300 **L&T**

A pair of lead planters, each side with floral garland decoration.

23in (57.5cm) wide

£300-500 **S&K**

A terracotta planter, with a moulded circular bowl raised on a pedestal and three herons, with a concave triform plinth, on a corresponding pedestal with lion's masks and a cavetto moulded plinth.

60in (150cm) high

£2,200-2,800 **L&T**

FOUNTAINS

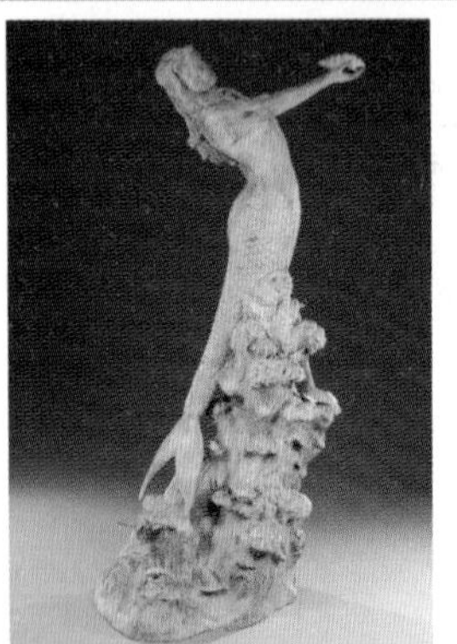

A bronze mermaid and dolphin fountain, the wave-form base encrusted with a turtle, a crab and various shells.

85in (212.5cm) high

£2,000-3,000 **S&K**

A patinated bronze fountain, cast with a putto holding a shell, with a turtle and a frog, within a circular basin with an anthemion rim, on a swan-form base.

49in (122.5cm) high

£1,200-1,800 **S&K**

A patinated bronze fountain, cast as a seated mermaid holding a shell.

31.5in (79cm) high

£500-800 **S&K**

A patinated bronze fountain, in two parts, the base cast with two mermaids on a hexagonal plinth supporting a cast figural upper section, with a mother and son on a rocky base.

82in (205cm) high

£4,500-5,500 **S&K**

FIGURES

One of a pair of English monumental cast stone rearing lions, each modelled grasping a shield carved with the arms of Wolsey, on later trapezoidal limestone plinths.

35in (89cm) wide

£6,000-9,000 pair **S&K**

A facing pair of cast lions, each standing with one front foot resting on a ball, on rectangular plinths.

29.5in (74cm) long

£600-900 L&T

A pair of bronze angels with outstretched arms, each in a flowing robe, on a rocky mound and a cut-corner base inscribed "Petrucci, Carli/1180 Wolfe/Montreal", marked "PETRUCCI-CARLI, MONTREAL".

66.75in (167cm) high

£8,000-12,000 NA

A cast-iron black painted setter.

52in (130cm) long

£4,000-6,000 NA

FURNITURE

A pair of mid-to late 19thC Rococo-revival cast-iron garden benches, attributed to Vulcan Iron Works, New Boston, Illinois, old crack to one bench.

The pattern of these benches is often referred to as the "White House" pattern, as benches of this design are in the Rose Garden of the White House. The design was patented in England in 1846. It was copied and manufactured by several foundries in the US until the end of the 19thC.

60.25in (153cm) wide

£3,000-4,000 FRE

A late 19thC Coalbrookdale lily-of-the-valley pattern polished iron bench, raised on foliate cast cabriole legs.

64in (160cm) wide

£1,800-2,200 S&K

A cast-iron garden bench, the back and arms cast with leafy s-curves and scrolls, on a pierced seat with a heart or palmette apron and shaped flora-form feet, marked "Peter Timmes Son Brooklyn, N. Y." and "Pat. May 7, 1895."

Benches of this design are found in the New York Botanical Garden, Bronx, New York.

43.5in (109cm) wide

£1,000-1,500 FRE

A nasturtium pattern garden bench, with pierced cast scroll back and sides, slatted wooden seat.

71in (180cm) wide

£800-1,200 L&T

A late 19th/early 20thC three-piece cream-painted cast-iron set of garden furniture, comprising a settee and two arm chairs.

42in (105cm) wide

£1,800-2,200 S&K

A Coalbrookdale wrought iron garden bench, the slightly curved back cast and pierced with nasturtium, above scrolled arms and a slatted wood seat, the whole raised on curved strap supports with cast panels to the ends, overpainted in green.

72in (183cm) wide

£500-800 L&T

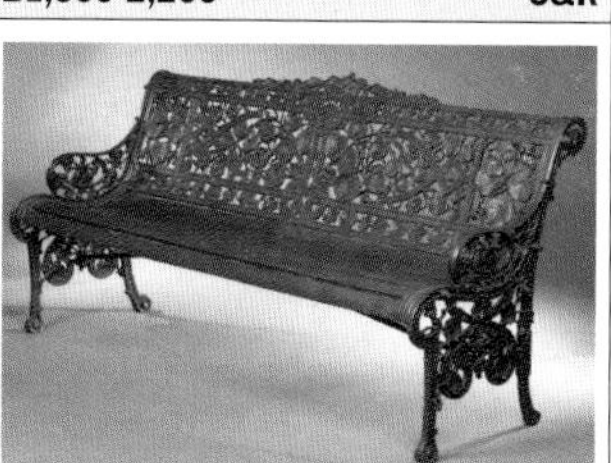

FIREPLACE ACCESSORIES

A pair of andirons, in hand forged iron with brass finials.

c1740

£500-700 **RAA**

A 19thC pair of French Neo-classical gilt-bronze chenets, modelled as foliate-draped helmets and plume-topped urns, a plinth base with four paw feet.

25in (62.5cm) high

£2,000-3,000 **S&K**

A pair of late 19thC Louis XV-style bronze chenets, of ornate pierced Rococo scroll form, each mounted with a seated cherub, one painting the other carving a marble bust, re-gilded.

16.5in (41cm) high

£800-1,200 **FRE**

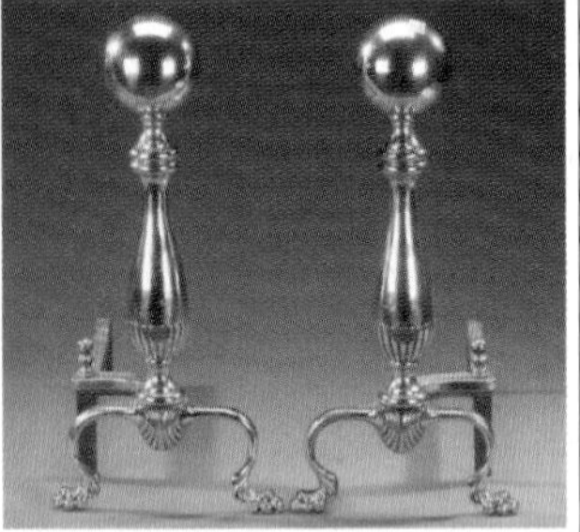

A pair of 20thC brass ball-top andirons, with baluster tapering standards on arched supports, on paw feet.

19in (47.5cm) high

£350-450 **S&K**

A pair of brass and iron ball-top andirons, with ball finials on octagonal shafts and spurred cabriole legs, ending in ball clawed feet.

22.75in (58cm) high

£500-700 **FRE**

A pair of diminutive brass and wrought-iron andirons, each with an acorn finial on a tapering, turned shaft and flattened openwork base.

7.5in (19cm) high

£400-600 **FRE**

A George III white-painted pine chimney piece, the inverted break-front ledge top above various mouldings, the break-front frieze decorated with foliate a centrepiece, swaya and wheatsheaves, the sides with oak leaves and acorns.

60in (152cm) wide

£800-1,200 **L&T**

A 19thC French-style Carara marble chimney piece, the serpentine mantel above a shaped panelled frieze, centred by scrolling foliate cabochon, supported by scrolled and moulded consoles, with acanthus and fruit carving and block plinths.

75.25in (188cm) wide

£4,500-5,500 **L&T**

An early 19thC George III cast-iron and brass fire grate, with a serpentine railed basket above a pierced brass frieze and a spread-wing eagle, on scrolled supports, vasiform finials and ball feet.

22.25in (55.5cm) high

£350-450 **S&K**

A 19thC cast-iron Franklin stove, with a floral rosette in a diamond cartouche, the back plate impressed "Wilson, New York", and with the initials "WE".

39in (97.5cm) high

£150-200 **S&K**

A wrought-iron and gilt-bronze tripartite firescreen, the trellis-back frame enclosing an oval cartouche, flanked by rearing lions and surmounted by a royal crown, suspending drapery swags, with a brass carrying handle.

44in (110cm) high

£700-1,000 **S&K**

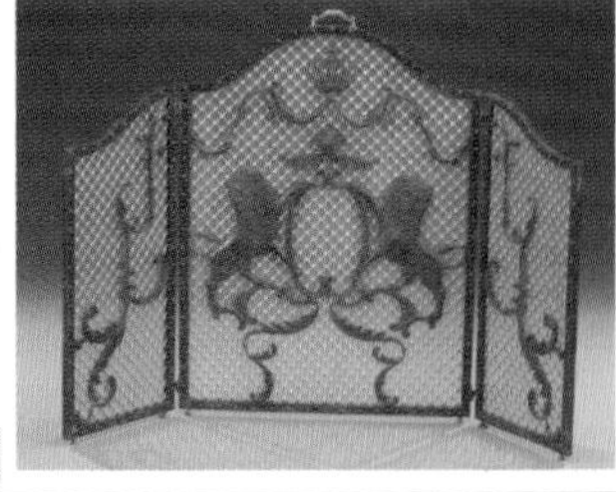

EDGED WEAPONS

An extremely rare Scottish medieval 15thC Knightly sword, in excavated blackened condition, long tang, a heavy thick oval pommel, quillons turned down towards the double edged blade, surviving remains of the tooled leather scabbard, the bronze, semi-circular chape decorated with radiating lines.

36in (90cm) blade

£10,000-15,000 **L&T**

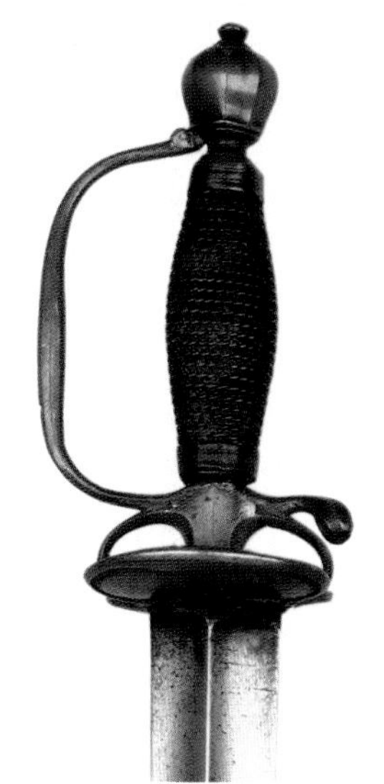

A brass hilted smallsword, with hollow ground colichemarde blade, large pas d'ane rings, reinforced borders to shell guards, swollen faceted quillon and pommel, wire bound grip.

c1725 blade 29.25in (74.5cm) long

£320-380 **W&W**

A massive 18thC Indian executioner's sword or tulwar, broad T-section blade, with traces of gold damascened inscription, steel hilt with silver damascened decoration overall.

blade 29in (74cm) long

£500-700 **W&W**

An 18thC naval boarding cutlass of American type, straight single-edged blade with narrow fuller, curved steel guard, ribbed one piece cast steel grip.

blade 26in (66cm) long

£300-400 **W&W**

A large Central Indian 18thC sword Patissa, straight blade with flared double-edged tip struck with maker's marks, traces of wootz pattern, steel hilt with silver damascened decoration.

£500-700 **W&W**

A heavy 18thC Indian tulwar of Sikh form, blade steel hilt of conventional form, swollen faceted quillons, radial solar disc to pommel with short faceted spike, thickly silver damascened overall.

blade 32.5in (82.5cm) long

£300-400 **W&W**

An unusual 18thC Moro kris, broad wavy bifullered blade, chiselled top engraved "622 SBO", silver mounted wooden hilt with carved pommel, inlaid ivory panels.

blade 19in (48.5cm) long

£280-320 **W&W**

A good hallmarked silver mounted smallsword by Thomas Foster, London, 1768, hollow ground colichemarde blade, pierced and chiselled, silver wire bound grip, in its silver mounted scabbard with later oil cloth covering, black polished, chape missing.

blade 31in (79cm) long

£1,000-2,000 **W&W**

A nielloed silver mounted Turkish Yataghan sword dated "AH 1210" (1796AD), blade struck with maker's mark, chiselled with two line inscription within foliate cartouche, and with star containing the date, hilt of silver with foliate chiselled gilt panels finely nielloed borders, flared pommel ears.

blade 18.5in (47cm) long

£300-400 **W&W**

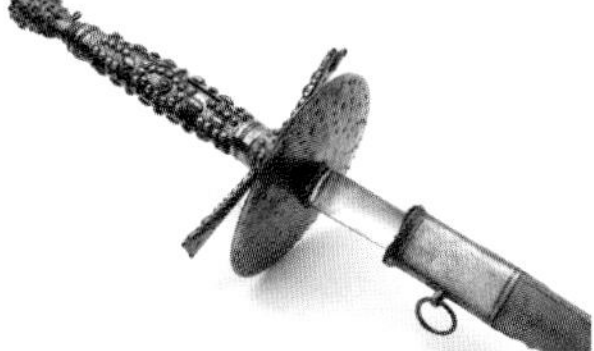

A late Georgian cut and polished steel hilted smallsword, hollow ground triangular section blade, steel mounted vellum covered scabbard with twin suspension rings.

blade 30in (76.5cm) long

£220-280 **W&W**

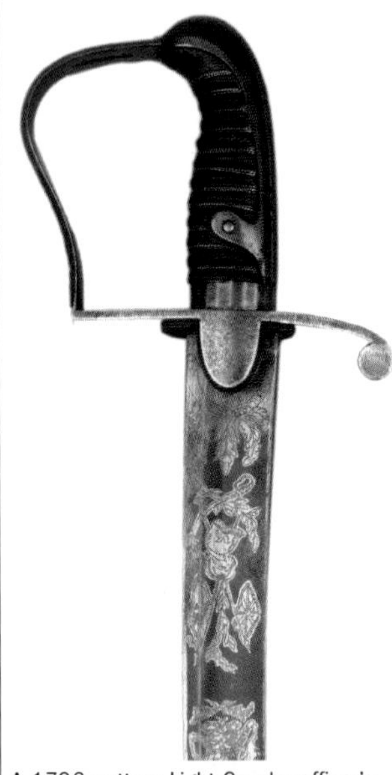

A 1796 pattern Light Cavalry officer's sword, curved, fullered blade etched "Osborn's" and "Warranted", pre-1801 Royal Arms, retaining most of the original blueing and gilding, regulation steel hilt and langets, wire bound leather covered grip, in its steel scabbard.

blade 32in (81.5cm) long

£1,200-1,800 **W&W**

A large Persian watered steel shamshir, broad blade of watered mechanical damascus steel, with maker's mark, with four gold damascened Islamic inscriptions, double-edged tip, later steel crosspiece, chequered wooden grips.

c1800 *blade 31in (79cm) long*

£700-800 **W&W**

An unusual early 19thC Tibetan shortsword, curved double-edged blade, sharkskin covered grip with brass mounts comprising ferrule, grip band and circular pommel with square button.

blade 17in (43.5cm) long

£100-150 **W&W**

A scarce 1822 Light Cavalry trooper's sword, regulation triple bar steel guard, stepped pommel, gripstrap, with steel scabbard engraved with Hussar indistinct regimental markings, twin hanging rings.

blade 35in (89cm) long

£300-400 **W&W**

A Victorian infantry officer's 1845 pattern sword, slightly curved blade by 'C Dyke. Princes S. W' etched with flat topped crowned VR cypher, wirebound fishskin covered grip, in its steel scabbard.

blade 33in (84cm) long

£180-220 **W&W**

A 19thC Persian Qjar 'Medieval Revival' sword, broad straight double-edged blade etched with 12 bust portraits upon a ground of Arabic Naskh inscriptions, steel hilt with down turned quillons, swollen grip and pommel.

blade 29.5in (75cm) long

£200-300 **W&W**

A 19thC Chinese River Pirate's sword, shallow diamond section blade inlaid with copper discs, faceted horn grip, cast with dragons and clouds, crosspieces in the form of a Makarra's head, sanded sharkskin scabbard.

blade 17in (43.5cm) long

£180-220 **W&W**

A 19thC Sumatran Klewang Pucok Meukawet, heavy, thick blade, square section at forte, with incised decoration, brass hilt cast with roped decoration and concentric circles, pommel surmounted by a bust in European style with tight coiffure and earrings.

27in (68.5cm) long

£220-280 **W&W**

A 19thC Chinese River Pirate's pair of swords, heavy single-edged blades, thick brass guards, wooden grips carved with foliage in relief with key pattern border, leather scabbard with silhouette decorated leather top.

blades 15in (38cm) long

£220-280 **W&W**

A scarce 1827 pattern Rifle Volunteer officer's sword of the Cornwall Rangers (Cornwall Rifles), blade by G. Smith, 12 Piccadilly London, etched with "Cornwall Rangers" and "Cornwall Rifles" within banners, wire bound fishskin grip, in its steel scabbard, top etched "TP12".

blade 32in (81.5cm) long

£300-400 **W&W**

A Victorian Volunteer Rifle Officer's 1827 pattern sword, slightly curved blade by Henry Wilkinson No 10208 (1860), strung bugle, wire bound fishskin grip, Wilkinson's records show it be the sword of William Carpmael, Lt (1860) 4th (Brixton) Surrey Rifle Vols.

blade 32in (81.5cm) long

£280-320 **W&W**

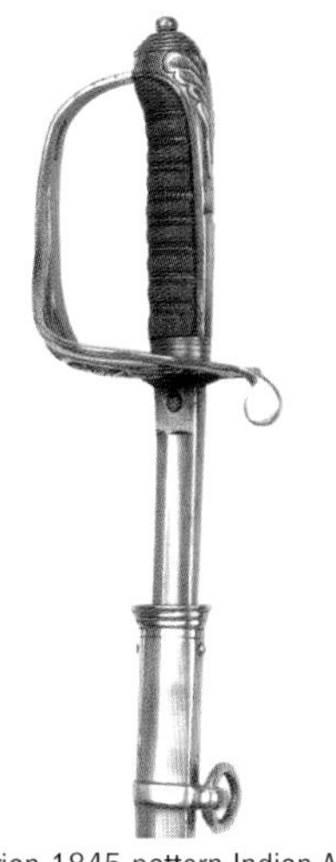

A Victorian 1845 pattern Indian Army officer's piquet weight sword, by Harman & Co, Calcutta, with crowned VRI, brass hilt pierced with crowned VRI, wire bound sharkskin grip, brass dress scabbard with twin hanging rings.

blade 33in (84cm) long

£350-400 **W&W**

An 1889 pattern naval cutlass, straight unfullered blade by Wilkinson Sword Company, date "92", steel mounted leather scabbard, blade reground, some pitting to hilt and scabbard.

blade 27.75in (70.5cm) long

£250-300 **W&W**

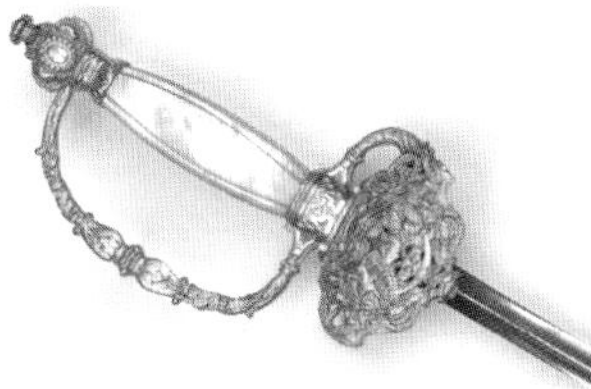

A post-1902 levee dress sword, blade etched with military trophies, brass hilt with bullion dress knot, brass mounted leather scabbard.

blade 31.75in (81cm) long

£300-400 **W&W**

A good Victorian courtsword, slender blade, etched with flat topped crowned VR cypher within floral scrolls, regulation gilt hilt with crosspiece, bullion dress knot, gilt mounted leather scabbard with cloth frog and webbing shoulder strap, in chamois lined oilskin cover.

blade 32in (81.5cm) long

£320-380 **W&W**

An unusual Indian Cavalry officer's sword by Wilkinson No 20255, for 1875, curved fullered blade stamped in Arabic "Wilkinson, London", large engraved and pierced steel guard of heavy cavalry officer's pattern, silver wire bound leather covered grip.

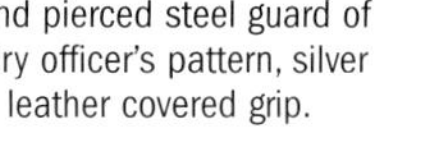

blade 31in (79cm) long

£400-450 **W&W**

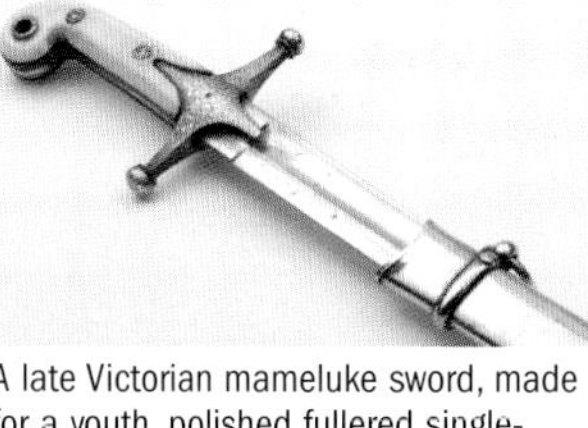

A late Victorian mameluke sword, made for a youth, polished fullered single-edged blade, brass crosspiece with ball finials, two piece ivory grips with ebony spacers and silvered gripstrap, brass scabbard with two hanging rings.

Allegedly, this sword was made for the Prince of Gwalior, India.

blade 22in (56cm) long

£220-280 **W&W**

A Persian shortsword Quama, broad slightly curved single edge blade with multi-fullers, with Arabic maker's stamp, two piece black horn polished grips, leather covered scabbard with steel hanging band, some wear.

The sword is dated 1295 and 1298 AH for 1878 and 1880AD.

blade 24in (61cm) long

£200-300 **W&W**

An unusual courtsword, probably late Victorian, polished hollow ground section blade marked "Jam. Holbeck, 21 Princes St, Hanover Sq, London", gilt brass with solid spiral grip, pommel chiselled with foliage, in its gilt brass mounted leather scabbard.

blade 30in (76.5cm) long

£220-280 **W&W**

An 1821 pattern light cavalry officer's undress sword by Wilkinson No 31892 (for 1892), straight fullered blade with crowned VR, Royal arms, POW plumes and foliage, back edge with centre of percussion, silver wire bound fishskin grip, worn, chequered grip.

blade 34.75in (88.5cm) long

£100-150 **W&W**

A George V 1897 pattern Infantry officer's sword, blade by Wilkinson No 44446, etched and polished with crowned GRI and "Capt C.W.G Walker from J.K.W.", scabbard with spare leather field service scabbard, leather sword bag, retaining all original polish.

blade 32in (81.5cm) long

£400-600 **W&W**

An Edwardian officer's sword of the Edinburgh City Royal Garrison Artillery Volunteers, blade by Hobson & Sons, London W, with crowned ER and regimental titles, fishskin grip, FS leather scabbard, frog stamped "Hobson & Sons 1902 London".

blade 33in (84cm) long

£180-200 **W&W**

An Edward VII officer's sword of the Royal Army Medical Corps, straight 1892 pattern blade, no maker's name, etched with crowned Edward VII cypher, gilt triple bar hilt incorporating crowned Edward VII cypher, wire bound fishskin covered grip, leather scabbard.

blade 32in (81.5cm) long

£280-320 **W&W**

An Imperial German artillery sword made for a boy, plated blade etched "Hans Schutze Aden, Weihnachten 1915", with trophies upon a dulled blued ground, regulation brass stirrup hit, lion's head pommel, crossed cannon on langet, in plated scabbard.

blade 19in (48.5cm) long

£180-220 **W&W**

An Indian Army Artillery trooper's sword, curved broad fullered blade stamped "Mole", steel triple bar guard, wire bound fishskin grip, back of quillon stamped "MA3-04" (probably Madras Artillery).

blade 30in (76.5cm) long

£180-220 **W&W**

An Indian army cavalry trooper's sword by Wilkinson with 1821 type hilt, curved blade with single fuller and false edge stamped "Wilkinson Pall Mall", triple bar steel guard, stepped pommel, wire bound grip.

blade 32in (81.5cm) long

£70-100 **W&W**

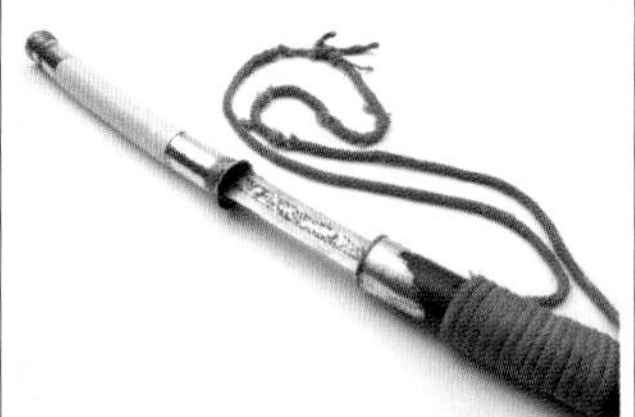

A silver mounted Burmese sword Dha, blade thickly silver damascened with figures, ivory hilt with silver mounts, foiled glass pommel, in its silver mounted wooden scabbard.

blade 24in (61cm) long

£500-800 **W&W**

A composite smallsword, hollow ground triangular section blade etched with scrolls, plated brass hilt with vertically fluted pommel and quillon block, ribbed knucklebow and edges to shell guards, later wire and tape bound grip.

blade 30in (76.5cm) long

£300-400 **W&W**

An Imperial German artillery officer's sword, plated fullered blade by C. Eickhorn, steel stirrup hilt with traces of gilding, lion's head pommel with red 'gem' eyes, lion's head quillon terminal, crossed cannon on langets, painted steel scabbard, some wear.

blade 30.5in (77.5cm) long

£150-200 **W&W**

A scarce Prussian M1852 cavalry troopers' sabre, fullered blade with WK & C trademark, etched "Firma I W Schoonman Stoel-Breda", "Izerhouwer", wire bound fishskin grip, brass mounted leather scabbard with leather frog, well worn, scabbard split.

blade 37in (94cm) long

£180-220 **W&W**

A French naval officer's M1837 dress sword, plain blade, gilt brass hilt with fouled anchor against flags on guard, folding sideguard, wire bound wooden grip, in its gilt brass mounted leather scabbard.

blade 29in (74cm) long

£180-220 **W&W**

A well-made late 16thC style Continental broadsword, straight broad double-edged fullered blade with maker's marks and stamps, with two guard rings, swollen flattened quillons, thumb ring and four rear bars to guard.

blade 36in (91.5cm) long

£1,200-1,800 **W&W**

A Continental military sidearm, curved blade, one piece plated brass hilt with ribbed grip and "Liberte" on crosspiece, patent leather scabbard with plated brass mounts, blade and scabbard worn.

blade 25in (63.5cm) long

£100-150 **W&W**

A Masonic sword, slender blade by G. Kenning & Son, London, Liverpool, Manchester and Glasgow, with masonic symbols, brass cruciform hilt, wire bound grip, in its brass mounted leather scabbard.

blade 27.75in (70.5cm) long

£120-180 **W&W**

A scarce Army Hospital Corps type private's sword, straight unfullered blade, ribbed iron grip with crowned GR mark and inspector's stamp, ribbed iron grip with brass guard, the crosspiece stamped "1/78", blade lightly pitted.

blade 27in (68.5cm) long

£150-200 **W&W**

An African Fang tribal shortsword Fa from the Gabon, with barbed forte, brass wire bound at root, with monitor lizard skin covered wooden sheath.

blade 13.5in (34.5cm) long

£180-220 **W&W**

An African Kuba tribal shortsword Ilwoon from Southern Congo, deep off set 'fullers', wooden hilt carved with cup-shaped pommel carved with two faces.

blade 18in (46cm) long

£150-200 **W&W**

A Chilean courtsword, hollow ground triangular section blade etched with military trophies, regulation gilt brass hilt, pierced guard, chiselled with arms of Chile, two-piece mother-of-pearl grips, leather scabbard.

blade 30.25in (77cm) long

£450-550 **W&W**

A nicely mounted Japanese sword Wakizashi, tsuba iron binding in imitation of tape, iron fuchi kashira chiselled as a catfish swallowing its tail, saya with copper bands, one missing, over fine fish skin covering with large iron kojiri.

blade 17.5in (44cm) long

£600-900 **W&W**

An Indian dagger katar, broad blade with raised central rib and thickened armour piercing tip, hilt sides pierced and with silver damascened decoration.

c1700 *10in (25.5cm) long*

£280-320 **W&W**

An early 18thC Indian watered steel katar, blade of finely watered oriental damascus steel with thickened armour piercing tip and raised ribs.

16in (41cm) long

£250-350 **W&W**

A midshipman's dirk, ivory handle with lion mask gilt metal finial, stiletto blade in a gilt metal sheaf cast in relief with the bust of a Classical warrior and an oval paterae.

c1800

£300-400 **GORL**

A 19thC Turkish watered steel dagger, blade of finely watered dark steel, chiselled at forte with gilt Islamic inscription and lion, gold inlaid brown jade hilt of three sections, Islamic inscriptions, velvet sheath with embossed gilt mounts.

blade 8in (20.5cm) long

£600-900 **W&W**

A Kamba Tribal knife Panga from Kenya, shaped blade, wooden hilt, leather covered sheath.

blade 13in (33cm) long

£30-50 **W&W**

A pair of Victorian pole axes, each with polished steel head engraved on either side with a boar's head and shield crest, steel straps enclose faceted oak poles terminating in turned steel caps.

11in (27.5cm) long

£1,000-1,500 **FRE**

A Mauser bayonet, blade stamped "Carl Eickhorn", and etched "SS II Panzer Division Das Reich" regulation hilt with wooden grips, backstrap etched "SS Das Reich", in its blued steel sheath, frog stud etched "SS".

blade 9in (23cm) long

£180-220 **W&W**

An African Guduf tribal throwing knife from Mandara Mountains, North Cameroon, crescent shaped top with lateral projection, leather covered grip.

25in (63.5cm) long

£150-200 **W&W**

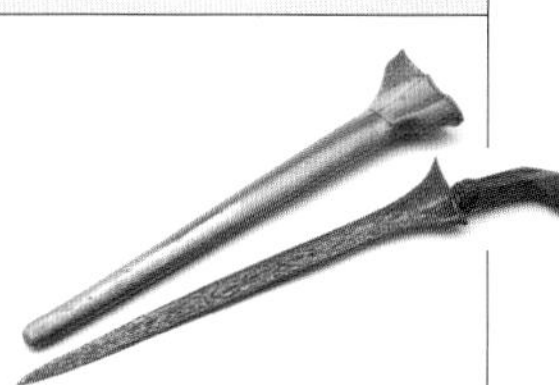

An early Javanese kris, straight swollen etched pamor watered blade, wooden hilt with silver filigree cup, in its sheath.

blade 14in (35.5cm) long

£100-150 **W&W**

An unusual Sumatran kris, early wavy blade of distinct pamor carved with a stylized naga, with gilt filigree cup, carved wooden hilt as Raksha, in carved wooden sheath.

£180-220 **W&W**

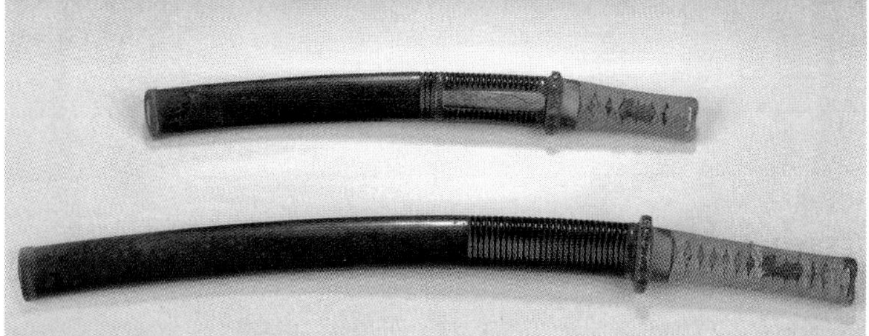

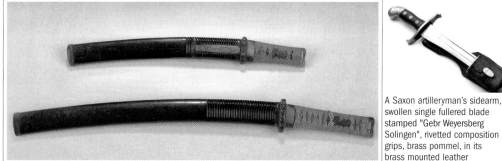

A fine set of Japanese Tanto short swords for a boy, the white rayskin grips bound with pale buff cord, with bronze hilt ornament, menuki, both with single edge watered blades, horn mounts and tsuba, lacquered scabbards, the smaller sword with skewer, kogai, the collar, habaki, decorated with gilt flame design.

larger 13in (33cm) long

£1,200-1,800 **L&T**

A Saxon artilleryman's sidearm, swollen single fullered blade stamped "Gebr Weyersberg Solingen", rivetted composition grips, brass pommel, in its brass mounted leather scabbard with frog.

blade 24in (61cm) long

£400-600 **W&W**

PISTOLS

A Continental early 18thC flintlock holster pistol, the lock signed "Corbau-A-Maastricht" with plain 13 bore barrel, brass fore-sight, spurred brass pommel, minor damage to spur tips, brass trigger guard, replacement ramrod and pipe, pale fruitwood full stock with carved shell behind tang.

19in (47.5cm) long

£17,000-20,000 **L&T**

A 22 bore Queen Anne cannon barrelled flintlock pistol by Lewis Barbar, turn-off barrel, with London and maker's proofs at breech, bulbous walnut butt, silver wire inlaid sideplate, and silver butt cap with raised edge.

c1710 *10in (25.5cm) long*

£1,200-1,800 **W&W**

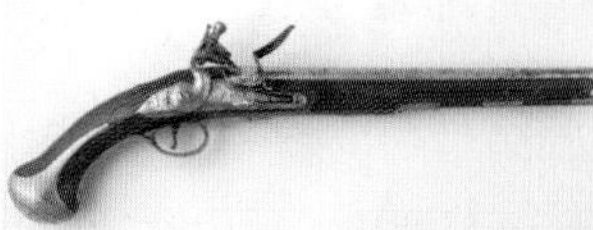

A scarce .56in Heavy Dragoon flintlock holster pistol to the Inniskilling Dragoons, barrel with Tower proofs and engraved "Inniskg. Drags", rounded lock, engraved with crowned GR and "Grice 1760", walnut fullstock, long spurred butt cap and wavy sideplate, ramrod replaced.

19in (48.5cm) long

£800-1,200 **W&W**

A pair of mid-18thC flintlock, box-lock, turn off cannon barrelled 'Queen Anne' pistols, the locks signed "Wilson London", with view and proof marks and maker's stamp, flat side dark walnut slat butts, inlaid with scrolled silver wire decoration.

c1760 *11in (27.5cm) long*

£2,500-3,000 **L&T**

A pair of brass barrelled and brass framed flintlock boxlock blunderbuss pistols with spring bayonets, by Waters & Co., stamped "Thos Gill", the frames engraved in script "Waters & Co, Patent", hallmarked Birmingham. 1780.

1780 *12.5in (32cm) long*

£3,800-4,200 **W&W**

A 24-bore cannon barrelled flintlock boxlock pistol, by Clarkson, turn-off barrel, London and maker's proofs at breech, walnut butt with simple silver wire inlay and silver grotesque mask buttcap, slight repairs.

c1780 *11.75in (30cm) long*

£800-1,200 **W&W**

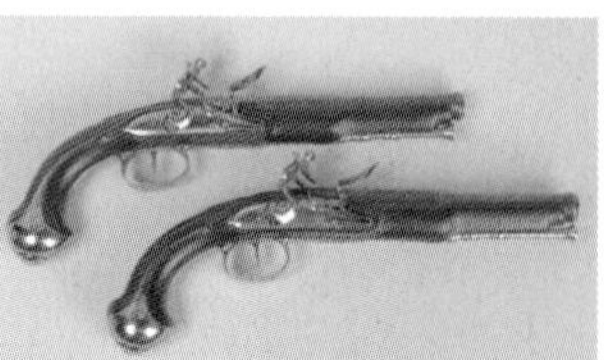

A pair of late 18thC French flintlock pistols, with blued steel barrels decorated with sun-eclipses covered by the moon, unsigned but probably by LePage.

c1790 *12.5in (32cm) long*

£18,000-20,000 **RN**

A cased pair of 30-bore flintlock duelling pistols by D. Egg, octagonal barrels with gold details and gold inlaid on top flat "D. Egg London", spurred trigger guards with single set triggers, in original case.

c1795 *15in (38.5cm) long*

£4,500-5,500 **W&W**

A good three barrelled 160-bore flintlock boxlock tap action pocket pistol, by Whalley, Macclesfield, turn-off barrels, numbered 1 to 3 and with Tower private proofs at breech, plain walnut butt.

c1800 *6.25in (16cm) long*

£1,200-1,800 **W&W**

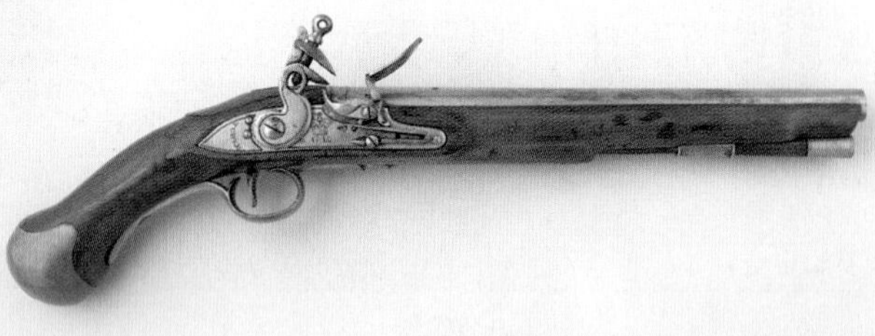

A .56in Tower long flintlock sea service pistol, barrel with Tower proofs, flat lock with engraved line border and crowned GR and Tower, pale walnut fullstock with clear 1806 store keeper's mark, regulation brass mounts, steel belt hook, brass tipped wooden ramrod.

19in (48.5cm) long

£2,800-3,200 **W&W**

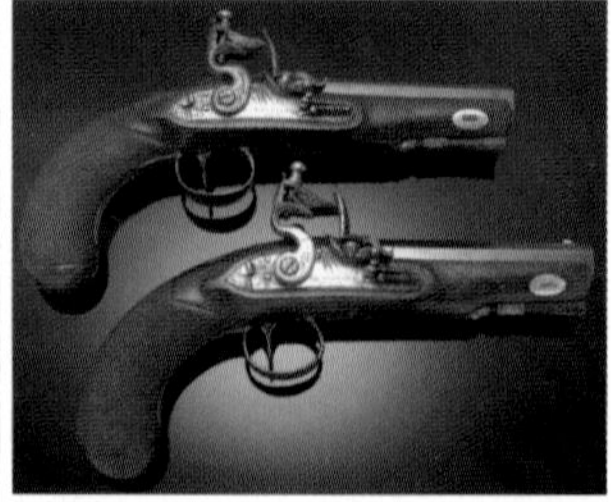

A pair of early 19thC flintlock travelling pistols, the flat sided stepped locks with safety slides, signed "W. Ketland", rain-proof pans, roller frizzen springs, octagonal Damacus barrels, engraved "LONDON", silver foresights, chequered walnut full stocks, original ramrods.

10in (25cm) long

£1,500-2,000 **L&T**

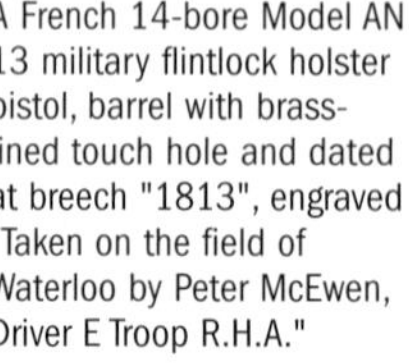

A French 14-bore Model AN 13 military flintlock holster pistol, barrel with brass-lined touch hole and dated at breech "1813", engraved "Taken on the field of Waterloo by Peter McEwen, Driver E Troop R.H.A."

14in (35.5cm) long

£1,200-1,800 **W&W**

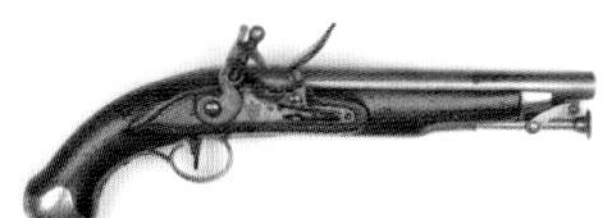

A .56in William IV Sea Service flintlock belt pistol, Tower military proofs, fullstocked, engraved with crowned WR, regulation brass mounts, swivel ramrod, sprung steel belt hook, stock struck with "BO" and broad arrow.

15.25in (39cm) long

£1,500-1,800 **W&W**

A .65in. William IV flintlock cavalry pistol of the Nottinghamshire Yeomanry, with Enfield military proofs, stepped bolted lock with crowned WR stamp, pale walnut fullstock, the trigger guard engraved "N-Y/D/78", swivel ramrod.

15in (38cm) long

£2,200-2,800 **W&W**

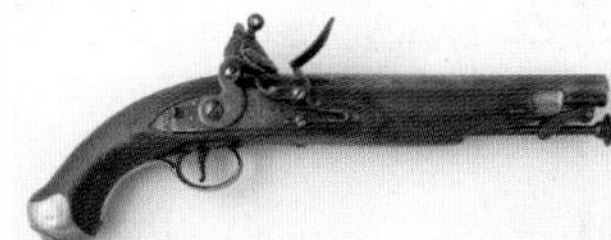

A .65in Tower New Land pattern flintlock holster pistol, barrel with Tower proofs, plain stepped lock with safety bolt, walnut fullstock, regulation brass mounts, the trigger guard numbered "83", swivel ramrod.

15in (38cm) long

£1,800-2,200 **W&W**

A 16 bore flintlock holster pistol by E. & W. Bond, London proved, stamped "Cornhill London", London civilian proofs, fullstocked, bolted lock engraved "E & W Bond", regulation brass mounts, brass tipped wooden ramrod.

14in (35.5cm) long

£600-900 **W&W**

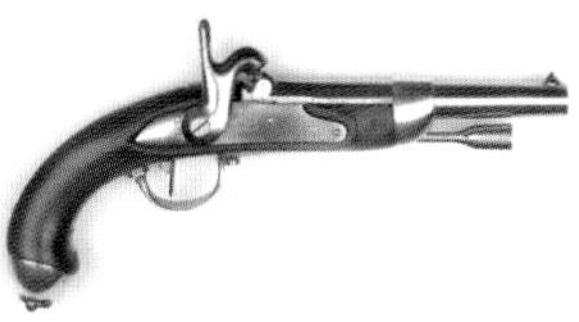

A 13 bore French Model 1822 percussion holster pistol, barrel tang etched "Mle 1822 bis", halfstocked, lock etched "Mre Impale de Chatellerault", stock with faint arsenal stamps including Chatell.

13.75in (35cm) long

£400-600 **W&W**

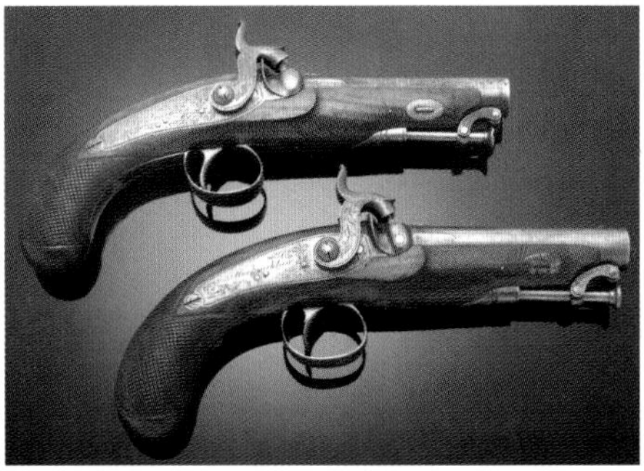

A 19thC pair of Scottish percussion travelling pistols, the back action locks signed "MacLauchlan", the barrels with gold line at the flase breech, engraved "Edinburgh", with captive swivel ram-rods, walnut full stocks.

8in (20cm) long

£1,200-1,800 **L&T**

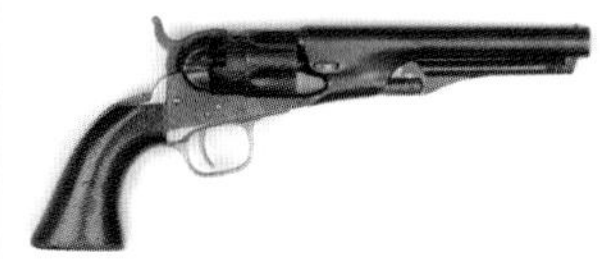

A five shot .36in. Colt Police SA percussion revolver, rebated cylinder stamped "Pat Sept 19th 1850", framed stamped "Colts Patent" brass backstrap and trigger guard stamped "36 Cal".

11in (28cm) long

£700-1,000 **W&W**

A six shot .44in Remington New Model Army single action percussion revolver, barrel number 122196, plain walnut grips, the left hand grip with inspector's initials "OVA".

13in (33cm) long

£1,800-2,200 **W&W**

A six shot .44in Starr Arms Co. double-action Army percussion revolver, barrel number 16920, inspector's stamp "B" on all parts, walnut butt with two sets of inspector's initials "GKC" and "CSL".

11in (28cm) long

£800-1,200 **W&W**

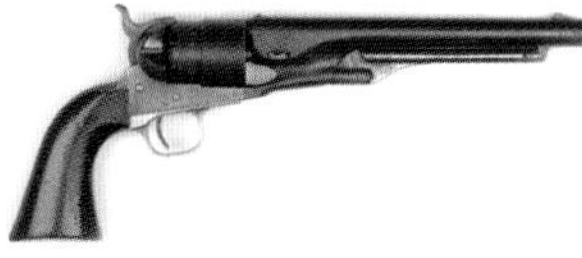

A six shot .44in Colt Army SA percussion revolver No 184025, round barrel stamped "Address Col Saml Colt New York US America" now fitted with an open rearsight, underlever rammer, rebated cylinder etched with naval engagement scene.

14in (35.5cm) long

£500-700 **W&W**

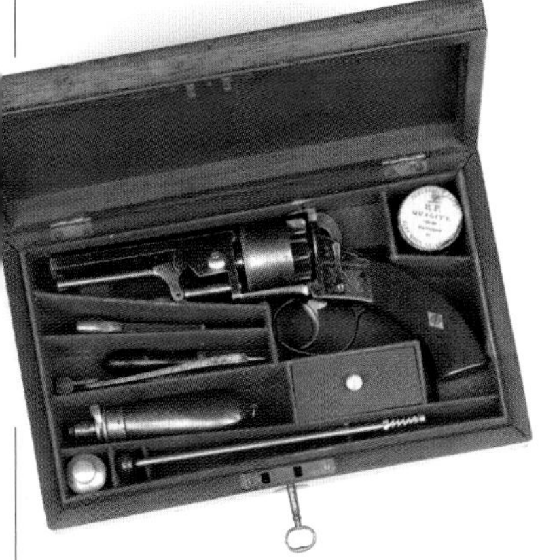

A six shot 60 bore Bentley type self-cocking open wedge frame percussion revolver, octagonal barrel engraved "S Booth & Co, London", Birmingham proved, numbered chambers, hinged rammer beneath barrel, in mahogany case, possibly non-original, with a Hawksley pistol flask, 60-bore steel pincher mould and other tools.

gun 9in (23cm) long

£1,200-1,800 **W&W**

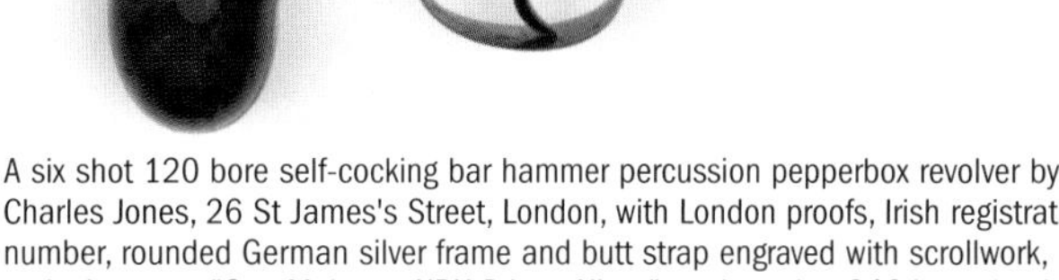

A six shot 120 bore self-cocking bar hammer percussion pepperbox revolver by Charles Jones, 26 St James's Street, London, with London proofs, Irish registration number, rounded German silver frame and butt strap engraved with scrollwork, maker's name, "Gun Maker to HRH Prince Albert", and number 246 in oval, raised knurled edge to frame, unusual external barrel locking catch.

7in (18cm) long

£1,200-1,800 **W&W**

A four-shot .30in RF Remington Elliot pocket pistol, stamped "Manufactured by E Remington & Sons Ilion NY", "Elliots' Patents May 29.1860 Oct 1 1861", ring trigger, traces of plating to frame, two-piece composition grips.

5in (13cm) long

£280-320 **W&W**

A scarce French 'Harmonica' pistol, 10 barrels with multi groove rifling, 7mm pinfire second-type Jarre's Patent self cocking, numbered "36" and stamped "A. Jarre Bte S G D G", boxlock action with unguarded hooked trigger.

5in (13cm) long

£2,500-3,000 **W&W**

A rare and important German custom-made broom handle Bolo Mauser pistol with attachable stock and leather holster, model 1896, barrel and frame highly engraved, rosewood military grips, matching elaborate leaf-carved oak case, automatic, 10 shot, with complete factory markings and matching serial numbers, marked "Waffenfabrik Mauser/ Oberndorf A. Neckar." serial no. 584888.

This piece appears never to have been fired. It was presented by the Mauser company to a member of the nobility or to high-ranking civil or military official.

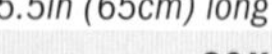

25.5in (65cm) long

£24,000-26,000 **S&K**

A scarce six-shot 'Apache' folding knuckleduster/dagger/revolver, a 5mm pinfire steel framed Dolne self-cocking weapon, with folding wavy blade, Liege proved, folding trigger.

7.75in (20cm) long

£1,500-2,000 **W&W**

A .41in. RF Remington Derringer DB pocket pistol, tip up barrels, stamped "Remington Arms Co Ilion NY" with ejector slide, sheathed trigger, swivel catch locks barrels.

4.75in (12cm) long

£400-600 **W&W**

A six-shot .30in RF Forehand & Wadsworth DA revolver, stamped "Patd Jun 27'71-Oct 28'73", stamped "Forehand & Wadsworth Double Action No. 32. Worcester Mass", fluted cylinder.

6in (15.5cm) long

£180-220 **W&W**

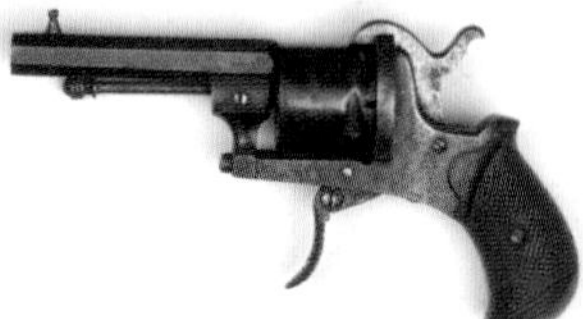

A five-shot 7mm PF DA revolver, 3in octagonal barrel engraved with retailer "E M Reilly & Co, 277 Oxford St, London", liege proofs, blued cylinder stamped "The Guardian American Model of 1878", sidegate loading, ejector rod.

6in (15.5cm) long

£150-200 **W&W**

A pre-war .22 'Webley Senior' slant grip air pistol, number S8907, standard markings and patent dates on air chamber, in case with trade label of "Edward Whistler, 11 Strand, Charing Cross, WC", containing an orange Webley .22in pellet tin and metal cleaning brush.

£300-500 **W&W**

A .41in RF Colt Derringer No 3 pistol No 25861, barrel 2in. London proved, stamped "Colt" with traces of original blued finish, brass frame with Colt trademark stamp, sheathed trigger.

4in (10.5cm) long

£380-420 **W&W**

A late 18thC flintlock, fowling-piece signed "BATE" in gold ovals on the lock and on the top flat of the two stage single browned barrel, octagonal at the breech with gold line at the false breech, with gold touch hole, steel furniture with acorn finial, full walnut stock, secured with four barrel bolts.

33.5in (85cm) long

£1,200-1,800 **L&T**

A rare 11mm Austrian Model 1799 officer's repeating air rifle by Contriner, Vienna, two-stage barrel, the breech section engraved "Contriner" and with broad gold band, tube magazine in right side of breech, engraved with trophy of flags and "in Wien" and initials "JC", brass frame, engraved brass trigger guard, leather covered butt/reservoir.

34in (86.5cm) long

£3,500-4,500 **W&W**

A 19thC 12 bore black powder, under-lever, hammer gun, the scroll engraved back action locks signed B. Woodward & Son, re-browned, side by side, Damascus barrels engraved "London laminated steel," possible replacement fore-end action.

barrel 27.25in (69.5cm) long

£320-380 **L&T**

A 19thC 28 bore side by side double barrel, back action, hammer sporting gun, signed "Joseph Bourne and Son, Birmingham", chequered walnut stock with Continental butt plate.

barrels 28in (71.5cm) long

£1,500-2,000 **L&T**

A 12 bore side by side double barrel hammer nose ejector sporting gun, number 4943, signed "Adams & Co." and "Adams Patent Small Arms Co. 391 Strand London", chequered walnut stock with leather cheekpiece, action re-blued trigger guard.

c1860 *barrel 30in (76.5cm) long*

£500-700 **L&T**

A James Purdey sporting gun, 12 bore under lever, side by side, hammer none ejector, signed "PURDEY", engraved "J. PURDEY 314, OXFORD STREET, LONDON", marked with serial number "7108" for which the makers confirm a date of 1865, chequered walnut stock.

£1,500-2,000 **L&T**

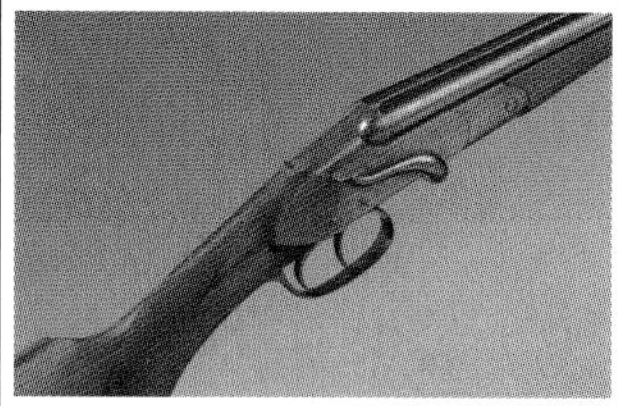

A .410 side by side blued double barrel sporting gun, chambered none ejector with side lever, with initials "DF" pierced with an arrow, Continental proof marks, horn cap and bone screw cover, cocking indicators.

barrel 29in (74cm) long

£300-400 **L&T**

A .577"/.450in Martini Henry action rifle, number 12402 by Westley Richards for the Zuid Afrikaans Republik, Birmingham proved, stamped "Westley Richards & CO. Henry Rifling" and "1897", ladder rearsight to 1200 yards, two steel barrel bands with bayonet lug on front band, steel cleaning rod.

50in (127cm) long

£500-800 **W&W**

A scarce 10 bore India Pattern Brown Bess flintlock musket, issued to the Shelburne Militia (Nova Scotia), barrel with Tower of London military proofmarks, the comb later carved on the left side with a cheekpiece presumably in Canada by or for the Militia.

55in (140cm) long

£1,500-2,000 **W&W**

A .54" Burnside 1st Model breech loading underlever falling block military percussion carbine, the falling breech block numbered "36871", back action lock marked "Burnshide Rifle Co, Providence RI".

39in (99cm) long

£600-900 **W&W**

A 12 bore percussion sporting gun, by Samual Nock, London, twist barrels with two platinum lines at breech, scroll engraved locks with fern to borders and maker's name in gothic script, grip safety catch, chequered wrist, steel mounts.

47in (119.5cm) long

£400-600 **W&W**

A single-barrel 12 bore percussion sporting gun, by John Manton & Son, London, two-stage twist barrel, engraved lock, detachable hammer nose, halfstocked with horn fore cap and chequered wrist, and silver barrel wedge plate.

46.25in (117.5cm) long

£600-900 **W&W**

A scarce 7mm Giffard's patent gas rifle, gold inlaid "Ste Stephanoise d'Armes St Etienne", with balloon trademark at breech, scroll engraved frame with revolving loading top, central hammer, adjustable trigger, walnut butt with chequered wrist.

41in (104.5cm) long

£400-500 **W&W**

HELMETS

A cabasset, formed in one piece, pear stalk finial, traces of armourer's stamp to brim with roped edge, brass rivet heads.

c1600

£500-800 **W&W**

A cabasset, formed in one piece, pear stalk finial, roped brim struck with armourer's mark, ornamental brass rivet heads.

c1600

£500-800 **W&W**

A cabasset, formed in one piece, pear stalk finial, etched with six groups of three vertical lines, traces of armourer's stamp to brim.

c1600

£500-800 **W&W**

A 17thC funerary helmet, two piece skull with tall comb and rivetted spike, visor fixed with four bars, sunken borders with ornamental rivet heads, two patched holes to skull covered overall with paint.

These helmets were made to hang as 'funerary achievements' over tombs inside churches, the spikes were fitted for securing to timber beams.

£1,500-2,000 **W&W**

A pre-1888 officer's busby of the Warwickshire Yeomanry (Hussars), white busby bag with silver braid trim and gimp button, silver-plated chin chain, ostrich and vulture feather plume in socket, with a framed photo of a Major in full dress marked "Earl of Warwick", service wear.

7.75in (19.5cm) high

£1,200-1,800 **W&W**

A Victorian OR's lance cap of The 17th (Duke of Cambridge's Own) Lancers, patent leather, rayed plated with battle honours to South Africa 1879, original chin chain with lion's head ear bosses, white hair plume, leather and oil-skin liner, "WD" stamp for 1901 inside.

£1,200-1,800 **W&W**

An officer's rifle green cloth spiked helmet, of the King's Own Light Infantry (South Yorkshire Regt), velvet-backed chin chain and ear rosettes, gilt and silver plated first pattern helmet plate, motto scroll and title scroll "The South Yorkshire Regiment", padded silk lining.

c1885

£800-1,200 **W&W**

A scarce Victorian OR's lance cap, of the 21st Lancers, black patent leather skull, peak and top, French grey and yellow cloth, brass mounts, rayed plated and chin chain with lion's head ear bosses, white hair plume in socket, leather and oil-skin liner.

c1895

£1,500-2,000 **W&W**

A post-1902 OR's lance cap of the 9th (Queen's Royal) Lancers, black patent leather skull, peak and top, blue cloth sides, brass ornamental band, chinstrap with lion's head ear bosses, black and white hair plume, leather and oilskin liner.

£800-1,200 **W&W**

A George V officer's lance cap of the 16th (The Queen's) Lancers, with gilt maker's stamp of Hawks & Co. Piccadilly, London.

£4,000-6,000 **W&W**

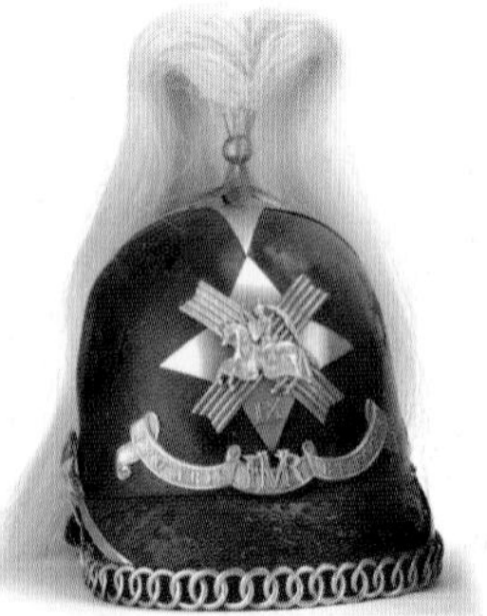

A scarce officer's black leather helmet of the Fife Mounted Rifles, brass and white metal regimental pattern four-pointed star and cross top mount, badge with Thane of Fife and ear rosettes, motto scroll, with "FMR" to the centre, white hair plume.

£500-700 **W&W**

An Imperial German Troopers helmet of the Saxon Garde Reiter Regiment, tombak skull, helmet plate of a silvered rayed star, with Saxony arms in the centre, brass leather-backed chinscales, lobster trailed neckguard, silvered lion parade crest supporting shield with Royal Chypher, leather lining.

£5,000-8,000 **W&W**

CERAMICS

Ceramicists have never been far from the cutting edge of the various fashions to have influenced the Decorative Arts, from the Aesthetic and Arts and Crafts movements, through Art Nouveau and Art Deco and on to Modernism and beyond. In all of these areas the emphasis has often been on craftsmanship, strength of design and experimentation with new materials.

Items which have been influential in the history of design will command high prices. The more elaborate aesthetics, for example Art Nouveau, do not always fit in with the current vogue for pared down interiors. The simpler lines of Art Deco, Modernist, and mid-20thC Scandinavian and Italian design are more in favour at present. Pottery by named designers will usually outperform generic pieces, although any item which represents a style or era particularly well is desirable.

CARLTON WARE

Not officially called 'Carlton Ware' until 1958, James Wiltshaw's company enjoyed great success during the inter-war period with the production of the highly collectable 'Tutenkahmen' and 'Mikado' ranges. Always finely attuned to popular taste and market trends, in 1929 the company became the first to manufacture 'oven to table' ceramics. Post-war investment in technology paid off and throughout the 1950s Carlton enjoyed high demand for its 'Royale' lustre ware and a wide range of hand-painted pieces. The 1970s 'Walking Ware' range was Carlton's last great popular success, but was insufficient to halt the period of decline ushered in by Cuthbert Wiltshaw's death in 1966. The firm is no longer trading.

A Carlton ware 'Prickly Pansy' vase and cover, pattern number 3449, printed and painted marks.

11in (28cm) high

£500-700 **WW**

A Carlton ware 'Bell' vase and cover, pattern number 3774, printed and painted marks, restored.

7in (18cm) high

£300-500 **WW**

A Carlton ware ginger jar, with floral 'Comets' pattern.

c1925 *5.25in (13.5cm) high*

£300-500 **TDG**

A Carlton ware 'Rouge Royale' ginger jar and cover, printed and painted with gilt and coloured enamels with a chinoiserie scene, printed marks.

8.75in (22cm) high

£180-220 **L&T**

A Carlton ware ginger jar with 'Dragon and Cloud' decoration.

c1925 *10.5in (26.5cm) high*

£400-600 **TDG**

A Carlton ware 'Crested Bird and Waterlily' jar and cover, printed and painted marks, paper label, hairline to cover.

6in (16cm) high

£280-320 **WW**

A Carlton ware 'Crested Bird and Waterlily' vase, pattern number 3530, printed and painted marks.

6.25in (16cm) high

£320-380 **WW**

A Carlton ware 'Paradise Bird and Tree with Cloud' vase, pattern number 3144, printed and painted mark.

6in (15.5cm) high

£300-500 **WW**

A Carlton ware 'Floral Comets' vase, pattern number 3422, printed and painted marks, minor wear to gilt top rim.

6in (15.5cm) high

£400-600 **WW**

A Carlton ware ovoid vase, decorated in the 'Sketching Bird' pattern, printed and painted marks.

7.5in (19cm) high

£280-320 **L&T**

A Carlton ware shouldered ovoid vase, with twin handles decorated in the 'Pagoda Landscape' pattern, on a green ground, printed and painted marks.

10.25in (25.5cm) high

£180-220 **L&T**

A Carlton ware 'Spider's Web' Rouge Royale twin-handled pedestal bowl, printed mark.

13in (33cm) wide

£150-200 **WW**

A Carlton ware 'Mandarins Chatting' pattern ovoid jug, pattern number 3654, printed and painted marks.

7.25in (18cm) high

£700-1,000 **L&T**

A Carlton ware 'Babylon' jug, pattern number 4163, printed and painted marks.

8in (20cm) high

£180-220 **WW**

A Carlton ware 'Devil's Copse' flower vase and brick, pattern number 3817, on matt turquoise ground, printed and painted mark.

8in (20cm) diam

£300-400 **WW**

A Carlton ware 'Floral Comets' powder bowl and cover, pattern number 3387, printed and painted marks.

5.5in (14cm) diam

£180-220 **WW**

A Carlton ware 'Tutenkahmen' bowl, printed and enamelled in colours and gilt, printed marks.

5.5in (14cm) diam

£220-280 **WW**

A Carlton ware 'Lace Cap Hydrangea' pattern twin-handled sandwich plate, printed and painted marks.

8.5in (21.5cm) wide

£70-100 **L&T**

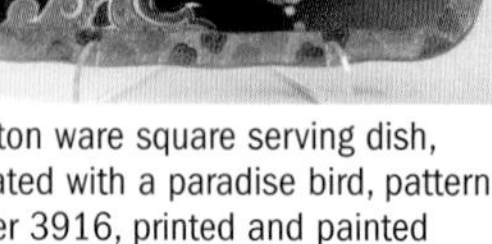

A Carlton ware square serving dish, decorated with a paradise bird, pattern number 3916, printed and painted marks.

9.75in (24cm) wide

£180-220 **L&T**

A Carlton ware 'Hollyhocks' circular bowl, pattern number 3973, printed and painted marks.

10in (25cm) diam

£80-120 **L&T**

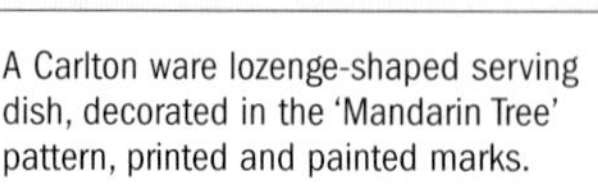

A Carlton ware lozenge-shaped serving dish, decorated in the 'Mandarin Tree' pattern, printed and painted marks.

12.25in (30.5cm) wide

£80-120 **L&T**

CLARICE CLIFF

A native of the Potteries, Clarice Cliff (1899-1972) started work as an enameller at the age of 13. At the age of 28 she launched her 'Bizarre Ware' range of tableware in colourful, geometric designs inspired by natural forms, fine art and the built environment. Although in stark contrast to the more sober taste of the time, 'Bizarre' was a runaway success throughout the 1930s and was followed by another range called 'Fantasque'. Cliff became Art Director of the Newport pottery in Burslem, responsible for the work of 1,000 potters and painters. Pottery bearing the Clarice Cliff name was produced until 1964.

A Clarice Cliff 'Circle Tree' vase, shape number 342.

7.75in (19cm) high

£800-1,200 **FRE**

A Clarice Cliff 'Pastel Melon' Bizarre vase, shape number 342, printed mark.

7.75in (20cm) high

£800-1,200 **WW**

A Clarice Cliff 'Whisper' Bizarre Isis vase, painted in colours, printed mark, restored.

10in (25cm) high

£400-600 **WW**

A Clarice Cliff 'Secrets' Bizarre Meiping vase, printed mark.

6.5in (16cm) high

£500-800 **WW**

A Clarice Cliff 'Orange Trees and Houses' Fantasque Meiping vase, decorated between blue borders, printed marks.

6.5in (16cm) high

£1,800-2,200 **WW**

A Clarice Cliff Fantasque flaring vase, decorated in the 'Orange Trees and House' pattern, printed marks.

8in (20cm) high

£500-800 **L&T**

A Clarice Cliff 'Inspiration Asters' Bizarre vase, printed and painted marks, sliver chip to base rim.

5.5in (13.5cm) high

£300-400 **WW**

A CLOSER LOOK AT A CLARICE CLIFF MINIATURE VASE

The Appliqué Lucerne pattern had two colourways. As well as the blue sky version shown here there was a version with orange sky. Although produced in similar quantities, collectors tend to prefer this blue version.

Probably a sample, this shape and size of vase would not have been available for general retail and so is very rare today.

The quality of the painting and the vibrancy of the colours is exceptional.

Clarice Cliff pottery with this pattern often commands very high prices at auction. An Appliqué Lucerne charger sold for nearly £10,000 in 2001.

A rare Clarice Cliff 'Appliqué Lucerne' miniature vase, printed factory mark.

The high quality of painting and the fact that the vase is a miniature would suggest that this is a tradesman's sample vase. The vase is painted with the whole Lucerne pattern between red, black and red bands.

3in (7.5cm) high

£2,200-2,800 **WW**

A Clarice Cliff 'Pastel Autumn' Bizarre vase, shape number 280, printed mark.

6in (15.5cm) high

£400-600 **WW**

A Clarice Cliff 'Original Bizarre' vase, painted with diamond motif, printed mark.

9.5in (24.5cm) high

£600-900 **WW**

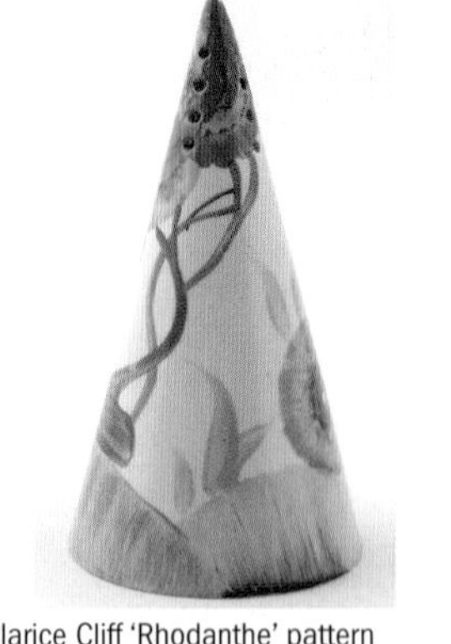

A Clarice Cliff 'Rhodanthe' pattern Bizarre conical sugar sifter, printed mark.

5.5in (14cm) high

£320-380 **WW**

A Clarice Cliff 'Orange Autumn' pattern Fantasque conical sugar sifter.

5.5in (14cm) high

£400-600 **GORL**

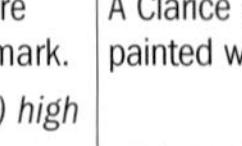

A Clarice Cliff 'Delecia' pattern conical sugar sifter.

5.5in (14cm) high

£400-600 **FRE**

A Clarice Cliff conical sugar sifter, painted in the 'Sandon' pattern, printed mark, staining and small chip.

5.5in (14cm) high

£220-280 **L&T**

A pair of Clarice Cliff 'Gay Day' pattern Bizarre book ends, retailed by Brice Rogers, printed marks, chip to back of one.

6.25in (16cm) high

£400-600 **WW**

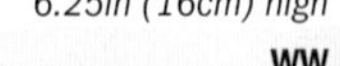

A Clarice Cliff 'Coral Firs' pattern Lynton sugar sifter.

5in (12.5cm) high

£400-600 **FRE**

A Clarice Cliff 'Original Bizarre' plate, printed mark.

10in (25.5cm) diam

£220-280 **WW**

A Clarice Cliff 'Original Bizarre' plate, printed mark.

10.5in (26.5cm) diam

£220-280 **WW**

A Clarice Cliff 'Young Ballerinas' Bizarre plate, designed by Dame Laura Knight, printed mark, restored rim.

9in (22.5cm) diam

£150-200 **WW**

A rare Clarice Cliff 'Appliqué Avignon' wall charger, painted with a radial design inside black borders, printed and painted mark, restored rim.

18in (46cm) diam

£6,000-8,000 **WW**

A Clarice Cliff 'Appliqué Idyll' Bizarre wall plaque, painted in colours, printed mark, minor paint loss to black band.

13.5in (34cm) diam

£2,000-3,000 **WW**

A Clarice Cliff green floral 'Nuage' pattern biscuit jar.

5.5in (14cm) high

£220-280 **FRE**

A Clarice Cliff 'Broth' Fantasque conical bowl, printed mark.

7.5in (19cm) diam

£1,200-1,800 **WW**

A Clarice Cliff 'Limberlost' Fantasque beehive honeypot and cover, printed marks, restored.

4in (10cm) high

£320-380 **WW**

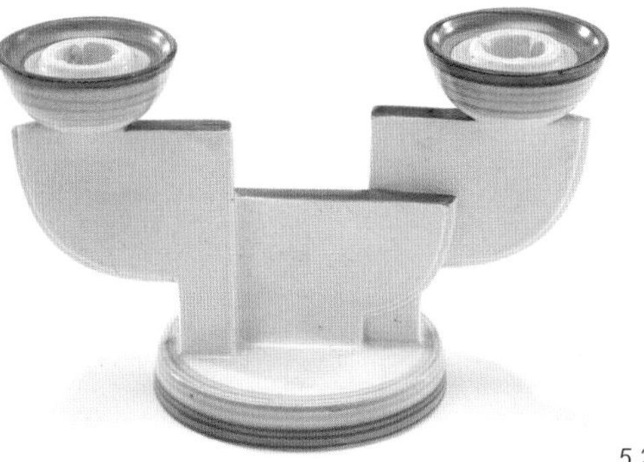

A Clarice Cliff double candlestick, shape number 609.

5.25in (13cm) high

£350-400 **FRE**

A Clarice Cliff 'May Avenue' Bizarre Crown jug, printed mark, restoration.

6in (16cm) wide.

£2,000-2,500 **WW**

A Clarice Cliff 'Orange House' Fantasque Crown jug, printed mark.

7.5in (19cm) wide

£800-1,200 **WW**

A Clarice Cliff 'Nasturtium' pattern lotus jug.

11.5in (29cm) high

£1,000-1,500 **FRE**

A Clarice Cliff 'Garland' pattern conical biscuit barrel, with silver plate handle.

9.5in (24cm) high

£800-1,200 **FRE**

A Clarice Cliff 'Appliqué Blue Lugano' Tankard coffee can and saucer, printed and painted marks.

2.5in (6.5cm) high

£1,000-1,500 **WW**

A Clarice Cliff 'Blue Crocus' pattern Bizarre globe teapot and cover, printed marks.

5in (12.5cm) high

£400-600 **WW**

A Clarice Cliff 'Secrets' pattern Fantasque clog, printed marks.

4.5in (11cm) wide

£350-400 **CHEF**

A Clarice Cliff 'The Laughing Cat' pattern Bizarre cat figure, painted with green, black and orange spots, printed mark.

4.75in (12cm) high

£600-900 **WW**

DOULTON

A Doulton Lambeth stoneware vase by Hannah Barlow, of tapered cylindrical form with tall rim, incised with a frieze of ponies, impressed and incised marks.

13.25in (33cm) high

£800-1,200 **L&T**

A Doulton Lambeth stoneware vase by Hannah Barlow, of cylindrical footed form with flared rim, incised with a frieze of children and donkeys, impressed and incised mark.

10.75in (27cm) high

£1,500-2,000 **L&T**

A Doulton Lambeth stoneware jug by Hannah Barlow, incised with a cat, restored rim, impressed and incised marks.

8in (20cm) high

£500-800 **L&T**

An early Doulton Lambeth jug by Hannah Barlow, incised with a duck and foliage, with silver rim, impressed mark and incised monogram.

9.25in (23.5cm) high

£1,000-1,500 **WW**

A large Royal Doulton classically shaped vase etched by Hannah Barlow, with mountain goats in a field, stamped marks.

15.5in (39.5cm) high

£1,500-2,000 **DRA**

A pair of Royal Doulton vases by Florence Barlow, painted with birds, with impressed mark and monogram.

10.75in (27.5cm) high

£1,500-2,000 **WW**

A pair of Doulton Lambeth stoneware vases by Florence Barlow, of baluster form with a frieze of sheep and geese.

7in (17.5cm) high

£1,200-1,800 **L&T**

A Doulton Lambeth stoneware vase by Edith Lupton, incised with stylised foliate cartouche, impressed mark.

1888 *11.75in (30cm) high*

£800-1,200 **WW**

A fine Doulton Lambeth tall pitcher, incised with floral medallions, marked "MA", small hole drilled in bottom.

8.5in (21.5cm) high

£70-100 **DRA**

A Doulton Lambeth stoneware tankard, depicting tooled leaves on a brown and beige ground, with hinged pewter lid, marked.

10.5in (26.5cm) high

£100-150 **DRA**

A Doulton Lambeth bulbous pitcher, carved with swirls of wheat in brown, blue, and green on a mottled amber ground, stamped and signed "RB".

7in (18cm) high

£220-280 **DRA**

A George Tinworth for Doulton Lambeth group, titled "The Fable of the Cat and Sparrows", the olive green glazed cat attacking one sparrow while another perches on its back above the blue domed rounded rectangular base, incised and impressed marks.

3.75in (9.5cm) high

£1,500-2,000 **CHEF**

A George Tinworth for Doulton stoneware group of a sea-blue mouse eating a currant from the top of a dark brown bun, incised marks.

2.25in (6cm) high

£1,500-2,000 **CHEF**

A Doulton Lambeth stoneware figure, depicting a brown bear seated with legs and arms astride a woven rush bowl of inverted beehive shape.

4in (10cm) high

£800-1,200 **CHEF**

A Royal Doulton tear-shaped 'Flambé' vase, with cottage by a river, stamped.

7in (18cm) high

£220-280 **DRA**

A Royal Doulton Titanian cylindrical 'Kingfisher' vase, by H.Allen, with a bird perched on a bamboo stalk in front of a pale blue sky, uncrazed, with ink stamp and signed by the artist.

10in (25.5cm) high

£500-700 **DRA**

A Royal Doulton bulbous vase, decorated with applied blue daisies on a mottled brown and bottle-green ground, restored chip to rim, stamped.

10.5in (26.5cm) high

£100-150 **DRA**

A rare Royal Doulton Arts and Crafts floor vase, incised and painted by Charles Noke with a monk taking a stroll amidst tall stylized trees, stamped and incised marks, signed by Noke to the body, some restoration.

Charles Noke (1858-1941) worked for Doulton from 1889. He was responsible for the range of 'Dickens' figures' which proved very popular as a collectable series.

24in (61cm) high

£1,800-2,200 **DRA**

A rare Doulton Chinese Jade covered jar by Charles Noke, with Madonna and Child finial to lid, marked in green ink to base.

4.25in (11cm) high

£600-900 **DRA**

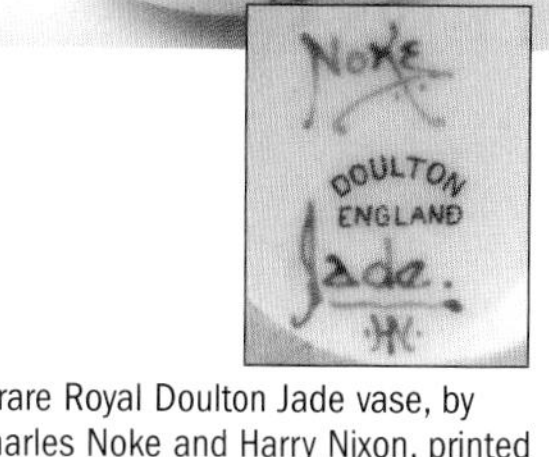

A rare Royal Doulton Jade vase, by Charles Noke and Harry Nixon, printed mark "Doulton England" and painted "Noke Jade" with HN monogram.

3.75in (9.5cm) diam

£400-600 **WW**

A Royal Doulton stoneware water jug, titled "The Old Sarum Kettle", embossed with symbol under a dark and light brown glaze, stamped.

10.75in (27.5cm) high

£100-150 **DRA**

A Royal Doulton figure, 'Tête-à-Tête', HN number 799, designed by Leslie Harradine, painted in colours, printed and painted marks, hairline to base.

£280-320 **WW**

A Royal Doulton figure, 'Willy-Won't-He', HN number 1561, designed by Leslie Harradine, printed and painted marks.

Leslie Harradine produced hundreds of figures for Doulton, many of which are still in production today. He is perhaps best known for his figures of children whose cherubic expressions make them perennially popular.

1933 *5.75in (14cm) high*

£220-280 **L&T**

A Royal Doulton bowl, with silver rim, marks for Birmingham 1921.

4.25in (11cm) diam

£70-100 **BJ**

A Royal Doulton Art Deco figure, 'Marietta', designed by L. Harradine, printed and painted marks "H.N.1341", damaged base.

8.25in (21cm) high

£220-280 **WW**

A Royal Doulton figure, 'Clemency', HN number 1634.

7in (18cm) high

£320-380 **L&T**

A CLOSER LOOK AT A ROYAL DOULTON FIGURE

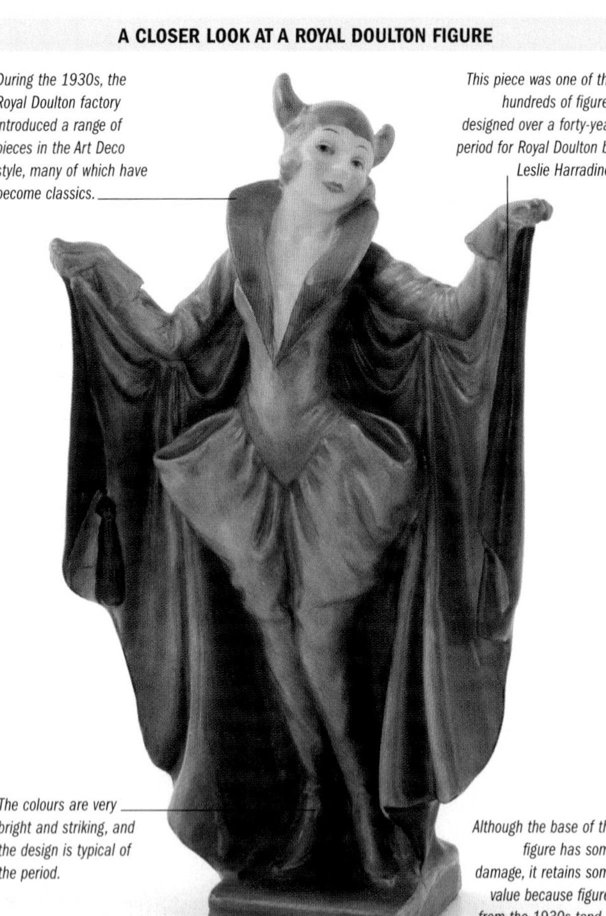

During the 1930s, the Royal Doulton factory introduced a range of pieces in the Art Deco style, many of which have become classics.
This piece was one of the hundreds of figures designed over a forty-year period for Royal Doulton by Leslie Harradine.
The colours are very bright and striking, and the design is typical of the period.
Although the base of the figure has some damage, it retains some value because figures from the 1930s tend to be popular.

A Royal Doulton Art Deco figure, 'Marietta', designed by L. Harradine, printed and painted marks "H.N.1446", damaged base.

8.25in (21cm) high

£320-380 **WW**

A Royal Doulton figure, 'The Apple Maid', HN number 2160.

6.5in (16.5cm) high

£150-200 **L&T**

A Royal Doulton figure, 'Jersey Milkmaid', HN number 2057.

6.5in (16.5cm) high

£80-120 **L&T**

A Royal Doulton figure, 'Pantalettes' HN number 1362.

7.75in (19.5cm) high

£120-180 **L&T**

A Royal Doulton figure, 'Mermaid', HN number 97.

7in (18cm) high

£200-250 **L&T**

A Royal Doulton figure, 'Jack Point', HN number 2080.

16.25in (40.5cm) high

£1,000-1,500 **L&T**

A Royal Doulton figure, 'The Jester', HN number 1702.

10in (25.5cm) high

£320-350 **L&T**

A Royal Doulton figure, 'The Pied Piper', HN number 2102.

8.5in (21.5cm) high

£120-180 **L&T**

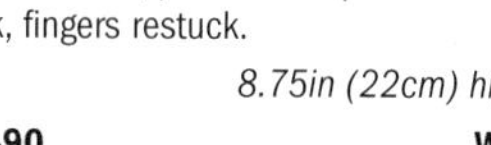

A Royal Doulton figure, 'Mendicant', HN number 1365, printed and painted mark, fingers restuck.

8.75in (22cm) high

£60-90 **WW**

A Royal Doulton figure, 'Recumbent Pig', printed mark, minor glaze loss.

6in (15cm) wide

£280-320 **WW**

A Doulton and Co. character jug, 'Robin Hood', with printed factory mark.

6.5in (16cm) high

£120-180 **L&T**

A Doulton and Co. character jug, 'Jarge', with printed factory mark "D6288".

6.5in (16cm) high

£120-180 **L&T**

A Royal Doulton figure, 'Flower Seller's Children' HN number 1342.

8in (20cm) high

£200-250 **L&T**

A Royal Doulton kingfisher dish, the bird sitting over the dish modelled as a pool enclosed by a rim of leaves, impressed marks.

6.25in (16cm) high

£280-320 **CHEF**

A Royal Doulton musical character jug, 'Tony Weller', printed marks "D.5888", restored.

6.5in (16cm) high

£120-180 **WW**

GOLDSCHEIDER

A Goldscheider figure by Dakon.

14in (35.5cm) high

£1,000-1,500 **BEV**

A Goldscheider Art Deco figure by Dakon, model number 6551, painted in colours, impressed marks and facsimile signature, restored.

15.75in (40cm) high

£1,000-1,500 **WW**

A Goldscheider Art Deco figure by Dakon, modelled as a girl seated on a hat box, impressed marks, facsimile signature, restored.

10.75in (27cm) high

£1,200-1,800 **WW**

A Goldscheider Art Deco figure of a female golfer by Dakon, impressed marks, restored ankles and club shaft.

10.75in (27cm) high

£800-1,200 **WW**

A Goldscheider figure of a dancer by Lorenzl, impressed marks, facsimile signature, plinth restored, minor restoration to back of hat.

13.75in (35cm) high

£800-1,200 **WW**

A Goldscheider pottery figure by Lorenzl, modelled as a seated Spanish lady, impressed marks, restored legs.

13.75in (35cm) high

£700-1,000 **WW**

A Goldscheider Art Deco pottery figure by Lorenzl, impressed "5902", facsimile signature, printed Goldscheider mark, restored waist.

14.25in (36cm) high

£1,800-2,200 **WW**

A Goldscheider figure, modelled as a young girl standing by a terrier dog, impressed marks "7274", restored.

10in (25.5cm) high

£400-600 **WW**

A Goldscheider figure group, by Dakon, modelled as a young clown and ballerina impressed marks and signature, restored.

8.75in (22.5cm) high

£180-220 **WW**

A CLOSER LOOK AT A GOLDSCHEIDER FIGURE

Goldscheider, established in Vienna in 1885, are well known for their striking 20thC figures.

The provocative pose and flamboyant dress of this figure are very representative of Art Deco sensibilities.

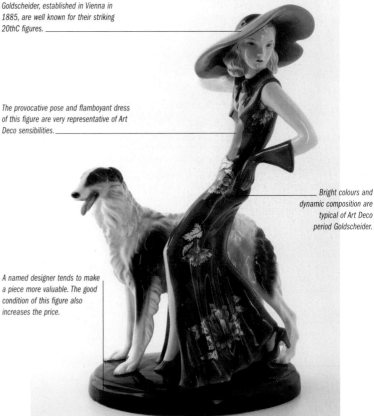

Bright colours and dynamic composition are typical of Art Deco period Goldscheider.

A named designer tends to make a piece more valuable. The good condition of this figure also increases the price.

A Goldscheider Art Deco pottery figure by Claire Herozeg, modelled as a lady in flowing blue dress and broad-rim sun hat walking a borzoi, impressed marks, facsimile signature, small glaze loss to dog's tongue.

17in (43cm) high

£1,500-2,000 **WW**

MAJOLICA

An English majolica fish jug, some damage, restored.

c1870 *8in (20.5cm) high*

£180-220 **DRA**

An English majolica jug, with a frieze of children and dogs on a cobalt blue ground, restored chip to rim.

c1865 *8in (20.5cm) high*

£220-280 **DRA**

A mid-Victorian Minton majolica mask jug, the baluster shape moulded with mistletoe and holly bands on a blue ground, separated by gadrooned yellow bands, the interior pink, impressed marks, date code obscured.

7in (18cm) high

£280-320 **CHEF**

A George Jones majolica sardine dish, cover and stand, moulded with flying pelicans, bamboo, flowers and swimming fish, with pelican knop, registration marks for 12th March 1875 and 23rd December 1871.

6in (15cm) wide

£3,000-4,000 **WW**

A Victorian Wedgwood majolica tortoise dish, the oval dish in the form of the body of a tortoise, the domed cover his shell, surmounted by seated hare, impressed mark and date code, some restoration to rim.

1878 *7.5in (19cm) long*

£6,000-8,000 **GORL**

A Victorian majolica butter dish and cover, moulded with ivy leaves against a brown ground, cover restored.

7in (17.5cm) wide

£80-120 **GORL**

A George Jones majolica game pie dish and cover, with a quail knop, the body moulded with rabbits amidst ferns on a turquoise ground, the interior pink, impressed factory and registration marks, the quail's beak chipped.

c1870 *8.5in (21.5cm) wide*

£3,000-4,000 **WW**

An English Victorian majolica jardiniere, in the Aesthetic taste, the yellow glazed scalloped top with pale purple interior, the deep relief decorated sides depicting daffodils, tulips and birds on three bold leaf cast feet, each foot with impressed Victorian registration mark "IVW".

17in (43cm) high

£6,000-8,000 **L&T**

A Wedgwood majolica oyster barrel, cover and stand, the coopered barrel with honey and caramel staves, the cover and underdish moulded with oysters impressed "Wedgwood Pearl", date letter for 1861.

1861 *12.5in (32cm) high*

£200-300 **CHEF**

A George Jones majolica nut dish, the rim with a fox's head peering in to the dish which is moulded with vine leaves, the exterior with a bushy tail, moulded and impressed marks, a small chip to one ear.

c1875 *10.25in (26cm) long*

£600-800 **WW**

A George Jones majolica nut dish, modelled with a squirrel, leaves and buds against a pale blue ground, chips and modifications to squirrel.

1869 *10.25in (25.5cm) high*

£220-280 **GORL**

A Joseph Holcroft majolica shell-shaped dish, painted in shades of blue, green and brown, supported on three shell feet, impressed marks, chipped feet.

c1880 *7in (18cm) wide*

£400-600 **DN**

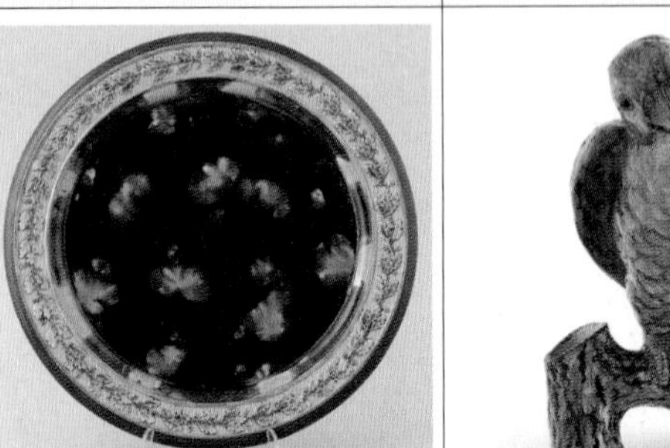

A mid-19thC Wedgwood majolica cheese bell base, with moulded and painted oak leaf band enclosing turquoise and deep blue mottling on a brown ground, impressed mark.

11.75in (30cm) diam

£100-150 **CHEF**

A Continental majolica model of a parrot, with glass eyes, brightly decorated in coloured enamels and perched on a branch.

11.25in (28.5cm) high

£280-320 **LFA**

A CLOSER LOOK AT A MAJOLICA OYSTER STAND

Green seaweed, seen on the moulding on this piece, was often used to decorate majolica. Other popular decoration included lilies, roses, fish and shells.

This Victorian oyster stand is ornate, impressive and unusual. It is in good condition, enhancing its value.

The stand revolves on a circular foot with a waved rim.

This piece was produced at a time of growing interest in elaborate cooking, culinary variety and attractive table presentation.

A Minton majolica oyster stand, modelled with four tapering tiers of oyster shells with white glazed interiors, brown exteriors and green seaweed, the finial formed of three fish and an eel, mounted to revolve on a circular foot with waved rim, unmarked, some rim chips.

c1865 *10.75in (27cm) high*

£5,000-6,000 **DN**

A late 19thC majolica pug dog stick stand, modelled standing on his hind legs and baring his teeth, all on a turquoise cushion, minor repairs.

21in (53cm) high

£1,800-2,200 **WW**

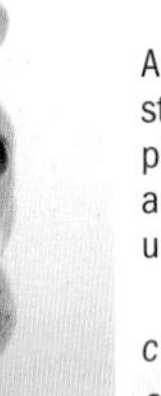

An unusual majolica hound's-head stirrup cup, in the form of a boxer dog, picked out in blue, brown and ochre, and wearing an ochre collar, chip to underside of one ear.

c1880 *4in (10cm) long*

£500-700 **LFA**

A Victorian majolica bracket, of scrolling corbel shape, moulded with an Elizabethan male portrait bust and ram's head, brightly painted, impressed patent mark.

18in (45cm) high

£150-200 **GORL**

A George Jones majolica dressing table tray, impressed monogram and registry mark, some damage.

1875 *13.25in (33.5cm) long*

£800-1,200 **DRA**

A Jean Baptiste Massier majolica vase, of waisted tapering form, with all-over iridescent glaze, with owl decoration, signed "Jerome Massier Fils, Vallauris, ANL".

10.25in (26cm) high

£4,000-5,000 **MACK**

MARTINWARE

A Martin Brothers stoneware bird jar and cover, modelled as a young chick with open outstretched beak, in shades of green, brown and ochre, incised to base "RW Martin & Bros London & Southall", the head rim incised "Martin Brothers London & Southall", restored.

7.75in 20cm high

£10,000-15,000 WW

A Martin Brothers stoneware bird, modelled standing and staring forward, glazed in shades of blue, green and brown, incised to head "RW Martin & Bros Southall", to base "1914", firing faults.

1914 9in (23cm) high

3,500-4,500 WW

A CLOSER LOOK AT A MARTIN BROTHERS BIRD

Like many of the grotesque birds produced by the Martin Brothers, this model has superb characterisation and a wry expression, making it appealing. Many of the birds are tobacco jars.

All Martin ware is signed with one of five different marks.

The bird is stoneware with a salt glaze. The natural, subdued colour is typical of the Martin Brothers, who are now considered to have been the first studio potters.

Martin Brothers ware is widely collected and highly sought-after. The birds are particularly popular, and can be hard to come across.

A Martin Brothers stoneware bird, modelled with a wry expression, incised to head "Martin Bros, London & Southall, 6-1897", to base "Martin Bros, London & Southall", small chips to rim of body.

1897 11in (28cm) high

£20,000-30,000 WW

A Martin Brothers 'Toby' stoneware dog, modelled seated with a collar, painted mark "Martin Bros London" to base, some damage.

4.75in (12cm) high

£10,000-15,000 WW

A Martin Brothers stoneware flask vase, of twin-handled form, incised with ferocious dragons, in shades of brown, incised mark "6-1903 Martin Bros London & Southall", small chips.

1903 7.25in (18.5cm) high

£800-1,200 WW

A Martin Brothers stoneware vase, of twin-handled form, incised with foliage, dragons and pomegranate, in shades of brown, incised signature and date mark.

1890 8.25in (21cm) high

£800-1,200 WW

A Martin Brothers stoneware ewer, the handle terminating in a Bacchanalian mask, incised and painted with grape and vine, incised marks.

1885 9.75in (25cm) high

£1,500-2,000 WW

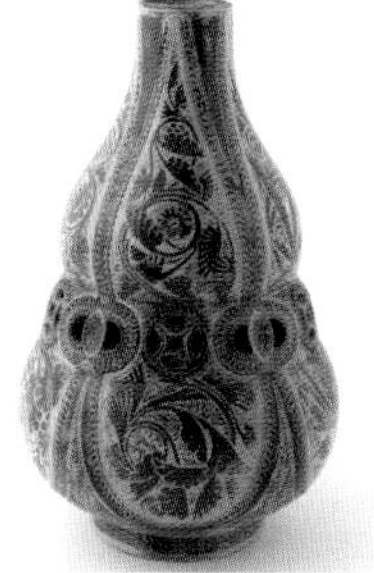

An early, large Martin Brothers stoneware vase, double gourd form with pierced band, incised with panels of flowers and scrolling foliage, incised marks.

1875 16.25in (41cm) high

£3,000-4,000 WW

A Martin Brothers stoneware vase, incised and painted with Turk's Cap lilies, incised "2-85 R W Martin & Bros London & Southall".

1885 9.5in (24cm) high

£1,000-1,500 WW

An early Martin Brothers stoneware beaker, with silver rim, incised with foliage, incised "RW Martin Fulham", stamped "London 1873", hairlines.

1873 5.5in (14cm) high

£220-280 WW

A Martin Brothers earthenware vase, of shaped square section with everted rim, incised with panels of exotic fish, incised signature and date mark.

9.75in (24.5cm) high

£2,500-3,000 L&T

MINTON

Thomas Minton founded his factory c1796 in Stoke-on-Trent. It produced everyday tableware, earthenware and bone china in styles typical of the period. Minton was famous for its blue and cream earthenware and majolica. Its marble-like parian porcelain was also very successful as it could be moulded into statues and figures without losing detail and had a high feldspar content which rendered a glaze unnecessary. Minton made copies of Japanese and Chinese pieces, including turquoise, pink and gold cloisonné ware.

When Herbert Minton took over the factory in 1836, following his father's death, he employed skilled artists and Minton became increasingly known for its decorative 'art' porcelain. A Sèvres process was used called pâte-sur-pâte, where layers of white slip – a mixture of clay and water – are built up on a coloured ground and then carved to create depth. During the 19thC, the Minton factory was commissioned by embassies and heads of state to produce made-to-order dinnerware. Many Minton pieces are marked, often with a date code.

A pair of Minton, Hollins and Co. ceramic tile panels, one with a blacksmith at his anvil, the other with a mother reading to her child, moulded marks.

12in (30.5cm) high

£280-320 **L&T**

A framed Minton tile, depicting a Middle-Eastern woman in colourful attire next to a large vessel in a self-standing metal and wooden frame, signed.

10in (25.5cm) high

£80-120 **JDJ**

A Minton porcelain plaque, painted with a brown and white hound in a landscape, signed lower right "W. Maguire" impressed marks recto, date code.

1909 *6in (15cm) wide*

£300-400 **DN**

A Minton buff earthenware round plaque, painted in coloured enamels in Aesthetic style with a young woman picking blossom from a tree, in a garden with lilies and roses, within a hatched band, impressed date mark.

1877 *15.25in (38.5cm) diam*

£600-900 **LFA**

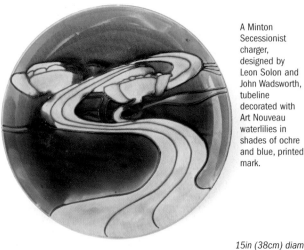

A Minton Secessionist charger, designed by Leon Solon and John Wadsworth, tubeline decorated with Art Nouveau waterlilies in shades of ochre and blue, printed mark.

15in (38cm) diam

£800-1,200 **WW**

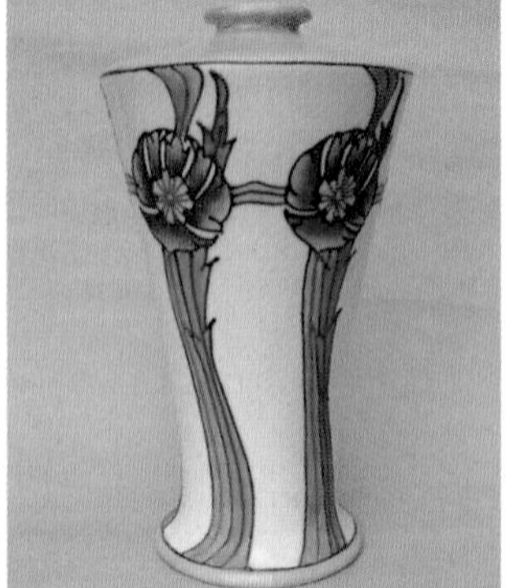

A Minton Secessionist vase of shouldered form, tubeline decorated in colours with stylized poppies against a white background.

10.5in (26.5cm) high

£600-800 **PC**

A Victorian Minton cloisonné vase, in the style of Christopher Dresser, boldly enamelled with butterflies and stylized foliage against a mid-blue ground, on a gilded base simulating fretwork, mould number 1384.

7.5in (19cm) high

£700-1,000 **GORL**

MOORCROFT

A William Moorcroft late Florian ware plate.

c1915 *8.5in (21.5cm) diam*

£1,000-1,200 **RUM**

A William Moorcroft Florian ware 'Freesia' pattern bowl.

c1900 *7in (17.5cm) diam*

£1,600-1,800 **RUM**

A Moorcroft Florian ware twin-handled bowl, of circular form, printed MacIntyre mark, signed in green, restored.

10.75in (27cm) wide

£1,000-1,500 **L&T**

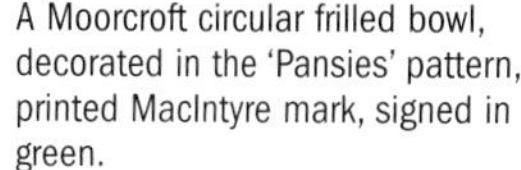

A Moorcroft circular frilled bowl, decorated in the 'Pansies' pattern, printed MacIntyre mark, signed in green.

8in (20cm) wide

£1,000-1,500 **L&T**

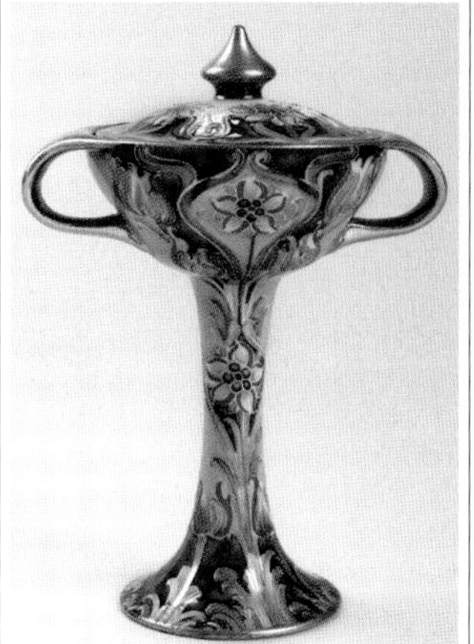

A Moorcroft Florian ware twin-handled chalice and cover, decorated with flowers and a blue and salmon pink ground, printed MacIntyre mark.

8.5in (21cm) high

£1,800-2,200 **L&T**

A William Moorcroft Florian ware 'Forget-me-not' pattern vase.

Moorcroft's later work for MacIntyre and Co. was retailed as 'Florian' ware.

c1900 *6in (15cm) high*

£3,000-4,000 **RUM**

A William Moorcroft green and gold Florian ware 'Tulips and Forget-me-nots' pattern vase.

c1900 *11.75in (30cm) high*

£1,500-2,000 **RUM**

A pair of Moorcroft Florian ware vases, each of baluster form, printed MacIntyre marks, initialled in green, restored.

12.5in (31.5cm) high

£2,200-2,800 **L&T**

A William Moorcroft Florian ware 'Poppy' pattern coffee pot, with milk jug and sugar bowl.

c1920 *6.75in (17cm) high*

£1,500-2,000 **RUM**

A William Moorcroft 'Tulip' pattern vase, on a rare stippled background.

c1900 *8.25in (21cm) high*

£3,000-4,000 **RUM**

A William Moorcroft 'Forget-me-not' pattern vase.

c1915 *7.75in (20cm) high*

£800-1,200 **RUM**

A William Moorcroft 'Cornflower' design vase, with powder blue ground.

c1930 *14in (35.5cm) high*

£1,800-2,200 **RUM**

A William Moorcroft 'Dawn' landscape pattern vase.

c1930 *3.25in (8.5cm) high*

£1,200-1,400 **RUM**

A William Moorcroft stylized 'Poppy' pattern vase.

c1930 *6in (15cm) high*

£750-850 **RUM**

A CLOSER LOOK AT A MOORCROFT VASE

Landscape designs became very popular in the 1920s and 30s and were used on many decorative ceramic pieces. William Moorcroft looked to the landscape as a source of design inspiration in the early 1920s and produced the 'Moonlit Landscape' design as well as a number of others, such as 'Eventide Landscape'.

This vase would have been made using a technique unique to Moorcroft. Pieces were hand thrown, painted, fired and then glazed and fired for a second time. The decoration on this vase was produced using blues and greens on a powder blue base.

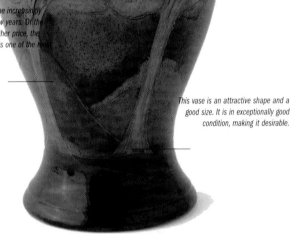

Moorcroft pottery has become increasingly sought-after over the last few years. Of the designs that command a higher price, the 'Moonlit Landscape' design is one of the most desirable and valuable.

This vase is an attractive shape and a good size. It is in exceptionally good condition, making it desirable.

A William Moorcroft 'Moonlit Landscape' pattern vase.

c1920 *12.5in (31.5cm) high*

£4,000-6,000 **RUM**

A William Moorcroft 'Orchid' pattern vase.

c1935 *7.75in (20cm) high*

£1,200-1,800 **RUM**

A William Moorcroft 'Vine' pattern vase, made for Liberty and Company.

c1905 *4.75in (12cm) high*

£1,200-1,800 **RUM**

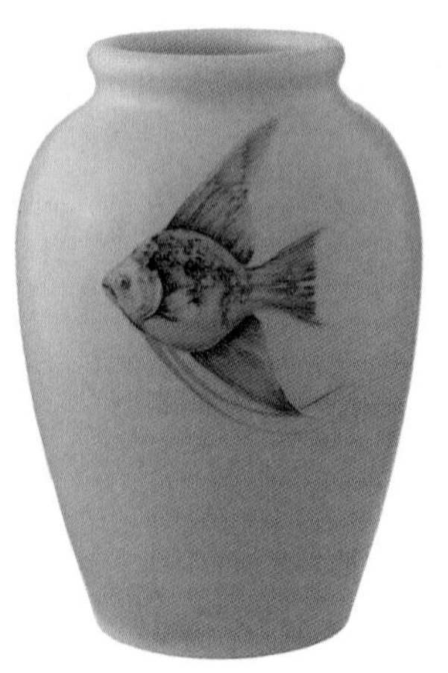

A William Moorcroft 'Fish' pattern vase.

c1930 *9.5in (24cm) high*

£1,200-1,800 **RUM**

A William Moorcroft 'Anemone' pattern vase.

c1935 *6.25in (16cm) high*

£350-400 **RUM**

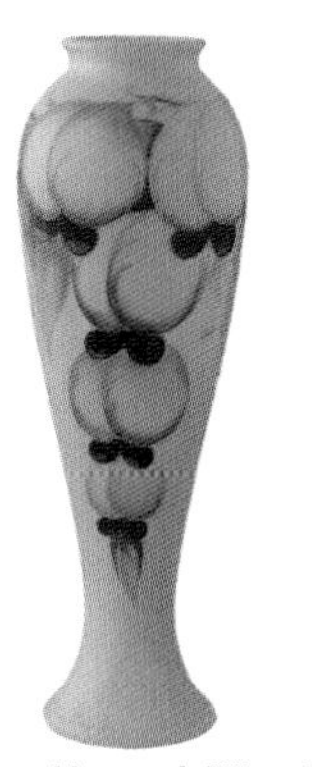

A William Moorcroft 'Wisteria' pattern vase.

c1930 *13in (33cm) high*

£1,800-2,200 **RUM**

A William Moorcroft 'Poppies and Forget-me-nots' pattern vase.

c1905 *8.75in (22cm) high*

£2,000-2,500 **RUM**

A William Moorcroft 'Tudor Rose' pattern vase, made for Liberty and Company.

c1910 *8.25in (21cm) high*

£1,200-1,800 **RUM**

A William Moorcroft green and gold Florian ware vase.

c1905 *9in (23cm) high*

£2,500-3,000 **RUM**

A William Moorcroft revived 'Cornflower' pattern vase.

c1925 *7.75in (20cm) high*

£3,500-4,500 **RUM**

A William Moorcroft 'Orchid' pattern vase.

c1915 *12.5in (32cm) high*

£3,000-5,000 **RUM**

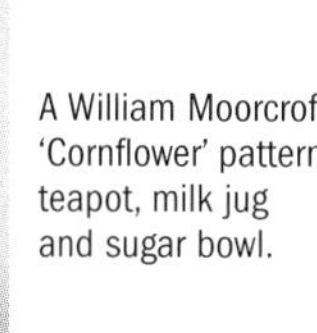

A William Moorcroft 'Cornflower' pattern teapot, milk jug and sugar bowl.

c1910 *6in (15cm) high*

£4,000-6,000 **RUM**

A William Moorcroft 'Roses Tulips and Forget-me-nots' pattern vase.

c1905 *7.5in (19cm) high*

£1,800-2,200 **RUM**

A Walter Moorcroft 'Spring Flowers' pattern vase.

c1955 *5in (12.5cm) high*

£300-350 **RUM**

A Walter Moorcroft 'Spring Flowers' pattern vase.

c1950 *7in (18cm) high*

£600-900 **RUM**

A Walter Moorcroft 'Orchid' pattern perfume bottle.

c1950 *5.75in (14.5cm) high*

£500-700 **RUM**

A Moorcroft shouldered cylindrical vase, decorated in the 'Striped Wisteria' pattern, restored rim, impressed mark, signed in blue.

8.5in (21cm) high

£400-600 **L&T**

A Moorcroft shouldered tapering vase, decorated with lilies and scrolling foliage, boxed, impressed marks, initialled in blue.

12.5in (31cm) high

£400-600 **L&T**

A Moorcroft shouldered tapering vase, decorated in the 'Lemon' pattern, impressed mark, initialled in green.

10in (25cm) high

£80-120 **L&T**

A Moorcroft Collectors Club 'Victoriana' vase, designed by Emma Bossons, painted and impressed marks.

c1995 *8.25in (21cm) high*

£200-250 **GORL**

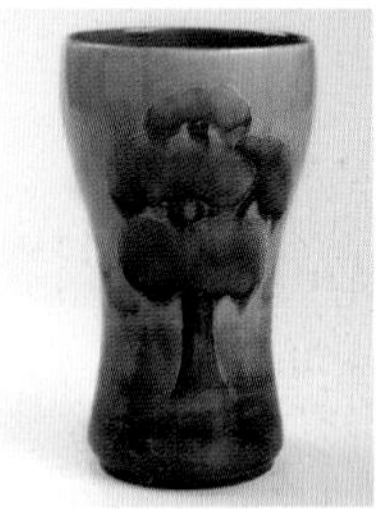

A Moorcroft tapered vase, decorated in the 'Hazeldene' pattern, printed registration mark, signed in green, restored rims.

8in (20cm) high

£700-1,000 **L&T**

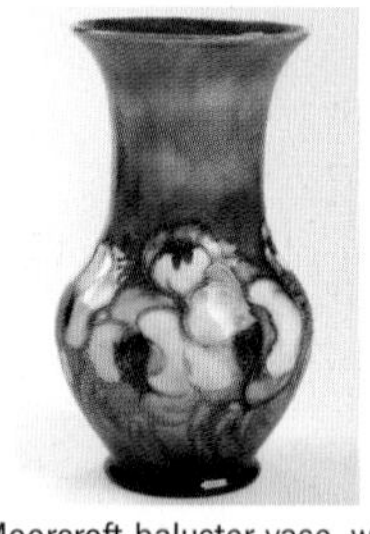

A Moorcroft baluster vase, with flaring rim, decorated in the 'Anemones' pattern, impressed facsimile signature, initialled in blue, with paper label.

10in (25cm) high

£320-380 **L&T**

A Moorcroft ovoid vase, decorated in the 'Swan' pattern, boxed, impressed marks, initialled in green.

6.5in (16.5cm) high

£220-280 **L&T**

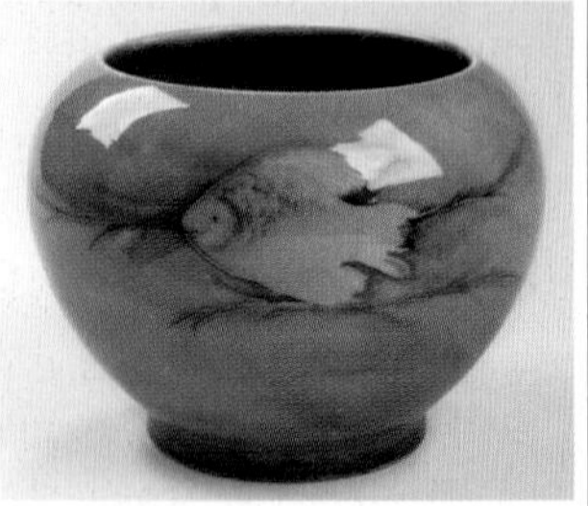

A Moorcroft ovoid vase, decorated in the 'Fish' pattern, pressed signature mark, signed in green.

6in (15cm) high

£1,000-1,500 **L&T**

A Moorcroft ovoid jardinière, decorated in the 'Orchids' pattern, impressed mark, initialled in blue.

6.5in (16.5cm) high

£350-400 **L&T**

A Moorcroft 'Leaf and Berries' pattern vase, with printed blue signature.

6.5in (16.5cm) high

£280-320 **WW**

A Moorcroft 'Leaf and Berries' pattern flambé vase, printed green signature.

6.5in (16.5cm) high

£400-600 **WW**

A Moorcroft cylindrical preserve jar and cover, decorated in the 'Plum Wisteria' pattern, impressed marks, initialled in green.

3.5in (9cm) high

£200-250 **L&T**

A Moorcroft circular 'Leaf and Berries' pattern flambé bowl, impressed marks, signed in blue.

10.25in (25.5cm) diam

£400-600 **L&T**

PILKINGTON'S

A fine and rare Pilkington's bulbous vessel painted with a large golden dragon on a shaded amber and red ground, a couple of minute flecks to rim, stamped "P/208/5/England".

10.5in (26.5cm) high

£1,500-2,000 **DRA**

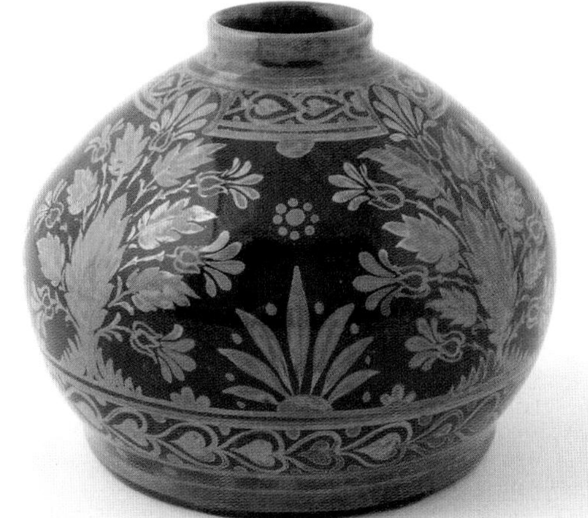

A Pilkington's Royal Lancastrian vase, by Richard Joyce, painted with foliate motif in shades of ruby and sand on a purple ground, impressed mark, artist cypher.

4.75in (12cm) high

£800-1,200 **WW**

A large Pilkington's Royal Lancastrian vase, by Richard Joyce, painted in copper lustre with toucans amongst pomegranate and foliage on a ruby lustre ground painted artist's cypher, impressed mark and date mark.

1918 *12.5in (32cm) high*

£8,000-10,000 **WW**

A Pilkington's Royal Lancastrian lustre shouldered tapering vase, with erected rim, painted by Richard Joyce, with all-over flowering rose branches on a dark blue ground, impressed marks and painted fish monogram.

8.5in (21cm) high

£1,200-1,800 **L&T**

A Pilkington's Royal Lancastrian vase, by Gordon M. Forsyth, painted in a rich ruby and copper lustre with bell flowers, on a flame orange ground, painted cypher, date mark.

1912 *13.5in (34.5cm) high*

£2,000-3,000 **WW**

A Pilkington's Royal Lancastrian twin-handled vase, of ovoid form, painted with opposed panels of flowering rose and peony plants by William S. Mycock, impressed marks, painted monogram and date mark.

1921 *9.75in (24.5cm) high*

£1,800-2,200 **L&T**

POOLE

A Carter, Stabler and Adams Poole shouldered vase, painted in colours with a floral frieze, impressed and painted marks.

7in (18cm) high

£300-350 **L&T**

A Carter, Stabler and Adams Poole vase, 'BX' pattern, painted in colours, impressed and painted marks.

10in (25.5cm) high

£350-400 **WW**

A Carter, Stabler and Adams Poole vase, painted with blue birds, serrated green leaves and flowers on a grey ground, artist's initials "AH" and "NT".

11.5in 29cm high

£400-600 **CHEF**

A large Poole Art Deco platter, painted by R. Sommerfelt with an antelope in front of a fruit tree, marked Poole, signed by the artist.

16in (40.5cm) diam

£300-500 **DRA**

A large Poole vase, of swollen cylindrical form painted with an all-over floral design, impressed and incised painted marks.

11.75in (27cm) high

£80-120 **L&T**

A large Poole baluster vase, painted with a frieze of flowering branches by Rene Hayes, impressed and incised painted marks.

10.5in (26cm) high

£150-200 **L&T**

A Poole pottery vase, of tapering cylindrical form with everted rim, painted in colours with gazelles leaping through flowering foliage on a white ground, impressed and painted marks.

7.5in (18.5cm) high

£180-220 **L&T**

A CLOSER LOOK AT A POOLE ROUNDEL

This Poole roundel was designed by Phoebe Stabler (1920-1955), during the successful period of the Carter, Stabler and Adams partnership.

The rarity of the roundel increases its market value.

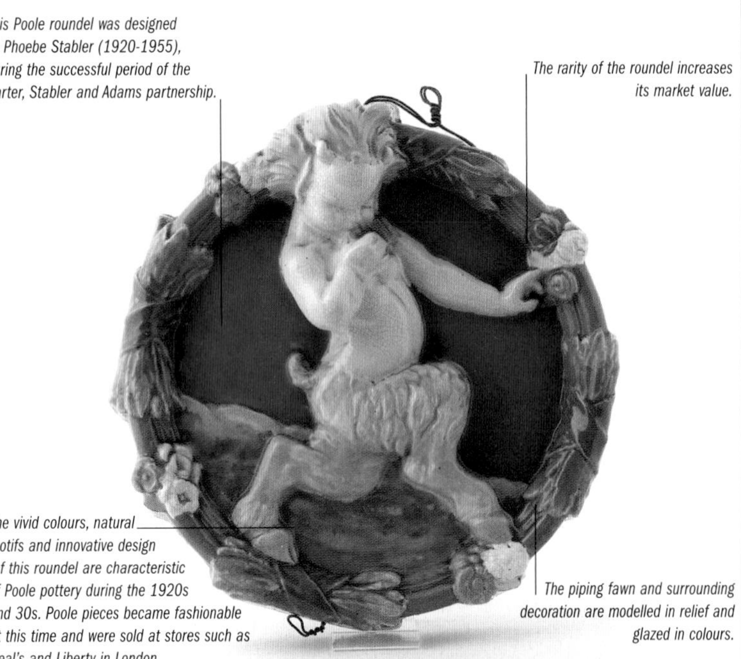

The vivid colours, natural motifs and innovative design of this roundel are characteristic of Poole pottery during the 1920s and 30s. Poole pieces became fashionable at this time and were sold at stores such as Heal's and Liberty in London.

The piping fawn and surrounding decoration are modelled in relief and glazed in colours.

A rare Carter, Stabler and Adams Poole 'Piping Fawn' roundel, designed by Phoebe Stabler, modelled in relief and glazed in colours, impressed factory mark, minor glaze nicks.

15.75in (40cm) diam

£2,000-2,500 **WW**

ROYAL DUX

A Royal Dux Bohemian ceramic figurine, depicting a woman with a lyre emerging from a shell.

c1905 *11in (28cm) wide*

£400-500 **TO**

A pair of Royal Dux Art Deco bookend figures, modelled as two pierrots, applied pink triangle mark, impressed mark "3077".

9.75in (24cm) high

£300-500 **L&T**

A Royal Dux Art Deco figure modelled by Schaff, of a young girl, applied pink triangle mark, impressed number "3251".

13in (32.5cm) high

£400-600 **L&T**

A Royal Dux Art Deco figure modelled by Schaff, of a dancing girl, applied pink triangle mark, impressed mark number "3602".

10.75in (27cm) high

£400-600 **L&T**

An Art Deco Royal Dux figurine.

£600-900 **TDG**

A pair of Royal Dux Art Deco bookends, each modelled as a kneeling dancer in Eastern dress, pink triangle mark, restored hands to one.

9in (23cm) high

£500-800 **WW**

ROYAL WORCESTER

A Royal Worcester teapot and cover, relief-moulded and gilded with flowering and fruiting branches.

1888 *7in (18cm) high*

£500-700 **WW**

A Royal Worcester teapot and cover, decorated with flower sprays on an ivory ground, the handle and spout gilded.

1888 *6in (15.5cm) high*

£200-300 **WW**

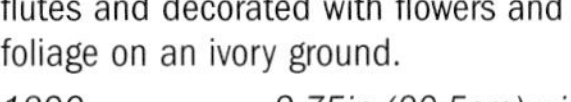

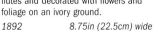

A Royal Worcester teapot and cover, shape number 1183, moulded with flutes and decorated with flowers and foliage on an ivory ground.

1892 *8.75in (22.5cm) wide*

£350-400 **WW**

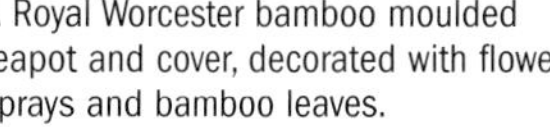

A Royal Worcester bamboo moulded teapot and cover, decorated with flower sprays and bamboo leaves.

1889 *7in (18cm) high*

£400-600 **WW**

A Royal Worcester oval teapot and cover, decorated with flowers and leaves on an ivory ground, printed mark.

1889 *8in (20.5cm) high*

£280-320 **WW**

A Royal Worcester blush ewer, painted with flowers, pattern number 1229.

1892 *6in (15cm) high*

£180-220 **GORL**

A Royal Worcester ewer, with moulded rim, decorated and gilt with floral sprays against a blushed ivory ground.

1897 *6in (15cm) high*

£80-120 **GORL**

A Royal Worcester ewer, the bottle shape net-moulded and painted with Iznik flowers, the brown organic shaped handles with spiky leaves and heart shaped buds, green printed marks, date mark.

1884 *13in (33cm) high*

£220-280 **CHEF**

A Royal Worcester ivory ground jug, painted and gilt with flowers, pattern number 1047.

1893 *9in (23cm) high*

£200-250 **GORL**

A Royal Worcester floral painted blush vase, with bulbous body and slender neck.

1953 *5.5in (14cm) high*

£180-220 **GORL**

A Royal Worcester ivory ground vase, painted with garden flowers, pattern number 1449.

1893 *12.5in (32cm) high*

£280-320 **GORL**

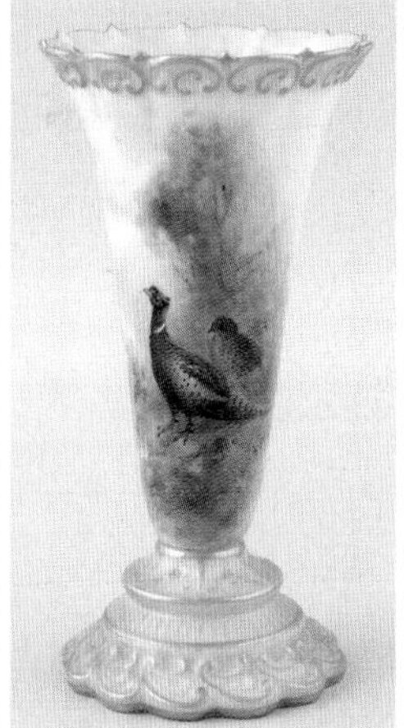

A Royal Worcester vase, painted by James Stinton, with a cock and a hen pheasant on its trumpet sides below a gilt barbed rim, with a blush stepped circular foot moulded with scrolls, printed marks, date code.

1915 *6.5in (16.5cm) high*

£800-1,200 **CHEF**

A Royal Worcester Persian shaped vase, decorated with flower stems, shape number 784.

1889 *7.25in (18.5cm) high*

£80-120 **WW**

One of a pair of Royal Worcester onion-shaped vases, painted with roses, green printed marks, signed "C.V. White".

1907 *10.25in (26cm) high*

£1,000-1,500 pair **WW**

A pair of Worcester (Kerr and Binns) two-handled urns and covers, each painted with a bust portrait panel, one of Ann Boleyn, the other of Edward VI, within gilt borders, printed marks, restored.

c1860 *8.25in (21cm) high*

£600-900 **DN**

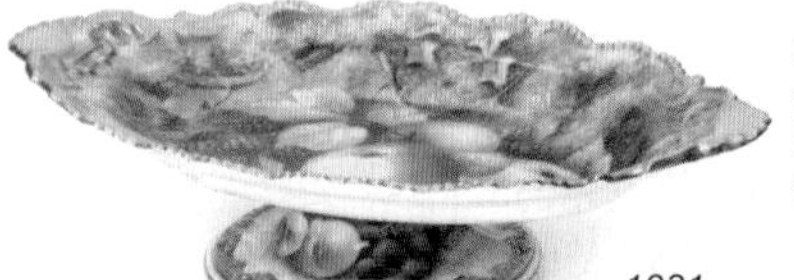

A Royal Worcester low oval stand, painted with fruit, the border and foot gilded, signed "T. Lockyer".

1931 *12.5in (32cm) high*

£500-700 **WW**

A CLOSER LOOK AT A ROYAL WORCESTER COFFEE SET

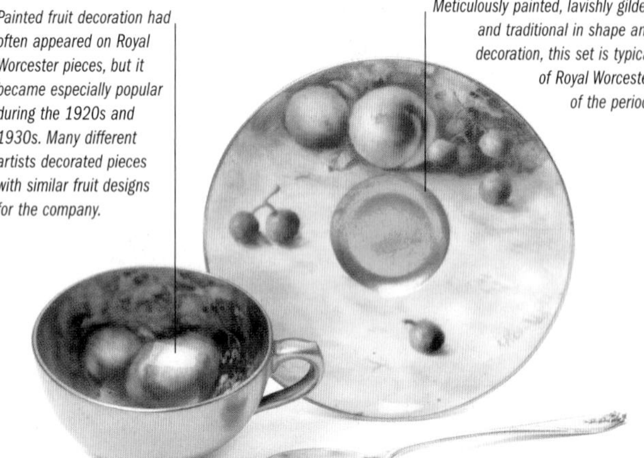

Painted fruit decoration had often appeared on Royal Worcester pieces, but it became especially popular during the 1920s and 1930s. Many different artists decorated pieces with similar fruit designs for the company.

Meticulously painted, lavishly gilded and traditional in shape and decoration, this set is typical of Royal Worcester of the period.

The set is complete with six silver spoons and a box, making it highly collectable.

A Royal Worcester boxed set of six coffee cups and saucers, painted with fruit and richly gilded, signed by Price, Austin and Flexman, with six silver spoons, one cup unsigned.

1920 *Saucer 4.5in (11.5cm) diam*

£2,500-3,000 set **WW**

A Royal Worcester model, 'Negro', by James Hadley, from a series of 'Countries of the World', painted in coloured bronzes, puce printed marks, date code.

1895 *6.25in (16cm) high*

£500-700 **DN**

A Royal Worcester model, 'Hindoo', by James Hadley, from a series of 'Countries of the World', painted in coloured bronzes, shape number 838, puce printed marks, date code.

1898 *6.75in (17cm) high*

£280-320 **DN**

A Royal Worcester model, 'John Bull', by James Hadley, from a series of 'Countries of the World', painted in coloured bronzes, shape number 851, green printed marks, date code.

1901 *6.75in (17cm) high*

£280-320 **DN**

A Royal Worcester model, 'Chinese', by James Hadley, from a series of 'Countries of the World', painted in coloured bronzes, shape number 837, puce printed marks, date code.

1904 *6.75in (17cm) high*

£400-600 **DN**

A Royal Worcester model, 'Scotchman', by James Hadley, from a series of 'Countries of the World', painted in coloured bronzes, date code.

1905 *5.5in (14cm) high*

£280-320 **DN**

A pair of Royal Worcester figures, 'Brigaree Indians', painted with bronzed colours, shape number 1243, green painted marks, date code.

1912 *9in (23cm) high*

£700-1,000 **DN**

A pair of Royal Worcester figures of the boy piper Strephon and his female companion playing a cymbal, shape number 1803, date code.

1920 *Female 6in (15cm) high*

£300-500 **DN**

A Royal Worcester glazed and tinted parian group, 'Peace blessing the Arts', impressed marks.

c1865 *11.5in (29.5cm) high*

£800-1,200 **DN**

A pair of Royal Worcester figures of Eastern water carriers, by Hadley, puce printed crowned circle mark and date code, impressed signature.

1892 *17.75in (44.5cm) high*

£500-800 **L&T**

A Royal Worcester figure of Peter Pan, modelled by F.G. Doughty.

8in (20.5cm) high

£150-200 **WW**

A Royal Worcester figure, 'Sister of the London Hospital', limited edition, in original box with paper label.

7in (18cm) high

£1,000-1,500 **GORL**

A Royal Worcester figure, 'Sister from University College Hospital', limited edition, in original box with paper label.

8.75in (22.5cm) high

£300-500 **GORL**

A Royal Worcester figure, 'Sister of St Thomas' Hospital', limited edition, in original box with paper label.

6.5in (16.5cm) high

£500-700 **GORL**

A Royal Worcester figure, 'British Red Cross Society V.A.D. Member', limited edition, in original box with paper label.

8.75in (22.5cm) high

£350-400 **GORL**

A Royal Worcester figure group, 'The Old Goat Woman', modelled by Phoebe Stabler, model number 2886, puce printed and script marks.

1936 *6in (15cm) high*

£220-280 **DN**

SÈVRES

A Sèvres tall porcelain vase, with enamelled trailing floral decoration on pale blue ground, black date stamp, russet circular stamp "Decoree à Sèvres 98" and signed "Mimard L".

1898 *16in (40.5cm) high*

£6,000-8,000 MACK

A Sèvres porcelain vase, decorated with trailing hair bells and gilt spider webs, blue factory stamp.

1900 *7in (17.5cm) high*

£2,000-2,500 MACK

A Sèvres tall porcelain vase, with enamelled yellow floral decoration and deep blue cartouche panels on a pale blue ground, date stamp.

1902 *17.25in 43.5cm high*

£7,000-10,000 MACK

A Sèvres porcelain and gilt bronze mounted vase and cover, with flower head finial above speckled blue glaze body, base with frog and lily pad decoration, stamped date code.

1897 *6.75in 17cm high*

£8,000-12,000 MACK

A Sèvres porcelain and gilt bronze mounted vase and cover, with raspberry finial above iridescent salmon glaze body, raspberry leaf base, stamped date code.

1906 *6.5in (16.5cm) high*

£8,000-12,000 MACK

A Sèvres porcelain vase, with bulbous neck above flared base with applied and painted all-over thistle decoration with gilt highlights, black date stamp and paper label.

1904 *8.75in (22.5cm) high*

£3,500-4,500 MACK

A Sèvres biscuit bust of General Kleber, with windswept cravat at the neck of his oak-leaf trimmed jacket, the blue glazed socle lined in gilt, printed and impressed marks, "VP" monogram and date mark.

1892 *15.75in (40cm) high*

£400-600 CHEF

A Sèvres white porcelain figure, by Theodore Riviere, modelled as a young woman wearing a cloak that opens to reveal her naked body, on a circular base, marked on the edge "Theodore Riviere", impressed "Sèvres" and with initials "LC", with fitted case marked "Manufacture Nationale de Sèvres".

6.5in (16.5cm) high

£500-700 DN

A pair of Sèvres bisque porcelain figurines, designed by Agathon Leonard, incised "Sèvres" and numbered.

Tallest 14.25in (36cm) high

£5,000-7,000 MACK

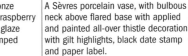

A Sèvres style saucer, painted with pink roses and blue and gilt ribbons, interlaced "L" marks.

4.5in (11.5cm) diam

£280-320 WW

A Sèvres Art Deco box and cover, with an odeonesque style plaque, printed mark "M.P. Sèvres".

c1925 *6.5in (16.5cm) diam*

£500-700 TDG

WEDGWOOD

A Wedgwood Fairyland Lustre 'Torches' vase, decorated with glowing torches along a stairway leading to a temple, with trees, vines, birds and fairies, marked to base with gold Wedgwood urn and "Wedgwood made in England".

11in (28cm) high

£3,500-4,500 **JDJ**

A Wedgwood Fairyland Lustre 'Butterfly Girl' trumpet vase, designed by Daisy Makeig-Jones, printed mark, restored base rim.

6in (15.5cm) high

£500-700 **WW**

A Wedgwood Fairyland Lustre 'Pillar' vase, of tall shouldered cylindrical form, printed and painted in gilt and coloured enamels, printed and painted marks, pattern number Z5360, restored.

14in (35cm) high

£800-1,200 **L&T**

A large Wedgwood Fairyland Lustre 'Ghostly Wood' vase, pattern number Z4968, printed mark.

12.75in (32.5cm) high

£3,000-5,000 **WW**

A Wedgwood Fairyland Lustre 'Jewelled Tree' vase, designed by Daisy Makeig-Jones, shape number 2351, printed and painted in colours and gilt, printed and painted marks.

Fairyland Lustre ware was designed exclusively for Wedgwood by Daisy Makeig-Jones, who joined the firm as a trainee decorator in 1909. Makeig-Jones combined the many commercially available lustre preparations with underglazes to create her innovative fairyland designs. She took some inspiration from leading fairytale illustrators at the time, such as Kay Nielsen and Edmund Dulac, but her design work was highly original and proved very popular.

As production increased, Makeig-Jones took on an increasingly supervisory role. Consequently, she did not decorate some later Fairyland Lustre pieces and collectors should check that pieces bear her original monogram and not one from an engraved plate. Makeig-Jones left Wedgwood in 1931 and production of Fairyland Lustre ceased.

The production process was expensive and comparatively few pieces were produced, so Fairyland Lustre in good condition is highly prized by collectors today.

9in (22.5cm) high

£4,000-6,000 **WW**

A large Wedgwood Fairyland Lustre footed bowl, printed and painted in gilt and coloured enamels with the 'Woodland Bridge' and 'Poplar Trees' patterns, printed and painted marks, pattern number Z4968.

11.5in (29cm) diam

£2,500-3,500 **L&T**

A Wedgwood 'Fairyland Lustre' octagonal bowl, printed and painted in gilt and coloured enamels with the 'Boxing Match' and 'Castle on a Road' patterns, pattern number Z3125, printed and painted marks, restored.

9.25in (23cm) diam

£500-800 **L&T**

A Wedgwood Fairyland Lustre bowl, designed by Daisy Makeig Jones, of octagonal form, printed and painted in colours with the 'Castle on a Road' and 'Fairy in a Cage' patterns, pattern number Z3125, printed and painted marks, cracked.

9in (23cm) diam

£500-800 **L&T**

A Wedgwood Fairyland Lustre 'Woodland Elves IV Big Eyes' malfrey pot and cover, designed by Daisy Makeig-Jones, printed mark, minor restoration.

3.75in (9.5cm) high

£600-900 **WW**

A pair of Wedgwood 'Dragon Lustre' baluster vases, each printed in gilt with dragons on a blue ground, printed and painted marks.

9in (22.5cm) high

£600-900 **L&T**

A Wedgwood lustre shouldered vase and cover, printed in gilt with humming birds with a mottled blue and turquoise ground, pattern number Z5088, printed and painted marks.

8in (20cm) high

£700-1,000 **L&T**

A Wedgwood lustre shouldered vase, printed in gilt with deer on a blue ground, printed and painted marks.

7.75in (19.5cm) high

£300-500 **L&T**

A Wedgwood lustre vase, printed with bluebells on a blue ground, printed marks.

7.75in (19.5cm) high

£150-200 **L&T**

A Wedgwood lustre 'Argus Pheasant' bowl, pattern number Z5486, printed and painted in gilt and coloured enamels, printed and painted marks.

9.25in (23cm) diam

£3,000-5,000 **L&T**

A Wedgwood lustre octagonal bowl, printed and painted in gilt and coloured enamels with fruits, printed and painted marks.

6.5in (16cm) wide

£150-200 **L&T**

A Wedgwood lustre bowl, of circular form, printed and painted in gilt and coloured enamels with moths and butterflies, printed and painted marks.

6.5in (16cm) diam

£220-280 **L&T**

A Wedgwood lustre vase, of flared tapering form with applied foot, printed in gilt with butterflies on a mottled ground, printed and painted marks.

8.75in (22cm) high

£600-900 **L&T**

A Wedgwood lustre footed punch bowl, of circular form, printed and painted in gilt and coloured enamels with bands of exotic foliage, printed and painted marks.

10.75in (27cm) diam

£800-1,200 **L&T**

A Wedgwood lustre footed bowl, with flaring rim, pattern number Z4832, printed and painted marks.

8.75in (22cm) diam

£500-700 **L&T**

A Wedgwood matt blue earthenware vase, designed by Keith Murray, printed mark, "KM" monogram.

7.5in (19cm) high

£400-600 **WW**

A Wedgwood 'Mirror Black' vase, designed by Keith Murray.

c1930 *8.5in (21cm) high*

£200-300 **AL**

A Wedgwood sculpture by John Skeaping, covered in an ochre glaze, impressed "Wedgwood J. Skeaping".

7in (18cm) high

£120-180 **WW**

STUDIO

A Richard Batterham bowl, cut sided form with green to grey glaze, unmarked.

5.5in (14.5cm) high

£180-220 **WW**

A Clive Bowen earthenware charger, lightly incised and painted with chevron and circle design in sand, ochre and green, unmarked.

15in (38cm) diam

£80-120 **WW**

An Emmanuel Cooper stoneware jug, of elliptical form, covered with pitted blue and white glaze, impressed "E" mark.

6in (15cm) high

£180-220 **WW**

A tall Swedish lamp base by Hans Folje Marian, manufactured by Tigmans Keramic, incised and painted with Classical gods, impressed and painted marks, dated.

1961 *27.5in (70cm) high*

£300-500 **WW**

A Shoji Hamada stoneware bowl, covered in a running temmoku glaze, impressed St Ives mark, artist's cypher.

6in (15cm) diam

£280-320 **WW**

A David Leach stoneware charger, comb decorated with a stylized willow tree under a temmoku glaze, impressed mark "DL".

13.5in (34cm) diam

£300-500 **WW**

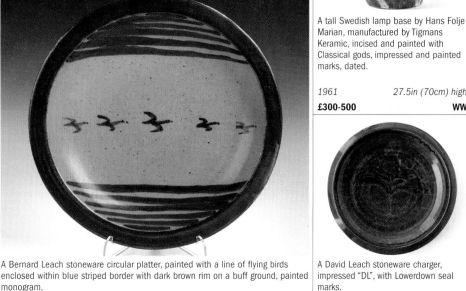

A Bernard Leach stoneware circular platter, painted with a line of flying birds enclosed within blue striped border with dark brown rim on a buff ground, painted monogram.

Bernard Leach studied at the Slade School and in Japan, where he met Shoji Hamada. Together they set up the St Ives Pottery in Cornwall in 1920. Their influence spread and many studio artists took apprenticeship under them.

12.5in (31cm) diam

£800-1,200 **L&T**

A David Leach stoneware charger, impressed "DL", with Lowerdown seal marks.

In 1933, David briefly took over the running of the St Ives Pottery from his father, Bernard Leach.

12.75in (32.5cm) diam

£400-600 **WW**

A Janet Leach stoneware slab vase, decorated with brush strokes of brown on a speckled blue, white and buff ground, impressed mark "JL".

Janet Leach, Bernard Leach's wife, was also a St Ives potter and took over the running of the St Ives Pottery in 1979, after her husband's death.

11in (27.5cm) high

£320-380 **WW**

A Malcolm Pepper stoneware charger, painted with abstract motif in brown on a crazed ground, impressed artist's cypher.

14in (35.5cm) diam

£180-220 **WW**

An Edition Picasso terracotta vase, painted with owls, impressed and painted marks, restored.

10.25in (26cm) high

£1,000-1,500 **WW**

OTHER CERAMICS

A Beswick pottery wall mask, 'Lady With Beret in Profile', impressed mark "277".

4.5in (11.5cm) high

£120-180 **WW**

An Alexander Bigot of Paris pottery and pewter mounted inkwell, designed by Gaillard, with green and brown glazes and applied pierced pewter cover and panels, with factory mark and inscribed "Gres De Bigot Paris D162".

6in (15cm) diam

£3,000-5,000 **MACK**

A rare French porcelain cream jug designed by Georges de Feure for Samuel Bing, cream white ground with painted trailing stylized floral decoration, green stamp "L' Art Nouveau Paris".

2.75in (7cm) high

£5,000-6,000 **MACK**

A Bough ovoid jug by Elizabeth Amour, painted with sprigs of flowers on a yellow striped and white ground, painted marks "E.A. 1920 Bough".

5in (12.5cm) high

£200-250 **L&T**

A rare Bough footed punch bowl by Katie Muir, painted to the interior with a band of daisies, with central daisy motif on a black ground, painted mark 'Bough K M 1914'.

1914 *10.25in (26cm) diam*

£120-180 **L&T**

A Bough circular plate, decorated by Elizabeth Amour with a central roundel of apples and blossom with a purple band with leaf border, painted marks dated.

1922 *9.5in (24cm) diam*

£120-180 **L&T**

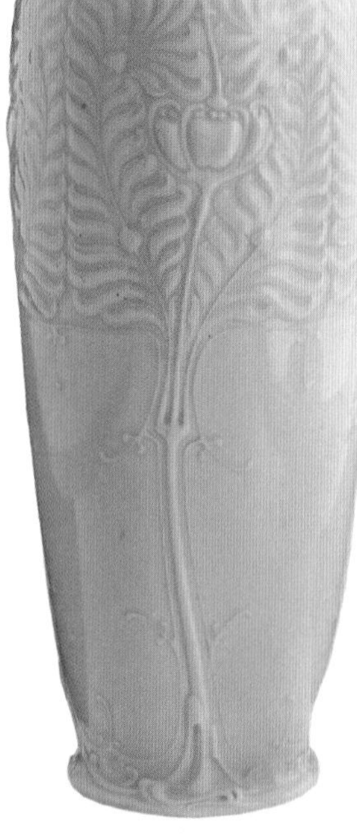

A rare French porcelain vase designed by Edward Colonna for Samuel Bing, made by G.D.A Limoges, the tapering circular body with relief decoration of trailing peacock feathers on cream ground, stamped for Colonna and marked "Leuconoe".

12.5in (31.5cm) high

£8,000-10,000 **MACK**

A large Brannam pottery vase, with multiple handles, decorated with coloured slips and sgraffito, with stylized birds and plant forms, by Frederick Braddon, dated.

1904 *20in (50cm) high*

£800-1,000 **PC**

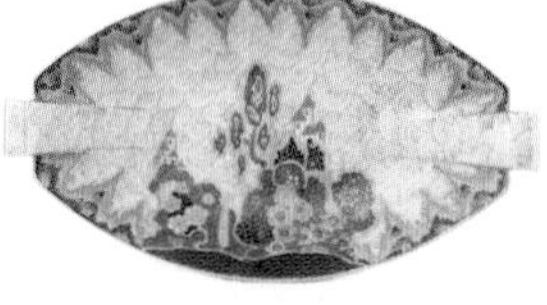

A Crown Derby 'Fairy Castle' tray, of scalloped form with painted pattern.

c1925 *12.5in (32cm) wide*

£500-700 **TDG**

A Crown Devon 'Fairy Castle' vase, printed and painted marks, restored.

6in (16cm) high

£180-220 **WW**

A Crown Devon 'Fairy Castle' tube-lined vase, printed and painted marks.

8.25in (21cm) high

£320-380 **WW**

A Crown Devon lustre vase with ram's head handles and floral pattern.

c1925 *7in (18cm) high*

£180-220 **TDG**

A Crown Devon 'Lightning' coffee service comprised of coffee pot, creamer, sugar bowl and six cups and saucers.

c1930 *Coffee pot 8in (20.5cm) high*

£500-700 **TDG**

One of a set of eight William de Morgan tiles, each painted in green and turquoise on a white ground with flowering sprigs in the 'Boston' design, with impressed Sands End marks.

£800-1,200 set **L&T**

A pair of Art Nouveau earthenware baluster vases, each painted and incised with a band of waterlilies on a deep brown ground marked "R. Dean", incised serial number to base.

10.25in (26cm) high

£320-380 **L&T**

A Denby twin-handled vase, of shouldered ovoid form covered with a streaky blue glaze, printed factory mark.

10in (24.5cm) high

£80-120 **L&T**

A French three piece tea set designed by Maurice Dufrene, comprising a teapot, sugar bowl and milk jug, each with flattened spherical body with arched scrolling handle, decorated with stylized leaves and flower heads in deep red and dark green, signed.

Teapot 5.25in (13.5cm) high

£3,000-4,000 **MACK**

A CLOSER LOOK AT A DE MORGAN PERSIAN TILE PANEL

This tile panel was made by the 19thC ceramicist William Frend de Morgan, regarded as one of the finest British art potters. This makes the panel a sought-after piece.

Peacocks have featured as decorative motifs since antiquity. They were popular during the late 19thC and are often found on William de Morgan's work.

A Persian influence can be seen in the use of blue, green and aubergine colours, as well as in the overall design of the frieze.

Despite cracks, chips and restoration, the piece is valuable due to the name of the maker, the size of the piece and its impressive design.

A William De Morgan Persian tile panel each three-tile frieze depicting a peacock above a vase of flowers, in shades of blue, green and aubergine, minor chips and restoration.

24in (61cm) high

£8,000-10,000 **WW**

An Eichwald jardinière and stand, of ovoid form, the jardinière moulded with roses and leafy swags, raised on a stand with three cylindrical columns moulded with roses and leaf swags on a spreading base, glazed in green, moulded and incised marks.

21in (53cm) high

£220-280 **L&T**

An Elton pottery double gourd vase, with incised decoration.

c1895 *9.5in (24cm) high*

£220-280 **HBK**

An Elton Art pottery jug.

c1910 *4.75in (12cm) high*

£220-280 **HBK**

An Elton Art pottery jug.

c1910 *10in (25.5cm) high*

£180-220 **HBK**

A pottery jug by Mary L. Fairgrieve, of tapering ovoid form painted with a band of flowers above a purple and amber chequer frieze reserved on a striped yellow and white ground, painted mark "MLF".

5.25in (13cm) high

£180-220 **L&T**

A Foley Intarsio ware twin-handled vase, designed by Frederick Rhead, transfer-decorated and painted in colours with poppies and foliage.

11in (27.5cm) high

£350-400 **PC**

A Grays pottery teapot and cover, of flattened ovoid form, painted with concentric bands of yellow, orange and yellow on a white ground, printed factory marks.

3.75in (9.5cm) high

£60-90 **L&T**

An Art Deco Hutschenreuther figure, modelled as a naked woman kneeling and adjusting her turban, highlighted in blue and gilt on a blanc-de-Chine ground, painted marks.

9.25in (23cm) high

£400-600 **L&T**

A Katzhütte Art Deco figure by Dakon, moulded as a young girl with a flowing dress and broad brim hat, printed monogram mark "H41".

16.75in (42cm) high

£350-400 **L&T**

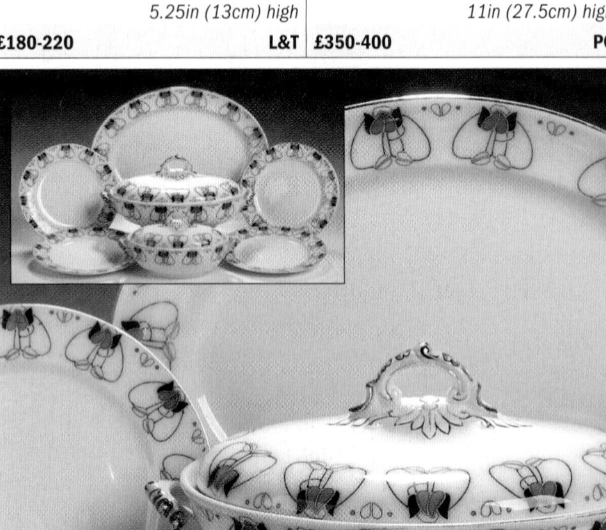

A Keeling and Co. Ltd 'Tulip' part dinner service designed by George Logan, comprising three oval platters, seven dinner plates, eight fish plates, two tureens with lids, a sauce tureen with lid and a sauce ladle, each printed with bands of stylized tulips on a blue and white ground with gilt highlights, printed marks.

£1,200-1,800 set **L&T**

A Jessie M. King oval dish, painted in blue, green and red with spring flowers, painted monogram, rabbit and green gate marks.

8.5in (21cm) wide

£400-600 **L&T**

A Laach terracotta paperweight of dished oval form, moulded with a Greek galleon in full sail and with the symbols 'A' and 'Ω' painted in colours, impressed marks "Laach Karlsruhe 95".

3.25in (8.5cm) diam

£30-40 **L&T**

A 1950's circular bowl, painted with primitive figures of huntsmen and their prey.

9.25in (23cm) diam

£20-30 **L&T**

A Lenci figure group, moulded as a baby playing with a ball, raised on a domed base, painted with floral rosettes, painted factory marks.

6.5in (16cm) high

£300-350 **L&T**

A Mak' Merry oval bowl, with deep tapering sides painted in columns with sprays of primroses on a yellow ground, painted mark "Mak' Merry".

10in (25cm) wide

£320-380 **L&T**

A Clement Massier ceramic figure of a seated ape, with a turquoise glaze, impressed factory marks.

3.5in (9cm) high

£120-180 **L&T**

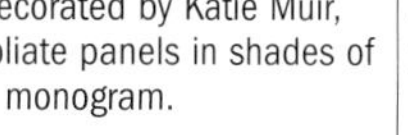

An ovoid jug decorated by Katie Muir, painted with foliate panels in shades of green, painted monogram.

5in (12cm) high

£30-40 **L&T**

An ovoid jug by Katie Muir painted in yellow and green with flowers buds, painted monogram.

4.5in (11.5cm) high

£30-40 **L&T**

A circular pottery bowl decorated by Mary A. Ramsay of Strathyre, with a band of flowering clematis on a cream ground, painted marks.

12.5in (32cm) diam

£320-380 **L&T**

An English china dessert service, by Royal Crown Derby, with Imari-style decoration, painted with pointed floral reserves and cobalt blue borders, comprising twelve dessert plates, side plates, coffee cups and saucers, a pair of circular compotes, a pair of oblong serving dishes, and a pair of shell-handled serving dishes, each with printed mark in red, the cups and smaller plates with painted number "1128", the compotes and plates with "1126", all impressed "DERBY", light wear to gilding.

Dessert plates 8.75in (22.5cm) diam

£1,800-2,200 set **FRE**

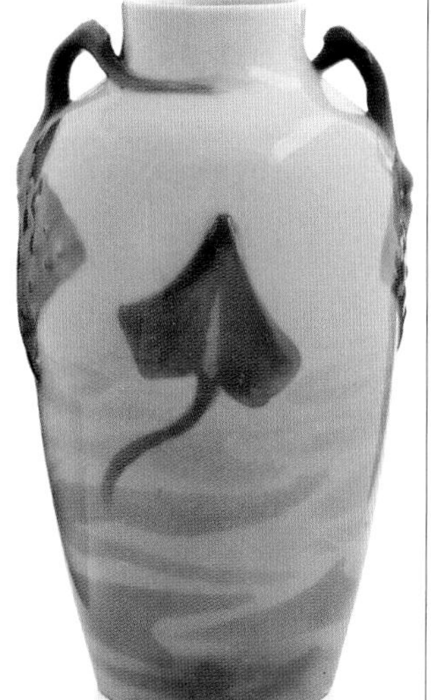

A Rorstrand porcelain vase in the manner of Alf Wallander, pale grey/blue field with manta ray decoration and handles, factory stamp.

9in (23cm) high

£2,500-3,000 **MACK**

A Holzer-Defanti porcelain figure, 'Korean Dance', produced by Porcelain Manufacture Selb, signed to base, green stamp and red painter's mark.

c1920 *15.75in (39.5cm) high*

£1,000-1,500 **DOR**

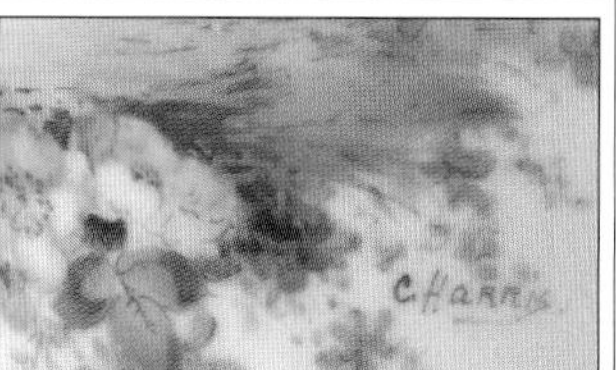

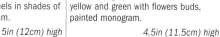

A Royal Crown Derby ewer in the Sèvres style, painted with vignettes of exotic birds and signed "C. Harris", within turquoise and and gilt borders, iron-red printed marks, date code, minute chip.

1906 *9in (23cm) high*

£800-1,200 **DN**

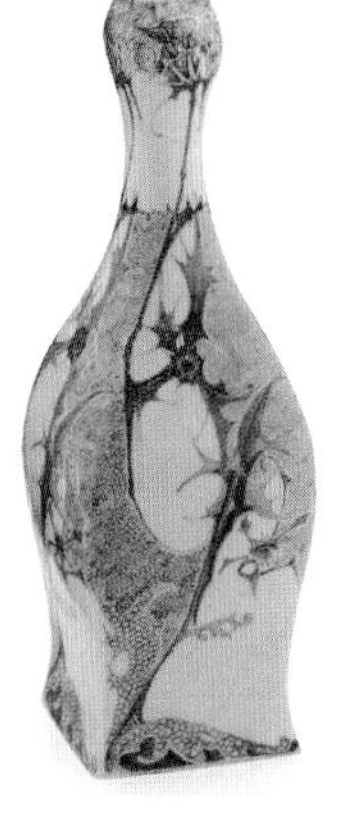

A Dutch eggshell porcelain vase, by Rozenburg, of shaped square section with all-over thistle decoration in yellow and orange, stamped in black with "Rozenburg den Haag", crown and heron marks.

10.75in 27cm high

£6,000-9,000 **MACK**

A Dutch eggshell porcelain vase by Rozenburg, single handle above flattened spherical body decorated with flower heads on a cream ground, factory stamp.

6im (15.5cm) high

£5,000-7,000 **MACK**

A Rozenburg earthenware vase, decorated with a raven and pomegranates on a swirling deep blue ground, signed "Rozenburg den Haag".

12in (30.5cm) high

£2,500-3,000 **MACK**

A pair of Rozenburg earthenware vases, each decorated with a floral design of lilies on a yellow and green ground with small red flower heads, each signed "Rozenburg den Haag".

c1890 *9.75in (25cm) high*

£2,000-4,000 **MACK**

A Rozenburg earthenware vase, with thin tapering neck above bulbous body decorated with red, purple and yellow flowers, factory mark and signed "J. Van Der Vet".

c1900 *15.25in 38.5cm high*

£5,000-7,000 **MACK**

A fine Ruskin barrel-shaped vase covered in a superior white, blue and rose mottled glaze with gunmetal and green speckles, oval Ruskin stamp, dated.

1903 *5.5in (14cm) high*

£1,500-2,000 **DRA**

A fine Ruskin tapering vase with silver overlay of fleshy poppies on a red and purple mottled ground, oval Ruskin stamp.

9.25in (23.5cm) high

£1,500-2,000 **DRA**

An art pottery vase, attributed to Ruskin, inlaid with engraved silver foliage against the mottled green brown ground.

4.25in (11cm) high

£120-180 **GORL**

A Salvini Art Nouveau faience plate with a woman's head in polychrome on a white ground, small chips and touch-ups to several points, signed "Salvin Italia".

6in (15cm) diam

£320-380 **DRA**

A Shelley three piece tea service designed by Mabel Lucie Attwell, comprising a teapot and cover, a milk jug and a sugar bowl, each forming the shape of a mushroom and painted in green, orange and yellow, with painted marks.

Teapot 5in (12.5cm) high

£280-320 **L&T**

A rare Shelley nursery figure, 'I's Shy', in original box with sign, designed by mabel Lucie Attwell, model number LA9, printed and painted marks.

6in (15cm) high

£3,000-5,000 **WW**

A Shelley ginger jar, with violet, emerald and orange decoration.

c1935 *6.5in (16.5cm) high*

£280-320 **TDG**

A CLOSER LOOK AT A TEPLITZ VASE

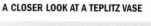

This piece belongs to a genre of vases called amphora, which were named after the slender Greek receptacles despite not always resembling them.
Squeezebagging is a method of piping or trailing decoration, in this case gilt, onto a piece of pottery.
The Glasgow Rose motif is indicative of how practitioners of the Art Nouveau style across Europe were influenced by each other's work.
Long-haired maidens with flawless features were popular subjects for Art Nouveau ceramics.

A fine Teplitz triangular vase, finely painted with a pre-Raphaelite maiden with golden hair, ornaments and Glasgow roses in gilded squeezebag, stamped "Teplitz Made in Austria", some damage.

5.75in (14.5cm) high

£1,500-2,000 **DRA**

A Belgian Art Nouveau pottery vase designed by Henry Van De Velde and attributed to Franz Ebenstei of Burgel, the circular tapering body with twisting sinuous abstract decoration in green and honey-coloured glazes, unmarked, minor repairs.

11.25in 28.5cm high

£4,000-6,000 **MACK**

C.VYSE
CHELSEA

A pottery figure by Charles Vyse, 'Clown', painted in colours, on ebonised wood base, impressed "Charles Vyse, Chelsea", restored finger.

13in (33cm) high

£3,000-5,000 **WW**

A group and two single ceramic figures, 'Pierrot and Pierrette', 'Lady With Garland' and 'Summer', painted in colours, with impressed marks.

c1910 *Tallest 12.25in (30.5cm) high*

£1,000-1,500 each **DOR**

A pottery figural group, 'Gypsy Dancers' by Charles Vyse of Chelsea, painted in colours and impressed "Charles Vyse, Chelsea".

11.5in (29cm) high

£3,000-5,000 **WW**

A pottery figure 'The Lavender Girl', by Charles Vyse, painted in colours, painted date mark.

Born in Staffordshire in 1882, Charles Vyse became apprenticed to Doulton as a designer and modeler, where his work proved very popular. He won a scholarship to the Royal College of Art to study sculpture in 1905 and was elected a member of the Royal Society of Sculptors in 1911.

By the 1920s he had set up a studio in Chelsea with his wife, Nell, where they began to create figures based on characters seen on the London streets around them. An expert in the chemistry of ceramics, Nell developed the glazes required to create Chinese Sung-style pottery which Charles also became interested in.

Vyse took up teaching at Farnham School of Art and after WWII, he began producing character figures with a former Farnham student called Barbara Waller.

Vyse exhibited his pieces through Walker's Gallery in London's Bond Street up until he retired in 1963. He died in 1971.

1921 *9in (22.5cm) high*

£400-600 **WW**

An Ernest Wahliss porcelain dressing table dish, moulded as an Art Nouveau maiden emerging from a waterlily pond smelling a rose, painted in gilt and coloured enamel on a cream ground, printed factory marks, impressed number "4706".

10.75in (27cm) wide

£220-280 **L&T**

A Michael Powolny putto, made by Vienna Ceramics, impressed monogram "MP", mark and number.

c1905 *29.5in (74cm) high*

£7,000-10,000 **DOR**

A Michael Powolny putto, 'Spring', made by Vienna Ceramics, impressed monogram "MP", marked "WK" and with model number "60/1".

c1905 *15.25in (38cm) high*

£7,000-10,000 **DOR**

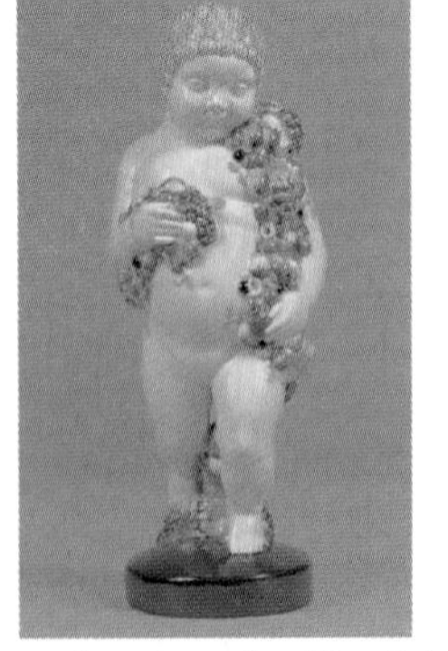

A Vienna Ceramics putto, with a garland of fruits, impressed maker's mark and model number "1635 50 3".

c1915 *17.75in (44.5cm) high*

£1,500-2,000 **DOR**

A Bristol part tea set by Louis Wain, comprising two cups and saucers, two side plates and a mug, each painted with a cat and a dog in various playful poses and marked, some damage.

£1,200-1,800 **L&T**

A CLOSER LOOK AT A ZSOLNAY PÉCS VASE

Zsolnay Pécs was a successful Hungarian decorative arts manufacturer. Pécs is the name of the town where the factory was based.

The organic lines of this stoppered vase are very evocative of the Art Nouveau period.

This piece showcases Zsolnay's work with iridescent ceramics, which became hugely influential.

This vase still has its original paper retailer's label, which makes it more valuable.

A rare Zsolnay Pécs vase and stopper, purple-red and iridescent blue glazed body with berry moulded stopper above serpentine floral relief moulded decoration with pierced top and foot, impressed factory mark and serial number "5745", paper label for "Gillman, Collamore & Co. New York".

10.75in (27cm) high

£30,000-50,000 **MACK**

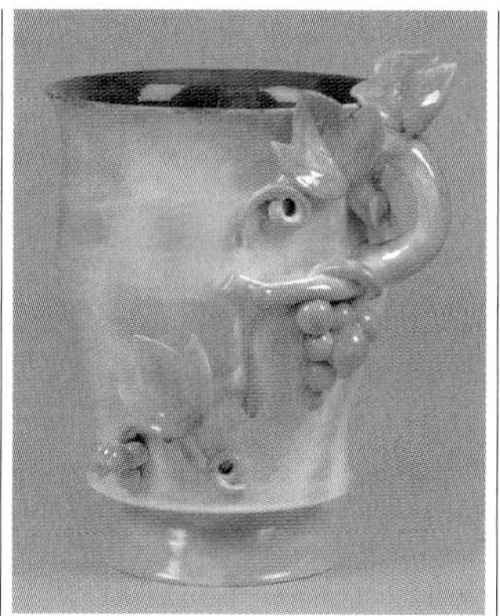

A tall Maria Likarz vase, made by Vienna Ceramics, turquoise and white exterior glaze and dark blue interior gaze, with applied grapevine motif, impressed monogram and number.

c1920 *14in (35cm) high*

£1,000-1,500 **DOR**

A faience vase by Zsolnay Pécs, with landscape decoration depicting a coastal night scene with trees, sailing boat and a swan, red, purple and green glaze, marked on base "Zsolnay Pécs".

c1900 *13.25in (33.5cm) high*

£6,000-8,000 **QU**

A Zsolnay Art Nouveau iridescent ceramic vase.

c1900 *9in (23cm) high*

£220-280 **AL**

A Zsolnay earthenware vase, the flattened ovoid body with bulbous neck, printed and painted in gilt and coloured enamels with bands of flora motifs, unmarked.

7.75in (19.5cm) high

£80-120 **L&T**

A German Art Nouveau porcelain comport, modelled as an Art Nouveau maiden and rearing horse, the maiden with diaphanous robes flowing into a curved wave forming the bowl, raised on curved tendril foot, painted in colours and highlighted in gilt, painted cross swords mark.

12.75in (32cm) wide

£320-380 **L&T**

A large vase in the Art Deco style, incised with stylized figures in profile under a lavender, green, black, and white glaze, no visible mark.

22in (56cm) high

£150-200 **DRA**

An English Art Deco jug, the handle modelled as a stylized saxophone player, impressed marks.

9.5in (24cm) high

£150-200 **WW**

An Art Deco porcelain figure of a dancing girl, wearing a long flowing green dress painted with flowers, printed marks.

10.25in (25.5cm) high

£280-320 **L&T**

An Amphora polar bear figural night-light, the bear standing on a naturalistic iceberg base, impressed and printed factory marks.

10.75in (27cm) high

£120-180 **L&T**

WEMYSS

A rare Wemyss inkwell, decorated with dolphins and a shell.

8in (20.5cm) long

£700-1,000 **RDER**

A Wemyss two-handled vase, hand-painted with roses.

12in (30.5cm) high

£500-800 **GCL**

A pair of Wemyss candlesticks, decorated with wild roses.

9.5in (24cm) high

£500-800 **RDER**

A Wemyss 'Roses' biscuit barrel and cover, painted with cabbage roses, the lid bearing the inscription "Biscuits", green painted mark "Wemyss".

4.5in (11cm) high

£200-300 **L&T**

A Wemyss 'Gordon' plate, decorated with yellow irises.

c1895 *8.25in (21cm) diam*

£500-700 **RDER**

A Wemyss three-handled tyg, decorated with irises, impressed factory mark, painted retailer's mark.

5.5in (14cm) high

£300-500 **L&T**

A Wemyss mug, decorated with thistles.

5.5in (14cm) high

£500-800 **RDER**

A small Wemyss pig, painted with flowering clover.

c1930 *6in (15cm) long*

£500-700 **RDER**

A rare Wemyss 'Gordon' plate, decorated with rag poppies, restored.

c1895 *8in (20.5cm) diam*

£500-700 **RDER**

A Wemyss 'Gordon' plate, decorated with buttercups.

8.25in (21cm) diam

£500-800 **RDER**

A Wemyss miniature basket, decorated with daffodils, small firing crack.

c1895 *6in (15cm) high*

£800-1,200 **RDER**

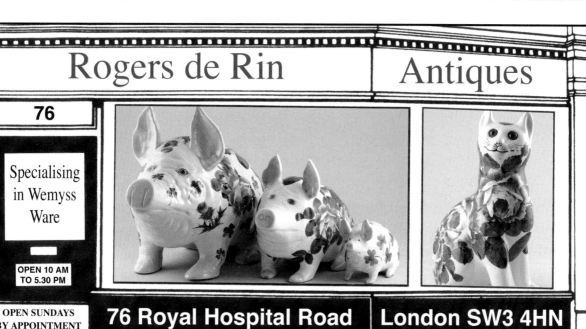

A Wemyss preserve pot, decorated with strawberries.

5in (13cm) high

£200-300 RDER

A Wemyss inkwell, decorated with strawberries, the ends replaced.

c1895 7in (18cm) wide

£400-600 RDER

A Wemyss loving cup, decorated with apples.

6.5in (16.5cm) high

£400-600 RDER

A Wemyss mug, decorated with apples.

c1900 5.75in (14.5cm) high

£500-700 RDER

A Wemyss biscuit barrel and cover, decorated with branches bearing plums.

6in (15cm) high

£200-250 L&T

A Wemyss 'Gordon' plate, decorated with plums.

8in (20.5cm) diam

£300-500 RDER

Two Wemyss plates, decorated with cherries.

c1895 5.5in (14cm) diam

£180-220 each RDER

A Wemyss mug, decorated with cherries, pink rim, restored chip.

c1890 *5.75in (14.5cm) high*

£500-800 **RDER**

A pair of Wemyss 'Cherries' beaker vases, painted and impressed marks.

7in (18cm) high

£220-280 **L&T**

A rare Wemyss 'Gordon' plate, decorated with red gooseberries.

c1895 *8.5in (21.5cm) diam*

£600-900 **RDER**

A small Wemyss plate, decorated with blackcurrants.

5.5in (14cm) diam

£300-400 **RDER**

A Wemyss preserve pot, decorated with oranges.

c1900 *5in (13cm) high*

£200-300 **RDER**

A Wemyss saucer, decorated with a brown cockerel.

c1900 *4.75in (12cm) diam*

£100-150 **RDER**

A Wemyss plate, painted with a pheasant.

4.75in (12cm) diam

£300-400 **RDER**

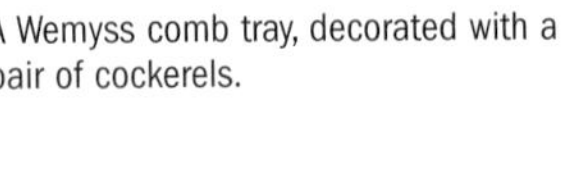

A Wemyss comb tray, decorated with a pair of cockerels.

c1900 *10in (25.5cm) wide*

£500-700 **RDER**

A Wemyss trumpet vase, decorated with dragonflies.

c1920 *7.5in (19cm) high*

£500-700 **RDER**

A Wemyss honey box with cover and stand, decorated with a hive and bees, with mark for Thomas Goode.

Stand 7.5in (19cm) wide

£500-800 **RDER**

A large Wemyss pig, with black and white sponged decoration, marked "Nekola Pinxt".

c1900 *18in (45.5cm) wide*

£2,200-2,800 **RDER**

DAUM

A Daum clear glass decanter with stopper, with enamel decoration.

c1890 *7.5in (19cm) high*

£200-300 **MW**

A Daum Nancy pitcher, frosted glass with cameo decoration and gold highlighted blossoms, leaves and branches, applied clear cameo glass handle, signed on base "Daum Nancy", damage to handle.

9.5in (24cm) high

£800-1,200 **JDJ**

A Daum Nancy small mug, of clear crystal glass with applied enamel decoration of flowers and gold highlights, signed in gold "Daum Nancy".

2.25in (5.5cm) high

£300-400 **JDJ**

A signed Daum Nancy pillow-shaped vase, mottled decoration of yellows, browns, greens, pink and mauve, signed on side of vase "Daum Nancy".

4.75in (12cm) high

£500-700 **JDJ**

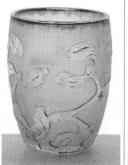

A Daum Nancy miniature tumbler vase.

c1900 *2in (5cm) high*

£300-400 **MW**

A Daum vase with original silver foot.

c1900 *4.25in (11cm) high*

£400-600 **MW**

A Daum triple coloured cameo glass.

c1895 *7.25in (18.5cm) high*

£1,000-2,000 **MW**

A Daum small cameo glass vase, with blue violets on a milky white ground with gilt detailing, signed "Daum Nancy" with Lorraine cross.

6.5in (16cm) high

£6,000-8,000 **MACK**

A Daum etched and enamelled 'Summer Scenic' glass vase, trees in landscape decoration, signed "Daum Nancy" with Lorraine cross.

c1900 *4in (10cm) high*

£3,000-3,500 **MACK**

A Daum bat vase, with an orange ground and black detail.

c1900 *9in (23cm) high*

£8,000-10,000 **MW**

A Daum cameo glass vase, applied pink glass bleeding hearts or dicentra decoration, signed "Daum Nancy" with Lorraine cross.

8in (20.5cm) high

£10,000-12,000 **MACK**

A Daum cameo glass vase, with cowslip decoration, signed "Daum Nancy France".

c1900 *5in (12.5cm) high*

£1,000-1,200 **TO**

A Daum etched and enamelled 'Winter landscape' glass vase, depicting a forest of winter trees against an early morning or evening sky and snow clad ground, signed "Daum Nancy" with Lorraine cross.

c1900 *7.5in (18.5cm) high*

£8,500-10,000 **MACK**

A Daum cameo glass vase, with red-purple poppy decoration on milky white ground, signed to base "Daum Nancy".

c1900 *6.5in (16.5cm) high*

£6,000-8,000 **MACK**

A Daum cornflower design green vase with overlay, signed "Daum Nancy".

c1900 *5.5in (14cm) high*

£3,000-4,000 **MW**

A Daum glass vase, with a rare 'Cornflower' pattern.

c1900 *3.5in (9cm) high*

£1,200-1,500 **STY**

A Daum twin-handled cameo glass vase, pink ground with trailing vine decoration, signed "Daum Nancy".

c1900 *8.25in (21cm) high*

£6,000-8,000 **MACK**

A Daum etched and enamelled twin-handled 'Champignons' vase, signed "Daum Nancy" with Lorraine cross.

9in (22.5cm) wide

£7,000-10,000 **MACK**

A Daum vase, with applied ears.

c1900 *6.75in (17cm) diam*

£3,000-4,000 **MW**

A Daum enamelled vase with a spring scene.

c1900 *6.75in (17cm) wide*

£2,000-3,000 **MW**

A Daum cameo glass bowl.

c1900 *6in (15cm) diam*

£1,200-1,400 **MW**

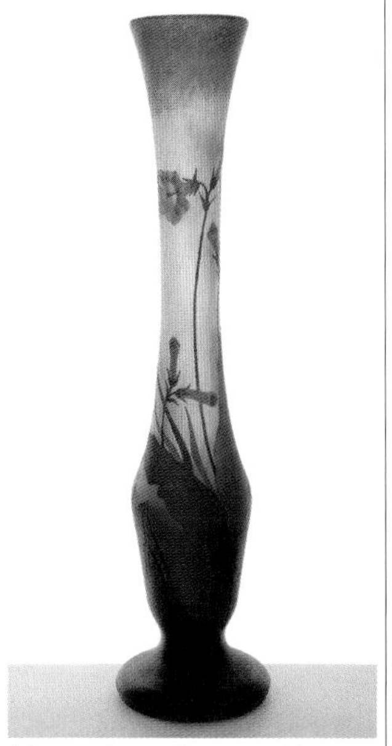

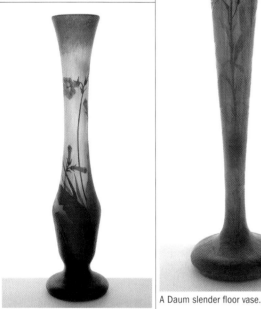

A Daum tobacco plant vase with hammering around the rim.

c1900 *23.75in (60cm) high*

£4,000-6,000 **MW**

A Daum Nancy enamelled bottle with stopper and seascape design.

c1900 *8in (20cm) high*

£1,200-1,400 **MW**

A Daum slender floor vase.

Provenance: Previously owned by Michael Caine.

c1900 *23.5in (59.5cm) high*

£8,000-10,000 **MW**

A Daum blackberry cameo vase.

c1905 *4.75in (12cm) high*

£1,400-1,600 **MW**

An organic Daum floor vase, with an extremely clear signature.

c1905 *24in (61cm) high*

£2,000-3,000 **MW**

A Daum enamelled vase.

c1905 *6in (15.5cm) high*

£3,000-4,000 **MW**

A Daum eucalyptus bowl.

c1910 *4.75in (12cm) diam*

£1,000-1,200 **MW**

A CLOSER LOOK AT A DAUM CAMEO VASE

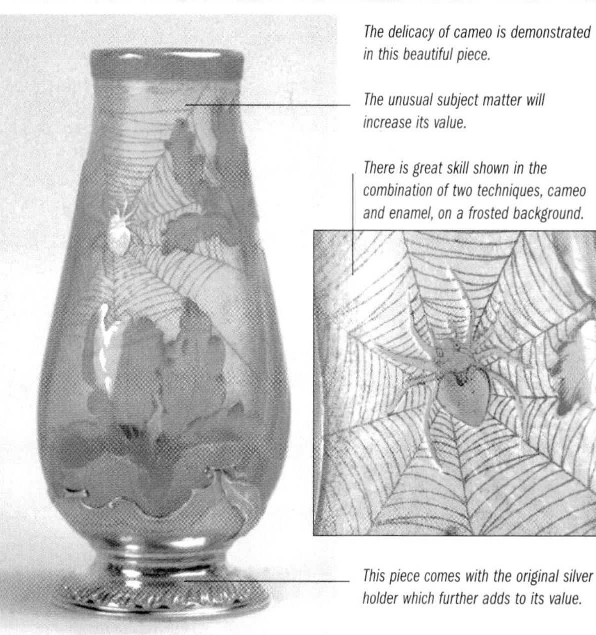

The delicacy of cameo is demonstrated in this beautiful piece.
The unusual subject matter will increase its value.
There is great skill shown in the combination of two techniques, cameo and enamel, on a frosted background.
This piece comes with the original silver holder which further adds to its value.

A rare Daum Nancy cameo spider web vase, with cameo decoration of green iris blossoms and leaves on a frosted chipped ice background, a cameo green spider rests on a gold enamel spider web, vase sits in original embossed silver holder, signed on base "Daum Nancy" in gold lettering.

9.25in (23.5cm) high

£3,000-4,000 **JDJ**

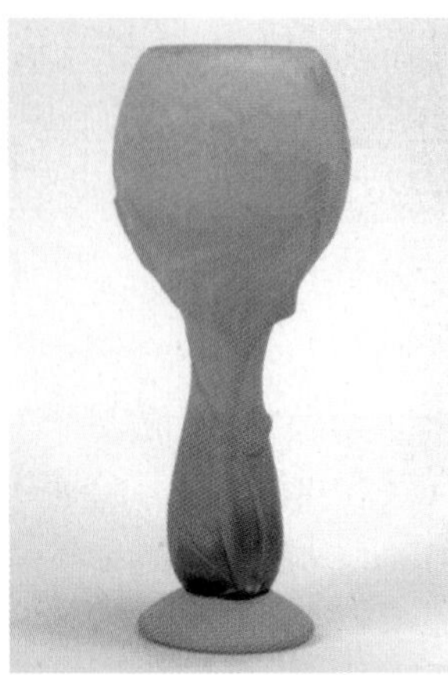

A Daum Nancy blown-out and cameo vase, decorated with blown-out blossom, leaf and stem with cameo leaf and vines, colours are green and brown on a frosted clear background, signed on side of vase "Daum Nancy".

10in (25.5cm) high

£9,000-12,000 **JDJ**

A Daum Nancy 'Feuilles de rosier à l'automne' vase of clear glass overlayed with yellow, red, green and purple enamels, decorated with etched rose branches, with Lorraine cross mark and "Daum Nancy" signature.

c1905 *7.25in (18cm) high*

£2,000-3,000 **QU**

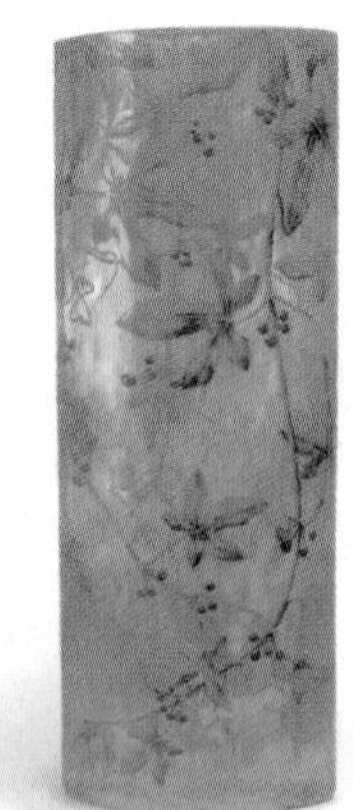

A Daum Nancy berry vase, cameo and enamel decoration of green leaves, ten applied red berries, signed "Daum Nancy".

13.75in (35cm) high

£6,000-8,000 **JDJ**

A Daum Nancy cameo and padded vase, the cameo decoration of green leaves and stems with two purple padded and wheelcarved gentian flower blossoms, signed on side of vase "Daum Nancy".

4in (10cm) high

£2,500-3,500 **JDJ**

A Daum Nancy cameo box, the cameo decoration of green leaves and red blossoms on a mottled orange and yellow background, matching cover also has green cameo leaves and red blossoms, signed "Daum Nancy" on base.

5in (12.5cm) long

£1,000-1,500 **JDJ**

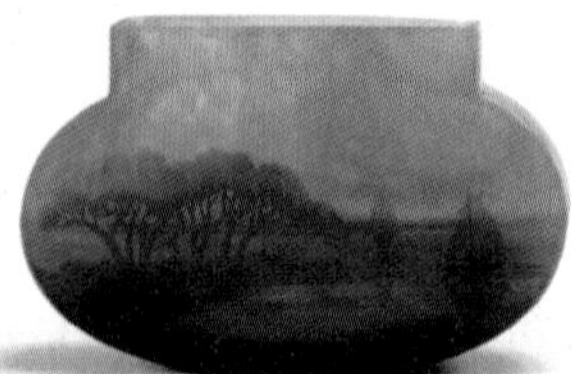

A Daum Nancy cameo vase, scenic cameo decoration with trees and boats in colours of brown, orange and yellow, pillow shaped with a square top, signed on side of vase "Daum Nancy", damage to rim.

7in (18cm) wide

£500-800 **JDJ**

A Daum Nancy miniature pitcher, with cameo and enamel decoration of flower blossoms and vines, applied crystal handle, signed on base "Daum Nancy" in gold lettering.

2.75in (7cm) high

£1,000-1,200 **JDJ**

A Joe Descomps for Daum pâte-de-verre vide poche, with snail decoration, signed "J Descomps, Daum Nancy".

Joe Descomps was an Art Nouveau sculptor who worked mainly in bronze.

9.75in (24.5cm) wide

£8,000-9,000 **MACK**

A CLOSER LOOK AT A DAUM PÂTE-DE-VERRE TRAY

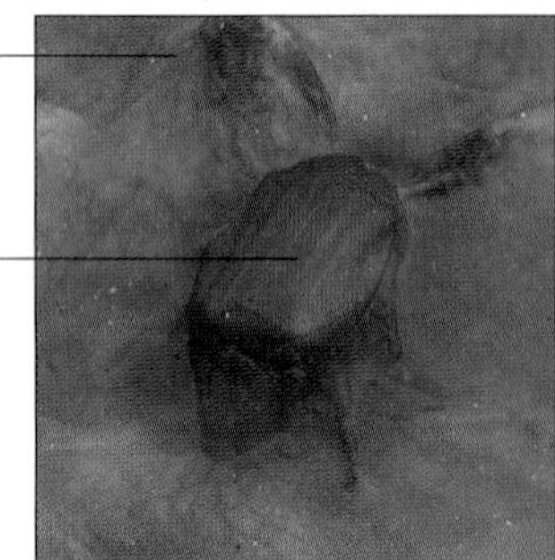

The naturalistic subject matter reflects the main inspiration of the Art Nouveau movement.

Pâte-de-verre allows for the precise placement of colour within a piece, as shown by this red beetle on the green and yellow leaf.

The pâte-de-verre technique, which casts ground glass paste, is a very expensive and demanding technique, and demonstrates the diversity of Daum's skills.

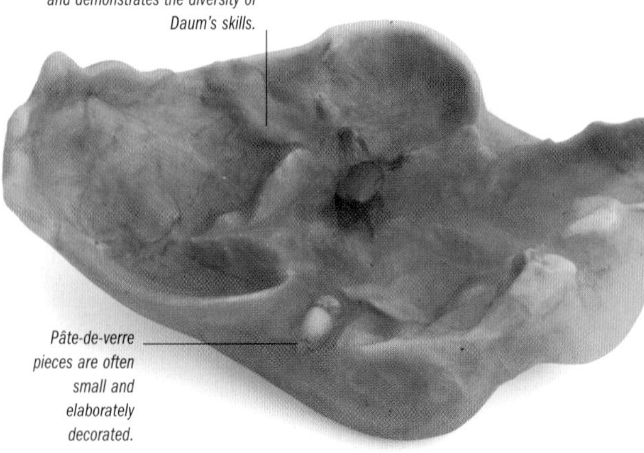

Pâte-de-verre pieces are often small and elaborately decorated.

A Daum pâte-de-verre tray, modelled with a small beetle on a yellow and green leaf background with acorns, signed "Daum Nancy".

8in (20.5cm) wide

£5,000-6,000 **MACK**

GALLE

A Gallé champagne glass, with gold enamel decoration with three coloured and faceted jewels on clear glass, the applied foot signed "E. Gallé" and connected with an opaque pink wafer.

4.5in (11.5cm) high

£1,500-2,000 **JDJ**

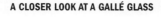

A CLOSER LOOK AT A GALLÉ GLASS

This piece is first period, made before Gallé began to work with cameo glass.
It demonstrates skillful use of two techniques – engraving and enamelling.
It also has an unusual early Gallé mark.

A Gallé first period clear glass, decorated with engraving then enamelling.

c1890 *5.5in (14cm) high*

£500-700 **MW**

A Gallé cordial glass, pale brown glass with enamelled decoration of cherries and gold highlighting, signed on foot "E Gallé".

2.75in (7cm) high

£600-900 **JDJ**

A rare Gallé enamel vase, with enamelled decoration of branches, blossoms, honeycomb and a bee on translucent brown ribbed glass, signed "Emile Gallé".

4.25in (11cm) high

£1,500-2,000 **JDJ**

A Gallé vase, with enamelled decoration of pink, brown and yellow orchids on a mottled transparent background, signed on base "Cristallerie d'Emile Gallé Nancy Modèle Depose".

8.25in (21cm) high

£1,800-2,200 **JDJ**

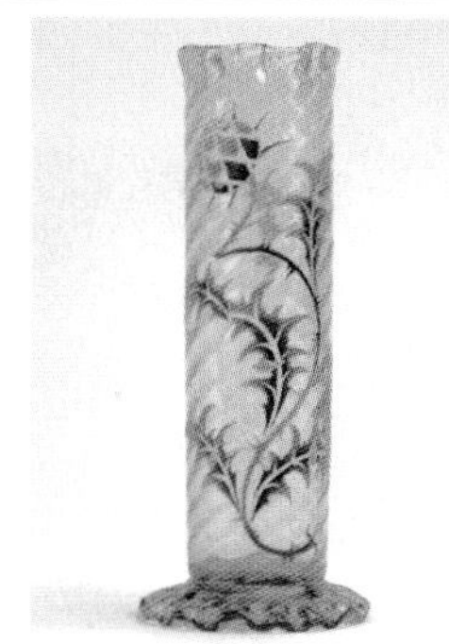

An enamelled Gallé cabinet vase, the cushion foot tapering to a narrow neck, applied and painted with flower on a stem with gilt highlights, signed in enamel "Cristallerie d'Emile Gallé a Nancy/Modèle et décor deposes".

c1895 *4.5in (11.5cm) high*

£1,100-1,500 **S&K**

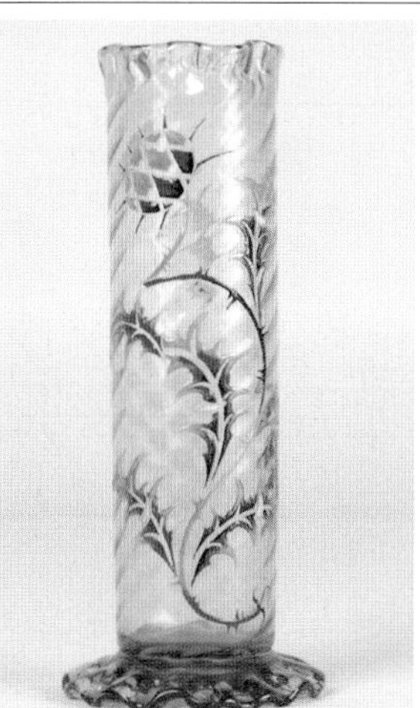

An early Gallé enamelled tube vase, with burgundy and mauve enamelled thistle on swirled clear amber glass, signed "E. GALLE Depose".

7.5in (19cm) high

£900-1,200 **JDJ**

A Gallé cameo trumpet vase, with cameo decoration of amethyst and blue blossoms and leaves on a frosted green background, signed on side of vase "Gallé".

14.25in (36cm) high

£3,500-4,500 **JDJ**

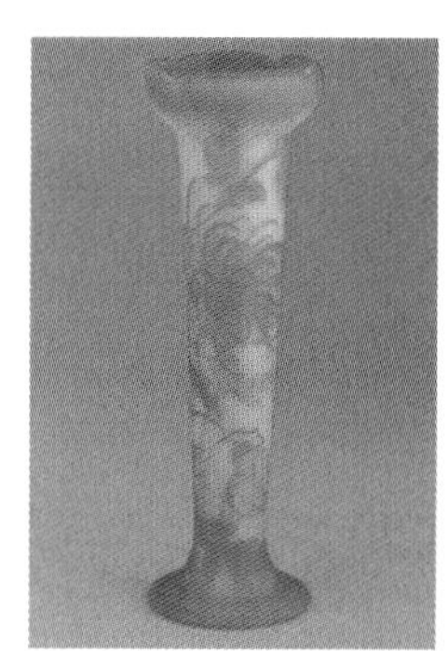

A tall Emile Gallé flaring vase with cupped rim, etched with orange spider chrysanthemums on a pearl grey ground, etched "GALLÉ".

5in (38cm) high

£1,200-1,800 **CR**

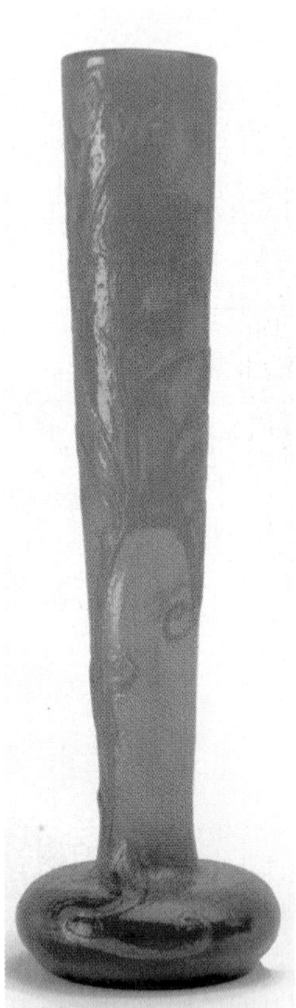

A Gallé cameo vase, with triple overlay.

c1900 *17.5in (44cm) high*

£3,000-4,000 **MW**

A Gallé fire-polished cameo vase, with a long neck, decorated with a floral design.

c1905 *14.5in (37cm) high*

£2,000-3,000 **MW**

A Gallé cameo rummer, decorated with etched and polished grapes, signed "Gallé" to the foot.

c1900 *10in (25cm) high*

£800-1,000 **DOR**

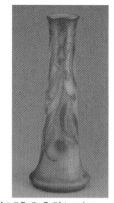

A tall Emile Gallé tapering vase, etched with a branch of olive green eucalyptus against a pearl grey ground, etched "GALLE".

25.5in (65cm) high

£2,200-2,800 **CR**

A Gallé wheelcarved cameo vase, with cameo decoration consisting of pink irises on green glass, glossy finish, signed on base "Cristallerie de Gallé" and "Modèle et Décor Depose".

15in (38cm) high

£20,000-25,000 **JDJ**

A Gallé triple overlay cameo vase, the cameo decoration of brown and beige blossoms, leaves and stems on a green and frosted background, signed "Gallé" on side of vase.

13.75in (35cm) high

£1,300-1,600 **JDJ**

A Gallé cameo vase, amethyst and green cameo decoration of iris blossoms, leaves and ferns on a mottled blue, yellow and orange background, signed on side of vase "Gallé".

14.75in (37.5cm) high

£3,600-4,200 **JDJ**

A Gallé cameo vase, the cameo decoration of green berries leaves and branches on an amber background, signed "Gallé" on the side, repair to foot.

14.25in (36cm) high

£1,800-2,200 **JDJ**

A Gallé triple overlay cameo vase, cameo decoration of brown and beige flower blossoms, leaves and stems on a green and frosted background, signed "Gallé" on side of vase.

13.75in (35cm) high

£2,600-3,200 **JDJ**

A Gallé cabinet vase, featuring cameo decoration of green thistles against a yellow ground.

c1900 *4in (10cm) high*

£400-600 **MW**

A Gallé cameo vase, the cameo decoration of green pods and leaves on a mottled green background, signed on the side "Gallé".

12in (30.5cm) high

£1,800-2,200 **JDJ**

A Gallé cameo vase, amethyst cameo decoration on a frosted salmon-coloured background, decoration consists of amethyst blossoms and leaves, signed "Gallé" on side of vase.

9.5in (24cm) high

£800-1,200 **JDJ**

A Gallé cameo vase, cameo decoration consists of red flower blossoms and leaves on a yellow background, signed "Gallé" on side of the vase.

10.75in (27.5cm) high

£3,500-4,000 **JDJ**

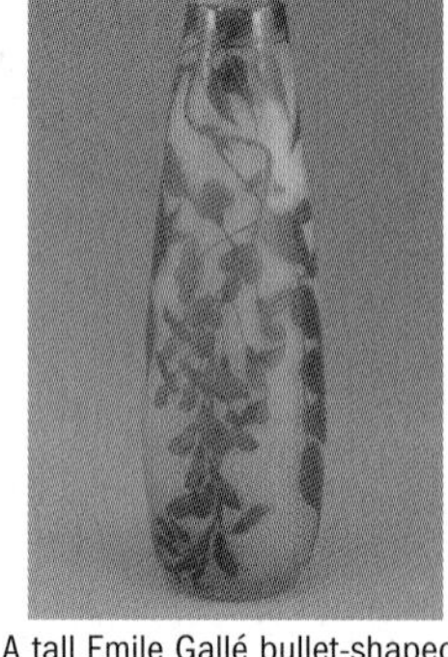

A tall Emile Gallé bullet-shaped vase, etched with branches of sweet peas in purple on a chartreuse and yellow ground, etched "Gallé", some scaling to rim.

14.5in (37cm) high

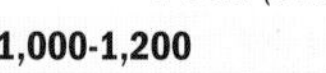

£1,000-1,200 **CR**

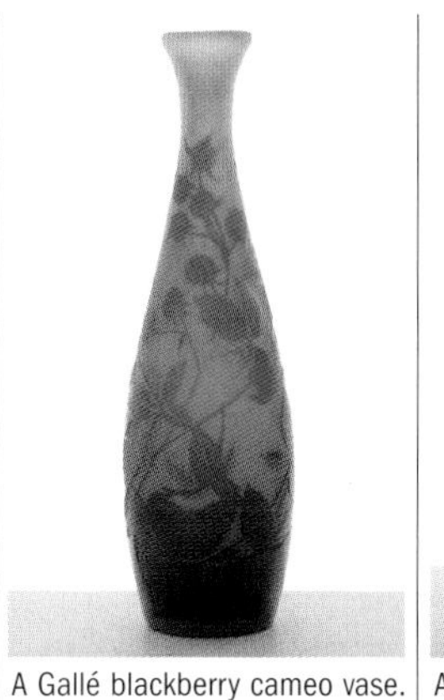

A Gallé blackberry cameo vase.

c1900 *7.75in (20cm) high*

£1,000-1,200 **MW**

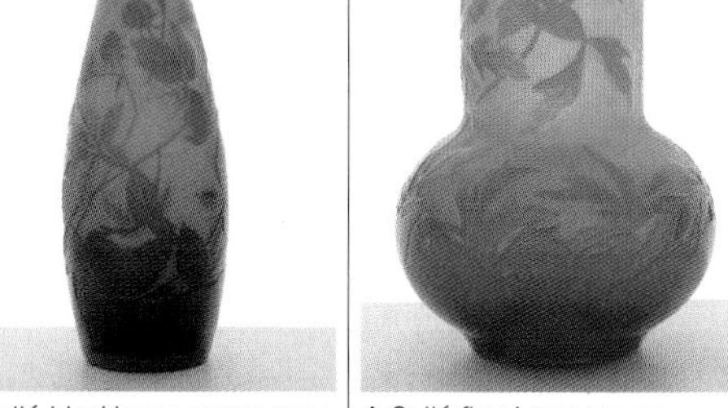

A Gallé floral cameo vase.

c1900 *6in (15.5cm) high*

£700-900 **MW**

A Gallé banjo cabinet vase.

c1900 *6.75in (17cm) high*

£700-900 **MW**

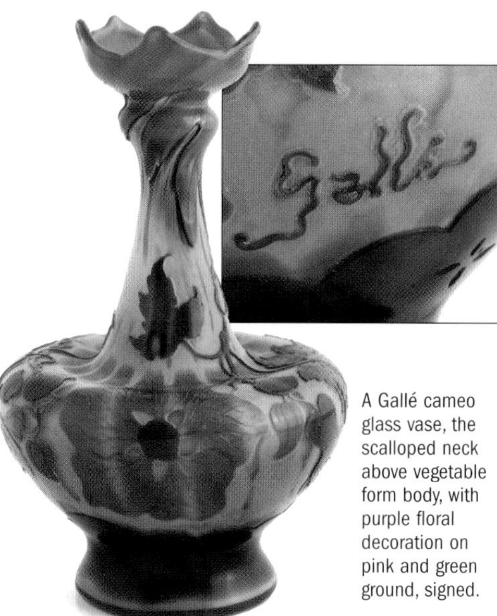

A Gallé cameo glass vase, the scalloped neck above vegetable form body, with purple floral decoration on pink and green ground, signed.

7.75in (20cm) high

£9,000-11,000 **MACK**

A Gallé floral design cabinet vase.

c1900 *4in (10cm) high*

£400-600 **MW**

A Gallé cameo vase, the cameo decoration of green leaves and berries on a pink frosted background, signed on the side of the vase "Gallé" with a star.

8.75in (22cm) high

£1,000-1,200 **JDJ**

A Gallé catkin flower vase.

c1905 *9in (23cm) high*

£1,500-2,000 **MW**

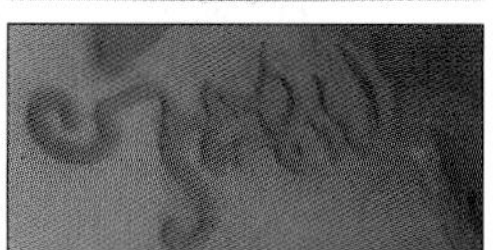

A Gallé cameo vase, with a floral design.

c1900 *8.25in (21cm) high*

£2,000-3,000 **MW**

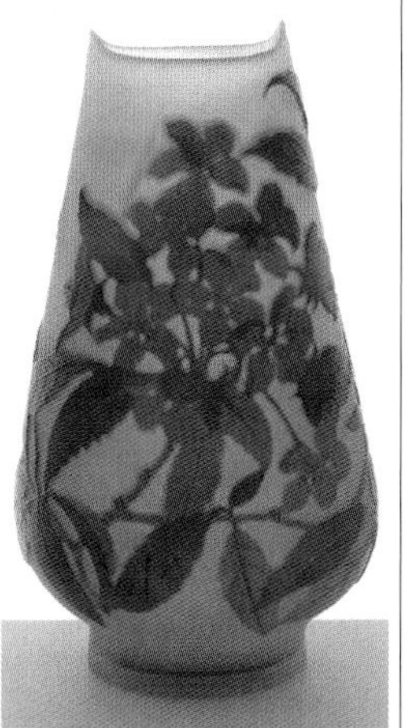

A Gallé floral cameo vase with pinched top.

c1900 *7.75in (20cm) high*

£2,000-3,000 **MW**

A Gallé floral cameo vase, with a standard Gallé signature.

c1900 *12.5in (31.5cm) high*

£7,000-8,000 **MW**

A Gallé cameo vase, relief decoration of oak leaves and acorns on a translucent green ground, signed "Gallé".

9.75in (25cm) high

£9,000-12,000 **MACK**

A signed Gallé cameo vase, the cameo decoration of green and amethyst flower blossoms and leaves on an orange and clear background, signed on side of vase "Gallé", ground rim.

18in (45.5cm) high

£1,200-1,800 **JDJ**

A Gallé cameo vase, crimped at the top, with pendulous foliage.

c1905 *9.5in (24.5cm) high*

£1,500-2,000 **MW**

A Gallé cameo vase, butterscotch yellow cameo decoration of leaves and berries with two applied cabochons, one red and one purple, signed on side of vase "Gallé".

4.25in (11cm) high

£1,200-1,600 **JDJ**

A Gallé blown vase of clear glass with a design of blue and purple hibiscus branches on a yellow ground, frosted finish, signed "Gallé".

c1925 *10in (25cm) high*

£10,000-12,000 **DOR**

A rare Gallé firepolished vase, the cameo decoration of amethyst on blue leaves and flower blossoms, all over a firepolished ground, signed "Gallé" on side of vase.

11in (28cm) high

£6,000-7,000 **JDJ**

A Gallé perfume bottle, cameo decoration of flowers and vines in amethyst and blue, matching amethyst stopper, signed within the design, one very minor pin nick on edge of bottle.

6in (15cm) high

£1,000-1,200 **JDJ**

A Gallé vase with a standard Gallé signature.

c1900 *6.75in (17.5cm) high*

£7,000-8,000 **MW**

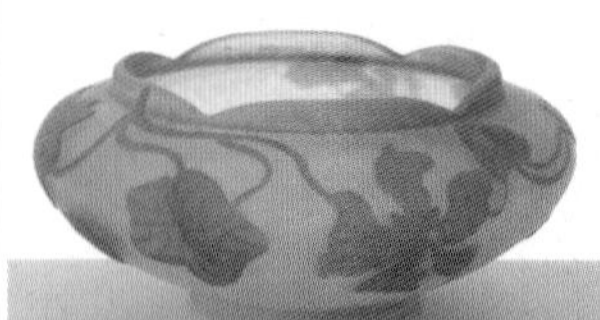

A Gallé orange cameo glass bowl, with a floral and foliate design.

c1905 *8.25in (21cm) wide*

£1,500-2,000 **MW**

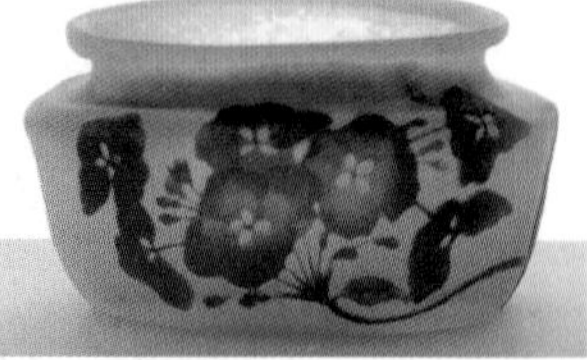

A Gallé, triple overlay cameo vase, with a floral design.

c1900 *7in (18cm) wide*

£1,500-2,000 **MW**

A Gallé bowl, made for the Paris World Fair in 1889, yellow glass with red and brown cameo design, signed "Emile Gallé ft Nancy", with Lorraine cross and "Exposition 1889" marks.

1889 *5in (12.5cm) diam*

£7,500-8,500 **DOR**

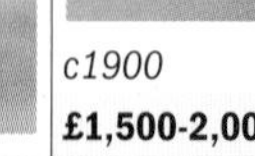

A standard Gallé cameo vase, with foliate design.

c1900 *5.5in (14cm) high*

£1,500-2,000 **MW**

A Gallé cameo thistle vase, green cameo thistle against a cream and pink background, signed on side "Gallé" in cameo, vase appears to have been cut down and has small chip to Gallé signature.

5.75in (14.5cm) high

£120-180 **JDJ**

A Gallé tricorn vase, cameo colours of brown and yellow on a clear and green frosted background, cameo decoration of flower blossoms and leaves with "Gallé" signature on side.

4in (10cm) high

£1,000-1,200 **JDJ**

A large Gallé centrepiece bowl, amethyst cameo decoration of blossoms, leaves and stems on a frosted background, signed on side "Gallé" with a star.

6.75in (17cm) wide

£900-1,200 **JDJ**

A rare Gallé covered box on a silver stand, box made of clear glass with engraving and enamelled flowers to the bottom, applied silver leaf and overlaid design of an orchid branch in polychrome to the upper part, the silver stand decorated with leaves, signed on the cover "Gallé".

c1895 *5in (12.5cm) wide*

£4,000-6,000 **DOR**

A Gallé cameo vase, cameo decoration of pond lilies in colours of amethyst and blue on a frosted background, signed within the design "Gallé", very good to excellent condition.

10.5in (26.5cm) high

£2,000-2,500 **JDJ**

A Gallé scenic vase, cameo decoration of trees and lake in colours of brown and green, signed on the side of vase "Gallé", very good condition.

12in (30.5cm) high

£1,600-2,000 **JDJ**

A Gallé cameo vase, green and brown scenic decoration, signed on side of vase.

9.5in (24cm) high

£1,200-1,800 **JDJ**

A Gallé cameo landscape vase.

c1900 *7in (18cm) high*

£1,000-1,500 **MW**

A CLOSER LOOK AT A GALLÉ CAMEO VASE

This early piece shows great skill in the use of cameo layers to create depth.
The Lake Como subject matter makes this a very unusual piece.
Earlier pieces have more layers, later pieces tend to use two.
The large size of this vase adds to its value.

A large Gallé Lake Como vase, cameo decoration consists of amethyst and blue over clear and amber background, decorated with trees, mountains, a castle and a peacock, signed "Gallé" within the design.

13.75in (35cm) high

£20,000-25,000 **JDJ**

LALIQUE

A Lalique 'Acanthes' vase, in clear and frosted glass with green patina, engraved Lalique mark.

c1920 *11in (29cm) high*

£1,500-2,000 **RDL**

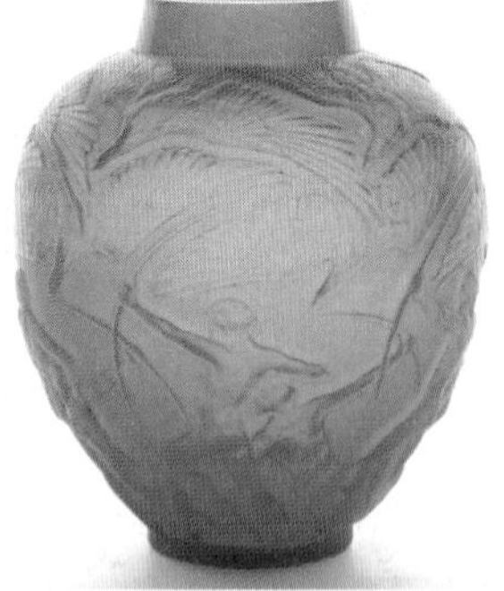

A Lalique 'Archers' vase in cased yellow glass, with a moulded "R. LALIQUE" mark, engraved "R. Lalique".

c1920 *10.25in (26cm) high*

£5,000-7,000 **RDL**

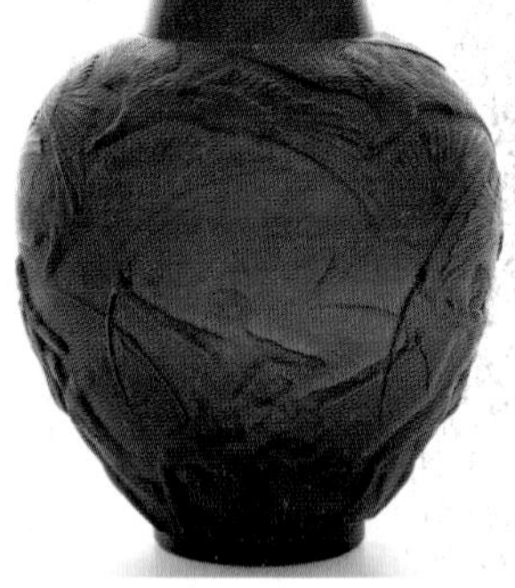

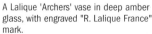

A Lalique 'Archers' vase in deep amber glass, with engraved "R. Lalique France" mark.

c1920 *10.25in (26cm) high*

£5,000-7,000 **RDL**

A Lalique 'Archers' vase, in clear and frosted glass with blue patina, a moulded "R. LALIQUE" mark.

c1920 *10.5in (26.5cm) high*

£3,000-4,000 **RDL**

A Lalique 'Archers' vase in clear and frosted glass with blue-grey patina, engraved "R. Lalique France" mark.

c1920 *10.5in (26.5cm) high*

£3,000-4,000 **RDL**

A Lalique 'Bacchantes' vase, in amethyst glass with sepia patina, a wheel-cut "R. LALIQUE FRANCE" mark.

c1925 *9.5in (25cm) high*

£5,000-7,000 **RDL**

A Lalique 'Camaret' vase, in opalescent glass, with an engraved "R. Lalique France No. 1010" mark.

c1930 *5.5in (14cm) high*

£700-1,000 **RDL**

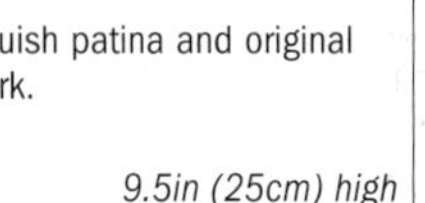

A Lalique 'Bacchantes' vase, in opalescent glass with bluish patina and original bronze base, with a wheel-cut "R. LALIQUE FRANCE" mark.

c1925 *9.5in (25cm) high*

£20,000-30,000 **RDL**

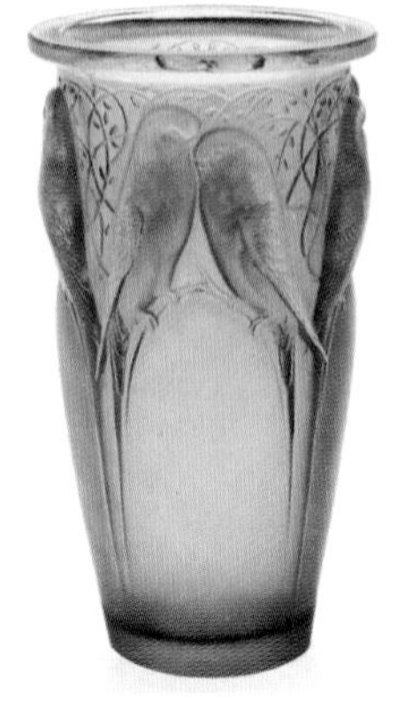

A Lalique 'Ceylan' vase, in opalescent glass with blue patina, a wheel-cut "R. LALIQUE FRANCE" mark.

c1925 *9.75in (25cm) high*

£5,000-7,000 **RDL**

A Lalique 'Chamonix' vase, in opalescent glass, stencilled "R. LALIQUE FRANCE" mark.

c1935 *6in (15cm) high*

£700-900 **RDL**

A Lalique 'Chardons' vase, in clear and frosted glass with sepia patina, engraved "R. Lalique France No. 929" mark.

c1920 *7.5in (19cm) high*

£500-700 **RDL**

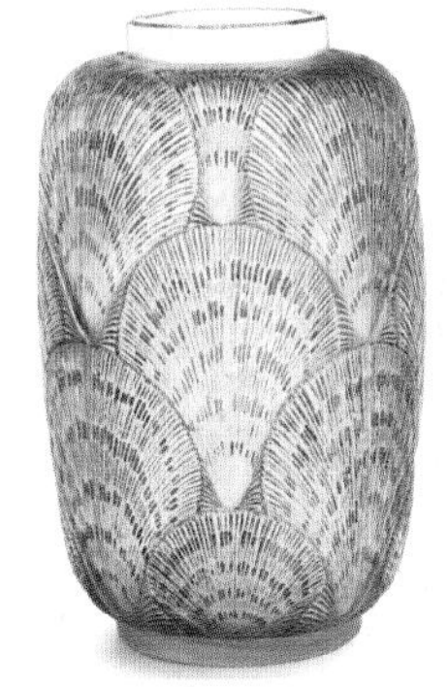

A Lalique 'Coquilles' vase, in clear and frosted glass with blue patina, with an "R. LALIQUE" moulded mark.

7.5in (18.8cm) high

£800-1,200 **RDL**

A Lalique 'Domremy' vase, in grey glass with sepia patina, moulded "R. LALIQUE" mark, and engraved "R. Lalique France" mark.

c1925 *9in (22cm) high*

£800-1,200 **RDL**

A Lalique 'Domremy' vase, in opalescent glass, engraved "R. Lalique France".

c1925 *9in (22cm) high*

£600-900 **RDL**

A Lalique 'Deux Pigeons' vase, in clear and frosted glass, with stencilled "R. LALIQUE FRANCE" mark.

c1930 *8in (20cm) high*

£1,200-1,800 **RDL**

A Lalique 'Dordogne' vase, in opalescent white glass with blue patina, moulded "R. LALIQUE" and engraved "R. Lalique France".

c1925 *7in (17.5cm) high*

£2,000-3,000 **RDL**

A Lalique 'Druides' vase, in opalescent glass with green patina, engraved "R. Lalique France No. 937" mark.

c1925 *7in (17.5cm) high*

£1,000-1,500 **RDL**

A Lalique 'Esterel' vase, in cased yellow glass with sepia patina, moulded with "R. LALIQUE" mark.

c1925 *6in (15cm) high*

£1,500-2,000 **RDL**

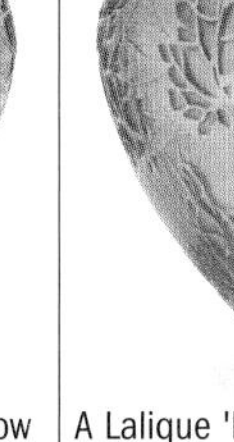

A Lalique 'Esterel' vase, in opalescent glass with blue patina, engraved with "R. Lalique France" mark.

c1925 *6in (15cm) high*

£700-900 **RDL**

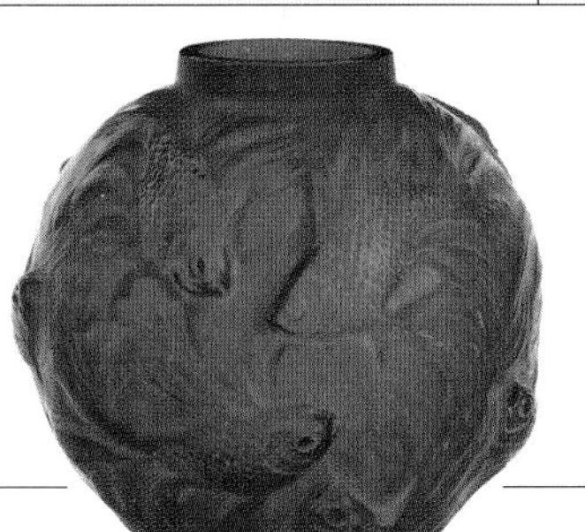

A Lalique 'Formose' vase, in red cased glass with whitish patina, with moulded "R. LALIQUE" mark.

c1925 *6.5in (18cm) high*

£5,000-7,000 **RDL**

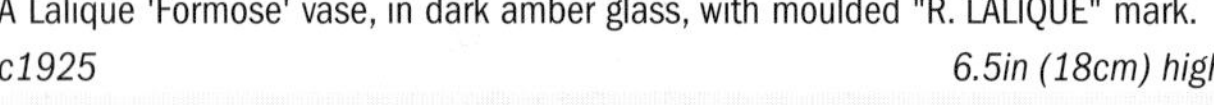

A Lalique 'Formose' vase, in dark amber glass, with moulded "R. LALIQUE" mark.

c1925 *6.5in (18cm) high*

£5,000-7,000 **RDL**

A Lalique 'Formose' vase, in opalescent glass with blue patina, engraved "R. Lalique France".

c1925 *6.5in (18cm) high*

£1,500-2,000 **RDL**

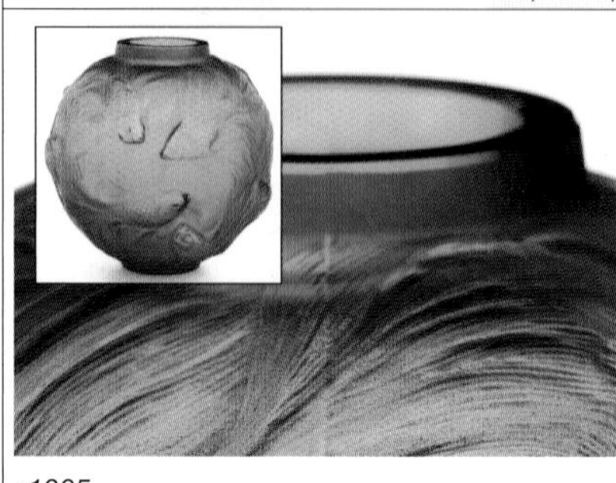

A Lalique 'Formose' vase, in emerald green glass, with stencilled mark "R. LALIQUE" and engraved "France".

These vases were made from moulded glass and the line of the mould can be seen here.

c1925 *6.5in (18cm) high*

£4,000-6,000 **RDL**

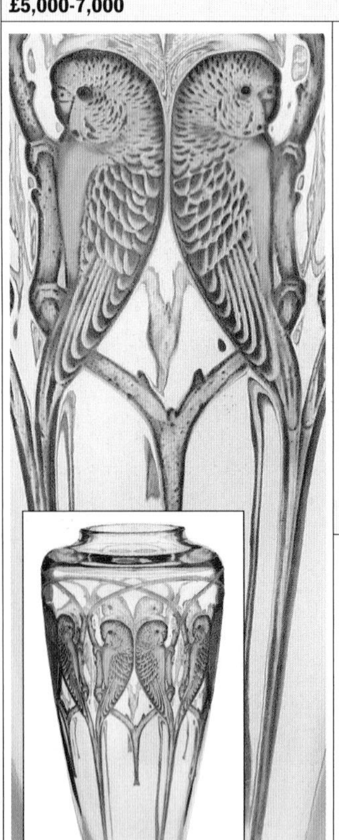

A rare Lalique 'Inseparables' vase, in clear and frosted glass with sepia patina, engraved "Lalique".

c1920 *13.5in (34cm) high*

£12,000-18,000 **RDL**

A Lalique 'Fougeres' vase, in clear and frosted glass with green patina, moulded "R. LALIQUE", engraved "R. Lalique France".

c1910 *6in (16cm) high*

£600-900 **RDL**

A rare Lalique 'Koudor' vase, in clear and frosted glass with black enamel, moulded "R. LALIQUE" mark, engraved with "R. Lalique France".

c1925 *7in (17.5cm) high*

£3,000-5,000 **RDL**

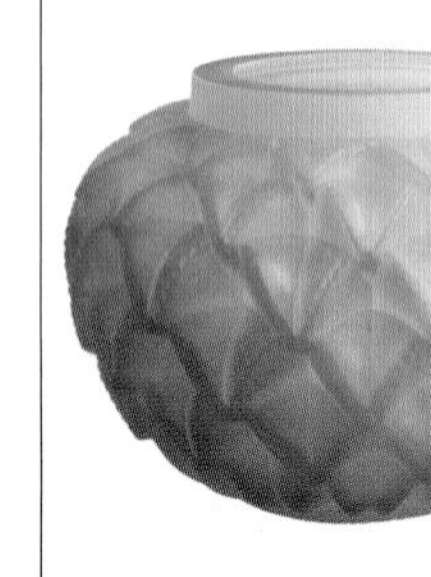

A Lalique 'Languedoc' vase, in opalescent glass, with stencilled "R. LALIQUE".

c1930 *11in (25.5cm) high*

£4,000-6,000 **RDL**

A Lalique 'Laurier' vase, in clear and frosted glass with sepia patina, engraved "R. Lalique France No. 947" mark.

c1920 *7in (17.5cm) high*

£700-1,000 **RDL**

A Lalique 'Malesherbes' vase, in opalescent glass with green patina, stencilled "R. LALIQUE" mark, engraved "France No. 1014".

c1925 *9in (22.5cm) high*

£1,500-2,000 **RDL**

A Lalique 'Moissac' vase, in amber glass, with stencilled "R. LALIQUE" mark, engraved "France".

c1925 *5in (13cm) high*

£1,800-2,200 **RDL**

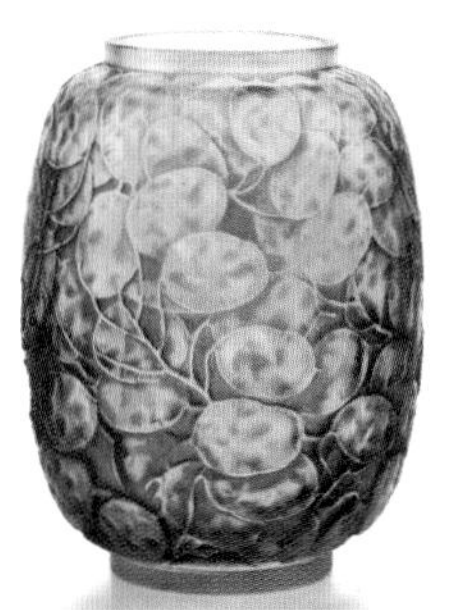

A Lalique 'Monnaie du Pape' vase, in clear and frosted glass with blue patina, moulded "R. LALIQUE" mark.

c1915 *9in (23cm) high*

£1,200-1,800 **RDL**

A Lalique 'Ormeaux' vase, in dark amber glass, with engraved "R. Lalique France No. 984" mark.

c1925 *6.75in (17cm) high*

£1,200-1,800 **RDL**

A Lalique 'Ormeaux' vase in clear and frosted glass, engraved "R. Lalique France".

c1925 *6in (17cm) high*

£600-900 **RDL**

A Lalique 'Penthievre' vase, in topaz glass with white patina, engraved "R. Lalique France No. 1011" mark.

c1930 *10.25in (26cm) high*

£4,000-6,000 **RDL**

A Lalique 'Perruches' vase, in electric blue glass, with moulded "R. LALIQUE" mark.

c1920 *10in (25cm) high*

£10,000-15,000 **RDL**

A Lalique 'Perruches' vase, in opalescent glass with blue patina, moulded "R. LALIQUE" mark, engraved "France" mark.

c1920 *10in (25cm) high*

£4,000-6,000 **RDL**

A CLOSER LOOK AT A LALIQUE 'PERRUCHES' VASE

'Perruches' is French for 'parakeets'. They were a motif favoured by Lalique.

Red Lalique vases are far more unusual and valuable than those in grey or clear glass.

The lip and the detailed mouldings are susceptible to chips. This vase is in good condition which makes it desirable.

The piece has a white patina, which is an attractive and desirable mark of the age.

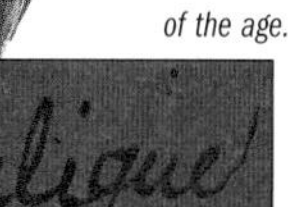

A Lalique 'Perruches' vase, in cased red glass with whitish patina, engraved "R. Lalique".

c1920 *10.25in (26cm) high*

£7,000-10,000 **DRA**

A Lalique 'Perruches' vase, in opalescent glass with green patina, with an engraved "R. Lalique France" mark, minor internal flaw to base.

c1920 *10in (25cm) high*

£1,800-2,200 **RDL**

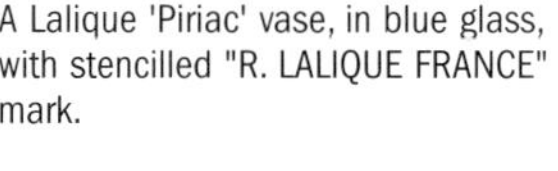

A Lalique 'Piriac' vase, in blue glass, with stencilled "R. LALIQUE FRANCE" mark.

c1930 *7in (17.5cm) high*

£3,000-5,000 **RDL**

A Lalique 'Pierrefonds' vase, in clear and frosted glass, with a wheel-cut R. "LALIQUE FRANCE" mark and engraved "No. 990" mark.

c1925 *6in (15cm) high*

£3,000-5,000 **RDL**

A Lalique 'Poissons' vase in deep red glass with white patina, moulded "R. LALIQUE" mark.

c1920 *9.5in (24cm) high*

£15,000-20,000 **RDL**

A Lalique 'Poissons' vase, in opalescent glass, with moulded "R. LALIQUE" mark, and engraved "Lalique" mark.

c1920 *9.5in (24cm) high*

£2,000-3,000 **RDL**

A Lalique 'Poissons' vase, in cased yellow glass with sepia patina, moulded "R. LALIQUE" mark.

c1920 *9.5in (23.5cm) high*

£7,000-10,000 **RDL**

A Lalique 'Prunes' vase, in clear and frosted glass with blue patina, marked with wheel-cut "R. LALIQUE FRANCE".

c1930 *6.75in (18cm) high*

£1,000-1,500 **RDL**

A Lalique 'Rampillon' vase, in opalescent glass with blue-grey patina, wheel-cut "R. LALIQUE FRANCE".

c1925 *5in (12.5cm) high*

£700-1,000 **RDL**

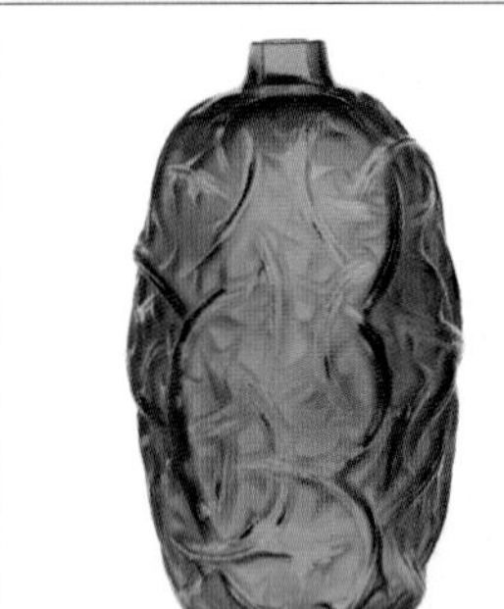

A Lalique 'Ronces' vase, in emerald green glass, moulded "R. LALIQUE", engraved "France".

c1920 *9.5in (24cm) high*

£3,500-4,500 **RDL**

A Lalique 'Ronces' vase, in cased butterscotch yellow glass, with moulded "R. LALIQUE" mark, engraved "Lalique France".

c1920 *9.5in (24cm) high*

£2,000-3,000 **RDL**

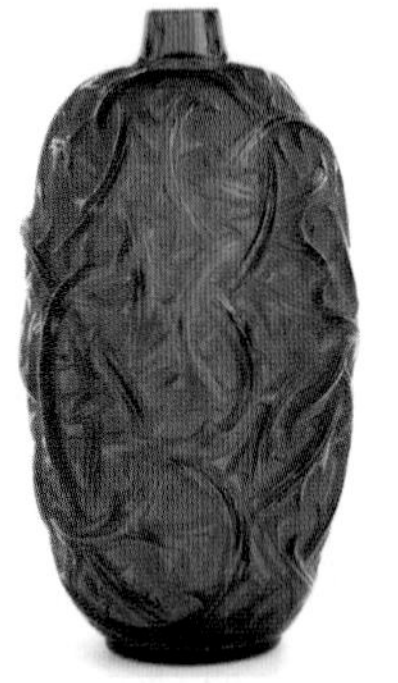

A Lalique 'Ronces' vase, in red glass, with moulded "R. LALIQUE" mark, and engraved "Lalique" mark.

c1920 *9.5in (24cm) high*

£3,500-4,500 **RDL**

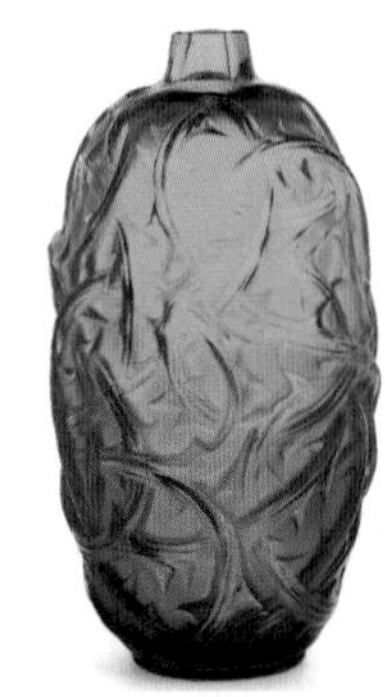

A Lalique 'Ronces' vase, in electric blue glass, with moulded "R. LALIQUE" mark, engraved Lalique France mark.

c1920 *9.5in (24cm) high*

£3,000-5,000 **RDL**

A Lalique 'Renoncules' vase, in clear and frosted glass, with stencilled "R. LALIQUE FRANCE" mark.

c1930 *6in (15cm) high*

£400-600 **RDL**

A Lalique 'Saint-Tropez' vase, in clear and frosted glass with blue patina, stencilled "R. LALIQUE FRANCE" mark.

c1935 *7.5in (19cm) high*

£1,200-1,800 **RDL**

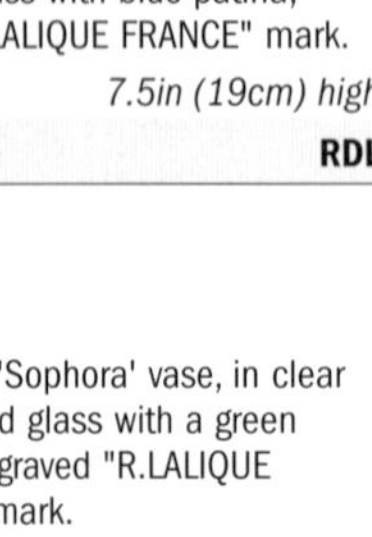

A Lalique 'Sophora' vase, in clear and frosted glass with a green patina, engraved "R.LALIQUE FRANCE" mark.

c1925 *11.5in (29cm) high*

£1,000-2,000 **RDL**

A CLOSER LOOK AT A LALIQUE 'SOPHORA' VASE

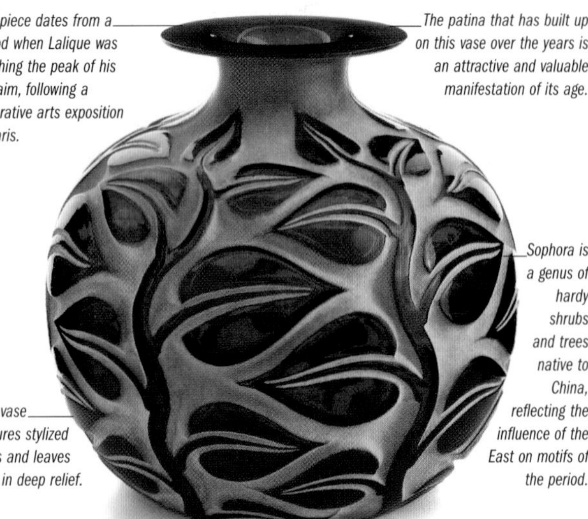

This piece dates from a period when Lalique was reaching the peak of his acclaim, following a decorative arts exposition in Paris.

The patina that has built up on this vase over the years is an attractive and valuable manifestation of its age.

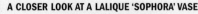

Sophora is a genus of hardy shrubs and trees native to China, reflecting the influence of the East on motifs of the period.

This vase features stylized vines and leaves cast in deep relief.

A Lalique 'Sophora' vase, in amber glass with whitish patina, engraved "R. Lalique France No. 977" mark.

c1925 *10in (26cm) high*

£6,000-9,000 **RDL**

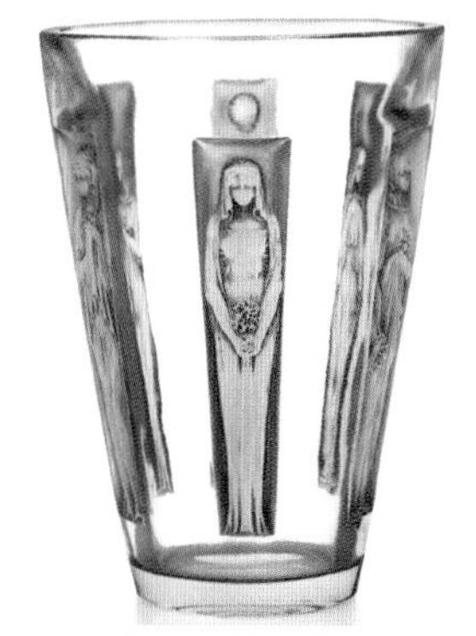

A Lalique 'Six Figurines' vase, in clear and frosted glass with sepia patina, engraved "R. Lalique France".

c1910 *7.5in (19cm) high*

£2,500-3,500 **RDL**

A Lalique 'Tourbillons' vase, in clear and frosted glass, with original bronze base, stencilled "R. LALIQUE" mark.

c1925 *8.5in (21.5cm) high*

£8,000-12,000 **RDL**

A Lalique 'Tournai' vase, in topaz glass with whitish patina, with moulded "R. LALIQUE" mark.

c1925 *5in (13cm) high*

£700-1,000 **RDL**

A Lalique 'Tulipes' vase, in opalescent glass with blue patina, engraved "R. Lalique France".

c1925 *8.25in (20.5cm) high*

£2,200-2,800 **RDL**

A Lalique 'Suzanne' statuette, in opalescent glass with a bronze peacock pattern illuminating base, moulded "R. LALIQUE", and engraved France.

c1925 *11in (28cm) high*

£15,000-20,000 **RDL**

A Lalique 'Thais' statuette, in clear and frosted glass, with engraved "R. Lalique" mark.

c1925 *8.25in (20.5cm) high*

£12,000-18,000 **RDL**

A Lalique 'Perruches' coupe, in opalescent glass with blue-green patina, with stencilled "R. LALIQUE FRANCE".

c1930 *9.5in (24.5cm) diam*

£2,500-3,500 **RDL**

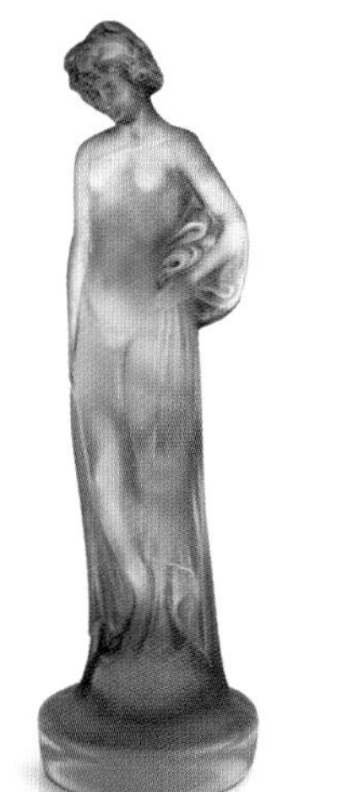

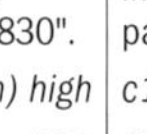

A Lalique 'Moyenne Nue' statuette, in opalescent glass with blue patina, engraved with "R. Lalique France No. 830".

c1910 *6in (15cm) high*

£3,500-4,500 **RDL**

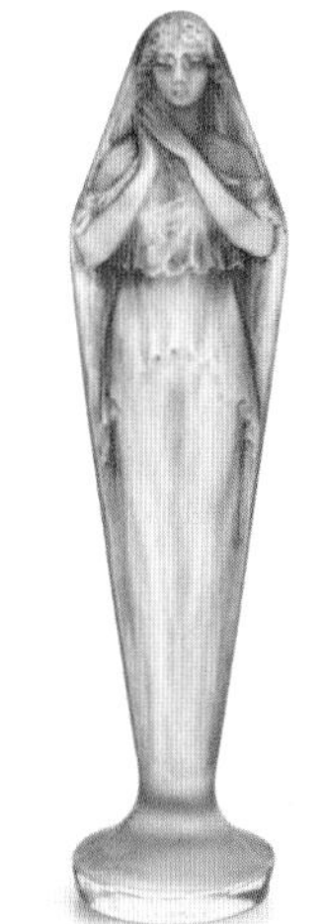

A Lalique 'Figurines Mains Jointes' seal, in clear and frosted glass with sepia patina, with engraved "R. Lalique".

c1920 *3.5in (9.5cm) high*

£1,200-1,800 **RDL**

A CLOSER LOOK AT A LALIQUE STATUETTE

This statuette, among Lalique's most celebrated, shares a name with his daughter, Suzanne.

Gently erotic subject matter like this is very evocative of the period.

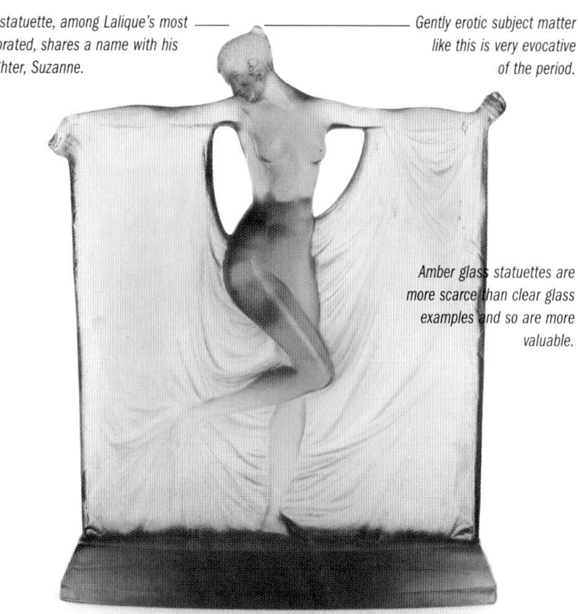

Amber glass statuettes are more scarce than clear glass examples and so are more valuable.

The inspiration for this piece seems to be the theatrical arts. Actresses such as Sarah Bernhardt were much lauded in this period.

A Lalique 'Suzanne' statuette in opalescent amber glass, with moulded "R. LALIQUE" mark.

c1925 *9in (23cm) high*

£15,000-20,000 **RDL**

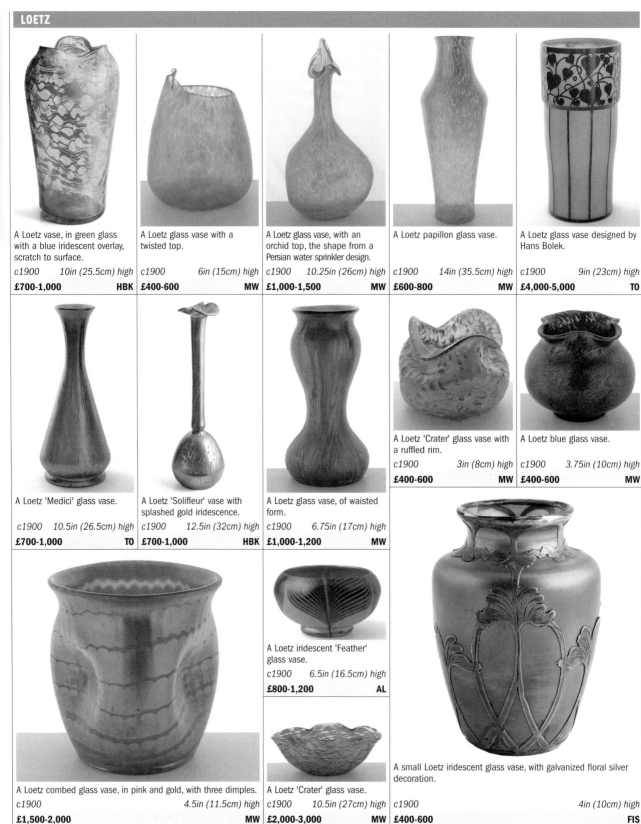

LOETZ

A Loetz vase, in green glass with a blue iridescent overlay, scratch to surface.

c1900 *10in (25.5cm) high*

£700-1,000 **HBK**

A Loetz glass vase with a twisted top.

c1900 *6in (15cm) high*

£400-600 **MW**

A Loetz glass vase, with an orchid top, the shape from a Persian water sprinkler design.

c1900 *10.25in (26cm) high*

£1,000-1,500 **MW**

A Loetz papillon glass vase.

c1900 *14in (35.5cm) high*

£600-800 **MW**

A Loetz glass vase designed by Hans Bolek.

c1900 *9in (23cm) high*

£4,000-5,000 **TO**

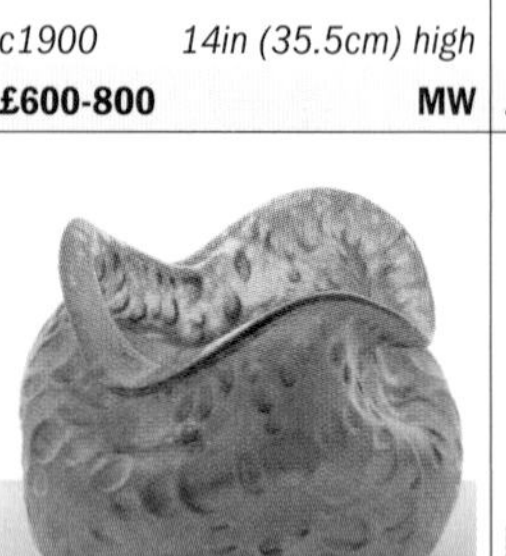

A Loetz 'Crater' glass vase with a ruffled rim.

c1900 *3in (8cm) high*

£400-600 **MW**

A Loetz blue glass vase.

c1900 *3.75in (10cm) high*

£400-600 **MW**

A Loetz 'Medici' glass vase.

c1900 *10.5in (26.5cm) high*

£700-1,000 **TO**

A Loetz 'Solifleur' vase with splashed gold iridescence.

c1900 *12.5in (32cm) high*

£700-1,000 **HBK**

A Loetz glass vase, of waisted form.

c1900 *6.75in (17cm) high*

£1,000-1,200 **MW**

A Loetz combed glass vase, in pink and gold, with three dimples.

c1900 *4.5in (11.5cm) high*

£1,500-2,000 **MW**

A Loetz iridescent 'Feather' glass vase.

c1900 *6.5in (16.5cm) high*

£800-1,200 **AL**

A Loetz 'Crater' glass vase.

c1900 *10.5in (27cm) high*

£2,000-3,000 **MW**

A small Loetz iridescent glass vase, with galvanized floral silver decoration.

c1900 *4in (10cm) high*

£400-600 **FIS**

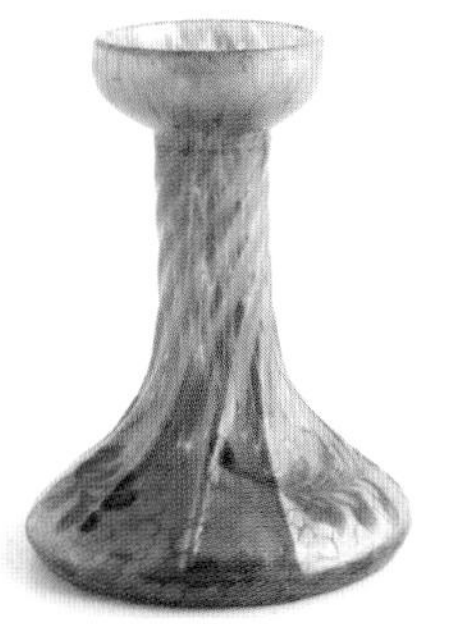

A Loetz iridescent glass vase, with a twisted bottle neck, in cameo glass with layers of iridescent yellow, green and honey-coloured shades, with green and amber leaf decoration.

c1900 *5.25in (13.5cm) high*

£320-380 **FIS**

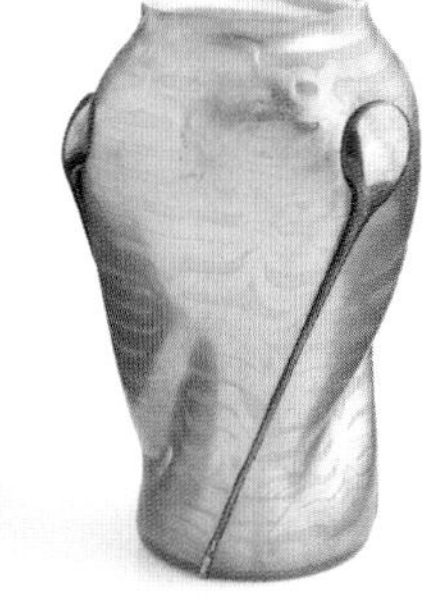

A Loetz iridescent glass vase, with gold and petrol blue bands and applied silver trailings, signed "Loetz Austria".

c1900 *6.5in (16.5cm) high*

£5,000-7,000 **MACK**

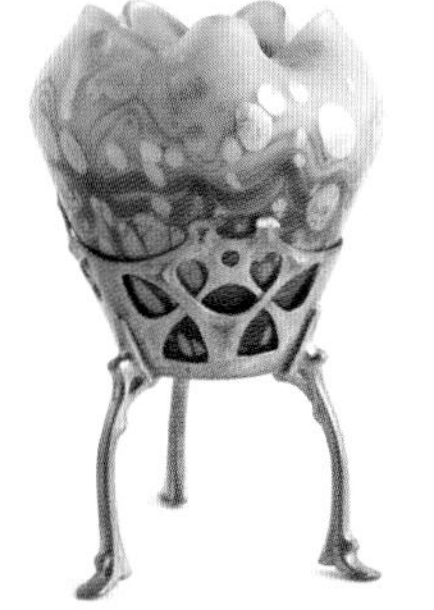

A rare Loetz 'Cytisus' glass vase, in yellow cameo glass with blue and silver, on a metal mount, marked and dated.

1902 *5.75in (14.5cm) high*

£1,000-1,500 **FIS**

A Loetz glass vase with a decorated interior, with three layers of painted glass.

c1905 *8in (20cm) high*

£1,500-2,000 **MW**

A CLOSER LOOK AT LOETZ VASE

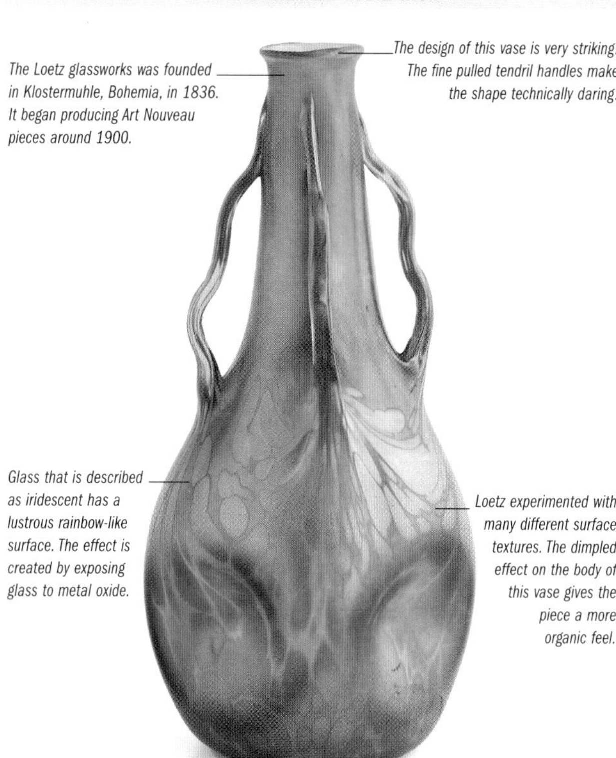

The Loetz glassworks was founded in Klostermuhle, Bohemia, in 1836. It began producing Art Nouveau pieces around 1900.

The design of this vase is very striking. The fine pulled tendril handles make the shape technically daring.

Glass that is described as iridescent has a lustrous rainbow-like surface. The effect is created by exposing glass to metal oxide.

Loetz experimented with many different surface textures. The dimpled effect on the body of this vase gives the piece a more organic feel.

A Loetz iridescent glass vase, with a pink and peach ground and four pulled tendril handles, the body dimpled.

c1900 *11.5in (29.5cm) high*

£10,000-15,000 **MACK**

A Loetz glass vase with a bronzed frame, designed by Karl Kellerman.

c1900 *10in (25.5cm) high*

£3,000-4,000 **TO**

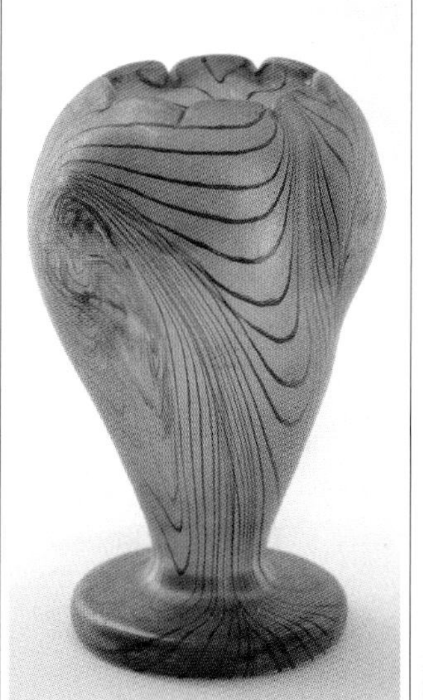

A Loetz glass vase, with swirling line decoration.

c1905 *7.5in (19cm) high*

£400-500 **TO**

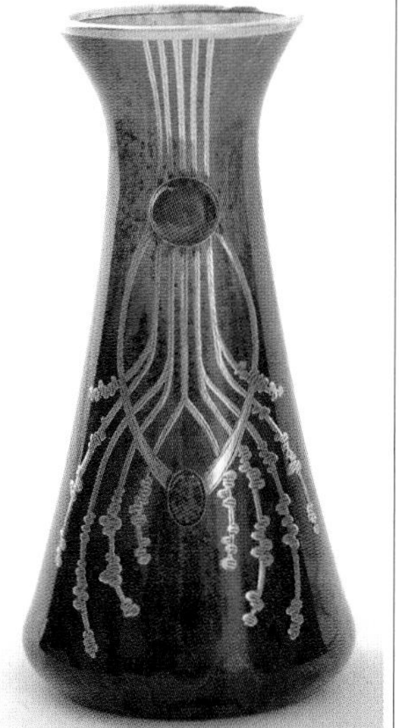

A Loetz glass vase with silver overlay.

c1905 *6in (15cm) high*

£600-800 **TO**

A Loetz bucket vase, graduating from clear to blue.

c1910 *8.25in (21cm) high*

£400-600 **MW**

A Loetz papillon glass bucket-shaped vase.

c1910 *7in (17.5cm) high*

£800-1,000 **MW**

A Loetz iridescent glass vase, with iridescent blue and gold waves on raisin coloured glass, with a flaring top, signed in pontil "Loetz Austria".

7.5in (19cm) high

£1,200-1,800 **JDJ**

A Loetz Art Glass vase, with iridescent blue swirls and dot decoration, on an iridescent gold background with purple highlights, the top ruffled, unsigned.

7in (18cm) high

£1,800-2,200 **JDJ**

A Loetz iridescent glass vase, decorated with iridescent blue swirls on amber glass, signed on bottom "Loetz Austria".

6in (15cm) high

£1,000-1,500 **JDJ**

A Loetz decorated glass vase, with iridescent blue pulled feather decoration on a green background, unsigned.

10.5in (26.5cm) high

£600-900 **JDJ**

A Loetz floriform glass vase, in iridescent blue with a crimped top and applied iridescent amber leaves.

12in (30.5cm) high

£1,800-2,200 **JDJ**

A Loetz papillon glass moulded balloon bowl.

c1900 *7.25in (18.5cm) diam*

£600-800 **MW**

An Austrian art glass bowl in the style of Loetz.

c1900 *5.25in (13.5cm) diam*

£200-300 **HBK**

A Loetz glass bowl, of ovoid form with inverted scrolled rim, the green glass body decorated with peacock iridescence.

6.5in (16.5cm) high

£300-500 **L&T**

A Loetz glass bowl with a ruffled rim, with blue papillon and a green centre.

c1900 *6.5in (17cm) diam*

£400-600 **MW**

A Loetz glass plate, the two sides showing different patterns, standard glass on the inside, papillon design on the base.

c1900 *12.75in (32.5cm) diam*

£500-700 **MW**

MONART AND VASART

A Monart tapering cylindrical glass vase, with a mottled orange and yellow body and an amethyst rim.

10.5in (26.5cm) high

£120-180 **L&T**

A Monart tapering cylindrical vase, the pale blue mottled body with a pale pink rim and a buff swirling band.

10.5in (26.5cm) high

£150-200 **L&T**

A Monart tapering cylindrical vase, with a waved and latticed mauve body and mica inclusions.

4in (10cm) high

£220-280 **L&T**

A Monart glass vase, of waisted cylindrical form with a flared rim, the clear glass with vertical blue stripes and mica inclusions, graduating to green at the rim.

6in (15cm) high

£150-200 **L&T**

A Monart flaring glass vase, with a swirling blue body, amethyst and aventurine inclusions to the rim.

9.25in (23cm) high

£150-200 **L&T**

A Monart shouldered glass vase, the mottled turquoise body with a cylindrical rim in blue, with pink swirls, the whole with aventurine inclusions, bears label "IV CC 261".

10in (25cm) high

£320-380 **L&T**

A Monart ovoid glass vase, with a mottled blue body, with aventurine and amethyst inclusions to the rim.

9.25in (23cm) high

£150-200 **L&T**

A Monart ovoid glass vase, with yellow, pink, green and aventurine swirling inclusions, bears paper label "No. IX.JA.480".

7in (17.5cm) high

£150-200 **L&T**

A Monart 'stoneware' glass vase, of ovoid form, the opaque white body overlaid with lemon glass, speckled inclusions and allover pumice surface.

8in (20cm) high

£300-350 **L&T**

A Monart ovoid glass vase, with a mottled blue body, with amethyst and aventurine inclusions to the rim.

7in (17.5cm) high

£100-150 **L&T**

A Monart glass vase, of ovoid form, with cylindrical neck, mottled orange and bubble inclusions.

10in (25cm) high

£120-180 **L&T**

A Monart ovoid glass vase, with cylindrical neck, the mottled orange body with aventurine inclusions to the rim, bears paper label "N.IV+".

8.75in (22cm) high

£120-180 **L&T**

A Monart rose bowl, of circular form with an inverted rim and a mottled orange body, with amethyst inclusions to the rim, bears paper label.

12in (30cm) diam

£150-200 **L&T**

A Monart ovoid glass vase, with a swirling white and yellow body, with multi-coloured pulled inclusions to the rim, bears paper label "No. VII*390".

6.5in (16cm) wide

£100-150 **L&T**

A rare Monart 'stoneware' glass bowl, of circular form in green and blue mottled glaze, with pulled up iridescent panels.

9.5in (24cm) diam

£1,000-1,500 **L&T**

A rare Monart glass vase, of tapering cylindrical form, the pale celadon body decorated with spiral bands in mottled green.

9.5in (23.5cm) high

£400-600 **L&T**

A Vasart glass vase, of cylindrical form with flared rim, the mottled pink body with swirling band graduating to green and pink mottling to the rim, with aventurine inclusions.

7.75in (19.5cm) high

£80-120 **L&T**

A Vasart waisted glass vase, the mottled pink and green body with a band of swirling inclusions, etched marks.

7.5in (19cm) high

£80-120 **L&T**

A Vasart glass lamp, with a tapering footed body, pulled decoration to the rim, the raspberry and amethyst colourway with aventurine inclusions.

11.5in (29cm) high

£400-500 **L&T**

A Vasart glass lamp, with a tulip shaped footed body, pulled decoration to the rim, the mottled celadon body with darker green inclusions to the rim.

10in (25cm) high

£180-220 **L&T**

A Vasart glass vase, of tapered cylindrical form, with orange, white and brown inclusions and whirl decoration, graduating to brown inclusions and white at the rim, etched mark.

7.5in (19cm) high

£100-150 **L&T**

SCHNEIDER

Charles Schneider (1881-1953) attended the Ecole des Beaux-Arts in Nancy, France. When he graduated, he specialized in glass and stone sculpture. He then joined his brother working for Daum.

In 1909 the brothers started their own factory specializing in electric light bulbs. After serving in WWI, the brothers reopened the factory and began producing cameo glass in the Art Nouveau style. They also produced vases with applied handles in contrasting colours and art glass. In 1918, Gallé's studios were destroyed by fire and a number of his artists moved to Schneider's factory to continue their work for Gallé. Here they taught Schneider the decorative technique of 'marqueterie de verre', where coloured glass shapes are pressed into glass of a different colour to form a pattern or image.

After the 1925 Paris Exhibition, Schneider's factory, now operating under the name Verrerie Schneider, expanded enormously and took on commissions from shops and perfumeries such as Coty. Schneider developed a technique using powders from metal oxides to create layers of coloured glass. A typical piece was then mould-blown and acid etched to show the layers. Selective polishing then left matt and shiny areas and the design often combined bubble or crackled glass with bands of Art Deco motifs.

Falling demand from the US after the Wall Street Crash and WWII spelled disaster. Charles and his son revived the factory in 1949 but produced only clear glass. Schneider died in 1953. The factory closed in 1981.

A 1920s Schneider glass vase, of tapering ovoid form, with an applied amethyst foot, etched mark.

13in (33cm) high

£600-900 **L&T**

A Schneider cameo glass vase, in orange, purple, yellow, pink and red, engraved "Schneider".

13.75in (35cm) high

£700-1,000 **FIS**

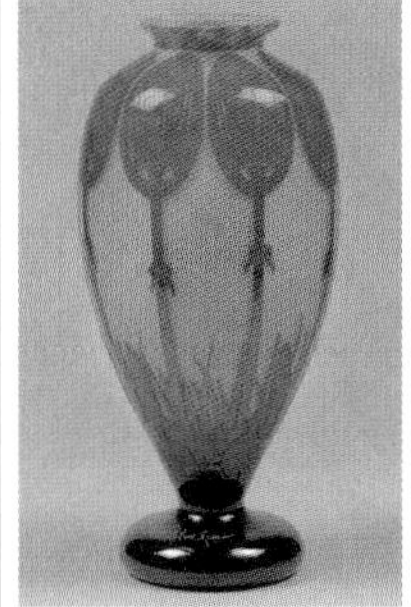

A large Schneider 'Champignons et Coprins' glass vase, signed "Le Verre Français".

17.75in (45cm) high

£1,800-2,200 **DOR**

A CLOSER LOOK AT A SCHNEIDER VASE

Schneider used clear glass coated in a powdered glass to make the body, with an outer layer of coloured glass, acid-etched, to make the decoration.

The peony motif repeats three times around the vase and is skillfully etched.

The etched marks "Le Verre Français" and "Charder" make this piece highly collectable. 'Charder' was a name made up from the first part of Charles and the second part of Schneider. It was sometimes marked on glass designed by Charles Schneider, particularly pieces in the Le Verre Français line.

Collectors should look for verifiable marks such as these as there are many fakes on the market.

A Verrerie Schneider 'Pivoine' glass vase, in cameo glass with layers of pink, white, purple and blue, with stylized floral decoration, etched mark "Le Verre Français".

c1925 *19.75in (50cm) high*

£1,000-1,500 **FIS**

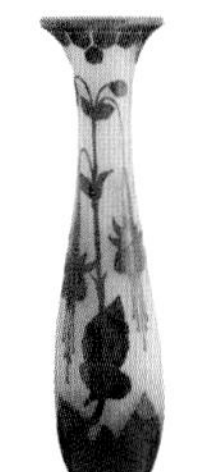

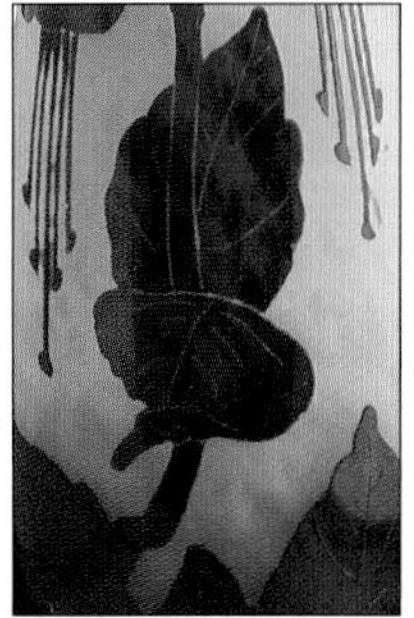

A Schneider 'Fuchsia' cameo glass vase, in blue, orange, turquoise and yellow, etched with fuchsia leaves, an etched mark 'Le Verre Français'.

c1925 *17.75in (45cm) high*

£1,000-1,500 **FIS**

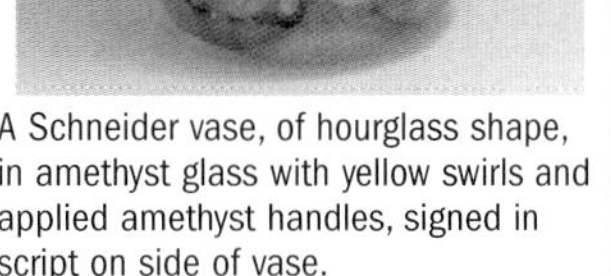

A Schneider vase, of hourglass shape, in amethyst glass with yellow swirls and applied amethyst handles, signed in script on side of vase.

8.25in (21cm) high

£400-600 **JDJ**

A Schneider glass vase, in mottled amethyst yellow and orange, with applied amethyst handles, signed "Schneider France Ovington", minor surface scratch.

7in (18cm) diam

£600-900 **JDJ**

A Schneider glass vase, in amethyst glass with Art Deco cameo decoration, signed on base in block letters "Schneider", one minor chip to design and a bruise to the side of the vase.

7.5in (19cm) high

£300-500 **JDJ**

STEVENS & WILLIAMS

The English glass-house Stevens & Williams was established in 1847 at the heart of the glass-producing region, at Brierley Hill, Stourbridge. After receiving the Royal Warrant in 1919, it became Royal Brierley. The company developed several new types of art glass, including Silveria and Alexandrite, as well as making fine engraved glass towards the end of the 19thC and cut glass using Keith Murray designs in the 1930s.

A Stevens & Williams double cased glass bowl.
c1895 10in (25cm) high
£600-800 AL

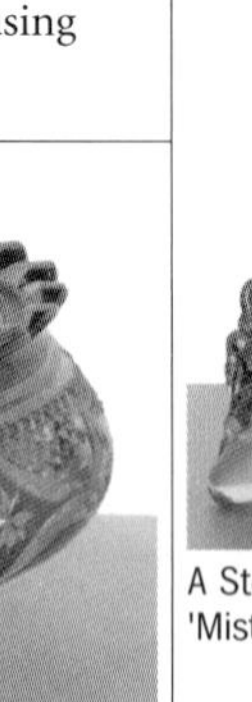

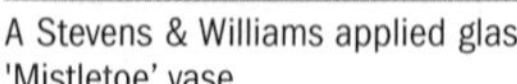

A Stevens & Williams applied glass 'Mistletoe' vase.
c1885 7in (18cm) high
£500-800 AL

A Stevens & Williams intaglio cut glass thistle decanter, with stopper.
c1890 9.25in (23.5cm) high
£500-800 AL

A tall Stevens & Williams silver mounted glass claret jug.
c1895 14in (36cm) high
£2,500-3,500 AL

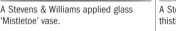

A Stevens & Williams double cased intaglio cut glass vase, probably by Frederick Carder.
c1900 12.25in (31cm) high
£1,500-2,500 AL

A Stevens & Williams Silveria glass pitcher, signed.
c1900 7.5in (17cm) high
£300-500 AL

A Stevens & Williams intaglio cut claret jug, with a silver mount.
c1905 11in (28cm) high
£500-800 AL

A cut glass decanter, attributed to Stevens & Williams, with a ruby flowing fan pattern, stamped, some damage.
10.5in (26.5cm) high
£2,800-3,200 JDJ

A Stevens & Williams cut glass decanter, of green cut to cranberry, sterling silver collar and stopper, stamped.
9in (23cm) high
£4,000-6,000 JDJ

An art glass perfume bottle, attributed to Stevens & Williams, in opaque blue glass with a clamshell top and stopper, unsigned.
4.75in (12cm) high
£220-280 JDJ

TIFFANY

Louis Comfort Tiffany (1848-1933), the son of Charles Lewis Tiffany who established Tiffany & Co., the New York firm of silversmiths and jewellers, began experimenting with glass in 1873.

He went on to establish the decorating company, Louis Tiffany & Associated Artists, which received many commissions, including the White House and Mark Twain's house.

However, the company was closed in 1883 and Tiffany established the Tiffany Glass & Decorating Company, which had its own furnace on Long Island. Here, Tiffany's famous iridescent 'Favrile' glass was created, named for the old English word 'fabrile' which means 'of a craftsman or his craft'.

Tiffany exhibited at the gallery of Siegfried Bing, the leading art critic and patron, and also at the 1900 Exposition Universelle in Paris, changing the company name at that point to Tiffany Studios. In 1902, when his father died, he became design director of Tiffany & Co., and began to design jewellery. From this point, all of Tiffany's wares were classed as Tiffany & Co. wares. Tiffany Studios continued to make Art Nouveau glass until 1924.

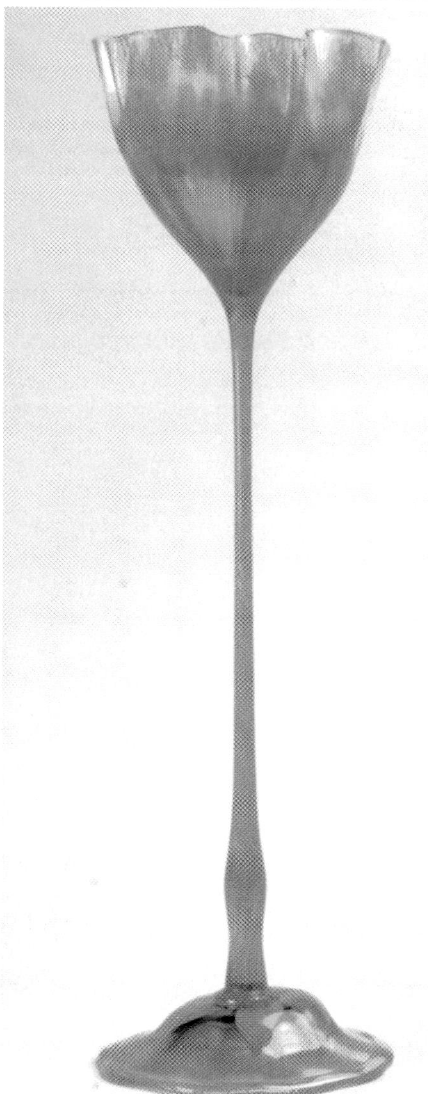

A Tiffany floriform glass vase, the gold iridescent foot with five curving leaves, a slender green stem with a subtle pulled design extending up to a subtle pulled design in the bowl, the bowl has rich orange iridescence terminating in opalescence, fading to a light green stretched rim, signed to base "LCT M3446", a line of dark inclusions from manufacture in the foot.

17.5in (44.5cm) high

£30,000-40,000 **JDJ**

A Tiffany floriform glass vase, with an iridescent green pulled feather design, on a creamy white background, the iridescent gold applied foot with blue and purple highlights, the interior in iridescent gold, signed "L.C.T.".

16in (40.5cm) high

£4,000-6,000 **JDJ**

An unusual Tiffany floriform glass vase, with gold iridescent foot and blue stem, with blue pulled feather leaves, the iridescent three-sided green crackle bowl dimpled, probably an experimental vase, with an open bubble.

10.25in (26cm) high

£1,800-2,200 **JDJ**

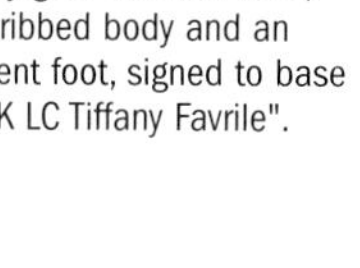

A Tiffany gold floriform vase, with a ribbed body and an iridescent foot, signed to base "1941K LC Tiffany Favrile".

11in (23cm) high

£1,800-2,200 **JDJ**

A CLOSER LOOK AT A TIFFANY VASE

This vase is a fine example of classic Tiffany golden iridescence. The effect was achieved by adding metallic oxides to the glass, which was then heated and sprayed.

Tiffany produced a variety of floriform pieces that depicted flowers at the different stages of their life cycle, from a bud to full bloom.

The glass has been hand blown by a skilled craftsman, who would have needed to work quickly to form the molten glass into the desired shape before it cooled.

This vase is signed "L.C. Tiffany". As the price of Tiffany increased, many pieces of art glass with fake Tiffany signatures, that were difficult to distinguish from the real mark, entered the market.

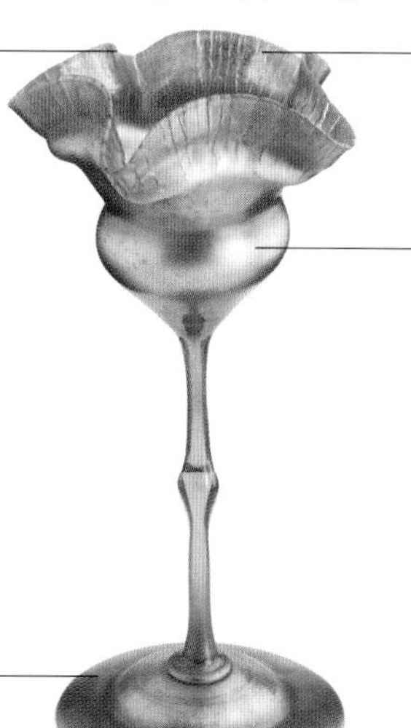

A Tiffany Favrile floriform glass vase, with a pinched flowerhead above a knopped stem, with a spreading circular base, signed "L.C.Tiffany".

10.5in (26.5cm) high

£5,000-8,000 **MACK**

A Tiffany floriform glass vase, with a gold iridescent foot and a transparent green stem, leading to a pulled feather bowl, possibly an experimental piece, with natural inclusions.

14in (35.5cm) high

£2,000-2,500 **JDJ**

A Tiffany floriform glass vase, with green and white pulled feather decoration and a ruffled top, an iridescent gold interior finish and iridescent gold applied foot, signed on base "LC Tiffany Inc. Favrile 1529-4337M".

5.75in (14.5cm) diam

£1,800-2,200 **JDJ**

A Tiffany iridescent vase, of butterscotch coloured double gourd form, the interior with an iridescent gold finish, signed to base "LC Tiffany Favrile 46802".

6.5in (16.5cm) high

£1,500-2,000 **JDJ**

A Tiffany Favrile and carved glass vase, of double gourd form with relief carved leaves and iridescent flowerheads, signed "L.C.Tiffany Favrile 3075H".

9.75in (25cm) high

£20,000-30,000 **MACK**

A Tiffany Favrile double gourd glass vase, the cream white neck trailing into a deep green iridescent finish, marked "W5812" and with Tiffany paper label.

c1900 *7.5in (19cm) high*

£6,000-9,000 **MACK**

A Tiffany Favrile paperweight glass vase, with an olive ground and trailing violet decoration, engraved "L.C.Tiffany Favrile, 9139C", with remains of Tiffany label.

12.25in (31cm) high

£15,000-20,000 **MACK**

A Tiffany decorated glass vase, with an iridescent blue finish and heart and vine decoration, a button pontil, signed on base "LC Tiffany Favrile. 244G".

7in (18cm) high

£2,000-2,500 **JDJ**

A monumental Tiffany decorated iridescent glass vase, with green decoration and dark green swirls, two intaglio cut beetles on the side, a button pontil, signed to base "LCT E159".

18.25in (46.5cm) high

£12,000-18,000 **JDJ**

A CLOSER LOOK AT TIFFANY PAPERWEIGHT VASE

Paperweight vases are among the rarest vases produced by Tiffany.

Floral paperweight vases were made with morning-glory, gladiola, narcissus, crocus and daffodil designs using millefiore canes to form the blossoms.

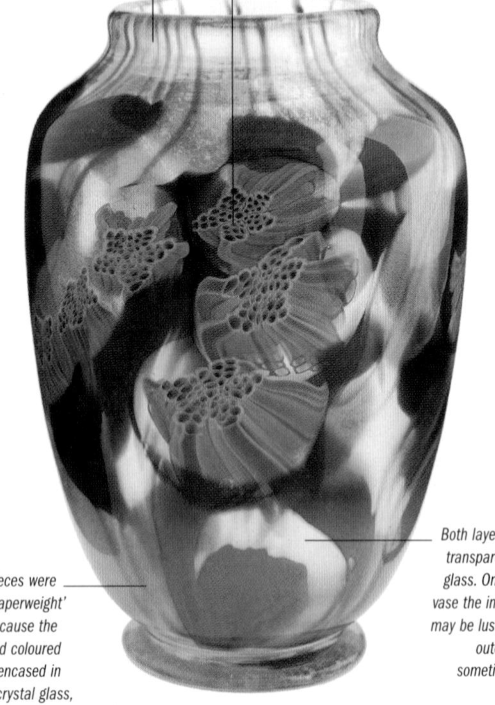

These pieces were called 'paperweight' vases because the decorated coloured glass is encased in smooth crystal glass, giving it the appearance of a paperweight.

Both layers consist of transparent coloured glass. On this type of vase the inside surface may be lustred and the outer surface is sometimes carved.

A rare Tiffany Favrile paperweight glass vase, with thick walls and trailing murrine floral decoration, signed "L.C.Tiffany Favrile 544E".

c1900 *10.5in (26.5cm) high*

£30,000-50,000 **MACK**

A Tiffany decorated glass vase, with iridescent finish, hooked feathers, a garland of rust and gold decoration around the shoulder, signed "LCT B1393".

6.75in (17cm) high

£2,200-2,800 **JDJ**

A Tiffany decorated glass vase, with green and gold wave decoration on the shoulder, gold chain decoration around the mid-section, signed "LCT B772", with paper label, interior staining.

5.5in (14cm) high

£1,500-2,000 **JDJ**

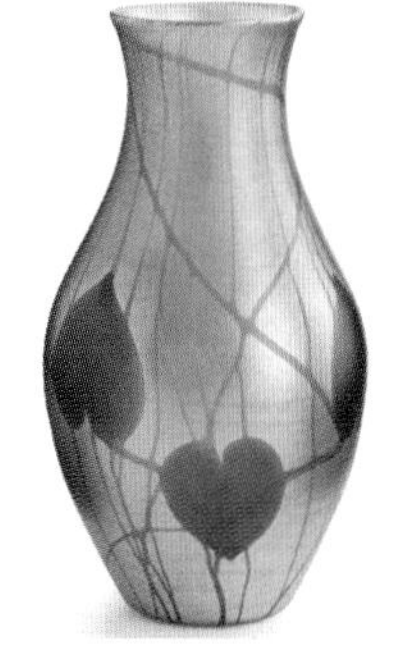

A Tiffany iridescent gold glass vase, decorated with heart-shaped green leaves and vines, signed "Louis C. Tiffany Furnaces, Inc, Favrile 1463".

8.75in (22cm) high

£5,000-8,000 **MACK**

A rare Tiffany 'Cypriote' glass vase, freeform with confetti style cypriote technique on a golden ground, signed "L.C.Tiffany", with a Tiffany Studios paper label to the base.

3.75in (9.5cm) high

£12,000-18,000 **MACK**

A pair of Tiffany glass vases in original bronze holders, the holders signed "Tiffany Studios New York 1049", both vases signed "LCT Favrile", damage to base on one vase.

14.25in (36cm) high

£1,500-2,000 **JDJ**

A Tiffany footed vase, in translucent glass with applied iridescent finish, vertical ribbing and a flaring top, signed "LCT V3177".

5.75in (14.5cm) high

£400-600 **JDJ**

A Tiffany bulbous stick glass vase, with iridescent gold finish, the body of double gourd form, with a long neck, signed on base "LC Tiffany-Favrile 9000G".

11.75in (30cm) high

£1,800-2,200 **JDJ**

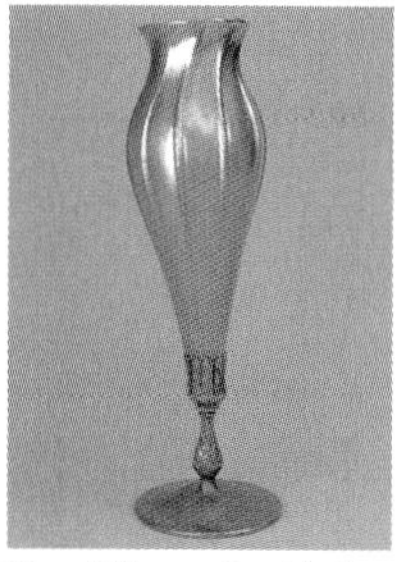

A Tiffany iridescent gold glass vase in a bronze holder, with vertical ribs and a scalloped top, damage to the holder, the holder unsigned.

15.75in (40cm) high

£500-800 **JDJ**

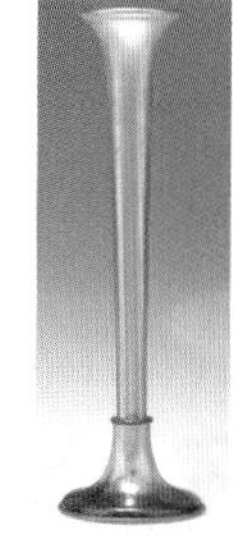

A Tiffany Favrile glass vase, with a trumpet-shaped copper foot, enamelled with red, blue and orange-yellow, signed to base "FAVRILE LOUIS C. TIFFANY FURNACES INC. 150".

18.75in (30cm) high

£1,200-1,800 **QU**

A Tiffany bud glass vase in a bronze holder, the iridescent blue stick with a flaring top, signed "LCT", the bronze holder signed "Tiffany Studios New York 717".

12in (30.5cm) high

£8,000-12,000 **JDJ**

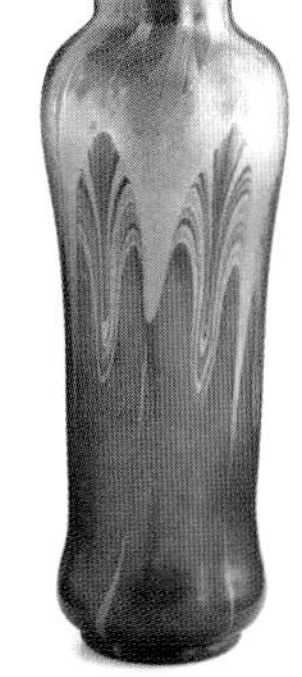

A Tiffany iridescent glass vase, with a deep honey ground and gilt trailed decoration, signed "L.C.Tiffany E1940".

9in (23cm) high

£6,000-9,000 **MACK**

A Tiffany Favrile 'Tel el Amarna' glass vase, with a deep blue ground and a band of simulated abalone to top, signed "L.C.Tiffany Favrile 6807 E".

8.25in (21cm) high

£8,000-12,000 **MACK**

A Tiffany 'Diatreta' vase, of pierced cage form, signed "L.C.Tiffany Favrile 5804 D".

4in (10cm) high

£15,000-20,000 **MACK**

A Tiffany small glass vase, with a green ground, bead and plait relief moulding, marked "02144".

c1900 *3in (7.5cm) high*

£3,000-5,000 **MACK**

A Tiffany opalescent drinking glass.

c1900 *8in (20cm) high*

£300-500 **AL**

A Tiffany bronze and iridescent 'turtleback' glass mounted revolving desk inkwell, the three wells with turquoise liners, a cylindrical body, marked "Tiffany Studios New York, 4218", engraved monogram.

6.75in (17.5cm) diam

£30,000-50,000 **MACK**

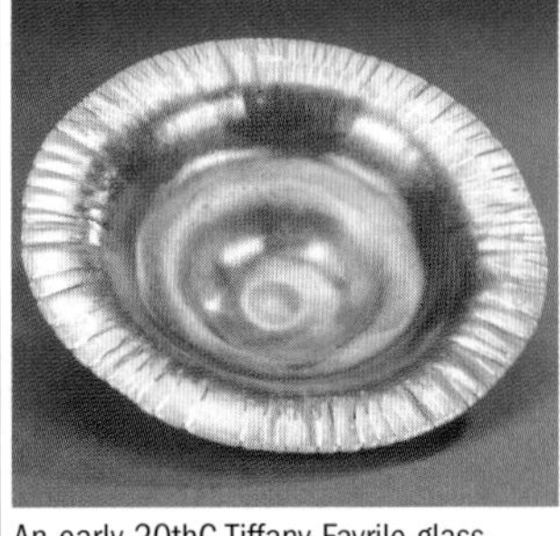

An early 20thC Tiffany Favrile glass bowl, with stepped sides and a flaring stretched rim, in amber glass with pink and gold iridescence, originally a compote, the stem broken off and polished.

7.25in (18.5cm) diam

£180-220 **S&K**

A Tiffany Favrile pastel glass bowl, the undulating sides in opalescent glass, shading to the purple rim, signed "L.C. Tiffany-Favrile V734".

c1905 *8.25in (21cm) diam*

£500-800 **S&K**

One of a pair of Tiffany gold iridescent finger bowls and under plates, the under plate with prunts, all signed "LCT".

6.5in (16.5cm) diam

£1,200-1,800 pair **JDJ**

A Tiffany Favrile glass bowl, on a round foot, in yellow and purple, signed and dated to base "1848 L.C. Tiffany - Favrile".

c1900 *7.75in (20cm) diam*

£1,200-1,800 **QU**

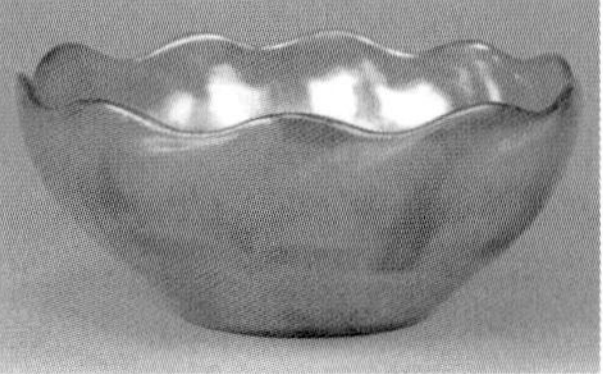

A Tiffany iridescent glass bowl, in gold with vertical ribs and a scalloped top, signed "LC Tiffany Favrile 1284", minor scratches.

8.25in (21cm) diam

£300-500 **JDJ**

A Tiffany pastel glass bowl, with diamond decoration, in pastel yellow and opalescent colouring, with an iridescent finish, applied foot, signed "LC Tiffany Inc Favrile 1576-3785".

9.5in (24cm) diam

£1,200-1,800 **JDJ**

A Tiffany pastel glass bowl, with opalescent pulled feather decoration and green pastel colouring, signed on foot "LC Tiffany Inc Favrile 5-1578".

8.25in (21cm) diam

£600-900 **JDJ**

A Tiffany glass tankard pitcher, signed on the base "LC Tiffany Favrile".

6.5in (16.5cm) high

£2,500-3,000 **JDJ**

A Tiffany pastel glass compote, signed "LCT Favrile 845T".

5.25in (13.5cm) high

£1,500-2,000 **JDJ**

An early 20thC Tiffany poinsettia table lamp, with mottled pale green background panels, the poinsettias in rich red variegated glass with the centre of each flower highlighted in amber, green and blue, deep green mottled and variegated glass stems, the base with a wide foot and a tapering stem, impressed with stylized flower buds and stems, in brown-green patina, signed "Tiffany Studios New York 1558".

26in (66cm) high

£30,000-50,000 **JDJ**

WHITEFRIARS

A Whitefriars seagreen ribbon trailed glass bowl by Barnaby Powell.

c1935 *6in (15cm) high*

£300-500 **AL**

An early 20thC Whitefriars cranberry threaded glass bowl by Harry Powell.

9in (23cm) diam

£500-800 **AL**

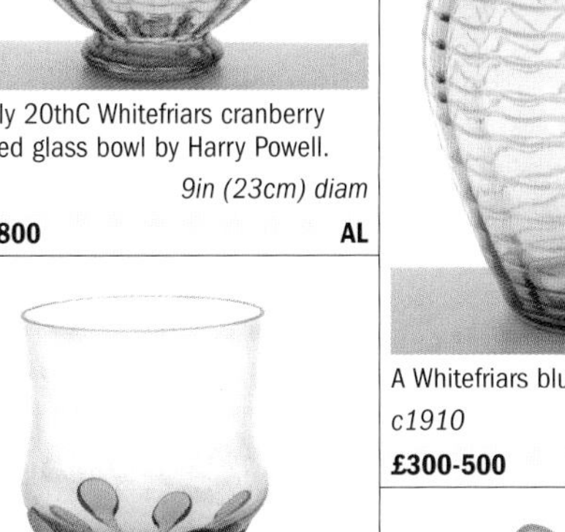

A Whitefriars blue threaded glass vase.

c1910 *8in (20cm) high*

£300-500 **AL**

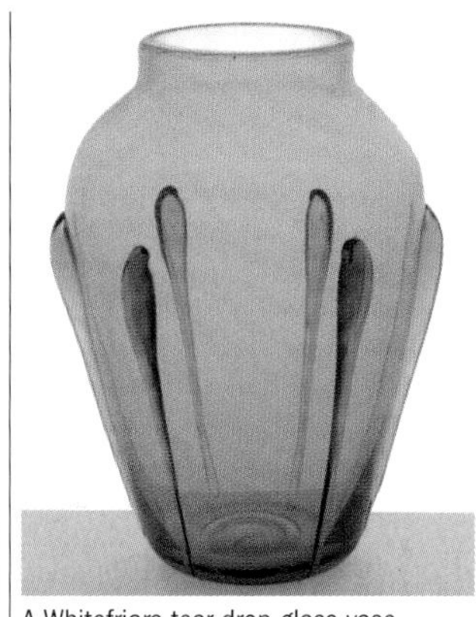

A Whitefriars tear drop glass vase.

c1930 *10.25in (26cm) high*

£400-500 **AL**

A Whitefriars straw opal footed bowl.

c1890 *9in (23cm) high*

£1,200-1,500 **AL**

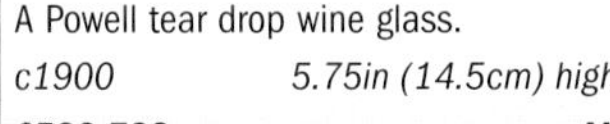

A Powell tear drop wine glass.

c1900 *5.75in (14.5cm) high*

£500-700 **AL**

A Powell vaseline glass vase.

c1905

£300-400 **MW**

MISCELLANEOUS

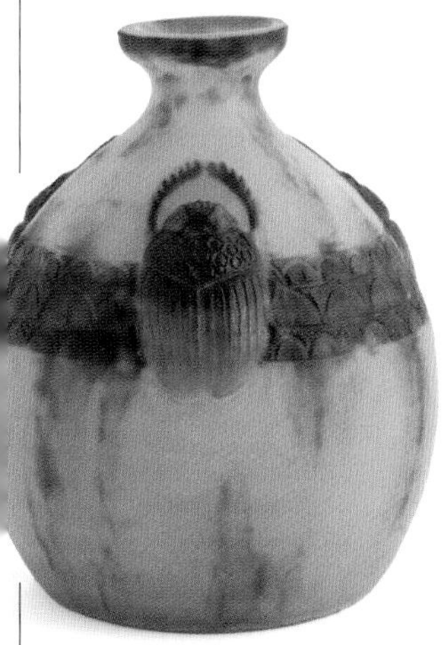

An Argy-Rousseau pâte-de-verre 'Scarabees' glass vase, the pale green ground with dark brown decoration, a red band and applied scarabs, signed.

6in (15cm) high

£10,000-15,000 **MACK**

A CLOSER LOOK AT AN ERNEST BAPTISTE-LEVEILLE VASE

Ernest Baptiste-Leveille was a pupil of highly regarded French glass artist Eugene Rousseau.

The Oriental lacquer-effect glass provides an effective foil to the Chinese subject matter.

The piece is technically daring and the result of highly skilled craftmanship.

This exquisite vase has a crackled glass body, overlaid with red glass to emulate cinnabar lacquer.

An Ernest Baptiste-Leveille glass vase, with deeply carved cinnabar-red glass overlaying a crackled glass ground, decorated to the front with four of the eight Chinese Scholars of Wisdom, mulberry trees to the sides of the vase and a bridge on the back, signed "Eleveille" and "1893" and "354".

6.25in (16cm) high

£20,000-30,000 **MACK**

An Argy-Rousseau pâte-de-verre glass vase, decorated with eight figures in russet and browns, signed on the side "G. Argy Rousseau".

6.25in (16cm) high

£7,000-10,000 **JDJ**

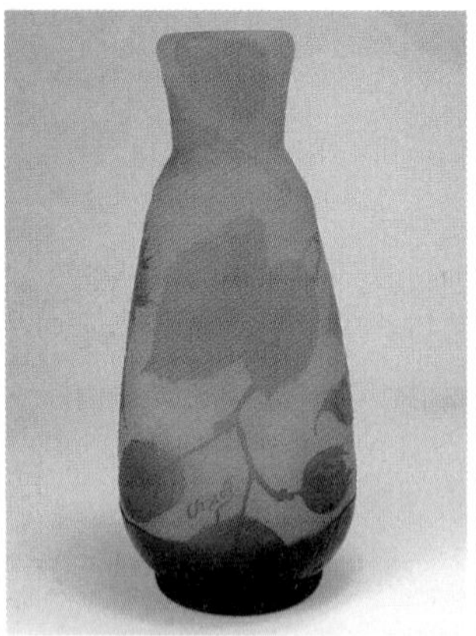

An Arsall cameo glass vase, in green over clear frosted glass, with a cameo decoration of leaves, vines and buds, signed on the side "Arsall".

11.75in (30cm) high

£400-600 **JDJ**

A d'Argental cameo glass vase, with a scenic decoration in browns on a frosted background, signed.

8in (20.5cm) high

£800-1,200 **JDJ**

A Daum Frères cameo glass vase, in brown, yellow and purple, with enamel etched decoration of berries and leaves, signed.

c1900 *14.75in (37.5cm) high*

£2,800-3,200 **FIS**

An Admedee de Caranza glass vase, decorated with cherries and leaves on a mustard ground, signed "A. de Caranza".

c1900 *6.25in (16cm) high*

£1,800-2,200 **MACK**

A DeVez cameo glass vase, with scenic decoration of a man and a gondola floating past a city in the distance, cameo colours of blue and yellow, framed by four arched columns, signed.

8in (20.5cm) high

£800-1,200 **JDJ**

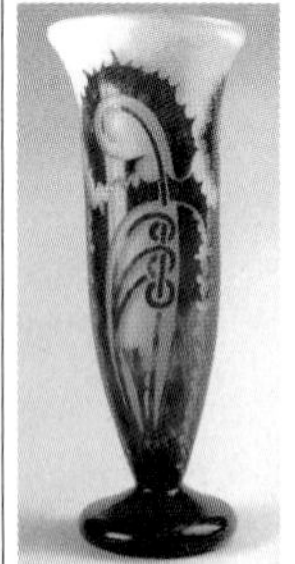

A monumental Degue cameo glass vase, with a rich, royal blue, cameo stylized design against a frosted background, engraved to the side "Degue" and engraved in the polished pontil "Made in France".

19in (48.5cm) high

£1,200-1,800 **JDJ**

A DeVez cameo glass vase, with a winter scene of a buck in a snow covered forest, lodges, and a moonlit sky, against a peach background, signed "DeVez", factory grinds to rim.

10in (25.5cm) high

£700-1,000 **JDJ**

A Fernandez cameo glass vase, decorated with cameo and enamel trees and fields, signed "Fernandez" and numbered "927/684".

5.25in (13.5cm) high

£500-800 **JDJ**

A rare Graflich Harrachsche Glasfabrik glass vase, with etched blossom leaves on a green ground, signed.

c1900 *14.25in (36cm) high*

£1,800-2,200 **FIS**

A French cameo glass vase, in green and white with an applied clear foot, signed "Editions d'Art des Cristalleries de Nancy Oeuvre de m. Guervcolas".

13in (33cm) high

£400-600 **JDJ**

A Continental Art Nouveau liqueur decanter and two glasses, probably by Harack.

c1900 *11.25in (28cm) high*

£300-500 **AL**

A set of Wilhelm Hoffman glass cream jugs on a tray, Carlsbad.

c1850 *Largest jug 4.25in (11cm) high*

£600-800 **AL**

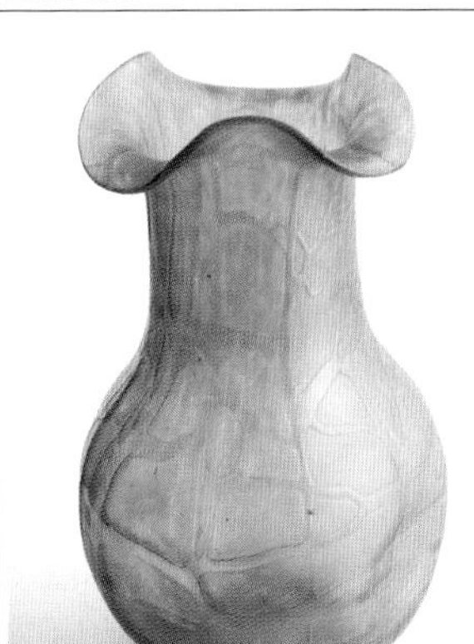

An Art Nouveau glass vase by Palline Konig.

c1905 *8.25in (21cm) high*

£320-380 **HBK**

A glass vase by Wilhelm Kralik Sohn, in clear glass with iridescent layers of silver, yellow and purple.

c1900 *17.25in (44cm) high*

£500-800 **FIS**

A French cameo glass vase, decorated in cameo and enamel with a country scene on a mottled white background, signed "Lamartine 327/530",

4.5in (11.5cm) high

£600-900 **JDJ**

A Bimini glass cocktail decanter and six glasses by Fritz Lampl.

c1930 *Jug 9.75in (24.5cm) high*

£600-800 **AL**

A signed Legras cameo glass vase, with decoration of red poppies with green and brown leaves, signed on base, bruise to inside of lip.

14in (35.5cm) high

£1,000-1,500 **JDJ**

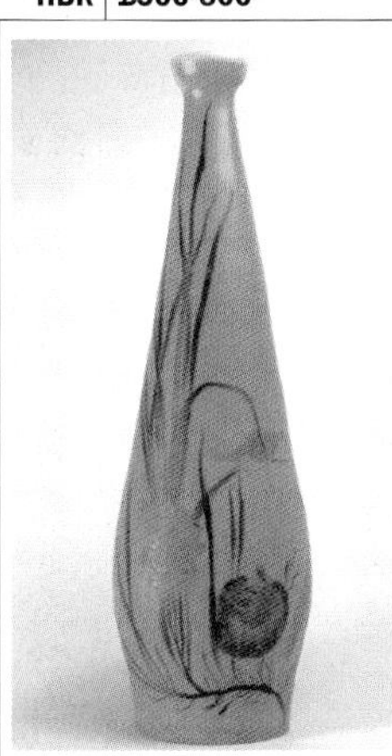

A monumental Legras cameo and enamel vase, with an underwater scene on an apricot background, signed "Legras", minor damage.

22in (56cm) high

£700-1,000 **JDJ**

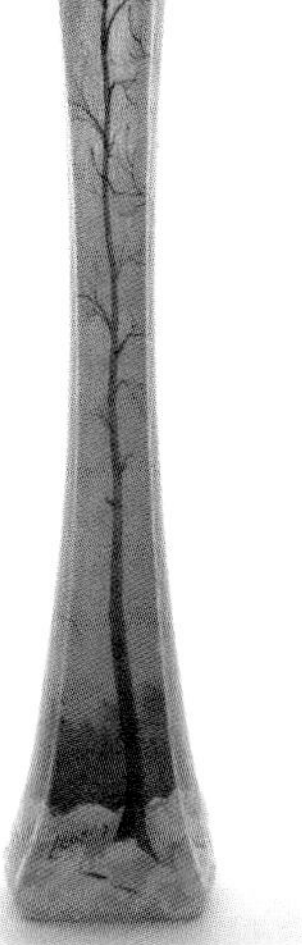

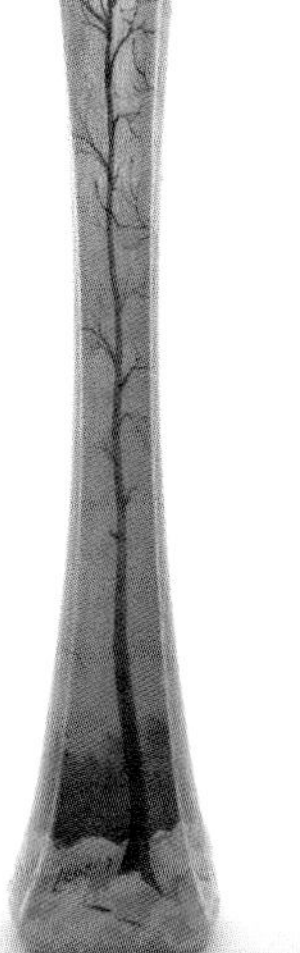

A Legras enamelled glass vase, with tree decoration.

c1900 *13.75in (35cm) high*

£200-300 **MW**

A Legras enamelled glass vase with a swan scene.

c1900 *10.75in (27cm) high*

£100-200 **MW**

A Le Verre Français cameo glass vase, with an orange and green cameo design of a shoal of swimming fish, on heavily bubbled frosted glass, signed "Le Verre Français France Ovington", crack to inside.

8.5in (21.5cm) high

£2,800-3,200 **JDJ**

A Le Verre Français cameo glass vase, the overlay flowers and leaves in orange and brown, on a mottled pink and white background, signed to base "Le verre Français".

8.5in (21.5cm) high

£1,200-1,800 **JDJ**

A Le Verre Français cameo glass vase, in mottled brown and white glass over amber, with an acid cut cameo decoration of leaves and vines, signed in script near base.

7.75in (19.5cm) high

£800-1,200 **JDJ**

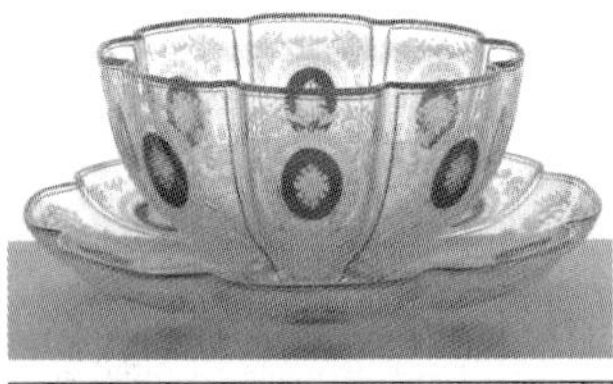

A set of six Lobmeyr glass bowls and underdishes.

c1875 *2.5in (6.5cm) high*

£600-800 set **AL**

An Art Deco green glass vase, by Jean Luce, signed.

c1930 *7.25in (18.5cm) high*

£600-900 **TDG**

An E. Michel wheel-carved cameo glass vase, the cameo decoration of green over pink over clear roses and leaves, on a hammered background, signed.

5.5in (14cm) high

£4,000-6,000 **JDJ**

A Moser acid cut cameo vase, signed.

c1925 *4.25in (10.5cm) high*

£800-1,200 **AL**

A Moser liqueur set.

c1870 *8.75in (22cm) high*

£500-800 **AL**

A Moser engraved purple floral glass vase.

c1905 *6in (15cm) high*

£200-300 **MW**

A large French enamel glass rose bowl, signed "Peynaud".

9.75in (25cm) diam

£300-400 **JDJ**

A CLOSER LOOK AT A MOSER VASE

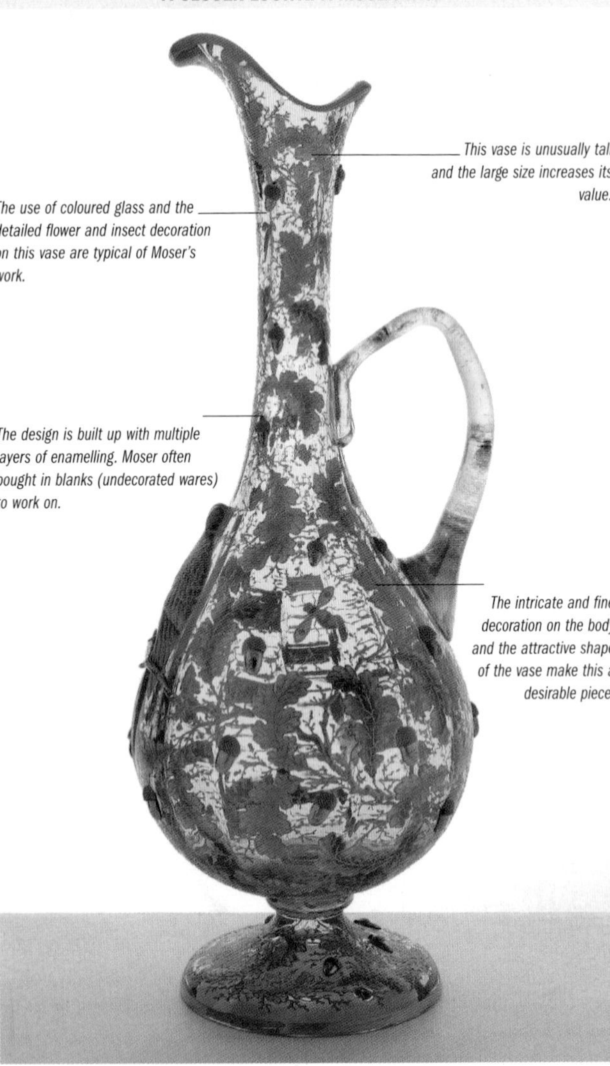

This vase is unusually tall and the large size increases its value.

The use of coloured glass and the detailed flower and insect decoration on this vase are typical of Moser's work.

The design is built up with multiple layers of enamelling. Moser often bought in blanks (undecorated wares) to work on.

The intricate and fine decoration on the body and the attractive shape of the vase make this a desirable piece.

An exceptionally tall Moser glass vase with applied acorns.

c1885 *17.5in (44.5cm) high*

£1,500-2,500 **AL**

A Richard cameo glass vase, decorated with a scene of farm buildings and two maidens surrounded by a lake, trees and mountains, in brown cameo against a yellow shading to orange background, signed on side in cameo "Richard".

14.25in (36cm) high

£1,000-1,500 **JDJ**

A French cameo vase by Villeroy and Boch, decorated with trees and landscape, by Edward Rigot.

c1930 *12.25in (31cm) high*

£1,800-2,000 **TO**

A late 19thC Richardson cameo vase.

c1890 *6.5in (16.5cm) high*

£600-900 **AL**

A Val St. Lambert footed glass tazza.

c1910 *15.25in (38.5cm) high*

£800-1,000 **AL**

A Val St. Lambert glass vase, with fluorogravure etched dragonfly and foliage decoration, signed "V S L".

10.75in (27.5cm) high

£4,000-6,000 **MACK**

A Val St. Lambert double-cased flared glass vase.

c1920 *11.25in (28.5cm) high*

£200-400 **AL**

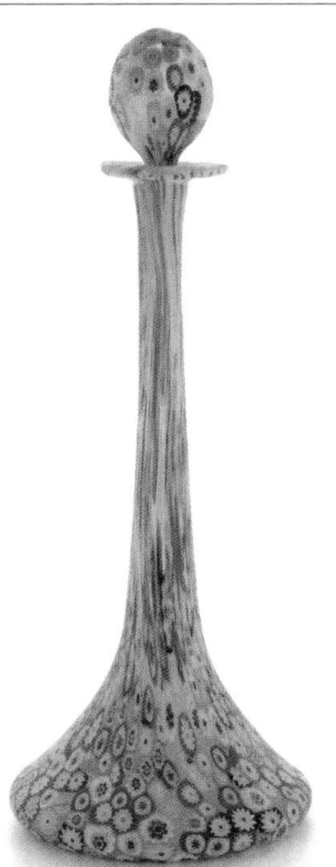

A Toso & Co. Venetian revival 'Millifiori' glass perfume bottle.

c1910 *11in (28cm) high*

£300-400 **AL**

A Le Verre Francais cameo vase, inscribed signature "Le Verre Francais France" and etched on the bottom "Ovington New York".

5in (26cm) diam

£300-500 **JDJ**

A Frederick Hale Thomson Varnish glass master salt, signed.

c1850 *4.5in (11.5cm) high*

£500-800 **AL**

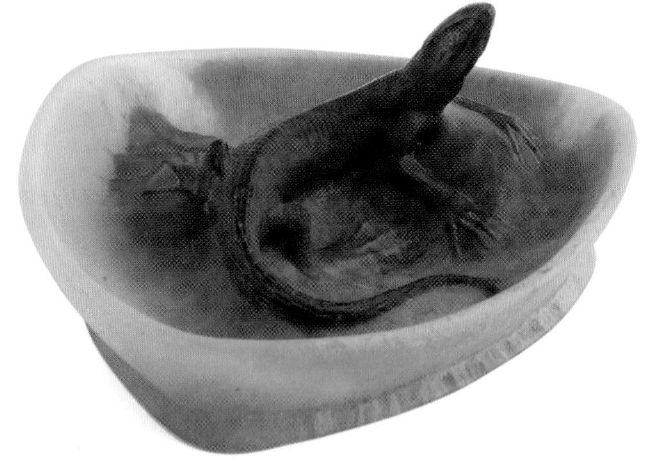

An Alméric Walter pâte-de-verre glass vide-poche, with an orange-green ground and central salamander figure, possibly modelled by Henri Berge, signed "A Walter".

c1900 *6.5in (16.5in) wide*

£10,000-15,000 **MACK**

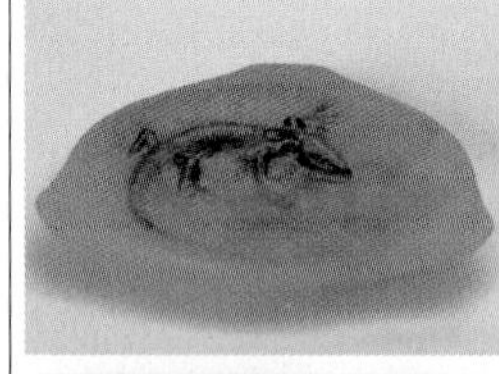

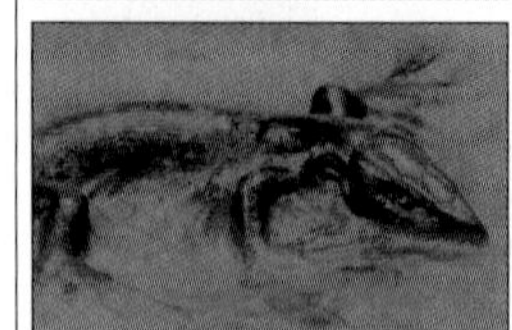

An Alméric Walter tray, with pâte-de-verre decoration of a lizard on leaves, signed "A. Walter Nancy".

6.75in (17cm) wide

£3,500-4,500 **JDJ**

A Webb peachblow vase, with a dark pink background fading to light pink, gold and pink highlighted flowers, with insects and butterflies, a creamy white interior, minor wear to gold.

7.5in (19cm) high

£80-120 **JDJ**

A Thomas Webb 'Bronze' glass vase, of tapering oviform with a flared neck, supported on a spreading circular foot, the predominantly black appearance relieved by violet, kingfisher-blue and golden iridescence.

5.5in (14cm) high

£80-120 **DN**

An Austrian iridescent green glass vase, an iridescent rippled finish with purple and blue highlights, four pinched-in sides and a ruffled top, unsigned.

13in (33cm) high

£180-220 **JDJ**

A Bohemian green glass vase, with galvanised copper mounts and three yellow vaseline glass cabochons.

c1900 *12in (30.5cm) high*

£500-700 **FIS**

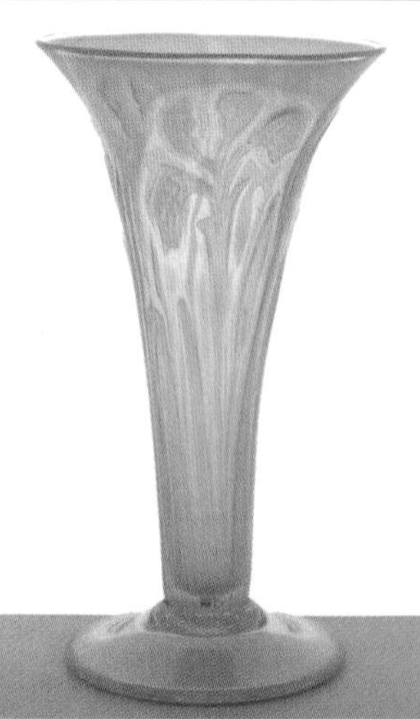

An English vaseline glass vase.

c1900 *10in (25cm) high*

£200-300 **MW**

A pair of English Art Nouveau 'twisted tear' glass vases.

c1900 *10in (25cm) high*

£300-400 **AL**

A 1930s ovoid smoked glass bowl, overlaid with silvered fish swimming near seaweed on a textured ground.

7in (18cm) high

£60-90 **L&T**

A Czechoslovakian art glass vase, the bowl in pastel pink glass with applied blue iridescent splotches on dark amethyst glass, the applied foot with blue iridescence, unsigned.

8.25in (21cm) diam

£600-900 **JDJ**

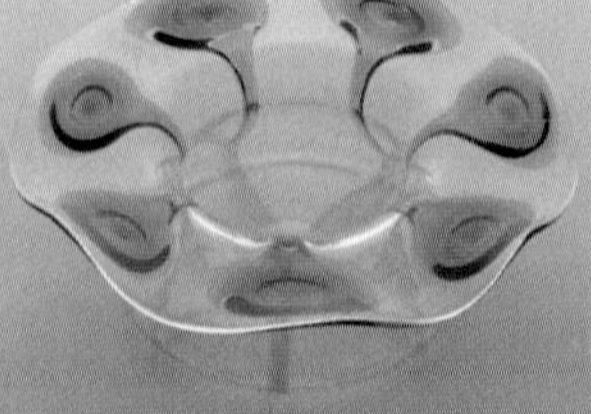

An English Peacock glass vase with green decoration.

c1910 *9.75in (25cm) high*

£300-400 **MW**

PERFUME BOTTLES

Perfume has been used for thousands of years to enhance the attractiveness of the wearer, and a huge variety of perfume bottles, especially those from the 19th and 20thC, are popular with collectors today. Most bottles dating from before the 20thC were sold empty by bottle makers to store perfume made at home or pre-mixed from a druggist. From the end of the 19thC, perfume manufacturers began to recognize the value of the bottle as a marketing tool and started to sell their perfumes in decorative containers, commissioned from glassmakers.

Collectors tend to focus on bottles from particular parfumiers, such as Coty, Caron and D'Orsay, or collect bottles from leading fashion houses such as Chanel, Dior and Schiaparelli. Containers from recognized glassmakers are also desirable and the perfume bottles of Lalique are especially sought-after, fetching anything from £40-40,000, depending on rarity, age and design.

Perfume bottles by famous brands produced in large numbers often have a lower price tag than rare and unusual pieces by less well-known companies, and an unopened bottle or one in its original box is generally more valuable. Visually attractive designs are popular, but a chip will detract from the value of most bottles, as will a missing or replacement stopper.

NINETEENTH CENTURY PERFUME BOTTLES

A Victorian double-ended scent bottle in ruby glass, divided for salts and vinaigrette, dented.

c1870 *4in (10cm) high*

£200-300 **RDL**

A Victorian double-ended novelty scent bottle in Bristol blue glass, of 'opera glass' style with brass mounts, lacking one stopper.

c1870 *5.75in (14.5cm) high*

£400-600 **RDL**

A rare Victorian scent bottle, in cut red crystal over mercury, with a hinged silver cover and a stopper, flaw.

c1870 *3.75in (9.5cm) high*

£500-800 **RDL**

A Victorian silvergilt mounted clear glass double-ended scent bottle, with a faceted, double tapering body and coral set mounts, monogrammed and contained in original fitted case, maker's mark only "G.B" for Beasley.

c1870 *5in (12.5cm) long*

£300-500 **WW**

A continental double-cased scent bottle, pink and white crystal cut to clear, with stopper and brass fittings.

c1890 *3.75in (9.5cm) high*

£300-500 **RDL**

A Victorian mounted glazed pottery scent flask, oval body with a screw cap, imitating three-colour jasperware, by Horton & Allday, Birmingham.

c1875 *3.25in (8.5cm) long*

£200-250 **WW**

A Belle Epoch cut crystal scent bottle, capped in 18 carat gold, set with approximately 0.60ct of rosecut diamonds surrounding a 13ct violet hued amethyst.

c1900 *3.25in (8cm) high*

£2,000-3,000 **RDL**

An early 19thC continental clear glass scent bottle, of faceted oviform with a bright-engraved silvergilt mount, the hinge opens to reveal a faceted stopper, the bottle contained in its original fitted case, unmarked, probably French.

2.5in (6.5cm) high

£500-800 **WW**

A French porcelain scent bottle, with enamelled detail and a metal crown sprinkler cap, marked "FRANCE HAND PAINTED".

c1920 *3in (7.5cm) high*

£200-300 **RDL**

A Victorian mounted cream coloured pottery scent flask, the fluted oval body heightened with gilt flowers and a butterfly, by Sampson Mordan & Co, London.

1887 *3.5in (9cm) high*

£150-200 **WW**

A Victorian scent bottle, in hand-decorated porcelain with a metal screw cap.

c1890 *2.25in (5.5cm) high*

£100-150 **RDL**

A Victorian scent bottle, in high relief silver with a hinged cover, a glass liner and a stopper, with maker's mark "SB&S".

c1885 *4.5in (11.5cm) high*

£350-450 **RDL**

A Russian scent bottle, in silver with cloisonné enamel, with maker's mark "BK" and "84".

c1900 *2.75in (7cm) high*

£700-1,000 **RDL**

An Edwardian perfume bottle contained in a silver sleeve by William Comyns of London, the body embossed with figures near a windmill.

c1900 *4.75in (12cm) high*

£70-100 **CHEF**

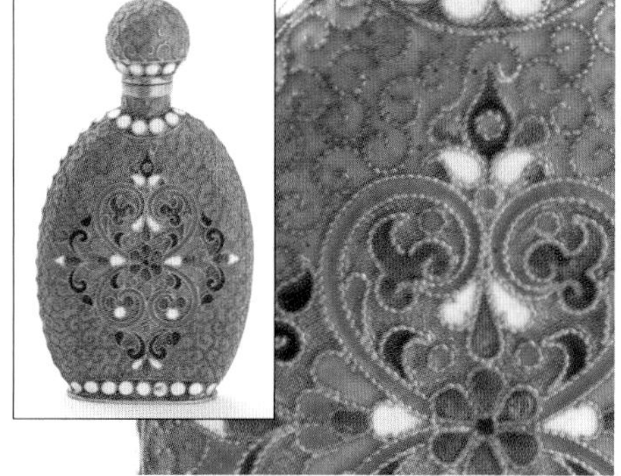

A late 19thC Russian cloisonné enamelled scent flask, with a globular screw cover and a flattened oval body, decorated in blues and foiled red within white pelleted borders, by an unascribed maker, with Russian state marks for Moscow.

c1895 *3in (7.5cm) high*

£700-1,000 **WW**

LALIQUE PERFUME BOTTLES

A Lalique 'Morabito No. 7' perfume bottle in cased yellow amber glass, with stencilled "LALIQUE FRANCE", minor flaw in neck.

4.5in (12.5cm) high

£1,800-2,200 **RDL**

A Lalique 'Ambre Antique' perfume bottle for Coty, in frosted glass with grey patina, side moulded "R. LALIQUE".

6in (15cm) high

£800-1,200 **RDL**

A Lalique 'Quatre Cigales' perfume bottle, in clear and frosted glass with blue patina, engraved "R. Lalique".

c1910 *5.25in (13cm) high*

£1,800-2,200 **RDL**

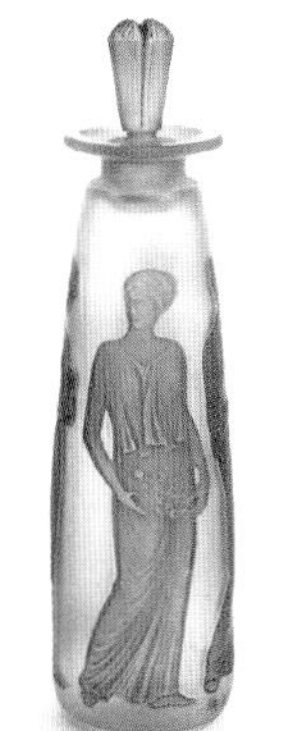

A Lalique 'Ambre Antique' perfume bottle for Coty, in clear and frosted glass with sepia patina, moulded "R. LALIQUE".

c1910 *6.25in (16cm) high*

£1,500-2,000 **RDL**

A Lalique 'Rosace Figurines' perfume bottle, in clear and frosted glass with sepia patina, engraved "R. Lalique".

c1910 4.5in (11cm) high

£1,500-2,000 **RDL**

A Lalique 'Deux Figurines, Bouchon Figurines' perfume bottle, in clear and frosted glass with sepia patina, engraved "R. Lalique France No. 490".
c1910 *5in (13.5cm) high*
£5,000-7,000 **RDL**

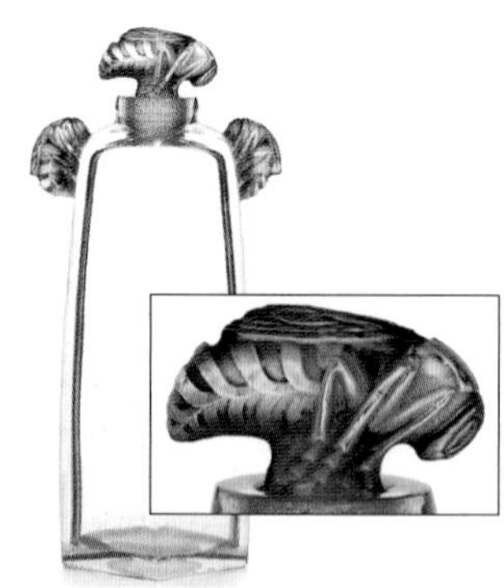

A Lalique 'Trois Guepes' perfume bottle, in clear and frosted glass with grey patina, engraved "R. Lalique France No. 498".
c1910 *5in (12cm) high*
£1,500-2,000 **RDL**

A Lalique 'Leurs Ames' perfume bottle for D'Orsay, in clear and frosted glass with sepia patina, moulded "LALIQUE" with extended "L", stopper barrel polished.
c1915 *5.25in (12.5cm) high*
£5,000-7,000 **RDL**

A Lalique 'Poesie' perfume bottle for D'Orsay, in clear and frosted glass with sepia patina, moulded "R. LALIQUE".
c1915 *6in (15cm) high*
£1,500-2,000 **RDL**

A Lalique 'Amphitrite' perfume bottle, in green glass, with engraved "R. Lalique France" mark.
c1920 *3.5in (9.5cm) high*
£2,500-3,500 **RDL**

A Lalique 'Serpent' perfume bottle, in clear and frosted glass with grey patina, moulded LALIQUE.
c1920 *3.5in (9cm) high*
£1,500-2,000 **RDL**

A Lalique 'Amphitrite' perfume bottle, in clear and frosted glass with blue patina, engraved "R. Lalique France No. 514" .
c1920 *3.75in (9.5cm) high*
£1,800-2,200 **RDL**

A Lalique 'Telline' perfume bottle, in clear and frosted glass with blue patina, engraved "R. Lalique France No. 508".
c1920 *4in (10cm) high*
£600-900 **RDL**

A Lalique 'Sirenes' perfume burner, in clear and frosted glass with blue patina, moulded "R. LALIQUE".
c1920 *7in (18cm) high*
£1,500-2,000 **RDL**

A Lalique 'La Phalene' perfume bottle for D'Heraud, in deep amber glass, moulded "R. LALIQUE" and "PHALENE" and bears unidentified gilt label for "Mona Lisa".
c1925 *3.5in (9cm) high*
£3,500-4,500 **RDL**

A Lalique 'Le Lys' perfume bottle for D'Orsay, in clear and frosted glass with sepia patina, with moulded "R. LALIQUE".

c1920 *7in (18.5cm) high*

£300-500 **RDL**

A Lalique 'Camille' perfume bottle, in blue glass, moulded "R. LALIQUE FRANCE" and engraved "R. Lalique France No. 516".

c1925 *2.25in (6cm) high*

£800-1,200 **RDL**

A Lalique 'Camille' perfume bottle, in clear and frosted glass with blue patina, engraved "R. Lalique France No. 516".

c1925 *2.5in (6cm) high*

£300-500 **RDL**

A Lalique 'Marquita' perfume bottle, in blue glass, with moulded "R. LALIQUE", and engraved "R. Lalique France No. 515".

c1925 *3.5in (8.8cm) high*

£1,200-1,800 **RDL**

A Lalique 'Amelie' perfume bottle, in clear and frosted glass with sepia patina, moulded "R. LALIQUE FRANCE" and engraved "R. Lalique France".

c1925 *3in (7.5cm) high*

£500-700 **RDL**

A Lalique 'Habanito' perfume bottle for Molinard, in clear and frosted glass with green patina, moulded "R. LALIQUE", engraved "Molinard MADE in France".

c1930 *4.75in (12cm) high*

£1,200-1,800 **RDL**

A CLOSER LOOK AT A LALIQUE 'LE BAISER DU FAUNE' PERFUME BOTTLE

The bottle is attractively displayed in an unusual leather case that allows light to shine through the glass body and highlight its shape and decoration.

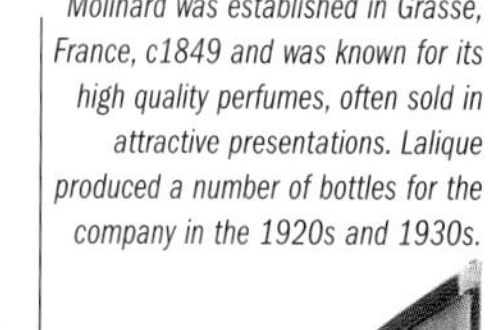

Molinard was established in Grasse, France, c1849 and was known for its high quality perfumes, often sold in attractive presentations. Lalique produced a number of bottles for the company in the 1920s and 1930s.

The circular central panel is engraved with a faun embracing a nude female figure. The perfume is stored in the surrounding ring.

The innovative design of the bottle and presentation, the quality of workmanship and the excellent condition of the bottle make it valuable.

A Lalique 'Le Baiser du Faune' perfume bottle for Molinard, in clear and frosted glass, a central moulded image, with a deluxe leather display case, signed "R. LALIQUE".

c1930 *6in (15cm) high*

£7,000-10,000 **RDL**

OTHER PERFUME BOTTLES

A Czechoslovakian perfume bottle, in green crystal, with blue and green jewelled metalwork, with stencilled oval "MADE in CZECHOSLOVAKIA" mark.

c1925 *5in (12.5cm) high*

£500-700 **RDL**

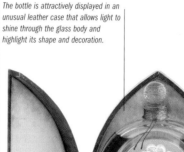

A Czechoslovakian perfume bottle, in blue crystal with a clear and frosted stopper, with enamelled and jewelled metalwork, a stencilled oval "MADE in CZECHOSLOVAKIA" mark and paper "MORLEE" label.

c1925 *6.25in (15.5cm) high*

£600-900 **RDL**

A Czechoslovakian perfume bottle, in purple crystal with enamelled and jewelled metalwork, a stencilled oval "MADE in CZECHOSLOVAKIA" mark.

c1925 *3.75in (9.5cm) high*

£400-600 **RDL**

A Hoffman perfume bottle, in opaque black crystal with a lemon stopper, with stencilled oval "MADE in CZECHOSLOVAKIA" mark.

c1925 *5.25in (13cm) high*

£400-600 **RDL**

A Hoffman perfume bottle, in clear and frosted crystal, with detailed decoration of foliage and female figures, with "HOFFMAN" intaglio mark.

c1925 *5.5in (13.5cm) high*

£400-600 **RDL**

A CLOSER LOOK AT A CZECH PERFUME BOTTLE

Stoppers often become separated from their bottles. This piece is complete with its unusual, original stopper which makes it more valuable.

Although made in large numbers, many perfume bottles were discarded once empty and so relatively few survive, making them desirable objects.

This figure's pose and the flowing fabric falling away from her body are typical of Czech aesthetic sensibilities of the period.

Hoffman's finely executed nude figures make his perfume bottles highly prized objects.

A Hoffman perfume bottle, in opaque turquoise crystal.

c1925 *8in (20cm) high*

£3,000-5,000 **RDL**

A Czechoslovakian 'Tiara' perfume bottle, in turquoise crystal, with stencilled circle "MADE in CZECHOSLOVAKIA" mark, and paper label marked "CRYSTAL".

c1935 *5.75in (14.5cm) high*

£400-600 **RDL**

A Czechoslovakian perfume bottle, in clear, frosted and engraved crystal.

c1935 *7in (17.5cm) high*

£300-500 **RDL**

BACCARAT PERFUME BOTTLES

A Baccarat 'Toujours Fidele', perfume bottle for D'Orsay, in clear and frosted crystal with grey stain in display box, the lid faded.

c1910 *3.5in (8.5cm) high*

£300-500 **RDL**

A Baccarat 'Ming Toy' figural perfume bottle for Forest, in clear crystal with enamelled details, with stencilled "BACCARAT" mark, inconsistencies in the gold decoration to face.

c1925 *4.5in (11cm) high*

£2,000-3,000 **RDL**

A Baccarat 'Mitsuko' large perfume bottle for Guerlain, in clear crystal with label and sealed, stencilled "BACCARAT" mark.

c1935 *8in (20cm) high*

£700-1,000 **RDL**

A Baccarat 'It's You', perfume bottle for Elizabeth Arden, in white crystal with enamel and gilded details, on a display stand, with stencilled "BACCARAT" mark, two scratches.

c1940 *6.5in (16.5cm) high*

£800-1,200 **RDL**

A 'Shocking' miniature perfume bottle for Schiaparelli, in glass, with tape and plastic dome.

c1935 *2in (5cm) high*

£250-350 **RDL**

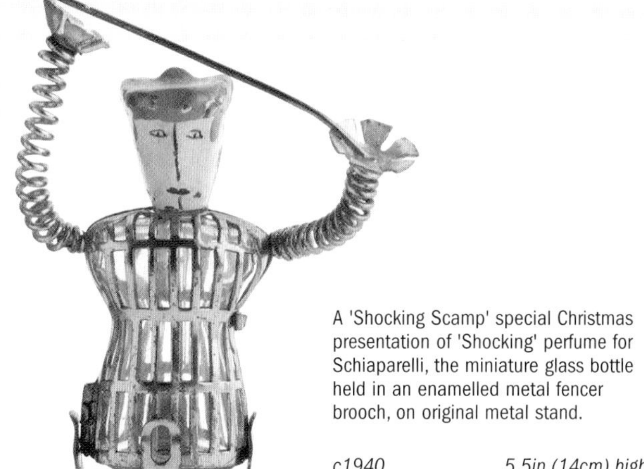

A 'Shocking Scamp' special Christmas presentation of 'Shocking' perfume for Schiaparelli, the miniature glass bottle held in an enamelled metal fencer brooch, on original metal stand.

c1940 *5.5in (14cm) high*

£1,200-1,800 **RDL**

A 'Shocking' perfume bottle for Schiaparelli, in clear glass bottle with pearlized glass flowers and paper tape, sealed in a glass dome and box.

c1945 *4.75in (12cm) high*

£250-350 **RDL**

NOVELTY PERFUME BOTTLES

A 'Golden Eagle' perfume presentation of 'Mitcham Lavender' for Potter & Moore, in clear glass and plastic, with a label in a card box.

c1925 *3in (7.5cm) high*

£250-350 **RDL**

A novelty perfume bottle by Schuco, in the form of a plush fabric bear, with a glass tube insert, minor wear.

c1925 *5in (12.5cm) high*

£300-500 **RDL**

A novelty perfume bottle by Schuco, in the form of a plush fabric monkey, with a glass tube insert and a rare Schuco hang tag, minor wear.

c1925 *3.5in (9cm) high*

£350-450 **RDL**

A 'Golliwogg Good Luck Perfume Pin' novelty for Vigny, in enamelled metal, with a hinged screen on reverse for scented cotton, on original card.

c1925 *3.5in (8.5cm) high*

£400-600 **RDL**

A 'Jack, Jill and Junior' presentation of 'Golliwogg' perfume for Vigny, clear and black glass bottles with enamel and fur details, sealed, with paper labels, and display box.

c1925 *2.75in (7cm) high*

£1,800-2,200 **RDL**

An 'Attention!' presentation set of 'Dashing' miniature perfume bottles for Lilly Dache, in composition over glass, with glass stoppers in an animated display box.

c1945 *3.5in (8.5cm) high*

£3,000-5,000 **RDL**

A 'Ze Zan' perfume bottle for Tuvache, in gilt glass with a wooden screw cap, on a wooden stand with a gold glazed ceramic display cover.

c1945 *4.25in (10.5cm) high*

£1,500-2,000 **RDL**

A 'Prince Douka' perfume bottle set for Marquay, in clear and frosted glass with jewelled fabric capes and neck labels, in plastic display box.

c1955 *3in (7.5cm) high*

£350-450 **RDL**

HANDEL

A Handel reverse-painted table lamp, depicting a moon with a scenic view of woods, fields and water, on painted base with double sockets and acorn pulls, shade signed "7107 Handel Com", paint chips.

24in (61cm) high

£4,000-6,000 **JDJ**

A Handel reverse-painted table lamp, with a chipped ice shade with border of pink roses, on a square ribbed Handel base, signed on the shade "Handel 6511", two new sockets and one missing.

22in (56cm) high

£3,500-4,000 **JDJ**

A Handel reverse-painted table lamp, with a scenic view of trees, water, fields and birds, the shade signed "Handel Lamps Pat'd no. 979664" and "Handel 7104", base wear and rewiring.

23.5in (60cm) high

£3,500-4,000 **JDJ**

A Handel knight table lamp, the shade with four reverse-painted panels, on a brass base with a double socket, repairs and discolouration to base.

20.5in (52cm) high

£1,200-1,800 **JDJ**

A Handel reverse-painted scenic desk lamp, with a tropical scene, on an adjustable base, the shade later ground and some damage.

14.5in (37cm) high

£1,000-1,500 **JDJ**

A Handel obverse-decorated table lamp, the shade with oak leaves and acorns on a chipped ice background, the base with three-socket cluster and acorn pulls, signed on the shade "Handel" and "Pat'd No. 979664".

22.5in (57cm) high

£2,500-3,000 **JDJ**

A Handel leaded glass table lamp, the shade with a honeycomb design and a slag glass top with poinsettia and leaf border, the base impressed "Handel" and the shade "Handel", damage and losses.

29in (73.5cm) high

£1,800-2,200 **JDJ**

A Handel leaded glass table lamp, the shade with carmel slag background panels and a flower and leaf border, on a base with double sockets and acorn pulls, the base with a cloth "Handel" label, the shade with a "Handel" tag.

20.5in (52cm) high

£1,200-1,800 **JDJ**

A Handel leaded table lamp, the shade with a green slag background and an irregular border of flowers and leaves, the base with an embossed design and three-socket cluster, signed "Handel" repairs.

21.5in (54.5cm) high

£1,000-1,500 **JDJ**

A rare Handel lava glass table lamp, the amber shade with white over turquoise lava glass, the base with a marble foot and a glass lava ball and a three-socket cluster, the shade signed "Handel Lamps".

25in (63.5cm) high

£8,000-12,000 **JDJ**

A Handel tropical sunset floor lamp, the shade with palm trees and islands backed with red striated sunset glass, with original Handel floor base.

64in (162.5cm) high

£8,000-12,000 **JDJ**

A Handel tulip floor lamp, the shade with green slag glass bent panels over white bent panels, on a harp floor base with an embossed design at the foot, signed "Handel", crack.

54in (137cm) high

£2,500-3,000 **JDJ**

TIFFANY

A CLOSER LOOK AT A TIFFANY CHANDELIER

This chandelier is a rare combination of Tiffany's 'Wisteria' blossom pattern and the colouring used on the 'Laburnum' mould.

The fragments of glass that have been used on the shade are especially small and are unusual on this type of piece.

The large circumference and irregular lower edge make this one of the most technically difficult shades produced by the Tiffany Studios.

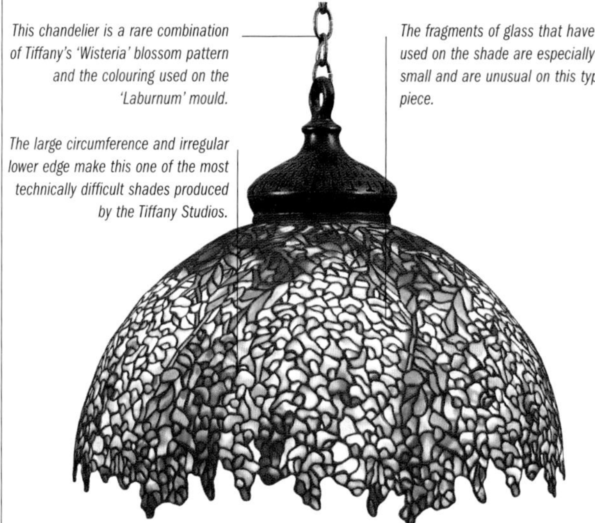

A rare and important Tiffany 'Wisteria Laburnum' leaded favrile glass chandelier, the domed shade of purple, blue and white mottled glass, with green and yellow leaves and stems and russet confetti glass branches, impressed "Tiffany Studios, New York".

Only two other examples of this shade are known, one from the Walter Chrysler collection which was sold at Sotheby's, New York in 1989, the other in a private collection of Michael and Lynn Lerner.

Provenance: *Property of Senator Edward W. Brooke.*

c1910 *24in (61cm) diam*

£250,000-300,000 **S&K**

A Tiffany nasturtium trellis hanging lamp, decorated with nasturtium and trellis pattern, with green striated and mottled leaves and stems and mottled blue-grey background glass, nasturtium flowers done in red, amber and lavender, the shade with numerous pieces of fracture or confetti glass, original mounting, hardware and bronze beaded trim around base, with six-socket cluster.

This is an outstanding piece very rarely found in today's market.

28in (71cm) diam

£50,000-70,000 **JDJ**

A Tiffany leaded daffodil table lamp, with mottled background panels and yellow daffodils, a Handel base fitted with Tiffany hardware, the shade signed on "Tiffany Studios New York 1449-2", and the base marked "Handel".

22in (56cm) high

£15,000-20,000 **JDJ**

A Tiffany 'Zodiac' turtleback desk lamp, with zodiac symbols surrounding the foot and a turtleback shade, patina shows deep browns and reds, marked on bottom "Tiffany Studios New York 541".

15in (38cm) high

£7,000-10,000 **JDJ**

A signed Tiffany harp desk lamp, with a gold iridescent, pulled feather shade signed "LCT" and "TIFFANY STUDIOS NEW YORK 419".

13.5in (34.5cm) high

£1,800-2,200 **JDJ**

A Tiffany 'Zodiac' harp desk lamp, with gold dore finish and zodiac symbols around the foot, a green pulled feather shade against a cream to orange background, shade signed "LCT" and base impressed "Tiffany Studios New York 661", minor wear.

13in (33cm) high

£2,500-3,000 **JDJ**

A Tiffany 'Zodiac' harp desk lamp, with impressed zodiac symbols around the foot, the damascene shade with a silver-green iridescent wave border, cracks.

17.5in (44.5cm) high

£3,000-4,000 **JDJ**

A Tiffany 'Zodiac' desk lamp, with zodiac symbols to top of shade, inside with several white reflector glass panels, green patina, minor wear to foot.

11in (28cm) wide

£1,800-2,200 **JDJ**

A Tiffany 'Zodiac' desk lamp, the zodiac design extending around the foot, the stem and to shade, with a rich brown-green patina, impressed to base "Tiffany Studios New York 668", some wear.

14in (35.5cm) high

£1,800-2,200 **JDJ**

A Tiffany bronze and glass candelabra, with green glass inserts, the bronze base signed "Tiffany Studios New York".

12.75in (32.5cm) high

£2,000-2,500 **JDJ**

A signed Tiffany pine needle lamp, the overlay shade with red and green sunset glass and a rich bronze patina, the bulbous bronze converted to electric and signed "Tiffany Studios New York 166", slight damage.

14in (35.5cm) high

£6,000-8,000 **JDJ**

A Tiffany 'Zodiac' leaded lamp, the base with a rich brown patina and zodiac design extending around the foot and up the stem of the base, leaded shade with mottled green glass in plain geometric panels.

16.5in (42cm) high

£5,000-7,000 **JDJ**

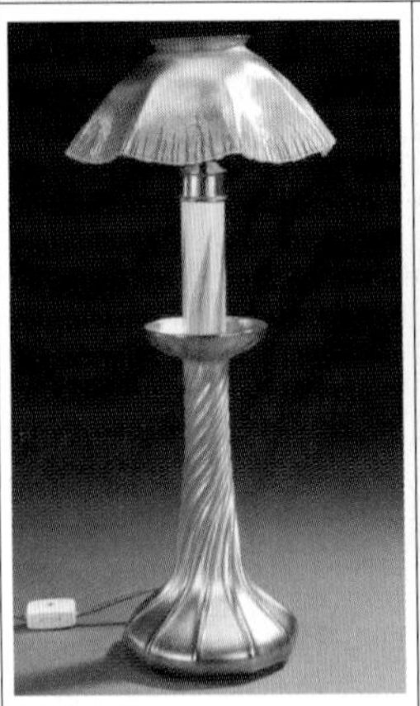

A Tiffany Favrile glass candlestick lamp, the spirally ribbed base of amber glass with blue and pink iridescence, fitted with an electric candle of white glass, surmounted by a gilt metal shade support and a ruffled shade of amber glass with gold and pink iridescence, base and shade signed "L.C.T".

16in (40.5cm) high

£1,200-1,800 **S&K**

A Tiffany Favrile glass floriform shade, the bulbous base with a flaring octagonal rim, in opalescent glass with gold and blue iridescent pulled feather decoration, inscribed "L.C.T. Favrile/2398"; together with a later wood and brass electrified base.

c1915 Shade 6in (15cm) high

£1,500-2,000 **S&K**

A large Tiffany hanging fixture, with an opal white background and gold pulled feather design decoration, suspended on three chains attached to a bronze collar, signed "LCT FAVRILE" missing decorative cap.

13in (33cm) diam

£4,000-5,000 **JDJ**

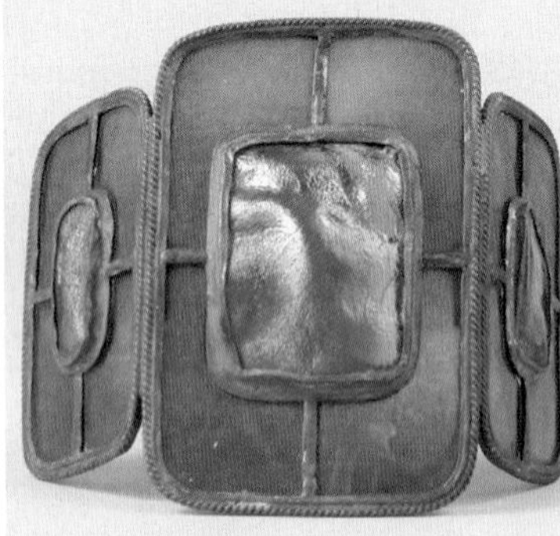

A Tiffany turtleback sconce shade, with lime green iridescent turtleback tiles on a rich amber ground, unsigned.

6in (15cm) h

£2,000-2,500 **JDJ**

A Tiffany linenfold shade, set with green linenfold glass, signed on interior "Tiffany Studios New York patent applied for", damage and repainting.

8in (20.5cm) diam

£2,500-3,000 **JDJ**

A Tiffany candlelamp lampshade, with iridescent green and gold King Tut pattern ruffled shade, unsigned.

6.5in (16.5cm) diam

£1,000-1,500 **JDJ**

A Tiffany candlelamp lampshade, with iridescent green and gold King Tut pattern ruffled shade, unsigned, chipped.

6.5in (16.5cm) diam

£700-1,000 **JDJ**

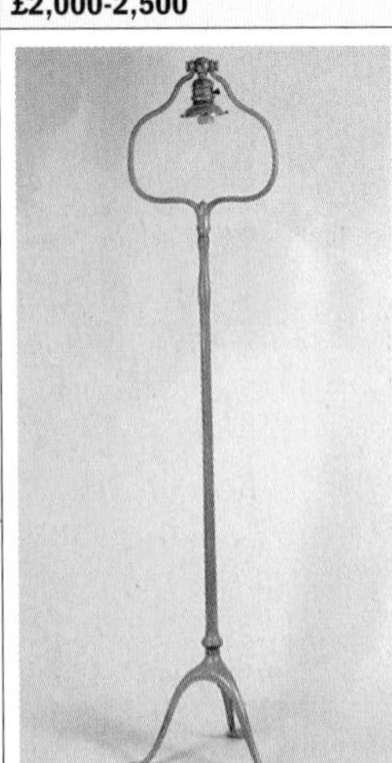

A Tiffany harp floor lamp base, with gold dore finish, signed on the foot "Tiffany Studios New York 428", some wear.

55in (139.5cm) high

£1,500-2,000 **JDJ**

A Tiffany 'Junior' floor lamp base, with five-legged foot and adjustable stem, signed on the foot "Tiffany Studios New York".

58.5in (148.5cm) high

£800-1,200 **JDJ**

OTHER MAKERS

A pair of Glasgow-style wall sconces, attributed to Agnes Bankier Harvey, each of rectilinear form and repoussé decorated with Art Nouveau maidens and stylized poppy heads above drip trays and nozzles.

12in (30cm) high

£1,500-2,000 **L&T**

A Benson lamp, with Powell shade.

c1900 *11.5in (20cm) high*

£800-1,000 **MW**

A Daum Frères Nancy table lamp, of stylized mushroom form, with a ribbed shade, clear overlay glass with greenish powder inclusions, rust-brown enamel detail, etched, signed.

c1905 *16.5in (41.5cm) high*

£2,000-3,000 **QU**

A table lamp by Daum Frères, Nancy, in clear purple overlay glass with yellow and red-orange powder enamels and acid etching, foot signed with "DN".

c1910 *32.25in (82cm) high*

£4,000-4,500 **FIS**

A pair of Durand lamps, with iridescent shades, gold applied threading and surface decorated hearts, gold interior, contemporary bases.

18.5in (47cm) high

£400-600 **JDJ**

One of a pair of Arts & Crafts wrought iron chandeliers by Thomas Hadden, each with three scrolled branches, decorated with fruiting berries, painted.

c1910 *32in (81cm) diam*

£700-1,000 pair **L&T**

A rare Daum Art Deco floor lamp, with amber-coloured cameo shade resting in a cast metal floor lamp base, cast in forms of oak leaves and acorns with birds resting on three extending tree limbs with climbing ivy, the domed foot hand hammered, the shade signed "Daum Nancy France" the base unsigned, possibly Majorelle.

64in (162.5cm) high

£6,000-9,000 **JDJ**

A French table lamp, by R. Jonkergouw, with colourful pâte-de-verre and bronze mounts, the shade formed as dragonflies, signed "R. Jonkergouw".

c1900 *17.25in (44cm) long*

£5,000-7,000 **DOR**

A Josef Hoffmann brass wand lamp, for Wiener Werkstätte, with a new white fabric shade, the arm with chain of pearls, electrified, monogram "JH", rose mark

c1912 *10.25in (25.5cm) long*

£1,500-2,000 **DOR**

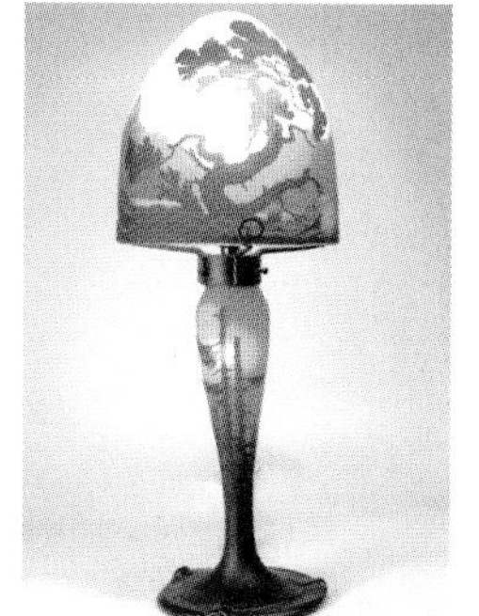

A Muller cameo lamp, with a scenic design of mountains and trees in amethyst, blue and orange on a pale yellow background, base and shade signed "Muller Fres Luneville".

20.25in (51.5cm) high

£6,000-9,000 **JDJ**

A KPM lithophane shade, each of the five panels showing a different scene.

6.5in (16.5cm) high

£500-700 **JDJ**

A pair of Smith Bros. vases, in silver-plated holders, with hand-painted scenes of birds, flowers, trees, with gold highlights, signed "Pairpoint".

11.5in (29cm) high

£1,000-1,500 **JDJ**

A fine Jessie Preston brass candlestick, with a tall flaring stem on a large circular base, stamped "A" in a triangle.

14in (35.5cm) high

£1,000-1,500 **DRA**

A French spelter figural lamp, with a spelter woman sitting on a tree stump with a bronze patina, the brass cat tails housing the light sockets and bulbs, the plaque inscribed "Pecheuse par Ferrand Recompense au Salon", replacement screws and damage.

40in (101.5cm) high

£800-1,200 **JDJ**

A Viennese table lamp, with a silver-plated metal base, and a Bohemian glass shade in clear, white matte and with irregularly applied green threads.

c1905 *14.75 in (37.5cm) high*

£1,000-1,500 **DOR**

An Arts and Crafts brass and copper hall lantern, the cylindrical clear glass shade with latticed moulding enclosed within banded frame with scrolling brackets and tapering surmount.

33in (84cm) high

£600-800 **L&T**

One of a pair of Arts and Crafts copper lanterns, each of cylindrical form with tapering stepped canopies, decorated with pierced motifs.

11.5in (29cm) high

£120-180 pair **L&T**

A pair of unusual Art Nouveau lamps, probably Austrian, with cypriot-type glass shades and iridescent swirl tops, on bronze patinated bases with beaded trim, damage.

19.5in (49.5cm) high

£1,500-2,000 **JDJ**

c1900

£1,500-2,000

A gilt bronze and marble naturalistic table lamp, cast as a bundle of chestnut branches, on a trefoil base.

24in (61cm) high

S&K

An Art Deco parrot lamp, featuring a cast metal parrot holding a cage containing a bulb, the stem with a glass ball and a fluted foot, some damage.

15.25in (39cm) high

£500-700 **JDJ**

An Art Deco bronze figural table lamp, cast as a naked girl holding a dish and raised on a stepped plinth, the associated shade of faceted form with glass panels painted with peacocks.

14.25in (36cm) high

£300-400 **L&T**

GUILD OF HANDICRAFT

Designer, architect, and major figure in the Arts and Crafts movement, Charles Robert Ashbee (1863-1942) founded the Guild of Handicraft in East London in 1888. Originally a school for crafts, the Guild soon became a community of artist craftsmen intent on producing high quality, handmade silverware, metalware and furniture. Some early pieces are marked with Ashbee's initials, 'CRA', whilst pieces produced after 1898, when the Guild became a limited company, are marked 'G of H Ltd'.

The Guild moved to Chipping Campden, in Gloucestershire in 1902, and closed in 1908, although some of the silversmiths, such as George Hart, continued to work as a loose guild until 1921. The mark 'G of H' continued to be used by George Hart and members of his family after 1912.

The Guild's metalwork mainly consists of small silver pieces decorated with enamel and hardstone cabochons. The best pieces are made from thin gauge metal and have hammered surfaces.

A Guild of Handicraft round silver box with enamel ship decoration, marks for London.

1901 *2.5in (96.5cm) high*

£3,500-5,500 **VDB**

A Guild of Handicraft round box, with cloisonné enamel ship, marker's mark, London.

1903 *3in (7.5cm) high*

£1,500-2,500 **VDB**

A Guild of Handicraft round silver box with enamel reindeer, London, restoration to small crack.

1903 *3in (7.5cm) high*

£1,500-2,500 **VDB**

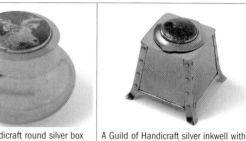

A Guild of Handicraft silver inkwell with enamel lid, London, minor faults to enamel.

1906 *2.5in (6.5cm) high*

£1,000-2,000 **VDB**

A Guild of Handicraft silver cut-out butter dish, designed by C.R. Ashbee, with hallmarks for London, dated, replacement glass liner.

1900 *8in (20cm) long*

£2,000-3,000 **VDB**

A Guild of Handicraft plated muffin dish and cover, with hot water reservoir in base, designed by C.R. Ashbee.

1900 *9.5in (24cm) diam*

£800-1,000 **VDB**

A Guild of Handicraft two-handled silver bowl set with cabochon stones, by C. R. Ashbee, marked "G of H Ltd", with hallmarks for London 1906.

4.25in (10.5cm) diam

£3,000-4,000 **VDB**

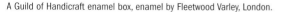

A Guild of Handicraft enamel box, enamel by Fleetwood Varley, London.

1904 *6.5in (16.5cm) high*

£3,000-4,000 **VDB**

A set of six Guild of Handicraft silver menu holders, marked "G of H London".

1908 *2.5in (6cm) high*

£4,000-6,000 **VDB**

GEORG JENSEN

The highly-regarded Danish silversmith, Georg Jensen (1866-1935) produced a wide range of decorative pieces in the Arts and Crafts and Art Nouveau styles during the late 19thC and early 20thC.

Jensen began his career as an apprentice to a Copenhagen goldsmith, and after taking art, engraving and modelling lessons, he studied at the Danish academy of Fine Arts. After working as a sculptor and a potter, Jensen opened his first workshop in Copenhagen in 1904. He initially produced jewellery inspired by nature, using silver and semi-precious stones, such as amber and opal. He soon expanded into silverware, taking inspiration from 18thC French silver. Pieces were rounded and simple in shape and had fruit, rose and tendril decoration. His organic, simple forms were an instant success.

Jensen collaborated with a number of talented designers, including Johan Rohde, Harald Neilsen and Torun Bulow-Hube. The firm's success continued after Jensen's death, employing silversmiths such as Henning Koppel.

Pieces are often marked with 'GJ' or 'GEORG JENSEN' and sometimes have a design number. His work remains popular and many of his designs are still produced by the Jensen firm today.

A Georg Jensen jug, designed by Johan Rohde, design no. 321.

c1920 *4in (10cm) high*

£1,000-1,500 **SF**

A Georg Jensen water jug, designed by Johan Rohde, design no. 432.

c1925 *9in (22.5cm) high*

£3,000-4,000 **SF**

A Georg Jensen jug, designed by Harald Nielsen, design no. 319.

c1930 *7in (18cm) high*

£3,000-4,000 **SF**

A Georg Jensen water pitcher, designed by Henning Koppel, design no. 992.

c1950 *11.75in (30cm) high*

£5,000-6,000 **SF**

A Georg Jensen lidded water pitcher, designed by Johan Rohde, design no. 45.

c1920 *9.5in (24cm) high*

£4,000-5,000 **SF**

A Georg Jensen ivory-handled chocolate pot, designed by Georg Jensen, design no. 235.

c1920 *8in (20.5cm) high*

£1,200-1,800 **SF**

A CLOSER LOOK AT A GEORG JENSEN WATER PITCHER

Henning Koppel is one of Jensen's most celebrated designers, known for his organic modernism and freeform style, as indicated by the form of this piece.
Water pitchers were one of the many 'hollow ware' items produced by Jensen.
Often dubbed 'the Pregnant Duck', this pitcher is Koppel's trademark design, its purity of form is unequalled by the rest of his work.
The satiny surface was achieved using a special technique developed by Jensen.

A Georg Jensen water pitcher, designed by Henning Koppel, design no. 1052.

c1950 *16.5in (42cm) high*

£7,000-10,000 **SF**

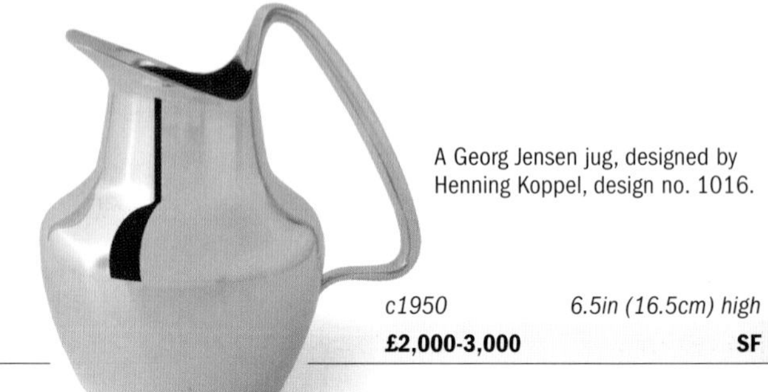

A Georg Jensen jug, designed by Henning Koppel, design no. 1016.

c1950 *6.5in (16.5cm) high*

£2,000-3,000 **SF**

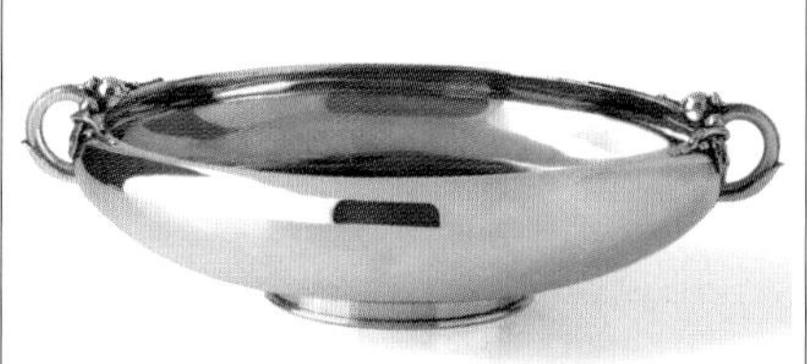

A Georg Jensen bowl, designed by Harald Nielsen, design no. 625.

c1920 *11.5in (29cm) wide*

£300-400 **SF**

A Georg Jensen bowl, designed by Sigvard Bernadotte, design no. 823.

c1930 *6.25in (16cm) wide*

£500-700 **SF**

A Georg Jensen bowl, designed by Harald Nielsen, design no. 622.

c1930 *13.75in (35cm) long*

£8,000-12,000 **SF**

A Georg Jensen 'Louvre' pattern bowl, designed by Georg Jensen, design no. 19.

c1940 *6.5in (16.5cm) high*

£1,500-2,500 **SF**

A Georg Jensen bowl, designed by Henning Koppel, design no. 980.

c1950 *15in (38cm) diam*

£8,000-12,000 **SF**

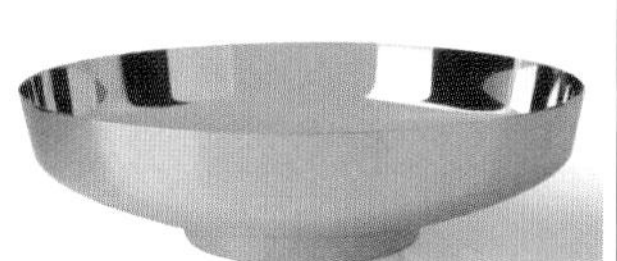

A Georg Jensen bowl, designed by Henning Koppel, design no. 1132.

c1950 *11.25 (28.5cm) diam*

£2,500-3,000 **SF**

A Georg Jensen side-handled serving bowl, designed by Georg Jensen, design no. 217.

c1920 *11.75 (30cm) long*

£1,000-1,500 **SF**

A Georg Jensen bonbonnière, designed by Georg Jensen, design no. 262.

c1915 *7.25in (18.5cm) wide*

£800-1,200 **SF**

A Georg Jensen pot, designed by Harald Nielsen, design no. 600.

c1920 *4.5in (11.5cm) high*

£700-1,000 **SF**

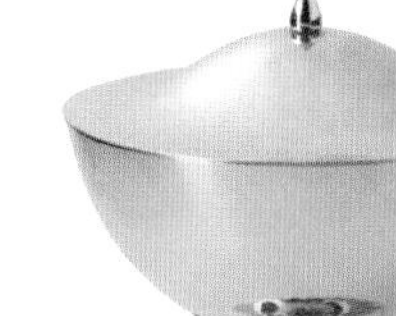

A Georg Jensen ball bonbonnière, designed by Johan Rohde, design no. 43.

c1920 *6.35in (15.5cm) high*

£2,000-2,500 **SF**

A Georg Jensen handled pot, designed by Harald Nielsen, design no. 685.

c1920 *8in (20.5cm) wide*

£2,000-3,000 **SF**

A Georg Jensen two-light candelabra, design no. 324.

c1920 *9in (23cm) high*

£5,000-7,000 **SF**

A Georg Jensen two-light candelabra, designed by Harald Nielsen, design no. 619.

c1920 *6.25in (16cm) high*

£3,000-4,000 **SF**

A Georg Jensen two-light candelabra, designed by Johan Rohde, design no. 481.

c1925 *17in (43cm) high*

£8,000-12,000 **SF**

A Georg Jensen five-light candelabra, designed by Johan Rohde, design no. 472.

c1925 *17in (43cm) high*

£10,000-15,000 **SF**

A Georg Jensen candle holder, designed by Harald Nielsen, design no. 604.

c1915 *4in (10cm) high*

£1,000-1,500 **SF**

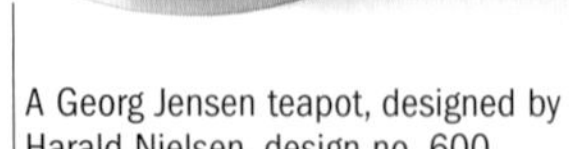

A Georg Jensen teapot, designed by Harald Nielsen, design no. 600.

c1920 *5.5in (14cm) high*

£3,000-3,500 **SF**

A Georg Jensen teapot, designed by Georg Jensen, design no. 80.

c1930 *11.5in (29cm) high*

£1,000-1,500 **SF**

A Georg Jensen teaset, designed by Harald Nielsen, design no. 917.

c1930 *Teapot 8in (20.5cm) high*

£4,000-6,000 **SF**

A Georg Jensen four-piece blossom tea set with tray, designed by Georg Jensen, design no. 2.

c1905 *Tray 18in (45.5cm) wide*

£12,000-18,000 **SF**

A Georg Jensen tray, designed by Harald Nielsen, design no. 600.

c1920 *7in (18cm) wide*

£2,000-2,500 **SF**

A Georg Jensen round platter, designed by Georg Jensen, design no. 232.

c1920 *13.5in (34.5cm) diam*

£2,000-2,500 **SF**

A Georg Jensen platter, designed by Georg Jensen, design no. 299.

c1920 *19.75in (50cm) long*

£1,500-2,000 **SF**

A Georg Jensen fish knife and fork, designed by Georg Jensen.

c1920 *Knife 8.75in (22cm) long*

£300-500 **SF**

Two Georg Jensen servers, designed by Georg Jensen, design no. 83.

c1920 *8in (20cm) long*

£300-500 **SF**

A Georg Jensen 'Pyramid' pattern five-piece place setting, designed by Harald Nielsen.

c1920 *Knife 8.75 (22cm) long*

£300-350 **SF**

A Georg Jensen 'Cactus' pattern salt and pepper, designed by Gundolph Albertus, design no. 629.

c1920 *2.75in (7cm) high*

£7,000-8,000 **SF**

A Georg Jensen salt and pepper, designed by Johan Rohde, design no. 741.

c1920 *3.5in (9cm) high*

£300-400 **SF**

A Georg Jensen sugar caster, designed by Georg Jensen, design no. 97.

c1915 *6.5in (16.5cm) high*

£1,000-1,500 **SF**

A Georg Jensen cocktail shaker, designed by Sigvard Bernadotte, design no. 819.

c1920 *7.5in (19cm) high*

£3,000-3,500 **SF**

A Georg Jensen cocktail shaker, designed by Harald Nielsen, design no. 462.

c1925 *10in (25.5cm) high*

£3,000-3,500 **SF**

A Georg Jensen grape goblet, designed by Georg Jensen, design no. 296.

c1920 *(9.5cm) high*

£1,000-1,500 **SF**

A Georg Jensen goblet, designed by Harald Nielsen, design no. 532.

c1920 *5.25in (13.5cm) high*

£300-500 **SF**

KAYSERZINN

The German pewterers J.P. Kayser & Sohne were leaders in their field from 1894 until 1925.

The company mass-produced a range of products in the Art Nouveau style. This range of pewter pieces included vases, dishes, ashtrays and lamps, and featured sinuous flower decoration and curvilinear shapes. All pieces were marked "KAYSERZINN" with a number between 4000 and 4999 in a circular or oval frame.

At the height of its popularity, the factory employed 800 workers and received a number of awards, including gold medals at the Paris Exhibition in 1900, the First Exhibition of Modern Art in Turin in 1902 and the St Louis Universal Exhibition in 1904.

Despite these successes, economic problems forced the factory to reduce its staff and output in 1906. The factory closed in 1925.

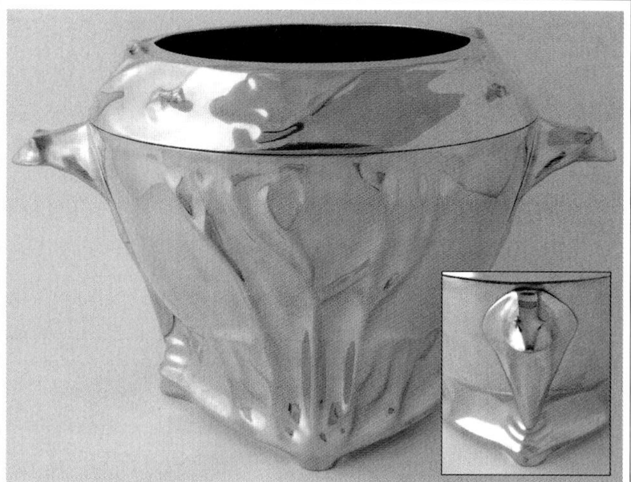

A Kayserzinn ice bucket or jardinière, designed by Hugo Levin.

c1900 *17.75in (45cm) wide*

£2,000-3,000 **STY**

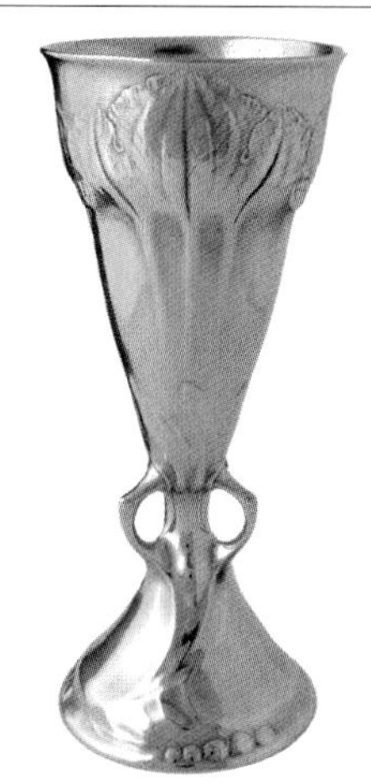

A Kayserzinn vase, designed by Hugo Levin.

c1900 *13.75in (35cm) high*

£800-1,200 **STY**

An unusual Kayserzinn 'Jugendstil' vase, designed by Hugo Levin, the square section embellished with organically inspired dimples, the pierced tapering shoulders surmounted by a circular disc with a central square aperture, all supported on four short feet, raised mark "Kayserzinn 4541" in a circle.

c1900 *7.25in (18.5cm) high*

£3,000-3,500 **DN**

A Kayserzinn jardinière, designed by Hugo Levin.

c1900 *10.5in (27cm) high*

£800-1,200 **STY**

An early 20thC Kayserzinn pewter liquor set, designed by Hugo Levin.

14in (35.5cm) wide

£400-500 **TO**

A Kayserzinn Art Nouveau pewter tankard, designed by Hugo Levin, of figural penguin form, stamped marks to base.

c1905 *11.25in (28.5cm) high*

£300-400 **FRE**

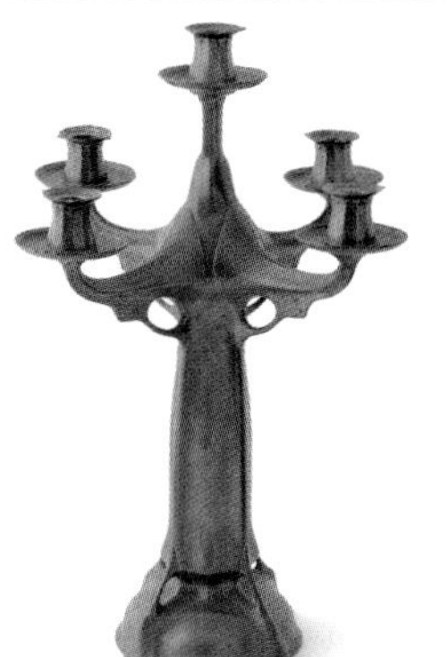

One of a pair of Kayserzinn pewter candelabra designed by Hugo Levin.

c1900 *19.5in (49.5cm) high*

£5,000-6,000 pair **TO**

A Kayserzinn flower pot.

c1900 *7in (18cm) high*

£700-1,000 **STY**

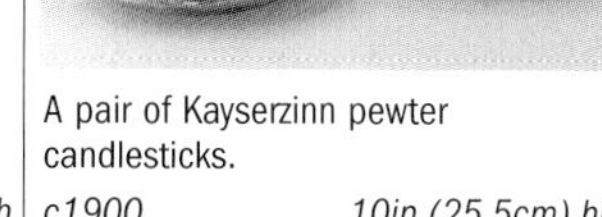

A pair of Kayserzinn pewter candlesticks.

c1900 *10in (25.5cm) high*

£500-600 **TO**

A Kayzerzinn pewter ink well.

c1905 *14in (35.5cm) wide*

£350-400 **TO**

LIBERTY Tudric & Cymric

A Liberty & Co. Tudric pewter hot water pot, designed by Archibald Knox.

c1900 *5.25in (13.5cm) high*

£200-250 **TO**

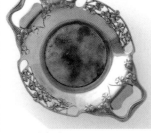

A Liberty & Co. Tudric pewter dish with enamelled plaque.

c1905 *11in (29cm) wide*

£200-250 **TO**

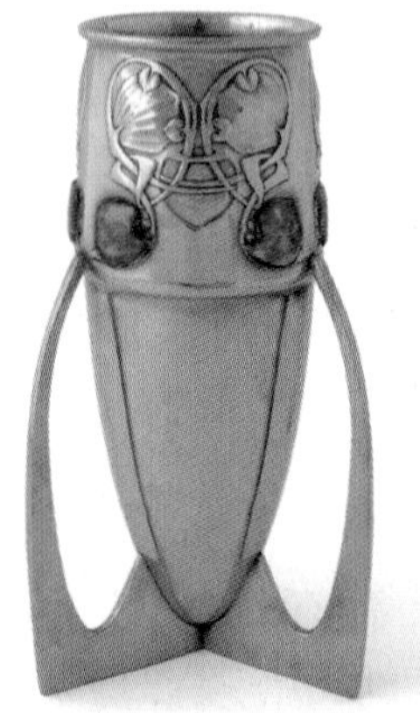

A Liberty & Co. Tudric pewter and enamelled vase designed by Archibald Knox.

c1905 *11.5in (29cm) high*

£1,500-2,000 **TO**

A Liberty & Co. Tudric pewter cigar box, with enamelled panel to lid.

12.25in (31cm) long

£1,500-2,500 **VDB**

A CLOSER LOOK AT A TUDRIC ENAMEL CLOCK

Tudric pieces are made from a type of pewter with a high proportion of silver.
The combination of interlacing patterns and turquoise enamelling epitomized Liberty style.
A major force behind Liberty's Tudric and Cymric wares, Knox took inspiration for them from swirling Celtic forms.
Stylized honesty leaves were a popular Art Nouveau motif.

A Liberty & Co. Tudric pewter and enamel clock designed by Archibald Knox, the case with honesty decoration around circular enamelled dial with exposed copper numerals, with French movement, marked "RS 468016, Made in England, English Pewter, 0609".

Featured in: "The Designs of Archibald Knox for Liberty & Co.", by A. J. Tilbrook, Ornament Press, Ltd., London, England, 1976, page 112, and "Archibald Knox", by Stephen A. Martin, Artmedia Press, 2001, pp. 10, 233.

c1900 *8.5in (21cm) high*

£8,000-12,000 **MACK**

A Liberty & Co. Tudric pewter box by Archibald Knox.

c1905 *3.75in (9.5cm) high*

£500-600 **TO**

An early 20thC Liberty & Co. Tudric pewter dish designed by Archibald Knox.

5.5in (14cm) diam

£100-150 **TO**

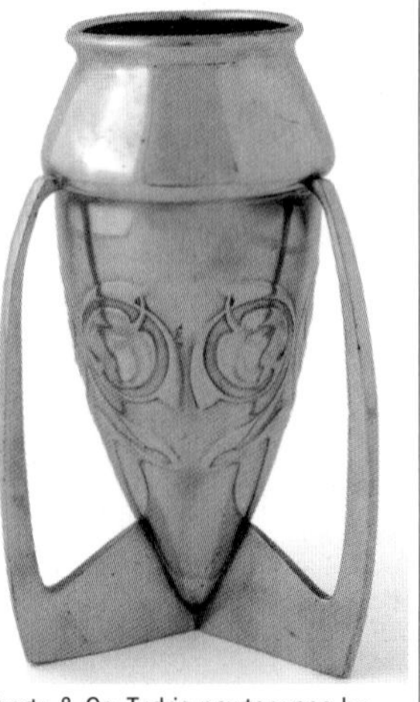

A Liberty & Co. Tudric pewter vase by Archibald Knox.

c1905 *7.5in (19cm) high*

£300-350 **TO**

A Liberty & Co. Tudric pewter and enamel mantel clock, designed by Archibald Knox.

c1900 *8in (20.5cm) high*

£4,000-5,000 **TO**

A Liberty and Co. hand-polished pewter ice bucket, designed by Archibald Knox, no. 0706, marked "Tudric".

c1905 *7.5in (19cm) high*

£2,500-3,500 **STY**

A fine Liberty & Co. Tudric pewter organic vase with band of blue and green enamelled cabochons, whiplash handles, stamped "Tudric/029/4".

9.75in (25cm) high

£1,000-1,500 **DRA**

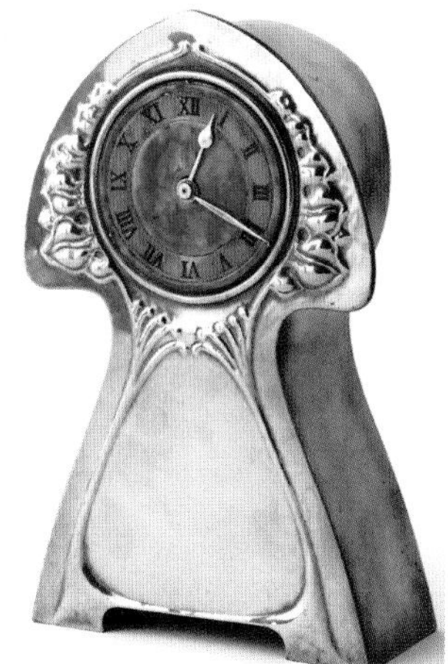

A Liberty & Co. Tudric pewter mantel clock, cast in low relief with foliate panels, the face enamelled in blue, model no. 0385, stamped marks.

7.75in (20cm) high

£2,000-3,000 **WW**

A Tudric pewter cigarette box, of rectangular form, the domed lid with hammered finish and a turquoise cabochon, the sides with applied bud decoration, stamped mark "078".

10.5in (20cm) long

£180-220 **L&T**

A Liberty & Co. Tudric pewter double inkstand, designed by Archibald Knox.

c1905 *10.5in (26.5cm) wide*

£1,200-1,500 **TO**

A twin-handled Tudric pewter vase, cast in low relief with stylized trees, inscribed with "For Old Times Sake", stamped marks, model no. 010.

7.75in (20cm) high

£700-1,000 **WW**

A Liberty & Co. Tudric twin-handled vase, designed by D. Veasey, cast with a frieze of honesty, bearing inscription "For Old Times Sake", stamped marks.

10.5in (20cm) high

£400-600 **L&T**

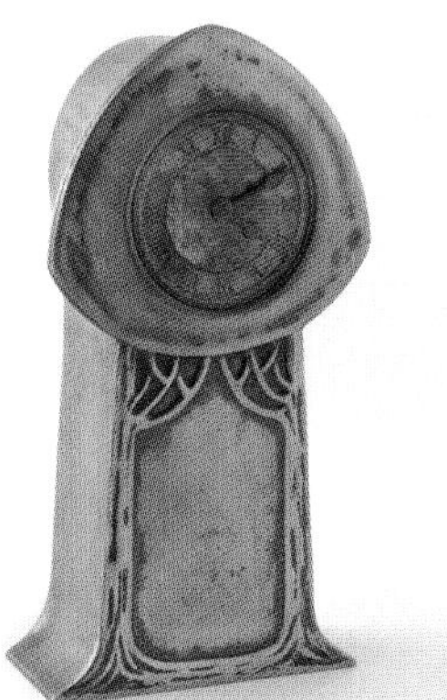

A Liberty & Co. Tudric pewter timepiece, the flared base embossed with stylized trees supporting the rounded triangular frame, centered with a hammered copper chapter ring with black Roman numerals, the German movement with cylinder escapement.

9in (23cm) high

£1,500-2,000 **DN**

One of a pair of Liberty & Co. Tudric pewter candlesticks, designed by Archibald Knox.

c1905 *9in (23cm) high*

£1,200-1,500 pair **TO**

A Tudric pewter three piece coffee set, comprising a coffee pot of tapering circular shape, hammered with high moulded girdle below a hinged cover, with a gothic arch finial over cane clad handle, marked 0232, together with the companion sugar basin and cream jug.

£80-120 **CHEF**

A Liberty & Co. pewter travel clock, designed by Archibald Knox, with a rounded square face, cast in low relief with stylized honesty, stamped marks, model no. 0482.

4in (10.5cm) high

£500-700 **WW**

A Liberty & Co. Cymric silver clock, Birmingham.

1903 *8.75in (22cm) high*

£1,500-1,800 **VDB**

A Liberty & Co. Cymric vase.

This is often thought to be the work of Archibald Knox, but is not.

1903 *9.5in (24cm) high*

£10,000-15,000 **VDB**

OTHER LIBERTY

A pair of Liberty & Co. hand-polished pewter candlesticks, designed by Archibald Knox.

c1905 *5.5in (14cm) high*

£1,200-1,500 **STY**

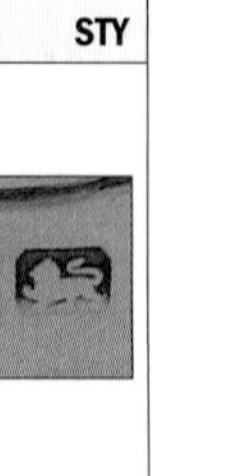

A W.H. Haseler for Liberty enamel coaster, designed by Archibald Knox, Birmingham.

1905 *3.5in (9cm) diam*

£1,000-2,000 **VDB**

A pair of Liberty & Co. silver candlesticks, designed by Archibald Knox.

1908 *8in (20.5cm) high*

£3,000-4,000 **TO**

A Liberty & Co. pewter and 'Clutha' glass bowl, designed by Archibald Knox, the mount pierced and embellished with leaf forms, on three legs above a circular base, the liner in pale green glass, with milky streaks and aventurine inclusions, marked "0276" and "8".

c1890 *6.5in (16.5cm) high*

£2,000-2,500 **DN**

A Liberty & Co. silver tea caddy, designed by Archibald Knox, Birmingham.

1906 *3.25in (8cm) high*

£2,000-3,000 **VDB**

A Liberty & Co. English pewter preserve pot, cover and spoon, designed by Archibald Knox, cast in low relief with a stylized bramble motif, stamped marks, model no. 0700.

5.75in (14.5cm) high

£1,000-1,500 **WW**

A Liberty & Co English pewter timepiece, designed by Archibald Knox, of oblong outline embossed with sinuous trailing stems and enamelled in shades of blue and green with honesty leaves, stamped verso, "English Pewter 0482" and "Solkets", restored enamel.

4in (10cm) high

£500-700 **DN**

ORIVIT

From 1901, Orivit pewter was produced by Rheinische Bronzegießerei in Germany. The factory produced a wide range of wares with the scrolling whiplash motifs typical of Art Nouveau design. The quality of the design and manufacture are key features of Orivit's pieces, which were stamped with the "ORIVIT" mark. The company was purchased by WMF in 1906.

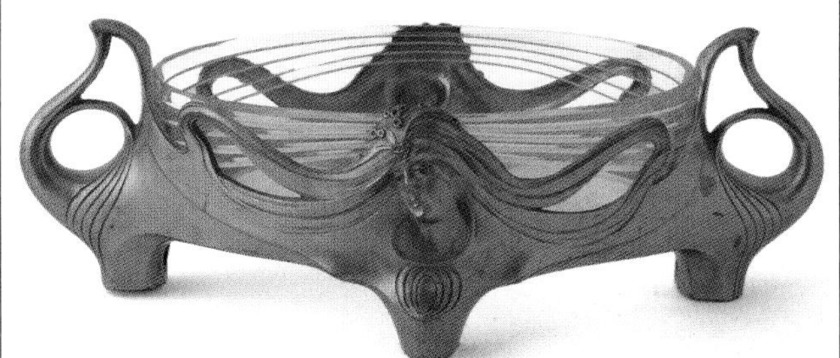

An Orivit centrepiece, with original gilding and liner.

c1900 *10.75in (27.5cm) long*

£550-650 **STY**

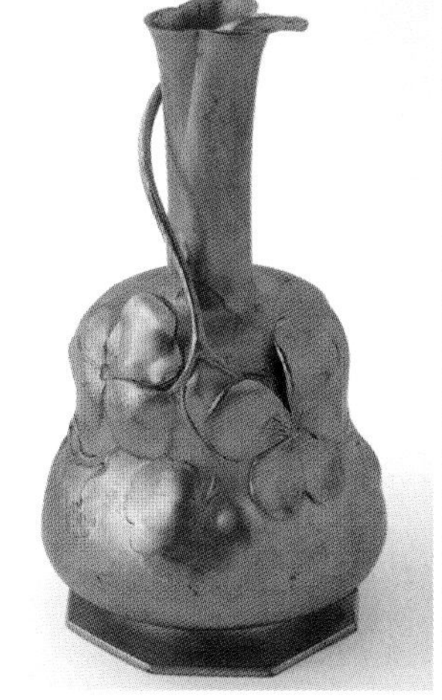

An Orivit gilded pewter vase.

c1900 *7.5in (19cm) high*

£200-250 **TO**

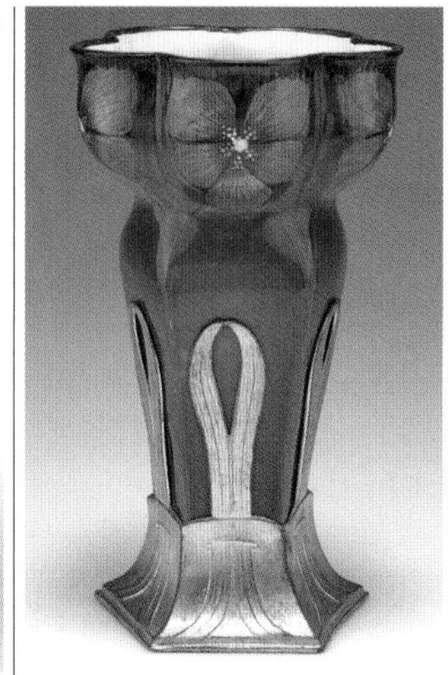

An Orivit vase in gilded pewter, with polychrome pansy decoration.

£400-600 **QU**

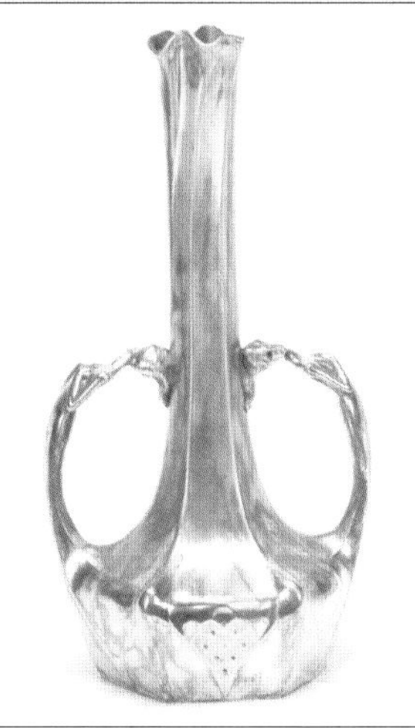

An Orivit Jugendstil pewter vase, the compressed lower body organically ribbed and with panels of stylized petals, the tall hexagonal neck twisting at the top, with twin handles of slender naked female form, with some traces of original gilding, stamped "Orivit" and numbered "2654".

15in (38cm) high

£300-500 **DN**

An Orivit pewter dressing table mirror.

c1905 *13.5in (34.5cm) high*

£1,200-1,500 **TO**

An Orivit metal and glass dish, decorated with geometric and floral designs, supported on four flat feet, signed "ORIVIT" and stamped "8582".

c1910 *9in (22.5cm) high*

£150-200 **QU**

An Orivit pewter tea set on tray.

c1905 *Tray 19.5in (49.5cm) wide*

£600-800 **TO**

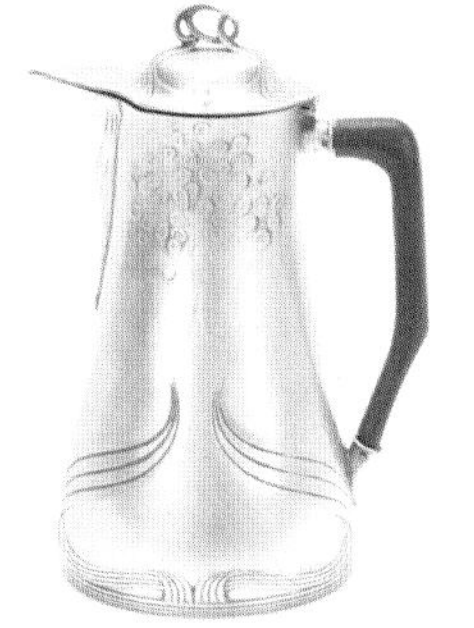

A German plated metal jug, attributed to Orivit, with tapering cylindrical body and hinged domed cover, embellished with stylized plant forms, with an ebonised handle, unmarked.

8.25in (21cm) high

£70-100 **DN**

One of a pair of Orivit pewter candlesticks, each with a sconce above a tapering stem, rising from a trefoil base with three lobed feet, marked on base.

5.5in (14cm) high

£150-200 pair **DN**

TIFFANY

A pair of Tiffany gilt bronze candle sticks, each with a detachable drip pan above pierced knop, naturalistic floral thin stem and circular foot, stamped "Tiffany Studios, New York".

10in (25.5cm) high

£1,200-1,800 **MACK**

A pair of Tiffany Studios gilt bronze candlesticks, each with a square sconce with enamelled edge, on a textured column rising from a spreading square base, decorated around the outer edge with an enamelled blue band resembling a mosaic, speckled with white and red, supported on ball feet, stamped with "LCT" monogram, "Louis C. Tiffany Furnaces Inc." and numbered "368".

£1,500-2,000 **DN**

A Tiffany bronze eight light table candelabrum, of pulled naturalistic form, the central handle with concealed snuffer, moulded circular foot, signed "L.C.Tiffany Studios, New York".

15in (38cm) high

£12,000-18,000 **MACK**

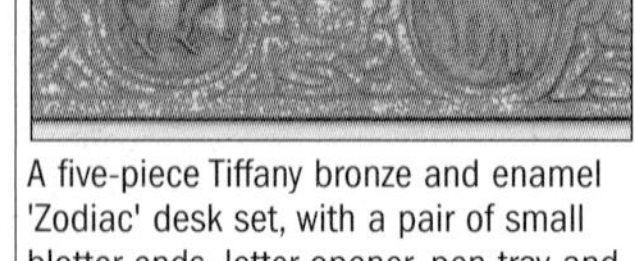

A five-piece Tiffany bronze and enamel 'Zodiac' desk set, with a pair of small blotter ends, letter opener, pen tray and rocker blotter, all in gold dore finish and marked "Tiffany Studios New York 990", some wear to dore finish.

£1,800-2,200 **JDJ**

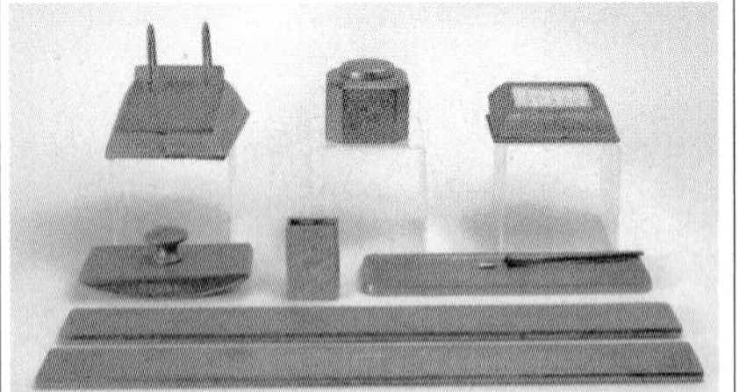

An eight-piece Tiffany 'Zodiac' desk set consisting of large blotter ends, pen tray, matchbox holder, inkwell with glass insert, rocker blotter, notepad holder and calendar, all with gold dore finish, all pieces show some wear to the finish.

Pen tray 10in (25.5cm) long

£800-1,200 **JDJ**

A rare Tiffany 'pine needle' pen, has bronze handle in the 'pine needle' pattern, some wear to brown patina from use.

6in (15cm) long

£400-600 **JDJ**

A Tiffany three-foot inkwell, with gold dore finish and original divided glass insert, the hinged cover has flower design, the three protruding legs end in paw feet, signed on bottom of one foot "Tiffany Studios New York 1086".

£1,200-1,800 **JDJ**

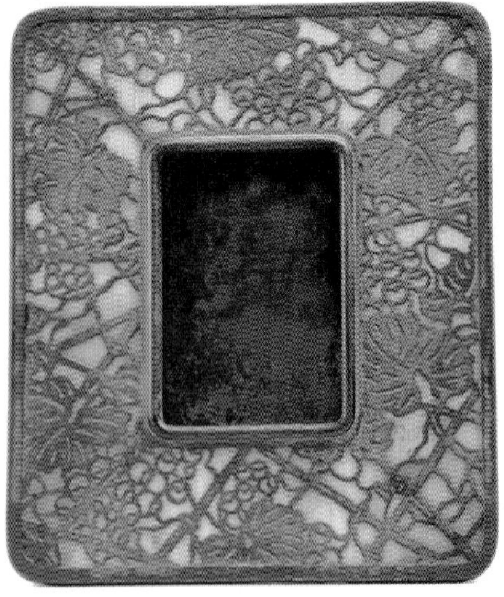

A rare Tiffany 'Grapevine' picture frame, with rounded corners and brown, green and red patina, backed with green slag glass, impressed on the back with "Tiffany Studios New York", in excellent condition.

7.25in (18.5cm) high

£1,800-2,200 **JDJ**

A Tiffany bronze picture frame, with braided swirl design, rich red-brown patina and green highlights, impressed on back "Tiffany Studios New York 914", in excellent condition.

9.75in (25cm) high

£1,200-1,800 **JDJ**

A Tiffany squat copper vessel decorated with abstract flowers and leaves in gold, over a bronzed patina, stamped "Tiffany & Co.", some overall wear.

10.25in (26cm) diam

£300-400 **DRA**

WMF

The Württemberg Metalwork Factory (WMF) was established in 1880 in Geislingen, Germany, by Daniel Straub, and is still in operation today.

Although it initially produced pieces in the Rococo style, it is best known for its highly commercial and decorative Art Nouveau items. Many pieces were mass-produced in an alloy known as Continental pewter, and decorated with Art Nouveau flowers, foliage and female figures with flowing hair. In the 1920s, WMF introduced a range of Art Deco pieces, including 'Ikora' metalware.

The company also made glass objects from 1883 until 1984, including a coloured glass 'Ikora' range with decorative bubbles, and an iridescent 'Myra' range.

A WMF hand-polished pewter visiting card tray.
c1900 *13in (33cm) wide*
£600-800 **STY**

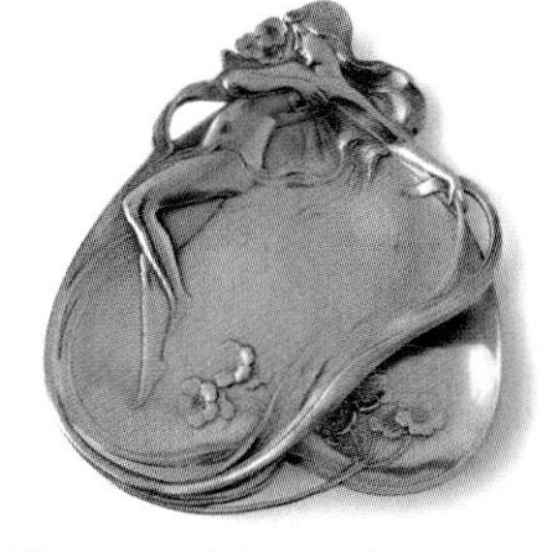

A WMF pewter visiting card tray.
c1900 *7.5in (19cm) wide*
£500-600 **STY**

A WMF pewter card tray.
c1905 *11.5in (29cm) wide*
£1,000-1,200 **TO**

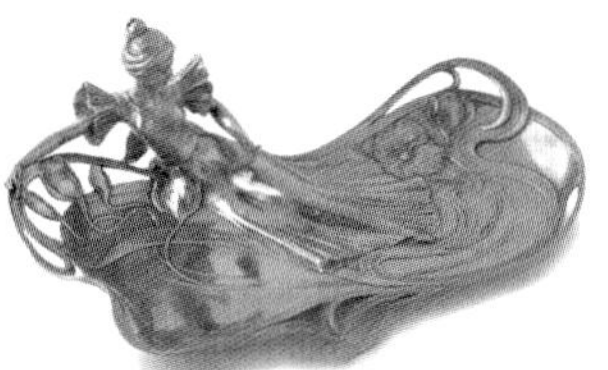

A WMF pewter card tray.
c1905 *13.5in (34.5cm) wide*
£1,000-1,200 **TO**

A large WMF silver-plated serving tray.
c1900 *24.75in (63cm) wide*
£1,000-1,200 **STY**

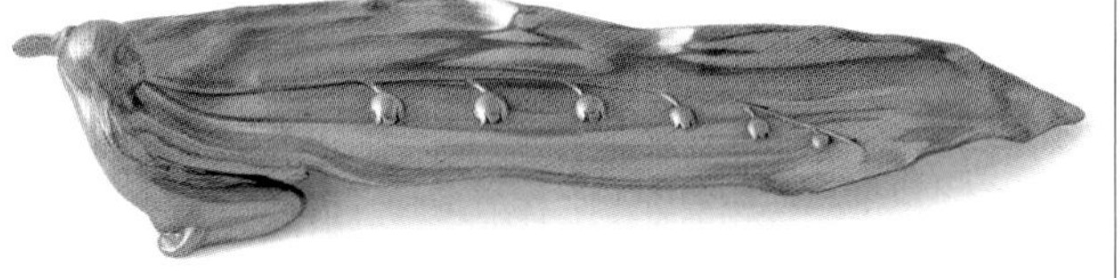

A WMF hand-polished pewter pen tray.
c1900 *10.5in (27cm) wide*
£300-400 **STY**

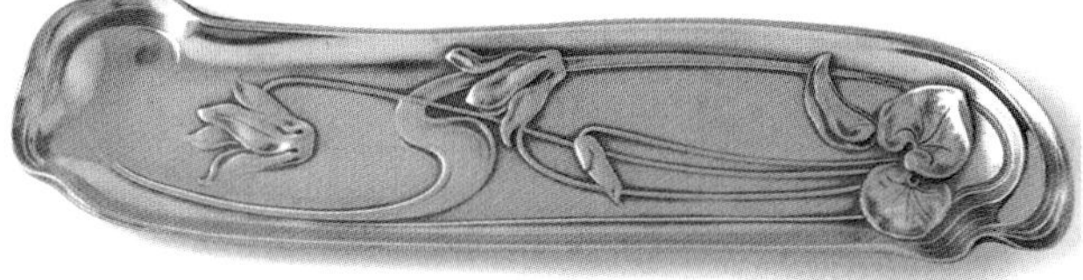

A WMF hand-polished pewter pen tray.
c1900 *11in (28cm) wide*
£150-250 **STY**

A WMF silver-plated tea tray.
c1905 *18.75in (47.5cm) wide*
£200-250 **TO**

A WMF Jugendstil hand-polished pewter picture frame.
c1905 *12.25in (31cm) high*
£1,200-1,500 **STY**

A WMF pewter dressing table mirror.
c1905 *20.5in (52cm) high*
£1,500-2,000 **TO**

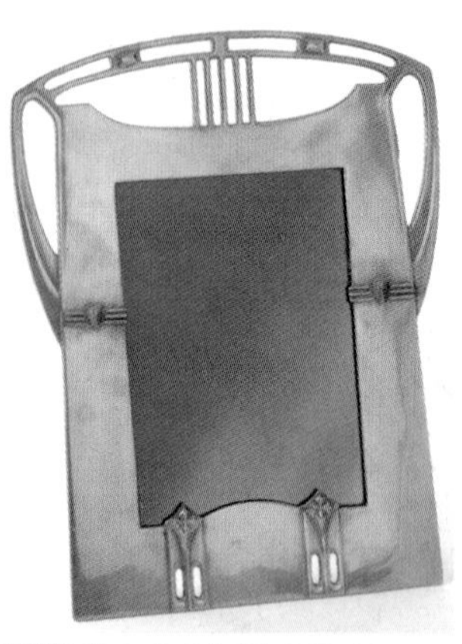

A WMF silver-plated picture frame.

c1905 *7.75in (19.5cm) high*

£400-500 **TO**

A WMF silver-plated dressing table mirror.

c1905 *20in (50.5cm) high*

£1,500-1,800 **TO**

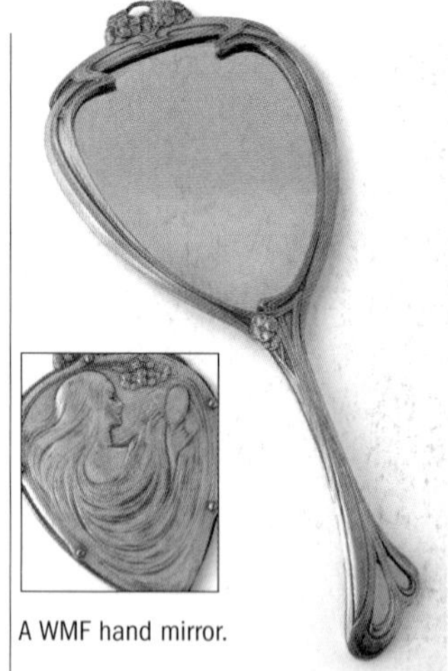

A WMF hand mirror.

c1900 *12.25in (31cm) high*

£400-500 **STY**

A WMF ewer, with mermaid handle.

c1900 *15.75in (40cm) high*

£1,200-1,800 **STY**

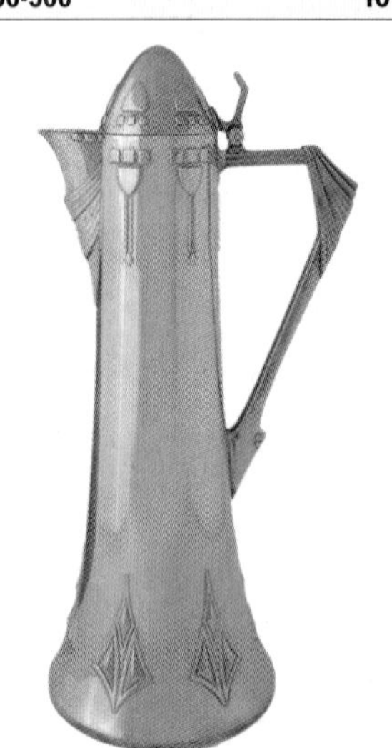

A WMF silver-plated claret jug.

c1905 *17.25in (44cm) high*

£900-1,000 **STY**

A WMF pewter claret jug.

c1900 *16in (41cm) high*

£600-800 **STY**

A CLOSER LOOK AT A WMF PUNCH BOWL

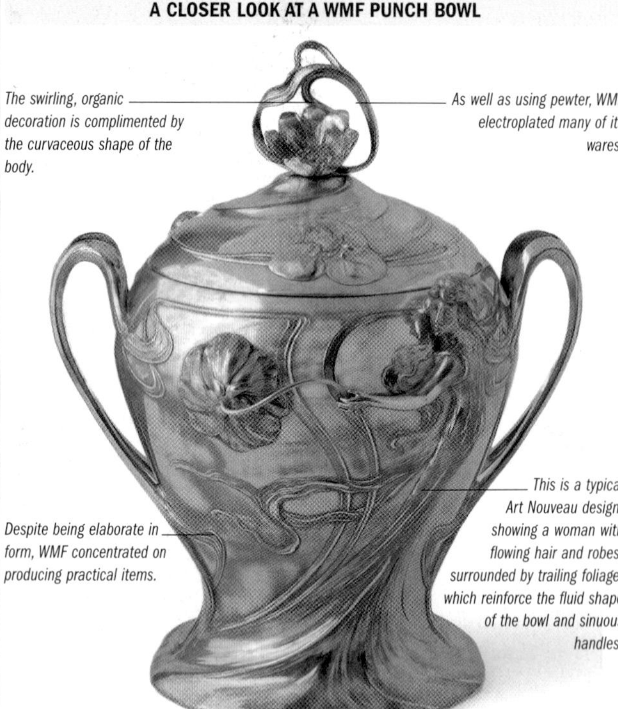

The swirling, organic decoration is complimented by the curvaceous shape of the body.
As well as using pewter, WMF electroplated many of its wares.
Despite being elaborate in form, WMF concentrated on producing practical items.
This is a typical Art Nouveau design, showing a woman with flowing hair and robes, surrounded by trailing foliage, which reinforce the fluid shape of the bowl and sinuous handles.

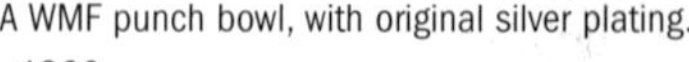

A WMF punch bowl, with original silver plating.

c1900 *13.5in (34cm) high*

£2,500-3,500 **STY**

A WMF glass and pewter claret jug.

c1905 *17in (43cm) high*

£800-1,000 **TO**

A WMF pewter champagne bucket.

c1905 *13in (33cm) high*

£1,800-2,200 **TO**

A WMF pewter champagne bucket.

c1905 *7.75in (19.5cm) high*

£300-400 **TO**

A WMF pewter bottle stand.

c1905 *4.25in (11cm) high*

£200-250 **TO**

A pair of WMF hand-polished pewter candlesticks.

c1900 *10.5in (27cm) high*

£1,300-1,800 **STY**

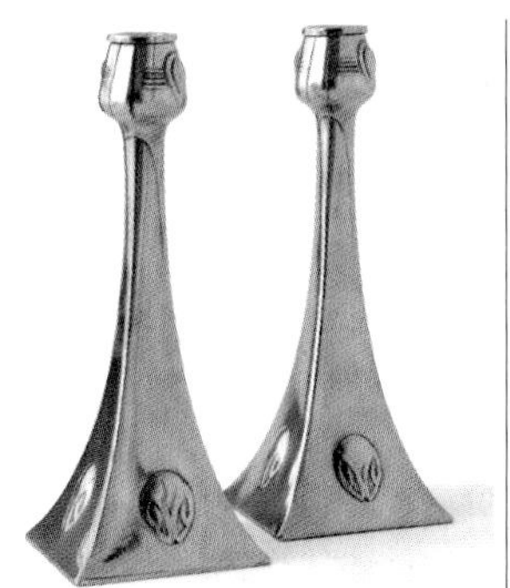

A pair of WMF pewter candlesticks, design attributed to Albin Muller.

c1905 *9in (23cm) high*

£700-800 **TO**

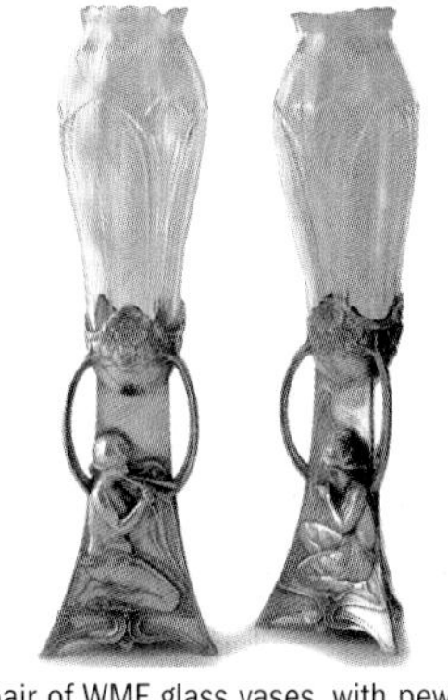

A pair of WMF glass vases, with pewter mounts.

c1905 *13.25in (33.5cm) high*

£800-1,000 **TO**

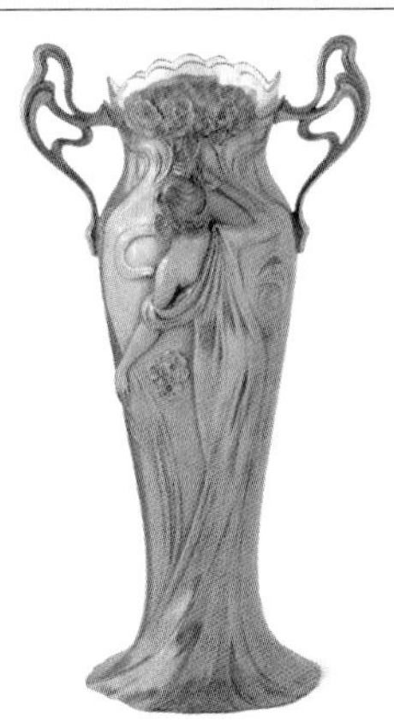

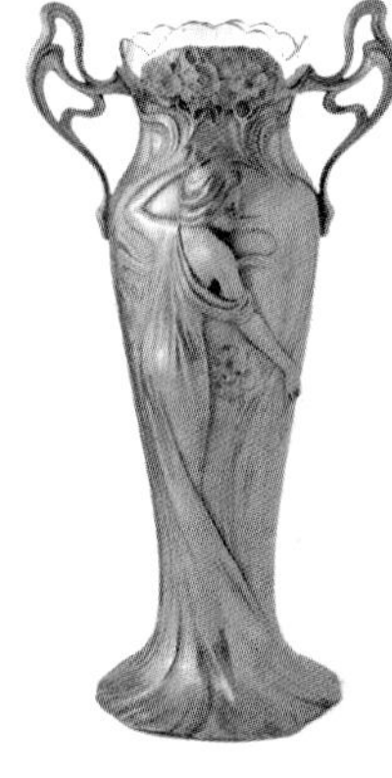

A WMF three piece garniture, with original glass and polished pewter.

A garniture was a set of three or five items which were designed as a decorative mantelpiece set.

c1900 *13.75in (35cm) high*

£7,000-8,000 **STY**

A WMF pewter clock.

c1900 *13in (33cm) high*

£900-1,200 **STY**

A WMF silver-plated tea caddy.

c1905 *5.5in (14cm) wide*

£200-250 **TO**

A WMF pewter wall plaque.

c1905 *20.25in (51.5cm) diam*

£1,500-1,800 **TO**

A WMF silver-plated photograph frame.

c1905 *6.75in (17cm) high*

£600-800 **STY**

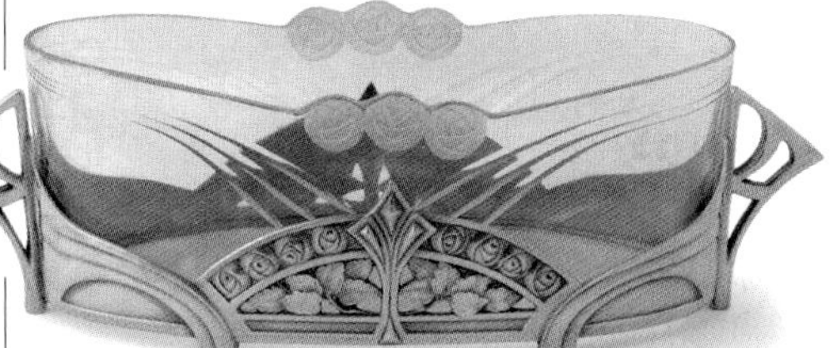

A WMF pewter and glass flower dish.

c1905 *11.75in (30cm) wide*

£300-400 **TO**

A WMF pewter hors d'oeuvres dish.

c1905 *11.25in (28.5cm) wide*

£800-1,000 **TO**

SILVER

An Albert Edward Jones silver bowl set with Ruskin pottery plaques, slight restoration to the two plaques, maker's mark, Birmingham.

1903 *7.25in (18cm) high*

£2,500-3,500 **VDB**

An Albert Edward Jones silver bowl on four feet, marks for Birmingham.

1906 *6.75in (17cm) diam*

£2,000-4,000 **VDB**

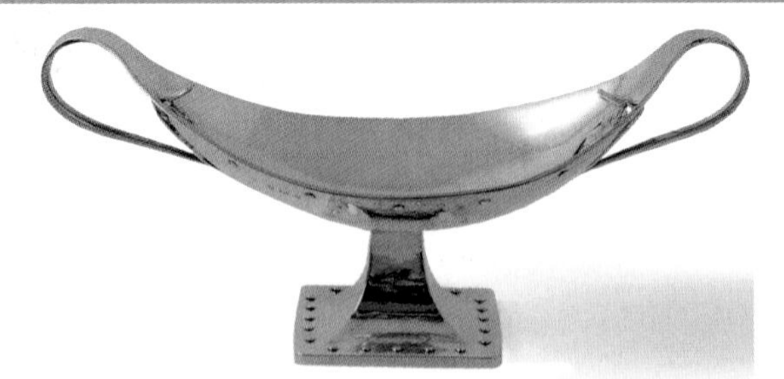

An Albert Edward Jones two handled silver comport, hallmarks for Birmingham.

1910 *12.5in (32cm) long*

£1,000-1,500 **VDB**

An Albert Edward Jones silver bowl decorated with roses, leaves and branches, Birmingham.

c1910 *8.5in (21.5cm) diam*

£3,000-4,000 **VDB**

An Albert Edward Jones silver centrepiece, marks for Birmingham.

1929 *9.5in (24cm) high*

£2,500-3,500 **VDB**

An Albert Edward Jones silver tea service, tray and water jug, maker's mark, Birmingham.

1930 *Coffee pot 7.5in (19cm) high*

£4,000-6,000 **VDB**

An Albert Edward Jones silver sugar castor, set with tiny Ruskin pottery stones, marks for Birmingham.

1905 *5in (12.5cm) high*

£400-600 **VDB**

An A. Jones silver inkwell, Birmingham.

1908 *4.75in (12cm) high*

£800-1,200 **VDB**

A William Hutton & Sons silver casket, London.

1904 *5.25in (13cm) wide*

£2,500-3,500 **VDB**

A William Hutton & Sons silver box and cover, the cover stamped in low relief with a knight in armour, stamped marks for London 1901, feet dented.

1901 *5in (12.5cm) wide*

£500-800 **WW**

A William Hutton silver box of circular form, the cover stamped with a spray of flowers, marks for London 1903.

1903 *2.75in (7cm) diam*

£200-250 **WW**

A William Hutton & Sons silver centrepiece, designed by Kate Harris, with maker's mark, London.

1899 *19.5in (50cm) high*

£3,500-5,000 **VDB**

A William Hutton silver and green glass vase, with pierced shoulder, stamped marks for London 1900.

1900 *7.75in (20cm) high*

£500-700 **WW**

An Omar Ramsden silver cup, the hammered inverted bowl on a waisted foot, stamped marks for London 1936, etched "Omar Ramsden Me Fecit".

1936 *7.5in (18.5cm) high*

£1,000-1,500 **WW**

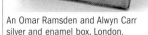

An Omar Ramsden and Alwyn Carr silver and enamel box, London.

1907 *3.75in (9.5cm) long*

£2,500-3,500 **VDB**

An Omar Ramsden and Alwyn Carr silver box and cover, set with blue and green enamel, London.

1901 *4.25in (11cm) high*

£800-1,500 **VDB**

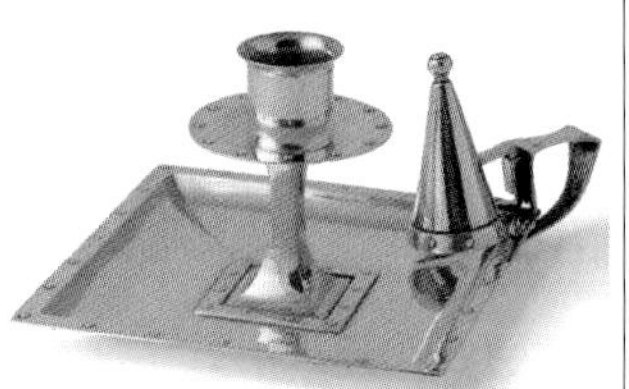

A James Dixon & Sons chamber stick and snuffer, marks for Sheffield.

1903 *4.5in (11.5cm) wide*

£1,500-2,500 **VDB**

An Omar Ramsden silver cup and cover, London.

1929 *10.5in (26.5cm) high*

£1,500-2,500 **VDB**

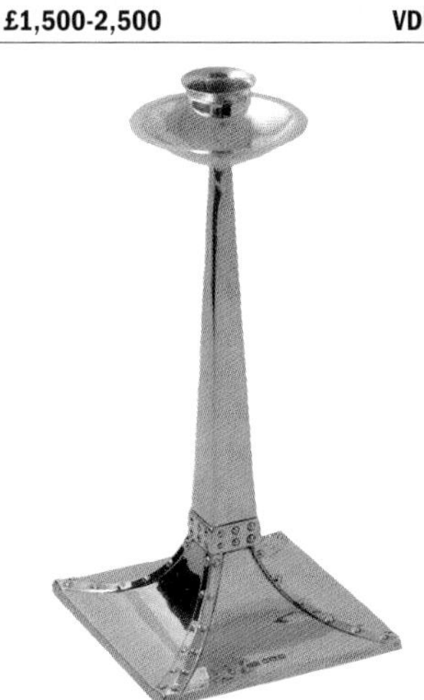

One of a pair of James Dixon & Sons silver candlesticks, marks for Sheffield.

1904 *8.75in (22cm) high*

£1,500-2,500 pair **VDB**

A CLOSER LOOK AT AN OMAR RAMSDEN VASE

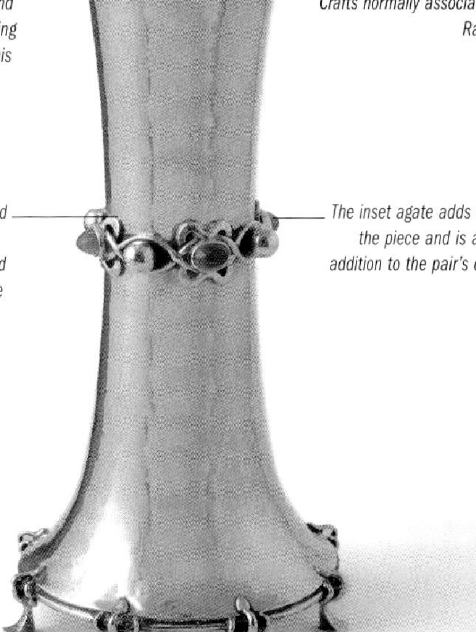

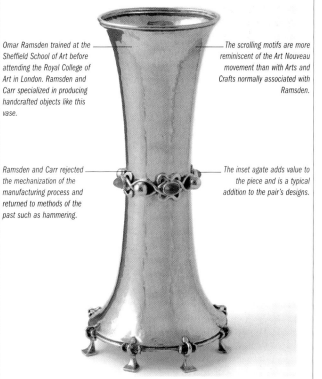

Omar Ramsden trained at the Sheffield School of Art before attending the Royal College of Art in London. Ramsden and Carr specialized in producing handcrafted objects like this vase.

The scrolling motifs are more reminiscent of the Art Nouveau movement than with Arts and Crafts normally associated with Ramsden.

Ramsden and Carr rejected the mechanization of the manufacturing process and returned to methods of the past such as hammering.

The inset agate adds value to the piece and is a typical addition to the pair's designs.

An Omar Ramsden and Alwyn Carr silver vase, set with green stained agate, marks for London.

1913 *11in (28cm) high*

£4,000-6,000 **VDB**

A pair of James Dixon and Sons Arts and Crafts silver candelabra.

1906 *8.75in (22cm) high*

£3,000-4,000 **VDB**

A pair of James Dixon and Sons silver candlesticks, the tapering circular section with bands of rivets, stamped "JD & S", mark for London 1928.

9in (23cm) high

£1,000-1,500 **WW**

A Gilbert Leigh Marks silver casket signed and dated, with maker's mark, London.

1898 *5in (13cm) long*

£5,000-7,000 **VDB**

A Gilbert Leigh Marks silver vase signed "Gilbert Marks", dated 1899, for London.

12.5in (32cm) high

£15,000-20,000 **VDB**

A Gilbert Leigh Marks silver dish, signed "Gilbert Marks", dated 1900, for London.

17.75in (45cm) high

£15,000-20,000 **VDB**

A pair of Adie Bros' Art Deco candelabra, designed by Harold Stabler.

c1935 *11.75in (30cm) high*

£4,000-6,000 **VDB**

A French silver-plated mermaid dish.

c1900 *7.75in (19.5cm) long*

£300-400 **STY**

One of a pair of Charles Robert Ashbee silver bowls, in a medieval style, marked with "CRA", London.

1900 *5in (12.5cm) diam*

£2,000-4,000 pair **VDB**

A silver pepper by George Angell, of baluster form, applied with lizard handles, stamped marks for GA London 1850.

Angell produced silver designs by William Burges in the mid-19thC including a decanter held in the Cecil Higgins Art Gallery collection, Bedford.

1865 *3.5in (8.5cm) high*

£300-500 **WW**

A pair of silver-plated candlesticks.

c1905 *6in (15cm) high*

£400-600 **STY**

An Irish silver and enamel chalice of medieval form, studded with blue and green enamel and stones, the rim inscribed with "Ah my beloved fill the cup that clears today of past regrets and future fears", from Edward Fitzgerald, in fitted case, with stamped harp mark, dated 1906.

1906 *6.5in (16cm) high*

£1,800-2,200 **WW**

A silver and enamel box and cover, of oval section, applied with scrolling borders, the sides applied with champlevé enamel panels of seagulls, the finial with a bluebird, unmarked.

6.25in (16cm) wide

£1,200-1,800 **WW**

An Alwyn Carr silver bowl and spoon, the bowl with an inscription and dated for 1903, the spoon dated for 1926, marks for London.

Bowl 8.25in (21cm) wide

£1,000-1,500 **VDB**

A silver milk jug, of tapering oval section, with flaring at the neck rim to form a lip, strap loop handle and plain surface, with gilded interior, marked "CFS" for Edinburgh 1941.

3.25in (8.5cm) high

£100-150 **DN**

An Arts and Crafts John Paul Cooper silver mounted shagreen box.

1918 *6in (15cm) long*

£4,000-6,000 **VDB**

A Bernard Cuzner silver wine cup, inscribed "And Still The Vine Her Ancient Ruby Yields", hallmark for Birmingham.

1903 *4in (10cm) high*

£900-1,500 **VDB**

A Bernard Cuzner silver bowl, twin-handled form, stamped with floral band, stamped mark for Birmingham 1909.

5.25in (13cm) diam

£120-180 **WW**

An Edith and Nelson Dawson silver bookmark with enamel of a ladybird, marked "N.D", London.

1905 *5in (12cm) long*

£300-500 **VDB**

A silver hand mirror stamped in low relief with a flower motif stamped "D & F", Birmingham 1902.

1902 *10.75in (27.5cm) long*

£150-200 **WW**

An Elkington & Co. Art Nouveau tea and coffee set, Birmingham.

1902 *Coffee pot 15.5in (39.5cm) high*

£6,000-10,000 **VDB**

A rare French silver water jug by Dufrenes, with a leaf shaped cover with thumbpiece above a body decorated with leaves and a drawn handle, stamped "Leverrier".

8in (20cm) high

£10,000-£15,000 **MACK**

A Sibyl Dunlop silver muffin dish, with maker's mark for London, dated.

1925 *7in (18cm) diam*

£1,000-2,000 **VDB**

A set of four Elkington & Co. silver candlesticks, all inscribed.

1906 *12.5in (32cm) high*

£15,000-20,000 **VDB**

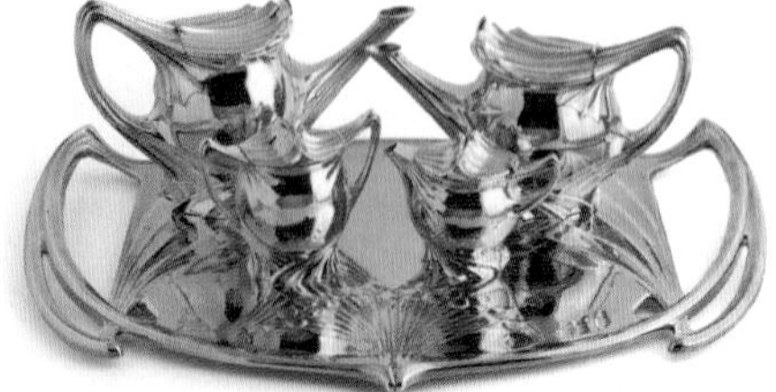

A rare Paul Follot silvered metal five piece tea and coffee service, comprising tray, coffee pot, teapot, sucrier and cream jug, each with raised arching spray band decoration, signed "Follot", Paris.

Tray 24.5in (62cm) wide

£30,000-50,000 **MACK**

A rare Eugene Feuillatre 'Azalees' silver and enamel pedestal cup and cover, bud terminal above azalea decorated cover and body, the stem with pale green enamel decoration continuing through to the pedestal foot, stamped three times, in original green leather fitted box.

1901 *Cup 9.75in (25cm) high*

£30,000-50,000 **MACK**

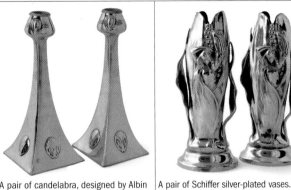

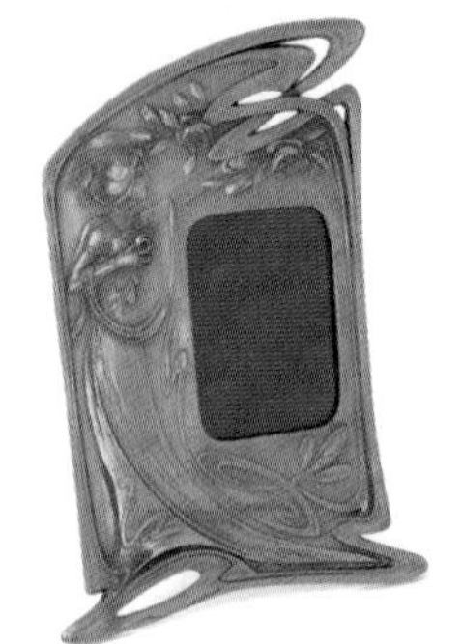

An Art Nouveau picture frame, designed by Max Heager.

c1900 *10.5in (27cm) high*

£600-800 **STY**

A silver cream jug, by I.F. & Son Ltd., of flared form with a broad curved edge forming the pouring lip, a solid, tapering handle, the whole supported on a short stem and flat circular foot, maker's mark for London 1957.

3.5in (9cm) high

£200-300 **DN**

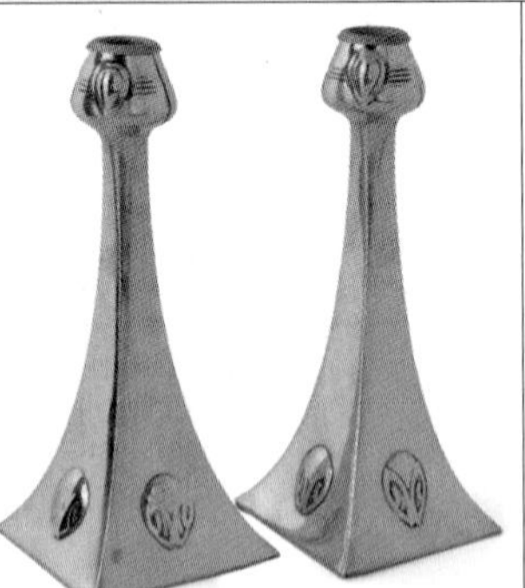

A pair of candelabra, designed by Albin Muller.

c1900 *8.75in (22cm) high*

£1,000-1,500 **STY**

A pair of Schiffer silver-plated vases.

c1910 *8.75in (22cm) high*

£500-600 **TO**

An Edwardian Art Nouveau fruit bowl, by Thomas Lawson & Son, Birmingham, oval decorated with pierced panels of stylized foliage between wave-pierced borders, on six panel feel, the D-shaped handles with stylized knots, with green glass liner.

1902 *9.5in (24cm) long*

£800-1,200 **BONS**

An Art Nouveau silver fruit bowl, with marks for Wilkens of Bremen, German.

7.5in (19cm) diam

£800-1,500 **VDB**

PEWTER

An English wall-hanging mirror with bevelled glass, its frame wrapped in sheet pewter and decorated with Ruskin pottery cabochons and stylized enamel decoration in green, blue and yellow, cracks to one cabochon.

15.5in (39.5cm) diam

£700-1,000 **DRA**

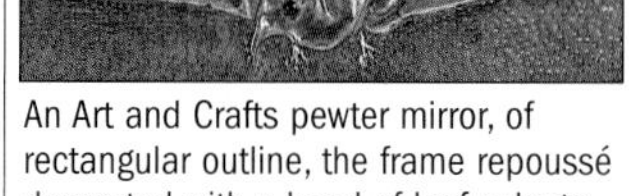

An Art and Crafts pewter mirror, of rectangular outline, the frame repoussé decorated with a band of leafy plants, with flying bird above, embellished with inset coloured cabochon stones.

17in (43cm) high

£500-800 **L&T**

An Argentor pewter dressing table mirror, of shaped rectangular form with foliate border, applied with two square jewel medallions, stamped marks.

19.75in (50cm) high

£300-600 **WW**

A Continental pewter picture frame, with easel support, cast in relief with an Art Nouveau maiden picking iris flowers, unmarked, minor damages.

17.75in (45cm) high

£1,500-2,000 **WW**

A Joseph Maria Olbrich hexagonal pewter plate, decorated with plant motifs.

c1900 *11.5in (29.2cm) wide*

£600-900 **QU**

A Joseph Maria Olbrich pewter plate, of circular form, with a wide rim decorated with roses.

c1900 *9.75in (25cm) diam*

£500-700 **QU**

A pair of Albert Reinneman, Germany, pewter candelabra.

c1900 *15.5in (39.5cm) high*

£1,200-1,500 **TO**

An 'Orion' pewter twin-light candelabrum, designed by Friedrich Adler, indistinct maker's mark to base.

8in (20cm) high

£200-250 **DN**

An Albin Muller pewter flagon, for E.Hueck, Germany.

c1900 *15.75in (40cm) high*

£1,000-1,200 **TO**

A German 'Jugendstil' ladle, by Bruckmann & Söhne, with a deep oval bowl, the slender handle with birds perched on branches, "800" standard marks and maker's mark.

7.75in (20cm) long

£150-200 **DN**

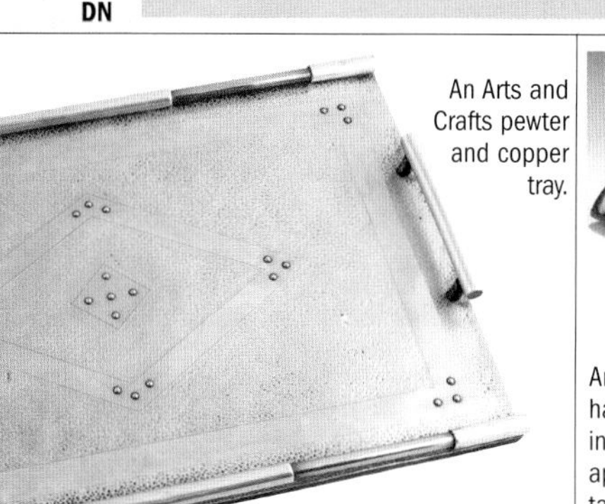

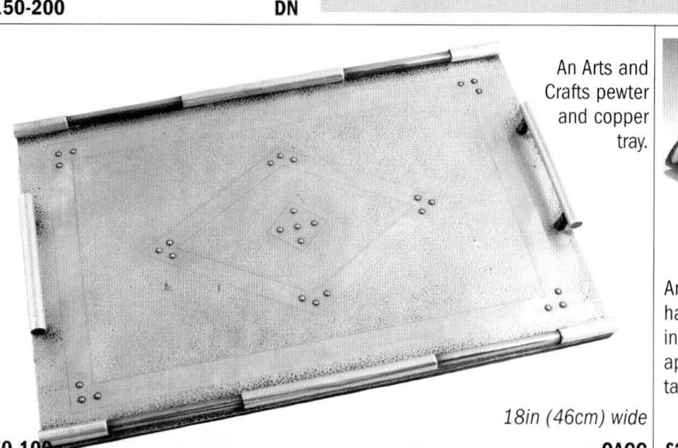

An Arts and Crafts pewter and copper tray.

18in (46cm) wide

£70-100 **OACC**

An Arts and Crafts pewter box, with hammered finish, the shaped hinged lid inset with turquoise cabochon, with applied decorative strapwork above tapered sides with rivet decoration.

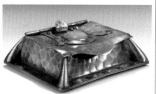

5.75in (14.5cm) wide

£280-320 **L&T**

COPPER

A Benham & Froud copper and brass kettle the design attributed to Dr Christopher Dresser, on cast iron stand with stamped mark.

33.5in (85cm) high

£280-320 **WW**

A Newton style copper wall sconce, in the manner of John Pearson, the single candle holder below a rectangular back plate repoussé decorated with entwined fish with a scalloped border.

12.5in (32cm) high

£200-300 **L&T**

A CLOSER LOOK AT A PAIR OF BENSON CANDLESTICKS

The elegant design is not as simple as more typical Benson pieces.

Copper and brass were inexpensive materials at the time so the piece was affordable to a wider market.

The sinuous shape reflects influences from both Arts and Crafts and Art Nouveau.

A pair of English Benson candlesticks, in copper and brass.

c1895 *11.75in (30cm) long*

£2,500-3,000 **STY**

A pair of Arts and Crafts copper lanterns, each of cylindrical form with tapering stepped canopies, decorated with pierced motifs.

11.5in (29cm) high

£100-200 **L&T**

An Arts and Crafts patinated copper lamp base, the simple turned column with curved handle on a tripod base, the angled supports terminating in pad feet.

13in (33cm) high

£50-80 **L&T**

An Arts and Crafts rectangular copper tray with a raised rim and embossed with four almost circular foliate panels against a stippled ground.

c1890 *22.5in (57cm) wide*

£100-150 **DN**

An Arts and Crafts oval copper tray, by Hugh Wallis of Altrincham, engraved in the centre with a flowering spray, heightened with silver patination, within a barbed panel, the upturned rim resembling ropework, stamped with "HW" in a square.

c1890 *17.25in (44cm) wide*

£150-200 **DN**

A Keswick School of Industrial Art copper tray, of rectangular galleried form repoussé, decorated with a band of flowering foliage, with stamped mark.

23.25in (59cm) wide

£200-300 **L&T**

A Keswick School of Industrial Art copper tray, of rectangular galleried form, repoussé decorated with all over foliate and floral designs, with stamped mark.

20in (51cm) wide

£200-300 **L&T**

An Arts & Crafts copper bowl by The Duchess of Sutherland Craft Guild, of lobed circular form and central repoussé decorated rosette, radiating fourteen spiral flutes with hammered finish, stamped marks.

c1860 *11.25in (28.5cm) wide*

£100-150 **L&T**

A WMF Art Nouveau copper dish, decorated with scrolls and flowers in relief, ostrich mark to base.

c1890 *7.5in (19cm) diam*

£30-50 **D**

An Arts & Crafts copper twin-handled jardinière, in the manner of John Pearson, the tapering cylindrical body repoussé decorated with opposed peacocks and arms issuing vines.

c1860 *8.25in (21cm) high*

£150-250 **L&T**

An Arts and Crafts copper plated stick stand, with ring handles, the cylindrical body repoussé decorated with stylized plant forms.

c1860 *22.5in (57cm) high*

£120-180 **L&T**

A brass and copper Arts and Crafts jug by Carl Defner.

c1900 *13.75in (35cm) high*

£300-350 **TDG**

An Edward Spencer electroplated copper box and cover, circular section, applied with a band of English roses, stamped mark 66, finial missing.

4.5in (13cm) diam

£400-600 **WW**

An embossed copper vase, possibly Belgian or Dutch, the globular vessel supported on a flared foot and embossed with stylized wheatsheaves, with stylized florets and scrolls with vertical flutes below.

7.25in (18.5cm) high

£30-50 **DN**

An Arts and Crafts copper casket, the rectangular hinged top with applied strapwork centred by a turquoise Ruskin cabochon, rounded with an applied cypher 'N', the body with applied riveted brackets to the angles.

7.5in (19cm) long

£250-300 **L&T**

An Aesthetic Movement copper and brass kettle, of domed and facetted form with alternating panels of brass and copper and with applied facetted spout, with scrolling lacquered wooden handle.

6.5in (16.5cm) high

£150-200 **L&T**

BRASS

A Scottish School Arts and Crafts brass wall mirror, of oval outline, repoussé decorated into sprays of roses and two oval Ruskin cabochons.

c1860 *3.25in (8.5cm) high*

£400-500 **L&T**

A Scottish School Arts and Crafts brass tray, of rectangular form with twin handles, repoussé decorated with fruiting cherries.

c1860 *25in (63.5cm) wide*

£150-200 **L&T**

A Scottish School Arts and Crafts brass jardinière, of oval outline with zinc liner and ring handles, repoussé decorated with a frieze of leaf tendrils bearing seed pods, raised on sphere feet.

14in (36cm) long

£100-150 **L&T**

A large Arts and Crafts brass and copper jug, possibly Masonic, the tapering cylindrical vessel with flared lip, embossed with lobes around the lower body, with an exaggerated scroll handle in copper, further decorated with beaten scrollwork attached by rivets and a plaque embossed with "Presented to Harry Lewis by The Brothers, 'Do Nothing' 365" and dated 1907.

23in (58.5cm) high

£400-500 **DN**

A Secessionist brass and copper caddy.

c1910 *3.25in (8cm) high*

£150-200 **HBK**

A Keswick School of Industrial Art brass plate, of circular form, repoussé decorated with opposed dragons, stamped marks.

8.5in (21.5cm) diam

£60-90 **L&T**

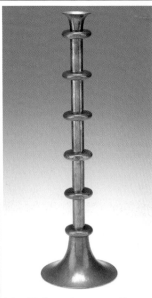

A Josef Hoffmann brass vase, with a cylindrical body on a bell-shaped base.

c1915 *13.5in (34cm) high*

£7,000-10,000 **QU**

A massive brass ewer probably manufactured by Benham & Froud to a design by Dr Christopher Dresser, unmarked.

22in (56cm) high

£4,000-5,000 **WW**

A Keswick school brass wall pocket by Mourson.

8.25in (21cm) long

£180-220 **HBK**

An Austrian rosewood and brass cased saucer dish, of circular form inlaid in brass and abalone with a dragonfly.

£80-120 **L&T**

BRONZE

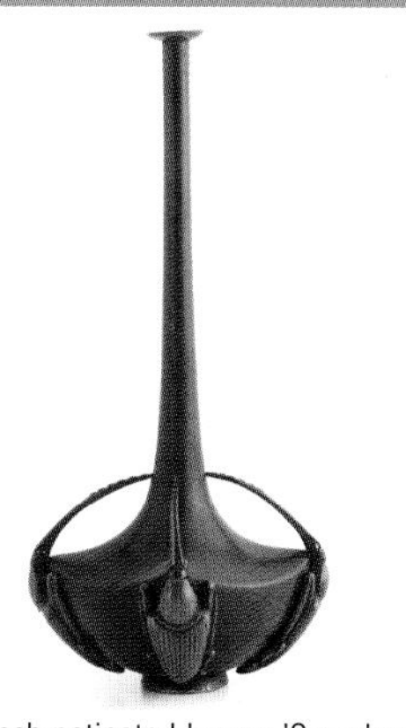

A French patinated bronze 'Scarabees' vase by Lucien Gaillard, thin tapering neck above bulbous body with applied scarabs, signed "Gaillard".

c1900 *9.5in (24cm) high*

£15,000-20,000 **MACK**

A French gilt bronze vase by Alexandre Vibert, with bulbous tapering body with relief poppy decoration, the stems forming twin handles to the sides, signed "A Vibert" and foundry mark for "Glisserei".

c1900 *9.5in (24cm) high*

£1,800-2,200 **MACK**

A French gilt bronze and enamel vase by Alexandre Vibert, with a scalloped neck above a tapering circular body, decorated all over with trailing peacock feather decoration with enamel feather 'eyes', signed.

c1900 *12.5in (32cm) high*

£6,000-9,000 **MACK**

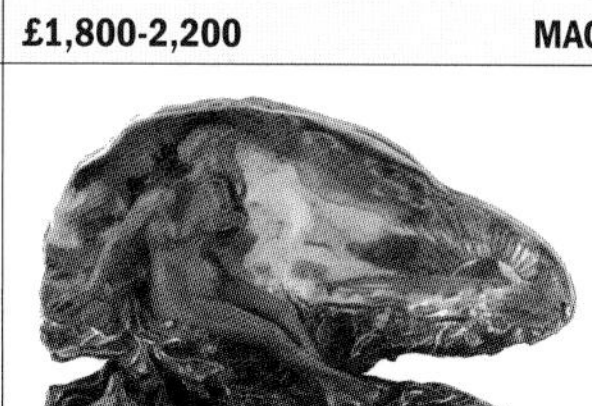

A French Art Nouveau bronze symbolist ink well, signed by Maillard with Jollet Paris Foundry mark.

c1905 *8in (20cm) wide*

£2,800-3,500 **STY**

A CLOSER LOOK AT A HECTOR GUIMARD VASE

Guimard is perhaps best known for his swirling cast iron entranceways to the Paris Metro. His distinctive style is evident in the design of this vase.

The architect's love of detail and his desire to use conventional materials in unexpected ways can be seen in the finely realized detailing.

Guimard made great use of decorative iron in his Art Nouveau buildings. A vase is a rare form.

The historical significance of the designer makes this a sought after piece and contributes to the high value.

A rare French bronze vase by Hector Guimard, attractive patina and all over whiplash decoration, unmarked.

c1900 *11in (28cm) high*

£60,000-90,000 **MACK**

Two WMF bronze vases, of ovoid form, one with inverted rim, decorated with trailing foliage on a verdigris ground, with stamped marks, the other decorated with red Autumn leaves, with stamped marks.

9in (23cm) high

£100-150 **L&T**

TIN

A Margaret Gilmour Glasgow-style tin box and cover, with tendrils and turquoise enamel, stamped monogram.

7in (17.5cm) long

£500-800 **L&T**

A Margaret Gilmour tin blotter, the angles with repoussé entwined Celtic knots, with stamped monogram.

17.75in (45cm) wide

£400-500 **L&T**

A Glasgow style tin-cased mantel clock, repoussé decorated with entwined foliate on a hammered ground.

6in (15cm) high

£300-400 **L&T**

A Scottish School Arts and Crafts tin jardinière, with ring handles, repoussé decorated fruiting vines, sphere feet.

15.5in (39cm) wide

£100-150 **L&T**

BRONZES

A French Art Nouveau bronze by Aloys.

c1900 *9in (22.5cm) high*

£700-1,000 **MW**

A French patinated gilt bronze figure, 'Nature Revealing Herself To Science', by Ernest-Louis Barrias, signed "E. Barrias Paris", with foundry mark for "Susse Freres".

9.5in (24cm) high

£8,000-12,000 **MACK**

A French gilt bronze figurine by A. Bartholome, depicting a seated woman concealing her face behind her draped clothes, signed "A. Bartholome", with foundry mark for "Siot Decauville Paris".

9.5in (24cm) high

£3,000-4,000 **MACK**

A gilt and silvered bronze group, 'Birth of Venus', depicting the goddess emerging from a sea shell, signed "Franz Bergman".

c1880 *24cm (9.5in) high*

£2,200-2,800 **RGA**

A cold-painted bronze figure by Franz Bergman, 'Snake Dancer', depicting a semi-naked dancer with snake, raised on a cream onyx plinth.

c1880 *7in (18cm) high*

£1,200-1,800 **RGA**

A Bessin Art Nouveau bronze bust.

c1905 *17.75in (45cm) high*

£1,000-1,500 **TO**

A CLOSER LOOK AT AN ART NOUVEAU FIGURAL LAMP

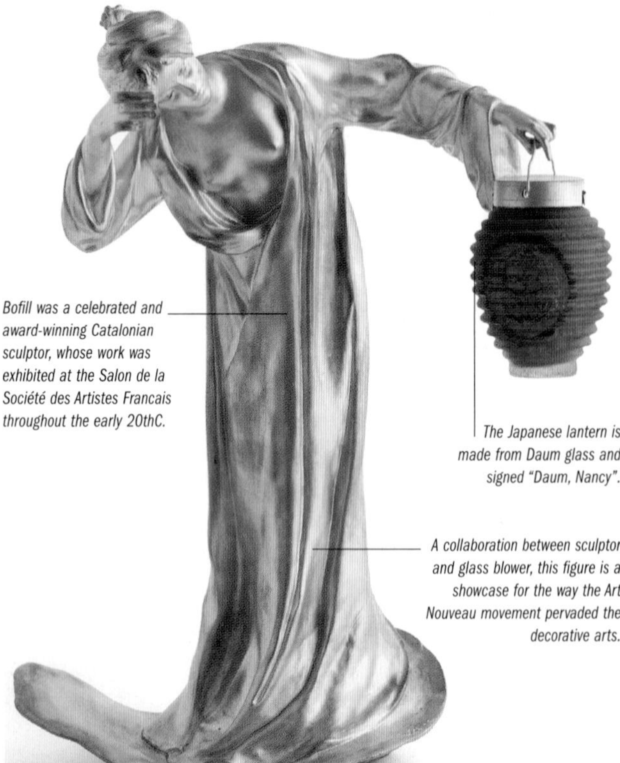

Bofill was a celebrated and award-winning Catalonian sculptor, whose work was exhibited at the Salon de la Société des Artistes Francais throughout the early 20thC.
The Japanese lantern is made from Daum glass and signed "Daum, Nancy".
A collaboration between sculptor and glass blower, this figure is a showcase for the way the Art Nouveau movement pervaded the decorative arts.

A rare French Art Nouveau gilt bronze figural lamp by Antonio Bofill, holding a red Japanese lantern, figure signed "Bofill", the lantern signed "Daum Nancy".

15in (38cm) high

£30,000-40,000 **MACK**

A French Art Nouveau gilt bronze and pewter planter by Maurice Bouval, with leaf-moulded handle and foot, with reclining nude to the side, signed.

13in (33cm) wide

£6,000-8,000 **MACK**

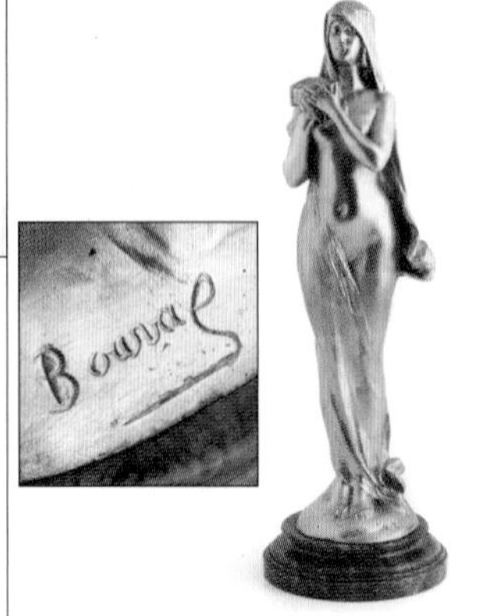

A French gilt bronze figure by Maurice Bouval, depicting a woman holding a box, standing on a stepped striated green marble base.

15in (38cm) high

£5,000-7,000 **MACK**

A French Art Nouveau gilt bronze pot and cover by Maurice Bouval, with seated nude female finial above leaf moulded body, signed, with foundry mark for "Jollet et Cie Paris".

6in (15cm) high

£6,000-8,000 **MACK**

A French Art Nouveau gilt bronze figural candlestick by Maurice Bouval, signed.

15.75in (40cm) high

£6,000-8,000 **MACK**

A German bronze female nude, the Classical parcel-gilt figure partially concealed by a drape, standing on a marble plinth.

c1925 *12.5in (32cm) high*

£600-900 **GORL**

A French gilt bronze figure by De La Grange, depicting a standing woman holding her long dress aloft, with scarab pendant, signed, with foundry mark.

15.25in (39cm) high

£10,000-12,000 **MACK**

An Austrian bronze inkstand by Gurschner, modelled as a mermaid looking at an amphora concealing a well, signed.

11.75in (30cm) wide

£4,000-6,000 **MACK**

A rare French large illuminated gilt bronze of the dancer Loie Fuller, by Raoul Larche, signed, with foundry mark for "Siot, Paris".

13in (33cm) high

£20,000-30,000 **MACK**

A French bronze figure of a female tambourine player by Agathon Leonard, attractive dark patina, signed, with foundry mark for "Susse Freres".

11in (28cm) high

£12,000-15,000 **MACK**

A large bronze Art Deco figure by Josef Lorenzl, modelled holding a clock, on an onyx base, signed "Lorenzl".

21.25in (54cm) high

£4,000-6,000 **WW**

A French bronze vase by F. Madurelli, of shaped bulbous form with relief decoration of a female face amongst scrolling waves, signed "F. Madurelli".

5.5in (14cm) high

£10,000-15,000 **MACK**

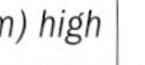

A bronze figure, 'Victory', cast from a model by Josef Lorenzl, on a stepped green onyx base, signed in the bronze "Lorenzl".

11.5in (29.5cm) high

£800-1,200 **WW**

A French gilt bronze female bust by Léopold Savine, the smiling face turned to the right with boldly modelled flowing hair, signed.

12.5in (32cm) high

£5,000-7,000 **MACK**

A French Art Nouveau gilt bronze figurine, 'Le Secret', by Pierre Fix Masseau, the hooded female figure holding a covered box, on a square pedestal base, signed, with foundry mark for "Siot Decauville Paris".

c1900 24.25in (61.5cm) high

£8,000-10,000 MACK

A bronze figure, 'Young Senorita', of a young lady in Spanish dress holding a fan, signed "Emil Meier", with foundry seal.

c1915 8in (20cm) high

£1,200-1,800 RGA

A French silvered bronze figure of a bust on a pedestal by Léopold Savine, the pedestal with relief-moulded peacock feather decoration and freestanding peacocks to the base, signed to rear "L Savine".

15.25in (39cm) high

£3,000-4,000 MACK

A bronze satyr figure by Francis Derwent Wood, modelled holding a wine sack, signed in the bronze.

Francis Derwent Wood (1871-1926) worked as an assistant to Alphonse Legros at the Slade School and was professor of sculpture at the Royal College of Art between 1918-23.

9.25in (23.5cm) high

£400-600 WW

A painted spelter figure of an Art Deco dancer, modelled standing, arms crossed, on an alabaster base, unsigned, damaged.

11in (28cm) high

£80-120 WW

BRONZE & IVORY

A silvered bronze ivory figure, in Egyptian stance, by Lorenzl.

9.5in (24cm) high

£2,000-2,500 DN

A gilt bronze and ivory figure by Lorenzl, signed.

12.5in (31.5cm) high

£1,800-2,200 DN

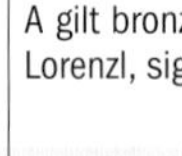

A gilt bronze and ivory figure by Lorenzl, signed.

8.75in (22cm) high

£500-700 DN

A small ivory figure after a model by Ferdinand Preiss, on a green onyx base, base incised "F Preiss".

4in (10cm) high

£1,200-1,800 WW

An over-painted Art Deco figure of a dancer, on a faceted onyx base.

14.5in (37cm) high

£200-300 L&T

A patinated bronze and ivory figure, resting against an onyx balustrade, the whole raised on an onyx stepped base, signed in the bronze.

10.5in (27cm) high

£700-1,000 L&T

GEORG JENSEN

Georg Jensen (1866-1935) is internationally known as one of the most talented silversmiths in history, but it was not until the age of 37 that he started to produce silverware. When he died 32 years later, his reputation had grown to such an extent that the New York Herald Tribune confidently named him "The greatest silversmith of the last 300 years".

Prior to founding his first silversmithy in Copenhagen in 1904, Georg Jensen became skilled in a variety of different media. His career began at the age of 14 as an apprentice to a goldsmith and, after taking lessons in art, engraving and modelling, he studied sculpture at the Danish Academy of Fine Arts. The first silver pieces to leave his studio were small decorative items, such as jewellery, hatpins and buckles, usually in organic shapes inspired by the Arts and Crafts and Art Nouveau movements. As the business grew more successful, coffee pots, cups, flatware and other larger items were made in ingenious and innovative designs, sometimes incorporating semi-precious stones and other materials, or decorated with distinctive oxidized satiny surfaces. His work remains popular and a number of his designs are still made by the Jensen company today.

A Georg Jensen bracelet, designed by Georg Jensen, design no. 14.

c1910 *7.5in (19cm) long*

£1,000-1,500 **SF**

A Georg Jensen bracelet, designed by Georg Jensen, design no. 3.

c1910 *7.5in (19cm) long*

£800-1,200 **SF**

A Georg Jensen bracelet, designed by Georg Jensen, design no. 15.

c1915 *7.5in (19cm) long*

£800-1,200 **SF**

A Georg Jensen bracelet, designed by Georg Jensen, design no. 23.

c1915 *7.5in (19cm) long*

£1,000-1,500 **SF**

A Georg Jensen bracelet, designed by Ibe Dahlquist, design no. 65.

c1930 *7.5in (19cm) long*

£1,500-2,000 **SF**

A Georg Jensen bracelet, designed by Harald Nielsen, design no. 86.

c1940 *7.5in (19cm) long*

£800-1,200 **SF**

A Georg Jensen bracelet, designed by Sigvard Bernadotte, design no. 74.

c1940 *7.5in (19cm) long*

£1,200-1,800 **SF**

A Georg Jensen bracelet, designed by Astrid Fog, design no. 169.

c1960 *7.5in (19cm) long*

£2,000-2,500 **SF**

A Georg Jensen necklace, designed by Georg Jensen, design no. 15.

c1910 *16in (41cm) long*

£800-1,200 **SF**

A Georg Jensen brooch, design no. 204.

c1910 *1.5in (4cm) long*

£300-500 **SF**

A Georg Jensen brooch, design no. 236B.

c1910 *1.5in (4cm) long*

£500-700 **SF**

A Georg Jensen brooch, design no. 100A.

c1915 *1.5in (3.5cm) long*

£400-600 **SF**

A Georg Jensen brooch, design no. 71.

c1915 *1.25in (3.5cm) long*

£400-600 **SF**

A Georg Jensen brooch, design no. 123.

c1915 *1.75in (4.5cm) long*

£200-250 **SF**

A Georg Jensen brooch, design no. 187.

c1915 *1.5in (4cm) wide*

£400-600 **SF**

A Georg Jensen brooch, designed by Hugo Liisberg, design no. 297.

c1915 *2.25in (5.5cm) long*

£300-350 **SF**

A pair of Georg Jensen cuff links, design no. 25B.

c1910 *0.75in (2cm) diam*

£200-250 **SF**

A pair of Georg Jensen earrings, design no. 101.

c1920 *0.75in (2cm) wide*

£300-500 **SF**

A CLOSER LOOK AT A PAIR OF GEORG JENSEN EARRINGS

Georg Jensen is a byword for high quality silver, from which these earrings are fashioned. Jensen was joined by some of the best designers and silversmiths.

These stones are cut from the mineral amazonite. In keeping with the ideals of the Arts and Crafts movement, Jensen favoured the use of semi-precious stones and minerals such as amber, opal and moonstone.

The bird motif is an iconic Georg Jensen design attributed to Mohl-Hansen. It appears on a wide range of Jensen products.

Despite the widespread use of bird designs on pieces such as brooches and bracelets, it is more unusual to see the motif on earrings, making them valuable.

A pair of Georg Jensen earrings, design no. 66.

c1915 *1in (2.5cm) long*

£800-1,200 **SF**

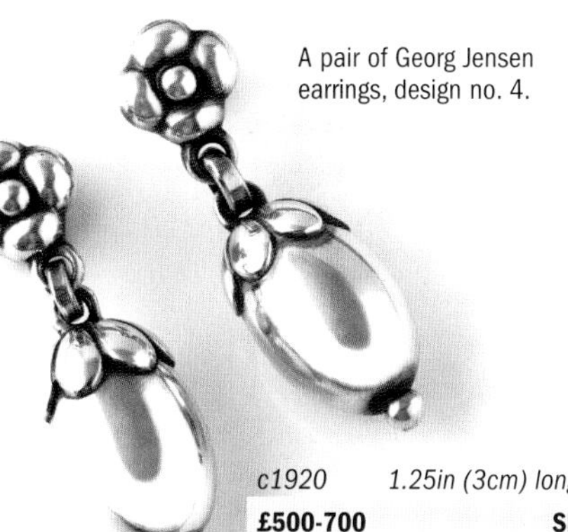

A pair of Georg Jensen earrings, design no. 4.

c1920 *1.25in (3cm) long*

£500-700 **SF**

A pair of Georg Jensen cuff links, design no. 10.

1in (2.5cm) long

£300-350 **SF**

A pair of Georg Jensen cuff links, designed by Henry Pilstrup, design no. 59D.

0.75in (2cm) wide

£200-250 **SF**

LIBERTY & CO.

Arthur Lazenby Liberty opened his store on Regent Street, London, in 1875 to sell high quality and affordable homewares and accessories from the Far East. It soon became one of the most fashionable places to shop in London and, by the 1890s, was renowned for its fine Arts and Crafts and Art Nouveau wares.

When demand outstripped supply, Liberty began to commission pieces from innovative British designers. As well as furniture, fabrics and ornaments, the Liberty range of jewellery was very popular in the early part of the 20thC. Pieces were typically of flowing metal designs, handcrafted in appearance and decorated with peacock blue and green stones or enamel. Archibold Knox, a leading figure in the Arts and Crafts Celtic revival movement, and the talented designer Jessie King, produced exceptional jewellery for the company, along with other currently sought-after makers, such as Oliver Baker and W. H. Haseler. The store is still thriving on Regent Street today.

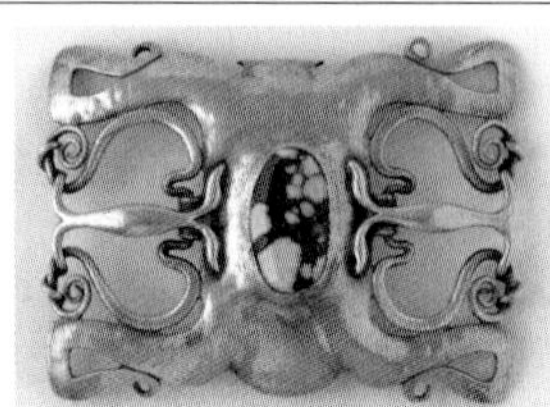

A Liberty & Co. silver buckle set with turquoise, attributed to Oliver Baker, Birmingham.

c1900 *2.75in (7cm) wide*

£800-1,200 **VDB**

A Liberty & Co. silver, gold and enamel brooch.

c1900 *1in (2.5cm) long*

£300-400 **VDB**

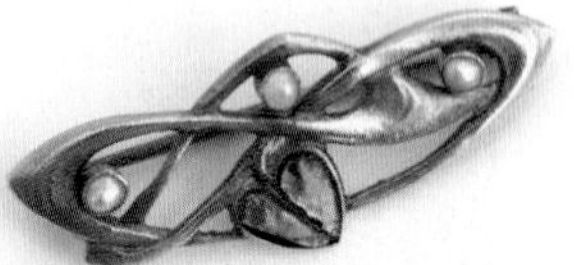

A Liberty & Co. 9ct gold brooch, with enamel and pearl, designed by Archibald Knox.

c1905 *1.25in (3.5cm) long*

£600-800 **RG**

A Liberty & Co. gold pendant, set turquoise stone and turquoise drop.

c1900 *2.25in (6cm) long*

£1,000-1,500 **VDB**

A Liberty & Co. silver buckle, with blue and green enamel, Birmingham.

1911 *3in (7.5cm) wide*

£800-1,200 **VDB**

A Liberty & Co. pendant with a central winter landscape by Charles Fleetwood Varley, surrounded by enamelled leaves, designed by Jessie King.

c1910 *18in (46cm) long*

£1,000-2,000 **VDB**

A Liberty & Co. silver pendant, with turquoise and pearl, unmarked.

c1910 *1.75in (4.5cm) long*

£300-350 **RG**

A CLOSER LOOK AT A LIBERTY & CO. NECKLACE

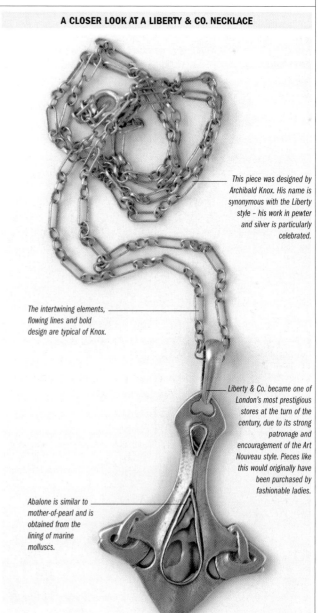

This piece was designed by Archibald Knox. His name is synonymous with the Liberty style - his work in pewter and silver is particularly celebrated.

The intertwining elements, flowing lines and bold design are typical of Knox.

Liberty & Co. became one of London's most prestigious stores at the turn of the century, due to its strong patronage and encouragement of the Art Nouveau style. Pieces like this would originally have been purchased by fashionable ladies.

Abalone is similar to mother-of-pearl and is obtained from the lining of marine molluscs.

A W.H. Haseler for Liberty & Co. silver pendant set with abalone, design attributed to Archibald Knox.

c1900 *Pendant 2in (5cm) long*

£1,200-1,500 **VDB**

MURRLE BENNETT & CO.

A Murrle Bennett & Co. 950 silver brooch, set with three opals with two opal drops.

c1900 *1.5in (3.5cm) long*

£300-400 **VDB**

A Murrle Bennett & Co. 950 silver brooch with blue enamel and a fresh water pearl drop.

c1900 *1.5in (3.5cm) long*

£1,000-1,500 **VDB**

A Murrle Bennett & Co. 950 silver brooch, set with a matrix stone and with a fresh water pearl drop.

c1900 *1.25in (3cm) diam*

£500-800 **VDB**

A Murrle Bennett & Co. Art Nouveau pin of goldwashed sterling silver with a central mottled green and brown semi-precious stone cabochon.

c1905 *1.75in (4.5cm) wide*

£250-300 **LYNH**

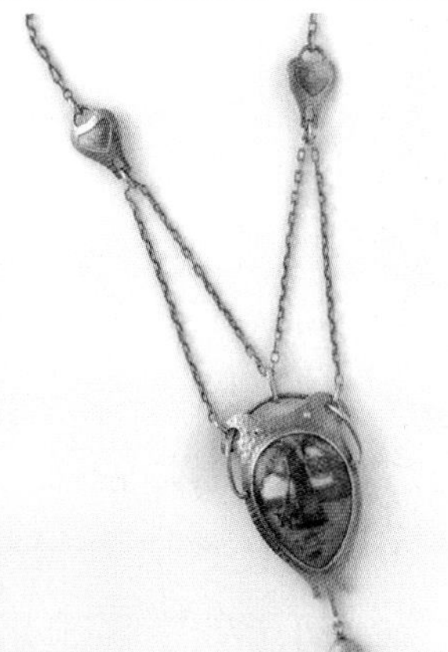

A Murrle Bennett & Co. necklace, set with blue enamel, with a plaque of a galleon, two enamelled spacers and a pearl drop.

c1900 *18.5in (47cm) long*

£1,200-1,500 **VDB**

A Murrle Bennett & Co. 15ct turquoise set pendant with three fresh water pearl drops.

c1900 *1.5in (4cm) long*

£1,200-1,500 **VDB**

A Murrle Bennett & Co. gold Jugendstil pendant, with turquoise and gold spacers.

c1900 *1.75in (4.5cm) long*

£1,000-2,000 **VDB**

A Murrle Bennett & Co. peridot set necklace, marks for 15ct gold.

c1900 *16.5in (42cm) long*

£2,000-3,000 **VDB**

A Murrle Bennett & Co. 950 silver and blue enamel necklace with two enamelled spaces and drop.

c1900 *Chain 17.75in (45cm) long*

£600-900 **VDB**

A Murrle Bennett & Co. 950 silver necklace, set with turquoise, with a turquoise drop and two silver spaces.

c1900 *16in (41cm) long*

£600-900 **VDB**

A Murrle Bennett & Co. 950 silver pendant, set with three amethysts.

c1900 *Chain 16.25in (41cm) long*

£400-700 **VDB**

A Murrle Bennett pendant, in silver gilt with mother of pearl and pearl, marked "MB Co 950".

c1905 *1.5in (4cm) long*

£450-500 **RG**

ARTS & CRAFTS

A James Fenton silver pendant, with blue and green enamel, with hallmarks for 1908.

2in (5cm) long

£250-300 **RG**

A James Fenton silver pendant, with purple and green enamel, with hallmarks for 1909.

1.5in (4cm) long

£350-400 **RG**

A James Fenton silver pendant, with yellow-green and blue enamel, marked "JF", with Birmingham hallmarks for 1909.

1.25in (3.5cm) long

£200-250 **RG**

A James Fenton silver bracelet, with blue and green enamel, marked "JF" with indistinguishable rubbed Birmingham hallmarks.

8in (20cm) long

£180-220 **RG**

A CLOSER LOOK AT AN ARTS AND CRAFTS NECKLACE

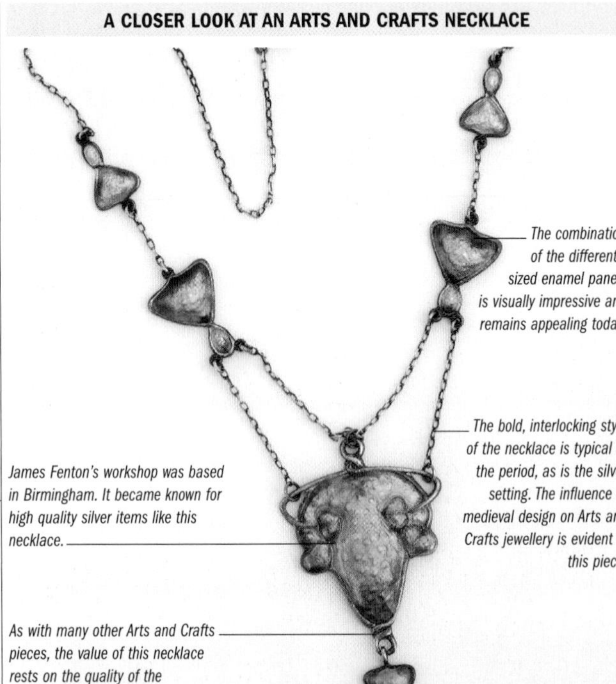
The combination of the differently sized enamel panels is visually impressive and remains appealing today.
The bold, interlocking style of the necklace is typical of the period, as is the silver setting. The influence of medieval design on Arts and Crafts jewellery is evident in this piece.
James Fenton's workshop was based in Birmingham. It became known for high quality silver items like this necklace.
As with many other Arts and Crafts pieces, the value of this necklace rests on the quality of the craftsmanship, rather than the use of expensive precious materials.

A James Fenton silver necklace, with blue and green enamel, hallmarks for 1909.

Pendant 2.25in (5.5cm) long

£450-500 **RG**

A 'mistletoe' gold, enamel and pearl necklace, by Mrs Newman.

c1890 *19in (48cm) long*

£6,000-7,000 **VDB**

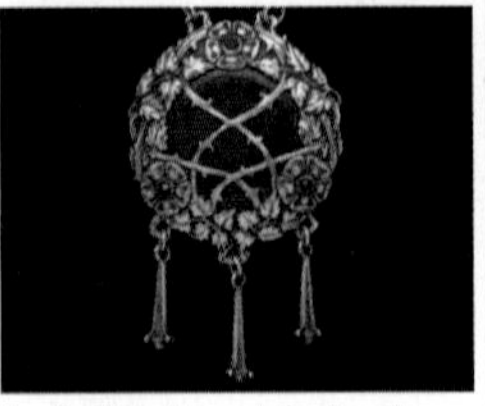

An English Art and Crafts silver and enamel pendant, by Omar Ramsden.

c1930 *1.5in (4cm) long*

£1,500-2,500 **VDB**

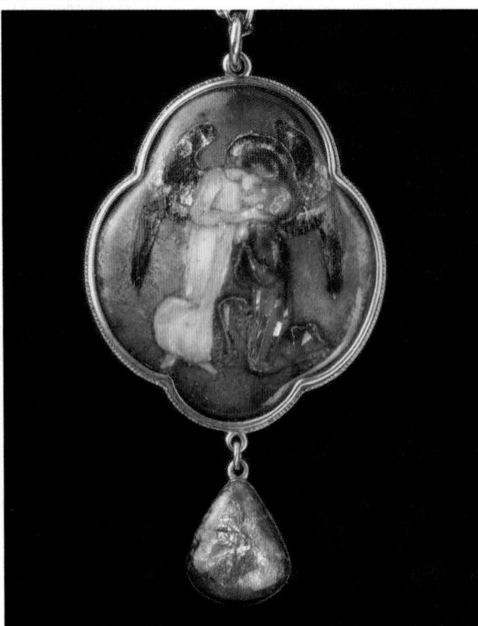

A pendant by Phoebe A. Traquair.

1906 *1.5in (4cm) long*

£7,000-10,000 **VDB**

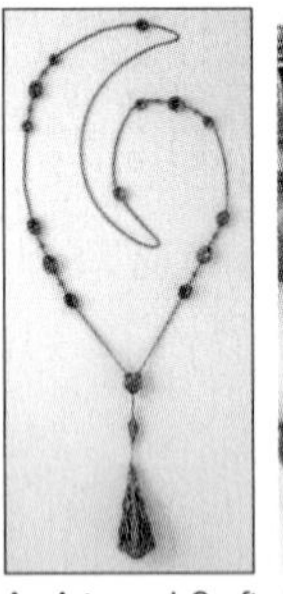

An Arts and Crafts long silver necklace, set with amethysts.

c1910 *Pendant 1.75in (4.5cm) long*

£2,000-3,000 **VDB**

A Danish Skonvirke Arts and Crafts brooch, by Kay Bojesen.

c1910 *4in (10cm) long*

£1,500-2,500 **VDB**

A pair of earrings, by Sibyl Dunlop.

c1930 *1.25in (3.5cm) long*

£3,000-4,000 **VDB**

ART NOUVEAU

A pair of English silver and coral cufflinks, marked "FW & Co".

c1910 *0.75in (2cm) diam*

£50-70 **RG**

An Edmond-Henri Becker gold pendant, depicting a lady with flowers, with a small pearl and gold chain and a pearl drop.

c1900 *Chain 14in (38cm) long*

£400-600 **VDB**

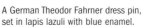

A German Theodor Fahrner dress pin, set in lapis lazuli with blue enamel.

c1900 *3.25in (8cm) long*

£1,000-2,000 **VDB**

A Danish William Fuglede silver brooch, set with amber, with three drops each set with enamel.

c1910 *3.25in (8cm) long*

£600-900 **VDB**

A Bertha L. Goff silver and green enamel necklace, the central plaque depicting "Leda And The Swan".

This necklace was one of the items submitted to a national competition by Bertha L. Goff of Holloway School of Art, for which she was awarded a silver medal.

1902 *Pendant 2.75in (7cm) long*

£2,500-3,500 **VDB**

A Gorham & Co. sterling silver belt buckle, with a Native American motif, with selected gold plating and a marbled turquoise cabochon.

c1900 *2in (5cm) high*

£300-350 **PC**

A Norwegian Marius Hammer brooch, with a carnelian setting and silver drops.

c1915 *3in (7.5cm) wide*

£600-900 **VDB**

A rare French Art Nouveau 18ct gold, enamel and briolette cut citrine pendant, attributed to Lucien Hirtz, with a triangular enamel panel decorated with a profile of young girl amidst flowers, within a 75ct diamond-set frame, the gold leaf border with suspended trailing leaves and citrines, with an enamelled necklace.

4.75in (12cm) high

£20,000-30,000 **MACK**

A very rare George Hunt silver and enamel brooch, English.

1928 *1.5in (4cm) long*

£300-400 **VDB**

A Liberty & Co. gold pendant, set with turquoise, with a turquoise drop.

c1900 *2.25in (6cm) long*

£1,300-1,500 **VDB**

A George Hunt enamelled brooch, depicting a lady, signed and dated.

1932 *2.75in (7cm) long*

£1,200-1,500 **VDB**

A George Hunt brooch, with an enamel centre depicting George and the dragon, signed and dated.

1937 *2.75in (7cm) wide*

£1,000-1,500 **VDB**

A Kerr & Co. Art Nouveau floral motif pin, in gold wash over sterling silver, with three faux moonstone cabochons.

c1900 *2.5in (6.25cm) wide*

£200-300 **PC**

A Kerr & Co. Art Nouveau double peacock motif belt buckle, in gold wash over sterling silver, set with ruby glass cabochons.

c1900 *3.5in (9cm) wide*

£300-400 **PC**

A La Pierre Art Nouveau sterling silver bangle, with stylized, elongated plant motifs around the perimeter.

c1900 *3in (7.5cm) diam*

£80-120 **PC**

A French 18ct gold and enamel pendant, by Leo Laporte-Blairsy, with a drop amethyst above an ivory carved head, within flower heads with seed pearl centres and rose cut diamond sprays, signed to back.

3in (7.5cm) high

£15,000-20,000 **MACK**

A Heinrich Levinger blue plique-à-jour enamel brooch, set with an opal stone.

c1900 *1.5in (4cm) long*

£1,000-2,000 **VDB**

A William Mark brooch, enamelled with a peacock eye motif.

c1910 *1in (2.5cm) long*

£400-600 **VDB**

A Meyle and Mayer mirror and locket, with a blue plique-à-jour enamel behind a Mucha style lady's drop.

c1900 *2in (5cm) long*

£1,000-2,000 **VDB**

A George Pierre carved horn butterfly pendant, with amber beads and gold foiled glass, on a silk cord, signed "GIP", repairs to back.

c1900 *Pendant 3in (8cm) long*

£250-300 **RG**

A Meyle & Mayer plique-à-jour brooch, depicting an Art Nouveau lady, with maker's mark.

c1900 *1.25in (3cm) long*

£1,000-2,000 **VDB**

A Danish Bernard Hertz Skonvirke brooch, with a set carnelian and a carnelian drop.

3in (7.5cm) long

£400-600 **VDB**

A Danish Skonvirke silver brooch, probably by Ferdinand Svinth, with a centrally set carnelian.

c1910 *2in (5cm) diam*

£300-400 **VDB**

A Skonvirke Evald Nielson silver brooch with dove amongst leaves, set with garnets, Denmark.

1930 *2in (5cm) long*

£250-350 **VDB**

An American brooch by Unger Bros., depicting a lady.

c1900 *3in (7.5cm) long*

£400-600 **VDB**

An Unger Bros brooch, depicting a lady.

c1900 *2in (5cm) long*

£350-550 **VDB**

An Unger Bros 'He Loves Me, He Loves Me Not' silver mirror, with maker's mark.

c1900 *8in (20cm) long*

£1,000-1,500 **VDB**

An Unger Bros. belt pin, with an Art Nouveau motif of a girl with sinuous, flowing hair, in sterling silver with a selected matt or 'French' finish gold plating.

1905 *1.75in (4.5cm) diam*

£400-600 **PC**

A CLOSER LOOK AT AN ART NOUVEAU BROOCH

Otto Prutscher was a Viennese architect who also designed products for companies including Wiener Werkstätte.

This brooch has an organic form reminiscent of a scarab, a popular Egyptian motif that was resurrected in the Art Nouveau period.

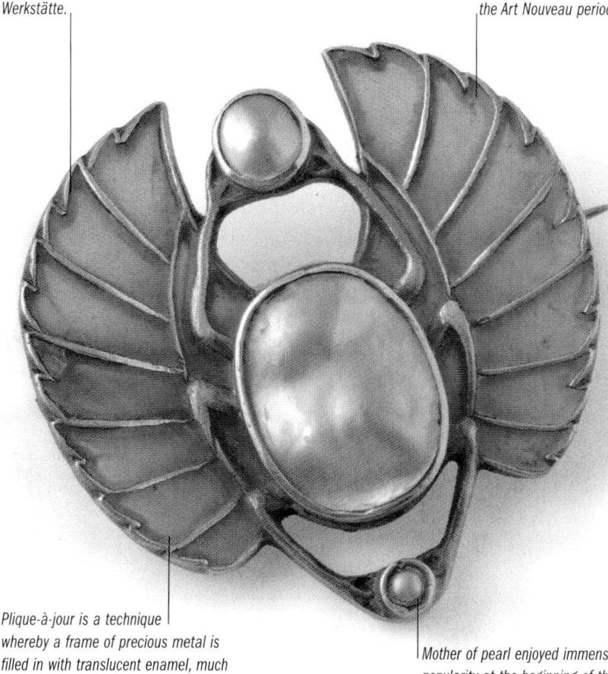

Plique-à-jour is a technique whereby a frame of precious metal is filled in with translucent enamel, much like a stained glass window.

Mother of pearl enjoyed immense popularity at the beginning of the 20thC.

An Otto Prutscher for Heinrich Levinger silver and plique-à-jour brooch, set with mother of pearl.

c1900 *1.25in (3cm) long*

£1,500-2,500 **VDB**

An English silver pendant, with enamel, mother of pearl and red paste.

c1905 *2in (5cm) long*

£180-220 **RG**

An English silver butterfly pendant, with enamel and opal, unmarked.

c1905 *1.5in (4cm) long*

£350-400 **RG**

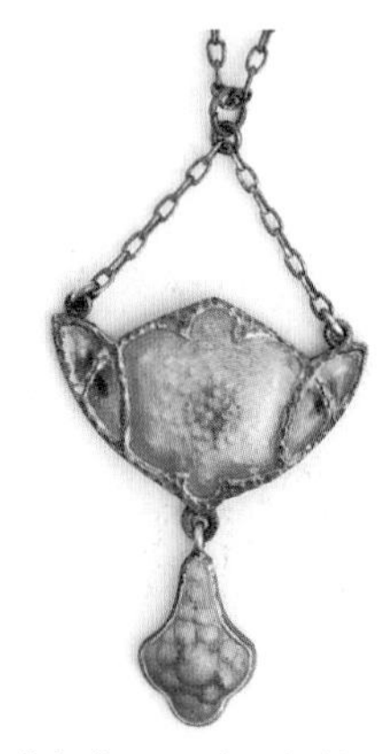

An English silver pendant, in blue and green, marked Sterling silver.

c1910 *2in (5cm) long*

£80-95 **RG**

A German Jugendstil silver and green onyx pendant.

c1905 *1.5in (3.5cm) long*

£100-120 **RG**

A Jugendstil silver chrysoprase and mother of pearl pendant, marked "800" and with an indistinguishable maker's mark.

c1905 *2.5in (6cm) long*

£180-220 **RG**

A German Jugendstil pendant, silver, rose quartz and pearl, unmarked.

c1905 *Pendant 2.5in (6cm) long*

£350-400 **RG**

A French Art Nouveau 18ct gold pendant, with blue plique-à-jour, rose cut diamond and seed pearl, showing a woman's head in profile looking at a small floral spray, on a green ground, with a seed pearl drop below.

1.5in (4cm) long

£2,500-3,000 **MACK**

An English silver necklace and brooch, by Bernard Instone, marked "Silver" and "BI".

c1920 *Necklace 16in (40cm) long*

£250-300 **RG**

An English silver bracelet, with a blue enamel curved design, marked "Sterling Silver".

c1910 *8in (20cm) long*

£120-150 **RG**

A 15ct gold Continental dragon pendant, with pearl drops, unmarked.

c1890 *Pendant 2in (4.5cm) long*

£300-350 **RG**

A French Art Nouveau 18ct gold brooch, with blue plique-à-jour enamel, depicting a laughing woman with a rose cut diamond mounted necklace, within a tree and foliage decorated frame.

1.25in (3cm) wide

£2,500-3,000 **MACK**

An Art Nouveau dragonfly pin with turquoise cabochons, enamelling and diamanté.

c1900 *2.75in (7cm) wide*

£250-450 **LYNH**

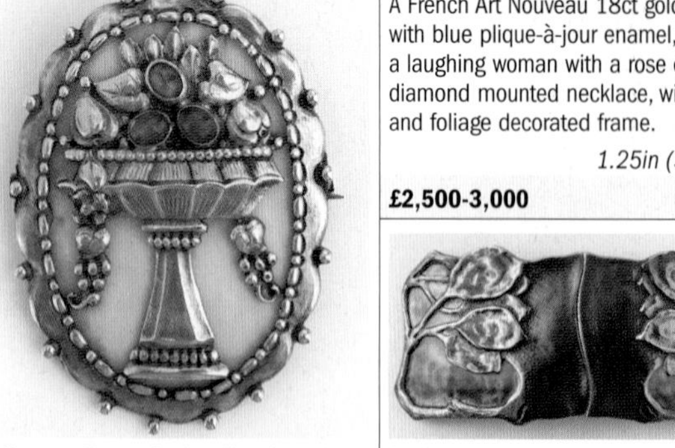

A German Secessionist silver brooch, with ivory and sapphires, unmarked.

c1910 *2in (5cm) long*

£350-400 **RG**

An Art Nouveau silver belt buckle, with foliate motifs and turquoise enamelling.

c1900 *3.25in (8.25cm) wide*

£300-500 **LYNH**

A Jugendstil silver and plique-à-jour brooch, set with stained agate and fresh water pearl, unmarked.

c1900 *1.25in (3cm) diam*

£700-1,000 **VDB**

ART DECO

A DRGM Art Deco bracelet with a safety chain, in Rhodium-plated alloy, set with clear crystal rhinestones.

c1925 *7in (18cm) circ*

£60-100 **MARA**

A DRGM bracelet with Art Deco geometric forms in Rhodium-plated alloy, set with clear crystal rhinestones.

c1925 *7in (18cm) circ*

£60-100 **MARA**

An American Art Deco sterling silver bracelet with engraved floral motifs.

c1925 *7.5in (19cm) long.*

£150-250 **JJ**

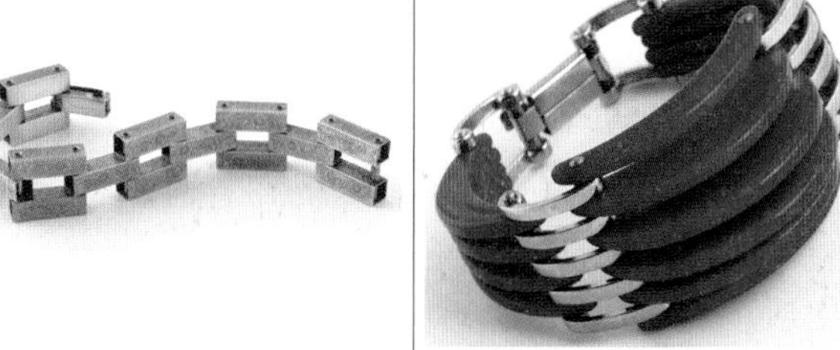

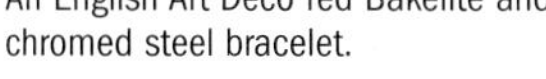

An English Art Deco red Bakelite and chromed steel bracelet.

c1925 *7.5in (19cm) circ*

£120-130 **RITZ**

An Art Deco African mask pin of black and red Bakelite with chromed steel eyebrows and mouth, unsigned.

c1925 *2.5in (6.5cm) long*

£160-190 **RITZ**

An English Art Deco necklace with a silver chain and a yellow and black Bakelite pendant.

c1925 *Pendant 2in (5cm) wide*

£140-160 **RITZ**

An English Art Deco necklace with triangular and shield-shaped sapphire blue faceted glass stones.

c1925 *15.5in (40cm) long*

£60-100 **ECLEC**

An English Art Deco necklace with geometric forms, in alternating silver, green and black Bakelite.

c1925 *14.75in (38cm) long*

£140-160 **RITZ**

A pair of Art Deco diamond set earrings.

1.5in (4cm) long

£6,000-7,000 **JHB**

A CLOSER LOOK AT AN ART DECO RING

Art Deco rings are often large and chunky with a clean and linear design.

Platinum was often used during this period because its strength allowed the settings to be pared down but still be secure enough to hold the diamonds.

The main diamond in this ring is 4.60 carats, of SI1 clarity and L colour. These classifications suggest the stone is large, light, but with a tint and has slight inclusions that would be clear to the naked eye. The other diamonds are estimated at 1.75 carats.

This is a baguette-cut diamond, rectangular in shape with step-like facets.

An Art Deco platinum ring, set with a baguette-cut diamond, with baguette diamonds to shoulders.

£28,000-32,000 **JHB**

AESTHETIC MOVEMENT

An Aesthetic Movement ebonised and gilt embellished armchair, the upholstered panel back enclosed by inlaid gilt embellished frame and surmounted by a spindle gallery with central rosette decoration, the padded arm with spindle-filled gallery above a stuffover seat on turned and blocked legs, linked by stretchers and terminating in brass caps and casters.

36in (91.5cm) high

£1,800-2,200 **L&T**

An Aesthetic Movement rocking chair, with lion's heads and floral leather decoration.

c1880 *35.5in (90cm) high*

£800-1,200 **TDG**

An Aesthetic Movement oak armchair, in the style of E.W. Godwin, the reeded top rail above curved spindle back and open arms linked to a baluster-turned upright, the ebonised leather upholstered panel seat above reeded rail and turned legs, linked by stretchers terminating in pot casters.

32in (81.5cm) high

£180-220 **L&T**

An Aesthetic Movement ebonised beech corner chair and side chair, in the manner of E.W. Godwin, the arms with ring-turned supports, and the rush seat on ring-turned legs linked by stretchers.

Largest 35in (89cm) high

£80-120 **L&T**

An Anglo-Japanese Aesthetic Movement mahogany writing cabinet by Gillows, the moulded top with pierced silvered gallery above central door with decorative drop handle, the central lacquer and ivory panel inlaid with the figure of a warrior, the three small drawers above a slide-out writing surface inlaid with tooled leather above a single drawer, inlaid with a panel of flowering branches, the drawer stamped "Gillow and Co. 1668" and with maker's label.

Gillow and Co. were an extremely successful firm of Lancaster cabinet makers. Their designs were popular with the provincial middle classes and they developed new types of furniture, such as the Davenport. They merged with S. J. Waring and Sons in 1900.

51.5in (131cm) high

£3,000-4000 **L&T**

An Aesthetic Movement ebonised mahogany Davenport desk, with gilt embellishments, carved in bas relief with flowering plant motifs, the hinged top similarly carved and supported by curved brackets, the sides opposed with four real and four false drawers, raised on a sledge base.

38in (95cm) high

£400-600 **L&T**

An Aesthetic Movement walnut side cabinet, manufactured by Frances and James Smith of Glasgow in the manner of Daniel Cottier, the reverse breakfront galleried cornice with flower-incised uprights, painted with flowering plants, with maker's label.

72in (183cm) long

£1,200-1,800 **L&T**

An Aesthetic Movement clock.

32in (81cm) high

£400-600 **TDG**

GOTHIC REVIVAL

One of a pair of Gothic Reform hall chairs, possibly by Bruce Talbert.

c1850 *36.5in (96cm) high*

£3,000-4,000 pair **TDG**

A Gothic Revival child's chair.

c1880 *44.5in (113cm) high*

£600-800 **TDG**

Two of a set of six Gothic Revival dining chairs, in pitch pine with King and Queen carvers.

c1880 *55.5in (141cm) high*

£2,000-3,000 set **TDG**

A set of eight 19thC Gothic Revival oak dining chairs, each with pierced and arched backs, carved in bas relief with foliate rosettes, the button-upholstered seats raised on turned and faceted legs terminating in brass caps and casters, stamped "Cope and Collinson Patent"

32in (81.5cm) high

£1,200-1,800 set **L&T**

A 19thC oak Gothic Revival cabinet, the rectangular top above trefoil-pierced frieze and two panelled doors with decorative iron hinges and lancet arched panels, enclosed by an arrangement of four open shelves and twelve short drawers, the whole raised on a plinth.

58.25in (148cm) long

£800-1,200 **L&T**

A CLOSER LOOK AT A GOTHIC REVIVAL TABLE

Centre tables were primarily ornamental and designed to be seen from all sides as the focal point of a room, so the tops were elaborately decorated.

This heavy piece, in rich walnut, is typical of the Gothic Revival period in the mid-19thC, which saw a return to heavy, highly decorated furniture with architectural details.

The large surface area of the tabletop allows the fine marquetry to be displayed without interruption.

The tilt-top design meant the table could be stored against a wall when not required, whilst still displaying its elaborate decoration.

A mid-19thC Gothic Reform marquetry-inlaid walnut centre table, the octagonal tilt top with burr panel and elaborate marquetry and specimen wood decoration, on triangular pedestal with carved and turned columns and strapwork decoration, on corresponding tripod base with moulded cabriole legs and scroll toes with casters.

27.5in (70cm) high

£4,000-6,000 **L&T**

A 19thC carved walnut Gothic side cabinet, the moulded cornice above a pair of panelled doors with applied lancet tracery and rosettes, enclosing a shelved interior on a plinth.

47in (120cm) long

£800-1,200 **L&T**

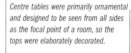

A late 19thC Gothic Revival mahogany four-tier corner shelf, with fretwork borders and sides, the finial missing.

41.5in (105.5cm) high

£700-900 **DN**

ARTS & CRAFTS

A fine and early Josef Hoffmann bentwood side chair, with bentwood back and tapering legs, four spheres under seat rail, and tacked-on brown leather upholstery to seat and back, unmarked.

38.75in (98.5cm) high

£1,000-1,500 **DRA**

A Scott Baillie large stained beech open armchair, the ladder back with downscrolled arms and bulbous octagonal supports, board seat and square section tapering legs joined by stretchers, bearing engraved brass plaque.

By long repute, this chair was used by Nicol Jarvie in his local tavern, the Clachlan Inn in Aberfoyle. Jarvie was one of Rob Roy MacGregor's closest friends and was of legendary size.

40in (100.5cm) high

£7,000-10,000 **L&T**

A Liberty and Co. mahogany 'Thebes' stool, on tripod legs with dished seat and applied Liberty label.

13in (33cm) high

£300-400 **WW**

One of a pair of beech and walnut armchairs, probably retailed by Liberty and Co., unmarked.

44.5in (113cm) high

£800-1,200 pair **WW**

A Liberty and Co. mahogany 'Thebes' stool, the rectangular slatted concave seat raised on square section legs linked by stretchers and further supported by slatted sides, bears lozenge-shaped label for Liberty.

14.5in (36.5cm) wide

£2,500-3,000 **L&T**

A stained wood 'Thebes' stool, probably retailed by Liberty and Co., with a square seat on four turned wooden legs.

17in (43cm) wide

£400-600 **WW**

A Liberty and Co. oak wing armchair, the three-quarter scroll-over upholstered top rail above ring-turned and blocked spandrels and upholstered panel, the upholstered panel seat enclosed by open arms with horizontal spandrels, raised on turned and blocked legs united by stretchers.

43in (109cm) high

£300-400 **L&T**

A pair of ebonised elm 'Suffolk' chairs by Morris and Co., each with backs comprising spindle-filled galleries and horizontal rails, the open arms with corresponding rails above rush seat.

£600-900 **L&T**

A Morris and Co. woven wool squab cushion, of rectangular form, double-sided with the 'Peacock and Dragon' pattern and raised on associated stained pine window seat.

68in (170cm) long

£300-500 **L&T**

A James Shoolbred oak chair, one of a set of six.

c1900 *43in (109cm) high*

£2,200-2,800 set **TDG**

A pair of Wylie and Lochhead oak side chairs, designed by E. A. Taylor, with, heart-shaped pierced top rails and rush seats, raised on square tapered legs united by stretchers.

43.5in (110.5cm) high

£220-280 **L&T**

A pair of Arts and Crafts tall-back chairs, each with cube-topped posts and cross-spindled back, brown leather upholstery to the seat, armrests and headrest decorated with winged griffin, some tears to the leather, unmarked.

57.5in (146cm) high

£600-900 **DRA**

A CLOSER LOOK AT AN ARTS AND CRAFTS CHAISE LONGUE

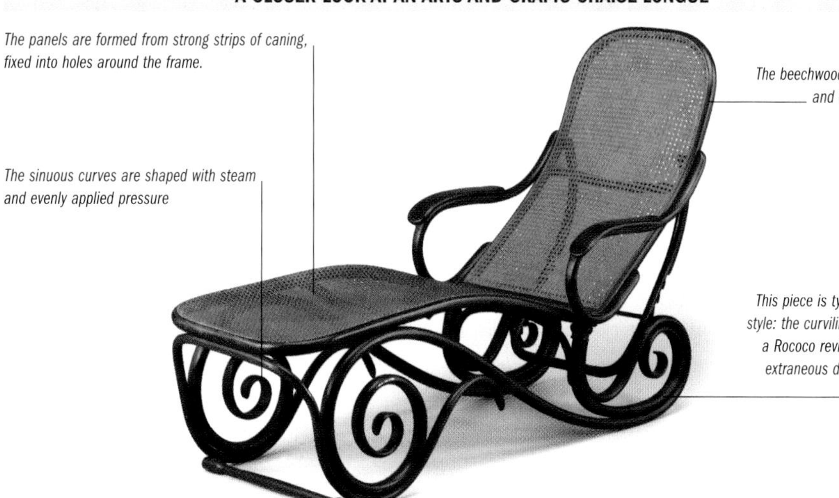

The panels are formed from strong strips of caning, fixed into holes around the frame.

The beechwood frame is strong and durable yet light.

The sinuous curves are shaped with steam and evenly applied pressure

This piece is typical of Thonet's style: the curvilinear lines reflect a Rococo revival influence but extraneous decoration is kept to a minimum.

A late 19thC Thonet bentwood chaise longue with caned seat and adjustable back, in fine condition, branded "Thonet".

57.5in (146cm) long

£1,000-1,500 **DRA**

A Scottish Arts and Crafts mahogany side chair, in the manner of George Walton, the serpentine top rail above a curved splat inset with heart-shaped silvered panel, repoussé-decorated with the face of an angel, the upholstered panel seat raised on square tapered legs linked by spindle-filled stretchers.

42in (106.5cm) high

£400-600 **L&T**

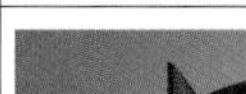

An Arts and Crafts oak hall settle, the arched slat-filled back above a hinged panel seat enclosed by scrolled open arms, the solid panel sides raised on shaped bracket feet.

48in (122cm) long

£300-400 **L&T**

An Arts and Crafts oak occasional table, the circular top carved in relief with a band of thistles raised above a turned column on tripod base with decorative pierced brackets.

18.5in (47cm) long

£120-180 **L&T**

An Arts and Crafts mahogany occasional table, the octagonal top above three twin tapering supports linked by a lower tier.

27.5in (69cm) high

£220-280 **L&T**

An Austrian Secessionist walnut card table, the circular top with radiating veneers above four pull-out guinea wells with attendant brass-capped supports on a hammered brass domed base.

29in (74cm) high

£1,500-2,000 **L&T**

A mahogany tea table with removable tray, with copper and pewter inlay to front and back.

c1905 *30in (76cm) high*

£800-1,200 **TDG**

A Swedish Biedermeier Revival oval table.

c1910 *47.25in (120cm) wide*

£700-1,000 **TDG**

A Liberty and Co. hexagonal table, with a moulded top on square tapering legs linked by pierced stretchers with pad feet.

28.75in (73cm) high

£500-800 **L&T**

A Liberty and Co. walnut dressing table, with two stepped drawers, all with original hinged copper handles.

71in (180cm) high

£400-600 **L&T**

An Arts and Crafts oak desk, in the Moorish style, the top with chequer stringing, three drawers decorated with blind fretwork and inlaid with marquetry panels, legs with chequer-inlaid angles, some alterations.

61in (152.5cm) wide

£1,000-1,500 **L&T**

A version of the Holland Cabinet, designed by George Walton for J.S. Henry, in mahogany with apron and double 'H'-stretcher.

c1900 *48in (122cm) high*

£1,800-2,200 **TDG**

A Glasgow-style mahogany side cabinet, attributed to James Salmon, serpentine ledge back, with three central drawers with stylized heart-shaped escutcheons and swing handles, with two panel doors, cabriole legs with block feet.

47.5in (119cm) wide

£800-1,200 **L&T**

An Arts and Crafts oak side cabinet, the serpentine leaf back with open shelf and panel carved in bas-relief with sunflowers, the sides with pierced decoration.

48.5in (123cm) long

£300-500 **L&T**

A Scottish Arts and Crafts oak corner cupboard, the design attributed to E.A. Taylor for Wylie and Lochhead, the panelled door marquetry-inlaid with a stylized flowering plant.

30.75in (77cm) high

£600-900 **L&T**

An Arts and Crafts oak and copper-mounted fire surround, the projecting mantel enclosing a copper panel repoussé-decorated, with tapering hood with rivet repoussé-decorated with heart shapes, with copper-clad fender.

75.25in (188cm) high

£500-800 **L&T**

A walnut fire surround by Wylie and Lochhead of Glasgow, the broad mantel with stepped panel above broad uprights on plinths, with marker's label.

50in (127cm) high

£120-180 **L&T**

An Arts and Crafts brass-studded and embossed jardinière trough, of stained beech.

c1900 *5.5in (14cm) high*

£500-700 **TDG**

A mahogany 'Thebes' planter, probably retailed by Liberty and Co., of tapering square section design.

41.75in (106cm) high

£300-500 **WW**

A pair of brass mounted steel andirons, designed by Edward Spencer for the Artificers Guild, each with pierced brass foliate roundels.

20.75in (52cm) high

£600-900 **L&T**

An Arts and Crafts mahogany open bookcase, in the manner of Morris and Co., panel sides with reeded edges, on stile supports with ogee cut-outs.

88in (220cm) high

£1,800-2,200 **L&T**

ART NOUVEAU

A rare Colonna mahogany elbow chair, with scroll-carved crested padded back above moulded arms with knuckle-scroll terminals, cabriole legs and distinctive low upholstered back, from a suite that also includes a settee and a side chair.

This particular Colonna suite design was exhibited at the Samuel Bing stand at the 1900 Paris Exposition Universelle.

£20,000-30,000 suite **MACK**

An Art Nouveau mahogany armchair, attributed to G.M. Ellwood for J.S. Henry, the moulded arched back inlaid with a stylized flowerhead, the serpentine upholstered seat with curved open arms and tapering uprights raised on square tapering supports terminating in block feet.

39in (96.5cm) high

£600-900 **L&T**

One of a pair of rare Gaillard cherry wood elbow chairs, each with curved padded back above curved splats, the curving arms on unusual cantilevered supports, the stuffover seat on delicate outsplayed legs.

c1900 *41in (104cm) high*

£20,000-30,000 pair **MACK**

One of a pair of rare Gaillard rosewood side chairs, each with scrolled raised wingback above padded back and stuffover seat, the frame and seat rail with delicate carved scroll decoration and outsplayed moulded legs.

c1900 *41.75in (106cm) high*

£15,000-25,000 pair **MACK**

A Gaillard carved walnut and bronze mounted chair, the original floral embossed leather upholstery within pierced floral carved frame, bronze mounts to the tops of the legs.

c1900 *38in (96.5cm) high*

£10,000-18,000 **MACK**

A pair of Josef Hoffmann beech seats, made by J. and J. Kohn of Vienna, with mahogany staining and original leather upholstery decorated with flowers and figures, with brass fittings throughout.

c1915 *35.25in (88cm) high*

£2,500-3,000 **DOR**

A Majorelle mahogany desk chair, with leather upholstered back and seat.

Initially trained as a painter, Louis Majorelle developed his father's cabinet making firm into one of the leading manufacturers of Art Nouveau furniture in France.

c1900 *36in (91.5cm) high*

£10,000-15,000 **MACK**

One of a pair of Majorelle mahogany chairs, each with rectangular padded back above overstuffed arms on back-curved supports and stuffover seat, on moulded legs.

c1900 *38.5in (98cm) high*

£15,000-25,000 pair **MACK**

A Majorelle mahogany elbow chair, with branch and leaf marquetry within spiral-turned spindles, moulded 'U'-shaped crinoline arms with duck-head terminals and stuffover seat on tapering legs.

37.75in (96cm) high

£12,000-18,000 **MACK**

A pair of oak armchairs, attributed to Joseph Maria Olbrich, with shaped toprail supporting five vertical splats, curved arms and tapering legs.

42.5in (108cm) high

£800-1,200 **WW**

An oak armchair, attributed to Joseph Maria Olbrich, with a shaped toprail supporting five vertical splats, curved arms and tapering legs.

42.5in (108cm) high

£800-1,200 **WW**

A rare chair by Thonet of Vienna, designed for the World Exhibition in Vienna, of twisted beechwood sticks with wickerwork seat and back.

c1870 *35.25in (89.5cm) high*

£1,500-2,000 **DOR**

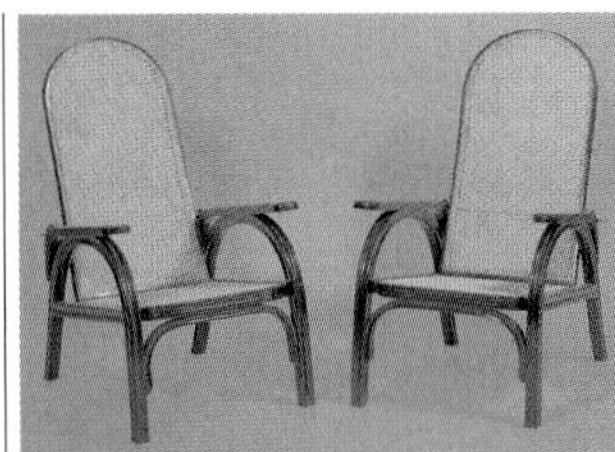

A pair of beechwood armchairs by Thonet of Vienna, design number 6392, stained in dark brown, with metal fittings and renewed wickerwork to seats and backs, restored.

c1905 *25in (63.5cm) wide*

£1,800-2,200 **DOR**

A beechwood rocking-chair, probably Viennese, stained in brown with wickerwork seat and back.

c1900 *36.75in (92cm) high*

£400-600 **DOR**

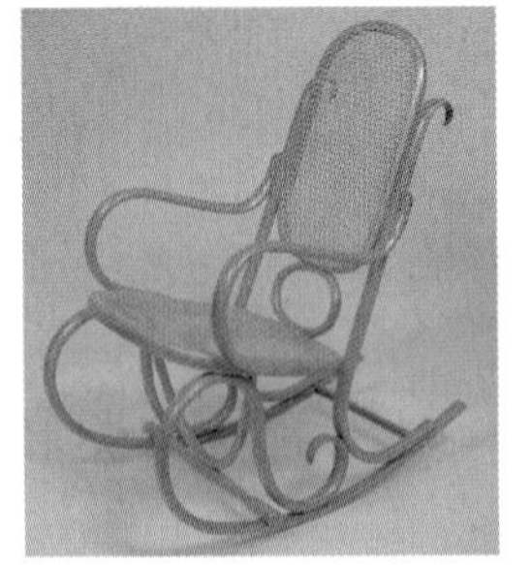

An Art Nouveau corner chair, the moulded top rail above splat-filled back and enclosing a rush seat, the whole raised on turned supports, linked by stretchers and terminating in bulbous feet.

£150-200 **L&T**

A Scottish Art Nouveau upholstered armchair, in the manner of George Walton, the tall tapered back above curved arms in the 'cacateuse' manner, the stuffover seat on square tapering legs, later plush fabric.

42in (106.5cm) high

£4,000-6,000 **L&T**

A Carlo Bugatti desk with walnut, brass and pewter stringing and gilt bronze mounting, the raised back with a pair of small shelved cupboards above a skiver-inset writing surface and a single frieze drawer on characteristic wheel-segment supports united by a block and turned stretcher, with all-over stylized floral decoration, mounted with dragonfly handles.

c1900 *36.5in (92.5cm) high*

£30,000-40,000 **MACK**

A CLOSER LOOK AT A GALLÉ TABLE

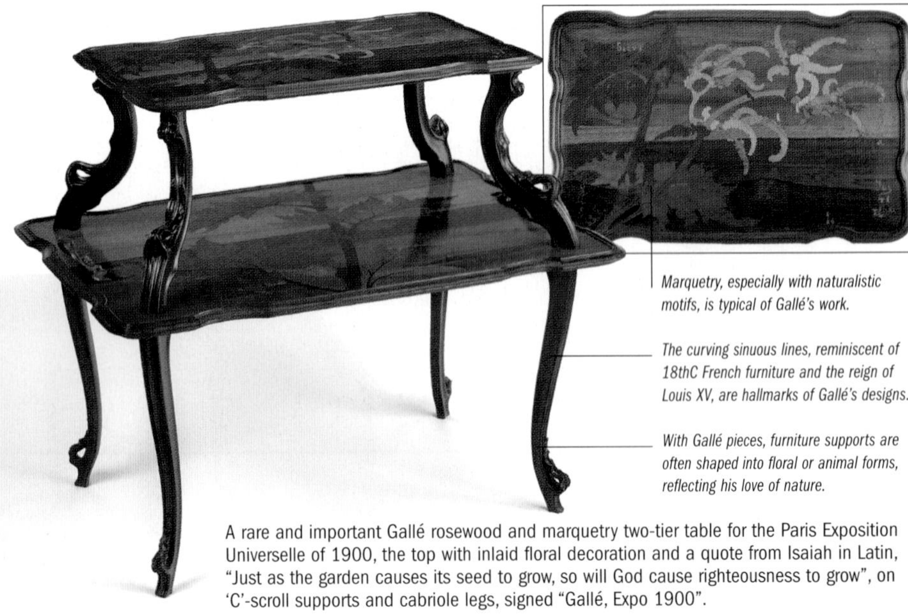

Marquetry, especially with naturalistic motifs, is typical of Gallé's work.

The curving sinuous lines, reminiscent of 18thC French furniture and the reign of Louis XV, are hallmarks of Gallé's designs.

With Gallé pieces, furniture supports are often shaped into floral or animal forms, reflecting his love of nature.

A rare and important Gallé rosewood and marquetry two-tier table for the Paris Exposition Universelle of 1900, the top with inlaid floral decoration and a quote from Isaiah in Latin, "Just as the garden causes its seed to grow, so will God cause righteousness to grow", on 'C'-scroll supports and cabriole legs, signed "Gallé, Expo 1900".

36.5in (93cm) wide

£20,000-25,000 **MACK**

A Georges De Feure Hungarian ash writing table, rectangular top with later inset tolled skiver, moulded edge above a pair of drawers, quarter-cut oak legs with leaf capitals and moulded square section legs with root carved block feet.

c1900 *43.25in (110cm) wide*

£15,000-20,000 **MACK**

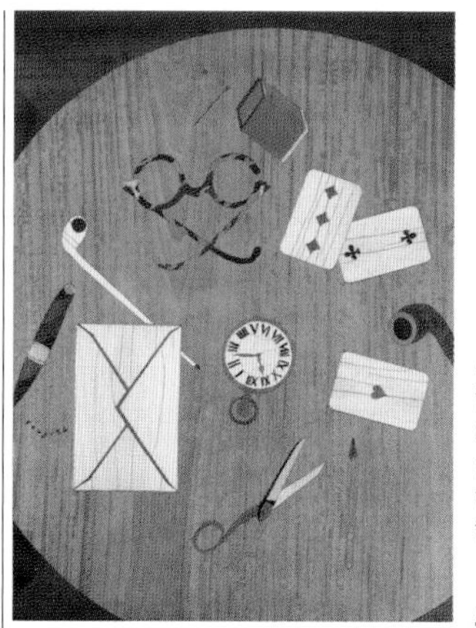

A rare Foujita mahogany low centre table, the square top with ivory and exotic woods trompe l'oeil marquetry of playing cards, smoking paraphernalia, watch and spectacles, on square tapering outsplayed legs, signed.

28in (71cm) wide

£28,000-32,000 **MACK**

A Gauthier mahogany and marquetry side table, the concave shaped rectangular top with floral marquetry above arched frieze with daffodil marquetry, on spiral carved tapering legs.

c1900 *32in (81cm) wide*

£10,000-15,000 **MACK**

A Gallé rosewood and marquetry two-tier table, each tier of shaped shield form with floral marquetry decoration, with three moulded legs, outsplayed open supports and scroll turned feet, signed.

c1900 *30.25in (77cm) high*

£12,000-18,000 **MACK**

A Gallé nest of four walnut and marquetry tables, each with dragonfly in wetland decoration, on pierced swelling dual standard supports united by stretchers, each signed.

Largest 28.25in (72cm) high

£12,000-15,000 **MACK**

A circular beechwood 'Fledermaus' table by Josef Hoffmann, made by J. and J. Kohn of Vienna, with paper label and stamp, some restoration.

c1905 *28.75in (73cm) high*

£1,000-1,500 **DOR**

A nest of four Secessionist black lacquered tables, the design attributed to Josef Hoffmann, each with rectangular top with rounded angles on turned spindle-filled supports with platform stretchers, the largest table with sphere-turned carving handles.

30.75in (77cm) high

£800-1,200 **L&T**

A rare extendable beechwood table, made by J. and J. Kohn of Vienna, the organic curvilinear feet with brass fittings and decorated with flutes, extendable, some restoration.

c1900 *52.2in (131cm) wide*

£3,000-4,000 **DOR**

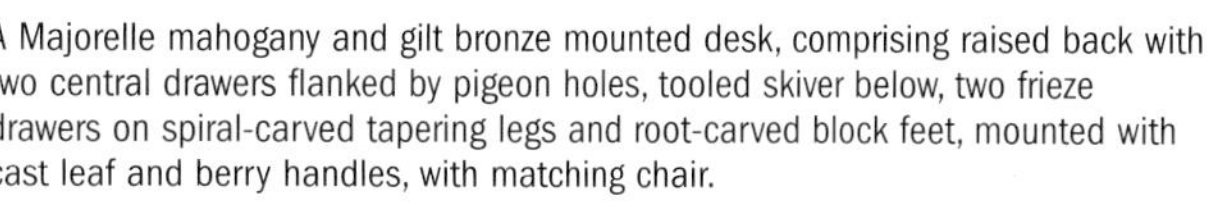

A Majorelle mahogany and gilt bronze mounted desk, comprising raised back with two central drawers flanked by pigeon holes, tooled skiver below, two frieze drawers on spiral-carved tapering legs and root-carved block feet, mounted with cast leaf and berry handles, with matching chair.

c1900 *122.75in (312cm) wide*

£20,000-25,000 the two **MACK**

A Majorelle mahogany two-tier table, with bronze foliate handles to the sides, dished rectangular upper tier with floral marquetry and 'palette' lower tier with similar decoration, the whole on dual carved and moulded 'W'-end supports united by a stretcher.

c1900 *35.25in (89.5cm) wide*

£12,000-16,000 **MACK**

A Majorelle gilt wood marble-topped side table, with inset mottled orange marble top within leaf and berry carved slip, wavy frieze above three moulded tapering legs with floral pierced tops and relief moulded decoration, united by arched stretcher, signed.

c1900 *30.75in (78cm) high*

£12,000-16,000 **MACK**

A beechwood case stand, by Thonet of Vienna, newly upholstered with turquoise leather, paper label on underside, some restoration.

c1890 *13.25in (78cm) wide*

£700-1,000 **DOR**

A mahogany veneer bar table, probably Viennese, with brass hinges, handles and feet, on tapering legs terminating in casters, top unfolds, some restoration.

c1905 *32.25in (80.5cm) wide*

£800-1,200 **DOR**

An Art Nouveau oak hall table, the rectangular moulded top above a single frieze drawer flanked by blank panels above a curved apron to four sides pierced with hearts, the whole raised on square tapering legs linked by stretchers and terminating with pad feet.

36in (91cm) long

£220-280 **L&T**

An Art Nouveau occasional table, the lobed top on three elaborately pierced supports linked by a shaped lower tier.

28.25in (70.5cm) high

£100-150 **L&T**

An Art Nouveau stained oak refectory table, the rectangular top with canted angles and moulded edge above curved supports of baluster outline, pierced with stylized flowerhead forms.

82in (205cm) long

£1,200-1,800 **L&T**

A Gallé ash, oak, calamander and marquetry cabinet, with carved floral cresting above a single glazed door enclosing shelved interior with marquetry decoration of a bird perched on trailing tree branches with leaf sprays, stepped asymmetric shelves to the sides on carved tree supports, and branch stretchers joining carved and moulded legs, signed.

61.5in (156cm) high

£30,000-40,000 **MACK**

A Gallé carved walnut, bird's-eye maple and exotic wood marquetry vitrine, with carved and pierced cresting of Japanese cherry flowers above a single glazed door, enclosing asymmetric stepped two-tier interior with glazed sides, pierced apron above outswept carved legs, signed.

c1900 *58.25in (148cm) high*

£20,000-30,000 **MACK**

A Gallé walnut, rosewood and marquetry vitrine, comprising glazed upper section with twin doors with leaf-carved surround above three plain shelves within moulded supports, pierced carved root apron and scroll-carved legs, signed.

c1900 *62.25in (158cm) high*

£20,000-30,000 **MACK**

A beechwood display cabinet, made by J. and J. Kohn of Vienna, design number 600, the upper part comprising polished glass doors enclosing two mahogany veneered shelves, and the lower part with two open compartments, with brass feet and clasps, some restoration.

c1905 *76in (190cm) high*

£3,000-4,000 **DOR**

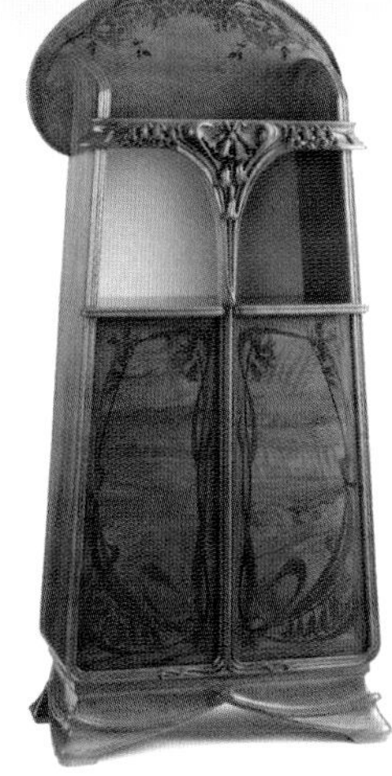

A Majorelle carved walnut and marquetry cabinet, the arched raised back with trailing floral inlay above a pair of part glazed and part marquetry panel doors divided by a richly carved central post with trailing floral capital, on swept short feet, signed.

25.5in (65cm) high

£40,000-50,000 **MACK**

An Art Nouveau mahogany hanging smokers cabinet, by Shapland and Petter, the projecting cornice above a glazed panelled door overlaid with a pierced copper filigree of stylized plant forms, the sides supporting open shelves with heart-shaped piercings and with ashtray and pipe rack below.

20.5in (51cm) high

£220-280 **L&T**

An Art Nouveau mahogany display cabinet, inlaid in copper, pewter and specimen wood with stylized flowerheads and leafy tendrils, with inlaid frieze and central mirrored panel, flanked by two glass doors, raised on square legs with bracket supports.

81.5in (207cm) high

£1,800-2,200 **L&T**

A Scottish Art Nouveau mahogany side cabinet, probably by Wylie and Lochhead of Glasgow, the serpentine top above three drawers with ring handles and square backplates enclosing two panel doors with marquetry inlay, raised on square tapering legs.

68in (172.5cm) wide

£320-380 **L&T**

An Art Nouveau mahogany display cabinet, the oval mirrored back enclosed by a shaped frame marquetry inlaid with flowers and whiplash tendrils below a moulded cornice supported by turned and curved uprights, the shaped and moulded top over marquetry inlaid frieze and twin leaded and glazed doors above a shaped undershelf, the moulded front supports with flower-carved capitals and spreading feet.

70.75in (177cm) high

£1,800-2,200 **L&T**

An Art Nouveau mahogany cabinet, the arched three-quarter surmount inlaid in copper, pewter and specimen woods with stylized flowers and tendrils, the projecting cornice above inlaid frieze and central mirrored panel flanked by two leaded glass doors, raised on square legs.

82.74in (207cm) high

£1,500-2,000 **L&T**

An Art Nouveau mahogany display cabinet, the spindle three-quarter gallery inset with a circular convex mirror enclosing marquetry inlaid stylized seed heads above twin glazed doors, each flanked by marquetry inlaid stylized plant forms, on square tapering supports.

68in (170cm) high

£600-900 **L&T**

An Art Nouveau oak and marquetry inlaid sideboard, with a three-quarter cushion-moulded cornice supported by square tapered columns, panelled back inlaid with stylized plant forms, and central bevelled mirror enclosed by pierced sides carved with stylized tulips, the base with two drawers above two inlaid panel doors.

66.5in (169cm) high

£700-1,000 **L&T**

An Emile Andre mahogany two-tier stand, with a shaped triangular top above arched pierced supports on three moulded legs united by a shaped triangular undertier.

51.5in (131cm) high

£12,000-15,000 **MACK**

A Gallé walnut and marquetry two-tier étagère, the two graduated tiers of shaped oval form with daffodil marquetry decoration, on bold 'C'-scroll supports and cabriole legs, signed.

36.25in (92cm) wide

£12,000-16,000 **MACK**

A Majorelle mahogany, satinwood, ash and marquetry three-tier étagère, three shaped tiers with floral marquetry on 'Y'-shaped front support and plain satinwood back with stile back supports, signed.

49.25in (125cm) high

£12,000-15,000 **MACK**

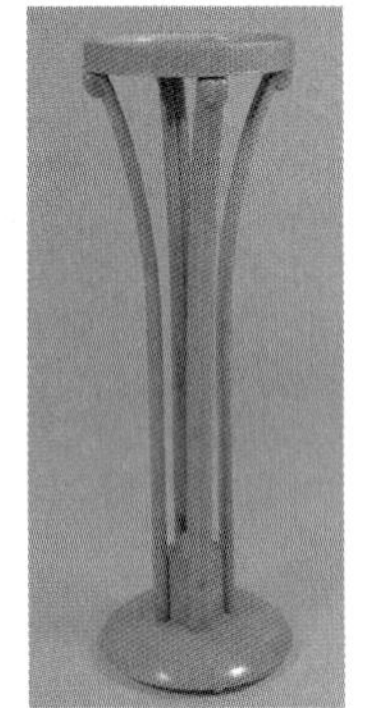

A beechwood flower stand by Otto Prutscher, made by Thonet of Vienna, stained light-brown.

c1915 *49in (122.5cm) high*

£1,500-2,000 **DOR**

A Selmersheim mahogany library stand, the square top with moulded edge above a compartmentalised shelf for books, shaped square mid-tier below on outsplayed moulded legs united by an 'X' stretcher.

c1900 *53.25in (135cm) high*

£12,000-16,000 **MACK**

A beechwood toiletry table made by Thonet of Vienna, stained in dark brown, on tripod stand, with three compartments, adjustable height, and tilting oval mirror, the two candle holders on the sides are missing, some restoration.

c1890 *61.25in (153 cm) high*

£2,200-2,800 **DOR**

A rare Colonna rosewood framed fire screen, retaining original Art Nouveau stylized floral material, the frame with delicate scrolling floral carving and dual standard ends.

c1900 *31.5in (80cm) high*

£800-1,200 **MACK**

An Art Nouveau mahogany firescreen, of shaped rectangular form with stylized elliptical and square piercings to the frame enclosing a silkwork panel of two figures under a fruiting tree, the whole raised on carved bracket supports.

39in (99cm) high

£100-150 **L&T**

A CLOSER LOOK AT AN ART NOUVEAU MIRROR

De Feure has chosen a Classical subject for his design - the Greek myth of Leda and the Swan.

Georges De Feure worked in various media and often mixed them as seen in this piece, which combines silver plate and mirrored glass.

This mirror's link with the seminal 1900 Paris Exposition gives it a strong historical context.

Despite the classical origin, De Feure has given his subject a very contemporary treatment. The maidens dress and pose are typical of the Art Nouveau style.

A Georges De Feure silver plated wall mirror from the 1900 Paris Exposition, with a relief-moulded scene of a woman in profile in a stylized landscape setting, within moulded oak frame, signed.

17.75in (45cm) wide

£12,000-16,000 **MACK**

ART DECO

An oak Art Deco drum table, in the manner of Betty Joel.

c1935 *24in (61cm) diam*

£400-600 **TDG**

A walnut Art Deco mirror table.

c1930 *23in (58.5cm) diam*

£300-400 **TDG**

An Art Deco chromium plated occasional table, the circular top inset with a black glass panel above three curved supports with circular ebonised base on flattened bun feet.

20.5in (51cm) high

£180-220 **L&T**

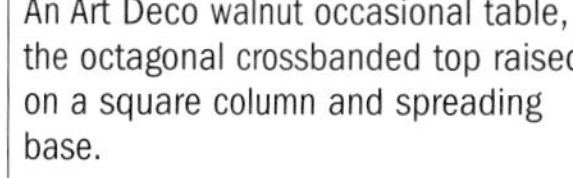

An Art Deco walnut occasional table, the octagonal crossbanded top raised on a square column and spreading base.

22in (55cm) high

£100-150 **L&T**

An Art Deco walnut veneered writing desk, the rectangular top with rounded angles and asymmetric pedestal to the side, with bowed door enclosing shelves, and twin frieze drawers above a kneehole.

48in (120cm) high

£1,000-1,500 **L&T**

An Art Deco sycamore chair, attributed to Ray Hille.

33.5in (85cm) high

£280-320 **TDG**

An Art Deco Calpan occasional table, and one of two tub chairs.

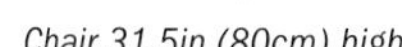

c1925 *Chair 31.5in (80cm) high*

£3,000-4,000 set **TDG**

A 1930s Art Deco sycamore chair, attributed to Ray Hille.

27.25in (69cm) high

£280-320 **TDG**

One of a pair of early 20thC red leather hall chairs.

46in (117cm) high

£1,200-1,800 pair **TDG**

Two of a set of six Art Deco walnut framed dining chairs, each with upholstered 'cloud' backs in deep pink plush, with square tapered legs.

£500-700 set **L&T**

A CLOSER LOOK AT AN ART DECO CABINET

At this stage in his career, Paul Follot was designing 'tranquil architecture' which adopted a more restrained style than his earlier work and typified the emerging Art Deco look.

With its simple, symmetrical design, this piece is typical of the Art Deco period.

Ivory, sourced from France's colonies, was often used decoratively at this time. Here, it is combined with golden amboyna wood to great effect.

The smooth, curved, unadorned doors draw attention to the curled grain of the wood.

A French Art Deco cabinet, in amboyna wood with ivory handles and inlay, designed and stamped by Paul Follot.

c1925 *60.25in (153cm) wide*

£8,000-12,000 **TDG**

Part of an Art Deco three-piece suite, comprising a two-seater sofa and two chairs, with walnut veneer.

c1930

£4,000-5,000 suite **TDG**

An Art Deco chromium fireplace surround, of rectangular outline with five stepped concentric bands enclosing the aperture, with associated ash guard.

48.75in (122cm) wide

£1,000-1,500 **L&T**

An Art Deco mahogany fire surround, with an open-shelved panel above panelled uprights, meeting a moulded cavetto surround.

46.5in (118cm) high

£80-120 **L&T**

An Art Deco black lacquer and burlwood veneer cabinet, with clip corner top, two glass doors and two interior glass shelves, over four small drawers with faceted brass pulls, unmarked.

c1920 *36.25in (92cm) wide*

£400-500 **DRA**

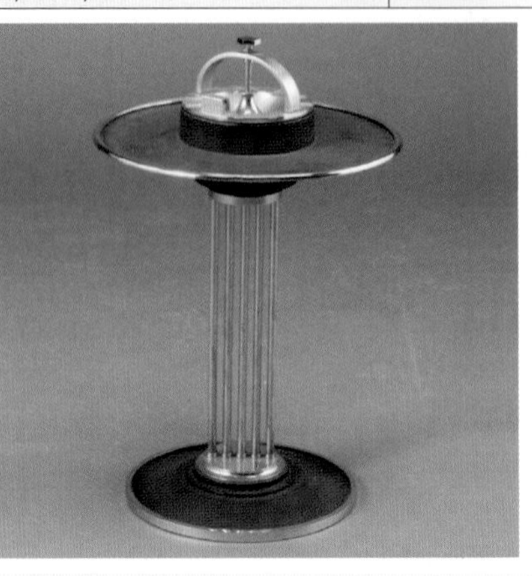

A Climax of Indiana Art Deco iron and chrome 'Cocktail Smoker', with revolving ashtray with matchholder and removable drinks tray, on a tubular pedestal shaft and circular base, from the '20th Century Limited' train, with Climax decals and patent numbers.

25in (63.5cm) high

£700-900 **DRA**

A fine G. Thew Art Deco bronze smoke stand, with removable ash receiver and figural penguin shaft, signed and dated.

1929 *23.75in (60cm) high*

£280-320 **DRA**

ARTS & CRAFTS

An Arts and Crafts Donegal carpet, attributed to Gavin Morton, designed with plant forms reserved on a madder ground.

179.25in (448cm) long

£600-900 **L&T**

A large Arts and Crafts Donegal carpet, probably designed by Gavin Morton, the rose field with a pattern of spaced flowersprays, within a rose floral vine border, between plain bands, repairs.

£1,000-1,500 **L&T**

A Turkish Arts and Crafts-style carpet, the green field with an overall pattern of large rose palmettes and cruciform motifs, within a rose, rosette and scrolling vine border, between yellow bands.

177in (442cm) wide

£2,000-3,000 **L&T**

A pair of William Morris Arts and Crafts 'Peacock and Dragon' woven woollen curtains and tiebacks, minor wear and losses.

William Morris, 1834-1896 *The name of English craftsman, designer and social reformer William Morris is synonymous with the British Arts and Crafts movement in the second half of the 19thC. As a major campaigner for the revival of craftsmanship in an industrial age, Morris was deeply opposed to factory production and sought a return to the skills employed by craftsmen since mediaeval times. His intention was to make hand-crafted goods for the masses, but because the production methods of the Industrial Revolution produced pieces that were far cheaper, his goods were only really available to the wealthy.*

Morris had his home, Red House, furnished and decorated by his craftsmen friends and from this association arose Morris, Marshall, Faulkner & Co. in 1861, which was renamed Morris & Co. in 1875.

Morris was best known for his textile and wallpaper designs, where design and simplicity were combined with functionality: he defined art as '"Man's expression of his joy in labour". The company produced furniture and furnishings until 1940.

Each curtain 94.5 x 63in (240 x 160cm) wide

£3,500-4,000 **WW**

An Arts and Crafts machine-woven carpet, the field with a foliate design on a blue ground.

£800-1,200 **L&T**

A 19thC William Morris 'Tulip and Rose' woven panel fragment, catalogue design No. 12, registered as a fabric 20th January 1876.

37 x 33in (94 x 84cm)

£500-700 **WROB**

An Arts and Crafts silkwork embroidered panel, in coloured silks with flowering and fruiting leafy stems on a buff-coloured lozenge ground.

25.25in (63cm) high

£450-550 **L&T**

ART NOUVEAU

A late 19thC French Art Nouveau mohair velvet panel, with a printed design of tulips.

118in (300cm) long

£1,200-1,800 **WROB**

An Art Nouveau printed velvet panel, probably Silver Studio, with the signature background motif.

c1900 170 x38in (432 x 96cm) long

£800-1,200 **WROB**

A late 19thC French woven silk panel with a fantastic design of ivy.

64 x 33in (162.5 x 84cm) long

£700-1,000 **WROB**

A 19thC Silver Studio printed cotton, with a red floral design.

The Silver Studio *Opened in 1880 by Arthur Silver, the Silver Studio of Design aimed to create designs for every form of home decoration. It became Britain's most important independent studio, selling to the UK and US, with influential clients such as Liberty, Sanderson and Warner & Sons, all of which commissioned Silver Studio designs for their own collections of wallpaper and textiles.*

The studio's ability to adapt to changing interior fashions, while producing beautifully drawn patterns, made it a commercial success.

Arthur's son Rex, who had run the studio after his father, died in 1965. Two years later the studio's contents, including over 40,000 textile and furnishing designs, was bequeathed to the University of Middlesex.

90 x 31in (228.5 x 78.5cm)

£600-700 **WROB**

A pair of late 19thC European Art Nouveau printed cottons, the pink of greater weight.

65.5in (166.5cm) long

£1,000-1,500 **WROB**

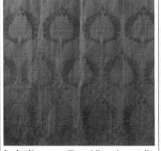

An Art Nouveau silk and linen brocatelle yardage, possibly American.

c1900 *144 x 50in (366 x 127cm)*

£2,200-2,800 **WROB**

A Dutch Art Nouveau mohair and velvet table carpet.

c1900 *120 x 60in (305cm x 152cm)*

£500-800 **WROB**

One of a pair of peacock-printed cotton panels.

c1890 *34 x 34in (86.5 x 86.5cm)*

£600-900 pair **WROB**

A green woven cotton, possibly Austrian.

c1905 *57.5 x 46in (146 x 117cm)*

£400-600 **WROB**

An Art Nouveau woven cotton and wool textile, mass produced in a popular design.

72 x 48.5in (183 x 123cm)

£280-320 **WROB**

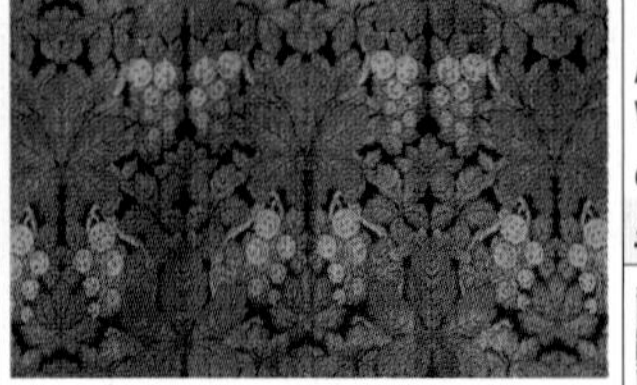

An early 20thC French Art Nouveau silk and metal panel, with a chestnut and leaf design, for the American market.

51 x 81in (129.5 x 205cm)

£2,000-2,500 **WROB**

WIENER WERKSTÄTTE

A Carl Otto Czeschka 'Waldidyll' (Forest Idyll) cotton sample, for Wiener Werkstätte, framed.

c1910 *8.5 x 15in (21.5 x 38cm) wide*

£700-1,000 **WROB**

A Josef Hoffmann 'Luchs' (Lynx) textile, for Wiener Werkstätte, preserved.

c1910 *37 x 29.5in (94 x 75cm)*

£1,500-2,000 **WROB**

A Arthur Berger, 'Mekka' (Mecca) silk, for Wiener Werkstätte, framed.

c1912 *37.5 x 8.75in (95 x 22.5cm)*

£600-900 **WROB**

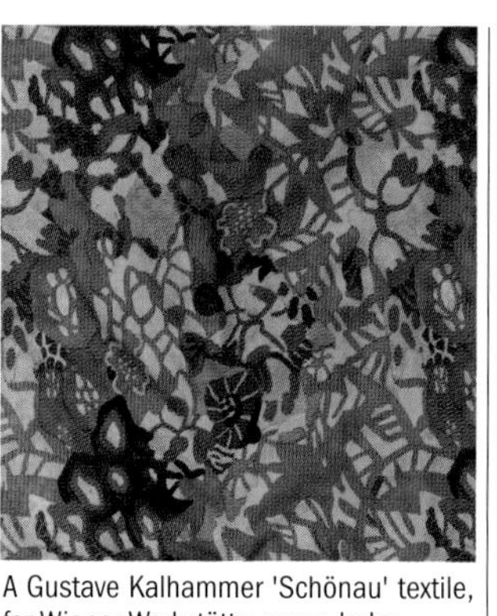

A Gustave Kalhammer 'Schönau' textile, for Wiener Werkstätte, some holes.

c1910 *23 x 46in (58.5 x 117cm)*

£400-600 **WROB**

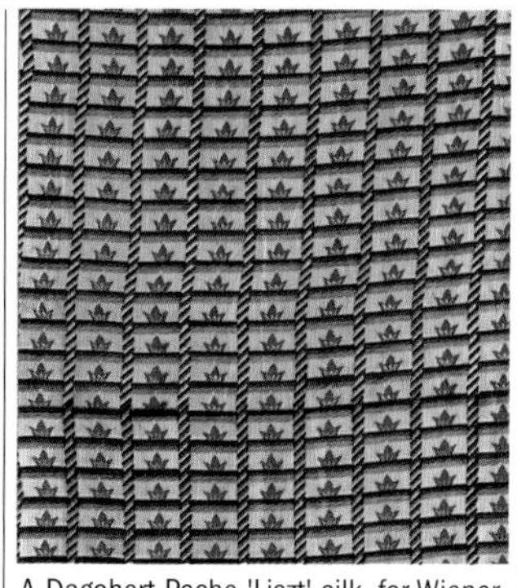

A Dagohert Peche 'Liszt' silk, for Wiener Werkstätte.

c1910 *40 x 18in (101.5 x 45cm)*

£800-1,000 **WROB**

A Julius Zimpel 'Bahia' fine silk, for Wiener Werkstätte, "WW" printed in selvage.

c1925 *29 x 12in (73.5 x 30.5cm)*

£600-700 **WROB**

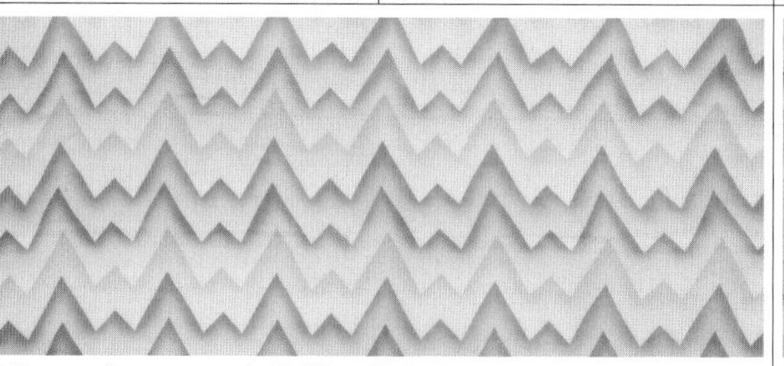

A Viennese fine cotton, probably Wiener Werkstätte, with a zigzag pattern.

42 x 29in (106 x 73cm)

£1,200-1,800 **WROB**

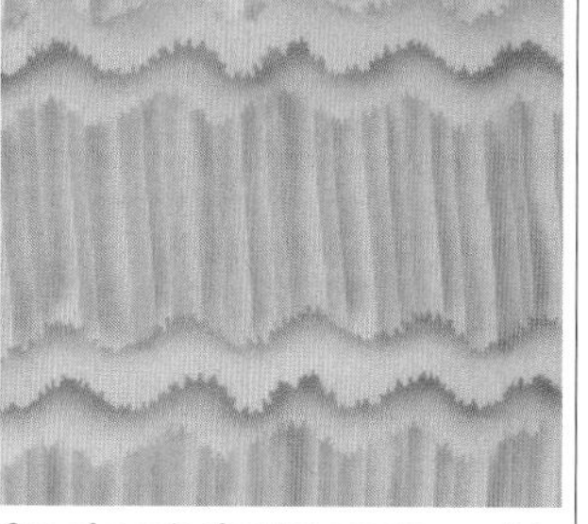

One of a pair of cotton panels, possibly Wiener Werkstätte.

21 x 112cm (53 x 284cm)

£1,700-1,900 pair **WROB**

ART DECO

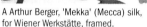

An Raoul Dufy Art Deco 'La Peche' cotton.

c1920 *50 x 48in (127 x 122cm)*

£1,200-1,800 **WROB**

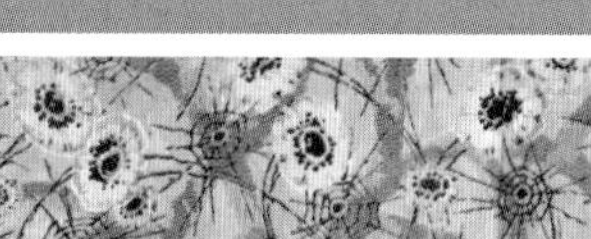

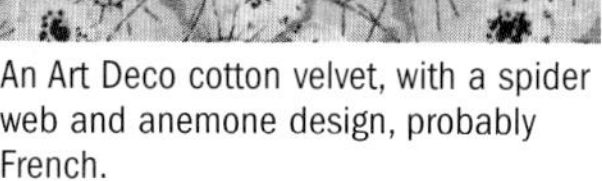

An Art Deco cotton velvet, with a spider web and anemone design, probably French.

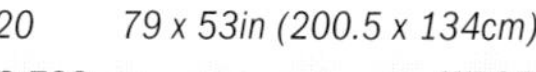

c1920 *79 x 53in (200.5 x 134cm)*

£500-700 **WROB**

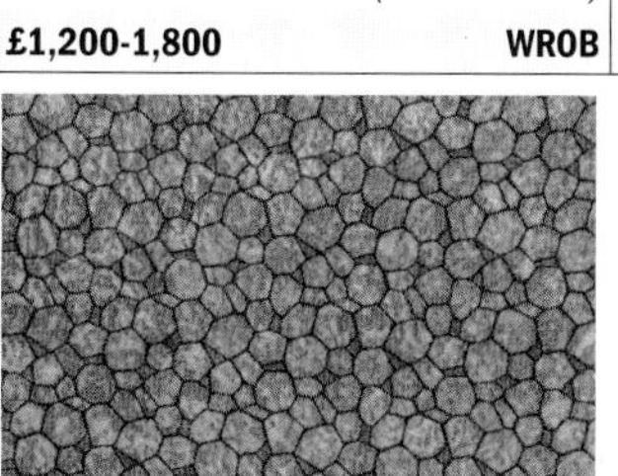

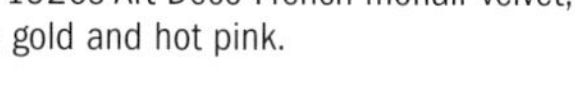

A 1920s Art Deco French mohair velvet, in gold and hot pink.

53 x 36in (134.5 x 91.5cm)

£500-700 **WROB**

An Art Deco printed double width cotton, probably American.

c1920 *80 x 60in (203 x 152cm)*

£250-350 **WROB**

A French Art Deco printed cotton velvet, in the Benedictus style.

c1920 *101 x 52in (256 x 131cm)*

£700-1,000 **WROB**

One of two 20thC French Art Deco printed cotton and velvet panels, possibly Martine Studios Paul Poiret, cut to make two panels.

110in (279.5cm) long

£600-900 each **WROB**

A Raoul Dufy Art Deco 'Nature Moret Aux Fruits' shawl.

Raoul Dufy, 1877-1953 *Born and educated in Le Havre and Paris, Raoul Dufy was a graphic artist, painter and textile designer who was heavily influenced by Matisse. He used bright colours and fluid, naturalistic designs in all of his work and bold brushstrokes in his painted designs. Best known for his watercolours, he produced over 3,000 works on paper, ceramic and textile, as well as his paintings. He worked with Catalan potter Josep Llorens Artigas in designing the ceramic blanks that he then decorated, marrying fluidity of the ceramic form with its painted decoration. Dufy also became influential in the fashion world.*

Dufy's talent with colour and the exuberance of execution make his decorative art as popular today as it was in the early 1900s.

c1925 *60 x 64in (152.5 x 162.5cm)*

£2,000-2,500 **WROB**

A French Art Deco velvet plush mohair panel.

118 x 52in (300 x 132cm)

£1,200-1,800 **WROB**

A French Art Deco woven panel, with pink and blue flowers,

c1930 *97 x 49.25in (246.5 x 125cm)*

£700-1,000 **WROB**

A French Art Deco printed cotton velvet, red and blue.

49 x 33in (124.5 x 84cm)

£700-1,000 **WROB**

A French Art Deco voided velvet coverlet, in the style of Paul Poiret and the Martine School.

86 x 82in (218.5 x 208.5cm)

£2,200-2,800 **WROB**

A French Art Deco voided velvet coverlet, in wool and silk, with a gold fountain design.

85 x 65in (216 x 165cm)

£2,200-2,800 **WROB**

An Art Deco machined wool carpet, with a central panel of an interlaced fan design in blue, green and pink within multiple borders.

109.5in (274cm) long

£200-300 **L&T**

A 1920s English printed cotton panel, with an oriental influence, with an original tag.

158 x 31in (401.5 x 78.5cm)

£400-600 **WROB**

A Japanese-influenced printed cotton panel, with an original fringe and passmenterie trim.

c1920 64 x 16in (162.5 x 40.5cm)

£500-800 **WROB**

A Mathilde Flögl 'Amazonas' fine silk, probably a scarf, all edges hand stitched, some damage.

c1930 36 x 36in (91.5 x 91.5cm)

£600-800 **WROB**

A spray printed silk, probably a scarf, hand-stitched edges, possibly hand painted by Gabriele Möschl-Lagus for Wiener Werkstätte, some damage.

18 x 56in (45.5 x 142cm)

£800-1,000 **WROB**

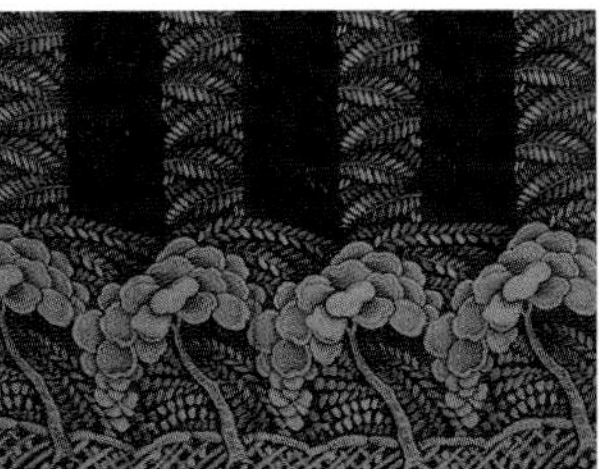

A French Art Deco silk and metal woven yardage, with a design of trees.

51.5 x 39in (131 x 99cm)

£700-1,000 **WROB**

An Art Deco Egyptianesque carpet, machine woven, the golden yellow field with a central medallion and polychrome faun motifs to the angles.

179.5in (449cm) long

£1,000-1,500 **L&T**

A CLOSER LOOK AT A WOOL RUG

Fernand Leger was a French Cubist painter and an expositor of modern urban and technological culture.

This rug is typical of Leger's style, which is characterised by tubular, fractured forms and bright colours.

The subjects of cubist paintings and sculpture were portrayed using abstract geometrical forms. The Cubist movement was influential during the early 20thC.

The muted colours of beige and grey, contrasted with a sleek black, were a feature of Art Deco design. Geometric rugs were a popular addition to an Art Deco home.

A wool art rug after a design by Fernand Léger, with a geometric Art Deco pattern in grey, black and shades of beige on a dark purple ground.

Fernand Léger (1881-1955), was a French Cubist painter. In 1927 Alfred H. Barr, Jr., who became The Museum of Modern Art's (New York City) first director, defined Léger as a "French Cubist whose forms are polished and cylindrical like steel, clangorous in red and black like new fire engines."

65.5in (166.5cm) long

£4,500-5,000 **SDR**

MODERN FURNITURE

A four door credenza 'Flirtation', by James Abbott, in African Wenge, teak and ebonised wood, carved on three sides with insects, flowers on swirling stems and a toadstool in high relief, on a floating base, unmarked.

71in (180.5cm) wide

£4,000-6,000 **SDR**

A fine trapezoidal single-door cabinet, by James Abbott, in African Wenge, teak and ebonised wood, carved on three sides with large panther and flowers in high relief, with interior shelves on floating base, unmarked.

59.5in (151cm) high

£1,200-1,800 **SDR**

A set of four chromium side chairs, by Harry Bertoia, for Knoll Associates, each with slightly curved mesh back and seat on tubular supports, the seats with black vinyl upholstered pads.

£600-900 **L&T**

Four steel and vinyl children's chairs, by Harry Bertoia for Knoll.

22in (55cm) high

£400-600 **FRE**

A pair of 'Diamond' chairs, designed by Harry Bertoia, for Knoll Associates from 1953, the chromium plated steel mesh seats on strut supports with white padded vinyl covers.

£300-500 **L&T**

A fine and rare Wendell Castle laminated walnut 'Crescent' armrocker, its seat frame with high chanelled back upholstered in brown leather, on a wishbone base with exposed joinery, signed "W. Castle/78".

1978 *39.5in (99cm) wide*

£18,000-20,000 **DRA**

An exceptional Wendell Castle post-modern bench, with elongated seat supported by seven simulated bamboo posts, mounted on a rectangular platform base, signed "W. Castle/1993".

1993 *88in (220cm) wide*

£10,000-12,000 **DRA**

A fine and large Wendell Castle laminated walnut executive desk, with two shallow drawers flanked by two pivoting consoles with black-leather interior, one with a television set and two drawers, the other with a telephone, clock and control panels for lights, drapes, and doors, signed "W.C./76".

1976 *103.5in (259cm) wide*

£12,000-14,000 **DRA**

A fine and large Wendell Castle stack-laminated walnut receptionist's desk of biomorphic form with curved apron, recessed work surface and two drawers on boot-shaped leg supports, unmarked.

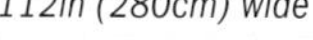

112in (280cm) wide

£11,000-13,000 **DRA**

A pair of Wendell Castle laminated walnut sculpture-front doors, each with sinuous organic design encasing a smoked mirror panel, with brass hardware, hinges and zebrawood backing, one signed "WC 76".

1976 *98.75in (247cm) high*

£12,000-14,000 **DRA**

CHARLES EAMES (1907-1978)

Born in 1907, Charles Eames developed an interest in engineering and architecture, which he studied at Washington University. In 1929, while travelling in Europe, he was influenced by the Modernist Movement through the works of Le Corbusier, Mies van der Rohe and Gropius.

In 1938 Eames began studying at Cranbrook Academy of Art, sponsored by Finnish architect Eliel Saarinen. There he met his future wife, Ray Kaiser.

Ray assisted Eames and Saarinen's son Eero on projects for 'The Organic Design in Home Furnishings' competition at New York Museum of Modern Art, held in 1940, where they won the two first prizes. Their exhibits utilised innovative manufacturing techniques including a method for moulding plywood.

Eames continued working on the plywood moulding technique, and developed the 'Kazam! Machine', a press for moulding plywood, which lead to a commission by the US Navy for limb splints.

Now married, the Eames' continued their work on plywood furniture, including a moulded plywood chair, which won the accolade 'chair of the century' from architectural critic, Esther McCoy. Herman Miller took on the production of this chair in the US and still produces Eames' designs today.

Other key pieces include the 'Lounge Chair and Ottoman' from 1956 and 'Tandem Sling Seating', which is still used in airports.

They continued their design work, and other major projects in architecture and film-making, into the 1970s. Charles died in 1978 and Ray in 1988.

An Eames fibreglass rocker, of fibreglass, steel, rubber and maple, with moulded Herman Miller mark.

26in (65cm) high

£400-600 **FRE**

A pair of Eames dowel-leg armshell chairs, of fibreglass, steel and maple, with moulded marks and paper labels, the wood bases are later production.

31in (77.5cm) high

£600-900 **FRE**

An Eames for Herman Miller wire chair, steel, maple, fabric, cloth tag to original bikini seat, fixed base.

32in (80cm) high

£300-500 **FRE**

An Eames for Herman Miller wire chair, of steel, maple and fabric, with a cloth tag to original bikini seat, swivel base.

32in (80cm) high

£400-600 **FRE**

An Eames '670' lounge chair and ottoman, of rosewood, aluminum, steel and leather, with circular Herman Miller metal tag to chair.

33in (82.5cm) high

£2,000-3,000 **FRE**

An early Charles Eames for Herman Miller first-series 'ESU-400', with black laminate shelves and drawer fronts, with enamelled masonite panels to back and sides, on angle iron frame, overall wear, early red/black/white Herman Miller label.

55in (137.5cm) high

£3,500-4,500 **DRA**

A Charles Eames for Herman Miller 'ESU-400', with four sliding dimpled plywood doors, three open shelves and three drawers with black laminate surfaces, and enamelled side and back panels, remnant of red/white Herman Miller label.

58.5in (156cm) high

£6,000-9,000 **DRA**

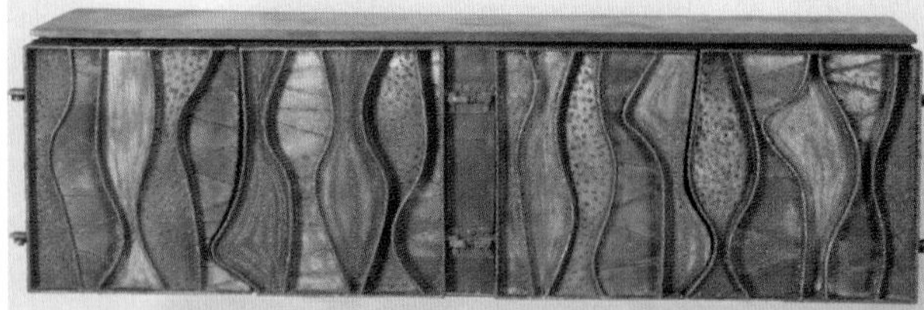

A rare 'Wavy Front' buffet by Paul Evans, with full-length slate top over-rivetted metal patchwork case with four doors sculpted in high relief with biomorphic shapes, concealing a red-painted interior, welded signature and date "PED 65".

This is one of Evans' rarest cabinet designs, it is believed that less than 60 were ever produced.

73in (185.5cm) wide

£12,000-14,000 **SDR**

A Paul Evans sculptured server, of metal, wood, composition and slate.

48in (120cm) wide

£250-350 **FRE**

A Paul Evans 'Directional' extension dining table, with broad exotic wood veneer top over brass-covered pedestal base, includes two leaves, unmarked.

60in (152.5cm) wide

£1,000-1,500 **SDR**

A Paul Evans steel sculptured iron side table, of patinated iron and slate.

24in (60cm) diam

£1,800-2,200 **FRE**

One of a set of six Paul Evans sculptured dining chairs, in metal, composition and fabric.

32in (80cm) high

£600-900 set **FRE**

A Paul Evans cube chair, the interior frame and loose seat cushions upholstered in gold velvet, the exterior with rivetted metal patchwork covered in copper, gold, silver and bronze patinas, on swivelling welded metal base, unmarked.

31.75in (80.5cm) wide

£1,000-1,500 **SDR**

A Paul Evans 'Directional' custom-designed, four-panel room screen in red lacquer finish, mounted with square and rectangular forms covered in patchwork chrome and brass.

80in (203cm) high

£2,200-2,800 **SDR**

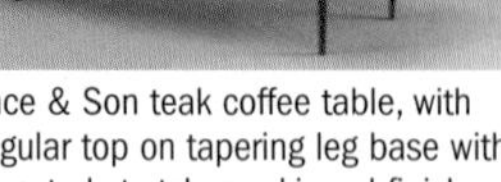

A France & Son teak coffee table, with rectangular top on tapering leg base with two corseted stretchers, skinned finish, tags for France & Son, plus John Stuart.

59in (150cm) wide

£220-280 **DRA**

A France & Son two-tiered teak corner table with V-shaped top on tapering dowel legs, some looseness, metal tag.

30in (76.5cm) wide

£150-200 **DRA**

A pair of Arne Jacobsen 'Grand Prix' teak and beech chairs, made by Fritz Hansen, Denmark, marks and labels.

31in (77.5cm) high

£400-600 **FRE**

An Arne Jacobsen 'Grand Prix' chair, made by Fritz Hansen, Denmark, of teak, beech and leather.

31in (77.5cm) high

£250-300 **FRE**

An Arne Jacobsen 'Drop-Chair', 'Kopenhagen', made by Fritz Hanzen, the plastic seat cushioned with foam, brown leather cover, the steel-tube legs copper-plated.

c1955 *33.75in (84.5cm) high*

£6,000-9,000 **QU**

ARNE JACOBSEN (1902-1971)

The Danish architect Arne Jacobsen was born in 1902 in Copenhagen. As a child he showed an extraordinary talent for drawing and depicting nature through scrupulous studies. At Nærum Boarding School, he met the Lassen brothers. Later, Flemming Lassen was to become his partner in a series of architectural projects. With him Jacobsen co-designed the 'House of the Future' project which helped introduce Modernism to Danish design.

Educated at the Royal Danish Academy of Fine Arts and the School of Architecture in Copenhagen, Jacobsen made prototypes for a range of items including furniture, textiles, wallpaper and silverware. His most famous designs became 'The Ant', 'Series 7', 'The Egg and The Swan', and the tableware 'Cylinda-Line'.

Jacobsen's architecture includes a considerable number of epoch-making buildings in Denmark, Germany and Great Britain. His most famous architectural works are the apartment blocks 'Bellavista' in Klampenborg, Bellevue Theatre, SAS Royal Hotel Copenhagen, Danmarks Nationalbank, and Saint Catherine's College in Oxford.

Jacobsen mastered the range of design from large, complex building projects to the teaspoon in a set of cutlery. His designs came into existence as brief sketches and were then modelled in plaster or cardboard in full size. He kept on working until his revolutionary ideas had been realised at the utmost perfection. 'The Ant' from 1952 became the starting point of his world fame as a furniture designer and became the first of a number of lightweight chairs with the seat and back in one piece of moulded wood. Model '3107' from 1955 is often merely called 'The Number Seven Chair'. It was launched in beech, black and white. '3107' has become the most important success in Danish furniture history - manufactured in more than 5 million copies.

During the 1960s Arne Jacobsen turned to forms such as the circle, cylinder, triangle and cube. His architectural knowledge often informed his other design work and the stainless steel tableware set 'Cylinda-Line' strongly reflects this.

Jacobsen began his career as a Roman Neo-classicist and later built a reputation as a functionalist interpreter of modernism in Denmark. His simple, elegant and functional designs have a remarkable, timeless appeal and have become international design classics.

Two of a set of six Fritz Hansen 'Oxford' chairs, by Arne Jacobsen, each with original yellow leather upholstery on swivelling steel base, Fritz Hansen labels and factory tags.

35.25in (89.5cm) diam

£2,500-3,000 set **SDR**

Two 'Oxford' armchairs, model '3291', designed by Arne Jacobsen for Fritz Hansen from 1965, each with upholstered moulded seat shell on swivelling cast aluminium base with casters.

£250-300 **L&T**

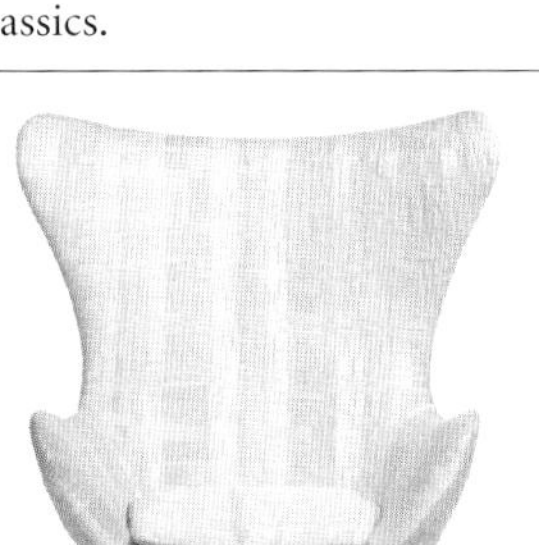

A Fritz Hansen 'Egg' chair, by Arne Jacobsen, with Fritz Hansen tag.

42in (106.5cm) high

£1,500-2,000 **SDR**

One of a pair of Arne Jacobsen 'Swan' chairs, of aluminum, steel, foam and wool, with Fritz Hansen labels.

32in (80cm) high

£1,000-1,500 pair **FRE**

An aluminium-framed 'Swan' sofa designed by Arne Jacobsen from 1957, for Fritz Hansen, lug arms, upholstered in an orange wool material and raised on rectangular supports, linked by a stretcher on trestle base, black plastic capped feet.

59.25in (148cm) wide

£450-550 **L&T**

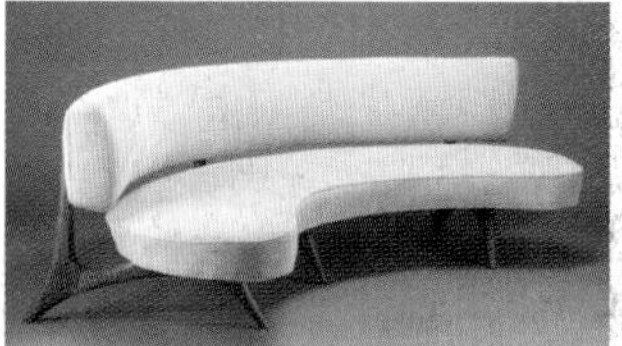

A fine Vladimir Kagan curvilinear sofa, upholstered in light beige chenille, on a sculpted walnut base with flaring legs, unmarked.

95in (237.5cm) wide

£10,000-12,000 **DRA**

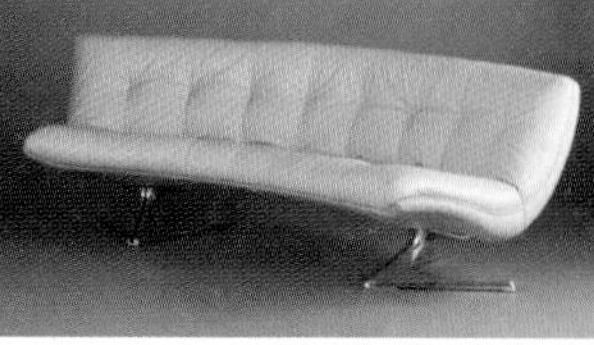

An exceptional Vladimir Kagan vintage 'Unicorn' sofa, newly-upholstered in a superior grade of tufted seafoam green Italian leather on a highly-sculptural steel base, unmarked.

102in (255cm) wide

£5,000-8,000 **DRA**

A fine biomorphic 'Cloud' sofa, by Vladimir Kagan, fully upholstered in lavender mohair, on wooden base, unmarked.

48in (122cm) wide

£5,000-8,000 **SDR**

A sofa upholstered in purple fabric, on short tapering legs, by Vladimir Kagan, reupholstered, unmarked.

82.5in (209.5cm) wide

£1,500-2,000 **SDR**

A cherry wood rocker and ottoman, by Vladimir Kagan, each on sculptural frames with fine and unusual woven leather tapestry in dark brown, unmarked.

41in (104cm) high

£6,000-9,000 **SDR**

A fine and rare Vladimir Kagan walnut-stained cherry rocker and ottoman, on biomorphic frames, each upholstered in fine burgundy leather, ottoman signed "Vladimir Kagan/1 of 6".

Chair 33.75in (84cm) high

£5,000-8,000 **DRA**

An extension dining table, by Vladimir Kagan, with curved edges and radiating grain pattern on top, sculpted walnut base, includes three leaves and centre leg for use with extension, unmarked.

62in (157.5cm) wide

£2,000-2,500 **SDR**

A prototype Isamu Noguchi rocking stool, with bevel-edged seat and base on a black-enamelled chrome wire shaft, missing one J-connector, unmarked.

This rare prototypical rocking stool is from the personal collection of Charles Niedringhaus, a former Knoll executive. Throughout his long career with Knoll, Mr. Niedringhaus often acted as an artistic liaison linking the inspired visions of designers such as Isamu Noguchi with Knoll's engineers, draughtsmen, and marketing departments. This confluence of art and business was fundamental to Knoll's identity and success.

14in (35cm) wide

£7,000-10,000 **DRA**

One of a set of four Knoll tall-back laminated bentwood chairs, by Frank Gehry, with aubergine enamelled finish, stamped signature and dated 9/1/92.

43in (109cm) high

£2,000-1,500 set **SDR**

A pair Florence Knoll for Knoll lounge chairs, chromium, wool, cloth labels, manufactured 1982.

32in (80cm) wide

£1,200-1,800 **FRE**

A rosewood circular dining table, probably designed by Peter Hvidt, for Knoll Associates, the circular top raised on four cluster column chromium supports.

42in (105cm) diam

£400-600 **L&T**

A 'Tulip' pedestal table, designed by Eero Saarinen for Knoll Associates from 1955, the circular white laminate top on slender pedestal with spreading base.

36in (90cm) diam

£400-600 **L&T**

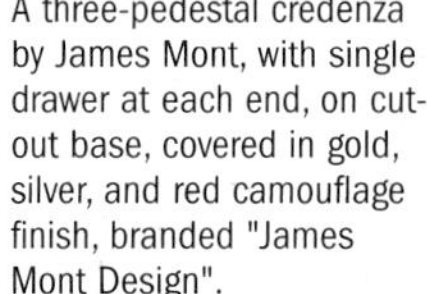

A three-pedestal credenza by James Mont, with single drawer at each end, on cut-out base, covered in gold, silver, and red camouflage finish, branded "James Mont Design".

100in (254cm) wide

£1,000-1,500 **SDR**

A large sofa by James Mont, with black lacquered frame and cross gate panels to back and sides, the seat cushion and back panel upholstered in garnet coloured fabric embossed with Oriental motif, unmarked.

116in (294.5cm) wide

£2,000-3,000 **SDR**

A wall-hanging display unit, by James Mont, with pagoda-shaped top and two panels carved with Chinese genre scenes, in a green-gold finish, marked "James Mont Design" on the back.

42in (106.5cm) high

£700-1,000 **SDR**

A George Nakashima walnut 'Conoid' lounge chair, of walnut and hickory.

33.75in (84cm) wide

£7,000-10,000 **FRE**

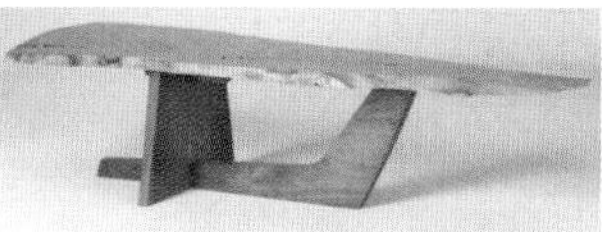

An English walnut coffee table, by George Nakashima, the free-edge top with single rosewood butterfly key, on a sled base, a rare and innovative Nakashima form, with a copy of the original sketch, signed "George Nakashima, June 2 1989".

67in (170cm) wide

£12,000-14,000 **SDR**

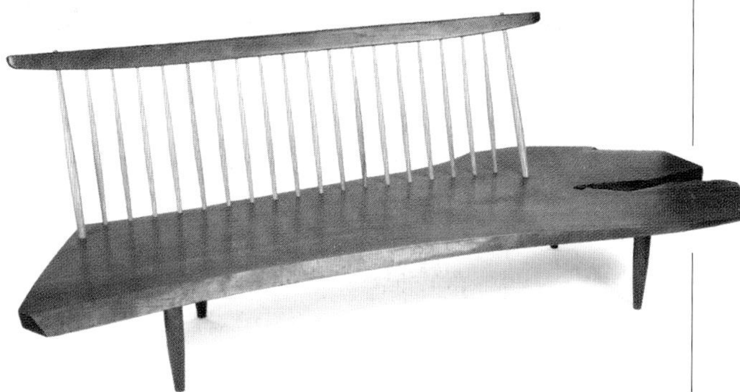

A fine 'Conoid' bench, by George Nakashima, with back in English walnut with hickory spindles, the free-edge seat with one crotch-figured end, on tapering dowel legs, unmarked.

83in (211cm) wide

£18,000-20,000 **SDR**

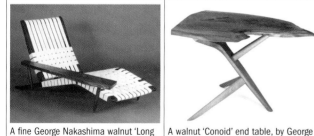

A fine George Nakashima walnut 'Long Chair', with free-edge slab arm, white cotton webbing, and front tapering legs, new webbing and pegs, both done by the Nakashima Studio, unmarked.

66in (165cm) wide

£8,000-12,000 **DRA**

A walnut 'Conoid' end table, by George Nakashima, its free-edge top with two rosewood butterfly keys, accompanied by a copy of the original sketch, signed "George Nakashima/June 2, 1989".

32.75in (83cm) wide

£7,000-10,000 **SDR**

A rare 'Minguren I' side table, by George Nakashima, with exceptional free-form buckeye burl top, with a signed and dated copy of the original drawing, unmarked.

1977 *33.25in (84.5cm) high*

£15,000-20,000 **SDR**

A fine and rare George Nakashima English walnut conoid dining table, signed "George Nakashima Nov 1969".

79in (197.5cm) wide

£30,000-40,000 **FRE**

An early 1970s unusual George Nakashima walnut long desk, with free-edge plank top and two three-drawer pedestals, on tapering dowel legs supports, unmarked.

102in (255cm) wide

£11,000-13,000 **DRA**

A fine walnut sideboard by George Nakashima, with pinned and dovetailed case construction, and three sliding doors enclosing six drawers and three shelves, marked with owner's name on back.

84in (213.5cm) wide

£18,000-20,000 **SDR**

A fine and rare George Nakashima walnut 'Kornbult' cabinet, with dovetailed case, two panelled doors with burl handle, and interior shelf, signed "George Nakashima/Oct. 17, 1985" on bottom of shelf, also marked "Studio" on bottom of case.

1985 *22in (55cm) high*

£10,000-12,000 **DRA**

An early Herman Miller 'Coconut' chair, by George Nelson, on polished metal base with first-production metal shell, newly upholstered in black glove-leather, unmarked.

41in (104cm) wide

£1,500-2,000 **SDR**

A Herman Miller 'Coconut' chair, by George Nelson, upholstered in white leather, unmarked.

41.5in (105.5cm) wide

£3,500-4,500 **SDR**

A fine and very rare Herman Miller coffee table, by George Nelson, with boat-shaped rosewood veneer top, on 'X' shaped legs of black enamelled wood with tubular steel rod supports, "Herman Miller" foil label.

60in (152.5cm) long

£1,200-1,800 **SDR**

GEORGE NELSON (1908-1986)

George Nelson (1908-1986) was one of the most powerful forces behind the development of the 20thC American design aesthetic. Nelson studied architecture at Yale and after graduating travelled through Europe where he met a number of modernist pioneers, including Walter Gropius and Le Corbusier.

Back in the US he became the first associate editor at 'Architectural Forum' and also published several books including "Tomorrow's House" and "How To See."

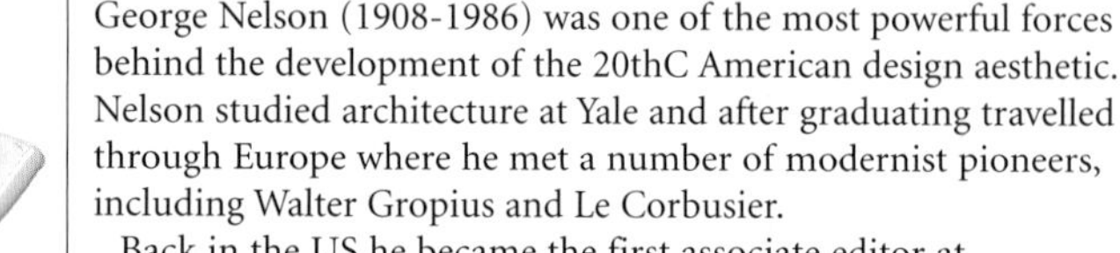

In the late 1940s Nelson came up with two popular inventions: the 'Grass of Main Street', which evolved into today's pedestrian mall, and the 'Storagewall' system. His innovative concepts attracted the attention of Herman Miller. He soon became Miller's design director and started a successful period of collaborations with Ray and Charles Eames, Harry Beroia, and Isamu Noguchi.

After establishing his own office, he went into partnership with Gordon Chadwick and became known as George Nelson & Associates.

His best known pieces show his keen eye for modern design, amongst them are the 1950 'Ball Clock', inspired by representations of the atom, the 1952 'Bubble Lamp' and the 1965 'Marshmallow' sofa, a grid of brightly coloured upholstered circles.

Nelson was an extremely talented and innovative designer as well as an early environmentalist and a powerful communicator of ideas through his writings and teaching.

A George Nelson plywood table, with aluminium legs.

42in (105cm) wide

£400-600 **FRE**

A Herman Miller walnut 'Home Office' desk by George Nelson, on tubular brushed metal frame, the raised cabinet with two leather-covered sliding doors, a fitted interior, the work surface flanked by hinged-top cabinet with tab pull, and mesh file basket, unmarked.

54.25in (138cm) wide

£3,000-4,000 **SDR**

A George Nelson for Herman Miller credenza in oak veneer, with single cabinet door and two sliding doors enamelled in grey, on tubular brushed metal legs, with orange-enamelled sliding door to reverse, and finished back, unmarked.

80in (203cm) wide

£2,000-3,000 **SDR**

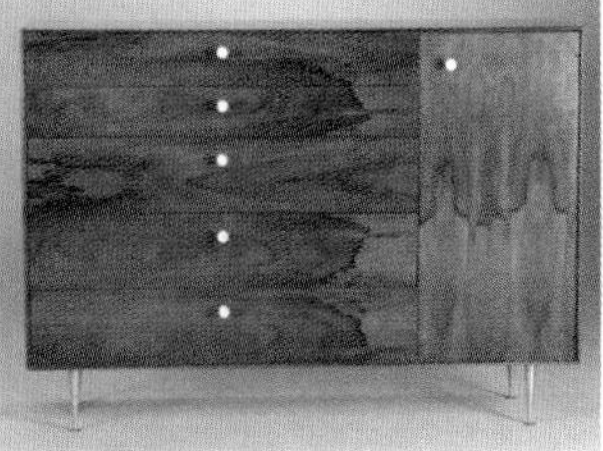

A fine Herman Miller 'Thin Edge' cabinet by George Nelson, in rosewood veneer, with five drawers flanking a cabinet door, with white porcelain pulls on tapering brushed metal legs, unmarked.

55.75in (141.5cm) wide

£3,000-4,000 **SDR**

A 'Heart' chair by Verner Panton, the frame and drop-in seat upholstered in original red fabric, on polished chrome star-shaped base, unmarked.

40in (101.5cm) high

£1,500-2,000 **SDR**

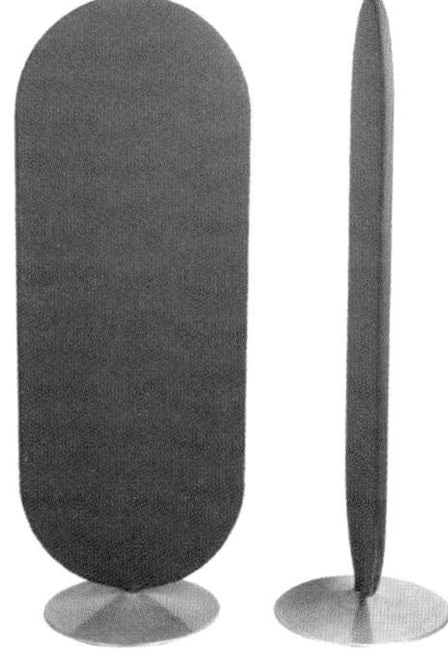

A set of three oval screens upholstered in dark blue-grey wool fabric, by Verner Panton, on circular metal base, unmarked.

62.5in (159cm) high

£800-1,200 set **SDR**

A fine two-piece breakfront, by Tommi Parzinger for Charak Modern, the illuminated top portion with three etched glass doors and mirrored interior, the bottom portion with inlaid door fronts and circular pulls with etched brass centres, stencilled "Charak Modern".

75in (187.5cm) high

£3,000-4,000 **DRA**

A Charak mahogany breakfront, by Tommi Parzinger, the top portion consisting of two glass-panelled cabinets with diamond-pattern latticework, resting on two single-door cabinets with etched brass sunburst pulls, unmarked.

80in (203cm) high

£1,800-2,200 **SDR**

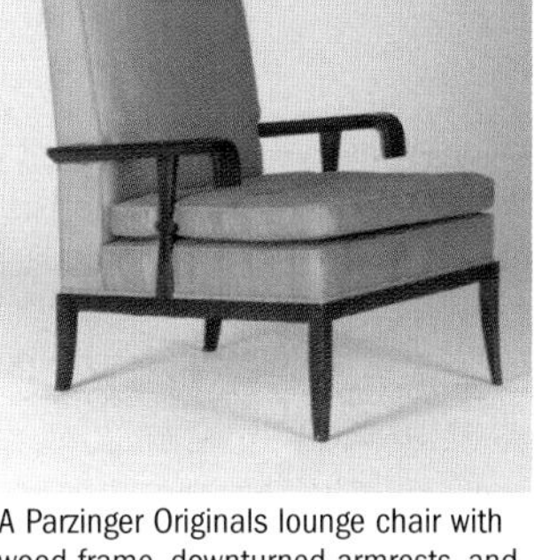

A Parzinger Originals lounge chair with wood frame, downturned armrests, and hourglass-shaped side rails, its frame and loose cushion upholstered in beige and green fabric, unmarked.

38.5in (98cm) high

£1,000-1,500 **SDR**

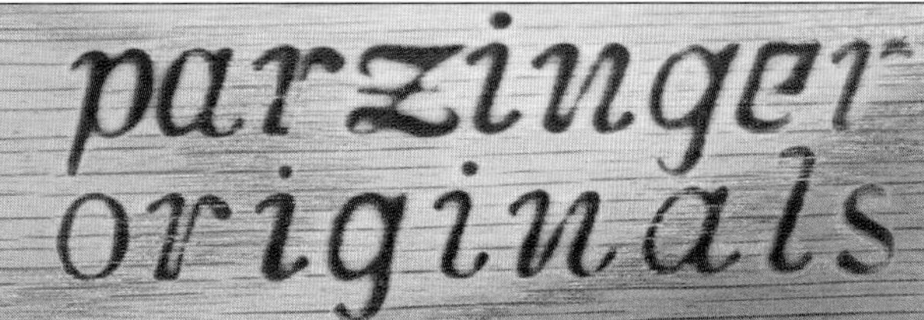

An exceptional custom-designed sideboard with orange lacquered finish, by Tommi Parzinger, with four cabinet doors concealing drawers and shelves, with brass corner brackets and etched brass pulls, strap hardware and bun feet, signed "Parzinger Originals".

84in (213.5cm) wide

£11,000-13,000 **SDR**

A custom-designed lacquered buffet by Tommi Parzinger, with four doors concealing single drawer and two adjustable shelves, with large matte chrome ring pulls on plinth base, marked "Parzinger Originals"

72in (183cm) wide

£5,000-7,000 **SDR**

A pair of iron floor lamps by Tommi Parzinger, each with four candlestick fixtures with brass bobeches and original white crêpe drum shades with black trim, unmarked.

72in (183cm) high

£5,000-8,000 **SDR**

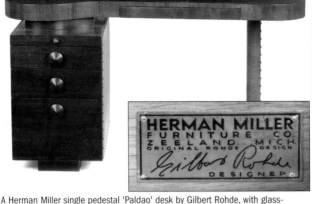

A Herman Miller single pedestal 'Paldao' desk by Gilbert Rohde, with glass-covered kidney shaped top and two shallow blind drawers, over pull-out shelf and drawers with carved wood pulls, and leatherette details, foil Herman Miller and Gilbert Rohde label.

52in (132cm) wide

£2,000-2,500 **SDR**

A fine Herman Miller single-pedestal desk with raised rectangular frame over drawers with horizontal off-centre pulls and birds-eye maple veneer fronts, missing glass insert for top, foil label "Herman Miller Furniture Co. Zeeland Michigan Original Rohde Design".

52in (132cm) wide

£1,200-1,800 **SDR**

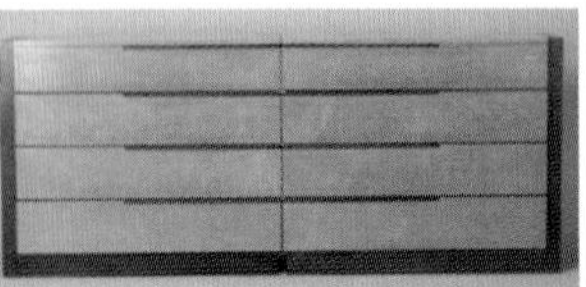

A pair of fine Herman Miller four drawer matched chests, by Gilbert Rohde, each with horizontal off-centre pulls and bird's eye maple veneer drawer fronts, on plinth base, foil label "Herman Miller Furniture Co. Zeeland Michigan Original Rohde Design".

43in (109cm) wide

£3,000-4,000 **SDR**

One of a pair of Herman Miller twin beds by Gilbert Rohde in walnut and bird's eye maple veneer.

79in (200.5cm) wide

£800-1,200 pair **SDR**

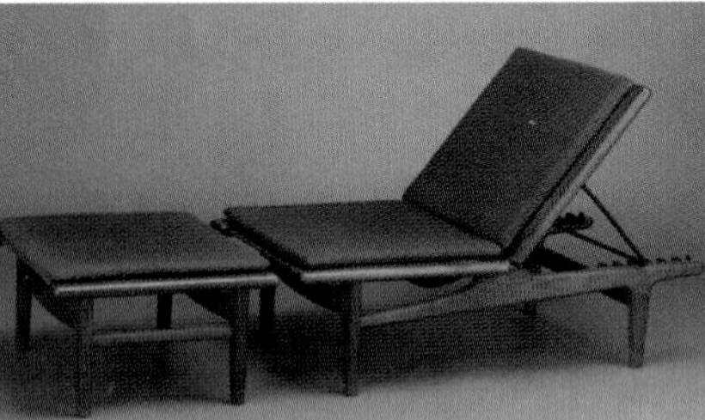

A Hans Wegner for Getama two-piece chaise lounge with adjustable, fold-down back that converts to a daybed, and green fabric-covered spring seat supports with cushions upholstered in blue wool, unmarked.

72.5in (181cm) wide

£1,500-2,000 **DRA**

A Johannes Hansen teak bench by Hans Wegner, with broad slats on top, on tapering plank legs, branded mark.

62.75in (159.5cm) wide

£2,500-3,000 **SDR**

A rare Johannes Hansen 'Valet' chair, by Hans Wegner, with contoured back, and hinged seat concealing small storage compartment, on tapering three-legged base, branded mark.

An icon of Danish Modern design, this chair encompasses a perfect blend of form and function.

38in (96.5cm) high

£2,500-3,500 **SDR**

A two-piece 'Drexel' black-lacquered breakfront in Chinese style, by Edward Wormley, the top portion with pen shelves and central cabinet door with caned back panel, the lower portion with four caned-panel doors, with square pulls, unmarked.

72.25in (183.5cm) high

£1,200-1,800 **SDR**

A 'Dunbar' bleached mahogany magazine tree, by Edward Wormley, with five shelves of graduated size, on base with shoe feet, branded "Dunbar" with "4764".

27.5in (70cm) high

£1,800-2,200 **SDR**

A fine Edward Wormley for Dunbar ebonised buffet with three drawers over three sliding doors with brass and woven walnut slats, on leather-wrapped plinth base, in pristine condition, brass Dunbar and paper factory tags.

61.5in (154cm) wide

£2,500-3,500 **DRA**

A Dunbar triangular magazine rack, by Edward Wormley, with marblized green leather side straps and inset panel to top, over lower shelf, brass "D" tag, factory label.

26.25in (66.5cm) high

£300-500 **SDR**

From top:

An Edward Wormley for Dunbar wooden candlestand.

24.5in (61cm) high

£1,800-2,200 **FRE**

An Edward Wormley for Dunbar 'Long John' stool, of mahogany and rosewood, with a green metal tag and paper label, losses.

12in (30cm) high

£300-500 **FRE**

An Edward Wormley for Dunbar 'Long John' bench, of mahogany and bentwood, with a green metal tag.

48in (120cm) wide

£700-1,000 **FRE**

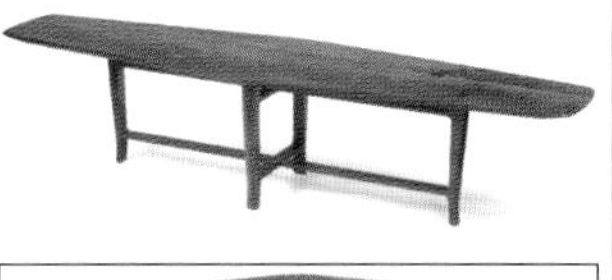

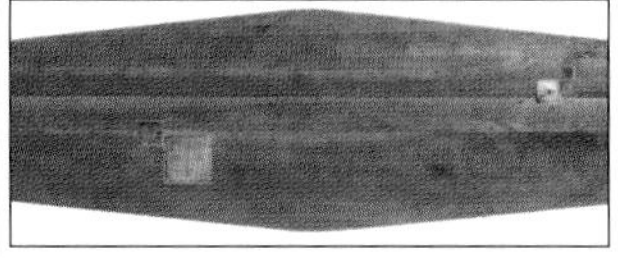

A rare Dunbar coffee table, by Edward Wormley, with six-sided top inset with square Tiffany lustred glass tiles, on base with double cruciform stretcher, brass "Dunbar" tag.

77in (195.5cm) wide

£5,000-8,000 **SDR**

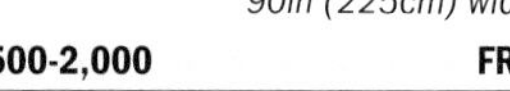

An Edward Wormley for Dunbar 'Angelo' sofa, of mahogany and upholstery.

90in (225cm) wide

£1,500-2,000 **FRE**

A rare and early 'Finnsven' lounge chair by Alvar Aalto, on laminated bentwood frame, with original orange tweed upholstery, unmarked.

31.5in (80cm) wide

£2,500-3,000 **SDR**

A 'Tank' chair by Alvar Aalto, with bent laminated birch sides and original tiger-skin fabric upholstery, unmarked.

30.5in (77.5cm) wide

£2,000-3,000 **SDR**

A Richard Artschwager chair, of red oak, formica, lacquered steel, covered with cowskin, artist's signature underneath the seat, "1990" and "27/100" in black pen.

1990 *40.5in (101.5cm) wide*

£5,000-7,000 **QU**

A set of six rosewood 'Scandia' dining chairs designed by Hans Brattrud, for Hove Moblier, Norway, each with bent-ply rosewood veneered slatted backs and seats on chromium supports, maker's labels.

£800-1,200 **L&T**

An early Marcel Breuer experimental student desk/drafting table, on trestle base with bentwood legs and shoe feet, unmarked.

c1940 *28in (70cm) wide*

£2,000-3,000 **DRA**

An early Marcel Breuer experimental student desk/drafting table, on cantilevered base, unmarked.

c1940 *27in (67.5cm) high*

£4,000-6,000 **DRA**

A set of three 'O.D. Mobler' bar stools, by Erik Buck, each with black leather upholstered seat on teak base with arched stretchers to front and back, and rosewood footrest, "O.D. Mobler OS" foil label.

c1965 *33.25in (84.5cm) high*

£700-1,000 **SDR**

An' Aeron' office chair designed by Donald Chadwick and William Stumpf, for Herman Miller from 1992, with recycled aluminium and fibreglass reinforced frame and base, the mesh and back raised on base with casters.

£280-320 **L&T**

A pair of orange plastic sectional tables designed by A. Castelli, for Kartell, each of rectangular form with cut-out apertures enclosing open shelves, moulded marks.

£60-90 **L&T**

A fine Michael Coffey prototype 'Variations' sculpted wall-hanging desk/cabinet of Mozambique and White Oak, with dovetail corner construction and drop-front door concealing drawers, paper and letter compartments, cork bulletin board, and task light, signed "M. Coffey".

42in (105cm) wide

£2,000-3,000 **DRA**

Two of a set of four very rare side chairs, by Luther Conover, each with broad plank seat and back mounted on tubular black iron frame with pyramidal base, unmarked.

31in (78.5cm) high

£2,500-3,500 set **SDR**

A 'Mae West Lips' sofa after a 1930s design by Salvador Dali, originally executed by Green and Abbot of London, and Jean-Michel Frank in Paris, this example with wood infrastructure, upholstered in linen, with tacks along the base, unmarked.

87in (221cm) wide

£3,500-4,500 **SDR**

A Donald Deskey double-sink with two stainless steel basins and serpentine centre, its wood frame covered in sheet aluminum with channelled surfaces to either side, unmarked.

80.5in (201cm) wide

£1,800-2,200 **DRA**

A Paul Frankl coffee table, made by Johnson Furniture, of cork and mahogany.

46in (115cm) wide

£1,500-2,000 **FRE**

A rare lounge chair, by A.J. Donahue, with bent plywood frame covered in dark brown enamel, and brown leather upholstered cushion, on tubular black iron base, unmarked.

Also called the 'Canadian Coconut' chair, this design stemmed from Donahue's post-war research into new building materials and had only a limited production.

c1945 *39in (99cm) high*

£1,200-1,800 **SDR**

A pair of white 'Egg' chairs designed by Peter Ghyczy, for Reuter Produkts from 1968, each with hinged lid enclosing upholstered seats, and a matching low table, the circular top with spreading base.

£1,000-1,500 **L&T**

In the manner of Diego Giacometti, a fine bronze dining table with overhanging rectangular plate glass top, the legs of its base modelled with unicorn heads and hoof feet, covered in a verdigris patina with stretcher, chip, bears the mark "Diego".

72in (180cm) wide

£12,000-14,000 **DRA**

A 1950s Daniel Jackson 'Fish' coffee table, Philadelphia, of walnut and glass.

71in (177.5cm) wide

£3,000-5,000 **FRE**

A fine bronze coffee table with scalloped top depicting scenes in a Chinese courtyard, on faceted pedestal base, signed "Philip & Kevin LaVerne".

36.75in (93.5cm) wide

£2,000-3,000 **SDR**

A fine and rare Finn Juhl 'Chieftain' chair with brown leather-upholstered armrests, seat and tufted back, on dowel-leg frame with sculpted backrails, missing one button, minor crackling to seat leather, unmarked.

The Chieftain chair, Finn Juhl's masterpiece, combines comfort with architectural sophistication.

40in (100cm) wide

£4,500-5,500 **DRA**

A Murano glass bar, with kidney-shaped stainless steel top, textured emerald green glass fixtures along top and bottom over fluorescent lighting, and glass panes along front and side depicting fish and sea plants, the back with pull-out stainless steel work shelf and three cabinet doors with circular glass pulls, on castered base, unmarked, minor repairs.

81in (205.5cm) wide

£11,000-13,000 **SDR**

A George Mann Neidecken rare side table, with square multi-layered top and faceted cross-pedestal base, unmarked.

Executed for the Edward R. Irving House in Decatur, IL, designed by Frank Lloyd Wright.

c1910 *30.5in (76cm) high*

£4,000-6,000 **DRA**

A Richard Scott Newman 'Hi-Lo' coffee table, with bevel-edged oval glass top mounted on an organic chip-carved tree trunk base with internal mechanism for adjusting height, a few chips to glass, unmarked.

c1975 *60in (150cm) wide*

£2,000-3,000 **DRA**

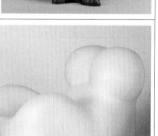

A B&B Italia 'Donna' foam lounge chair and ottoman by Gaetano Pesce, from the 'UP' series, each fully upholstered in yellow stretch fabric, "B&B Italia" label.

£1,800-2,200 **SDR**

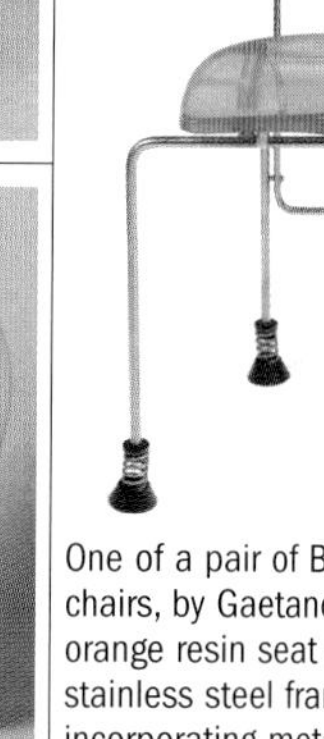

One of a pair of Bernini '543 Broadway' chairs, by Gaetano Pesce, each with orange resin seat and back, on stainless steel frame with nylon feet incorporating metal springs, embossed mark.

28.75in (73cm) high

£800-1,200 pair **SDR**

A 'Plana' folding table, designed by Giancarlo Piretti for Castelli, with four hinged and moulded black panels opening to form a square top, slender columns on four strut supports, with maker's mark.

33.5in (85.5cm) wide

£400-600 **L&T**

A Gio Ponti dining table, with wood trestle and green marble base with brass trim, unmarked.

c1940 *78.5in (199.5cm) wide*

£3,000-4,000 **SDR**

A fine and rare Phil Powell dining table, with original oval slate top, on pedestal base of stack-laminated walnut with gilded apron, unmarked.

Phil Powell was one of the New Hope School's most innovative and talented designers, who helped to pioneer organic design through the use of stack-laminated furniture construction.

66in (167.5cm) wide

£6,000-8,000 **SDR**

One of a set of six Phil Powell laminated walnut armchairs, with sculpted frame and black upholstery to back and seat pad, with nylon webbed seat support, two professionally restored, unmarked.

Powell was an eclectic designer and railed against the conformity of matching sets. It is therefore very unusual to find a set of Powell chairs. This particular form is also very rare.

34.25in (87cm) high

£2,000-3,000 set **SDR**

A rare child's-size settee, by John Risley, with the figures of a man and a woman, the drop-in seat pad covered in black and grey striped cotton fabric, marked with initials on side.

35.25in (89.5cm) high

£1,200-1,800 **SDR**

Two chrome and black-enamelled side tables, one two-tiered circular by Royal, the other with rectangular top and base, with two columnar supports, one marked with metal tag.

£200-300 **DRA**

A 'Relax' armchair by Jean Royere, with spring seat support, frame and loose seat cushion reupholstered in dark brown mohair, on cylindrical blond wood feet, unmarked.

40in (101.5cm) high

£6,000-8,000 **SDR**

A post-modern stainless steel armchair by Johnathan Singleton, with brown leather upholstered seat cushion, signed on bottom, with numbers.

41in (104cm) high

£3,000-5,000 **SDR**

A coffee table by Karl Springer, with amoeba-shaped top, asymmetrically placed on a conforming pedestal base with brass trim, covered in an ivory and brown lacquered finish, unmarked.

59in (150cm) wide

£600-900 **SDR**

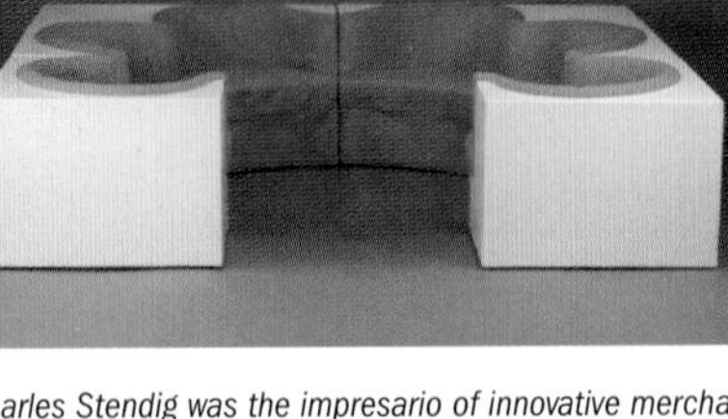

A rare and important late 1960s 'Safari' modular sofa, designed by Archizoom Associati for Poltronova, comprising four fibreglass components fitting together to form a scalloped interior, original tweed upholstery over latex foam, imported by Stendig, Inc. for the US market, Stendig label.

Charles Stendig was the impresario of innovative merchandising, introducing to the US modern designs from Italy and Scandinavia, over forty years ago. His selective eye is apparent in this piece, which combines Pop-Art, kitsch and the spirit of the times.

104in (260cm) wide

£7,000-10,000 **DRA**

Two of a set of six plywood chairs by The Architectural Collaborative, each with orange enamelled back and white enamelled seat, restored to their original colours, unmarked.

30.75in (78cm) high

£1,200-1,800 set **SDR**

A rare carved wood music stand by Smokey Tunis, with red, green and orange painted finish, crooked spine, and two lower shelves, on canted base, unmarked.

56.5in (143.5cm) high

£1,500-2,000 **SDR**

A fine post-modern media cabinet by Bruce Volz, of dyed exotic wood veneer with gold leaf and applied sunburst motif on doors, with two panels, two shelves and electrical box to interior, and inlaid geometric design on base, signed "Bruce Volz 92".

1992 *67.25in (171cm) high*

£1,500-2,000 **SDR**

An Arne Vodder loveseat, with contoured frame reupholstered in umber fabric with light confetti-pattern in teal, orange and yellow green, and loose seat cushion, covered in olive green leather, on flared dowel-leg base, branded "George Tanier Selection".

c1965 *65in (165cm) wide*

£400-600 **DRA**

An L. Woodard & Son armrocker with soldered metal barrel frame and oak arms, backrest and rockers, seat upholstered in original floral vinyl, unmarked.

32in (81cm) high

£200-300 **DRA**

A fine 'Heywood Wakefield' end table by Russel Wright, in contrasting veneers, its two drawers with broad horizontal polished chrome pulls, flanked by open shelves, unmarked.

28.5in (72.5cm) wide

£7,000-10,000 **SDR**

One of a pair of 1950s maple spoon-back chairs with ebonised decoration.

36in (91.5cm) high

£5,500-6,500 pair **B&I**

A Windsor-style settee, by L. Woodward & Son, Minnesota, with horizontal plank back, spindled wrought iron frame and cream-coloured vinyl seat cushion, unmarked.

59.25in (150.5cm) wide

£450-550 **DRA**

A Robert Worth settee and table, Philadelphia.

Robert Worth, a graduate of the Rochester Institute of Technology, was chairman of the Philadelphia College of Art (University of the Arts) woodworking department. This piece featured in Philadelphia Magazine, August 1982.

c1980

£1,200-1,800 **FRE**

Two 1920s French club chairs with original leather upholstery, one in brown and the other in reddish-brown, with loose seat cushions, tacks to back and wood feet, unmarked.

34in (86.5cm) high

£1,500-2,000 **SDR**

A 1960s circular glass-topped table on four decorated sabre supports and a circular plinth base with splayed brass border.

46in (117cm) diam

£3,000-5,000 **BL**

A blond bird's-eye maple chest of drawers, Italian, with two short and three long drawers with circular knob handles and projecting splayed apron on recessed square tapered legs.

c1955 *47in (119.5cm) wide*

£1,800-2,200 **BL**

A three-seat sofa with tubular bright chrome and black metal frame, loose seat and back cushions upholstered in red and royal blue vinyl and black enamelled armrests, unmarked.

69.5in (176.5cm) wide

£700-1,000 **DRA**

A tubular metal-frame sofa and armchair with bright chrome finish, black enamelled wood armrests and loose grey vinyl-upholstered seat and back cushions, unmarked.

Sofa 69in (175cm) wide

£500-800 **DRA**

A four-drawer chest, accompanied by a wall-hanging mirror, unmarked.

50in (127cm) wide

£1,200-1,800 **SDR**

A bronze and ebonised wood side chair on zoomorphic frame, unmarked.

41in (104cm) high

£600-900 **SDR**

A rosewood sewing chest with centre-hinged top, with a plastic fitted insert, over a brown suede bin on cylindrical wooden legs with stretcher, foil tag reading "Prize 1 Norwegian Design Competition 1962, Des-Rastad Og Relling Prod Rasmus Solberg".

23.5in (59.5cm) diam

£700-1,000 **SDR**

MODERN GLASS

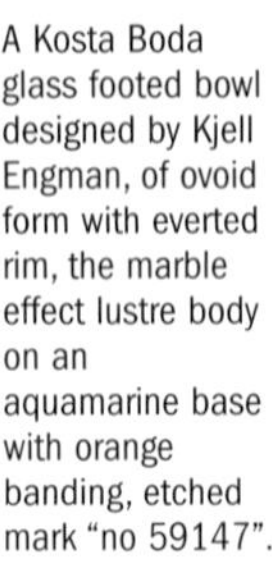

A Kosta Boda glass footed bowl designed by Kjell Engman, of ovoid form with everted rim, the marble effect lustre body on an aquamarine base with orange banding, etched mark "no 59147".

10in (26cm) high

£150-200 **L&T**

A Vicke Lindstrand 'Unica' vase, by Kosta, in cream glass with red strands.

c1960 *20cm high*

£300-400 **JH**

A Kosta 1950s Vicke Lindstrand vase, 'The Bath', marked "LG150J95"4.

8.25in (21cm) high

£180-220 **JH**

An Ernest Gordon sandblasted and cut bowl, for Kosta.

1954 *4.5in (11cm) high*

£400-500 **JH**

A Kosta glass vase designed by Vicke Lindstrand, the undulating clear glass tapered body etched with birds, perched on leafy branches, etched mark "Kosta * * 268".

12in (30cm) high

£400-600 **L&T**

A Kosta clear glass vase, of teardrop outline with alternating concave and convex panels, the interior with concentric blue and yellow ovoid inclusions, etched mark "Kosta ss 172".

4.5in (11cm) high

£200-250 **L&T**

MURANO

A large vase with lobed base by Dino Martens, in transparent tortoise-shell and coloured glass, with aventurine highlights, some minor scratches to the body, unmarked.

13in (33cm) high

£6,000-9,000 **SDR**

A tall Aureliano Toso 'Oriente' glass vase by Dino Martens, of organic shape embedded with multi-coloured forms, zanfirico canes, and aventurine highlights, paper label with "Made in Italy".

15in (38cm) high

£5,000-7,000 **SDR**

An Aureliano Toso 'Oriente' vase, design by Dino Martens, Murano.

1952 *11in (28cm) high*

£3,000-4,000 **FIS**

A vase designed by Ansolo Fuga for AVEM, Murano, the clear glass with murrine and cane inserts.

c1960 *10in (25cm) high*

£2,000-3,000 **FIS**

A fine AVEM tall vase by Guilio Radi, with protruding mid-section and internal latticework decoration in black and gold encased in green and amber glass, unmarked.

c1950 *13.75in (35cm) high*

£1,500-2,000 **SDR**

A rare AVEM promotional showpiece, by Emilio Nason.

This was made by Nason for use on display stands or in a shop as an advertising display piece in the first years of the AVEM (Arte Vetraria Muranese) factory.

1932-1934 *16.5in (42cm) high*

£8,000-10,000 **VET**

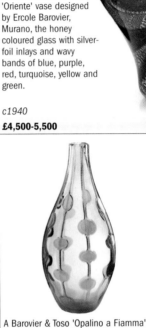

A rare Barovier & Toso 'Oriente' vase designed by Ercole Barovier, Murano, the honey coloured glass with silver-foil inlays and wavy bands of blue, purple, red, turquoise, yellow and green.

c1940 *7.25in (18cm) high*

£4,500-5,500 **FIS**

A Barovier & Toso 'Opalino a Fiamma' vase designed by Ercole Barovier, Murano, clear glass with vertical stripes and opalescent dot pattern.

c1955 *16.25in (40.5cm) high*

£800-1,200 **FIS**

A tesserae bowl, designed and made by Ercole Barovier for Barovier & Toso, bearing his inscribed signature to the base.

c1955 *9.5in (24.5cm) diam*

£2,000-3,000 **VET**

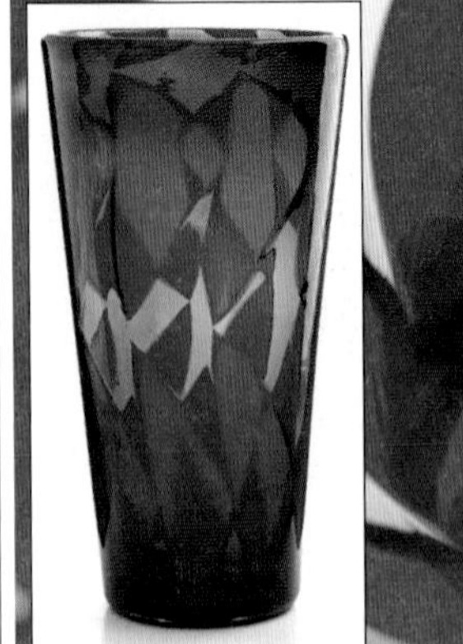

A Barovier & Toso 'Intarsio' vase designed by Ercole Barovier, Murano, clear glass with mosaic triangle pattern in red and brown.

1961 *12.5in (31cm) high*

£1,800-2,200 **FIS**

An Ercole Barovier bowl 'Sidereo', cylindrical wall on lentil-shaped base, produced by Barovier & Toso, Murano, clear glass with melted on rings of clear glass with white core, signed "Ercole Barovier Murano".

1966 *8in (20cm) diam*

£400-600 **QU**

A rare Barovier & Toso 'Athena Cattedrale' vase designed by Ercole Barovier, Murano, clear glass with blue and green murrine 'Athena' pattern.

1967 *12.5in (33cm) high*

£4,500-5,500 **FIS**

An aventurine murrine and pietini vase, designed and made by Vittorio Ferro at the Fratelli Pagnin factory from glass made at the De Majo factory.

2000 *9in (23cm) high*

£3,000-3,500 **PC**

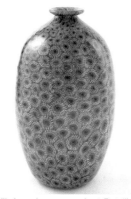

A 'Kiku' murrine vase made at Fratelli Toso with murrines designed and made by Ulderico Moretti.

c1930 *9.5in (24.5cm) high*

£5,500-6,500 **VET**

A Fratelli Toso 'Stellato' vase designed by Pollio Perelda, Murano, clear glass with multicoloured star-shaped 'aventurine' decoration, original label.

1953 *11.25in (28.5cm) high*

£2,500-3,500 **FIS**

A 'Kiku' murrine vase designed by Ermanno Toso and made at the Fratelli Toso factory.

c1950 *10.25in (26cm) high*

£5,500-6,500 **VET**

A 1960s concentric circle murrine vase, made at the Fratelli Toso factory.

7.75in (20cm) high

£700-1,000 **VET**

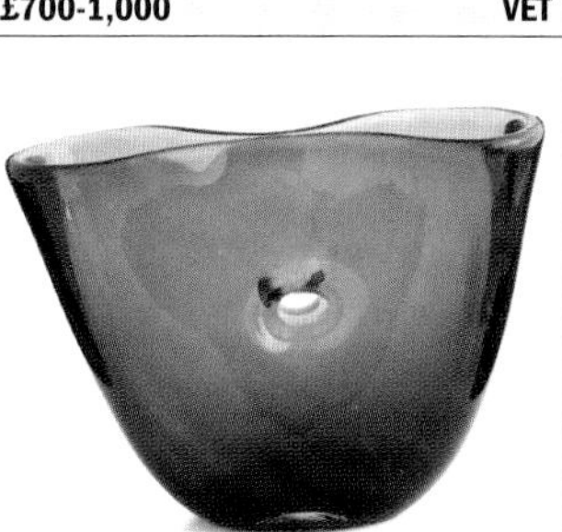

A Venini 'Forato' vase, designed by Fulvio Bianconi, Murano, clear glass with a purple underlay, signed.

1951 *10.25in (19.5cm) high*

£700-1,000 **FIS**

An important Venini 'Pezzato' vase designed by Fulvio Bianconi, Murano, clear glass with red, blue, beige and green 'tesserae' pattern, signed.

1950 *8in (20.5cm) high*

£4,500-5,500 **FIS**

A Venini vase designed by Fulvio Bianconi, Murano, with red and blue bands bands on clear glass, signed.

1951 *9.5in (24cm) high*

£2,000-3,000 **FIS**

A Venini 'Occhi' vase, designed by Carlo Scarpa, Murano, red mosaic tile pattern on clear glass.

c1960 *8.75in (22cm) high*

£1,000-1,500 **FIS**

A late 1950s I.V.R. Mazzego 'Egyptian wine bearer' figurine, designed or inspired by Fulvio Bianconi.

The use of a red interior on the amphora and the speckled white glass of the body relates to other pieces known to have been designed by Bianconi when he worked at the Venini and Cenedese factories.

15in (38cm) high

£5,500-6,000 **VET**

A late 1950s Venini decanter.

£600-900 **JH**

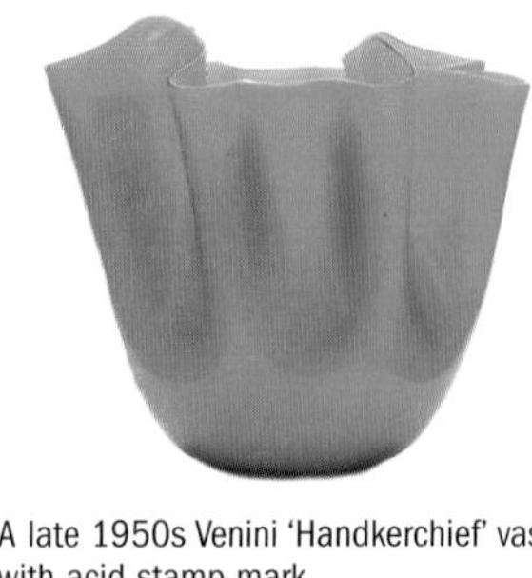

A late 1950s Venini 'Handkerchief' vase, with acid stamp mark.

The fact that the vase was marked with an acid stamp means it was made before 1960.

6in (12cm) high

£180-220 **JH**

A pezzato vase designed and made by Vittorio Ferro, signed "VITTORIO FERRO V&A MURANO".

2000 *10in (25cm) high*

£1,200-1,800 **VET**

A large blue and green 'Windy' murrine vase cased in clear glass, designed and made by Vittorio Ferro and signed to the base "Vittorio Ferro".

These murrines are known as 'Windy' as they are slightly blurred, giving the impression of movement in the wind.

2002 *12.5in (31.5cm) high*

£2,200-2,800 **VET**

A green and red 'flattened drop' shaped murrine vase designed and made by Vittorio Ferro, signed on the base "VITTORIO FERRO".

This piece is in the Corning Museum of Glass collection.

2002 *18.5in (47cm) high*

£1,500-2,000 **VET**

A large green, orange, blue and yellow baluster murrine vase designed and made by Vittorio Ferro, with iridescent areas between the murrines, signed on the base "VITTORIO FERRO".

2002 *14.5in (37cm) high*

£2,200-2,800 **VET**

A Seguso Vetri d'Arte 'Sommerso' vase designed by Flavio Poli, with original label, model number '13886'.

c1950 *14.75in (37cm) high*

£1,000-1,500 **FIS**

An Edward Harald for Orrefors vase, engraved with feathers, designed 1953.

1954 *5in (13cm) high*

£450-500 **JH**

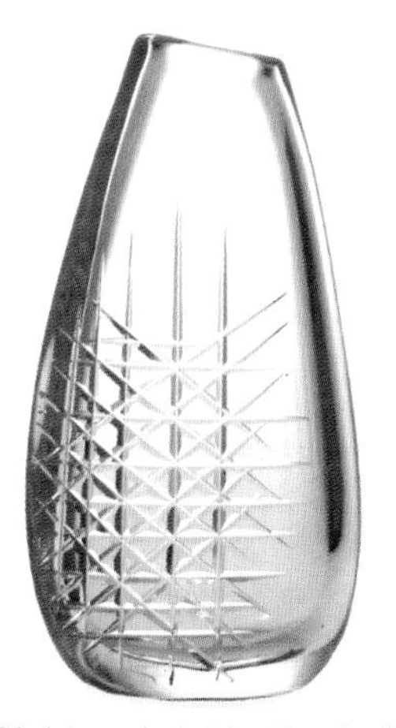

A 'Toledo' vase by Ingeborg Lunden for Orrefors.

10.5in (26.5cm) high

£140-180 **JH**

An Orrefors 'Ariel' bowl.

c1950

£300-400 **JH**

A 1960s Orrefors 'Kraka' vase.

6in (15.5cm) high

£550-650 **JH**

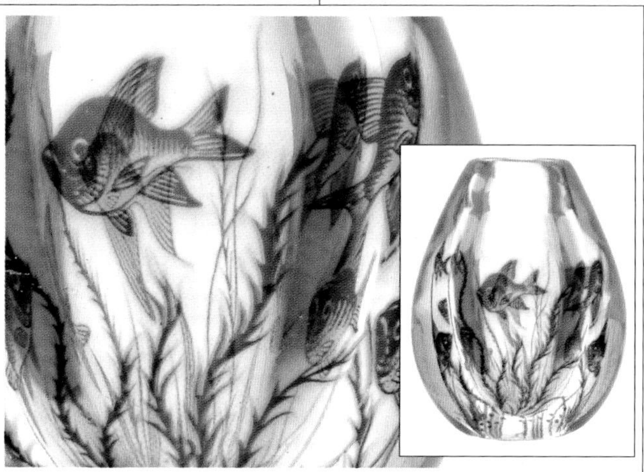

An Orrefors fish 'Graal' vase.

The reflections and refractions in the glass mean there appear to be twice as many fish. The vase was first designed in 1937 and was made for many decades. However quality decreased as time went on.

c1950 *7.75in (20cm) high*

£600-800 **JH**

A 1950s John Luxton for Stuart vase.

This design was originally intended for the US market, as a joint venture with Royal Worcester's agent.

10in (25cm) high

£300-400 **JH**

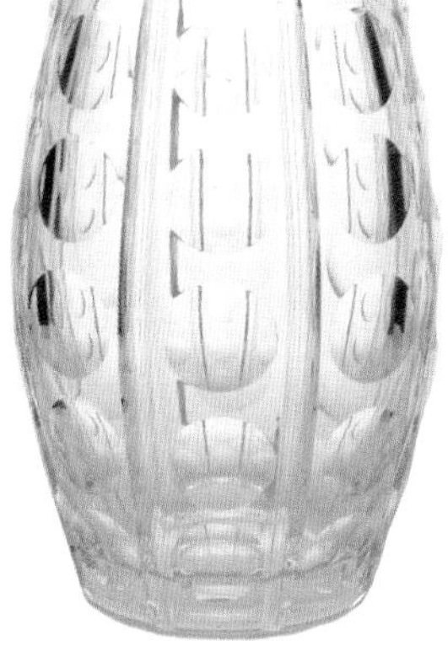

A John Luxton design for Stuart, a barrel vase with seven panels of four polished lenses between vertical flutes, marked "Stuart England".

c1950 *7.5in (19cm) high*

£500-700 **JH**

A 1950s Webb vase with alternating panels of mitre cut and engraved leaf motifs, designed by David Hammond, pattern number 52873/5256, marked "Webbs England".

This was one of the rarest designs: "Echo" is more common. The 1950s price was 50/-.

8.5in (21.5cm) high

£500-700 **JH**

A late 1940s Webb cut bowl, the heavy cut vase designed by Tom Pitchford.

10in (25.5cm) diam

£400-600 **JH**

A mid-1950s Webb Corbett tall cut glass vase with daffodil motifs, designed by David Smith.

11in (28cm) high

£400-600 **JH**

A Webb Corbett barrel vase with five bands of polished circles between triple horizontal cuts, designed by Irene Stevens, circle mark.

c1950 *8.75in (22.5cm) high*

£500-600 **JH**

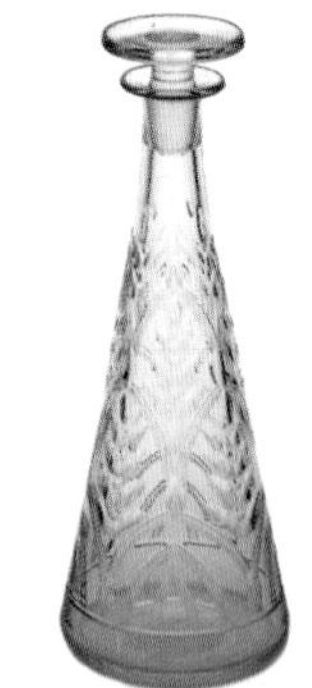

A mid-1930s Webb Corbett cut decanter, with leaf design, with flat stopper, probably by Herbert Webb.

11.75in (30cm) high

£300-400 **JH**

A small Whitefriars textured 'Drunken Bricklayer' vase in indigo designed by Geoffrey Baxter, pattern no. 9673.

1967 *8.5in (21.5cm) high*

£200-250 **TCS**

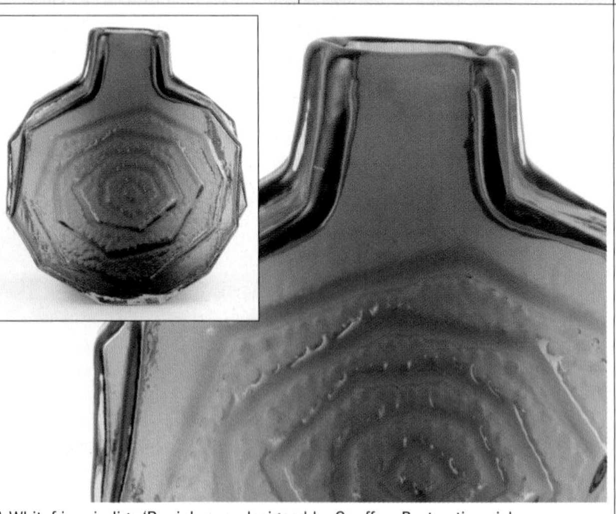

A Whitefriars indigo 'Banjo' vase, designed by Geoffrey Baxter, tiny nicks.

12.25in (31cm) high

£1,000-1,500 **WW**

A Whitefriars tangerine 'Hoop' vase, designed by Geoffrey Baxter.

11.5in (29cm) high

£200-300 **WW**

A Whitefriars new 'Studio' range gold amber cylinder vase with silver nitrate strapping to centre designed by Geoffrey Baxter, pattern 9882.

c1980 *10in (25.5cm) high*

£520-580 **TCS**

A Whitefriars 'Studio' range 'Peacock' ancient urn vase, silver nitrate random strapwork centre band, designed by Peter Wheeler, pattern no. S13.

c1970 *11.5in (29cm) high*

£700-1,000 **TCS**

A Whitefriars peacock-blue lamp base with wave rib.

c1930 *10.5in (27cm) high*

£320-380 **TCS**

A large bowl by Hadelands, mould blown with moulded diamond pattern and folded rim, designed by Arne Jon Jutrem.

c1960 *9.5in (24cm) diam*

£400-500 **JH**

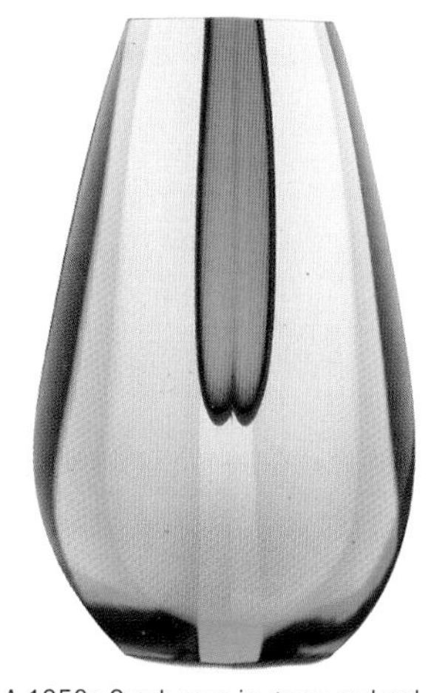

A 1950s Czech vase in green and red, probably by Pavel Hlava.

c1935 *8.25in (21cm) high*

£700-900 **JH**

A French red, cut glass vase for the 250th anniversary of St Louis Glassworks, acid stamped on the base.

1982 *15.5in (39cm) high*

£300-400 **JH**

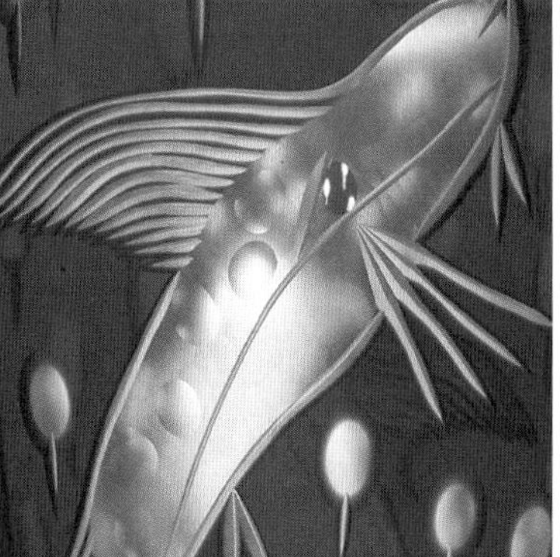

A 1950s Waterford clear and cased carved blue glass vase.

8.75in (22cm) high

£200-300 **JH**

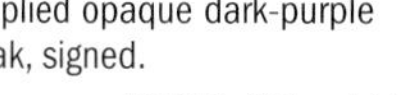

A Egidio Costantini, Fucina degli Angeli 'Colomba' vase designed by Pablo Picasso, clear glass with red overlay, decoration of applied opaque dark-purple bands of glass which mark the dove feathers and beak, signed.

1962 *12.25in (31cm) high*

£6,000-9,000 **FIS**

A Stourbridge cut glass vase with floral design with stylized clover and grass, designed by Harry Cuneen, maker Tudor England.

c1950 *10in (25.5cm) high*

£500-700 **JH**

A 1950s Czech cut glass dish.

14.25in (36cm) diam

£1,200-1,500 **JH**

The floral and maritime motifs that infuse Chihuly's work are informed by his seaside childhood in Tacoma, Washington. He was formally trained in glassblowing at the University of Wisconsin and went on to further study at Rhode Island School of Design, where he founded the glass programme in 1969. Two years later, Chihuly was also involved in the establishment of the world's foremost institution for the education of glass artists, the Pilchuck Glass School.

Since an injury sustained to his left eye in 1976 left him unable to blow glass, Chihuly has directed teams of glassblowers working on his projects. This practice has enabled Chihuly to realise ever larger and more ambitious installation and environmental pieces. His pioneering installation work has earned him a reputation as the man who took studio glass out of the studio and into public space, an achievement perhaps best encapsulated by the 'Chihuly Bridge of Glass', opened in his hometown of Tacoma in 2002. Chihuly has collections on display across the world including at the Corning Museum of Glass, New York and the Victoria & Albert Museum, London.

A Dale Chihuly 'Yellow Bloom', a wall installation composed of two 'Seaforms', one in yellow glass with amber chevron stripes, black lip and mauve iridescence on back, the other in cobalt blue and red striped glass with red lip, unsigned.

Provenance: *Gift from the artist to the current owner.*

c1995 *34in (85cm) high*

£10,000-15,000 **S&K**

A Dale Chihuly 'Seaform', in purple, amber and clear striped glass, dark green lip, signed and dated.

1993 *13in (32.5cm) wide*

£2,500-3,000 **S&K**

A Dale Chihuly 'Ribbed Trumpet-Form Vessel', in blue glass with green stripes and white threading, red lip, unsigned.

6in (15cm) wide

£600-900 **S&K**

A Dale Chihuly 'Ribbed Trumpet-Form Vessel with Baluster-Form Base', in blue and silver striped glass with white threading, red lip, unsigned.

12in (30cm) high

£600-900 **S&K**

A Dale Chihuly 'Ribbed Trumpet-Form Vessel with Flattened Ovoid Base and Ovoid Bulb in Stem', in blue and green striped glass cased in amber, unsigned.

9.5in (24cm) high

£600-900 **S&K**

A Dale Chihuly 'Ribbed Flask-Form Vessel', amber shading to green and blue glass with red stripes banded in white and with blue shading to silvery purple iridescence, red lip, unsigned.

5.5in (14cm) high

£800-1,200 **S&K**

A Dale Chihuly 'Two Ribbed Glass Globular Vessels', one in blue, clear and dark red stripes with black lip, the other with yellow and clear stripes and blue lip, unsigned.

4in (10cm) diam

£800-1,200 **S&K**

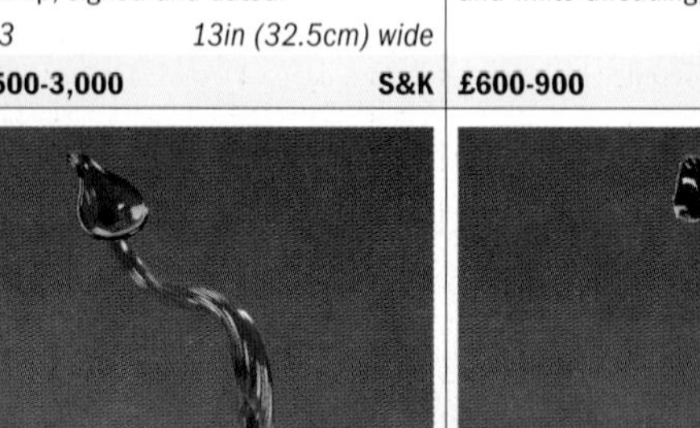

A Dale Chihuly 'Ribbed Rosewater Sprinkler', in blue glass with dark red and clear stripes and a black lip, unsigned.

14.5in (36cm) long

£600-900 **S&K**

A Dale Chihuly 'Ribbed Rosewater Sprinkler with Flattened Triple Gourdform Base', in amber shading to green and blue glass with a red stripe banded in white, silvery blue iridescence at neck, red lip, unsigned.

19.25in (48cm) high

£700-1,000 **S&K**

A late 1980s Keith Brocklehurst pâte de verre bowl, legs cast with the piece, yellow and light blue.

7.75in (19.5cm) diam

£1,200-1,800 **JH**

A Neil Drobnis bird figure, in hand-blown aqua glass with stylized bird with applied wings and head, wings, head and base have sand textured finish, signed on base "NEIL DROBNIS '92".

14in (35.5cm) high

£1,500-2,000 **JDJ**

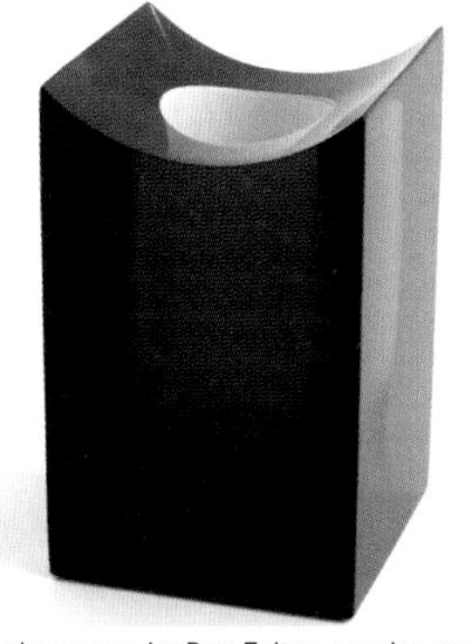

A glass vase by Petr Foltyn, smoky-grey glass with opaque white underlay, signed.

1978 *5in (13cm) high*

£200-250 **FIS**

A vase by Pavel Hlava, clear and coloured glass, cut, polished and glued, signed.

1989 *11.75in (30cm) high*

£2,000-3,000 **FIS**

A glass cube with the portrait of Rainer Maria Rilke, by Jiri Harcuba, signed.

1988 *5in (12.5cm) wide*

£800-1,200 **FIS**

A glass cube with the portraits of Franz Kafka by Jiri Harcuba, signed.

1991 *8.5in (21.5cm) wide*

£1,200-1,800 **FIS**

A glass object 'Quartett Smetana' by Bohuslav Horacek, clear glass, signed.

1987 *9.5in (24.5cm) wide*

£600-900 **FIS**

A tall W.A. Hunting vase, multicoloured layers cased in clear glass, with murrine and cane inserts, signed.

c1985 *14.5in (37cm) high*

£800-1,200 **FIS**

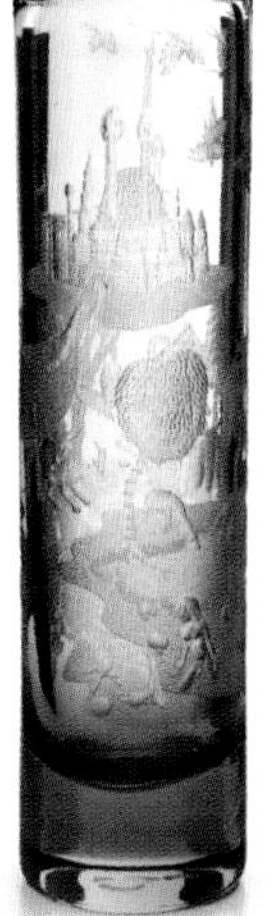

A cylindrical vase 'The dream of five jugglers' by Kristian Klepsch, Neuzeug-Siernig, signed.

1993 *11.75in (30cm) high*

£400-600 **FIS**

A glass object 'Bird', by Vladimir Klein, two parts, clear, light purple and uran-green glass, cut, polished, glued, signed.

1989 *8in (20.5cm high*

£800-1,200 **FIS**

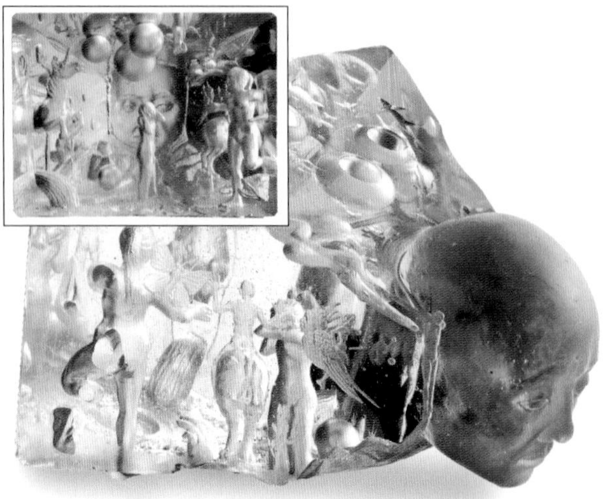

A glass-sculpture by Kristian Klepsch, Neuzeug-Sierning, clear glass, slightly damaged, signed.

1984 *7.75in (20cm) high*

£300-500 **FIS**

A sculpture entitled 'Maternity II' by Aristide Najean, signed near the base "Baolioli M. najean 4 VIII 02".

2002 *16in (41cm) high*

£1,500-2,000 **VET**

A sculpture entitled 'Female Toreador', by Aristide Najean, signed "LXII 93 najean - M. Baolioli 1/1".

1993 *17in (43cm) high*

£2,000-3,000 **VET**

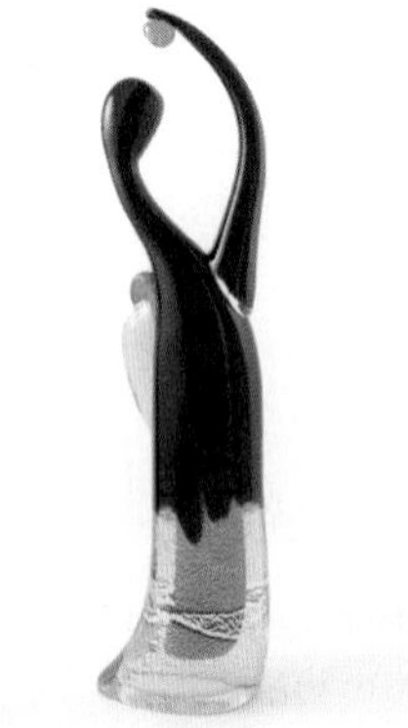

A sculpture entitled 'Mother & Child' by Aristide Najean, signed near the bottom "Baolioli M. najean 3 VIIII 02".

2002 *20.25in (51.5cm) high*

£2,500-3,000 **VET**

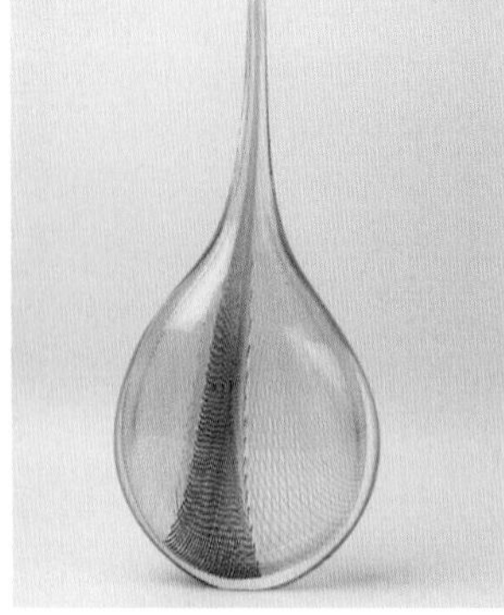

A Lino Tagliapietra vase, banjo-shaped, highlighted with lines of coloured glass, signed "LINO TAGLIAPIETRA".

22.5in (57cm) high

£6,000-9,000 **JDJ**

A Hiroshi Yamano fish vase, with cased glass of blue over white sands on applied frosted three-legged foot, decorated with applied gold background and silver fish, the glass stopper has leaf decoration and is topped by cast bronze scaled fish.

c1990 *21in (53.5cm) high*

£6,000-9,000 **JDJ**

An incalmo reticello and zanfirico vase, designed and made by Andrea Zilio, signed on the base "Zilio Andrea Anfora Murano '97".

1997 *17in (43cm) high*

£3,000-3,500 **ANF**

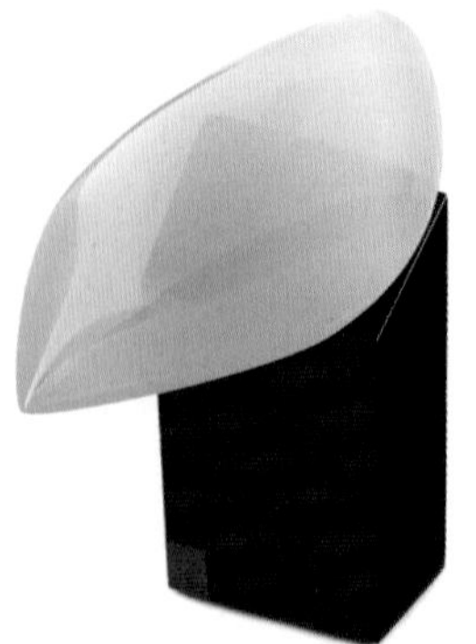

A glass sculpture by Vladimir Tom, of two parts in ruby and opal glass, cut and polished, signed.

1990 *7.25in (18.5cm) high*

£500-700 **FIS**

A green glass vase by Frantisek Vizner, signed.

1991 *11.75in (29.5cm) high*

£3,500-4,000 **FIS**

MODERN CERAMICS

A large F. Carlton Ball/Aaron Bohrod bulbous vase, decorated with incised and painted nudes balancing on horses, in white on a brown and ivory ground, signed by both artists.

13.25in (33.5cm) high

£2,500-3,500 **DRA**

A Dorothy Becker red clay figural sculpture, 'Onlooker', of a crouching man wearing a basketball cap, incised "D. Becker/92", with title.

1992 *16in (40.5cm) high*

£150-200 **DRA**

A fine and unusual Richard DeVore bowl-form, with an interior crater-like opening covered by a tier, with deep firing lines in matte grey faux-crackled glaze, unmarked.

12.75in (32.5cm) wide

£3,000-4,000 **DRA**

A fine flaring stoneware vessel by Richard Devore, with melt fissures and three layered openings to interior, covered in reddish-brown glaze with brown exterior, unmarked.

9in (23cm) high

£2,000-3,000 **SDR**

A Ken Ferguson flaring stoneware bowl incised with crouching female nude and covered in a grey and oxblood glaze, square stamp with "F".

12in (30.5cm) diam

£350-450 **DRA**

A Matilda Flogi for Wiener Werkstätte glazed faience sculpture of a rider on rearing horse, restoration to horse, leg and whip, stamped "WW/Made in Austria/252", with impressed star or flower.

8.5in (21.5cm) high

£500-800 **DRA**

A rare Maija Grotell stoneware flaring bowl, with heavy grog covered in a sheer white matte glaze, unmarked.

9.75in (25cm) wide

£600-900 **DRA**

A Richard Ginore Italian espresso set, comprising seventeen cups with saucers, each with circus acrobats and animals, signed.

2.5in (6.5cm) high

£800-1,200 **FRE**

A fine Maija Grotell hand-thrown porcelain large bowl, with a banded wave pattern in coral on a teal and cobalt matte glaze, incised "MG".

11in (28cm) wide

£3,000-5,000 **DRA**

A Karen Karnes stoneware vessel, with fissured rim and two dimpled sides, with embossed dots, covered in a brown and light green speckled glaze, with white glazed interior, stamped "KK".

9.25in (23.5cm) wide

£700-1,000 **DRA**

A large Karen Karnes wheel-thrown stoneware covered vessel, with sheer ivory matte, with reduction flashes, the lid sculpted, with tooling and lined, with umber glaze, incised "KK".

14in (35.5cm) high

£2,500-3,500 **DRA**

An early Wiener Keramos faience centrebowl with attached flower frog, on three penguin support covered in polychrome glaze, impressed "WK mark/Austria" and numbered, repairs.

10in (25.5cm) high

£400-600 **DRA**

A Howard Kottler earthenware sculpture, 'Paisley Cup', depicting a coffee cup embedded in a rectangular block, with blue paisley decal decoration, marked "S-72".

6.5in (16.5cm) wide

£2,500-3,500 **DRA**

A David Leach earthenware flagon, decorated with Willow motif, impressed "DL" seal, hairlines to neck.

15.25in (39cm) high

£80-120 **WW**

A Lenci ceramic figure of a seated nude woman with hand-painted face, her legs crossed and a towel draped over her arm, covered in polychrome glaze, restoration, Lenci/Torini paper label.

11.75 (30cm) high

£700-1,000 **DRA**

An Edger Littlefield bowl, slip-decorated in the Persian style with a stylized peacock within a lotus medallion, in turquoise and purple, signed "EL/1942".

1942 *13in (33cm) wide*

£700-1,000 **DRA**

A Joe Mariscal glazed earthenware sculpture, "nodding off" of a man with tattoos of a purple rose on his chest and the words "El Parandero" on his arm, a couple of firing lines to back, small repair, incised 84/Mariscal on back.

1984 *11.75in (30cm) high*

£500-700 **DRA**

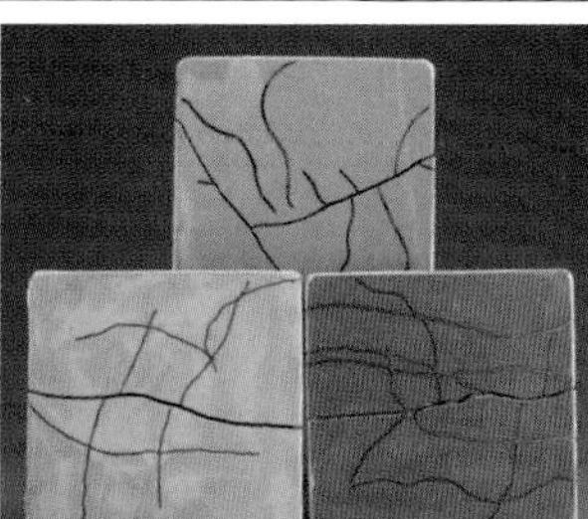

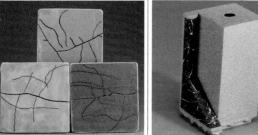

A set of three Jim Melchert glazed earthenware tiles, with fissures and random linear patterns in green and blue, mahogany and silver, terracotta and black, all mounted on plywood, chips to edges, signed and dated on reverse.

1991 *12in (30.5cm) wide*

£1,200-1,800 **DRA**

A Ron Nagle Post-Modern bud vase with four-sided structure attached to an angled one, with rough cement texture covered in orange, cobalt, yellow and gray glazes, small chip to one corner, unmarked.

6.75in (17cm) wide

£3,500-4,500 **DRA**

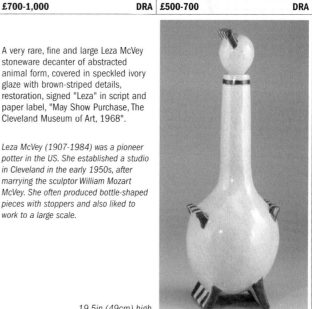

A very rare, fine and large Leza McVey stoneware decanter of abstracted animal form, covered in speckled ivory glaze with brown-striped details, restoration, signed "Leza" in script and paper label, "May Show Purchase, The Cleveland Museum of Art, 1968".

Leza McVey (1907-1984) was a pioneer potter in the US. She established a studio in Cleveland in the early 1950s, after marrying the sculptor William Mozart McVey. She often produced bottle-shaped pieces with stoppers and also liked to work to a large scale.

19.5in (49cm) high

£7,000-10,000 **DRA**

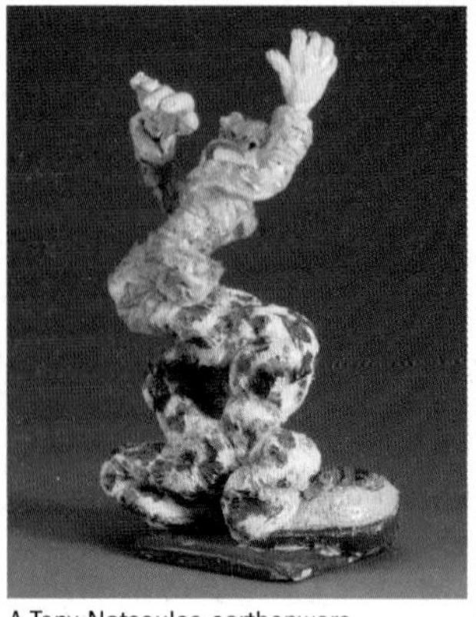

A Tony Natsoulos earthenware sculpture, 'Deflation', of a collapsing figure with exaggerated features and contorted limbs, in polychrome glazes, signed and dated on botton.

1991 *22.25in (56.5cm) high*

£350-450 **DRA**

A fine straight-walled vessel covered in volcanic verdigris glaze, signed in ink, "G+O Natzler".

6in (15cm) high

£1,800-2,200 **SDR**

GERTRUD AND OTTO NATZLER

Born in Vienna, Austria in 1908, Gertrud and Otto Natzler met during the early 1930s and fled the Nazi annexation of Austria together. They moved to Los Angeles, California and set up their first studio. The couple worked together, with Gertrud throwing and synthesising the clay into form and Otto glazing and acting as firing technician.

Gertrud's forms are simple and classic, with a concentration on bowls and vases and provide an excellent vehicle for Otto's unusual glazes. Otto had a thorough understanding of the chemical and physical properties of the glazes and mystical control of the firing process. The couple perfected their glazes and refined the forms over three decades, from 1939 to 1971.

Gertrud's elegant forms echo the Art Nouveau movement and are the epitome of weightless grace and refinement. Many of the Natzlers' works are a subtle vision of form and colour, close to the fragile beauty of Japanese and Chinese ceramics. They believed in a purist's natural approach to form. While traditional in format, the couple's vessels are subtly modulated to create poetic objects of rare beauty. They are famous for their jewel-like colours suspended in rich, luminous glazes.

The Natzlers worked collaboratively until Gertrud's death in 1971. Otto and Gertrud Natzler were one of the leading couples of the modern ceramic movement.

A large hemispheric bowl by Natzler, covered in a gunmetal and deep purple crystalline glaze, with oxblood flashes to exterior, "Natzler" in ink, typed label with "0036" and a red square.

The red square indicates that this piece was in the personal collection of the Natzlers.

7.75in (19.5cm) high

£6,000-9,000 **SDR**

An exceptional and early Natzler bell-shaped vessel, with small opening, covered in a striated orange and caramel volcanic glaze, inscribed "Natzler" in ink, with typed inventory label "M299".

6.75in (17cm) high

£6,000-9,000 **SDR**

A John Pearson serving dish, painted in pink and silver lustres and in shades of blue and green, painted verso with a exotic fish with a monogram mark.

11.5in (29cm) wide

£600-900 **L&T**

A Pablo Picasso for Madoura figural vessel, painted with a woman's head in black on a white semi-matte ground, restoration to chips at base, stamped and in ink, "Edition Picasso", with "Madoura".

11.25in high

£2,500-3,000 **DRA**

A Pillin footed vase decorated with a horse, dancer and woman playing a mandolin, in polychrome, signed 'Pillin'.

7in (18cm) high

£700-1,000 **DRA**

A Pillin ovoid vase with stylized horses in charcoal, ochre and black on a mottled grey ground, signed "Pillin", small touch ups.

7in (18cm) high

£300-400 **DRA**

A large Poole 'Delphis' circular charger, painted in colours with the bust of a girl, printed and painted marks.

14.5in (36cm) wide

£120-180 **L&T**

An Antonio Prieto ovoid vase with small opening, decorated in sgraffito with a scale-like pattern covered in thick matte yellow glaze over gunmetal ground, signed "Prieto".

10.25in (26cm) high

£1,500-2,000 **DRA**

A Daniel Rhodes hand-built stoneware footed vessel, with spherical top, with small opening surrounded by modelled clay formations, with gunmetal-glazed interior and applied flared base, signed "Rhodes".

c1975 *9.5in (24cm) high*

£1,200-1,800 **DRA**

A Richard Shaw porcelain sculpture, 'Basketful for John', painted and transfer-printed with icons from his career: a deck of cards, pack of cigarettes and matches, poker chips, paint and a cruise ship in a woven basket, signed and dated on base, with label from Braunstein/Quay Gallery Gallery in San Frencisco.

1992 *15.25in (38.5cm) wide*

£3,000-4,000 **DRA**

A Richard Shaw bisque porcelain sculpture, 'Lawrence Bottle', comprising stacked forms with overglaze transfers, accompanied by a copy of the exhibition catalogue, 'Robert Hudson and Richard Shaw: New Ceramic Sculpture', held in 1998 at the Addison Gallery of American Art, Philips Academy, Andover, MA, which features this piece on the corner, unmarked.

1997 *18.5in (47cm) high*

£3,000-4,000 **DRA**

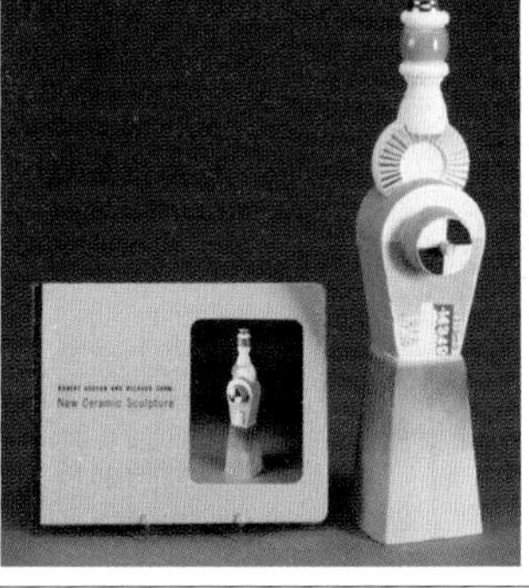

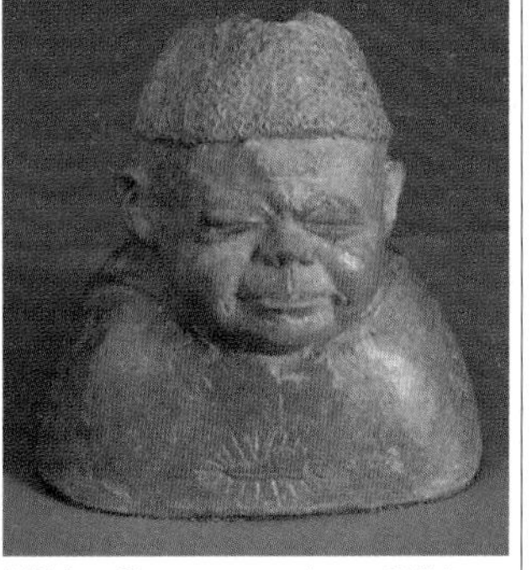

A Walter Sinz terracotta bust of Nikita Kruschev with modelled and incised details including a shoe incised on his chest, signed "Walter Sinz" on reverse.

6.5in (16.5cm) high

£300-400 **DRA**

A tall raku vase, by Paul Soldner, with irregular rim and combed texture, in white with oxide spray, signed with a chop mark.

15.5in (39.5cm) high

£500-800 **SDR**

A large Edith Sonne Brun for Saxbo tapered and faceted vessel, with collared rim, covered in a green and umber matte glaze, stamped "Saxbo/Denmark", with "Sonne" in script.

11in (28cm) high

£400-600 **DRA**

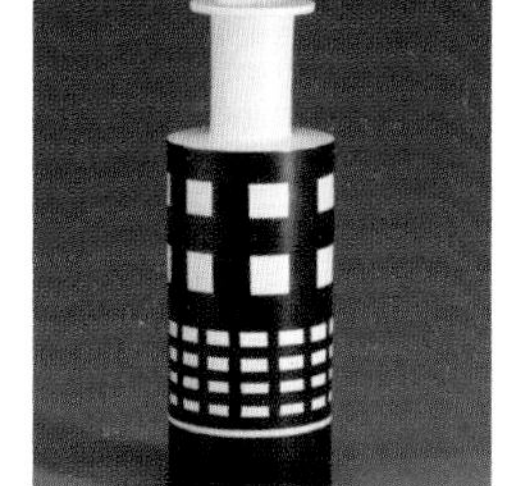

An Ettore Sottsass tall cylindrical vase, painted with white squares on matte black, under a white cylindrical neck, signed "Sottsass/ Bitossi/ Montelupo".

1967 *18in (45.5cm) high*

£600-900 **DRA**

A Toshiko Takaezu stoneware bowl, with straight sides, painted, with a random olive green stroke on matte grey ground, incised "TT".

7in (18cm) wide

£2,000-3,000 **DRA**

A fine Toshiko Takaezu wheel-thrown stoneware vessel, with sheer ivory matte and dripping umber glazes, hairline to rim, incised "TT".

9.5in (24cm) wide

£4,000-6,000 **DRA**

A Toshiko Takaezu wheel-thrown stoneware vessel, with dipped and poured white matte, teal, and umber glazes, incised "TT".

10in (25.5cm) wide

£700-1,000 **DRA**

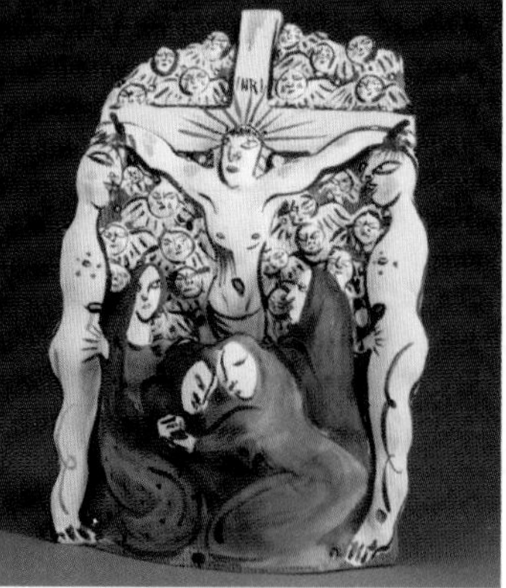

An Akio Takamori homoerotic faience sculpture, 'Crucifixion', with two naked men flanking a crowd of people witnessing a crucifixion scene, and outline of bloodied cross on reverse, signed "Akio".

21in (53cm) high

£3,000-5,000 **DRA**

An Anna Thompson large charger, enamel-decorated with fish and sea plants in polychrome on a dark brown ground, stamped "A.L.T./OE/Made in Sweden".

17.25in (44cm) diam

£500-800 **DRA**

A Peter Voulkos stoneware ice bucket, with torn and flattened rim, its body indented, with three fissured areas covered in a cobalt blue glaze, signed "Voulkos/73" on base.

1973 *7in (18cm) wide*

£5,000-8,000 **DRA**

A fine and large Peter Voulkos stoneware charger, with torn, carved, and applied pieces in dark brown clay, in glaze "Voulkos 95".

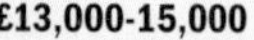

1995 *21.25in (53cm) diam*

£13,000-15,000 **DRA**

A Carl Walters tin-glazed flaring bowl, with salmon and teal animals and leaves on a glossy buff ground, small flecks, incised "cipher/Walters/1925".

10.5in (27cm) diam

£500-800 **DRA**

A Beatrice Wood footed bowl with straight walls, covered in a raspberry and light green lustred glaze, a couple of minor flecks, signed "Beato", with "BW564C".

5in (12.5cm) high

£700-1,000 **DRA**

A Beatrice Wood flaring bowl covered, with sheer yellow and brown flambé glazes on redware body, small chip below outer rim, "BEATO" in ink.

10in (25.5cm) diam

£3,000-4,000 **DRA**

An unusual bulbous urn by Beatrice Wood, covered in a cratered chocolate brown over mahogany glossy glaze, signed "Beato".

9.25in (23.5cm) high

£700-1,000 **SDR**

A large Betty Woodman flaring stoneware bowl, with two applied ribbon handles, covered in a speckled green glaze, with random mahogany, brown and white brush strokes, impressed "WOODMAN".

14.75in (37.5cm) wide

£1,000-1,500 **DRA**

A large Betty Woodman salt-glazed stoneware footed vessel, with folded rim and applied ribbon handles covered in umber, cobalt and green sponged glazes on a glossy celadon ground, impressed "WOODMAN".

17.75in (45cm) wide

£1,800-2,200 **DRA**

A Russel Wright for Bauer pillow vase, covered in white semi-matte glaze, two tight lines from rim, stamped "Russel Wright/Bauer".

10in (25.5cm) wide

£1,500-2,000 **DRA**

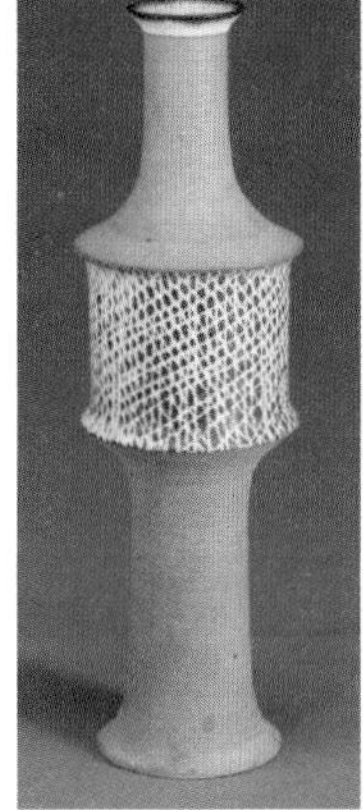

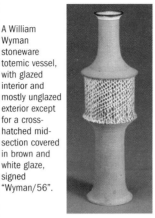

A William Wyman stoneware totemic vessel, with glazed interior and mostly unglazed exterior except for a cross-hatched mid-section covered in brown and white glaze, signed "Wyman/56".

1956 *14.75in (37.5cm) high*

£3,000-4,000 **DRA**

A Martine Bedin for Memphis 'Super' lacquered fibreglass table lamp, a hemispheric form on rubber wheels, with six cylindrical fixtures, in polychrome, Memphis metal tag.

1981 *20.5in (52cm) wide*

£800-1,200 **DRA**

MODERN LIGHTING

An Arredoluce 'Eye' lamp, with central adjustable fixture on magnetic socket and polished chrome shaft, mounted on black enamelled metal base, "Arredoluce Moza" paper label.

24.5in (62cm) high

£1,000-1,500 **SDR**

A fine 'Triennale' floor lamp by Arteluce, with shades enamelled in red, white and black, on polished chrome tripod base, die-stamped mark.

67in (170cm) high

£2,200-2,800 **SDR**

An extremely rare and important James Harvey Crate 'Heifetz T-3-C' table lamp, of tripod form with spring-mounted reflector, over black enamelled metal and spun aluminium components, with ball finials and feet in cork, unmarked.

24.25in (61.5cm) high

£10,000-12,000 **SDR**

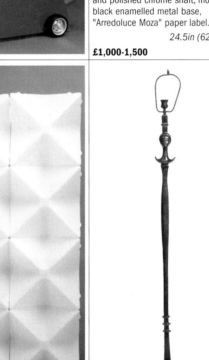

A Tom Dixon for Eurolounge 'Octo' modular light sculpture comprised of sixty free-standing and individually wired moulded plastic star-shaped cubes that can be stacked to form a variety of configurations, unmarked.

15in (37.5cm) high

£2,200-2,800 **DRA**

A bronze 'Tete du Femme' floorlamp with verdigris patina, after a design by Diego and Alberto Giacometti for Jean-Michel Frank, and cast for Frank in Argentina by Comte Ltda between 1940 and 1960.

56.5in (143.5cm) high

£3,000-5,000 **SDR**

A Solar (Denmark) 'Verona' hanging light fixture with spun copper and white enamelled finish, in the style of Poul Henningsen, paper label.

15.5in (39cm) diam

£300-500 **DRA**

A James Mont carved wood baluster table lamp, with single socket, its base incised with abstracted flowers under a rubbed red and gold finish, with matching finial and silk drum shade with gold brocade trimming, unmarked.

35in (89cm) high

£180-220 **DRA**

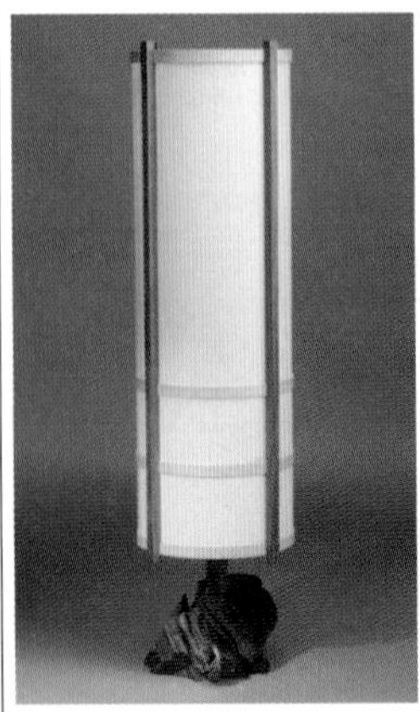

A fine and rare George Nakashima Kent Hall lamp with interesting free-form walnut base, cylindrical shade with parchment liner and holly rings, marked with owner's name on bottom.

58.75in (147cm) high

£7,000-10,000 **DRA**

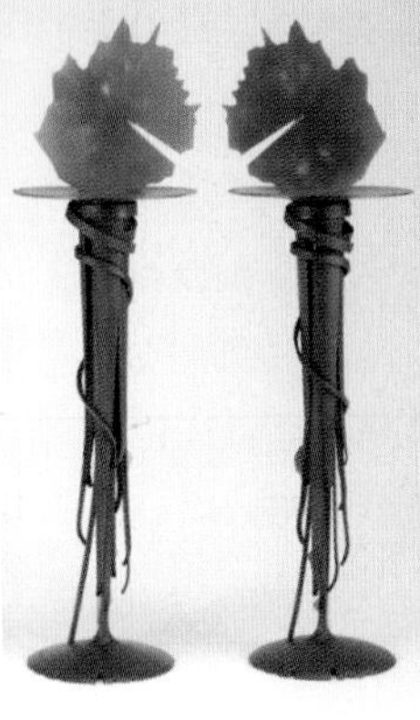

A pair of 'Sunset' tall candlesticks, of forged and fabricated steel with brass insert, stamped "Albert Paley 1993" numbered "27" and "43" out of an edition of 50, additionally stamped "Helped ABT".

21.5in (54.5cm) high

£1,500-2,000 **SDR**

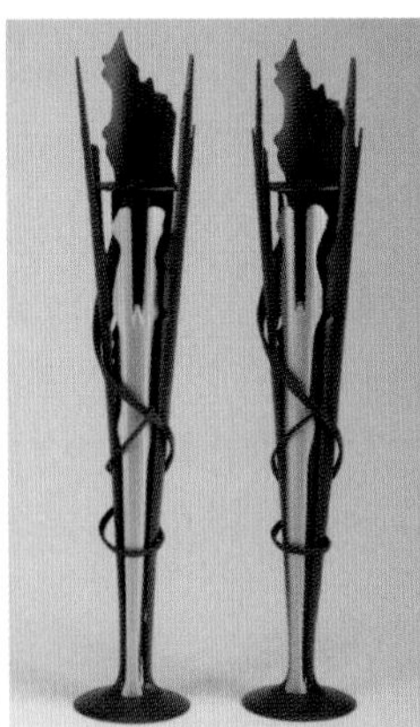

A pair of 'Vulcan' tall candlesticks of forged and fabricated steel and brass, stamped "Albert Paley 1994".

20.25in (51.5cm) high

£2,200-2,800 **SDR**

A Vernon Panton for J. Luber AG 'Fun 1 DM' ceiling lamp, unmarked.

24in (61cm) high

£1,000-1,500 **DRA**

A Verner Panton ceiling lamp 'Moon', consisting of nine revolvable, flexible rings, produced by Louis Poulsen & Co, Copenhagen, with white lacquered metal rings and metal mountings.

£400-600 **QU**

A pair of early Jorge Pensi for B. Lux 'Regina' aluminium desk lamps, each with double-rod shaft to accommodate adjustable-height shade and fixture, on weighted base, B. Lux labels.

22.5in (57.5cm) high

£500-800 **DRA**

A Stiffel brass and enamelled metal table lamp, with silk-covered parchment shade on a slightly bulbous shaft, with star-shaped base, small stain to shade, unmarked.

31.25in (79.5cm) high

£1,200-1,800 **DRA**

A Yugoslavian wall-hanging light fixture, with wooden cap and mount, and bulbous frosted glass shade, stamped mark.

21in (53.5cm) high

£400-600 **DRA**

A brass desk lamp with flaring fibreglass shade on pivoting tubular shaft and circular base with brushed finish, stamped 'P' in square.

19.25in (49cm) high

£60-90 **DRA**

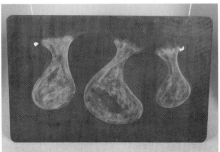

MODERN SCULPTURE

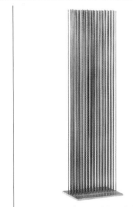

A large copper panel Harry Bertoia sculpture, with four planes of alternating squares welded to a central shaft, on square base, unmarked.

65in (165cm) high

£16,000-18,000 **SDR**

A Harry Bertoia sonambient in beryllium copper, with five rows of slender rods mounted on a rectangular base, unmarked.

28in (71cm) high

£13,000-15,000 **SDR**

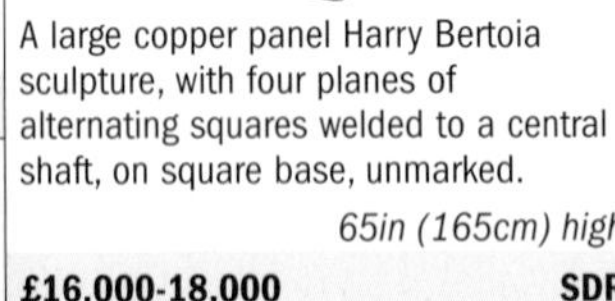

A fine and rare 'Yin-Yang' gong by Harry Bertoia, consisting of a sawn out silicon bronze plate with three biomorphic forms in verdigris, accompanied by mallet, unmarked.

48in (122cm) wide

£22,000-24,000 **SDR**

HARRY BERTOIA

Harry Bertoia (1915-1978) was born in Italy and moved to the US in 1930. He studied at the Cass Technical High School in Detroit and then trained at the Cranbrook Academy of Art, Michigan. During this time he began experimenting with jewellery forms and explored ideas that would later emerge into his sculptures. Ten years later he set up a metal workshop and began to teach.

In 1943 he worked with Charles and Ray Eames and later on established his own studio in Pennsylvania. At that time he introduced his famous 'Diamond' chair made of welded steel lattice work. During the 1950s Bertoia joined Knoll International and designed chairs that brought him wide acclaim.

He was a man of a vast energy and worked as a designer of furniture, decorative arts, sculpture and jewellery. He enjoyed a very successful career creating furniture, metal sculptures, sounding pieces, and kinetic works of art in metal as well as monoprints and table-sculptures. He also started the exploration of tonal and sounding sculptures. Many of Bertoia's pieces were wire structures or screens. Examples of his sculptural work include a structural screen for the Manufacturers Hanover Trust Company, New York City, and a bronze panel at Dulles International Airport, Washington, D.C.

Harry Bertoia died in in 1978 in Barto, Pennsylvania.

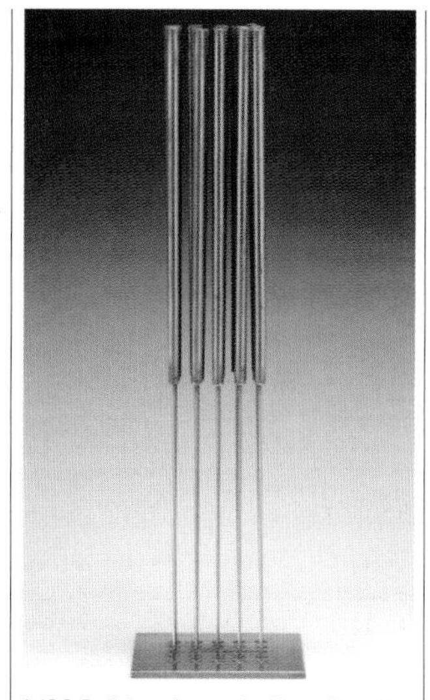

A '36 Bells' sculpture by Harry Bertoia, beryllium copper and brass, consisting of thirty six rods.

22in (55cm) high

£12,000-14,000 **FRE**

A monumental 'Willow' sculpture by Harry Bertoia, composed of stainless steel rods mounted atop a steel base, unmarked.

This is one of only two made in this extraordinary size.

96in (244cm) high

£42,000-50,000 **SDR**

A Hagenauer olive wood horse head sculpture with carved features mounted on a flat rectangular brass base, stamped "Hagenauer Wein/Made in Austria/WHW/Handmade".

13in (33cm) high

£500-800 **DRA**

A Hagenauer polished chrome sculpture of a woman's head in profile with stylized features, wearing a beaded choker, stamped "WHW/Hagenauer Wien/ Made in Austria".

26in (53cm) high

£4,000-6,000 **DRA**

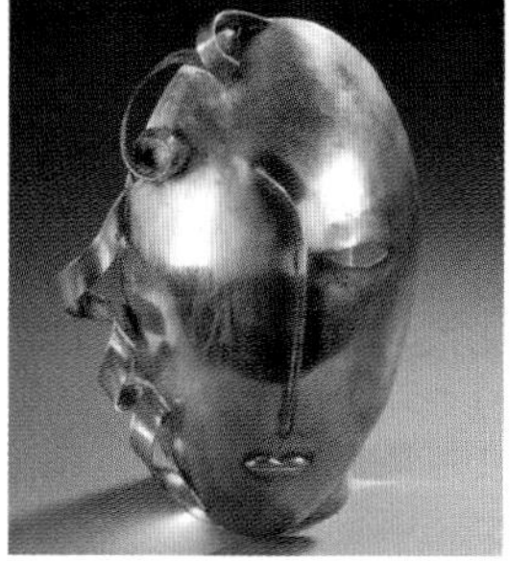

A bronze Hagenauer mask, depicting a stylized female face, the reverse with hammered surface, stamped with "wHw" Hagenauer Vienna workshop mark.

10in (25.5cm) high

£1,500-2,000 **S&K**

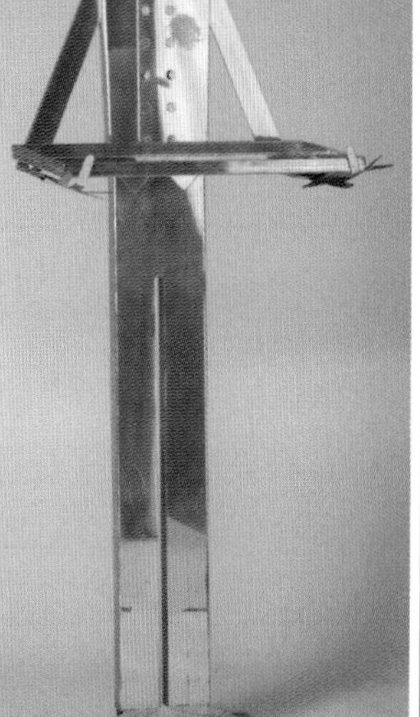

A very rare, life-size Hagenauer brass sculpture of a waiter, with applied and embossed details, with a removable tray, some separation to decoration on cap, and minor finish wear, marked "Hagenauer Wien/Made in Austria", under epaulets.

65in (162.5cm) high

£12,000-14,000 **DRA**

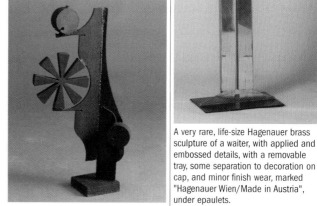

A chrome tabletop 'Z'-form mirror by Franz Hagenauer, inset with rectangular glass, stamped "WHW FRANZ Hagenauer Wien Made in Austria".

26in (66cm) high

£3,000-5,000 **SDR**

An Alexander Lieberman welded steel abstract sculpture, of vertical composition with dark patina, signed and dated.

Born in Kiev, Russia, Lieberman moved to the United States in 1941 where he painted and sculpted in abstract style, often using the circle which he asserted was the ideal shape.

1966 *30.75in (78cm) high*

£700-1,000 **DRA**

An Alexander Lieberman welded steel abstract sculpture, with a series of five forms arranged horizontally on a rectangular base with dark patina, signed and dated.

1966 *40in (101.5cm) long*

£1,500-2,000 **DRA**

A grey plastic figure of an elephant designed by Eduardo Paolozzi, for Nairn Floors Ltd, 1972.

The plastic geometric form has a removable lid enclosing a compartment for brochures on Nairn products and the production of the elephant.

12in (30cm) high

£600-900 **L&T**

A Tommi Parzinger for Dorlyn Silversmiths brass and stainless steel tall coffee pot, die-stamped "Dorlyn Silversmiths".

16.5in (42cm) high

£100-150 **DRA**

A Jonathan Shahn stoneware bust of the 19thC French poet Charles Baudelaire, titled 'Head', mounted on a square black-enamelled wood base, firing line near base, signed in ink.

This bust is accompanied by a letter of provenance/authentication from the artist dated May 26, 1967.

1962 *16.25in (41.5cm) high*

£1,500-2,000 **DRA**

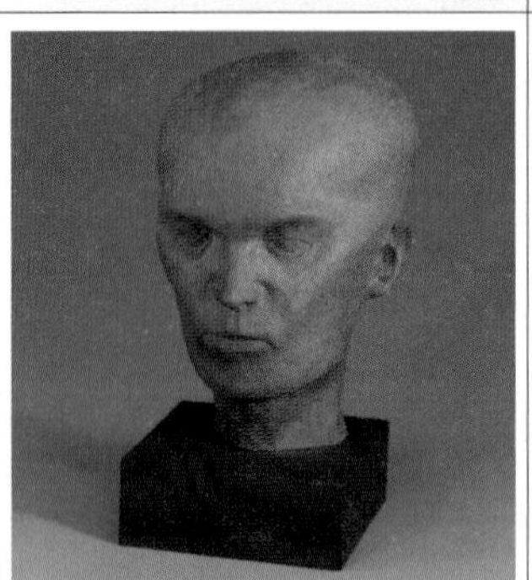

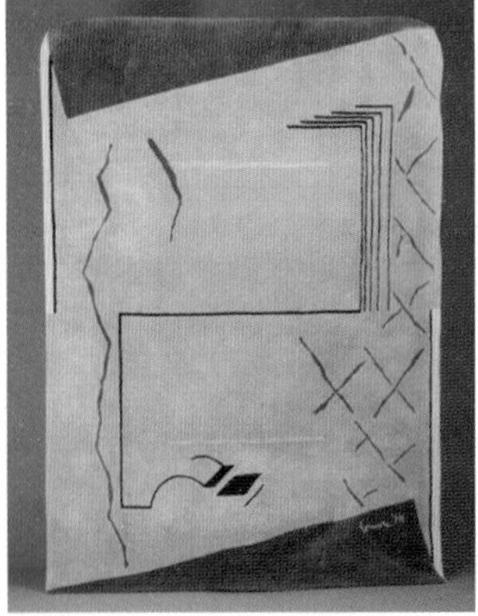

A Michael Graves cut-pile abstract area rug, in shades of grey, burgundy and cream, minor staining, signed and dated "Graves 79".

1979 *86in (218.5) long*

£700-1,000 **DRA**

A fine and rare Edwin and Mary Scheier woven wool tapestry, 'Man in Fish,' depicting a man and woman inside a fish, in ivory on dark brown ground, unmarked.

1964 *90in (228.5cm) long*

£400-600 **DRA**

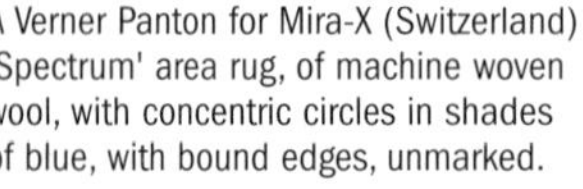

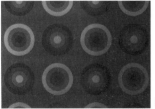

A Verner Panton for Mira-X (Switzerland) 'Spectrum' area rug, of machine woven wool, with concentric circles in shades of blue, with bound edges, unmarked.

From the interior of 'Europa Grand Hotel', Lac Lugano, Switzerland.

c1970 *79.5in (202cm) wide*

£450-550 **DRA**

OTHER MODERN WORKS

A Zofia Butrymowic carpet, 'Slonce Szafirowe', in wool and mixed fabric, mounted on wood, signed "ZB" in the weave, stamped marks to reverse.

c1970 *81in (206cm) long*

£280-320 **FRE**

A mid- to late 20thC contemporary art rug.

93in (236cm) long

£200-300 **S&K**

A fine and large flaring wooden bowl, by Richard Devore, with melt fissures and four small openings at rim, covered in a rich matte frogskin glaze, unmarked.

14.25in (36cm) diam

£1,200-1,800 **SDR**

A fine walnut flaring bowl by Mark Lindquist, "Ascending Conoid #1", with fissures and deeply-carved decoration, signed, dated and titled on bottom.

15.25in (38.5cm) diam

£500-800 **SDR**

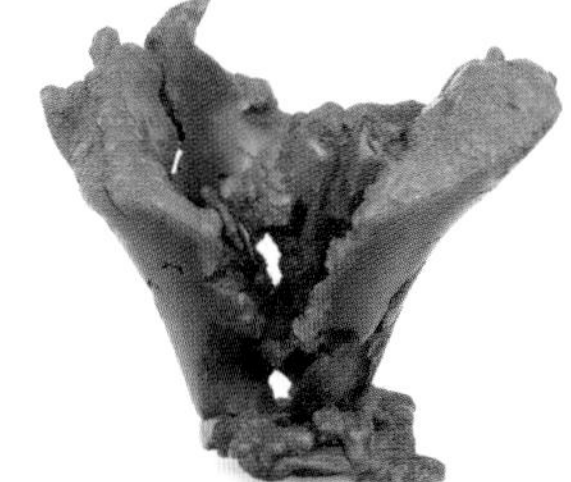

An extraordinary 'Old Indian Bowl #3' by Melvin Lindquist, carved from manzanita Burl, fully marked on bottom.

1983 *17in (43cm) high*

£3,000-5,000 **SDR**

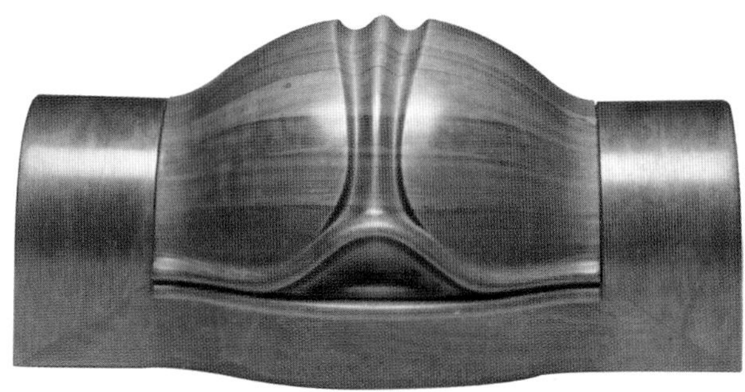

An Alphonse Mattia cherrywood humidor, cherry, mixed media, with electrical components inside.

Alphonse Mattia is a graduate of the Philadelphia College of Art and the Rhode Island School of Design, where he currently teaches. This early work expresses the playful and humourous elements common in his oeuvre. It received first prize at the Philadelphia Craft Show in 1974.

28.5in (71cm) wide

£1,200-1,800 **FRE**

A large wild cherry turned wood vessel, by Philip Moulthrop, with closed-in rim, artist signed with cipher.

14.5in (37cm) diam

£1,200-1,800 **SDR**

A 'Madrone' turned vessel of spherical form, by Philip Moulthrop, artist signed with cipher.

8.5in (21.5cm) diam

£1,000-1,500 **SDR**

An exceptional and large free-form bowl, by Peter Petrochko, constructed from North American spalted crimson maple, fully marked on the bottom.

1983 *15.5in (39.5cm) high*

£1,000-1,500 **SDR**

A Jens Quistgaard for Dansk Wenge wood hat-shaped salad bowl, from Dansk's 1962 'Rare Woods' series, with inlaid design, slight split, stamped "Dansk Designs/Denmark".

16in (40.5cm) diam

£500-800 **DRA**

An exceptional Harry Bertoia woodcut print on rice paper, 'Grape Harvest', with four registers of scenes with figures, mounted in carved wood frame, signed and dated in pencil lower right, "Harry V. Bertoia, 1941".

This is one of only five known copies of this image, which along with "Corn Harvest", is one of the only two woodblock prints made by Bertoia. This piece was produced early in his career while he was attending Cranbrook Academy of Art, in Bloomfield Hills, MI. These prints also mark the only time Bertoia was known to sign his work with his full name. The "Grape Harvest" was a gift from Bertoia to the owner.

10in (25cm) high

£12,000-15,000 **DRA**

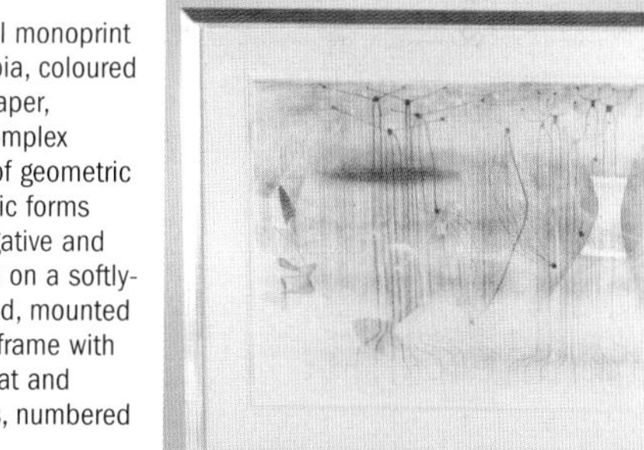

An exceptional monoprint by Harry Bertoia, coloured inks on rice paper, depicting a complex arrangement of geometric and biomorphic forms floating in negative and positive space on a softly-textured ground, mounted in a gold leaf frame with silk pongee mat and museum glass, numbered "672".

c1945 *23.75in (60.5cm) wide*

£3,000-5,000 **SDR**

A fine Albert Paley wall relief, pictured in situ, of forged and fabricated bronze, comprising four large uprights with overhanging scalloped tops, intersecting a series of horizontal elements, all with polished brass finish, custom installation required, unmarked.

180in (450cm) wide

£16,000-18,000 **DRA**

'Cycles Humber', by Henriette Bressler, Paris.

c1900 *59.5in (151cm) high*

£1,500-2,000 **SWA**

'Pur Champagne Damery', by Leonetto Cappiello, Paris.

c1900 *53.25in (135cm) high*

£3,000-4,000 **SWA**

'Toiles Fraudet', by Leonetto Cappiello, Paris.

1910 *62in (157.5cm) high*

£3,500-4,500 **SWA**

'Tabarin', by Ernst Deutsch, Berlin.

c1910 *37.5in (95.5cm) high*

£1,800-2,200 **SWA**

'Fata Morgana', by Joseph Frank, with an Art Nouveau depiction of a performer with snake bracelets, surrounded by caravans, sheiks and a swirl of exotic pink flowers, some damage, wooden dowels affixed to top and bottom margins.

1911 *47.25in (120cm) high*

£1,200-1,800 **SWA**

'Women's Edition Courier', by Alice Russel Glenny, some repaired tears.

This is one of only two posters designed by Glenny, and is highly regarded because the depiction of an 'Art Nouveau woman' is less rigid than in other US images.

c1895 *27in (68.5in) high*

£1,500-2,000 **SWA**

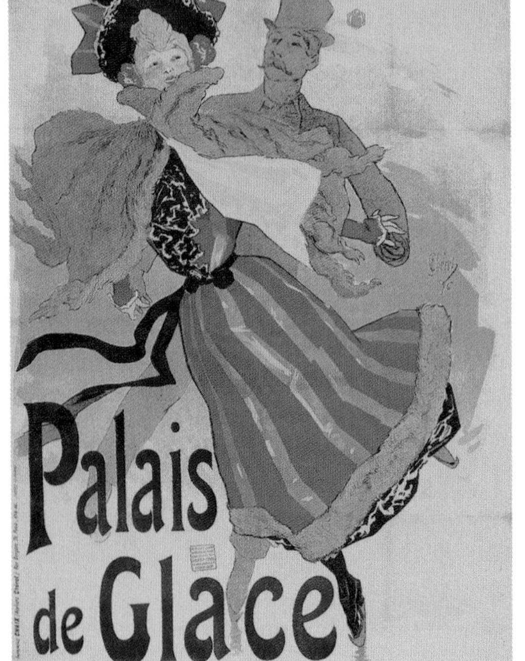

'Palais de Glace', Jules Cheret, Paris.

c1895 *47in (119cm) high*

£4,000-6,000 **SWA**

'Salon des Cent', by Eugene Grasset, from a a limited edition of 100 without lettering, Paris.

c1900 *24.75 (63cm) high*

£4,000-6,000 **SWA**

'Palais de Glace', by Albert Guillame, Paris.

c1895 *45.5in (115.5cm) high*

£3,000-5,000 **SWA**

'Il Vystava Spolku Manes', by Arnost Hoffbauer, Prague.

c1900 *42.5in (108cm) high*

£2,800-3,200 **SWA**

'Café Plendl', by Ludwig Holwein, Munich.

c1910 *47in (119cm) high*

£3,000-4,000 **SWA**

'Parfumerie Tochtermann', by Ludwig Holwein, Munich, with elegant women smelling flowers, minor restoration.

c1910 *46.75in (119cm) high*

£8,000-12,000 **SWA**

'Exposition Internationale Bruxelles', by Privat Livemont, depicting a woman holding a shield and overlooking a multicultural crowd entering the Brussel's World Fair, in three sheets, French version, some damage and foxing, on old linen.

1897 *108in (275cm) high*

£1,500-2,000 **SWA**

'Martingay', designed by Charles Loupot, printed by Sonor, Geneva, depicting an elegant lady listening to the birds in a cage, creamy background.

c1920 *50.5in (126cm) high*

£5,000-7,000 **SWA**

'Fleurs de Mousse', by Leopoldo Metlicovitz, Milan.

c1900 *42in (107cm) high*

£2,500-3,000 **SWA**

'Flouvella', by Leopoldo Metlicovitz, with a woman in soft pastels, advertising French perfume manufacturer Sauze, some losses, Milan.

c1910 *43in (109.5cm) high*

£2,800-3,200 **SWA**

'Cycles Perfecta', by Alphonse Mucha.

This is Mucha's most graphic poster and, unusually, is on white paper.

c1900 *61in (155cm) high*

£12,000-18,000 **SWA**

'La Plume', designed by Alphonse Mucha, printed by F. Champenois, Paris, one of two decorative panels from the set 'Plume et Primevere', the symbolic figure with aureoles around her head and adorned with filigree diadems in her hair.

29in (72.5cm) high

£4,000-6,000 **SWA**

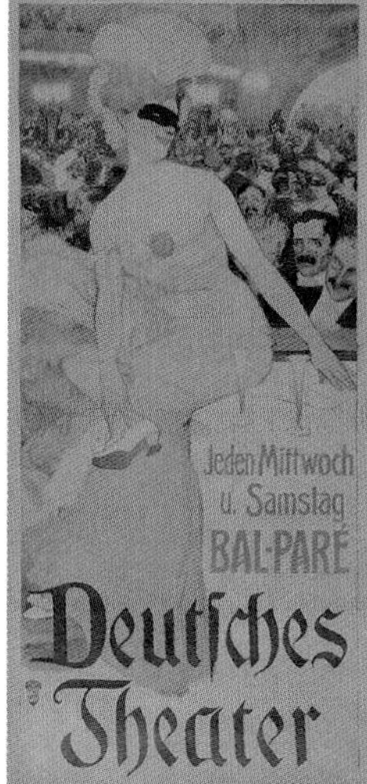

'Bal Pare Deutsches Theater', by Aldolf Münzer, Munich.

c1905 *82.5in (209.5cm) high*

£2,000-3,000 **SWA**

'Humber bicycles', by Louis Oury, with a woman in a black and green outfit holding a black bicycle against a red and grey patterned background, with green lettering.

62in (157.5cm) wide

£3,500-4,500 **SWA**

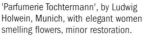

'Pan-American Exposition / Buffalo', by Evelyn Rumsey Cary, restored losses and overpainting.

Although unsigned, this American Art Nouveau classic poster is based on the painting 'Spirit of Niagra' by Evelyn Rumsey Cary. A prominent member of Buffalo's society, Cary's paintings and portraits were regularly exhibited at the Buffalo Fine Arts Academy and at annual exhibitions held by the Buffalo Society of Artists.

1901 *47.5in (120.5cm) high*

£2,500-3,000 **SWA**

'Odeon Casino', designed by Walter Schnakenberg, with a call girl and her patron, Munich.

c1910 *47.5in (120.5cm) high*

£8,000-12,000 **SWA**

'Lait pur Sterilise', by Theophile-Alexandre Steinlen, depicting the artist's daughter, outlined in green to create a soft image, Paris.

c1895 *53.35in (135.5cm) high*

£10,000-15,000 **SWA**

'La Traite des Blanches', by Theophile-Alexandre Steinlen, Paris.

c1900 *60.5in (154cm) high*

£8,000-12,000 **SWA**

'Tournee du Theatre de la Renaissance / Montmartre', by Ange Supparo, Paris.

62.5in (159cm) high

£7,000-10,000 **SWA**

'Mele', by Aleardo Terzi, Milan.

c1910 *55.75 (141.5cm) high*

£4,000-6,000 **SWA**

'El Dorado Aristide Bruant dans son Cabaret', by Henri de Toulouse-Lautrec, lithograph, with titled monogrammed lower right and mounted on canvas.

57in (145cm) high

£1,500-2,000 **POOK**

'May Belfort', by Henri de Toulouse Lautrec, depicting the Irish performer.

c1895 *32in (81.5cm) high*

£10,000-15,000 **SWA**

'Le Sillon', by Fernand Toussaint, for the circle of decorative realists known as 'Le Sillon', Brussels.

c1895 *40in (101.5cm) high*

£8,000-12,000 **SWA**

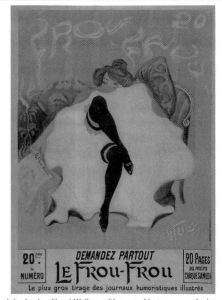

'Le Frou Frou', by Lucien Henri Weiluc, with a smoking woman, designed for risqué magazine 'Le Frou Frou', Asnieres.

c1900 *61.75in (157cm) high*

£15,000-20,000 **SWA**

'Zoologischer Garten Zürich', designed by Otto Baumberger, printed by Brothers Fretz, Zürich.

c1930 *48.75in (122cm) high*

£1,200-1,800 **SWA**

'Prunier', two maquettes designed by Alexey Brodovitch, to advertise cavier, one showing an open tin, the other a sturgeon, matted and framed.

c1925 *11.75in (29cm) wide*

£8,000-12,000 **SWA**

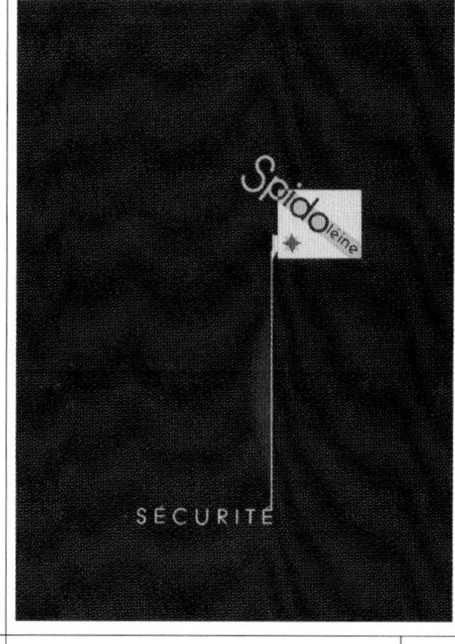

'Spidoléine', designed by Adolphe Mouron Cassandre, with a minimal image of yellow oil pouring from a can and forming the word "sécurité", against a black background, signed.

The sans-serif typography, and the play with typographic size and colour, show Cassandre's familiarity with Bauhaus avant-garde design principles.

c1930 *63in (157.5cm) high*

£25,000-30,000 **SWA**

'Vera Mint', designed by Adolphe Mouron Cassandre, printed by Courbet, Paris, with a minimal image suggesting a corner of a table and the outline of a glass, to advertise an apperitif.

1930 *80in (200cm) high*

£15,000-20,000 **SWA**

'André Renaud', designed by Paul Colin, printed by H. Chachoin, Paris.

Colin was one of the most important French Art Deco graphic artists of the period.

c1930 *62in (155cm) high*

£8,000-12,000 **SWA**

'Champagne Devaux', designed by Ernest Deutsch Dryden, printed by Joseph-Charles, Paris, for a small Champagne company, depicting a gentleman in tails, lighting a cigar in front of an oversized champagne glass.

c1940 *61in (152.5cm) high*

£2,000-2,500 **SWA**

'Arnold Constable', designed by Jean Dupas, printed by Tolmer, Paris, in the Art Deco style, depicting three women dressed in fashions of the past, present and future, amid surrealistic scenery.

c1930 *46.5in (116cm) high*

£3,000-4,000 **SWA**

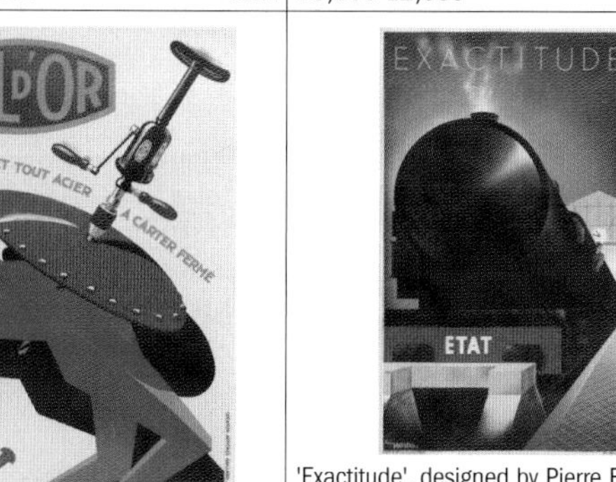

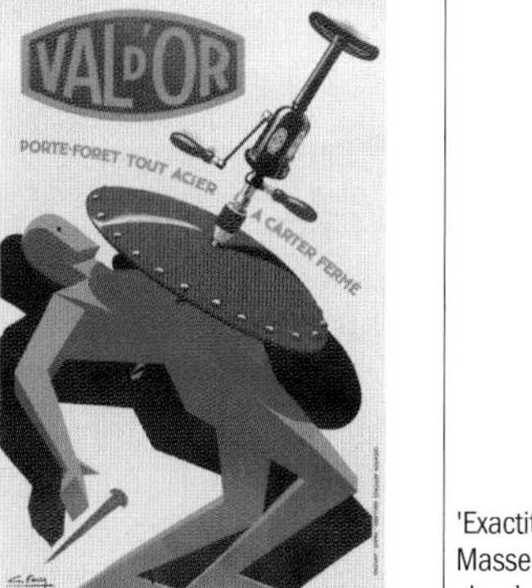

'Val D'Or', designed by G. Favre, printed by Gaillard, Paris, with a cubistically rendered green character and shadow.

c1930 *58.25in (145.5cm) high*

£500-800 **SWA**

'Exactitude', designed by Pierre Fix-Masseau, printed by Edita, Paris, the classic Art Deco railroad image with a triangular station roof, circular train front, and geometric platform, in warm colours.

c1930 *39.5in (99cm) high*

£7,000-10,000 **SWA**

'Chez Victor', designed by Paolo Federico Garetto, printed by Dureysen, Clichy.

Chez Victor was a fashionable Cannes restaurant in the heyday of the Riviera.

c1935 *62.25in (155.5cm) high*

£700-1,000 **SWA**

'Jaarbeurs Utrecht', designed by Franz Ter Gast, printed by Lankhout, the typography and rigid layout in the Art Nouveau style and the Ziggurat in a modernist, Art Deco style, Dutch.

1920 *46.25in (115.5cm) high*

£600-900 **SWA**

'BP Ethyl', designed by Edward McKnight Kauffer, with an electric flash cuting the poster in half and a photograph integrated on the right evoking 'horse power'.

c1935 *44in (110cm) wide*

£4,500-5,500 **SWA**

'Das neue Heim', designed by Ernst Keller, printed by J.C. Müller, Zürich, with bold, sans-serif typography, and black rectangles.

1928 *50.25in (125.5cm) high*

£1,800-2,200 **SWA**

'Cycles Automoto' designed by Marton Lajos, with a strong and simple close-up image of the front fork of a bicycle against a vividly coloured background.

c1930 *37.25in (93cm) high*

£1,000-1,500 **SWA**

'Pisces', designed by Charles Loupot, depicting two fish with their astronomical symbol and a cup, in a minimalist style, surrounded by stars.

c1930 *12.25in (30.5cm) high*

£2,000-2,500 **SWA**

'Stop-Fire', designed by Charles Loupot, printed by Les Belles Affiches, Paris, advertising a fire extinguisher, hand-drawn lettering, unsigned, "LBA" monograph.

c1930 *47.25in (118cm) high*

£3,000-5,000 **SWA**

'Bündnis Moskau Berlin Bringt Rettung', designed by Lazlo Peri, printed by Fides, Berlin.

c1925 *37.25in (93cm) high*

£1,800-2,200 **SWA**

'DSB / Chemins De Fer De L'Etat Danois', designed by Aage Rasmussen, printed by Andreasen & Lachmann, Copenhagen.

c1935 *39.25in (98cm) high*

£1,000-1,500 **SWA**

'Festa Major', designed by J. Vilarrasa, printed by Barral Herms, Barcelona, the Art Deco design with the red and yellow colours of the Catalan flag combined with sheets from a daily calendar, to announce a series of fiestas.

1932 *46.75in (117cm) high*

£800-1,200 **SWA**

One of 20 plates in a 'Dessins' portfolio, showing designs for fabric, wallpaper and graphic designs, by Paris' Russian immigrant artist community and others.

c1925 *14in (35.5cm) high*

£2,000-3,000 set **SWA**

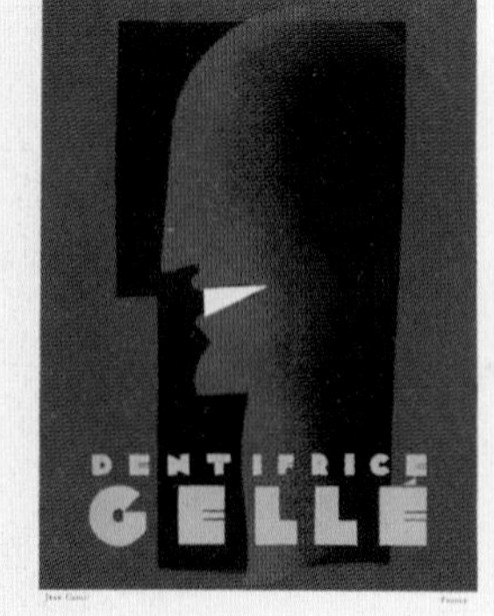

One of 49 plates in the 'Publicité' portfolio, printed by Charles Moreau, Paris, from the important Art Deco series of 15 portfolios titled 'L'Art International d'Aujour d'Hui'.

c1930 *13in (32.5cm) high*

£1,800-2,200 set **SWA**

'Reklame Schau', designed by Lucian Bernhard, printed by Hans Pusch, Berlin, depicting a 'look and listen' image, stylistically playing with light and colour.

1929 *32.5in (81cm) high*

£1,500-2,000 **SWA**

'Aixafem El Feixisme', designed by Roca Catala, printed by La Comissaria de Propaganda de la Generalitat de Catalunya, with a photograph of a foot in an espandrille crushing a swastika, with the caption, in Catalan, "Smash Fascism".

c1935 *39.25in (98cm) high*

£1,500-2,000 **SWA**

'Manthey', designed by Margarethe Friedländer, printed by Ernst Max, Berlin, with an elaborate rendering of a woman playing the piano.

c1910 *36.75in (92cm) wide*

£1,000-1,500 **SWA**

'Internationale Photographische Ausstellung', designed by Wilhelm Hartz, with a peacock-like bird over highly stylized typography.

1909 *38in (95cm) high*

£1,200-1,800 **SWA**

'Metropolis', designed by Werner Graul, printed by Eckert, Berlin, advertising Fritz Lang's 1927 science fiction movie, depicting the film's central character, Maria, as a robot in an hypnotic image of stylized realism.

The world premiere of 'Metropolis' was on January 10, 1927 at Berlin's Ufa-Palast am Zoo. The next day the film moved to the Ufa-Pavillion am Nollendorf, where it ran from January 11, 1927 to May 13, 1927. This poster advertises the four month run at the Pavillion. It was then inexplicably withdrawn from the theatre and edited.

c1925 *27.25in (68cm) high*

£25,000-30,000 **SWA**

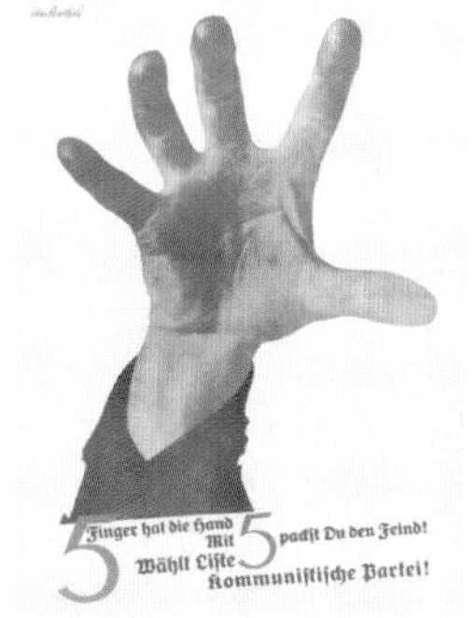

'5 Finger hat die Hand', designed by John Heartfield, promoting the Communist ballot 'List Five' in the upcoming elections.

c1970 *38in (95cm) high*

£1,000-1,500 **SWA**

'Olivetti Typewriters', designed by Frederic Henri Kay Henrion, a post-Surrealist image of an eye above a typewriter.

119.5in (299cm) high

£1,500-2,000 **SWA**

'Café Odeon und Billard Akademie', designed by Ludwig Hohlwein, printed by G. Schuh, Munich, depicting a dandy sitting on a billiard table being served by a young, liveried boy.

c1910 *46.75in (117cm) high*

£2,500-3,000 **SWA**

'Marco-Polo Tee', designed by Ludwig Hohlwein, printed in Leipzig, depicting a wizened Chinese Mandarin with tea bags in his lap, with watercolours.

c1915 *43.25in (108cm) high*

£2,800-3,200 **SWA**

'Blue Star Line', by Marcal Artkaud, printed by Ed. Alepee, Paris, in the style of A. M. Cassandre, slight damage.

35.5in (90cm) high

£1,000-1,500 **SWA**

'New York Central Building', by Achesley Bonestell, printed by Latham Lith & Ptg., New York, with an evening scene of the Central Building above Grand Central Station, mounted on board, some wear.

c1930 *36in (91.5cm) high*

£1,200-1,800 **SWA**

'Egypt / Savoy Hotel', by Mario Borgoni, printed by Richter, Naples, minor restored losses and repaired tears in margins, horizontal fold.

c1910 *56.5in (143.5cm) high*

£2,000-3,000 **SWA**

'La Plage de Monte Carlo', by Michel Bouchaud, printed by Publicité Vox, Tolmer, with a fashionable couple at the confluence of the bay and a pool, framed.

c1930 *46.5in (118cm) high*

£2,200-2,800 **SWA**

'Meeting D'Aviation / Nice', by Charles Leonce Brosse, printed by Robaudy, Cannes, repaired tears and creases.

This poster was also issued with extra text at the bottom advertising train tickets.

1910 *42in (107cm) high*

£6,000-9,000 **SWA**

'World Cruise', by J.F. Butler, depicting a giant liner beneath a map of the world, some damage, mounted on old linen.

1924 *42.5in (108cm) high*

£1,500-2,000 **SWA**

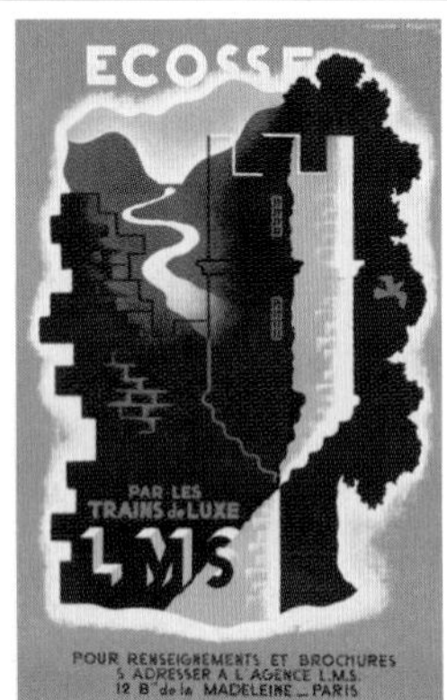

'Ecosse', by Adolphe Mouron Cassandre, printed by Bemrose & Sons, Derby, depicting a castle and river.

c1930 *40in (101.5cm) high*

£2,000-3,000 **SWA**

'Bordeaux', designed by Jean Dupas, printed by Rousseau, for Dupas' birthplace, to promote the city's harbour, wine and monuments.

c1935 *39in (97.5cm) high*

£3,000-5,000 **SWA**

'Ski Canada' designed by Peter Ewart, depicting a skier on vertical descent, leaving a trail of snow.

35.5in (89cm) high

£1,500-2,000 **SWA**

AEROPOSTALE

SERVIÇO POSTAL AEREO

EUROPA _ AFRICA _ SUL AMERICA

Cie Gle Aéropostale. 50, Av. Rio Branco. Rio de Janeiro

'Aeropostale', by 'F', Brazilian, depicting a night flight over jungle, advertising newly opened intercontinental routes, minor restoration to left margin.

c1930 *32in (81cm) high*

£3,000-4,000 **SWA**

'Wein / Imperial Feigenkaffe', by Ernst Ludwig Franke, printed by Obpacher, Munich, advertising coffee, restoration.

Franke was co-founder of the Union of Austrian Graphic Designers, with Joseph Binder, Leo Pernitsch and others.

c1940 *47.25in (120cm) wide*

£1,000-1,500 **SWA**

'Terranova', by Ludwig Hohlwein, printed by Terranova Verwetung, Vienna, creases.

c1910 *34.5in (88cm) high*

£2,000-3,000 **SWA**

'Au Maroc Par Avion / Aeropostale', by Jean Jacquelin, printed by Step, Paris.

c1930 *31.5in (80cm) high*

£1,500-2,000 **SWA**

'Dartmouth Winter Carnival', designed by H.M. Joanethis, with a close up view from below, of a skier.

c1940 *33.75in (84cm) high*

£1,500-2,000 **SWA**

'Belgie De Kunst', designed by Leo Marfurt, printed by Les Créations Publicitaires, Brussels, for the Belgian tourist board, the sandcastle bearing a Belgian flag.

c1940 *38.75in (97cm) high*

£1,200-1,800 **SWA**

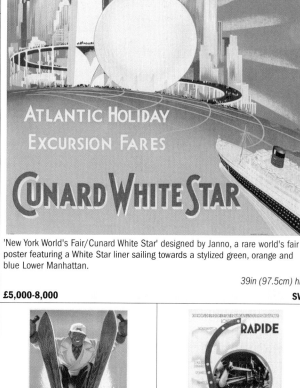

'New York World's Fair/Cunard White Star' designed by Janno, a rare world's fair poster featuring a White Star liner sailing towards a stylized green, orange and blue Lower Manhattan.

39in (97.5cm) high

£5,000-8,000 **SWA**

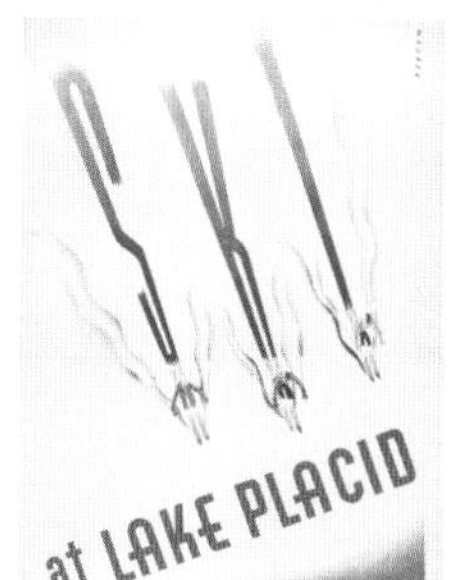

'Ski Lake Placid', designed by Sascha Maurer, printed by The Ultman Co., depicting downhill skiing with a typographic conceit.

c1940 *24.5in (61cm) high*

£3,000-5,000 **SWA**

'Flexible Flyer / Hogback Mountain Ski Area', designed by Sascha Maurer.

One in a series of popular advertisements for Flexible Flyer skis which were printed with a blank space at the bottom to be used by different advertisers.

37in (92.5cm) high

£2,000-3,000 **SWA**

'Ski / The New Haven R.R.' designed by Sascha Maurer, with a skier taking to the air over the poster's title.

c1940 *42in (105cm) high*

£3,000-5,000 **SWA**

Rapide / Cote D'Émeraude Pyrénées' designed by 'N.', printed by Périn-Dufour, Paris, with an image of locomotive wheels.

c1930 *39in (97.5cm) high*

£1,000-1,500 **SWA**

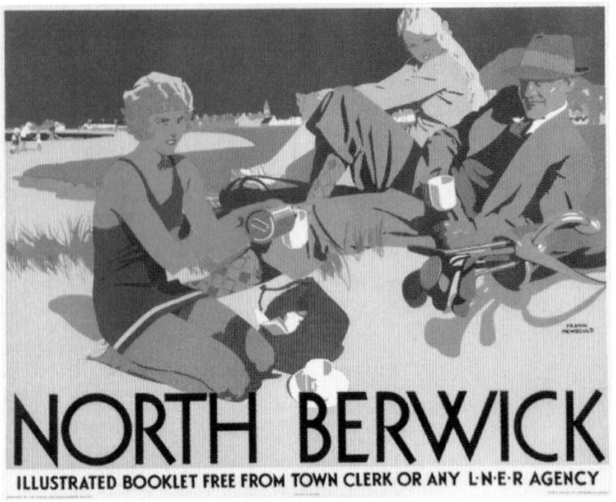

'North Berwick', by Frank Newbould, printed by Dobson Molle, Edinburgh, slight damage and repair, framed.

c1930 *49.5in (125.5cm) wide*

£4,000-6,000 SWA

'Simplon-Orient-Express', by Joseph de la Neziere, printed by Lucien Serre, Paris, depicting the train passing the Acropolis and other Greek ruins.

c1925 *41.5in (105.5cm) high*

£1,800-2,200 SWA

'Say it Fast...Often...In Color / Subway Posters', designed by Eric Nitsche, with a semi-abstract vision of a subway passing a wall of posters.

c1945 *45in (112.5cm) high*

£2,200-2,800 SWA

'Delahaye', designed by Roger Perot, printed by Les Ateliers A. B. C., Paris, the typography mirroring the angle of the roadster's front wheels.

c1935 *61in (152.5cm) high*

£3,000-4,000 SWA

'Wings Of A Century / World's Fair Chicago', probably by Weimer Pursell, printed by Neely Printing Company, Chicago, advertising an individual attraction, rare, repairs and restoration.

1934 *41in (104cm) high*

£2,000-3,000 SWA

'Rails To Sales / Subway Posters' designed by Otis Shepard, with Cassandre-style rail in a tunnel hurtling towards advertisements.

c1945 *45in (112.5cm) high*

£3,000-4,000 SWA

'Gateway to the Mount Mansfield Winter Sports Country', designed by Stephen J. Vorhees, one in a series by the artist for the Central Vermont Railway.

30in (75cm) high

£1,500-2,000 SWA

'East African Airways', printed by Galvin & Sales, Cape Town, with Mt. Kilimanjaro rising above the clouds.

39.5in (100.5cm) high

£600-900 SWA

'Visitez Le Maroc', printed by Le Novateur, Paris, with a stylized ship and buildings.

39.25in (100cm) high

£1,000-1,500 SWA

'Cuba / Habana', depicting pre-Castro Cuba, rare, creases and minor restoration.

c1950 *33in (84cm) high*

£2,500-3,500 SWA

'Air France', printed by P. Chanove, Courbevoie, with a Dewoitine D-333 flying through a sunburst and people from around the world, wear.

38in (96.5cm) high

£400-600 SWA

'Veedol Motor Oil', a poster-portrait of the famous German Zeppelins, the Hindenburg and the Graf Zeppelin, to advertise motor oil, restored.

1936 *42in (107cm) high*

£3,000-4,000 SWA

'LMS Express and Cunard Liner', slight damage and restoration.

An effort to cross-market two formidable transportation companies by highlighting their elegant, streamlined flagships.

39in (99cm) high

£2,000-3,000 SWA

'Carry On! Buy Liberty Bonds To Your Utmost', by Edwin Howland Blashfield, printed by Heyward, Strasser and Voight, rare, three-sheet poster, restored.

c1915 *77.25in (196cm) high*

£2,000-3,000 **SWA**

'Help Your Country Stop This / Enlist In The Navy', by Frank Brangwyn, printed by American Lithographic Co., New York, a lithographic portrait of the survivors of a U-boat attack, restoration.

c1915 *77.25in (196cm) wide*

£800-1,200 **SWA**

'Put Strength In The Final Blow / Buy War Bonds', by Frank Brangwyn, printed by Avenue Press, London, restored.

c1915 *60.5in (153.5cm) high*

£500-800 **SWA**

'America's answer! Production', by Jean Carlu, printed by US Government Printing Office, restored.

c1940 *40.25in (102cm) wide*

£1,200-1,800 **SWA**

'Give Us The Faith And Courage Of Our Forefathers', by Howard Chandler Christy, printed by Recruiting Publicity Bureau, U. S. Army, depicting Uncle Sam seeking divine strength.

1950 *35.25in (89.5cm) high*

£800-1,200 **SWA**

'The Motor Corps', by Howard Chandler Christy, a young US with a corpswoman carrying a stretcher, restored.

c1915 *43in (109cm) high*

£1,500-2,000 **SWA**

'If You Want To Fight Join The Marines', by Howard Chandler Christy, over-painting, restoration.

c1915 *40.5in (103cm) high*

£1,000-1,500 **SWA**

'Gee! I Wish I Were A Man I'd Join The Navy', by Howard Chandler Christy, depicting a woman in a naval outfit, wear.

c1920 *41.25in (105cm) high*

£1,200-1,800 **SWA**

'Und Ihr?' ('And You?'), by Frtiz Erler, printed by Hollerbaum & Schmidt, two-sheet, depicting a wounded soldier.

c1915 *55.25in (140cm) high*

£800-1,200 **SWA**

'Wake Up America!', by James Montgomery Flagg, printed by The Hegeman Print, New York, restored losses and tears.

Flagg designed two of these images to prepare the US for involvement in WWI. Here in an allegory of a country unprepared, Columbia is sleeping on her front porch, while behind her the flames and smoke of war can be seen in the distance.

c1915 *39.5in (100cm) high*

£6,000-8,000 **SWA**

'I Want You', by James Montgomery Flagg, printed by Leslie Judge, New York, restored.

Because this poster was so universally known, it was reissued during WWII with different text. The classic image is actually a self-portrait of the artist, and the pose was adopted from an earlier British poster featuring Lord Kitchener.

c1915 *40.25in (102cm) high*

£7,000-10,000 **SWA**

'Nieder mit den Kriegshetzern!', designed by John Heartfield, printed by Westdeutsche Buchdruck Werkstätten, Düsseldorf, extolling the people to vote Communist "Down with the war mongers! Fight for the Soviet Union!".

c1930 *29in (72.5cm) high*

£5,000-7,000 **SWA**

'Treat 'Em Rough! / Join The Tanks', by Angiet Hutaf, printed by National Printing and Engraving Co, New York, repair.

'Black Tom' was the tank corp mascot.

c1915 *41.25in (105cm) high*

£800-1,200 **SWA**

'Fulfillment of the 5 Year Plan', designed by Gustav Klutsis, with a crowd of workers, factories and a large image of Stalin.

c1930 *58in (145cm) high*

£3,500-4,500 **SWA**

'N.E.P. Russia Will Become Socialist Russia', attributed to Gustav Klutsis, a photomontage in the form of a picture-poem.

c1930 *33.25in (83cm) high*

£3,500-4,500 **SWA**

'With the Efforts of Millions of Workers Involved in the Socialist Competition, We Will Convert the Five-Year Plan into a Four-Year One', designed by Gustav Klutsis, with cranes and a workman in the foreground and asymmetrical typography.

c1930 *41.5in (104cm) high*

£2,000-3,000 **SWA**

'This Is The Enemy', by Karl Koehler & Victor Ancona, printed by Grinnell, New York.

Winner of the National War Poster Competition at the Museum of Modern Art, New York.

c1940 *34.5in (88cm) high*

£3,000-5,000 **SWA**

'Make More Tanks', designed by El Lissitsky, a political photomontage poster of a young boy and girl, with a factory, tank and an aeroplane, Russian.

c1940 *35in (87.5cm) high*

£5,000-8,000 **SWA**

'War Loan / Forward For Victory', by A. Maksimov, to raise money for involvement with WWI, with a medieval Russian knight carrying a flag bearing the Romanov Coat-of-Arms, restoration.

c1915 *38in (97cm) high*

£400-600 **SWA**

'You / How Have You Helped The Front?', by Dmitri Moor, to encourage participation in the war effort, restored.

c1940 *35in (89cm) high*

£700-1,000 **SWA**

'Enlist', by Paxton & Hall, printed by Sackett & Wilhelms, New York, in four-sheets, damage.

109.5in (278cm) high

£1,200-1,800 **SWA**

'U. Hajók Elöre!', by Lipot Satori, printed by Seidner, Budapest, featuring a submarine to advertise a movie, restored.

49.25in (125cm) high

£800-1,200 **SWA**

'SI', designed by Xanti Schwawinsky, printed by Alfieri & Lacroix, Milan, photomontage celebrating the 12th year of the Italian Fascist regime.

1934 *37.5in (94cm) high*

£1,500-2,000 **SWA**

'From Workers to Farmers... Thanks!', designed by Ben Shahn, printed by L.I.P. & B.A., New York.

c1945 *39.5in (99cm) high*

£1,200-1,800 **SWA**

'En Belgique Les Belges Ont Faim', by Theophile-Alexandre Steinlen, printed by I. Lapina, Paris, promoting a raffle for starving Belgians, restoration.

c1915 *51in (130cm) high*

£600-900 **SWA**

'U.S. Navy / Over There', by Albert Sterner, printed by American Lithographic Co., New York, restored.

c1915 *56.75in (144cm) high*

£500-800 **SWA**

'The Motherland Is Calling', by Irakli M. Toidze, with Mother Russia holding a broadside bearing the text of the Russian military oath in many of the languages of the former Soviet Union, restored.

c1940 *40in (101.5cm) high*

£400-600 **SWA**

'Buy War Bonds', by N. C. Wyeth, printed by U.S. Government Printing Office, repaired tears and restoration.

One of America's greatest illustrators, Wyeth gave exciting visual life to more than a century of classic adventure stories. For WWII, Wyeth utilizes his most heroic style to depict a stirring version of Uncle Sam urging America's troops onward. This is the largest and rarest of three different sizes.

c1940 *60in (152cm) high*

£1,500-2,000 **SWA**

'The Jews The World Over', printed by Montreal Litho Co., a rare Canadian WWI image calling on Jews to enlist in the army, restoration.

An extraordinary call to arms, employing three separate persuasive techniques: patronizing expectation ("Britain expects every son of Israel to do his duty"); historical association ("The Jews the world over love liberty, have fought for it & will fight for it"); and following a visual example (the man pictured is saying "you have cut my bonds and set me free-now let me help you set others free!"). This poster was also printed in a Yiddish language version.

c1915 *40.75in (103.5cm) high*

£2,000-3,000 **SWA**

'Britain Needs You At Once', printed by Spottiswoode, London, an early recruitment poster featuring St. George battling the dragon.

Britain didn't introduce mandatory conscription until 1916. Several different countries used this same motif for their war posters.

c1915 *30in (76cm) high*

£700-1,000 **SWA**

KEY TO ILLUSTRATIONS

EVERY ANTIQUE ILLUSTRATED in *DK Antiques Price Guide 2005* by Judith Miller has a letter code which identifies the dealer or auction house that sold it. The list below is a key to these codes. In the list, auction houses are shown by the letter Ⓐ and dealers by the letter Ⓓ. Some items may have come from a private collection, in which case the code in the list is accompanied by the letter Ⓟ. Inclusion in this book in no way constitutes or implies a contract or a binding offer on the part of any of our contributors to supply or sell the goods illustrated, or similar items, at the prices stated.

AA Ⓓ
Albert Amor
37 Bury Street, St James's, London SW1Y 6AU
Tel: 020 7930 2444
Fax: 020 7930 9067
info@albertamor.co.uk
www.albertamor.co.uk

AAC Ⓐ
Sanford Alderfer Auction Company
501 Fairgrounds Road, Hatfield, PA 19440, USA
Tel: 001 215 393 3000
info@alderferauction.com
www.alderferauction.com

ABIJ Ⓓ
Aurora Bijoux
525 Perkiomen Avenue, Lansdale,
PA 19446, USA
Tel: 001 215 872 7808
www.aurorabijoux.com

AD Ⓓ
Andrew Dando
34 Market Street,
Bradford on Avon BA15 1LL
Tel: 01225 865 444
andrew@andrewdando.co.uk
www.andrewdando.co.uk

AG Ⓓ
Antique Glass at Frank Dux Antiques
33 Belvedere, Lansdown Road, Bath, BA1 5HR
Tel: 01225 312 367
Fax: 01225 312 367
m.hopkins@antique-glass.co.uk
www.antique-glass.co.uk

AHL Ⓓ
Andrea Hall Levy
Antique Collections, Inc., 28 West
25th Street, New York, NY 10010
Tel: 001 646 441 1726

AL Ⓓ
Andrew Lineham Fine Glass
Stand G19, The Mall, Camden Passage,
London N1 8ED
Tel: 020 7704 0195
Fax: 01243 576241
Andrew@AndrewLineham.co.uk
www.antiquecolouredglass.co.uk

ANA Ⓓ
Ancient Art
85 The Vale, Southgate,
London N14 6AT
Tel: 020 8882 1509
Fax: 020 8886 5235
ancient.art@btinternet.com
www.ancientart.co.uk

ANF Ⓓ
Anfora Glass Factory
Contact through Vetri & Arte Gallery
Calle del Cappeller 3212, Dorsoduro,
Venice 30123, Italy
Tel: 0039 041 522 8525

ATK Ⓐ
Auction Team Köln
Postfach 50 11 19,
D-50971 Cologne, Germany
Tel: 00 49 (0)221 38 70 49
Fax: 00 49 (0)221 37 48 78
Auction@Breker.com
www.Breker.com

ATL Ⓓ
Antique Textiles and Lighting
34 Belvedere, Lansdowne Road, Bath BA1 5HR
Tel: 01225 310 795
www.antiquetextilesandlighting.com

B Ⓐ
Dreweatte Neate (Formely Bracketts)
Auction Hall, The Pantiles, Tunbridge Wells,
Kent TN2 5QL
Tel: 01892 544 500
Fax: 01892 515 191
tunbridgewells@dnfa.co.uk
www.dnfa.co.uk

B&I Ⓓ
Burden & Izett
180 Duane Street, New York,
NY 10013, USA
Tel: 001 212 941 8247
Fax: 001 212 431 5018
info@burdenandizett.net
www.burdenandizett.net

BCAC Ⓓ
Bucks County Antique
Centre Route 202, 8 Skyline Drive,
PA 18914, USA
Tel: 001 215 794 9180

BEJ Ⓓ
Bébés & Jouets
c/o Post Office, 165 Restalrig Road,
Edinburgh EH7 6HW
Tel: 0131 332 5650
bebesetjouets@u.genie.co.uk

BEV Ⓓ
Beverley Adams
30 Church Street, London, NW8 8EP
Tel: 020 7262 1576
Mob: 07776 136003

BJ Ⓓ
Barbara Johnson at Heritage
6 Market Place, Woodstock, Oxon, OX20 1TA
Tel: 01993 811 332

BL Ⓓ
Blanchard Ltd.
86/88 Pimlico Road, London SW1W 8PL
Tel: 020 7823 6310
Fax: 020 7823 6303
piers@jwblanchard.com

BMN Ⓐ
Auktionshaus Bergmann
Möhrendorfer Str. 4, 91056, Erlangen, Germany
Tel: 00 49 (0)9131 45 06 66
Fax: 00 49 (0)9131 45 02 04
www.auction-bergmann.de

BONS Ⓐ
Bonhams, Bond Street
101 New Bond Street, London W1S 1SR
Tel: 020 7629 6602
Fax: 020 7629 8876
info@bonhams.com
www.bonhams.com

BP Ⓓ
The Blue Pump
178 Davenport Road, Toronto,
M5R 1J2, Canada
Tel: 001 416 944 1673
www.thebluepump.com

BY Ⓓ
Bonny Yankauer
bonnyy@aol.com

CATO Ⓓ
Lennox Cato Antiques
1 The Square, Church Street, Edenbridge,
Kent TN8 5BD
Tel: 01732 865 988
cato@lennoxcato.com
www.lennoxcato.com

CHEF Ⓐ
Cheffins
1-2 Clifton Road, Cambridge CB1 7EA
Tel: 01223 213 343
Fax: 01223 271 949
fine.art@cheffins.co.uk
www.cheffins.co.uk

CLV Ⓐ
Clevedon Salerooms The Auction Centre,
Kenn Road, Clevedon, Bristol BS21 6TT
Tel: 01934 830 111
Fax: 01934 832 538
info@clevedon-salerooms.com
www.clevedon-salerooms.com

CO Ⓐ
Cooper Owen
10 Denmark Street,
London WC2H 8LS
Tel: 020 7240 4132
Fax: 020 7240 4339
auctions@cooperowen.com
www.cooperowen.com

CRIS Ⓓ
Cristobal 26 Church Street, London NW8 8EP
Tel/Fax: 020 7724 7230
steven@cristobal.co.uk
www.cristobal.co.uk

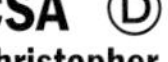
CSA Ⓓ
Christopher Sykes Antiques
The Old Parsonage, Woburn,
Milton Keynes, MK17 9QJ
Tel: 01525 290 259/290 467
Fax: 01525 290 061
www.sykes-corkscrews.co.uk

CSAY Ⓓ
Charlotte Sayers
Stand 313-315 Grays Antique Markets,
58 Davies Street, London W1K 5LP
Tel: 020 7499 5478

D Ⓐ
Dickins Auctioneers
Calvert Court, Middle Claydon,
Bucks, MK18 2EZ
Tel: 01296 714 434
Fax: 01296 714 492
info@dickins-auctioneers.com
www.dickins-auctioneers.com

DAW Ⓐ
Dawson's & Nye Auctioneers & Appraisers
128 American Road, Morris Plains,
NJ 07950, USA
Tel: 001 973 984 6900
Fax: 001 973 984 6956
info@dawsons.org
www@dawsons.org

DB Ⓓ
David Bowden
Stand 107, Grays Antique Markets,
58 Davies Street, London W1K 5LP
Tel / Fax: 020 7495 1773

DL Ⓓ
David Love
10 Royal Parade, Harrogate HG1 2SZ
Tel: 01423 565 797
Fax: 01423 525567

DN Ⓐ
Dreweatt Neate
Donnington Priory Salerooms, Donnington,
Newbury, Berkshire RG14 2JE
Tel: 01635 553 553
Fax: 01635 553 599
fineart@dnfa.co.uk
www.dnfa.co.uk

DOR Ⓐ
Dorotheum
Palais Dorotheum, A-1010 Vienna,
Dorotheergasse 17
Tel: 0043 1 515 600
Fax: 0043 1 515 60443
kundendienst@dorotheum.at
www.dorotheum.com

DR Ⓓ
Derek Roberts Fine Antique Clocks & Barometers
25 Shipbourne Road, Tonbridge, Kent TN10 3DN
Tel: 01732 358 986
Fax: 01732 771 842
drclocks@clara.net
www.qualityantiqueclocks.com

DRA Ⓐ
David Rago Auctions
333 North Main Street, Lambertville,
NJ 08530, USA
Tel: 001 609 397 9374
Fax: 001 609 397 9377
info@ragoarts.com
www.ragoarts.com

ECLEC Ⓓ
Eclectica
2 Charlton Place, Islington, London N1 8AJ
Tel: 020 7226 5625
liz@eclectica.biz
www.eclectica.biz

EP Ⓓ
Elaine Phillips Antiques
1 & 2 Royal Parade, Harrogate,
North Yorkshire HG1 2SZ
Tel: 01423 569 745
ep@harrogateantiques.com

ET Ⓓ
Early Technology
Monkton House, Old Craighall,
East Lothian, Scotland
Tel: 0131 665 5753
www.earlytech.com

F Ⓐ
Fellows & Sons
Augusta House, 19 Augusta Street, Hockley,
Birmingham, B18 6JA
Tel: 0121 212 2131
Fax: 0121 212 1249
info@fellows.co.uk
www.fellows.co.uk

FAN Ⓓ
Fantiques
Tel: 020 8840 4761
Mob: 07956 242 540
paula.raven@ntlworld.com

FIS Ⓐ
Dr Fischer
Trappensee-Schlösschen,
D-74074 Heilbronn, Germany
Tel: 00 49 (0)7131 15 55 7 0
Fax: 00 49 (0)7131 15 55 7 2
info@auctions-fischer.de
www.auctions-fischer.de

FM Ⓓ
Francesca Martire
F131-137, Alfies Antique Market, 13 Church Street, Marylebone, London NW8 8DT
Tel: 020 7724 4802

FRE Ⓐ
Freeman's
1808 Chestnut Street, Philadelphia,
PA 19103, USA
Tel: 001 215 563 9275
Fax: 001 215 563 8236
info@freemansauction.com
www.freemansauction.com

GAS Ⓓ
Alan Sharp at The Ginnel
The Ginnel Antiques Centre, off Parliament Street, Harrogate, North Yorkshire, HG1 2RB
Tel: 01423 508 857
www.redhouseyork.co.uk

GCL Ⓓ
Claude Lee at The Ginnel
The Ginnel Antiques Centre, off Parliament Street, Harrogate,
North Yorkshire, HG1 2RB
Tel: 01423 508 857
www.redhouseyork.co.uk

GEW Ⓓ
Eileen Wilson at The Ginnel
The Ginnel Antiques Centre, off Parliament Street, Harrogate,
North Yorkshire, HG1 2RB
Tel: 01423 508 857
www.redhouseyork.co.uk

GFA Ⓓ
Fiona Aston at The Ginnel
The Ginnel Antiques Centre, off Parliament Street, Harrogate,
North Yorkshire, HG1 2RB
Tel: 01423 508 857
www.redhouseyork.co.uk

GHA Ⓓ
Hawkswood Antiques at The Ginnel
The Ginnel Antiques Centre, off Parliament Street, Harrogate,
North Yorkshire, HG1 2RB
Tel: 01423 508 857
www.redhouseyork.co.uk

GHOU Ⓐ
Gardiner Houlgate
Bath Auction Rooms, 9 Leafield Way,
Corsham, Nr Bath, SN13 9SW
Tel: 01225 812 912
Fax: 01225 817 777
auctions@gardiner-houlgate.co.uk

GMC Ⓓ
Mary Cooper at The Ginnel
The Ginnel Antiques Centre, off Parliament Street, Harrogate,
North Yorkshire, HG1 2RB
Tel: 01423 508 857
www.redhouseyork.co.uk

GOL Ⓓ
Nancy Goldsmith
Tel: 212 696 0831

GORL Ⓐ
Gorringes
15 North Street, Lewes BN7 2PD
Tel: 01273 472 503
Fax: 01273 479 559
clientservices@gorringes.co.uk
www.gorringes.co.uk

GRO Ⓓ
Mary Wise and Grosvenor Antiques
27 Holland Street, London W8 4NA
Tel: 020 7937 8649
Fax: 020 7937 7179
www.wiseantiques.com

GS Ⓓ
Goodwins Antiques
15 & 16 Queensferry Street,
Edinburgh EH2 4QW
Tel: 0131 225 4717
Fax: 0131 2201412

H&G Ⓓ
Hope and Glory
131A Kensington Church Street, London W8 7LP
Tel: 020 7727 8424

HAMG Ⓐ
Hamptons
Baverstock House,
93 High Street, Godalming, Surrey GU7 1AL
Tel: 01483 423 567
Fax: 01483 426 392
fineart@hamptons-int.com
www.hamptons.co.uk

HBK Ⓓ
Hall-Bakker at Heritage
Heritage, 6 Market Place, Woodstock,
Oxon, OX20 1TA
Tel: 01993 811332

HD Ⓓ
Halcyon Days
14 Brook Street,
London W1S 1BD
Tel: 020 7629 8811
Fax: 020 7409 7901
info@halcyondays.co.uk
www.halcyondays.co.uk

HGS Ⓓ
Harper General Store
10482 Jonestown Road, Annville,
PA 17003, USA
Tel: 001 717 865 3456
Fax: 001 717 865 3813
lauver5@comcast.net
www.harpergeneralstore.com

HP Ⓓ
Hilary Proctor
Advintage, Shop E20, Grays Antiques Market,
1-7 Davies Mews, London, W1Y 2PL
Tel: 020 7499 7001
hproctor@antiquehandbags.fs.net.co.uk
www.advintageuk.com

JBS Ⓓ
John Bull Silver
139A New Bond Street, London W1S 2TN
Tel: 020 7629 1251
Fax: 020 7495 3001
www.jbsilverware.co.uk

JDJ Ⓐ
James D Julia Inc
PO Box 830, Fairfield,
Maine 04937, USA
Tel: 001 207 453 7125
www.juliaauctions.com

JF Ⓓ
Jill Fenichell
305 East 61st Street,
New York, NY, USA
Tel: 001 212 980 9346
jfenichell@yahoo.com

JH Ⓓ
Jeanette Hayhurst Fine Glass
32A Kensington Church St.,
London W8 4HA
Tel: 020 7938 1539
www.antiqueglasslondon.com

JHB Ⓓ
Joseph H Bonnar
72 Thistle Street, Edinburgh, EH2 1EN
Tel: 0131 226 2811
Fax: 0131 225 9438

JHD Ⓓ
John Howard at Heritage
6 Market Place, Woodstock, Oxon, OX20 1TA
Tel: 0870 444 0678
john@johnhoward.co.uk
www.antiquepottery.co.uk

JHOR Ⓓ
Jonathan Horne
66c Kensington Church Street,
London W8 4BY
Tel: 020 7221 5658
Fax: 020 7792 3090
JH@jonathanhorne.co.uk
www.jonathanhorne.co.uk

JJ Ⓓ
Junkyard Jeweler
937 West Beech Street, Suite 49,
Long Beach, NY 11561, USA
www.tias.com/stores/thejunkyardjeweler

JK Ⓓ
John King
74 Pimlico Road, London SW1W 8LS
Tel: 020 7730 0427
Fax: 020 7730 2515
kingj896@aol.com

JV Ⓓ
June Victor
Vintage Modes, Grays Antiques Market, 1-7
Davies Mews, London, W1Y 2PL
Tel: 020 7629 7034
info@vintagemodes.co.uk
www.vintagemodes.co.uk

JW Ⓓ
Wadsworth's Marehill, Pulborough,
West Sussex RH20 2DY
Tel: 01798 873 555
Fax: 01798 872 333
info@wadsworthrugs.com

KBON Ⓐ
Bonhams Knowle
The Old House, Station Road, Knowle, West
Midlands, B93 0HT
Tel: 01564 776 151
info@bonhams.com
www.bonhams.com

L&T Ⓐ
Lyon and Turnbull Ltd.
33 Broughton Place, Edinburgh EH1 3RR
Tel: 0131 557 8844
Fax: 0131 557 8668
info@lyonandturnbull.com
www.lyonandturnbull.com

LB Ⓓ
Linda Bee
Grays Antique Market, 58 Davies Street,
London, W1Y 2LP
Tel: 020 7629 5921

LFA Ⓐ
Law Fine Art Ltd.
Ash Cottage, Ashmore Green Road
Ashmore Green, Newbury
Berkshire, RG18 9ER
Tel: (01635) 860033
Fax: (01635) 860036
info@lawfineart.co.uk
www.lawfineart.co.uk

LNXG Ⓓ
Lennox Gallery Ltd.
Grays Antique Market, 58 Davies Street,
London, W1K 5LP
Tel: 020 7491 0091

LPZ Ⓐ
Lempertz
Neumarkt 3, 50667 Cologne, Germany
Tel 00 49 (0)221 925 72 90
Fax: 00 49 (0)221 925 72 96
www.lempertz.com

LYNH Ⓓ
Lynn & Brian Holmes
Tel: 020 7368 6412

MACK Ⓓ
Macklowe Gallery
667 Madison Avenue, New York,
NY 10021, USA
Tel: 001 212 644 6400
Fax: 001 212 755 6143
email@macklowegallery.com
www.macklowegallery.com

MARA Ⓓ
Marie Antiques
G107 & 136-7, Alfies Antique Market,
13 Church Street, London NW8 8DT
Tel: 020 7706 3727
www.marieantiques.co.uk

MB Ⓓ
Mostly Boxes
93 High Street, Eton,
Windsor, Berkshire SL4 6AF
Tel: 01753 858 470
Fax: 01753 857 212

MILLB Ⓓ
Million Dollar Babies
47 Hyde Blvd., Ballston Spa, NY 12020, USA
Tel: 001 518 885 7397

MW Ⓓ
Mike Weedon
7 Camden Passage, Islington,
London N1 8EA
Tel: 020 7226 5319
Fax: 020 7700 6387
info@mikeweedonantiques.com
www.mikeweedonantiques.com

NA Ⓐ
Northeast Auctions
93 Pleasant Street, Portsmouth,
NH 03801, USA
Tel: 001 603 433 8400
Fax: 001 603 433 0415
contact@northeastauctions.com
www.northeastauctions.com

NAG Ⓐ
Nagel
Neckarstrasse 189-191, 70190 Stuttgart,
Germany
Tel: 0049 711 649 690
Fax: 0049 711 649 69696
contact@auction.de
www.auction.de

NOA Ⓓ
Norman Adams Ltd.
8-10 Hans Road, London SW3 1RX
Tel: 020 7589 5266
Fax: .020 7589 1968
antiques@normanadams.com
www.normanadams.com

OACC Ⓓ
Otford Antiques and Collectors Centre
26-28 High Street, Otford, Kent TN14 5PQ
Tel: 01959 522 025
www.otfordantiques.co.uk

PC Ⓟ
Private Collection

PH Ⓓ
Pantry and Hearth
PO Box 268,
121 East 35th Street,
New York, NY 10016, USA
Tel: 001 212 532 0535
gail.lettick@prodigy.net
www.nhada.org/pantryhearth.htm

POOK Ⓐ
Pook and Pook
463 East Lancaster Avenue,
Downington, PA 19335, USA
Tel: 001 610 269 4040/0695
Fax: 001 610 269-9274
info@pookandpook.com
www.pookandpook.com

PST Ⓓ
Patricia Stauble Antiques
180 Main Street, PO Box 265,
Wiscasset, ME 04578, USA
Tel: 001 207 882 6341

QU Ⓐ
Quittenbaum Kunstauktionen München
Hohenstaufenstraße 1, D-80801,
Munich, Germany
Tel: 00 49 (0)89 33 00 75 6
www.quittenbaum.de

RAA Ⓓ
Axtell Antiques
1 River Street, Deposit, New York 13754 USA
Tel: 001 607 467 2353
rsaxtell@msn.com
www.axtellantiques.com

R&GM Ⓓ
R & G McPherson Antiques
40 Kensington Church Street, London W8 4BX
Tel: 020 7937 0812
Fax: 020 7938 2032
rmcpherson@orientalceramics.com
www.orientalceramics.com

RB Ⓓ
Roger Bradbury
Church Street, Coltishall, Norwich,
Norfolk NR12 7DJ
Tel: 01603 737 444

RBRG Ⓓ
RBR Group at Grays
175, Grays Antique Market, 58 Davies Street,
London, W1Y 5LP
Tel: 020 7629 4769

RDER Ⓓ
Rogers de Rin
76 Royal Hospital Road,
Paradise Walk, Chelsea,
London SW3 4HN
Tel: 020 7352 9007
rogersderin@rogersderin.co.uk
www.rogersderin.co.uk

RDL Ⓐ
David Rago/Nicholas Dawes Lalique Auctions
333 North Main Street, Lambertville,
NJ 08530 USA
Tel: 001 609 397 9374
Fax: 001 609 397 9377
info@ragoarts.com
www.ragoarts.com

RG Ⓓ
Richard Gibbon
34/34a Islington Green,
London N1 8DU
Tel: 020 7354 2852

RGA Ⓓ
Richard Gardner Antiques
Swan House, Market Square,
Petworth, West Sussex GU28 0AN
Tel: 01798 343 411
rg@richardgardnerantiques.co.uk
www.richardgardnerantiques.co.uk

RITZ Ⓓ
Ritzy
7 The Mall Antiques Arcade, 359 Upper Street,
London, N1 0PD
Tel: 020 7704 0127

RN Ⓓ
Raymond E. Nordberg
102 Belcher Road, Blairstown,
NJ 07825, USA
Tel: 001 908 362 9667

ROX Ⓓ
Roxanne Stuart
Langhorne, PA, USA
Tel: 001 215 750 8868
gemfairy@aol.com

RUM Ⓓ
Rumours
4 The Mall Antiques Arcade,
359 Upper Street, London, N1 0PD
Tel: 020 7704 6549

RR Ⓓ
Red Roses
Vintage Modes, Grays Antiques Market,
1-7 Davies Mews, London, W1Y 2PL
Tel: 020 7629 7034
www.vintagemodes.co.uk

SA Ⓓ
Stockspring Antiques
114 Kensington Church Street,
London W8 4BH
Tel/Fax: 020 7727 7995
stockspring@antique-porcelain.co.uk
www.antique-porcelain.co.uk

S&K Ⓐ
Sloans & Kenyon
4605 Bradley Boulevard
Bethesda, Maryland 20815, USA
Tel: 001 301 634-2330
Fax: 001 301 656-7074
www.sloansandkenyon.com

SAPH Ⓓ
Galerie Saphir
69, rue du Temple,
75003 Paris, France
Tel: 0033 01 42 72 61 19
galerie-saphir@wanadoo.fr

SDR Ⓐ
John Sollo/David Rago
333 North Main Street, Lambertville,
NJ 08530 USA
Tel: 001 609 397 9374
Fax: 001 609 397 9377
info@ragoarts.com
www.ragoarts.com

SF Ⓓ
The Silver Fund
1 Duke of York Street, London SW1Y 6JP
Tel: 0207 839 7664
Fax: 020 7839 8935
www.thesilverfund.com

SG Ⓓ
Sidney Gecker
226 West 21st Street, New York, NY 10011, USA
Tel: 001 212 929 8769

SK Ⓐ
Skinner
63 Park Plaza, Boston, MA 02116, USA &
357 Main Street, Bolton, MA 01740, USA
Tel: 001 617 350 5400
Fax: 001 617 350 5429
www.skinnerinc.com

SSP Ⓓ
Sylvie Spectrum
Stand 372, Grays Antique Market, 58 Davies
Street, London, W1K 5LP
Tel: 020 7629 3501
Fax: 020 8883 5030
spectrum@grays.clara.net

STE Ⓓ
Stephanie's Antiques
28 West 25th Street, New York NY 10010, USA
Tel: 212 633 6563

STY Ⓓ
Style Gallery
10 Camden Passage, London, N1 8ED
Tel: 020 7359 7867
www.styleantiques.co.uk

SUM Ⓓ
Sue Mautner Costume Jewellery
Stand A18-19, Antiquarius, 135 King's Road,
London, SW3 4PW
Tel: 020 7352 7155

SWA Ⓐ
Swann Galleries Inc
104 East 25th Street
New York, New York 10010, USA
Tel: 001 212 254 4710
Fax: 001 212 979 1017
www.swanngalleries.com

TA Ⓐ
333 Auctions LLC
333 North Main Street, Lambertville,
NJ 08530 USA
Tel: 001 609 397 9374
Fax: 001 609 397 9377
info@ragoarts.com
www.ragoarts.com

TAB Ⓓ
Take-A-Boo Emporium
1927 Avenue Road, Toronto, Ontario, Canada
Tel: 001 416 785 4555
Fax: 001 416 785 4594
swinton@takeaboo.com
www.takeaboo.com

TAG Ⓓ
Tagore Ltd
302, Grays Antique Market,
58 Davies Street, London, W1K 5LP
Tel: 020 7499 0158
Fax: 020 7499 0158
tagore@grays.clara.net

TCS Ⓓ
The Country Seat
Huntercombe Manor Barn,
nr Henley on Thames, Oxon RG9 5RY
Tel: 01491 641349
Fax: 01491 641533
www.thecountryseat.com

TCT Ⓓ
The Calico Teddy
330 Tunbridge Road,
Baltimore, MD 21212, USA
Tel: 001 410 433 9202
Fax: 001 410 433 9203
calicoteddy@aol.com
www.calicoteddy.com

TDG Ⓓ
The Design Gallery
5 The Green, Westerham
Kent TN16 1AS
Tel: 01959 561 234
sales@thedesigngallery.uk.com
www.thedesigngallery.uk.com

TO Ⓓ
Titus Omega
Shop 21, The Mall, Camden Passage,
London N1 0PD
Tel: 020 7688 1295
info@titusomega.com
www.titusomega.com

TR Ⓓ
Terry Rodgers & Melody
1050 2nd Avenue, New York,
NY 10022, USA
Tel: 001 212 758 3164
melodyjewelnyc@aol.com

VDB Ⓓ
Van Den Bosch
Shop 1, Georgian Village, Camden Passage,
Islington N1 8DU
Tel: 020 7226 4550
info@vandenbosch.co.uk
www.vandenbosch.co.uk

VET Ⓓ
Vetri & Arte Gallery (V&A Gallery)
Calle del Cappeller 3212, Dorsoduro,
Venice 30123, Italy
Tel: 0039 041 522 8525
contact@venicewebgallery.com
www.venicewebgallery.com

W&W Ⓐ
Wallis and Wallis
West Street Auction Galleries, Lewes,
East Sussex BN7 2NJ
Tel: 01273 480 208
Fax: 01273 476 562
auctions@wallisandwallis.co.uk
www.wallisandwallis.co.uk

WAD Ⓐ
Waddington's
111 Bathurst Street,
Toronto, Ontario, Canada M5V 2R1
Tel: 001 416 504 9100
info@waddingtonsauctions.ca
www.waddingtonsauctions.ca

WAIN Ⓓ
William Wain at Antiquarius
Stand J6, Antiquarius, 135 King's Road,
Chelsea, London SW3 4PW
Tel: 020 7351 4905
w.wain@btopenworld.com

WROB Ⓓ
Junnaa & Thomi Wroblewski
78 Marylebone High Street, Box 39,
London W1U 5AP
Tel: 020 7499 7793

WW Ⓐ
Woolley and Wallis
51-61 Castle Street, Salisbury, Wiltshire SP13SU
Tel: 01722 424 500
Fax: 01722 424 508
enquiries@woolleyandwallis.co.uk
www.woolleyandwallis.co.uk

NOTE

For valuations, it is advisable to contact the dealer in advance to confirm that they will perform this service and whether any charge is involved. Telephone valuations are not possible, so it will be necessary to send details, including a photograph, of the object to the dealer, along with a stamped addressed envelope for response. While most dealers will be happy to help you with an enquiry, do remember that they are busy people. Please mention *DK Antiques Price Guide 2005* by Judith Miller when making an enquiry.

DIRECTORY OF AUCTIONEERS

This is a list of auctioneers that conduct regular sales. Auction houses that would like to be included in the next edition should contact us by 1 February 2005.

London

Bonhams
101 New Bond Street
W1S 1SR
Tel: 020 7629 6602
Fax: 020 7629 8876

Bonhams
Montpelier Street,
Knightsbridge
SW7 1HH
Tel: 020 7393 3900
Fax: 020 7393 3905
info@bonhams.com
www.bonhams.com

Christie's
8 King Street, St. James's
SW1Y 6QT
Tel: 020 7839 9060
Fax: 020 7839 1611

Christie's South Kensington
85 Old Brompton Road
SW7 3LD
Tel: 020 7581 7611
Fax: 020 7321 3311
info@christies.com
www.christies.com

Cooper Owen
10 Denmark Street
WC2H 8LS
Tel: 020 7240 4132
Fax: 020 7240 4339
customerservice@cooperowen.com
www.cooperowen.com

Lots Road Galleries
71-73 Lots Road, Chelsea
SW10 0RN
Tel: 020 7376 6800
Fax: 020 7376 6899
www.lotsroad.com

Sotheby's
34-35 New Bond Street
W1A 2AA
Tel: 020 7293 5000
Fax: 020 7293 5989
www.sothebys.com

Avon

Aldridges of Bath
Newark House,
26-45
Cheltenham Street,
Bath BA2 3EX
Tel: 01225 462830
Fax: 01225 311319
www.invaluable.co.uk/aldridgesof-bath

Clevedon Salerooms
Herbert Road, Clevedon
BS21 7ND
Tel: 01275 876699
Fax: 01275 343765
clevedon.salerooms@cableinet.co.uk
www.clevedon-salerooms.co.uk

Gardiner Houlgate
9 Leafield Way, Corsham,
Bath SN13 9SW
Tel: 01225 812912
Fax: 01225 811777
auctions@gardiner-houlgate.co.uk
www.gardiner-houlgate.co.uk

Bedfordshire

W. & H. Peacock
The Auction Centre, 26 Newnham St,
Bedford MK40 3JR
Tel: 01234 266366
www.peacockauctions.co.uk
info@peacockauctions.co.uk

Berkshire

Dreweatt Neate
Donnington Priory, Donnington,
Nr Newbury RG14 2JE
Tel: 01635 553553
Fax: 01635 553599
fineart@dreweatt-neate.co.uk
www.auctions.dreweatt-neate.co.uk

Law Fine Art Ltd.
Firs Cottage, Church Lane,
Brimpton RG7 4TJ
Tel: 0118 971 0353
Fax: 0118 971 3741
info@lawfineart.co.uk
www.lawfineart.co.uk

Special Auction Services
The Coach House, Midgham Park,
Reading RG7 5UG
Tel: 0118 9712949

Buckinghamshire

Dickins Auctioneers
The Claydon Saleroom, Claydon
House Park, Calvert Rd,
Middle Claydon,
MK18 2EZ
Tel: 01296 714 434
Fax: 01296 714492
info@dickins-auctioneers.com
www.dickins-auctioneers.com

Cambridgeshire

Cheffins
The Cambridge Saleroom, 2 Clifton
Road, Cambridge CB1 4BW
Tel: 01223 213343
www.cheffins.co.uk

Hyperion Auctions Ltd
Station Road, St. Ives PE27 5BH
Tel: 01480 464140
Fax: 01480 497552
enquiries@hyperionauctions.co.uk
www.hyperionauctions.co.uk

Maxey & Son
Auction Hall, Cattle Market Chase,
Wisbech PE13 1RD
Tel: 01945 584609
www.maxeyandson.co.uk

Rowley Fine Art Auctioneers & Valuers
The Old Bishop's Palace,
Little Downham, Ely CB6 2TD
Tel: 01353 699177
Fax: 01353 699088
www.rowleyfineart.com

Cheshire

Frank R. Marshall and Co.
Marshall House, Church Hill,
Knutsford WA16 6DH
Tel: 01565 653284
Fax: 01565 652341
antiques@frankmarshall.co.uk
www.frankmarshall.co.uk

Halls Fine Art
Booth Mansion, 30 Watergate
Street, Chester CH1 2LA
Tel: 01244 312300
Fax: 01244 312112

Maxwells of Wilmslow
133A Woodford Road, Woodford,
Cheshire, SK7 1QD
Tel: 01614395182

Peter Wilson Fine Art Auctioneers
Victoria Gallery, Market Street,
Nantwich CW5 5DG
Tel: 01270 623878
Fax: 01270 610508
auctions@peterwilson.co.uk
www.peterwilson.co.uk

Wright Manley Auctioneers
Beeston Castle Salerooms,
Tarporley CW6 9NZ
Tel: 01829 262150
Fax: 01829 262110

Cornwall

W. H. Lane & Son
Jubilee House, Queen Street,
Penzance TR18 4DF
Tel: 01736 361447
Fax: 01736 350097
Graham.Bazley@excite.com

David Lay
The Penzance Auction House,
Alverton, Penzance TR18 4RE
Tel: 01736 361414

Cumbria

James Thompson
64 Main Street, Kirkby Lonsdale
LA6 2AJ
Tel: 01524 271555
Fax: 01524 272939
sales@jthompsonauctioneers.co.uk
www.jthompson-auctioneers.co.uk

Derbyshire

Noel Wheatcroft & Son
Matlock Auction Gallery,
The Old Picture Palace, Dale Road,
Matlock DE4 3LU
Tel: 01629 57460
Fax: 01629 57956
www.wheatcroft-noel.co.uk

Devon

Bearne's
St Edmund's Court, Okehampton
Street, Exeter EX4 1LX
Tel: 01392 207000

Hampton & Littlewood
The Auction Rooms,
Alphin Brook Road, Alphington,
Exeter EX2 8TH
Tel: 01392 413100
Fax: 01392 413110
www.hamptonandlittlewood.co.uk

Taylor's
Honiton Galleries, 205 High Street,
Honiton EX14 1LQ
Tel: 01404 42404

S. J. Hales Auctioneers
Tracey House Salerooms, Newton
Road, Bovey Tracey,
Newton Abbot TQ13 9AZ
Tel: 01626 836 684
Fax: 01626 836 318
info@sjhales.com
www.sjhales.com

Dorset

Cottees
The Market, East Street,
Wareham BH20 4NR
Tel: 01929 552826
Fax: 01929 554916

Dalkeith Auctions Bournemouth
Dalkeith Hall, Dalkeith Steps, Rear
of 81 Christchurch Road BH1 1YL
Tel: 01202 292905
www.dalkeith-auctions.co.uk

Hy. Duke and Son
Fine Art Salerooms, Weymouth
Avenue, Dorchester DT1 1QS
Tel: 01305 265080
Fax: 01305 260101

Wm. Morey and Sons
Salerooms, St. Michael's Lane,
Bridport DT6 3RB
Tel: 01308 422078
www.wmoreyandsons.co.uk

Riddetts of Bournemouth
177 Holdenhurst Road,
Bournemouth BH8 8DQ
Tel: 01202 555686
Fax: 01202 311004

Durham

Vectis Auctions Limited
Fleck Way, Thornaby,
Stockton on Tees TS17 9JZ
Tel: 01642 750 616
Fax: 01642 769 478
enquiries@vectis.co.uk
www.vectis.co.uk

Essex

Chalkwell Auctions Ltd. (EADA)
The Arlington Rooms, 905 London
Road, Leigh-on-Sea
Tel: 01702 710383
www.ridgeweb.co.uk

Cooper Hirst Auctions
The Granary Salerooms, Victoria
Road, Chelmsford CM2 6LH
Tel: 01245 260535

G.E. Sworder and Sons
14 Cambridge Road, Stansted
Mountfitchet CM24 8BZ
Tel: 01279 817778
Fax: 01279 817779
www.sworder.co.uk

Gloucestershire

Bristol Auction Rooms Ltd
St. John's Place, Apsley Road,
Clifton, Bristol BS8 2ST
Tel: 0117 973 7201
Fax: 0117 973 5671
info@bristolauctionrooms.com
www.bristolauctionrooms.com

Fraser Glennie and Partners
The Coach House, Upper
Siddington, Cirencester GL7 6HL
Tel: 01285 659667
Fax: 01285 642256

Mallams Fine Art Auctioneers and Valuers
26 Grosvenor Street,
Cheltenham GL52 2SG
Tel: 01242 235712
Fax: 01242 241943

Moore, Allen & Innocent
The Salerooms, Norcote,
Cirencester GL7 5RH
Tel: 01285 646050
www.mooreallen.com/cat

Specialised Postcard Auctions
25 Gloucester Street,
Cirencester,
GL7 2DJ
Tel: 01285 659 057

Wotton Auction Rooms Ltd
Tabernacle Road,
Wotton-under-Edge GL12 7EB
Tel: 01453 844733
Fax: 01453 845448
www.wottonauctionrooms.co.uk

Hampshire

Andrew Smith & Son
The Auction Rooms
Manor Farm, Itchen Stoke
SO24 0QT

Jacobs and Hunt Fine Art Auctioneers
Lavant Street, Petersfield GU32 3EF
Tel: 01730 233 933
Fax: 01730 262 323

May and Son
18 Bridge Street, Andover
SP10 1BH
Tel: 01264 323417
Fax: 01264 338841
mayandson@enterprise.net

Herefordshire

Brightwells
The Fine Art Saleroom, Ryelands
Road, Leominster HR6 8NZ
Tel: 01568 611122
Fax: 01568 610519

Hertfordshire

Brown and Merry – Tring Market Auctions
Brook Street, Tring HP23 5EF
Tel: 01442 826 446
Fax: 01442 890 927

Isle of Wight

Shanklin Auction Rooms
79 Regent Street, Shanklin
PO37 7AP
Tel: 01983 863 441
Fax: 01983 863 890
shanklin.auction@tesco.net
www.shanklinauctionrooms.co.uk

Ways
The Auction House, Garfield Road,
Ryde PO33 2PT
Tel: 01983 562 255
Fax: 01983 565 108
ways@waysauctionrooms.fsbusiness.co.uk
www.waysauctionrooms.fsbusiness.co.uk

Kent

B.J. Norris
The Quest, West Street,
Harrietsham, Maidstone ME17 1JD
Tel: 01622 859515
norrisoz@globalnet.co.uk
www.antiquesbulletin.com/bjnorris

Dreweatt Neate
Auction Hall, Pantiles,
Tunbridge Wells TN2 5QL
Tel: 01892 544 500
Fax: 01892 515 191
www.bfaa.co.uk

G.W. Finn and Son Auctioneers
Canterbury Auction Market, Market
Way, Canterbury CT2 7JG
Tel: 01227 767751
www.thesaurus.co.uk/gwfinn

Gorringes
15 The Pantiles, Tunbridge Wells
TN2 5TD
Tel: 01892 619 670
Fax: 01892 619 671
auctions@gorringes.co.uk
www.gorringes.co.uk

Lambert and Foster Auction Sale Rooms
102 High Street, Tenterden
TN30 6HU
Tel: 01580 762083
Fax: 01580 764317

Mervyn Carey
Twysden Cottage, Benenden,
Cranbrook TN17 4LD
Tel: 01580 240283

Parkinson Auctioneers
46 Beaver Road, Ashford TN23 7RP
Tel: 01233 624426
Fax: 01233 624426
www.parkinson-uk.com

Lancashire

Capes Dunn & Co Fine Art
Auctioneers & Valuers, The Auction
Galleries, 38 Charles Street,
Manchester M1 7DB
Tel: 0161 273 1911
Fax: 0161 273 3474

Leicestershire

Gilding's Auctioneers and Valuers
Roman Way, Market Harborough
LE16 7PQ
Tel: 01858 410414
www.gildings.co.uk

Heathcote Ball & Co
Castle Auction Rooms, 78 St.
Nicholas Circle, Leicester LE1 5NW
Tel: 0116 2536789
Fax: 0116 2538517
heathcote-ball@clara.co.uk

Lincolnshire

Eleys Auctioneers
26 Wide Bargate, Boston PE21 6RX
Tel: 01205 361687
Fax: 01205 351091
sales@j-eley.co.uk
www.j-eley.co.uk/eleys/

Thomas Mawer & Son Ltd
Dunstan House, Portland Street,
Lincoln LN5 7NN
Tel: 01522 524984
Fax: 01522 535 600

Marilyn Swain
The Old Barracks, Sandon Road,
Grantham NG31 9AS
Tel: 01476 568861
Fax: 01476 576100

Naylors Auctions
The Hall Meadow Lane, South
Hykeham, Lincoln LN6 9PF
Tel: 01522 696496

John Taylors
The Wool Mart, Kidgate,
Louth LN11 9EZ
Tel: 01507 611107
enquiries@johntaylors.com
www.invaluable.com/johntaylors

Merseyside

Cato & Crane & Co
6 Stanhope Street, Liverpool
L8 5RF
Tel: 0151 709 5559
www.cato-crane.co.uk

J. Kent (Auctioneers) Ltd
2/6 Valkyrie Road
Wallasey L45 4RQ
Tel: 0151 638 3107
Fax: 0151 512 2343

Outhwaite and Litherland
Kingsway Galleries, Fontenoy Street,
Liverpool L3 2BE
Tel: 0151 236 6561
Fax: 0151 236 1070
auction@lots.uk.com
www.lots.uk.com

Norfolk

Thos. Wm. Gaze and Son
Diss Auction Rooms, Roydon Road,
Diss IP22 4LN
Tel: 01379 650306
Fax: 01379 644313
www.twgaze.com

Horners Auctions
North Walsham Sale Rooms,
Midland Road, North Walsham
NR28 9JR
Tel: 01692 500603
Fax: 01692 500975
auction@horners.co.uk
www.horners.co.uk

G.A. Key Auctioneers & Valuers
8 Market Place, Aylsham NR11 6EH
Tel: 01263 733195
www.aylshamsalerooms.co.uk

Knights Sporting Auctions
The Thatched Gallery,
The Green, Aldborough,
Norwich NR11 7AA
Tel: 01263 768 488
Fax: 01263 768 788
www.knights.co.uk

Great Yarmouth Sale Rooms
Beevor Road,
Great Yarmouth NR30 3PS
Tel: 01493 332 668

Northamptonshire

Heathcote Ball & Co.
Albion Auction Rooms, Commercial
Street, Northampton NN1 1PJ
Tel: 01604 622735

Merry's Auctions
Northampton Auction & Sales
Centre, Liliput Road, Brackmills
NN4 7BY
Tel: 01604 769 990
Fax: 01604 763 155

Nottinghamshire

Arthur Johnson and Sons (Auctioneers)
The Nottingham Auction Centre,
Meadow Lane, Nottingham
NG2 3GY
Tel: 0115 9869128
Fax: 0115 9862139

Mellors & Kirk Fine Art Auctioneers
Gregory Street, Nottingham
NG7 2NL
Tel: 0115 9790000
melkirk@dircon.co.uk
www.mellors-kirk.co.uk

Neales
192-194 Mansfield Road,
Nottingham NG1 3HU
Tel: 0115 9624141
Fax: 0115 9856890
fineart@neales.co.uk
www.neales.co.uk

John Pye & Sons Auctioneers & Valuers
James Shipstone House, Radford
Road, Nottingham NG7 7EA
Tel: 0115 9706060
Fax: 0115 9420100
ap@johnpye.co.uk
www.johnpye.co.uk

Northgate Auctions Ltd.
17 Northgate, Newark NG24 1EX
Tel: 01636 605 905
Fax: 01636 640 051

T Vennett-Smith Auctioneers and Valuers (FSB)
11 Nottingham Road, Gotham,
Nottingham NG11 0HE
Tel: 0115 9830541
Fax: 0115 9830114
info@vennett-smith.com
www.vennett-smith.com

Oxfordshire

Holloways
49 Parsons Street, Banbury OX16
5PF
Tel: 01295 817777
Fax: 01295 817701
enquiries@hollowaysauctioneers.co.uk
www.hollowaysauctioneers.co.uk

Mallams Fine Art Auctioneers
Bocard House, 24a St. Michael's
Street, Oxford OX1 2EB
Tel: 01865 241358
Fax: 01865 725 483
www.mallams.co.uk/fineart

Simmons and Sons
32 Bell Street, Henley-on-Thames
RG9 2BH
Tel: 01491 571111
Fax: 01491 579833
www.simmonsandsons.com

Soames Country Auctions
Pinnocks Farm Estate, Northmoor,
Witney OX8 1AY
Tel: 01865 300626
soame@email.msn.com
www.soamesauctioneers.co.uk

Shropshire

Mullock & Madeley (RICS ISVA)
The Old Shippon, Wall under
Heywood, Church Stretton
SY6 7DS
Tel: 01694 771771
Fax: 01694 771772
info@mullockmadeley.co.uk
www.mullock-madeley.co.uk

Walker Barnett and Hill
Cosford Auction Rooms, Long Lane,
Cosford TF11 8PJ
Tel: 01902 375555
Fax: 01902 375556

Somerset

Greenslade Taylor Hunt Fine Art
Magdelene House, Church Square,
Taunton TA1 1SB
Tel: 01823 332525
Fax: 01823 353120

Lawrence's Fine Art Auctioneers Ltd.
South Street, Crewkerne TA18 8AB
Tel: 01460 73041
Fax: 01460 74627
enquiries.@lawrences.co.uk
www.lawrences.co.uk

The London Cigarette Card Co. Ltd
Sutton Road, Somerton TA11 6QP
Tel: 01458 273452
Fax: 01458 273515
cards@londoncigcard.co.uk
www.londoncigcard.co.uk

Wells Auction Rooms
66-68 Southover, Wells BA5 1UH
Tel: 01749 678094

Woodspring Auctions
Churchill Road, Weston-super-Mare
BS23 3HD
Tel: 01934 628419

Staffordshire

Hall and Lloyd Auctioneers
South Street, Stafford ST16 2DZ
Tel: 01785 258176

Louis Taylor Fine Art Auctioneers
Britannia House, 10 Town Road,
Hanley, Stoke-on-Trent ST1 2QG
Tel: 01782 214111
Fax: 01782 215 283

Potteries Specialist Auctions
271 Waterloo Road, Cobridge,
Stoke-on-Trent ST6 3HR
Tel: 01782 286622
Fax: 01782 213777
enquires@potteriesauctions.com
www.potteriesauctions.com

Richard Winterton Auctioneers and Valuers
School House Auction Rooms,
Hawkins Lane, Burton-on-Trent
DE14 1PT
Tel: 01283 511224

Wintertons
Lichfield Auction Centre, Fradley
Park, Fradley, Lichfield WS13 8NF
Tel: 01543 263256
www.wintertons.co.uk

Suffolk

Abbotts Auction Rooms
Campsea Ashe, Nr. Woodbridge
IP13 0PS
Tel: 01728 746323
Fax: 01728 748173

Durrant's
The Auction Rooms, Gresham Road,
Beccles NR34 9QN
Tel: 01502 713490
durrants.auctionrooms@virgin.
net.co.uk
www.durrantsauctionrooms.com

Dyson & Son
The Auction Room, Church Street,
Clare CO10 8PD
Tel: 01787 277 993
Fax: 01787 277 996
info@dyson-auctioneers.co.uk
www.dyson-auctioneers.co.uk

Lacy Scott and Knight Fine Art & Furniture
10 Risbygate Street,
Bury St. Edmunds IP33 3AA
Tel: 01284 748600
Fax: 01284 748620

Neal Sons and Fletcher
26 Church Street, Woodbridge
IP12 1DP
Tel: 01394 382263
Fax: 01394 383030
enquiries@nsf.co.uk
www.nsf.co.uk

Surrey

Clarke Gammon Fine Art Auctioneers
The Guildford Auction Rooms,
Bedford Road, Guildford GU1 4SJ
Tel: 01483 880915
Fax: 01483 880918

Crows Auction Gallery
Rear of Dorking Halls, Reigate
Road, Dorking RH4 1SG
Tel: 01306 740382

Ewbank Auctioneers
Burnt Common Auction Rooms,
London Road, Send,
Woking GU23 7LN
Tel: 01483 223101
Fax: 01483 222171
www.ewbankauctioneers.co.uk

Hamptons International
Baverstock House, 93 High Street,
Godalming GU7 1AL
Tel: 01483 423567
Fax: 01483 426392
fineart@hamptons-int.com

Lawrences' Auctioneers Limited
Norfolk House, 80 High Street,
Bletchingley RH1 4PA
Tel: 01883 743323
Fax: 01883 744578
www.lawrencesbletchingley.co.uk

Richmond and Surrey Auctions
The Old Railway Parcels Depot,
Kew Road, Richmond TW9 2NA
Tel: 020 8948 6677
Fax: 020 8948 2021

P.F. Windibank Fine Art Auctioneers & Valuers
Dorking Halls, Reigate Road,
Dorking RH4 1SG
Tel: 01306 884556/876280
Fax: 01306 884669
sjw@windibank.co.uk
www.windibank.co.uk

East Sussex

Gorringe's Auction Galleries
Terminus Road,
Bexhill-on-Sea, TN39 3LR
Tel: 01424 212994
Fax: 01424 224035
bexhill@gorringes.co.uk
www.gorringes.co.uk

Gorringe's Auction Galleries
15 North Street, Lewes BN7 2PD
Tel: 01273 472503
auctions@gorringes.co.uk
www.gorringes.co.uk

Graves, Son and Pilcher Fine Arts
Hove Street, Hove BN3 2GL
Tel: 01273 735266
info@gsp.uk.com
www.gravessonandpilcher.com

John Nicholson
The Auction Rooms Longfield
Haslemere
GU27 3EF
Tel: 01428 653727

Raymond P. Inman
The Auction Galleries, 35 and 40
Temple Street, Brighton BN1 3BH
Tel: 01273 774777
Fax: 01273 735660

Rye Auction Galleries
Rock Channel,
Rye TN31 7HL
Tel: 01797 222124

Wallis and Wallis
West Street Auction Galleries,
Lewes BN7 2NJ
Tel: 01273 480 208
Fax: 01273 476 562
grb@wallisandwallis.co.uk
www.wallisandwallis.co.uk

West Sussex

John Bellman Ltd
New Pound, Wisborough Green,
Billingshurst RH14 0AZ
Tel: 01403 700858
Fax: 01403 700059
enquiries@bellmans.co.uk
www.bellmans.co.uk

Denham's
The Auction Galleries, Warnham,
Nr. Horsham RH12 3RZ
Tel: 01403 255699
Fax: 01403 253837
denhams@lineone.net
www.catalogs.icollector.com/denhams

Rupert Toovey & Co.
Star Road, Partridge Green,
Horsham RH13 8RA
Tel: 01403 711744
Fax: 01403 711919
auctions@rupert-toovey.com
www.rupert-toovey.com

Worthing Auction Galleries
Fleet House, Teville Gate,
Worthing BN11 1UA
Tel: 01903 205565
www.worthing-auctions.co.uk

Tyne and Wear

Anderson and Garland
Fine Art Salerooms, Marlborough
House, Marlborough Crescent,
Newcastle-upon-Tyne NE1 4EE
Tel: 0191 232 6278
Fax: 0191 261 8665
agarland@compuserve.com
www.auction-net.co.uk

Boldon Auction Galleries
24a Front Street, East Boldon
NE36 0SJ
Tel: 0191 537 2630
Fax: 0191 536 3875
enquiries@boldonauctions.co.uk
www.boldonauctions.co.uk

Corbitts
5 Mosley Street, Newcastle-upon-Tyne NE1 1YE
Tel: 0191 232 7268
Fax: 0191 261 4130
collectors@corbitts.com
www.corbitts.com

Warwickshire

Bigwood Auctioneers Ltd
The Old School, Tiddington,
Stratford-upon-Avon
CV37 7AW
Tel: 01789 269415
www.bigwoodauctioneers.co.uk

Locke and England
18 Guy Street, Leamington Spa
CV32 4RT
Tel: 01926 889100
valuers@leauction.co.uk
www.catalogs.icollector.com/locke

Warwick and Warwick Ltd
Chalon House, Scar Bank,
Millers Road, Warwick
CV34 5DB
Tel: 01926 499031
Fax: 01926 491906

West Midlands

Biddle & Webb
Ladywood, Middleway,
Birmingham B16 0PP
Tel: 0121 455 8042
Fax: 0121 454 9615
antiques@biddleandwebb.freeserve.co.uk
www.invaluable.com/biddle&webb

Bonhams
The Old House, Station Road,
Knowle, Solihull B93 0HT
Tel: 01564 776151
Fax: 01564 778069
knowle@bonhams.com
www.bonhams.com

Fellows and Sons
Augusta House, 19 Augusta Street,
Hockley, Birmingham B18 6JA
Tel: 0121 212 2131
Fax: 0121 212 1249
www.fellows.co.uk

Walker Barnett and Hill
Waterloo Road Salerooms,
Clarence Street,
Wolverhampton WV1 4JE
Tel: 01902 773531
www.thesaurus.co.uk/wbh

Weller & Dufty Ltd
141 Bromsgrove Street,
Birmingham B5 6RQ
Tel: 0121 692 1414
Fax: 0121 622 5605
www.wellerandduftv.co.uk

Wiltshire

Atwell Martin
Chippenham Auction Rooms,
St. Mary's Street,
Chippenham SN15 3JM
Tel: 01249 462222
www.invaluable.com/atwell

The Hilditch Auction Rooms (NAVA)
Gloucester Road Trading Estate,
Malmesbury SN16 9JT
Tel: 01666 822577
Fax: 01666 825597
sales@hilditchauctions.co.uk
www.hilditchauctions.co.uk

Woolley and Wallis
Salisbury Salerooms Ltd,
51-61 Castle Street,
Salisbury SP1 3SU
Tel: 01722 424500
Fax: 01722 424508
enquiries@woolleyandwallis.co.uk
www.woolleyandwallis.co.uk

Worcestershire

Andrew Grant Fine Art Auctioneers
St. Marks Close,
Worcester WR5 3DL
Tel: 01905 357547
fine.art@andrew-grant.co.uk
www.andrew-grant.co.uk

Griffiths and Charles
57 Foregate Street,
Worcester WR1 1DZ
Tel: 01905 26464
info@griffiths-charles.co.uk
www.griffiths-charles.co.uk

Philip Laney – FRICS – Fine Art
Malvern Auction Centre,
Portland Road, off Victoria Road,
Malvern WR14 2TA
Tel: 01684 893933
Fax: 01684 577948
philiplaney@compuserve.com
www.thesaurus.co.uk/philiplaney

Philip Serrell Auctioneers & Valuers
The Malvern Sale Room,
Barnards Green Road,
Malvern WR14 3LW
Tel: 01684 892314
Fax: 01684 569832
www.serrell.com

East Yorkshire

Gilbert Baitson
The Edwardian Auction Galleries,
Wiltshire Road, Hull HU4 6PG
Tel: 01482 500500
Fax: 01482 500501
www.gilbert-baitson.co.uk

Clegg & Son
68 Aire Street, Goole DN14 5QE
Tel: 01405 763140
gooleoffice@cleggandson.co.uk
www.cleggandson.co.uk

Dee Atkinson & Harrison
Agricultural and Fine Arts,
The Exchange Saleroom,
Driffield YO25 7LJ
Tel: 01377 253151
Fax: 01377 241041
exchange@dee-atkinson-harrison.co.uk
www.dee-atkinson-harrison.co.uk

North Yorkshire

Bairstow Eves Fine Art
West End Rooms, The Paddock,
Whitby YO21 3AX
Tel: 01947 820033/820011

David Dugleby Fine Art
The Vine Street Salerooms,
Scarborough YO11 1XN
Tel: 01723 507111
www.thesaurus.co.uk/david-dugleby

Malcolm's No. 1 Auctioneers and Valuers
The Chestnuts, 16 Park Avenue,
Sherbern in Elmet,
Nr. Leeds, LS25 6EF
Tel: 01977 684 971
Fax: 01977 681 046
info@malcolmsno1auctions.co.uk
www.malcolmsno1auctions.co.uk

Morphets of Harrogate
6 Albert Street, Harrogate HG1 1JL
Tel: 01423 530030
Fax: 01423 500717
www.morphets.co.uk

Tennants
The Auction Centre, Leyburn
DL8 5SG
Tel: 01969 623780
Fax: 01969 624281
www.tennants.co.uk

South Yorkshire
BBR Auctions
Elsecar Heritage Centre,
Nr. Barnsley S74 8AA
Tel: 01226 745156
Fax: 01226 361561
www.bbrauctions.co.uk

A.E. Dowse and Son Sheffield
Cornwall Galleries, Scotland Street,
Sheffield S3 7DE
Tel: 0114 2725858
Fax: 0114 2490550

ELR Auctions Ltd
The Sheffield Saleroom,
The Nichols Building,
Shalesmoor,
Sheffield S3 8UJ
Tel: 0114 2816161
Fax: 0114 2816162
liz.dashper@virgin.net
www.elrauctions.com

Peter Young Auctioneers
Doncaster Road, Bawtry,
Doncaster DN10 6NQ
Tel: 01302 711770
peter@auction.demon.co.uk
www.auction.demon.co.uk

West Yorkshire

De Rome
12 New John Street, Westgate,
Bradford BD1 2QY
Tel: 01274 734116/9

Andrew Hartley Fine Arts
Victoria Hall Salerooms,
Little Lane, Ilkley LS29 8EA
Tel: 01943 816363
Fax: 01943 816363
info@andrewhartleyfinearts.co.uk
www.invaluable.com/andrew-hartley

John Walsh & Co. Auctioneers & Valuers
55 Jenkin Road, Horbury,
Wakefield WF4 6DP
Tel: 01924 271710
Fax: 01924 267758
valuations@john-walsh.co.uk
www.john-walsh.co.uk

Scotland

Bonhams
65 George Street,
Edinburgh EH2 2JL
Tel: 0131 225 2266
Fax: 0131 220 2547
edinburgh@bonhams.com
www.bonhams.com

Christie's Scotland
164-166 Bath Street,
Glasgow G2 4TB
Tel: 0141 332 8134
www.christies.com

Finlays Auctioneers Ltd (NAVA)
Central Auction Hall, Bankside,
Falkirk Central FK2 7XR
Tel: 01324 623000
www.finlays.uk.com

Loves Auction Rooms
52-54 Canal Street, Perth,
Perthshire PH2 8LF
Tel: 01738 633337
Fax: 01738 629830

Lyon and Turnbull Ltd.
33 Broughton Place, Edinburgh
EH1 3RR
Tel: 0131 557 8844
Fax: 0131 557 8668
info@lyonandturnbull.com
www.lyonandturnbull.com

Lyon and Turnbull Ltd.
4 Woodside Place,
Glasgow G3 7QF.
Tel: 0141 353 5070
Fax: 0141 332 2928
info@lyonandturnbull.com
www.lyonandturnbull.com

MDS Auction Co.
15-17 Smeaton Industrial
Estate, Kirkcaldy,
Fife KY1 2HE
Tel: 01592 640969
Fax: 01592 640969
sales@scotlandauction.co.uk
www.scotlandauction.co.uk

D.J. Manning Auctioneers
Carriden, Bo'ness, West Lothian
EH51 9SF
Tel: 01506 827693
Fax: 01506 826495
info@djmanning.co.uk
www.djmanning.co.uk

McTear's
Clydeway Business Centre,
8 Elliot Place,
Glasgow G3 8EP
Tel: 0141 221 4456
Fax: 0141 204 5035
enquiries@mctears.co.uk
www.mctears.co.uk

Taylor's Auction Rooms
11 Panmure Row, Montrose,
Angus DD10 8HH
Tel: 01674 672775
enquiries@scotlandstreasures.co.uk
www.scotlandstreasures.co.uk

Thomson, Roddick & Medcalf Ltd.
60 Whitesands, Dumfries,
Dumfriesshire DG1 2RS
Tel: 01387 279879

Thomson, Roddick & Medcalf Ltd.
44/3 Hardengreen Business Park,
Eskbank, Edinburgh
EH22 3NX
Tel: 0131 454 9090
Fax: 0131 454 9191

Wales

Bonhams
7-8 Park Place, Cardiff,
Glamorgan CF10 3DP
Tel: 02920 727980
Fax: 02920 727989
cardiff@bonhams.com
www.bonhams.com

Bonhams
Napier House, Spilman Street,
Carmarthen SA31 1JY
Tel: 01267 238231
Fax: 02920 727989
carmarthen@bonhams.com
www.bonhams.com

Evans Bros (ISVA)
Mart Office, Llanybydder,
Dyfed SA40 9UE
Tel: 01570 480 444
Fax: 01570 480 988
www.evansbros.com

Peter Francis
Curiosity Salerooms,
19 King Street,
Carmarthen,
South Wales SA31 1BH
Tel: 01267 233456
Fax: 01267 233458
www.peterfrancis.co.uk

Jones & Llewelyn (NAEA)
Llandeilo Auction Rooms,
21 New Road, Llandeilo,
Dyfed SA19 6DE
Tel: 01558 823430
Fax: 01558 822004
www.jonesllewelyn.freeserve.co.uk

Rogers-Jones & Co.
33 Abergele Road,
Colwyn Bay, Clwyd LL29 7RU
Tel: 01492 532176
www.rogersjones.ukauctioneers.com

Welsh Country Auctions
2 Carmarthen Road,
Cross Hands, Llanelli,
Dyfed SA14 6SP
Tel: 01269 844428
Fax: 01269 844428

DIRECTORY OF SPECIALISTS

SPECIALISTS THAT WOULD LIKE TO BE INCLUDED in the next edition, or have a change of address or telephone number, should contact us by 1 February 2005.

Readers should contact dealers by telephone before visiting them to avoid a wasted journey.

Antiquities

Ancient Art
85 The Vale, Southgate,
London N14 6AT
Tel: 020 8882 1509
ancient.art@btinternet.com
www.ancientart.co.uk

Bath Antiquities Centre
4 Bladud Buildings, Bath BA1 5LS
Tel: 01225 460 408
artefacts@bathantiquities.freeserve.co.uk

David Aaron Ancient Arts & Rare Carpets
22 Berkeley Sq, Mayfair,
London W1X 7DD
Tel: 020 7491 9588

Finch & Co
Suite No 744, 2 Old Brompton Road, London SW7 3DQ
Tel: 020 7413 9937

G Oliver & Sons
Guildford, Surrey
Open by appointment only
Tel: 01428 652220

Helios Gallery
292 Westbourne Grove,
London W11 2PS
Tel: 07711 955 997
mail@heliosgallery.com
www.heliosgallery.com

John A Pearson
Horton Lodge, Horton Road, Horton, Near Slough, Berkshire SL3 9NU
Tel: 01753 682136

Oxford Forum of Ancient Art
3 North Parade, Banbury Road, Oxford, Oxfordshire OX2 6LX
Tel: 01865 316366
vpurcell@oxfordforum-ancientart.com
www.oxfordforum-ancientart.com

Rupert Wace Ancient Art Limited
14 Old Bond Street, London
W1X 3DB
Tel: 020 7495 1623
rupert.wace@btinternet.com

Architectural

Crowther of Syon Lodge
Busch Corner, London Road,
Isleworth,
Middlesex TW77 5BH
Tel: 0208 5607978
Fax: 0208 5687572

D & R Blissett
c/o Coutts & Co, PO Box 1EE,
16 Cavendish Square, London
W1A 1EE
Tel: 01264 771768

Joanna Booth
247 King's Road, London SW3 5EL
Tel: 020 7352 8998
joannabooth@London.web.net
www.joannabooth.co.uk

LASSCO
St. Michael's, Mark St, London
EC2A 4ER
Tel: 020 7749 9944
www.lassco.co.uk

Sweerts de Landas
Dunsborough Park, Ripley,
Surrey GU23 6AL
Tel: 01483 225366
garden.ornament@lineone.net

Carpets & Rugs

Alexander Juran & Co
Nathan Azizollahoff, OCC, Building A, 105 Eade Road, London N4 1TJ
Tel: 020 8809 5505
Tel: 020 7435 0280

Atlantic Bay Gallery
5 Sedley Place, London W1R 1HH
Tel: 020 7355 3301
atlanticbaygallery@btinternet.com

C John (Rare Rugs) Ltd.
70 South Audley Street,
London W1Y 5FE
Tel: 020 7493 5288
cjohn@dircon.co.uk

Clive Loveless
54 St Quintin Avenue, London
W10 6PA
Tel: 020 8969 5831

Gallery Yacou
127 Fulham Road, London
SW3 6RT
Tel: 020 7584 2929

Gideon Hatch
1 Port House, Plantation Wharf,
Battersea, London SW11 3TY
Tel: 020 7223 3996
info@gideonhatch.co.uk

John Eskenazi Ltd.
15 Old Bond Street,
London W1X 4JL
Tel: 020 7409 3001
john.eskenazi@john-eskenazi.com

Karel Weijand
Lion & Lamb Courtyard, Farnham,
Surrey GU9 7LL
Tel: 01252 726215
karelweijand@btinternet.com

Lindfield Galleries
62 High Street, Lindfield,
West Sussex RH16 2HL
Tel: 01444 483817
david@orientalandantiquerugs.com
www.orientalandantiquerugs.com

Richard Purdon Antique Carpets
158 The Hill, Burford, Oxfordshire
OX18 4QY
Tel: 01993 823777
antiquerugs@richardpurdon.demon.co.uk
www.purdon.com

Wadsworth's
Marehill, Pulborough,
West Sussex RH20 2DY
Tel: 01798 873 555
Mob: 07770 942 489

Boxes

Alan & Kathy Stacey
PO Box 2771 Chapel Lane,
Yeovil, Somerset
BA22 7DZ
Tel: 01963 441 333
www.antiqueboxes.uk.com

Mostly Boxes
93 High Street, Eton,
Windsor, Berkshire SL4 6AF
Tel: 01753 858 470

Ceramics

Albert Amor Ltd.
37 Bury St, St. James's,
London SW1Y 6AU
Tel: 020 7930 2444

Andrew Dando
34 Market Street, Bradford-on-Avon
BA15 1LL
Tel: 01225 422 702
andrew@andrewdando.co.uk
www.andrewdando.co.uk

Brian & Angela Downes
PO Box 431, Chippenham,
Wiltshire SN14 6SZ
Tel: 01454 238134

Clive & Lynne Jackson
Cheltenham, Gloucestershire
Open by appointment only
Tel: 01242 254 3751
Mob: 07710 23935

E & H Manners
66A Kensington Church Street,
London W8 4BY
Tel: 020 7229 5516
manners@europeanporcelain.com
www.europeanporcelain.com

Earle D Vandekar of Knightsbridge Inc
13 Laburnum Grove, Ruislip,
Middlesex HA4 7XF
Tel: 01895 638311

Gillian Neale Antiques
PO Box 247, Aylesbury,
Buckinghamshire HP20 1JZ
Tel: 01296 423754
gillianneale@btconnect.com
www.gilliannealeantiques.co.uk

Highgate Antiques
PO Box 10060, London N6 5JH
Tel: 020 8340 9872

Hope and Glory
131a Kensington Church Street,
London W8 7LP
Tel: 020 7727 8424

John Howard @ Heritage
19 High Street, Woodstock,
Oxon OX20 1TE
Tel: 0870 444 0678
john@ johnhoward.co.uk
www.antiquepottery.co.uk

Janice Paull
Beehive House, 125 Warwick Road,
Kenilworth, Warwickshire CV8 1HY
Tel: 01926 855253
janicepaull@btinternet.com
www.masonsironstone.com

Jonathan Horne Antiques Ltd.
66b and 66c Kensington Church Street, London W8 4BY
Tel: 020 7221 5658
jh@jonathanhorne.co.uk
www.jonathanhorne.co.uk

Klaber & Klaber
PO Box 9445, London NW3 1WD
Tel: 020 7435 6537
info@klaber.com
www.klaber.com

Mary Wise and Grosvenor Antiques
Grosvenor Antiques, 27 Holland
Street, London W8 4NA
Tel: 020 7937 8649

Rennies
13 Rugby Street,
London WC1 3QT
Tel: 020 7405 0220
info@rennart.co.uk
www.rennart.co.uk

Robyn Robb
43 Napier Avenue, London
SW6 3PS
Tel: 020 7731 2878

Roderick Jellicoe
3A Campden Street, London
W8 7EP
Tel: 020 7727 1571
jellicoe@englishporcelain.com
www.englishporcelain.com

Rogers de Rin
76 Royal Hospital Road, Paradise
Walk, Chelsea, London SW3 4HN
Tel: 020 7352 9007
rogersderin@rogersderin.co.uk
www.rogersderin.co.uk

Roy W. Bunn Antiques
Tel: 01282 813703
www.roywbunnantiques.co.uk
freeserve.co.uk

Simon Spero
109 Kensington Church Street,
London W1 7LN
Tel: 020 7727 7413

Steppes Hill Farm Antiques
Steppes Hill Farm, Stockbury,
Sittingbourne, Kent ME9 7RB
Tel: 01795 842205

Stockspring Antiques
114 Kensington Church Street,
London, W8 4BH
Tel: 020 7727 7995
stockspring@antique-porcelain.
co.uk
www.antique-porcelain.co.uk

T C S Brooke
The Grange, 57 Norwich Road,
Wroxham, Norfolk NR12 8RX
Tel: 01603 782644

Thrift Cottage Antiques
PO Box 113, Bury St Edmunds,
Suffolk IP33 2RQ
Tel: 01284 702470

Valerie Main
PO Box 92, Carlisle, Cumbria
CA5 7GD
Tel: 01228 711342
valerie.main@btinternet.com

W Agnew & Company Ltd.
58 Englefield Road,
London N1 4HA
Tel: 020 7254 7429

W W Warner Antiques
The Green, High Street, Brasted,
Kent TN16 1JL
Tel: 01959 563698

Yvonne Adams Antiques
Worcestershire
Open by appointment only
Tel: 01386 858016/852584
antiques@adames.demon.co.uk

Clocks and Watches

Alan Walker
Halfway Manor, Halfway, Nr
Newbury, Berkshire RG20 8NR
Tel: 01488 657670

Aubrey Brocklehurst
124 Cromwell Road, South
Kensington, London SW7 4ET
Tel: 020 7373 0319

Baskerville Antiques
Saddlers House, Saddlers Row,
Petworth, West Sussex GU28 0AN
Tel: 01798 342067

Bobinet Ltd.
PO Box 2730, London NW8 9PL
Tel: 020 7266 0783

Campbell & Archard Ltd.
Maple House, Market Place,
Lechlade-on-Thames,
Gloucestershire, GL7 3AB
Tel: 01367 252267

Campbell & Archard Ltd.
Lychgate House, Church Street,
Seal, Kent TW15 0AR
Tel: 01367 252267

David Gibson
PO Box 301, Axminster, Devon
EX13 7YJ
Tel: 01297 631179

Derek and Tina Rayment Antiques
Orchard House, Barton Road,
Barton, Nr. Farndon, Cheshire
SY14 7HT
Tel: 01829 270429

Derek Roberts Fine Antique Clocks & Barometers
25 Shipbourne Road, Tonbridge,
Kent TN10 3DN
Tel: 01732 358986
drclocks@clara.net
www.quallityantiqueclocks.com

G E Marsh (Antique Clocks) Ltd.
32a The Square, Winchester,
Hampshire SO23 9EX
Tel: 01962 844443
gem@marshclocks.co.uk
www.marshclocks.co.uk

Jeffrey Formby Antiques
Orchard Cottage, East Street,
Moreton-in-Marsh, Gloucestershire
GL56 0LQ
Tel: 01608 650558
jeff@formby-clocks.co.uk
www.formby-clocks.co.uk

Jillings Antiques
Croft House, 17 Church Street,
Newent, Gloucestershire GL18 1PU
Tel: 01531 822100
clocks@jillings.com

John Carlton-Smith
17 Ryder Street, London SW1Y 6PY
Tel: 020 7930 6622
www.fineantiqueclocks.com

Montpellier Clocks
13 Rotunda Terrace, Montpellier
Street, Cheltenham, Gloucestershire
GL50 1SW
Tel: 01242 242178

Patric Capon
350 Upper Street, Islington,
London N1 0PD
Tel: 020 7354 0487

Pendulum of Mayfair
51 Maddox Sreet, London W1
Tel: 020 7629 6606
pendulumclocks@aol.com
www.pendulumofmayfair.co.uk

Raffety & Walwyn
79 Kensington Church St.,
London W8 4BG
Tel: 020 7938 1100
www.raffetyantiqueclocks.com

Somlo Antiques
7 Piccadilly Arcade,London SW1Y 6NH
Tel: 020 7499 6526

Strike One
48A Highbury Hill,
London N5 1AP
Tel: 020 7354 2790
www.strikeone.co.uk

The Watch Gallery
129 Fulham Road,
London SW3 6RT
Tel: 020 7581 3239

Weather House Antiques
Foster Clough, Hebden Bridge,
West Yorkshire HX7 5QZ
Tel: 01422 882808/886961
kymwalker@btinternet.com

Anthony Woodburn Ltd.
PO Box 2669, Lewes,
East Sussex BN7 3JE
Tel: 01273 486666
anthonywoodburn@compuserve.com
www.artnet.com/awoodburn.html

Horological Workshops
204 Worplesdon Road, Guildford,
Surrey GU2 6UY
Tel: 01483 576496
mdtooke@aol.com

Costume Jewellery

Cristobal
26 Church Street, London NW8 8EP
Tel: 020 7724 7230
steven@cristobal.co.uk
www.cristobal.co.uk

Eclectica
2 Charlton Place, Islington,
London N1 8AJ
Tel: 020 7226 5625

Richard Gibbon
34/34a Islington Green, London N1 8DU
Tel: 020 7354 2852
neljeweluk@aol.com

Ritzy
7 The Mall Antiques Arcade, 359
Upper Street, London N1 0PD
Tel: 020 7351 5353

William Wain at Antiquarius
Stand J6, Antiquarius,
135 King's Road,
Chelsea, London SW3 4PW
Tel: 020 7351 4905

Decorative Arts

Adrian Sassoon
Rutland Gate, London, SW7 1BB
Tel: 020 7581 9888
ads@asassoon.demon.co.uk
www.adriansassoon.com

Aesthetics
Stand V2, Antiquarius, 131-141
Kings Road, London SW3 4PW
Tel: 020 7352 0395

Arenski Fine Arts Ltd.
The Coach House, Ledbury Mews
North, Notting Hill, London W11 2AF
Tel: 020 7727 8599
arenski@netcomuk.co.uk
www.arenski.com

Art Deco Etc
73 Upper Gloucester Road,
Brighton, Sussex BN1 3LQ
Tel: 01273 329 268
Mob: 07971 268 302
johnclark@artdecoetc.co.uk

Art Nouveau Originals c.1900
5 Pierrepont Row Arcade, Camden
Passage, Islington, London N1 8EF
Tel: 020 7359 4127

Beth Adams at Alfies Antique Market
Stand G43/44, 13-25 Church St.
London NW8
Tel: 020 7723 5613

Beverly
30 Church Street, London NW8 8EP
Tel: 020 7262 1576

Charles Edwards
19a Rumbold Road, (off King's Road) London SW6 2DY
Tel: 020 7736 7172
charles@charles edwards.com

Chevertons Of Edenbridge Ltd.
Taylour House, 69 High Street, Edenbridge, Kent TN8 5AL
Tel: 01732 863196
chevertons@msn.com
www.chevertons.com

Fay Lucas Gallery
50 Kensington Church Street, London W8 4DA
Tel: 020 7938 3763
info@faylucas.com

Gallery 1930 - Susie Cooper Ceramics
18 Church Street, London NW8 8EP
Tel: 020 7723 1555
gallery1930@aol.com
www.susiecooperceramics.com

H Blairman & Sons Ltd.
119 Mount Street, London W1Y 5HB
Tel: 020 7493 0444
blairman@atlas.co.uk

Halcyon Days Ltd.
4 Royal Exchange, London EC3V 3LL
Tel: 020 7626 1120

Halcyon Days Ltd.
14 Brook Street, London W1Y 1AA
Tel: 020 7629 8811
info@halcyondays.co.uk
www.halcyondays.co.uk

Harris Lindsay
67 Jermyn Street, London SW1Y 6NY
Tel: 020 7839 5767

Keshishian
73 Pimlico Road, London SW1 8NE
Tel: 020 7730 8810

Mike Weedon
7 Camden Passage, Islington, London N1 8EA
Tel: 020 7226 5319
info@mikeweedonantiques.com
www.mikeweedonantiques.com

Rainer Zietz Ltd.
1a Prairie Street, London SW8 3PX
Tel: 020 7498 2355
rainer.zietz@btinternet.com

Richard Gardner Antiques
Swan House, Market Square, Petworth, West Sussex GU28 0AN
Tel: 01798 343 411
rg@richardgardenerantiques.co.uk
www.richardgardenerantiques.co.uk

Robert Bowman Ltd.
8 Duke Street, St James's, London SW1Y 6BN
Tel: 020 7839 3100
bowmanart@msn.com
www.artnet.com/rbowman.html

Rumours
4 The Mall Antiques Arcade, 359 Upper Street, London N1 0PD
Tel: 020 7704 6549

Sladmore Sculpture Gallery Ltd.
32 Bruton Place, Berkeley Square, London W1X 7AA
Tel: 020 7499 0365
www.sladmore.com

Spencer Swaffer Antiques
Spencer Swaffer Antiques, 30 High Street, Arundle, West Sussex BN18 9AB
Tel: 01903 882132
spencerswaffer@btconnect.com

Style Gallery
10 Camden Passage, London N1 8ED
Tel: 020 7359 7867
www.styleantiques.co.uk

Tadema Gallery
10 Charlton Place, Camden Passage, London N1 8AJ
Tel: 020 7359 1055

The Coach House London, Ltd.
185 Westbourne Grove, London W11 2SB
Tel: 020 7229 8311
arenski@netcomuk.co.uk

The Country Seat
Huntercombe Manor Barn, nr Henley on Thames, Oxen RG9 5RY
Tel: 01491 641349
www.thecountryseat.com

The Design Gallery
5 The Green, Westerham Kent TN16 1AS
Tel: 01959 561 234
Mob: 07974 322 858
sales@thedesigngallery.uk.com
www.thedesigngallery.uk.com

Tim Stothert
Calder Mount, Calder House Lane, Garstang, Lancashire PR3 1QB
Tel: 01995 605384
tim@stothert.co.uk
www.stothert.co.uk

Titus Omega
Shop 21, The Mall, Camden Passage, Islington N1 8DU
Tel: 020 7688 1295
www.titusomega.com

Van Den Bosch
1 Georgian Village, Camden Passage, Islington, London N1 8DU
Tel: 020 7226 4550
Fax: 020 8348 5410
info@vandenbosch.co.uk
www.vandenbosch.co.uk

Dolls and Toys

Bébés & Jouets
c/o Post Office, 165 Restalrig Road, Edinburgh EH7 6HW
Tel: 0131 332 5650
bebesetjouets@u.genie.co.uk

Collectors Old Toy Shop and Antiques
89 Northgate, Halifax, West Yorkshire HX1 1XF
Tel: 01422 360434/822148

Sue Pearson
13 1/2 Prince Albert St, Brighton, East Sussex BN1 1HE
Tel: 01273 329247

Victoriana Dolls
101 Portobello Rd, London W11 2BQ
Tel: 01737 249 525
heather.bond@totalserve.co.uk

Jewellery

N. Bloom & Son Ltd.
12 Piccadilly Arcade, London SW1Y 6NH
Tel: 020 7629 5060
nbloom@nbloom.com
www.nbloom.com

J H Bonnar
72 Thistle Street, Edinburgh
Tel: 0131 226 2811

Furniture

Adrian Alan
66/67 South Audley Street, London W1Y 5FE
Tel: 020 7495 2324
enqurіes@adrianalan.com
www.adrianalan.com

Alistair Sampson Antiques Ltd.
120 Mount Street, London W1Y 5HB
Tel: 020 7409 1799
info@alistairsampson.com
www.alistairsampson.com

Anthemion
Cartmel, Grange-over-Sands, Cumbria LA11 6QD
Tel: 015395 36295

Anthony Outred (Antiques) Ltd.
46 Pimlico Road, London SW1W 8LP
Tel: 020 7730 4782
antiques@outred.co.uk
www.outred.co.uk

The Antiques Warehouse
25 Lightwood Road, Buxton, Derbyshire SK17 7BJ
Tel: 01298 72967

Antoine Cheneviere Fine Arts Ltd.
27 Bruton Street, London W1X 7DB
Tel: 020 7491 1007

Antony Preston Antiques Ltd.
The Square, Stow-on-the-Wold, Gloucestershire GL54 1AB
Tel: 01451 831586

Apter Fredericks Ltd.
265-267 Fulham Road, London SW3 6HY
Tel: 020 7352 2188
antiques@apter-fredericks.demon.co.uk

Arthur Brett & Sons Ltd.
42 St Giles Street, Norwich, Norfolk NR2 1LW
Tel: 01603 628171

Avon Antiques
25, 26, 27 Market Street, Bradford-on-Avon, Wiltshire BA15 1LL
Tel: 01225 862052

Baggott Church Street Ltd
Church Street, Stow-on-the-Wold, Gloucestershire GL54 1BB
Tel: 01451 830 370

Blanchard
86/88 Pimlico Road, London SW1W 8PL
Tel: 020 7823 6310

Brian Rolleston (Antiques) Ltd.
104a Kensington Church Street, London W8 4BU
Tel: 020 7229 5892

Carlton Hobbs Ltd.
8 Little College Street, London SW1P 3SH
Tel: 020 7340 1000

Charles Lumb & Sons Ltd.
2 Montpellier Gardens, Harrogate, North Yorkshire HG1 2TF
Tel: 01423 503776

Christopher Buck Antiques
56-60 Sandgate High Street, Sandgate, Folkestone, Kent CT20 3AP
Tel: 01303 221 229
chrisbuck@throwley.freeserve.co.uk

Christopher Hodsoll Ltd.
89-91 Pimlico Road, London
SW1W 8PH
Tel: 020 7730 3370
c.hodsoll@btinternet.com
www.hodsoll.com

Clifford Wright Antiques Ltd.
104-106 Fulham Road,
London SW3 6HS
Tel: 020 7589 0986

Country Antiques (Wales)
Old Castle Mill, Kidwelly,
Carmarthenshire SA17 4UU
Tel: 01554 890534
richardbebb@countryan-
tiqueswales.fsnet.co.uk
www.richardbebb.com

County Antiques
PO Box 1, Wem, Shropshire SY4
5WD
Tel: 07801 190972

David H Dickinson
High Barn, Cocksheadhey Road,
Bollington, Macclesfield, Cheshire
SK10 5QZ
Tel: 01625 560821

David J Hansord (Antiques)
6/7 Castle Hill, Lincoln,
Lincolnshire LN1 3AA
Tel: 01522 530044

David Love
10 Royal Parade, Harrogate,
North Yorkshire HG1 2SZ
Tel: 01423 565797

De Montfort
Tel: 01403 713 388
Mob: 07860 632 822
alexander@demontfortantiques.co.uk
www.demontfortantiques.co.uk

Denzil Grant
Drinkstone House, Drinkstone, Bury
St Edmunds, Suffolk IP30 9TG
Tel: 01449 736576
nickygrant@excite.co.uk
www.denzilgrant.com

Didier Aaron (London) Ltd.
21 Ryder Street, London SW1Y 6PX
Tel: 020 7839 4716
didaaronuk@aol.com
www.didieraaron.com

Douglas Bryan
The Old Bakery, St David's Bridge,
Cranbrook, Kent TN17 3HN
Tel: 01580 713103

Elaine Phillips Antiques Ltd.
1/2 Royal Parade, Harrogate,
North Yorkshire HG1 2SZ
Tel: 01423 569745
antiques@heliscott.co.uk

Freeman & Lloyd
44 Sandgate High Street,
Sandgate, Folkestone,
Kent CT20 3AP
Tel: 01303 248986
freemanlloyd@ukgateway.net
www.freemanandlloyd.com

Georgian Antiques
10 Pattison St., Leith Links,
Edinburgh EH6 7HF Scotland
Tel: 0131 553 7286
georgianantiques@btconnect.com
www.georgianantiques.net

Godson & Coles
92 Fulham Road, London SW3 6HR
Tel: 020 7584 2200

H C Baxter & Sons
40 Drewstead Road,
London SW16 1AB
Tel: 020 8769 5869/5969

H W Keil Ltd.
Tudor House, Broadway,
Worcestershire WR12 7DP
Tel: 01386 852408

Heath Bullocks
8 Meadrow, Godalming,
Surrey GU7 3HN
Tel: 01483 422 562

Hotspur Ltd.
14 Lowndes Street,
London SW1X 9EX
Tel: 020 7235 1918
Fax: 020 7235 4371
hotspurLtd@msn.com

Huntington Antiques Ltd
Church Street, Stow-on-the-wold,
Gloucestershire GL54 1BE
Tel: 01451 830 842
Fax: 01451 832 211
info@huntington-antiques.com
www.huntington-antiques.com

Jacob Stodel
Flat 53, Macready House, 75
Crawford Street, London W1H 1HS
Tel: 020 7723 3732
jacobstodel@aol.com

Jeremy Ltd.
29 Lowndes Street,
London SW1X 9HX
Tel: 020 7823 2923
Fax: 020 7245 6197
jeremy@jeremique.co.uk
www.jeremy.ltd.uk

John Bly
27 Bury Street, St James's,
London SW1Y 6AL
Tel: 020 7930 1292
Fax: 020 7839 4775
john@johnbly.com
www.johnbly.com

John Hobbs Ltd.
105/107A Pimlico Road,
London SW1W 8PH
Tel: 020 7730 8369
Fax: 020 7730 8369
www.hobbs.co.uk

John King
74 Pimlico Road,
London SW1W 8LS
Tel: 020 7730 0427
Fax: 020 7730 2515
johnking21@virgin.net

Lennox Cato
1 The Square, Church Street,
Edenbridge, Kent TN8 5BD
Tel: 01732 865988
cato@lennoxcato.com
www.lennoxcato.com

Lewis & Lloyd
65 Kensington Church Street,
London W8 4BA
Tel: 020 7938 3323
Fax: 020 7361 0086
www.lewisandlloyd.co.uk

Lucy Johnson
PO Box 84, Carterton DO, Burford,
Oxfordshire OX18 4AT
Tel: 07071 881232
Fax: 07071 881233
lucy-johnson@lucy-johnson.com

M & D Seligmann
37 Kensington Church Street,
London W8 4LL
Tel: 020 7937 0400
Fax: 020 7722 4315

Mac Humble Antiques
7-9 Woolley Street, Bradford-on-
Avon, Wiltshire BA15 1AD
Tel: 01225 866329
Fax: 01225 866329
mac.humble@virgin.net
www.machumbleantiques.co.uk

Michael Foster
118 Fulham Road, London SW3 6HU
Tel: 020 7373 3636
Fax: 020 7373 4042

Michael Norman Antiques Ltd.
Palmeira House, 82 Western Road,
Hove, East Sussex BN3 1JB
Tel: 01273 329 253
Fax: 01273 206 556

Oswald Simpson
Mannings, The Green,
Elmsett, Ipswich, Suffolk IP7 6NA
Tel: 01473 658 444

Owen Humble Antiques
11-12 Clayton Road, Jesmond,
Newcastle Upon Tyne, Tyne and
Wear NE2 4RT
Tel: 0191 281 4602
Fax: 0191 281 9076
antiques@owenhumble.fsnet.co.uk

Patrick Sandberg Antiques
150-152 Kensington Church Street,
London W8 4BN
Tel: 020 7229 0373
Fax: 020 7792 3467
psand@antique.net
www.antique.net

Paul Hopwell Antiques
30 High Street, West Haddon,
Northamptonshire NN6 7AP
Tel: 01788 510636
Fax: 01788 510044
hopwell@aol.com
www.antiqueoak.co.uk

Peter A Crofts
Briar Patch, 117 Elm High Road,
Elm, Wisbeach, Cambridgeshire
PE14 0DN
Tel: 01945 584614

Peter Bunting
Harthill Hall, Alport, Bakewell,
Derbyshire DE45 1LH
Tel: 01629 636203
Fax: 01629 636 101
www.countryoak.co.uk

Peter Foyle Hunwick
The Old Malthouse,
15 Bridge Street, Hungerford,
Berkshire RG17 0EG
Tel: 01488 682209
Fax: 01488 682209
hunwick@oldmalthouse30.free-
serve.co.uk

Peter Lipitch Ltd.
120 & 124 Fulham Road,
London SW3 6HU
Tel: 020 7373 3328
Fax: 020 7373 8888
lipitcha1@aol.com

Philip Andrade
White Oxen Manor, Rattery,
South Brent, Devon TQ10 9JX
Tel: 01364 72454
Fax: 01364 73061

Phillips of Hitchin (Antiques) Ltd.
The Manor House, Hitchin,
Hertfordshire SG5 1JW
Tel: 01462 432067
Fax: 01462 441368

R G Cave & Sons Ltd.
Walcote House, 17 Broad Street,
Ludlow, Shropshire SY8 1NG
Tel: 01584 873568
Fax: 01584 875050

R Green
Ashcombe Coach House Antiques,
Brighton Road, Lewes, East Sussex
BN7 3JR
Tel: 01273 474794
Fax: 01273 705959/707700
anglocont@applied-tech.com

R N Myers & Son
Endsleigh House, High Street,
Gargrave, Skipton, North Yorkshire
BD23 3LX
Tel: 01756 749587
Fax: 01756 749 322
rnmyersson@aol.com

Randolph
97-99 High Street, Hadleigh,
Suffolk IP7 5EJ
Tel: 01473 823789
Fax: 01473 823867

Reindeer Antiques Ltd.
81 Kensington Church Street,
London W8 4BG
Tel: 020 7937 3754
Fax: 020 7937 7199
www.reindeerantiques.co.uk

Reindeer Antiques Ltd.
43 Watling Street, Potterspury,
Northamptonshire NN12 7QD
Tel: 01908 542407
Fax: 01908 542121
www.reindeerantiques.co.uk

Richard Courtney Ltd.
112-114 Fulham Road, South
Kensington, London SW3 6HU
Tel: 020 7370 4020
Fax: 020 7370 4020

Richard J Kingston
95 Bell Street, Henley-on-Thames,
Oxfordshire RG9 2BD
Tel: 01491 574535
Fax: 01491 574535

Robert Dickson &
Lesley Rendall Antiques
263 Fulham Road, London SW3 6HY
Tel: 020 7351 0330
Fax: 020 7352 0078

Robert E Hirschhorn
83 Camberwell Grove,
London SE5 8JE
Tel: 020 7703 7443
Fax: 020 7703 7443

Robert Harman Antiques
Church Street, Ampthill,
Bedfordshire MK45 2PL
Tel: 01525 402322
Fax: 01525 756177

Robert Morrison & Son
Trentholme House, 131 The Mount,
York, North Yorkshire YO24 1DU
Tel: 01904 655394
www.york-antiques.com

Robert Young Antiques
68 Battersea Bridge Rd.,
London SW11 3AG
Tel: 020 7228 7847
Fax: 020 7585 0489
office@robertyoungantiques.com
www.robertyoungantiques.com

Robin Butler
20 Clifton Road, Bristol BS8 1AQ
Tel: 0117 973 3017
Fax: 0117 973 2415
robin.butler@ukgateway.net

Robin Shield
New Inn, 27 Station Road, Castle
Bytham, Lincolnshire NG33 4SB
Tel: 01476 550892

Roderick Butler
Marwood House, Honiton,
Devon EX14 1PY
Tel: 01404 42169

Ronald Phillips Ltd.
26 Bruton Street, London W1J 6LQ
Tel: 020 7493 2341
Fax: 020 7495 0843
ronphill@aol.com

S J Webster-Speakman
52 Halesworth Road, Reydon,
Southwold, Suffolk IP18 6NR
Tel: 01502 722252

Stair & Company Ltd.
14 Mount Street, London W1Y 5RA
Tel: 020 7499 1784
Fax: 020 7629 1050
stairandcompany@talk21.com

Suffolk House Antiques
High Street, Yoxford, Saxmundham,
Suffolk IP17 3EP
Tel: 01728 668122
Fax: 01728 668122

Oliver Charles Antiques Ltd.
Lombard Street, Petworth,
West Sussex GU28 0AG
Tel: 01798 344443

Thomas Coulborn & Sons
Vesey Manor, 64 Birmingham Road,
Sutton Coldfield, West Midlands
B72 1QP
Tel: 0121 354 3974
Fax: 0121 354 4614

Tobias Jellinek Antiques
20 Park Road, East Twickenham,
Middlesex TW1 2PX
Tel: 020 8892 6892
Fax: 020 8744 9298
toby@jellinek.com

Town & Country Antiques
34 Market Street, Bradford-on-
Avon, Wiltshire BA15 1LL
Tel: 01225 867877
Fax: 01225 867877

Turpin's Antiques
17 Bridge Street, Hungerford,
Berkshire RG17 0EG
Tel: 01488 681886

Turpin's Antiques
Old Manor Cottage, Little Bedwyn,
Nr Marlborough, Wiltshire SN8 3JG
Tel: 01672 870727

Ulla Stafford
Binfield Lodge, Binfield,
Berkshire RG42 5QB
Tel: 0118 934 3208
Fax: 0118 934 3208

Victor Mahy
Netherhampton House,
Netherhampton, Salisbury,
Wiltshire SP2 8PU
Tel: 01722 743131
johnparnaby@netherhampton
house.co.uk
www.netherhamptonhouse.co.uk

W A Pinn & Sons
124 Swan Street, Sible Hedingham,
Essex CO9 3HP
Tel: 01787 461127

W R Harvey & Co
(Antiques) Ltd.
86 Corn Street, Witney, Oxfordshire
OX8 7BU
Tel: 01993 706501
Fax: 01993 706601
antiques@wrharvey.co.uk
www.wrharvey.co.uk

Wakelin & Linfield
PO Box 48, Billingshurst, West
Sussex RH14 0YZ
Tel: 01403 700004
Fax: 01403 700004
wakelin_linfield@lineone.net

William H Stokes
The Cloisters, 6/8 Dollar Street,
Cirencester, Gloucestershire
GL7 2AJ
Tel: 01285 653907
Fax: 01285 653907

William Redford
PO Box 17770, London W8 5ZB
Tel: 020 7376 1825
Fax: 020 7376 1825

Witney Antiques
96-100 Corn Street, Witney,
Oxfordshire OX8 7BU
Tel: 01993 703902
Fax: 01993 779852
witneyantiques@community.co.uk
www.witneyantiques.com

General

Alfies Antique Market
13-25 Church Street, Marylebone,
London NW8 8DT
Tel: 020 7723 6066
Fax: 020 7724 0999

All Our Yesterdays
6, Park Road, Kelvinbridge,
Glasgow G4 9JG
Tel: 0141 334 7788
Fax: 0141 339 8994
antiques@allouryesterdays.fsnet.co.uk

Antiquarius
131-141 Kings Road,
London SW3 4PW
Tel: 020 7351 5353

Below Stairs of Hungerford
103 High Street, Hungerford,
Berkshire RG17 0NB
Tel: 01488 682 317
Fax: 01488 684 294
hofgartner@belowstairs.co.uk
www.belowstairs.co.uk

Branksome Antiques
370 Poole Road, Branksome, Poole,
Dorset BH12 1AW
Tel: 01202 763 324
Fax: 01202 763 643

Christina Bertrand Collection
tineke@rcn.com

Christopher Sykes
The Old Parsonage
Woburn, Milton Keynes, MK17 9QL
Tel: 01525 290259
Fax: 01525 290061

Early Technology
Monkton House, Old Craighall,
East Lothian, Scotland
Tel: 0131 665 5753
www.earlytech.com

Grays Antique Market
58 Davies St,
London W1K 5LP
Tel: 020 7629 7034
Email: info@graysantiques.com

Heritage
6 Market Place
Woodstock
Oxfordshire
OX20 1TA
Tel: 01993 811332

Otford Antiques and Collectors Centre
26-28 High Street, Otford,
Kent TN15 9DF
Tel: 01959 522025
Fax: 01959 525858
www.otfordantiques.co.uk

Jean Scott Collection
Stanhope Collectors' Club,
42 Frankland Crescent, Parkstone,
Poole, Dorset BH14 9PX
jean@stanhopes.info
www.stanhopes.info

Pantiles Spa Antiques
Pantiles Spa Antiques,
4-6 Union House, The Pantiles,
Tunbridge Wells, Kent TN4 8HE
Tel: 01892 541377
Fax: 01435 865660
psa.wells@btinternet.com
www.antiques-tun-wells-kent.co.uk

The Ginnel Antiques Centre
Off Parliament Street,
Harrogate HG1 2RB
Tel: 01423 508857

Glass

Andrew Lineham Fine Glass
The Mall, Camden Passage,
London N1 8ED
Tel/Fax: 01243 576241
Mob: 07767 702722
andrew@andrewlineham.co.uk
www.andrewlineham.co.uk

Antique Glass @ Frank Dux Antiques
33 Belvedere, Lansdown Road
Bath BA1 5HR
Tel: 01225 312367

Christine Bridge Antiques
78 Castelnau, London
SW13 9EX
Tel: 07000 445277
Fax: 07000 329 45277
christine@bridge-antiques.com
www.bridge-antiques.com
www.antiqueglass.co.uk

Delomosne & Son Ltd.
Court Close, North Wraxall,
Chippenham, Wiltshire SN14 7AD
Tel: 01225 891505
Fax: 01225 891907
www.delomosne.co.uk

Gerald Sattin
PO Box 20627, London
NW6 7GA
Tel: 020 8451 3295
Fax: 020 8451 3295
gsattin@compuserve.com

Jeanette Hayhurst Fine Glass
32A Kensington Church St,
London W8 4HA
Tel: 020 7938 1539
www.antiqueglasslondon.com

Mum Had That
info@mumhadthat.com
www.mumhadthat.com

Oriental and Asian

Arthur Millner
2 Campden Street, Off Kensington
Church Street, London W8 7EP
Tel: 020 7229 3268
Mob: 07900 248 390
info@arthurmillner.com
www.arthurmillner.com

Guest & Gray
1-7 Davies Mews,
London W1K 5AB
Tel: 020 7408 1252
Fax: 020 7499 1445
info@chinese-porcelain-art.com
www.chinese-porcelain-art.com

Ormonde Gallery
156 Portobello Road,
London W11 2EB
Tel: 020 7229 9800

Roger Bradbury
Church Street,
Coltishall, Norwich,
Norfolk NR12 7DJ
Tel: 01603 737 444

R & G McPherson Antiques
40 Kensington Church Street,
London W8 4BX
Tel: 020 7937 0812
Fax: 020 7938 2032
Mob: 07768 432 630
rmcpherson@orientalceramics.com
www.orientalceramics.com

Silver

B. Silverman
Tel: 020 7242 3269
Fax: 020 7404 0635
silver@silverman-london.com
www.silverman-london.com

C. & L. Burman
5 Vigo Steet,
London W1S 3HF
Tel: 020 7439 6604
Fax: 020 7439 6605

Didier Antiques
58-60 Kensington Church Street
London W8 4DB
Tel: 020 7938 2537
didier.antiques@virgin.net

Fay Lucas Artmetal
Christies Fine Art Securities
42 Ponton Road,
London SW8 5BA
Tel: 020 7371 4404
info@faylucas.com
www.faylucas.com

Goodwins Antiques Ltd
15 & 16 Queensferry Street,
Edinburgh EH2 4QW
Tel: 0131 225 4717
Fax: 0131 220 1412

Hannah Antiques
Tel: 01844 351 935
Fax: 07831 800 774

John Bull Silver
139A New Bond Street, London
W1S 2TN
Tel: 020 7629 1251
www.jbsilverware.co.uk

J. H. Bourdon Smith Ltd
24 Mason's Yard, Duke Street,
St James's, London SW1Y 6BU
Tel: 020 7839 4714
Fax: 020 7839 3951

Marks
49 Curzon Street, London W1J 7UN
Tel: 020 7499 1788
Fax: 020 7409 3183
marks@marksantiques.com
www.marksantiques.com

Mary Cooke Antiques
12 The old Power Station,
121 Mortlake Highstreet,
London SW14 8SN
Tel: 020 8876 5777
Fax: 020 8876 1652
silver@marycooke.co.uk
www.marycooke.co.uk

Nicholas Shaw Antiques
Virginia Cottage, Lombard Street,
Petworth, West Sussex GU28 0AG
Tel: 01798 345 146
silver@nicholas-shaw.com
www.nicholas-shaw.com

Paul Bennett
48a George Street, London W1U 7DY
Tel: 020 7935 1555
Fax: 020 7224 4858
paulbennett@ukgateway.net
www.paulbennett.ukgateway.net

Payne & Son (Goldsmiths) Ltd
131 High Street, Oxford OX1 4DH
Tel: 01865 243 787
Fax: 01865 793 241
silver@payneandson.co.uk
www.payneandson.co.uk

Peter Cameron Antique Silver
PO Box LB739, London W1A 9LB
petercameron@idnet.co.uk

Peter Szuhay
325 Grays Antiques,58 Davies Street,
London W1Y 2LB
Tel: 020 7408 0154
Fax: 020 8993 8864
pgszuhay@aol.com

Sanda Lipton
28a Devonshire Street,
London W1G 6PS
Tel: 020 7431 2688
Fax: 020 7431 3224
sanda@antique-silver.com
www.antique-silver.com

S & J Stodel
Vault 24,
London Silver Vaults,
Chancery Lane,
London WC2A 1QS
Tel: 020 7405 7009
Fax: 020 7242 6366
stodel@msn.com
www.chinesesilver.com

Shapiro & Company
380 Grays Antiques, 58 Davies
Street, London W1K 5LP
Tel: 020 7491 2710

Smith & Robinson
Tel: 020 8994 3783
cwsmith@ukonline.co.uk

Steppes Hill Farm Antiques
The Hill Farm, South Street,
Stockbury, Sittingbourne,
Kent ME9 7RB
Tel: 01795 842 205

The Silver Fund
1 Duke of York Street, London
SW1Y 6JP
Tel: 020 7839 8935
www.thesilverfund.com

Van Den Bosch
1 Georgian Village,
Camden Passage,
Islington,
London N1 8DU
Tel: 020 7226 4550
Fax: 020 8348 5410
info@vandenbosch.co.uk
www.vandenbosch.co.uk

Textiles

Antique Textiles and Lighting
34 Belvedere, Lansdowne Road,
Bath BA1 5HR
Tel: 01225 310 795
Fax: 01225 443 884
joannaproops@aol.co.uk

Fantiques
30 Hastings Road, Ealing, London
W13 8QH
Tel: 020 8840 4761
paulajraven@aol.com

Junnaa & Thomi Wroblewski
78 Marylebone High Street, Box 39
London W1U 5AP
Tel: 020 7499 7793

Vintage to Vogue
28 Milsom Street,
Bath BA1 1DG
Tel: 01225 337 323
www.vintagetovoguebath.com

Tribal Art

Elms Lesters
Painting Rooms,
Flitcroft Street,
London WC2H 8DH
Tel: 020 7836 6747
Fax: 020 7379 0789
gallery@elms-lesters.demon.co.uk
www.elms-lesters.demon.co.uk

Jean-Baptiste Bacquart
www.AfricanAndOceanicArt.com

GLOSSARY

A

acanthus A popular leaf motif, often carved or inlaid.

acid etching A technique using acid to produce a matt or frosted effect on glass.

alberello jar An Italian tin-glazed earthenware pharmacy jar.

appliqué Decoration which is formed separately and then applied or stitched to a piece.

apron/skirt The strip of wood beneath the seat rail of a chair or settee, or to the base of a table or chest.

architrave The moulding around a door or aperture on a piece of furniture.

ashet A large plate or dish.

astragal Architechtural moulding with a semi-circular section.

B

Bakelite An early synthetic plastic which was patented in 1907.

balance An escape mechanism that is used in clocks without pendulums.

baluster A curved form with a bulbous base and slender neck.

Baroque An ornate and extravagant decorative style which was popular in the 17th and 18thC.

bébé The French term for a doll that represents a baby.

bergère The French term for an upholstered armchair.

bezel The groove or rim on the inside of the cover or lid on vessels such as teapots.

biscuit Porcelain that has been fired once and has a characteristic matt white body.

bisque A type of unglazed porcelain used for making dolls' heads from 1860 to 1925.

bob The metal weight at the end of a pendulum rod.

bombé A swollen curving form.

bone china A type of very white porcelain which has dried ox bone added to the body.

boulle case A type of marquetry that includes tortoiseshell and metal.

bow front An outwardly curving shape typically on case furniture.

bracket clock A spring-driven clock originally designed to stand on a wall bracket and later on a shelf.

bracket foot A square-shaped foot often found on 18thC furniture.

break-front A term for furniture with a projecting centre section.

C

cabochon A French term for a smooth domed gem.

cabriole leg A leg with two gentle curves that create an S-shape.

cameo Hardstone, coral or shell that has been carved to show a design in a contrasting colour.

cameo glass Glass made from differently coloured layers, carved to reveal the colour beneath.

canterbury A small stand with dividers for storing sheet music.

cartouche A framed panel, often in the shape of a paper scroll.

caryatid An architechtural column in the form of a woman.

casting The process of forming a solid object by pouring a liquid into a mould and letting it set.

centre seconds hand A seconds hand that is pivoted at the centre of the dial.

champlevé A type of decoration where enamel is applied to stamped hollows in metal.

chapter ring The ring of hour and minute numbers on a clock dial.

chinoiserie Oriental-style lacquered or painted decoration featuring figures and landscapes.

chronometer Timekeeper used for calculating longitude at sea.

clock garniture A matching clock and candelabra set.

collet setting A jewellery setting where the gem sits on a mount.

commode A decorated low chest of drawers with a curved form.

composition A mixture of wood pulp, plaster and glue and used for dolls' heads and bodies.

core forming An early form of glass-making where molten glass is wound around a mud core.

crackle A deliberate crazed effect found in the glaze of Chinese Song dynasty and later porcelain.

craze A network of fine cracks in the glaze caused by uneven shrinking during firing.

credenza The Italian term for a side cabinet with display shelves at both ends.

crewelwork A linen embroidery technique using wool.

D

davenport A small writing desk. In America, a large parlour sofa.

dentils Small teeth-like blocks that form a border under a cornice.

Deutsche Blumen Flower decoration found on 18thC faience and porcelain.

diaper A repeating pattern of geometric shapes.

diecast Objects made by pouring molten metal into a closed metal die or mould.

E

earthenware A type of porous pottery that requires a glaze to make it waterproof.

enamel Coloured glass paste that is applied to surfaces to create a decorative effect.

escapement The part of a clock that regulates the transfer of energy from the weights or spring to the movement.

escutcheon A protective plate fixed over a keyhole.

F

faïence The French name for tin-glazed earthenware.

Fazackerly A style of floral painting found on English delft.

finial A decorative knob on a terminal or cover of a vessel.

flatware A general term for cutlery.

fretwork Geometric pierced decoration.

frieze A long piece of wood used to support a table top or cornice.

frit Powdered glass added to white clay to produce a soft-paste porcelain. Also describes impurites found in old glass.

fusee A grooved device found in clocks that offsets the force of the spring as it runs down.

G

gadroon A decorative border of flutes or reeds.

gesso A paste mixture applied to timber then carved and gilded.

gilding Applying a gold coating to silver or other materials.

glaze The glassy coating applied to porous ceramics to make them stronger and waterproof.

Greek key A Classical motif of interlocking lines.

grosse point A stitch that crosses two warp and two weft threads.

ground The base or background colour of ceramics.

guilloché enamel Enamel applied over engraved metal.

H

hard-paste porcelain Porcelain made from kaolin, petuntse and quartz.

harlequin set A set of ceramics or furniture, in which the pieces are similar rather than identical.

hippogryph A mythical creature.

I J K

inclusion Naturally occuring flaw within a gemstone.

inlay A pattern of wood, ivory or other materials that has been sunk into a wooden surface.

intaglio Cut or engraved decoration on glass.

jasperware A hard and refined stoneware produced by Wedgwood c1775.

japanning The process of coating objects with layers of coloured varnish in imitation of lacquer.

kaolin A fine white china clay used as the main ingredient in hard-paste porcelain.

knop The knob on lids and covers and also the bulge on the stem of a candlestick or glass.

kovsh A Russian shallow drinking vessel with a handle.

L

lead glass or crystal A particularly clear type of glass with a high lead oxide content.

lead glaze A clear glaze with a lead based component.

longcase clock A weight-driven, free-standing clock.

lustre An iridescent finish found on pottery and produced using metallic oxides.

M

manganese A mineral used to produce a purple glaze.

maiolica Italian tin-glazed earthenware produced from the 14thC.

majolica 19thC heavily modelled earthenware with lead glazes.

marquetry A decorative veneer made up from coloured woods.

married A term uses to describe a piece that is composed of parts that were not originally together.

moulding Decorative strips formed from wood, metal or plaster.

movement The entire time-keeping mechanism of a clock or watch.

N O

netsuke A carved toggle used in traditional Japanese dress.

ogee An S-shaped shallow curve.

opaline glass A translucent white glass made with the addition of oxides and bone ash.

open work Pierced decoration.

ormolu Bronze gilding used in 18thC and early 19thC France as decorative mounts.

overglaze Enamel or transfer-printed decoration on porcelain that is applied after firing.

ovolo A quarter-circle shaped moulding.

P

parian A semi-matt type of porcelain made with feldspar that does not require a glaze.

parure A jewellery set usually comprising a matching necklace, earrings, a pair of bracelets and a brooch.

paste The mixture of ingredients that make up porcelain. Also a compound of glass used to make imitation gemstones.

patera An oval or circular motif with a floral or fluted centre.

pâte-sur-pâte A form of cameo-like low relief decoration produced by carving through layered slip.

patina A surface sheen on objects that is produced over time through polishing and handling.

pavé setting A method of mounting jewels so that each stone is set close to the next.

pearlware English earthenware with a blue tinted glaze, developed by Wedgwood.

pediment The gabled form on top of a cornice.

pembroke table A small table with two flaps and four legs.

penny toys Small and simple toys designed to be sold for a penny.

petit point Finely worked embroidery with stitches that cross one warp or weft thread.

petuntse The Chinese name for china stone. A feldspar which is mixed with kaolin to form hard-paste porcelain.

pinion A small toothed gear within a clock movement.

piqué Form of decoration where metal is inlaid into tortoiseshell or ivory.

plique-à-jour Technique where enamel is set into an openwork metal frame to create an effect similar to stained glass.

polychrome Decoration in more than two colours.

prattware Creamware decorated with a high-fired palette of blue, green and yellow.

press-moulded Ceramic or glass objects formed by pressing the substance into a mould.

Q R S

relief moulding Moulded decoration that is raised above the background surface.

repoussé Embossed relief decoration on metal.

rhinestone Clear quartz used for costume jewellery. Also costume pieces mounted with paste.

rhodium A white metal used in metalwork and jewellery.

rococo An ornamental French style popular in the 18thC.

sabot The metal 'shoe' on the end of cabriole legs.

sabre leg A leg shaped like the curved blade of a sabre.

salver A flat serving dish with a border, often with small feet.

scagliola Imitation marble made with plaster.

serpentine A curved form with a projecting middle.

sgraffito A pattern of scratched decoration that reveals a contrasting colour beneath.

silver gilt Silver with a thin layer of gold.

slip A mixture of clay and water used to decorate pottery and to produce slip-cast wares.

slip-casting Method of making thin-bodied vessels by pouring slip into a mould.

soft-paste porcelain Porcelain made from kaolin, powdered glass, soapstone and clay.

spandrel The triangular bracket found at the top of legs.

splat The central upright in a chair back.

squab A stuffed cushion.

stoneware A type of ceramic made of high-fired clay mixed with stone such as feldspar, which makes it non-porous.

stretchers The bar between two legs on tables and chairs used to stablise the structure.

stuff-over seat A chair with an upholstered seat rail.

swan-neck cresting or pediment Formed when two S-shaped curves almost meet.

T

tantulus A lockable frame holding cut-glass spirit decanters.

tazza A shallow bowl or cup on a pedestal foot.

tin-glaze An opaque tin oxide glaze used on earthenware.

tinplate Toys made from thin steel covered with a coating of tin to guard against rust.

torchère A portable stand for supporting a candle or lamp.

train A set of wheels and pinions that transfers energy from the spring or wheel to the escape mechanism in a clock.

transfer printing A method of printing ceramics that involves transferring a design from an inked engraving to a vessel.

transitional The Chinese period around the transition from the Ming to the Qing dynasty.

U

underglaze Decoration painted on to a biscuit body before glazing.

ushabti Figurines in the form of mummies.

A

B

C

D

E

F

G

H

I

M

N